IF FOUND, please notify and arrange return to owner. This text is important for the owner's preparation for the Uniform Certified Public Accountant Examination.

Name of CPA Candidate ______________________________

Address ______________________________

City, State, Zip ______________________________

Telephone (   ) ______________________________

Additional texts are available at your local bookstore

or directly from John Wiley and Sons, Inc.

Order information and order forms can be found at the back of the book

CPA

EXAMINATION REVIEW

VOLUME II

PROBLEMS and SOLUTIONS

11th EDITION

Irvin N. Gleim, Ph.D., CPA
University of Florida
Gainesville, Florida

&

Patrick R. Delaney, Ph.D., CPA
Northern Illinois University
DeKalb, Illinois

JOHN WILEY & SONS

New York Chichester Brisbane Toronto Singapore

Permissions

The following items copyright © by the American Institute of Certified Public Accountants, Inc. are reprinted with permission:

1. *Uniform CPA Examination Questions and Unofficial Answers,* 1973, 1974, 1975, 1976, 1977, 1978, 1979, 1980, 1981, 1982, 1983, and 1984. Those which have been adapted are so identified.
2. Definitions, example schedules, etc., from *Accounting Research Bulletins, APB Opinions, APB Statements,* and *The Code of Professional Ethics.*

Reproduction and adaption of pronouncements, copyright © Financial Accounting Standards Board, High Ridge Park, Stamford, Connecticut 06905 with permission.

Certified Internal Auditor Examination, May 1979, Principles of Internal Auditing Question No. 33, copyright © 1979 by the Institute of Internal Auditors, Inc., 249 Maitland Avenue, Altamonte Springs, Florida 33701 U.S.A. Reprinted with permission.

Material from the *Certificate in Management Accounting Examination,* copyright © 1979 and 1981, by the National Association of Accountants is reprinted with permission.

The following problems in this volume were taken, with permission, from *Intermediate Accounting,* Fourth Edition, by Donald E. Kieso and Jerry J. Weygandt, John Wiley and Sons, Inc., 1983.

1. Problem 7 in Module 28.
2. Problem 1 in Module 29, Debt Restructure.
3. Problem 6 in Module 30.

ISBN 0-471-80082-1

10 9 8 7 6 5 4 3 2 1

PREFACE

The first purpose of Volume II is to provide CPA candidates with recent examination problems/questions organized by topic, e.g., internal control, consolidations, secured transactions, etc. This text includes over 1,950 objective questions (largely 1981 to date). The multiple choice questions are an effective means of studying the material tested on past exams; however, it is also necessary to work with practice problems and essay questions to develop the solutions approach (the ability to solve CPA essay questions and practice problems efficiently).

The second objective of this volume is to explain the AICPA unofficial answers to the examination problems/questions included in this text. The AICPA publishes past CPA examinations and unofficial answers. No explanation is made, however, of the procedures that should have been applied to the examination problem to obtain the unofficial answers. Relatedly, the unofficial answers to objective questions provide no justification and/or explanation. This text provides explanations of both how to work problems and the unofficial answers to multiple choice questions.

This text is designed to be used in conjunction with Volume I, Outlines and Study Guides, but may be used with or without any other study source. Both volumes are organized into 44 manageable study units (modules) to assist candidates in organizing their study programs. The multiple choice questions in this volume are grouped into topical categories which correspond to the sequencing of material as it appears in Volume I.

Multiple Choice questions from the November 1983 (virtually all) and May 1984 (all) examinations have been added to this Eleventh Edition. Also many of the essay questions/practice problems from both 1983 exams are included. As new questions and problems are added, older problems are deleted. New problems are not added just for the sake of change. Rather, new problems emphasize more current topics, pronouncements, etc. They also illustrate the most current type and format of problems being used on the examination. Changes in the Board of Examiners, their philosophy, and most important, the AICPA examination staff, result in changing types and formats of questions and problems.

A Sample Examination for each of the four parts of the exam is included in the Appendix at the end of this volume. The questions and problems for these exams were selected on the basis of a statistical analysis of the last six exams.

The authors are indebted to the American Institute of Certified Public Accountants, the Institute of Management Accounting of the National Association of Accountants, and the Institute of Internal Auditors for permission to reproduce and adapt examination materials from past certification examinations. This edition includes three problems from Kieso and Weygandt, *Intermediate Accounting*, Fourth Edition, John Wiley & Sons, Inc. These problems deal with topics which have not been tested in comprehensive problems subsequent to the issuance of pronouncements dealing with these topics.

The authors deeply appreciate the enthusiastic and dedicated attitude of the many CPA candidates with whom the authors have had the pleasure to work. As always, the authors welcome any comments concerning materials contained in or omitted from this text. Please send these to Patrick R. Delaney, c/o CPA Examination Review, P.O. Box 886, DeKalb, Illinois 60115.

Please carefully read Chapter One "How to Use This Book."

Good Luck on the Exam,

Irvin N. Gleim
Patrick R. Delaney
May 15, 1984

ABOUT THE AUTHORS

Patrick R. Delaney is Chair and Professor of Accountancy at Northern Illinois University. He received his PhD in Accountancy from the University of Illinois. He is past president of the Rockford Chapter, National Association of Accountants; is a member of the Illinois CPA Society's Accounting Principles Committee; and has served on numerous other professional committees. He is a member of the American Accounting Association, American Institute of Certified Public Accountants, and National Association of Accountants. Professor Delaney has published in *The Accounting Review* and is a recipient of NIU's Excellence in Teaching Award. He has been involved in NIU's CPA Review Course as director and instructor and has served as an instructor of NASBA's Critique Program.

Irvin N. Gleim is Professor of Accounting at the University of Florida and is a CPA, CIA and CMA. He received his PhD in Accountancy from the University of Illinois. He is a member of the American Institute of Certified Public Accountants, Florida Institute of Certified Public Accountants, American Accounting Association, American Business Law Association, Institute of Internal Auditors, Institute of Management Accounting, and National Association of Accountants. He has published professional articles in the *Journal of Accountancy, The Accounting Review,* and *The American Business Law Journal.* He has developed and taught both proprietary and university CPA review courses. He is author of *CIA Examination Review* and *CMA Examination Review*, both published by Accounting Publications, Inc.

TABLE OF CONTENTS

**As explained in Chapter 1, this volume is organized into 44 modules (manageable study units). Volume I is organized in a parallel fashion. For easy reference, both Volumes I and II have numbered index tabs indicating the first page of each module.*

3/3
3/17

ABOUT THE CONTRIBUTORS

John C. Borke, MAS, CPA, is Assistant Professor of Accounting at the University of Wisconsin-Platteville. He has worked as a staff auditor with Peat, Marwick, Mitchell & Co. Professor Borke prepared multiple choice answer explanations and solution guides for the practice problems in Cost and Financial Accounting.

Maryellen Burns, JD, CPA, is a member of the Illinois and Federal Bars and an Instructor of Business Law at Northern Illinois University. She has served as an Editor-in-Chief of the Recent Decisions Section of the *Illinois Bar Journal* and is currently pursuing a LLM at the University of Illinois. Ms. Burns has also taught in NIU's CPA Review Course. She prepared answer explanations for the multiple choice questions from the Business Law examination.

Philip DiMarzio, JD, LLM, is an Assistant Professor of Business Law at Northern Illinois University. He has nine years experience in the practice of law including both criminal and civil litigation. He teaches in NIU's Executive MBA Program. Mr. DiMarzio prepared answer explanations for the multiple choice questions from the Business Law examination.

John H. Engstrom, DBA, CPA, is an Associate Professor of Accountancy at Northern Illinois University. He prepared and reviewed solutions to problems in Governmental and Nonprofit Accounting.

Edward C. Foth, PhD, CPA, is an Associate Professor and Administrator of the Master of Science in Taxation Program at DePaul University. He has public accounting experience with Arthur Andersen & Co. and teaches in their Basic and Intermediate U.S. Tax Schools. Professor Foth is the author of Commerce Clearing House's *Study Guide for Federal Tax Course* and coauthor of their *S Corporation Guide.* Professor Foth prepared the answer explanations to the multiple choice questions in Income Taxes, selected the problem material in that area, and updated items to reflect revisions in the tax law.

Kurt Pany, PhD, CPA, is an Associate Professor of Accounting at Arizona State University. He is a member of the American Institute of Certified Public Accountants and the American Accounting Association. Prior to entering academia he worked as a staff auditor for Touche Ross & Co. Professor Pany prepared the answer explanations for the multiple choice questions and selected the problem material in Auditng, Chapter 2.

John R. Simon, PhD, CPA, is Associate Professor of Accountancy at Northern Illinois University and is a recipient of NIU's Excellence in Teaching Award. He has taught in NIU's CPA Review Course for the past eight years and is presently the director of the course. Professor Simon selected and updated the problem material in Inflation Accounting.

Harold Wright, JD, is Coordinator and Assistant Professor of Business Law at Northern Illinois University. He has taught in NIU's CPA Review Course for the past eleven years, has served as an instructor of NASBA's Critique Program, and is a recipient of NIU's Excellence in Teaching Award. Professor Wright prepared answer explanations for the multiple choice questions and selected problem material in Business Law, Chapter 3.

Acknowledgements

Writing an annualized text is always a publishing event and a rejuvenating human experience. The authors are most grateful to the many users of previous editions, both instructors and students who have so generously shared with us their satisfaction with our work and their suggestions for changes and improvements. We hope that this will continue for we have benefited from those communications.

This work continues to be a "community effort." In addition to those colleagues cited as contributors above, we would like to acknowledge and thank those many friends who gave us so many devoted hours to bring this 11th annualized edition to you so quickly after the May 1984 Examination: Diane Babich, Mary Ann Babich, Bruce Barron, David Charbonneau, Sandy Donnelly, Lee Gampfer, Ona Golden, Rudy Knappmeyer, Paula Krueger, Pam Miller, Nancy Thompson, Eileen Thorsen, Lester Welles, and Ray Wisbrock.

The authors are indebted to the following individuals who read parts of the manuscript and made helpful suggestions: Katherine B. Frazier, University of Colorado, Karola Jungbacker, University of Wisconsin–Oshkosh, James Marshall, Michigan State University, J. Hal Reneau, Arizona State University, S. Jay Sklar, Temple University, and G. William Glezen, University of Arkansas.

Several of our colleagues allowed us to use their charts or summaries in the text; these credits are noted with their contributions.

OTHER CONTRIBUTORS AND REVIEWERS

David R. Ackerman, MAS, CPA, is employed by Coopers & Lybrand. Mr. Ackerman drafted answer explanations for multiple choice questions in Governmental and Nonprofit Accounting.

Michael L. Baker, BA, is a candidate for the MBA degree. Mr. Baker has worked as a staff auditor and senior tax specialist for Peat, Marwick, Mitchell & Co. He drafted and reviewed answer explanations for the multiple choice questions from the Theory and Practice examinations.

Katherine H. Casavant, BS, has accepted employment with Peat, Marwick, Mitchell & Co. Ms. Casavant drafted and reviewed answer explanations for the multiple choice questions from the Theory and Practice examinations.

Lynn A. Duttlinger, BS, is a candidate for the MAS degree. Ms. Duttlinger drafted and reviewed answer explanations for the multiple choice questions from the Theory and Practice examinations.

Stephen J. Gilmour, MAS, CPA, is an Instructor of Accountancy at Northern Illinois University. He has public accounting experience with Peat, Marwick, Mitchell & Co. Mr. Gilmour reviewed and revised Chapter 1 of this volume and drafted answer explanations for the multiple choice questions in Cost Accounting. He also selected the problem material for the Cost Accounting modules.

Bill Griesenauer, MAS, CPA, has accepted employment with Ernst & Whinney. Mr. Griesenauer drafted and reviewed answer explanations for the multiple choice questions from the Theory and Practice examinations.

Darrel S. Grove, BS, CPA, is employed by Touche Ross & Co. Mr. Grove reviewed answer explanations for the multiple choice questions in Auditing.

William R. Hartig, MBA, CPA. Mr. Hartig drafted and reviewed answer explanations for the multiple choice questions from the Theory and Practice examinations.

Cindy L. Johnson, MAS, CPA, is an Instructor of Accountancy at Northern Illinois University. Ms. Johnson drafted answer explanations for multiple choice questions in Managerial Accounting.

Michael S. Kelly, BS, has accepted employment with Arthur Andersen & Co. Mr. Kelly drafted and reviewed answer explanations for the multiple choice questions from the Theory and Practice examinations.

Carol Krenek, MAS, CPA, is an Instructor of Accountancy at Northern Illinois University. Ms. Krenek drafted answer explanations for multiple choice questions from the Theory and Practice examinations.

Kevin M. Weber, BS, is employed by Peat, Marwick, Mitchell & Co. Mr. Weber drafted answer explanations for the multiple choice questions from the Business Law examination.

Randall Wosilus, BS, CPA, is a candidate for the MAS degree. Mr. Wosilus drafted and reviewed answer explanations for the multiple choice questions from the Theory and Practice examinations.

CHAPTER ONE

HOW TO USE THIS BOOK

This volume is a collection of recent CPA Problem and Solutions. The text is designed and organized to be used in conjunction with Volume I CPA EXAMINATION REVIEW: OUTLINES AND STUDY GUIDES, but may be used with or without any other study source. Each module in this volume corresponds to a module in Volume I. In this Volume, a module consists of

1. Multiple choice questions.
2. Practice problems and/or essay questions.
3. Unofficial answers with the authors' explanations for the multiple choice questions.
4. Unofficial answers prefaced by solution guides for practice problems.
5. Unofficial answers prefaced by answer outlines for essay questions.

Also included at the end of this volume is a complete sample CPA examination. It is included to enable candidates to gain experience in taking a "realistic" exam. While studying the modules, the candidate can become accustomed to concentrating on fairly narrow topics. By working through the sample examination near the end of their study program, candidates will be better prepared for taking the actual examination.

Before you begin working the recent CPA problems in this volume, peruse the table of contents and scan through the book, noting the manner in which the chapters and modules are organized. The schedule at the beginning of each chapter provides an index to the essay questions and practice problems appearing in each module. Some questions have been modified to reflect recent changes in law or practice. For a complete analysis of recent examinations and the *AICPA Content Specification Outlines* of future examinations, see Volume I, *Outlines and Study Guides.*

Multiple Choice Questions

The multiple choice questions, answers, and explanations to answers can be used in many ways. First, they may be used as a diagnostic evaluation of your knowledge. For example, before beginning to review statistical sampling you may wish to answer 10 to 15 multiple choice questions to determine your ability to answer CPA examination questions on statistical sampling. The apparent difficulty of the questions and the correctness of your answers will allow you to determine the necessary breadth and depth of your review. Additionally, exposure to examination questions prior to review and study of the material should provide motivation. You will develop a feel for your level of proficiency and an understanding of the scope and difficulty of past examination questions. Moreover, your review materials will explain concepts encountered in the diagnostic multiple choice questions.

Second, the multiple choice questions can be used as a post-study or post-review evaluation. You should attempt to understand all concepts mentioned (even in incorrect answers) as you answer the questions. Refer to the explanation of the answer for discussion of the alternatives even though you selected the correct response. Thus, you should read the explanation of the unofficial answer unless you completely understand the question and all of the alternative answers.

Third, you may wish to use the multiple choice questions as a primary study vehicle. This is probably the quickest, but least thorough, approach. Make a sincere effort to understand the question and to select the correct reply before referring to the unofficial answer and explanation. In many cases the explanations will appear inadequate because of your unfamiliarity with the topic.

The multiple choice questions in Volume II are grouped into topical categories. These categories correspond to the sequencing of material as it appears within each of the corresponding modules in Volume I. In the answer explanations for the multiple choice questions in Volume II, we have included headings which provide cross-references to the text material in Volume I. For example, in Module 26, Fixed Assets, a heading appears above the answers to those dealing with depreciation. This heading is identified by the letter "F." To find the topical coverage of depreciation in Volume I, the candidate would refer to the Table of Contents for Financial Accounting (Chapter 9) and look under the module title (Fixed Assets) for the letter "F." Across the page on the line marked "F" would be the appropriate page number in Fixed Assets related to depreciation.

As you work through the multiple choice questions in each module of this volume, you will notice that all of the questions from the latest exam (May exam preceding publication of this volume) that pertain to a given module are grouped together at the end of the module. Among these questions you will encounter some which are identified as **REPEAT QUESTIONS.** The AICPA uses some questions verbatim and other questions are changed slightly (e.g., the numbers in an accounting practice question that appeared in an earlier exam may all be doubled or halved). These questions and the related answer explanations are not included in this volume because they are so similar to questions appearing earlier in the respective modules that such inclusion would be redundant.

The multiple choice questions outnumber the essay questions/practice problems by greater than 10 to 1 in this book. This is similar to a typical CPA exam. Recent exams have contained:

	Multiple choice	*Essay/ Problem*
Auditing	60	4
Business Law	60	4
Practice I	60	2
Practice II	60	2
Theory	60	4
Totals	300	16

The numbers are somewhat misleading in that many essay questions/practice problems contain multiple (and often unrelated) parts.

One difficulty with so many multiple choice questions is that you may overemphasize them. Candidates generally prefer to work multiple choice questions because they are:

1. Shorter and less time consuming,
2. Solvable with less effort, and
3. Less frustrating than essay questions and practice problems.

Essay questions require the ability to organize and compose a solution, as well as knowledge of the subject matter. Remember, working essay questions/practice problems from start to finish is just as important as, if not more important than, working multiple choice questions.

Another difficulty with the large number of multiple choice questions is that you may tend to become overly familiar with the questions. The result may be that you may begin reading the facts and assumptions of previously studied questions into the questions on your examination. Guard against this potential problem by reading each multiple choice question with **extra** care.

Although not as critical as for essay questions and practice problems, the solutions approach (a systematic problem solving methodology) is relevant to multiple choice questions. The solutions approach for multiple choice questions consists of the following steps:

1. **Work individual questions in order.**
   a. If a question appears lengthy or difficult, skip it until you can determine that extra time is available. Put a big question mark in the margin to remind you to return to questions you have skipped or need to review.
2. **Cover the answers before reading each question**
   a. The answers are frequently ambiguous which may cause you to misread or misinterpret the question.

3. **Read each question carefully to determine the topical area.**
   a. Study the requirements first so you know which data are important.
   b. Underline keywords.
   c. Be especially careful to note when the requirement is an **exception**, e.g., "Which of the following is **not** an attribute of variables sampling?"
   d. If a set of data is the basis for two or more questions, read the requirements of each of the questions before beginning to work the first question (sometimes it is more efficient to work the questions out of order or simultaneously).
4. **Anticipate the answer before looking at the alternative answers.**
   a. Recall the applicable principle (e.g., change in estimate); the applicable model (e.g., net present value); or the applicable code section (e.g., 1245).
   b. If Accounting Practice question(s) deal with a complex area like earnings per share, set them up like full-blown problems on scratch paper, if necessary, using abbreviations that enable you to follow your work (remember these questions are graded by machine).
5. **Read the answers and select the best alternative.**
   a. For Accounting Practice questions, if the answer you have computed is not among the choices, quickly check your math and the logic of your solution. If you don't arrive at one of the given answers in the allotted time, make an educated guess.
6. **Mark the correct (or best guess) answer on the examination itself.**
7. **After completing all of the individual questions in an overall question, transfer the answers to the machine gradeable answer sheet with extreme care.**
   a. Be very careful not to fall out of sequence with the answer sheet. A mistake would cause most of your answers to be wrong. SINCE THE AICPA USES ANSWER SHEETS WITH DIFFERENT FORMATS, IT WOULD BE VERY EASY TO GO ACROSS THE SHEET INSTEAD OF DOWN OR VICE VERSA.
   b. Review to check that you have transferred the answers correctly.
   c. Do not leave this step until the end of the exam as you may find yourself with too little time to transfer your answers to the answer sheet. THE PROCTORS ARE NOT PERMITTED TO GIVE YOU EXTRA TIME TO TRANSFER THEM.

Practice Problems

The solutions approach to practice problems is more critical than for multiple choice or essay questions. Many candidates have trouble with Accounting Practice due to their inability to "put a handle on" or "gain control of" practice problems. Without an efficient solutions approach, it is easy to spin your wheels and/or be overwhelmed by many of the practice problems.

To develop a solutions approach for practice problems, you have to work problems from start to finish under examination conditions. There are many possible series of solution steps. A series of solution steps is outlined below. Candidates should develop and adapt a series of specific steps to fit their individual needs. They may find that some of the steps are occasionally unnecessary, or that certain additional procedures increase their problem-solving efficiency. A solutions approach should be developed and practiced on recent CPA questions and problems prior to taking the CPA examination.

1. **Glance over the problem.** Only scan the problem. Get a feel for the type or category of problem. Do not read it. Until you understand the requirements, you cannot discriminate important data from irrelevant data.
2. **Study the requirements.** "Study" as differentiated from "read." Candidates continually lose points due to misunderstanding the requirements. Underline key phrases and words.

2a. **Visualize the solution format.** Determine the expected format of the required solution. Develop an awareness of "schedule and statement format." Put headings on the required statements and schedules. Often a single requirement will require two or more statements, schedules, etc. A common example is a question followed by "why" or "explain." Explicitly recognize multiple requirements by numbering or lettering them on your examination booklet, expanding on the letters already assigned to problem parts.

3. **Outline the required procedures mentally.** Interrelate the data within the text of the problem to the expected solution format, mentally noting a "to do" list. Determine what it is you are going to do before you get started doing it.

3a. **Review applicable principles, knowledge.** Before immersing yourself in the details of the problem, quickly (30-60 seconds) review and organize the principles and your knowledge applicable to the problem. Jot down any acronyms, formulas, or other memory aids relevant to the topic of the question. Otherwise, the details of the problem will confuse and overshadow your previous knowledge of the applicable principles.

4. **Study the text of the problem.** Read the problem carefully. With the requirements in mind, you now can begin to sort out relevant from irrelevant data. Underline and circle important data. The data necessary for answering each requirement may be scattered throughout the problem. As you study the text, use arrows, etc. to connect data pertaining to a common requirement. List the requirements (a,b, etc.) in the margin alongside the data to which they pertain. Use a wild colored pen to mark up the problem. Heavy colored underlining and comments are attention getting and give you confidence.

4a. **Prepare intermediary solutions as you study the problem.** E.g., calculate goodwill, reconstruct accounts, prepare time diagrams, etc. You are able to perceive these required intermediary solutions because you already understand the problem requirements. These intermediary solutions, underlining and notes in the text of the problem will drastically decrease re-reading time.

5. **Prepare the solution.** You now are in a position to write a neat, complete, organized, labeled solution. Label computations, intermediary solutions, assumptions made, etc., on your scratch sheets and turn them in with your solution (note: not necessary for multiple choice questions).

6. **Proofread and edit.** Do not underestimate the utility of this step. Just recall all of the "silly" mistakes you made on undergraduate examinations. Corrections of errors and completion of oversights during this step can easily be the difference between passing and failing.

7. **Review the requirements.** Assure yourself that you have answered them all.

It is not recommended that candidates consult the solution guides and unofficial answers before substantially completing the practice problems.

Essay Questions

Essay questions appear on the auditing, business law, and theory portions of the examination. While multiple choice questions can often be answered by guessing or by "recognizing" a correct answer, essay questions require more extensive knowledge of the subject matter.

Such knowledge, while necessary, is not sufficient in itself to insure proper answering of essay questions. In addition, candidates must be able to organize and present a well-written answer in a limited time period. The solutions approach to essay questions will assist candidates in developing the necessary skills to successfully answer essay questions on the CPA exam. This approach must be practiced and refined by answering essay questions from previous CPA exams until you are confident of your ability to organize and present well-written answers to the graders of the CPA exam.

The major difference between the solutions approach for practice problems and essay questions is the use of a **keyword** outline. The **keyword** outline in the essay solutions approach takes the place of the intermediary solution in the problem solutions approach. Substitute the following two steps for step 4a. "Prepare intermediary solutions as you study the problem" in the practice problem "solutions approach."

4a. **Write down keywords (concepts).** Jot down a list of keywords (grading concepts) in the margin of the examination. The proximity of the keywords to the text of the question will be more efficient than making notes on a separate sheet of paper which may be misplaced.

4b. **Organize the keywords into a solution outline.** After you have noted all of the grading concepts which bear on the requirements, reorganize the outline for the entire answer. Make sure that you respond to each requirement and do not preempt answers to other requirements.

Next, write up your solution and edit as needed. If you have time later, review your solution again.

Plan ahead when writing your answer. You may wish to revise certain sections or add explanations if time permits you to review your answer. Writing on every other line and leaving a portion of each page blank will make it easier for you to proofread and edit. Also, your solution will be easier for the grader to read.

Note: you **must** write out the answers to the essay questions. Keyword outlines are not sufficient. THE AICPA EXPECTS THE GRADING CONCEPTS TO BE EXPLAINED IN CLEAR, CONCISE, WELL-ORGANIZED SENTENCES. The paragraphs can be numbered in an outline format similar to that of the unofficial answers.

The essay questions and unofficial answers may also be used for study purposes without preparation of answers. Before turning to the unofficial answers, study the question and outline the solution (either mentally or in the margin of the book). Look at the answer outline and compare it to your own. Next, read the unofficial answer, underlining keywords and phrases. The underlining should reinforce your study of the answer content and also assist you in learning how to structure your solutions. On the next page, the unofficial answer to an auditing internal control question is underlined to illustrate the technique.

Answer outlines which summarize the major concepts contained in the unofficial answer are provided for each auditing, business law, and theory essay question. These outlines will facilitate your study of essay questions.

Diagnose Your Weaknesses Prior to the Exam

This volume of problems and solutions provides you with an opportunity to diagnose and correct any exam-taking weaknesses prior to your taking the examination. Continuously analyze the contributing factors to incomplete or incorrect solutions to CPA problems prepared during your study program. General categories of candidates' weaknesses include:

1. Failure to understand the requirements.
2. Misunderstanding the text of the problem.
3. Lack of knowledge of material tested.
4. Inability to apply the solutions approach.
5. Lack of an exam strategy, e.g., time budgeting.
6. Sloppiness, computational errors, etc.
7. Failure to proofread and edit.

Additional Study Aids

A more complete discussion of the solutions approach, including illustrations thereof, appears in Chapter 3 of Volume I, *Outlines and Study Guides*. Additionally, use of "note cards" as an integral part of your study program is discussed and illustrated in Chpater 1 of Volume I. Chapter 4 of Volume I includes a detailed checklist to assist candidates with their last minute preparation and to provide guidance concerning the actual taking of the exam.

NOW IS THE TIME
TO MAKE A COMMITMENT

ANSWER OUTLINE

Problem 7 Purchasing Department Controls

a. Effective internal accounting control procedures
   1. Purchase requisition prepared when goods needed
   2. Purchase requisition copy on file in stores department
   3. Responsible person in stores dept. approves requisitions
      Based on need for goods
      Clearly indicates approval on requisition
   4. Purchase orders can be issued only after proper approval
   5. Vendors are requested to confirm purchase orders
   6. Purchase requisitions are filed with purchase orders
   7. Copies of purchase orders sent to receiving department
      But do not include quantities ordered
   8. Purchase orders are numbered and all numbers accounted for
   9. Receiving dept. only accepts goods per purchase orders

b. 1. The time to order is determined by
      Quantities on hand
      Expected rate of use
      Time it takes to receive goods (lead time)
      Cost of owning versus cost of stock-out
   2. The order quantity of supplies, etc., is based on
      Expected use
      Order costs
      Ability to receive goods
      Ability to pay for goods
      Set-up costs
      Storage costs
      Interest on investment
      Risk of obsolescence
      Quantity discounts
      Shipping costs
   Calculated by economic order quantity

UNOFFICIAL ANSWER

Problem 7 Purchasing Department Controls

a. Those internal accounting control procedures that Long would expect to find if Maylou's system of internal accounting control over purchases is effective are as follows:

- Purchase requisitions are prepared and/or approved only after there has been a proper determination of the need for the goods requested. One copy of the purchase requisition is maintained on file in the stores department.
- Purchase requisitions are approved by a responsible person in the stores department. Approval is given only after that person is satisfied that a need exists and that the requisition is properly prepared. Approval is clearly indicated on requisitions.
- Purchase orders are issued only after they are approved by persons given the specific responsibility to make such approval.
- Vendors are requested to confirm purchase orders. This indicates acceptance and constitutes a contractual commitment.
- Purchase requisitions are filed with purchase orders, and both are maintained in an orderly file in the purchase office.
- Copies of purchase orders sent to the receiving department do not include the quantities of merchandise ordered.
- All purchase orders are numbered, and all numbers are accounted for. This allows control over purchase orders canceled or rejected by vendors.
- Receiving department accepts only those goods for which a purchase order is on hand.

b.

1. The question when to order depends primarily on quantities on hand, rate of use, and the lead time between order placement and receipt of goods. Other factors include the trade-off between the cost of owning and storing merchandise versus the risk of being out of stock.

2. Factors considered in determining how much to order include expected use, costs of placing an order, receiving and paying for what has been purchased, set-up costs, storage costs, interest on investment, risk of obsolescence or deterioration, quantity discounts, and shipping costs. The determination is made judgmentally or mathematically by arriving at an economic order quantity.

CHAPTER TWO

AUDITING PROBLEMS AND SOLUTIONS

Auditing is tested on Thursday morning from 8:30 to 12:00. The exam traditionally includes 60 multiple choice questions (60% of the auditing grade) and 4 essay questions (each 10% of the auditing grade).

The exam will most likely include questions on the subject matter in each of the six modules. A complete analysis of recent examinations and the *AICPA Content Specification Outlines* appear in Volume I, *Outlines and Study Guides*.

Explanations to auditing answers contain references to *AICPA Professional Standards, Volumes I and II*, published by Commerce Clearing House. Volume I contains the standards for Auditing (AU), Management Advisory Services (MS), Tax Practice (TX), and Accounting and Review Services (AR). Volume II contains the standards for Ethics (ET) and Quality Control (QC). Candidates are strongly urged to refer to **current** editions of these volumes.

Each question is coded as to month, year, section, problem number, and multiple choice question number. For example, (583,A1,31) indicates May 1983, audit problem 1, and question number 31. Questions are also marked as being from the Certified Internal Auditor Examination (CIA) or the Certificate in Management Accounting Examination (CMA).

AUDITING PROBLEMS INDEX

Multiple Choice Questions (1–60)

1. Which of the following best describes what is meant by generally accepted auditing standards?
   a. Acts to be performed by the auditor.
   b. Measures of the quality of the auditor's performance.
   c. Procedures to be used to gather evidence to support financial statements.
   d. Audit objectives generally determined on audit engagements.

2. Which of the following statements **best** describes the primary purpose of Statements on Auditing Standards?
   a. They are guides intended to set forth auditing procedures which are applicable to a variety of situations.
   b. They are procedural outlines which are intended to narrow the areas of inconsistency and divergence of auditor opinion.
   c. They are authoritative statements, enforced through the code of professional ethics, and are intended to limit the degree of auditor judgment.
   d. They are interpretations which are intended to clarify the meaning of "generally accepted auditing standards."

3. The first general standard requires that a person or persons have adequate technical training and proficiency as an auditor. This standard is met by
   a. An understanding of the field of business and finance.
   b. Education and experience in the field of auditing.
   c. Continuing Professional Education.
   d. A thorough knowledge of the Statements on Auditing Standards.

4. To emphasize auditor independence from management, many corporations follow the practice of
   a. Appointing a partner of the CPA firm conducting the examination to the corporation's audit committee.
   b. Establishing a policy of discouraging social contact between employees of the corporation and the staff of the independent auditor.
   c. Requesting that a representative of the independent auditor be on hand at the annual stockholders' meeting.
   d. Having the independent auditor report to an audit committee of outside members of the board of directors.

5. Which of the following underlies the application of generally accepted auditing standards, particularly the standards of field work and reporting?
   a. The elements of materiality and relative risk.
   b. The element of internal control.
   c. The element of corroborating evidence.
   d. The element of reasonable assurance.

6. The primary responsibility for the adequacy of disclosure in the financial statements of a publicly held company rests with the
   a. Partner assigned to the audit engagement.
   b. Management of the company.
   c. Auditor in charge of the field work.
   d. Securities and Exchange Commission.

7. A CPA's license to practice will ordinarily be suspended or revoked automatically for
   a. Committing an act discreditable to the profession.
   b. Conviction of willful failure to file personal income tax returns.
   c. Refusing to respond to an inquiry by the AICPA practice review committee.
   d. Accepting compensation while honoring a subpoena to appear as an expert witness.

8. Auditing interpretations, which are issued by the staff of the AICPA Auditing Standards Division in order to provide timely guidance on the application of pronouncements of the Auditing Standards Board, are
   a. Less authoritative than a pronouncement of the Auditing Standards Board.
   b. Equally authoritative as a pronouncement of the Auditing Standards Board.
   c. More authoritative than a pronouncement of the Auditing Standards Board.
   d. Nonauthoritative opinions which are issued without consulting members of the Auditing Standards Board.

9. The AICPA Code of Professional Ethics recognizes that the reliance of the public, the government and the business community on sound financial reporting imposes particular obligations on CPAs. The code derives its authority from
   a. Public laws enacted over the years.
   b. General acceptance of the code by the business community.
   c. Requirements of governmental regulatory agencies such as the Securities and Exchange Commission.
   d. Bylaws of the American Institute of Certified Public Accountants.

10. An auditor is about to commence a recurring annual audit engagement. The continuing auditor's independence would ordinarily be considered to be impaired if the prior year's audit fee
  a. Was only partially paid and the balance is being disputed.
  b. Has **not** been paid and will **not** be paid for at least twelve months.
  c. Has **not** been paid and the client has filed a voluntary petition for bankruptcy.
  d. Was settled by litigation.

11. A CPA, while performing an audit, strives to achieve independence in appearance in order to
  a. Reduce risk and liability.
  b. Become independent in fact.
  c. Maintain public confidence in the profession.
  d. Comply with the generally accepted standards of fieldwork.

12. A CPA who performs primary actuarial services for a client would normally be precluded from expressing an opinion on the financial statements of that client if the
  a. Fees for actuarial services have **not** been paid.
  b. Actuarial services are a major determinant of the pension expense.
  c. Client is an insurance company.
  d. Actuarial assumptions used are **not** in accordance with generally accepted auditing standards.

13. The concept of materiality would be least important to an auditor in determining the
  a. Transactions that should be reviewed.
  b. Need for disclosure of a particular fact or transactions.
  c. Scope of the CPA's audit program relating to various accounts.
  d. Effects of direct financial interests in the client upon the CPA's independence.

14. An auditor who accepts an audit engagement and does not possess the industry expertise of the business entity, should
  a. Engage financial experts familiar with the nature of the business entity.
  b. Obtain a knowledge of matters that relate to the nature of the entity's business.
  c. Refer a substantial portion of the audit to another CPA who will act as the principal auditor.
  d. First inform management that an unqualified opinion cannot be issued.

15. In determining estimates of fees, an auditor may take into account each of the following, **except** the
  a. Value of the service to the client.
  b. Degree of responsibility assumed by undertaking the engagement.
  c. Skills required to perform the service.
  d. Attainment of specific findings.

16. A CPA who is seeking to sell an accounting practice must
  a. Not allow a peer review team to look at working papers and tax returns without permission from the client prior to consummation of the sale.
  b. Not allow a prospective purchaser to look at working papers and tax returns without permission from the client.
  c. Give all working papers and tax returns to the client.
  d. Retain all working papers and tax returns for a period of time sufficient to satisfy the statute of limitations.

17. Which of the following is required for a firm to designate itself "Member of the American Institute of Certified Public Accountants" on its letterhead?
  a. At least one of the partners must be a member.
  b. The partners whose names appear in the firm name must be members.
  c. All partners must be members.
  d. The firm must be a dues paying member.

18. The AICPA Code of Professional Ethics provides, where a CPA is required to express an opinion on combined or consolidated financial statements which include a subsidiary, branch, or other component audited by another independent public accountant, that the CPA may
  a. Insist on auditing any such component which the CPA judges necessary to warrant the expression of an opinion.
  b. Insist only on performing a review of any such component.

c. Not insist on auditing any such component but may request copies of all worksheets relevant to the other independent public accountant's examinations.
d. Not insist on auditing any such component or reviewing worksheets belonging to the other independent public accountant.

19. Inclusion of which of the following statements in a CPA's advertisement is **not** acceptable pursuant to the AICPA Code of Professional Ethics?
a. Paul Fall
Certified Public Accountant
Fluency in Spanish and French
b. Paul Fall
Certified Public Accountant
J.D., Evans Law School 1964
c. Paul Fall
Certified Public Accountant
Free Consultation
d. Paul Fall
Certified Public Accountant
Endorsed by AICPA

20. Inclusion of which of the following in a promotional brochure published by a CPA firm would be most likely to result in a violation of the AICPA rules of conduct?
a. Names and addresses, telephone numbers, number of partners, office hours, foreign language competence, and date the firm was established.
b. Services offered and fees for such services, including hourly rates and fixed fees.
c. Educational and professional attainments, including date and place of certification, schools attended, dates of graduation, degrees received, and memberships in professional associations.
d. Names, addresses and telephone numbers of the firm's clients, including the number of years served.

21. A CPA's retention of client records as a means of enforcing payment of an overdue audit fee is an action that is
a. **Not** addressed by the AICPA Code of Professional Ethics.
b. Acceptable if sanctioned by the state laws.
c. Prohibited under the AICPA rules of conduct.
d. A violation of generally accepted auditing standards.

22. Below are the names of four CPA firms and pertinent facts relating to each firm. Unless otherwise indicated, the individuals named are CPAs and partners, and there are no other partners. Which firm name and related facts indicates a violation of the AICPA Code of Professional Ethics?
a. Arthur, Barry, and Clark, CPAs (Clark died about five years ago; Arthur and Barry are continuing the firm).
b. Dave and Edwards, CPAs (The name of Fredricks, CPA, a third active partner, is omitted from the firm name).
c. Jones & Co., CPAs, P.C. (The firm is a professional corporation and has ten other stockholders who are all CPAs).
d. George and Howard, CPAs (Howard died three years ago; George is continuing the firm as a sole proprietorship).

23. Hawkins requested permission to communicate with the predecessor auditor and review certain portions of the predecessor auditor's working papers. The prospective client's refusal to permit this will bear directly on Hawkins' decision concerning the
a. Adequacy of the preplanned audit program.
b. Ability to establish consistency in application of accounting principles between years.
c. Apparent scope limitation.
d. Integrity of management.

24. Early appointment of the independent auditor will enable
a. A more thorough examination to be performed.
b. A proper study and evaluation of internal control to be performed.
c. Sufficient competent evidential matter to be obtained.
d. A more efficient examination to be planned.

25. The independent auditor's plan for an examination in accordance with generally accepted auditing standards is influenced by the possibility of material errors. The auditor will therefore conduct the examination with an attitude of
a. Professional skepticism.
b. Subjective mistrust.
c. Objective indifference.
d. Professional responsiveness.

26. It would **not** be appropriate for the auditor to initiate discussion with the audit committee concerning
   a. The extent to which the work of internal auditors will influence the scope of the examination.
   b. Details of the procedures which the auditor intends to apply.
   c. The extent to which change in the company's organization will influence the scope of the examination.
   d. Details of potential problems which the auditor believes might cause a qualified opinion.

27. A CPA may reduce the audit work on a first-time audit by reviewing the working papers of the predecessor auditor. The predecessor should permit the successor to review working papers relating to matters of continuing accounting significance such as those that relate to
   a. Extent of reliance on the work of specialists.
   b. Fee arrangements and summaries of payments.
   c. Analysis of contingencies.
   d. Staff hours required to complete the engagement.

28. If, during an audit examination, the successor auditor becomes aware of information that may indicate that financial statements reported on by the predecessor auditor may require revision, the successor auditor should
   a. Ask the client to arrange a meeting among the three parties to discuss the information and attempt to resolve the matter.
   b. Notify the client and the predecessor auditor of the matter and ask them to attempt to resolve it.
   c. Notify the predecessor auditor who may be required to revise the previously issued financial statements and auditor's report.
   d. Ask the predecessor auditor to arrange a meeting with the client to discuss and resolve the matter.

29. In connection with the element of inspection, a CPA firm's system of quality control should ordinarily provide for the maintenance of
   a. A file of minutes of staff meetings.
   b. Updated personnel files.
   c. Documentation to demonstrate compliance with its policies and procedures.
   d. Documentation to demonstrate compliance with peer review directives.

30. A CPA establishes quality control policies and procedures for deciding whether to accept a new client or continue to perform services for a current client. The primary purpose for establishing such policies and procedures is
   a. To enable the auditor to attest to the integrity or reliability of a client.
   b. To comply with the quality control standards established by regulatory bodies.
   c. To lessen the exposure to litigation resulting from failure to detect irregularities in client financial statements.
   d. To minimize the likelihood of association with clients whose management lacks integrity.

31. Dickens, a CPA firm's personnel partner, periodically studies the CPA firm's personnel advancement experience to ascertain whether individuals meeting stated criteria are assigned increased degrees of responsibility. This is evidence of the CPA firm's adherence to prescribed
   a. Standards of due professional care.
   b. Quality control standards.
   c. Supervision and review standards.
   d. Standards of fieldwork.

32. Which of the following is **not** an element of quality control?
   a. Documentation.
   b. Inspection.
   c. Supervision.
   d. Consultation.

33. Within the context of quality control, the primary purpose of continuing professional education and training activities, is to enable a CPA firm to provide personnel within the firm with
   a. Technical training that assures proficiency as an auditor.
   b. Professional education that is required in order to perform with due professional care.
   c. Knowledge required to fulfill assigned responsibilities and to progress within the firm.
   d. Knowledge required in order to perform a peer review.

34. Williams & Co., a large international CPA firm, is to have an "external peer review." The peer review will most likely be performed by
   a. Employees and partners of Williams & Co. who are **not** associated with the particular audits being reviewed.

b. Audit review staff of the Securities and Exchange Commission.
c. Audit review staff of the American Institute of Certified Public Accountants.
d. Employees and partners of another CPA firm.

35. Which of the following is not an element of quality control that should be considered by a firm of independent auditors?
a. Assigning personnel to engagements.
b. Consultation with appropriate persons.
c. Keeping records of quality control policies and procedures.
d. Supervision.

36. The auditor is most likely to presume that a high risk of a defalcation exists if
a. The client is a multinational company that does business in numerous foreign countries.
b. The client does business with several related parties.
c. Inadequate segregation of duties places an employee in a position to perpetrate and conceal thefts.
d. Inadequate employee training results in lengthy EDP exception reports each month.

37. Which of the following statements best describes the auditor's responsibility regarding the detection of fraud?
a. The auditor is responsible for the failure to detect fraud only when such failure clearly results from nonperformance of audit procedures specifically described in the engagement letter.
b. The auditor must extend auditing procedures to actively search for evidence of fraud in all situations.
c. The auditor must extend auditing procedures to actively search for evidence of fraud where the examination indicates that fraud may exist.
d. The auditor is responsible for the failure to detect fraud only when an unqualified opinion is issued.

38. If an illegal act is discovered during the audit of a publicly held company, the auditor should
a. Notify the regulatory authorities.
b. Determine who was responsible for the illegal act.
c. Intensify the examination.
d. Report the act to high level personnel within the client's organization.

39. If the auditor considers an illegal act to be sufficiently serious to warrant withdrawing from the engagement, then the auditor should
a. Notify all parties who may rely upon the company's financial statements of the company's illegal act.
b. Consult with legal counsel as to what other action, if any, should be taken.
c. Return all incriminating evidence and working papers to the client's audit committee for follow-up.
d. Contact the successor auditor to make the successor aware of the possible consequences of relying on management's representations.

40. An auditor who finds that the client has committed an illegal act would be most likely to withdraw from the engagement when the
a. Illegal act affects the auditor's ability to rely on management representations.
b. Illegal act has material financial statement implications.
c. Illegal act has received widespread publicity.
d. Auditor can **not** reasonably estimate the effect of the illegal act on the financial statements.

41. Generally, the decision to notify parties outside the client's organization regarding an illegal act is the responsibility of the
a. Independent auditor.
b. Management.
c. Outside legal counsel.
d. Internal auditors.

42. The AICPA Rules of Conduct will ordinarily be considered to have been violated when the CPA represents that specific consulting services will be performed for a stated fee and it is apparent at the time of the representation that the
a. Actual fee would be substantially higher.
b. Actual fee would be substantially lower than the fees charged by other CPAs for comparable services.
c. Fee was a competitive bid.
d. CPA would **not** be independent.

43. A management advisory service consultation, as opposed to a management advisory service engagement, generally involves advice or information given by a CPA that is based upon
a. Existing personal knowledge about the client.

b. An analytical approach and process.
c. Information obtained during an examination of the client's financial statements.
d. The results of an operational audit.

44. A CPA should **not** undertake a management advisory service engagement that includes continued participation through implementation, unless
a. The CPA accepts overall responsibility for implementation of the chosen course of action.
b. The CPA acquires an overall knowledge of the client's business that is equivalent to that possessed by management.
c. Upon implementation the client's personnel will have the knowledge and ability to adequately maintain and operate such systems as may be involved.
d. Upon implementation a new study and evaluation of the system of internal control is performed.

45. An audit independence issue might be raised by the auditor's participation in management advisory services engagements. Which of the following statements is **most** consistent with the profession's attitude toward this issue?
a. Information obtained as a result of a management advisory services engagement is confidential to that specific engagement and should **not** influence performance of the attest function.
b. The decision as to loss of independence must be made by the client based upon the facts of the particular case.
c. The auditor should **not** make management decisions for an audit client.
d. The auditor who is asked to review management decisions is also competent to make these decisions and can do so without loss of independence.

46. During the course of an audit, independent CPAs are often called upon to give informal advice on many diverse questions. This type of service differs from management advisory services in that this type of service is informal and therefore
a. The independent CPA does **not** make any warranties with respect to the competence of the extemporaneous advice.
b. The independent CPA is **not** exposed to liability as a consequence of the extemporaneous advice.
c. No presumption should exist that all pertinent facts have been identified and considered.
d. No presumption should exist that the advice will impact upon the operations of the business enterprise.

47. Which of the following is **not** a Management Advisory Service Practice Standard?
a. In performing management advisory service, a practitioner must act with integrity and objectivity and be independent in mental attitude.
b. The management advisory services engagement is to be performed by a person or persons having adequate technical training as a management consultant.
c. Management advisory service engagements are to be performed by practitioners having competence in the analytical approach and process, and in the technical subject matter under consideration.
d. Before undertaking a management advisory service engagement, a practitioner is to notify the client of any reservations regarding anticipated benefits.

48. Jones, CPA, prepared Smith's 1982 federal income tax return and appropriately signed the preparer's declaration. Several months later Jones learns that Smith improperly altered several figures before mailing the tax return to the IRS. Jones should communicate disapproval of this action to Smith and
a. Take no further action with respect to the 1982 tax return but consider the implications of Smith's actions upon any future relationship.
b. Inform the IRS of the unauthorized alteration.
c. File an amended tax return.
d. Refund any fee collected, return all relevant documents, and refuse any further association with Smith.

49. Which of the following is implied when a CPA signs the preparer's declaration on a federal income tax return?
a. The tax return is **not** misleading based on all information of which the CPA has knowledge.
b. The tax return and supporting schedules were prepared in accordance with generally accepted accounting principles.

c. The tax return was examined in accordance with standards established by the AICPA's Federal Tax Division.

d. The tax return was prepared by a CPA who maintained an impartial attitude.

50. Which of the following is **not** an acceptable manner of designating that an estimated figure was used in preparing a federal income tax return?

a. State expressly that an amount has been estimated.

b. Use a round amount.

c. Use an amount suggested in a treasury department guideline.

d. Modify the tax preparer's declaration on the return before signing the tax return.

51. In tax practice, which of the following would **not** be considered reasonable support for taking a position contrary to the Internal Revenue Code?

a. Proposed regulations advocated by the IRS.

b. Legal opinions as to the constitutionality of a specific provision.

c. Possible conflicts between two sections of the Internal Revenue Code.

d. Tax court decisions **not** acquiesced to by the IRS.

52. According to the AICPA rules of conduct, contingent fees are permitted by CPAs engaged in tax practice because

a. This practice establishes fees which are commensurate with the value of the services.

b. Attorneys in tax practice customarily set contingent fees.

c. Determinations by taxing authorities are a matter of judicial proceedings which do not involve third parties.

d. The consequences are based upon findings of judicial proceedings or the findings of tax authorities.

53. In accordance with the AICPA Statements On Responsibilities In Tax Practice, where a question on a federal income tax return has not been answered, the CPA should sign the preparer's declaration only if

a. The CPA can provide reasonable support for this omission upon examination by IRS.

b. The information requested is not available.

c. The question is not applicable to the taxpayer.

d. An explanation of the reason for the omission is provided.

54. In accordance with the AICPA Statements On Responsibilities In Tax Practice, if after having provided tax advice to a client there are legislative changes which affect the advice provided, the CPA

a. Is obligated to notify the client of the change and the effect thereof.

b. Is obligated to notify the client of the change and the effect thereof if the client was not advised that the advice was based on existing laws which are subject to change.

c. Cannot be expected to notify the client of the change unless the obligation is specifically undertaken by agreement.

d. Cannot be expected to have knowledge of the change.

55. A CPA while performing tax services for a client may learn of a material error in a previously filed tax return. In such an instance the CPA should

a. Prepare an affidavit with respect to the error.

b. Recommend compensating for the prior year's error in the current year's tax return where such action will mitigate the client's cost and inconvenience.

c. Advise the client to file a corrected return regardless of whether or not the error resulted in an overstatement or understatement of tax.

d. Inform the IRS of the error.

56. Which of the following reports is an indication of the changing role of the CPA that calls for an extension of the auditor's attest function?

a. Report on annual comparative financial statements.

b. Report on internal control based on an audit.

c. Report on separate balance sheet of a holding company.

d. Report on balance sheet and statements of income, retained earnings, and changes in financial position prepared from incomplete financial records.

May 1984 Questions

57. The **least** important evidence of a CPA firm's evaluation of its system of quality controls would concern the CPA firm's policies and procedures with respect to

a. Employment (hiring).
b. Confidentiality of audit engagements.
c. Assigning personnel to audit engagements.
d. Determination of audit fees.

58. A difference of opinion concerning accounting and auditing matters relative to a particular phase of the audit arises between an assistant auditor and the auditor responsible for the engagement. After appropriate consultation, the assistant auditor asks to be disassociated from the resolution of the matter. The working papers would probably be

a. Silent on the matter since it is an internal matter of the auditing firm.
b. Expanded to note that the assistant auditor is completely disassociated from responsibility for the auditor's opinion.
c. Expanded to document the additional work required, since all disagreements of this type will require expanded substantive testing.
d. Expanded to document the assistant auditor's position, and how the difference of opinion was resolved.

59. A CPA engaged in tax practice

a. May take a position contrary to a specific section of the IRS Code without disclosure.
b. May take a position contrary to Internal Revenue Service interpretations of the IRS Code without disclosure.
c. Must disclose any position contrary to Treasury Department regulations concerning the IRS Code.
d. Must **not** take a position contrary to Internal Revenue Service interpretations of the IRS Code without disclosure.

60. Which of the following is responsible for the fairness of the representations made in financial statements?

a. Client's management.
b. Independent auditor.
c. Audit committee.
d. AICPA.

Repeat Questions

(584,A1,40) Identical to item 46 above

(584,A1,51) Identical to item 5 above

Problems

Problem 1 Audit Committees (1178,A2)

(15 to 25 minutes)

For many years the financial and accounting community has recognized the importance of the use of audit committees and has endorsed their formation.

At this time the use of audit committees has become widespread. Independent auditors have become increasingly involved with audit committees and consequently have become familiar with their nature and function.

Required:

a. Describe what an audit committee is.

b. Identify the reasons why audit committees have been formed and are currently in operation.

c. What are the functions of an audit committee?

Problem 2 Audit Deficiencies (578,A2)

(15 to 25 minutes)

Brown, CPA, received a telephone call from Calhoun, the sole owner and manager of a small corporation. Calhoun asked Brown to prepare the financial statements for the corporation and told Brown that the statements were needed in two weeks for external financing purposes. Calhoun was vague when Brown inquired about the intended use of the statements. Brown was convinced that Calhoun thought Brown's work would constitute an audit. To avoid confusion Brown decided not to explain to Calhoun that the engagement would only be to prepare the financial statements. Brown, with the understanding that a substantial fee would be paid if the work were completed in two weeks, accepted the engagement and started the work at once.

During the course of the work, Brown discovered an accrued expense account labeled "professional fees" and learned that the balance in the account represented an accrual for the cost of Brown's services. Brown suggested to Calhoun's bookkeeper that the account name be changed to "fees for limited audit engagement." Brown also reviewed several invoices to determine whether accounts were being properly classified. Some of the invoices were missing. Brown listed the missing invoice numbers in the working papers with a note indicating that there should be a follow-up on the next engagement. Brown also discovered that the available records included the fixed asset values at estimated current replacement costs. Based on the records available, Brown prepared a balance sheet, income statement and statement of stockholder's equity. In addition, Brown drafted the footnotes but decided that any mention of the replacement costs would only mislead the readers. Brown suggested to Calhoun that readers of the financial statements would be better informed if they recieved a separate letter from Calhoun explaining the meaning and effect of the estimated replacement costs of the fixed assets. Brown mailed the financial statements and footnotes to Calhoun with the following note included on each page:

"The accompanying financial statements are submitted to you without complete audit verification."

Required:

Identify the inappropriate actions of Brown and indicate what Brown should have done to avoid each inappropriate action.

Organize your answer sheet as follows:

Inappropriate Action	What Brown Should Have Done To Avoid Inappropriate Action

Problem 3 Violations of GAAS (1176,A6)

(15 to 25 minutes)

Ray, the owner of a small company, asked Holmes, CPA, to conduct an audit of the company's records. Ray told Holmes that an audit is to be completed in time to submit audited financial statements to a bank as part of a loan application. Holmes immediately accepted the engagement and agreed to provide an auditor's report within three weeks. Ray agreed to pay Holmes a fixed fee plus a bonus if the loan was granted.

Holmes hired two accounting students to conduct the audit and spent several hours telling them exactly what to do. Holmes told the students not to spend time reviewing the controls, but instead to concentrate on proving the mathematical accuracy of the ledger accounts, and summarizing the data in the accounting records that support Ray's financial statements. The students followed Holmes' instructions and after two weeks gave Holmes the financial statements which did not include footnotes. Holmes reviewed the statements and prepared an unqualified auditor's report. The report, however, did not refer to generally accepted accounting principles nor to the year-to-year application of such principles.

Required:

Briefly describe each of the generally accepted auditing standards and indicate how the action(s) of Holmes resulted in a failure to comply with each standard.

Organize your answer as follows:

Brief Description of Generally Accepted Auditing Standards	Holmes' Actions Resulting in Failure to Comply with Generally Accepted Auditing Standards

Problem 4 EDP Services (580, A2)

(15 to 25 minutes)

Savage, CPA, has been requested by an audit client to perform a non-recurring engagement involving the implementation of an EDP information and control system. The client requests that in setting up the new system and during the period prior to conversion to the new system, that Savage:

- Counsel on potential expansion of business activity plans.
- Search for and interview new personnel.
- Hire new personnel.
- Train personnel.

In addition, the client requests that during the three months subsequent to the conversion, that Savage:

- Supervise the operation of new system.
- Monitor client-prepared source documents and make changes in basic EDP generated data as Savage may deem necessary without concurrence of the client. Savage responds that he may perform some of the services requested, but not all of them.

Required:

a. Which of these services may Savage perform and which of these services may Savage not perform?

b. Before undertaking this engagement, Savage should inform the client of all significant matters related to the engagement. What are these siginficant matters?

c. If Savage adds to his staff an individual who specializes in developing computer systems, what degree of knowledge must Savage possess in order to supervise the specialist's activities?

Multiple Choice Answers

1.	b	13.	d	25.	a	37.	c	49.	a
2.	d	14.	b	26.	b	38.	d	50.	d
3.	b	15.	d	27.	c	39.	b	51.	d
4.	d	16.	b	28.	a	40.	a	52.	d
5.	a.	17.	c	29.	c	41.	b	53.	d
6.	b	18.	a	30.	d	42.	a	54.	c
7.	b	19.	d	31.	b	43.	a	55.	c
8.	a	20.	d	32.	a	44.	c	56.	b
9.	d	21.	c	33.	c	45.	c	57.	d
10.	b	22.	d	34.	d	46.	c	58.	d
11.	c	23.	d	35.	c	47.	b	59.	b
12.	c	24.	d	36.	c	48.	a	60.	a

Multiple Choice Answer Explanations

A. General Standards and Rules of Conduct

A.1. General Standards

1. (1181,A1,23) (b) The requirement is to determine the meaning of generally accepted auditing standards. Answer (b) is correct because auditing standards are concerned with measures of the quality of the auditor's performance of acts known as procedures (para 150.01).

2. (581,A1,41) (d) The requirement is to determine the primary purpose of Statements on Auditing Standards. Statements on Auditing Standards are interpretations of generally accepted auditing standards (Section 100). While answers (a), (b), and (c) may all, to some extent, be the result of Statements on Auditing Standards, none of them can be considered to be the primary purpose.

3. (1179,A1,48) (b) The first general standard of GAAS recognizes that a person must obtain proper education and experience in the field of auditing (para 210.02). Answer (a) is incorrect because understanding of the field of business and finance is a necessary but not sufficient condition. Presumably people obtain an understanding of the field of business and finance in the course of obtaining education experience in auditing. Answers (c) and (d) are incorrect because continuing professional education and knowledge of SAS are only parts of the knowledge and experience, i.e., the answers are incomplete.

4. (577,A1,14) (d) The requirement is a method to emphasize auditor independence from management. Having the independent auditor report to an audit committee made up of nonmanagement members of the board of directors emphasizes the auditor's independence from management. Corporate audit committees made up of outside board members also helps overcome the internal control limitation whereby top management may be able to circumvent or ignore internal controls. For example, if the CPA reports to the chief operating officer and the chief operating officer has been using the corporate plane for personal business, internal control is inoperative. Answer (a) is incorrect because the CPA firm's independence would be impaired if a partner served on the corporation's audit committee (specifically prohibited per Ethics Rule 101). Answer (b) is incorrect because discouraging social contact between corporate employees and the independent auditor does not relate to the auditor's independence from management. Answer (c) is incorrect because the CPA on hand for the stockholders' meeting usually sits with corporate management, and thus does not emphasize independence.

5. (579,A1,27) (a) The elements of materiality and relative risk underlie the application of all the standards, particularly the standards of field work and reporting (para 150.03). Answers (b), internal control, and (c), corroborating evidence, are incorrect because GAAS are concerned with measures of quality of performance rather than with elements of audit evidence. Answer (d) is incorrect because reasonable assurance is a basic concept of internal control, which recognizes that the cost of internal control should not exceed the benefits expected to be derived (para 320.32).

6. (1178,A1,28) (b) Financial statements are the representations of management, and management has responsibility for producing proper financial statements (para 110.02 of SAS 1). The partner assigned to the audit engagement (answer (a)) has responsibility for expressing an opinion as to fairness of the financial statements. The auditor in charge of field work (answer (c)) has the responsibility to gather audit evidence regarding the fairness of the financial statements. The SEC (answer (d)) has the responsibility for enforcing the Securities Acts which does not include primary responsibility for disclosure in the financial statements of particular companies.

A.2.b. Overall Review of the Code of Ethics

7. (1183,A1,56) (b) The requirement is to determine the situation in which a CPA's license to practice will ordinarily be suspended or revoked automatically. Conviction of a felony (which failure to file personal income tax returns is) is considered by most states as sufficient cause for certificate suspension or revocation. Answers (a) and (c) are not as accurate as (b) since in such circumstances disciplinary actions are taken by individual states on a case by case basis. Answer (d) is incorrect because a CPA may accept compensation while serving as an expert witness.

8. (1180,A1,5) (a) Section 9000 states that auditing interpretations, issued by the staff of the Auditing Standards Division, are not as authoritative as a pronouncement by the Auditing Standards Board. Note, however, that a member may have to justify a departure from an interpretation if the quality of the member's work is questioned.

9. (1177,A1,9) (d) The AICPA code of ethics has been adopted by the membership of the AICPA. Relatedly, the bylaws of the AICPA provide that the trial board may admonish, suspend, or expel a member who is found guilty of infringing on the bylaws or the code of ethics. Thus, there are no public laws which enforce the AICPA's code of ethics. It should be noted that many state public accountancy statutes incorporate various aspects of the AICPA's code of ethics. The general acceptance of the AICPA's code of ethics by the business community does not give authority to the code. Finally, while the SEC has provided impetus to the development of professional ethics, particularly in the area of independence, the SEC does not provide authority for the AICPA's code of ethics.

A.2.c.1) Independence

10. (1183,A1,55) (b) The requirement is to determine the situation in which events related to an audit fee will affect auditor independence. Auditor independence is impaired if the prior year's (material) audit fee has not been paid when the current year's audit report is to be issued; thus, the twelve month delay will impair independence (ET 191.103). Answer (a) is incorrect since the existence of litigation does not, in all cases, result in a lack of independence (ET 191.089). Answer (c) is incorrect since last year's fee may be paid before this year's audit report is issued. Answer (d) is incorrect because, depending upon the specific facts of the situation, past litigation may or may not result in a loss of independence (ET 101.07).

11. (583,A1,58) (c) The requirement is to determine the reason for a CPA's concern with independence in appearance. The appearance of independence is necessary to maintain public confidence in the profession. The profession uses the criterion of whether reasonable men, having knowledge of all the facts and taking into consideration normal strength of character and normal behavior under the circumstances, would conclude that a specified relationship between a CPA and a client poses an unacceptable threat to the CPA's integrity or objectivity (ET 52.09). Answer (a) is incorrect because, while it may be a side benefit of perceived independence, reducing risk and liability is not the primary reason for the standard. Answer (b) is incorrect because independence in appearance does not imply independence in fact. Answer (d) is incorrect because independence is the second general standard, not a field standard.

12. (1181,A1,19) (c) The requirement is to determine the circumstance which would normally preclude the expression of an opinion on the financial statements of a client. Answer (c) is the best choice because the Public Oversight Board *(Scope of Services by CPA Firms,* 1979, p. 71) has taken the position that a CPA firm should not render actuarially oriented advisory services involving the determination of policy reserves for insurance companies unless such clients utilize their own actuaries or third party actuaries to provide management with the primary actuarial capabilities. Answer (a) is incorrect because at the time a member issues a report on the client's financial statements, the client may be indebted to the member for one year's professional services fees (ET 191.104). Answer (b) is incorrect because an auditor may provide actuarial services in circumstances in which the actuarial services are a major determinant of the pension expense (ET 191.103-.104). Answer (d) is a nonsense answer because actuarial assumptions do not follow generally accepted auditing standards.

13. (580,A1,39) (d) The concept of materiality is not relevant to a CPA's direct financial interest in a client per Ethics Rule 101 which requires an appearance of independence as well as independence in fact. Elsewhere in auditing the concept of materiality is generally inherent (see para 150.04). Answer (a) is incorrect because the materiality of various transactions would help determine which would be reviewed by the auditor. Answer (b) is incorrect because the need for disclosure of particular fact or transaction would be determined by its materiality. Answer (c) is incorrect because the scope of an audit program would be affected by the materiality of the various accounts.

A.2.c.2) General and Technical Standards

14. (1179,A1,11) (b) An auditor who accepts an audit engagement and does not possess industry expertise of the new client should obtain the knowledge of matters that relate to the nature of the entity's business organization and its operating characteristics. These include types of products and services, capital structure, related parties, locations, and production, distribution, and compensation methods. Also, the auditor should become acquainted with the economic conditions, government regulations, changes in technology relating to the industry in which the entity operates. See para 311.06-.08. Answer (a) is incorrect because audit expertise rather than financial expertise is required. Presumably the auditor will be able to obtain competence with respect to the industry of the new client. Answer (c) is incorrect because there is no requirement to refer a substantial portion of the audit to another principal auditor. Answer (d) is incorrect because audit opinions are not qualified or disclaimed due to lack of capability of the auditor. If the auditor does not have the competence to undertake the engagement, the auditor should decline the engagement. Rule 201 of the Code of Professional Ethics requires CPAs to complete all engagements with professional competence, which includes adequate planning and supervision. It is within the planning aspect of an audit that the auditor should obtain a level of knowledge about the client's business that will enable the auditor to plan and perform the examination per GAAS.

A.2.c.3) Responsibilities to Clients

15. (583,A1,44) (d) The requirement is to determine the basis on which an auditor may **not** base fees. A fee based on certain findings is considered contingent and such fees are not considered ethical (ET 302.01). Answers (a), (b), and (c) all represent factors which may be considered in the determination of fees (ET 56.06–.07).

16. (582,A1,25) (b) The requirement is to determine the proper treatment of working papers when a CPA is selling an accounting practice. Permission must be obtained for both audit working papers and tax returns. Answer (a) is incorrect because the confidential client information rule does not apply to peer reviews (ET 301.01). Answer (c) is incorrect because client permission must first be obtained. Answer (d) is incorrect because if the practice is sold, the working papers and tax returns for which permission has been obtained may be given to the CPA who has purchased the practice.

A.2.c.5) Other Responsibilities

17. (1181,A1,1) (c) The requirement is to determine when a firm may designate itself "Member of the American Institute of Certified Public Accountants" on its letterhead. Answer (c) is correct because Section ET 505.01 of the Code of Professional Ethics requires that all partners or shareholders be members of the Institute for a firm to so designate itself.

18. (1181,A1,5) (a) The requirement is to determine whether CPAs may insist on auditing a portion of combined or consolidated financial statements which have already been audited by another CPA. Answer (a) is correct because although the Code of Professional Ethics prohibits encroachment (ET 55.05), auditing such a component as is considered necessary to warrant the expression of an opinion is allowed (para 543.13). Answer (b) is incorrect because a CPA may do more than a review. Answers (c) and (d) are incorrect because the CPA may insist on auditing such a component.

19. (1181,A1,43) (d) The requirement is to identify the advertisement which is not acceptable under the AICPA's Code of Professional Ethics. Rule 502 prohibits advertising which is false, misleading or deceptive. Foreign language competence [answer (a)], schools attended [answer (b)] and fees charged [answer (c)] are all acceptable (see ET 502.02). Answer (d) is correct because the AICPA has no formal endorsement procedures.

20. (581,A1,49) (d) The requirement is to determine which information in a recruiting brochure might result in a code of ethics violation. Answers (a), (b), and (c) are presented in the code of ethics as acceptable forms of advertising (ET 502.02). Answer (d) is questionable. For example, the mere engagement of a CPA firm is often confidential and thus its disclosure might violate the code of ethics (ET 391.014).

21. (1180,A1,26) (c) The retention of client records as a means of enforcing payment of an overdue audit fee is considered to be an act discreditable to the profession (ET 501.02). Since the Code of Professional Ethics explicitly prohibits the retention of records, answers (a) and (b) are incorrect. Answer (d) is inferior to answer (c) since the issue is addressed only in the Code.

22. (1178,A1,27) (d) The requirement is to identify the CPA firm name which is in violation of Rule 505 of the Code of Professional Ethics. CPAs are not permitted to practice under a firm name that is misleading about form of organization. Here, an individual is practicing as a sole proprietor in the name of a partnership.

Note that Rule 505 does permit an individual to practice in the name of the former partnership for up to two years. Here the former partner died three years ago. Answer (a) does not constitute an ethics violation as the partnership name does not contain any fictitious names and is not misleading about the form of organization. Answers (b) and (c) are not violations of the code of ethics as all partners or stockholders do not have to have their names in the partnership name. Answer (c) is not a violation of ethics as the result of being a professional corporation, as it conforms to the professional corporation characteristics per AICPA Council.

B. Control of the Audit

B.1. Planning and Supervision

23. (1181,A1,14) (d) The requirement is to determine the effect of a prospective client's refusal to allow a potential successor auditor to review certain of the predecessor auditor's working papers. Answer (d), integrity of management, is correct since obtaining evidence relative to the integrity of management is one of the objectives to be accomplished during such a review (para 315.05-.06). Answer (a), adequacy of the preplanned audit program, is incorrect since such a program will not exist before the prospective client is accepted. Answer (b), ability to establish consistency, might be a concern in certain circumstances but is usually not a problem due to the availability of prior year financial statements and accounting records. Answer (c) is incorrect since it is not actually a scope limitation since the potential successor has not yet accepted the prospective client.

24. (581,A1,15) (d) The requirement is to determine an advantage of early appointment of the auditor. The early appointment of the independent auditor enables the auditor to plan his/her work so that it may be done expeditiously and to determine the extent to which it can be done before the balance sheet date. Such preliminary work by the auditor permits the examination to be performed in a more efficient manner and to be completed at an early date after the year end (para 310.03). Answer (a) is incorrect because the overall scope of the examination must remain the same regardless of appointment date. Answer (b) is incorrect because a proper study and evaluation of internal control may be performed even without early appointment. Answer (c) similarly is incorrect because sufficient competent evidential matter must be obtained regardless of the appointment date.

25. (581,A1,58) (a) The requirement is to determine the auditor's attitude when conducting an examination. The auditor should plan and perform his/her examination with an attitude of professional skepticism, recognizing that the application of his/her auditing procedures may produce evidential matter indicating the possibility of errors or irregularities (para 327.06). Answers (b) and (c) are incorrect because the auditor does not approach an audit with mistrust or indifference. Answer (d) is less accurate than answer (a) when an auditor is considering material errors.

26. (1180,A1,53) (b) While an auditor may reply to audit committee questions concerning the detailed procedures to be applied, initiating the discussion is generally not necessary. Intitiating discussion on the work of internal auditors, answer (a), may be helpful in gaining assistance which will lead to a more efficient audit. Discussing overall effects on audit scope of changes in the company's organization, answer (c), is also acceptable and desirable so as to allow the audit committee to obtain a better understanding of the audit. Answer (d), discussing details of potential problems, is also acceptable since the audit committee as representatives of the stockholders may be able to correct for the problems and, as a minimum, should be aware of them.

27. (578,A1,33) (c) Para 9 of SAS 7 provides two examples of matters of continuing accounting significance which are usually provided to successor auditors by predecessor auditors. The two examples are working paper analysis of balance sheet accounts and matters surrounding contingencies. These are items which would facilitate the predecessor's audit. Answers (a), (b), and (d) relate to the predecessor firm's auditing philosophy rather than to data underlying the client's financial statements as indicated in answer (c), i.e., analysis of contingencies.

28. (578,A1,44) (a) When a successor auditor becomes aware of information indicating a predecessor auditor may have to take steps to have prior financial statements revised, the successor auditor cannot contact the predecessor auditor directly due to the confidential relationship to the client. Accordingly, the CPA should request that the client arrange a meeting among the three parties to discuss the potential problems and seek their resolution. See para 10 of SAS 7. Answers (b), (c), and (d) are incorrect because the CPA must have the client's permission before discussing the matter with the predecessor auditor.

B.2. Quality Control

29. (1183,A1,48) (c) The requirement is to determine what **inspection**, an element of quality control, should include. Answer (c) is the most accurate because

it provides for maintenance of documentation of the various quality control policies and procedures. Thus, it is all encompassing. Answers (a), (b), and (d), while desirable, relate to more specific areas and are thus less complete than (c).

30. (583,A1,34) (d) The requirement is to determine the primary purpose of establishing quality control policies and procedures for determining whether or not to accept a new client or to continue to perform services for a current client. Such policies and procedures should be established to minimize the likelihood of association with a client whose management lacks integrity (QC 90.23). Answer (a) is incorrect because an auditor does not **attest** to the integrity or reliability of a client. Answer (b) is incorrect because a professional does not meet the standards merely for compliance purposes. Answer (c) is incorrect because, while such policies may lessen exposure to litigation, it is not the main objective of the quality control policy.

31. (583,A1,45) (b) The requirement is to determine what periodic studies of a CPA firm's personnel advancement experience provide evidence of. The procedure of monitoring personnel advancement is the quality control element of advancement (QC 90.21). "The purpose of a firm's considering the elements of quality control and adopting quality control policies and procedures is to provide reasonable assurance that it is conforming with GAAS" (QC 200.03) in its practice as a whole. Answers (a), (c), and (d) relate more directly to the performance of individual audits.

32. (583,A1,57) (a) The requirement is to determine which answer is **not** an element of quality control. Answer (a), documentation, is not one of the nine elements of quality control (QC 10.07).

33. (582,A1,34) (c) The requirement is to determine the primary purpose of continuing professional education and training activities. Continuing professional education and training activities enable a firm to provide personnel with the knowledge required to fulfill responsibilities assigned to them and to advance within the firm (QC 10.07 f). Answer (a) is incorrect because it is less complete than (c) and because the quality control standards apply to all auditing, accounting and review services — not only auditing. Answer (b) is incorrect because it is less complete than (c). Answer (d) is incorrect because the emphasis of such education is not primarily on obtaining peer review skills.

34. (582,A1,59) (d) The requirement is to determine which parties are most likely to perform an external peer review. Peer review teams are made up of employees and partners of one or more CPA firms. Answer (a) is incorrect because Williams & Co. personnel may not do the review. Answers (b) and (c) are also incorrect since neither the Securities and Exchange Commission or the American Institute of Certified Public Accountants has an audit review staff available for peer reviews.

35. (578,A1,47) (c) QC 10.07 suggests 9 considerations in establishing policies to provide assurance that CPA firms will comply with GAAS. The 9 considerations include those concerned with assigning personnel to engagements, consultations with appropriate persons, and supervision. QC 10.09 specifically points out that keeping records concerning quality control policies and procedures may be convenient, but is not in itself an element of quality control.

C. Other Responsibilities

C.1. Detection of Errors and Irregularities

36. (1183,A1,50) (c) The requirement is to determine the situation which will cause an auditor to presume that a high risk of a defalcation exists. Incompatible functions for internal accounting control purposes are those that place any person in a position to perpetrate and to conceal errors or irregularities (e.g., thefts) in his/her normal course of duties (AU 320.36). Answer (a) is incorrect since the mere operation in numerous foreign countries is not necessarily an indication of potential defalcations. Answer (b) is incorrect because doing business with related parties may be entirely proper. Answer (d) is incorrect because lengthy exception reports do not necessarily indicate that defalcations probably exist.

37. (1179,A1,33) (c) Auditors should extend audit procedures to detect fraud when the examination indicates that fraud may exist per para 327.14. Answer (a) is incorrect because engagement letters do not specify audit procedures. Answer (b) is incorrect because while the auditor plans the examination with the attitude of skepticism, special audit procedures to detect fraud are not routinely made unless the examination indicates that material errors or irregularities may exist (para 327.05 and .14). Answer (d) is incorrect because issuance of an opinion other than an unqualified opinion does not relieve the auditor of his responsibility to detect fraud if it should be detected in complying with GAAS.

C.2. Illegal Acts by Clients

38. (1183,A1,44) (d) The requirement is to determine an auditor's responsibility when an illegal act has been discovered during the audit of a publicly held company. When an illegal act has occurred, the auditor should report the circumstances to personnel within

the client's organization who are at a level in authority high enough that appropriate action can be taken by the client (AU 328.13). Answer (a) is incorrect because deciding whether there is a need to notify parties other than personnel within the client's organization of an illegal act is the responsibility of management (AU 328.18). Answer (b) is incorrect because although the auditor may upon discovering the act know who was responsible, in many cases an investigation by representatives of the firm is necessary to determine the person(s) responsible. Answer (c) is incorrect since it is management's role to investigate the matter; the auditor should review the adequacy of management efforts.

39. (1183,A1,60) (b) The requirement is to determine an auditor's responsibility when s/he becomes aware of an illegal act sufficiently serious to warrant withdrawing from the engagement. The auditor should consult with legal counsel as to what other action, if any, should be taken (AU 328.19). Answer (a) is incorrect because deciding whether there is a need to notify parties other than personnel within the client's organization is the responsibility of management (AU 328.18). Answer (c) is incorrect because there is no requirement that all evidence be returned to the client's audit committee. Answer (d) is incorrect because any responsibility for communication between predecessor and successor auditor must be initiated, with client approval, by the successor auditor (AU 315).

40. (583,A1,8) (a) The requirement is to determine the circumstances under which an auditor's discovery of an illegal act would be most likely to result in withdrawal from the engagement. The auditor must consider the effects of illegal acts on his/her ability to rely on management's representations and the possible effects of continuing his/her association with the client (AU 328.18). Answer (b) is incorrect because a material illegal act need not always result in resignation (AU 328.18). Answer (c) is incorrect because according to the professional standards (AU 328), publicity is not directly related to a decision to withdraw. Answer (d) is incorrect because while an inability to estimate the effect of an illegal act may lead to report modification, it need not lead to withdrawal.

41. (583,A1,48) (b) The requirement is to determine whose responsibility it is to notify parties outside the client's organization regarding illegal acts. The professional standards state that the decision, whether there is a need to notify parties other than personnel within the client's organization of an illegal act, is the responsibility of management (AU 328.19).

C.3. Responsibilities in Management Advisory Services

42. (1183,A1,46) (a) The requirement is to determine the situation in which the AICPA Rules of Conduct will ordinarily be considered violated when a CPA is performing consulting services. Answer (a) represents a violation since misrepresenting the likely actual fee violates a CPA's responsibility to his/her clients to be fair and candid (ET 54). Answer (b) is incorrect because a CPA may provide services for substantially lower fees than other CPAs (ET 56.06 covers factors related to fees). Answer (c) is incorrect because fees may be competitively awarded. Answer (d) is incorrect because independence is not required in MAS or tax practice (ET 52.11).

43. (1183,A1,49) (a) The requirement is to determine the nature of a MAS consultation. In a MAS consultation a CPA bases replies largely, if not entirely, on existing personal knowledge about the client, circumstances, technical matters involved, and mutual intent of the parties (MS 11.04). Answer (b) is incorrect because an analytical approach and process is applied in a MAS engagement (MS 11.04). Answer (c) is incorrect because such knowledge typically extends beyond that obtained during an examination of the client's financial statements. Answer (d) is incorrect because a consultation usually is **not** based on the results of an operational audit.

44. (583,A1,56) (c) The requirement is to determine the condition which is necessary for a CPA to undertake a management advisory service that includes continued participation through implementation. A CPA will need to determine that the client's personnel will be able to maintain and operate the system; otherwise, the client will have received a service with no real value. Answer (a) is incorrect because the client may also assume responsibility for implementation. Answer (b) is incorrect because a CPA will often have a very limited knowledge of a client's business when compared to that possessed by management. Answer (d) is incorrect because there is no such requirement that internal control be evaluated.

45. (1182,A1,2) (c) The requirement is to determine the statement which is most consistent with the profession's attitudes toward management advisory services. An MAS practitioner should not assume the role of management (make management decisions); see MS 11.06. Answer (a) is incorrect because information obtained as a result of a management advisory services engagement may influence the performance of an audit. Answer (b) is incomplete because the client

is only one party which must consider the possible loss of auditor independence. Answer (d) is incorrect because the profession does not believe that auditors should make management decisions for their clients.

46. (582,A1,37) (c) The requirement is to determine the most accurate statement with respect to informal advice provided by CPAs during the course of an audit. In such a situation there is no presumption that an extensive study has been performed to identify and consider all pertinent facts and alternatives (MS 430.24). Answer (a) is incorrect because a CPA should not provide such informal advice without having the competence. Answer (b) is incorrect because a CPA may be exposed to liability as a consequence of such advice. Answer (d) is incorrect because such advice will often impact upon the operations of the enterprise.

47. (1180,A1,33) (b) The eight Management Advisory Services Practice Standards are included in the Statements on Management Advisory Services (MS 101.04). While answers (a), (c) and (d) are Standards, answer (b) is not.

C.4. Responsibilities in Tax Practice

48. (1183,A1,53) (a) The requirement is to determine a CPA's responsibility, in addition to communicating disapproval to the client, when a client has altered figures on a CPA prepared tax return. Professional standards require the CPA to consider the implications of the client's failure to correct the return on future relationships with the client (TX 161.05). Answer (b) is incorrect because a CPA is neither obligated to inform the IRS nor may s/he do so without client permission (TX 161.04). Answer (c) is incorrect because a CPA cannot file the return without client permission. Answer (d) is also incorrect because it suggests actions which the professional standards referred to above do not require.

49. (1182,A1,45) (a) The requirement is to determine what is implied when a CPA signs the preparer's declaration on a federal income tax return. A CPA should not sign the preparer's declaration on a misleading tax return. Answer (b) is incorrect because the tax return and supporting schedules will be prepared based on income tax principles as opposed to generally accepted accounting principles. Answer (c) is incorrect because no such standards are established by the AICPA. Answer (d) is incorrect because a CPA may resolve reasonable doubt in favor of a client (ET 131.07).

50. (1181,A1,41) (d) The requirement is to determine which answer is **not** an acceptable manner of designating an estimated figure on a federal income tax return. Answer (d) is unacceptable since a CPA who prepares a federal return should sign it without modifying the declaration (TX 191.13). Stating expressly that an amount has been estimated [answer (a)], using a round amount [answer (b)] and using an amount suggested in a treasury department guideline [answer (c)] are all acceptable (TX 151.03).

51. (581,A1,38) (a) The requirement is to determine a circumstance which would **not** be considered to be reasonable support for taking a position contrary to the Internal Revenue Code. The existence of proposed regulations is not sufficient support. Answers (b), (c), and (d) are all considered adequate (TX 201).

52. (1180,A1,13) (d) The requirement is the rationale underlying the AICPA rules of conduct allowing contingent fees for CPAs engaged in tax practice. ET 302 indicates that contingent fees are acceptable because they are based on the results of judicial proceedings or the findings of governmental agencies. Answer (a) is incorrect because there is no reason to believe that it is true in all tax practice situations. Answer (b) is incorrect because CPAs do not, in general, base their fees on what other professions charge. Answer (c) is incorrect since judicial proceedings often do involve third parties, and because the existence of a third party is not considered a criterion for permitting contingent fees.

53. (580,A1,2) (d) Statement on Responsibilities in Tax Practice No. 3 requires CPAs to make sure that a reasonable effort has been made to answer all questions on a tax return before the CPA signs the return. If data are not readily available and the question/answer is not significant to the tax liability, the answer may be omitted if the reason for the unanswered question is stated. Answer (a) is incorrect because the explanation of the omission should be provided on the return rather than held for an IRS examination. Answer (b) is incorrect because even if an answer is omitted because the data are not readily available, an explanation of the reason for the omission of an answer should be provided. Answer (c) is incorrect because if a question is not applicable to a taxpayer, the question can be answered "not applicable."

54. (580,A1,22) (c) After providing tax advice to a client, the CPA cannot be expected to notify the client of any subsequent legislative changes which affect the advice previously provided per Statement On Responsibilities In Tax Practice No. 8. If, however, the obligation for the subsequent notification is specifically undertaken by the CPA, the CPA is obviously expected to

notify the client of any such changes. Answer (a) is incorrect because the obligation does not exist unless the CPA specifically undertakes the obligation. Answer (b) is incorrect because the CPA is not required to disclaim responsibility for subsequent notification of any changes affecting the advice. Answer (d) is incorrect because the CPA should be expected to have knowledge of all changes if the CPA maintains competence in the area of taxes.

55. (1179, A1,20) (c) When a CPA learns of a material error in a previously filed tax return of a tax client, the CPA should advise the client of the error and recommend that the client correct the error in an appropriate manner per AICPA Statement of Responsibilities in Tax Practice No. 6, "Knowledge of Error: Return Preparation." Answer (a) is incorrect because the CPA's responsibility is to advise the client orally or in writing, and an affidavit with respect to the errors is not necessary. Answer (b) is incorrect because the error needs to be corrected per IRS regulations rather than based on mitigation of client cost and inconvenience. Answer (d) is incorrect because the CPA may not inform the IRS without permission per Statement No. 6 and ethics rule 301 prohibiting disclosure of confidential client information without consent of client.

C.5. Continuing Professional Education and Current Topics

56. (1181,A1,50) (b) The requirement is to determine a report which is an indication of the changing role of the CPA that calls for an extension of the auditor's attest function. Answer (b) is correct since reports on internal control based on an audit have led to publicly available attestation reports on internal control (Section 642). Reports on comparative financial statements [answer (a)], reports on separate balance sheets of holding companies [answer (c)], and reports based on incomplete financial records [answer (d)] all represent types of audit reports which have not directly led to extension of the attest function.

May 1984 Answers

57. (584,A1,8) (d) The requirement is to determine the **least** important evidence obtained during a CPA firm's evaluation of its system of quality controls. The determination of audit fees is less directly related to the objective than are the alternative answers. Answers (a) and (c) are two of the profession's nine quality control standards (QC 10.07). The objective of quality control standards is to provide reasonable assurance that engagements are performed in accordance with professional standards (QC 10.05). Thus, answer (b) is incorrect because the profession's standards require a confidential relationship between a CPA and his/her client.

58. (584,A1,33) (d) The requirement is to determine the proper handling of a difference of opinion concerning accounting and auditing matters in which the assistant auditor has asked to be disassociated from the resolution of the matter. The quality control standards require procedures for resolving differences of professional judgment and documentation of the considerations involved in the resolution of a difference of opinion (QC 90.14). Answer (a) is incorrect because it simply ignores the situation and does not resolve the difference of opinion. Answer (b) is incorrect because merely noting the disassociation does not resolve the difference. Answer (c) is incorrect because **all** such disagreements may not require expanded substantive testing.

59. (584,A1,38) (b) The requirement is to determine the proper statement relating to a CPA's responsibility in tax practice. The standards state that a position contrary to an IRS interpretation may be made without disclosure, if there is reasonable support for the position (TX 201.02). Answer (a) is incorrect because disclosure is necessary when a CPA takes a position contrary to a specific section of the IRS Code (TX 201.03). Answer (c) is incorrect because the standards do not require disclosure of positions contrary to Treasury Department regulations (TX 201.02). Answer (d) is incorrect because disclosure is not necessary when a CPA takes a position contrary to IRS interpretations.

60. (584,A1,54) (a) The requirement is to determine who is responsible for the fairness of the representations made in financial statements. The fairness of the representations made through financial statements is an implicit and integral part of management's responsibility; the financial statements are the representations of management (AU 110.02). Answer (b) is incorrect because an independent auditor's responsibility is to issue an opinion on whether the financial statements are in conformity with GAAP (AU 110.01); the auditor is not responsible for the fairness of the financials. Answer (c) is incorrect because client management is responsible for the fairness of the financials, and the audit committee is normally composed of outside board of directors members. Answer (d) is incorrect because the AICPA is not responsible for the fairness of any specific set of financial statements (except its own).

Answer Outline

Problem 1 Audit Committees

a. Audit committee is part of company organizational structure
   - Special committee formed by board of directors
   - Ideally a group of outside directors
   - Provides liaison between the CPA and board of directors
   - Helps fulfill public financial reporting responsibility

b. Audit committee helps board of directors exercise due care
   - Improves responsiveness to financial reporting duty
   - Recognizes reporting responsibility to the public investor
   - Reinforces auditor independence from management

c. Audit committee functions may include:
   1. Select auditor and review audit fee and engagement letter
   2. Review auditor's overall audit plan
   3. Review preliminary annual financial statements
   4. Review results of audit, e.g.,
      - Restrictions
      - Cooperation received
      - Audit findings
      - Audit recommendations
   5. Review auditor's evaluation of internal control
   6. Review company's accounting, financial, and operating controls
   7. Review internal audit reports
   8. Review preliminary interim financial reports
   9. Review policies on unethical and illegal procedures
   10. Review financial statements for regulatory agencies
   11. Review auditor's observations of company personnel
   12. Participate in the selection of accounting policies
   13. Review impact of proposed accounting pronouncements
   14. Review company's insurance program
   15. Review auditor's management letter

Unofficial Answer

Problem 1 Audit Committees

a. An audit committee is an important part of a company's organizational structure. It is a special committee formed by the board of directors. It is ideally a group of outside directors who have no active day-to-day operations role and who are a liaison between the independent auditor and the board of directors. The audit committee assists and advises the full board of directors, and, as such, aids the board in fulfilling its responsibility for public financial reporting.

b. Audit committees have been formed to satisfy the shareholders' need for assurance that directors are exercising due care in the performance of their duties. They were formed so that a company can be more responsive to the needs of those interested in financial reporting. Their formation, itself, is a recognition of the responsibilities of both the corporation and its auditor to the public investor. Also, they have been formed to reinforce auditor independence, particularly the appearance of independence, from the management of a company whose financial statements are being examined by the auditor.

c. The functions of an audit committee may include the following:

- Select the independent auditor; discuss audit fee with the auditor; review auditor's engagement letter.
- Review the independent auditor's overall audit plan (scope, purpose, and general audit procedures).
- Review the annual financial statements before submission to the full board of directors for approval.
- Review the results of the auditor's examination including experiences, restrictions, cooperation received, findings, and recommendations. Consider matters that the auditor believes should be brought to the attention of the directors or shareholders.
- Review the independent auditor's evaluation of the company's internal control systems.
- Review the company's accounting, financial, and operating controls.
- Review the reports of internal audit staff.
- Review interim financial reports to shareholders before they are approved by the board of directors.

• Review company policies concerning political contributions, conflicts of interest, and compliance with federal, state, and local laws and regulations, and investigate compliance with those policies.

• Review financial statements that are part of prospectuses or offering circulars; review reports before they are submitted to regulatory agencies.

• Review independent auditor's observations of financial and accounting personnel.

• Participate in the selection and establishment of accounting policies; review the accounting for specific items or transactions as well as alternative treatments and their effects.

• Review the impact of new or proposed pronouncements by the accounting profession or regulatory bodies.

• Review the company's insurance program.

• Review and discuss the independent auditor's management letter.

Answer Outline

Problem 2 Audit Deficiencies

1. Accepted engagement without determining intended use of statements
   Discuss the intended statement use with client
   Indicate alternative services available
2. Allowed client confusion about type of services to be provided
   Explain preparation of statements in contrast to audit
3. Accepted client without investigation of client
   Make inquiry of client to insure client integrity
4. Accepted engagement without confirming in writing
   Prepare an engagement letter and send to client
5. Performed work on a contingent fee basis
   Accept fee based upon work to be performed
6. Used account name "Fees for Limited Audit Engagement"
   Do not use word "audit" in nonaudit engagements
   Use the term "accounting services"
7. Ignored missing invoices
   Advise client of missing invoices
   Encourage investigation of missing invoices
8. Prepared incomplete set of financial statements
   Prepare a statement of changes in financial position
   If not presented, disclose in disclaimer of opinion
9. Failed to disclose noncompliance with GAAP in footnotes
   Insist on appropriate revision of statements
   If not revised, disclose noncompliance in disclaimer of opinion
10. Failed to indicate clearly that statements were unaudited
    "Without complete audit verification" implies some audit performed
    Indicate statements are not audited and no opinion is expressed
    Mark each page "unaudited"

Unofficial Answer

Problem 2 Audit Deficiencies

Inappropriate Action	What Brown Should Have Done to Avoid Inappropriate Action
• Brown should not have accepted the assignment without determining the intended use of the financial statements.	• Brown should have discussed with Calhoun the intended use of the statements. • Brown should have appraised Calhoun's needs and expectations and should have advised Calhoun about the types of professional services appropriate in light of Calhoun's objectives.
• Brown should not have ignored Calhoun's confusion about the services provided.	• Brown should have explained to Calhoun that preparation of financial statements is normally an engagement for accounting services and not an audit of financial statements.

Inappropriate Action	What Brown Should Have Done to Avoid Inappropriate Action
• There is no indication that Brown considered policies and procedures with regard to acceptance of this new client.	• Brown should have made appropriate inquiries to minimize any likelihood of association with a client whose management lacks integrity.
• Brown should not have accepted a verbal engagement without confirming it in writing.	• The verbal commitment should have been followed up with an engagement letter that included a description, as specific as possible, of the nature and extent of the accounting service to be performed.
• Brown should not have accepted the contingent fee arrangement.	• Brown should have accepted a fee arrangement that was based on the work to be performed, not on a contingency such as finishing within a certain time period.
• Brown should not have suggested that the account name be changed to "fees for limited audit engagement."	• The word "audit" should not be used on nonaudit engagements. Brown should not have suggested any change or should have persuaded Calhoun to use the words "accounting services" and should have made certain that Calhoun understood the difference between an accounting service and an audit examination of the financial statements in accordance with generally accepted auditing standards.
• Brown should not have ignored the missing invoices.	• Brown should have advised Calhoun of the missing invoices. • Brown should have suggested that Calhoun expedite an investigation of the missing invoices, or, if Calhoun so desired, Brown could have investigated the matter as an additional accounting service.
• Brown should not have prepared an incomplete set of financial statements.	• Brown should have prepared a statement of changes in financial position, which APB Opinion no. 19 requires to be presented whenever a balance sheet and income statement are presented. • If Calhoun did not wish to include a statement of changes in financial position with the other basic statements, Brown should have appropriately referred to the incomplete presentation in the disclaimer of opinion.
• Brown should not have prepared a footnote that failed to disclose lack of conformity with generally accepted accounting principles.	• Brown should have insisted on appropriate revision of the unaudited statements so that they no longer reflect assets at replacement costs. • If Calhoun did not wish to make revisions, Brown should set forth reservations in the disclaimer of opinion with respect to the unacceptable accounting and lack of disclosure and the dollar effect.

Inappropriate Action	What Brown Should Have Done to Avoid Inappropriate Action
• Brown's attempt at a disclaimer did not clearly indicate that the statements had not been audited.	• Brown should have avoided using the words "without complete audit verification." These words imply that some type of audit was performed, and, because of them, Brown may be assuming more responsibility than originally intended. • Brown's disclaimer of opinion should have stated that the financial statements "were not audited by me and accordingly I do not express an opinion on them." • In addition each page of the financal statements should have been clearly and conspicuously marked as "unaudited."

Answer Outline

Problem 3 Violations of GAAS

1. Adequate technical training and auditing proficiency
   Students had neither
2. Independence
   Contingent fee nullifies
3. Due professional care
   Lack of review and supervision
   Failure to comply with GAAS
4. Adequate planning and supervision
   Inadequate planning and no supervision
5. Proper study and evaluation of internal control
   None undertaken
6. Sufficient competent evidential matter
   None obtained
7. In accordance with GAAP
   No reference in report
   No basis for assertion
8. GAAP consistently applied
   No reference in report
   No basis for assertion
9. Adequate informative disclosure
   No statement footnotes
   No exception in report
10. Expression of opinion on statements as a whole
    Given but not on basis of proper audit

Unofficial Answer

Problem 3 Violations of GAAS

Brief Description of Generally Accepted Auditing Standards	Holme's Actions Resulting in Failure to Comply With Generally Accepted Auditing Standards
General Standards	
(1) The examination is to be performed by a person or persons having adequate technical training and proficiency as an auditor.	(1) It was inappropriate for Holmes to hire two students to conduct the audit. The examination must be conducted by persons with proper education and experience in the field of auditing. Although a junior assistant has not completed his formal education he may help in the conduct of the examination as long as there is proper supervision and review.

Brief Description of Generally Accepted Auditing Standards	Holmes's Actions Resulting in Failure to Comply With Generally Accepted Auditing Standards
(2) In all matters relating to the assignment, an independence in mental attitude is to be maintained by the auditor or auditors.	(2) To satisfy the second general standard, Holmes must be without bias with respect to the client under audit. Holmes has an obligation for fairness to the owners, management, and creditors who may rely on the report. Because of the financial interest in whether the bank loan is granted to Ray, Holmes is independent in neither fact nor appearance with respect to the assignment undertaken.
(3) Due professional care is to be exercised in the performance of the examination and the preparation of the report.	(3) This standard requires Holmes to perform the audit with due care, which imposes on Holmes and everyone in Holmes's organization a responsibility to observe the standards of field work and reporting. Exercise of due care requires critical review at every level of supervision of the work done and the judgments exercised by those assisting in the examination. Holmes did not review the work or the judgments of the assistants and clearly failed to adhere to this standard.
Standards of Field Work	
(1) The work is to be adequately planned and assistants, if any, are to be properly supervised.	(1) This standard recognizes that early appointment of the auditor has advantages for the auditor and the client. Holmes accepted the engagement without considering the availability of competent staff. In addition, Holmes failed to supervise the assistants. The work performed was not adequately planned.
(2) There is to be a proper study and evaluation of the existing internal control as a basis for reliance thereon and for the determination of the resultant extent of the tests to which auditing procedures are to be restricted.	(2) Holmes did not study the system of internal control nor did the assistants conduct such a study. There appears to have been no audit examination at all. The work performed was more an accounting service than it was an auditing service.
(3) Sufficient, competent evidential matter is to be obtained through inspection, observation, inquiries, and confirmations to afford a reasonable basis for an opinion regarding the financial statements under examination.	(3) Holmes acquired no evidence that would support the financial statements. Holmes merely checked the mathematical accuracy of the records and summarized the accounts. Standard audit procedures and techniques were not performed.

Brief Description of Generally Accepted Auditing Standards	Holmes's Actions Resulting in Failure to Comply With Generally Accepted Auditing Standards
Standards of Reporting	
(1) The report shall state whether the financial statements are presented in accordance with generally accepted accounting principles.	(1) Holmes's report made no reference to generally accepted accounting principles. Because Holmes did not conduct a proper examination, the report should state that no opinion can be expressed as to the fair presentation of the financial statements in accordance with generally accepted accounting principles.
(2) The report shall state whether such principles have been consistently observed in the current period in relation to the preceding period.	(2) Holmes's report makes no reference to the consistent application of accounting principles. Holmes's improper examination would not enable such an expression on consistency.
(3) Informative disclosures in the financial statements are to be regarded as reasonably adequate unless otherwise stated in the report.	(3) Management is primarily responsible for adequate disclosure in the financial statements, but when the statements do not contain adequate disclosures the auditor should make such disclosures in the auditor's report. In this case both the statements and the auditor's report lack adequate disclosures.
(4) The report shall either contain an expression of opinion regarding the financial statements taken as a whole or an assertion to the effect that an opinion cannot be expressed. When an overall opinion cannot be expressed, the reasons therefor should be stated. In all cases where an auditor's name is associated with financial statements, the report should contain a clear-cut indication of the character of the auditor's examination, if any, and the degree of responsibility he is taking.	(4) Although the Holmes report contains an expression of opinion, such opinion is not based on the results of a proper audit examination. Holmes should disclaim an opinion because he failed to conduct an examination in accordance with generally accepted auditing standards.

Answer Outline

Problem 4 EDP Services

a. Services that Savage may perform
   1. Counsel on potential expansion plans
   2. Search for and interview new personnel
   3. Train personnel

   Services that Savage may not perform
   1. Hire new personnel
   2. Instruct and train new personnel
   3. Supervise operation of system
   4. Monitor client's source documents and make changes in EDP generated data without client concurrence

b. Significant matters of which client should be informed
   1. Engagement objectives
   2. Scope
   3. Approach
   4. Role of personnel
   5. Manner in which results are to be communicated
   6. Timetable
   7. Fee

c. Degree of knowledge necessary to supervise specialist
   Ability to define tasks
   Ability to evaluate end product

Unofficial Answer

Problem 4 EDP Services

a.

Services that Savage may perform	*Services that Savage may not perform*
Counsel on potential expansion plans. Search for and interview new personnel. Train personnel.	Hire new personnel. Supervise the operation of the system. Monitor client-prepared source documents and make changes in basic EDP generated data without concurrence of the client.

b. The significant matters related to an engagement generally include (a) the engagement's objectives, (b) the scope, (c) the approach, (d) the role of all personnel, (e) the manner in which results are to be communicated, (f) the timetable, and (g) the fee.

c. Savage must be qualified to supervise and evaluate the work of specialist employees. Although supervision does not require that Savage be qualified to perform each of the specialist's tasks, Savage should be able to define the tasks and evaluate the end product.

Multiple Choice Questions (1–79)

1. In the evaluation of internal accounting control, the auditor is basically concerned that the system provides reasonable assurance that

a. Controls have **not** been circumvented by collusion.
b. Errors have been prevented or detected.
c. Operational efficiency has been achieved in accordance with management plans.
d. Management can **not** override the system.

2. The primary purpose of the auditor's study and evaluation of internal control is to provide a basis for

a. Determining whether procedures and records that are concerned with the safeguarding of assets are reliable.
b. Constructive suggestions to clients concerning improvements in internal control.
c. Determining the nature, extent, and timing of audit tests to be applied.
d. The expression of an opinion.

3. For good internal control, which of the following functions should **not** be the responsibility of the treasurer's department?

a. Data processing.
b. Handling of cash.
c. Custody of securities.
d. Establishing credit policies.

4. Which of the following internal control features would an auditor be **least** likely to review?

a. Segregation of the asset-handling and record-keeping functions.
b. Company policy regarding credit and collection efforts.
c. Sales and cost records classified by products.
d. Authorization of additions to plant and equipment.

5. Which of the following would be **least** likely to be considered an objective of a system of internal control?

a. Checking the accuracy and reliability of accounting data.
b. Detecting management fraud.
c. Encouraging adherence to managerial policies.
d. Safeguarding assets.

6. Which of the following sets of duties would ordinarily be considered basically incompatible in terms of good internal control?

a. Preparation of monthly statements to customers and maintenance of the accounts receivable subsidiary ledger.
b. Posting to the general ledger and approval of additions and terminations relating to the payroll.
c. Custody of unmailed signed checks and maintenance of expense subsidiary ledgers.
d. Collection of receipts on account and maintaining accounts receivable records.

7. Which of the following would **not** be considered an internal control feature?

a. Use of the double-entry system.
b. An internal audit staff.
c. Competent personnel.
d. A comparison-shopping staff.

8. Which of the following is an administrative control?

a. Authorizing credit terms.
b. Execution of transactions.
c. Recording original data.
d. Accountability over source data.

9. When considering internal control, an auditor must be aware of the concept of reasonable assurance which recognizes that

a. The employment of competent personnel provides assurance that the objectives of internal control will be achieved.
b. The establishment and maintenance of a system of internal control is an important responsibility of the management and not of the auditor.
c. The cost of internal control should not exceed the benefits expected to be derived from internal control.
d. The segregation of incompatible functions is necessary to obtain assurance that the internal control is effective.

10. Which of the following would be **least** likely to suggest to an auditor that the client's management may have overridden the internal control system?

a. Differences are always disclosed on a computer exception report.
b. Management does **not** correct internal control weaknesses that it knows about.
c. There have been two new controllers this year.
d. There are numerous delays in preparing timely internal financial reports.

11. An auditor engaged to report on internal accounting control, distinguishes between primary control procedures and secondary control procedures. Primary control procedures are designed to achieve one or more specific objectives of a system of internal accounting control. Which of the following would be a primary control procedure?
   a. Comparison of receiving reports with vendor invoices prior to payment.
   b. Comparison of budgeted costs for direct labor with actual costs for direct labor.
   c. Comparison of actual costs for raw materials with standard costs for raw materials.
   d. Comparison of the cost of goods sold with credit sales.

12. Of the following statements about an internal control system, which one is **not** valid?
   a. No one person should be responsible for the custodial responsibility and the recording responsibility for an asset.
   b. Transactions must be properly authorized before such transactions are processed.
   c. Because of the cost/benefit relationship, a client may apply control procedures on a test basis.
   d. Control procedures reasonably insure that collusion among employees can **not** occur.

13. Proper segregation of functional responsibilities calls for separation of the
   a. Authorization, approval, and execution functions.
   b. Authorization, execution, and payment functions.
   c. Receiving, shipping, and custodial functions.
   d. Authorization, recording, and custodial functions.

14. Effective internal control requires organizational independence of departments. Organizational independence would be impaired in which of the following situations?
   a. The internal auditors report to the audit committee of the board of directors.
   b. The controller reports to the vice president of production.
   c. The payroll accounting department reports to the chief accountant.
   d. The cashier reports to the treasurer.

15. Which of the following best describes the inherent limitations that should be recognized by an auditor when considering the potential effectiveness of a system of internal accounting control?
   a. Procedures whose effectiveness depends on segregation of duties can be circumvented by collusion.
   b. The competence and integrity of client personnel provides an environment conducive to accounting control and provides assurance that effective control will be achieved.
   c. Procedures designed to assure the execution and recording of transactions in accordance with proper authorizations are effective against irregularities perpetrated by management.
   d. The benefits expected to be derived from effective internal accounting control usually do not exceed the costs of such control.

16. A system of internal accounting control normally would include procedures that are designed to provide reasonable assurance that
   a. Employees act with integrity when performing their assigned tasks.
   b. Transactions are executed in accordance with management's general or specific authorization.
   c. Decision processes leading to management's authorization of transactions are sound.
   d. Collusive activities would be detected by segregation of employee duties.

17. The Foreign Corrupt Practices Act requires that
   a. Auditors engaged to examine the financial statements of publicly-held companies report all illegal payments to the SEC.
   b. Publicly-held companies establish independent audit committees to monitor the effectiveness of their system of internal control.
   c. U.S. firms doing business abroad report sizable payments to non U.S. citizens to the Justice Department.
   d. Publicly-held companies devise and maintain an adequate system of internal accounting control.

18. The auditor observes client employees during the review of the system of internal control in order to
   a. Prepare a flowchart.

b. Update information contained in the organization and procedure manuals.
c. Corroborate the information obtained during the initial review of the system.
d. Determine the extent of compliance with quality control standards.

19. Which of the following statements regarding auditor documentation of the client's system of internal control is correct?
a. Documentation must include flow charts.
b. Documentation must include procedural write-ups.
c. No documentation is necessary although it is desirable.
d. No one particular form of documentation is necessary, and the extent of documentation may vary.

20. Which of the following would be **inappropriate** during a preliminary evaluation of the system of internal control?
a. Completion of an internal control questionnaire.
b. Use of attribute sampling.
c. Oral inquiries.
d. Review of an accounting manual prepared by the client.

21. Compliance testing is performed in order to determine whether or not
a. Controls are functioning as designed.
b. Necessary controls are absent.
c. Incompatible functions exist.
d. Material dollar errors exist.

22. After finishing the review phase of the study and evaluation of internal control in an audit engagement, the auditor should perform compliance tests on
a. Those controls that the auditor plans to rely upon.
b. Those controls in which material weaknesses were identified.
c. Those controls that have a material effect upon the financial statement balances.
d. A random sample of the controls that were reviewed.

23. A CPA examines a sample of copies of December and January sales invoices for the initials of the person who verified the quantitative data. This is an example of a
a. Compliance test.
b. Substantive test.
c. Cutoff test.
d. Statistical test.

24. The objective of the tolerable rate in sampling for compliance testing on an internal control system is to
a. Determine the probability of the auditor's conclusion based upon reliance factors.
b. Determine that financial statements taken as a whole are not materially in error.
c. Estimate the reliability of substantive tests.
d. Estimate the range of procedural deviations in the population.

25. Which of the following would be **least** likely to be included in an auditor's tests of compliance?
a. Inspection.
b. Observation.
c. Inquiry.
d. Confirmation.

26. Which of the following audit tests would be regarded as a test of "compliance?"
a. Tests of the specific items making up the balance in a given general ledger account.
b. Tests of the inventory pricing to vendors' invoices.
c. Tests of the signatures on cancelled checks to board of director's authorizations.
d. Tests of the additions to property, plant, and equipment by physical inspections.

27. The reliance placed on substantive tests in relation to the reliance placed on internal control varies in a relationship that is ordinarily
a. Parallel.
b. Inverse.
c. Direct.
d. Equal.

28. An independent auditor has concluded that the client's records, procedures, and representations can be relied upon based on tests made during the year when internal control was found to be effective. The auditor should test the records, procedures, and representations again at year-end if
a. Inquiries and observations lead the auditor to believe that conditions have changed significantly.
b. Comparisons of year-end balances with like balances at prior dates revealed significant fluctuations.

c. Unusual transactions occurred subsequent to the completion of the interim audit work.
d. Client records are in a condition that facilitate effective and efficient testing.

29. Tracing copies of sales invoices to shipping documents will provide evidence that all
a. Shipments to customers were recorded as receivables.
b. Billed sales were shipped.
c. Debits to the subsidiary accounts receivable ledger are for sales shipped.
d. Shipments to customers were billed.

30. Which of the following is **not** a universal rule for achieving strong internal control over cash?
a. Separate the cash handling and record-keeping functions.
b. Decentralize the receiving of cash as much as possible.
c. Deposit each day's cash receipts by the end of the day.
d. Have bank reconciliations performed by employees independent with respect to handling cash.

31. When a customer fails to include a remittance advice with a payment, it is a common practice for the person opening the mail to prepare one. Consequently, mail should be opened by which of the following four company employees?
a. Credit manager.
b. Receptionist.
c. Sales manager.
d. Accounts receivable clerk.

32. To verify that all sales transactions have been recorded, a test of transactions should be completed on a representative sample drawn from
a. Entries in the sales journal.
b. The billing clerk's file of sales orders.
c. A file of duplicate copies of sales invoices for which all prenumbered forms in the series have been accounted for.
d. The shipping clerk's file of duplicate copies of bills of lading.

33. For effective internal control, the billing function should be performed by the
a. Accounting department.
b. Sales department.
c. Shipping department.
d. Credit and collection department.

34. Which one of the following would the auditor consider to be an incompatible operation if the cashier receives remittances from the mailroom?
a. The cashier prepares the daily deposit.
b. The cashier makes the daily deposit at a local bank.
c. The cashier posts the receipts to the accounts receivable subsidiary ledger cards.
d. The cashier endorses the checks.

35. Which of the following would be the best protection for a company that wishes to prevent the "lapping" of trade accounts receivable?
a. Segregate duties so that the bookkeeper in charge of the general ledger has no access to incoming mail.
b. Segregate duties so that no employee has access to both checks from customers and currency from daily cash receipts.
c. Have customers send payments directly to the company's depository bank.
d. Request that customers' payment checks be made payable to the company and addressed to the treasurer.

36. Which of the following internal control procedures will most likely prevent the concealment of a cash shortage resulting from the improper write-off of a trade account receivable?
a. Write-offs must be approved by a responsible officer after review of credit department recommendations and supporting evidence.
b. Write-offs must be supported by an aging schedule showing that only receivables overdue several months have been written off.
c. Write offs must be approved by the cashier who is in a position to know if the receivables have, in fact, been collected.
d. Write-offs must be authorized by company field sales employees who are in a position to determine the financial standing of the customers.

37. The **least** crucial element of internal control over cash is
a. Separation of cash record keeping from custody of cash.
b. Preparation of the monthly bank reconciliation.
c. Batch processing of checks.
d. Separation of cash receipts from cash disbursements.

38. An auditor compares information on canceled checks with information contained in the cash disbursement journal. The objective of this test is to determine that

a. Recorded cash disbursement transactions are properly authorized.
b. Proper cash purchase discounts have been recorded.
c. Cash disbursements are for goods and services actually received.
d. **No** discrepancies exist between the data on the checks and the data in the journal.

39. Which of the following is an effective internal accounting control measure that encourages receiving department personnel to count and inspect all merchandise received?

a. Quantities ordered are excluded from the receiving department copy of the purchase order.
b. Vouchers are prepared by accounts payable department personnel only after they match item counts on the receiving report with the purchase order.
c. Receiving department personnel are expected to match and reconcile the receiving report with the purchase order.
d. Internal auditors periodically examine, on a surprise basis, the receiving department copies of receiving reports.

40. A client's materials-purchasing cycle begins with requisitions from user departments and ends with the receipt of materials and the recognition of a liability. An auditor's primary objective in reviewing this cycle is to

a. Evaluate the reliability of information generated as a result of the purchasing process.
b. Investigate the physical handling and recording of unusual acquisitions of materials.
c. Consider the need to be on hand for the annual physical count if this system is not functioning properly.
d. Ascertain that materials said to be ordered, received, and paid for are on hand.

41. Which of the following is an effective internal accounting control over cash payments?

a. Signed checks should be mailed under the supervision of the check signer.
b. Spoiled checks which have been voided should be disposed of immediately.
c. Checks should be prepared only by persons responsible for cash receipts and cash disbursements.
d. A check-signing machine with two signatures should be utilized.

42. The physical count of inventory of a retailer was higher than shown by the perpetual records. Which of the following could explain the difference?

a. Inventory items had been counted but the tags placed on the items had **not** been taken off the items and added to the inventory accumulation sheets.
b. Credit memos for several items returned by customers had **not** been recorded.
c. No journal entry had been made on the retailer's books for several items returned to its suppliers.
d. An item purchased "FOB shipping point" had **not** arrived at the date of the inventory count and had **not** been reflected in the perpetual records.

43. A client's physical count of inventories was higher than the inventory quantities per the perpetual records. This situation could be the result of the failure to record

a. Sales.
b. Sales discounts.
c. Purchases.
d. Purchase returns.

44. Apex Manufacturing Corporation mass produces eight different products. The controller who is interested in strengthening internal controls over the accounting for materials used in production would be most likely to implement

a. An economic order quantity (EOQ) system.
b. A job order cost accounting system.
c. A perpetual inventory system.
d. A separation of duties among production personnel.

45. When evaluating inventory controls with respect to segregation of duties, a CPA would be **least** likely to

a. Inspect documents.
b. Make inquiries.
c. Observe procedures.
d. Consider policy and procedure manuals.

46. Which of the following is an internal control weakness for a company whose inventory of supplies consists of a large number of individual items?

a. Supplies of relatively little value are expensed when purchased.
b. The cycle basis is used for physical counts.
c. The storekeeper is responsible for maintenance of perpetual inventory records.
d. Perpetual inventory records are maintained only for items of significant value.

47. To minimize the opportunities for fraud, unclaimed cash payroll should be
a. Deposited in a safe deposit box.
b. Held by the payroll custodian.
c. Deposited in a special bank account.
d. Held by the controller.

48. A large retail enterprise has established a policy which requires that the paymaster deliver all unclaimed payroll checks to the internal auditing department at the end of each payroll distribution day. This policy was **most** likely adopted in order to
a. Assure that employees who were absent on a payroll distribution day are **not** paid for that day.
b. Prevent the paymaster from cashing checks which are unclaimed for several weeks.
c. Prevent a bona fide employee's check from being claimed by another employee.
d. Detect any fictitious employee who may have been placed on the payroll.

49. Proper internal control over the cash payroll function would mandate which of the following?
a. The payroll clerk should fill the envelopes with cash and a computation of the net wages.
b. Unclaimed pay envelopes should be retained by the paymaster.
c. Each employee should be asked to sign a receipt.
d. A separate checking account for payroll be maintained.

50. A CPA reviews a client's payroll procedures. The CPA would consider internal control to be less than effective if a payroll department supervisor was assigned the responsibility for
a. Reviewing and approving time reports for subordinate employees.
b. Distributing payroll checks to employees.
c. Hiring subordinate employees.
d. Initiating requests for salary adjustments for subordinate employees.

51. Effective internal accounting control over the payroll function should include procedures that segregate the duties of making salary payments to employees and
a. Controlling unemployment insurance claims.
b. Maintaining employee personnel records.
c. Approving employee fringe benefits.
d. Hiring new employees.

52. Effective internal control over the payroll function would include which of the following?
a. Total time recorded on time-clock punch cards should be reconciled to job reports by employees responsible for those specific jobs.
b. Payroll department employees should be supervised by the management of the personnel department.
c. Payroll department employees should be responsible for maintaining employee personnel records.
d. Total time spent on jobs should be compared with total time indicated on time-clock punch cards.

53. With respect to an internal control measure that will assure accountability for fixed asset retirements, management should implement a system that includes
a. Continuous analysis of miscellaneous revenue to locate any cash proceeds from sale of plant assets.
b. Periodic inquiry of plant executives by internal auditors as to whether any plant assets have been retired.
c. Continuous utilization of serially numbered retirement work orders.
d. Periodic observation of plant assets by the internal auditors.

54. Which of the following is the most important internal control procedure over acquisitions of property, plant and equipment?
a. Establishing a written company policy distinguishing between capital and revenue expenditures.
b. Using a budget to forecast and control acquisitions and retirements.
c. Analyzing monthly variances between authorized expenditures and actual costs.
d. Requiring acquisitions to be made by user departments.

55. A company holds bearer bonds as a short-term investment. Responsibility for custody of these bonds and submission of coupons for periodic interest collections probably should be delegated to the

a. Chief Accountant.
b. Internal Auditor.
c. Cashier.
d. Treasurer.

56. Where no independent stock transfer agents are employed and the corporation issues its own stocks and maintains stock records, cancelled stock certificates should

a. Be defaced to prevent reissuance and attached to their corresponding stubs.
b. Not be defaced but segregated from other stock certificates and retained in a cancelled certificates file.
c. Be destroyed to prevent fraudulent reissuance.
d. Be defaced and sent to the secretary of state.

57. In order to avoid the misappropriation of company-owned marketable securities, which of the following is the best course of action that can be taken by the management of a company with a large portfolio of marketable securities?

a. Require that one trustworthy and bonded employee be responsible for access to the safekeeping area, where securities are kept.
b. Require that employees who enter and leave the safekeeping area sign and record in a log the exact reason for their access.
c. Require that employees involved in the safekeeping function maintain a subsidiary control ledger for securities on a current basis.
d. Require that the safekeeping function for securities be assigned to a bank that will act as a custodial agent.

58. A company has additional temporary funds to invest. The board of directors decided to purchase marketable securities and assigned the future purchase and sale decisions to a responsible financial executive. The best person(s) to make periodic reviews of the investment activity should be

a. The investment committee of the board of directors.
b. The treasurer.
c. The corporate controller.
d. The chief operating officer.

59. The use of fidelity bonds protects a company from embezzlement losses and also

a. Minimizes the possibility of employing persons with dubious records in positions of trust.
b. Reduces the company's need to obtain expensive business interruption insurance.
c. Allows the company to substitute the fidelity bonds for various parts of internal accounting control.
d. Protects employees who made unintentional errors from possible monetary damages resulting from such errors.

60. A secondary objective of the auditor's study and evaluation of internal control is that the study and evaluation provide

a. A basis for constructive suggestions concerning improvements in internal control.
b. A basis for reliance on the system of internal accounting control.
c. An assurance that the records and documents have been maintained in accordance with existing company policies and procedures.
d. A basis for the determination of the resultant extent of the tests to which auditing procedures are to be restricted.

61. The auditor who becomes aware of a material weakness in internal control is required to communicate this to the

a. Audit committee and board of directors.
b. Senior management and board of directors.
c. Board of directors and internal auditors.
d. Internal auditors and senior management.

62. In general, a material internal control weakness may be defined as a condition in which material errors or irregularities would ordinarily **not** be detected within a timely period by

a. An auditor during the normal study and evaluation of the system of internal control.
b. A controller when reconciling accounts in the general ledger.
c. Employees in the normal course of performing their assigned functions.
d. The chief financial officer when reviewing interim financial statements.

63. When an auditor issues an unqualified opinion on an entity's system of internal accounting control, it is implied that the

a. Entity has **not** violated provisions of the Foreign Corrupt Practices Act.
b. Likelihood of management fraud is minimal.
c. Financial records are sufficiently reliable to permit the preparation of financial statements.
d. Entity's system of internal accounting control is in conformity with criteria established by its audit committee.

64. A CPA's study and evaluation of the system of internal accounting control in an audit

a. Is generally more limited than that made in connection with an engagement to express an opinion on the system of internal accounting control.
b. Is generally more extensive than that made in connection with an engagement to express an opinion on the system of internal accounting control.
c. Is generally identical to that made in connection with an engagement to express an opinion on the system of internal accounting control.
d. Will generally result in the CPA expressing an opinion on the system of internal accounting control.

65. Which of the following **best** describes how the detailed audit program of the CPA who is engaged to audit the financial statements of a large publicly held company compares with the audit client's comprehensive internal audit program?

a. The comprehensive internal audit program is more detailed and covers areas that would normally **not** be reviewed by the CPA.
b. The comprehensive internal audit program is more detailed although it covers less areas than would normally be covered by the CPA.
c. The comprehensive internal audit program is substantially identical to the audit program used by the CPA because both review substantially identical areas.
d. The comprehensive internal audit program is less detailed and covers less areas than would normally be reviewed by the CPA.

66. In connection with the examination of financial statements by an independent auditor, the client suggests that members of the internal audit staff be utilized to minimize audit costs. Which of the following tasks could most appropriately be delegated to the internal audit staff?

a. Selection of accounts receivable for confirmation, based upon the internal auditor's judgment as to how many accounts and which accounts will provide sufficient coverage.
b. Preparation of schedules for negative accounts receivable responses.
c. Evaluation of the internal control for accounts receivable and sales.
d. Determination of the adequacy of the allowance for doubtful accounts.

67. An independent auditor might consider the procedures performed by the internal auditors because

a. They are employees whose work must be reviewed during substantive testing.
b. They are employees whose work might be relied upon.
c. Their work impacts upon the cost/benefit tradeoff in evaluating inherent limitations.
d. Their degree of independence may be inferred by the nature of their work.

68. Taylor Sales Corp. maintains a large full-time internal audit staff which reports directly to the chief accountant. Audit reports prepared by the internal auditors indicate that the system is functioning as it should and that the accounting records are reliable. The independent auditor will probably

a. Eliminate compliance testing.
b. Increase the depth of the study and evaluation of administrative controls.
c. Avoid duplicating the work performed by the internal audit staff.
d. Place limited reliance on the work performed by the internal audit staff.

May 1984 Questions

69. The auditor would be **least** likely to be concerned about internal control as it relates to

a. Land and buildings.
b. Common stock.
c. Shareholder meetings.
d. Minutes of board of directors' meetings.

70. Which of the following is **not** an auditing procedure that is commonly used in performing compliance tests?

a. Inquiring.
b. Observing.
c. Confirming.
d. Inspecting.

71. The accountant's report expressing an opinion on an entity's system of internal accounting control should state that the

a. Establishment and maintenance of the system of internal control are the responsibility of management.
b. Objectives of the client's system of internal accounting control are being met.
c. Study and evaluation of the system of internal control was conducted in accordance with generally accepted auditing standards.
d. Inherent limitations of the client's system of internal accounting control were examined.

72. When reviewing the system of internal control, the auditor would ordinarily prepare and obtain answers to an internal control questionnaire based upon a tentative flowchart of the system. The next step should ordinarily be to

a. Determine the extent of audit work necessary to form an opinion.
b. Arrive at a decision regarding the effectiveness of the internal control system.
c. Gather enough evidence to determine if the internal control system is functioning as described.
d. Make a preliminary evaluation of the internal control system assuming satisfactory compliance.

73. The accountant's report expressing an opinion on an entity's system of internal accounting control would **not** include a

a. Description of the scope of the engagement.
b. Specific date that the report covers, rather than a period of time.
c. Brief explanation of the broad objectives and inherent limitations of internal accounting control.
d. Statement that the entity's system of internal accounting control is consistent with that of the prior year after giving effect to subsequent changes.

74. After the study and evaluation of a client's system of internal accounting control has been completed, an auditor might decide to

a. Increase the extent of compliance and substantive testing in areas where the system of internal accounting control is strong.
b. Reduce the extent of compliance testing in areas where the system of internal accounting control is strong.
c. Reduce the extent of both substantive and compliance testing in areas where the system of internal accounting control is strong.
d. Increase the extent of substantive testing in areas where the system of internal accounting control is weak.

75. Which of the following is the correct order of performing the auditing procedures A through C below?

A = Compliance tests.
B = Preparation of a flowchart depicting the client's system of internal control.
C = Substantive tests.

a. ABC
b. ACB
c. BAC
d. BCA

76. In a properly designed internal accounting control system, the same employee should **not** be permitted to

a. Sign checks and cancel supporting documents.
b. Receive merchandise and prepare a receiving report.
c. Prepare disbursement vouchers and sign checks.
d. Initiate a request to order merchandise and approve merchandise received.

77. The proper use of prenumbered termination notice forms by the payroll department should provide assurance that all

a. Uncashed payroll checks were issued to employees who have **not** been terminated.
b. Personnel files are kept up to date.
c. Employees who have **not** been terminated receive their payroll checks.
d. Terminated employees are removed from the payroll.

78. A well prepared flowchart should make it easier for the auditor to

a. Prepare audit procedure manuals.
b. Prepare detailed job descriptions.

c. Trace the origin and disposition of documents.
d. Assess the degree of accuracy of financial data.

79. A well functioning system of internal control over the inventory/production functions would provide that finished goods are to be accepted for stock only after presentation of a completed production order and a(n)

a. Shipping order.
b. Material requisition.
c. Bill of lading.
d. Inspection report.

Problems

Problem 1 Purchase Orders (1183, A2)

(15 to 25 minutes)

Properly designed and utilized forms facilitate adherence to prescribed internal accounting control policies and procedures. One such form might be a multicopy purchase order, with one copy intended to be mailed to the vendor. The remaining copies would ordinarily be distributed to the stores, purchasing, receiving and accounting departments.

The following purchase order is currently being used by National Industrial Corporation:

PURCHASE ORDER

SEND INVOICE ONLY TO:

297 HARDINGTEN DR., BX., NY 10461

TO ______________________________ **SHIP TO** ______________________________

______________________________ ______________________________

______________________________ ______________________________

DATE TO BE SHIPPED	SHIP VIA	DISC. TERMS	FREIGHT TERMS	ADV. ALLOWANCE	SPECIAL ALLOWANCE

QUANTITY	DESCRIPTION

PURCHASE CONDITIONS

1. Supplier will be responsible for extra freight cost on partial shipment, unless prior permission is obtained.
2. Please acknowledge this order.
3. Please notify us immediately if you are unable to complete order.
4. All items must be individually packed.

Required:

a. In addition to the name of the company, what other necessary information would an auditor recommend be included in the illustrative purchase order?

b. What primary internal control functions are served by the purchase order copies that are distributed to the stores, purchasing, receiving and accounting departments?

Problem 2 Purchases and Disbursements Flowchart (583,A5)

(15 to 25 minutes)

The following illustrates a Manual System for Executing Purchases and Cash Disbursements Transactions.

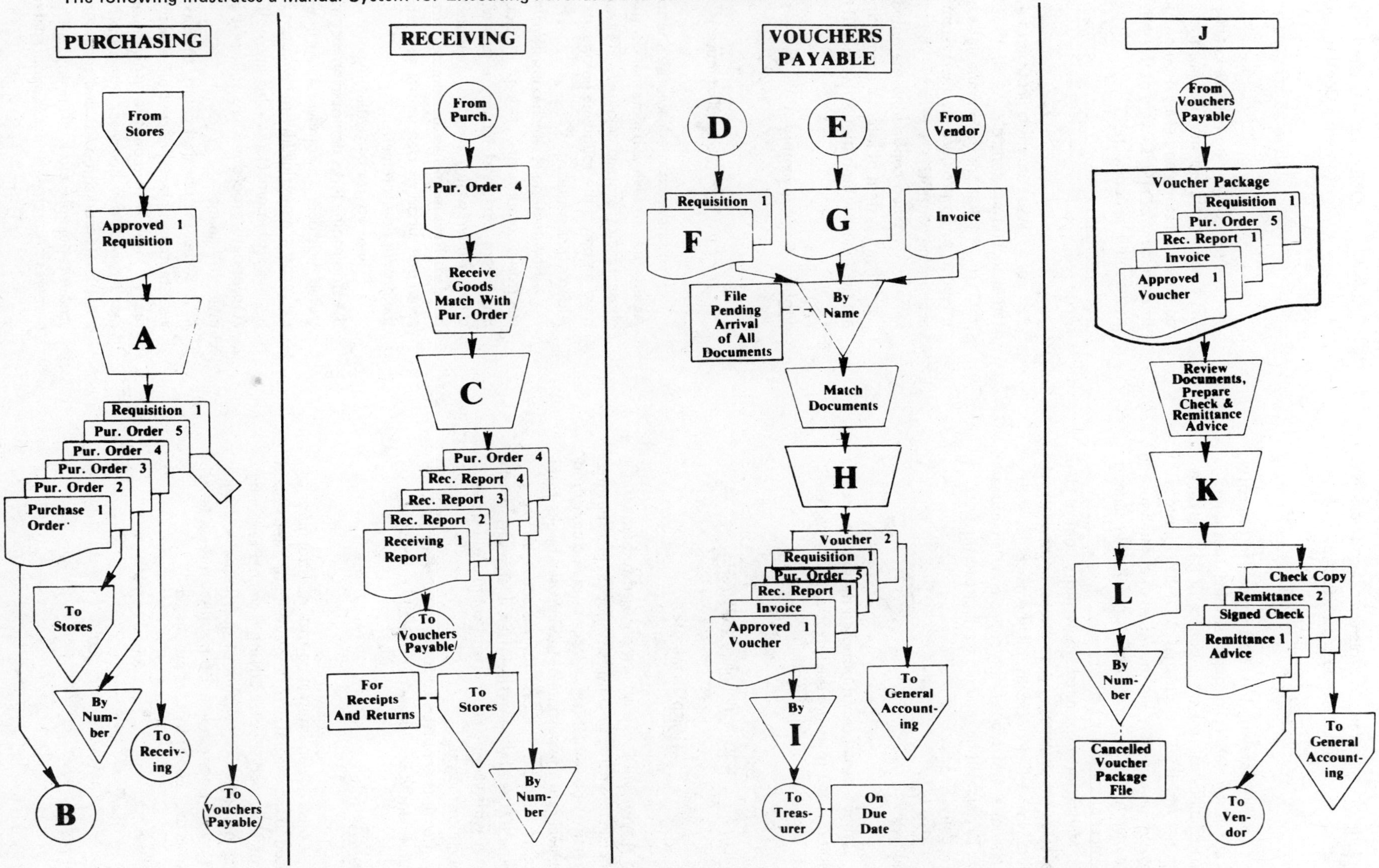

Required: Indicate what each of the letters (A) through (L) represent. Do not discuss adequacies or inadequacies in the system of internal control.

Problem 3 Internal Controls Over Cash Receipts and Warehousing (1182,A3)

(15 to 25 minutes)

Trapan Retailing Inc., has decided to diversify operations by selling through vending machines. Trapan's plans call for the purchase of 312 vending machines which will be situated at 78 different locations, within one city, and the rental of a warehouse to store merchandise. Trapan intends to sell only canned beverages at a standard price.

Management has hired an inventory control clerk to oversee the warehousing functions, and two truck drivers who will periodically fill the machines with merchandise, and deposit cash collected at a designated bank. Drivers will be required to report to the warehouse daily.

Required:

What internal controls should the auditor expect to find in order to assure the integrity of the cash receipts and warehousing functions?

Problem 4 IC Questionnaire (581,A4)

(15 to 25 minutes)

Taylor, a CPA, has been engaged to audit the financial statements of University Books, Incorporated. University Books maintains a large revolving cash fund exclusively for the purpose of buying used books from students for cash. The cash fund is active all year because the nearby university offers a large variety of courses with varying starting and completion dates throughout the year.

Receipts are prepared for each purchase and reimbursement vouchers are periodically submitted.

Required:

Construct an internal control questionnaire to be used in the evaluation of the system of internal control of University Book's buying segments revolving cash fund. The internal control questionnaire should elicit a yes or no response. **Do not discuss the internal controls over books that are purchased.**

Problem 5 Objectives and Limitations of Systems of Internal Control (582,A3)

(15 to 25 minutes)

Jones, CPA, who has been engaged to examine the financial statements of Ajax Inc., is about to commence a study and evaluation of Ajax's system of internal control and is aware of the inherent limitations that should be considered.

Required:

a. What are the objectives of a system of internal accounting control?

b. What are the reasonable assurances that are intended to be provided by the system of internal accounting control?

c. When considering the potential effectiveness of any system of internal accounting control what are the inherent limitations that should be recognized?

Problem 6 Inventory IC Weaknesses (1173,A6)

(25 to 30 minutes)

You have been engaged by the management of Alden, Inc., to review its internal control over the purchase, receipt, storage, and issue of raw materials. You have prepared the following comments which describe Alden's procedures.

Raw materials, which consist mainly of high-cost electronic components, are kept in a locked storeroom. Storeroom personnel include a supervisor and four clerks. All are well trained, competent, and adequately bonded. Raw materials are removed from the storeroom only upon written or oral authorization of one of the production foremen.

There are no perpetual-inventory records; hence, the storeroom clerks do not keep records of goods received or issued. To compensate for the lack of perpetual records, a physical-inventory count is taken monthly by the storeroom clerks who are well supervised. Appropriate procedures are followed in making the inventory count.

After the physical count, the storeroom supervisor matches quantities counted against predetermined reorder level. If the count for a given part is below the reorder level, the supervisor enters the part number on a materials-requisition list and sends this list to the accounts-payable clerk. The accounts-payable clerk prepares a purchase order for a predetermined reorder quantity for each part and mails the purchase order to the vendor from whom the part was last purchased.

When ordered materials arrive at Alden, they are received by the storeroom clerks. The clerks count the merchandise and agree the counts to the shipper's bill of lading. All vendors' bills of lading are initialed, dated, and filed in the storeroom to serve as receiving reports.

Required:

Describe the weaknesses in internal control and recommend improvements of Alden's procedures for the purchase, receipt, storage, and issue of raw materials. Organize your answer sheet as follows:

Weaknesses	Recommended Improvements

Problem 7 Payroll IC Weaknesses (580,A5)

(15 to 25 minutes)

A CPA's audit working papers contain a narrative description of a **segment** of the Croyden Factory, Inc., payroll system and an accompanying flowchart as follows:

NARRATIVE

The internal control system with respect to the personnel department is well-functioning and is **not** included in the accompanying flowchart.

At the beginning of each work week payroll clerk No. 1 reviews the payroll department files to determine the employment status of factory employees and then prepares time cards and distributes them as each individual arrives at work. This payroll clerk, who is also responsible for custody of the signature stamp machine, verifies the identity of each payee before delivering signed checks to the foreman.

At the end of each work week the foreman distributes payroll checks for the preceding work week. Concurrent with this activity, the foreman reviews the current week's employee time cards, notes the regular and overtime hours worked on a summary form, and initials the aforementioned time cards. The foreman then delivers all time cards and unclaimed payroll checks to payroll clerk No. 2.

Required:

a. Based upon the narrative and accompanying flowchart, what are the weaknesses in the system of internal control?

b. Based upon the narrative and accompanying flowchart, what inquiries should be made with respect to clarifying the existence of **possible additional weaknesses** in the system of internal control?

Note: Do not discuss the internal control system of the personnel department.

Flowchart appears on following page

Problem 8 Cash Receipts IC Weaknesses (1180,A4)

(15 to 25 minutes)

The Art Appreciation Society operates a museum for the benefit and enjoyment of the community. During hours when the museum is open to the public, two clerks who are positioned at the entrance collect a five dollar admission fee from each nonmember patron. Members of the Art Appreciation Society are permitted to enter free of charge upon presentation of their membership cards.

At the end of each day one of the clerks delivers the proceeds to the treasurer. The treasurer counts the cash in the presence of the clerk and places it in a safe. Each Friday afternoon the treasurer and one of the clerks deliver all cash held in the safe to the bank, and receive an authenticated deposit slip which provides the basis for the weekly entry in the cash receipts journal.

The board of directors of the Art Appreciation Society has identified a need to improve their system of internal control over cash admission fees. The board has determined that the cost of installing turnstiles, sales booths or otherwise altering the physical layout of the museum will greatly exceed any benefits which may be derived. However, the board has agreed that the sale of admission tickets must be an integral part of its improvement efforts.

Smith has been asked by the board of directors of the Art Appreciation Society to review the internal control over cash admission fees and provide suggestions for improvement.

Required:

Indicate weakness in the existing system of internal control over cash admission fees, which Smith should identify, and recommend one improvement for each of the weaknesses identified.

Organize the answer as indicated in the following illustrative example:

Problem 7 *(continued)*

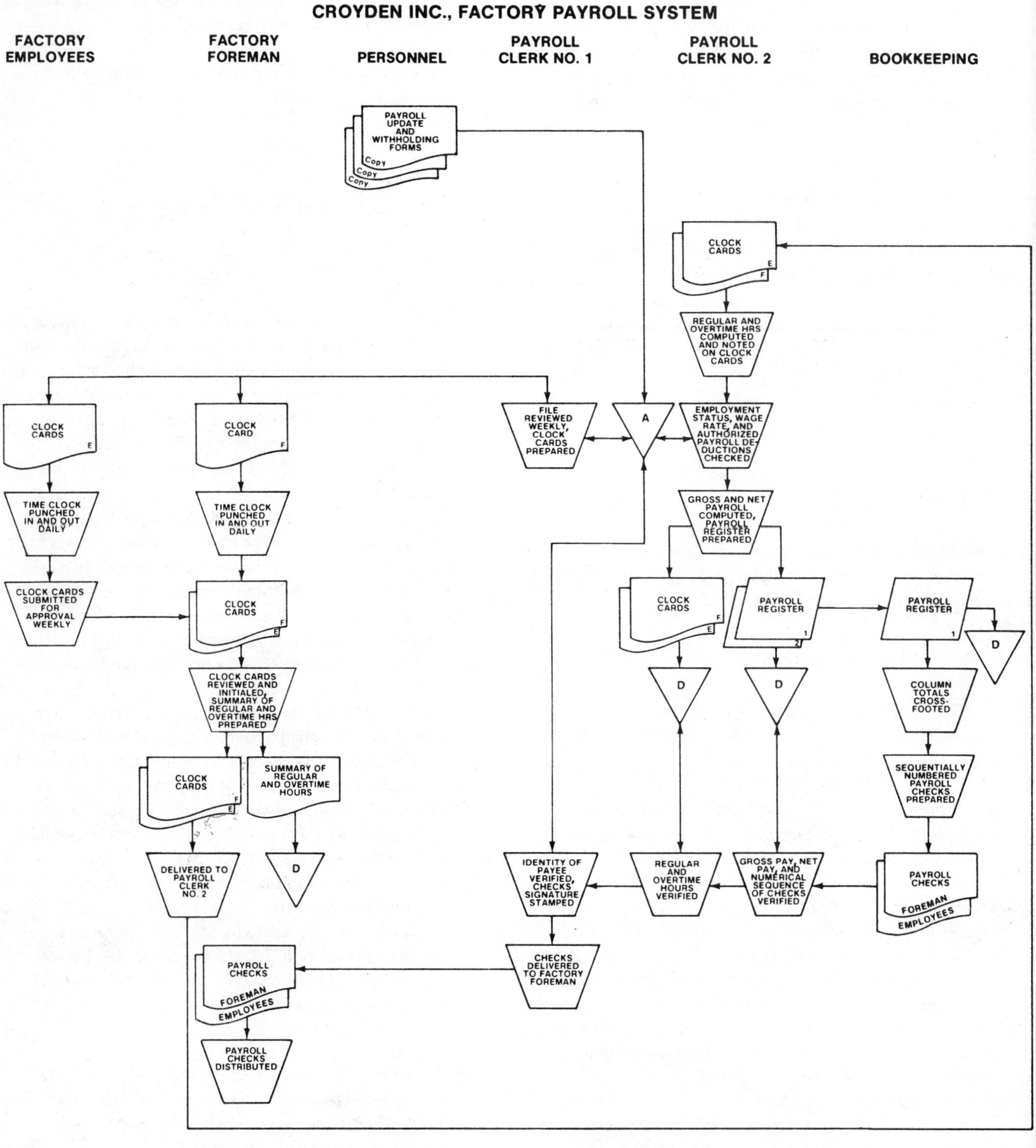

Weakness	Recommendation
1. There is no basis for establishing the documentation of the number of paying patrons.	*1. Prenumbered admission tickets should be issued upon payment of the admission fee.*

Problem 9 Purchasing Function Flowchart (1175,A6)

(20 to 25 minutes)

Anthony, CPA, prepared the flowchart on the following page which portrays the raw materials purchasing function of one of Anthony's clients, a medium-sized manufacturing company, from the preparation of initial documents through the vouching of invoices for payment in accounts payable. The flowchart was a portion of the work performed on the audit engagement to evaluate internal control.

Required:

Identify and explain the systems and control weaknesses evident from the flowchart on the following page. Include the internal control weaknesses resulting from activities performed or not performed. All documents are prenumbered.

Flowchart appears on following page

Problem 10 Inventory Weaknesses (CMA,679,PRS 8)

(30 minutes)

The Jameson Co. produces a variety of chemical products for use by plastics manufacturers. The plant operates on two shifts, five days per week with maintenance work performed on the third shift and on Saturdays as required.

An audit conducted by the staff of the new corporate internal audit department has recently been completed and the comments on inventory control were not favorable. Audit comments were particularly directed to the control of raw material ingredients and maintenance materials.

Raw material ingredients are received at the back of the plant, signed for by one of the employees of the batching department and stored near the location of the initial batching process. Receiving tallies are given to the supervisor during the day and he forwards the tallies to the Inventory Control Department at the end of the day. The Inventory Control Department calculates ingredient usage using weekly reports of actual production and standard formulas. Physical inventories are taken quarterly. Purchase requisitions are prepared by the Inventory Control Department and rush orders are frequent. In spite of the need for rush orders the Production Superintendent regularly gets memos from the Controller stating that there must be excess inventory because the ingredient inventory dollar value is too high.

Maintenance parts and supplies are received and stored in a storeroom. There is a storeroom clerk on each of the operating shifts. Storeroom requisitions are to be filled out for everything taken from the storeroom; however, this practice is not always followed. The storeroom is not locked when the clerk is out because of the need to get parts quickly. The storeroom is also open during the third shift for the maintenance crews to get parts as needed. Purchase requisitions are prepared by the storeroom clerk and physical inventory is taken on a cycle count basis. Rush orders are frequent.

Required:

a. 1. Identify the weaknesses in Jameson Company's internal control procedures used for

- Ingredients inventory.
- Maintenance material and supplies inventory.

2. Recommend improvements which should be instituted for each of these areas.

b. What procedures would the internal auditors use to identify the weaknesses in Jameson Company's inventory control?

Problem 11 Sales System Flowchart (579,A2)

(15 to 25 minutes)

A partially-completed charge sales systems flowchart follows. The flowchart depicts the charge sales activities of the Bottom Manufacturing Corporation.

A customer's purchase order is received and a six-part sales order is prepared, therefrom. The six copies are initially distributed as follows:

Copy No. 1 – Billing copy - to billing department.
Copy No. 2 – Shipping copy - to shipping department.
Copy No. 3 – Credit copy - to credit department.
Copy No. 4 – Stock request copy - to credit department.
Copy No. 5 – Customer copy - to customer.
Copy No. 6 – Sales order copy - file in sales order department.

Problem 9 *(continued)*

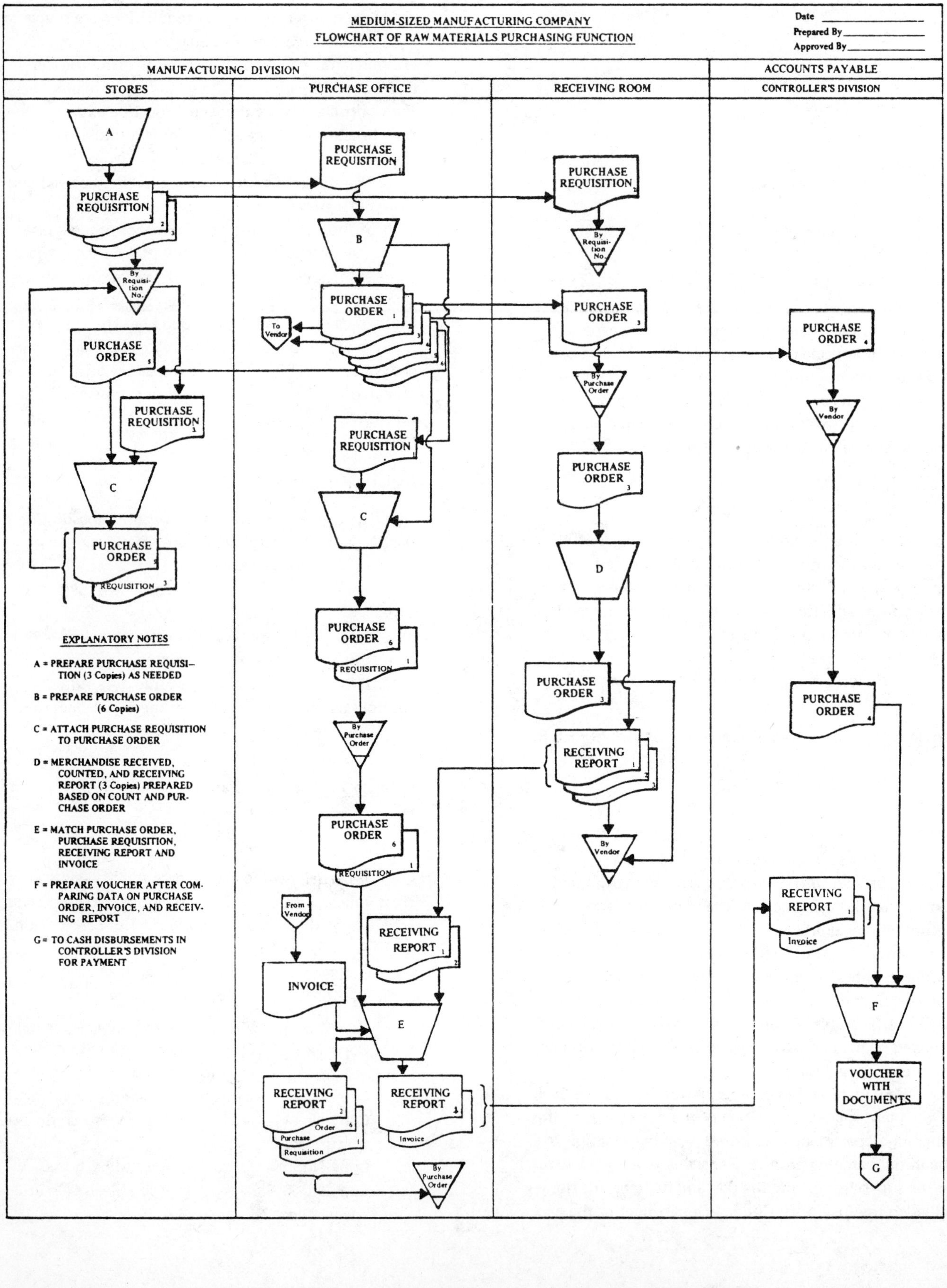

When each copy of the sales order reaches the applicable department or destination it calls for specific internal control procedures and related documents. Some of the procedures and related documents are indicated on the flowchart. Other procedures and documents are labeled letters a to r.

Required:

List the procedures or the internal documents that are labeled letters c to r in the flowchart of Bottom Manufacturing Corporation's charge sales system.

Organize your answer as follows (note that an explanation of the letters a and b which appear in the flowchart are entered as examples):

Flowchart Symbol Letter	Procedures or Internal Document
a.	Prepare six-part sales order.
b.	File by order number.

BOTTOM MANUFACTURING CORPORATION

Flowchart of Credit Sales Activities

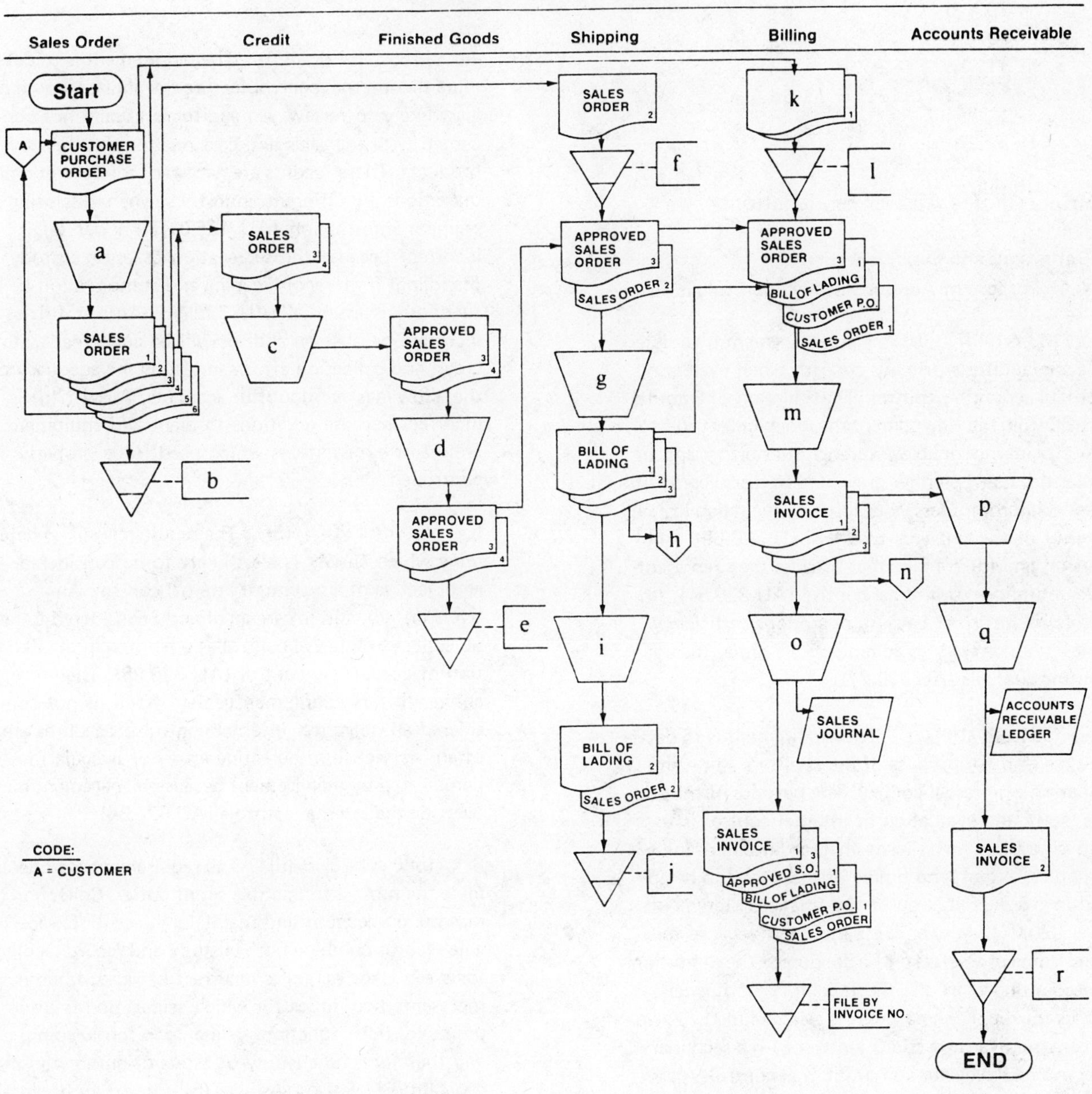

Multiple Choice Answers

1. b	17. d	33. a	49. c	65. a
2. c	18. c	34. c	50. b	66. b
3. a	19. d	35. c	51. d	67. b
4. c	20. b	36. a	52. d	68. d
5. b	21. a	37. c	53. c	69. c
6. d	22. a	38. d	54. b	70. c
7. d	23. a	39. a	55. d	71. a
8. a	24. d	40. a	56. a	72. d
9. c	25. d	41. a	57. d	73. d
10. a	26. c	42. b	58. a	74. d
11. a	27. b	43. c	59. a	75. c
12. d	28. a	44. c	60. a	76. c
13. d	29. b	45. a	61. b	77. d
14. b	30. b	46. c	62. c	78. c
15. a	31. b	47. c	63. c	79. d
16. b	32. d	48. d	64. a	

Multiple Choice Answer Explanations

A. Definitions and Basic Concepts

A.1. Purpose of Auditor's Study and Evaluation

1. (1183,A1,43) (b) The requirement is to determine the auditor's primary concern when evaluating internal accounting control. The function of internal control, from the viewpoint of the independent auditor, is to provide reasonable assurance that errors and irregularities may be either prevented or discovered with reasonable promptness, thus assuring the reliability and integrity of the financial records (AU 320.68). Answers (a) and (d) are incorrect because they represent basic limitations of internal control (AU 320.34). Answer (c) is incorrect because operational efficiency relates more directly to administrative rather than accounting controls (AU 320.27).

2. (581,A1,7) (c) The requirement is to determine the primary purpose of the auditor's study and evaluation of internal control. The purpose of the auditor's study and evaluation of internal control is to establish a basis for reliance thereon in determining the nature, extent, and timing of audit tests to be applied in the examination of the financial statements (para 320.06). Answer (a) is incorrect because the safeguarding of assets is only a portion of the definition of accounting controls; the reliability of financial records for reporting purposes is also included. Providing constructive suggestions (answer b) is a secondary objective of the evaluation of internal control. Answer (d) is incorrect because in the normal financial statement audit the expression of an opinion is based only in part on the results of the evaluation of internal control.

A.2. Definitions and Basic Concepts

3. (1183,A1,15) (a) The requirement is to determine the function which should **not** be the responsibility of the treasurer's department. Data processing should **not** be a responsibility of the treasurer's department because it is a recordkeeping function which is incompatible with the treasurer's department's custodial responsibility. Answers (b) and (c) are incorrect because under a good system of internal control the treasurer's department is typically responsible for the custody over cash and securities. Answer (d) is incorrect because the treasurer, as an officer, will often be involved in establishing credit policies.

4. (1183,A1,42) (c) The requirement is to determine the internal control feature the auditor would be least likely to review. An auditor is usually not concerned with the sales and cost records classified by products. These records are necessary for determining operations in different industries when disclosing segment information (AU 435.01). Answer (a) is incorrect because the segregation of asset custody (handling) from recordkeeping and authorization functions is essential (AU 320.36). Answer (b) is incorrect because an auditor will be concerned with credit and collection efforts in testing the adequacy of the allowance for doubtful accounts. Answer (d) is incorrect because additions to plant and equipment are major expenditures which need to be properly controlled.

5. (583,A1,20) (b) The requirement is to determine which answer is **least** likely to be considered an objective of a system of internal control. Answers (a), (c), and (d) are all directly considered to be objectives of internal control as presented in the definition of accounting control (AU 320.28). Therefore, answer (b), detecting management fraud, is not considered an objective. Internal control procedures are often ineffective at detecting errors or irregularities perpetrated by management because management may override the internal controls (AU 320.34).

6. (583,A1,23) (d) The requirement is to determine the most incompatible set of duties. Collection of receipts on account and maintaining accounts receivable records combine both custody and recordkeeping for assets. Answer (a) is incorrect because, while it represents two duties for which segregation is often desirable, both functions relate to recordkeeping, and therefore, no custody of assets or authorization capability is involved. Answer (b) is incorrect because no custody of assets is involved. Answer (c) is incorrect

because while the individuals will have both custody of assets (the checks) and recordkeeping responsibility, they relate to different areas.

7. (583,A1,39) (d) The requirement is to determine the item which would **not** be considered an internal control feature. Answer (d), a comparison-shopping staff, is best since while such a staff may be desirable, it is unlikely that it will increase internal control. Answers (a), (b), and (c) all relate to internal accounting controls (see AU 320.28).

8. (583,A1,60) (a) The requirement is to determine the example of an administrative control. AU 320.26–.29 divides internal controls into administrative and accounting controls. Authorizing credit terms is an administrative control because such controls relate to the plan of organization and the procedures and records that are concerned with the decision processes leading to management's authorization of transactions (AU 320.27). Answers (b), (c), and (d) are all incorrect because they are examples of accounting controls relating to safeguarding assets and the reliability of financial records (AU 320.28).

9. (1182,A1,24) (c) The requirement is to identify the meaning of the concept of reasonable assurance. Reasonable assurance recognizes that the cost of internal control should not exceed the benefits expected to be derived (AU 320.32). Answers (a), (b), and (d) all represent statements which are not part of the definition of the concept of reasonable assurance.

10. (1182,A1,26) (a) The requirement is to determine the situation which would be **least** likely to be indicative of the fact that the client's management may have overriden the internal control system. Differences noted on computer exception reports are expected and will be followed up on. Answer (b) may be indicative of management override because the failure to correct known weaknesses raises questions as to management's desire to prepare accurate financial information. Answer (c) is consistent with management override of the system since one must question why two controllers (responsible for the recordkeeping function) have been replaced. Answer (d) is also consistent with management override because a delay in report preparation may result when management is overriding the system.

11. (1182,A1,51) (a) The requirement is to determine the example of a primary internal control procedure. Primary control procedures are designed to achieve one or more specific control objectives and are generally applied at points where errors or irregularities could occur in the processing of transactions and the handling of assets (AU 642.24). Such errors could occur if receiving reports were not compared with vendor invoices prior to payment. Answers (b), (c) and (d) are all incorrect because they represent examples of secondary control procedures which contribute **primarily** to the achievement of broader management control objectives (see AU 642.24).

12. (582,A1,44) (d) The requirement is to determine which statement concerning an internal control system is **not** valid. Procedures whose effectiveness depends on segregation of duties can be circumvented by collusion (AU 320.34). Answer (a) is a valid statement since custody and recording responsibility should be segregated. Answer (b) is a valid statement because transactions should be properly authorized (AU 320.37). Answer (c) is also a valid statement because under the concept of reasonable assurance the cost/benefit relationship may be considered (AU 320.32).

13. (580,A1,7) (d) Proper segregation of the functional responsibilities requires separation of (1) authorization, (2) recording, and (3) custodial functions. Per para 320.36 incompatible functions are those that place any person in a position both to perpetrate and to conceal errors and irregularities. Thus, those that authorize transactions must be separated from those who account for the transactions and from those who have custody of any related assets. Answers (a), (b), and (c) are incorrect because they do not include the required accounting (or recording) function.

14. (579,A1,42) (b) The requirement is a situation causing the impairment of organizational independence. The controller, who is in charge of accounting, should be independent of the production function. Since the accounting function reports on the production function, there would be a conflict of interest if the controller reported to the vice president of production. Answer (a) is incorrect because internal auditors typically report to the audit committee of the board of directors. Answer (c) is incorrect because the payroll department should report to the chief accountant, as the chief accountant has responsibility for the payroll accounting function. Answer (d) is incorrect because cashiers typically account and report to the treasurer because the treasurer has responsibility for cash custodianship.

15. (577,A3,42) (a) The requirement is the best description of the inherent limitations concerning a system of internal control. Para 320.34 of SAS 1

describes inherent limitations that can render a system of internal control ineffective. Included are the possibilities of misunderstanding instructions, mistakes of judgment, personal carelessness, distraction, fatigue, collusion among employees whose duties are segregated, and perpetrations by management. Answers (b), (c), and (d) describe basic concepts of internal control and are found in para 320.35, 320.37, and 320.32 respectively.

16. (1178,A1,58) (b) Internal accounting control has two major objectives: safeguarding assets and promoting reliability of financial records. As a result, a system of internal accounting control provides reasonable assurances that 1) transactions are recorded per management's authorization, 2) transactions are recorded as necessary, 3) access to assets is permitted only with management's authorization, 4) recorded accountability of assets is compared with physical assets periodically (para 320.28 of SAS 1). Answer (a) is incorrect because an internal control system assumes that employees act with integrity and determines the contrary when irregularities occur. Answer (c) is incorrect because the decision processes leading to management's authorization concern internal administrative control rather than internal accounting control (para 320.27). Answer (d) is incorrect because one of the limitations of internal control systems is that they may be circumvented by collusion (para 320.34).

A.3. Additional Considerations

17. (582,A1,11) (d) The requirement is to determine what the Foreign Corrupt Practices Act requires. The act's provisions prohibit illegal foreign payments and require publicly-held companies to devise and maintain an adequate system of internal accounting control. Answers (a), (b), and (c) are not required by the Act.

B. Study and Evaluation of the System of Internal Control

B.1. Review of Internal Control

18. (582,A1,8) (c) The requirement is to determine why the auditor observes client employees during the review of the system of internal control. The effectiveness of procedures which leave no audit trail is corroborated through inquiries **and** observation (AU 320.59). Answer (a) is incorrect because a flowchart is prepared during the preliminary review of internal control based primarily on **inquiries** of key personnel. Answer (b) is incorrect because the auditor does not typically update information in the client's organization and procedure manuals. Answer (d) is incorrect because quality control standards refer to those practices used by CPA firms to assure quality.

B.2. Preliminary Evaluation of Internal Control

19. (1183,A1,52) (d) The requirement is to determine the correct statement with respect to the auditor's required documentation of the client's system of internal control. An auditor may document his/her understanding of the system and his/her conclusions about the design of that system in the form of answers to a questionnaire, narrative memorandums, flowcharts, decision tables, or any other form that the auditor considers appropriate in the circumstances (AU 320.58). Also, in situations in which the auditor does not plan to rely on the system of internal control to restrict substantive tests, his/her documentation may be limited to a record of reasons for deciding not to extend the review of internal control (AU 320.54). Answers (a) and (b) are, thus, incorrect because they suggest restrictions which do not exist in practice. Answer (c) is incorrect since at a minimum a list of reasons for nonreliance must be provided.

20. (1181,A1,6) (b) The requirement is to determine a procedure which is inappropriate during the preliminary evaluation of the system of internal control. Answer (b), attribute sampling, is inappropriate in the preliminary evaluation which consists of procedures such as the completion of an internal control questionnaire [answer (a)], oral inquiries [answer (c)] and the review of an accounting manual [answer (d)]. Attribute sampling may be used during tests of compliance which are performed subsequent to the preliminary evaluation to test whether accounting control procedures are being applied as prescribed (para 320.55 and SAS 39, para 31-37).

B.3. Tests of Compliance

21. (1183,A1,10) (a) The requirement is to determine the purpose of compliance testing. The purpose of tests of compliance is to provide reasonable assurance that the internal accounting control procedures are being applied as prescribed (AU 320.59). Answers (b) and (c) are incorrect because the existence of necessary controls (which may or may not be working properly) and of incompatible functions is primarily determined during the preliminary evaluation of internal control. Answer (d) is incorrect because substantive tests more directly address the existence of material dollar errors than compliance tests do.

22. (583,A1,40) (a) The requirement is to determine the correct statement with respect as to when an auditor will perform compliance tests. Compliance tests are only performed on controls that the auditor plans to rely upon (AU 320.55). Answer (b) is incorrect because the auditor is unlikely to test controls in which material weaknesses exist since they cannot be relied upon. Answer (c) is incorrect because, even though some controls have a material effect upon financial statement balances, they may not be relied upon because substantive testing may be more efficient (AU 320.73). Answer (d) is incorrect because the decision whether or not to perform compliance tests is determined by employing professional judgment based upon the results of the preliminary review, not by a random sample.

23. (581,A1,39) (a) The requirement is to determine what type of test an auditor applies in examining initials on sales invoices. Tests of compliance provide reasonable assurance that accounting control procedures are being applied as prescribed (para 320.55). Examining the initials of the individual who verified the quantitative data on the sales invoices tests firm compliance with the prescribed control. Answer (b) is incorrect because the test does not substantiate the validity and propriety of accounting treatment of transactions and balances. Answer (c) is incorrect since cutoff tests relate to testing dates on such invoices at year-end to determine whether they have been recorded in the proper period. Answer (d) is incorrect since the test may or may not be performed using statistical sampling.

24. (581,A1,60) (d) The requirement is to determine the objective of precision in sampling. Precision is calculated to determine the range of procedural deviations in the population (para 33 of SAS 39). Answer (a) is incorrect because probabilities relate more directly to reliability. Answer (b) is incorrect because errors on financial statements in materiality terms relate to variables sampling. Answer (c) is incorrect because it does not accurately indicate the relationship between reliability and precision.

25. (1180,A1,2) (d) Auditors perform compliance tests to provide reasonable assurance that prescribed accounting control procedures are being followed. Inspection procedures [answer (a)] are used to test whether and by whom control procedures were performed and to permit an evaluation of the propriety of their performance (para 320.58). Observation [answer (b)] and inquiry [answer (c)] may be used, for example, to test controls which leave no audit trail (para 320.59). Confirmation [answer (d)] is used primarily to enable the auditor to substantiate the existence of an account balance; it is, therefore, considered a substantive test.

26. (580,A1,47) (c) The requirement is the audit test which would be considered a test of compliance. Tests of compliance are primarily concerned with "were the necessary procedures performed, how were they performed, and by whom were they performed?" per para 320.57. Tests of signatures on cancelled checks will determine whether the checks were signed by those authorized by the board of directors. Answer (a) is incorrect because tests of specific items making up a balance in a ledger account would be a transactions test. Answer (b) is incorrect because tests of inventory pricing to vendors' invoices also is a transactions test. Answer (d) is incorrect because tests of additions of property, plant, and equipment would also be a transactions test.

B.4. Reevaluation of Internal Control

27. (1182,A1,27) (b) The requirement is to determine the relationship between reliance on internal control and reliance on substantive tests. Inverse (AU 320.73) is correct because as internal control is relied upon to a lesser extent substantive tests are relied upon to a greater extent.

28. (579,A1,16) (a) The requirement is the situation in which auditors should retest records and procedures as well as apply new compliance tests at year end, when these tests have already been done during the year and internal control has been found to be effective. Auditors should retest records and transactions if year-end inquiries and observations lead the auditor to believe conditions have changed significantly (para 310.06). Answer (b) is incorrect because significant fluctuations in account balances are acceptable if they can be explained by a change in business conditions. If, however, the conditions of the records and internal control systems have changed, additional year-end work is required. Answer (c) is incorrect because unusual transactions subsequent to the interim audit work should be examined on an individual basis (para 310.06). Answer (d) is incorrect because significantly changed conditions would require retesting whether or not client records are in a condition to facilitate the retesting.

C. Accounting Cycles

C.1. Sales, Receivables, and Cash Receipts

29. (583,A1,12) (b) The requirement is to determine the purpose of tracing copies of sales invoices to shipping documents. Sales invoices will often serve as "bills," and by tracing them to shipping documents, the auditor discovers whether those "bills" are supported by shipments. Answers (a) and (c) are incorrect because no examination of receivables has taken place. Answer (d) is incorrect because to test whether shipments to customers were billed, the auditor would trace from the shipping documents to the sales invoices (the opposite direction).

30. (583,A1,15) (b) The requirement is to determine which answer is **not** a universal rule for achieving strong internal control over cash. Decentralization of receiving cash generally would not increase internal control; in fact, the additional points of cash receipt may well be more difficult to control. Answer (a) is incorrect because separation of cash handling and recordkeeping separates custody from recordkeeping, thereby enhancing internal control. Answer (c) is incorrect because the daily deposit of cash receipts helps to deter irregularities and thefts. Answer (d) is incorrect because separating reconciliation from handling of cash is a proper segregation within the recordkeeping function.

31. (1182,A1,19) (b) The requirement is to determine who should prepare a remittance advice when the customer fails to include one with a remittance. Remittances should be opened by an individual such as a receptionist who is independent of the sales function. That individual will prepare any needed remittance advices. The credit manager [answer (a)], the sales manager [answer (c)], and the accounts receivable clerk [answer (d)] are all incorrect because all of these individuals perform functions related to sales.

32. (1182,A1,55) (d) The requirement is to determine how an auditor may verify that **all** sales transactions have been recorded. Items actually shipped (as evidenced by bills of lading) represent the firm's sales. Answer (a) is incorrect because the sales journal only reflects sales which have already been recorded. Answer (b) is incorrect because only sales for which the billing clerk has received a copy of the sales order will be tested. Answer (c) is incorrect because the sales invoices only reflect those sales which have properly reached the invoice stage.

33. (582,A1,51) (a) The requirement is to determine which department should perform the billing function so as to have effective accounting control. The accounting department serves a recording function: billing is an example of a recording function. Answer (b) is incorrect because the sales department will often authorize sales — recording and authorization would not be segregated if billing were also performed. Answer (c) is incorrect because shipping is primarily a custodial function. Answer (d) is incorrect because credit and collections authorize credit and make collections.

34. (1181,A1,15) (c) The requirement is to determine an incompatible operation for a cashier who receives remittances from the mailroom. Answer (c), posting the receipts to the accounts receivable subsidiary ledger cards, is incompatible because it provides the cashier with recordkeeping as well as custodial responsibilities. Preparing the daily deposit [answer (a)], making the daily deposit [answer (b)] and endorsing the checks [answer (d)] are all a part of the cashier's custodial function.

35. (578,A1,9) (c) Lapping of trade accounts receivable is an abstraction of funds and subsequent delay in crediting receipts to accounts receivable. If the customers sent payments directly to a depository bank, there is no opportunity for abstractions or subsequent misapplication. Answer (a) is incorrect because lapping involves incorrect entries in the subsidiary ledgers, not the general ledger. Answers (b) and (d) are incorrect because lapping can occur by forging checks, i.e., there is no requirement that abstraction be made directly from cash.

36. (578,A1,32) (a) If A/R write offs must be approved by an officer on the basis of credit department recommendations including supporting evidence, there is very little likelihood of improper write offs to conceal cash shortages. Answer (b) is incorrect because receivables overdue by several months is not a basis for write off; uncollectibility is. Answer (c) is incorrect because the cashier could conceal cash shortages by approving A/R write offs. Answer (d) is incorrect because sales employees could accept payments from customers and then authorize the accounts to be written off.

C.2. Purchases, Payables, and Cash Disbursements

37. (1183,A1,38) (c) The requirement is to determine the **least** crucial element of internal control over cash. Answer (c) is least crucial because, while the batch processing of checks may be efficient, the specific

circumstances involved will determine whether it has strong (weak) internal control. Unlike the other choices given, it is not an element of internal control over cash. Answer (a) is incorrect because for cash (and other assets) recordkeeping should be separated from the custodial and authorization functions (AU 320.36). Answer (b) is incorrect because a monthly bank reconciliation can detect a variety of errors. Answer (d) is incorrect because of the potential for defalcation when one individual controls both receipts and disbursements.

38. (1182,A1,52) (d) The requirement is to determine why an auditor would compare information on cancelled checks with information contained in the cash disbursement journal. Such discrepancies can be found by this simple comparison. Answer (a) is incorrect because a test of authorization is not being performed. Answer (b) is incorrect because purchase discounts are not being recalculated. Answer (c) is incorrect because no evidence of whether the goods have been received (e.g., a receiving report) is being examined.

39. (577,A1,7) (a) The requirement is the internal control measure to encourage receiving department personnel to count and inspect all merchandise received. If the quantities ordered are not known to the receiving department personnel, they will have to count and inspect the incoming merchandise without prejudice. In other words, they will not count to an expected number. Answer (b) is incorrect because it does not relate to the requirement, i.e., counting and inspecting. Answer (c) is incorrect because receiving department personnel should only count and inspect and not perform reconciliations. Answer (d) is incorrect because an examination of the receiving report will not indicate whether counts were made by receiving department personnel. It will only indicate that numbers were recorded by receiving department personnel.

40. (577,A2,22) (a) The CPA's primary objective in reviewing the materials purchasing cycle is to evaluate the reliability of the information generated as a result of the purchasing process. This is in accordance with the second standard of field work which requires there is to be a "proper study and evaluation of existing internal control as a basis for reliance thereon. . ." Thus, answer (a) also encompasses answers (b), (c), and (d).

41. (1178,A1,2) (a) The requirement is the effective internal accounting control over cash payments. The person signing checks should supervise or control the mailing of the checks. The check signer reviews the supporting documentation and authorizes the requested disbursement. By controlling the mailing of the checks, there is reasonable assurance that the payee will receive the payment. If the payee is not due the money, presumably the payee will contact the payor. If the signed checks were returned to the person preparing the checks, that person could prepare checks to false payees or abscond with checks to bona fide payees without collusion with others. Answer (b) is incorrect because voided checks should be retained as proof that they have not been (or will not be) issued. Answer (c) is incorrect because persons preparing checks should not have access to cash receipts and disbursements, e.g., to eliminate opportunities for kiting. Answer (d) is incorrect because a check signing machine with two signatures provides little control unless separate persons, responsible for authorizing individual payments, control the signature plates.

C.3. Inventories and Production

42. (583,A1,36) (b) The requirement is to determine why the physical count of inventory might be higher than that shown by the perpetual records. If credit memos for items had not been recorded they would be included in the count and not in the perpetual records. Answer (a) is incorrect because if the tags had not been taken off the items, the count would be less than the perpetual records. Answer (c) is incorrect because items returned to suppliers would not be counted, and therefore, if no book entries had been made, the books would exceed the count. Answer (d) is incorrect because items which had not been received would not be included in either the count or the perpetual records; therefore, both totals would be understated by the same amount.

43. (583,A1,50) (c) The requirement is to determine the situation which could cause a client's physical count of inventories to be higher than the inventory **quantities** per the perpetual records. Failure to record purchases will result in a situation in which the item will be included in the count yet the perpetual records will not reflect the item. Answer (a) is incorrect because the failure to record sales (and therefore, cost of goods sold) will result in a situation in which the physical count is lower than the perpetual records. Answer (b) is incorrect because sales discounts relate to the selling price and not to the quantity of items in inventory. Answer (d) is incorrect because unrecorded returns of a firm's purchases to its suppliers will result in a lower physical count than is reflected in the perpetual records.

44. (582,A1,57) (c) The requirement is to determine the best method for strengthening internal controls over the accounting for materials used in production in a firm which mass produces eight different products. A perpetual inventory system will show when and where materials are being used. Answer (a) is incorrect because an EOQ system is a control system that controls ordering and storage cost, but not usage. Answer (b) is incorrect since the corporation mass produces the products. Answer (d) is incorrect because the separation of duties among production personnel does not affect the **accounting** for the materials being used in production.

45. (581,A1,59) (a) The requirement is to determine the **least** likely inventory audit procedure relating to segregation of duties. Because many aspects of the segregation of duties leave no audit trail of documentary evidence, inspecting documents is least likely (para 320.59). The auditor will make inquiries [answer (b)], observe procedures [answer (c)], and consider policy and procedure manuals [answer (d)] to determine both how the duties are purported to be and actually are segregated.

46. (578,A1,21) (c) If the storekeeper, who is involved in physical control, is also allowed to keep inventory records, there is an internal control weakness. One of the basic concepts of internal control is segregation of functional responsibilities. See para 320.36 of SAS 1. Answers (a), (b), and (d) describe normal operating procedures.

C.4. Personnel and Payroll

47. (582,A1,32) (c) The requirement is to determine the best method to minimize the opportunities for fraud for unclaimed cash in a **cash** payroll system. For a **cash** payroll the best control is to get the unclaimed cash out of the firm's physical control and into the bank. Answer (a) is incorrect because maintaining the accountability for cash which is in a safe deposit box is difficult. Answers (b) and (d) are incorrect because the cash need not be kept by the firm.

48. (582,A1,55) (d) The requirement is to determine the reason why unclaimed payroll checks are delivered to the internal auditing department at the end of each payroll distribution day. The issuance of payroll checks for individuals who either never did work for the firm or did work for the firm and have resigned may be detected by this procedure since no one will pick up the check. The unclaimed checks should be investigated by someone independent from the authorization, recordkeeping and custodial functions of payroll. The most obvious independent group to perform this activity would be the internal auditors. A better procedure to prevent the paymaster from cashing checks [answer (b)] would be to redeposit these checks in a special checking account on a daily basis. Internal auditors can cash checks as well as the paymaster. Answer (a) is incorrect since the timekeeping function will not typically be performed by internal auditors. Answer (c) is incorrect because this is a control only over unclaimed checks.

49. (1179,A1,54) (c) If payment of wages were to be in cash, each employee receiving payment should be required to sign a receipt for the amount of pay received. Thus, there would be control over the total amount disbursed as well as amounts disbursed to each individual employee. Answer (a) is incorrect because if a signed receipt is not received from each employee paid, there would be no proof of payment. Even though the pay envelopes include both cash and a computation of net wages, the employees should have the opportunity to count the cash received before signing a payroll receipt. Answer (b) is incorrect because unclaimed pay envelopes should not be retained by the paymaster, but rather deposited in a bank account by the cashier. Answer (d) is incorrect because the wage payment will be made in cash and not by check. Accordingly, a receipt must be obtained for each cash payment.

50. (1179,A1,59) (b) The payroll department supervisor should not distribute payroll checks to employees, because the payroll supervisor would be in a position to prepare checks to ficticious employees and keep the checks. Answer (a) is incorrect because the payroll department supervisor should review approved time reports for those employees in the payroll department under the supervisor's supervision. Answer (c) is incorrect because as supervisor, the supervisor should hire subordinate employees. Answer (d) is incorrect because the supervisor should initiate requests for salary adjustments for subordinate employees.

51. (578,A1,41) (d) The payroll function should be separated from the hiring function. Hiring new employees effectively authorizes pay. The functional responsibilities of payroll authorization and payroll payment should be separated. Payroll functions commonly include controlling unemployment claims, maintaining personnel records, and approving fringe benefits (answers (a), (b), and (c)).

52. (579,A1,37) (d) The requirement is an effective internal control technique over the payroll function. Note that you are looking for the best answer of the four alternatives. Total time spent on individual jobs should be compared with total time per the time clock. This will insure that all time is properly allocated to individual jobs, and excess time was not incurred that was not chargeable to specific jobs. Answer (a) is incorrect because employees should not be permitted to reconcile or check their own job reports, i.e., there should be a separate review. Answers (b) and (c) are incorrect because the payroll department and the personnel department should be separate, as they have separate functional responsibilities. The personnel department authorizes the hiring and pay levels of employees whereas the payroll department expends funds. These functional responsibilities should be separate, and neither department should supervise the other department.

C.5. Property, Plant, and Equipment

53. (1180,A1,35) (c) All four answers may, in certain circumstances, assure accountability for fixed assets retirements. Answer (c) is best because continuous utilization of serially numbered retirement orders will assist in control of all retirements (possibly limited by a materiality factor) since, if used properly, they will help assure that only properly authorized retirements will be made. Answer (a) is less complete since it will only help for assets which are sold. The unsystematic nature of the controls in answers (b) and (d) is likely to limit their effectiveness.

54. (578,A1,5) (b) Note that the requirement is the most important internal control procedure over acquisitions of property. Answer (b) is correct, because using budgets to control acquisitions implies a follow-up analysis of budget variances as suggested by answer (c). The use of budgets also permits the level of authorized expenditures to be controlled which does not occur with answer (c). Thus answer (b) is better than (c). Answer (a) is incorrect because a written policy distinguishing capital and revenue expenditures will not provide a control over acquisitions of property. Answer (d) is incorrect because further delegation of acquisitions to user departments will weaken controls over property acquisitions rather than strengthen them.

C.6. Overall Internal Control Checklists

55. (1182,A1,30) (d) The requirement is to determine who should have responsibility for custody of short-term bearer bond investments and the submission of coupons for periodic collections of interest. The treasurer authorizes such transactions. Answer (a) is incorrect because the chief accountant, who is in charge of the recordkeeping function, should not also maintain custody of the bonds. Answer (b) is incorrect because the internal auditor should not be directly involved as such involvement would make an independent review of the system impossible. Answer (c) is incorrect because the cashier function is more directly involved with details such as endorsing, depositing and maintaining records of cash receipts.

56. (1179,A1,42) (a) Cancelled stock certificates should be defaced and attached to corresponding stubs as is done with voided checks. The objective of the control is to prevent reissuance. Answer (b) is incorrect because failure to deface permits reissuance. Answer (c) is incorrect because destruction of the certificates would preclude their control, i.e., their existence after defacing provides assurance that they cannot be reissued. If the certificates were destroyed, one or more might be reissued without any proof that such occurred. Answer (d) is incorrect because the Secretary of State has no interest in receiving defaced and cancelled stock certificates.

57. (578,A1,26) (d) The best control against misappropriation of marketable securities is to assign the custodial responsibilities to a bank. If securities are lost or missing, the bank will be responsible, i.e., the client will not have to be concerned with misappropriation of securities. Answer (a) is incorrect because even trustworthy bonded employees may misappropriate assets. Answer (b) is incorrect because employees who enter the safekeeping area can still misappropriate securities even though they are required to record the reason for their entry in a log. Answer (c) is incorrect because requiring persons with custodial responsibilities also to keep records does not provide much additional control. Remember that the functional responsibilities of custodianship and recordkeeping are to be separated.

58. (579,A1,10) (a) The requirement is the person(s) to make periodic reviews of investment activity delegated by the board of directors to a financial executive. The review should be made by an investment committee of the board of directors, as the authority was delegated by the board of directors. Answers (b), treasurer, (c), corporate controller, and (d), chief operating officer, are incorrect because they did not make the delegation and therefore should not make the periodic reviews. Also the treasurer has custodial functional responsibility and the controller

has accounting functional responsibility, which would further preclude them from authorization functional responsibility.

General

59. (582,A1,24) (a) The requirement is to determine a benefit of fidelity bonds. Bonding companies will typically investigate the backgrounds of new employees. Answer (b) is incorrect since business interruption insurance relates to events which temporarily stop the firm's production, e.g., strikes. Answer (c) is incorrect because even with the existence of fidelity bonds internal controls must be maintained. Answer (d) is incorrect because fidelity bonds deal with irregularities and because fidelity bonds insure the company, not the employees.

D. Other Considerations

D.1. Required Communication of Material Weaknesses

60. (583,A1,16) (a) The requirement is to determine which choice states the secondary objective of the auditor's study and evaluation of internal control. The communication to management of material weaknesses in internal control is a secondary objective in the study and evaluation of internal controls (AU 320.06–.08). The primary objective is to establish a basis for reliance on internal controls and ultimately to determine the nature, extent, and timing of substantive audit tests which will be required to express an opinion on the financial statements. Answers (b) and (d) are incorrect because they relate to the auditor's primary objective. Answer (c) is incorrect because it describes the purpose of compliance tests (AU 320.55–.58). Compliance tests are the second phase in the study and evaluation of internal controls and are an integral part of achieving the auditor's primary objective.

61. (1182,A1,42) (b) The requirement is to determine to whom the auditor is required to communicate material weaknesses in internal control. AU 323.01 requires the auditor to communicate to senior management and the board of directors or its audit committee material weaknesses in internal control that come to his/her attention during the examination of financial statements.

62. (1181,A1,17) (c) The requirement is to determine a segment of the definition of a material internal control weakness. Answer (c) is correct because para 323.01 defines a material internal accounting control weakness as a condition in which the specific control procedures or the degree of compliance therewith do not reduce to a relatively low level the risk that errors or irregularities in amounts that would be material in relation to the financial statements being audited may occur and not be detected within a timely period by **employees in the normal course of performing their assigned functions.**

D.2. Reports on Internal Control

63. (1182,A1,59) (c) The requirement is to determine what an unqualified opinion on an entity's system of internal accounting control implies. The broad objectives of internal accounting control (AU 320.28) are to render reasonable assurance that assets are safeguarded from unauthorized use or disposition and that financial records are sufficiently reliable to permit the preparation of financial statements. Answer (a) is incorrect because compliance with the Foreign Corrupt Practices Act is a legal question not addressed by such an opinion. Answer (b) is incorrect since the likelihood of management fraud may be at a higher than minimal level. Answer (d) is incorrect because typically auditors do not address whether audit committee criteria have been met.

64. (1181,A1,60) (a) The requirement is to determine the true statement with respect to a CPA's study and evaluation of internal accounting control as a part of an audit. Answer (a) is correct because when expressing an opinion on the system of internal control an auditor will perform compliance tests on all important controls. In the case of an audit, compliance testing may be omitted in certain areas due to reasons such as an auditor's desire to rely on substantive testing (para 642.09-.11). Answer (b) is incorrect because, as indicated, the review under an audit is less extensive. Answer (c) is incorrect because compliance tests need not be performed in all areas for an audit. Answer (d) is incorrect because a CPA will not express an opinion on internal accounting control as a result of an audit.

D.6. Effects of an Internal Audit Function

65. (1183,A1,35) (a) The requirement is to determine the statement which best describes how a CPA's audit program compares with the audit client's comprehensive internal audit program. The internal audit program is often more detailed and gives more consideration to achieving administrative control objectives than does a CPA's program. Answer (b) is incorrect because the internal auditor's program will not generally cover less areas than normally are covered by the CPA's. Answer (c) is incorrect because of the internal auditor's

emphasis on administrative controls. Answer (d) is incorrect because it understates the scope of the internal audit program's coverage.

66. (583,A1,41) (b) The requirement is to determine the most appropriate task for internal auditors to perform to assist CPAs. Because decision making responsibility is not involved, the CPA may review the work of the internal auditor relating to the preparation of schedules for negative accounts receivable responses. Answer (a) is incorrect because the CPA must make decisions pertaining to the scope of receivable confirmations. Answer (c) is incorrect because the CPA is responsible for making an evaluation of internal control. Similarly, answer (d) is incorrect because a CPA may not delegate the responsibility for the determination of the adequacy of the allowance for doubtful accounts (or, for that matter, other accounts).

67. (582,A1,54) (b) The requirement is to determine the correct statement with respect to an independent auditor's relationship to internal auditors. When an auditor reviews the competence and objectivity of internal auditors, decisions may be made as to the degree of reliance upon their work (Section 322). Answer (a) is incorrect because the work of internal auditors need not be reviewed during substantive testing. Answer (c), while partially correct, is not as accurate as (b). Answer (d) is incorrect because the independent auditor primarily considers the organizational level to which internal auditors report to establish their degree of objectivity (AU 322.07).

68. (1181,A1,53) (d) The requirement is to determine the effect of the existence of an internal audit staff, which reports to the chief accountant, on the scope of an audit. Answer (d), placing limited reliance on the work performed by internal auditors, is correct as indicated in Section 322 which suggests that CPAs must review the competence and objectivity of internal auditors to determine the extent to which they may be relied upon. Answer (a) is incorrect because a CPA will not completely rely on internal auditors and completely eliminate compliance testing. Answer (b) is incorrect since there is no reason to believe that the existence of internal auditors should increase the CPA's study and evaluation of administrative controls. Answer (c) is incorrect because differing objectives of internal auditors as well as the results of the CPA's analysis of internal auditor competence and objectivity may result in duplication of work.

May 1984 Answers

69. (584,A1,5) (c) The requirement is to determine the area in which the auditor would consider internal control least important. A client's internal control system will not relate as directly to shareholder meetings as to the other answers. CPAs will often attend the shareholder meetings and be aware of what has transpired, but important matters at such meetings are generally publicly available. Answers (a) and (b) are incorrect because land, buildings, and common stock all relate to a firm's double entry bookkeeping system which attempts to safeguard assets and the reliability of financial records. Answer (d) is incorrect because the minutes of board of directors must be received in their complete form by the auditor so the auditor may be aware of matters such as contractual agreements.

70. (584,A1,16) (c) The requirement is to determine the auditing procedure that is **not** commonly used in performing compliance tests. Confirmation is used almost exclusively as a substantive procedure and not as a compliance testing procedure. Inquiring, observing, and inspecting [answers (a), (b), and (d)] are compliance procedures described throughout AU 320.

71. (584,A1,20) (a) The requirement is to determine which statement is included in an accountant's report expressing an opinion on an entity's system of internal accounting control. Such a report is provided in AU 642.39. Answer (a) is the only listed statement included in the report. Answer (b) is incorrect because the report concludes only that in the auditor's **opinion** the internal accounting control system meets the objectives insofar as they pertain to the prevention or detection of material errors or irregularities. Answer (c) is incorrect because the report states that the review was conducted in accordance with the AICPA's standards for a review of internal control. Answer (d) is incorrect because although a statement is made suggesting that inherent limitations exist, no mention is made of an examination of these limitations.

72. (584,A1,25) (d) The requirement is to determine the step which follows the completion of an internal control questionnaire. A preliminary evaluation must be made to determine whether compliance testing is cost justified. Answer (a) is incorrect because a determination of work necessary to form an opinion cannot be made at this point. Answer (b) is incorrect because compliance tests must be performed before a decision on internal control effectiveness can be made. Answer (c) is incorrect because compliance tests may not be performed in certain circumstances.

73. (584,A1,37) (d) The requirement is to determine which statement is **not** made in an accountant's report expressing an opinion on internal accounting control. A statement is not made regarding consistency (AU 642.39). Answer (a) is incorrect because the standard report states the study and evaluation was conducted in accordance with AICPA standards. Answer (b) is incorrect because a specific date is mentioned in the report. Answer (c) is incorrect because the report does describe objectives and limitations. See AU 642.39 for the standard form report on internal accounting control.

74. (584,A1,41) (d) The requirement is to determine the correct statement with respect to changes in planned audit procedures based on the results of the study and evaluation of internal control. Additional substantive tests will be necessary if internal controls are not working properly. When the study and evaluation of internal controls has been completed (as the question specifies), all desired compliance testing has been performed. Thus answers (a), (b), and (c) are incorrect because they specify either an increase or decrease in compliance test.

75. (584,A1,44) (c) The requirement is to determine the correct order of compliance tests, flowchart preparation, and substantive tests. Flowcharts are prepared in conjunction with the review of internal controls; then compliance tests are performed to test internal controls; and, finally, substantive tests are performed to audit specific account balances. This sequence is described throughout AU 320, but especially 320.51-.73.

76. (584,A1,47) (c) The requirement is to determine the set of **incompatible** duties under a good system of internal control. A good system of internal control will segregate recording, custody, and authorization duties. Therefore, answer (c) is correct because the preparation of disbursement vouchers and signing of checks places an individual in a position in which s/he can both prepare erroneous vouchers and then pay them. Answer (a) is incorrect because the person signing the checks should cancel supporting documents to avoid a second payment. Answer (b) is incorrect because the individual receiving the merchandise should prepare a receiving report so as to establish control over the goods. Answer (d) is incorrect because the person requesting the merchandise will be able to determine whether the appropriate merchandise has been received and should, therefore, approve it.

77. (584,A1,48) (d) The requirement is to determine the proper use **by the payroll department** of prenumbered termination notice forms. The payroll department, entrusted with preparing the payroll, must determine that terminated employees do not continue receiving payroll checks. Answer (a) is incorrect because the termination notices will only relate to terminated, not continuing, employees. Answer (b) is incorrect because the personnel department, not the payroll department, must keep the personnel files up to date. Answer (c) is incorrect because such termination notices, as indicated above, do not relate to current employees.

78. (584,A1,55) (c) The requirement is to determine a benefit of a well-prepared flowchart. A flowchart may be used to document the auditor's understanding of the flow of transactions and documents (AU 320.51-.58). Answer (a) is incorrect because while an audit procedures manual may suggest the use of flowcharts, flowcharts will not in general be used to prepare such a manual. Answer (b) is less accurate than (c) because while it may be possible to obtain general information on various jobs, the flowchart will not allow one to obtain a **detailed** job description. Answer (d) is incorrect because a flowchart does not directly address actual accuracy of financial data within a system.

79. (584,A1,56) (d) The requirement is to determine what, in addition to a production order, should accompany finished goods being accepted for stock. Answer (d) is correct because finished goods should be inspected to determine their condition before leaving the production department. Answer (a) is incorrect because a shipping order will not be received until the good has been sold and is to be shipped. Answer (b) is incorrect because a material requisition will be used during the production process to requisition materials with which to produce the goods. Answer (c) is incorrect because a bill of lading will not be prepared until the item is sold.

Unofficial Answer*
(Author Modified)

Problem 1 Purchase Orders

a. Purchase orders may vary in format and style. However, all purchase orders should include areas for insertion of the following information which was not included in the illustration:

- Price
- Purchase order number
- Purchase order execution date
- Authorization signature

b. In the stores department purchase orders serve to:

- Verify that the purchase order was executed as authorized.
- Verify that the quantities reported as received in the receiving department are correct.

In the purchasing department purchase orders serve as:

- A control copy of outstanding orders until the order is received.
- A control copy that accounts for the numerical sequence of all purchase orders (to detect unauthorized use).

In the receiving department purchase orders serve to:

- Authorize acceptance of specified merchandise.
- Establish an independent verification of quantities received (usually by compelling a blind count).

In the accounting department purchase orders serve to:

- Verify that the acquisition was authorized.
- Verify the accuracy of the terms of the vendor's invoice.
- Authorize payment upon proof of delivery.

**Because the requirements of this question could be answered by lists of items, we have not included an outline of the solution.*

Unofficial Answer*

Problem 2 Purchases and Disbursements Flowchart

A. Prepare purchase order
B. To vendor
C. Prepare receiving report
D. From purchasing
E. From receiving
F. Purchase order No. 5
G. Receiving report No. 1
H. Prepare and approve voucher
I. Unpaid voucher file, filed by due date
J. Treasurer
K. Sign checks and cancel voucher package documents
L. Cancelled voucher package

**Because the requirements of this question could be answered by lists of items we have not included an outline of the solution.*

Unofficial Answer*

Problem 3 Internal Controls Over Cash Receipts and Warehousing

The system of internal control should provide for:

- Drivers to count and then sign for all merchandise received.
- Daily verification of each driver's ending inventory.
- Cash to be deposited daily by each driver.
- Daily return of duplicate deposit slips by each driver.
- Reconciliation of cash deposits with the daily net change in inventory.
- Provision for explanation of overages and shortages.
- A periodic independent surprise check of machines to verify that
  - a. machines contain only authorized Trapan-purchased merchandise.
  - b. machines are mechanically programmed to charge the authorized prices.
  - c. cash and merchandise in machines equal a predetermined (imprest) total.
- Bonding of employees.
- Alternate driver routes and required vacations.
- Restricting access to the warehouse.
- The warehouseman to count and sign for all items going into or out of the warehouse.
- Maintenance of perpetual inventory records.
- Periodic physical inventory count of merchandise in the warehouse.
- Analytical review of collections.

**Because the requirements of this question could be answered by lists of items we have not included an outline of the solution.*

Answer Outline

Problem 4 IC Questionnaire

Internal control questionnaire for revolving fund
- Custody
  - Is fund responsibility vested in one person?
  - Is physical access to the fund denied to others?
  - Is custodian independent of others who handle cash?
  - Is custodian bonded?
  - Is custodian denied access to other cash funds?
- Receipts
  - Are receipts unalterable?
  - Are receipts prenumbered?
  - Is the integrity of the prenumbered sequence periodically verified?
  - Are receipts signed by the book seller?
- Reimbursement Vouchers
  - Are receipts attached to reimbursement vouchers?
  - Are vouchers submitted for reimbursement approved by someone other than the custodian?
  - Are reimbursement vouchers cancelled after payment?
- Disbursements from Fund
  - Is fund used only for the repurchase of books?
- Non-Custodian Control
  - Is fund periodically reconciled by someone other than the custodian?
  - Is fund maintained on an imprest basis?
  - Is size of the fund suitable for the purpose intended?

Unofficial Answer

Problem 4 IC Questionnaire

University Books Incorporated
Revolving Cash Fund
Internal Control Questionnaire

Question	Yes	No
Is responsibility for the fund vested in one person?		
Is physical access to the fund denied to all others?		
Is the custodian independent of other employees who handle cash?		
Is the custodian bonded?		
Is the custodian denied access to other cash funds?		
Are receipts unalterable?		
Are receipts prenumbered?		
Is the integrity of the prenumbered sequence periodically accounted for?		
Does the seller sign receipts?		
Are receipts attached to reimbursement vouchers?		
Are vouchers that are submitted for reimbursement approved by someone other than the custodian?		
Are reimbursement vouchers and attachments (receipts) cancelled after reimbursement?		
Is the fund used exclusively for the acquisition of books?		
Is the fund periodically counted and reconciled by someone other than the custodian?		
Is the fund maintained on an imprest basis?		
Is the size of the fund appropriate for the purpose intended?		

Unofficial Answer*
(Author Modified)

Problem 5 Objectives and Limitations of Systems of Internal Control

a. Objectives of a system of internal accounting control are to (AU 320.28):
   1. Safeguard assets.
   2. Provide reliable financial records.

b. A system of internal accounting control provides reasonable assurance that (AU 320.28):
   1. Transactions are executed per management's authorization.
   2. Transactions are recorded so as to provide a basis for preparation of the financial statements per GAAP or other applicable criteria and to maintain accountability over assets.
   3. Access to assets is controlled.
   4. Assets are compared periodically with recorded accountability.

c. Inherent limitations of a system of internal accounting control include (AU 320.34):
   1. Misunderstanding of instructions.
   2. Mistakes in judgment.

**Because the requirements of this question could be answered by lists of items we have not included an outline of the solution.*

3. Personal carelessness.
4. Distraction or fatigue.
5. Possibility of collusion.
6. Perpetrations by management.
7. Changes in conditions.
8. Deteriorating degree of compliance.

Answer Outline

Problem 6 Inventory IC Weaknesses

1. Raw materials may be obtained by oral authorization
   Proper written authorization should be required
2. Perpetual inventory system does not exist
   Periodic method may allow stockouts or overstocks
   Establish adequate perpetual inventory system
3. Raw material purchases do not vary with production demands
   Purchases should be based upon production schedules
4. Purchasing function and invoice payment are combined
   Require centralized purchasing with prenumbered purchase orders
   Separate purchasing and payment functions
5. The same vendor is always used
   Use competitive bids
6. There is no receiving department
   Establish receiving department
7. There is no inspection of goods upon receipt
   Establish inspection department with inspection reports

Unofficial Answer

Problem 6 Inventory IC Weaknesses

Weaknesses	Recommended Improvements
1. Raw materials may be removed from the storeroom upon oral authorization from one of the production foremen.	1. Raw materials should be removed from the storeroom only upon written authorization from an authorized production foreman. The authorization forms should be prenumbered and accounted for, list quantities and job or production number, and be signed and dated.
2. Alden's practice of monthly physical-inventory counts does not compensate for the lack of a perpetual-inventory system. Quantities on hand at the end of one month may not be sufficient to last until the next month's count. If the company has taken this into account in establishing reorder levels, then it is carrying too large an investment in inventory.	2. A perpetual-inventory system should be established under the control of someone other than the storekeepers. The system should include quantities and values for each item of raw material. Total inventory value per the perpetual records should be agreed to the general ledger at reasonable intervals. When physical counts are taken they should be compared to the perpetual records. Where differences occur they should be investigated, and if the perpetual records are in error they should be adjusted. Also, controls should be established over obsolescence of stored materials.
3. Raw materials are purchased at a predetermined reorder level and in predetermined quantities. Since production levels may often vary during the year, quantities ordered may be either too small or too great for the current production demands.	3. Requests for purchases of raw materials should come from the production-department management and be based on production schedules and quantities on hand per the perpetual records.

Weaknesses	Recommended Improvements
4. The accounts-payable clerk handles both the purchasing function and payment of invoices. This is not a satisfactory separation of duties.	4. The purchasing function should be centralized in a separate department. Prenumbered purchase orders should originate from and be controlled by this department. A copy of the purchase order should be sent to the accounting and receiving departments. Consideration should be given to whether the receiving copy should show quantities.
5. Raw materials are always purchased from the same vendor.	5. The purchasing deparment should be required to obtain competitive bids on all purchases over a specified amount.
6. There is no receiving department or receiving report. For proper separation of duties, the individuals responsible for receiving should be separate from the storeroom clerk.	6. A receiving department should be established. Personnel in this department should count or weigh all goods received and prepare a prenumbered receiving report. These reports should be signed, dated, and controlled. A copy should be sent to the accounting department, purchasing department, and storeroom.
7. There is no inspection department. Since high-cost electronic components are usually required to meet certain specifications, they should be tested for these requirements when received.	7. An inspection department should be established to inspect goods as they are received. Prenumbered inspection reports should be prepared and accounted for. A copy of these reports should be sent to the accounting department.

Answer Outline

Problem 7 Payroll IC Weaknesses

a. Weaknesses in system of internal control
a1. Lack of approval of foreman's clock card
a2. Computation of regular and overtime hours by payroll clerk no. 2 not compared with foreman's summary
a3. Computations and rates of pay not checked by independent person
a4. Payroll checks not reconciled to payroll register
a5. Payroll clerk should not have custody of signature-stamp machine and blank checks
a6. Payroll not approved by officer
a7. Payroll checks should not be distributed by foreman
a8. Unclaimed checks not held by independent employee
a9. Comparison of hours on check with hours on clock card should not be done by clerk who did original computation
a10. Comparison of payroll on check with register should not be done by clerk who prepared register

b. Inquiries concerning possible additional weaknesses
b1. Are clock cards checked for foreman's approval?
b2. Is overtime on clock cards approved?
b3. Is data in payroll files checked with personnel files?
b4. Is clock card punching observed by timekeeper?
b5. Are other mitigating internal controls in existence, e.g., bonding, required vacations?

Unofficial Answer

Problem 7 Payroll IC Weaknesses

a. Weaknesses in the system of internal control are the following:

1. Lack of approval of the foreman's clock card by an appropriate supervisor is an unsound practice. Employees should not be permitted to maintain their own time records and submit them without approval.

2. The computation of regular and overtime hours prepared by payroll clerk no. 2 that is used in the preparation of the payroll register is not compared with the summary of regular and overtime hours prepared by the foreman.

3. Arithmetic computations and rates of pay used in the preparation of the payroll register are not checked by a person who is independent of their preparation and payroll register columns are not verified (re-added) by a person other than the preparer of the payroll register.

4. Payroll checks are not reconciled to the payroll register in order to prevent improper disbursements.

5. A signature-stamp machine should not be in the custody of any payroll clerk who has access to unsigned checks.

6. Payroll is not approved by an officer of the company.

7. Since the paymaster should be independent of the payroll process, signed payroll checks should not be distributed by the foreman.

8. Unclaimed payroll checks should be in the custody of an employee who is independent of the payroll process.

9. The comparison of (regular and overtime) hours indicated on payroll check (or attachments) with (regular and overtime) hours indicated on clock cards should not be performed by the clerk who is responsible for the original computation of (regular and overtime) hours indicated on clock cards.

10. The comparison of gross and net payroll indicated on payroll check (or attachments) with gross and net payroll indicated in the payroll register should not be performed by the clerk who is responsible for preparing the payroll register.

b. One should inquire whether:

1. Payroll clerk no. 2 checks clock cards for the foreman's written approval.

2. Approved overtime is indicated on clock cards.

3. Employment, wage, and related data in payroll files are periodically crosschecked with personnel files for agreement.

4. The punching of clock cards is observed by a timekeeper.

5. Other mitigating internal control measures (for example, bonding, required vacations, and so forth) are in existence.

Answer Outline

Problem 8 Cash Receipts IC Weaknesses

Weaknesses in and Recommended Improvements for Internal Control

1. No segregation of duties between persons collecting admission fees and persons authorizing admission
   - One clerk (collection clerk) should collect admission fees and issue prenumbered tickets
   - Another clerk (admission clerk) should authorize admission upon receipt of ticket or proof of membership
2. No independent count made of paying patrons
   - Admission clerk should retain a portion of the prenumbered admission ticket
3. No proof of accuracy of amounts collected by the clerks
   - Each day treasurer should reconcile admission ticket stubs with cash collected by treasurer
4. Cash receipts records not promptly prepared
   - Collection clerk should record cash collections daily
   - Recording should be a permanent record to serve as first record of accountability
5. Cash receipts are not promptly deposited
   - Deposit cash at least once a day
6. No proof of accuracy of amounts deposited
   - Compare authenticated deposit slips with daily cash collections
   - Investigate and resolve discrepancies promptly
   - Treasurer should establish policy including analytical review of cash collections
7. No record of internal accountability for cash
   - Treasurer should issue signed receipt for all proceeds received from collection clerk
   - Maintain receipts and periodically check against cash collection and deposit records

Unofficial Answer

Problem 8 Cash Receipts IC Weaknesses

	Weakness		*Recommendation*
1.	There is no segregation of duties between persons responsible for collecting admission fees and persons responsible for authorizing admission.	1.	One clerk (hereafter referred to as the collection clerk) should collect admission fees and issue prenumbered tickets. The other clerk (hereafter referred to as the admission clerk) should authorize admission upon receipt of the ticket or proof of membership.
2.	An independent count of paying patrons is not made.	2.	The admission clerk should retain a portion of the prenumbered admission ticket (admission ticket stub).
3.	There is no proof of accuracy of amounts collected by the clerks.	3.	Admission ticket stubs should be reconciled with cash collected by the treasurer each day.
4.	Cash receipts records are not promptly prepared.	4.	The cash collections should be recorded by the collection clerk daily on a permanent record that will serve as the first record of accountability.
5.	Cash receipts are not promptly deposited. Cash should not be left undeposited for a week.	5.	Cash should be deposited at least once each day.
6.	There is no proof of accuracy of amounts deposited.	6.	Authenticated deposit slips should be compared with daily cash collection records. Discrepancies should be promptly investigated and resolved. In addition, the treasurer should establish policy that includes an analytical review of cash collections.
7.	There is no record of the internal accountability for cash.	7.	The treasurer should issue a signed receipt for all proceeds received from the collection clerk. These receipts should be maintained and should be periodically checked against cash collection and deposit records.

Answer Outline

Problem 9 Purchasing Function Flowchart

Question requires identification and explanation of control problems. Only improvements are listed below.

- Require proper approval of purchase requisitions
- Delete purchase requisition copy sent to receiving room
- Compare purchase requisitions and purchase orders
- Separate file for unmatched purchase requisitions
- Review need prior to preparing purchase order
- Negotiate with different vendors for best price
- Purchase office to review invoice prior to approving for payment
- Do not show quantities on purchase orders sent to receiving room
- Establish procedures for vendors' misshipments
- Send copy of receiving report to stores department
- Establish control over number of vouchers submitted for payment
- Establish control over dollars of vouchers submitted for payment

Examine documents prior to voucher preparation
Treasurer, not controller, should be responsible for cash disbursements
Establish procedures for purchase returns
Establish procedures for reconciling discrepancies
Establish control over prenumbered forms

Unofficial Answer

Problem 9   Purchasing Function Flowchart

The identification and explanation of the systems and control problems are as follows:

1. The purchase requisition is not approved. The purchase requisition should be approved by a responsible person in the stores department. The approval should be indicated on the purchase requisition after the approver is satisfied that it was properly prepared based on a need to replace stores or the proper request from a user department.

2. Purchase requisition number two is not required. Purchase requisitions are unnecessarily sent from the stores department to the receiving room. The receiving room does not make any use of the purchase requisitions and no purpose seems to exist for the receiving room to obtain a copy. A copy of the requisition might be sent from stores directly to accounts payable where it can be compared to the purchase order to verify that the merchandise requisitioned by an authorized employee has been properly ordered.

3. Purchase requisitions and purchase orders are not compared in the stores department. Although purchase orders are attached to purchase requisitions in the stores department, there is no indication that any comparison is made of the two documents. Prior to attaching the purchase order to the purchase requisition the requisitioner's function should include a check that –

   a. Prices are reasonable.
   b. The quality of the materials ordered is acceptable.
   c. Delivery dates are in accordance with company needs.
   d. All pertinent data on the purchase order and purchase requisition (e.g., quantities, specifications, delivery dates, etc.) are in agreement.

Since the requisitioner will be charged for the materials ordered, the requisitioner is the logical person to perform the steps.

4. Purchase orders and purchase requisitions should not be combined and filed with the unmatched purchase requisitions, in the stores department. A separate file should be maintained for the combined and matched documents. The unmatched purchase requisitions file can serve as a control over merchandise requisitioned but not yet ordered.

5. Preliminary review should be made before preparing purchase orders. Prior to preparation of the purchase order the purchase office should review the company's need for the specific materials requisitioned and approve the request.

6. The purchase office should attempt to obtain the highest quality merchandise at the lowest possible price, and the procedures that are followed to achieve this should be included on the flowchart. There is no indication that the purchase office submits purchase orders to competitive bidding when appropriate. That office should be directly involved with vendors in determining the cost of materials ordered and should be primarily responsible for deciding at what price materials should be ordered and which vendor should be used.

7. The purchase office does not review the invoice prior to processing approval. The purchase office should review the vendor's invoice for overall accuracy and completeness, verifying quantity, prices, specifications, terms, dates, etc., and if the invoice is in agreement with the purchase order, receiving report, and purchase requisition, the purchase office should clearly indicate on the invoice that it is approved for payment processing. The approval invoice should be sent to the accounts payable department.

8. The copy of the purchase order sent to the receiving room generally should not show quantities ordered, thus forcing the department to count goods received. In addition to counting the merchandise received from the vendor, the receiving department personnel should examine the condition and quality of the merchandise upon receipt.

9. There is no indication of the procedures in effect when the quantity of merchandise received differs from what was ordered. Procedures for handling over-shipments and short-shipments should be clearly outlined and included on the flowchart.

10. The receiving report is not sent to the stores department. A copy of the receiving report should be sent from the receiving room directly to the stores department with the materials received. The stores department, after verifying the accuracy of the receiving report, should indicate approval on that copy and send it to the accounts payable department. The copy sent to accounts payable will serve as proof that the materials ordered were received by the company and are in the user department.

11. There is no indication of control over vouchers in the accounts payable department. In the accounts payable department a record of all vouchers

submitted to the cashier should be maintained, and a copy of the vouchers should be filed in an alphabetical vendor reference file.

12. There is no indication of control over dollar amounts on vouchers. Accounts payable personnel should prepare and maintain control sheets on the dollar amounts of vouchers. Such sheets should be sent to departments posting transactions to general and subsidiary ledgers.

13. There is no examination of documents prior to voucher preparation. In addition to the matching procedure, the mathematical accuracy of all documents should be verified prior to preparation of vouchers.

14. The controller should not be responsible for cash disbursements. The cash disbursement function should be the responsibility of the treasurer, not the controller, so as to provide proper division of responsibility between the custody of assets and the recording of transactions.

15. There is no indication of the company's procedures for handling purchase returns. Although separate return procedures may be in effect and included on a separate flowchart, some indications of this should be included as part of the purchases flowchart.

16. Discrepancy procedures are not indicated. The flowchart should indicate what procedures are followed whenever matching reveals a difference between the information on the documents compared.

17. There is no indication of any control over prenumbered forms. All prenumbered documents should be accounted for.

Unofficial Answer*

Problem 10 Inventory Weaknesses

a. *Ingredients inventory*

1. Weaknesses	*2. Recommended improvements*
• Failure to delegate authority for receiving material.	• If feasible a separate receiving department should be established. At a minimum specific employees should be given responsibility for receiving merchandise.
• Receivers are currently accepting whatever is delivered and simply taking some sort of count or tally.	• Receivers should be given a copy of purchase orders with complete descriptions except quantities. These copies should be used instead of tallies.
• Ingredients inventory is stored in the production area.	• Ingredients inventory should be placed in a protected storage area which has controlled access.
• Apparently only a periodic inventory system is being employed.	• A perpetual system should be installed if possible.
• No mention is made of adjustment and reconciliation of book inventory to physical including appropriate cut-off procedures.	• All differences between physical and book inventory should be reviewed and investigated when deemed appropriate.

**Because the requirements of this question could be answered by lists of items we have not included an outline of the solution.*

Maintenance materials and supplies inventory

1. Weaknesses	*2. Recommended improvements*
• There appears to be a lack of accountability for inventory throughout the production process.	• Ingredients inventory items should only be released from stores upon written requisition. Appropriate documentation should follow the inventory throughout the production process.
• Access to inventory is unrestricted at various times during the first two shifts and during the entire third shift and Saturday.	• The room should be locked and a clerk present at all times when the room is open. Requisitions should be required for all withdrawals of materials and supplies.
• A periodic inventory system appears to be in effect.	• A perpetual system should be used if possible.
• No indication is given of book to physical inventory adjustments.	• Book to physical inventory adjustments should be made, and investigated when appropriate.

b. The internal auditors should review and evaluate the formally documented company procedures which have been established for the purchasing, receiving, storing, issuing, and costing of inventories. This review and evaluation is accomplished through review of procedures manuals and oral questioning of top management.

Once the procedures have been reviewed and evaluated, compliance testing should be performed to see if the procedures are in fact being followed. A partial list of these procedures would include: comparison of receiving reports with purchase orders noting appropriate signatures; observing physical inventories and making test counts; observing and questioning operating personnel as to their duties and procedures followed: review book to physical inventory adjustments.

Any shortcomings in established procedures should be eliminated. Any lack of compliance with procedures should be evaluated to determine if it is an isolated incident or a breakdown in internal control. If it is determined to be a breakdown of internal control, recommendations should be made for appropriate action to be taken by management.

Unofficial Answer*

Problem 11 Sales System Flowchart

Flowchart symbol letter	*Internal control procedure or internal document*
c.	Approve customer credit and terms.
d.	Release merchandise to shipping department.
e.	File by sales order number.
f.	File pending receipt of merchandise.
g.	Prepare bill of lading.
h.	Copy of bill of lading to customer.
i.	Ship merchandise to customer.
j.	File by sales order number.
k.	Customer purchase order and sales order.
l.	File pending notice of shipment.
m.	Prepare three-part sales invoice.
n.	Copy of invoice to customer.
o.	Post to (or enter in) sales journal.
p.	Account for numerical sequence.
q.	Post to customer accounts.
r.	File by (payment due) date.

**Because the requirements of this question could be answered by lists of items we have not included an outline of the solution.*

Multiple Choice Questions (1–111)

1. Which of the following **best** describes the primary purpose of audit procedures?
   a. To detect error or irregularities.
   b. To comply with generally accepted accounting principles.
   c. To gather corroborative evidence.
   d. To verify the accuracy of account balances.

2. Each of the following might, in itself, form a valid basis for an auditor to decide to omit a test **except** the
   a. Relative risk involved.
   b. Relationship between the cost of obtaining evidence and its usefulness.
   c. Difficulty and expense involved in testing a particular item.
   d. Degree of reliance on the relevant internal controls.

3. Audit evidence can come in different forms with different degrees of persuasiveness. Which of the following is the **least** persuasive type of evidence?
   a. Vendor's invoice.
   b. Bank statement obtained from the client.
   c. Computations made by the auditor.
   d. Prenumbered client invoices.

4. Which of the following statements relating to the competence of evidential matter is always true?
   a. Evidential matter gathered by an auditor from outside an enterprise is reliable.
   b. Accounting data developed under satisfactory conditions of internal control are more relevant than data developed under unsatisfactory internal control conditions.
   c. Oral representations made by management are **not** valid evidence.
   d. Evidence gathered by auditors must be both valid and relevant to be considered competent.

5. Which of the following is the **least** persuasive documentation in support of an auditor's opinion?
   a. Schedules of details of physical inventory counts conducted by the client.
   b. Notation of inferences drawn from ratios and trends.
   c. Notation of appraisers' conclusions documented in the auditor's working papers.
   d. Lists of negative confirmation requests for which **no** response was received by the auditor.

6. Which of the following elements ultimately determines the specific auditing procedures that are necessary in the circumstances to afford a reasonable basis for an opinion?
   a. Auditor judgment.
   b. Materiality.
   c. Relative risk.
   d. Reasonable assurance.

7. Whenever negative assurance is provided by a CPA it is based upon
   a. An absence of nullifying evidence.
   b. A presence of substantiating evidence.
   c. An objective examination in accordance with generally accepted auditing standards.
   d. A judgmental determination in accordance with guidelines promulgated by the AICPA.

8. With respect to the auditor's planning of a year-end examination, which of the following statements is always true?
   a. An engagement should **not** be accepted after the fiscal year end.
   b. An inventory count must be observed at the balance sheet date.
   c. The client's audit committee should **not** be told of the specific audit procedures which will be performed.
   d. It is an acceptable practice to carry out substantial parts of the examination at interim dates.

9. To test for unsupported entries in the ledger, the direction of audit testing should be from the
   a. Ledger entries.
   b. Journal entries.
   c. Externally generated documents.
   d. Original source documents.

10. Which of the following procedures is **least** likely to be performed before the balance sheet date?
    a. Observation of inventory.
    b. Review of internal control over cash disbursements.
    c. Search for unrecorded liabilities.
    d. Confirmation of receivables.

11. When examining a client's statement of changes in financial position, for audit evidence, an auditor will rely primarily upon
    a. Determination of the amount of working capital at year-end.

b. Cross-referencing to balances and transactions reviewed in connection with the examination of the other financial statements.
c. Analysis of significant ratios of prior years as compared to the current year.
d. The guidance provided by the APB Opinion on the statement of changes in financial position.

12. Which of the following procedures is not included in a review engagement of a nonpublic entity?
a. Inquiries of management.
b. Inquiries regarding events subsequent to the balance sheet date.
c. Any procedures designed to identify relationships among data that appear to be unusual.
d. A study and evaluation of internal control.

13. Which of the following is ordinarily designed to detect possible material dollar errors on the financial statements?
a. Compliance testing.
b. Analytical review.
c. Computer controls.
d. Post audit working paper review.

14. An auditor compares 1981 revenues and expenses with those of the prior year and investigates all changes exceeding 10%. By this procedure the auditor would be most likely to learn that
a. An increase in property tax rates has **not** been recognized in the client's accrual.
b. The 1981 provision for uncollectible accounts is inadequate, because of worsening economic conditions.
c. Fourth quarter payroll taxes were **not** paid.
d. The client changed its capitalization policy for small tools in 1981.

15. Which of the following analytical review procedures should be applied to the income statement?
a. Select sales and expense items and trace amounts to related supporting documents.
b. Ascertain that the net income amount in the statement of changes in financial position agrees with the net income amount in the income statement.
c. Obtain from the proper client representatives, the beginning and ending inventory amounts that were used to determine costs of sales.
d. Compare the actual revenues and expenses with the corresponding figures of the previous year and investigate significant differences.

16. An inventory turnover analysis is useful to the auditor because it may detect
a. Inadequacies in inventory pricing.
b. Methods of avoiding cyclical holding costs.
c. The optimum automatic reorder points.
d. The existence of obsolete merchandise.

17. One reason why the independent auditor makes an analytical review of the client's operations is to identify probable
a. Weaknesses of a material nature in the system of internal control.
b. Unusual transactions.
c. Non-compliance with prescribed control procedures.
d. Improper separation of accounting and other financial duties.

18. In the context of an audit of financial statements, substantive tests are audit procedures that
a. May be eliminated under certain conditions.
b. Are designed to discover significant subsequent events.
c. May be either tests of transactions, direct tests of financial balances, or analytical tests.
d. Will increase proportionately with the auditor's reliance on internal control.

19. Those procedures specifically outlined in an audit program are primarily designed to
a. Gather evidence.
b. Detect errors or irregularities.
c. Test internal systems.
d. Protect the auditor in the event of litigation.

20. In the course of the examination of financial statements for the purpose of expressing an opinion thereon, the auditor will normally prepare a schedule of unadjusted differences for which the auditor did not propose adjustment when they were uncovered. What is the primary purpose served by this schedule?
a. To point out to the responsible client officials the errors made by various company personnel.
b. To summarize the adjustments that must be made before the company can prepare and submit its federal tax return.

c. To identify the potential financial statement effects of errors or disputed items that were considered immaterial when discovered.
d. To summarize the errors made by the company so that corrections can be made after the audited financial statements are released.

21. In planning an audit engagement, which of the following is a factor that affects the independent auditor's judgment as to the quantity, type, and content of working papers?
a. The estimated occurrence rate of attributes.
b. The preliminary evaluations based upon initial substantive testing.
c. The content of the client's representation letter.
d. The anticipated nature of the auditor's report.

22. Which of the following is **not** a primary purpose of audit working papers?
a. To coordinate the examination.
b. To assist in preparation of the audit report.
c. To support the financial statements.
d. To provide evidence of the audit work performed.

23. Which of the following eliminates voluminous details from the auditor's working trial balance by classifying and summarizing similar or related items?
a. Account analyses.
b. Supporting schedules.
c. Control accounts.
d. Lead schedules.

24. Assuming an excellent system of internal control exists, which of the following audit procedures would be **least** likely to be performed?
a. Physical inspection of a sample of inventory.
b. Search for unrecorded cash receipts.
c. Obtain a client representation letter.
d. Confirmation of accounts receivable.

25. Which of the following is one of the better auditing techniques that might be used by an auditor to detect kiting?
a. Review composition of authenticated deposit slips.
b. Review subsequent bank statements and cancelled checks received directly from the banks.
c. Prepare a schedule of bank transfers from the client's books.
d. Prepare year-end bank reconciliations.

26. A cash shortage may be concealed by transporting funds from one location to another or by converting negotiable assets to cash. Because of this, which of the following is vital?
a. Simultaneous confirmations.
b. Simultaneous bank reconciliations.
c. Simultaneous verification.
d. Simultaneous surprise cash count.

27. The auditor should ordinarily mail confirmation requests to all banks with which the client has conducted any business during the year, regardless of the year-end balance, since
a. The confirmation form also seeks information about indebtedness to the bank.
b. This procedure will detect kiting activities which would otherwise not be detected.
c. The mailing confirmation forms to all such banks is required by generally accepted auditing standards.
d. This procedure relieves the auditor of any responsibility with respect to nondetection of forged checks.

28. To establish illegal "slush funds," corporations may divert cash received in normal business operations. An auditor would encounter the greatest difficulty in detecting the diversion of proceeds from
a. Scrap sales.
b. Dividends.
c. Purchase returns.
d. C.O.D. sales.

29. With respect to contingent liabilities, the Standard Bank Confirmation Inquiry form approved jointly by the AICPA and the Bank Administration Institute requests information regarding notes receivable
a. Held by the bank in a custodial account.
b. Held by the bank for collection.
c. Collected by the bank.
d. Discounted by the bank.

30. Which of the following statements regarding the examination of negotiable notes receivable is correct?
a. Confirmation from the customer of a note is **not** an acceptable alternative to inspection.
b. Notes receivable discounted without recourse are confirmed via the standard bank confirmation form used in the audit of cash.

c. Physical inspection of a note by the auditor provides conclusive evidence.
d. Notes receivable discounted with recourse need **not** be confirmed.

31. An auditor confirms a representative number of open accounts receivable as of December 31, 1982, and investigates respondents' exceptions and comments. By this procedure the auditor would be most likely to learn of which of the following?
a. One of the cashiers has been covering a personal embezzlement by lapping.
b. One of the sales clerks has **not** been preparing charge slips for credit sales to family and friends.
c. One of the EDP control clerks has been removing all sales invoices applicable to his account from the data file.
d. The credit manager has misappropriated remittances from customers whose accounts have been written off.

32. During the process of confirming receivables as of December 31, 1982, a positive confirmation was returned indicating the "balance owed as of December 31 was paid on January 9, 1983." The auditor would most likely
a. Determine whether there were any changes in the account between January 1 and January 9, 1983.
b. Determine whether a customary trade discount was taken by the customer.
c. Reconfirm the zero balance as of January 10, 1983.
d. Verify that the amount was received.

33. An auditor reconciles the total of the accounts receivable subsidiary ledger to the general ledger control account, as of October 31, 1982. By this procedure, the auditor would be most likely to learn of which of the following?
a. An October invoice was improperly computed.
b. An October check from a customer was posted in error to the account of another customer with a similar name.
c. An opening balance in a subsidiary ledger account was improperly carried forward from the previous accounting period.
d. An account balance is past due and should be written off.

34. Which of the following is the best argument against the use of negative accounts receivable confirmations?
a. The cost-per-response is excessively high.
b. There is **no** way of knowing if the intended recipients received them.
c. Recipients are likely to feel that in reality the confirmation is a subtle request for payment.
d. The inference drawn from receiving no reply may **not** be correct.

35. Customers having substantial year-end past due balances fail to reply after second request forms have been mailed directly to them. Which of the following is the most appropriate audit procedure?
a. Examine shipping documents.
b. Review collections during the year being examined.
c. Intensify the study of the client's system of internal control with respect to receivables.
d. Increase the balance in the accounts receivable allowance (contra) account.

36. The negative form of accounts receivable confirmation request is particularly useful **except** when
a. Internal control surrounding accounts receivable is considered to be effective.
b. A large number of small balances are involved.
c. The auditor has reason to believe the persons receiving the requests are likely to give them consideration.
d. Individual account balances are relatively large.

37. Which of the following is **not** a primary objective of the auditor in the examination of accounts receivable?
a. Determine the approximate realizable value.
b. Determine the adequacy of internal controls.
c. Establish validity of the receivables.
d. Determine the approximate time of collectibility of the receivables.

38. Johnson is engaged in the audit of a utility which supplies power to a residential community. All accounts receivable balances are small and internal control is effective. Customers are billed bi-monthly. In order to

determine the validity of the accounts receivable balances at the balance sheet date, Johnson would most likely

a. Examine evidence of subsequent cash receipts instead of sending confirmation requests.
b. Send positive confirmation requests.
c. Send negative confirmation requests.
d. Use statistical sampling instead of sending confirmation requests.

39. From the auditor's point of view, inventory counts are more acceptable prior to the year end when

a. Internal control is weak.
b. Accurate perpetual inventory records are maintained.
c. Inventory is slow-moving.
d. Significant amounts of inventory are held on a consignment basis.

40. Purchase cut-off procedures should be designed to test whether or not all inventory

a. Purchased and received before the year end was recorded.
b. On the year end balance sheet was carried at lower of cost or market.
c. On the year end balance sheet was paid for by the company.
d. Owned by the company is in the possession of the company.

41. Which of the following situations would **most** likely require special audit planning by the auditor?

a. Some items of factory and office equipment do **not** bear identification numbers.
b. Depreciation methods used on the client's tax return differ from those used on the books.
c. Assets costing less than $500 are expensed even though the expected life exceeds one year.
d. Inventory is comprised of precious stones.

42. An auditor has accounted for a sequence of inventory tags and is now going to trace information on a representative number of tags to the physical inventory sheets. The purpose of this procedure is to obtain assurance that

a. The final inventory is valued at cost.
b. All inventory represented by an inventory tag is listed on the inventory sheets.
c. All inventory represented by an inventory tag is bona fide.
d. Inventory sheets do **not** include untagged inventory items.

43. An internal control questionnaire indicates that an approved receiving report is required to accompany every check request for payment of merchandise. Which of the following procedures provides the **greatest** assurance that this control is operating effectively?

a. Select and examine receiving reports and ascertain that the related cancelled checks are dated **no** earlier than the receiving reports.
b. Select and examine receiving reports and ascertain that the related cancelled checks are dated **no** later than the receiving reports.
c. Select and examine cancelled checks and ascertain that the related receiving reports are dated **no** earlier than the checks.
d. Select and examine cancelled checks and ascertain that the related receiving reports are dated **no** later than the checks.

44. The accuracy of perpetual inventory records may be established, in part, by comparing perpetual inventory records with

a. Purchase requisitions.
b. Receiving reports.
c. Purchase orders.
d. Vendor payments.

45. When title to merchandise in transit has passed to the audit client, the auditor engaged in the performance of a purchase cutoff will encounter the greatest difficulty in gaining assurance with respect to the

a. Quantity.
b. Quality.
c. Price.
d. Terms.

46. An auditor will usually trace the details of the test counts made during the observation of the physical inventory taking to a final inventory schedule. This audit procedure is undertaken to provide evidence that items physically present and observed by the auditor at the time of the physical inventory count are

a. Owned by the client.
b. Not obsolete.
c. Physically present at the time of the preparation of the final inventory schedule.
d. Included in the final inventory schedule.

47. The auditor tests the quantity of materials charged to work in process by tracing these quantities to

a. Cost ledgers.
b. Perpetual inventory records.

c. Receiving reports.
d. Material requisitions.

48. When auditing a public warehouse, which of the following is the most important audit procedure with respect to disclosing unrecorded liabilities?
a. Confirmation of negotiable receipts with holders.
b. Review of outstanding receipts.
c. Inspection of receiving and issuing procedures.
d. Observation of inventory.

49. Apex Incorporated issued common stock to acquire another company, in an acquisition that was accounted for as a pooling of interest. The auditor examining this transaction would be **least** interested in ascertaining
a. The net book value of the acquired company.
b. The par value of the stock that was issued.
c. Whether or **not** the acquisition was approved by the board of directors of Apex Incorporated.
d. Whether the fair market value of the acquired assets were independently appraised.

50. Jones was engaged to examine the financial statements of Gamma Corporation for the year ended June 30, 1980. Having completed an examination of the investment securities, which of the following is the **best** method of verifying the accuracy of recorded dividend income?
a. Tracing recorded dividend income to cash receipts records and validated deposit slips.
b. Utilizing analytical review techniques and statistical sampling.
c. Comparing recorded dividends with amounts appearing on federal information forms 1099.
d. Comparing recorded dividends with a standard financial reporting service's record of dividends.

51. In verifying the amount of goodwill recorded by a client, the most convincing evidence which an auditor can obtain is by comparing the recorded value of assets acquired with the
a. Assessed value as evidenced by tax bills.
b. Seller's book value as evidenced by financial statements.
c. Insured value as evidenced by insurance policies.
d. Appraised value as evidenced by independent appraisals.

52. Which of the following is **not** one of the auditor's primary objectives in an examination of marketable securities?
a. To determine whether securities are authentic.
b. To determine whether securities are the property of the client.
c. To determine whether securities actually exist.
d. To determine whether securities are properly classified on the balance sheet.

53. In the examination of property, plant, and equipment, the auditor tries to determine all of the following **except** the
a. Adequacy of internal control.
b. Extent of property abandoned during the year.
c. Adequacy of replacement funds.
d. Reasonableness of the depreciation.

54. For which of the following ledger accounts would the auditor be **most** likely to analyze the details?
a. Service Revenue.
b. Sales.
c. Repairs and maintenance expense.
d. Sales salaries expense.

55. In violation of company policy, Lowell Company erroneously capitalized the cost of painting its warehouse. The auditor examining Lowell's financial statements would most likely detect this when
a. Discussing capitalization policies with Lowell's controller.
b. Examining maintenance expense accounts.
c. Observing, during the physical inventory observation, that the warehouse had been painted.
d. Examining the construction work orders supporting items capitalized during the year.

56. Which of the following accounts should be reviewed by the auditor to gain reasonable assurance that additions to property, plant, and equipment are **not** understated?
a. Depreciation.
b. Accounts payable.

c. Cash.
d. Repairs.

57. Treetop Corporation acquired a building and arranged mortgage financing during the year. Verification of the related mortgage acquisition costs would be least likely to include an examination of the related
a. Deed.
b. Cancelled checks.
c. Closing statement.
d. Interest expense.

58. The auditor is least likely to learn of retirements of equipment through which of the following?
a. Review of the purchase return and allowance account.
b. Review of depreciation.
c. Analysis of the debits to the accumulated depreciation account.
d. Review of insurance policy riders.

59. When an auditor selects a sample of items from the vouchers payable register for the last month of the period under audit and traces these items to underlying documents, the auditor is gathering evidence primarily in support of the assertion that
a. Recorded obligations were paid.
b. Incurred obligations were recorded in the correct period.
c. Recorded obligations were valid.
d. Cash disbursements were recorded as incurred obligations.

60. Unrecorded liabilities are most likely to be found during the review of which of the following documents?
a. Unpaid bills.
b. Shipping records.
c. Bills of lading.
d. Unmatched sales invoices.

61. Which of the following procedures relating to the examination of accounts payable could the auditor delegate entirely to the client's employees?
a. Test footings in the accounts payable ledger.
b. Reconcile unpaid invoices to vendors' statements.
c. Prepare a schedule of accounts payable.
d. Mail confirmations for selected account balances.

62. Which of the following audit procedures is **least** likely to detect an unrecorded liability?
a. Analysis and recomputation of interest expense.
b. Analysis and recomputation of depreciation expense.
c. Mailing of standard bank confirmation form.
d. Reading of the minutes of meetings of the board of directors.

63. An examination of the balance in the accounts payable account is ordinarily **not** designed to
a. Detect accounts payable which are substantially past due.
b. Verify that accounts payable were properly authorized.
c. Ascertain the reasonableness of recorded liabilities.
d. Determine that all existing liabilities at the balance sheet date have been recorded.

64. The auditor is **most** likely to verify accrued commissions payable in conjunction with the
a. Sales cutoff review.
b. Verification of contingent liabilities.
c. Review of post balance sheet date disbursements.
d. Examination of trade acccounts payable.

65. Which of the following is the **best** audit procedure for determining the existence of unrecorded liabilities?
a. Examine confirmation requests returned by creditors whose accounts appear on a subsidiary trial balance of accounts payable.
b. Examine unusual relationships between monthly accounts payable balances and recorded purchases.
c. Examine a sample of invoices a few days prior to and subsequent to year-end to ascertain whether they have been properly recorded.
d. Examine a sample of cash disbursements in the period subsequent to year-end.

66. Auditor confirmation of accounts payable balances at the balance sheet date may be unnecessary because
a. This is a duplication of cutoff tests.
b. Accounts payable balances at the balance sheet date may not be paid before the audit is completed.

c. Correspondence with the audit client's attorney will reveal all legal action by vendors for nonpayment.
d. There is likely to be other reliable external evidence to support the balances.

67. During an examination of a publicly-held company, the auditor should obtain written confirmation regarding debenture transactions from the
a. Debenture holders.
b. Client's attorney.
c. Internal auditors.
d. Trustee.

68. The auditor's program for the examination of long-term debt should include steps that require the
a. Verification of the existence of the bondholders.
b. Examination of any bond trust indenture.
c. Inspection of the accounts payable subsidiary ledger.
d. Investigation of credits to the bond interest income account.

69. Several years ago Conway, Inc., secured a conventional real estate mortgage loan. Which of the following audit procedures would be **least** likely to be performed by an auditor examining the mortgage balance?
a. Examine the current years' cancelled checks.
b. Review the mortgage amortization schedule.
c. Inspect public records of lien balances.
d. Recompute mortgage interest expense.

70. An audit program for the examination of the retained earnings account should include a step that requires verification of the
a. Market value used to charge retained earnings to account for a two-for-one stock split.
b. Approval of the adjustment to the beginning balance as a result of a write-down of an account receivable.
c. Authorization for both cash and stock dividends.
d. Gain or loss resulting from disposition of treasury shares.

71. All corporate capital stock transactions should ultimately be traced to the
a. Minutes of the Board of Directors.
b. Cash receipts journal.
c. Cash disbursements journal.
d. Numbered stock certificates.

72. In the audit of a medium-sized manufacturing concern, which one of the following areas would be expected to require the least amount of audit time?
a. Owners' equity.
b. Revenue.
c. Assets.
d. Liabilities.

73. If management refuses to furnish certain written representations that the auditor believes are essential, which of the following is appropriate?
a. The auditor can rely on oral evidence relating to the matter as a basis for an unqualified opinion.
b. The client's refusal does **not** constitute a scope limitation that may lead to a modification of the opinion.
c. This may have an effect on the auditor's ability to rely on other representations of management.
d. The auditor should issue an adverse opinion because of management's refusal.

74. Which of the following auditing procedures is ordinarily performed last?
a. Reading of the minutes of the directors' meetings.
b. Confirming accounts payable.
c. Obtaining a management representation letter.
d. Testing of the purchasing function.

75. The date of the management representation letter should coincide with the
a. Date of the auditor's report.
b. Balance sheet date.
c. Date of the latest subsequent event referred to in the notes to the financial statements.
d. Date of the engagement agreement.

76. When an examination is made in accordance with generally accepted auditing standards, the independent auditor must
a. Utilize statistical sampling.
b. Employ analytical review procedures.
c. Obtain certain written representations from management.
d. Observe the taking of physical inventory on the balance sheet date.

77. In which of the following instances would an auditor be **least** likely to require the assistance of a specialist?
   a. Assessing the valuation of inventories of art works.
   b. Determining the quantities of materials stored in piles on the ground.
   c. Determining the value of unlisted securities.
   d. Ascertaining the assessed valuation of fixed assets.

78. When an outside specialist has assumed full responsibility for taking the client's physical inventory, reliance on the specialist's report is acceptable if
   a. The auditor is satisfied through application of appropriate procedures as to the reputation and competence of the specialist.
   b. Circumstances made it impracticable or impossible for the auditor either to do the work personally or observe the work done by the inventory firm.
   c. The auditor conducted the same audit tests and procedures as would have been applicable if the client employees took the physical inventory.
   d. The auditor's report contains a reference to the assumption of full responsibility.

79. In which of the following instances would it be appropriate for the auditor to refer to the work of an appraiser in the auditor's report?
   a. An unqualified opinion is expressed and the auditor wishes to place emphasis on the use of a specialist.
   b. A qualified opinion is expressed because of a major uncertainty unrelated to the work of the appraiser.
   c. An adverse opinion is expressed based on a difference of opinion between the client and the outside appraiser as to the value of certain assets.
   d. A disclaimer of opinion is expressed due to a scope limitation imposed on the auditor by the appraiser.

80. An auditor will ordinarily examine invoices from lawyers primarily in order to
   a. Substantiate accruals.
   b. Assess the legal ramifications of litigation in progress.
   c. Estimate the dollar amount of contingent liabilities.
   d. Identify possible unasserted litigation, claims, and assessments.

81. An attorney is responding to an independent auditor as a result of the audit client's letter of inquiry. The attorney may appropriately limit the response to
   a. Asserted claims and litigation.
   b. Matters to which the attorney has given substantive attention in the form of legal consultation or representation.
   c. Asserted, overtly threatened, or pending claims and litigation.
   d. Items which have an extremely high probability of being resolved to the client's detriment.

82. The letter of audit inquiry addressed to the client's legal counsel will **not** ordinarily be
   a. Sent to a lawyer who was engaged by the audit client during the year and soon thereafter resigned the engagement.
   b. A source of corroboration of the information originally obtained from management concerning litigation, claims, and assessments.
   c. Limited to references concerning only pending or threatened litigation with respect to which the lawyer has been engaged.
   d. Needed during the audit of clients whose securities are **not** registered with the SEC.

83. When obtaining evidence regarding litigation against a client, the CPA would be **least** interested in determining
   a. An estimate of when the matter will be resolved.
   b. The period in which the underlying cause of the litigation occurred.
   c. The probability of an unfavorable outcome.
   d. An estimate of the potential loss.

84. A lawyer's response to an auditor's request for information concerning litigation, claims, and assessments will ordinarily contain which of the following?
   a. An explanation regarding limitations on the scope of the response.
   b. A statement of concurrence with the client's determination of which unasserted possible claims warrant specification.
   c. Confidential information which would be prejudicial to the client's defense if publicized.
   d. An assertion that the list of unasserted possible claims identified by the client represent all such claims of which the lawyer may be aware.

85. Auditors often request that the audit client send a letter of inquiry to those attorneys who have been consulted with respect to litigation, claims, or assessments. The primary reason for this request is to provide the auditor with

a. An estimate of the dollar amount of the probable loss.
b. An expert opinion as to whether a loss is possible, probable or remote.
c. Information concerning the progress of cases to date.
d. Corroborative evidential matter.

86. A CPA has received an attorney's letter in which no significant disagreements with the client's assessments of contingent liabilities were noted. The resignation of the client's lawyer shortly after receipt of the letter should alert the auditor that

a. Undisclosed unasserted claims may have arisen.
b. The attorney was unable to form a conclusion with respect to the significance of litigation, claims and assessments.
c. The auditor must begin a completely new examination of contingent liabilities.
d. An adverse opinion will be necessary.

87. An auditor refers to significant related party transactions in a middle paragraph of the report. If the ensuing opinion paragraph contains the words, "with the foregoing explanation," the auditor's report would be considered a(n)

a. Unqualified opinion with appropriate reference to the middle paragraph.
b. Example of inappropriate reporting.
c. Adverse opinion.
d. Negative assurance opinion.

88. Which of the following would **not** necessarily be a related party transaction?

a. Sales to another corporation with a similar name.
b. Purchases from another corporation that is controlled by the corporation's chief stockholder.
c. Loan from the corporation to a major stockholder.
d. Sale of land to the corporation by the spouse of a director.

89. Governmental auditing often extends beyond examinations leading to the expression of opinion on the fairness of financial presentation and includes audits of efficiency, effectiveness, and

a. Internal control.
b. Evaluation.
c. Accuracy.
d. Compliance.

90. A typical objective of an operational audit is for the auditor to

a. Determine whether the financial statements fairly present the entity's operations.
b. Evaluate the feasibility of attaining the entity's operational objectives.
c. Make recommendations for improving performance.
d. Report on the entity's relative success in attaining profit maximization.

91. When auditing contingent liabilities, which of the following procedures would be **least** effective?

a. Reading the minutes of the board of directors.
b. Reviewing the bank confirmation letter.
c. Examining customer confirmation replies.
d. Examining invoices for professional services.

92. A common audit procedure in the audit of payroll transactions involves tracing selected items from the payroll journal to employee time cards that have been approved by supervisory personnel. This procedure is designed to provide evidence in support of the audit proposition that

a. Only bona fide employees worked and their pay was properly computed.
b. Jobs on which employees worked were charged with the appropriate labor cost.
c. Internal controls relating to payroll disbursements are operating effectively.
d. All employees worked the number of hours for which their pay was computed.

93. Patentex developed a new secret formula which is of great value because it resulted in a virtual monopoly. Patentex has capitalized all research and development costs associated with this formula. Greene, CPA, who is examining this account, will probably

a. Confer with management regarding transfer of the amount from the balance sheet to the income statement.
b. Confirm that the secret formula is registered and on file with the county clerk's office.

c. Confer with management regarding a change in the title of the account to "goodwill."
d. Confer with management regarding ownership of the secret formula.

94. Once satisfied that the balance sheet and income statement are fairly presented in accordance with generally accepted accounting principles, an auditor who is examining the statement of changes in financial position would be most concerned with details of transactions in
a. Cash.
b. Trade receivables.
c. Notes payable.
d. Dividends payable.

May 1984 Questions

95. The auditor faces a risk that the examination will not detect material errors in the financial statements. In regard to minimizing this risk, the auditor primarily relies on
a. Substantive tests.
b. Compliance tests.
c. Internal control.
d. Statistical analysis.

96. In the confirmation of accounts receivable the auditor would most likely
a. Request confirmation of a sample of the inactive accounts.
b. Seek to obtain positive confirmations for at least 50% of the total dollar amount of the receivables.
c. Require confirmation of all receivables from agencies of the federal government.
d. Require that confirmation requests be sent within one month of the fiscal year end.

97. Which of the following expressions is **least** likely to be included in a client's representation letter?
a. No events have occurred subsequent to the balance sheet date that require adjustment to, or disclosure in, the financial statements.
b. The company has complied with all aspects of contractual agreements that would have a material effect on the financial statements in the event of noncompliance.
c. Management acknowledges responsibility for illegal actions committed by employees.
d. Management has made available all financial statements and related data.

98. As one of the year-end audit procedures, the auditor instructed the client's personnel to prepare a standard bank confirmation request for a bank account that had been closed during the year. After the client's treasurer had signed the request, it was mailed by the assistant treasurer. What is the major flaw in this audit procedure?
a. The confirmation request was signed by the treasurer.
b. Sending the request was meaningless because the account was closed before the year end.
c. The request was mailed by the assistant treasurer.
d. The CPA did **not** sign the confirmation request before it was mailed.

99. Auditors may use positive and/or negative forms of confirmation requests for accounts receivable. An auditor most likely will use
a. The positive form to confirm all balances regardless of size.
b. A combination of the two forms, with the positive form used for large balances and the negative form for the small balances.
c. A combination of the two forms, with the positive form used for trade receivables and the negative form for other receivables.
d. The positive form when controls related to receivables are satisfactory, and the negative form when controls related to receivables are unsatisfactory.

100. An auditor should obtain written representations from management concerning litigation claims and assessments. These representations may be limited to matters that are considered either individually or collectively material provided an understanding on the limits of materiality for this purpose has been reached by
a. The auditor and the client's lawyer.
b. Management and the auditor.
c. Management, the client's lawyer, and the auditor.
d. The auditor independently of management.

101. Of the following, which is the **least** persuasive type of audit evidence?
a. Documents mailed by outsiders to the auditor.
b. Correspondence between auditor and vendors.
c. Copies of sales invoices inspected by the auditor.
d. Computations made by the auditor.

102. As a result of analytical review procedures, the independent auditor determines that the gross profit percentage has declined from 30% in the preceding year to 20% in the current year. The auditor should
- a. Document management's intentions with respect to plans for reversing this trend.
- b. Evaluate management's performance in causing this decline.
- c. Require footnote disclosure.
- d. Consider the possibilty of an error in the financial statements.

103. The auditor notices significant fluctuations in key elements of the company's financial statements. If management is unable to provide an acceptable explanation, the auditor should
- a. Consider the matter a scope limitation.
- b. Perform additional audit procedures to investigate the matter further.
- c. Intensify the examination with the expectation of detecting management fraud.
- d. Withdraw from the engagement.

104. Analytical review procedures are
- a. Substantive tests designed to evaluate a system of internal control.
- b. Compliance tests are designed to evaluate the validity of management's representation letter.
- c. Substantive tests designed to evaluate the reasonableness of financial information.
- d. Compliance tests designed to evaluate the reasonableness of financial information.

105. The auditor may refer to and identify a specialist in the auditor's report if the auditor
- a. Expresses an unqualified opinion.
- b. Believes it will facilitate an understanding of the reason for modification of the report.
- c. Wishes to indicate a division of responsibility.
- d. Wishes to emphasize the thoroughness of the audit.

106. The auditor is most likely to seek information from the plant manager with respect to the
- a. Adequacy of the provision for uncollectible accounts.
- b. Appropriateness of physical inventory observation procedures.
- c. Existence of obsolete machinery.
- d. Deferral of procurement of certain necessary insurance coverage.

107. Which of the following is **not** a specialist upon whose work an auditor may rely?
- a. Actuary.
- b. Appraiser.
- c. Internal auditor.
- d. Engineer.

108. Of the following, which is the most efficient audit procedure for verification of interest earned on bond investments?
- a. Tracing interest declarations to an independent record book.
- b. Recomputing interest earned.
- c. Confirming interest rate with the issuer of the bonds.
- d. Vouching the receipt and deposit of interest checks.

109. An unrecorded check issued during the last week of the year would most likely be discovered by the auditor when the
- a. Check register for the last month is reviewed.
- b. Cutoff bank statement is reconciled.
- c. Bank confirmation is reviewed.
- d. Search for unrecorded liabilities is performed.

110. Refusal by the client's legal counsel to furnish certain requested information would most likely be considered
- a. A limitation in the scope of the auditor's examination.
- b. Indicative of the existence of material unasserted loss contingencies.
- c. A characteristic of untrustworthy management.
- d. Evidence of an inability to formulate an opinion regarding the outcome of pending litigation.

111. The letter of inquiry that is ordinarily sent to lawyers with whom management consulted concerning litigation, claims, and assessments is the auditor's method of
- a. Identifying all possible unasserted claims.
- b. Obtaining admissions of irregularities which are safeguarded by privileged communications laws.
- c. Obtaining corroboration of information furnished by the client.
- d. Identifying impaired assets and incurred liabilities.

Problems

Problem 1 Audit Program for Accounts Payable (1183,A4)

(15 to 25 minutes)

Taylor, CPA, is engaged in the audit of Rex Wholesaling for the year ended December 31, 1982. Taylor performed a proper study of the system of internal accounting control relating to the purchasing, receiving, trade accounts payable and cash disbursement cycles and has decided not to proceed with compliance testing. Based upon analytical review procedures Taylor believes that the trade accounts payable balance on the balance sheet as of December 31, 1982, may be understated.

Taylor requested and obtained a client-prepared trade accounts payable schedule listing the total amount owed to each vendor.

Required:

What additional substantive audit procedures should Taylor apply in examining the trade accounts payable?

Problem 2 Objectives and Audit Program for Noncurrent Assets (1183,A5)

(15 to 25 minutes)

Kent, CPA, who is engaged in the audit of the financial statements of Bass Corporation for the year ended December 31, 1982, is about to commence an audit of the noncurrent investment securities. Bass' records indicate that the company owns various bearer bonds, as well as 25% of the outstanding common stock of Commercial Industrial Inc. Kent is satisfied with evidence that supports the presumption of significant influence over Commercial Industrial Inc. The various securities are at two locations as follows:

- Recently acquired securities are in the company's safe in the custody of the treasurer.
- All other securities are in the company's bank safe deposit box.

All of the securities in Bass' portfolio are actively traded in a broad market.

Required:

a. Assuming that the system of internal control over securities is satisfactory and may be relied upon, what are the objectives of the examination of these noncurrent investment securities?

b. What audit procedures should be undertaken by Kent with respect to the examination of Bass' noncurrent investment securities?

Problem 3 Representation Letter (583,A2)

(15 to 25 minutes)

During the examination of the annual financial statements of Amis Manufacturing, Inc., the company's president, R. Alderman, and Luddy, the auditor, reviewed matters that were supposed to be included in a written representation letter. Upon receipt of the following client representation letter, Luddy contacted Alderman to state that it was incomplete.

To E.K. Luddy, CPA

In connection with your examination of the balance sheet of Amis Manufacturing, Inc. as of December 31, 1982, and the related statements of income, retained earnings, and changes in financial position for the year then ended, for the purpose of expressing an opinion as to whether the financial statements present fairly the financial position, results of operations, and changes in financial position of Amis Manufacturing, Inc. in conformity with generally accepted accounting principles, we confirm, to the best of our knowledge and belief, the following representations made to you during your examination. There were no:

- Plans or intentions that may materially affect the carrying value or classification of assets and liabilities.
- Communications from regulatory agencies concerning noncompliance with, or deficiencies in, financial reporting practices.
- Agreements to repurchase assets previously sold.
- Violations or possible violations of laws or regulations whose effects should be considered for disclosure in the financial statements or as a basis for recording a loss contingency.
- Unasserted claims or assessments that our lawyer has advised are probable of assertion and must be disclosed in accordance with Statement of Financial Accounting Standards No. 5.
- Capital stock repurchase options or agreements or capital stock reserved for options, warrants, conversions, or other requirements.

• Compensating balance or other arrangements involving restrictions on cash balances.

R. Alderman, President
Amis Manufacturing, Inc.

March 14, 1983

Required:

Identify the other matters that Alderman's representation letter should specifically confirm.

Problem 4 Cash Audit Procedures (583,A4)

(15 to 25 minutes)

The following client-prepared bank reconciliation is being examined by Kautz, CPA, during an examination of the financial statements of Cynthia Company:

Cynthia Company
Bank Reconciliation
Village Bank Account 2
December 31, 1982

Balance per bank (a)		$18,375.91
Deposits in Transit (b)		
12/30	1,471.10	
12/31	2,840.69	4,311.79
Subtotal		22,687.70
Outstanding checks (c)		
837	6,000.00	
1941	671.80	
1966	320.00	
1984	1,855.42	
1985	3,621.22	
1987	2,576.89	
1991	4,420.88	(19,466.21)
Subtotal		3,221.49
NSF check returned 12/29 (d)		200.00
Bank charges		5.50
Error Check No. 1932		148.10
Customer note collected by the bank ($2,750 plus $275 interest) (e)		(3,025.00)
Balance per books (f)		$ 550.09

Required:

Indicate one or more audit procedures that should be performed by Kautz in gathering evidence in support of each of the items (a) through (f) above.

Problem 5 Procedures for Notes Payable (1182,A4)

(15 to 25 minutes)

Andrews, CPA, has been engaged to examine the financial statements of Broadwall Corporation for the year ended December 31, 1981. During the year, Broadwall obtained a long-term loan from a local bank pursuant to a financing agreement which provided that the:

1. Loan was to be secured by the company's inventory and accounts receivable.
2. Company was to maintain a debt to equity ratio not to exceed two to one.
3. Company was not to pay dividends without permission from the bank.
4. Monthly installment payments were to commence July 1, 1981.

In addition, during the year the company also borrowed, on a short-term basis, from the president of the company, including substantial amounts just prior to the year end.

Required:

a. For purposes of Andrews' audit of the financial statements of Broadwall Corporation, what procedures should Andrews employ in examining the described loans? **Do not discuss internal control.**

b. What are the financial statement disclosures that Andrews should expect to find with respect to the loans from the president?

Problem 6 Insurance Schedule Procedures (1181,A2)

(15 to 25 minutes)

During an examination of the financial statements of Gole Inc., Robbins, CPA requested and received a client-prepared property casualty insurance schedule which included appropriate premium information.

Required:

a. Identify the type of information, in addition to the appropriate premium information, that would ordinarily be expected to be included in a property casualty insurance schedule.

b. What are the basic audit procedures which Robbins should perform in examining the client-prepared property casualty insurance schedule?

Problem 7 Subsequent Events (581,A2)

(15 to 20 minutes)

Windek, a CPA, is nearing the completion of an examination of the financial statements of Jubilee, Inc., for the year ended December 31, 1980. Windek is currently concerned with ascertaining the occurrence of subsequent events that may require adjustment or disclosure essential to a fair presentation in conformity with generally accepted accounting principles.

Required:

a. Briefly explain what is meant by the phrase "subsequent event."

b. How do those subsequent events which require financial statement adjustment differ from those that require financial statement disclosure?

c. What are the procedures which should be performed in order to ascertain the occurrence of subsequent events?

Problem 8 Audit Tests and Analytical Review (581,A5)

(15 to 25 minutes)

Decker, CPA, is performing an examination of the financial statements of Allright Wholesale Sales, Inc., for the year ended December 31, 1980. Allright has been in business for many years and has never had its financial statements audited. Decker has gained satisfaction with respect to the ending inventory and is considering alternative audit procedures to gain satisfaction with respect to management's representations concerning the beginning inventory which was not observed.

Allright sells only one product (bottle brand X beer), and maintains perpetual inventory records. In addition, Allright takes physical inventory counts monthly. Decker has already confirmed purchases with the manufacturer and has decided to concentrate on evaluating the reliability of perpetual inventory records and performing analytical review procedures to the extent that prior years' unaudited records will enable such procedures to be performed.

Required:

What are the audit tests, including analytical review procedures, which Decker should apply in evaluating the reliability of perpetual inventory records and gaining satisfaction with respect to the January 1, 1980, inventory?

Problem 9 Payroll Input Verification and; Examination Procedures (1180,A5)

(15 to 25 minutes)

James, who was engaged to examine the financial statements of Talbert Corporation, is about to audit payroll. Talbert uses a computer service center to process weekly payroll as follows:

Each Monday Talbert's payroll clerk inserts data in appropriate spaces on the preprinted service center prepared input form, and sends it to the service center via messenger. The service center extracts new permanent data from the input form and updates master files. The weekly payroll data are then processed. The weekly payroll register and payroll checks are printed and delivered by messenger to Talbert on Thursday.

Part of the sample selected for audit by James includes the following input form and payroll register:

See following page

Required:

a. Describe how James should verify the information in the payroll input form shown on the following page.

b. Describe (but do **not** perform) the procedures that James should follow in the examination of the November 12, 1979, payroll reigster shown on the following page.

Problem 10 Procedures for Loss Contingencies (579,A4)

(15 to 25 minutes)

During an audit engagement Harper, CPA, has satisfactorily completed an examination of accounts payable and other liabilities and now plans to determine whether there are any loss contingencies arising from litigation, claims, or assessments.

Required:

What are the audit procedures that Harper should follow with respect to the existence of loss contingencies arising from litigation, claims, and assessments? Do not discuss reporting requirements.

Problem 9 *(continued)*

Talbert Corporation Payroll Input — Week Ending Friday, Nov. 23, 1979

— Employee Data — Permanent File —				—Current Week's Payroll Data —				
		W-4	Hourly	Hours		Special Deductions		
Name	Social Security	Information	Rate	Reg	OT	Bonds	Union	Other
A. Bell	999-99-9991	M-1	10.00	35	5	18.75		
B. Carr	999-99-9992	M-2	10.00	35	4			
C. Dawn	999-99-9993	S-1	10.00	35	6	18.75	4.00	
D. Ellis	999-99-9994	S-1	10.00	35	2		4.00	50.00
E. Frank	999-99-9995	M-4	10.00	35	1		4.00	
F. Gillis	999-99-9996	M-4	10.00	35			4.00	
G. Hugh	999-99-9997	M-1	7.00	35	2	18.75	4.00	
H. Jones	999-99-9998	M-2	7.00	35			4.00	25.00
J. King	999-99-9999	S-1	7.00	35	4		4.00	
New Employee								
J. Smith	999-99-9990	M-3	7.00	35				

Talbert Corporation Payroll Register — Nov. 23, 1979

Employee	Social Security	Hours Reg	Hours OT	Payroll Reg	Payroll OT	Gross Payroll	Taxes Withheld FICA	Taxes Withheld Fed	Taxes Withheld State	Other Withheld	Net Pay	Check No.
A. Bell	999-99-9991	35	5	350.00	75.00	425.00	26.05	76.00	27.40	18.75	276.80	1499
B. Carr	999-99-9992	35	4	350.00	60.00	410.00	25.13	65.00	23.60		296.27	1500
C. Dawn	999-99-9993	35	6	350.00	90.00	440.00	26.97	100.90	28.60	22.75	260.78	1501
D. Ellis	999-99-9994	35	2	350.00	30.00	380.00	23.29	80.50	21.70	54.00	200.51	1502
E. Frank	999-99-9995	35	1	350.00	15.00	365.00	22.37	43.50	15.90	4.00	279.23	1503
F. Gillis	999-99-9996	35		350.00		350.00	21.46	41.40	15.00	4.00	268.14	1504
G. Hugh	999-99-9997	35	2	245.00	21.00	266.00	16.31	34.80	10.90	22.75	181.24	1505
H. Jones	999-99-9998	35		245.00		245.00	15.02	26.40	8.70	29.00	165.88	1506
J. King	999-99-9999	35	4	245.00	42.00	287.00	17.59	49.40	12.20	4.00	203.81	1507
J. Smith	999-99-9990	35		245.00		245.00	15.02	23.00	7.80		199.18	1508
Totals		350	24	3,080.00	333.00	3,413.00	209.21	540.90	171.80	159.25	2,331.84	

Problem 11 Cutoff Tests (1171,A3)

(25 to 30 minutes)

In connection with his examination of the financial statements of Houston Wholesalers, Inc. for the year ended June 30, 1971, a CPA performs several cutoff tests.

Required:

a. 1. What is a cutoff test?
   2. Why must cutoff tests be performed for both the beginning and the end of the audit period?

b. The CPA wishes to test Houston's sales cutoff at June 30, 1971. Describe the steps he should include in this test.

c. The CPA obtains a July 10, 1971, bank statement directly from the bank. Explain how he will use this cutoff bank statement:
   1. In his review of the June 30, 1971, bank reconciliation.
   2. To obtain other audit information.

Problem 12 Client Representation Letters (1172,A5)

(25 to 30 minutes)

The major written understandings between a CPA and his client, in connection with an examination of financial statements, are the engagement (arrangements) letter and the client's representation letters.

Required:

a. 1. What are the objectives of the engagement (arrangements) letter?
   2. Who should prepare and sign the engagement letter?
   3. When should the engagement letter be sent?
   4. Why should the engagement letter be renewed periodically?

b. 1. What are the objectives of the client's representation letters?
   2. Who should prepare and sign the client's representation letters?
   3. When should the client's representation letters be obtained?
   4. Why should the client's representation letters be prepared for each examination?

c. A CPA's responsibilities for providing accounting services sometimes involve his association with unaudited financial statements. Discuss the need in this circumstance for:
   1. An engagement letter.
   2. Client's representation letters.

Problem 13 Audit Programs (1177,A2)

(15 to 25 minutes)

Part a. The first generally accepted auditing standard of field work requires, in part, that "the work is to be adequately planned." An effective tool that aids the auditor in adequately planning the work is an audit program.

Required:

What is an audit program, and what purposes does it serve?

Part b. Auditors frequently refer to the terms "Standards" and "Procedures." Standards deal with measures of the quality of the auditor's performance. Standards specifically refer to the ten generally accepted auditing standards. Procedures relate to those acts that are performed by the auditor while trying to gather evidence. Procedures specifically refer to the methods or techniques used by the auditor in the conduct of the examination.

Required:

List at least eight different types of procedures that an auditor would use during an examination of financial statements. For example, a type of procedure that an auditor would frequently use is the observation of activities and conditions. Do not discuss specific accounts.

Problem 14 Inventory Audit Procedures (1176,A4)

(15 to 25 minutes)

Ace Corporation does not conduct a complete annual physical count of purchased parts and supplies in its principal warehouse but uses statistical sampling instead to estimate the year-end inventory. Ace maintains a perpetual inventory record of parts and supplies and believes that statistical sampling is highly effective in determining inventory values and is sufficiently reliable to make a physical count of each item of inventory unnecessary.

Required:

a. Identify the audit procedures that should be used by the independent auditor that change or are in addition to normal required audit procedures when a client utilizes statistical sampling to determine inventory value and does not conduct a 100 percent annual physical count of inventory items.

b. List at least ten normal audit procedures that should be performed to verify physical quantities whenever a client conducts a periodic physical count of all or part of its inventory.

Problem 15 Objectives – Tests Relationships: Cash (CIA,579,PIA33)

(15 minutes)

As an internal auditing manager, you assigned one of your supervisors to audit the acquisition and payment cycle of a new subsidiary. The key internal controls for acquiring goods and services appear adequate. However, the controls over cash disbursements are of concern to you, so you give the supervisor in charge of the audit special instructions. One objective of the audit is to determine if disbursements are recorded on a timely basis. One test to achieve this audit objective is to compare dates on a sample of cancelled checks to dates in the cash disbursements journal.

Required:

a. List **three** additional objectives for the audit of cash disbursements.

b. For **each** objective listed in a., give **one** test to achieve the audit objective. List the test in b. beside the appropriate objective in a.

Problem 16 Audit Procedures for Marketable Securties (582,A4)

(15 to 25 minutes)

The following schedule was prepared by the controller of World Manufacturing Inc., for use by the independent auditors during their examination of World's year-end financial statements. All procedures performed by the audit assistant were noted at the bottom "Legend" section, and it was properly initialed, dated and indexed, and then submitted to a senior member of the audit staff for review. Internal control was reviewed and is considered to be satisfactory.

World Manufacturing, Inc.
Marketable Securities
Year Ended December 31, 1981

Description of security			*Serial no.*	*Face value of bonds*	*Gen. ledger 1/1*	*Purch. in 1981*	*Sold in 1981*	*Cost*	*Gen. ledger 12/31*	*12/31 market*	*Dividend & interest: Pay date(s)*	*Amt. rec.*	*Accruals 12/31*
Corp. bonds	*%*	*Yr. due*											
											1/15	300 b,d	
A	6	91	21-7	10000	9400a				9400	9100	7/15	300 b,d	275
D	4	83	73-0	30000	27500a				27500	26220	12/1	1200 b,d	100
G	9	98	16-4	5000	4000a				4000	5080	8/1	450 b,d	188
Rc	5	85	08-2	70000	66000a		57000b	66000					
Sc	10	99	07-4	100000		100000e			100000	101250	7/1	5000 b.d	5000
					106900	100000	57000	66000	140900	141650		7250	5563
					a,f	f	f	f	f,g	f		f	f
Stocks													
											3/1	750 b,d	
P 1,000 shs. Common			1044		7500a				7500	7600	6/1	750 b,d	
											9/1	750 b,d	
											12/1	750 b,d	250
U 50 shs. Common			8530		9700a				9700	9800	2/1	800 b,d	
											8/1	800 b,d	667
					17200				17200	17400		4600	917
					a,f				f,g	f		f	f

Legends and comments relative to above

a = Beginning balances agreed to 1980 working papers
b = Traced to cash receipts
c = Minutes examined (purchase and sales approved by the board of directors)
d = Agreed to 1099
e = Confirmed by tracing to broker's advice
f = Totals footed
g = Agreed to general ledger

Required:

a. What information that is essential to the audit of marketable securities is missing from this schedule?

b. What are the essential audit procedures that were not noted as having been performed by the audit assistant?

Multiple Choice Answers

1. c	24. b	46. d	68. b	90. c
2. c	25. b	47. d	69. c	91. c
3. d	26. c	48. c	70. c	92. d
4. d	27. a	49. d	71. a	93. a
5. a	28. a	50. d	72. a	94. c
6. a	29. d	51. d	73. c	95. a
7. a	30. a	52. a	74. c	96. a
8. d	31. a	53. c	75. a	97. c
9. a	32. d	54. c	76. c	98. c
10. c	33. c	55. d	77. d	99. b
11. b	34. d	56. d	78. c	100. b
12. d	35. a	57. a	79. c	101. c
13. b	36. d	58. a	80. d	102. d
14. d	37. d	59. c	81. b	103. b
15. d	38. c	60. a	82. c	104. c
16. d	39. b	61. c	83. a	105. b
17. b	40. a	62. b	84. a	106. c
18. c	41. d	63. b	85. d	107. c
19. a	42. b	64. a	86. a	108. b
20. c	43. d	65. d	87. b	109. b
21. d	44. b	66. d	88. a	110. a
22. c	45. b	67. d	89. d	111. c
23. d				

Multiple Choice Answer Explanations

A. Audit Evidence — General

A.1. Competent and Sufficient Evidential Matter

1. (1183,A1,47) (c) The requirement is to determine the primary purpose of audit procedures. Audit procedures are primarily designed to gather corroborative audit evidence which becomes the basis of the auditor's report. Answer (a) is incorrect because dedetecting errors and irregularities, while a benefit of an audit, is not the primary objective. Answer (b) is incorrect because under GAAP there is no requirement that audit procedures be performed. Answer (d) is incorrect because it is limited to account balances disclosures and omits other information such as footnote disclosures.

2. (583,A1,19) (c) The requirement is to determine the reason which is **not** valid for omitting an audit test. Difficulty and expense are not justifiable reasons for such omission (AU 326.21). If the test is important to the formation of an opinion it must be performed, regardless of difficulty and expense. Answer (a) is incorrect because when a very low relative risk is involved less audit procedures will be necessary than when risk is high. Answer (b) is incorrect because there should be a rational relationship between the cost of obtaining evidence and its usefulness (AU 326.21). Answer (d) is incorrect because an inverse relationship exists between the amount of substantive test reliance (and therefore the scope of audit procedures) and reliance on internal control (AU 320.73).

3. (1182,A1,28) (d) The requirement is to determine the **least** persuasive type of audit evidence. Prenumbered client invoices are least persuasive because they represent a form of evidence secured solely within the entity as contrasted to evidence secured from independent sources (see AU 326.18). Answers (a) and (b) are incorrect because a vendor's invoice and a bank statement are both externally prepared. Answer (c), computations made by the auditor, are considered more persuasive because the independent auditor's direct personal knowledge obtained in such a manner is more persuasive than information obtained indirectly (AU 326.18).

4. (582,A1,6) (d) The requirement is to determine the correct statement with respect to the competence of evidential matter. To be competent, evidence must be both valid and relevant (AU 326.18). Answer (a) is incorrect because while externally generated evidence is generally considered to provide greater assurance of reliability, there are important exceptions, e.g., the confirmation erroneously returned with no exception when one actually exists. Answer (b) is incorrect because while evidence so gathered is typically considered to provide greater assurance concerning reliability (AU 326.18), no similar generalization can be made about its relevance.

5. (1181,A1,22) (a) The requirement is to determine the least persuasive documentation in support of an auditor's opinion. Answer (a), schedules of details of physical inventory counts conducted by the client, is least persuasive because it is developed solely within the entity (para 326.18). Answer (b) is incorrect because inferences drawn by the auditor from self-computed ratios and trends are more persuasive than those from the client's data. Answer (c) is incorrect because an independent third party's conclusions are considered more persuasive than internal firm sources. Answer (d) is incorrect because **no** reply to a negative confirmation from an independent third party is considered to be support for the accuracy of the accounts receivable.

6. (1181,A1,47) (a) The requirement is to determine the element which ultimately determines the auditing procedures which are necessary in specific cir-

cumstances. Answer (a) is correct because the measure of the validity of audit evidence, for audit purposes, lies in the judgment of the auditor (para 326.02). This auditor judgment is used to estimate levels of materiality [answer (b)], and relative risk [answer (c)]. Answer (d) is incorrect because reasonable assurance is the general concept which states that the cost of internal controls should not exceed their expected benefit.

7. (1181,A1,58) (a) The requirement is to determine the nature of negative assurance. Answer (a), an absence of nullifying evidence, is correct because negative assurance consists of a statement by accountants to the effect that as a result of specified procedures, nothing came to their attention that caused them to believe that specified matters do not meet a specified standard. Answer (b) is incorrect because the limited nature of the procedures makes substantiation impossible. Answer (c) is wrong because a positive opinion as opposed to negative assurance is issued in the case of a normal audit performed in accordance with generally accepted auditing standards. Answer (d) is incorrect because while judgment is necessary to determine whether negative assurance may be issued, the answer is less complete than answer (a).

A.2. Types of Evidence

8. (582,A1,35) (d) The requirement is to determine the correct statement pertaining to audit planning. It is an acceptable practice for the auditor to carry out substantial parts of the examination at interim dates (AU 310.05). Typically the "substantial parts of the examination" performed at an interim date consist of planning and internal control procedures. In addition, tests of transactions are often performed at interim dates. If internal control cannot be relied upon, this determination is usually made at an interim date. Answer (a) is incorrect because while early appointment of the independent auditor is advantageous to both the auditor and the client, an engagement can be accepted near or after the close of the fiscal year (AU 310.04). Answer (b) is incorrect because the auditor's observation procedures may be performed either during or after the end of the period under audit in cases of well-kept perpetual inventory records (AU 331.10). Further, the inventory count need not be observed if it is impracticable; however, the auditor must bear in mind that s/he has the burden of justifying the use of alternative procedures (AU 331.01). Answer (c) is incorrect because in certain circumstances the audit committee may be told of specific audit procedures.

9. (582,A1,3) (a) The requirement is to determine the direction of audit testing to test for unsupported entries in the ledger. In these tests, entries will be tested **from** the ledger **to** the original source documents. The auditor will thus attempt to determine whether the items in the ledger are supported. Answer (b) is incorrect since it would only test whether there is support for journal entries. Answer (c) is incorrect because externally generated documents will generally be source documents which will provide support for entries in the ledger. Answer (d) is incorrect because tracing from orginal source documents to the ledger will only help the auditor to determine that all transactions have been recorded.

10. (1180,A1,34) (c) The search for unrecorded liabilities is performed near the completion of the audit to determine that proper cutoffs have been made and to give the auditor additional information in his evaluations of accounts as of the balance sheet date. While the observation of inventory [answer (a)] and the confirmation of receivables [answer (d)] are frequently done at the date of the balance sheet, strong internal controls may allow the auditor to perform both of these procedures earlier. The review of internal controls over cash receipts [answer (b)] is frequently performed prior to year-end.

11. (1180,A1,54) (b) Because audit tests have been performed on balance sheet and income statement accounts the auditor ordinarily will be able to cross-reference balances on the statement of changes in financial position to these other statements. Answer (a) is incorrect because determination of the amount of working capital is only one check needed in cases in which the statement is prepared on that basis. Answer (c) is incorrect since the pertinent ratios have already been calculated in auditing the balance sheet and income statement. Answer (d) is incorrect since no **auditing** guidance is provided in APB 19 on the statement of changes in financial position.

12. (580,A1,13) (d) The requirement is the procedure that is not part of a review engagement of a nonpublic entity. Section 100 (SSARS 1) provides the necessary standards and procedures applicable to a review of a nonpublic entity. AR 100.04 states that a review provides the accountant with a reasonable basis for expressing limited assurance that there are no material modifications that should be made to the statements to bring them into conformity with GAAP. Since the objective of a review differs from the objective of an examination made in accordance with GAAS, audit procedures such as a study and evalua-

tion of internal control, tests of accounting records, inspection, observation, confirmation, and certain other procedures are not performed. Specifically included per para AR 100.27 are review procedures such as inquiries of management [answer (a)], inquiries regarding subsequent events [answer (b)], and procedures to identify unusual relationships among data [answer (c)].

B.1.a. Analytical Review

13. (583,A1,46) (b) The requirement is to determine the audit procedure which is ordinarily designed to detect possible material dollar errors on the financial statements. Analytical review procedures are substantive tests which can aid in the detection of material errors by identifying unexpected fluctuations or the absence of expected fluctuations in the relationships between data (see AU 318). Answer (a) is incorrect because compliance testing is used to test whether controls work as prescribed (AU 320.56–.57). Answer (c) is incorrect because computer controls are a subset of internal controls [answer (a)]. Answer (d) is incorrect because a post audit working paper review is used to test whether the audit has been performed in conformity with GAAS.

14. (582,A1,12) (d) The requirement is to determine the types of events or transactions which an investigation of variances of greater than 10% from 1980 revenues and expenses would discover. A change in a capitalization policy is likely to have a large dollar effect – even for small tools. Answer (a) is incorrect because the lack of recognition of an increase in property tax rates is likely to make 1981 tax expenses approximately equal to the prior year and therefore no investigation will occur. Answer (b) is incorrect because if no adjustment for the worsening economic conditions has been made the 1980 and 1981 bad debt expense for each will approximate one another. Answer (c) is incorrect because it pertains to a liability account – not a revenue or expense account.

15. (1180,A1,50) (d) Analytical review procedures are used to gather evidence relative to relationships among various accounting and nonaccounting data. The procedure of comparison of the financial information with information of prior periods [answer (d)] is a suggested analytical review procedure per para 318.06a. Answer (a) is incorrect since it is an example of a test of details of transactions and balances. Answer (b), while desirable, is not a required analytical review procedure for the income statement. Answer (c) is incorrect since the inventory information suggested is available through balance sheet review procedures.

16. (1179,A1,22) (d) Inventory turnover analysis may be useful to the auditor in detecting existence of obsolete merchandise. As the proportion of obsolete merchandise to total inventory grows, the inventory turnover would decrease. Answer (a) is incorrect because the mispricing of inventory would have to be very material to effect the inventory turnover ratio. Recall that the inventory turnover ratio is cost of goods sold divided by the average inventory. Thus, the inventory would have to be substantially incorrect to effect the turnover ratio to a noticeable degree. Answers (b) and (c) are incorrect because the auditor's first concern is with the fairness of presentation of the financial statements rather than control over inventory holding and inventory order costs.

17. (1179,A1,27) (b) A major reason for an analytical review of client operations is to identify unexpected fluctuations or transactions per para 318.04. Analytical review procedures are substantive tests of financial information made by study and comparison of relationships among the data per para 318.02. Thus, they are not tests of internal control, and therefore would not identify major weaknesses in internal control [answer (a)], noncompliance with control procedures [answer (c)] or improper separation of functional responsibilities [answer (d)].

B.1.b. Tests of Details of Transactions and Balances

18. (1181,A1,27) (c) The requirement is to find the statement which describes substantive audit tests. Answer (c) is correct because substantive tests are defined as tests of transactions, direct tests of financial balances, or analytical tests (para 320.70). Answer (a) is incorrect because substantive tests may not be eliminated due to the limitations of internal control (para 320.71). Answer (b) is incorrect since substantive tests primarily directly test ending financial statement balances, not subsequent events. Answer (d) is incorrect because substantive tests **decrease** with increased reliance on internal control (para 320.73).

B.2. Preparing Substantive Test Audit Programs

19. (580,A1,14) (a) The requirement is the primary purpose of the procedures listed in an audit program. Audit procedures are *primarily* designed to gather audit evidence which becomes the basis of the auditor's report. Audit programs are required per para 311.05. Completion of the audit program and any additional audit procedures should provide sufficient competent evidential matter for an opinion on the financial statements as required by the third standard of fieldwork. Answer (b), detection of errors and irregularities, an-

swer (c), tests of internal systems, and answer (d) protection in the event of litigation are all benefits of completing an audit program but are not the primary objective.

B.3. Documentation

20. (1181,A1,2) (c) The requirement is to determine the primary purpose of a schedule of unadjusted differences for which the auditor did not propose adjustment when discovered. Answer (c) is correct because the auditor uses such a schedule to aggregate the effects of individually immaterial items for the purpose of determining whether the total effect on the financial statements is material. Answer (a) is incorrect because, depending upon their perceived importance, these immaterial errors may or may not be pointed out to client officials. Answer (b) is incorrect because there is no requirement that such immaterial adjustments be reflected on the federal tax return. Answer (d) is incorrect because the immaterial nature of the errors or disputed items made their posting at year-end unnecessary.

21. (1181,A1,13) (d) The requirement is to determine the factor which affects the auditor's judgment as to the quantity, type and content of working papers. Answer (d) is correct because the **nature of the auditor's report**, the nature of the financial statements, the nature and condition of the client's records and internal control, and the needs of personnel involved on the audit for supervision and review are the factors affecting the quantity, type and content of working papers (para 338.05).

22. (1181,A1,37) (c) The requirement is to determine which answer is **not** a primary purpose of audit working papers. Working papers serve mainly to (1) aid the auditor in the conduct of his/her work and (2) to provide important support for the audit opinion (para 338.02). Answers (a) and (b) represent examples of aid to the auditor in the conduct of the audit. Answer (d) represents support for the audit opinion. Answer (c) is correct since the underlying accounting system and **not** the working papers of the audit should support the financial statements.

23. (1180,A1,46) (d) Lead schedules serve to accumulate similar or related information before it is transferred to the working trial balance. Answer (a) is incorrect because account analyses show the changes in accounts during the year which normally would not appear on a working trial balance. Answer (b) is incorrect since supporting schedules are normally included in account analyses. Answer (c), control accounts, eliminate details from the clients' general ledger.

C. Other Specific Evidence Topics

C.1. Cash

24. (583,A1,24) (b) The requirement is to determine the auditing procedure which is most likely to be omitted when internal control is strong. There is no requirement that a search for unrecorded cash receipts be performed; in cases of good internal control an auditor **may** decide to omit it. Observation of inventories [answer (a)] and confirmation of accounts receivable [answer (d)] are generally accepted auditing procedures which the auditor will generally not omit since their omission must be justified (AU 331.01). Similarly, a representation letter [answer (c)] is required (AU 333).

25. (1181,A1,40) (b) The requirement is to determine the best method of detecting kiting. Answer (b), the review of subsequent bank statements and cancelled checks is best because unrecorded checks and corresponding bank deposits will be detected. Answer (a) is incorrect because simply reviewing deposit slips would not detect the kiting as the deposit has actually been made. Answer (c) is incorrect because the schedule of bank transfers must be made by using bank statements prior to and subsequent to year-end in addition to any available client records. Answer (d) is incorrect because a bank reconciliation prepared separately for each bank for the last month of the year might not detect kiting.

26. (1181,A1,46) (c) The requirement is to determine an approach for detecting the concealing of a cash shortage by transporting funds from one location to another or by converting negotiable assets to cash. Answer (c) is correct because the timing of the performance of auditing procedures involves the proper synchronizing of their application and thus comprehends the possible need for simultaneous examination of, for example, cash on hand and in banks, securities owned, bank loans, and other related items (para 310.08). Simultaneous confirmations [answer (a)], bank reconciliations [answer (b)], and cash count [answer (d)], while all are desirable, are incomplete in and of themselves.

27. (581,A1,17) (a) The requirement is to determine why an auditor should normally mail confirmations to all banks with which the client has conducted business during the year. The standard bank confirmation form elicits information on actual liabilities, contingent liabilities, and security agreements under

the Uniform Commercial Code in addition to year-end cash balance information. The confirmation is therefore helpful in detecting unrecorded and contingent liabilities. Answer (b) is incorrect because the confirmation is of limited assistance in detecting kiting since only the bank's year end balance for cash is included (an inter-bank transfer schedule is more helpful for detecting kiting). Answer (c) is incorrect because generally accepted auditing standards do not explicitly require the confirmation of all accounts. Answer (d) is incorrect because the procedure will not, in and of itself, relieve the auditor of responsibility for forged checks.

28. (581,A1,56) (a) The requirement is to determine the area in which an auditor will have the most difficult time detecting an illegal diversion of proceeds. Because scrap sales are generally irregular in nature, they often are inadequately controlled by the internal control system. Answers (b), (c), and (d) are all typical, frequently recurring business transactions which are under the internal control system.

29. (1179,A1,15) (d) The standard bank confirmation form requests:

1. Balances to the credit of the client
2. Direct liabilities for client's loans
3. Client contingent liability on endorsed or discounted notes
4. Other direct or contingent liabilities, open letters of credit, etc.
5. Security agreements under the UCC

Thus with respect to contingent liabilities, concern regarding notes receivable is on those discounted by the bank. Answers (a), (b), and (c) are incorrect because they are not contingent liabilities of the client.

C.2. Receivables

30. (1183,A1,23) (a) The requirement is to determine the correct statement with respect to the examination of **negotiable** notes receivable. The negotiable nature of the notes limits the usefulness of confirmation since, unknown to the customer, the notes may be in the process of sale at year end. Answer (b) is incorrect because the bank confirmation form asks for notes on which the firm has a contingent liability; the "without recourse" provision eliminates the contingent liability. Answer (c) is incorrect because an auditor will perform other procedures in addition to physical inspection (e.g., valuation tests). Answer (d) is incorrect because the contingent liability due to the "with recourse" provision will generally result in confirmation procedures being used.

31. (1183,A1,24) (a) The requirement is to determine what the confirmation of a number of **open** receivables is most likely to achieve. Lapping slows down the recording of customers' payments. Therefore, confirmations may detect lapping when an auditor receives replies in which customers state that they have paid the receivable well before year end. Answer (b) is incorrect because it is doubtful that such accounts will be confirmed since they will generally have low dollar or zero book balances; also, if confirmations are sent one would not expect family and friends to disclose the fraud with which they are involved. Answer (c) is incorrect because the EDP control clerk also is not likely to self-report the fraud. Answer (d) is incorrect because it relates to accounts which have been written off and not to **open** accounts.

32. (1183,A1,25) (d) The requirement is to determine the proper audit procedure related to a reply on a confirmation stating that the balance had been paid after year end. Auditors trace such "gratuitous" information to the accounting records to avoid later embarrassment if the amount is never recorded and to assist in testing the valuation assertion. Answer (a) is incorrect because there is not a general need to audit all transactions in the subsequent year's first nine days. Answer (b) is incorrect because an auditor's primary objective of forming an opinion on the financial statements is not directly related to whether the customer took an available discount. Answer (c) is incorrect because there is no need to reconfirm.

33. (583,A1,32) (c) The requirement is to determine the error which reconciling the total of the accounts receivable subsidiary ledger to the general ledger control account is most likely to disclose. The improper carrying forward of an opening balance in the subsidiary ledger will result in a difference between that ledger and the general ledger account. Answer (a) is incorrect because the improper computation of an invoice will affect both the subsidiary and the general ledger accounts. Answer (b) is incorrect because, while the improper posting of a receipt will cause the two subsidiary accounts to be in error, the total of the subsidiary ledger will equal the general ledger control account. Answer (d) is incorrect because past due accounts will also be included in both ledgers.

34. (582,A1,10) (d) The requirement is to determine the best argument against the use of negative accounts receivable confirmations. When no reply is received, the auditor assumes that the debtor agrees that the account is correct – other assumptions are plausible. Answer (a) is incorrect since the cost-per-response

should be no higher than that for positive confirmations. Answer (b) is incorrect because the auditor may control for non-delivered confirmations through insertions of his/her firm's address in the return address portion of the envelope in which the confirmation is enclosed. Answer (c) is incorrect since there is no reason to believe that recipients will consider this a subtle request for payment any more than any other form of confirmation.

35. (582,A1,14) (a) The requirement is to determine the most appropriate audit procedure for nonreplies to second confirmation requests of receivables. These accounts may be in dispute and support on whether the proper items and quantities have been shipped may be obtained from shipping documents. Answer (b) is incorrect because collections made during the year will provide only limited assurances as to the proper valuation of the account. Answer (c) is incorrect because there is no reason at this point to believe that the internal control system has broken down. Answer (d) is incorrect because, although subsequent audit procedures may indicate the need for an increase in the allowance account, no reason to make the entry exists at this point.

36. (1181,A1,48) (d) The requirement is to determine the situation in which negative confirmations are **not** particularly useful. Answer (d) is correct since positive confirmations are suggested for large account balances (para 331.05). Strong internal control [answer (a)], a large number of small balances [answer (b)] and the auditor's belief that persons receiving the requests for confirmation are likely to give them consideration [answer (c)] are all circumstances which may lead the auditor to the use of the negative form of confirmation (para 331.05).

37. (581,A1,4) (d) The requirement is to determine which is **not** a primary objective in the examination of accounts receivable. Determining the approximate time of collection is not a primary objective; it is a method for determining whether the accounts are properly valued. Answers (a), (b), and (c) all represent primary objectives of the auditor in the examination of accounts receivable.

38. (580,A1,29) (c) The requirement is the verification technique for accounts receivable from residential customers during the audit of an electric utility. Per para 331.05 negative confirmations are particularly useful when internal control is effective and there is a large number of small balances. Additionally they are used when the auditor believes the recipients are not likely to give them much consideration which is probably the case with confirmation of utility bills. Answer (a) is incorrect because confirmation requests should be sent per para 331.01. Answer (b) is incorrect because para 331.05 indicates that negative rather than positive confirmation requests are more appropriate in this case. Answer (d) is incorrect because if statistical sampling were used, it would only be used to select the accounts to confirm and evaluate the results of the confirmation, i.e., would help implement the confirmation plan but not be a substitute.

C.3. Inventory

39. (1183,A1,6) (b) The requirement is to determine when inventory counts prior to year end are most acceptable. When well-kept perpetual records are maintained, the auditor's observation procedures usually can be performed either during or after the end of the period under audit (AU 331.10). Answer (a) is incorrect because weak internal control will often necessitate a year-end count; the auditor does not have sufficient confidence that the accounting system has properly handled transactions subsequent to the inventory count. Answer (c) is incorrect because there is no necessary relationship between inventory turnover and when a count is to be made; for example, when weak internal controls exist errors may occur after the inventory count for either high or low turnover items. Similarly, answer (d) is incorrect because the timing of the counting of consigned inventory is contingent upon the strength of internal control.

40. (1183,A1,14) (a) The requirement is to determine what purchase cutoff procedures should be designed to test. Inventory items which have been purchased and received before year end should be included in year-end inventory; title has passed to the purchaser. (More completely, purchase cutoff procedures for inventory should be designed to test whether all inventory items to which the firm holds title at year end are recorded.) Answer (b) is incorrect because cutoff procedures do not directly address whether the balance is carried at the lower of cost or market. Answer (c) is incorrect because under accrual basis accounting the items need not be paid for at year end to be included in inventory. Answer (d) is incorrect because all inventory need not be in the possession of the company (e.g., consigned inventory).

41. (1183,A1,40) (d) The requirement is to determine the situation **most** likely to require special audit planning by the auditor. Answer (d) is correct because when an inventory is comprised of precious stones a specialist may be needed (and arranged for in advance)

to assist in gathering evidence related primarily to the valuation assertion (see AU 336.02 for information on the decision to use the work of a specialist). Answer (a) is incorrect because while inconvenient, the lack of identification numbers on some factory and office equipment is normal and to be expected. Answer (b) is incorrect because the use of differing depreciation methods for tax and book purposes in many cases simply requires a knowledge of tax deferral principles. Answer (c) is incorrect because the auditor will either accept the policy as being reasonable or, less likely, recommend that certain items be capitalized.

42. (583,A1,33) (b) The requirement is to determine the purpose of tracing information on inventory tags to the physical inventory sheets. When an auditor begins with the inventory tags and traces to the inventory sheets, an inventory completeness check is being performed; that is, the auditor is testing whether the inventory counted has been included on the inventory sheets. Answer (a) is incorrect because the tags will generally include quantity and not cost information. Answer (c) is incorrect because to determine whether an inventory item which is represented by an inventory tag is bona fide an auditor will examine the item. Answer (d) is incorrect because an auditor will trace information from the physical inventory sheets to the tags (opposite direction) to determine whether untagged inventory items have been included.

43. (1181,A1,16) (d) The requirement is to determine the audit procedure providing the most assurance that an approved receiving report accompanies each check request for payment of merchandise. Answer (d) is correct because a receiving report evidencing the receipt of the goods should be prepared before the check is issued. Answer (a) is incorrect because it tests only those items for which receiving reports have been filled out. Answer (b) is incorrect for the same reason as (a) and because the date on the cancelled check should not be earlier than the one on the receiving report. Answer (c) is incorrect because checks should not be issued before items are received.

44. (581,A1,16) (b) The requirement is to determine an audit step to establish the accuracy of perpetual inventory records. The receiving report will indicate the quantity actually received. Answers (a) and (c) are incorrect because they deal with the quantity ordered; this may differ from the quantity received. The actual payment to the vendor, answer (d), will not be as helpful as the receiving report because it will be difficult to convert the amount of the payment to individual items received. In addition to the payment, the vendor's invoice and/or the receiving report will be needed.

45. (1180,A1,58) (b) The vendor's invoice may be used in a purchase cutoff. The invoice will assist the auditor in obtaining information on quantity [answer (a)], price [answer (b)] and terms [answer (d)]. It will give limited assistance on the quality of the item which is in transit and is thus not available.

46. (580,A1,15) (d) Tracing the test counts from the observation of physical inventory to the final inventory schedule determines that items observed by the auditor are included in the final inventory schedule. Answers (a) and (b) are incorrect because tracing the test count data to the final inventory schedule provides no evidence of the ownership or the obsolescence of the inventory. Answer (c) is incorrect because while the inventory was present for the auditor's observation and test count, it may have been shipped prior to the auditor's tracing the test count data to the final inventory schedule.

47. (1179,A1,4) (d) The requirement is supporting documentation for quantities of materials charged to work in process. Material requisitions by production departments would be the basis for charging materials to work in process. Answer (a) is incorrect because cost ledgers include the work-in-process account, and therefore are not a source of supporting information to initiate transactions which would be recorded later in the cost ledger. Answer (b) is incorrect because perpetual inventory records are maintained based upon supporting or initiating documentation such as material requisitions. Answer (c) is incorrect because receiving reports are generally prepared by the receiving department when received from third parties at the plant itself. Generally, receiving reports are not prepared in addition to the material requisitions for movement.

48. (1179,A1,51) (c) The requirement is the most important audit procedure for disclosing unrecorded liabilities of a public warehouse. Warehouse receipts are issued upon storage of goods. They may be negotiable or non-negotiable and are regulated by either the UCC or the Uniform Warehouse Receipts Act. Goods represented by negotiable warehouse receipts can be released only by surrender of the receipt, but goods represented by non-negotiable receipt may be released upon valid instructions of the holder of the receipt. Inspection of receiving and issuing procedures will permit the auditor to thoroughly evaluate the internal control system over the custodial responsibilities of the

warehousemen. If the custodial responsibilities are not properly discharged, there may be significant unrecorded liabilities (para 901.18). Answer (a) is incorrect because confirmation of negotiable instruments may be impractical due to nonidentifiability of the holder of the negotiable receipt. Answer (b) is incorrect because a review of outstanding receipts cannot be made because the auditor has no knowledge of who may hold "unrecorded" receipts. Answer (d) is incorrect because an observation of inventory will only determine what is on hand. The amount of inventories on hand must be coupled with a review of outstanding warehouse receipts to determine any unrecorded liabilities.

C.4. Marketable Securities

49. (1183,A1,28) (d) The requirement is to determine the information with which the auditor will be **least** interested when reviewing a pooling of interests. The fair market value of the acquired assets has more relevance in a transaction accounted for as a purchase than in one treated as a pooling of interests. In a pooling of interests the acquired firm's assets are recorded at book values. Therefore, answers (a) and (b) are incorrect since the auditor will need to consider book value and par value of stock that was issued. Answer (c) is incorrect since legal and disclosure issues will exist if the acquisition was not properly approved.

50. (1181,A1,4) (d) The requirement is to determine the best method of verifying the accuracy of recorded dividend income from investment securities. Answer (d) is correct because references should be made to a standard financial reporting service's record of dividends to determine that all dividends have been recorded and received. Answer (a) is incorrect because it does not provide evidence that all dividends have been recorded. Answer (b) is incorrect because of its generality and because of the fact that statistical sampling does not have to be used. Answer (c) is incorrect because the client has control over 1099's.

51. (1181,A1,44) (d) The requirement is to determine the most convincing evidence with respect to recorded goodwill. Answer (d) is correct because identifiable assets acquired in a "purchase" business combination should be recorded at their appraised values (APB 16, para 88). Answer (a) is incorrect because assessed tax values may deviate from the value to be recorded under generally accepted accounting principles. Answer (b) is incorrect because the seller's book value is not relevant to the value at which the purchaser should record the assets. Answer (c) is incorrect because for valid business reasons a firm may insure its assets for other than their cost.

52. (1180,A1,38) (a) In an examination of investments auditors must establish existence (answer (c)), ownership (answer (b)), cost, carrying amount, and any related disclosures required (e.g., balance sheet classification (answer (d)). Authenticity, answer (a) is not a **primary** objective.

C.5. Property, Plant, and Equipment

53. (1183,A1,45) (c) The requirement is to determine which answer is **not** a primary objective of the auditor in the examination of property, plant, and equipment. Determining whether adequate replacement funds exist is not a primary objective because it does not bear directly on the fairness of presentation in conformity with GAAP. Answer (a) is incorrect because an auditor will test the adequacy of internal control. Answer (b) is incorrect because abandoned property needs to be properly reflected in the financial statements. Similarly, answer (d) is incorrect because an auditor must determine that the firm's depreciation is reasonable.

54. (583,A1,42) (c) The requirement is to determine the income statement account for which the auditor would be most likely to analyze the details. Expensing capital acquisitions is a frequent accounting error. The other answers, service revenue (a), sales (b), and salaries expense (d) are all more frequently tested through analytical review and compliance test procedures.

55. (583,A1,52) (d) The requirement is to determine how an auditor might find an item which has been erroneously capitalized in violation of company policy. The cost which was erroneously capitalized will be included in the population of construction work orders which were capitalized during the year. Answer (a) is incorrect because it is unlikely that a mere discussion of capitalization policies will cause the controller both to realize and to disclose the error. Answer (b) is incorrect because information on the capitalized item will not be included in the maintenance expense accounts. Answer (c) is incorrect because merely noting that the warehouse has been painted will not necessarily lead the auditor to the testing of whether the cost has been properly handled in the accounting records.

56. (582,A1,38) (d) The requirement is to determine the account which would be reviewed to assist the auditor in determining that additions to property, plant, and equipment are **not** understated. The repairs expense account may include additions that have been erroneously expensed. Answer (a) is incorrect because

it is unlikely that depreciation will be taken on assets which have not been capitalized. Answer (b), while possible, is not as complete as (d) because even if the item has been set up in accounts payable, it may not have been capitalized properly — the debit portion of the entry may be in the repairs expense account. Answer (c) is incorrect because most entries to cash will be for payment of accounts payable which have already been established.

57. (580,A1,28) (a) The requirement is the document least likely to provide evidence regarding mortgage acquisition costs. Deeds generally consist of a legal conveyance of rights to use real property. Frequently the sales price is not even specified and the related mortgage acquisition costs are much less likely to be stated in a deed. Answer (b) is incorrect because cancelled checks would provide verification of mortgage acquisition costs. Answer (c) is incorrect because the closing statement would provide a detailed listing of the costs of acquiring the real property, including possible mortgage acquisition costs. Answer (d) is incorrect because examination of interest expense would also relate to the mortgage acquisition costs.

58. (580,A1,31) (a) The requirement is the least likely means to learn of retirements of equipment. The purchase return and allowance account is credited upon the return of merchandise purchased by the client. Since there is no relationship between merchandise returned and equipment and there are no entries related to purchase returns upon retirement of equipment, review of the purchase return and allowance account would provide no evidence of the equipment retirements. Answer (b) is incorrect because equipment retirements will reduce depreciation. Answer (c) is incorrect because debits to the accumulated depreciation account arise when equipment is retired. Answer (d) is incorrect because insurance policy riders are often added for new equipment, and new equipment often replaces old equipment which has been retired.

C.7. Payables (Current)

59. (1183,A1,5) (c) The requirement is to determine the assertion which is being tested when an auditor traces items for the last month from the vouchers payable register to the underlying documents. The existence of support for the recorded transactions will help the auditor to determine that the recorded obligations are valid. Answer (a) is incorrect because the items in the vouchers payable register recorded during the last month may or may not have been paid when an auditor is performing the audit. Answer (b) is not as accurate as answer (c) because such a test provides a very limited test of whether the obligations were recorded in the correct period. A more complete test would be to trace from the actual vouchers to the vouchers register to determine that they had been properly posted, both prior to year end and subsequent to year end. Answer (d) is incorrect because to test whether cash disbursements are properly recorded an auditor would need to use the cash disbursements journal.

60. (1183,A1,20) (a) The requirement is to determine the situation in which unrecorded liabilities are most likely to be found. When an auditor reviews unpaid bills, items which should have been recorded as of year end, but were not, are often discovered. Answers (b), (c), and (d) all relate to a firm's sales and, therefore, to receivable and inventory cutoffs.

61. (1182,A1,16) (c) The requirement is to determine what procedure relating to accounts payable an auditor could delegate entirely to the client's employees. Preparation of a schedule of accounts payable is a client's accounting function necessary to corroborate the accounts payable control account. Answer (a) is incorrect since an auditor tests the various footings. Answer (b) is incorrect because, while client assistance may be obtained in such reconciliation of invoices to statements, the auditor will generally wish to review such work. Answer (d) is incorrect because the auditor should mail the confirmation to determine that they are actually sent to the debtor.

62. (1182,A1,18) (b) The requirement is to determine the audit procedure least likely to detect an unrecorded liability. An analysis and recomputation of depreciation expense is based on transactions which have already been recorded (in this case an equipment purchase). Answer (a) is incorrect because unrecorded debt may be discovered through recomputation of interest expense. Answer (c) is incorrect because the standard bank confirmation form explicitly asks for information on liabilities. Answer (d) is incorrect because the minutes of the meetings of the board of directors may include discussions of major liabilities incurred by the firm.

63. (582,A1,40) (b) The requirement is to determine the statement that is **not** an objective of the **examination of the balance** in the accounts payable account. Answers (a), (c), and (d) all relate to substantive tests performed by the auditor to verify the balance in accounts payable. Answer (a) is an objective because the firm makes assertions as to the appropriate presentation and disclosure of such liabilities

(AU 326.08). Answer (c) is an objective because the reasonableness of recorded liabilities pertains to the existence assertion (AU 326.04). Answer (d) is also an objective since determining that all existing liabilities are recorded pertains to the completeness assertion (AU 326.05). Answer (b) is the correct answer because proper authorization is an internal control principle that an auditor examines by compliance testing. Proper authorization only suggests that related account balances are more likely to be correct. Based on this reliance the auditor adjusts his/her substantive tests of account balances accordingly. Additionally, account balances may be correct whether they are properly authorized or not.

64. (1180,A1,19) (a) Commissions are directly related to sales in verifying accrued commission payable; the auditor seeks to determine that both are recorded in the proper period. Answer (b) is incorrect because contingent liabilities generally have little to do with commissions; in most cases, the liability exists when the sale occurs. Answer (c) is incorrect because the overall general nature of the post balance sheet review makes discovery difficult, although certainly possible. Answer (d) is incorrect because the examination trade accounts payable will be of assistance in verifying accrued commissions only in those cases in which there are classification errors.

65. (1180,A1,51) (d) The search for unrecorded liabilities is performed near the completion of the audit to determine that proper cutoffs have been made and to give the auditor additional information in his/her evaluations of account balances as of the balance sheet date. One of the principal procedures used to accomplish this objective is the examination of a sample of cash disbursements in the period subsequent to year-end [answer (d)]. Answer (a) is incorrect since it will only be effective for creditors already recorded in the accounts payable ledger. Answer (b) is incorrect since for unrecorded items it is likely that both the purchases account and the accounts payable account will be understated. Answer (c) is of limited assistance because of the few days involved.

66. (580,A1,52) (d) The requirement is why confirmation of accounts payable is unnecessary. Accounts payable are usually not confirmed because there is better evidence available to the auditor, i.e., examination of cash payments subsequent to the balance sheet date. If the auditor reviews all cash payments for a sufficient time after the balance sheet date for items pertaining to the period under audit and finds no such payments which were not recorded as liabilities at year end, the auditor is reasonably assured that accounts payable were not understated.

C.8. Long-Term Debt

67. (581,A1,10) (d) The requirement is to determine from whom the auditor should obtain written confirmation for debenture transactions of a publicly-held company. Firms will almost always utilize the services of an independent trustee when debentures are outstanding. The trustee will maintain records on the bond transactions during the year. Answer (a) is incorrect because debenture holders will generally be able to confirm only balances (as opposed to transactions) at any one point in time. The client's attorney, answer (b), does not generally maintain detailed transaction records pertaining to debentures. Internal auditors, answer (c), will in general have no more detailed information on the debentures than that already available to the auditor from the firm being audited. Also, internal auditors provide internally generated evidence which is not in general considered as reliable as externally generated evidence.

68. (581,A1,43) (b) The requirement is to identify a procedure which would be used in examining long-term debt. The auditor will examine the bond trust indenture to obtain an understanding of the material aspects of the debt. Due to the existence of a trustee for bond transactions, the confirmation and verification [answer (a)] of the existence of the bondholders will not be necessary in most circumstances. Answer (c) is incorrect because accounts payable will frequently be associated with normal current trade accounts. Answer (d) is incorrect because long-term debt is not related to bond interest income.

69. (1180,A1,42) (c) It is unlikely that public records will have the required current mortgage balance. Answer (a) describes a procedure, the examination of cancelled checks, that provides evidence that the payments have been made. Answers (b) and (d), reviewing the amortization schedule and recomputing interest expense, gives the portions of the payments representing principle (reduction of mortgage balance) and interest.

C.9. Owners' Equity

70. (581,A1,14) (c) The requirement is to determine a likely step in the audit program for retained earnings. The legality of a dividend depends in part on whether it has been properly authorized (state laws differ on specific requirements). Thus, the auditor must determine that proper authorization exists, as both cash and stock dividends affect retained earnings. Answer (a) is incorrect since only a memo entry is required for a stock split. Answer (b) is incorrect because

the write-down of an account receivable will not, in general, be recorded in retained earnings. Answer (d) is incorrect because gains from the disposition of treasury shares are recorded in paid-in capital accounts.

71. (1180,A1,7) (a) Answer (a) is correct since only the Minutes will show whether the stock issuance or retirement has been properly authorized. Although the auditor may examine cash receipts (for issuances) and cash disbursements (retirements), the requirement specifies "ultimately traced to" thus, neither answers (b) and (c) meet the requirement. Answer (d) is incorrect; once the stock is issued, the stockholders possess the stock certificates.

72. (580,A1,12) (a) The requirement is the area which would require the least amount of time in an audit of a medium-sized manufacturing concern. The number of transactions affecting owners' equity are few in number relative to transactions affecting revenue, assets, and liabilities. Generally only dividend payments, sales of stock, treasury stock transactions, and stock dividends affect owners' equity. Thus all owners' equity transactions can be verified in relatively little time.

C.11. Client Representation Letters

73. (1183,A1,18) (c) The requirement is to determine the correct statement relating to the situation in which management refuses to furnish certain essential written representations. Management's refusal to furnish such written representations constitutes a scope limitation which is sufficient to preclude an unqualified opinion and which causes the auditor to consider whether s/he can rely on other representations of management (AU 333.11). Answer (a) is incorrect since the written evidence is considered necessary. Answer (b) is incorrect because such refusal does constitute a scope limitation that may lead to a modification of the opinion. Answer (d) is incorrect because the auditor is not in a position to know whether the information is incorrect. Therefore, a qualified opinion or a disclaimer would be more appropriate than an adverse opinion.

74. (583,A1,38) (c) The requirement is to determine the audit procedure which is ordinarily performed last. A management representation letter should be received and dated as of the last day of field work (the date of the auditor's report) – see AU 333.09. Answer (a) is incorrect because the minutes will often reveal matters requiring further investigation and should, therefore, be read early in the engagement during the planning phase. Answers (b) and (d) are incorrect because substantive and compliance tests are normally performed at an interim date or as of year end with the results being subject to subsequent analytical review.

75. (1182,A1,25) (a) The requirement is to determine the date of the management representation letter. AU 333.09 states that the management representation letter should be dated the same as the auditor's report.

76. (580,A1,45) (c) Audits per GAAS require the auditor to obtain certain written representations for management per para 333.01. Answer (a) is incorrect because the use of statistical sampling is permissive rather than mandatory under GAAS per para 350.4. Answer (b) is incorrect because analytical review procedures are not required per para 318.01. Answer (d) is incorrect because inventory observation on the balance sheet date is not required per para 331.09 through para 331.13.

C.12. Using the Work of a Specialist

77. (583,A1,49) (d) The requirement is to determine when an auditor will be **least** likely to require the assistance of a specialist. It is unlikely that an auditor will have to deal with the assessed valuation of fixed assets. The professional standards suggest the use of a specialist to help in the valuation of works of art [answer (a)], mineral reserves [answer (b)], and unlisted securities [answer (c)] – see AU 336.03.

78. (1182,A1,10) (c) The requirement is to determine the acceptable statement with respect to a situation in which a CPA wishes to rely on an outside specialist who has assumed full responsibility for taking a client's physical inventory. Answer (c) is correct because when a CPA has conducted the same tests as s/he would have if client employees had taken the inventory, sufficient evidence will normally have been collected. In fact, in many such circumstances the CPA may reduce the extent of his/her work (AU 9509.06). Answer (a) is incorrect because even if the reputation and competence of the specialist have been evaluated some test counts will be necessary (AU 9509.06). Answer (b) is also incorrect because of the need for test counts. Answer (d) is incorrect because, ordinarily, the audit report need not refer to the specialist.

79. (581,A1,26) (c) The requirement is to determine the circumstance in which it is appropriate for an auditor to refer to the work of a specialist. When an auditor decides to modify his/her opinion as a result of the findings of a specialist, reference to the specialist

may be made in the auditor's report (para 336.12). When an unqualified opinion is given, as in answer (a), the auditor should not refer to the work of the specialist (para 336.11). Answer (b) is incorrect because the qualification is unrelated to the work of the appraiser. Answer (d) is incorrect because the appraiser will not, in general, be imposing scope limitations on the auditor.

C.13. Inquiry of a Client's Lawyer

80. (1183,A1,51) (d) The requirement is to determine the primary reason auditors examine invoices from lawyers. An auditor may learn of litigation, claims, and assessments on which an attorney has worked when the attorney lists them on an invoice (AU 337.05c). Answer (a) is incorrect because such accruals are typically of a lesser concern than the litigation, claims, and assessments. Answers (b) and (c) are incorrect because legal ramifications and estimates of contingent liabilities will be obtained primarily through use of lawyers' letters and through discussions with management.

81. (583,A1,51) (b) The requirement is to determine the proper statement with respect to an attorney's letter. An attorney may limit his/her responses to matters to which s/he has given substantive attention in the form of legal consultation or representation (AU 337.09b). Answers (a) and (c) are incorrect because an attorney will also comment on unasserted claims and litigation subject to the same limitations in answer (b). Answer (d) is incorrect because, as indicated above, items in addition to those with an extremely high probability of being resolved to the client's detriment are also addressed by the attorney.

82. (1182,A1,6) (c) The requirement is to determine a characteristic which will **not** exist in the letter of audit inquiry addressed to the client's legal counsel. Such a letter will seek information on claims, litigation, assessments, and unasserted claims as well as on pending or threatened litigation. Answer (a) is incorrect because such an inquiry will be sent to the attorney regardless of whether he has resigned. Answer (b) is incorrect because such a letter does corroborate information supplied by management on litigation, claims, and assessments. Answer (d) is incorrect because such a letter is used for both SEC and non-SEC reporting firms.

83. (1182,A1,31) (a) The requirement is to determine the type of evidence regarding litigation against a client that the CPA would be **least** interested in determining. The accounting treatment accorded the litigation is more dependent upon the factors [answers (b), (c), and (d)] which the applicable standards (AU 337.04) require an auditor to obtain evidential matter on.

84. (1181,A1,57) (a) The requirement is to determine which answer is accurate with respect to a lawyer's response to an auditor's request for information concerning litigation, claims, and assessments. Answer (a) is correct because a lawyer whose response is limited should so indicate (para 337.12-.14 & para 337.4). Answer (b) is incorrect because the lawyer will not provide a statement of concurrence with the client's determination of which **unasserted** claims warrant specification (para 337.09). Answer (c) is incorrect because there is no reason to believe that a lawyer's response will **ordinarily** include confidential information prejudicial to the client's defense — although this may possibly occur. Answer (d) is incorrect because a lawyer will **not** state that the list of unasserted claims is complete (para 337.09).

85. (1180,A1,21) (d) CPAs use a letter of audit inquiry to the client's lawyer as the primary means of corroborating information outlined by the client concerning litigations, claims and assessments (para 337.08). While answers (a), (b), and (c) are all partially correct, since such information may be provided by the lawyer, they are all more limited and incomplete than is (d) which includes all of them.

86. (580,A1,11) (a) If a client's lawyer resigned shortly after the receipt of an attorney's letter which indicated no significant disagreements with the client's assessment of contingent liabilities, the auditor should inquire why the attorney resigned. The auditor's concern is whether any undisclosed unasserted claims have arisen. Per para 337.11 a lawyer may be required to resign if his advice concerning reporting for litigation, claims, and assessments is disregarded by the client. Accordingly, the resignation shortly after issuance of an attorney's letter may indicate a problem. Answer (b) is incorrect because the attorney issued a letter indicating no significant disagreement with the client's assessment of contingent liabilities. Answers (c) and (d) are incorrect because para 337.11 only suggests that the auditor should consider the need for inquiries, i.e., para 337.11 does not require a complete new exam of contingent liabilities or an adverse opinion.

C.14. Related Party Transactions

87. (1183,A1,17) (b) The requirement is to determine the correct statement concerning the phrase "with the foregoing explanation" when referring to a

middle paragraph which emphasizes a related party transaction. Such phrases should not be used in the opinion paragraph when a matter has been emphasized (AU 509.27). Answer (a) is incorrect because, as indicated above, such reference is not appropriate when an unqualified opinion is being issued. Answer (c) is incorrect because the phrase is not used in adverse opinions (AU 509.43). Similarly, answer (d) is incorrect because the phrase is not used when negative assurance is being provided (e.g., letters for underwriters, Section 631).

88. (1183,A1,39) (a) The requirement is to determine the situation which would **not necessarily** be a related party transaction. Numerous corporations, often unrelated, have similar names. Answers (b), (c), and (d) are all necessarily related party transactions since AU 335 defines related parties to include the reporting entity, its affiliates, principal owners, management, and members of their immediate families (among others).

C.15. Operational Auditing

89. (583,A1,53) (d) The requirement is to determine the scope of governmental auditing in addition to audits of efficiency and effectiveness. Compliance audits are frequently performed by governmental auditors (e.g., compliance with legislative restrictions on the use of funds). Answer (a) is incorrect because governmental auditors infrequently directly examine internal control (although CPAs sometimes perform such analyses — see AU 642). Answers (b) and (c), evaluation and accuracy, are terms which are not typically used to describe types of audits.

90. (1182,A1,44) (c) The requirement is to determine a typical objective of an operational audit. Operational audits typically address the efficiency and effectiveness with which some function is being performed, and result in recommendations for improving such performance. Therefore, answer (c) is correct. Answer (a) is incorrect because determining whether the financial statements fairly present the entity's operations relates to financial statement auditing. Answer (b) is less accurate than answer (c) because evaluating the feasibility of attaining operational objectives is not as directly addressed in an operational audit as are recommendations for improving performance. Answer (d) is incorrect due to the difficulties in determining criteria for attaining and measuring profit maximization.

Other

91. (582,A1,22) (c) The requirement is to determine the audit procedure which would be least effective for auditing contingent liabilities. While any of the four choices may locate a contingent liability, answer (c) is least likely because customers are not asked directly about contingencies and because customers represent only one possible source of contingent liabilities. Answer (a) is a likely source of information on contingent liabilities because the board of directors typically discusses such matters. Answer (b) represents a good source because the standard bank confirmation explicitly requests information on contingent liabilities. Answer (d) is a good source because professional services such as those of lawyers may relate to contingent liabilities.

92. (581,A1,28) (d) The requirement is to determine the purpose of tracing selected items from the payroll journal to employee time cards during the audit of payroll. The employee time card will generally include information such as the employee's name, number, and hours worked. A properly approved time card will thus provide evidence that the number of hours paid was the number of hours worked. Answer (a) is incorrect because the auditor will generally need sources other than the time card to determine the pay rate. Answer (b) is incorrect because the individual product job card is not being examined. Answer (c) is incorrect, because simply examining the time card will not directly test the payroll disbursements.

93. (581,A1,40) (a) The requirement is to determine proper procedures relating to research and development costs. The proper accounting for research and development costs is to expense them in the period incurred. Therefore, the firm's capitalization of the expenditures [answer (a)] is likely to be of concern to the auditor. Answer (b) is incorrect since the county clerk will probably not have registered the secret formula. Answer (c) is incorrect since the costs do not qualify as goodwill. Answer (d) is incomplete since the fact that Patentex developed the formula would indicate that ownership is not the primary topic of concern here.

94. (580,A1,44) (c) The requirement is the account that the auditor would be concerned with in the examination of the statement of changes in financial position after the auditor is satisfied with the balance sheet and income statement. The auditor would examine notes payable (a noncurrent account) to determine financing and investing activities that occurred, i.e., changes in noncurrent accounts. If the statement of changes in

financial position is based upon the cash format, the net change in trade receivables and the net change in dividend payables (both current items) are each included as an item affecting operations. Each transaction involving notes payable, however, is generally considered a financing and investing activity which is generally disclosed. The auditor's interest in notes payable is equally true when the statement of changes in financial position is based on a working capital approach. Answer (a) is incorrect because the auditor analyzes the changes in the noncurrent accounts rather than the cash account if a working capital format is used. If a cash format is used, the auditor also analyzes the individual changes in the noncurrent accounts and additionally the gross changes in the current accounts.

May 1984 Answers

95. (584,A1,2) (a) The requirement is to determine the method by which the auditor minimizes the risk of not detecting material errors in the financial statements. Substantive tests are used to control the risk of incorrect acceptance of a population which is materially in error (AU 350.12). Answer (b) is incorrect because compliance tests relate more directly to overreliance or underreliance on internal accounting control (AU 350.12). Answer (c) is incorrect because the audit client depends on internal control to minimize the risk of errors, although a CPA through compliance testing might rely on this system of internal control. Answer (d) is incorrect because it is less complete than (a) in that not all audit tests use statistical analysis.

96. (584,A1,6) (a) The requirement is to determine the most likely characteristic relating to accounts receivable confirmations. Answer (a) is best because auditors generally confirm a sample of inactive accounts to assist in detecting lapping as well as to ascertain amounts in dispute in the case of open, inactive accounts. Answer (b) is incorrect because no requirement of 50% dollar coverage through confirmations exists; in the case of firms with many small receivables (e.g., utilities) such coverage may not be necessary. Answer (c) is incorrect because there is no requirement for governmental receivables. Answer (d), while often true, is not necessary, especially in cases of good internal control in which receivables may be confirmed more than one month prior to year end.

97. (584,A1,11) (c) The requirement is to determine the **least** likely expression to be included in a client's representation letter. Answer (c) is least likely (and therefore correct) because it would seem unreasonable to expect management to acknowledge responsibility for **any** illegal acts committed by employees. Answers (a), (b), and (d) are all items suggested to be included in the representation letter (AU 333.04).

98. (584,A1,12) (c) The requirement is to determine the inappropriate procedure relating to the preparation and mailing of a bank confirmation. Allowing the client to mail the confirmation has taken it out of the auditor's control. The auditor is unable to ascertain whether it reached the proper confirming party. Answer (a) is incorrect because the treasurer (or some appropriate client representative) needs to sign the confirmation request, thereby authorizing the bank to respond directly to the CPA. Answer (b) is incorrect because additional information may be gathered with respect to the account or to the various other questions on a confirmation (e.g., debt outstanding to bank). Answer (d) is incorrect because CPAs do not sign bank confirmations.

99. (584,A1,19) (b) The requirement is to determine the correct statement with respect to positive and negative confirmation of accounts receivable. The professional standards suggest the use of positive confirmations for large balances and negatives for small balances (AU 331.06). Answer (a) is incorrect because negative confirmations are permissible. Answer (c) is incorrect because there is no requirement that positives be used for trade receivables or that negatives be used for other receivables. Answer (d) is incorrect because positive confirmations are suggested in cases of bad internal control (AU 331.05).

100. (584,A1,22) (b) The requirement is to identify the parties which determine the limits of materiality for statements made in the representation letter. Materiality is to be determined by management and the auditor (see both AU 333.05 and 337.09). The client's lawyer only becomes involved when an inquiry has been directed to him/her (AU 337.12).

101. (584,A1,23) (c) The requirement is to determine the **least** persuasive type of audit evidence. Copies of sales invoices represent internally generated evidence, which is considered less reliable than externally generated evidence received directly by the auditor (AU 326.18a). Answers (a) and (b) are incorrect because they represent externally generated evidence received directly by the auditor. Answer (d) is incorrect because computations made by the auditor represent direct personal knowledge, which is also considered more persuasive than internally generated evidence (AU 326.18c).

102. (584,A1,26) (d) The requirement is to determine what action an auditor should take when s/he has noted a large decline in gross profit percentage during the analytical review stage of the audit. Such fluctuations should be investigated (AU 318.08) since it may indicate there is an error in the financials. Answers (a) and (b) are incorrect because the objective of a financial statement audit is not to directly evaluate management's intentions or performance. Answer (c) is incorrect because, depending upon the situation involved, footnote disclosure may not be necessary.

103. (584,A1,27) (b) The requirement is to determine the auditor's responsibility when management is unable to explain significant fluctuations in key elements of the company's financial statements. The auditor should investigate fluctuations that are not expected. The investigation would ordinarily begin with inquiries of management. If management is unable to provide an acceptable explanation, the auditor should perform additional procedures to investigate the fluctuation further (AU 318.08). Answer (a) is incorrect because management has not restricted the scope of the audit—management simply can't explain the fluctuations. Answer (c) is incorrect because management fraud is only one of many possible explanations. Answer (d) is incorrect because no information is given which would indicate the need for withdrawal.

104. (584,A1,29) (c) The requirement is to determine the correct statement with respect to analytical review procedures. Analytical review procedures are substantive tests of financial information made by a study of relationships among data (AU 318.02). When a relationship does not seem reasonable, further investigation is necessary. Answer (a) is incorrect because compliance tests, not analytical review procedures, are used to evaluate internal control. Answers (b) and (d) are incorrect because analytical review procedures are substantive tests and not compliance tests.

105. (584,A1,31) (b) The requirement is to determine when an auditor may refer to and identify a specialist in the auditor's report. Answer (b) is correct because such reference is appropriate only when a report modification is being made as a result of the report or findings of the specialist (AU 336.11). Answer (a) is incorrect because in an unqualified opinion the auditor should not refer to the findings of the specialist as this may be misunderstood to be a qualification of the auditor's opinion or a division of responsibility (AU 336.11). Answer (c) is incorrect because a division of responsibility, as defined in the standards, involves other auditors, not a specialist (AU 336.01). Answer (d) is incorrect because the thoroughness of the audit is not expressed in such a manner. The thoroughness of the audit is determined by whether the examination was made in accordance with GAAS and is expressed in the opinion paragraph.

106. (584,A1,34) (c) The requirement is to determine the information an auditor is most likely to seek from the plant manager. The plant manager comes into day-to-day contact with the machinery when producing a product; that contact is likely to provide information on its condition and usefulness. Answers (a) and (d) are incorrect because the plant manager will generally not have detailed knowledge as to the adequacy of the provision for uncollectible accounts or the amount of insurance which is desirable. Answer (b) is incorrect because the plant manager will have limited knowledge concerning physical inventory observation procedures and their appropriateness.

107. (584,A1,35) (c) The requirement is to determine which individual is **not** considered a **specialist** upon whose work an independent auditor may rely. The professional standards relating to using the work of a specialist do not apply to using the work of an internal auditor (AU 336.01—footnote 2). The other answers (actuary, appraiser, engineer) are all examples of specialists per the professional standards (AU 336.01). Note here that the question and its reply do not imply that a CPA cannot use the work of an internal auditor. What is being suggested is that an internal auditor is not considered a specialist under the professional standards.

108. (584,A1,36) (b) The requirement is to determine the most efficient audit procedure for verification of interest earned on bond investments. An auditor may quickly and easily recompute the amount of interest which has been earned. Answer (a) is incorrect because, in the case of interest earned, interest declarations will not be generally available. Answer (c) is incorrect because information on the interest rate is easily available from the bond agreement. Answer (d) is incorrect because vouching the receipt and deposit of interest checks will test interest received and recorded as contrasted to interest earned.

109. (584,A1,49) (b) The requirement is to determine the technique which is most likely to lead to discovery of an unrecorded check issued during the last week of the year. The cutoff bank statement will include the cancelled check which is not reflected on the books. Answer (a) is incorrect because by definition an unrecorded check would not be included in the last month check register. Answer (c) is incorrect

because a bank confirmation will simply provide a month end balance per the bank's records. Although this could lead to discovery of the check if it has already cleared the bank at year end, this is doubtful given the fact that it was written during the last week. Answer (d) is incorrect because the search for unrecorded liabilities will only detect this check if it is recorded after year end.

110. (584,A1,50) (a) The requirement is to determine the nature of refusal by the client's legal counsel to furnish certain requested information. Answer (a) is correct because the professional standards consider this to be a scope limitation (AU 337.13). Answer (b) is incorrect because the matter may not relate to unasserted loss contingencies. Answer (c) is also not necessarily true since a refusal by the client's legal council may or may not be indicative of management's trustworthiness. Answer (d) is partially correct, but this information in and of itself may not preclude an unqualified opinion.

111. (584,A1,60) (c) The requirement is to determine the basic purpose of a letter of inquiry sent to lawyers. Answer (c) is most complete and, therefore, correct because the purpose is to corroborate the information furnished by the client (AU 337.08). Answer (a) is incorrect because **all** possible unasserted claims are unlikely to be disclosed—the inquiry only requests information on those probable of assertion and, if asserted, reasonably possible to result in liability. Answer (b) is also inaccurate as information concerning irregularities is only one type of information received. Answer (d) is incorrect because the information from the lawyer may not all relate to impaired assets or incurred liabilities.

Unofficial Answer*
(Author Modified)

Problem 1 Audit Program for Accounts Payable

Taylor should perform the following additional substantive audit procedures.

- Foot the client-prepared schedule.
- Tie the general ledger accounts payable control account to the client-prepared accounts payable schedule.
- Examine vendors' statements in support of items on the client-prepared schedule.
- Examine other documents (such as approved vouchers) in support of items on the client-prepared schedule.
- Review the general ledger control account for noncash debits or unusual items, and investigate them.
- Confirm, with positive confirmation requests, account balances from vendors with account balances and vendors with zero account balances.
- Examine unpaid invoices on hand (to ascertain whether any were erroneously omitted from the client-prepared schedule of accounts payable).
- Examine documents in support of invoices paid subsequent to the year end (to ascertain whether the payable was recorded in the appropriate year).
- Inspect receiving reports to (test the accuracy of the year-end cutoff).
- Ascertain whether year-end outstanding checks to vendors were returned with the cutoff bank statement.
- Review correspondence files with respect to disputed items.
- Review open purchase orders for unusual or old items that may have been received but not recorded.
- Examine unmatched receiving reports.
- Make certain that the client representation letter includes the proper assertions concerning accounts payable.
- Investigate and resolve confirmation exceptions and other matters requiring follow-up.

**Because the requirements of this question could be answered by lists of items, we have not included an outline of the solution.*

Unofficial Answer*
(Author Modified)

Problem 2 Objectives and Audit Program for Noncurrent Assets

a. The auditor's objectives during the examination of noncurrent investment securities are to obtain evidence regarding the

- Existence of the investment securities at the balance sheet date.
- Ownership of the investment securities.
- Cost and carrying value of the investment securities.
- Proper presentation and disclosure of the investment securities in the financial statements.
- Proper recognition of interest income.
- Proper recognition of investment gains and losses.

b. The following audit procedures should be undertaken by Kent in order to fulfill the audit objectives referred to above in response to part a.

- Inspect and count securities in the company's safe and safe deposit box.
- Examine brokers' statements to obtain assurance that all transactions were recorded.
- Examine documents in support of purchases and sales of investment securities.
- Obtain market quotations for all investment securities as of the balance sheet date.
- Inspect minutes of the board of directors meeting.
- Review the audited financial statements of the (25%) investee.
- Verify that the equity method of accounting was used for the carrying value of the investment in Commercial Industrial.
- Obtain a client representation letter which confirms the client's representations concerning the noncurrent investment securities.
- Verify the calculation of interest income.
- Review the propriety of the presentation and disclosure of the securities in the financial statements.

**Because the requirements of this question could be answered by lists of items, we have not included an outline of the solution.*

Solution Outline

Problem 3 Representation Letter

Additional matters that representation letter should specifically confirm include whether or not
- Management acknowledges responsibility for fair presentation in financial statements (FSs) in conformity with GAAP
  - Or other comprehensive basis of accounting
- All material transactions properly treated in FSs
- Other material liabilities or gain (loss) contingencies requiring accrual/disclosure exist
- Satisfactory title exists for all owned assets and whether
  - Liens or encumbrances placed on these assets
  - Any assets pledged
- Disclosure made in FSs of related party transactions or related A/R and A/P
- Contractual agreements for which noncompliance would have material FS effect complied with
- Subsequent events require adjustment to, or disclosure in, FSs
- Accountant advised of all stockholder and board of directors actions affecting FSs
- All financial records and data available
- Management aware of irregularities that could
  - Materially affect FSs
  - Involve management or employees having important roles in IC system
- Excess/obsolete inventories written down to NRV
- Material loss in connection with fulfillment (or inability to fulfill) sales commitments provided for
- Material loss in connection with purchase commitments provided for
  - Quantities > Normal requirements
  - Prices > Prevailing market prices

Unofficial Answer

Problem 3 Representation Letter

Other matters that Alderman's representation letter should specifically confirm include whether or not:

- Management acknowledges responsibility for the fair presentation in the financial statements of financial position, results of operations, and changes in financial position in conformity with generally accepted accounting principles (or other comprehensive basis of accounting).
- All material transactions have been properly reflected in the financial statements.
- There are other material liabilities or gain or loss contingencies that are required to be accrued or disclosed.
- The company has satisfactory title to all owned assets, and whether there are liens or encumbrances on such assets or any pledging of assets.
- There are related party transactions or related amounts receivable or payable that have not been properly disclosed in the financial statements.
- The company has complied with all aspects of contractual agreements that would have a material effect on the financial statements in the event of noncompliance.
- Events have occurred subsequent to the balance sheet date that would require adjustment to, or disclosure in, the financial statement.
- The accountant has been advised of all actions taken at meetings of stockholders, board of directors, and committees of the board of directors (or other similar bodies, as applicable) that may affect the financial statements.
- All financial records and data were made available.
- Management is aware of irregularities that could have a material effect on the financial statements, or involve management or employees who have significant roles in the system of internal control.
- Provision, when material, has been made to reduce excess or obsolete inventories to their estimated net realizable value.
- Provision has been made for any material loss to be sustained in the fulfillment, or from inability to fulfill, any sales commitments.
- Provision has been made for any material loss to be sustained as a result of purchase commitments for inventory quantities in excess of normal requirements or at prices in excess of the prevailing market prices.

Unofficial Answer*

Problem 4 Cash Audit Procedures

Basic audit procedures that should be performed by Kautz in gathering evidence in support of each of the items (a) through (f) are as follows:

<u>Balance per bank (item a)</u>

1. Confirm by direct written communication with bank.

**Because the requirements of this question could be answered by lists of items we have not included an outline of the solution.*

2. Obtain and inspect a January 1983 cutoff bank statement directly from the bank (examine opening balance).

<u>Deposit in transit (item b)</u>

1. Verify that the deposit was listed in the January 1983 cutoff bank statement on a timely basis.
2. Trace to the cash receipts journal.
3. Inspect the client's copy of the deposit slip for the date of deposit.

<u>Outstanding checks (item c)</u>

1. Trace to the cash disbursements journal.
2. Examine all supporting documents for those outstanding checks that were not returned with the cutoff bank statement.
3. Examine checks accompanying the January 1983 cutoff bank statement and trace all 1982, or prior, checks to the outstanding check list.
4. Ascertain why check number 837 is still outstanding, if possible.

<u>NSF check returned (item d)</u>

1. Follow up on the ultimate disposition of the NSF check.
2. Examine all supporting documents.

<u>Note collected (item e)</u>

1. Examine bank credit memo.

<u>Balance per books (item f)</u>

1. Foot this total and compare this balance with the general ledger balance.

Unofficial Answer*

(Author Modified)

Problem 5 Procedures for Notes Payable

a. Andrews should use following procedures
   - Send standard bank confirmation
     Direct liabilities
     Security agreements
   - Examine notes for terms, provisions, etc.
   - Review board meeting minutes
     Authority for transactions
     Dividends declared
   - Determine compliance with bank loan provisions
   - Consider effects of president's loans on debt/equity
   - Investigate business purpose of loan
   - Trace loan proceeds to cash receipts records
   - Trace interest and principal payments to cash disbursements records
   - Recompute and verify interest expense and accrual computations
   - Consider balance sheet presentation/disclosure
     Current/noncurrent portions
     Assets pledged as collateral
     Related party
   - Obtain management representation letter

b. Broadwell's financials should include following related party disclosures
   - Nature of party's relationship
   - Description of the transaction
   - Dollar volume of the loans
   - Amounts due to president and terms of settlement

Unofficial Answer*

Problem 6 Insurance Schedule Procedures

a. Types of information, other than premium information, that would ordinarily be included in an insurance schedule are as follows:
   - Name of the insurance company
   - Insurance policy number
   - Type of coverage
   - Amount of coverage
   - Time periods covered
   - Coinsurance percentage
   - Any unusual riders or specified obligations

b. Basic audit procedures which Robbins should perform in examining the client-prepared insurance schedule are:
   - Analytically review insurance
   - Determine whether all major assets and risks are covered by insurance
   - Compare current values of assets with the insured values
   - Confirm that insurance is in force
   - Vouch information on the insurance schedule to the insurance policies
   - Vouch amount of premiums to client records
   - Foot appropriate columns
   - Reconcile prepaid insurance and insurance expenses per the insurance schedule with the client's ledger account
   - Determine whether management periodically reviews the insurance coverage

* *Because the requirements of this question could be answered by lists of items we have not included an outline of the solution.*

Answer Outline

Problem 7 Subsequent Events

a. Subsequent event is occurrence after balance sheet date, but before issuance of financial statements and auditor's report

b. Subsequent events requiring financial statement adjustment
   Provide additional evidence concerning conditions existing at balance sheet date
   Affect estimates used in preparation of financial statements
   Subsequent events requiring disclosure
   Provide evidence concerning conditions arising after the balance sheet date
   Would cause financial statements to be misleading if not disclosed
   Best supplemented with pro forma statements

c. Procedures to help ascertain the occurrence of subsequent events
   Read interim financial statements
   Determine whether interim financials were prepared on same basis as statements under examination
   Question management on existence of contingent liabilities or commitments
   Discuss with management changes in capital stock, long-term debt, or working capital since balance sheet date
   Discuss with management status of financial statement items accounted for on a tentative basis
   Read minutes pertaining to subsequent period
   Obtain letters of inquiry from company's outside legal counsel
   Obtain representation letter from management
   Ask management if any unusual adjustments were made during subsequent period
   Additional procedures as considered necessary to dispose of questions concerning subsequent events

Unofficial Answer

Problem 7 Subsequent Events

a. A subsequent event is an event or transaction that occurs subsequent to the balance sheet date but prior to the issuance of the financial statements and auditor's report that has a material effect on the financial statements and therefore requires adjustment or disclosure in the financial statements.

b. The occurrence of subsequent events that provide additional evidence regarding conditions that existed at the date of the balance sheet and affect the estimates inherent in the process of preparing financial statements necessitate financial statement adjustment. Those events that provide evidence regarding conditions that did not exist at the date of the balance sheet being reported on but arose subsequent to that date ordinarily would not result in adjustment of the financial statements.

Some of these latter events, however, may be such that disclosure of them is required to keep the financial statements from being misleading. Occasionally such an event may be so significant that disclosure can best be made by supplementing the historical financial statements with pro forma financial data giving effect to the event as if it had occurred on the balance sheet date.

c. The specific procedures that should be performed in order to ascertain the occurrence of subsequent events are these:

- Read the latest available interim financial statements, compare them with the financial statements being reported upon, and make any other comparisons considered appropriate in the circumstances. Inquire of officers and other executives having responsibility for financial and accounting matters whether the interim statements have been prepared on the same basis as that used for the statements under examination.
- Inquire of and discuss with officers and other executives having responsibility for financial and accounting matters (limited, where appropriate, to major locations) regarding:
  a. Whether any substantial contingent liabilities or commitments existed at the date of the balance sheet being reported on or at the date of inquiry.
  b. Whether there was any significant change in the capital stock, long-term debt, or working capital to the date of inquiry.
  c. The current status of items in the financial statements being reported on that were accounted for on the basis of tentative, preliminary, or inconclusive data.
  d. Whether any unusual adjustments have been made during the period from the balance sheet date to the date of inquiry.

- Read the available minutes of meetings of stockholders, directors, and appropriate committees; inquire about matters dealt with at meetings for which minutes are not available.
- Obtain from the client's legal counsel a description and evaluation of any litigation, impending litigation, claims, and contingent liabilities (of which counsel has knowledge) that existed at the date of the balance sheet being reported on, together with a description and evaluation of any additional matters of such nature that have come to counsel's attention up to the date the information is furnished.
- Obtain a letter of representations, dated as of the date of the auditor's report, from appropriate officials (generally the chief executive officer and chief financial officer) regarding whether any events occurred subsequent to the date of the financial statements being reported on by the independent auditor that, in the officer's opinion, would require adjustment or disclosure in these statements.
- Make such additional inquiries or perform such procedures as considered necessary and appropriate to dispose of questions that arise in carrying out the foregoing procedures, inquiries, and discussions.

Answer Outline

Problem 8 Audit Tests and Analytical Review

Audit procedures to apply in evaluating perpetual inventory records (exclusive of analytical review)
  Trace entries in perpetual records
    To and from receiving reports
    To and from shipping reports
  Compare records of physical counts with perpetual records
  Determine whether perpetual records are adjusted to monthly counts
  Test arithmetic accuracy of perpetual records
  Reconcile beginning and ending inventory quantities
  Evaluate consistency of cost and market value determination
  Compare unit costs on inventory listings with paid vouchers
  Apply other procedures as deemed necessary
Analytical review procedures to apply in evaluating perpetual inventory records
  Comparison of financial data with prior period data
  Comparison of financial data with expected results
  Study of relationships of elements of financial data expected to conform to a predictable pattern
  Comparison of financial data with similar industry data
  Study of relationships between financial data and relevant nonfinancial information

Unofficial Answer

Problem 8 Audit Tests and Analytical Review

The tests, including analytical review procedures, that Decker should apply are as follows:

- Trace entries to perpetual inventory records from receiving reports and shipping reports.
- Trace entries from perpetual inventory records to receiving reports and shipping reports.
- Compare records of monthly physical counts with perpetual inventory records.
- Ascertain whether perpetual inventory records have been adjusted based upon physical counts.
- Test arithmetic accuracy of perpetual inventory records.
- Reconcile beginning inventory quantities with ending inventory quantities.
- Ascertain the consistency of the methods of determining cost and market value.
- Compare unit costs on inventory listings with paid vouchers (purchase orders and vendor's invoices).
- Compare financial information with information for comparable prior periods (for example, inventory turnover, gross profit percentage, dollar and unit sales, and so forth).
- Compare financial information with anticipated results (based upon budgets, forecasts, trends analysis, long term agreements, commitments, and so forth).
- Study the relationships of elements of financial information that would be expected to conform to a predictable pattern based upon the entity's experience (for example, perform a comparison of statistical data from sales departments with accounting records or relationships between changes in sales and changes in accounts receivable balances).
- Compare the financial information with similar information regarding the industry in which the entity operates (for example, government publications, trade association data, and so forth).
- Study relationships of the financial information with relevant nonfinancial information (for example, relate insurance coverage to inventory amounts, compare inventory quantities with storage capactiy of storage facilities, and so forth).
- Apply other appropriate audit procedures which may be deemed necessary in the circumstances.

Answer Outline

Problem 9 Payroll Input Verification and Examination Procedures

a. To verify the information in the input form James should
a1. Compare name, social security number, and withholding data on input form with W-4 forms
a2. Compare names with employment authorizations
a3. Compare pay rates with wage authorizations and union contracts
a4. Compare number of hours worked (regular and overtime) with approved time sheets or other supportive records
Recompute regular and overtime hours
a5. Inspect employee authorization forms for "special deductions."
b. Procedures to be performed examining the November 12, 1979, payroll register
b1. Compare input information with information in payroll register and information on issued payroll checks
E.g., spelling of names, correctness of social security numbers, hours, rates, and deductions
b2. Test payroll deductions using withholding tax tables to recompute social security and withholding taxes
b3. Manually compute gross and net pays and compare with computer printed figures
b4. Compare payroll summary totals with other pay periods; investigate unusual variations among periods
b5. Check footings and crossfooting in payroll register
b6. Perform other related auditing procedures deemed necessary in circumstances

Unofficial Answer

Problem 9 Payroll Input Verification and Examination Procedures

a. In order to verify the information in the input form James should—

- Compare name, social security number, and withholding data on the input form with W-4 forms.
- Compare names with employment authorizations.
- Compare pay rates with wage authorizations and union contracts.
- Compare number of hours worked (regular and overtime) with approved time sheets or other supportive reports; recompute regular and overtime hours.
- Inspect employee authorization forms for "special deductions."

b. James should perform the following procedures in the examination of the November 23, 1979, payroll register:

- Compare information on the input form with information in the payroll register and information on issued payroll checks (for example, spelling of names, correctness of social security numbers, hours, rates, and deductions).
- Test payroll deductions by using withholding tax tables to recompute social security and withholding taxes.
- Manually compute gross and net pays and compare with computer printed figures.
- Compare payroll summary totals with other pay periods; investigate any unusual variations among periods.
- Check footings and crossfootings in the payroll register.
- Perform other related basic auditing procedures that may be deemed necessary in accordance with the circumstances.

Answer Outline

Problem 10 Procedures for Loss Contingencies

Procedures for loss contingencies from litigation, claims, etc.
1. Discuss with client the client policies and procedures to
   Identify, evaluate, and account
   For litigation, claims, and assessments
2. Obtain client description and evaluation of litigations, claims, etc.
   As of balance sheet date
   From balance sheet date to time information received
   Also matters referred to counsel
   Management assurance of disclosure per SFAS 5
   Usually in representation letter
3. Examine client document re litgations, claims, etc.
   Including correspondence and invoices from attorneys

4. Obtain written client representation that
   All unasserted claims probable of assertion
      Have been disclosed per GAAP
      After consultation with attorneys
5. With client's permission, inform attorney of the assurance
6. Have client send letter of inquiry to attorneys
7. Other sources of information re claims, assessments, etc.
   Minutes of appropriate committees
   Contracts, loan agreements, leases, etc.
   Correspondence from governmental agencies
   Bank confirmation forms for client guarantees

Unofficial Answer

Problem 10 Procedures for Loss Contingencies

Since the events or conditions that should be considered in the financial accounting for and reporting of litigation, claims, and assessments are matters within the direct knowledge, and often, control of management of an entity, management is the primary source of information about such matters. Accordingly, the independent auditor's procedures with respect to the existence of loss contingencies arising from litigation, claims, and assessments should include the following:

1. Inquire of and discuss with management the policies and procedures adopted for identifying, evaluating, and accounting for litigation, claims, and assessments.

2. Obtain from management a description and evaluation of litigation, claims, and assessments that existed at the date of the balance sheet being reported on, and during the period from the balance sheet date to the date the information is furnished, including an identification of those matters referred to legal counsel, and obtain assurances from management, ordinarily in the form of representation letters that they have disclosed all such matters required to be disclosed by generally accepted accounting principles (Statement of Financial Accounting Standards No. 5).

3. Examine documents in the client's possession concerning litigation, claims, and assessments, including correspondence and invoices from lawyers.

4. Obtain assurance from management, ordinarily in the form of a client representation letter, that they have disclosed all unasserted claims that the lawyer has advised them are probable of assertion and must be disclosed in accordance with generally accepted accounting principles (Statement of Financial Accounting Standards no. 5).

In addition, the auditor, with the client's permission, should inform the lawyer that the client has given the auditor this assurance. This client representation may be communicated by the client in the inquiry letter or by the auditor in a separate letter. The auditor should request the client's management to send a letter of inquiry to those lawyers with whom they consulted concerning litigation, claims, and assessments. Examples of other procedures undertaken for different purposes that might also disclose litigation, claims, and assessments are the following:

Reading minutes of stockholders, directors, and appropriate committee meetings held during and subsequent to the period being examined.

Reading contracts, loan agreements, leases, and correspondence from taxing or other governmental agencies, and similar documents.

Obtaining information concerning guarantees from bank confirmation forms.

Inspecting other documents for possible guarantees by the client.

Answer Outline

Problem 11 Cutoff Tests

a1. Cutoff date is last day of reporting period
    Cutoff test assures proper application of cutoff date
a2. Cutoff tests at beginning and end of period
    Assure proper reporting of expense and revenue
    On continuing engagements, no retest of beginning cutoff
b. Sales cutoff test should
    Determine cutoff policy and reasonableness
    Select a sample of sales invoices around cutoff date
    Trace invoices to shipping documents to verify proper treatment
    Determine proper costing of sales
    Select a sample of shipping documents
       Trace to the sales invoice
       Insure proper recording
    Review cutoff for sales returns and allowances
c1. The bank cutoff statement is used to determine if
    Opening balance agrees with prior "balance per bank"
    Returned checks dated prior to July 1 were outstanding on reconciliation
    Deposits in transit cleared
    Interbank transfers were properly reported
    Other reconciling items are cleared up

c2. Other audit procedures include
- Investigating unusual entries on cutoff statement
- Examining canceled checks
- Reviewing other documents received with bank statement

These procedures might point out
- Irregular payments or other items
- Unrecorded transactions near year-end
- Abnormal sales returns in new year
- NSF checks applicable to old year
- Material expenditures during cutoff period

Unofficial Answer

Problem 11 Cutoff Tests

a. 1. The cutoff date is the date that a company stops transaction flow for purposes of financial closing. Most often this will coincide with the balance sheet date, but it may be a few days before or after. The period between cutoff and the balance sheet date should not include abnormal activity. A company may not use the same cutoff date for all transactions, but it should be consistent between accounting periods. A cutoff test generally involves the examination (on a test basis) of underlying support for transactions recorded during short periods before and after the balance sheet date (or other cutoff date). The auditor performs a cutoff test to determine whether transactions are recorded in the proper accounting period, establish that cutoff was consistent between periods, and determine that activity was normal between cutoff and the balance sheet date.

2. The auditor must perform cutoff tests at the beginning and end of the audit period in order to assure himself that cutoff was consistent at the two dates and that a single period's revenues and expenses have been recorded within the period. If the auditor examined the prior year's statements, he would not repeat his beginning cutoff tests.

b. The CPA's test of the sales cutoff at June 30, 1971, should include the following steps:

1. Determine what Houston's cutoff policy is, review the policy for reasonableness and compare it to the prior year for consistency.
2. Select a sample of sales invoices (including the last serial invoice number) from those recorded in the last few days of June and the first few days of July.
3. Trace these sales invoices to shipping documents and determine that sales have been recorded in the proper period in accordance with company cutoff policy.
4. Determine that the cost of the goods sold has been recorded in the period of sale.
5. Select a sample of shipping documents for the same period and trace these to the sales invoice. Determine that the sale and the cost of goods sold have been recorded in the proper period.
6. Review the cutoff for sales returns and allowances, determine that it has been based upon a consistent policy and that there have not been abnormal sales returns and allowances in July; this might indicate either an overstatement of sales during the audit period or the need for a valuation account at June 30, 1971, to provide for future returns and allowances.

c. 1. The CPA will use the July 10, 1971, cutoff bank statement in his review of the June 30, 1971, bank reconciliation to determine whether:
   a. The opening balance on the cutoff bank statement agrees with the "balance per bank" on the June 30, 1971, reconciliation.
   b. The June 30, 1971, bank reconciliation includes those canceled checks that were returned with the cutoff bank statement and are dated or bear bank endorsements prior to July 1.
   c. Deposits in transit cleared within a reasonable time.
   d. Interbank transfers have been considered properly in determining the June 30, 1971, adjusted bank balance.
   e. Other reconciling items which had not cleared the bank at June 30, 1971, (such as bank errors) clear during the cutoff period.

2. The CPA may obtain other audit information by:
   a. Investigating unusual entries on the cutoff bank statement.

b. Examining canceled checks, particularly noting unusual payees or endorsements.
c. Reviewing other documentation supporting the cutoff bank statement.

Among the transactions or circumstances which these procedures might disclose are:
a. Irregular payments or payments related to matters which the CPA should investigate. For example, he would want to learn the reason for an unusual legal fee or a payment to a company officer.
b. Borrowings in the new fiscal year or repayment of recorded or unrecorded loans outstanding at year-end.
c. Abnormal sales returns during the new fiscal year.
d. NSF checks applicable to the year ended June 30, 1971.
e. Material expenditures during the cut-off period.

Answer Outline

Problem 12 Client Representation Letters

a1. Objectives of the client engagement letter
 Assure agreement between client and CPA
 Inform client about CPA's work and expected results
 Written record of CPA's responsibilities
a2. Engagement letters follow up verbal understandings
 Client should endorse a copy and return to CPA
a3. Engagement letter is appropriate at the beginning of the engagement
a4. Engagement letter is most useful on first engagements
 But should be used in subsequent engagements
 May be changes in circumstances
b1. Objectives of client's representation letter
 Written documentation of client's replies to inquiries
 Avoid misunderstandings about client representations
 Reminder that client has primary responsibility for statements
 Complements CPA's examination of statements
b2. Representation letters should be on client's stationery and signed by client
 CPA usually drafts letter
b3. All representations should be obtained before concluding field work
 Subsequent event letter as of last day of field work
b4. Client letters are important evidence
 Should be prepared for each examination
c1. Engagement letter is very important for unaudited engagements
 Due to potential client misunderstanding
c2. Client representations complement, not substitute, audit procedures
 Thus limit usefulness on unaudited engagements

Unofficial Answer

Problem 12 Client Representation Letters

a. 1. The objectives of the engagement letter are to
 (a) Make sure that the CPA and his client are in agreement as to the nature of the engagement.
 (b) Inform the client about the scope of the CPA's work and what may be expected to result.
 (c) Provide a written record of the responsibilities assumed by the CPA and those retained by the client. (This understanding protects both the CPA and his client.)
2. The CPA usually prepares the engagement letter as a follow-up to a verbal understanding that he and his client have reached. It is desirable that the client endorse and return an approved copy of the engagement letter to the CPA. It also is acceptable for the client to prepare his own letter summarizing his understanding of the nature of the engagement.
3. Preferably the engagement letter should be sent at the beginning of the engagement so that misunderstandings, if any, can be remedied.
4. Obviously, the engagement letter will be most useful in clarifying misunderstandings on a first engagement. But it is desirable that the letter be renewed periodically. Client personnel or the nature of the engagement may change, and the resubmission of the letter gives both parties an opportunity to review the circumstances. Accordingly, for recurring examinations of financial statements, it is appropriate to

prepare an engagement letter at the start of each examination. For other continuing engagements, the engagement letter also should be updated periodically—probably on a yearly basis.

b. 1. The objectives of the client's representation letter are to
   (a) Provide written documentation for the client's replies to inquiries made by the CPA in the course of his examination of the client's financial statements. This is particularly important for information that is not shown in the accounting records or might not otherwise be discovered.
   (b) Avoid misunderstandings as to client representations and force the client to consider the correctness of his representations.
   (c) Remind the client of his primary responsibility for the financial statements.
   (d) Complement (rather than substitute for) the CPA's examination of the financial statements.

2. Representation letters should be prepared on the client's stationery and signed by appropriate officers and employees. In most cases the CPA will draft the representation letter, but the officer or employee must accept the statements in the letter as his own representations.

   It is important that the representation letter be signed by one or more officers or responsible employees who are knowledgeable about the particular area or activity reported upon. For example (and depending on the circumstances), the company secretary might prepare the presentation concerning minutes of the board of directors, the controller might affirm the fair presentation of the financial statements and recording of liabilities, and the purchasing agent might report on purchase commitments.

3. All client representations should be obtained before the end of field work. If the representation letter refers to events occurring in the subsequent period, it is appropriate that the letter be signed, dated, and delivered to the auditor on the last day of field work.

4. Client representation letters are evidential matter supporting the auditor's opinion. Accordingly, they should be prepared for each succeeding examination of financial statements. If the auditor's report is updated, he should obtain from the client an additional representation as to events occurring subsequent to the date of his previous report.

c. 1. The CPA definitely should prepare an engagement letter if his responsibilities involve unaudited financial statements. Many individuals do not understand the varied nature of the CPA's work and misinterpret any rendering of accounting services as implying that an audit has been performed. The engagement letter will provide additional clarification at a propitious time, before the work is done. Also, the engagement letter protects the CPA against later claims that he agreed to perform an audit.

2. Client representations are intended only to complement the auditor's procedures, not to substitute for them. Accordingly, there usually will be little advantage in obtaining them in connection with unaudited financial statements. In certain cases, however, it may be advisable to obtain client representations, but if the CPA has reservations about unaudited financial statements with which he is associated, he cannot rely upon a client's representation to relieve him of responsibility for describing these reservations in his disclaimer of opinion.

Answer Outline

Problem 13 Audit Programs

a. Audit program – list of audit procedures
   Record of work performed
   Proof of compliance with GAAS
   Outline of evidence gathering procedures
      Of actual transactions
      Of account balances

b. Types of audit procedures
- Observation of activity
- Physical (test) counts
- Confirmation
- Inspection of documents
- Recomputation
- Retracing, bookkeeping procedures, etc.
- Scanning
- Inquiry of client personnel (including review of minutes)
- Examination and corroboration of subsidiary records
- Correlation with related information
  - I.e., reasonableness
  - Ratio and trend analysis
- Use of sampling to test transactions
- Review of subsequent events
- Attorney's letter and other legal representations
- Reliance on outside experts

Unofficial Answer

Problem 13 Audit Programs

a. An audit program is a set of the auditor's logically planned examination procedures. The audit program is the auditor's plan of action. It serves as an outline of those evidence-gathering procedures that the auditor will following during the examination. An audit program serves as a record of the work performed during the examination. It represents evidence that the examination was conducted in accordance with generally accepted auditing standards. It is a list of the detailed procedures or techniques that the auditor will follow in connection with authentication work. Since an audit program typically includes steps to gain corroborative evidence, it serves as a list of procedures necessary to test actual transactions and resulting balances. A typical audit program would include steps that require the auditor to perform certain techniques.

b. Types of procedures that would be used by the auditor during an examination of financial statements are the following.

(1) Observation of activities and conditions.

(2) Physical examination and count.

(3) Confirmation.

(4) Inspection of authoritative documents.

(5) Recomputation (including footings, cross-footings, extensions, recalculations, etc.).

(6) Retracing (including tracing bookkeeping procedures, walking through the system, checking data processing flow, agreeing evidence to accounting records, flowcharting, checking audit trails, vouching, etc.).

(7) Scanning (including skimming).

(8) Inquiry (including discussion, questioning, etc.)

(9) Examination and corroboration of subsidiary records (including reconciliation or tie-in to control accounts).

(10) Correlation with related information (including ratio and trend analysis, analytic review, analytic comparisons of actual data with expected results or norms, etc.).

(11) Testing (including sampling, tests of transactions).

(12) Review of subsequent events (including cutoff examination of cash receipts and disbursements in subsequent events period).

(13) Reliance on outside experts.

(14) Examination of legal letters (including obtaining legal representations).

Answer Outline

Problem 14 Inventory Audit Procedures

a. Audit procedures peculiar to statistical sampling
- Review client procedures to ascertain reliability
- Become satisfied that the sampling plan has statistical validity
  - It will be properly applied
  - Precision and reliability are reasonable
- Ensure all parts are included in the perpetual inventory record
- Observe drawing of sample
- Observe actual physical counts and client counting procedures
- Review the statistical evaluation

b. Audit procedures for physical inventory count
- Review client inventory procedures
- Observe physical count
- Make test counts
- Trace count data to inventory records
- Trace items from inventory records to count data
- Trace random items from the warehouse to perpetual records
- Verify footings of inventory records
- Compare physical inventory records with subsidiary ledger records
- Ascertain proper purchase and sales cutoff
- Review merchandise in transit and consigned goods
- Confirm inventory in warehouses
- Perform overall analytical review of inventories
- Account for all inventory count sheets
- Review classification of inventory items
- Review for obsolete merchandise

Unofficial Answer

Problem 14 Inventory Audit Procedures

a. When a client uses statistical sampling to estimate inventories, the auditor should perform procedures similar to the following:

(1) The auditor should review the client's procedures and methods for determining inventories to ascertain that they are sufficiently reliable to produce results substantially the same as those that would be obtained by a 100% inventory count.

(2) The auditor should be satisfied that the statistical sampling plan to be used by the client has statistical validity, that it will be properly applied, and the planned precision and reliability, as defined statistically, will be reasonable in the circumstance.

(3) The auditor should ascertain that proper steps have been taken to ensure that all parts and supplies in the warehouse are included in the perpetual inventory record. This would normally be checked in advance of the physical count.

(4) The auditor should be present when the sample is drawn to make sure that the requirements for random selection are properly observed and that all items in the inventory have an equal or determinable probability of selection.

(5) The auditor must be present to observe counts and must be satisfied with the client's counting procedures. The inventory observation can be made either during or after the year end of the period under audit it if well-kept perpetual records are maintained and the client makes periodic comparison of physical counts with such records.

(6) The auditor should review the statistical evaluation and be satisfied that the estimated value of the precision at a given level of reliability meets the materiality requirements set for the audit.

b. In addition to the above, the following standard audit procedures for verification of physical quantities should be performed whether the client conducts a periodic physical count for all or part of its inventory:

(1) Review and be satisfied with the client's physical inventory-taking procedures.

(2) Observe the physical count.

(3) Make test counts where appropriate.

(4) Trace selected count data to the inventory compilation.

(5) Select items from compilation and trace them to original count data.

(6) Select items from the warehouse at random and trace these items to the perpetual inventory record.

(7) Verify footings.

(8) Compare inventory compilation amounts to the subsidiary ledger control and investigate significant differences.

(9) Ascertain that there was a proper purchases and sales cutoff.

(10) Review the treatment of merchandise in transit and consigned merchandise.

(11) Confirm merchandise in warehouses.

(12) Perform an overall analytic review of inventories.

(13) Account for all client inventory count sheets.

(14) Be sure inventory items are properly classified, in good condition, and of proper quality.

Unofficial Answer*

Problem 15 Objectives—Tests Relationships: Cash

<u>Objectives and Tests</u>

I. Determine if cash disbursements are for goods and services actually received.

- Test for approval system that requires verification of disbursement validity through matching of purchase invoices with supporting documents prior to check signing by comparing cancelled checks to supporting documents such as purchase orders and receiving reports, noting agreement of name, description, quantity, and amount.
- Test for segregation of duties between acacounts payable and custody of signed checks by discussion with personnel and observation of activities.
- Trace cancelled checks to purchase journal and compare payee's name and amount.
- Examine cancelled checks for authorized signature and proper endorsement.
- Investigate large or unusual amounts found in review of cash-disbursements journal.

**Because the requirements of this question could be answered by lists of items we have not included an outline of the solution.*

II. Determine if all cash disbursements are properly authorized or approved.

- Examine supporting documents for authorized approval prior to check signing.
- Trace vendor's name to the approved master-vendors' list.
- Compare authorized signatures to lists of authorized approvers.

III. Determine if all existing cash disbursements were recorded.

- Evaluate the procedure for properly accounting for checks by discussion with personnel and by observation.
- Account for a sequence of checks to determine if they are prenumbered and used in numerical order.
- Examine bank reconciliations and observe their preparation to determine if they are prepared monthly by an employee with no conflicting duties.
- Perform a proof of cash disbursements by reconciling the recorded cash disbursements with the cash disbursements on the bank statement.
- Confirm selected disbursements and vendor.
- Reconcile the bank accounts independently.

IV. Determine if cash disbursements were recorded in the proper amount.

- Compare the entries in the check register to the cancelled checks and vendors' invoices by noting agreement of check number, payee, and amount.
- Compare the vendor's invoice to the other supporting documents (P.O., requisition and receiving report) and note agreement of date, vendor's name and address, product description, terms, quantities, and amount.
- Examine purchase invoices for evidence of internal verification of calculations and amounts.
- Test the clerical accuracy of invoice footings and extensions.
- Recompute cash discounts.
- Prepare a proof of cash disbursements.

V. Determine if cash disbursements are properly classified in the accounts.

- Examine the procedures manual and the chart of accounts to determine if proper classification methods are used.
- Examine for internal verification of classification.
- Test for proper classifications by comparing purchase-journal entries with purchase invoices and chart of accounts.

VI. Determine if cash-disbursement transactions are properly summarized and posted in the general ledger.

- Foot the check register, voucher register, expense register, or other appropriate registers. Trace the posting to the general ledger and accounts payable subsidiary.
- Foot selected general ledger accounts.

Unofficial Answer*
(Author Modified)

Problem 16 Audit Procedures for Marketable Securities

a. Missing information that is essential to the audit of marketable securities includes:
   1. General ledger account numbers.
   2. Dates securities acquired and sold.
   3. Interest earned (accrual/receipt) on R prior to the date of sale.
   4. Interest due (accrual/payment) on S to the date of purchase.
   5. Support for accrual of dividends.
   6. Data related to income accruals, 12/31/80.
   7. Handling of bond discount.
   8. Data necessary to determine classification of securities.

b. Essential audit procedures that were not noted as having been performed are:
   1. Physically examine and count securities on hand. Compare data on securities such as name registered, maturity dates, interest rates, and serial numbers to similar data listed on schedule for agreement. Compare such data

**Because the requirements of this question could be answered by lists of items we have not included an outline of the solution.*

for current year to last year's work papers noting any exceptions. Follow up any exceptions.

2. Confirm securities held by others.
3. Inquire whether any securities are pledged.
4. Compare proceeds for bonds sold with broker's advice.
5. Recalculate gain (loss) on the sale of securities by verifying original cost and trace amount of gain (loss) to general ledger account.
6. Trace disbursement for bonds purchased to cash disbursements.
7. Trace dollar amount of each security held to the general ledger balance.
8. Trace the accruals to receivable accounts.
9. Trace the total interest and dividends to income accounts.
10. Cross foot the 12/31 general ledger column.
11. Check extension of the amounts in the 12/31 general ledger columns.
12. Compare market prices of bonds and common stock with a published source.
13. Check the extension of amounts in 12/31 market column.
14. Compare dividends received/accrued and interest received/accrued to published record such as Moody's.
15. Recompute bond interest received and accrued.
16. Recompute dividends received and accrued.
17. Perform analytical review procedures for income and accrued receivable amounts.
18. Determine if the Allowance for the Excess of Cost over Market of Marketable Securities needs adjustment to zero since market value of securities is greater than cost.
19. Make inquiries of management concerning classification of securities.

Multiple Choice Question (1–89)

1. The first standard of reporting requires that, "the report shall state whether the financial statements are presented in accordance with generally accepted accounting principles." This should be construed to require

a. A statement of fact by the auditor.
b. An opinion by the auditor.
c. An implied measure of fairness.
d. An objective measure of compliance.

2. The fourth reporting standard requires the auditor's report to contain either an expression of opinion regarding the financial statements, taken as a whole, or an assertion to the effect that an opinion cannot be expressed. The objective of the fourth standard is to prevent

a. The CPA from reporting on one basic financial statement and **not** the others.
b. Misinterpretations regarding the degree of responsibility the auditor is assuming.
c. The CPA from expressing different opinions on each of the basic financial statements.
d. Management from reducing its final responsibility for the basic financial statements.

3. If a separate statement of changes in stockholders' equity accounts accompanies the traditional financial statements, the auditor must

a. Make no mention of this additional statement in the auditor's report.
b. Mention this additional statement in the opinion paragraph.
c. Mention this additional statement in the scope paragraph.
d. Mention this additional statement in both the scope and opinion paragraphs.

4. Which of the following **best** describes the reference to the expression "taken as a whole" in the fourth generally accepted auditing standard of reporting?

a. It applies equally to a complete set of financial statements and to each individual financial statement.
b. It applies only to a complete set of financial statements.
c. It applies equally to each item in each financial statement.
d. It applies equally to each material item in each financial statement.

5. For reporting purposes, the independent auditor should consider each of the following types of financial presentation to be a financial statement, **except** the statement of

a. Changes in owners' equity.
b. Operations by product lines.
c. Changes in the elements of working capital.
d. Cash receipts and disbursements.

6. A CPA's report on a client's balance sheet, income statement, and statement of changes in financial position was sent to the stockholders. The client now wishes to present only the balance sheet along with an appropriately modified auditor's report in a newspaper advertisement. The auditor may

a. Permit the publication as requested.
b. Permit only the publication of the originally issued auditor's report and accompanying financial statements.
c. Not permit publication of a modified auditor's report.
d. Not permit publication of any auditor's report in connection with a newspaper advertisement.

7. Which of the following will **not** result in modification of the auditor's report due to a scope limitation?

a. Restrictions imposed by the client.
b. Reliance placed on the report of another auditor.
c. Inability to obtain sufficient competent evidential matter.
d. Inadequacy in the accounting records.

8. When restrictions that significantly limit the scope of the audit are imposed by the client, the auditor generally should issue which of the following opinions?

a. "Except for."
b. Disclaimer.
c. Adverse.
d. "Subject to."

9. Skates, an independent auditor, was engaged to perform an examination of the financial statements of Apex Incorporated one month after its fiscal year had ended. Although the inventory count was not observed by Skates, and accounts receivable were not confirmed by direct communication with creditors, Skates was able to gain satisfaction by applying alternative auditing procedures. Skates' auditor's report will probably contain

a. An "except for" qualification.
b. An unqualified opinion and an explanatory middle paragraph.

c. Either a qualified opinion or a disclaimer of opinion.
d. A standard unqualified opinion.

10. It is **not** appropriate for the auditor's report to refer a reader to a financial statement footnote for details regarding a (an)
a. Change in accounting principle.
b. Limitation in the scope of the audit.
c. Uncertainty.
d. Related party transaction.

11. Management's refusal to furnish a written representation on a matter which the auditor considers essential constitutes
a. Prima facie evidence that the financial statements are **not** presented fairly.
b. A violation of the Foreign Corrupt Practices Act.
c. An uncertainty sufficient to preclude an unqualified opinion.
d. A scope limitation sufficient to preclude an unqualified opinion.

12. Stone was asked to perform the first audit of a wholesale business that does **not** maintain perpetual inventory records. Stone has observed the current inventory but has **not** observed the physical inventory at the previous year-end date and concludes that the opening inventory balance, which is **not** auditable, is a material factor in the determination of cost of goods sold for the current year. Stone will probably
a. Decline the engagement.
b. Express an unqualified opinion on the balance sheet and income statement except for inventory.
c. Express an unqualified opinion on the balance sheet and disclaim an opinion on the income statement.
d. Disclaim an opinion on the balance sheet and income statement.

13. An auditor's report contains the following sentences:

> We did not examine the financial statements of B Company, a consolidated subsidiary, which statements reflect total assets and revenues constituting 20 percent and 22 percent, respectively, of the related consolidated totals. These statements were examined by other auditors whose report thereon has been furnished to us, and our opinion expressed herein, insofar as it relates to the amounts included for B Company, is based solely upon the report of the other auditors.

These sentences
a. Disclaim an opinion.
b. Qualify the opinion.
c. Divide responsibility.
d. Are an improper form of reporting.

14. If the principal auditor decides to make reference to the other auditor's examination, the scope paragraph must specifically indicate the
a. Magnitude of the portion of the financial statements examined by the other auditor.
b. Name of the other auditor.
c. Name of the consolidated subsidiary examined by the other auditor.
d. Type of opinion expressed by the other auditor.

4

15. Morgan, CPA, is the principal auditor for a multinational corporation. Another CPA has examined and reported on the financial statements of a significant subsidiary of the corporation. Morgan is satisfied with the independence and professional reputation of the other auditor, as well as the quality of the other auditor's examination. With respect to Morgan's report on the consolidated financial statements, taken as a whole, Morgan
a. Must **not** refer to the examination of the other auditor.
b. Must refer to the examination of the other auditor.
c. May refer to the examination of the other auditor.
d. May refer to the examination of the other auditor, in which case Morgan must include in the auditor's report on the consolidated financial statements a qualified opinion with respect to the examination of the other auditor.

16. Thomas, CPA, has examined the consolidated financial statements of Kass Corporation. Jones, CPA, has examined the financial statements of the sole subsidiary which is material in relation to the total examined by Thomas. It would be appropriate for Thomas to serve as the principal auditor, but it is impractical for Thomas to review the work of Jones. Assuming an unqualified opinion is expressed by Jones, one would expect Thomas to

a. Refuse to express an opinion on the consolidated financial statements.
b. Express an unqualified opinion on the consolidated financial statements and not refer to the work of Jones.
c. Express an unqualified opinion on the consolidated financial statements and refer to the work of Jones.
d. Express an "except for" opinion on the consolidated financial statements and refer to the work of Jones.

17. When the client fails to include information that is necessary for the fair presentation of financial statements in the body of the statements or in the related footnotes, it is the responsibility of the auditor to present the information, if practicable, in the auditor's report and issue a(n)
a. Qualified opinion or a disclaimer of opinion.
b. Qualified opinion or an adverse opinion.
c. Adverse opinion or a disclaimer of opinion.
d. Qualified opinion or an unqualified opinion.

18. Higgins Corporation is required to but does not wish to prepare and issue a statement of changes in financial position along with its other basic financial statements. In these circumstances, the independent auditor's report on the Higgins' financial statements should include a (an)
a. Unqualified opinion with a statement of changes in financial position prepared by the auditor and included as part of the auditor's report.
b. Qualified opinion with a middle paragraph explaining that the company declined to present the required statement.
c. Adverse opinion stating that the financial statements, taken as a whole, are **not** fairly presented because of the omission of the required statement.
d. Disclaimer of opinion with a separate explanatory paragraph stating why the company declined to present the required statement.

19. Late in December, Tech Products Company sold its marketable securities which had appreciated in value and then repurchased them the same day. The sale and purchase transactions resulted in a large gain. Without the gain the company would have reported a loss for the year. Which of the following statements with respect to the auditor is correct?
a. If the sale and repurchase are disclosed, an unqualified opinion should be rendered.
b. The repurchase transaction is a sham and the auditor should insist upon a reversal or issue an adverse opinion.
c. The auditor should withdraw from the engagement and refuse to be associated with the company.
d. A disclaimer of opinion should be issued.

20. When an adverse opinion is expressed, the opinion paragraph should include a direct reference to
a. A footnote to the financial statements which discusses the basis for the opinion.
b. The scope paragraph which discusses the basis for the opinion rendered.
c. A separate paragraph which discusses the basis for the opinion rendered.
d. The consistency or lack of consistency in the application of generally accepted accounting principles.

21. A CPA engaged to examine financial statements observes that the accounting for a certain material item is not in conformity with generally accepted accounting principles, and that this fact is prominently disclosed in a footnote to the financial statements. The CPA should
a. Express an unqualified opinion and insert a middle paragraph emphasizing the matter by reference to the footnote.
b. Disclaim an opinion.
c. Not allow the accounting treatment for this item to affect the type of opinion because the deviation from generally accepted accounting principles was disclosed.
d. Qualify the opinion because of the deviation from generally accepted accounting principles.

22. In which of the following circumstances would an adverse opinion be appropriate?
a. The auditor is not independent with respect to the enterprise being audited.
b. An uncertainty prevents the issuance of an unqualified opinion.
c. The statements are **not** in conformity with APB Opinion No. 8 regarding pension plans.
d. A client-imposed scope limitation prevents the auditor from complying with generally accepted auditing standards.

23. The management of Stanley Corporation has decided **not** to account for a material transaction in accordance with the provisions of a recent statement of

the FASB. They have set forth their reasons in note "B" to the financial statements which clearly demonstrates that due to unusual circumstances the financial statements would otherwise have been misleading. The auditor's report will probably contain a (an)

a. Consistency exception and a reference to note "B".
b. Unqualified opinion and an explanatory middle paragraph.
c. "Subject to" opinion and an explanatory middle paragraph.
d. "Except for" opinion and an explanatory middle paragraph.

24. Raider, Inc. uses the last-in, first-out method of valuation for half of its inventory and the first-in, first-out method of valuation for the other half of its inventory. Assuming the auditor is satisfied in all other respects, under these circumstances the auditor will issue a(n)

a. Opinion modified due to inconsistency.
b. Unqualified opinion with an explanatory middle paragraph.
c. Qualified or adverse opinion depending upon materiality.
d. Unqualified opinion.

25. The objective of the consistency standard is to provide assurance that

a. There are **no** variations in the format and presentation of financial statements.
b. Substantially different transactions and events are **not** accounted for on an identical basis.
c. The auditor is consulted before material changes are made in the application of accounting principles.
d. The comparability of financial statements between periods is **not** materially affected by changes in accounting principles without disclosure.

26. Which of the following should be recognized as a consistency modification in the auditor's report, whether or **not** the item is fully disclosed in the financial statements?

a. A change in accounting estimate.
b. A change from an unacceptable accounting principle to a generally accepted one.
c. Correction of an error **not** involving a change in accounting principle.
d. A change in classification.

27. If a client makes a change in accounting principle that is inseparable from the effect of a change in estimate, this material event should be accounted for as a change in

a. Estimate and the auditor would report a consistency exception.
b. Principle and the auditor would report a consistency exception.
c. Estimate and the auditor would **not** modify the report.
d. Principle and the auditor would **not** modify the report.

28. A company has changed its method of inventory valuation from an unacceptable one to one in conformity with generally accepted accounting principles. The auditor's report on the financial statements of the year of the change should include

a. No reference to consistency.
b. A reference to a prior period adjustment.
c. A middle paragraph explaining the change.
d. A justification for making the change and the impact of the change on reported net income.

29. A material change in an accounting estimate

a. Requires a consistency modification in the auditor's report and disclosure in the financial statements.
b. Requires a consistency modification in the auditor's report but does **not** require disclosure in the financial statements.
c. Affects comparability and may require disclosure in a note to the financial statements but does **not** require a consistency modification in the auditor's report.
d. Involves the acceptability of the generally acceptable accounting principles used.

30. For financial reporting purposes, a change from straight-line to an accelerated depreciation method was disclosed in a note to the financial statements and has an **immaterial** effect on the current financial statements. It is expected, however, that the change will have a significant effect on future periods. The auditor should express a (an)

a. Consistency exception.
b. Adverse opinion.
c. Unqualified opinion.
d. "Subject to" opinion.

31. When there is a change in accounting principle with which the auditor concurs, what modification, if any, should be made to the auditor's report?

a. Modify the consistency phrase and remain silent regarding concurrence.
b. Modify the consistency phrase and explicitly express concurrence.
c. Not modify the consistency phrase and remain silent regarding concurrence.
d. Not modify the consistency phrase but explicitly express concurrence.

32. In a first audit of a new company the auditor's report will
a. Remain silent with respect to consistency.
b. State that the accounting principles have been applied on a consistent basis.
c. State that accounting principles have been applied consistently during the period.
d. State that the consistency standard does not apply because the current year is the first year of audit.

33. Which of the following requires recognition in the auditor's opinion as to consistency?
a. Changing the salvage value of an asset.
b. Changing the presentation of prepaid insurance from inclusion in "other assets" to disclosing it as a separate line item.
c. Division of the consolidated subsidiary into two subsidiaries which are both consolidated.
d. Changing from consolidating a subsidiary to carrying it on the equity basis.

34. An auditor need not mention consistency in the audit report if
a. The client has acquired another company through a "pooling of interests."
b. An adverse opinion is issued.
c. This is the first year the client has had an audit.
d. Comparative financial statements are issued.

35. A lawyer limits a response concerning a litigated claim because the lawyer is unable to determine the likelihood of an unfavorable outcome. Which type of opinion should the auditor express if the litigation is adequately disclosed and the range of potential loss is material in relation to the client's financial statements considered as a whole?
a. Adverse.
b. Unaudited.
c. Qualified.
d. Unqualified.

36. A note to the financial statements of the First Security Bank indicates that all of the records relating to the bank's business operations are stored on magnetic discs, and that there are no emergency back-up systems or duplicate discs stored since the First Security Bank and their auditors consider the occurrence of a catastrophe to be remote. Based upon this, one would expect the auditor's report to express
a. A "subject to" opinion.
b. An "except for" opinion.
c. An unqualified opinion.
d. A qualified opinion.

37. When financial statements are prepared on the basis of a going concern and the auditor believes that the client may not continue as a going concern, the auditor should issue
a. A "subject to" opinion.
b. An unqualified opinion with an explanatory middle paragraph.
c. An "except for" opinion.
d. An adverse opinion.

38. An auditor includes a middle paragraph in an otherwise unqualified report in order to emphasize that the entity being reported upon is a subsidiary of another business enterprise. The inclusion of this middle paragraph
a. Is appropriate and would **not** negate the unqualified opinion.
b. Is considered a qualification of the report.
c. Is a violation of generally accepted reporting standards if this information is disclosed in footnotes to the financial statements.
d. Necessitates a revision of the opinion paragraph to include the phrase "with the foregoing explanation."

39. A CPA is associated with client-prepared financial statements, but is not independent. With respect to the CPA's lack of independence, which of the following actions by the CPA might confuse a reader of such financial statements?
a. Stamping the word "unaudited" on each page of the financial statements.
b. Disclaiming an opinion and stating that independence is lacking.
c. Issuing a qualified auditor's report explaining the reason for the auditor's lack of independence.
d. Preparing an auditor's report that included essential data that was not disclosed in the financial statements.

40. A closely-held manufacturing company must disclose all of the following information in audited financial statements **except**

a. Replacement cost of inventory.
b. Any pledged inventory.
c. LIFO reserves.
d. Any changes in methods of accounting for inventory.

41. Basic financial statements which would otherwise receive an unqualified opinion do not contain certain supplementary information that is required to be presented pursuant to an FASB pronouncement. The auditor must identify, in an additional paragraph, the supplementary information that is omitted and express a (an)

a. "Except for" opinion.
b. Disclaimer of opinion.
c. Adverse opinion.
d. Unqualified opinion.

42. When financial statements examined by the independent auditor contain notes which are captioned "unaudited" or "not covered by the auditor's report," the auditor

a. May refer to these notes in the auditor's report.
b. Has **no** responsibility with respect to information contained in these notes.
c. Must refer to these notes in the auditor's report.
d. Is precluded from referring to these notes in the auditor's report.

43. An auditor's decision concerning whether or not to "dual date" the audit report is based upon the auditor's willingness to

a. Extend auditing procedures.
b. Accept responsibility for subsequent events.
c. Permit inclusion of a footnote captioned: event (unaudited) subsequent to the date of the auditor's report.
d. Assume responsibility for events subsequent to the issuance of the auditor's report.

44. Karr has examined the financial statements of Lurch Corporation for the year ended December 31, 1980. Although Karr's field work was completed on February 27, 1981, Karr's auditor's report was dated February 28, 1981, and was received by the management of Lurch on March 5, 1981. On April 4, 1981, the management of Lurch asked that Karr approve inclusion of this report in their annual report to stockholders which will include unaudited financial statements for the first quarter ended March 31, 1981. Karr approved of the inclusion of this auditor's report in the annual report to stockholders. Under the circumstances Karr is responsible for inquiring as to subsequent events occuring through

a. February 27, 1981.
b. February 28, 1981.
c. March 31, 1981.
d. April 4, 1981.

45. If a complete set of financial statements is presented on a comparative basis for two years, the auditor's opinion as it applies to the results of operations and changes in financial position would contain which of the following phrases?

a. The two years then ended.
b. The years then ended.
c. Each of the two years ended.
d. Each of the years in the two year period ended.

46. When comparative financial statements are presented but the predecessor auditor's report is **not** presented, the current auditor should do which of the following in the audit report?

a. Disclaim an opinion on the prior year's financial statements.
b. Identify the predecessor auditor who examined the financial statements of the prior year.
c. Make **no** comment with respect to the predecessor auditor's examination.
d. Indicate the type of opinion expressed by the predecessor auditor.

47. During the current examination, an auditor who issued an unqualified report on the prior year's financial statements becomes aware of a material unresolved uncertainty that affects the prior year financial statements presented with the current year financial statements. The auditor should

a. Qualify or disclaim an opinion in the updated report on the prior year's financial statements.
b. Not change the opinion on the prior year's financial statements because the uncertainty remains unresolved.
c. Express an adverse opinion in the updated report on the prior year's financial statements.
d. Express an opinion only on the current year's financial statements.

48. When financial statements of a prior period are presented on a comparative basis with financial statements of the current period, the continuing auditor is responsible for

a. Expressing dual dated opinions.
b. Updating the report on the previous financial statements only if there has **not** been a change in the opinion.
c. Updating the report on the previous financial statements only if the previous report was qualified and the reasons for the qualication no longer exist.
d. Updating the report on the previous financial statements regardless of the opinion previously issued.

49. An auditor's report on comparative financial statements should be dated as of the date of the

a. Issuance of the report.
b. Completion of the auditor's recent field work.
c. Latest financial statements being reported on.
d. Last subsequent event disclosed in the statements.

50. The annual report of a publicly held company presents the prior year's financial statements which are clearly marked "unaudited" in comparative form with current year audited financial statements. The auditor's report should

a. Express an opinion on the audited financial statements and contain a separate paragraph describing the responsibility assumed for the financial statements of the prior period.
b. Disclaim an opinion on the unaudited financial statements, modify the consistency phrase, and express an opinion on the current year's financial statements.
c. State that the unaudited financial statements are presented solely for comparative purposes and express an opinion only on the current year's financial statements.
d. Express an opinion on the audited financial statements and state whether the unaudited financial statements were compiled or reviewed.

51. After issuance of the auditor's report, the auditor has **no** obligation to make any further inquiries with respect to audited financial statements covered by an auditor's report unless a

a. Contingency is resolved.
b. Development occurs which may affect the client's ability to continue as a going concern.
c. Material defalcation ensues.
d. History of significant non-arms-length related party transactions is discovered.

52. After an auditor has issued an audit report on a nonpublic entity, there is no obligation to make any further audit tests or inquiries with respect to the audited financial statements covered by that report **unless**

a. New information comes to the auditor's attention concerning an event which occurred prior to the date of the auditor's report which may have affected the auditor's report.
b. Material adverse events occur after the date of the auditor's report.
c. Final determination or resolution was made on matters which had resulted in a qualification in the auditor's report.
d. Final determination or resolution was made of a contingency which had been disclosed in the financial statements.

53. Under which of the following circumstances may audited financial statements contain a note disclosing a subsequent event which is labeled unaudited?

a. When the subsequent event does **not** require adjustment of the financial statements.
b. When the event occurs after completion of fieldwork and before issuance of the auditor's report.
c. When audit procedures with respect to the subsequent event were **not** performed by the auditor.
d. When the event occurs between the date of the auditor's original report and the date of the reissuance of the report.

54. Which event that occurred after the end of the fiscal year under audit but prior to issuance of the auditor's report would not require disclosure in the financial statements?

a. Sale of a bond or capital stock issue.
b. Loss of plant or inventories as a result of fire or flood.
c. A major drop in the quoted market price of the stock of the corporation.
d. Settlement of litigation when the event giving rise to the claim took place after the balance-sheet date.

55. A CPA who is associated with the financial statements of a public entity, but has **not** audited or reviewed such statements, should
   a. Insist that they be audited or reviewed before publication.
   b. Read them to determine whether there are obvious material errors.
   c. State these facts in the accompanying notes to the financial statements.
   d. Issue a compilation report.

56. When an independent CPA is associated with the financial statements of a publicly held entity, but has **not** audited or reviewed such statements, the appropriate form of report to be issued must include a (an)
   a. Negative assurance.
   b. Compilation opinion.
   c. Disclaimer of opinion.
   d. Explanatory paragraph.

57. During a review of the financial statements of a nonpublic entity, the CPA finds that the financial statements contain a material departure from generally accepted accounting principles. If management refuses to correct the financial statement presentations, the CPA should
   a. Disclose the departure in a separate paragraph of the report.
   b. Issue an adverse opinion.
   c. Attach a footnote explaining the effects of the departure.
   d. Issue a compilation report.

58. Which of the following procedures is **not** included in a review engagement of a nonpublic entity?
   a. Inquiries of management.
   b. Inquiries regarding events subsequent to the balance sheet date.
   c. Any procedures designed to identify relationships among data that appear to be unusual.
   d. A study and evaluation of internal control.

59. When an auditor performs a review of interim financial statements which of the following steps would **not** be part of the review?
   a. Review of computer controls.
   b. Inquiry of management.
   c. Review of ratios and trends.
   d. Reading the minutes of the stockholders' meetings.

60. When the financial statements of a nonpublic entity for a prior period have **not** been audited and are presented, for comparative purposes, with current period statements that have been audited,
   a. The auditor should request removal of the unaudited statements since it is improper to present them for comparative purposes with audited statements.
   b. The auditor should identify the financial statements that were **not** examined in a separate paragraph in the auditor's report accompanying the current statements.
   c. The unaudited statements do **not** need to be marked "unaudited" as this may confuse the users of the statements.
   d. The auditor's report accompanying the statements should **not** mention that the prior period statements are unaudited, but the unaudited statements should be marked "unaudited."

61. An accountant's compilation report should be dated as of the date of
   a. Completion of fieldwork.
   b. Completion of the compilation.
   c. Transmittal of the compilation report.
   d. The latest subsequent event referred to in the notes to the financial statements.

62. A CPA who is **not** independent may issue a
   a. Compilation report.
   b. Review report.
   c. Comfort letter.
   d. Qualified opinion.

63. A modification of the CPA's report on a review of the interim financial statements of a publicly-held company would be necessitated by which of the following?
   a. An uncertainty.
   b. Lack of consistency.
   c. Reference to another accountant.
   d. Inadequate disclosure.

64. A CPA has audited financial statements and issued an unqualified opinion on them. Subsequently the CPA was requested to compile financial statements for the same period that omit substantially all disclosures and are to be used for comparative purposes. In these circumstances the CPA may report on comparative compiled financial statements that omit such disclosures provided the
   a. Missing disclosures are immaterial in amount.

b. Financial statements and notes appended thereto are not misleading.
c. Accountant's report indicates the previous audit and the date of the previous report.
d. Previous auditor's report accompanies the comparative financial statement.

65. When reporting on financial statements prepared on a comprehensive basis of accounting other than generally accepted accounting principles, the independent auditor should include in the report a paragraph that

a. States that the financial statements are **not** intended to be in conformity with generally accepted accounting principles.
b. Justifies the comprehensive basis of accounting being used.
c. Refers to the authoritative pronouncements that explain the comprehensive basis of accounting being used.
d. States that the financial statements are **not** intended to have been examined in accordance with generally accepted auditing standards.

66. Negative assurance is **not** permissible in

a. Letters required by security underwriters for data pertinent to SEC registration statements.
b. Reports relating to the results of agreed upon procedures to one or more specified elements, accounts, or items of a financial statement.
c. Reports based upon a review engagement.
d. Reports based upon an audit of the interim financial statements of a closely-held business entity.

67. Which of the following statements with respect to an auditor's report expressing an opinion on a specific item on a financial statement is correct?

a. Materiality must be related to the specified item rather than to the financial statements taken as a whole.
b. Such a report can only be expressed if the auditor is also engaged to audit the entire set of financial statements.
c. The attention devoted to the specified item is usually less than it would be if the financial statements taken as a whole were being audited.
d. The auditor who has issued an adverse opinion on the financial statements taken as a whole can never express an opinion on a specified item in these financial statements.

68. An auditor is reporting on cash-basis financial statements. These statements are best referred to in his opinion by which one of the following descriptions?

a. Financial position and results of operations arising from cash transactions.
b. Assets and liabilities arising from cash transactions, and revenue collected and expenses paid.
c. Balance sheet and income statement resulting from cash transactions.
d. Cash balance sheet and the source and application of funds.

69. Whenever special reports, filed on a printed form designed by authorities, call upon the independent auditor to make an assertion that the auditor believes is not justified, the auditor should

a. Submit a short-form report with explanations.
b. Reword the form or attach a separate report.
c. Submit the form with questionable items clearly omitted.
d. Withdraw from the engagement.

70. If the auditor believes that financial statements which are prepared on a comprehensive basis of accounting other than generally accepted acounting principles are not suitably titled, the auditor should

a. Modify the auditor's report to disclose any reservations.
b. Consider the effects of the titles on the financial statements taken as a whole.
c. Issue a disclaimer of opinion.
d. Add a footnote to the financial statements which explains alternative terminology.

71. The term "special reports" may include all of the following, **except** reports on financial statements

a. Of an organization that has limited the scope of the auditor's examination.
b. Prepared for limited purposes such as a report that relates to only certain aspects of financial statements.

c. Of a not-for-profit organization which follows accounting practices differing in some respects from those followed by business enterprises organized for profit.
d. Prepared in accordance with historical cost/constant dollar accounting.

72. A financial forecast is an estimate of financial position, results of operations, and changes in financial position that, to the best of management's knowledge, is
a. At the midpoint of a given precision range.
b. At the low point of a given precision range.
c. Conservative.
d. Most probable.

73. When a CPA is associated with the preparation of forecasts, all of the following should be disclosed **except** the
a. Sources of information.
b. Character of the work performed by the CPA.
c. Major assumptions in the preparation of the forecasts.
d. Probability of achieving estimates.

May 1984 Questions

74. When the audited financial statements of the prior year are presented together with those of the current year, the continuing auditor's report should cover
a. Both years.
b. Only the current year.
c. Only the current year, but the prior year's report should be presented.
d. Only the current year, but the prior year's report should be referred to.

75. An auditor's report on financial statements that are prepared in accordance with a comprehensive basis of accounting other than generally accepted accounting principles should preferably include all of the following, **except**
a. Disclosure of the fact that the financial statements are **not** intended to be presented in conformity with generally accepted accounting principles.
b. An opinion as to whether the use of the disclosed method is appropriate.
c. An opinion as to whether the financial statements are presented fairly in conformity with the basis of accounting described.
d. An opinion as to whether the disclosed basis of accounting has been applied in a manner consistent with the preceding period.

76. Each page of the financial statements compiled by an accountant should include a reference such as
a. See accompanying accountant's footnotes.
b. Unaudited, see accountant's disclaimer.
c. See accountant's compilation report.
d. Subject to compilation restrictions.

77. During a review of financial statements of a nonpublic entity, the CPA would be **least** likely to
a. Perform analytical procedures designed to identify relationships that appear to be unusual.
b. Obtain written confirmation from management regarding loans to officers.
c. Obtain reports from other accountants who reviewed a portion of the total entity.
d. Read the financial statements and consider conformance with generally accepted accounting principles.

78. If the auditor believes there is minimal likelihood that resolution of an uncertainty will have a material effect on the financial statements, the auditor would issue a(n)
a. "Except for" opinion.
b. Adverse opinion.
c. Unqualified opinion.
d. "Subject to" opinion.

79. The principal auditor is satisfied with the independence and professional reputation of the other auditor who has audited a subsidiary. To indicate the division of responsibility, the principal auditor should modify
a. Only the scope paragraph of the report.
b. Only the opinion paragraph of the report.
c. Both the scope and opinion paragraphs of the report.
d. Only the opinion paragraph of the report and include an explanatory middle paragraph.

80. The predecessor auditor, who is satisfied after properly communicating with the successor auditor, has reissued a report because the audit client desires comparative financial statements. The predecessor auditor's report should make
a. No reference to the report or the work of the successor auditor.

b. Reference to the work of the successor auditor in the scope and opinion paragraphs.
c. Reference to both the work and the report of the successor auditor only in the opinion paragraph.
d. Reference to the report of the successor auditor only in the scope paragraph.

81. Jones, CPA, examined the 1983 financial statements of Ray Corp. and issued an unqualified opinion on March 10, 1984. On April 2, 1984, Jones became aware of a 1983 transaction that may materially affect the 1983 financial statements. This transaction would have been investigated had it come to Jones' attention during the course of the examination. Jones should
a. Take **no** action because an auditor is **not** responsible for events subsequent to the issuance of the auditor's report.
b. Contact Ray's management and request their cooperation in investigating the matter.
c. Request that Ray's management disclose the possible effects of the newly discovered transaction by adding an unaudited footnote to the 1983 financial statements.
d. Contact all parties who might rely upon the financial statements and advise them that the financial statements are misleading.

82. When, in the auditor's judgment, the financial statements are **not** presented fairly in conformity with generally accepted accounting principles, the auditor will issue a(n)
a. Qualified opinion.
b. Special report.
c. Disclaimer of opinion.
d. Adverse opinion.

83. An auditor's examination reveals a misstatement in segment information that is material in relation to the financial statements taken as a whole. If the client refuses to make modifications to the presentation of segment information, the auditor should issue a(n)
a. "Except for" opinion.
b. "Subject to" opinion.
c. Unqualified opinion.
d. Disclaimer of opinion.

84. Which of the following material events occurring subsequent to the December 31, 1983, balance sheet would **not** ordinarily result in an adjustment to the financial statements before they are issued on March 2, 1984?
a. Write-off of a receivable from a debtor who had suffered from deteriorating financial condition for the past 6 years. The debtor filed for bankruptcy on January 23, 1984.
b. Acquisition of a subsidiary on January 23, 1984. Negotiations had begun in December of 1983.
c. Settlement of extended litigation on January 23, 1984, in excess of the recorded year-end liability.
d. A 3 for 5 reverse stock split consummated on January 23, 1984.

85. If an accounting change has **no** material effect on the financial statements in the current year, but the change is reasonably certain to have a material effect in later years, the change should be
a. Treated as a consistency modification in the auditor's report for the current year.
b. Disclosed in the notes to the financial statements of the current year.
c. Disclosed in the notes to the financial statements and referred to in the auditor's report for the current year.
d. Treated as a subsequent event.

86. An auditor's report included an additional paragraph disclosing that there is a difference of opinion between the auditor and the client for which the auditor believed an adjustment to the financial statements should be made. The opinion paragraph of the auditor's report most likely expressed a(n)
a. Unqualified opinion.
b. "Except for" opinion.
c. "Subject to" opinion.
d. Disclaimer of opinion.

87. When comparative financial statements are presented, the fourth standard of reporting, which refers to financial statements "taken as a whole," should be considered to apply to the financial statements of the
a. Periods presented plus one preceding period.
b. Current period only.
c. Current period and those of the other periods presented.
d. Current and immediately preceding period only.

88. When an auditor submits a document containing audited financial statements to a client, the auditor has a responsibility to report on
a. Only the basic financial statements included in the document.

b. The basic financial statements and only that additional information required to be presented in accordance with provisions of the Financial Accounting Standards Board.
c. All of the information included in the document.
d. Only that portion of the document which was audited.

89. An auditor's standard report expresses an unqualified opinion and includes a middle paragraph that emphasizes a matter included in the notes to the financial statements. The auditor's report would be deficient if the middle paragraph states that the entity

a. Is a component of a larger business enterprise.
b. Has changed from the completed-contract method to the percentage-of-completion method for accounting for long-term construction contracts.
c. Has had a significant subsequent event.
d. Has accounting reclassifications that enhance the comparability between years.

Problems

Problem 1 Report with Predecessor Auditor Involvement (1183,A3)

(15 to 25 minutes)

Ross, Sandler & Co., CPAs, completed an examination of the 1982 financial statements of Fairfax Corporation on March 17, 1983, and concluded that an unqualified opinion was warranted. Because of a scope limitation arising from the inability to observe the January 1, 1981, inventory, the predecessor auditors, Smith, Ellis & Co., issued a report which contained an unqualified opinion on the December 31, 1981, balance sheet and a qualified opinion with respect to the statements of income, retained earnings, and changes in financial position for the year then ended.

The management of Fairfax Corporation has decided to present a complete set of comparative (1982 and 1981) financial statements in their annual report.

Required:

Prepare an auditor's report assuming the March 1, 1982, auditor's report of Smith, Ellis & Co. is not presented.

Problem 2 Report Deficiencies (583,A3)

(15 to 25 minutes)

The following report was drafted by an audit assistant at the completion of an audit engagement and was submitted to the auditor with client responsibility for review. The auditor has reviewed matters thoroughly and has properly concluded that the scope limitation was not client-imposed and was not sufficiently material to warrant a disclaimer of opinion although a qualified opinion was appropriate.

To Carl Corporation Controller:

We have examined the accompanying financial statements of Carl Corporation as of December 31, 1982. Our examination was made in accordance with generally accepted auditing standards, and accordingly included such auditing procedures as we considered necessary in the circumstances.

On January 15, 1983, the company issued debentures in the amount of $1,000,000 for the purpose of financing plant expansion. As indicated in note 6 to the financial statements, the debenture agreement restricts the payment of future cash dividends to earnings after December 31, 1982.

The company's unconsolidated foreign subsidiary did not close down production during the year under examination for physical inventory purposes and took no physical inventory during the year. We made extensive tests of book inventory figures for accuracy of calculation and reasonableness of pricing. We did not make physical tests of inventory quantities. Because of this, we are unable to express an unqualified opinion on the financial statements taken as a whole. However:

Except for the scope limitation regarding inventory, in our opinion the accompanying balance sheet presents the financial position of Carl Corporation at December 31, 1982, subject to the effect of the inventory on the carrying value of the investment. The accompanying statements of income and of retained earnings present the incomes and expenses and the result of transactions affecting retained earnings in accordance with generally accepted accounting principles.

December 31, 1982

Pate & Co., CPAs

Required:

Identify all of the deficiencies in the above draft of the proposed report.

Problem 3 Report on a Review (1182,A5)

(15 to 25 minutes)

For the year ended December 31, 1980, Novak & Co., CPAs, audited the financial statements of Tillis Ltd., and expressed an unqualified opinion dated February 27, 1981.

For the year ended December 31, 1981, Novak & Co., were engaged by Tillis Ltd., to review Tillis Ltd.'s financial statements, i.e., "look into the company's financial statements and determine whether there are any obvious modifications that should be made to the financial statements in order for them to be in conformity with generally accepted accounting principles."

Novak made the necessary inquiries, performed the necessary analytical procedures, and performed certain additional procedures that were deemed necessary to achieve the requisite limited assurance. Novak's work was completed on March 3, 1982, and the financial statements appeared to be in conformity with generally accepted accounting principles which were consistently applied. The report was prepared on March 5, 1982. It was delivered to Jones, the controller of Tillis Ltd., on March 9, 1982.

Required:

Prepare the properly addressed and dated report on the comparative financial statements of Tillis Ltd., for the years ended December 31, 1980 and 1981.

Problem 4 Report on Engagement Involving Agreed-Upon Procedures (582,A5)

(15 to 25 minutes)

In order to obtain information that is necessary to make informed decisions, management often calls upon the independent auditor for assistance. This may involve a request that the independent auditor apply certain audit procedures to specific accounts of a company which is a candidate for acquisition and report upon the results. In such an engagement, the agreed-upon procedures may constitute a scope limitation.

At the completion of an engagement performed at the request of Uclean Corporation which was limited in scope as explained above, the following report was prepared by an audit assistant and was submitted to the auditor for review:

To: Board of Directors of Ajax Corporation

We have applied certain agreed-upon procedures, as discussed below, to accounting records of Ajax Corporation, as of December 31, 1981, solely to assist Uclean Corporation in connection with the proposed acquisition of Ajax Corporation.

We have examined the cash in banks and accounts receivable of Ajax Corporation as of December 31, 1981, in accordance with generally accepted auditing standards and, accordingly, included such tests of the accounting records and such other auditing procedures as we considered necessary in the circumstances.

In our opinion, the cash and receivables referred to above are fairly presented as of December 31, 1981, in conformity with generally accepted accounting principles applied on a basis consistent with that of the preceding year. We therefore recommend that Uclean Corporation acquire Ajax Corporation pursuant to the proposed agreement.

Signature

Required:

Comment on the proposed report describing those assertions that are:

a. Incorrect or should otherwise be deleted.
b. Missing and should be inserted.

Problem 5 Assurances Given (1180,A3)

(15 to 25 minutes)

The auditor should obtain a level of knowledge of the entity's business, including events, transactions, and practices, that will enable the planning and performance of an examination in accordance with generally accepted auditing standards. Adhering to these standards enables the auditor's report to lend credibility to financial statements by providing the public with certain assurances.

Required:

a. How does knowledge of the entity's business help the auditor in the planning and performance of an examination in accordance with generally accepted auditing standards?

b. What assurances are provided to the public when the auditor states that the financial statements "present fairly . . . in conformity with generally accepted accounting principles applied on a consistent basis?"

Problem 6 Write Report (1180,A2)

(15 to 25 minutes)

Rose & Co., CPAs, has satisfactorily completed the examination of the financial statements of Bale & Booster, a partnership, for the year ended December 31, 1979. The financial statements which were prepared on the entity's income tax (cash) basis include footnotes which indicate that the partnership was involved in continuing litigation of material amounts relating to alleged infringement of a competitor's patent. The amount of damages, if any, resulting from this litigation could not be determined at the time of completion of the engagement. The prior years' financial statements were not presented.

Required:

Based upon the information presented, prepare an auditor's report which includes appropriate explanatory disclosure of significant facts.

Multiple Choice Answers

1.	b	19.	a	37.	a	55.	b	73.	d
2.	b	20.	c	38.	a	56.	c	74.	a
3.	c	21.	d	39.	c	57.	a	75.	b
4.	a	22.	c	40.	a	58.	d	76.	c
5.	c	23.	b	41.	d	59.	a	77.	b
6.	a	24.	d	42.	a	60.	b	78.	c
7.	b	25.	d	43.	a	61.	b	79.	c
8.	b	26.	b	44.	b	62.	a	80.	a
9.	d	27.	a	45.	b	63.	d	81.	b
10.	b	28.	b	46.	d	64.	c	82.	d
11.	d	29.	c	47.	a	65.	a	83.	a
12.	c	30.	c	48.	d	66.	d	84.	b
13.	c	31.	b	49.	b	67.	a	85.	b
14.	a	32.	a	50.	a	68.	b	86.	b
15.	c	33.	d	51.	d	69.	b	87.	c
16.	c	34.	b	52.	a	70.	a	88.	c
17.	b	35.	c	53.	d	71.	a	89.	b
18.	b	36.	c	54.	c	72.	d		

Multiple Choice Answer Explanations

A. Financial Statement Audit Report — General

1. (1183,A1,16) (b) The requirement is to determine the meaning of the first standard of reporting. The standard is construed **not** to require a statement of fact [answer (a)] but an opinion as to whether the financial statements are presented in conformity with GAAP (AU 410.02). Answers (c) and (d) are both incorrect because they are less encompassing than answer (b).

2. (583,A1,14) (b) The requirement is to determine the objective of the fourth reporting standard which requires either an opinion or an assertion to the effect that an opinion cannot be expressed. This standard states that the objective is to prevent misinterpretation of the degree of responsibility the auditor is assuming when his/her name is associated with financial statements (AU 509.05). Answer (a) is incorrect because an auditor may report on one statement (AU 509.13). Answer (c) is incorrect because differing opinions can be issued on each of the financial statements (e.g., if the beginning inventory has not been counted, an auditor may disclaim an opinion on the income statement and yet express an unqualified opinion on the balance sheet). Answer (d) is incorrect since preventing management from reducing its responsibility for the financial statements is not directly addressed in the standard.

3. (1182,A1,21) (c) The requirement is to determine where mention of a separate statement of changes in stockholders' equity accounts is made in an audit report. Answer (c) is correct because AU 509.06 states that mention need be made only in the scope paragraph.

4. (1182,A1,58) (a) The requirement is to determine the meaning of the expression "taken as a whole" in the fourth generally accepted auditing standard of reporting. AU 509.05 states that "taken as a whole" applies equally to a complete set of financial statements and to an individual financial statement.

5. (582,A1,60) (c) The requirement is to determine which of the financial presentations listed is not a financial statement for reporting purposes. The changes in the elements of working capital is not a complete statement — the other three statements [answers (a), (b), (d)] are all mentioned in AU 621.02.

6. (1179,A1,8) (a) The issue is whether a client may utilize only a balance sheet and an appropriately modified auditor's report in a newspaper advertisement when the auditor originally issued an audit report on all the financial statements. First, ethics ruling 86 on "other responsibilities" permits a CPA to be engaged to verify financial data used in a client's advertising and the CPA's name be used in such advertising. Thus, presentation of the modified auditor's report in a newspaper advertisement is not an ethics problem. Second, auditor reissuance of a report on only a balance sheet would be permissable per para 509.13 which indicates that reporting on one basic financial statement and not the others involves limited reporting objectives rather than a limitation in scope. Here, there apparently was no limitation in scope as a complete audit was done in all the statements. Thus, answer (b) is incorrect because an appropriately modified report can be issued per para 509.13. Answers (c) and (d) are incorrect because there is no ethics violation.

B. Financial Statement Audit Report — Detailed

B.1.a. Scope Limitations

7. (1183,A1,31) (b) The requirement is to determine which situation will **not** result in modification of the auditor's report due to a scope limitation. Reliance on the report of another auditor does not constitute a qualification of the auditor's opinion (AU 509.14). Answer (a) is incorrect because restrictions imposed by the client are considered scope limitations (AU 509.10-.13). Answer (c) is incorrect because the inability to obtain sufficient competent evidential matter is the basis for a scope limitation. Answer (d) is incorrect

because inadequate accounting records are considered a scope limitation imposed by circumstance (AU 509.10–.13).

8. (583,A1,30) (b) The requirement is to determine the report which will generally be issued when a **significant, client-imposed** scope restriction occurs. When a significant, client-imposed scope restriction occurs, the auditor should generally disclaim an opinion on the financial statements (AU 509.12). Answer (a) is incorrect because, when the scope restriction is significant and client-imposed, a disclaimer, not an "except for" qualification, is usually appropriate. Answer (c) is incorrect because adverse opinions are issued when the auditor knows a departure from GAAP exists (AU 509.41). Answer (d) is incorrect because "subject to" qualifications are issued when a material uncertainty exists and the outcome thereof cannot be reasonably estimated (AU 509.24).

9. (1182,A1,37) (d) The requirement is to determine the type of opinion to be issued when an auditor has neither observed the inventory count nor confirmed accounts receivable but has applied alternate procedures to gain satisfaction that the accounts are properly stated. Answer (d) is correct because in such circumstances a standard unqualified opinion may be issued (AU 509.10, footnote 4). Answers (a), (b) and (c) are all incorrect because no qualification, explanatory middle paragraph or disclaimer of opinion is necessary.

10. (1182,A1,43) (b) The requirement is to determine the situation in which it is **not** appropriate for the auditor's report to refer the reader to a financial statement footnote for details. The footnotes to the financial statements refer to accounting matters affecting the financial statements as opposed to matters affecting the scope of the auditor's examination. Answers (a), (c) and (d) are all incorrect because they relate to accounting matters which will be described in the footnotes and referred thereto in the auditor's report.

11. (582,A1,49) (d) The requirement is to determine the effect on an audit report of management's refusal to furnish a written representation on an essential matter. AU 333.11 defines this as a situation in which the scope limitation is sufficient to preclude an unqualified opinion. Answer (a) is incorrect because the auditor does not know whether the financial statements are fairly presented. Answer (b) is incorrect because the Foreign Corrupt Practices Act contains no provision requiring management to furnish such written representation. Answer (c) is incorrect because the term "uncertainty" refers to uncertainties facing the firm — not necessarily scope limitations.

12. (1180,A1,9) (c) For the case described in this question, the auditor will be able to gather evidence on all year-end balances. However, evidence with respect to the beginning inventory is lacking making the verification of Cost of Goods Sold, an income statement element, impossible. If no other problems arise, the auditor will be able to issue an unqualified opinion on the balance sheet and a disclaimer on the income statement (para. 509.05). Answer (a) is incorrect since no reason is given for declining the engagement. Answer (b) is incorrect since it describes a form of audit report not permitted under GAAS. Answer (d) is incorrect since the auditor may render an opinion on the year-end balance sheet.

B.1.b. Opinion Based, in part, on Report of Another Auditor

13. (1183,A1,58) (c) The requirement is to determine the purpose of the two sentences which indicate the existence of another auditor. The sentences are those suggested in cases in which an auditor has decided to make reference to the examination of other auditors (AU 543.09). Answers (a) and (b) are incorrect since such a report need not be a disclaimer or a qualified opinion. Answer (d) is incorrect because the sentences are recommended in the referred to standard.

14. (583,A1,26) (a) The requirement is to determine a principal auditor's reporting responsibility when s/he makes reference to another auditor's examination. An auditor must make reference to the magnitude of the other auditor's examination in the scope paragraph (AU 543.07). Answer (b) is incorrect because the name of the other auditor will only be included in cases in which that auditor's report is to be presented (AU 543.07). Answer (c) is incorrect because there is no requirement that the subsidiary examined by the other auditor be named. Answer (d) is incorrect because the principal auditor may decide that any exceptions in the other auditor's report may be immaterial to the firm as a whole (AU 543.15).

15. (1182,A1,23) (c) The requirement is to determine the principal auditor's reporting responsibility in the situation in which a part of the examination was made by another auditor. The principal auditor may determine whether to make reference in his/her report to the examination of the other auditor (AU 543.02). Answers (a) and(b) are incorrect because the principal auditor does have the choice of whether to refer to the other auditor. Answer (d) is incorrect because such referral to the other auditor does not require a qualified opinion with respect to the other auditor (AU 543.08).

16. (581,A1,54) (c) The requirement is to determine principal auditor reporting responsibility when s/he finds it impractical to review the work of another auditor. In such cases, the principal auditor will make reference to the examination of the other auditor and issue an unqualified report (para 543.06). Answer (a) is incorrect because if it is appropriate for Thomas to be the principal auditor, and if Jones has issued an unqualified report, there is no reason to refuse to express an opinion. Answer (b) is incorrect because additional procedures are required when a decision is made not to make reference to the other auditor (para 543.12-.13). Answer (d) is incorrect because the division of responsibility within an audit report is not considered an "except for" qualified opinion.

B.1.c. Departure from a Generally Accepted Accounting Principle

17. (583,A1,28) (b) The requirement is to determine the appropriate types of audit reports when a client omits information necessary for fair presentation of financial statements. When financial statements are materially affected by a departure from generally accepted accounting principles either a qualified or an adverse opinion is appropriate (AU 509.15). Answers (a) and (c) are incorrect because a disclaimer of opinion is not appropriate. Answer (d) is incorrect because the omission of necessary information makes an unqualified opinion inappropriate.

18. (1182,A1,5) (b) The requirement is to determine the auditor's reporting responsibility when a client does not include a statement of changes in financial position with its other basic financial statements. In such circumstances the appropriate standards (AU 545.04-.05) require a qualified opinion with the omission being noted in a middle paragraph to the report. The other answers are all incorrect because they relate to other than a qualified opinion.

19. (582,A1,56) (a) The requirement is to determine the effect of a sale and subsequent repurchase of marketable securities. The accounting treatment described for these transactions is in conformity with GAAP (note that disclosure of these transactions is also necessary). Answer (b) is incorrect since transactions have occurred. Answer (c) is incorrect since there is no information provided suggesting the need to withdraw – GAAP has been followed. Answer (d) is incorrect because the transaction is in accordance with GAAP.

20. (580,A1,48) (c) The opinion paragraph of an adverse opinion should refer to a separate paragraph which discusses the basis for the opinion rendered per para 509.43. Answer (a) is incorrect because the auditor (not the client) should disclose all the substantive reasons for the adverse opinion and the principal effects on the financial position and results of operation per para 509.42. Answer (b) is incorrect because no mention of the nonconformity with GAAP is made in the scope paragraph. Answer (d) is incorrect because adverse opinions are only issued when the financial statements taken as a whole do not present fairly per GAAP. Generally there is no reference to consistency unless the auditor has specific exceptions as to consistency (para 509.44).

21. (1181,A1,31) (d) The requirement is to determine the effect of a departure from generally accepted accounting principles on an auditor's opinion. Answer (d) is correct because when financial statements are materially affected by a departure from generally accepted accounting principles an auditor should issue either a qualified (except for) or an adverse opinion (para 509.15). Therefore, answers (a) and (b) are wrong since they suggest other types of reports. Answer (c) is incorrect because auditors do not make decisions on the types of accounting principles to be followed by their clients.

22. (581,A1,33) (c) The requirement is for a circumstance in which an adverse opinion would be appropriate. An adverse opinion may be necessary in cases in which financial statements depart from generally accepted accounting principles, in this case, pension plan accounting. Answer (a) is incorrect because a lack of independence will lead to a disclaimer. Answer (b) is incorrect because uncertainties lead to "subject to" qualifications or disclaimers. Answer (d) is incorrect because an auditor will generally disclaim an opinion in cases in which significant client-imposed scope restrictions exist.

B.1.d. Departure from a Promulgated Accounting Principle

23. (1181,A1,11) (b) The requirement is to determine the type of audit report to issue when unusual circumstances have caused the client to depart from the provisions of a promulgated accounting principle so as to avoid the issuing of misleading financial statements. Answer (b), an unqualified opinion with an explanatory middle paragraph, is correct in such a situation (para 509.18-.19). Answer (a), a consistency exception, is not correct because there is no indication that the financial statements are inconsistent with those of the prior year. Answers (c) and (d) are incorrect because an unqualified report is issued in these circumstances (para 509.18-.19).

B.1.e. Consistency

24. (1183,A1,26) (d) The requirement is to determine the effect on an audit report of a client's use of LIFO on one-half of its inventory and FIFO on the other half. An unqualified opinion is correct since there is no requirement under GAAP that a client use only one inventory valuation method. Different flow assumptions may be used for different inventory items. Answer (a) is incorrect because nothing in the facts of the question implies a lack of consistency with the prior year. Answer (b) is partially correct in the sense that an auditor may choose to add an explanatory middle paragraph to emphasize the matter (AU 509.27). However, there is no such requirement of a middle paragraph. Answer (c) is incorrect because there is no departure from GAAP involved here which would lead to either a qualified or an adverse opinion.

25. (1183,A1,54) (d) The requirement is to determine the objective of the consistency standard. The objective is (1) to give assurance that the comparability of financial statements between periods has not been materially affected by changes in accounting principles, or (2) if comparability has been materially affected by such changes, to require appropriate reporting by the independent auditor regarding such changes (AU 420.02). Answer (a) is incorrect since there may be variations in format and presentation of financial statements. Answer (b) is incorrect since the consistency standard only requires the communication of the fact that a lack of consistency exists in the handling of items between periods. Answer (c) is incorrect because there is no requirement that an auditor be consulted before material changes are made in the application of accounting principles (although this may be done if the client so desires).

26. (583,A1,17) (b) The requirement is to determine which answer describes a situation in which a consistency modification is necessary. A change from an unacceptable accounting principle to an acceptable one results in a consistency exception (AU 420.10). Answer (a) is incorrect because a change in estimate requires no consistency modification (AU 420.12). Answer (c) is incorrect because an error not involving a principle (e.g., a clerical error) is treated as a prior period adjustment with no consistency exception (AU 420.13). Answer (d) is incorrect because changes in classification do not result in consistency exceptions (AU 420.14).

27. (583,A1,29) (a) The requirement is to determine the proper accounting and audit reporting when a client makes a change in accounting principle that is inseparable from the effect of a change in estimate. AU 420.11 states that a consistency exception is necessary since a change in principle is involved, even though the accounting for such a change is the same as the accounting for a change in estimate.

28. (583,A1,37) (b) The requirement is to determine the proper statement with respect to a change in method of inventory valuation from an unacceptable one to one in conformity with GAAP. The correction of an error in principle is treated as a correction of an error which is accounted for as a prior period adjustment (AU 420.10). Answer (a) is incorrect because a consistency exception is required (AU 420.10). Answer (c) is incorrect because a consistency exception does not normally require an explanatory middle paragraph (AU 546.02). Answer (d) is incorrect because neither the justification for nor the impact of the change is reported in the auditor's report.

29. (1182,A1,17) (c) The requirement is to determine the auditing and reporting treatment of a material change in an accounting estimate. While a consistency modification is not necessary, footnote disclosure is required (AU 420.12). Answers (a) and (b) are incorrect because they state that a consistency modification is necessary. Answer (d) is incorrect because a change in accounting principles has not occurred.

30. (582,A1,50) (c) The requirement is to determine the effect on an audit report of a change in accounting principles which is immaterial this year but expected to be material in the future. AU 420.18 states that an unqualified opinion is appropriate in such circumstances.

31. (1181,A1,32) (b) The requirement is to determine the effect on an audit report of a change in accounting principle with which the auditor concurs. Answer (b) is the method required by para 546.01 and is, therefore, correct.

32. (580,A1,26) (a) In the first audit of a new company, the auditor's report should remain silent with respect to consistency because no previous period exists with which to make a comparison. See para 420.21. Answer (b) is incorrect because there is no basis to state that accounting principles have been applied on a consistent basis. Answer (c) is incorrect because there is an implication that accounting principles have been applied consistently during a period unless so stated. Answer (d) is incorrect because the consistency standard applies within the current year (no mention is necessary) even though the current year is the first year of operations.

33. (580,A1,42) (d) The requirement is the accounting change which requires recognition in the auditor's opinion as to consistency. Changing from consolidating a subsidiary to carrying on the equity basis is a change in reporting entity per para 420.07. Changes in reporting entities, changes in accounting principles, correction of errors, and changes in principles inseparable from changes in estimates all affect consistency and must be referred to in the auditor's opinion. Answer (a) is incorrect because changing the salvage value of an asset is considered a change in an accounting estimate which does not affect consistency per para 420.12. Answer (b) is incorrect because changing the presentation of prepaid insurance from inclusion in other assets to a separate item is a change in classification which does not affect consistency per para 420.14. Answer (c) is incorrect because division of a consolidated subsidiary into two consolidated subsidiaries is a change in classification not affecting consistency per para 420.14.

34. (580,A1,53) (b) The requirement is when does an auditor need not mention consistency. Per para 509.44 auditors should not refer to consistency when an adverse opinion is issued because consistency implies the application of GAAP. Answer (a) is incorrect because if a pooling of interests is not applied retroactively to comparative financial statements, the financial statements are not per GAAP (see APB 16 and para 546.12). Answer (c) is incorrect because in the first year of an audit the auditor can compare the accounting principles used in the current period to those applied in the prior period. Only when the client is in the first year of operations, there is no mention of consistency per para 420.21. Answer (d) is incorrect because the second standard of reporting requires that the audit opinion state whether GAAP have been applied consistently.

B.1.f. Uncertainties

35. (583,A1,13) (c) The requirement is to determine the effect on an audit report of a lawyer's limited response concerning a litigated claim in which the lawyer is unable to determine the likelihood of an unfavorable outcome. When uncertainty over a material amount exists, an auditor will ordinarily conclude that a qualified (or possibly a disclaimer of opinion) opinion will be necessary (AU 337.14 and AU 509.21–.26). Answer (a) is incorrect because adverse opinions are used when an auditor knows that the statements are misleading. Answer (b) is incorrect because "unaudited" is not a type of audit opinion. Answer (d) is incorrect because if the effect on the financial statements could be material, the auditor will ordinarily conclude that an unqualified opinion is inappropriate (AU 337.14). Note that this would not preclude an unqualified opinion in certain circumstances.

36. (1180,A1,22) (c) Because the likelihood of loss is remote, there is no need to modify the audit report (para 509.21). Answer (a) is only appropriate when there is significant uncertainty involved. Answer (b) is incorrect since there is no departure from generally accepted accounting principles. Answer (d) is incorrect since the use of both types of qualifications, subject to and except for, are not permitted per GAAS.

37. (1179,A1,46) (a) When an auditor believes that the client may not continue as a going concern, he should express a qualified "subject to" opinion. See para 509.35. Answer (b) is incorrect because a significant uncertainty with respect to the going concern assumption requires a qualified opinion. See para 509.23. Answer (c) is incorrect because an "except for" opinion is used in all qualified opinions except for those being qualified due to an uncertainty (para 509.35). Answer (d) is incorrect because an adverse opinion is to be expressed if the financial statements do not fairly represent. Here the problem specified that there may be a going concern problem, not that there is one.

B.1.g. Emphasis of a Matter

38. (1181,A1,24) (a) The requirement is to determine the effect of including a middle paragraph to emphasize a matter in an audit report. Answer (a) is correct because the report is still considered unqualified (para 509.27). Answer (b) is incorrect for the same reason that (a) is correct. Answer (c) is incorrect because footnote disclosure of such an emphasis of a matter is allowed. Answer (d) is incorrect because para 509.27 also explicitly states that the words "with the foregoing explanation" should not be added to the opinion paragraph.

B.1.h. Lack of Independence

39. (578,A1,54) (c) Auditors who are not independent should disclaim and disclose that there is a lack of independence. There should be no discussion of the reason for lack of independence, because such discussion may confuse the reader concerning the importance of the impairment of independence. See section 517 in SAS 1. Answer (a) is incorrect because the word "unaudited" should appear on each page of unaudited

statements (para 517.03). Answer (b) is incorrect because disclaiming an opinion for nonindependence without explanation is the correct procedure. Answer (d) is incorrect because even though the CPA is not independent and disclaims an opinion, the auditor is obligated to set forth any reservations concerning the financial statements (para 517.06). As of 7/1/79, SSARS 1, "Compilation and Review of Financial Statements," will set standards for unaudited engagements.

B.1.j. Additional Information Included with Basic Financial Statements

40. (583,A1,27) (a) The requirement is to determine the information which need not be disclosed relating to inventory of a closely-held manufacturing company. Replacement cost of inventory need not be disclosed because GAAP does not require the information. Pledged inventory, LIFO reserves, and accounting changes all must be disclosed in order for the financial statements to follow GAAP. Therefore, answers (b), (c), and (d) are incorrect.

41. (582,A1,31) (d) The requirement is to determine the form of audit report which is to be issued when supplementary information required by an FASB pronouncement has been omitted. An unqualified opinion is appropriate because this information is not audited and is not a required part of the basic financial statements (AU 553.08). "Except for" opinions (a), disclaimer (b), and adverse opinions (c) all pertain to information which is to be audited.

42. (1181,A1,42) (a) The requirement is to determine the audit report treatment of "unaudited" footnotes in audited financial statements. Answer (a) is correct since an auditor may refer to these notes if supplementary information required by the FASB is omitted, if the auditor has concluded that the reported supplementary information departs materially from FASB guidelines, or if the auditor is unable to complete required procedures on these disclosures (para 533.08). Answer (b) is incorrect since an auditor does have responsibility with respect to the disclosures as noted above (see also the required procedures outlined in para 553.07). Answer (c) is incorrect because the auditor is not required in all cases to refer to the notes. Answer (d) is incorrect since the circumstances cited above outline situations in which the auditor's report does include mention of these notes.

B.2.a. Dating the Report

43. (1181,A1,59) (a) The requirement is to determine the basis for deciding whether to dual date an audit report. Answer (a) is correct because if the auditor does not wish to dual date, certain audit procedures must be extended (para 560.12). Answer (b) is incorrect since the auditor must accept responsibility for the known subsequent event regardless of whether dual dating is used. Answer (c) is incorrect because such known subsequent events are to be audited. Answer (d) is incorrect because the auditor, with or without dual dating, need not assume responsiblity for events subsequent to the issuance of the auditor's report.

44. (581,A1,12) (b) The requirement is to determine the date through which the auditor is responsible for inquiring as to subsequent events. The auditor is required to perform audit procedures relating to subsequent events through the date of the audit report (February 28 in this question). Answer (a) is incorrect because the report is outstanding and, for some reason, the auditor chose not to date it the last day of field work (e.g., possibly due to the existence of a subsequent event). Answers (c) and (d) are incorrect because the auditor's responsibility with respect to information in documents containing audited financial statements does not extend beyond the financial information identified in his/her report and the auditor has no obligation to perform any procedures to corroborate the other information contained in the annual report. The auditor need only read the other information and consider whether it appears inconsistently or incorrectly, see para 550.04.

B.2.b. Comparative Statements

45. (1183,A1,57) (b) The requirement is to determine the appropriate phrase which is used in a comparative statements audit report. Answer (b) is correct as stated in AU 505.03.

46. (583,A1,9) (d) The requirement is to determine a successor auditor's reporting responsibility when a predecessor auditor's report is not being presented with comparative statements. In such situations the successor auditor should mention that the prior period's statements were examined by other auditors, provide the date of the successor's report, **its type**, and, if that report is other than unqualified, the reasons therefor (AU 505.12). Answer (a) is incorrect because disclaiming an opinion might lead others to believe that no audit had been performed in the prior year. Answer (b) is incorrect because identification of the predecessor auditor is unnecessary (AU 505.12–.13). Answer (c) is incorrect because, as discussed above, the successor auditor must comment on the predecessor auditor's examination.

47. (583,A1,43) (a) The requirement is to determine the proper reporting of a material unresolved uncertainty that had been omitted from the prior year's report. When an auditor becomes aware of an uncertainty that affects the prior-period financial statements, s/he should modify the opinion or disclaim an opinion in the updated report on those statements (AU 505.06). Answer (b) is incorrect because the uncertainty makes an unqualified opinion inappropriate. Answer (c) is incorrect because adverse opinions are not issued in such uncertainty conditions. Answer (d) is incorrect because such comparative statements require a two year audit report.

48. (1182,A1,36) (d) The requirement is to determine the continuing auditor's responsibility with respect to an audit report based on comparative statements. The report on the previous statements must be updated regardless of the opinion previously issued (AU 505.02). Answer (a) is incorrect because such an opinion is not dual dated; it should be dated as of the completion of this year's field work. Answers (b) and (c) are both incorrect due to the need to update regardless of the previously issued report.

49. (1181,A1,35) (b) The requirement is to determine the appropriate date for an audit report based on comparative financial statements. Answer (b) is correct since para 505.02 states that ordinarily such a report should be dated as of the date of completion of the most recent examination.

50. (1180,A1,15) (a) A separate paragraph decribing the responsibility taken is required (para 504.15). Answer (b) is incorrect since there is no indication that the accounting principles have not been consistently applied. Answer (c) is incorrect because the auditor may not restrict the use of the financial statements to comparative analysis. Answer (d) is incorrect since the statements were not compiled or reviewed; these forms of auditor association are for non-public firms.

B.3. Subsequent Events and Subsequent Discovery of Facts Existing at the Date of the Audit Report

51. (1183,A1,59) (d) The requirement is to determine the situation in which an auditor has an obligation to make further inquiries after a report has already been issued. Answer (d) is correct because it represents a situation in which the auditor has become aware of facts that may have existed at the balance sheet date which might have affected his/her audit report had s/he then been aware of such facts (AU 561.01). Answer (a) is incorrect because if the contingency had been disclosed in the financial statements no further action is necessary. Answers (b) and (c) are incorrect because the situations have developed subsequent to the release of the financial statements.

52. (1182,A1,35) (a) The requirement is to determine the situation in which an auditor is required to make further audit tests once an audit report has been issued. An auditor who becomes aware of new information on an event which occurred prior to the date of the auditor's report, which may have affected that report, must extend procedures (AU 561.01). Answers (b), (c), and (d) are all incorrect because they describe situations for which AU 561.03 states that the auditor is under no obligation to make further inquiry upon discovery.

53. (1180,A1,16) (d) The type of events in answers (a), (b) and (c) need to be audited (para 509.10—.13). However, when a report is being reissued the subsequent event may be labeled unaudited (para 530.08 and para 9509.24).

54. (579,A1,1) (c) The requirement is the type of subsequent event that would not require disclosure in financial statements. Para 560.06 provides examples of items requiring disclosure in statements that include answers (a), (b), and (d). If any of these items had occurred in the period under audit, they would be reflected in the financial statements. If any of these items occurred in the subsequent period before the last day of field work, they should be disclosed in the footnotes to the financial statements. Answer (c) however, a major drop in the quoted market price of the corporation stock, would not have affected the financial statements and accordingly would not have to be disclosed as a subsequent event.

C. Auditor Association Other Than Audits

C.1. Other Forms of Auditor Association with Historical Financial Statements

C.1.a. Unaudited Statements

55. (582,A1,9) (b) The requirement is to determine a CPA's responsibility with respect to financial statements of a **public entity**, with which s/he is associated, which have not been audited or reviewed. The CPA is required to read the statements to determine whether obvious material errors exist (AU 504.05). Answer (a) is incorrect because it is not the CPA's role to insist that financial statements be audited or reviewed.

Answer (c) is incorrect because while the financial statements should be conspicuously marked as unaudited, no more detail is required. Answer (d) is incorrect since a compilation need not be performed and since compilations are primarily for non-public firms (AR 100.01).

56. (1180,A1,17) (c) In this situation, the requirement is the proper form of the auditor's report to be issued when an independent CPA is associated with a public entity's financial statements that he has not audited or reviewed. A disclaimer is issued in this situation per para 504.05 . Answer (a) is incorrect since the required disclaimer should include no assurance, positive or negative. Answer (b) is incorrect since compilations are limited to nonpublic firms (AR 100). Answer (d) is incorrect since no explanatory paragraph is added.

C.1.b. Compiled or Reviewed Statements

57. (1183,A1,30) (a) The requirement is to determine the effect on a nonpublic company **review** report of a material departure from GAAP. If the accountant concludes that modification is appropriate, the departure should be disclosed in a separate paragraph of his/her report (AR 100.40). Answer (b) is incorrect because adverse opinions are only appropriate for audits. Answer (c) is incorrect because it is not the role of the CPA to attach footnotes to his/her client's reports. Answer (d) is incorrect because a review has been performed.

58. (1183,A1,33) (d) The requirement is to determine the procedure that is **not** part of a review engagement of a nonpublic entity. AR 100 provides the necessary standards and procedures applicable to a review of a nonpublic entity. AR 100.04 states that a review provides the accountant with a reasonable basis for expressing limited assurance that there are no material modifications that should be made to the statements to bring them into conformity with GAAP. Since the objective of a review differs from the objective of an examination made in accordance with GAAS, audit procedures such as a study and evaluation of internal control, tests of accounting records, inspection, observation, confirmation, and certain other procedures are not performed. Specifically included per AR 100.27 are review procedures such as inquiries of management [answer (a)], inquiries regarding subsequent events [answer (b)], and procedures to identify unusual relationships among data [answer (c)].

59. (583,A1,31) (a) The requirement is to determine the procedure which is **not** a part of an interim review. Answer (a) is not a part of an interim review because a review of computer controls relates to the review of internal control; such procedures are not performed during reviews. Answers (b), (c), and (d) are all procedures suggested in the appropriate standards (AU 722.06).

60. (583,A1,55) (b) The requirement is to determine the auditor's reporting responsibility when comparative statements for a nonpublic entity are being issued and the prior period has **not** been audited. In such circumstances the auditor may add a separate paragraph to the audit report and identify the financial statements (AU 504.15—.17). Answer (a) is incorrect because the unaudited statements need not be removed. Answer (c) is incorrect because the unaudited statements must be marked "unaudited" (AU 504.15). Answer (d) is incorrect because the auditor's report should mention that the prior statements are unaudited (AU 504.17).

61. (1182,A1,41) (b) The requirement is to determine the appropriate date for an auditor's compilation report. AR 100.5 requires that the date of completion of the compilation should be used.

62. (1181,A1,56) (a) The requirement is to determine the type of report which a CPA who is not independent may issue. Answer (a) is correct since AR 100.22 allows a compilation to be performed by a CPA who is not independent. Answer (b) is incorrect because an accountant is precluded from issuing a review report on the financial statements of an entity with respect to which the CPA is not independent (AR 100.38). Answer (c) is incorrect because independence is necessary for letters to underwriters, or "comfort letters" (para 631.12). Answer (d) is incorrect because a qualified opinion presupposes the performance of an audit; audits must be performed by independent auditors (para 150.02).

63. (581,A1,53) (d) The requirement is to determine the circumstance which will lead to a modification of an interim report. Departures from generally accepted accounting principles, which include adequate disclosure, require modification of the accountant's report (para 721.20). Normally neither an uncertainty [answer (a)] nor a lack of consistency [answer (b)] would cause a report modification (para 721.20). Reference to another accountant [answer (c)] is not considered a modification (para 721.19).

64. (1180,A1,45) (c) A CPA may report on compiled financial statements which omit substantially all disclosures and use them for comparative purposes with previously audited financial statements if an additional paragraph indicating the previous audit and the date of the previous report is included (AR 200.29). Answer (a) is incorrect because there is no requirement that the missing disclosures be immaterial. Answer (b) is correct only in circumstances in which the CPA has knowledge that the omission of disclosures is undertaken with the intention of misleading users (AR 100.19). Answer (d) is incorrect since there is no requirement that the previous auditor's report accompany the comparative statements.

C.2.a. Special Reports

65. (583,A1,10) (a) The requirement is to determine what an auditor needs to disclose in a separate paragraph in his/her audit report on financial statements prepared on a comprehensive basis of accounting other than GAAP. The explanatory middle paragraph should indicate that the financial statements are not intended to be presented in conformity with GAAP, and should also refer the reader to a note in the financial statements which describes the basis of accounting and how it differs from GAAP (AU 621.05b). Answer (b) is incorrect because the auditor need not justify the comprehensive basis being used. Answer (c) is incorrect because no such referral to authoritative pronouncements is advised in the standards (AU 621.02–.08). Answer (d) is incorrect because audits of such statements are to follow GAAS (AU 621.05a).

66. (1182,A1,1) (d) The requirement is to determine the situation in which negative assurance is **not** acceptable. Negative assurance consists of a statement by accountants to the effect that, as a result of specified procedures, nothing came to their attention that caused them to believe that specified matters do not meet a specified standard (AU 631.02, footnote 2). When an audit is performed, negative assurance is not to be provided. Answer (a) is incorrect because letters required by security underwriters may include negative assurance (AU 504.19). Answer (b) is incorrect because negative assurance is allowed for specified elements (AU 622.05). Answer (c) is incorrect because the review report issued includes negative assurance with respect to the financial statements (AR 100.35).

67. (1180,A1,28) (a) When issuing a special report on a specific financial statement item, the measurement of materiality must be related to that item (para 621.11). Answer (b) is incorrect since an auditor may report on a single item without performing a complete financial statement audit (para 621.09). Answer (c) is incorrect; the materiality threshhold is lower for a single item than it would be for an overall audit causing the examination for a single item to be more extensive (para 621.11). Answer (d) is correct only in cases in which such reporting would be tantamount to expressing a piecemeal opinion (para 621.12).

68. (580,A1,20) (b) The preferable titles when reporting on cash basis financial statements are assets and liabilities arising from cash transactions, and revenue collected and expenses paid. See para 621.07. Terms such as balance sheet, statement of financial position, statement of income, statement of operations, and statement of changes in financial position should be avoided. Accordingly, answers (a), (c), and (d) are incorrect.

69. (582,A1,26) (b) If printed forms or schedules include wording which is unacceptable to the auditor, the auditor should reword the form or attach a separate report (para 621.21) so that it is consistent with his responsibility concerning applicable reporting standards. Answer (a) is incorrect because a short-form report is not required and may not be appropriate, e.g., a report on a comprehensive basis of accounting other than GAAP. Answer (c) is incorrect because the auditor's report should be consistent with his responsibilities under the circumstances. Answer (d) is incorrect because the auditor would only withdraw from the engagement if the rewording or separate report is unacceptable to the client.

70. (1179,A1,13) (a) If the auditor believes that financial statements prepared per a comprehensive basis other than GAAP are not suitably titled, he should modify his report to disclose any reservations per para 621.07. Titles such as balance sheet, income statement, etc., generally only apply to financial statements per GAAP. Financial statements per the cash basis or income tax basis should be suitably described. Answer (b) is incorrect because the auditor has determined the effects of the titles as being not suitable per the problem. Answer (c) is incorrect because a disclaimer should only be issued when the auditor is not expressing an opinion on the financial statements. Here, the titles were found to be not suitable, and thus the CPA must express his reservations in an unqualified or adverse opinion. Answer (d) is incorrect because the financial statements and related footnotes are the representations of management rather than the auditor. Thus, the auditor's reservations belong in the audit report rather than in the statements.

71. (1182,A1,20) (a) The requirement is to determine the situation in which a special report will **not** be issued. Scope limitation situations are not a form of special report. Special reports only include financial information based on (1) a comprehensive basis of accounting other than GAAP, (2) specified elements, (3) compliance with various agreements, and (4) prescribed forms (see AU 621). Answer (b) is incorrect because such limited purpose reports are included under the "specified elements" category of special reports. Answer (c) is incorrect because not-for-profit statements are a form of comprehensive basis of accounting other than GAAP. Answer (d) is incorrect because historical cost/constant dollar reports are also an alternate comprehensive basis of accounting.

C.2.c. Reviewed Forecasts

72. (1183,A1,29) (d) The requirement is to determine the basis on which a financial forecast is prepared. A financial forecast for an entity is an estimate of the most probable financial position, results of operations, and changes in financial position for one or more future periods (AICPA, *Guide for a Review of a Financial Forecast,* p. 1). A financial **projection** for an entity is an estimate of financial results based on assumptions that are not necessarily the most likely. Thus, while a projection could be based on answers (a), (b), and (c), a forecast must be based on the most probable assumptions.

73. (1181,A1,30) (d) The requirement is for the information which need **not** be disclosed in a forecast. Answer (d) is correct because the Professional Code of Ethics in ET 201.03 requires the disclosure of sources of information [answer (a)], the character of the work performed by the CPA [answer (b)] and the forecast's major assumptions [answer (c)].

May 1984 Answers

74. (584,A1,3) (a) The requirement is to determine an auditor's reporting responsibility when financial statements for two periods are being presented together. Answer (a) is correct because the reporting standards for such comparative statements require that one audit report cover both years (AU 505.03). Answers (b), (c), and (d) are all incorrect because the report must refer to both years.

75. (584,A1,4) (b) The requirement is to determine the information **not** included in an audit report of a client using a comprehensive basis of accounting other than GAAP. Answer (b) is correct because no comment need be made concerning the appropriateness of the disclosed method (AU 621.05). The professional standards (AU 621.05) require disclosure of the information suggested in answers (a), (c), and (d).

76. (584,A1,9) (c) The requirement is to determine the statement which must appear on each page of financial statements which have been compiled by an accountant. Answer (c) is correct as per the requirements of AR 100.16. Answer (a) is incorrect because the footnotes are not those of the accountant who performed the compilation. Answer (b) is incorrect because the statements are not considered "unaudited"—see AU 504 for unaudited statements of a public company. Answer (d) is incorrect because the phrase "subject to compilation restrictions" is not recommended in AR 100.

77. (584,A1,17) (b) The requirement is to determine the **least** likely procedure during a review of a nonpublic entity. Answer (b) is least likely and, therefore, correct because it is not a procedure indicated by the appropriate standards—AR 100.27. Answers (a), (c), and (d) are all review procedures listed under AR 100.27.

78. (584,A1,18) (c) The requirement is to determine the effect on an audit report of an uncertainty which has a minimal likelihood of having a material effect on the financial statements. Answer (c), an unqualified report, is correct because SFAS 5, para 10 only requires footnote disclosure of uncertainties which have at least a reasonable possibility of occurrence. Answers (a), (b), and (d) are all incorrect because generally accepted accounting principles have been followed; therefore, no report modification is necessary.

79. (584,A1,28) (c) The requirement is to determine the appropriate modifications which need to be made to an audit report when another auditor's work is to be referred to in the principal auditor's report. Answer (c) is correct because both the scope and opinion paragraphs need to be modified (AU 543.07); also, no explanatory middle paragraph is necessary.

80. (584,A1,39) (a) The requirement is to determine the proper statement with respect to the form of a predecessor auditor's report which is to be reissued with that of the successor auditor. No reference to the work of the successor auditor is to be made in this situation (AU 505.09-.11). Answers (b), (c), and (d) are incorrect because they all suggest the need to make reference to the report of the successor auditor.

81. (584,A1,42) (b) The requirement is to determine an accountant's responsibility when s/he has become aware of a material transaction which may materially affect financial statements on which s/he has already reported. Per AU 561.04, the first step is to contact the firm's management and request cooperation in investigation of the matter. Answer (a) is incorrect because the auditor must take action and **is** responsible for the subsequent discovery of facts existing at the date of the auditor's report. Answer (c) is incorrect because the "possible effects" of this newly discovered transaction should be investigated further to determine whether the financials may need revision in lieu of footnote disclosure. Answer (d) is impractical because it is impossible to contact all parties who might rely upon the financial statements.

82. (584,A1,43) (d) The requirement is to determine the appropriate type of report to be issued when financial statements are **not** presented in conformity with GAAP. Professional standards require an adverse opinion (AU 509.41). Answer (a) is incorrect because a qualified opinion, in the case of a departure from GAAP, is given when there is a departure but when the overall financial statements do follow accepted principles. Answer (b) is incorrect because special reports may or may not pertain to GAAP (see AU 621.01 for a presentation of the four types of special reports). Answer (c) is incorrect because a disclaimer of opinion is issued when an accountant does not have an opinion as to whether the financial statements follow GAAP.

83. (584,A1,45) (a) The requirement is to determine the type of audit report to be issued when a client's segmental disclosure is misstated. Answer (a) is correct because this, like other departures from GAAP leads to either a qualified "except for" opinion or an "adverse" opinion (AU 435.09). Note that an adverse opinion is not a choice here. Answers (b), (c), and (d) all suggest types of reports which are inappropriate, given the professional standards.

84. (584,A1,46) (b) The requirement is to determine the event occurring after year end which would **not** result in an adjustment to the financial statements before they are issued. The condition (purchase of a subsidiary) did not come into existence until after year end. Footnote disclosure of this transaction, however, is necessary (AU 560.06). Answer (a) is incorrect because the debtor's deteriorating financial condition was in existence at year end, thus requiring a journal entry adjustment (AU 560.04). Answer (c) is incorrect because all such information on extended litigation should be used to adjust an estimated liability account (AU 560.04). Answer (d) is incorrect because APB 15, para 48 requires retroactive adjustment for such stock splits.

85. (584,A1,52) (b) The requirement is to determine the proper accounting and audit report effects of a change in accounting principles which is immaterial during the year of change but is expected to have a material effect in later years. AU 420.17 suggests that in such circumstances the change should be disclosed in the notes to the financial statements of the year of change and that an unqualified audit report should be issued. Answers (a) and (c) are incorrect because no consistency modification is necessary. Answer (d) is incorrect because this is not an example of a subsequent event (see AU 560 for information on subsequent events).

86. (584,A1,53) (b) The requirement is to determine the type of opinion paragraph which is most likely when an audit report includes an additional paragraph which discloses a difference of opinion between the auditor and the client. Answer (b), an "except for" opinion, is most likely because such a difference of opinion will generally relate to what the auditor believes to be a departure from GAAP (AU 509.36). Answer (a) is incorrect because, if the difference of opinion is important to note, an unqualified opinion would not seem appropriate. Answer (c) is incorrect because "subject to" opinions relate to uncertainties facing the firm. Answer (d) is unlikely because a disclaimer of opinion will not generally be used where a difference of opinion exists between the auditor and client.

87. (584,A1,57) (c) The requirement is to determine the meaning of "taken as a whole" in an audit report on comparative financial statements. The professional standards state that this term should be considered to apply not only to the financial statements of the current period but also to those of one or more prior periods that are presented on a comparative basis with those of the current period (AU 505.02). Answer (a) is incorrect because "taken as a whole" does not relate to the financial statements of a preceding period that are not presented with those of the current period. Answers (b) and (d) are incorrect because all periods presented need to be considered.

88. (584,A1,58) (c) The requirement is to determine an auditor's reporting responsibility on information accompanying the basic financial statements in auditor-submitted documents. You may recall that this information in the past was referred to as "long-form reports." Answer (c) is correct because the professional

standards require that when an auditor submits a document containing audited financial statements to his/her client or to others, s/he has a responsibility to report on all the information included in the document (AU 551.04). Note that while all information is to be reported on, it need not all be audited (some of it may be "unaudited"). Answers (a), (b), and (d) are all less complete than the requirements of the standard referred to above.

89. (584,A1,59) (b) The requirement is to determine which information in a middle paragraph is inconsistent with the issuance of an unqualified audit opinion. Answer (b) is inconsistent with an unqualified opinion and, therefore, correct because a change in accounting principles will result in a consistency modification in the opinion paragraph (AU 420.06). Answers (a) and (c) are incorrect because they represent items which the standards explicitly suggest that an auditor **may** choose to emphasize in a middle paragraph and yet express an unqualified opinion (AU 509.27). Answer (d) is incorrect because accounting reclassifications will not in general result in modification of the opinion paragraph (AU 420.14) and because an auditor **may** choose to emphasize them in a middle paragraph (AU 509.27).

Answer Outline

Problem 1 Report with Predecessor Auditor Involvement

Address to shareholders and board of directors
Financial statements examined
  Balance sheet as of 12/31/82
  Statements of income, retained earnings, and changes in financial position for year ended 12/31/82
Reference to GAAS
Reference to tests of accounting records
Reference to other auditing procedures as considered necessary
Financial statements for year ended 12/31/81 examined by other auditors
  Other auditors' report dated 3/1/82
Report by other auditors expressed unqualified opinion on balance sheet
Report by other auditors expressed qualified opinion on statements of income, retained earnings, and changes in financial position
1/1/81 (beginning) physical inventory not observed
  Qualification due to inability to determine effects on 1981 statements of adjustments required (if any) had physical inventory been observed
Opinion refers to fair presentation of statements per GAAP
  Financial position as of 12/31/82
  Results of operations and changes in financial position for year ended 12/31/82
Reference to consistency
Signed in name of firm
Report dated 3/17/83

Unofficial Answer

Problem 1 Report with Predecessor Auditor Involvement

To the shareholders and board of directors, Fairfax Corporation:

We have examined the balance sheet of Fairfax Corporation as of December 31, 1982, and the related statements of income, retained earnings, and changes in financial position for the year then ended. Our examination was made in accordance with generally accepted auditing standards and, accordingly, included such tests of the accounting records and such other auditing procedures as we considered necessary in the circumstances. The financial statements of Fairfax Corporation for the year ended December 31, 1981, were examined by other independent auditors, whose report dated March 1, 1982, on those statements expressed an unqualified opinion on the balance sheet as of December 31, 1981, and a qualified opinion with respect to the statements of income, retained earnings, and changes in financial position for the year then ended due to an inability to determine the effects on these 1981 financial statements of such adjustments, if any, as might have been determined to be necessary had the January 1, 1981, physical inventory been observed.

In our opinion, the 1982 financial statements referred to above present fairly the financial position of Fairfax Corporation as of December 31, 1982, and the results of its operations and the changes in its financial position for the year then ended, in conformity with generally accepted accounting principles applied on a basis consistent with that of the preceding year.

Ross, Sandler & Co.

March 17, 1983

Answer Outline

Problem 2 Report Deficiencies

Deficiencies in auditor's report prepared by audit assistant
  Scope paragraph **did not**
    Identify financial statements (FSs) examined
    Identify time period covered by FSs
    Mention that tests were made of accounting records
    Refer reader to second middle paragraph
  Second middle paragraph
    Should have been explanatory
    Incorrectly disclaimed opinion on FSs overall
  Opinion paragraph **did not**
    Express opinion on results of operations and changes in financial position
    Identify time period covered by FSs
    State that BS presented in conformity with GAAP
    Refer to consistent application of GAAP
    Properly express qualified opinion
      Reason for qualification required in both
        Scope paragraph
        Opinion paragraph
      Language used should state qualification referred to possible FS effects
        Not with scope limitation per se
      "Subject to" usage incorrect
  Address
    Should have been to Board of Directors, Stockholders, or Corporation
  Date
    As of last day of fieldwork

Unofficial Answer

Problem 2 Report Deficiencies

Deficiencies in the auditor's report, as drafted by the audit assistant, may be categorized as follows:

- The scope paragraph did not specifically identify the financial statements that were examined or the period of time which they covered. Further, the scope paragraph did not specifically state that the examination included tests of accounting records, and it did not refer the reader to the second middle paragraph.
- The second middle paragraph, which should have been explanatory, improperly disclaimed an opinion on the financial statements taken as a whole.
- The opinion paragraph did not express an opinion on the results of operations and changes in financial position for the period, and the period covered by these financial statements was not identified. Further, it did not state that the balance sheet was presented fairly in conformity with generally accepted accounting principles, and it did not refer to the consistent application of generally accepted accounting principles.

If the intent was to express a qualified opinion, the reason for the qualification should have been referred to in both the scope and opinion paragraphs and the wording in the opinion paragraph should have indicated that the qualification pertained to the possible effects on the financial statements and not the scope limitation itself. Further, the "subject to" phrase should not have been used.

- The report should have been addressed to the Board of Directors; Stockholders; or Corporation.
- The date of the report should have been as of the last date of the field work.

Answer Outline

Problem 3 Report on a Review

Report (dated March 3, 1982, and addressed to the Board of Directors) setting forth the following

Paragraph 1
- Review performed in accordance with AICPA standards
- Financial statements are representations of management

Paragraph 2
- Review procedures consist of inquiry and analytical review
- Review less in scope than audit
- No opinion is expressed

Paragraph 3
- Not aware of material modifications needed to be in conformity with GAAP

Paragraph 4
- Prior years statements were examined
- Expressed unqualified opinion
- Date of previous report
- No procedures performed after date of previous report

Unofficial Answer

Problem 3 Report on a Review

To: The Board of Directors of Tillis Ltd.

We have reviewed the accompanying balance sheet of Tillis Ltd. as of December 31, 1981; and the related statements of income, retained earnings, and changes in financial position for the year then ended, in accordance with standards established by the American Institute of Certified Public Accountants. All information included in these financial statements is the representation of the management of Tillis Ltd.

A review consists principally of inquiries of company personnel and analytical procedures applied to financial data. It is substantially less in scope than an examination in accordance with generally accepted auditing standards, the objective of which is the expression of an opinion regarding the financial statements taken as a whole. Accordingly, we do not express such an opinion.

Based on our review, we are not aware of any material modifications that should be made to the accompanying 1981 financial statements in order for them to be in conformity with generally accepted accounting principles.

The financial statements for the year ended December 31, 1980, were examined by us, and we expressed an unqualified opinion on them in our report dated February 27, 1981, but we have not performed any auditing procedures since that date.

Novak & Co.

March 3, 1982

Unofficial Answer*
(Author Modified)

Problem 4 Report on Engagement Involving Agreed-Upon Procedures

a. The assertions that are incorrect or should otherwise be deleted are the following (AU 622.04 & 622.06):
  1. Report should be addressed to Unclean Corporation's Board of Directors.
  2. Delete the entire paragraph describing the scope except for the reference to cash in banks and accounts receivable.
  3. Delete the opinion rendered on cash in banks and accounts receivables.
  4. Delete the recommendation to acquire Ajax.

b. The assertions that are missing and should be inserted are the following (AU 622.04 & 622.06):
  1. Date of the report.
  2. Statement limiting the distribution of the report to Unclean's management.
  3. Description of the procedures performed.
  4. Statement that the agreed-upon procedures applied are not adequate to constitute a GAAS examination.
  5. Description of the accountant's findings.
  6. Disclaimer of an opinion concerning cash in banks and accounts receivable.
  7. Statement limiting the report only to cash in banks and accounts receivable and indicating that the report does not extend to the financials taken as a whole.

**Because the requirements of this question could be answered by lists of items we have not included an outline of the solution.*

Answer Outline

Problem 5 Assurances Given

a. Knowledge of an entity's business assists the auditor in
a1. Identifying areas of special consideration
a2. Assessing conditions under which accounting data are produced, processed, reviewed, and accumulated within the organization
a3. Evaluating the reasonableness of estimates, e.g., valuation of inventories, depreciation, allowances for doubtful accounts, and percentage of completion of long-term contracts
a4. Evaluating reasonableness of management representations
a5. Making judgments about appropriateness of accounting principles applied and adequacy of disclosures
a6. Perceiving conflicts of interest and planning of internal control evaluations
b. Assurances provided by the statement that financial statements are presented "fairly . . . in conformity with generally accepted accounting principles applied on a consistent basis." include
b1. Accounting principles selected and applied have general acceptance
b2. Accounting principles are appropriate in the circumstances
b3. Financial statements, including the related notes, are informative of matters that may affect their use, understanding and interpretation
b4. Information presented in financial statements is classified and summarized in a reasonable manner (neither too detailed nor too condensed)
b5. Financial statements reflect underlying events and transactions within a range of acceptable limits
b6. Comparability of financial statements between periods has not been materially affected by changes in accounting principles

Unofficial Answer

Problem 5 Assurances Given

a. Knowledge of the entity's business helps the auditor in—

- Identifying areas that may need special consideration.
- Assessing conditions under which accounting data are produced, processed, reviewed, and accumulated within the organization.
- Evaluating the reasonableness of estimates, such as valuation of inventories, depreciation, allowances for doubtful accounts, and percentage of completion of long-term contracts.
- Evaluating the reasonableness of management representations.
- Making judgments about the appropriateness of the accounting principles applied and the adequacy of disclosures.
- Perceiving conflicts of interest and planning internal control evaluations.

b. When the auditor states that the financial statements are presented "fairly . . . in conformity with generally accepted accounting principles applied on a consistent basis," the public is assured that in the auditor's judgment—

- The accounting principles selected and applied have general acceptance.
- The accounting principles are appropriate in the circumstances.
- The financial statements, including the related notes, are informative of matters that may affect their use, understanding, and interpretation.
- The information presented in the financial statements is classified and summarized in a reasonable manner (neither too detailed nor too condensed).
- The financial statements reflect the underlying events and transactions within a range of acceptable limits.
- The comparability of financial statements between periods has not been materially affected by changes in accounting principles.

Answer Outline

Problem 6 Write Report

a. Address to partnership (Bale & Booster)
b. Financial statements examined
b1. Statement of assets, liabilities, and capital: income tax (cash) basis as of 12-31
b2. Statement of revenues and expenses and changes in partners' capital accounts: income tax (cash) basis for year ended 12-31
c. Reference to GAAS
d. Reference to tests of accounting records
e. Reference to other auditing procedures as considered necessary
f. Explanation of income tax (cash basis)
f1. Certain revenue and related assets recognized when cash received
f2. Certain expenses recognized when paid
g. Financial statements not in accordance with GAAP
h. Separate paragraph disclosing patent infringement litigation
h1. Damage not subject to estimate
i. Opinion refers to fair presentation of statements on income tax (cash) basis
i1. Statement of assets, liabilities, and capital as of 12-31
i2. Statement of revenues and expenditures and changes in partners' capital accounts for year ended 12-31
j. Auditor should refer to footnote describing income tax (cash) basis
k. Opinion should refer to consistency

Unofficial Answer

Problem 6 Write Report

Addressee:

We have examined the statement of assets, liabilities, and capital [income tax (cash) basis] of Bale & Booster, a partnership, as of December 31, 1979, and the related statement of revenue and expenses [income tax (cash) basis] and the statement of changes in partners' capital accounts [income tax (cash) basis] for the year then ended. Our examination was made in accordance with generally accepted auditing standards and, accordingly, included such tests of the accounting records and such other auditing procedures as we considered necessary in the circumstances.

As described in note X, the partnership's policy is to prepare its financial statements on the accounting basis used for income tax purposes; consequently, certain revenue and related assets are recognized when received rather than when earned, and certain expenses are recognized when paid rather than when the obligation is incurred. Accordingly, the accompanying financial statements are not intended to present financial position and results of operations in conformity with generally accepted accounting principles.

In addition, the company is involved in continuing litigation relating to patent infringement. The amount of damages, if any, resulting from this litigation cannot be determined at this time.

In our opinion, the financial statements referred to above present fairly the assets, liabilities, and capital of the Bale & Booster partnership as of December 31, 1979, and its revenue and expenses and changes in its partners' capital accounts for the year then ended, on the income tax (cash) basis of accounting as described in note X, which basis has been applied in a manner consistent with that of the preceding year.

Date *Firm Name*

Multiple Choice Questions (1–31)

1. Which of the following is an element of sampling risk?
   a. Choosing an audit procedure that is inconsistent with the audit objective.
   b. Choosing a sample size that is too small to achieve the sampling objective.
   c. Failing to detect an error on a document that has been inspected by the auditor.
   d. Failing to perform audit procedures that are required by the sampling plan.

2. The application of statistical sampling techniques is **least** related to which of the following generally accepted auditing standards?
   a. The work is to be adequately planned and assistants, if any, are to be properly supervised.
   b. In all matters relating to the assignment, an independence in mental attitude is to be maintained by the auditor or auditors.
   c. There is to be a proper study and evaluation of the existing internal control as a basis for reliance thereon and for the determination of the resultant extent of the tests to which auditing procedures are to be restricted.
   d. Sufficient competent evidential matter is to be obtained through inspection, observation, inquiries and confirmations to afford a reasonable basis for an opinion regarding the financial statements under examination.

3. Given random selection, the same sample size, and the same precision requirement for the testing of two unequal populations, the risk of overreliance on the smaller population is
   a. Higher than the risk of overreliance on the larger population.
   b. Lower than the risk of overreliance on the larger population.
   c. The same as the risk of overreliance on the larger population.
   d. Indeterminable relative to the risk of overreliance on the larger population.

4. If the achieved precision range of a statistical sample at a given reliability level is greater than the desired range this is an indication that the
   a. Standard deviation was larger than expected.
   b. Standard deviation was less than expected.
   c. Population was larger than expected.
   d. Population was smaller than expected.

5. In which of the following cases would the auditor be most likely to conclude that all of the items in an account under consideration should be examined rather than tested on a sample basis?

	The measure of tolerable error is	*Error frequency is expected to be*
a.	Large	Low
b.	Small	High
c.	Large	High
d.	Small	Low

6. Which of the following best illustrates the concept of sampling risk?
   a. A randomly chosen sample may **not** be representative of the population as a whole on the characteristic of interest.
   b. An auditor may select audit procedures that are **not** appropriate to achieve the specific objective.
   c. An auditor may fail to recognize errors in the documents examined for the chosen sample.
   d. The documents related to the chosen sample may **not** be available for inspection.

7. In attribute sampling, a 10% change in which of the following factors normally will have the **least** effect on the size of a statistical sample?
   a. Population size.
   b. Precision (confidence interval).
   c. Reliability (confidence level).
   d. Standard deviation.

8. An auditor initially planned to use unrestricted random sampling with replacement in the examination of accounts receivable. Later, the auditor decided to use unrestricted random sampling without replacement. As a result only of this decision, the sample size should
   a. Increase.
   b. Remain the same.
   c. Decrease.
   d. Be recalculated using a binomial distribution.

9. Which of the following statistical selection techniques is **least** desirable for use by an auditor?
   a. Systematic selection.
   b. Stratified selection.
   c. Block selection.
   d. Sequential selection.

10. What is the primary objective of using stratification as a sampling method in auditing?

a. To increase the confidence level at which a decision will be reached from the results of the sample selected.
b. To determine the occurrence rate for a given characteristic in the population being studied.
c. To decrease the effect of variance in the total population.
d. To determine the precision range of the sample selected.

11. There are many kinds of statistical estimates that an auditor may find useful, but basically every accounting estimate is either of a quantity or of an error rate. The statistical terms that roughly correspond to "quantities" and "error rate", respectively, are
a. Attributes and variables.
b. Variables and attributes.
c. Constants and attributes.
d. Constants and variables.

12. An advantage of using statistical sampling techniques is that such techniques
a. Mathematically measure risk.
b. Eliminate the need for judgmental decisions.
c. Define the values of precision and reliability required to provide audit satisfaction.
d. Have been established in the courts to be superior to judgmental sampling.

13. If certain forms are not consecutively numbered
a. Selection of a random sample probably is not possible.
b. Systematic sampling may be appropriate.
c. Stratified sampling should be used.
d. Random number tables cannot be used.

14. In the application of statistical techniques to the estimation of dollar amounts, a preliminary sample is usually taken primarily for the purpose of estimating the population
a. Variability.
b. Mode.
c. Range.
d. Median.

15. If all other factors specified in an attribute sampling plan remain constant, changing the specified precision from 6% to 10%, and changing the specified reliability from 97% to 93%, would cause the required sample size to
a. Increase.
b. Remain the same.
c. Decrease.
d. Change by 4%.

16. Use of the ratio estimation sampling technique to estimated dollar amounts is **inappropriate** when
a. The total book value is known and corresponds to the sum of all the individual book values.
b. A book value for each sample item is unknown.
c. There are some observed differences between audited values and book values.
d. The audited values are nearly proportional to the book values.

5

17. The major reason that the difference and ratio estimation methods would be expected to produce audit efficiency is that the
a. Number of members of the populations of differences or ratios is smaller than the number of members of the population of book values.
b. Beta risk may be completely ignored.
c. Calculations required in using difference or ratio estimation are less arduous and fewer than those required when using direct estimation.
d. Variability of the populations of differences or ratios is less than that of the populations of book values or audited values.

18. Which of the following sampling plans would be designed to estimate a numerical measurement of a population, such as a dollar value?
a. Numerical sampling.
b. Discovery sampling.
c. Sampling for attributes.
d. Sampling for variables.

19. An auditor examining inventory may appropriately apply sampling for attributes in order to estimate the
a. Average price of inventory items.
b. Percentage of slow-moving inventory items.
c. Dollar value of inventory.
d. Physical quantity of inventory items.

20. The tolerable rate of deviations for a compliance test is generally
a. Lower than the expected rate of errors in the related accounting records.

b. Higher than the expected rate of errors in the related accounting records.
c. Identical to the expected rate of errors in the related accounting records.
d. Unrelated to the expected rate of errors in the related accounting records.

21. If the auditor is concerned that a population may contain exceptions, the determination of a sample size sufficient to include at **least** one such exception is a characteristic of
a. Discovery sampling.
b. Variables sampling.
c. Random sampling.
d. Dollar-unit sampling.

22. An auditor plans to examine a sample of 20 checks for countersignatures as prescribed by the client's internal control procedures. One of the checks in the chosen sample of 20 cannot be found. The auditor should consider the reasons for this limitation and
a. Evaluate the results as if the sample size had been 19.
b. Treat the missing check as a deviation for the purpose of evaluating the sample.
c. Treat the missing check in the same manner as the majority of the other 19 checks, i.e., countersigned or not.
d. Choose another check to replace the missing check in the sample.

23. Which of the following sampling methods is most useful to auditors when testing for compliance?
a. Stratified random sampling.
b. Attribute sampling.
c. Variable sampling.
d. Unrestricted random sampling with replacement.

24. When performing a compliance test with respect to control over cash disbursements, a CPA may use a systematic sampling technique with a start at any randomly selected item. The biggest disadvantage of this type of sampling is that the items in the population
a. Must be recorded in a systematic pattern before the sample can be drawn.
b. May occur in a systematic pattern, thus destroying the sample randomness.
c. May systematically occur more than once in the sample.
d. Must be systematically replaced in the population after sampling.

25. In estimation sampling for attributes, which one of the following must be known in order to appraise the results of the auditor's sample?
a. Estimated dollar value of the population.
b. Standard deviation of the values in the population.
c. Actual occurrence rate of the attribute in the population.
d. Sample size.

26. When using statistical sampling for tests of compliance an auditor's evaluation of compliance would include a statistical conclusion concerning whether
a. Procedural deviations in the population were within an acceptable range.
b. Monetary precision is in excess of a certain predetermined amount.
c. The population total is not in error by more than a fixed amount.
d. Population characteristics occur at least once in the population.

27. In connection with his test of the accuracy of inventory counts, a CPA decides to use discovery sampling. Discovery sampling may be considered a special case of
a. Judgmental sampling.
b. Sampling for variables.
c. Stratified sampling.
d. Sampling for attributes.

May 1984 Questions

28. Statistical sampling provides a technique for
a. Exactly defining materiality.
b. Greatly reducing the amount of substantive testing.
c. Eliminating judgment in testing.
d. Measuring the sufficiency of evidential matter.

29. At times a sample may indicate that the auditor's planned degree of reliance on a given control is reasonable when, in fact, the true compliance rate does not justify such reliance. This situation illustrates the risk of
a. Overreliance.
b. Underreliance.
c. Incorrect precision.
d. Incorrect rejection.

30. The theoretical distribution of means from all possible samples of a given size is a normal distribution

and this distribution is the basis for statistical sampling. Which of the following statements is **not** true with respect to the sampling distribution of sample means?

a. Approximately 68% of the sample means will be within one standard deviation of the mean for the normal distribution.

b. The distribution is defined in terms of its mean and its standard error of the mean.

c. An auditor can be approximately 95% confident that the mean for a sample is within two standard deviations of the population mean.

d. The items drawn in an auditor's sample will have a normal distribution.

31. In examining cash disbursements, an auditor plans to choose a sample using systematic selection with a random start. The primary advantage of such a systematic selection is that population items

a. Which include irregularities will **not** be overlooked when the auditor exercises compatible reciprocal options.

b. May occur in a systematic pattern, thus making the sample more representative.

c. May occur more than once in a sample.

d. Do **not** have to be prenumbered in order for the auditor to use the technique.

Problems

<u>Problem 1</u> Steps in a Sampling Plan (1182,A2)

(15 to 25 minutes)

Jiblum, CPA, is planning to use attribute sampling in order to determine the degree of reliance to be placed on an audit client's system of internal accounting control over sales. Jiblum has begun to develop an outline of the main steps in the sampling plan as follows:

1. State the objective(s) of the audit test (e.g. to test the reliability of internal accounting controls over sales).
2. Define the population (define the period covered by the test; define the sampling unit, define the completeness of the population).
3. Define the sampling unit (e.g. client copies of sales invoices).

Required:

a. What are the remaining steps in the above outline which Jiblum should include in the statistical test of sales invoices? **Do not present a detailed analysis of tasks which must be performed to carry out the objectives of each step. Parenthetical examples need not be provided.**

b. How does statistical methodology help the auditor to develop a satisfactory sampling plan?

<u>Problem 2</u> Statistical Judgment (572,A3)

(25 to 30 minutes)

The use of statistical sampling techniques in an examination of financial statements does not eliminate judgmental decisions.

Required:

a. Identify and explain four areas where judgment may be exercised by a CPA in planning a statistical sampling test.

b. Assume that a CPA's sample shows an unacceptable error rate. Describe the various actions that he may take based upon this finding.

c. A nonstratified sample of 80 accounts payable vouchers is to be selected from a population of 3,200. The vouchers are numbered consecutively from 1 to 3,200 and are listed, 40 to a page, in the voucher register. Describe four different techniques for selecting a random sample of vouchers for review.

Multiple Choice Answers

1. b	8. c	14. a	20. b	26. a
2. b	9. c	15. c	21. a	27. d
3. b	10. c	16. b	22. b	28. d
4. a	11. b	17. d	23. b	29. a
5. b	12. a	18. d	24. b	30. d
6. a	13. b	19. b	25. d	31. d
7. a				

Multiple Choice Answer Explanations

A. Basic Statistical Auditing Concepts

1. (1183,A1,7) (b) The requirement is to determine an element of sampling risk. Sampling risk arises from the possibility that, when a compliance or a substantive test is restricted to a sample, the auditor's conclusions may be different from the conclusions s/he would reach if the test were applied in the same way to all items in the account balance or class of transactions (AU 350.10). For example, the items in the selected sample might not disclose an error. Answers (a), (c), and (d) are all incorrect because they represent nonsampling risk examples which are unrelated to the mathematics of the sampling process (AU 350.11).

2. (1183,A1,8) (b) The requirement is to determine the standard to which the use of statistical sampling techniques is **least** related. The requirement that the auditor be independent is absolute and is not subject to sampling. Answer (a) is incorrect because statistical sampling techniques will often be considered during the planning of an audit. Answer (c) is incorrect because compliance tests to evaluate existing internal control may be performed using statistical sampling techniques (AU 350). Answer (d) is incorrect because statistical sampling techniques may be used to help obtain sufficient competent evidential matter.

3. (1183,A1,9) (b) The requirement is to determine the effect of population size on the risk of overreliance (on internal accounting control). When sample size and precision are held constant a lower risk will exist for the smaller population. For example, sampling 30 of a population of 100 items will lead to less risk than sampling 30 of a population of 100,000 items. Because of this basic relationship between sample size and population size answers (a), (c), and (d) are all incorrect.

4. (1183,A1,12) (a) The requirement is to determine what can cause greater achieved precision range than had been desired, given a reliability level. Precision about the mean is equal to the reliability factor times the standard deviation divided by sample size. [Precision = (Reliability factor x Standard deviation) ÷ Sample size]. Holding constant the reliability and the sample size, the only factor which may increase the precision is an increased standard deviation [answer(a)]. Precision about the population's total estimated value is obtained by multiplying the above precision about the mean times population size. Thus, it might be argued that a larger population will result in a larger precision range about the total value [answer (c)]. But answer (c) is not as complete as answer (b) because one must also assume that the auditor made the error of not incorporating the increased population size into the determination of the required sample size; it is, therefore, only correct in limited circumstances, while answer (a) is always correct. Answers (b) and (d) are incorrect because both are opposites of the proper mathematical relationships.

5. (583,A1,1) (b) The requirement is to determine the situation in which an auditor is most likely to conclude that all population items, not a sample, need to be tested. Both a small tolerable error and a high error frequency increase an auditor's required sample size. A small tolerable error requires a larger sample size to insure reducing the allowance for sampling risk (precision) to a level smaller than the tolerable error. A high error frequency may lead an auditor to reconsider and decrease reliance on internal control and therefore increase the extent of substantive testing through increasing sample size (AU 350.28). A higher error frequency will also increase the necessary allowance for sampling risk by increasing the variance and standard deviation of the sample. Answers (a) and (c) are incorrect, since a larger tolerable error permits a larger allowance for sampling risk and therefore a smaller required sample size. Answer (d) is incorrect because a low frequency of errors will reduce the required allowance for sampling risk and therefore permit use of a smaller sample size.

6. (583,A1,6) (a) The requirement is to determine which answer represents the concept of sampling risk. Sampling risk arises from the possibility that an auditor's conclusions based upon a sample would differ from the conclusions which would be drawn from examining the entire population, i.e., the risk that the sample examined is not representative of the population. Answers (b), (c), and (d) are all incorrect because they relate to errors which could occur even if 100% of the population were examined, i.e., nonsampling risk (see AU 350.11 for a discussion of nonsampling risk).

7. (1182,A1,54) (a) The requirement is to determine which factor, if changed by 10%, would least

affect sample size in attribute sampling. Changes in population size have a very minor effect on sample size. Changes in precision [answer (b)], reliability [answer (c)] and standard deviation [answer (d)] all have a larger effect on the required sample size.

8. (582,A1,2) (c) The requirement is to determine the effect on sample size of a change from unrestricted random sampling with replacement to unrestricted random sampling without replacement. When sampling without replacement, a finite correction factor will be used which will decrease sample size. Answers (a) and (b) are therefore incorrect. Answer (d) is incorrect because a binomial distribution will not generally be used.

9. (1181,A1,12) (c) The requirement is to determine the least desirable statistical selection technique. Answer (c), block selection, is correct because, ideally, a sample should be selected from the entire set of data to which the resulting conclusions are to be applied (para 320.61). When block sampling is used the selection of blocks often precludes items from being so selected. In most cases, systematic [answer (a)], stratified [answer (b)], and sequential [answer (d)] selection techniques all provide a better representation of the entire population than does block selection.

10. (575,A1,18) (c) Stratified sampling is a technique of breaking the population down into subpopulations and applying different sample selection methods to the subpopulations. Stratified sampling is used to minimize the variance within the overall population. Recall that as variance increases, so does the required sample size (because of the extreme values). Thus stratification allows the selection of subpopulations to reduce the effect of dispersion in the population.

11. (575,A2,39) (b) Statistical sampling accounting applications are either based on variables sampling or attribute sampling. Variables sampling is measurement of a continuous variable, i.e., a variable such as number of items in inventory or amount of accounts receivable. The variable being estimated can take on a continuum of values, e.g., zero to infinity. Variable sampling is based upon the normal distribution. Attribute sampling is based on the binomial distribution and sample items must be binary in nature, i.e., right or wrong, correct or incorrect, etc. Attribute sampling is most applicable to tests of compliance and variables sampling is most applicable to substantive tests.

B. Planning for Audit Sampling

12. (581,A1,11) (a) The requirement is to determine an advantage of statistical sampling. The distinguishing feature of statistical sampling is that it provides a means for measuring mathematically the degree of uncertainty that results from examining only a part of the data (SAS 39, para 45). Answer (b) is incorrect since statistical sampling still requires the auditor to make judgmental decisions (e.g., set appropriate precision and reliability levels). While answer (c) is a correct statement insofar as it relates to auditor responsibility, it cannot be considered an advantage of statistical sampling. The courts have not definitively ruled on the merits of statistical vs. judgmental sampling, thus, answer (d) is incorrect.

13. (580,A1,5) (b) The requirement is the correct statement concerning a statistical sampling application where the population consists of forms which are not consecutively numbered. Answer (b) is correct because it is not incorrect, i.e., all the other answers are incorrect. Systematic sampling is a procedure where a random start is obtained and then every n^{th} item is selected. For example, a sample of forty from a population of a thousand would require selecting every 25th item after obtaining a random start between items 1 through 25. Answer (a) is incorrect because selection of a random sample is possible even though the population is not consecutively numbered. Answer (c) is incorrect because there is no special reason for using stratified sampling. Stratified sampling breaks down the population into subpopulations and applies different selection methods to each subpopulation. This selection method is used when the population consists of different types of items, e.g., large balances and small balances. Answer (d) is incorrect because random number tables can be used even though the forms are not consecutively numbered. If random numbers are selected for which there are no forms, they are ignored. This is the same as if there were 86,000 items in a consecutively numbered population and random numbers selected between 86,000 and 99,999 are ignored.

C. Variables Based Sampling

14. (1183,A1,13) (a) The requirement is to determine the purpose of taking a preliminary sample when one uses statistical techniques. It is necessary to obtain an estimate of a population's standard deviation (variability) when calculating the required sample size and when using sampling techniques. Answers (b), (c), and (d) are incorrect because, in most statistical techniques used by auditors, the mode (most frequent bal-

ance), the median (middle balance) and the range (difference between the highest and lowest values) are not used.

15. (582,A1,1) (c) The requirement is to determine the net effect on the required sample size in an attribute sampling plan of an increase in specified precision and a decrease in specified reliability, if all other factors remain constant. Both an increase in specified precision and a decrease in reliability cause decreases in sample size. Answers (a) and (b) are incorrect because sample size will not increase or stay the same. Answer (d) is incorrect because the size of the change in sample size need not be exactly 4% — it will depend upon population size.

16. (1180,A1,41) (b) The ratio estimation sampling technique is based on comparing the ratio of the book value to the audited value of the sampled items. Answer (b) is the answer because the method cannot be used when there is no book value to make the comparison. The circumstances described in answers (a) and (c) are necessary for ratio point and interval estimation. Answer (d) describes the circumstances in which the use of ratio estimation will be efficient in terms of required sample size.

17. (580,A1,43) (d) Difference and ratio estimation methods are statistical sampling methods. They measure the difference between audit and book values or the ratio of audit to book values. As these differences should not be great, the population of these differences will have little variance. In statistical sampling the less variation in a population, the smaller the required sample to provide an estimate of the population. In other words, difference and ratio estimation methods are more efficient because the differences between audit and book values are expected to vary less than the actual items in the population. Answer (a) is incorrect because the number of members in the population for differences or ratio methods would be the same as the number of items in the population for a direct estimation method. In difference sampling, many items would be zero because audit and book are the same, and in ratio sampling, many of the members would be 1 for the same reason. Answer (b) is incorrect because beta risk can never be ignored, as beta risk is the risk of accepting an incorrect (unacceptable) population. Answer (c) is incorrect because the calculations required in difference and ratio sampling are similar to those used in direct estimation sampling.

18. (579,A1,18) (d) The requirement is the sampling plan which would estimate a numerical measurement of a population, such as a dollar value. Sampling for variables or estimation of variables sampling is designed to estimate the mean item in the population from which the total value of the population can be estimated. Answer (a) is incorrect because numerical sampling is a nonsense term. All quantitative sampling must be numerical. Answers (b) and (c) are incorrect because discovery sampling is a special case of sampling for attributes. Sampling for attributes samples binary data, i.e., right or wrong, error or nonerror, good or bad, etc.

D. Attribute Sampling

19. (1183,A1,32) (b) The requirement is to determine an inventory application of sampling for attributes. Answer (b) is an example of attribute sampling because it deals with the attribute of an item either being or not being slow-moving. Answers (a), (c), and (d) all represent applications of variables sampling.

20. (583,A1,2) (b) The requirement is to determine the correct relationship between the tolerable rate of deviations and the expected rate of deviations for a compliance test. The tolerable rate of deviations is the maximum rate of deviations from a prescribed control procedure that an auditor would be willing to accept and, unless the expected error rate is lower, reliance on internal control is not justified. Answer (a) is incorrect because if the tolerable rate of deviations is less than the expected rate, the auditor would not plan to rely on internal control and would therefore omit compliance tests (AU 320.59). Answer (c) is incorrect because compliance testing is inappropriate if the expected rate of errors equals the tolerable rate of deviations (mathematically, the precision of zero makes the sample size equal to population size). Answer (d) is incorrect because, as indicated above, to perform compliance tests one must assume that the tolerable rate of deviations is more than the expected error rate.

21. (583,A1,5) (a) The requirement is to determine the type of sampling which is most directly related to finding at least one exception. Discovery sample sizes and related discovery sampling tables are constructed to measure the probability of at least one error occurring in a sample if the error rate in the population exceeds the tolerable rate. Answer (b) is incorrect because variables sampling need not include at least one exception (mean per unit sampling, for example, needs no errors). Answer (c) is incorrect since random sampling only deals with the technique used to select items to be included in the sample. Answer (d) is incorrect because dollar-unit sampling results are not directly related to finding at least one exception.

22. (583,A1,7) (b) The requirement is to determine the proper method of handling a sample item which cannot be located for evaluation purposes. An auditor would ordinarily consider the selected item to be a deviation (AU 350.39). Answer (a) is incorrect because it ignores the missing check and bases results on the remaining 19 checks. Answer (c) is incorrect because treating the check similarly to the majority is unjustified because, since it cannot be found, it is quite different than the remaining 19 checks. Answer (d) is also incorrect because to be justified one would have to assume that the replacement check had the same pertinent characteristics as the one which cannot be located.

23. (582,A1,46) (b) The requirement is to determine the sampling method most useful to auditors when testing for compliance. Compliance tests utilize attribute sampling. Attribute sampling allows the auditor to estimate how frequently the tested control is working properly. Answers (a) and (d) are incorrect because they are sample selection methods rather than sampling methods. Stratified random sampling is the stratification of the population, and then application of random sampling to each strata. Stratified random sampling is typically more useful for variable sampling (e.g., selecting primarily large receivables to confirm). Unrestricted random sampling with replacement is a sampling method where population items can be reselected, and is only one of the possible ways of implementing attribute sampling. Answer (c) is incorrect because variable sampling is used primarily for substantive tests.

24. (1181,A1,29) (b) The requirement is to determine a disadvantage of systematic sampling. Systematic sampling consists of drawing every n^{th} item from a population beginning with a random start. Answer (b) is correct because if there is any cyclic or periodic arrangement of the disbursements which is related to the attributes being measured or tested, a bias can result; i.e., the sample will not be random and thus the results of the test will not be valid. Answer (a) is incorrect because a systematic pattern would bias the sample. Answers (c) and (d) are incorrect because a particular disbursement will be selected only once when systematic sampling is used, because the auditor will make one pass through the population (disbursements) selecting every nth item.

25. (581,A1,18) (d) The requirement is to determine the information necessary to appraise the results of an attribute sample. Sample size is needed to evaluate the results. Answer (a) is incorrect because the estimated dollar value of the population is used only in variables sampling. Answer (b), the standard deviation of the values in the population, also deals with variables sampling. Answer (c) is incorrect since the auditor will not know the **actual** occurrence rate of the attribute in the population unless she/he audits the entire population.

26. (578,A1,56) (a) In compliance tests the auditor is concerned with the population error rate. Thus the auditor wishes to determine that the error rate is within an acceptable range. Answer (b) is incorrect because compliance tests are not concerned with monetary amounts but rather with error rates. Answer (c) is incorrect because auditor concern is with the error rate, not the absolute number of error rates in a given population. Answer (d) is a nonsense answer—"population characteristics occur at least once in the population."

27. (573,A2,19) (d) Both discovery sampling and acceptance sampling are special cases of sampling for attributes. Discovery sampling is a special case of acceptance sampling. In discovery sampling there should be no opportunity to observe more than one occurrence, because it is designed to sample for serious or critical errors. Once a critical or serious error is discovered, the sampling plan will probably be abandoned and a more comprehensive examination undertaken.

May 1984 Answers

28. (584,A1,7) (d) The requirement is to determine the correct statement with respect to statistical sampling. Answer (d) is correct because the use of statistical sampling allows the auditor to objectively quantify results and thus measure the sufficiency of evidential matter. Answer (a) is incorrect because the auditor must judgmentally determine a level of materiality. Answer (b) is incorrect because the use of statistical sampling may or may not reduce the amount of substantive testing. Answer (c) is incorrect because statistical sampling does not eliminate judgment—it quantifies judgment.

29. (584,A1,10) (a) The requirement is to determine the risk which relates to the situation in which an auditor relies on a control when, in fact, the true compliance rate does not justify such reliance. The risk of overreliance on internal accounting control is the risk that the sample supports the auditor's planned degree of reliance on the control when the true compliance rate would not support such reliance (AU 350.12). An-

swer (b) is incorrect because the risk of underreliance pertains to the situation in which the sample does not support the auditor's planned degree of reliance on the control when the true compliance rate supports such reliance. Answer (c) is incorrect because it does not relate directly to the planned degree of reliance on controls. Answer (d) is incorrect because the risk of incorrect rejection relates to substantive tests.

30. (584,A1,21) (d) The requirement is to determine the statement which is **not** true with respect to the sampling distribution of sample means from a normal distribution. Answer (d) is not true and, therefore, is the correct answer, because in skewed populations the items drawn in a sample may not have a normal distribution. Answer (a) is an incorrect response since approximately 68% of the sample means will be within one standard deviation (also referred to as standard error) of the mean. Answer (b) is an incorrect response because a normal distribution is defined in terms of the mean and standard error. Answer (c) is an incorrect response because approximately 95% of the time the sample means will be within two standard deviations of the population mean.

31. (584,A1,30) (d) The requirement is to determine the primary advantage of systematic sampling of population items. Answer (d) is correct because the items need not be prenumbered—the auditor will simply select every n^{th} item. Answer (a) is incorrect as irregularities may be overlooked. Answer (b) is a disadvantage of systematic sampling in the sense that its results may be biased if a systematic pattern exists in the population being sampled. Answer (c) is incorrect since an auditor using every n^{th} item will not include one item in a sample more than once.

Unofficial Answer*

Problem 1 Steps in a Sampling Plan

a. The remaining steps are as follows:

4. Define the attributes (characteristics) of interest to be tested (including the criteria for establishing the existence of errors or deviant conditions).
5. Set the maximum rate of deviations from a prescribed control procedure that would support the planned reliance on the control (tolerable rate).
6. Select a confidence level (quantify the risk of over-reliance).
7. Estimate the population error rate (deviation rate).
8. Determine the sample size.
9. Choose a method for randomly selecting a sample.
10. Perform the compliance audit procedures.
11. Perform error analysis (calculate the deviation rate and consider the qualitative aspects of the deviations).
12. Interpret sample results (calculate a population deviation rate).
13. Decide on the acceptability of the results of the sample.

b. Statistical sampling methodology helps the auditor (a) to design an efficient sample, (b) to measure the sufficiency of the evidential matter obtained, and (c) to evaluate the sample results. By using a statistical sampling methodology the auditor can quantify sampling risk to assist in limiting it to an acceptable level.

**Because the requirements of this question could be answered by lists of items we have not included an outline of the solution.*

Answer Outline

Problem 2 Statistical Judgment

a. Sampling decisions requiring auditor judgment
- Sample design
- Sample method
- Sample selection technique
- Specified precision (confidence interval)
- Specified reliability (confidence level)

b. Alternatives available to an unacceptable error rate
- Enlarge sample
- Isolate type of error
- Have client reprocess the data
- Qualify opinion

c. Nonstratified random sample selection techniques
- Random sample
  - Table of random numbers
  - Terminal digits
  - Random number generator
- Systematic sample
  - Every n^{th} item
  - Randomly varying sample interval
  - Every random n^{th} item
- Cluster sample

Unofficial Answer

Problem 2 Statistical Judgment

a. Areas where judgment may be exercised by a CPA in planning a statistical sampling test include:

1. The sample design—the CPA must define the population in terms of its size, the characteristics of significance to the audit and what constitutes an error.
2. Sampling method—the CPA must determine the type of sampling method to be used (e.g., sampling for attributes, discovery sampling, acceptance sampling) and the most efficient means of selecting the sample.
3. Selection technique—the CPA must decide which sampling selection process is to be used (e.g., stratified sampling, cluster sampling, systematic sampling).
4. Specified precision (confidence interval)—this is the range within which the sample statistic (e.g., error rate) may fall and still be acceptable to the CPA. It will be based upon the materiality of the account or activity being examined and the nature of the error or other characteristic.
5. Specified reliability (confidence level)—this is the probability that the sample statistic will fall within the specified precision limits if the population error rate is acceptable. It will be based upon the materiality of the account or activity being examined, the nature of the error and the reliance placed upon internal control.

b. If the CPA's sample shows an unacceptable error rate, he may take the following actions:

1. He may enlarge his sample or select another sample. If his sample design has been sound, additional sampling will confirm his original findings in most cases. But the auditor may wish to have greater statistical accuracy if the sample is to be the basis of a recommended adjustment.
2. He may isolate the type of error and expand his examination as it relates to the transactions that give rise to that type of error.
3. He may ask the client to reprocess the data and prepare an adjusting journal entry and then make an appropriate review of the client's work. In some cases it may be satisfactory to prepare the adjusting journal entry based upon the auditor's sample—this approach is most applicable when stratified sampling was used or both the specified precision and specified reliability were high.
4. If the client refuses to accept or investigate the auditor's finding or error, or if it is impracticable to determine the overall degree of error with acceptable precision, the CPA should evaluate the necessity of opinion qualification. This determination will depend upon materiality—the nature of the error and its effects upon financial statement presentation. Based upon the degree of materiality, the CPA may render an unqualified, a qualified ("except for") or adverse opinion; a "subject to" opinion is not justified. The CPA will disclaim an opinion if his scope is so limited that he cannot form an opinion on the fairness of presentation of the financial statements as a whole.

c. Techniques for selecting a nonstratified random sample of accounts-payable vouchers include the following:

Random Sample. A random sample is a sample of a given size drawn from a population in a manner such that every possible sample of that size is equally likely to be drawn. Items may be selected randomly by:

1. Table of Random Numbers. Use one of a number of published tables. Using four columns in the table, select the first 80 numbers which fall within the range 1 to 3,200. The starting point in the table should be selected randomly and the path to be followed through the table should be set in advance and followed consistently.
2. Terminal Digits. Select two two-digit numbers randomly and examine all vouchers ending in this number. Select one more two-digit number randomly and examine every other voucher ending in this number, making the initial selection (from the first hundred or second hundred vouchers) on a random basis.
3. Random Number Generator. Using a utility computer program, generate a list of 80 random numbers.

Systematic Sample. A systematic sample is drawn by selecting every n^{th} item beginning with a random start.

1. Every n^{th} Item. Select every 40th voucher after selecting the initial voucher (from 1 to 40) randomly.
2. Randomly Varying Sample Interval. Select an initial item randomly and after the selection of each sample item obtain a random number between 1 and 80 and add it to the number of the previously selected item to obtain the number of the next item.
3. Every Random n^{th} Item. Select a number from a random number table between 1 and 40 and select that item from among the first 40 items. A second random number between 1 and 40 (plus 40) would be used to select the item within the second group of 40 items, etc.

Cluster Sample. Instead of drawing individual sample items, select groups of contiguous sample items. For example, using a random number table, select two pages within the voucher register and review all vouchers on those pages. (A disadvantage of this method is that consecutive vouchers may be for similar expenditures and the sample may not provide adequate coverage of the range of expenditures.)

Multiple Choice Questions (1–37)

1. One of the major problems in an EDP system is that incompatible functions may be performed by the same individual. One compensating control for this is use of
   a. A tape library.
   b. A self-checking digit system.
   c. Computer generated hash totals.
   d. A computer log.

2. Which of the following would lessen internal control in an electronic data processing system?
   a. The computer librarian maintains custody of computer program instructions and detailed listings.
   b. Computer operators have access to operator instructions and detailed program listings.
   c. The control group is solely responsible for the distribution of all computer output.
   d. Computer programmers write and debug programs which perform routines designed by the systems analyst.

3. More than one file may be stored on a single magnetic memory disc. Several programs may be in the core storage unit simultaneously. In both cases it is important to prevent the mixing of data. One way to do this is to use
   a. File integrity control.
   b. Boundary protection.
   c. Interleaving.
   d. Paging.

4. A procedural control used in the management of a computer center to minimize the possibility of data or program file destruction through operator error includes
   a. Control figures.
   b. Crossfooting tests.
   c. Limit checks.
   d. External labels.

5. The use of a header label in conjunction with magnetic tape is **most** likely to prevent errors by the
   a. Computer operator.
   b. Keypunch operator.
   c. Computer programmer.
   d. Maintenance technician.

6. When erroneous data are detected by computer program controls, such data may be excluded from processing and printed on an error report. The error report should most probably be reviewed and followed up by the
   a. EDP control group.
   b. System analyst.
   c. Supervisor of computer operations.
   d. Computer programmer.

7. In a daily computer run to update checking account balances and print-out basic details on any customer's account that was overdrawn, the overdrawn account of the computer programmer was never printed. Which of the following control procedures would have been most effective in detecting this irregularity?
   a. Use of the test-deck approach by the auditor in testing the client's program and verification of the subsidiary file.
   b. Use of a running control total for the master file of checking account balances and comparison with the printout.
   c. A program check for valid customer code.
   d. Periodic recompiling of programs from documented source decks, and comparison with programs currently in use.

8. Which of the following is a computer test made to ascertain whether a given characteristic belongs to the group?
   a. Parity check.
   b. Validity check.
   c. Echo check.
   d. Limit check.

9. When an on-line, real-time (OLRT) electronic data processing system is in use, internal control can be strengthened by
   a. Providing for the separation of duties between keypunching and error listing operations.
   b. Attaching plastic file protection rings to reels of magnetic tape before new data can be entered on the file.
   c. Preparing batch totals to provide assurance that file updates are made for the entire input.
   d. Making a validity check of an identification number before a user can obtain access to the computer files.

10. A control feature in an electronic data processing system requires the central processing unit (CPU) to send signals to the printer to activate the print mechanism for each character. The print mechanism, just

prior to printing, sends a signal back to the CPU verifying that the proper print position has been activated. This type of hardware control is referred to as

a. Echo control.
b. Validity control.
c. Signal control.
d. Check digit control.

11. In the weekly computer run to prepare payroll checks, a check was printed for an employee who had been terminated the previous week. Which of the following controls, if properly utilized, would have been most effective in preventing the error or ensuring its prompt detection?

a. A control total for hours worked, prepared from time cards collected by the timekeeping department.
b. Requiring the treasurer's office to account for the numbers of the prenumbered checks issued to the EDP department for the processing of the payroll.
c. Use of a check digit for employee numbers.
d. Use of a header label for the payroll input sheet.

12. Auditing by testing the input and output of an EDP system instead of the computer program itself will

a. Not detect program errors which do **not** show up in the output sampled.
b. Detect all program errors, regardless of the nature of the output.
c. Provide the auditor with the same type of evidence.
d. Not provide the auditor with confidence in the results of the auditing procedures.

13. To replace the human element of error detection associated with manual processing, a well-designed automated system will introduce

a. Dual circuitry.
b. Programmed limits.
c. Echo checks.
d. Read after write.

14. If a control total were to be computed on each of the following data items, which would best be identified as a hash total for a payroll EDP application?

a. Gross pay.
b. Hours worked.
c. Department number.
d. Number of employees.

15. Which of the following is likely to be of **least** importance to an auditor in reviewing the internal control in a company with automated data processing?

a. The segregation of duties within the EDP center.
b. The control over source documents.
c. The documentation maintained for accounting applications.
d. The cost/benefit ratio of data processing operations.

16. When testing a computerized accounting system, which of the following is **not** true of the test data approach?

a. Test data are processed by the client's computer programs under the auditor's control.
b. The test data must consist of all possible valid and invalid conditions.
c. The test data need consist of only those valid and invalid conditions in which the auditor is interested.
d. Only one transaction of each type need be tested.

17. Which of the following is likely to be **least** important to an auditor who is reviewing the internal controls surrounding the automated data processing function?

a. Ancillary program functions.
b. Disposition of source documents.
c. Operator competence.
d. Bit storage capacity.

18. The auditor's preliminary understanding of the client's EDP system is primarily obtained by

a. Inspection.
b. Observation.
c. Inquiry.
d. Evaluation.

19. After a preliminary phase of the review of a client's EDP controls, an auditor may decide not to perform compliance tests related to the control procedures within the EDP portion of the client's internal control system. Which of the following would not be a valid reason for choosing to omit compliance tests?

a. The controls appear adequate.
b. The controls duplicate operative controls existing elsewhere in the system.
c. There appear to be major weaknesses that would preclude reliance on the stated procedure.
d. The time and dollar costs of testing exceed the time and dollar savings in substantive testing if the compliance tests show the controls to be operative.

20. Accounting control procedures within the EDP activity may leave no visible evidence indicating that the procedures were performed. In such instances, the auditor should test these accounting controls by

a. Making corroborative inquiries.
b. Observing the separation of duties of personnel.
c. Reviewing transactions submitted for processing and comparing them to related output.
d. Reviewing the run manual.

21. An independent auditor studies and evaluates a client's electronic data processing system. The auditor's study portion includes two phases: (1) a review or investigation of the system and (2) tests of compliance. The latter phase might include which of the following?

a. Examination of systems flowcharts to determine whether they reflect the current status of the system.
b. Examination of the systems manuals to determine whether existing procedures are satisfactory.
c. Examination of the machine room log book to determine whether control information is properly recorded.
d. Examination of organization charts to determine whether electronic data processing department responsibilities are properly separated to afford effective control.

22. Which of the following client electronic data processing (EDP) systems generally can be audited without examining or directly testing the EDP computer programs of the system?

a. A system that performs relatively uncomplicated processes and produces detailed output.
b. A system that affects a number of essential master files and produces a limited output.
c. A system that updates a few essential master files and produces no printed output other than final balances.
d. A system that performs relatively complicated processing and produces very little detailed output.

23. Auditors often make use of computer programs that perform routine processing functions such as sorting and merging. These programs are made available by electronic data processing companies and others and are specifically referred to as

a. Compiler programs.
b. Supervisory programs.
c. Utility programs.
d. User programs.

24. Hitech, Inc., has changed from a conventional to a computerized payroll clock card system. Factory employees now record time in and out with magnetic cards and the EDP system automatically updates all payroll records. Because of this change

a. The auditor must audit through the computer.
b. Internal control has improved.
c. Part of the audit trail has been lost.
d. The potential for payroll related fraud has been diminished.

25. Which of the following is **not** a characteristic of a batch processed computer system?

a. The collection of like transactions which are sorted and processed sequentially against a master file.
b. Keypunching of transactions, followed by machine processing.
c. The production of numerous printouts.
d. The posting of a transaction, as it occurs, to several files, without intermediate printouts.

26. An electronic data processing technique, which collects data into groups to permit convenient and efficient processing, is known as

a. Document-count processing.
b. Multi-programming.
c. Batch processing.
d. Generalized-audit processing.

27. What is the computer process called when data processing is performed concurrently with a particular activity and the results are available soon enough to influence the particular course of action being taken or the decision being made?

a. Batch processing.
b. Realtime processing.
c. Integrated data processing.
d. Random access processing.

28. Which of the following symbolic representations indicate that a file has been consulted?

a. 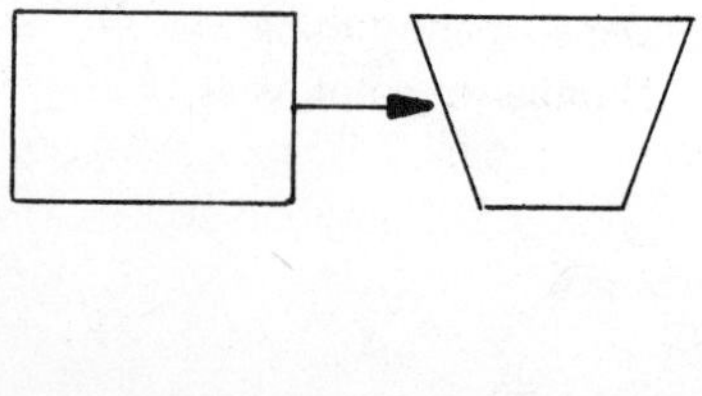

b. 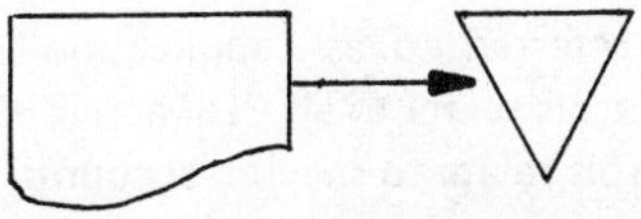

c. 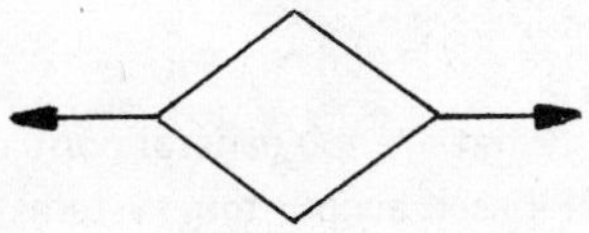

d. 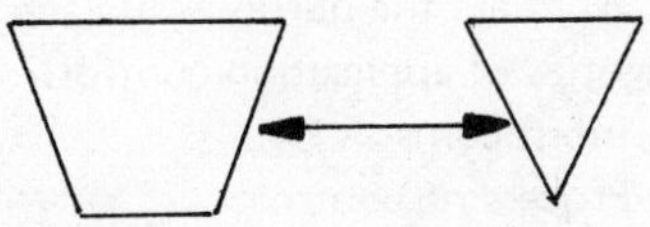

29. The program flowcharting symbol representing a decision is a
 a. Triangle.
 b. Circle.
 c. Rectangle.
 d. Diamond.

30. The machine language for a specific computer
 a. May be changed by the programmer.
 b. Is the same as all other computer languages.
 c. Is determined by the engineers who designed the computer.
 d. Is always alphabetic.

31. In a computerized system, procedure or problem-oriented language is converted to machine language through a (an)
 a. Interpreter.
 b. Verifier.
 c. Compiler.
 d. Converter.

32. Where disc files are used, the grandfather-father-son updating backup concept is relatively difficult to implement because the
 a. Location of information points on discs is an extremely time consuming task.
 b. Magnetic fields and other environmental factors cause off-site storage to be impractical.
 c. Information must be dumped in the form of hard copy if it is to be reviewed before used in updating.
 d. Process of updating old records is destructive.

33. An auditor should be familiar with a client's electronic data processing hardware and software. An important element of the client's software is the program. Another element of software is the
 a. Cathode ray tube (CRT).
 b. Central processing unit (CPU).
 c. Magnetic tape drive.
 d. Compiler.

May 1984 Questions

34. Adequate technical training and proficiency as an auditor encompasses an ability to understand an EDP system sufficiently to identify and evaluate
 a. The processing and imparting of information.
 b. Essential accounting control features.
 c. All accounting control features.
 d. The degree to which programming conforms with application of generally accepted accounting principles.

35. Which of the following constitutes a weakness in the internal control of an EDP system?
 a. One generation of backup files is stored in an off-premises location.
 b. Machine operators distribute error messages to the control group.
 c. Machine operators do **not** have access to the complete systems manual.
 d. Machine operators are supervised by the programmer.

36. First Federal S & L has an online real-time system, with terminals installed in all of its branches. This system will not accept a customer's cash withdrawal instructions in excess of $1,000 without the use of a "terminal audit key." After the transaction is authorized by a supervisor, the bank teller then processes the transaction with the audit key. This control can be strengthened by
 a. Online recording of the transaction on an audit override sheet.
 b. Increasing the dollar amount to $1,500.
 c. Requiring manual, rather than online, recording of all such transactions.
 d. Using parallel simulation.

37. Totals of amounts in computer-record data fields which are **not** usually added for other purposes but are used only for data processing control purposes are called
 a. Record totals.
 b. Hash totals.
 c. Processing data totals.
 d. Field totals.

Repeat Questions

(584,A1,14) Identical to item 1 above

(584,A1,32) Identical to item 6 above

Problems

Problem 1 Computerized Audit Programs (580,A3)

(15 to 25 minutes)

After determining that computer controls are valid, Hastings is reviewing the sales system of Rosco Corporation in order to determine how a computerized audit program may be used to assist in performing tests of Rosco's sales records.

Rosco sells crude oil from one central location. All orders are received by mail and indicate the preassigned customer identification number, desired quantity, proposed delivery date, method of payment and shipping terms. Since price fluctuates daily, orders do not indicate a price. Price sheets are printed daily and details are stored in a permanent disc file. The details of orders are also maintained in a permanent disc file.

Each morning the shipping clerk receives a computer printout which indicates details of customers' orders to be shipped that day. After the orders have been shipped, the shipping details are inputted in the computer which simultaneously updates the sales journal, perpetual inventory records, accounts receivable, and sales accounts.

The details of all transactions, as well as daily updates, are maintained on discs which are available for use by Hastings in the performance of the audit.

Required:

a. How may a computerized audit program be used by Hastings to perform substantive tests of Rosco's sales records in their machine readable form? **Do not discuss accounts receivable and inventory.**

b. After having performed these tests with the assistance of the computer, what other auditing procedures should Hastings perform in order to complete the examination of Rosco's sales records?

Problem 2 EDP Controls (579,A3)

(15 to 25 minutes)

When auditing an electronic data processing (EDP) accounting system, the independent auditor should have a general familiarity with the effects of the use of EDP on the various characteristics of accounting control and on the auditor's study and evaluation of such control. The independent auditor must be aware of those control procedures that are commonly referred to as "general" controls and those that are commonly referred to as "application" controls. General controls relate to all EDP activities and application controls relate to specific accounting tasks.

Required:

a. What are the general controls that should exist in EDP-based accounting systems?

b. What are the purposes of each of the following categories of application controls?

1. Input controls
2. Processing controls
3. Output controls

Problem 3 Audit of Computerized A/R (1179,A4)

(15 to 25 minutes)

In the past, the records to be evaluated in an audit have been printed reports, listings, documents and written papers, all of which are visible output. However, in fully computerized systems which employ daily updating of transaction files, output and files are frequently in machine-readable forms such as cards, tapes, or disks. Thus, they often present the auditor with an opportunity to use the computer in performing an audit.

Required:

Discuss how the computer can be used to aid the auditor in examining accounts receivable in such a fully computerized system.

Problem 4 EDP Controls (1181,A4)

(15 to 25 minutes)

Johnson, CPA, was engaged to examine the financial statements of Horizon Incorporated which has its own computer installation. During the preliminary review, Johnson found that Horizon lacked proper segregation of the programming and operating functions. As a result, Johnson intensified the study and evaluation of the system of internal control surrounding the computer and concluded that the existing compensating general controls provided reasonable assurance that the objectives of the system of internal control were being met.

Required:

a. In a properly functioning EDP environment, how is the separation of the programming and operating functions achieved?

b. What are the compensating general controls that Johnson most likely found? **Do not discuss hardware and application controls.**

Problem 5 Payroll System Flowchart (1174,A7)

(20 to 25 minutes)

You are reviewing audit work papers containing a narrative description of the Tenney Corporation's factory payroll system. A portion of that narrative is as follows:

> Factory employees punch time clock cards each day when entering or leaving the shop. At the end of each week the timekeeping department collects the time cards and prepares duplicate batch-control slips by department showing total hours and number of employees. The time cards and original batch-control slips are sent to the payroll accounting section. The second copies of the batch-control slips are filed by date.
>
> In the payroll accounting section payroll transaction cards are keypunched from the information on the time cards, and a batch total card for each batch is keypunched from the batch-control slip. The time cards and batch-control slips are then filed by batch for possible reference. The payroll transaction cards and batch total card are sent to data processing where they are sorted by employee number within batch. Each batch is edited by a computer program which checks the validity of employee number against a master employee tape file and the total hours and number of employees against the batch total card. A detail printout by batch and employee number is produced which indicates batches that do not balance and invalid employee numbers. This printout is returned to payroll accounting to resolve all differences.

In searching for documentation you found a flowchart of the payroll system which included all appropriate symbols (American National Standards Institute, Inc.) but was only partially labeled. The portion of this flowchart described by the above narrative appears below.

Required:

a. Number your answer 1 through 17. Next to the corresponding number of your answer, supply the appropriate labeling (document name, process description, or file order) applicable to each numbered symbol on the flowchart.

b. Flowcharts are one of the aids an auditor may use to determine and evaluate a client's internal control system. List advantages of using flowcharts in this context.

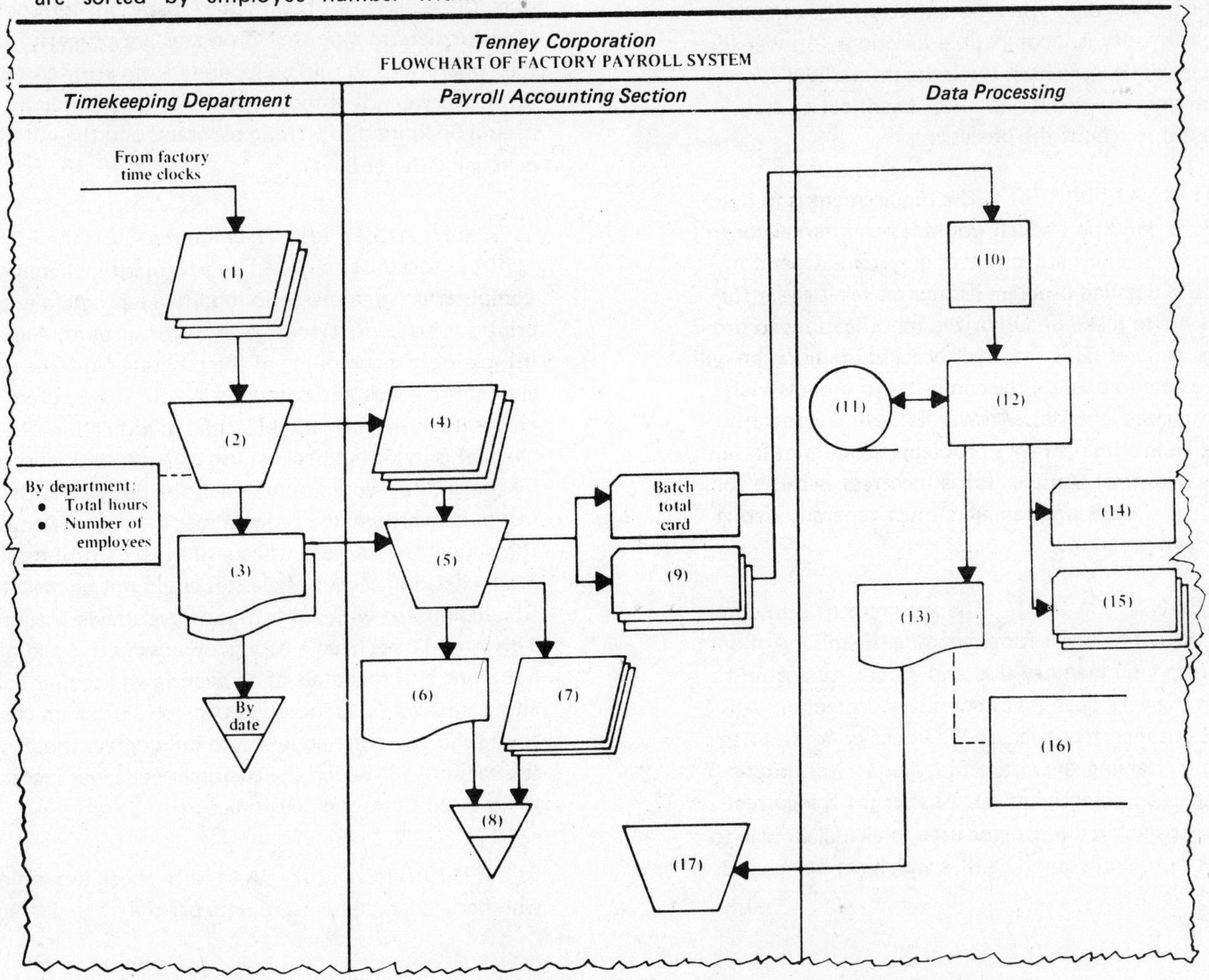

Multiple Choice Answers

1.	d	9.	d	17.	d	24.	c	31.	c
2.	b	10.	a	18.	c	25.	d	32.	d
3.	b	11.	a	19.	a	26.	c	33.	d
4.	d	12.	a	20.	c	27.	b	34.	b
5.	a	13.	b	21.	c	28.	d	35.	d
6.	a	14.	c	22.	a	29.	d	36.	a
7.	d	15.	d	23.	c	30.	c	37.	b
8.	b	16.	b						

Multiple Choice Answer Explanations

I.A. General EDP Controls

1. (1182,A1,32) (d) The requirement is to determine a compensating control in an EDP system to consider the problem of incompatible functions being performed by the same individual. Answer (d) is correct because the use of a computer log will allow a review of an individual's access to the system. Answer (a) is incorrect because a tape library is likely to be effective only in situations in which the library is effectively controlled (AU 321.15). Answer (b) is incorrect since a self-checking digit system is unlikely to be effective if the difficulty is incompatible functions. Answer (c) is incorrect because hash totals are primarily a control to determine that data have not been lost or transformed throughout the processing.

2. (1182,A1,50) (b) The requirement is to determine the condition which would **lessen** internal control in an electronic data processing system. Operator access to detailed program listings makes it easier for operators to make unauthorized modifications to programs. Answer (a) is incorrect because the librarian will not be able to operate the computer to process such unauthorized changes. Answer (c), while probably resulting in administrative problems, would not lessen internal control. Answer (d) is incorrect because for practical reasons programmers must generally debug their own programs.

3. (582,A1,27) (b) The requirement is to determine the control best for preventing the mixing of data on a magnetic memory disc and a core storage unit. This is the very purpose of boundary protection. Answer (a) is incorrect because file integrity control deals with maintaining the entire file. Answer (c), interleaving, is a nonsense answer. Answer (d) is incorrect because paging is a technique used in virtual storage to segment programs and data files which are being used.

4. (581,A1,34) (d) The requirement is to determine an EDP control to prevent file destruction by the operator. External labels will prevent file destruction by properly identifying the file. Answers (a), (b), and (c) are all incorrect because they address the accuracy of information on a file, not the physical security of a program file.

5. (581,A1,35) (a) The requirement is to determine whose errors a header label on a header tape is likely to prevent. Since the header label is actually on the magnetic tape, it is the computer operator whose errors will be prevented. Answer (b) is incorrect because the keypunch operator deals with punch cards. Answer (c) is incorrect because the programmer will write the programs and not run them under a good system of internal control. Answer (d) is incorrect because the maintenance technician will not run the magnetic tape.

6. (1180,A1,3) (a) An error report should be reviewed and followed up by the EDP control group whose responsibility it is to supervise and monitor the input, operations, and distribution of output. Answer (b) is incorrect because the systems analyst is responsible for designing the system. Answer (c) is incorrect since the supervisor of computer operations is responsible for determining that programs are properly run (i.e., operations should be separate from error correction). Answer (d) is incorrect since the programmer should be limited to writing programs and the initial debugging thereof.

7. (580,A1,21) (d) The requirement is the EDP control procedure to detect an irregularity whereby a computer programmer who modified a program not to print out his own personal overdrawn account. Answer (d), periodic recompiling of the program from the original source deck and comparison with the program currently in use, would detect the modification. Answer (a) is incorrect because use of a test-deck approach by the auditor would only detect the problem if the test data overdrew the programmer's account. Answer (b) is incorrect because using a running control total of all checking account balances could not be meaningfully compared with a printout of overdrawn accounts. This would have been a very good answer if it had been a running control totals of all overdrawn account balances. Answer (c) is incorrect because a program check for a valid customer code would only detect those transactions for which the customer code was incorrectly inputted or no such customer existed.

8. (1179,A1,2) (b) A validity check determines whether a character is legitimate per the given charac-

ter set. Note the validity check determines whether a given character is within the desired group. Answer (a) is incorrect because a parity check is a summation check in which the binary digits of a character are added to determine whether the sum is odd or even. Another bit, the parity bit, is turned on or off so the total number of bits will be odd or even as required. Answer (c) is incorrect because an echo check is a hardware control wherein data is transmitted back to its source and compared to the original data to verify the transmission correctness. Answer (d) is incorrect because a limit or reasonableness check is a programmed control based on specified limits. For example, a calendar month cannot be numbered higher than 12, or a week cannot have more than 168 hours.

9. (1178,A1,11) (d) The requirement is an internal control procedure relevant to online real-time systems (OLRT). Online refers to a terminal or input device that is in direct communication with the CPU. Real-time refers to the immediate, timely response by the CPU to the process being monitored. Only on real-time systems can a validity check be processed to determine whether a user is authorized to have access to computer files. Answers (a), (b), and (c) do not apply to OLRT as they imply lack of direct communication with the CPU. Answer (a) is concerned with the separation of keypunching and error listing operations. Answer (b) is concerned with file protection rings on magnetic tapes. Answer (c) concerns batch totals. These are appropriate control measures for a batch processing system.

10. (1178,A1,18) (a) An echo check or control consists of transmitting data back to the source unit for comparison with the original data that were transmitted. In this case, the print command is sent to the printer and then returned to the CPU to verify that the proper command was received. A validity check consists of the examination of a bit pattern to determine that the combination is legitimate for the system character set, i.e., that the character represented by the bit combination is valid per the system. Answer (c), a signal control or signal check, appears to be a nonsense term. Answer (d), check digit control, is a programmed control wherein the last character or digit can be calculated from the previous digits.

11. (1183,A1,22) (a) The requirement is to determine a control which could prevent the issuance of a check for an employee who had been terminated the previous week. Answer (a) is correct because the payroll, which included the erroneous check, would have been calculated using more total hours than the hours on the time cards. The control total would thus differ from the payroll. Answer (b) is incorrect because simply accounting for the sequence of checks would not disclose the fact that one of the checks should not have been printed. Answer (c) is incorrect because a check digit most frequently only addresses whether the employee's number is an appropriate number which can be used by the firm as opposed to whether that number is currently being used. Answer (d) is incorrect because a header label will simply summarize what is on the input sheet, regardless of whether the information is correct or incorrect.

12. (1183,A1,27) (a) The requirement is to determine the correct statement with respect to testing inputs and outputs of an EDP system instead of testing the actual computer program itself. Answer (a) is correct because portions of the program which have errors not reflected on the output will be missed. Thus, if a "loop" in a program is not used in one application, it is not tested. Answer (b) is incorrect because the lack of an understanding of the entire program precludes the detection of all errors. Answer (c) is incorrect because while auditing inputs and outputs can provide valuable evidence, it will often be different than the evidence obtained by testing the program itself. Answer (d) is incorrect because such auditing of inputs and outputs may well satisfy the auditor.

13. (1180,A1,47) (b) Programmed limits in a computer program replace the human element of error detection by having the computer test inputs for reasonableness (e.g., no hourly employee's input hourly wage rate should be higher than some established, known limit). Answer (a) is incorrect since dual circuitry is a double-wiring of the equipment to assure no malfunctioning. Answer (c) is incorrect since echo checks are a hardware control which involve transmitting data received by an output unit back to the source unit (e.g., to test whether the printer is operating). Answer (d) is incorrect; read after write does not take the place of human error detection since it is a procedure in which information is returned to the sending unit for review of its accuracy.

14. (580,A1,38) (c) The requirement is which data item would be best identified as a hash total. A hash total is a meaningless control total such as total of all invoice numbers in a batch of sales invoices. Hash totals are utilized to determine if any data items are lost. Here the department numbers of all employees added together would provide such a "meaningless"

total which would indicate whether anyone's data items were omitted. Answers (a), (b), and (d) are incorrect because totals of gross pay, hours worked and number of employees are all meaningful totals.

15. (1183,A1,21) (d) The requirement is to determine the **least** important item to an auditor when reviewing the internal control of a company with automated data processing. The cost/benefit ratio of data processing operations is least important because it relates to administrative and not to accounting controls. Answers (a), (b), and (c) are accounting controls which are emphasized during financial statement audits (AU 320.29).

16. (1183,A1,41) (b) The requirement is to determine which statement is **not** true of a test data approach for auditing a computerized accounting system. The auditor need not test all possible valid and invalid conditions. For example, certain controls may exist in the program which the auditor need not rely on (e.g., administrative controls). Answer (a) is incorrect because the test data is processed by the client's computer program under the auditor's control. Answer (c) is incorrect because test data need only be used to test conditions in which the auditor is interested. Answer (d) is incorrect because in a computer program the control (if precisely enough defined) will either work or not work—a sample of one is sufficient.

17. (1181,A1,10) (d) The requirement is to determine the least important aspect to an auditor who is reviewing internal controls over the data processing function. Answer (d), bit storage capacity, is least important because it deals with the overall storage capacity of the computer which is not typically considered a part of internal control. Answer (a) is incorrect because ancillary program functions need to be tested and understood. Answer (b), disposition of source documents, is important to provide support for the information being processed. Answer (c), operator competence, is incorrect since the competence of those involved with the data processing function needs to be considered when determining the scope of audit tests.

18. (1180,A1,12) (c) The requirement is the means by which an auditor obtains a "preliminary understanding" of the client's EDP system. As indicated in para 321.25, the auditor's preliminary understanding is ordinarily obtained by inquiry. Inspection [answer (a)], observation [answer (b)], and evaluation [answer (d)], are procedures performed in subsequent compliance testing (para 320.58–.59).

19. (580,A1,54) (a) The requirement is an invalid reason for choosing to omit compliance tests of EDP controls after a review of the system had been completed. If the controls appear adequate, the auditor tests compliance unless (1) the costs of compliance testing are expected to exceed the savings in substantive tests, which is answer (d), or (2) the EDP controls are redundant to other internal control procedures, which is answer (b); see para 321.26. Answer (c) is incorrect because the auditor should not expend the effort on the tests of compliance if the review of the system indicates that there are major weaknesses which would preclude reliance on the system irrespective of the outcome of the tests of compliance.

20. (1179,A1,23) (c) The requirement is the method of testing accounting controls for an EDP activity that leaves no visible evidence that the control procedures were performed. When EDP control procedures leave no visible evidence indicating the procedures have been performed, the auditor should test these controls by reviewing transactions submitted for processing and by comparing them with the related output. The objective is to determine that no transactions tested with unacceptable conditions went unreported and without appropriate resolution. This procedure can be undertaken by submitting for comparison actual client live data or dummy transactions (see para 321.29). Answer (a) is incorrect because corroborative inquiries will not test the accounting controls per se. Answer (b) is incorrect because observing the separation of functional responsibilities is less applicable to an EDP activity because frequently many previously separated functions are combined in an EDP activity as discussed in para 321.12. Answer (d) is incorrect because the run manual consists of program documentation including the problem statement, system flowchart, operating instructions, record layouts, program flowcharts, program listing, test data, and an approval and change sheet. Reviewing the run manual would be part of the review of the system's controls and not part of the test of the system.

21. (1177,A1,39) (c) Answers (a), (b), and (d) all refer to review or investigation of the system. The review of the system indicates the controls that are supposed to be in effect. The second phase, tests of compliance, is designed to determine if the purported controls are in effect, e.g., examination of log books to determine whether information is properly recorded.

22. (579,A1,46) (a) The requirement is the type of EDP system that can be audited without examining or directly testing EDP computer programs, i.e., auditing around the system. Auditing around the system is possible if the system performs uncomplicated processes and produces detailed output, i.e., is a fancy bookkeeping machine. Answers (b), (c), and (d) all describe more complicated EDP systems that produce only limited output. In these more complicated systems, the data and related controls are within the system, and thus the auditor must examine the system itself.

Per para 321.04, auditors must identify and evaluate the accounting controls in all EDP systems. Further, complex EDP systems require auditor specialized expertise to perform the necessary procedures.

23. (1181,A1,38) (c) The requirement is to determine the type of computer programs which auditors use to assist them in functions such as sorting and merging. Answer (c) is correct because a utility program is a standard routine for performing commonly required processing such as sorting, merging, editing, and mathematical routines. Answer (a) is incorrect because compiler programs translate programming languages such as COBOL or FORTRAN to machine-language. Answer (b) is incorrect because supervisory programs or "operating systems" consist of a series of programs that perform functions such as scheduling and supervising the application programs, allocating storage, controlling peripheral devices, and handling errors and restarts. Answer (d) is incorrect because user or "application programs" perform specific data processing tasks such as general ledger, accounts payable, accounts receivable, and payroll. Application programs make use of utility routines.

II. Unique Characteristics of Specific EDP Systems

24. (1183,A1,4) (c) The requirement is to determine the effect of a change from a conventional to a computerized payroll clock card system. The system no longer includes a time card which summarizes the hours worked; thus, a part of the audit trail has been lost. Answer (a) is incorrect because while an auditor may choose to audit through the computer, it may not be necessary. Answer (b) is incorrect because the change's effect on internal control is dependent on the controls existing in the new system. Answer (d) is incorrect because the EDP system's effect on the likelihood of fraud is also not determinable without further information on specific controls currently in existence.

25. (1182,A1,38) (d) The requirement is to determine which answer is **not** a characteristic of a batch processed computer system. Simultaneous posting to several files is most frequently related to an online real-time system, not a batch system. Answer (a) is incorrect since a batch system may process sequentially against a master file. Answer (b) is incorrect because keypunching is followed by machine processing in batch systems. Answer (c) is incorrect because the numerous batches ordinarily result in numerous printouts.

26. (1177,A1,23) (c) Batch processing groups transactions together until a sufficient number is accumulated to permit efficient processing. Multiprogramming is a systems configuration which permits more than one program to be worked on by a given computer at one time. Answers (a), document count processing, and (d), generalized-audit processing, appear to be nonsense terms.

27. (579,A1,51) (b) Online, real-time systems are those in which processing is performed as data is inputted and the results are immediately outputted to influence operations or decisions. Answer (a) is incorrect because batch processing describes systems in which records are collected into groups (batches) before processing. Then entire groups of records are processed on a regular basis. Answer (c) is incorrect because integrated data processing refers to a system, batch or realtime, in which duplicate records and duplicate operations are minimized. Answer (d), random access processing, is incorrect because it is a method of data access, e.g., random versus sequential, not a method of processing.

III. Flowcharting

28. (583,A1,54) (d) The requirement is to determine the symbolic representations that indicate that a file has been consulted. Answer (d) indicates that a manual operation (the trapezoid symbol) is accessing data from a file and returning the data to the file, i.e., "consulting" the file. Answer (a) is incorrect because it represents a processing step (the rectangle) being followed by a manual operation. Answer (b) is incorrect because it represents a document being filed. Answer (c) is incorrect because the diamond symbol represents a decision process.

29. (580,A1,10) (d) The flowcharting symbol which represents a decision is a diamond. On a flowchart it indicates which alternative path is to be followed. Answer (a) is incorrect because a triangle represents offline storage. Answer (b) is incorrect because a circle with a straight line pointing to the right at the bottom of the circle represents a magnetic tape. Answer (c) is

incorrect because a rectangle represents an operation which is a process resulting in a change in the information or in the flow direction.

IV. EDP Definitions

30. (1183,A1,3) (c) The requirement is to determine the correct statement with respect to the machine language for a specific computer. The machine language must be designed for the computer. Answer (a) is incorrect because a programmer may not be able to write a program which will change the computer's machine language. Answer (b) is incorrect (1) because machine languages differ and (2) because machine languages differ from user programs (e.g., written in BASIC, COBOL). Answer (d) is incorrect because the machine language is never alphabetic; it is of a binary form.

31. (582,A1,53) (c) The requirement is to determine the item which converts problem oriented language to machine language. A compiler produces a machine-language object program from a source-program (i.e., problem oriented) language. Answer (a) is incorrect because an interpreter is used to make punched cards easily readable to people. Answer (b) is incorrect because a verifier is used to test whether key punching errors exist on punched cards. Answer (d) is incorrect because a converter changes a program from one form of problem oriented language to another, related form (e.g., from one form of COBOL to another form of COBOL).

32. (1181,A1,8) (d) The requirement is to determine why the grandfather-father-son updating backup concept is relatively difficult to implement for disc files. Answer (d) is correct because updating destroys the old records. Answer (a) is incorrect because the location of information points on discs is **not** an extremely time consuming task if the discs have been properly organized and maintained. Answer (b) is incorrect because off-site storage through discs is possible, though costly. Answer (c) is incorrect because information need not be dumped in the form of hard copy.

33. (581,A1,3) (d) The requirement is an element of software. Compilers are software. The compiler program translates a source program (written in FORTRAN, COBOL, etc.) into an object program which is machine-readable, i.e., instructions to be followed by the CPU. Answer (a) is incorrect because a cathode ray tube is a television-like device (hardware) to display input or output data. Answer (b) is incorrect because the CPU (central processing unit, mainframe) is the principal hardware component of a computer containing the mathematic unit, primary storage, and a control unit. Answer (c) is incorrect because a magnetic tape drive is a hardware unit which reads and writes on magnetic tape, i.e., a storage device, as well as an input and output device.

May 1984 Answers

34. (584,A1,1) (b) The requirement is to determine the extent of technical training and proficiency which an auditor needs to understand an EDP system. Answer (b) is correct because AU 321.04 requires a knowledge of essential accounting control features. Answer (a) is incorrect because a detailed knowledge of the processing and imparting of information may not be necessary when controls are not being relied upon. Note, however, that during the preliminary phase of an auditor's review s/he must obtain an understanding of the flow of transactions through the accounting system (AU 321.24). Answer (c) is incorrect because **all** accounting control features need not be identified and evaluated, especially in cases in which the control is not of significant importance. Answer (d) is incorrect because the programming itself may not directly relate to generally accepted accounting principles.

35. (584,A1,13) (d) The requirement is to determine the situation which constitutes an internal control weakness in an EDP system. Answer (d) is correct because machine operators should not be supervised by the programmers; good internal control in an EDP system requires that operators, programmers, and library function be segregated. Answer (a) is incorrect because storing backup files off-premises will improve internal control (reconstruction of files, if necessary, will be possible). Answer (b) is incorrect because machine operators will, by nature of operating the system, have access to error messages and will distribute them to the control group. Answer (c) is incorrect because not providing operators with access to the manual improves internal control through not allowing them to have complete information on the operation (and weaknesses) of the overall system.

36. (584,A1,15) (a) The requirement is to determine a control which will strengthen an online real-time cash withdrawal system. Answer (a) is correct because documentation of all situations in which the "terminal audit key" has been used will improve the audit trail. Answer (b) is incorrect because increasing the dollar amount required for use of the key will simply reduce the number of times it is used (and allow larger withdrawals to be made without any required

special authorization). Answer (c) is incorrect because there is no reason to believe that a manual system will be more effective than an online system. Answer (d) is incorrect because parallel simulation, running the data through alternate software, would seem to have no particular advantage for processing these large withdrawals.

37. (584,A1,24) (b) The requirement is to determine the type of total not generally added for purposes other than for data processing control. Answer (b) is correct because a hash total represents an otherwise meaningless control total, such as the summation of invoice numbers in a batch of sales invoices, used to determine if data have been lost. Answer (a) is incorrect because a firm may want a record total (number of records processed) for various purposes. Answers (c) and (d) are incorrect because processing data totals and field totals often are posted in the accounting system.

Answer Outline

Problem 1 Computerized Audit Programs

a. Use of computer to perform substantive tests of sales records
   1. Test extensions and footings
   2. Verify accuracy of postings
   3. Determine that all documents are accounted for
   4. Select sales transactions for review
   5. Print a list of items selected and relevant data
   6. Select all debits to sales account and postings to sales account not from sales journal
   7. Analytical review
   8. Compare duplicate data in separate files
   9. Examine records for quality

b. Other procedures to complete audit of sales records
   1. Trace postings from journal to invoices
   2. Trace data from invoices to journal
   3. Compare dates of recorded transactions with shipping records
   4. Determine that all shipping documents are accounted for
   5. Examine documents for approval
   6. Determine extent and nature of transactions with major customers
   7. Verify sales cutoffs
   8. Compare invoices to daily price list

Unofficial Answer

Problem 1 Computerized Audit Programs

a. Based upon the information given the computer may be used by Hastings to do the following:

- Test extensions and footings of computerized sales records that serve as a basis for the preparation of the invoices and sales journal.
- Verify the mathematical accuracy of postings from the sales journal to appropriate ledger accounts.
- Determine that all sales invoices and other related documents have been accounted for (for example, by accounting for the integrity of the numerical sequence).
- Select sales transactions for review (based upon predetermined criteria) through a review of the sales journal or the accounts receivable subsidiary ledger.
- Print a workpaper that lists each item selected, with relevant data inserted in applicable columns.
- Select all debits posted to the sales account and all postings to the sales account from a source other than the sales journal.
- Analytically review recorded sales by use of predetermined criteria (percentage relationships, gross margin, trends, and so forth, on a periodic or annual basis).
- Compare duplicate data maintained in separate files for correctness. For example, the computer may be used to compare the client's records of quantities sold with the client's records of quantities shipped.
- Examine records for quality (completeness, consistency, and so forth). [The quality of visible records is readily apparent to the auditor. Sloppy record-keeping, lack of completeness, and so on, are observed by the auditor in the normal course of the audit. If machine-readable records are evaluated manually, a complete printout is needed to examine their quality. Hastings may choose to use the computer to examine these records for quality].

b. In addition to the procedures outlined above, Hastings should do the following:

- Trace postings from the sales journal to invoice copies.
- Trace data from sales invoices to the sales journal.
- Compare dates of recorded sales transactions with dates on shipping records.
- Determine that all shipping documents have been accounted for (for example, by accounting for the integrity of the numerical sequence).
- Examine documents for appropriate approval (for example, grant of credit, shipment of goods, and determination of price and billing).
- Determine the extent and nature of business transacted with major customers (for indications of previously undisclosed relationships—related parties—and for determination of applicability of disclosure requirements required by generally accepted accounting principles).
- Verify the sales cutoff at the beginning and end of the period to determine whether the recorded sales represent revenues of the period.
- Test pricing by comparing invoices to daily price list.

Answer Outline

Problem 2 EDP Controls

a. General EDP controls
1. Plan of organization and operation
2. Procedures for documenting, reviewing, testing, and approving new programs and program changes
3. Hardware controls
4. Access controls to equipment and data files
5. Other data and procedural controls

b1. Input controls provide reasonable assurance that inputted data
Have been properly authorized
Are converted into machine sensible form
Have not been lost, suppressed, added, duplicated, or altered

b2. Processing controls provide reasonable assurance
EDP has been performed as intended, e.g.,
All transactions processed as authorized
No authorized transactions are omitted
No unauthorized transactions are added

b3. Output controls provide reasonable assurance
Of the accuracy of processing results
E.g., account listings, reports, magnetic files, etc.
That only authorized personnel receive the output

Unofficial Answer

Problem 2 EDP Controls

a. General control features in most EDP-based accounting systems are classified in Statement on Auditing Standards no. 3 as follows:
1. The plan or organization and operation of the EDP activity.
2. The procedures for documenting, reviewing, testing, and approving systems or programs and changes thereto.
3. Controls built into the equipment (i.e., hardware controls).
4. Controls over access to equipment and data files.
5. Other data and procedural controls affecting overall EDP operations.

b. 1. Input controls are designed to provide reasonable assurance that data received for processing by EDP have been properly authorized and converted into machine-sensible form and identified and that data (including data transmitted over communication lines) have not been lost, suppressed, added, duplicated, or otherwise improperly changed.

2. Processing controls are designed to provide reasonable assurance that electronic data processing has been performed as intended for the particular application (i.e., that all transactions are processed as authorized, that no authorized transactions are omitted, and that no unauthorized transactions are added).

3. Output controls are designed to assure the accuracy of the processing result (such as account listings or displays, reports, magnetic files, invoices, or disbursement checks) and to assure that only authorized personnel receive the output.

Answer Outline

Problem 3 Audit of Computerized A/R

Computer uses in auditing accounts receivable

1. Recomputing extensions and footings to test for accuracy
2. Selecting and printing confirmation requests
3. Examining records for completeness, consistency, validity
4. Summarizing data and analyses useful to the auditor
5. Selecting and printing audit samples
6. Comparing duplicate data for correctness and consistency
7. Comparing confirmation information with company records
8. Listing accounts confirmed with relevant data
9. Comparing account balances to credit limits

Unofficial Answer

Problem 3 Audit of Computerized A/R

- Testing Extensions and Footings.

The computer can be used to perform simple summations and other computations to test the correctness of extensions and footings. The auditor may choose to perform tests on all records instead of just on samples, since the speed and low cost per computation of the computer enable this at only a small extra amount of time and expense.

• Selecting and Printing Confirmation Requests.
The computer can select and print out confirmation requests on the basis of quantifiable selection criteria. The program can be written to select the accounts according to any set of criteria desired and using any sampling plan.

• Examining Records for Quality (Completeness, Consistency, Valid Conditions, etc.).
The quality of visible records is readily apparent to the auditor. Sloppy record-keeping, lack of completeness, and so on, are observed by the auditor in the normal course of the audit. If machine-readable records are evaluated manually, however, a complete printout is needed to examine their quality. The auditor may choose to use the computer for examining these records for quality.

If the computer is to be used for the examination, a program is written to examine the record for completeness, consistency among different items, valid conditions, reasonable amounts, and so forth. For instance, customer file records might be examined to determine those for which no credit limit is specified, those for which account balances exceed credit limit, and those for which credit limits exceed a stipulated amount.

• Summarizing Data and Performing Analyses Useful to the Auditor.
The auditor frequently needs to have the client's data analyzed and/or summarized. Such procedures as aging accounts receivable or listing all credit balances in accounts receivable can be accomplished with a computer program.

• Selecting and Printing Audit Samples.
The computer may be programmed to select audit samples by the use of random numbers or by systematic selection techniques. The sample selection procedure may be programmed to use multiple criteria, such as the selection of a random sample of items under a certain dollar amount plus the selection of all items over a certain dollar amount. Other considerations can be included, such as unusual transactions, dormant accounts, and so forth.

• Comparing Duplicate Data (Maintained in Separate Files) for Correctness and Consistency.
Where there are two or more separate records having identical data fields, the computer can be used to test for consistency—for instance, to compare catalogue prices with invoice prices.

• Comparing Confirmation Information with Company Records.
For example, the computer can be used to compare payment dates indicated on customer confirmations with client cash receipts records.

• The computer may be programmed to print a workpaper listing of each account selected, with relevant data inserted in applicable columns.

• The computer may be programmed to compare the customer's account balance with the customer's history of purchases or to determine whether credit limits have been exceeded.

Answer Outline

Problem 4 EDP Controls

a. Separation of programming and operating functions is achieved by preventing
  - Programmer access to the computer except during designated testing periods
  - Programmer access to input documents
  - Programmer access to output documents
  - Operator access to operating program documentation
  - Operator from writing programs
  - Operator from changing programs

b. Mitigating controls which Johnson most likely found include
  - Joint operation by two or more operators
  - Rotation of operator duties
  - Use of a computer activity log book
  - Comparison of actual computer times to an average or norm
  - Investigation of all excess computer time (errors)
  - Adequate supervision of all EDP operations
  - Periodic comparison of program code value to a control value
  - Periodic comparison of all programs with control copies
  - Required vacations for all employees

Unofficial Answer

Problem 4 EDP Controls

a. The primary internal control objectives in separating the programming and operating functions are achieved by preventing programmer access to the computer (except during designated testing periods) or to input or output documents and by preventing operator access to operating programs and operating program documentation, or by preventing operators from writing or changing programs.

b. Johnson is likely to find the following mitigating controls that are particularly important and that should exist when the programming and operating functions are not separated:

- Joint operation by two or more operators
- Rotation of operator duties
- Use of a computer activity log book
- Comparison of computer times to an average or norm
- Investigation of all excess computer time (errors)
- Adequate supervision of all EDP operations
- Periodic comparison of program code value to a control value
- Periodic comparison of all programs with control copies
- Required vacations for all employees

Unofficial Answer*

Problem 5 Payroll System Flowchart

a. (1) Time cards
(2) Prepare batch-control slips
(3) Batch-control slips (the numbers 1 and 2 should be added to indicate first and second copy)
(4) Time cards
(5) Keypunch
(6) Batch-control slip (the number 1 should be added to indicate first copy)
(7) Time cards
(8) By batch
(9) Payroll transaction cards
(10) Sort by employee number within batch
(11) Master employee file
(12) Edit and compare batch total hours and number of employees
(13) Batch listing and exception report
(14) Batch total card
(15) Payroll transaction cards
(16) Exceptions noted:
- Unbalanced batch
- Invalid employee number

(17) Resolve differences

b. Advantages of a flowchart:

1. It insures a more comprehensive survey since incomplete information is more evident when it is being recorded on flowcharts.
2. It is readily tailored to specific client system.
3. It enables the system to be more quickly understood by the audit staff since the information is presented in a concise, graphic manner which is easy to comprehend and visualize.
4. It creates more interest on the part of the audit staff because they can better appreciate the functioning of the system and hence the reasons for tests.
5. It produces more valuable and realistic recommendations to clients on internal controls and system efficiency because of increased awareness of accounting systems, relationships and document flows.
6. It emphasizes those areas of the internal control system (and related accounts) which require more or less attention and therefore assists in better use of audit time.
7. It increases client goodwill because new audit staff members usually require less time for system orientation, and interference with the client's staff is kept to a minimum.

**Because the requirements of this question could be answered by lists of items we have not included an outline of the solution.*

CHAPTER THREE

BUSINESS LAW PROBLEMS AND SOLUTIONS

Business law is tested on Friday morning from 8:30 to 12:00. Recent business law exams have consisted of 60 multiple choice questions (60% of the business law grade) and 4 essay questions (each 10% of the business law grade). Essay questions generally contain 2 to 4 parts, frequently unrelated, even to the point of testing unrelated topics, e.g., part "a" tests antitrust and part "b" tests bankruptcy.

Recent business law exams have covered subject matter from almost all of the 16 business law modules (May 1980 did cover all 16 modules). A complete analysis of recent examinations and the *AICPA Content Specification Outlines* appear in Volume I, *Outlines and Study Guides*.

CPA candidates tend to overemphasize multiple choice questions in business law, even more so than in other sections of the examination, due to unfamiliarity with business law topics relative to accounting topics. Special attention should be directed to law essay questions because they often require yes-no type decisions at the beginning of the answers in addition to a well-organized, complete answer presentation as in auditing and theory.

A recent development is the testing of tax theory concepts on the law section, e.g., what are the tax consequences of issuing preferred stock instead of debt? Candidates preparing for the business law section of the examination may wish to also glance through the taxation modules.

Each question is coded as to month, year, section, problem number, and multiple choice question number, e.g., (1183, L1,43): where 1183 is November 1983; L1 is law problem 1; and 43 is the multiple choice question number. Some questions were altered to make them applicable due to changes in the law.

BUSINESS LAW INDEX

Multiple Choice Questions (1–51)

1. In determining whether a bilateral contract has been created, the courts look primarily at
   a. The fairness to the parties.
   b. The objective intent of the parties.
   c. The subjective intent of the parties.
   d. The subjective intent of the offeror.

2. Flaxx, a sales representative of Dome Home Sites, Inc., escorted Mr. & Mrs. Grand through several acres of Dome's proposed subdivision and showed the Grands various one-acre lots for sale at $27,000 each. Upon conclusion of the tour, the Grands expressed interest in purchasing a lot in the near future. Flaxx urged them to show their good faith and sign a letter of intent, which stated: "We, the undersigned, having decided to purchase a lot from Dome Home Sites in the future, deliver to the corporation's agent one hundred dollars ($100) earnest money." This was signed by the Grands at the bottom of the form and the $100 was delivered to Flaxx by the Grands. Under the circumstances
   a. The Grands have made an offer to buy a lot from Dome.
   b. If all the lots are sold by Dome, the Grands have a cause of action for breach of contract.
   c. If no deal is ever consummated, the Grands have the right to the return of the $100.
   d. The $100 constitutes liquidated damages and will be forfeited in the event the Grands do not purchase a lot.

3. Harris wrote Douglas a letter which might be construed alternatively as an offer to sell land, an invitation to commence negotiations, or merely an invitation to Douglas to make an offer. Douglas claims that the communication was a bona fide offer which he has unequivocally accepted according to the terms set forth therein. In deciding the dispute in question, the court will
   a. Look to the subjective intent of Harris.
   b. Use an objective standard based on how a reasonably prudent businessman would have interpreted the letter to Douglas.
   c. Decide that an offer had **not** been made if any of the usual terms were omitted.
   d. Decide on the basis of what Douglas considered the writing to be.

4. Love granted Nelson a written option to buy a tract of land in an industrial park. The option stated that it was irrevocable for 11 days and was given for $20 and other valuable consideration. The $20 was not paid and there was no other valuable consideration. Which of the following is a correct statement regarding the option in question?
   a. Since real property is involved, Nelson's acceptance must be contained in a signed writing if Nelson is to enforce it against Love.
   b. It is an option contract enforceable for the 11-day period.
   c. Acceptance must be received at Love's place of business before expiration of the 11 days.
   d. It is unenforceable because it lacks consideration.

5. West sent a letter to Baker on October 18, 1983, offering to sell a tract of land for $70,000. The offer stated that it would expire on November 1, 1983. Baker sent a letter on October 25, indicating the price was too high and that he would be willing to pay $62,500. On the morning of October 26, upon learning that a comparable property had sold for $72,500, Baker telephoned West and made an unconditional acceptance of the offer at $70,000. West indicated that the price was now $73,000. Baker's letter offering $62,500 arrived the afternoon of October 26. Under the circumstances
   a. West's letter was a firm offer as defined under the Uniform Commercial Code.
   b. Baker validly accepted on the morning of October 26.
   c. There is **no** contract since Baker's acceptance was not in a signed writing.
   d. The parol evidence rule will preclude Baker from contradicting his written statements with oral testimony contra to his letter of October 25.

6. Starbuck Corporation sent Crane Company an offer by a telegram to buy its patent on a calculator. The Starbuck telegram indicated that the offer would expire in ten days. The telegram was sent on February 1, 1982, and received on February 2, 1982, by Crane. On February 8, 1982, Starbuck telephoned Crane and indicated it was withdrawing the offer. Crane telegraphed an acceptance on the 11th of February. Which of the following is correct?
   a. Starbuck's withdrawal of the offer was ineffective because it was **not** in writing.
   b. The offer was an irrevocable offer, but Crane's acceptance was too late.
   c. No contract arose since Starbuck effectively revoked the offer on February 8, 1982.
   d. Since Crane used the same means of communication, acceptance was both timely and effective.

7

7. Dustin received a telephone call on Monday from his oil supplier. The supplier offered him 1,000 barrels of heating oil at $48 a barrel, the current price in a rapidly changing market. Dustin said he would take the offer under advisement. The next day, the market price rose to $50 a barrel and Dustin sent the supplier a letter late that afternoon accepting the offer at $48 a barrel. The letter arrived in the usual course on Thursday morning, by which time the market price had moved to $56 a barrel. The supplier called Dustin and said it would not accept his order. Dustin insisted that he had a contract. Which of the following is correct?

a. Acceptance took place on dispatch of Dustin's letter.
b. Acceptance did **not** take place upon dispatch as the offer had already expired.
c. Acceptance did **not** take place because the only means of acceptance Dustin could use was the phone.
d. Acceptance could only be made by a signed writing.

8. Justin made an offer to pay Benson $1,000 if Benson would perform a certain act. Acceptance of Justin's offer occurs when Benson

a. Promises to complete the act.
b. Prepares to perform the act.
c. Promises to perform and begins preliminary performance.
d. Completes the act.

9. Luxor wrote Harmon offering to sell Harmon Luxor's real estate business for $200,000. Harmon sent a telegram accepting the offer at $190,000. Later, learning that several other parties were interested in purchasing the business, Harmon telephoned Luxor and made an unqualified acceptance on Luxor's terms. The telegram arrived an hour after the phone call. Under the circumstances

a. Harmon's telegram effectively terminated the offer.
b. Harmon's oral acceptance is voidable, because real estate is involved.
c. The offer was revoked as a result of Harmon's learning that others were interested in purchasing the business.
d. Harmon has made a valid contract at $200,000.

10. On October 1, 1982, Arthur mailed to Madison an offer to sell a tract of land located in Summerville for $13,000. Acceptance was to be not later than October 10. Madison posted his acceptance on the 6th of October. The acceptance arrived on October 7th. On October 4th, Arthur sold the tract in question to Larson and mailed to Madison notice of the sale. That letter arrived on the 6th of October, but after Madison had dispatched his letter of acceptance. Which of the following is correct?

a. There was a valid acceptance of the Arthur offer on the day Madison posted his acceptance.
b. Arthur's offer was effectively revoked by the sale of the tract of land to Larson on the 4th of October.
c. Arthur could **not** revoke the offer to sell the land until after October 10th.
d. Madison's acceptance was **not** valid since he was deemed to have notice of revocation prior to the acceptance.

11. Water Works had a long-standing policy of offering employees $100 for suggestions actually used. Due to inflation and a decline in the level and quality of suggestions received, Water Works decided to increase the award to $500. Several suggestions were under consideration at that time. Two days prior to the public announcement of the increase to $500, a suggestion by Farber was accepted and put into use. Farber is seeking to collect $500. Farber is entitled to

a. $500 because Water Works had decided to pay that amount.
b. $500 because the suggestion submitted will be used during the period that Water Works indicated it would pay $500.
c. $100 in accordance with the original offer.
d. Nothing if Water Works chooses **not** to pay since the offer was gratuitous.

12. Marglow Supplies Inc., mailed a letter to Wilson Distributors on September 15, 1981, offering a three-year franchise dealership. The offer stated the terms in detail and at the bottom stated that the offer would not be withdrawn prior to October 1, 1981. Which of the following is correct?

a. The statute of frauds would **not** apply to the proposed contract.
b. The offer is an irrevocable option which can **not** be withdrawn prior to October 1, 1981.
c. The offer can **not** be assigned to another party by Wilson if Wilson chooses **not** to accept.
d. A letter of acceptance from Wilson to Marglow sent on October 1, 1981, but **not** received until October 2, 1981, would **not** create a valid contract.

13. Wilcox mailed Norriss an unsigned contract for the purchase of a tract of real property. The contract represented the oral understanding of the parties as to the purchase price, closing date, type of deed, and other details. It called for payment in full in cash or certified check at the closing. Norriss signed the contract, but added above his signature the following:

> This contract is subject to my (Norriss) being able to obtain conventional mortgage financing of $100,000 at 13% or less interest for a period of not less than 25 years.

Which of the following is correct?

a. The parties had already made an enforceable contract prior to Wilcox's mailing of the formalized contract.
b. Norriss would **not** be liable on the contract under the circumstances even if he had **not** added the "conventional mortgage" language since Wilcox had **not** signed it.
c. By adding the "conventional mortgage" language above his signature, Norriss created a condition precedent to his contractual obligation and made a counteroffer.
d. The addition of the "conventional mortgage" language has **no** legal effect upon the contractual relationship of the parties since it was an implied condition in any event.

14. Fernandez is planning to attend an auction of the assets of Cross & Black, one of his major competitors who is liquidating. In the conduct of the auction, which of the following rules applies?

a. Such a sale is without reserve unless the goods are explicitly put up with reserve.
b. A bidder may retract his bid at any time until the falling of the hammer.
c. The retraction of a bid by a bidder revives the previous bid.
d. If the auction is without reserve, the auctioneer can withdraw the article at any time prior to the fall of the hammer.

15. Lally sent Queen Supply Company, Inc., a telegram ordering $700 of general merchandise. Lally's telegram indicated that immediate shipment was necessary. That same day Queen delivered the goods to the Red Freight Company. The shipment was delayed due to a breakdown of the truck which was transporting the goods. When the merchandise did not arrive as promptly as expected, Lally notified Queen that it revoked the offer and was purchasing the goods elsewhere. Queen indicated to Lally that the merchandise had been shipped the same day Lally had ordered it and Lally's revocation was not good. Which of the following statements best describes the transaction?

a. The statute of frauds will be a defense on any action by Queen to enforce the contract.
b. Prompt shipment of the merchandise by Queen constituted an acceptance.
c. Lally's revocation of the offer was effective since Lally had not received a notice of acceptance.
d. Lally's order was an offer to Queen to enter into a bilateral contract which could be accepted only by a promise.

16. Dougal is seeking to avoid performing a promise to pay Clark $500. Dougal is relying upon lack of consideration on Clark's part sufficient to support his promise. Dougal will prevail if he can establish that

a. The contract is executory.
b. Clark's asserted consideration is worth only $100.
c. Prior to Dougal's promise, Clark had already performed the requested act.
d. Clark's only claim of consideration was the relinquishment of a legal right.

17. Williams purchased a heating system from Radiant Heating, Inc., for his factory. Williams insisted that a clause be included in the contract calling for service on the heating system to begin not later than the next business day after Williams informed Radiant of a problem. This service was to be rendered free of charge during the first year of the contract and for a flat fee of $200 per year for the next two years thereafter. During the winter of the second year, the heating system broke down and Williams promptly notified Radiant of the situation. Due to other commitments, Radiant did not send a man over the next day. Williams phoned Radiant and was told that the $200 per year service charge was uneconomical and they could not get a man over there for several days. Williams in desperation promised to pay an additional $100 if Radiant would send a man over that day. Radiant did so and sent a bill for $100 to Williams. Is Williams legally required to pay this bill and why?

a. No, because the pre-existing legal duty rule applies to this situation.
b. No, because the statute of frauds will defeat Radiant's claim.
c. Yes, because Williams made the offer to pay the additional amount.
d. Yes, because the fact that it was uneconomical for Radiant to perform constitutes economic duress which freed Radiant from its obligation to provide the agreed-upon service.

18. Martinson Services, Inc., agreed to rent two floors of office space in Jason's building for five years. An escalation clause in the lease provided for a $200 per month increase in rental in the fifth year of occupancy by Martinson. Near the end of the fourth year, during a serious economic recession, Martinson's business was doing very poorly. Martinson called upon Jason to inform him that Martinson could not honor the lease if the rent was increased in the fifth year. Jason agreed in a signed writing to allow Martinson to remain at the prior rental, and Martinson did so. At the end of the fifth year Martinson moved to another office building. Then, Jason demanded payment of $2,400 from Martinson.

What is the legal standing of the parties involved?

a. A binding accord and satisfaction has resulted between the parties.
b. The agreed upon rent reduction is valid due to the increased burden of performance as a result of events beyond Martinson's control.
c. Martinson's relinquishment of the legal right to breach the contract provides the consideration for the reduction in rent.
d. The writing signed by Jason does not bind him to the agreed reduction in rent.

19. Fairbanks, an author, was approached by Nickle Corporation to ghostwrite the history of Nickle for $15,000. Larson, the president of Nickle, told Fairbanks the job was his if he would agree to cleverly defame its leading competitor, Mogul Corporation, using sly innuendo and clever distortion of the facts. Fairbanks wrote the history. It turned out that the Mogul passages were neither sly nor clever and Mogul obtained a judgment against Nickle. Fairbanks is seeking to collect the final $5,000 installment on the contract. Nickle refuses to pay and seeks to recover the $10,000 it has already paid. In the event of a lawsuit

a. Fairbanks will recover $5,000.
b. The court will deny relief to either party.
c. Nickle will recover $10,000.
d. Fairbanks will recover in quantum meruit for the value of his services.

20. Glass Co. telephoned Hourly Company and ordered 2,000 watches at $2 each. Glass agreed to pay 10% immediately and the balance within ten days after receipt of the entire shipment. Glass forwarded a check for $400 and Hourly shipped 1,000 watches the next day, intending to ship the balance by the end of the week. Glass decided that the contract was a bad bargain and repudiated it, asserting the Statute of Frauds. Hourly sued Glass. Which of the following will allow Hourly to enforce the contract in its entirety despite the Statute of Frauds?

a. Glass admitted in court that it made the contract in question.
b. Hourly shipped 1,000 watches.
c. Glass paid 10% down.
d. The contract is **not** within the requirements of the Statute.

21. The Statute of Frauds

a. Codified common law rules of fraud.
b. Requires that formal contracts be in writing and signed by the parties to the contract.
c. Does **not** apply if the parties waive its application in the contract.
d. Sometimes results in a contract being enforceable by only one party.

22. Certain oral contracts fall outside the Statute of Frauds. An example would be a contract between

a. A creditor and a friend of the debtor, providing for the friend's guaranty of the debt in exchange for the creditor's binding extension of time for payment of the debt.
b. A landlord and a tenant for the lease of land for ten years.
c. A school board and a teacher entered into on January 1, for nine months of service to begin on September 1.
d. A retail seller of television sets and a buyer for the sale of a TV set for $399 C.O.D.

23. A salesman for A & C Company called upon the purchasing agent for Major Enterprises, Inc., and offered to sell Major 1,500 screwdriver sets at $1.60 each. Major's purchasing agent accepted and the following day sent A & C a purchase order which bore Major's name and address at the top and also had the purchasing agent's name and title stamped at the bottom with his initials. The purchase order recited the agreement reached orally the prior day. Subsequently, Major decided it did not want the screwdriver sets since it was overstocked in that item. Major thereupon repudiated the contract and asserted the statute of frauds as a defense. Under the circumstances, which of the following is correct?

a. The statute of frauds does not apply to this transaction since performance is to be completed within one year from the date of the making of the contract.

b. Major will lose but only if its purchasing agent's authority to make the contract was in writing.
c. The fact that an authorized agent of A & C did not sign the purchase order prevents its use by A & C against Major to satisfy the statute of frauds.
d. The purchase order is sufficient to satisfy the statute of frauds even though the purchasing agent never signed it in full.

24. Under what conditions will the statute of frauds be a defense under the Uniform Commercial Code where there is a contract for the sale of goods worth more than $500?
a. The seller has completed goods specially manufactured for the buyer which are not salable in the ordinary course of the seller's business.
b. The written memorandum omits several important terms but states the quantity, and it is signed by the party to be charged.
c. The party asserting the statute of frauds admits under oath to having made the contract.
d. The goods in question are fungible and actively traded by merchants in the business community.

25. Elrod is attempting to introduce oral evidence in court to explain or modify a written contract he made with Weaver. Weaver has pleaded the parol evidence rule. In which of the following circumstances will Elrod **not** be able to introduce the oral evidence?
a. The modification asserted was made several days after the written contract had been executed.
b. The contract indicates that it was intended as the "entire contract" between the parties, and the point is covered in detail.
c. There was a mutual mistake of fact by the parties regarding the subject matter of the contract.
d. The contract contains an obvious ambiguity on the point at issue.

26. With respect to written contracts, the parol evidence rule applies
a. Exclusively to the purchase or sale of goods.
b. To subsequent oral modifications.
c. Only to prior or contemporaneous oral modifications.
d. To modifications by prior written or oral agreements.

27. Silvers entered into a contract which contains a substantial arithmetical error. Silvers asserts mistake as a defense to his performance. Silvers will prevail
a. Only if the mistake was a mutual mistake.
b. Only if the error was **not** due to his negligence.
c. If the error was unilateral and the other party knew of it.
d. If the contract was written by the other party.

28. Smith, an executive of Apex Corporation, became emotionally involved with Jones. At the urging of Jones, and fearing that Jones would sever their relationship, Smith reluctantly signed a contract which was grossly unfair to Apex. Apex's best basis to rescind the contract would be
a. Lack of express authority.
b. Duress.
c. Undue influence.
d. Lack of consideration.

29. In order to establish a common law action for fraud, the aggrieved party must establish that
a. Although the defendant did **not** in fact know that his statements were false, he made the false statements with a reckless disregard for the truth.
b. The contract entered into is within the Statute of Frauds.
c. There was a written misrepresentation of fact by the defendant.
d. The plaintiff acted as a reasonably prudent businessman in relying upon the misrepresentation.

30. Paul filed a $20,000 fire loss claim with the Williams Fire Insurance Company. Dickerson, Williams' adjuster, called Paul on the phone and invited him to come to his hotel room to settle the claim. Upon Paul's entry to the room, Dickerson locked the door and placed the key in his pocket. He then accused Paul of having set the building on fire and of having been involved in several previous suspicious fire claims. Dickerson concluded by telling Paul that unless he signed a release in exchange for $500, he would personally see to it that Paul was prosecuted by the company for arson. Visibly shaken by all this, Paul

signed the release. Paul has subsequently repudiated the release. The release is **not** binding because of

a. Fraud.
b. Lack of consideration.
c. Undue influence.
d. Duress.

31. Which of the following is **not** required in order for the plaintiff to prevail in an action for innocent misrepresentation?

a. That the misrepresentation was intended to induce reliance.
b. That the misrepresentation amounted to gross negligence.
c. That the plaintiff acted promptly and offered to restore what was received.
d. That the plaintiff relied upon the misrepresentation.

32. The assignment of a contract right

a. Will **not** be enforceable if it materially varies the obligor's promise.
b. Is invalid unless supported by consideration.
c. Gives the assignee better rights against the obligor than the assignor had.
d. Does not create any rights in the assignee against the assignor until notice is given to the obligor.

33. Walton owed $10,000 to Grant. Grant assigned his claim against Walton to the Line Finance Company for value on October 15, 1982. On October 25, 1982, Hayes assigned his matured claim for $2,000 against Grant to Walton for value. On October 30, 1982, Line notified Walton of the assignment to them of the $10,000 debt owed by Walton to Grant. Line has demanded payment in full. Insofar as the rights of the various parties are concerned

a. Walton has the right of a $2,000 set-off against the debt which he owed Grant.
b. Walton must pay Line in full, but has the right to obtain a $2,000 reimbursement from Grant.
c. Line is a creditor beneficiary of the debt owed by Walton.
d. The claimed set-off of the Hayes claim for $2,000 is invalid since it is for an amount which is less than the principal debt.

34. Conrad is seeking to avoid liability on a contract with Fuld. Conrad can avoid liability on the contract if

a. A third party has agreed to perform his duty and has for a valuable consideration promised to hold Conrad harmless on the obligation to Fuld.
b. The entire contract has been assigned.
c. There has been a subsequent unexecuted accord between Fuld and himself.
d. He has been discharged by a novation.

35. Fennell and McLeod entered into a binding contract whereby McLeod was to perform routine construction services according to Fennell's blueprints. McLeod assigned the contract to Conerly. After the assignment

a. Fennell can bring suit under the doctrine of anticipatory breach.
b. McLeod extinguishes all his rights and duties under the contract.
c. McLeod extinguishes all his rights but is **not** relieved of his duties under the contract.
d. McLeod still has all his rights but is relieved of his duties under the contract.

36. Monroe purchased a ten-acre land site from Acme Land Developers, Inc. He paid 10% at the closing and gave his note for the balance secured by a 20-year mortgage. Three years later, Monroe found it increasingly difficult to make payments on the note and finally defaulted. Acme Land threatened to accelerate the loan and foreclose if he continued in default. It told him either to get the money or obtain an acceptable third party to assume the obligation. Monroe offered the land to Thompson for $1,000 less than the equity he had in the property. This was acceptable to Acme and at the closing Thompson paid the arrearage, executed a new mortgage and note, and had title transferred to his name. Acme surrendered Monroe's note and mortgage to him. The transaction in question is a (an)

a. Assignment and delegation.
b. Third party beneficiary contract.
c. Novation.
d. Purchase of land subject to a mortgage.

37. Nancy is asserting rights as a third party donee beneficiary on a contract made by Johnson and Harding. In order to prevail, Nancy must prove that

a. The contract specifically named her as the beneficiary.
b. She gave consideration for the donative promise.
c. She is related by blood or marriage to the promisee.
d. The terms of the contract and surrounding circumstances manifest a clear intent to benefit her.

38. Wilson sold his factory to Glenn. As part of the contract, Glenn assumed the existing mortgage on the property which was held by Security Bank. Regarding the rights and duties of the parties, which of the following is correct?

a. The promise by Glenn need **not** be in writing to be enforceable by Security.
b. Security is a creditor beneficiary of Glenn's promise and can recover against him personally in the event of default.
c. Security is a mere incidental beneficiary since it was **not** a party to the assignment.
d. Wilson has **no** further liability to Security.

39. Stone engaged Parker to perform personal services for $1,000 a month for a period of three months. The contract was entered into orally on August 1, 1983, and performance was to commence January 1, 1984. On September 15, Parker anticipatorily repudiated the contract. As a result, Stone can

a. Obtain specific performance.
b. Not assign her rights to damages under the contract to a third party.
c. Immediately sue for breach of contract.
d. Not enforce the contract against Parker since the contract is oral.

40. Kent Construction Company contracted to construct four garages for Magnum, Inc., according to specifications provided by Magnum. Kent deliberately substituted 2 x 4s for the more expensive 2 x 6s called for in the contract in all places where the 2 x 4s would not be readily detected. Magnum's inspection revealed the variance and Magnum is now withholding the final payment on the contract. The contract was for $100,000, and the final payment would be $25,000. Damages were estimated to be $15,000. In a lawsuit for the balance due, Kent will

a. Prevail on the contract, less damages of $15,000, because it has substantially performed.
b. Prevail because the damages in question were not substantial in relation to the contract amount.
c. Lose because the law unqualifiedly requires literal performance of such contracts.
d. Lose all rights under the contract because it has intentionally breached it.

41. Smith contracted to perform for $500 certain services for Jones. Jones claimed that the services had been performed poorly. Because of this, Jones sent Smith a check for only $425. Marked clearly on the check was "payment in full". Smith crossed out the words "payment in full" and cashed the check. Assuming that there was a bona fide dispute as to whether Smith had in fact performed the services poorly, the majority of courts would hold that

a. The debt is liquidated, and Smith can collect the remaining $75.
b. The debt is liquidated, but Jones by adding the words "payment in full" cancelled the balance of the debt owed.
c. The debt is unliquidated and the cashing of the check by Smith completely discharged the debt.
d. The debt is unliquidated, but the crossing out of the words "payment in full" by Smith revives the balance of $75 owed.

42. Marblehead Manufacturing, Inc., contracted with Wellfleet Oil Company in June to provide its regular supply of fuel oil from November 1 through March 31. The written contract required Marblehead to take all of its oil requirements exclusively from Wellfleet at a fixed price subject to an additional amount not to exceed 10% of the contract price and only if the market price increases during the term of the contract. By the time performance was due on the contract, the market price had already risen 20%. Wellfleet seeks to avoid performance. Which of the following will be Wellfleet's best argument?

a. There is no contract since Marblehead was not required to take any oil.
b. The contract fails because of lack of definiteness and certainty.
c. The contract is unconscionable.
d. Marblehead has ordered amounts of oil unreasonably disproportionate to its normal requirements.

43. The Johnson Corporation sent its only pump to the manufacturer to be repaired. It engaged Travis, a local trucking company, both to deliver the equipment to the manufacturer and to redeliver it to Johnson promptly upon completion of the repair. Johnson's entire plant was inoperative without this pump, but the trucking company did not know this. The trucking company delayed several days in its delivery of the repaired pump to Johnson. During the time it expected to be without the pump, Johnson incurred $5,000 in lost profits. At the end of that time Johnson rented a replacement pump at a cost of $200 per day. As a result of these facts, what is Johnson entitled to recover from Travis?

a. The $200 a day cost incurred in renting the pump.
b. The $200 a day cost incurred in renting the pump plus the lost profits.

c. Actual damages plus punitive damages.
d. Nothing because Travis is not liable for damages.

44. Myers entered into a contract to purchase a valuable rare coin from Eisen. Myers tendered payment which was refused by Eisen. Upon Eisen's breach, Myers brought suit to obtain the coin. The court will grant Myers

a. Compensatory damages.
b. Specific performance.
c. Reformation.
d. Restitution.

45. The Balboa Custom Furniture Company sells fine custom furniture. It has been encountering difficulties lately with some customers who have breached their contracts after the furniture they have selected has been customized to their order or the fabric they have selected has been cut or actually installed on the piece of furniture purchased. The company therefore wishes to resort to a liquidated damages clause in its sales contract to encourage performance or provide an acceptable amount of damages. Regarding Balboa's contemplated resort to a liquidated damages clause, which of the following is correct?

a. Balboa may not use a liquidated damages clause since it is a merchant and is the preparer of the contract.
b. Balboa can simply take a very large deposit which will be forfeited if performance by a customer is not made for any reason.
c. The amount of the liquidated damages stipulated in the contract must be reasonable in light of the anticipated or actual harm caused by the breach.
d. Even if Balboa uses a liquidated damages clause in its sales contract, it will nevertheless have to establish that the liquidated damages claimed did not exceed actual damages by more than 10%.

46. When a lengthy delay has occurred between the breach of a contract and the commencement of the lawsuit, the statute of limitations defense may be raised. The statute

a. Is three years irrespective of the type of legal action the plaintiff is bringing.
b. Does **not** apply to an action brought in a court of equity.
c. Is a defense to recovery if the requisite period of time has elapsed.
d. Fixes a period of time in which the plaintiff must commence the action or be barred from recovery, regardless of the defendant's conduct during the period.

May 1984 Questions

47. Mix entered into a contract with Small which provided that Small would receive $10,000 if he stole trade secrets from Mix's competition. Small performed his part of the contract by delivering the trade secrets to Mix. Mix refuses to pay Small for his services. Under what theory may Small recover?

a. Quasi contract, in order to prevent the unjust enrichment of Mix.
b. Promissory estoppel, since Small has changed his position to his detriment.
c. None, due to the illegal nature of the contract.
d. Express contract, since both parties bargained for and exchanged promises in forming the contract.

48. Pam orally agreed to sell Jack her used car for $400. At the time the contract was entered into, the car had been stolen and its whereabouts were unknown. Neither party was aware of these facts at the time the contract was formed. Jack sues Pam for her failure to deliver the car in accordance with their agreement. Pam's best defense would be that the

a. Agreement was unenforceable because it was **not** evidenced by a writing.
b. Risk of loss for the car was on Jack.
c. Agreement is unconscionable.
d. Parties were under a mutual mistake of a material fact at the time the contract was entered into.

49. Which of the following requires consideration in order to be binding on the parties?

a. Material modification of a sale of goods contract under the UCC.
b. Ratification of a contract by a person after reaching the age of majority.
c. Material modification of a contract involving the sale of real estate.
d. A written promise signed by a merchant to keep an offer to sell goods open for 10 days.

50. Pine Co. published circulars containing price quotes and a description of products which it would like to sell. Bean, a prospective customer, demands the right to purchase one of the products at the quoted price. Which of the following statements is correct under general contract law?

a. Pine has made an offer.
b. Bean has made an offer.
c. Pine must sell the product which Bean demands at the quoted price.
d. Bean has accepted Pine's firm offer to sell.

51. Which of the following statements is correct with regard to an auction of goods?

   a. The auctioneer may withdraw the goods at any time prior to completion of the sale unless the goods are put up without reserve.
   b. A bidder may retract his bid before the completion of the sale only if the auction is without reserve.
   c. A bidder's retraction of his bid will revive the prior bid if the sale is with reserve.
   d. In a sale with reserve, a bid made while the hammer is falling automatically reopens the bidding.

Repeat Question

(584,L1,13) Identical to item 34 above

Problems

Problem 1 Wrongful Interference with Contractual Relationship; Illegal Agreement (1183,L4)

(15 to 20 minutes)

Bar Manufacturing and Cole Enterprises were arch rivals in the high technology industry and both were feverishly working on a new product which would give the first to develop it a significant competitive advantage. Bar engaged Abel Consultants on April 1, 1983, for one year, commencing immediately, at $7,500 a month to aid the company in the development of the new product. The contract was oral and was consummated by a handshake. Cole approached Abel and offered them a $10,000 bonus for signing, $10,000 a month for nine months, and a $40,000 bonus if Cole was the first to successfully market the new product. In this connection, Cole stated that the oral contract Abel made with Bar was unenforceable and that Abel could walk away from it without liability. In addition, Cole made certain misrepresentations regarding the dollar amount of its commitment to the project, the stage of its development, and the expertise of its research staff. Abel accepted the offer.

Four months later, Bar successfully introduced the new product. Cole immediately dismissed Abel and has paid nothing beyond the first four $10,000 payments plus the initial bonus. Three lawsuits ensued: Bar sued Cole, Bar sued Abel, and Abel sued Cole.

Required:

Answer the following, setting forth reasons for any conclusions stated.

Discuss the various theories on which each of the three lawsuits is based, the defenses which will be asserted, the measure of possible recovery, and the probable outcome of the litigation.

Problem 2 Preexisting Contractual Duty; Elements of Fraud (582,L4)

(15 to 20 minutes)

Part a. Craig Manufacturing Company needed an additional supply of water for its plant. Consequently, Craig advertised for bids. Shaw Drilling Company submitted the lowest bid and was engaged to drill a well. After a contract had been executed and drilling begun, Shaw discovered that the consistency of the soil was much harder than had been previously encountered in the surrounding countryside. In addition, there was an unexpected layer of bedrock. These facts, unknown to both Craig and Shaw when the contract was signed, significantly increased the cost of performing the contract. Therefore, Shaw announced its intention to abandon performance unless it was assured of recovering its cost. Craig agreed in writing to pay the amount of additional cost if Shaw would continue to drill and complete the contract. Shaw, on the strength of this written promise, completed the job. The additional cost amounted to $10,000 which Shaw now seeks to recover. Craig refuses to pay and asserts that the additional burden was a part of the risk assumed and that the only reason it agreed to pay the additional amount was that it needed the additional water supply on time as agreed.

Shaw has commenced legal action to recover the $10,000 in dispute. Craig denies liability.

Required:

Answer the following, setting forth reasons for any conclusions stated.

1. What is the legal liability of Craig as a result of the facts described above?

2. Suppose the contract had been for the purchase of computer parts and the manufacturer had encountered a significant increase in labor cost which it wished to pass on to the purchaser. Would the purchaser's subsequent written promise to make an additional payment have been binding?

Part b. Ogilvie is a wealthy, prominent citizen of Clarion County. Most of his activities and his properties are located in Vista City, the county seat. Among his holdings are large tracts of farmland located in the outlying parts of Clarion. He has not personally examined large portions of his holdings due to the distance factor and the time it would take. One of his agents told him that 95% of the land was fertile and could be used for general farming. Farber, a recent college graduate who inherited a modest amount of money decided to invest in farmland and raise avacados. He had read certain advertising literature extolling the virtues of avocado farming as an investment. He called upon Ogilvie and discussed the purchase of his land. In the process, Ogilvie praised his land as a great investment for the future. He stated that the land was virtually all splendid farmland and that it would be suitable for avocado growing. Farber entered into a contract of purchase and made a deposit of 10% on the purchase price.

On the eve of the closing, Farber learned of the presence of extensive rock formations at or near the surface of the land. These rock formations make avocado growing virtually impossible but still permit limited use for some other types of farming. These rock formations are partially visible and could have been seen if Farber had examined the property. They cover approximately 25% of the land.

Accordingly, Farber refused to perform the original contract and demanded that the unsuitable 25% of the land be severed from the contract and the price diminished accordingly.

Ogilvie asserted that "a contract is a contract" and that the doctrine of caveat emptor is applicable in the sale of land. Specifically, he stated that he committed no fraud because:

1. Nothing he said was a statement of fact. It was opinion or puffing.
2. His statements were not material since most of the land is okay, and the balance can be used for some types of farming.
3. He had not lied since he had no knowledge of the falsity of his statements.
4. Farber could have and should have inspected and by failing to do so he was negligent and cannot recover.

Farber then commenced legal proceedings against Ogilvie based on fraud.

Required:

Answer the following, setting forth reasons for any conclusions stated.

In separate paragraphs, discuss the validity of each of Ogilvie's four assertions that he committed no fraud.

Problem 3 Substantial Performance; Effectiveness of Acceptance (580,L3a&b)

(15 to 20 minutes)

Part a. Smithers contracted with the Silverwater Construction Corporation to build a home. The contract contained a detailed set of specifications including the type, quality, and manufacturers' names of the building materials that were to be used. After construction was completed, a rigid inspection was made of the house and the following defects were discovered.

1. Some of the roofing shingles were improperly laid.

2. The ceramic tile in the kitchen and three bathrooms was not manufactured by Disco Tile Company as called for in the specifications. The price of the alternate tile was $325 less than the Disco but was of approximately equal quality.

3. The sewerage pipes that were imbedded in concrete in the basement were also not manufactured by the specified manufacturer. It could not be shown that there was any difference in quality and the price was the same.

4. Various minor defects such as improperly hung doors.

Silverwater has corrected defects 1 and 4 but has refused to correct defects 2 and 3 because the cost would be substantial. Silverwater claims it is entitled to recover under the contract and demands full payment. Smithers is adamant and is demanding literal performance of the contract or he will not pay.

Required:

Answer the following, setting forth reasons for any conclusions stated.

1. If the dispute goes to court, who will prevail, assuming Silverwater's breach of contract was intentional?

2. If the dispute goes to court, who will prevail, assuming Silverwater's breach of contract was unintentional?

Part b. Jane Anderson offered to sell Richard Heinz a ten acre tract of commercial property. Anderson's letter indicated the offer would expire on March 1, 1980, at 3:00 p.m. and that any acceptance must be received in her office by that time. On February 29, 1980, Heinz decided to accept the offer and posted an acceptance at 4:00 p.m. Heinz indicated that in the event the acceptance did not arrive on time, he would assume there was a contract if he did not hear anything from Anderson in five days. The letter arrived on March 2, 1980. Anderson never responded to Heinz's letter. Heinz claims a contract was entered into and is suing thereon.

Required:

Answer the following, setting forth reasons for any conclusions stated.

Is there a contract?

Multiple Choice Answers

1. b	12. c	22. d	32. a	42. d
2. c	13. c	23. d	33. a	43. a
3. b	14. b	24. d	34. d	44. b
4. d	15. b	25. b	35. c	45. c
5. b	16. c	26. d	36. c	46. c
6. c	17. a	27. c	37. d	47. c
7. b	18. d	28. c	38. b	48. d
8. d	19. b	29. a	39. c	49. c
9. d	20. a	30. d	40. d	50. b
10. a	21. d	31. b	41. c	51. a
11. c				

Multiple Choice Answer Explanations

A. Classification of Contracts

1. (583,L1,6) (b) In determining whether a contract has been created, the courts look primarily at the objective intent of the parties. The courts look to see what a reasonable person in the respective positions of each of the parties would be led to believe by the words and conduct of the other party, disregarding the parties' secret thoughts and subjective intent. Therefore, answers (c) and (d) are incorrect. Answer (a) is incorrect because while the courts do consider the fairness to the parties in examining a contract, this is not the primary factor in deciding whether a contract has been created.

B.1.a. Offer

2. (1183,L1,27) (c) The Grands' letter of intent does not constitute an offer. It lacks definiteness in that it does not specify which lot is to be purchased. Answer (a) is, therefore, incorrect. Since the letter does not qualify as an offer, there is no contract. A court would not enforce an agreement which is this vague. Answers (b) and (d) are, therefore, incorrect since both of those answers are premised on the assumption that a contract exists. Because there is no contract and because the Grands did not intend to make a gift to the corporation, they have the right to the return of the $100.

3. (1182,L1,2) (b) In determining whether a communication qualifies as an offer, the law uses an objective standard based on how a reasonably prudent businessman would have interpreted the communication. The subjective intent of Harris would be immaterial, as would Douglas' opinion, in deciding whether this letter constituted an offer. Therefore, answers (a) and (d) are incorrect. Answer (c) is incorrect because only the essential terms must be present in the communication, and even if some of these are missing, the needed terms can be added in later negotiations.

B.1.b. Termination of an Offer

4. (1183,L1,28) (d) When the option stated that it was given for $20 and the $20 was not paid and no other valuable consideration was present, the option is unenforceable because it lacks consideration. Under common law an option which creates an irrevocable offer is only present when the offeree gives consideration to keep the offer open for the stated time period. Therefore, answer (b) is incorrect. Answer (a) is incorrect because to enforce the option against Love, Nelson would only need a writing signed by Love, the party to be charged. Answer (c) is incorrect because the acceptance, if sent by reasonable means of communication, would be effective when sent not when received at Love's place of business. Consequently, an acceptance sent by Nelson on the ninth day that did not arrive until the twelfth day would be effective if sent by reasonable means.

5. (1183,L1,29) (b) A rejection is never effective until communicated to the offeror. Consequently, Baker's letter of rejection was not effective until received by West. Thus, Baker's acceptance by phone on October 26 creates a contract. Answer (a) is incorrect because the Uniform Commercial Code only applies to contracts for the sale of goods. This contract involves the sale of real property. A firm offer is only present when a merchant offeror makes a written offer concerning the sale of goods stating that the offer will not be withdrawn. Answer (c) is incorrect because the Statute of Frauds would demand a writing signed only by the party to be charged, not both parties. Even if the agreement did not comply with the Statute of Frauds, there would still be a contract although it would be an unenforceable agreement. Answer (d) is incorrect because the parol evidence rule only applies if the two parties intend the written agreement to be the complete final expression of their contract. Obviously, Baker's written statements were not intended as the final expression of the agreement. Also, the parol evidence rule would not exclude evidence that occurred subsequent to the writing.

6. (1182,L1,3) (c) The offeror may terminate an offer by communicating a revocation to the offeree before acceptance occurs unless the offer is an option or a firm offer. The offer is not an option because it is not supported by consideration from the offeree, Crane. Starbuck's offer is not a firm offer because it does not involve the sale of goods; consequently, the UCC does not apply. Therefore, when Starbuck communicated its revocation before Crane's acceptance, the offer was terminated. Thus, answers (b) and (d) are

incorrect. Answer (a) is incorrect because a revocation is effective when communicated orally, as well as in writing, to the offeree.

7. (1181,L1,1) (b) The offeree's opportunity to accept may be terminated by a lapse of time. If no time is stated in the offer, acceptance must be within a reasonable period of time given the surrounding facts, circumstances and subject matter of the contract. The barrels of heating oil are characterized by a rapidly fluctuating price market; therefore, a reasonable time for acceptance had elapsed and the offer had already expired. Answers (c) and (d) are incorrect because the U.C.C. states that unless otherwise indicated by the language or circumstances, an offer to make a contract shall be construed as inviting acceptance in any manner and by any medium reasonable in the circumstances.

B.1.c. Acceptance

8. (583,L1,8) (d) Acceptance of an offer for a unilateral contract can only occur by full performance of the act demanded, in exchange for the promise made by the offeror. Therefore, answer (a) is incorrect since a promise to perform the act does not constitute a valid acceptance of an offer for a unilateral contract. Answer (b) is incorrect because the preparation to perform the act is not a valid acceptance. Answer (c) is incorrect because the act must be completely performed in order for acceptance to occur in a unilateral contract.

9. (583,L1,9) (d) Harmon's telegram accepting the offer at $190,000 was a counteroffer that constituted a rejection of Luxor's original offer. However, a rejection is never effective until communicated to the offeror, and prior to Luxor receiving Harmon's telegram, Harmon telephoned an acceptance of the original terms. Therefore, the telephone acceptance was effective, resulting in a valid contract at $200,000. Consequently, answer (a) is incorrect. Answer (b) is incorrect because the sale of a real estate business does not constitute the sale of an interest in land, and therefore, does not need to be in writing under the section of the Statute of Frauds concerning real property. Answer (c) is incorrect because knowledge by the offeree that others were interested in the offer does not constitute a revocation of the offer. If Harmon had learned of the sale of the business to another party, this would have constituted a revocation of the offer.

10. (1182,L1,1) (a) Madison's acceptance was valid as soon as the letter left Madison's hands on the 6th since he used a reasonable means of communication to send the acceptance. Arthur could have stipulated a specific means of acceptance or required that the acceptance be received before becoming effective; but when this was not required, the acceptance was effective as soon as it was sent by a reasonable means. A revocation is never effective until communicated to the offeree. Consequently, Madison's acceptance was effective before Arthur's revocation was communicated on the 6th. Answer (b) is incorrect because Arthur's sale of the land would not revoke the offer until Madison learned of the sale. Answer (c) is incorrect because Arthur's offer was not an option, since it was not supported by consideration from Madison, nor was it a firm offer since sale of land is involved and the UCC would not apply.

11. (1181,L1,7) (c) An offeree cannot accept an offer unless the offeree knows of the existence of the offer; otherwise there is no objective meeting of the minds. Farber does not know of the increase of the monetary award to $500, and submitted his suggestion as an acceptance to the terms of the offer of which he knew, i.e., the $100. Even though Water Works later raised the amount and will use the suggestion in the later period, Farber only has a right to receive $100. Thus answers (a) and (b) are incorrect. Answer (d) is incorrect because Water Works' offer was not gratuitous; it was a manifestation of an intent to enter a contract. The offer was definite and certain and possessed the requisite essentials to make it operative; therefore, Water Works must perform its promise of remuneration for Farber's accepted and used suggestion.

12. (1181,L1,10) (c) Offers to contract may only be accepted by the person to whom they were made. Offers are not assignable to others unless the offeror consents to such assignment. Answer (a) is incorrect because this proposed contract falls within the provisions of the Statute of Frauds, since by its terms it is not capable of being performed within one year. Answer (b) is incorrect because an option is only created when the offeree gives something of value to keep the offer open for a stated period of time. Therefore, no option was created, and Marglow can revoke its offer any time prior to acceptance by Wilson. Answer (d) is incorrect because acceptance is effective when it leaves the hands of the offeree if sent by a reasonable means of communication. In this problem mail would be considered a proper means; therefore, a valid contract would be created.

13. (581,L1,13) (c) The acceptance of an offer must conform exactly to the terms of the offer. If a party intends to accept an offer, but includes additional or different terms which are intended to become part of the contract, this constitutes a counteroffer and not an acceptance (a possible exception to this exists with

contracts made between two merchants concerning the sale of goods). Norriss' additional term is a condition precedent and constitutes a counteroffer. Answer (a) is incorrect because a contract for the sale of real property must be in writing (under the Statute of Frauds) to be enforceable unless the doctrine of partial performance applies. Answer (b) is incorrect since a valid contract need only be signed by the party to be charged with performance. Answer (d) is untrue because the addition of a condition precedent has a significant effect on the contractual relationship since it prevents a contract from being formed unless Wilcox accepts the new term.

14. (1180,L1,14) (b) The correct answer is (b). In an auction, the offer is accepted when the hammer goes down and the bidder can retract his bid until this time. The law presumes the sale is with reserve unless the owner announces the auction is without reserve, making answer (a) incorrect. Answer (d) is incorrect because an auction without reserve implies that the owner must sell to the highest bidder. Answer (d) describes an auction with reserve. Answer (c) is incorrect since the retraction of a bid does not revive the previous bid.

15. (1179,L1,9) (b) An offer which is ambiguous as to whether or not the offeror is bargaining for shipment of merchandise or the promise to ship can be accepted by the offeree doing either. Thus, the prompt shipment of the merchandise by Queen constitutes an acceptance and also passes the risk of loss (or delay as here) to the buyer, Lally. Answer (a) is incorrect because the statute of frauds has been satisfied by the telegram and by the fact that due to ambiguity the nature of the contract is unilateral requiring only that Queen ship the goods. Answer (c) is incorrect because Lally's revocation was not effective because it was received after acceptance. The absence of a notice of acceptance was a risk that Lally assumed in making a unilateral offer. Answer (d) is incorrect because Lally's order was an offer to enter into a unilateral contract since a reasonable reading of Lally's telegram was that they were bargaining for the act of immediate shipment and not a promise to ship.

B.2. Consideration

16. (583,L1,7) (c) Past consideration is not valid consideration. Past consideration is present when something done in the past is given for a present promise. This type of consideration lacks the bargained for element. Thus, if Clark had performed the act prior to Dougal's promise to pay, Dougal's promise was made in exchange for past consideration and Dougal will prevail. Answer (a) is incorrect because the fact that a contract is executory does not allow a party to avoid performance of the agreement; an executory contract is still a binding agreement. Answer (b) is incorrect because the value of the consideration is not considered by the court in determining whether the agreement has sufficient consideration. The court looks merely for the presence of consideration and not for its adequacy. Answer (d) is incorrect because the relinquishment of a legal right is sufficient to act as consideration. Consideration is legally sufficient if it is either a legal benefit to the promisor or a legal detriment to the promisee. The promisee suffers a legal detriment if s/he promises to refrain from doing something s/he has a legal right to do.

17. (579,L1,9) (a) As part of the original contract Radiant agreed to service the heating system purchased by Williams for a flat rate of $200 per year. Thus, Radiant was under a pre-existing legal duty to perform the maintenance work and any subsequent promise to pay for such services is without consideration and unenforceable. Answer (b) is incorrect because the Statute of Frauds is not applicable to this problem. The dispute is over a service arrangement and not the sale of goods. Answer (c) is incorrect because the offer to pay the additional amount makes no difference with respect to the requirement of consideration. Answer (d) is incorrect because an uneconomical contract does not free a party from a contract unless significant unforeseen difficulties are encountered.

18. (575,L1,7) (d) In the absence of a controlling statute Jason is not bound by the writing because he received no consideration to support it. Martinson did not have the legal right to breach, and thus refraining from the breach is not legal forbearance. Neither is the promise to remain and pay the reduced rent for the fifth year consideration, because this was an obligation of the original contract and is therefore a pre-existing duty. A change in economic conditions is not an excuse for non-performance nor for a rent reduction.

B.4. Legality

19. (583,L1,10) (b) The contract between Fairbanks and Nickle Corporation violates public policy and, therefore, is an illegal agreement. The courts will not aid either party to the illegal agreement unless one party is less to blame than the other, or the agreement has not been performed and the party seeking recovery repents. Neither of these exceptions is present, consequently the court will deny relief to either party. Thus,

answers (a) and (c) are incorrect. Answer (d) is incorrect because the courts allow no recovery under the quantum meruit theory (quasi-contract) concerning illegal agreements.

B.5. Conformity with the Statute of Frauds

20. (583,L1,11) (a) Even though a contract for the sale of goods for greater than, or equal to, $500 must be in writing under the Statute of Frauds; a contract which is oral, but has been acknowledged in court by the defendant, is legally binding to the extent of the admission. Thus, since Glass admitted in court the contract with Hourly, this agreement will be enforced in its entirety. Answer (b) is incorrect because the shipment of 1,000 watches would not cause the contract to be enforceable in its entirety, but merely to the extent that goods have been delivered and accepted, in this case to the extent of the 1,000 watches. Answer (c) is incorrect since a down payment will only cause the contract to be enforceable to the extent of the payment made and accepted by Hourly, and not in the contract's entirety. Answer (d) is incorrect because the amount of the contract is $4,000, and any contract involving the sale of goods for $500 or more is within the requirements of the Statute of Frauds.

21. (583,L1,12) (d) The Statute of Frauds may result in a contract being enforceable by only one party. A writing sufficient to satisfy the Statute of Frauds need only be signed by the party to be charged (the defendant) and not by both parties to the agreement. Therefore, if a written contract is signed by one party, it complies with the Statute, but is only enforcable against the party that signed the agreement. Answer (a) is incorrect because the Statute stipulates what agreements must be in writing and does not codify common law fraud. Answer (b) is incorrect because formal contracts are those for which the law, not the Statute of Frauds, requires a particular set of formalities, such as negotiable instruments. Answer (c) is incorrect because the parties to a contract cannot waive the application of the Statute of Frauds to the agreement.

22. (583,L1,13) (d) Contracts involving the sale of goods for less than $500 fall outside the Statute of Frauds. Answer (a) is incorrect because it constitutes the promise to pay the debt of another, which falls within the Statute of Frauds. Answer (b) is incorrect because, although a lease is not considered to be the sale of an interest in real property, a ten-year lease is within the Statute of Frauds because it is not capable of being performed within one year. Answer (c) is incorrect because although the duration of the services to be performed under the contract will only be nine months, when determining whether a contract is capable of being performed within one year, the time period starts the day the contract was formed. Therefore, this agreement falls within the Statute of Frauds because it cannot be performed within one year from January 1. It will not be completed until May 31 of the following year.

23. (1179,L1,8) (d) The purchase order which recited the oral agreement of the prior day is known under the UCC as a confirmation. For UCC cases, written confirmations satisfy the provision of the statute of frauds. The stamped name, title, and initials of the agent at the bottom of the purchase order would constitute a sufficient "signature" and therefore would indicate that Major Corporation's agent intended to authenticate the document. Answer (a) is incorrect because the statute of frauds does apply to this transaction since it involves the sale of goods in excess of $500. Answer (b) is incorrect because the purchasing agent's authority to make this particular contract need not be in writing but may be considered to be implied or apparent from his position. In general, there is no requirement that the authority of agents be in writing. Answer (c) is incorrect because the statute of frauds is satisfied if the party against whom the action is brought has signed. Thus, the absence of a signature by A & C is of no importance in so far as enforcement against Major is concerned. In any event, a confirmation which is binding on the sender is also binding on the receiver unless objected to by the receiver. Hence the confirmation satisfies the statute of frauds for both parties.

24. (1176,L1,5) (d) The general rule is an agreement for the sale of goods for $500 or more is required to be in writing. Fungible goods actively traded by merchants comes within this rule as would other goods. A contract for specially manufactured goods not suitable for sale in the ordinary course of the seller's business is an exception to the general rule if the seller has made a substantial start in their manufacture. No special form is required for the writing except that it must be signed by the party sought to be charged and quantity is the one term that cannot be left out under the UCC. As a practical matter, the other important terms, e.g., price, should be included. Another exception to the statute of frauds is if the party asserting the statute admits the contract in court.

B.5.e. Parol Evidence Rule

25. (583,L1,16) (b) The parol evidence rule states that once an agreement is reduced to a writing intended as the complete contract, the parties may not introduce oral or written evidence in an attempt to alter or contradict the terms of the agreement. Thus, Elrod would not be able to introduce the evidence if the contract indicates that it was intended as the entire contract, and the disputed point is covered in detail in the agreement. Answer (a) is incorrect because the parol evidence rule applies only to evidence arising prior to the formation of the written contract; evidence which arises after the formation of the contract is admissable. Answer (c) is incorrect since the parol evidence rule does not bar from admission any evidence which will prove that a contract is invalid. Therefore, evidence in support of the contention that a mutual mistake is present would be admissable. Answer (d) is incorrect because the parol evidence rule does not bar evidence which will clarify an ambiguous point in the written contract.

26. (583,L1,41) (d) The parol evidence rule does apply to prior written or oral modifications of a written agreement. It also applies to contemporaneous oral or written modifications. Answer (a) is incorrect because the parol evidence rule does not apply exclusively to contracts for the sale of goods, but can be applied to all written contracts intended as the final and complete expression of the agreement. Answer (b) is incorrect because the parol evidence rule does not apply to subsequent modifications of a written contract. Such modifications are admissible in court to alter the written agreement. Answer (c) is incorrect because the parol evidence rule does not only apply to prior or contemporaneous oral modifications, but also applies to prior or contemporaneous written modifications as well.

C. Reality of Consent

27. (583,L1,14) (c) When a contract contains a unilateral mistake which the other party knew of, or had reason to know of, the party making the mistake can avoid the contract. Thus, answer (a) is incorrect. Answer (b) is incorrect because negligence while a criterion is not the only criteria for deciding whether a mistake will cause the agreement to be voidable. The additional criteria which must be present is whether or not the other party had knowledge of, or reason to know of, the mistake. Answer (d) is incorrect because the issue of what party transcribed the contract is not relevant when deciding whether a mistake is present that will create a voidable agreement.

28. (583,L1,15) (c) Undue influence occurs when a party entering into a contract is so greatly influenced by the second party because of their relationship with that party, that the party does not exercise free will in entering into the contract. In this case, Smith was unduly influenced by Jones because of their close personal relationship. Even though Smith, as an executive, is only an agent of Apex, it is as if the undue influence were exerted over Apex, the principal. Thus, Apex will be able to avoid the contract. Answer (a) is incorrect because even if express authority to enter into the contract had not been given to Smith, as an executive he would have either implied or apparent authority to do so, and accordingly, Apex would be bound to the contract. Answer (b) is incorrect because duress does not apply to the situation in which one party influences another by using the relationship existing between the two parties. Duress involves the use of a threat to overcome a party's free will and force the individual into a contract. Answer (d) is incorrect because there is no indication that a lack of consideration is present. Even though the contract is grossly unfair to Apex, the court is not primarily concerned with the adequacy of consideration. However, the fact that the contract was grossly unfair to Apex will help prove undue influence is present.

29. (1182,L1,9) (a) In order to establish a common law action for fraud, the plaintiff must prove either the defendant knew the falsity of his statements or the false statements were made with a reckless disregard for the truth. Answer (b) is incorrect because the Statute of Frauds stipulates what contracts must be in writing to be enforceable and has no relevance in establishing an action for fraud. Answer (c) is incorrect because an oral misrepresentation of fact, as well as a written misrepresentation, can be the basis of fraud. Answer (d) is incorrect because in order to establish fraud there must be proof of justifiable reliance upon the misrepresentation by the plaintiff.

30. (582,L1,14) (d) Duress is the threat of harm to a party or to a member of the party's family, which deprives the party of free will and causes him to enter into a contract. Duress is present when one party uses the threat of criminal prosecution to force the second party to enter into an agreement. Dickenson's threat to prosecute Paul for arson would create a voidable contract at Paul's option due to duress. Consequently, answer (d) is correct while answers (a), (b), and (c) are incorrect.

C.2. Innocent Misrepresentation

31. (1182,L1,10) (b) An innocent misrepresentation is a misstatement of fact made with an honest and justifiable belief (in good faith), without intent to defraud (scienter). Therefore, a plaintiff is not required to prove that the misrepresentation amounted to gross negligence to prevail in an action for innocent misrepresentation. Answer (a) is incorrect because the misrepresentation, although innocent, must have been a substantial factor in inducing the plantiff to enter into the contract. Answer (c) is incorrect because in an action for innocent misrepresentation, any benefits received by the parties must be returned in order to restore each party to his/her precontractual position. Answer (d) is incorrect because the plaintiff must show that there was justifiable reliance upon a representation made with an intent to be relied upon.

D. Assignment and Delegation

32. (583,L1,18) (a) A contract right cannot be assigned if the assignment materially varies the obligor's promise. It would be unjust to enforce a contract against an obligor who, after agreeing to the terms of one contract, becomes subject to materially different terms merely because the other party assigned the rights to the contract. The obligor never really assented to the terms of the contract as changed by the assignment, thus the contract as assigned would be unenforceable against the obligor. Answer (b) is incorrect because the assignment of rights to a contract need not be supported by consideration. An assignment can be made with the intent of conferring a gift upon the assignee. Answer (c) is incorrect because an assignee generally steps into the shoes of the assignor and will have no better rights than the assignor had in the contract. Answer (d) is incorrect because knowledge by the obligor need not be present for a valid assignment to occur. However, if an obligor has no knowledge of the assignment, he can perform the contract by rendering performance to the assignor without suffering any liability to the assignee. In any case, the assignee will always have rights against the assignor provided that the assignment was valid and was not gratuitous in nature, in which case the assignment may be revoked.

33. (1182,L1,13) (a) Assignee takes the assignment subject to not only defenses or counterclaims which existed between the original parties at the time of the assignment, but also subject to additional defenses and counterclaims that arise subsequent to the assignment but before the obligor has knowledge of such assignment. Therefore, since Walton acquired the $2,000 claim against Grant prior to having notice of the assignment (from Grant to Line), Walton has the right to assert this counterclaim as a set-off against Line. Answer (b) is incorrect because since Walton's claim arose before he had knowledge of the assignment he acquires the right to set-off. If the counterclaim arose after notice of the assignment, then Walton must pay Line in full, but would have the right to obtain a $2,000 reimbursement from Grant. Answer (c) is incorrect because a third party beneficiary contract is an agreement whereby the two contracting parties intend to benefit a third party. Line is not a creditor beneficiary, since at the time of contracting, Walton and Grant did not intend to benefit Line. Walton's debt to Line arose out of the assignment by Grant. Answer (d) is incorrect because the fact that the set-off amount of $2,000 is less than the assigned principal debt does not make the set-off claim invalid.

34. (1182,L1,14) (d) A novation substitutes a new party and discharges one of the original parties to the contract. Consequently, a new contract is created with the same terms as the original one, wherein only the parties are changed. Therefore, Conrad can avoid liability on the contract if he has been discharged by a novation. Answer (a) is incorrect because the fact that the third party has agreed to hold Conrad harmless does not discharge Conrad from his contractual liability to Fuld, in the event that the third party does not perform. Answer (b) is incorrect because even though Conrad assigned the entire contract, he still remains liable for any default in the performance of his original contractual duties. Answer (c) is incorrect because since the accord is unexecuted (executory), the new substituted rights and duties have not yet come into being, and Conrad's liability under the old contract still exists.

35. (1181,L1,5) (c) An assignment of a contract is taken to mean both assignment of the rights and delegation of the duties. There can be a delegation without the other party's consent as long as a special skill is not needed to perform the duty or a materially different performance would result. McLeod can delegate his duty to Conerly, if qualified, since no special skill, other than following a set of blueprints, is involved. This assignment extinguishes McLeod's rights, but the delegation does not eliminate McLeod's obligation under the contract, unless there is a novation. Thus answers (b) and (d) are incorrect. Answer (a) is incorrect because a delegation of duties is not an anticipatory breach.

36. (1181,L1,6) (c) A novation substitutes a new party and discharges one of the original parties to the contract. Consequently a new contract is created with the same terms as the original one wherein only

the parties are changed. In order to constitute a novation, there must be an agreement on the part of the creditor to substitute the new debtor in place of the original debtor and an agreement to release and discharge the original debtor. Therefore, this transaction constitutes a novation with Thompson being substituted for Monroe and a new contract being created. Answer (a) is incorrect because under an assignment and delegation, Monroe would still be liable under the mortgage contract. But in this case, Monroe is released and discharged of his obligation. Answer (b) is incorrect because a third party beneficiary contract is created when the two parties enter a contract that benefits a third person who is not a party to the agreement. But in this case, Thompson is a party to the contract with Acme. Answer (d) is incorrect because the novation releases Monroe from liability on the mortgage, making Thompson the party liable for payment of the obligation. Whereas, if this had been a purchase subject to the mortgage, Monroe, not Thompson, would have personal liability on the mortgage.

E. Third-Party Beneficiary Contracts

37. (583,L1,17) (d) In the third party donee beneficiary contract, the donee beneficiary can assert rights to the contract if the beneficiary can prove that the terms of the contract and surrounding circumstances manifest a clear intent to benefit her. The donee beneficiary need not prove that the contract specifically named her as the beneficiary. Thus, answer (a) is incorrect. Answer (b) is incorrect because a donee beneficiary does not have to establish that she gave consideration for the benefit conferred in the agreement. The nature of a third party donee beneficiary contract is such that a gift is being conferred on the donee beneficiary, with no consideration being given in exchange. Answer (c) is incorrect because a donee beneficiary need not prove that they are related to the promisee by blood or marriage. This has no relevance in deciding whether a third party donee beneficiary can enforce the contract.

38. (1182,L1,12) (b) Wilson intended to discharge his debt owed to Security by the agreement he entered into with Glenn. Since Wilson and Glenn obviously intended Security to benefit from their agreement, Security is a creditor beneficiary with the right to recover against Glenn personally in the event of a default. Answer (a) is incorrect because the Statute of Frauds would apply since the agreement involves the sale of an interest in land and also because Glenn's promise would constitute a promise to answer for the debt of another. Consequently, Glenn's promise must be in writing. Answer (c) is incorrect because an incidental beneficiary is a third party whom the contract was not intended to benefit. Wilson and Glenn did intend to benefit Security; therefore, Security is not an incidental beneficiary. Answer (d) is incorrect because the fact the buyer assumes personal liability on the mortgage does not release the seller, the original mortgagor. An assumption of the mortgage creates a surety relationship, with the buyer being the principal debtor and the seller acting as the surety. Wilson's liability is terminated only when Security, the mortgagee, specifically releases Wilson.

F. Discharge of Contracts

39. (1183,L1,30) (c) When Parker anticipatorily repudiated a contract, Stone could immediately sue for breach of contract or wait for performance on the appointed date, and then sue for breach if performance was not rendered. Answer (a) is incorrect because specific performance is not available as a remedy for breach of personal service contract. It would violate the constitutional amendment prohibiting involuntary servitude. Answer (b) is incorrect because it is not illegal to assign your damages under a contract to a third party. However, it is illegal when one party pays another's costs and expenses in bringing a case to court with the understanding that if the case is successful, the party putting up the money will share in the proceeds (champerty). Answer (d) is incorrect because the oral agreement is enforceable since the agreement is capable of being performed within one year.

40. (583,L1,19) (d) Under the doctrine of substantial performance, a contract obligation may be discharged even though the performance tendered was not in complete conformity with the terms of the agreement. Under this doctrine, if it can be shown that the defect in performance was only minor in nature, that a good faith effort was made to conform completely with the terms of the agreement, and if the performing party is willing to accept a decrease in compensation equivalent to the amount of the minor defect in performance, the contractual obligation will be discharged. Since Kent did not make a good faith effort to conform to the terms of the agreement, but in fact intentionally breached it, their obligation will not be discharged and they will lose all rights under the contract. Therefore, answers (a) and (b) are incorrect. Answer (c) is incorrect because the law does not demand literal performance of contracts, but will allow the discharge of an obligation to a contract when it has been substantially performed as described above under the doctrine of substantial performance.

41. (581,L1,7) (c) At the time the contract was made, the debt was liquidated since the amount was certain ($500). However, the bona fide dispute changed the debt to an unliquidated debt. Payment of a lesser sum to discharge an unliquidated debt will be effective if accepted as payment in full since each party gives consideration in the form of forfeiting a claim to dispute the amount of the debt. Smith's cashing of the check was acceptance of a settlement for the full amount of the debt. Answers (a) and (b) are incorrect since they refer to liquidated debts and this debt is unliquidated. Answer (d) is incorrect since the fact that Smith crossed out the words "paid in full" has no effect. The check must be accepted in the manner offered and Smith's cashing of the check discharges the entire unliquidated debt.

42. (580,L1,29) (d) The agreement involved is a requirements contract; thus Marblehead's ordering of unreasonably disproportionate amounts of oil would be a breach by them. A requirements contract is considered definite and both parties are viewed as having provided consideration, thus answers (a), (b), and (c) are incorrect.

43. (578,L1,22) (a) The trucking company was engaged to redeliver the pump promptly upon completion of the repair. The delay in returning the pump was a breach of contract. The $200/day pump rental is Johnson Corporation's actual damages which are recoverable. Answer (b) is incorrect because the lost profits are not recoverable. The lost profits were not foreseeable, i.e., the trucking company did not know the special circumstances of Johnson's plant. Answer (c) is incorrect because punitive damages are not normally allowed for breach of contract. Answer (d) is incorrect because in any breach of contract, the nonbreaching party is liable for a minimum of nominal damages.

H. Remedies

44. (583,L1,20) (b) The court will grant specific performance of a contract as a remedy if money damages will not be adequate to compensate the nonbreaching party. Since the coin is rare (unique) and cannot be readily purchased in the market, the court will grant specific performance to Myers. Thus, answer (a) is incorrect. Answer (c) is incorrect because reformation applies to written contracts containing ambiguities and would not be an appropriate remedy in this fact situation. Answer (d) is also incorrect because restitution involves both parties to a contract returning whatever they have received under the agreement. In this question, neither party rendered any performance, therefore restitution would be an inappropriate remedy.

45. (1180,L1,13) (c) A liquidated damage provision is a contractual provision which states the amount of damages that will occur if either party breaches the contract. If the amount is reasonable in light of the anticipated or actual harm caused by the breach, it is enforceable. Answer (c) is correct. Answer (a) is incorrect because the fact that the preparer of the contract is a merchant has no bearing on the use of a liquidated damage clause. Answer (b) is incorrect because retaining a large deposit could be considered unconscionable and unenforceable. The reasonableness of a liquidated damage clause is judged in light of anticipated harm, not by a set percentage by which the liquidated damages exceed the actual damages.

I. Statute of Limitations

46. (1181,L1,2) (c) The statute of limitations prescribes the time period in which a plaintiff must initiate the lawsuit, declaring that no suit shall be maintained on such causes of action unless brought within a specified period of time after the right accrued. The statute constitutes a defense to recovery once the requisite period of time has lapsed. Answer (a) is incorrect because there is no standard prescribed period of time for all cases. The time period fluctuates according to type of case involved (i.e., contracts, tort). Answer (b) is incorrect because the statute of limitations is equally applicable to actions brought in courts of equity as in courts of law. Answer (d) is incorrect because the running of the statutory period may be stopped if the defendent becomes absent from the court's jurisdiction during the period, effectively making it impossible for the plaintiff to institute a lawsuit.

May 1984 Answers

47. (584,L1,11) (c) The agreement to steal trade secrets is illegal and, therefore, unenforceable. Because both parties are guilty (pari delicto), the courts will not aid either Mix or Small in recovering the consideration exchanged. Consequently, Small will not be permitted to recover the $10,000 under any theory. Answers (a), (b), and (d) are, therefore, incorrect.

48. (584,L1,12) (d) Because both parties were unaware of the fact that the car had been stolen, Pam and Jack entered the contract under a mutual mistake of a material fact. Consequently, the contract is voidable at the option of either party. Answer (a) is incorrect because the Statute of Frauds under the UCC re-

quires written evidence of the contract only for the sale of goods for $500 or more. Answer (b) is incorrect because under the UCC, absent any breach, the risk of loss passes from a nonmerchant seller to the buyer on tender of delivery. Answer (c) is incorrect because there is no evidence to support the theory that Jack has a superior bargaining position or has otherwise taken unfair advantage of Pam.

49. (584,L1,14) (c) At common law, which applies to the sale of real property, the modification of an existing contract must be supported by consideration. Under the UCC, however, a contract for the sale of goods may be modified either orally or in writing without consideration. Furthermore, a merchant's firm offer under the UCC does not require consideration. Accordingly, answers (a) and (d) are incorrect. A contract entered into by a minor is voidable by that minor. The minor may ratify the contract within a reasonable time after reaching the age of majority, and no consideration is required to support such a ratification. Answer (b) is, therefore, incorrect.

50. (584,L1,15) (b) A published circular quoting prices is merely an invitation to submit an offer and is not an offer in itself. Consequently, Pine has not made an offer, firm or otherwise, but only initiated preliminary negotiations. Answers (a) and (d) are, therefore, incorrect. Answer (c) is incorrect because Pine will not be bound until it accepts Bean's offer.

51. (584,L1,50) (a) In an auction with reserve, the auctioneer may withdraw the goods at any time until he announces completion of the sale. If the auction is without reserve, the article cannot be withdrawn once the auctioneer calls for bids unless no bid is made within a reasonable time. Under the UCC, unless otherwise specified, auctions are presumed to be held with reserve. Answer (d) is incorrect because when a bid is made at the moment the hammer is falling, the auctioneer may, at his discretion, either reopen the bidding or close the sale on the bid on which the hammer was falling. Regardless of whether the auction is with or without reserve, a bidder may retract his bid until the auctioneer announces completion of the sale. A bidder's retraction does not revive any previous bid. Accordingly, answers (b) and (c) are incorrect.

Answer Outline

Problem 1 Wrongful Interference with Contractual Relationship; Illegal Agreement

Bar will prevail against Cole
  Cole knowingly interfered with a valid contractual relationship which constitutes intentional tort of wrongful interference with a contractual relationship
Bar could recover actual damages suffered, i.e., consulting fees incurred in excess of Abel's
  Since Cole committed intentional tort, recovery of punitive damages possible
Bar should prevail against Abel for breach of contract
  However, if Bar collects actual damages from Cole, he cannot collect from Abel also
  Punitive damages are rarely available in contract action
Abel's lawsuit against Cole would be based on fraud and breach of contract
  However, contract between Abel and Cole was illegal contract—requiring Abel to commit a tort
  Thus, Abel will be denied recovery since both Abel and Cole are considered wrongdoers

Unofficial Answer

Problem 1 Wrongful Interference with Contractual Relationship; Illegal Agreement

Bar's lawsuit against Cole will be based upon the intentional tort of wrongful interference with a contractual relationship. The primary requirements for this cause of action are a valid contractual relationship with which the defendant knowingly interferes. This requirement is met in the case of Cole. The contract is not required to be in writing since it is for exactly a year from the time of the making thereof and is therefore valid even though oral. Cole's knowledge of the contract is obvious. The principal problem, however, is damages. Since Bar was the first to successfully market the product, it would appear that damages are not present. It is possible there were actual damages incurred by Bar, e.g., it hired another consulting firm at an increased price. It also might be possible that some courts would permit the recovery of punitive damages since this is an intentional tort.

Bar's cause of action against Abel would be for breach of contract. Once again, damages would appear to be a serious problem. Furthermore, punitive damages would rarely be available in a contract action. Finally, Bar cannot recover the same damages twice. Hence, if it proceeds against Cole and recovers damages caused by Abel's breach of contract, it will not be able to recover a second time.

Abel's lawsuit against Cole will be based upon fraud and breach of contract. There were fraudulent statements made by Cole with the requisite intent and possibly to Abel's detriment. The breach of contract by Cole is obvious. However, the contract which Cole induced Abel to enter into and which it subsequently breached was an illegal contract, i.e., one calling for the commission of a tort. Therefore, both parties are likely to be treated as wrongdoers and Abel will be denied recovery.

Answer Outline

Problem 2 Preexisting Contractual Duty; Elements of Fraud

Part a.

1. Modification of preexisting contract under common law
    Normally, if no new consideration
      Modification is not binding
    Shaw gave no additional consideration
      Because he has preexisting legal duty
  Some courts recognize exception concerning construction contracts
    Where one party encounters unforeseen substantial difficulty not in the parties' contemplation at time of contracting
2. Modification of preexisting contract for sale of goods
    Apply the Uniform Commercial Code
    No new consideration needed to make modification binding
    Complies with Statute of Frauds
    Modification in writing
      Signed by party charged

Part b.

Fraud in the inducement
Statement of fact vs. opinion
  Ogilvie engaged in a statement of fact concerning suitability of land for avocado growing
Materiality of misrepresentation was significant
  Reason Farber purchased the land
Ogilvie made the representations negligently
  With reckless disregard for the truth
  Negligent as well as intentional misrepresentation
    Qualifies as proper basis for fraud in the inducement

Justifiable reliance will not demand inspection of this property
  Considering seller's inability to engage in such inspection
    Due to vast holdings, distance factor, and time needed

Unofficial Answer

(Author Modified)

Problem 2 Preexisting Contractual Duty; Elements of Fraud

Part a.

1. The described fact situation deals with the sale of services, not the sale of goods. Consequently, the common law, not the Uniform Commercial Code applies. The general rule under common law is that a modification of an existing contract needs new consideration before it is binding. Shaw gave no additional consideration for Craig's promise to bear the additional cost. Thus, normally Craig would not be liable for the additional $10,000 because Shaw is merely promising to complete the well in the modification which he was already obligated to do under the original contract (i.e. a preexisting legal duty).

However, recently, several courts have recognized an exception to this rule, with regard to construction contracts, even under common law. The exception relates to the situation where one party upon beginning performance discovers a substantial difficulty which is unforseen and not in the contemplation of the parties at the time of contracting. If this situation is present, these courts allow enforcement of the modification even though there is no new consideration. This exception would apply in the given fact situation, since Shaw Drilling Company discovered a substantially harder soil consistency than was expected and initially contemplated by both Shaw and Craig at the time of contracting. Therefore, Craig's promise to pay the additional money to Shaw falls within the exception and would be enforceable in courts that recognize this exception, thusly resulting in Craig's liability for the additional cost of $10,000.

2. Yes. If the purchase of computer parts were involved in the agreement, it would constitute a contract for the sale of goods. Instead of applying common law, as we did in the above question, the Uniform Commercial Code would now govern. Under the Uniform Commercial Code, a modification of a pre-existing contract for the sale of goods does not require new consideration to be binding. Thus, even though the manufacturer is merely promising to perform what it was already obligated to do under the original contract, the modification would be binding.

Another issue would be whether the Statute of Frauds applies to the modification. It appears the modification would involve the sale of goods for $500 or more. Consequently, the Statute of Frauds would require the modification to be in writing. Since the question states the purchaser engaged in a subsequent written promise, this would satisfy the Statute of Frauds requirement, in that the writing is signed by the party to be charged (the purchaser).

Part b.

Ogilvie's first assertion is invalid. Since Ogilvie is the seller of real property, many of his statements could be construed to be opinion and "puffing" in an attempt to promote the sale of his land. But Ogilvie did engage in a statement of fact when he stated that the land was suitable for avocado growing. This is a representation which is definite, objective and verifiable. Since the land was not suitable for avocado growing, Ogilvie's statement was false. Therefore, the first requirement for establishing fraud, a misstatement of fact, has been met.

Ogilvie's second assertion that his statements were not material is also invalid. In determining the materiality of a representation, courts look to the impression made upon the mind of the party to whom it was made. The representation must relate to something of sufficient substance to induce reliance. Since Farber purchased the land for the exclusive use of growing avocados, Ogilvie's representation that the land was suitable for avocado growing was material in nature.

Ogilvie's third assertion that he had not lied is invalid. Ogilvie had not personally examined the farmland in question, so he apparently had little basis for making the representations he made. But this lack of knowledge of the facts does not excuse Ogilvie. A party has imputed knowlege (thereby satisfying the knowledge requirement necessary to establish fraud) if s/he makes the representations negligently, with a reckless disregard and indifference as to their truthfulness. Many courts have imputed such knowledge to a party, such as Ogilvie, and have held him responsible where the means of his knowledge was such as to make it his duty to know the truth or falsity of his representations. Ogilvie who represents something as being true based on his own knowledge, but who is in fact completely ignorant of the subject, is treated in the law as knowingly making a false statement, thereby satisfying the scienter (knowledge) requirement of establishing fraud.

The final assertion deals with the reliance requirement necessary to establish fraud. Ogilvie asserts that Farber cannot justifiably rely on Ogilvie's representations since if Farber would have inspected the land he would have discovered the rock formations. Normally, where the accuracy of the seller's statements can be verified, and it would be feasible to do so, justifiable reliance requires such verification. But in this fact situation, the seller was unable to personally examine the land due to the distance factor and the time it would take. Therefore, the buyer can not be expected to do something which the seller did not do. To allow Ogilvie's assertion to be a valid defense would result in the promotion of engaging in fraud, because a person who makes a misrepresentation with intent to induce action could simply state that the buyer should have looked for himself/herself.

Answer Outline

Problem 3 Substantial Performance; Effectiveness of Acceptance

a. Result if dispute goes to court
   Common-law requires literal performance; anything less is a breach releasing either party from duty to perform
   Courts have developed doctrine of substantial performance as an exception concerning construction contracts
   If breach is immaterial; party who breached may recover, less damages. Party who breached must prove
   1. Defect was not structural in nature
   2. Breach was minor relative to total job (95% is a guide courts use)
   3. Breach was not intentional

   Elements 1 and 2 appear to be met in this case
   Satisfaction of element 3 is not determinable from facts given
      Would be met if substitutions were due to mistake or mere negligence, and Silverwater would prevail
      If substitution was willful, no recovery by Silverwater

b. No contract for sale of real property
   Offer is governed by common law of contracts
   Offer stipulations stated that acceptance must be received before effective
      Negated possibility of acceptance being effective even though sent by same means
   Purported acceptance was counteroffer
      Had to be accepted to create contract
   Silence does not constitute acceptance unless
   1. Parties intended silence as acceptance
   2. Prior dealing indicates silence is acceptable
   3. Custom of industry recognizes silence as acceptance

   Above exceptions do not apply, and there is no contract

Unofficial Answer

Problem 3 Substantial Performance; Effectiveness of Acceptance

Parts a1. and a2.

The general common-law rules require literal performance by a party to a contract. Failure to literally perform constitutes a breach. Since promises are construed to be dependent upon each other, the failure by one party to perform releases the other. However, a strict and literal application of this type of implied condition often results in unfairness and hardship, particularly in cases such as this. Therefore, the courts developed some important exceptions to the literal performance doctrine. The applicable rule is known as the substantial performance doctrine, which applies to construction contracts and is a more specific statement of the material performance rule that applies to contracts other than construction contracts. The general rule holds that if the breach is immaterial, the party who breached may nevertheless recover under the contract, less damages caused by the breach. The substantial performance doctrine requires the builder (party breaching) to prove the following facts.

a. The defect was not a structural defect.
b. The breach was relatively minor in relation to the overall performance of the contract. The courts and texts sometimes talk in terms of a 95 percent or better performance.
c. The breach must be unintentional or, to state it another way, the party breaching must have been acting in good faith.

It would appear that requirements a and b are clearly satisfied on the basis of the facts. Requirement c cannot be determined on the facts given. If Silverwater deliberately (with knowledge) substituted the improper and cheaper tile or sewerage pipes, then it may not be entitled to the benefit of the substantial performance exception. On the other hand, if these breaches were the result of an innocent oversight or mere negligence on its part, recovery should be granted. The recovery must be decreased by the amount of the damages caused by the breach. The substitute of sewer pipe of like quality and value would be considered substantial performance.

Part b.

No. The offer for the sale of real property is governed by the common law of contracts.

Anderson's letter constituted an offer that stated it would expire at a given time. In addition to stating the time, the letter indicated that acceptance "must be received in her (Anderson's) office" by said time. This language is clear and unambiguous and effectively negated the rule whereby acceptance may take place upon dispatch. Thus, despite use of the same means of communication, acceptance was not effective until receipt by Anderson on March 2, 1980. This was too late. Thus, the purported acceptance was a mere counteroffer by Heinz and had to be accepted in order to create a contract. Silence does not usually constitute acceptance. In fact, the common-law exceptions to this rule are limited in nature and narrowly construed. The law clearly will not permit a party to unilaterally impose silence upon the other as acceptance. The narrow exceptions are the following:

1. The parties intended silence as acceptance.
2. Prior dealing indicates that silence is an acceptable method of acceptance.
3. The custom of the trade or industry recognizes silence as acceptance.

It is clear that our case is not within any of the exceptions; hence, silence does not constitute acceptance, and there is no contract.

Multiple Choice Questions (1–38)

1. Which of the following requirements must be met for modification of a sales contract under the Uniform Commercial Code?
   a. The modification must satisfy the Statute of Frauds if the contract as modified is within its provisions.
   b. There must be consideration present if the contract is between merchants.
   c. The parol evidence rule applies and thus a writing is required.
   d. There must be a writing if the original sales contract is in writing.

2. In order to have an irrevocable offer under the Uniform Commercial Code, the offer must
   a. Be made by a merchant to a merchant.
   b. Be contained in a signed writing which gives assurance that the offer will be held open.
   c. States the period of time for which it is irrevocable.
   d. Not be contained in a form supplied by the offeror.

3. A claim has been made by Donnegal to certain goods in your client's possession. Donnegal will be entitled to the goods if it can be shown that Variance, the party from whom your client purchased the goods, obtained them by
   a. Deceiving Donnegal as to his identity at the time of the purchase.
   b. Giving Donnegal his check which was later dishonored.
   c. Obtaining the goods from Donnegal by fraud, punishable as larceny under criminal law.
   d. Purchasing goods which had been previously stolen from Donnegal.

4. Wilson Corporation entered into a contract to sell goods to Marvin who has a place of business in the same town as Wilson. The contract was clear with respect to price and quantity, but failed to designate the place of delivery. Which of the following statements is correct?
   a. The contract is unenforceable because of indefiniteness.
   b. The place for delivery must be designated by the parties within five days or the contract is voidable.
   c. The seller's place of business is the proper place for delivery.
   d. The buyer's place of business is the proper place for delivery.

5. On October 1, Baker, a wholesaler, sent Clark, a retailer, a written signed offer to sell 200 pinking shears at $9 each. The terms were F.O.B. Baker's warehouse, net 30, late payment subject to a 15% per annum interest charge. The offer indicated that it must be accepted no later than October 10, that acceptance would be effective upon receipt, and that the terms were not to be varied by the offeree. Clark sent a telegram which arrived on October 6, and accepted the offer expressly subject to a change of the payment terms to 2/10, net/30. Baker phoned Clark on October 7, rejecting the change of payment terms. Clark then indicated it would accept the October 1 offer in all respects, and expected delivery within 10 days. Baker did not accept Clark's oral acceptance of the original offer. Which of the following is a correct statement?
   a. Baker's original offer is a firm offer, hence irrevocable.
   b. There is **no** contract since Clark's modifications effectively rejected the October 1 offer, and Baker never accepted either of Clark's proposals.
   c. Clark actually created a contract on October 6, since the modifications were merely proposals and did **not** preclude acceptance.
   d. The statute of frauds would preclude the formation of a contract in any event.

8

6. Calvin Poultry Co. offered to sell Chickenshop 20,000 pounds of chicken at 40 cents per pound under specified delivery terms. Chickenshop accepted the offer as follows:

   "We accept your offer for 20,000 pounds of chicken at 40 cents per pound per city scale weight certificate."

   Which of the following is correct?
   a. A contract was formed on Calvin's terms.
   b. Chickenshop's reply constitutes a conditional acceptance, but **not** a counteroffer.
   c. Chickenshop's reply constitutes a counteroffer and **no** contract was formed.
   d. A contract was formed on Chickenshop's terms.

7. Darrow purchased 100 sets of bookends from Benson Manufacturing, Inc. Darrow made substantial prepayments of the purchase price. Benson is insolvent and the goods have not been delivered as promised. Darrow wants the bookends. Under the circumstances, which of the following will prevent Darrow from obtaining the bookends?

a. The fact that he did **not** pay the full price at the time of the purchase even though he has made a tender of the balance and holds it available to Benson upon delivery.
b. The fact that he can obtain a judgment for damages.
c. The fact that he was **not** aware of Benson's insolvency at the time he purchased the bookends.
d. The fact that the goods have **not** been identified to his contract.

8. Wexford Furniture, Inc., is in the retail furniture business and has stores located in principal cities in the United States. Its designers created a unique cocktail table. After obtaining prices and schedules, Wexford ordered 2,000 tables to be made to its design and specifications for sale as a part of its annual spring sales promotion campaign. Which of the following represents the earliest time Wexford will have an insurable interest in the tables?
a. At the time the goods are in Wexford's possession.
b. Upon shipment of conforming goods by the seller.
c. When the goods are marked or otherwise designated by the seller as the goods to which the contract refers.
d. At the time the contract is made.

9. Hack Company owned 100 tires which it deposited in a public warehouse on April 25, receiving a negotiable warehouse receipt in its name. Hack sold the tires to Fast Freight Co. On which of the following dates did the risk of loss transfer from Hack to Fast?
a. May 1—Fast signed a contract to buy the tires from Hack for $15,000. Delivery was to be at the warehouse.
b. May 2—Fast paid for the tires.
c. May 3—Hack negotiated the warehouse receipt to Fast.
d. May 4—Fast received delivery of the tires at the warehouse.

10. In deciding a controversy involving the question of who has the risk of loss, the court will look primarily to
a. The intent of the parties manifested in the contract.
b. The shipping terms used by the parties.
c. Whether title has passed.
d. The insurance coverage of the parties.

11. Under a contract for sale on approval, unless otherwise agreed, what happens to "risk of loss" and "title" upon delivery to the buyer?
a. Risk of loss but not title passes to buyer.
b. Title but not risk of loss passes to buyer.
c. Risk of loss and title pass to buyer.
d. Neither risk of loss nor title pass to buyer.

12. Falcon, by telegram to Southern Wool, Inc., ordered 30 bolts of cloth, first quality, 60% wool and 40% dacron. The shipping terms were F.O.B. Falcon's factory in Norwalk, Connecticut. Southern accepted the order and packed the bolts of cloth for shipment. In the process it discovered that one half of the bolts packed had been commingled with cloth which was 50% wool and 50% dacron. Since Southern did not have any additional 60% wool cloth, it decided to send the shipment to Falcon as an accommodation. The goods were shipped and later the same day Southern wired Falcon its apology informing Falcon of the facts and indicating that the 15 bolts of 50% wool would be priced at $15 a bolt less. The carrier delivering the goods was hijacked on the way to Norwalk. Under the circumstances, who bears the risk of loss?
a. Southern, since they shipped goods which failed to conform to the contract.
b. Falcon, since the shipping terms were F.O.B. Falcon's place of business.
c. Southern, because the order was **not** a signed writing.
d. Falcon, since Falcon has title to the goods.

13. Hall is suing the manufacturer, the wholesaler, and the retailer for bodily injuries caused by a lawnmower Hall purchased. Under the theory of strict liability
a. Privity will be a bar insofar as the wholesaler is concerned if the wholesaler did **not** have a reasonable opportunity to inspect.
b. Contributory negligence on Hall's part will always be a bar to recovery.
c. The manufacturer will avoid liability if it can show it followed the custom of the industry.
d. Hall may recover despite the fact that he can **not** show that any negligence was involved.

14. Gold sold Sable ten fur coats. The contact contained no specific provision regarding title warranties. It did, however, contain a provision which indicated that the coats, were sold "with all faults and defects." Two of the coats sold to Sable had been stolen and were reclaimed by the rightful owner. Which of the following is a correct statement?

a. The implied warranty of title is eliminated by the parol evidence rule.
b. The contract automatically contained a warranty that the title conveyed is good and can only be excluded by specific language.
c. Since there was **no** express title warranty, Sable assumed the risk.
d. The disclaimer "with all faults and defects" effectively negates any and all warranties.

15. The Uniform Commercial Code provides for a warranty against infringement. Its primary purpose is to protect the buyer of goods from infringement of the rights of third parties. This warranty
a. Only applies if the sale is between merchants.
b. Must be expressly stated in the contract or the Statute of Frauds will prevent its enforceability.
c. Protects the seller if the buyer furnishes specifications which result in an infringement.
d. Can **not** be disclaimed.

16. Target Company, Inc. ordered a generator from Maximum Voltage Corporation. A dispute has arisen over the effect of a provision in the specifications that the generator have a 5,000 kilowatt capacity. The specifications were attached to the contract and were incorporated by reference in the main body of the contract. The generator did not have this capacity but instead had a maximum capacity of 4,800 kilowatts. The contract had a disclaimer clause which effectively negated both of the implied warranties of quality. Target is seeking to avoid the contract based upon breach of warranty and Maximum is relying on its disclaimer. Which of the following is a correct statement?
a. The 5,000 kilowatt term contained in the specifications does not constitute a warranty.
b. The disclaimer effectively negated any and all warranty protection claimed by Target.
c. The description language (5,000 kilowatt) contained in the specifications is an express warranty and has not been effectively disclaimed.
d. The parol evidence rule will prevent Target from asserting the 5,000 kilowatt term as a warranty.

17. The Uniform Commercial Code implies a warranty of merchantability to protect buyers of goods. To be subject to this warranty the goods need **not** be
a. Fit for all of the purposes for which the buyer intends to use the goods.
b. Adequately packaged and labeled.
c. Sold by a merchant.
d. In conformity with any promises or affirmations of fact made on the container or label.

18. In general, disclaimers of implied warranty protection are
a. Permitted if they are explicit and understandable and the buyer is aware of their existence.
b. Not binding on remote purchasers with notice thereof.
c. Void because they are against public policy.
d. Invalid unless in writing and signed by the buyer.

19. The Uniform Commercial Code's position on privity of warranty as to personal injuries
a. Resulted in a single uniform rule being adopted throughout most of the United States.
b. Prohibits the exclusion on privity grounds of third parties from the warranty protection it has granted.
c. Applies exclusively to manufacturers.
d. Allows the buyer's family the right to sue only the party from whom the buyer purchased the product.

20. Webster purchased a drill press for $475 from Martinson Hardware, Inc. The press has proved to be defective and Webster wishes to rescind the purchase based upon a breach of implied warranty. Which of the following will preclude Webster's recovery from Martinson?
a. The press sold to Webster was a demonstration model and sold at a substantial discount; hence, Webster received no implied warranties.
b. Webster examined the press carefully, but as regards the defects, they were hidden defects which a reasonable examination would **not** have revealed.
c. Martinson informed Webster that they were closing out the model at a loss due to certain deficiencies and that it was sold "with all faults."
d. The fact that it was the negligence of the manufacturer which caused the trouble and that the defect could **not** have been discovered by Martinson without actually taking the press apart.

21. Marvin contracted to purchase goods from Ling. Subsequently, Marvin breached the contract and Ling is seeking to recover the contract price. Ling can recover the price if

a. Ling does **not** seek to recover any damages in addition to the price.
b. The goods have been destroyed and Ling's insurance coverage is inadequate, regardless of risk of loss.
c. Ling has identified the goods to the contract and the circumstances indicate that a reasonable effort to resell the goods at a reasonable price would be to no avail.
d. Marvin anticipatorily repudiated the contract and specific performance is **not** available.

22. Sanders Hardware Company received an order for $900 of assorted hardware from Richards & Company. The shipping terms were F.O.B. Lester Freight Line, seller's place of business, 2/10, net/30. Sanders packed and crated the hardware for shipment and it was loaded upon Lester's truck. While the goods were in transit to Richards, Sanders learned that Richards was insolvent in the equity sense (unable to pay its debts in the ordinary course of business). Sanders promptly wired Lester's office in Denver, Colorado, and instructed them to stop shipment of the goods to Richards and to store them until further instructions. Lester complied with these instructions. Regarding the rights, duties, and liabilities of the parties, which of the following is correct?

a. Sanders' stoppage in transit was improper if Richards' assets exceeded its liabilities.
b. Richards is entitled to the hardware if it pays cash.
c. Once Sanders correctly learned of Richards' insolvency, it had no further duty or obligation to Richards.
d. The fact that Richards became insolvent in no way affects the rights, duties, and obligations of the parties.

23. Kent, a wholesale distributor of cameras, entered into a contract with Williams. Williams agreed to purchase 100 cameras with certain optional attachments. The contract was made on October 1, 1976, for delivery by October 15, 1976; terms: 2/10, net 30. Kent shipped the cameras on October 6, and they were delivered on October 10. The shipment did not conform to the contract, in that one of the attachments was not included. Williams immediately notified Kent that he was rejecting the goods. For maximum legal advantage Kent's most appropriate action is to

a. Bring an action for the price less an allowance for the missing attachment.
b. Notify Williams promptly of his intention to cure the defect and make a conforming delivery by October 15.
c. Terminate his contract with Williams and recover for breach of contract.
d. Sue Williams for specific performance.

24. On February 1, 1983, Nugent Manufacturing, Inc. contracted with Costello Wholesalers to supply Costello with 1,000 integrated circuits. Delivery was called for on May 1, 1983. On March 15, 1983, Nugent notified Costello that it would not perform and that Costello should look elsewhere. Nugent had received a larger and more lucrative contract on February 27, 1983, and its capacity was such that it could not fulfill both orders. The facts

a. Are **not** sufficient to clearly establish an anticipatory repudiation.
b. Will prevent Nugent from retracting its repudiation of the Costello contract.
c. Will permit Costello to sue immediately after March 15, 1983, even though the performance called for under the contract was not until May 1, 1983.
d. Will permit Costello to sue only after May 1, 1983, the latest performance date.

25. Brown ordered 100 cases of Delicious Brand peas at list price from Smith Wholesaler. Immediately upon receipt of Brown's order, Smith sent Brown an acceptance which was received by Brown. The acceptance indicated that shipment would be made within ten days. On the tenth day Smith discovered that all of its supply of Delicious Brand peas had been sold. Instead it shipped 100 cases of Lovely Brand peas, stating clearly on the invoice that the shipment was sent only as an accommodation. Which of the following is correct?

a. Smith's shipment of Lovely Brand peas is a counteroffer, thus **no** contract exists between Brown and Smith.
b. Smith's note of accommodation cancels the contract between Smith and Brown.
c. Brown's order is a unilateral offer, and can only be accepted by Smith's shipment of the goods ordered.
d. Smith's shipment of Lovely Brand peas constitutes a breach of contract.

26. Gibbeon Manufacturing shipped 300 designer navy blue blazers to Custom Clothing Emporeum. The blazers arrived on Friday, earlier than Custom had an-

ticipated and on an exceptionally busy day for its receiving department. They were perfunctorily examined and sent to a nearby warehouse for storage until needed. On Monday of the following week, upon closer examination, it was discovered that the quality of the linings of the blazers was inferior to that specified in the sales contract. Which of the following is correct insofar as Custom's rights are concerned?

a. Custom can reject the blazers upon subsequent discovery of the defects.
b. Custom must retain the blazers since it accepted them and had an opportunity to inspect them upon delivery.
c. Custom's only course of action is rescission.
d. Custom had no rights if the linings were of merchantable quality.

27. Cox Manufacturing repudiated its contract to sell 300 televisions to Ruddy Stores, Inc. What recourse does Ruddy Stores have?

a. It can obtain specific performance by the seller.
b. It can recover punitive damages.
c. It must await the seller's performance for a commercially reasonable time after repudiation if it wishes to recover anything.
d. It can "cover," that is, procure the goods elsewhere and recover any damages.

28. Devold Manufacturing, Inc., entered into a contract for the sale to Hillary Company of 2,000 solid-state CB radios at $27.50 each, terms 2/10, N/30, FOB Hillary's loading platform. After delivery of the first 500 radios, a minor defect was discovered. Although the defect was minor, Hillary incurred costs to correct the defect. Hillary sent Devold a signed memorandum indicating that it would relinquish its right to recover the costs to correct the defect, provided that the balance of the radios were in conformity with the terms of the contract and the delivery dates were strictly adhered to. Devold met these conditions. Shortly before the last shipment of radios arrived, a dispute between the parties arose over an unrelated matter. Hillary notified Devold that it was not bound by the prior generous agreement and would sue Devold for damages unless Devold promptly reimbursed Hillary. In the event of litigation, what would be the result and the basis upon which the litigation would be decided?

a. Devold will lose in that Hillary's relinquishment of its rights was not supported by a consideration.
b. Devold will win in that the defect was minor and the substantial performance doctrine applies.
c. Hillary will lose in that the communication constituted a waiver of Hillary's rights.
d. Hillary will win in that there was a failure to perform the contract, and Hillary suffered damages as a result.

29. Dodd Company sold Barney & Company 10,000 ball point pens. The shipment, upon inspection, was found to be nonconforming and Barney rejected the pens. Barney purchased the pens elsewhere at a price which was $525 more than the contract price. The Dodd sales contract contained a clause which purported to reduce the statute of limitations provision of the Uniform Commercial Code to one year. Barney has done nothing about the breach except to return the pens and demand payment of the $525 damages. Dodd has totally ignored Barney's claim. The statute of limitations

a. Is four years according to the Uniform Commercial Code and can **not** be reduced by the original agreement.
b. Will totally bar recovery unless suit is commenced within the time specified in the contract.
c. May be extended by the parties but **not** beyond five years.
d. Can **not** be reduced by the parties to a period less than two years.

30. Johnstone purchased all the inventory, machinery, and fixtures of Lomax. Johnstone failed to comply with the requirements of the Bulk Transfers Article of the Uniform Commercial Code. Dark subsequently purchased some of the used machinery from Johnstone. Dark

a. Must give notice to Lomax's creditors who sold the machinery to Lomax.
b. Will take free of the claims of Lomax's creditors irrespective of Dark's good faith or notice since the creditors must seek recourse from Johnstone exclusively.
c. Will have a voidable title even if he took in good faith and without notice.
d. Takes subject to any title defect if he had notice of Johnstone's failure to comply.

31. The Bulk Transfers Article of the Uniform Commercial Code applies to

a. A general assignment for the benefit of creditors.
b. A sale of substantially all assets by auction.

c. A transfer of the bulk of the inventory to settle a lien or other security interest.
d. A transfer of assets to a receiver.

May 1984 Questions

32. Which of the following will render a bulk transfer ineffective as to a creditor of the transferor?
    a. Failure by the transferee to require the transferor to furnish a list of the transferor's existing creditors.
    b. Failure to file in the county clerk's office a schedule of the property to be transferred at least 10 days prior to the transfer.
    c. Failure by the transferor to preserve the list of creditors and schedule of property for at least six months after the transfer.
    d. Without the knowledge of the transferee, the transferor fails to prepare a complete and accurate list of the transferor's creditors.

33. Nat purchased a typewriter from Rob. Rob is not in the business of selling typewriters. Rob tendered delivery of the typewriter after receiving payment in full from Nat. Nat informed Rob that he was unable to take possession of the typewriter at that time, but would return later that day. Before Nat returned, the typewriter was destroyed by a fire. The risk of loss
    a. Passed to Nat upon Rob's tender of delivery.
    b. Remained with Rob, since Nat had **not** yet received the typewriter.
    c. Passed to Nat at the time the contract was formed and payment was made.
    d. Remained with Rob, since title had **not** yet passed to Nat.

34. Under the UCC, the warranty of title for the sale of goods
    a. May **not** be excluded by the seller.
    b. May be excluded by the phrase "as is."
    c. Will vest title absolutely in a bona fide purchaser for value provided that the seller is a merchant.
    d. Will apply regardless of whether it is provided in the contract unless it is specifically excluded.

35. Olsen purchased a used van from Super Sales Co. for $350. A clause in the written contract in boldface type provided that the van was being sold "as is." Another clause provided that the contract was intended as the final expression of the parties' agreement. After driving the van for one week, Olsen realized that the engine was burning oil. Olsen telephoned Super and requested a refund. Super refused but orally gave Olsen a warranty on the engine for six months. Three weeks later the engine exploded. Super's oral warranty
    a. Is invalid since the modification of the existing contract required additional consideration.
    b. Is invalid due to the statute of frauds.
    c. Is valid and enforceable.
    d. Although valid, proof of its existence will be inadmissible because it contradicts the final written agreement of the parties.

36. Park purchased from Derek Truck Sales a truck which had serious mechanical problems. Park learned of the defects six months after the date of sale. Five years after the date of sale Park commenced an action for breach of warranty against Derek. Derek asserts the statute of limitations as a defense. Which of the following statements made by Derek is correct?
    a. A clause in the original contract reducing the statute of limitations to nine months is enforceable.
    b. Park was required to bring the action within the statute of limitation as measured from Derek's tender of delivery.
    c. Park was required to bring the action within the statute of limitation as measured from the time the breach was discovered or should have been discovered.
    d. Park is precluded from asserting under any circumstances that the statute of limitations stopped running.

37. The UCC Sales Article applies
    a. Exclusively to the sale of goods between merchants.
    b. To the sale of real estate between merchants.
    c. To the sale of specially manufactured goods.
    d. To the sale of investment securities.

38. Which of the following factors will be most important in determining if an express warranty has been created?
    a. Whether the promises made by the seller became part of the basis of the bargain.
    b. Whether the seller intended to create a warranty.
    c. Whether the statements made by the seller were in writing.
    d. Whether the sale was made by a merchant in the regular course of business.

Repeat Questions

(584,L1,47)	Identical to item 7 above
(584,L1,49)	Identical to item 12 above
(584,L1,51)	Identical to item 22 above

Problems

Problem 1 Bulk Sale (1181,L5a)

(8 to 10 minutes)

Part a. A client engaged its CPA to perform services in connection with the proposed acquisition of the entire inventory of a company that decided to terminate its business and dissolve. Among the services requested was the examination of the seller's inventory schedules which describe the subject matter of the sale. In addition, the client-buyer obtained from the seller a list of the seller's creditors and requested the CPA to make an examination of the seller's accounts payable ledger to verify the accuracy of the list. The sale was consummated on March 1, 1981, and the examination of the inventory schedules and the accounts payable ledger was completed 20 days prior to that date. The CPA performed the services as agreed and the schedules of inventory and the list of the seller's creditors appeared to be proper and were accepted by the client-buyer.

Required:

Answer the following, setting forth reasons for any conclusions stated.

1. What is the legal nature of the proposed acquisition described above?
2. There are certain legal procedures necessary to make the transaction described above valid and effective against any creditor. What are the major procedures and what do they attempt to prevent?
3. Were the two precautions taken by the buyer in connection with the purchase necessary in order to protect its rights?

Problem 2 Option Contract, Risk of Loss (1178,L5a & b)

(12 to 15 minutes)

Part a. Clauson Enterprises, Inc., was considering adding a new product line to its existing lines. The decision was contingent upon its being assured of a supply of an electronic component for the product at a certain price and a positive market study which clearly justified the investment in the venture.

Clauson's president approached Migrane Electronics and explained the situation to Migrane's president. After much negotiation, Migrane agreed to grant Clauson an option to purchase 12,000 of the necessary electronic components at $1.75 each or at the prevailing market price, whichever was lower. Clauson prepared the option below incorporating their understanding.

Option Agreement
Clauson Enterprises/Migrane Electronics

Migrane Electronics hereby offers to sell Clauson Enterprises 12,000 miniature solid state electronic breakers at $1.75 each or at the existing market price at the time of delivery, whichever is lower, delivery to be made in 12 equal monthly installments beginning one month after the exercise of this option. This option is irrevocable for six months from January 1, 1978.

Clauson Enterprises agrees to deliver to Migrane its market survey for the product line in which the component would be used if it elects not to exercise the option.

Both parties signed the option agreement and Migrane's president signed Migrane's corporate name alongside the last sentence of the first paragraph. On May 1, 1978, Migrane notified Clauson that it was revoking its offer. The market price for the component had increased to $1.85. On May 15, 1978, Clauson notified Migrane that it accepted the offer and that if Migrane did not perform, it would be sued and held liable for damages. Migrane replied that the offer was not binding and was revoked before Clauson accepted. Furthermore, even if it were binding, it was good for only three months as a matter of law.

Upon receipt of Migrane's reply, Clauson instituted suit for damages.

Required:

Answer for following, setting forth reasons for any conclusions stated.

Who will prevail? Discuss all the issues and arguments raised by the fact situation.

Part b. On May 30, 1978, Hargrove ordered 1,000 spools of nylon yarn from Flowers, Inc., of Norfolk, Virginia. The shipping terms were "F.O.B., Norfolk & Western RR at Norfolk." The transaction was to be a cash sale with payment to be simultaneously exchanged for the negotiable bill of lading covering the goods. Title to the goods was expressly reserved in Flowers. The yarn ordered by Hargrove was delivered to the railroad and loaded in a boxcar on June 1, 1978. Flowers obtained a negotiable bill of lading made out to its own order. The boxcar was destroyed the next day while the goods were in transit. Hargrove refused to pay for the yarn and Flowers sued Hargrove for the purchase price.

Required:

Answer the following, setting forth reasons for any conclusions stated.

Who will prevail?

Problem 3 Consignments (580,L4a)

(7 to 10 minutes)

Part a. After much study and deliberation, the marketing division of Majestic Enterprise, Inc., has recommended to the board of directors that the corporation market its products almost exclusively via consignment arrangements instead of other alternate merchandising-security arrangements. The board moved favorably upon this proposal.

Required:

Answer the following, setting forth reasons for any conclusions stated.

What are the key legal characteristics of a consignment?

Problem 4 Breach of Warranty; Breach of Sales Contract (582,L5)

(15 to 20 minutes)

Part a. Sure Rain Apparel, Inc., manufactures expensive, exclusive rain apparel. One model is very popular and sold widely throughout the United States. About six months after their initial sale to distributors, Sure started receiving complaints that there was a noticeable fading of the color of the material. Many of the distributors seek to return the goods, recover damages, or both. Sure denies liability on the following bases: (1) there was an "Act of God," (2) there was no breach of warranty since the fading was to be expected in any event, and (3) any and all warranty protection was disclaimed unless expressly stated in the contract.

The contract contained the following provisions relating to warranty protection:

First: The manufacturer warrants that the material used to make the raincoats is 100% Egyptian long fiber cotton.

Second: The manufacturer guarantees the waterproofing of the raincoat for one year if the directions as to dry cleaning are followed.

Third: There are no other express warranties granted by the seller, except those indicated above. This writing is intended as a complete statement and integration of all express warranty protection.

Fourth: The manufacturer does not purport to give any implied warranty of merchantability in connection with this sale. The express warranties above enumerated are granted in lieu thereof.

Fifth: There are no warranties which extend beyond the description above.

The fourth and fifth provisions were conspicuous and initialed by the buyers.

Several buyers have commenced legal actions against Sure based upon implied warranties and express oral warranties made prior to the execution of the contract.

Required:

Answer the following, setting forth reasons for any conclusions stated.

Is Sure liable for breach of warranty?

Part b. Nielson Wholesalers, Inc., ordered 1,000 scissors at $2.50 a pair from Wilmot, Inc., on February 1, 1982. Delivery was to be made not later than March 10. Wilmot accepted the order in writing on February 4. The terms were 2/10, net/30, F.O.B. seller's loading platform in Baltimore. Due to unexpected additional orders and a miscalculation of the backlog of orders, Wilmot subsequently determined that it could not perform by March 10. On February 15, Wilmot notified Nielson that it would not be able to perform, and cancelled the contract. Wilmot pleaded a reasonable mistake and impossibility of performance as its justification for cancelling. At the time the notice of cancellation was received, identical scissors were available from other manufacturers at $2.70. Nielson chose not to purchase the 1,000 scissors elsewhere, but instead notified Wilmot that it rejected the purported cancellation and would await delivery as agreed. Wilmot did not deliver on March 10, by which time the price of the scissors had risen to $3.00 a pair. Nielson is seeking to recover damages from Wilmot for breach of contract.

Required:

Answer the following, setting forth reasons for any conclusions stated.

1. Will Nielson prevail and, if so, how much will it recover?

2. Would Nielson be entitled to specific performance under the circumstances?

3. Assuming that Wilmot discovers that Nielson was insolvent, will this excuse performance?

Multiple Choice Answers

1. a	9. c	17. a	25. d	32. a
2. b	10. a	18. a	26. a	33. a
3. d	11. d	19. b	27. d	34. d
4. c	12. a	20. c	28. c	35. c
5. b	13. d	21. c	29. b	36. b
6. d	14. b	22. b	30. d	37. c
7. d	15. c	23. b	31. b	38. a
8. c	16. c	24. c		

Multiple Choice Answer Explanations

A. Contracts for Sale of Goods

1. (1183,L1,50) (a) A modification of a contract for the sale of goods must be in writing if, as modified, the agreement falls within the provisions of the Statute of Frauds (i.e., involves the sale of goods, $500 or more). Answer (b) is incorrect because no consideration is needed for a modification of a contract for the sale of goods. It is an exception to the rule that consideration must be present to create a binding agreement. Answer (c) is incorrect because the Statute of Frauds, not the parol evidence rule, demands certain contracts be in writing to be enforceable. The parol evidence rule excludes the admission of certain evidence that occurred prior to or contemporaneously with the complete written expression of the parties' agreement. Answer (d) is incorrect because in deciding whether the modification must be in writing, it is irrelevant that the original contract was written. If the contract as modified is not within the Statute of Frauds' provisions, an oral modification would be enforceable.

2. (1183,L1,51) (b) In order to have an irrevocable offer (firm offer) under the UCC, the offer must be made by a merchant offeror in a signed writing which gives assurances that the offer will be held open. There is no requirement that the offeree also be a merchant. A firm offer does not need to state the period of time for which it is irrevocable. If no time period is stated it is irrevocable for a reasonable period of time. Normally, a firm offer would be contained in a form provided by the offeror; however, it could be contained in a form provided by the offeree if the merchant offeror signs outside the paragraph that contains the firm offer. Therefore, answers (a), (c), and (d) are incorrect.

3. (582,L1,47) (d) Donnegal will be entitled to return of the goods if the goods have been stolen from him. A thief has no power to transfer a good title in goods to a good faith purchaser. However, a person with a voidable title may transfer good title in the goods to a good faith purchaser. A person has a voidable title when the goods have been delivered under a transaction of purchase and (1) the transferor was deceived as to the identity of the purchaser, or (2) the delivery was in exchange for a check which is later dishonored, or (3) the delivery was procured through fraud punishable as larceny under criminal law. Therefore, answers (a), (b), and (c) are incorrect.

4. (578,L1,43) (c) Open terms will not cause a contract for the sale of goods to fail for indefiniteness if there was an intent to contract and a reasonable basis for establishing a remedy is available. If the place of delivery is left open, the UCC provides that the seller's place of business shall be the proper place of delivery. Answer (a) is incorrect because the Code supplies the omitted delivery terms. Answer (b) is incorrect because no rule requires the parties to designate place of delivery within 5 days. Nor is the buyer's place of business [answer (d)] the proper place of delivery unless so stated in the contract.

A.2.d. Battle of Forms

5. (1183,L1,53) (b) Clark's telegram of October 6 does not operate as an effective acceptance of Baker's offer because Clark's acceptance was expressly conditioned on the change in payment terms. Consequently, the battle of the forms exception does not apply. This telegram is actually a counteroffer which Baker expressly rejected in the October 7 telephone conversation. Clark's subsequent offer to honor the terms as originally expressed on October 1 was never accepted by Baker and, therefore, there is no contract between the parties. Answer (c) is incorrect because Clark expressly conditioned his acceptance on the modifications. If, in fact, Clark's changes were mere proposals, the modifications would still not have become part of the contract since this transaction was between merchants, and Baker expressly stated that the terms in his offer were not to be varied. Answer (d) is incorrect because under the Uniform Commercial Code a writing will satisfy the Statute of Frauds as long as it indicates a contract has been made, is signed by the party to be bound, and states the quantity. Assuming Clark is seeking to enforce the contract against Baker, Baker's written signed offer of October 1 stating a quantity of 200 pinking shears complies with the Statute of Frauds. Answer (a) is incorrect because Baker's original offer does not satisfy the requirements for a firm offer. Under the Uniform Commercial Code a merchant cannot revoke a written signed offer to buy or sell goods if he gives assurances that the offer will be held open. Such an offer is irrevocable for the stated time, up to a maximum of 3

months. If no period is specified, then a reasonable time is implied. Baker's offer is not a firm offer because it does not contain assurances that it will be held open. The statement that the offer "must be accepted no later than October 10" only establishes the expiration date of the offer. Baker has determined when the offer will lapse without expressly committing himself to keeping the offer open until October 10.

6. (1182,L1,4) (d) Between merchants, additional and different terms become part of the contract unless they materially alter it, notification of objection to them is given within a reasonable time, or the original offer expressly limited acceptance to the terms of the offer. The additional and different term added by Chickenshop is neither material nor contrary to the terms of the original offer. And the original offer did not expressly limit acceptance to its terms. Therefore, a contract was formed on Chickenshop's terms. Answer (a) is incorrect since the additional and different term added by Chickenshop becomes part of the contract. Answer (b) is incorrect because Chickenshop's reply was an unconditional, effective acceptance. The reply manifested an intent to accept and enter into a contract, and was not conditional upon assent to the additional terms included in the acceptance. Under common law, the additional term in offeree's acceptance would operate as a counteroffer, which is an automatic rejection of the offer. However, since the facts in this question dictate application of the "battle of the forms" rule, under the Uniform Commercial Code, the additional term becomes a part of the contract. Therefore, answer (c) is incorrect.

A.5. Identification

7. (581,L1,20) (d) Upon identification of the goods that relate to a contract, several specific rights are granted to the buyer of these goods. Among these is the right to take delivery of goods upon insolvency of the seller if full or partial payment was made at the time of the purchase and any balance due is tendered to the seller. Since the question asks which condition will prevent recovery of the goods, lack of identification is correct because identification must occur before any rights of repossession accrue to the buyer. It is not necessary that the full price be paid at the time of purchase (a) as long as tender of the balance due is made to the seller. Answers (b) and (c) are incorrect since the fact that a buyer may obtain a judgment for damages to the goods by third parties or that a buyer is not aware of a seller's insolvency will not prevent the buyer from gaining possession of the goods.

8. (578,L1,14) (c) Under the UCC, the buyer obtains an insurable interest in goods when they are identified to the contract. In the case of future goods, identification occurs when the goods are shipped, marked, or otherwise designated by the seller as the goods to which the contract refers. Answer (d) is incorrect because the insurable interest is not obtained at the time the contract is made. Answer (a) is incorrect because an insurable interest can arise before the goods are in the buyer's possession. Answer (b) is incorrect because an insurable interest will be obtained before shipment when the goods are identified for shipment.

A.6. Risk of Loss

9. (1183,L1,46) (c) Provided there is no agreement to the contrary and neither party is in breach, risk of loss to goods, which are held in a warehouse for delivery without being moved, will pass at the time the document of title is properly negotiated to the buyer. If the document of title is nonnegotiable, then the risk of loss passes a reasonable time after the buyer receives the document. Where there is no document of title representing the goods, risk of loss will pass once the warehouseman acknowledges the buyer's right to the goods. Answers (a), (b), and (d) are incorrect since Hack Company has a negotiable document of title which is properly negotiated to Fast Freight Company on May 3.

10. (1183,L1,56) (a) The UCC rules concerning risk of loss only apply if the parties have not allocated risk of loss in their contract. Consequently, shipping terms used and insurance coverage of the parties would not be relevant in allocating risk of loss if the parties had manifested their intent in the contract. Therefore, answers (b) and (d) are incorrect. Answer (c) is incorrect because the fact that title of the goods has passed to the buyer does not mean that risk of loss has also passed, and vice versa. The UCC allocates risk of loss irrespective of title. One party may have title to the goods, while the other party has risk of loss.

11. (577,L3,42) (d) Under the UCC both title and risk of loss remain with the seller until the buyer accepts the goods if it is a contract for "sale on approval." These contracts are used between sellers and consumers. Goods bought for resale may be bought under a contract for "sale or return." Under "sale and return," the seller retains title but the buyer has risk of loss.

12. (1182,L1,48) (a) The UCC places risk of loss on the breaching party. Since Southern shipped non-

conforming goods, they breached the contract and would have risk of loss until the nonconforming goods were accepted by the buyer. Answer (b) is incorrect because the shipping term FOB would only control passage of risk of loss if conforming goods had been shipped. However, even if conforming goods had been shipped under "FOB Falcon's factory," risk of loss would not have shifted to Falcon until the goods arrived at the factory. Answer (c) is incorrect because Falcon's telegram would act as a signed writing. Answer (d) is incorrect because Falcon does not have title to the goods. However, even if title had passed, Southern would still have risk of loss because title to the goods has no relevance in allocating risk of loss.

A.7. Product Liability

13. (1183,L1,60) (d) Under strict liability a seller engaged in the business of selling a product is held liable for injuries caused by that product, provided he sold it in a defective and unreasonably dangerous condition. A seller is, therefore, liable regardless of whether he was negligent or at fault for the defective condition of the product. Finally, a seller engaged in the business of selling the product is defined to include not only the buyer's immediate seller, but also the prior sellers in the distribution chain such as the wholesaler and manufacturer. Answers (a), (b), and (c) are incorrect because the only defenses available in strict liability are misuse and assumption of the risk. An individual misuses a product when he uses it for some purpose other than for which the product was originally intended. Assumption of the risk exists when an individual proceeds to use a product in disregard of a known danger associated with that product. Contributory negligence, compliance with industry standards or custom, and lack of privity of contract are not defenses to strict liability. Although the fact that the wholesaler did not have a reasonable opportunity to inspect the goods may be of importance under the negligence theory of product liability, it is irrelevant in strict liability since the showing of fault is not required to impose liability on a seller.

A.7.c.1) Warranty of Title

14. (1183,L1,52) (b) In every contract for the sale of goods it is implied that the seller has the right to transfer the goods, that he is conveying good title, and that the goods are free from any encumbrance. This warranty of title may be disclaimed either by specific language in the contract or by such circumstances which put the buyer on notice that the seller is not claiming good title. Answer (d) is incorrect because a general disclaimer does not affect the warranty of title. Answer (c) is incorrect because the warranty of title is granted automatically in every sale of goods unless disclaimed. Answer (a) is incorrect because the parol evidence rule would not affect the warranty of title in any manner.

15. (581,L1,14) (c) In a sale by a merchant, the merchant warrants that the goods are free from a rightful claim of infringement of patent or trademark by third parties. (A seller will be protected against liability under a warranty against infringement if the buyer furnishes the specifications used to manufacture the product that infringes upon another party's patent or trademark rights.) Answer (a) is incorrect because only the seller need be a merchant. Answer (b) is incorrect because a warranty against infringment is granted along with the warranty of title and thus, does not need to be expressly stated in the contract to be enforceable. Like the warranty of title, a warranty against infringement can be disclaimed by specific language or circumstances that indicate that this warranty is not extended. Therefore, answer (d) is incorrect.

A.7.c.2) Express Warranties

16. (580,L1,32) (c) The "5000 kilowatt" term is a statement of fact made as part of the basis of the bargain; thus it qualifies as an express warranty. Only the implied warranties were disclaimed, thus answer (c) is correct and answers (a) and (b) are incorrect. Answer (d) is incorrect because the parol evidence rule excludes oral statements from evidence when the agreement is in writing. The "5000 kilowatt" term was part of the written agreement, therefore the parol evidence rule would not exclude this term from the agreement.

A.7.c.3) Implied Warranties

17. (1183,L1,54) (a) Every merchant seller of goods impliedly warrants that the goods sold are fit for the ordinary purposes for which such goods are used, are adequately packaged and labeled, and conform to promises or affirmations of fact made on the package or label. This implied warranty of merchantability does not guarantee that the goods are fit for all possible purposes for which the buyer might use the goods. Accordingly, answers (b), (c), and (d) are incorrect.

18. (583,L1,39) (a) Disclaimers of implied warranty protection are statements by the seller that purport to modify or completely exclude the implied warranty. The UCC seeks to protect a buyer from unexpected and unbargained-for language of disclaimers by permitting the exclusion of implied warranties only by clear and conspicuous language or other circum-

stances that protect the buyer from surprise. To disclaim the implied warranty of merchantability, the language must mention the word "merchantability," and if the disclaimer is written, it must be conspicuous. To disclaim the implied warranty of fitness for particular purpose, the exclusion must be in conspicuous writing and must be understandable and explicit. Answer (b) is incorrect because a disclaimer of implied warranties, which satisfies the aforementioned requirement(s), will be binding on remote purchasers with notice thereof. Answer (c) is incorrect because disclaimers are not against public policy. Disclaimers are one of several shields afforded the seller against the considerable potential liability inherent in warranties. Answer (d) is incorrect because a disclaimer need not be in writing unless it is attempting to disclaim the implied warranty of fitness for particular purpose; a disclaimer need not be signed by the buyer.

19. (583,L1,40) (b) The Uniform Commercial Code, being consumer oriented, has broadened the basis of liability and modified the concept of privity of contract, thereby allowing warranties to extend to parties other than the purchaser. The UCC prohibits the exclusion on privity grounds of third parties from the warranty protection it has granted. Answer (a) is incorrect because there is no single uniform rule, rather there is disagreement over how far warranty liability should extend. In order to satisfy opposing views of the various states, the drafters of the UCC proposed three alternatives for warranty liability to third parties. Answer (c) is incorrect because the UCC's position on privity of warranty also applies to retail sellers and the ultimate purchaser or consumer. Answer (d) is incorrect because the buyer's family could sue the manufacturer as well as the retail seller from whom the buyer purchased the product. Most courts have abolished the requirement of vertical privity in actions for breach of warranty.

20. (1182,L1,47) (c) When goods are sold "as is" or "with all faults", all implied warranties are disclaimed including the implied warranty of merchantability. Normally, a disclaimer of the implied warranty of merchantability must contain some form of the word "merchantability" to be effective. However, goods sold "with all faults" is an exception to that rule. Answer (a) is incorrect because selling a demonstration model at a substantial discount would not disclaim the implied warranties. Answer (b) is incorrect because offering an inspection of the goods to a buyer only disclaims the implied warranties concerning patent defects, not concerning latent (hidden) defects in the goods. Answer (d) is incorrect because a merchant seller of goods gives an implied warranty that the goods are fit for ordinary purposes, regardless of which party caused the defect in the goods. The breach of warranty theory is not based on negligence.

B.3. Seller's Remedies

21. (1183,L1,58) (c) The seller can recover the full contract price if the buyer has accepted the goods before breaching the contract, the goods have already been identified to the contract and the seller is unable to resell them at a reasonable price, or the goods are lost or destroyed after the risk of loss has passed to the buyer. Accordingly, answer (b) is incorrect. Answer (a) is incorrect because the seller is entitled to seek incidental damages in addition to the full contract price. Answer (d) is incorrect because, even if one assumes that Marvin anticipatorily repudiated the contract, the seller has the choice of either suing at once or waiting until the time for performance. In any event, the seller is entitled to the usual contract remedies. However, Ling could only sue for the full contract price if one of the above mentioned three situtations is present.

22. (1182,L1,50) (b) Even though Sanders, the seller, learns of Richards' insolvency before the goods are delivered, Richards, the buyer, is entitled to performance if it pays cash. Therefore, answer (c) is incorrect. Answer (a) is incorrect because the seller's right to stoppage in transit is available if the buyer is insolvent in the equity sense (unable to pay its debts when due) even though the buyer is still solvent in the bankruptcy sense (assets exceed liabilities). Answer (d) is incorrect because the insolvency of the buyer allows the seller to refuse to perform under the terms of the agreement (2/10, net/30), and instead, demand cash upon delivery of the goods.

23. (1176,L1,9) (b) Under the UCC, a seller has the right to cure nonconforming goods within the original time of the contract if he notifies the buyer. This would put Kent in the position of having fulfilled the contract and having complied with the UCC. Then Williams would be the one in breach of the contract if he does not pay on time.

If on the other hand, Kent does not cure the defect and brings an action for the price less an allowance, Williams would have the defense that the goods were nonconforming and he had the right to reject them. Then Kent could not recover for breach of contract, because it was he who breached it by tendering non-conforming goods. In the case of duplicatable cameras, specific performance would not be available to either party.

B.4. Buyer's Remedies

24. (583,L1,42) (c) Anticipatory repudiation occurs when a party renounces the duty to perform the contract before the party's obligation to perform arises. Therefore, because Nugent Manufacturing notified Costello of its intent not to perform, it has engaged in anticipatory repudiation. Anticipatory repudiation discharges the nonrepudiating party (Costello) from the contract and allows this party to sue for breach immediately. However, if commercially reasonable, the nonrepudiating party can ignore the repudiation and await performance at the appointed time. If the nonrepudiating party chooses this latter course of action, the repudiating party may retract the renunciation and perform as promised. Therefore, answers (a), (b), and (d) are incorrect.

25. (581,L1,15) (d) Shipment of a different brand of peas, even as an accommodation, constitutes a breach of contract because the terms of the contract have not been complied with. Answer (a) is incorrect because the shipment cannot be considered a counteroffer since there was already a contract in existence between Brown and Smith. Answer (b) is untrue because only the promised performance will discharge Smith, unless Brown accepts the accommodation. Answer (c) is incorrect since Brown's offer to Smith constitutes a bilateral offer which was accepted by Smith's communication to Brown. This bilateral offer could have been accepted by delivery of the specified goods as well.

26. (1180,L1,12) (a) Answer (a) is correct since the buyer has a reasonable time in which to reject defective goods. Discovering the defect on Monday would be considered within a reasonable time, considering the goods had been delivered on Friday. Answer (d) is incorrect since the specification concerning the linings in the sales contract would be an express warranty which was breached when the linings were found to be inferior to what had been stated. Thus, the merchantable quality of the linings would be irrelevant.

27. (1179,L1,1) (d) The nonbreaching party under a contract for sale can attempt to mitigate damages by "cover," that is, by procuring the goods elsewhere and recovering as damages the difference between the contract price and the price of cover. Answer (a) is incorrect because specific performance is available only upon the damaged party showing that money damages are inadequate or other unique conditions exist which require actual performance. There is nothing here to indicate that the televisions are unavailable in the market or other unique conditions exist. Answer (b) is incorrect because punitive damages are never recoverable for breach of contract. Answer (c) is incorrect since a nonbreaching party need not wait after a breach occurs to begin proceedings to recover.

28. (578,L1,41) (c) The communication constituted a waiver of Hillary's rights which is not retractable if it would be unjust because Devold relied on it. Waivers of claims arising out of an alleged breach of contract require no consideration to be valid under the UCC. Thus answer (a) is incorrect under the Code, although it would be correct under common law. Answer (b) is incorrect because the doctrine of substantial performance provides that performance is satisfied if deviations have been minor. However, damages would still be available except that Hillary waived his right to them. Answer (d) is incorrect because Hillary would win had he not, under the rules of the Code, waived his claim to damages.

B.5. Statute of Limitations

29. (1183,L1,59) (b) Under the Uniform Commercial Code the statute of limitations for the sale of goods is four years. Although the parties may not extend this period, they may agree to reduce it to a period of not less than one year. If an action for breach of contract is not commenced within the limitations period, then recovery will be totally barred. Accordingly, answers (a), (c), and (d) are incorrect.

C. Bulk Sales

30. (583,L1,29) (d) Failure to comply with the Bulk Transfers Article of the UCC makes the sale ineffective against the seller's creditors. The creditors may enforce their claims against the goods in possession of the buyer (transferee). A subsequent bona fide purchaser (one who takes from the bulk buyer for value and without knowledge) has valid title to the goods and takes free of creditors' claims. If Dark had notice of Johnstone's failure to comply with the UCC Bulk Sale Provisions, (i.e., therefore Dark not being a bona fide purchaser), then Dark takes subject to any title defects, and Lomax's creditors may seek recourse from Dark. Therefore, answers (b) and (c) are incorrect. Answer (a) is incorrect because Johnstone, the original buyer, not Dark, must obtain a list of all of the seller's (Lomax's) existing creditors and give them notice at least 10 days before he makes payment or takes possession, whichever comes first. This would

include the creditors who sold the machinery to Lomax but the notice requirement would not be limited to these creditors.

31. (582,L1,26) (b) The Bulk Transfers Article of the UCC applies to a bulk transfer even though the transfer is by sale at auction. Persons who direct, control or are responsible for the auction must solicit a list of the owner's creditors and give notice of the auction to these creditors at least 10 days prior to the sale. If these persons (collectively called the auctioneer) fail to meet these requirements, and they know the auction constitutes a bulk transfer, they are liable to the creditors up to the net proceeds of the auction. Answers (a), (c), and (d) are incorrect because transfers to receivers, general assignments for the benefit of creditors, and transfers to give security are all specifically exempted from the Bulk Transfers Article of the UCC.

May 1984 Answers

32. (584,L1,20) (a) In order for a bulk transfer to be valid, the transferee must require the transferor to supply a list of existing creditors. If the transferee does not comply with this requirement, the sale is invalidated and the buyer must return the goods or satisfy the claims of the bulk seller's creditors. Answer (b) is incorrect because there is no requirement that a schedule of the property to be transferred must be filed in the county clerk's office at least 10 days prior to the transfer. The transferee need only notify the transferor's creditors of the bulk sale at least 10 days prior to taking physical possession of the goods or making payment for the goods, whichever comes first. Answer (c) is incorrect because there is no requirement which states that the transferor must preserve the list of creditors and schedule of property for at least 6 months after the transfer. Answer (d) is incorrect since the transferee is required to notify only the listed creditors and other persons the transferee knows are owed money by the transferor. Thus, if the transferee was unaware of the unlisted creditor, the sale is effective.

33. (584,L1,48) (a) The risk of loss rules under the UCC operate independently of any transfer of title. Specifically, the UCC states that absent any breach, the risk of loss passes from a nonmerchant seller to the buyer on tender of delivery. Accordingly, answers (b), (c), and (d) are incorrect.

34. (584,L1,52) (d) Under the UCC every seller warrants good title, rightful transfer, and freedom from any security interest or lien of which the buyer has no actual knowledge. This warranty of title may only be disclaimed by specific language or such circumstances which give the buyer reason to know that he is not receiving full title. A general disclaimer of all warranties or such language as "as is" is insufficient. A breach of the warranty of title does not vest good title in a bona fide puchaser but, instead, allows the purchaser to sue for breach of warranty. Answers (a), (b), and (c) are, therefore, incorrect.

35. (584,L1,53) (c) The parol evidence rule states that a written agreement intended by the parties to be final and complete is binding on the parties and may not be contradicted by proof of prior or contemporaneous oral agreements. Subsequent modifications (i.e., a later oral agreement), however, may be proven provided the Statute of Frauds, if applicable, is met. In this case, the Statute of Frauds is of no concern since the sale of the van is not for $500 or more. Moreover, under the UCC, the modification of an existing contract does not require additional consideration. Accordingly, Super's subsequent oral warranty is valid and enforceable, and answers (a), (b), and (d) are incorrect.

36. (584,L1,54) (b) When a warranty explicitly extends to the future performance of the goods, a cause of action for breach of that warranty must be brought within the Statute of Limitations period as measured from the time the breach was discovered or should have been discovered. If the warranty does not explicitly extend to future performance, a cause of action for breach accrues at tender of delivery. Derek Truck Sales, a merchant, has sold a truck with serious mechanical problems, thereby breaching the implied warranty of merchantability—such a defective truck is not fit for its ordinary purposes. An implied warranty, by definition, is not explicit; and, therefore, Park's cause of action for breach of the implied warranty of merchantability accrued when delivery of the truck was tendered. Since the parties did not agree to otherwise reduce the statutory period, the four-year limitations period established by the UCC controls; and Park must, therefore, file his lawsuit within four years of tender of delivery. Accordingly, answer (c) is incorrect. Answer (a) is incorrect because the parties may, in their original contract, agree to reduce the UCC statutory period of four years to a period of not less than one year. Under no circumstances, however, may the parties extend the Statute of Limitations. Answer (d) is incorrect because a plaintiff may, in proper circumstances (i.e., disability of plaintiff to sue or defendant's absence from the jurisdiction), claim that the running of the Statute of Limitations has been tolled (stopped).

37. (584,L1,55) (c) The Sales Article of the UCC applies to the sale of goods, specially manufactured or otherwise. Although certain provisions apply only to transactions between merchants, the general scope of the Article extends to sales by nonmerchants as well. By UCC definition, the term "goods" does not include investment securities. Goods is defined as all things (including specially manufactured goods) which are moveable at the time of identification to the contract, except money, investment securities, intangible property, contract rights, or accounts receivable. Goods include the unborn young of animals, growing crops, and standing timber to be cut. The sale of investment securities is, therefore, covered by a separate Article. The sale of real estate is governed by common law, not Article 2 of the UCC. Answers (a), (b), and (d) are, therefore, incorrect.

38. (584,L1,56) (a) Any seller, not only a merchant seller, may create an express warranty by making any affirmation of fact or promise which forms part of the basis of the bargain. Such a warranty may be made either orally or in writing and will exist regardless of the seller's intent. Answers (b), (c) and (d) are, therefore, incorrect.

Answer Outline

Problem 1 Bulk Sale

a1. Transaction qualifies as a bulk sale
As covered by Article 6 of the U.C.C.
Seller's entire inventory being sold, not a sale, in ordinary course of business

a2. Bulk sale is ineffective against any of transferor's creditors unless
Transferee requires transferor to furnish list of existing creditors and property transferred
Transferee gives notice of the bulk sale to the creditors at least 10 days prior to the transfer
Legal procedures are employed to prevent wrongful sales
Merchant selling to favored buyer at unrealistically low prices
Merchant selling in bulk and disappearing with proceeds

a3. Yes, with respect to inventory examination
An accurate description of the inventory is both parties' responsibility
Examination of inventory schedule was required to protect buyer's rights
No, with respect to list of creditors
An accurate list of creditors is solely transferor's responsibility
Transferee not required to incur cost to verfiy it
Transferee has right to rely upon it
Unless transferee has knowledge of inaccuracies

Unofficial Answer

Problem 1 Bulk Sale

Part a.

1. The transaction is a bulk sale as described in Article 6, Bulk Transfers, of the Uniform Commercial Code, because the seller's entire inventory is being sold in other than the ordinary course of business.

2. The Uniform Commercial Code provides that the following procedures must be followed for a bulk transfer to be valid and effective against any creditor:

- The transferee (bulk purchaser) must require the transferor to furnish a list of his existing creditors and amounts due.
- The parties must prepare a schedule of the property transferred sufficient to identify it.
- At least 10 days prior to taking possession or paying for the goods, the transferee must give notice to the creditors.

The bulk sale provisions are aimed at preventing two types of wrongful sales by a dishonest, financially distressed merchant. The merchant either sells in bulk at unrealistically low prices to a favored buyer and his creditors receive very little, or he sells and disappears with the proceeds.

3. Yes, with respect to the inventory; no, with respect to the list of creditors. A full and accurate description of the inventory is the responsibility of the parties; hence, the examination of the seller's inventory schedules was required. The preparation of the list of creditors is exclusively the responsibility of the bulk transferor. The purchaser is not required to incur the cost to verify the accuracy of the list of creditors and has the right to rely upon it unless he knows otherwise.

Answer Outline

Problem 2 Option Contract, Risk of Loss

a. Clauson will prevail. If no consideration, firm offer rule of UCC Article 3 applies
Offer by merchant
Signed writing
Assurance that offer is not revocable
Limited in all cases to three months
Three-month limit not applicable due to consideration
I.e., a binding contract exists
Clauson's acceptance was lawful and timely
Clauson is entitled to recover damages

b. Flowers will prevail
Risk of loss on Hargrove per shipping terms
Terms specified FOB N&W RR at Norfolk
I.e., specified shipper and FOB shipping point
Risk of loss passed to Hargrove when delivered to N&W
Reservation of title has no effect on risk of loss

Unofficial Answer

Problem 2 Option Contract, Risk of Loss

Part a.

Clauson Enterprises will prevail. The option in question is supported by consideration and consequently is a binding contract. The offer is definite and certain despite the fact that the pricing terms are not presently determinable. The Uniform Commercial Code is extremely liberal regarding satisfaction of the pricing terms.

Except for the presence of consideration in the form of the promise by Clauson to deliver the market survey to Migrane, the option would not have been binding beyond three months and Migrane would have prevailed. Section 2-205 of the Uniform Commercial Code provides as follows:

> An offer by a merchant to buy or sell goods in a signed writing which by its terms gives assurance that it will be held open is not revocable, for lack of consideration, during the time stated or if no time is stated for a reasonable time, but in no event may such period of irrevocability exceed three months; but any such term of assurance on a form supplied by the offeree must be separately signed by the offeror.

It is apparent from the wording of this section that the option was valid without consideration, but only for three months. It was an offer by a merchant contained in a signed writing and clearly stated its irrevocability. Furthermore, the separately signed requirement where the form is supplied by the offeree was satisfied. But the section is inapplicable to the facts of this case since bargained-for consideration was present. The Uniform Commercial Code's three-month limitation does not apply to options where consideration is present. Hence, Clauson's acceptance was valid, and if Migrane refuses to perform, Clauson will be entitled to damages.

Part b.

Flowers will prevail because Hargrove has the risk of loss. The shipping terms determine who had the risk of loss. Section 2-509(1) of the Uniform Commercial Code provides that "Where the contract requires or authorizes the seller to ship the goods by carrier, (a) if it does not require him to deliver at a particular destination, the risk of loss passes to the buyer when the goods are duly delivered to the carrier, even though the shipment is under reservation . . ."

The facts that title was reserved by Flowers and that Flowers retained the negotiable bill of lading do not affect the determination of who is to bear the risk of loss. The code makes it clear that title is irrelevant in determining the risk of loss.

Answer Outline

Problem 3 Consignments

a. Key legal characteristics of consignments
  - Consignor — owner of goods
  - Consignee — agent who is to sell goods

  Characteristics
  1. Title stays with consignor
  2. Consignee has no obligation to purchase or pay for goods
  3. Consignee is paid a commission for goods sold
  4. Proceeds are consignor's

Unofficial Answer

Problem 3 Consignments

Part a.

A consignment is a selling arrangement between the owner, called the *consignor*, and the party who is to sell the goods, called the *consignee*. The consignee is appointed the agent to sell the owner's merchandise. The following are the key characteristics.

1. Title to the goods remains at all times with the consignor.
2. The consignee is at no time obligated to buy or pay for the goods.
3. The consignee receives a commission for the goods sold.
4. The proceeds belong to the consignor.

Answer Outline

Problem 4 Breach of Warranty; Breach of Sales Contract

Part a.

No. Sure not liable for breach of warranty
- Sure did not give any implied warranties
  - Disclaimed implied warranty of merchantability
    - Disclaimer mentioned "merchantability"
  - Disclaimed implied warranty of fitness of purpose
    - Disclaimer was in writing and was conspicuous
- Contract was considered final expression of agreement
  - Parol evidence rule negates prior express warranties

Part b.

1. Yes. Wilmot's defenses for nonperformance are without merit
   Wilmot engaged in anticipatory repudiation
      Buyer can sue for difference between contract price and market value at time learned of breach
2. No. Monetary damages are adequate
   Puts Nielson in same position as if performance had occurred
3. No. Upon seller's learning of buyer's insolvency
   Seller need only perform if buyer pays with cash
   Seller also has right to demand written assurances

Unofficial Answer

(Author Modified)

Problem 4 Breach of Warranty; Breach of Sales Contract

Part a.

No. Both implied and express warranties may be present in a sale of goods. In the described fact situation, it appears that the fading of the coats could be considered a breach of both the implied warranty of merchantability and the implied warranty of fitness of purpose. However, due to the disclaimers contained in provisions four and five of the sales contract, Sure did not extend these warranties in this sale of goods. For the seller to disclaim the implied warranty of merchantability, the disclaimer, if in writing, must be conspicuous and contain some form of the word "merchantability". Provision four meets both of these requirements, and consequently would operate to disclaim the implied warranty of merchantability.

To disclaim the implied warranty of fitness of purpose, the seller need not use the exact language (i.e., fitness of purpose). The seller must use a conspicuous written statement that would alert the reasonable buyer to the fact that this warranty is being disclaimed. Provision five would meet this requirement. Consequently, in this sale of goods, neither implied warranty has been granted by Sure.

In deciding whether Sure breached the oral express warranties, the parol evidence rule must be applied, since Sure and its distributors intended the written contract as a complete and final expression of their agreement. The parol evidence rule states that a final writing intended by the parties as their complete agreement may not be changed, modified, altered or varied by any oral or written evidence occuring prior to, or contemporaneously with the signing of the agreement. Consequently, any express oral warranties made by Sure prior to the execution of this contract would have no legal effect.

Thus, the only warranties granted by Sure would be those contained in the first and second provisions of the written contract, and neither of these have been breached. Therefore, Sure would not be liable for breach of warranty.

Part b.

1. Yes. It appears that Wilmot is attempting to assert the defense of mistake of an existing fact which, if present, would destroy the reality of consent needed for a binding agreement and create an unenforceable contract. However, in the described situation, there is no mistake of an existing fact, only poor business judgement which would not discharge Wilmot's contractual obligation.

Wilmot is also claiming impossibility as a defense. Objective impossibility, if present, does discharge a party's contractual duty to perform. Objective impossibility occurs when: (1) needed subject matter is destroyed, (2) subsequent statute makes activity involved in contract illegal, (3) incapacitation of individual whose services are needed. None of these three situations are present in the described facts. Wilmot's impossibility would be subjective impossibility, which does not discharge the party's duty to perform. Thus, Wilmot breached the contract when he attempted to cancel on February 15.

Wilmot's cancellation constituted anticipatory repudiation. Upon such repudiation by the seller, the buyer may immediately terminate the contract and sue for the appropriate remedy (in this problem—monetary damages). However, if commercially reasonable, the buyer also has the option of ignoring the seller's repudiation, and waiting for the seller to perform at the appointed time (by March 10). If seller's performance does not occur at that time, then the buyer is able to sue for breach.

Nielson engaged in this latter course of action. This presents an issue as to which market value of the goods should be used in computing the buyer's damages, market value at time of cancellation ($2.70) or market value at date for performance ($3.00). The rule states that the market value at the time the buyer learned of the breach should be used in computing the buyer's damages. However, the Uniform Commercial Code is not exactly clear on what this means with regard to anticipatory repudiation. Section 2-723 of the Uniform Commercial Code states that if the action based on anticipatory repudiation comes to trial before time for performance, the market price used to compute the buyer's damages is the price prevailing at the time the buyer learned of the repudiation. However, the Uniform Commercial Code states nothing concerning an action coming to court after the date for performance (March 15). Thus, one could argue that if the buyer was adhering to the duty to mitigate one's damages by awaiting the contract time for performance, the court should use the market value at the time of performance to compute the buyer's damages. If this situation existed in the stated problem, Nielson would then collect $.50 per pair of scissors [the difference between the contract price ($2.50) and the market value at time of performance ($3.00)] plus incidental and consequential damages minus any expenses saved due to the seller's breach. However, if it was not commercially reasonable to await performance, then Nielson could only collect $.20 per pair [the difference between the contract price ($2.50) and the market value at time Nielson learned of breach ($2.70)].

2. No. Specific performance is only available in a breach of contract action when monetary damages would be inadequate to redress the injury that the nonbreaching party suffered. In this problem, monetary damages would be adequate to put Nielson in the same position it would have occupied if Wilmot had performed as promised.

3. No. When the seller discovers that the buyer is insolvent before delivering the goods, the seller must still perform if the insolvent buyer is willing to pay cash. Also, when Wilmot learned of Nielson's insolvency, it could have demanded written assurances of performance. The Uniform Commercial Code states that when reasonable grounds for insecurity concerning the other party's performance are learned, the aggrieved party can suspend their performance and demand adequate assurances of performance from the other party. If Nielson does not provide these assurances within a reasonable period of time, Wilmot may consider the agreement breached.

Multiple Choice Questions (1–51)

1. The following question concerns an instrument which Alex & Co. has in its possession:

> October 5, 1982
>
> To: Henry Futterman Suppliers
> 281 Cascade Boulevard
> Spokane, Washington 99208
>
> $950.00
>
> Pay to the order of Alex & Co.
> Nine hundred fifty and 00/100 dollars
> one month after acceptance.
>
> Alex & Co.
>
> By *Charles Alex*
> Managing Partner
>
> Alex & Co.
> 264 Liberty Avenue
> Philadelphia, Pa. 19117
>
> Accepted by: *Laura Futterman,* TREASURER
> Henry Futterman Suppliers
>
> Date: October 15, 1982

The above instrument is

a. Nonnegotiable since the payee is also the drawer.
b. A time promissory note.
c. A trade acceptance which imposes primary liability upon Henry Futterman Suppliers after acceptance.
d. A negotiable investment security under the Uniform Commercial Code.

2. An instrument complies with the requirements for negotiability contained in the Commercial Paper Article of the Uniform Commercial Code. The instrument contains language expressly acknowledging the receipt of $10,000 by the First Bank of Grand Rapids and an agreement to repay principal with interest at 15% one year from date. This instrument is

a. Nonnegotiable because of the additional language.
b. A negotiable certificate of deposit.
c. A banker's draft.
d. A banker's acceptance.

3. The following question concerns an instrument which Alex & Co. has in its possession:

> No. 003
> Nov.1, 1982 62-105/251
>
> Pay to the order of *Alex & Co.* $1,000.00
>
> *One Thousand and 00/100* Dollars
>
> *Ten days after presentment*
>
> Security Trust Company
> Austin, Texas
>
> Memo: For purchases
> of securities
>
> *Herbert Stein*
> Herbert Stein

The above instrument is

a. Nonnegotiable.
b. A draft.
c. A trade acceptance.
d. A check.

9

4. Ash Company has in its possession the following note:

> October 15, 1982
>
> I, Joseph Gorman, promise to pay or deliver to Harold Smalley or to his order ONE THOUSAND DOLLARS ($1,000) or at his option to deliver an amount of stock in the Sunrise Corporation which, on the due date of this instrument, is worth not less than ONE THOUSAND DOLLARS ($1,000). This note is due and payable on the 1st of November, 1982.
>
> *Joseph Gorman*
> Joseph Gorman

This note is

a. Not commercial paper, but instead a negotiable investment security.
b. A negotiable promissory note since it is payable to Smalley's order and contains an

unconditional promise to pay $1,000 if the holder so elects.

c. Nonnegotiable since it gives Smalley the option to take stock instead of cash.

d. Nontransferable.

5. Below is a note which your client, Robinson Real Estate, Inc., obtained from Grant in connection with Grant's purchase of a homesite located in Bangor, Maine. The note was given for the balance due on the purchase and was secured by a first mortgage on the homesite.

> $17,000.00 Bangor, Maine
> November 1, 1982
>
> For value received, five years after date, I promise to pay to the order of Robinson Real Estate, Inc., SEVENTEEN THOUSAND and 00/100 DOLLARS with interest at 15% compounded annually until fully paid. This instrument arises out of the sale of land located in Maine and the law of Maine is to be applied to any question which may arise. It is secured by a first mortgage on the land conveyed. It is further agreed that:
>
> 1. Purchaser will pay the costs of collection including attorney's fees upon default.
> 2. Purchaser may repay the amount outstanding on any anniversary date of this note.
> 3. This note is subject to such implied conditions as are applicable to such notes.
>
> Robert Grant

This note is a

a. Nonnegotiable promissory note since it is secured by a first mortgage.

b. Nonnegotiable promissory note since it permits prepayment and requires the maker's payment of the costs of collection and attorney's fees.

c. Negotiable promissory note.

d. Negotiable investment security under the Uniform Commercial Code.

6. The following instrument has been received by your client:

> October 15, 1981
>
> To: Bill Souther
> Rural Route 1
> Waverly, Iowa
>
> Pay to the order of James Olson six hundred dollars.
>
> Robert Smythe

Which of the following is correct?

a. The instrument is payable on demand.

b. The instrument is a negotiable note.

c. As Bill Souther is the drawer, he is primarily liable on the instrument.

d. As Bill Souther is the drawee, he is secondarily liable on the instrument.

7. Which of the following provisions contained in an otherwise negotiable instrument will cause it to be nonnegotiable?

a. It is payable in Mexican pesos.

b. It contains an unrestricted acceleration clause.

c. It grants to the holder an option to purchase land.

d. It is limited to payment out of the entire assets of a partnership.

8. A client has in its possession the instrument below.

> I, Margaret Dunlop, hereby promise to pay to the order of Caldwell Motors five thousand dollars ($5,000) upon the receipt of the final distribution from the estate of my deceased uncle, Carlton Dunlop. This negotiable instrument is given by me as the down payment on my purchase of a 1981 Lincoln Continental to be delivered in two weeks.
>
> Margaret Dunlop

The instrument is

a. Negotiable.

b. Not negotiable as it is undated.

c. Not negotiable in that it is subject to the two week delivery term regarding the purchase of the Lincoln Continental.

d. Not negotiable because it is **not** payable at a definite time.

9. The following three indorsements appear on the back of a negotiable promissory note made payable to Harold Dawson. The note is in the possession of Maxim Company.

> Pay to James Edwards
> *Harold Dawson*
>
> Without Recourse
> *James Edwards*
>
> *Gilbert Olsen*

The instrument has been dishonored after due presentment by Maxim. Proper notice of dishonor has been given to all parties. Which of the following is correct?

a. James Edwards' signature on the instrument was **not** necessary.

b. James Edwards has effectively negated all warranty liability to any subsequent party except Gilbert Olsen.

c. James Edwards has neither contractual nor warranty liability as a result of his indorsing without recourse.

d. Gilbert Olsen's signature was **not** necessary to effectively negotiate the instrument to Maxim.

10. Drummond broke into the Apex Drug Store and took all of the cash and checks which were in the cash register. The checks reflect payments made to Apex for goods sold. Drummond disposed of the checks and has disappeared. Apex is worried about its ability to recover the checks from those now in possession of them. Which of the following is correct?

a. Apex will prevail as long as its signature was necessary to negotiate the checks in question.

b. Since there was no valid transfer by Apex to Drummond, subsequent parties have no better rights than the thief had.

c. Apex will prevail only if the checks were payable to cash.

d. Apex will not prevail on any of the checks since it was the only party that could have prevented the theft.

11. Hoover is a holder in due course of a check which was originally payable to the order of Nelson or bearer and has the following indorsements on its back:

> Nelson
> Pay to the order of Maxwell
> Duffy
> Without Recourse
> Maxwell
> Howard

Which of the following statements about the check is correct?

a. It was originally order paper.

b. It was order paper in Howard's hands.

c. Maxwell's signature was **not** necessary for it to be negotiated.

d. Presentment for payment must be made within seven days after indorsement to hold an indorser liable.

12. Balquist sold a negotiable instrument payable to her order to Farley. In transferring the instrument to Farley, she forgot to indorse it. Accordingly

a. Farley qualifies as a holder in due course.

b. Farley has a specifically enforceable right to obtain Balquist's unqualified indorsement.

c. Farley obtains a better right to payment of the instrument than Balquist had.

d. Once the signature of Balquist is obtained, Farley's rights as a holder in due course relate back to the time of transfer.

13. Filmore had a negotiable instrument in its possession which it had received in payment of certain equipment it had sold to Marker Merchandising. The instrument was originally payable to the order of Charles Danforth or bearer. It was indorsed specially by Danforth to Marker which in turn negotiated it to Filmore via a blank indorsement. The instrument in question, along with some cash and other negotiable instruments, was stolen from Filmore on October 1, 1981. Which of the following is correct?

a. A holder in due course will prevail against Filmore's claim to the instrument.

b. Filmore's signature was necessary in order to further negotiate the instrument.

c. The theft constitutes a common law conversion which prevents anyone from obtaining a better title to the instrument than the owner.

d. Once an instrument is bearer paper it is always bearer paper.

14. Johnson lost a check that he had received for professional services rendered. The instrument on its face was payable to Johnson's order. He had indorsed it on the back by signing his name and printing "for deposit only" above his name. Assuming the check is found by Alcatraz, a dishonest person who attempts to cash it, which of the following is correct?

a. Any transferee of the instrument must pay or apply any value given by him for the instrument consistent with the indorsement.
b. The indorsement is a blank indorsement and a holder in due course who cashed it for Alcatraz would prevail.
c. The indorsement prevents further transfer or negotiation by anyone.
d. If Alcatraz simply signs his name beneath Johnson's indorsement, he can convert it into bearer paper and a holder in due course would take free of the restriction.

15. Industrial Factors, Inc., discounted a $4,000 promissory note, payable in two years, for $3,000. It paid $1,000 initially and promised to pay the balance ($2,000) within 30 days. Industrial paid the balance within the 30 days, but before doing so learned that the note had been obtained originally by fraudulent misrepresentation in connection with the sale of land which induced the maker to issue the note. For what amount will Industrial qualify as a holder in due course?

a. None because the 25% discount is presumptive or prima facie evidence that Industrial is **not** a holder in due course.
b. $1,000.
c. $3,000.
d. $4,000.

16. Who among the following can personally qualify as a holder in due course?

a. A payee.
b. A reacquirer who was not initially a holder in due course.
c. A holder to whom the instrument was negotiated as a gift.
d. A holder who had notice of a defect but who took from a prior holder in due course.

17. Your client, Globe, Inc., has in its possession an undated instrument which is payable 30 days after date. It is believed that the instrument was issued on or about August 10, 1980, by Dixie Manufacturing, Inc., to Harding Enterprises in payment of goods purchased. On August 13, 1980, it was negotiated to Desert Products, Inc., and thereafter to Globe on the 15th. Globe took for value, in good faith and without notice of any defense. It has been learned that the goods shipped by Harding to Dixie are defective. Which of the following is correct?

a. Since the time of payment is indefinite, the instrument is non-negotiable and Globe can **not** qualify as a holder in due course.
b. By issuing an undated instrument payable 30 days after date, Dixie was reserving the right to avoid liability on it until it filled in or authorized the filling in of the date.
c. Since the defense involves a rightful rejection of the goods delivered, it is valid against Globe.
d. Globe can validly fill in the date and will qualify as a holder in due course.

18. Barber has in his possession a negotiable instrument which he purchased in good faith and for value. The drawer of the instrument stopped payment on it and has asserted that Barber does not qualify as a holder in due course since the instrument is overdue. In determining whether the instrument is overdue, which of the following is incorrect?

a. A reasonable time for a check drawn and payable in the United States is presumed to be 30 days after issue.
b. A reasonable time for a check drawn and payable in the United States is presumed to be 20 days after the last negotiation.
c. All demand instruments, other than checks, are not overdue until a reasonable time after their issue has elapsed.
d. The instrument will be deemed to be overdue if a demand for payment had been made and Barber knew this.

19. Ajax, Inc., sold a refrigerator to Broadway Bill's Restaurant and accepted Broadway's negotiable promissory note for $600 as payment. The note was payable to Ajax's order one year after the date of issue. Thirty days after receiving the note, Ajax indorsed the note with a blank indorsement and sold it to National Bank for $550. National credited Ajax's checking account with $550, which brought Ajax's balance to $725. Ajax drew checks for a total of $675 which National honored. National then learned that the refrigerator had not been delivered by Ajax. The note is now due and unpaid. When National brings suit, Broadway pleads lack of consideration on the note. Which of the following is a valid statement with respect to the above facts?

a. The discount on the note is so great as to impugn National's taking in good faith.
b. In ascertaining the extent to which value had been given by National, the FIFO rule will apply to checks or notes deposited and the proceeds withdrawn.
c. Broadway has no liability on the note since it never received the refrigerator.
d. Broadway has only secondary liability on the note in question.

20. Marlin ordered merchandise from Plant to be delivered the following day and gave Plant a check payable to its order drawn on Marlin's account in First Bank. It was agreed that the check would not be transferred unless delivery was received and accepted. The goods were not delivered and Marlin notified Plant that he exercised his right to rescind. Plant, nevertheless, negotiated the check for full value to Rose who took it in good faith and without notice of any defense. Rose then negotiated it for full value to Quirk who knew of Plant's breach of the agreement. Marlin promptly stopped payment on the check and refuses to pay it. Under these circumstances, which of the following statements is correct?
a. Marlin would have a valid defense in a suit by Rose for the amount of the check.
b. Marlin would have a valid defense in a suit by Quirk for the amount of the check.
c. Despite the fact that Quirk can not personally qualify as a holder in due course, he can assert Rose's standing as such.
d. A stop payment order will not prevent a holder in due course from collecting from the bank.

21. Cindy Lake is a holder in due course of a negotiable promissory note for $1,000. Which of the following defenses of the maker may be validly asserted against her?
a. A total failure of consideration on the part of the party to whom it was issued.
b. A wrongful filling in of the amount on the instrument by the party to whom it was issued.
c. Nonperformance of a condition precedent to its transfer by the party to whom it was issued.
d. Infancy of the maker to the extent that it is a defense to a simple contract.

22. Harrison obtained from Bristow his $11,500 check drawn on the Union National Bank in payment for bogus uranium stock. He immediately negotiated it by a blank indorsement to Dunlop in return for $1,000 in cash and her check for $10,400. Dunlop qualified as a holder in due course. She deposited the check in her checking account in the Oceanside Bank. Upon discovering that the stock was bogus, Bristow notified Union National to stop payment on his check, which it did. The check was returned to Oceanside Bank, which in turn debited Dunlop's account and returned the check to her. Which of the following statements is correct?
a. Dunlop can collect from Union National Bank since Bristow's stop payment order was invalid in that the defense was only a personal defense.
b. Oceanside's debiting of Dunlop's account was improper since she qualified as a holder in due course.
c. Dunlop can recover $11,500 from Bristow despite the stop order, since she qualified as a holder in due course.
d. Dunlop will be entitled to collect only $1,000.

23. Dodger fraudulently induced Tell to issue a check to his order for $900 in payment for some nearly worthless securities. Dodger took the check and artfully raised the amount from $900 to $1,900. He promptly negotiated the check to Bay who took in good faith and for value. Tell, upon learning of the fraud, issued a stop order to its bank. Which of the following is correct?
a. Dodger has a real defense which will prevent any of the parties from collecting anything.
b. The stop order was ineffective against Bay since it was issued after the negotiation to Bay.
c. Bay as a holder in due course will prevail against Tell but only to the extent of $900.
d. Had there been no raising of the amount by Dodger, the bank would be obligated to pay Bay despite the stop order.

24. Dilworth, an employee of Excelsior Super Markets, Inc., stole his payroll check from the cashier before it was completed. The check was properly made out to his order but the amount payable had not been filled in because Dilworth's final time sheet had not yet been received. Dilworth filled in an amount which was $300 in excess of his proper pay and cashed it at the Good Luck Tavern. Good Luck took the check in good faith and without suspecting that the instrument had been improperly completed. Excelsior's bank paid the instrument in due course. Excelsior is demanding that

the bank credit its account for the $300 or that it be paid by Good Luck. Which of the following is correct?

a. Good Luck has **no** liability for the return of the $300.
b. Excelsior's bank must credit Excelsior's account for the $300.
c. A theft defense would be good against all parties including Good Luck.
d. Only in the event that negligence on Excelsior's part can be shown will Excelsior bear the loss.

25. Kirk made a check payable to Haskin's order for a debt she owed on open account. Haskin negotiated the check by a blank indorsement to Carlson who deposited it in his checking account. The bank returned the check with the notation that payment was refused due to insufficient funds. Kirk is insolvent. Under the circumstances

a. Kirk has a real defense assertable against all parties including Carlson, a holder in due course.
b. If Kirk files for bankruptcy, Haskin or Carlson could successfully assert that there had been an assignment of whatever funds were in Kirk's checking account.
c. If there is a proper presentment, and notice is properly given by Carlson to Haskin, Carlson may recover the amount of the check from Haskin.
d. Haskin or Carlson can correctly assert the standing of a secured creditor.

26. Franklin sold her grain business to Hobson for $150,000 and received a check drawn on Farmer's Bank for that amount. In addition, she entered into a contract for the purchase of a ranch for the same amount. The closing on the ranch is to take place in five days. The sales contract regarding the ranch requires payment by cash, by buyer's certified check, or by certified check payable to the buyer's order and indorsed to the seller. Franklin intends to have Hobson's check certified by Farmer's Bank and use it as payment. Which of the following is correct?

a. If the bank refuses to certify the check it has been dishonored.
b. If Hobson's account has sufficient funds to honor the check, Franklin has the right to have it certified.
c. Certification by the bank will discharge Hobson from liability as the drawer.
d. Only Hobson can obtain certification of the check.

27. Your client, Ensign Factors Corporation, has purchased the trade acceptance shown below from Mason Art Productions, Inc. It has been properly indorsed in blank on the back by Mason.

October 15, 1981

Adams Wholesalers, Inc.
49 Buena Vista Avenue
Santa Monica, California

Pay to the order of Mason Art Productions, Inc., ten thousand and 00/100 dollars ($10,000.00).

Gilda Loucksi, Pres.
Gilda Loucksi, President
Mason Art Productions, Inc.

Accepted October 24, 1981
Adams Wholesalers, Inc.
By Charles Lurch, President

As to the rights of Ensign, which of the following is correct?

a. The instrument is nonnegotiable, hence Ensign is an assignee.
b. Until acceptance, Mason had primary liability on the instrument.
c. After acceptance by Adams Wholesalers, Adams is primarily liable and Mason is secondarily liable.
d. After acceptance by Adams, Mason is primarily liable, and Adams is secondarily liable.

28. Smith buys a TV set from the ABC Appliance Store and pays for the set with a check. Later in the day Smith finds a better model for the same price at another store. Smith immediately calls ABC trying to cancel the sale. ABC tells Smith that they are holding him to the sale and have negotiated the check to their wholesaler, Glenn Company, as a partial payment on inventory purchases. Smith telephones his bank, the Union Trust Bank, and orders the bank to stop payment on the check. Which of the following statements is correct?

a. If Glenn can prove it is a holder in due course, the drawee bank, Union Trust, must honor Smith's check.
b. Union Trust is **not** bound or liable for Smith's stop payment order unless the order is placed in writing.

c. If Union Trust mistakenly pays Smith's check two days after receiving the stop order, the bank will **not** be liable.
d. Glenn can **not** hold Smith liable on the check.

29. Marshall Franks purchased $1,050 worth of inventory for his business from Micro Enterprises. Micro insisted on the signature of Franks' former partner, Hobart, before credit would be extended. Hobart reluctantly signed. Franks delivered the following instrument to Micro:

> January 15, 1980
>
> We, the undersigned, do hereby promise to pay to the order of Micro Enterprises, Inc., One Thousand and Fifty Dollars ($1,050.00) on the 15th of April, 1980.
>
> Marshall Franks
>
> Marshall Franks
>
> Norman Hobart
>
> Norman Hobart
>
> Memo:
> N. Hobart signed as an
> accommodation for Franks

Franks defaulted on the due date. Which of the following is correct?

a. The instrument is non-negotiable.
b. Hobart is liable on the instrument but only for $525.
c. Since it was known to Micro that Hobart signed as an accommodation party, Micro must first proceed against Franks.
d. Hobart is liable on the instrument for the full amount and is obligated to satisfy it immediately upon default.

30. Gomer developed a fraudulent system whereby he could obtain checks payable to the order of certain repairmen who serviced various large corporations. Gomer observed the delivery trucks of repairmen who did business with the corporations, and then he submitted bills on the bogus letterhead of the repairmen to the selected large corporations. The return envelope for payment indicated a local post office box. When the checks arrived, Gomer would forge the payees' signatures and cash the checks. The parties cashing the checks are holders in due course. Who will bear the loss assuming the amount cannot be recovered from Gomer?

a. The defrauded corporations.
b. The drawee banks.
c. Intermediate parties who indorsed the instruments for collection.
d. The ultimate recipients of the proceeds of the checks even though they are holders in due course.

31. An otherwise valid negotiable bearer note is signed with the forged signature of Darby. Archer, who believed he knew Darby's signature, bought the note in good faith from Harding, the forger. Archer transferred the note without indorsement to Barker, in partial payment of a debt. Barker then sold the note to Chase for 80% of its face amount and delivered it without indorsement. When Chase presented the note for payment at maturity, Darby refused to honor it, pleading forgery. Chase gave proper notice of dishonor to Barker and to Archer. Which of the following statements best describes the situation from Chase's standpoint?

a. Chase can **not** qualify as a holder in due course for the reason that he did **not** pay face value for the note.
b. Chase can hold Barker liable on the ground that Barker warranted to Chase that neither Darby nor Archer had any defense valid against Barker.
c. Chase can hold Archer liable on the ground that Archer warranted to Chase that Darby's signature was genuine.
d. Chase can **not** hold Harding, the forger, liable on the note because his signature does **not** appear on it and thus, he made no warranties to Chase.

32. Mask stole one of Bloom's checks. The check was already signed by Bloom and made payable to Duval. The check was drawn on United Trust Company. Mask forged Duval's signature on the back of the check and cashed the check at the Corner Check Cashing Company which in turn deposited it with its bank, Town National Bank of Toka. Town National proceeded to collect on the check from United. None of the parties mentioned was negligent. Who will bear the loss assuming the amount cannot be recovered from Mask?

a. Bloom.
b. Duval.
c. United Trust Company.
d. Corner Check Cashing Company.

33. Robb stole one of Markum's blank checks, made it payable to himself, and forged Markum's signature to it. The check was drawn on the Unity Trust Company.

Robb cashed the check at the Friendly Check Cashing Company which in turn deposited it with its bank, the Farmer's National. Farmer's National proceeded to collect on the check from Unity Trust. The theft and forgery were quickly discovered by Markum who promptly notified Unity. None of the parties mentioned was negligent. Who will bear the loss, assuming the amount cannot be recovered from Robb?

a. Markum.
b. Unity Trust Company.
c. Friendly Check Cashing Company.
d. Farmer's National.

34. Thieves broke into the warehouse of Monogram Airways and stole a shipment of computer parts belonging to Valley Instruments. Valley had in its possession a negotiable bill of lading covering the shipment. The thieves transported the stolen parts to another state and placed the parts in a bonded warehouse. The thieves received a negotiable warehouse receipt which they used to secure a loan of $20,000 from Reliable Finance. These facts were revealed upon apprehension of the thieves. Regarding the rights of the parties

a. Reliable is entitled to a $20,000 payment before relinquishment of the parts.
b. Monogram will be the ultimate loser of the $20,000.
c. Valley is entitled to recover the parts free of Reliable's $20,000 claim.
d. Valley is **not** entitled to the parts but may obtain damages from Monogram.

35. The Uniform Commercial Code deals differently with negotiable documents of title than with commercial paper. Which of the following will prevent a due negotiation of a negotiable document of title?

a. The transfer by delivery alone of a title document which has been endorsed in blank.
b. The receipt of the instrument in payment of an antecedent money obligation.
c. The taking of a bearer document of title from one who lacks title thereto.
d. The fact that the document of title is more than one month old.

36. Under the Uniform Commercial Code's rule, a warehouseman

a. Is liable as an insurer.
b. Will **not** be liable for the nonreceipt or misdescription of the goods stored even to a good faith purchaser for value of a warehouse receipt.
c. Can **not** limit its liability in respect to loss or damage to goods while in its possession.
d. Is liable for damages which could have been avoided through the exercise of due care.

37. In order to qualify as an investment security under the Uniform Commercial Code, an instrument must be

a. Issued in registered form, and **not** bearer form.
b. Of a long-term nature not intended to be disposed of within one year.
c. Only an equity security or debenture security, and **not** a secured obligation.
d. In a form that evidences a share, participation or other interest in property or in an enterprise, or evidences an obligation of the issuer.

38. Dwight Corporation purchased the following instrument in good faith from John Q. Billings:

> No. 7200 ●●●REGISTERED●●● $10,000
> Magnum Cum Laude Corporation
>
> Ten year 14% Debenture, Due May 15, 1990
>
> Magnum Cum Laude Corporation, a Delaware Corporation, for value received, hereby promises to pay the sum of TEN THOUSAND DOLLARS ($10,000) to JOHN Q. BILLINGS, or registered assigns, at the principal office or agency of the Corporation in Wilmington, Delaware.

On the reverse side of the instrument, the following appeared:

"For value received, the undersigned sells, assigns, and transfers unto DWIGHT CORPORATION, (signed) JOHN Q. BILLINGS." Billings' signature was guaranteed by Capital Trust Company.

Magnum's 14% debentures are listed on the Pacific Coast Exchange. The instrument is

a. A registered negotiable investment security which Dwight took free of adverse title claims.
b. Nonnegotiable since the instrument must be registered with Magnum to be validly transferred.
c. Negotiable commercial paper.
d. A nonnegotiable investment security since the instrument lacks the words of negotiability, "to the order of or bearer."

39. While auditing the common stock ledger of Sims Corporation a CPA uncovers the following situation. An investor has purchased a certificate representing 500 shares of common stock of the Sims Corporation from a former clerk of the corporation. It was the duty of the clerk to prepare stock certificates from a supply of blanks for signature of the corporate secretary. The clerk forged the corporate secretary's signature on a bearer certificate and delivered the certificate for value to the investor who did not have notice of the forgery and who now demands a reissued certificate in the investor's name from the corporation. The corporation asserts that it has no liability to reissue a certificate in the name of the investor and that the investor's bearer certificate is null and void. Which of the following is correct?

a. The certificate is valid and the investor is entitled to a reissued certificate.
b. The certificate issued is invalid and the corporation has **no** liability to reissue.
c. An appropriate recourse of the investor is to sue the corporation and clerk for dollar damages and to sue the clerk for the crime of forgery.
d. The corporation is required to reissue a certificate only if appropriately compensated by the investor.

40. Wilberforce & Company has in its possession certain securities which it took in good faith and for value from Dunlop. An adverse claim or defense has been asserted against the securities. Which of the following warranties may Wilberforce validly assert against Dunlop, its prior transferor?

a. There is **no** defect in the prior chain of title.
b. The securities are genuine and have **not** been materially altered.
c. There is **no** defect which might impair the validity of the securities.
d. Dunlop will defend the purchasers' title from adverse claim or defects which would impair the validity of the securities.

May 1984 Questions

Items 41 through 50 involve commercial paper under Article 3 of the Uniform Commercial Code.

41. Assuming each of the following instruments is negotiable, which qualifies as commercial paper?

a. Bearer documents of title.
b. Investment securities endorsed in blank.
c. Foreign currency.
d. A foreign draft.

42. Assuming each of the following is negotiable, which qualifies as a draft?

a. A bearer bond.
b. A trade acceptance.
c. A certificate of deposit.
d. A demand promissory note.

43. The requirements in order for an instrument to qualify as negotiable commercial paper

a. Are the same as the requirements for a bill of lading.
b. Permit some substitution or variance from the literal language of the UCC.
c. May be satisfied by a statement in the instrument that it is to be considered negotiable despite its omission of one or more requirements.
d. May be waived by the parties in a signed writing.

44. Your client has in its possession the following instrument:

> $700.00 Provo, Utah June 1, 1983
>
> Thirty days after date I promise to pay to the order of
>
> Cash
>
> Seven hundred Dollars
>
> at Boise, Idaho
>
> Value received with interest at the rate of ten percent per annum.
> This instrument is secured by a conditional sales contract.
>
> No. 20 Due July 1, 1983 Lyn Bowie

This instrument is

a. A negotiable time draft.
b. A nonnegotiable note since it states that it is secured by a conditional sales contract.
c. Not negotiable until July 1, 1983.
d. A negotiable bearer note.

45. The difference between an assignment to a good faith purchaser and negotiation to a holder in due course is

a. That the holder in due course obtains the instrument free of the defense of lack of consideration whereas one who takes as an assignee does **not**.
b. Mainly procedural in nature.

c. Primarily important insofar as the methods of transfer are concerned.
d. Relatively unimportant from a legal standpoint.

46. Ed Moss has a negotiable draft in his possession. The draft was originally payable to the order of John Davis. The instrument was endorsed as follows:

(1) Carl Bass
(2) John Davis
(3) Pay to the order of Nix & Co.
(4) Pay to Ed Moss, without recourse,
Nix & Co. per Jane Kirk, President
(5) For deposit, Ed Moss

Which of the following is correct regarding the above endorsements?

a. Number 1 prevents further negotiation since Bass is not the payee.
b. Number 2 does **not** change the instrument to bearer paper since it was originally payable to the order of Davis.
c. Number 4 eliminates all the contractual liability of the endorser.
d. Number 5 prevents any further negotiation.

47. In order to be a holder of a bearer negotiable instrument, the transferee must

a. Give value for the instrument.
b. Have physical possession of the instrument.
c. Take the instrument before receipt of notice of a defense.
d. Take in good faith.

48. Which of the following will **not** constitute value in determining whether a person is a holder in due course?

a. The taking of a negotiable instrument for a future consideration.
b. The taking of a negotiable instrument as security for a loan.
c. The giving of one's own negotiable instrument in connection with the purchase of another negotiable instrument.
d. The performance of services rendered the payee of a negotiable instrument who endorses it in payment for services.

49. Which of the following defenses may be successfully asserted by the maker against a holder in due course?

a. Wrongful filling in of an incomplete instrument by a prior holder.
b. Total failure to perform the contractual undertaking for which the instrument was given.
c. Fraudulent misrepresentations as to the consideration given by a prior holder in exchange for the negotiable instrument.
d. Discharge of the maker of the instrument in bankruptcy proceedings.

50. Regarding certification of a check,

a. Certification by a bank constitutes an acceptance of the check.
b. Certification of a check obtained by the drawer releases the drawer.
c. A bank is obligated to certify a customer's check if a holder demands certification and there are sufficient funds in the drawer's account.
d. If a holder obtains certification of a check, all prior endorsers are discharged, but the drawer remains liable.

51. Woody Pyle, a public warehouseman, issued Merlin a negotiable warehouse receipt for fungible goods stored. Pyle

a. May **not** limit the amount of his liability for his own negligence.
b. Will be absolutely liable for any damages in the absence of a statute or a provision on the warehouse receipt to the contrary.
c. May commingle Merlin's goods with similar fungible goods of other bailors.
d. Is obligated to deliver the goods to Merlin despite Merlin's improper refusal to pay the storage charges due.

Problems

Problem 1 Trade Acceptance; Nonnegotiable Instrument; Holder in Due Course (1183,L2b)

(7 to 10 minutes)

Part b. Hardy & Company was encountering financial difficulties. Melba, a persistent creditor whose account was overdue, demanded a check for the amount owed to him. Hardy's president said that this was impossible since the checking account was already overdrawn. However, he indicated he would be willing to draw on funds owed by one of the company's customers. He drafted and presented to Melba the following instrument.

October 1, 1983

TO:
Stitch Fabrications, Inc.
2272 University Avenue
Pueblo, Colorado 81001

Pay Hardy & Company, ONE THOUSAND and no/100 dollars ($1,000.00) 30 days after acceptance, for value received in connection with our shipment of August 11, 1983.

Hardy & Company

by Charles Hardy, President

242 Oak Lane Drive
Hinsdale, Illinois 60521

Accepted by: ______________________

Hardy endorsed the instrument on the back as follows:

Pay to the order of Walter Melba

Hardy & Company
Charles Hardy, President

Melba asserts that he is a holder in due course.

Required:

Answer the following, setting forth reasons for any conclusions stated.

1. What type of instrument is the above? How and in what circumstances is it used?

2. Is it negotiable?

3. Assume that the instrument is negotiable and accepted by Stitch, but prior to payment, Stitch discovers the goods are defective. May Stitch successfully assert this defense against Melba to avoid payment of the instrument?

Problem 2 Rights of Holder in Due Course; Unauthorized Signatures; Liability of Drawee Bank (581,L2)

(15 to 20 minutes)

Part a. Oliver gave Morton his 90-day negotiable promissory note for $10,000 as a partial payment for the purchase of Morton's business. Morton had submitted materially false unaudited financial statements to Oliver in the course of establishing the purchase price of the business. Morton also made various false statements about the business' value. For example, he materially misstated the size of the backlog of orders. Morton promptly negotiated the note to Harrison who purchased it in good faith for $9,500, giving Morton $5,000 in cash, a check for $3,500 payable to him which he indorsed in blank and an oral promise to pay the balance within 5 days. Before making the final payment to Morton, Harrison learned of the fraudulent circumstances under which the negotiable promissory note for $10,000 had been obtained. Morton has disappeared and the balance due him was never paid. Oliver refuses to pay the note.

Required:

Answer the following, setting forth reasons for any conclusions stated.

In the subsequent suit brought by Harrison against Oliver, who will prevail?

Part b. McCarthy, a holder in due course, presented a check to the First National Bank, the drawee bank named on the face of the instrument. The signature of the drawer, Williams, was forged by Nash who took the check from the bottom of Williams' check book along with a cancelled check in the course of burglarizing Williams' apartment. The bank examined the signature of the drawer carefully, but the signature was such an artful forgery of the drawer's signature that only a handwriting expert could have detected a difference. The bank therefore paid the check. The check was promptly returned to Williams, but he did not discover the forgery until thirteen months after the check was returned to him.

Required:

Answer the following, setting forth reasons for any conclusions stated.

1. Williams seeks to compel the bank to credit his account for the loss. Will he prevail?

2. The facts are the same as above, but you are to assume that the bank discovered the forgery before returning the check to Williams and credited his account. Can the bank in turn collect from McCarthy the $1,000 paid to McCarthy?

3. Would your answers to 1 and 2 above be modified if the forged signature was that of the payee or an indorser rather than the signature of the drawer?

Problem 3 Shelter Rule; Secondary Liability (583,L5a)

(7 to 10 minutes)

Part a. Dunhill fraudulently obtained a negotiable promissory note from Beeler by misrepresentation of a material fact. Dunhill subsequently negotiated the note to Gordon, a holder in due course. Pine, a business associate of Dunhill, was aware of the fraud perpetrated by Dunhill. Pine purchased the note for value from Gordon. Upon presentment, Beeler has defaulted on the note.

Required:

Answer the following, setting forth reasons for any conclusions stated.

1. What are the rights of Pine against Beeler?
2. What are the rights of Pine against Dunhill?

Multiple Choice Answers

1.	c	12.	b	22.	c	32.	d	42.	b
2.	b	13.	a	23.	c	33.	b	43.	b
3.	b	14.	a	24.	a	34.	c	44.	d
4.	c	15.	b	25.	c	35.	b	45.	a
5.	c	16.	a	26.	c	36.	d	46.	c
6.	a	17.	d	27.	c	37.	d	47.	c
7.	c	18.	b	28.	c	38.	a	48.	a
8.	d	19.	b	29.	d	39.	a	49.	d
9.	d	20.	c	30.	a	40.	b	50.	a
10.	a	21.	d	31.	b	41.	d	51.	c
11.	d								

Multiple Choice Answer Explanations

B. Types of Negotiable Instruments

1. (1182,L1,37) (c) This instrument is a trade acceptance. A trade acceptance is a draft drawn by the seller of goods on the buyer and accepted by the buyer. The buyer, Henry Futterman Suppliers, has primary liability on the instrument after their acceptance. Answer (a) is incorrect because the fact the payee is also the drawer does not destroy the negotiable aspect of an instrument. Answer (b) is incorrect because this instrument contains an order not a promise. Consequently, it does not qualify as a promissory note. Answer (d) is incorrect because the instrument is obviously not a negotiable investment security (stocks and bonds) which would be governed by Article 8 of the UCC.

2. (1182,L1,39) (b) A negotiable certificate of deposit is an instrument that complies with the requirements of a negotiable instrument and contains an acknowledgement of receipt of money by a bank with an agreement to repay it. The acknowledgement of the receipt of money by the bank on the face of the instrument does not destroy the negotiable aspect of the instrument. Therefore, answer (a) is incorrect. Answer (c) is incorrect because a banker's draft is a check drawn by one bank against funds deposited in its account in another bank. Answer (d) is incorrect because a banker's acceptance is a draft drawn on and accepted by a bank.

C. Requirements of Negotiability

3. (1182,L1,36) (b) The instrument is a negotiable draft since it meets all the requirements of a negotiable instrument and is a three party instrument that contains an order on its face. Stein is the drawer, Security Trust is the drawee and Alex & Company is the payee; therefore, answer (a) is incorrect. Answer (c) is incorrect because this instrument is not a trade acceptance since it is not drawn on and accepted by the buyer. Answer (d) is incorrect because before an instrument can qualify as a check it must be payable on demand. This instrument is not payable on demand, but payable ten days after presentment.

4. (1182,L1,41) (c) This instrument is nonnegotiable since it gives Smalley the option to take stock instead of cash. A negotiable promissory note must be payable only in money. The provision granting the payee the option to select stock as a second medium of payment would destroy the negotiable aspect of the instrument since it is possible to pay this instrument in something besides money. Therefore, answer (b) is incorrect. Answer (a) is incorrect because an investment security would not contain a promise to pay a sum certain in money. Answer (d) is incorrect because even though the instrument is nonnegotiable, Smalley could assign the instrument. Such a transfer would be governed by the law of assignments, not Article 3 of the UCC.

5. (1182,L1,40) (c) The instrument meets all the requirements needed for a negotiable instrument. It is a two party instrument that contains a promise. Consequently, it is a negotiable promissory note. The three provisions listed at the bottom of the instrument would not destroy the negotiable character of the instrument. Answer (a) is incorrect because a negotiable instrument may contain a second promise (another promise besides the unconditional promise to pay a sum certain in money), if the second promise provides security for the instrument. Answer (b) is incorrect because a provision requiring the maker's payment of the cost of collection does not destroy the sum certain needed for a negotiable instrument. Also a negotiable instrument may contain a prepayment provision. Answer (d) is incorrect since the instrument is obviously not a negotiable investment security (stocks and bonds) which would be governed by Article 8 of the UCC.

6. (582,L1,35) (a) The negotiable instrument in question is a draft payable on demand. If an instrument has no stated time for payment it is payable on demand. Answer (b) is incorrect because the instrument is a three-party instrument containing an order (a draft). A note is a two-party instrument that contains a promise. Answer (c) is incorrect because Souther is the drawee, not the drawer. Also, a drawer is secondarily liable on the instrument. This means the holder must first present the instrument to the drawee, the instrument must be dishonored and notice of dishonor must be given to the drawer before his secondary liability comes into effect. Answer (d)

is incorrect because Souther, as the drawee, would have no liability on the instrument until he accepted the draft and then he would have primary liability.

7. (582,L1,43) (c) Generally, if an instrument contains a promise to do any act in addition to the payment of money, it is nonnegotiable. An exception to this rule occurs when the additional promise concerns providing security for the instrument. Granting to the holder an option to purchase land is an additional promise that does not concern the providing of security. Consequently, this second promise would destroy the negotiable aspect of the instrument. Answer (a) is incorrect because an instrument that is payable in foreign currency is considered to be a sum certain in money even though the exchange rate might fluctuate from day to day. Answer (b) is incorrect because a negotiable instrument may be made payable at a definite time subject to acceleration at the option of the holder. Answer (d) is incorrect because a negotiable instrument must contain an unconditional promise or order. Normally a promise or order is conditional if the instrument states that it is to be paid only out of a particular fund. However, there is an exception to the particular fund rule that allows a partnership to issue a negotiable instrument that limits payment to the entire assets of the partnership.

8. (1181,L1,40) (d) One of the requirements for negotiability is that the instrument be payable on demand or at a definite time. An instrument which by its terms is otherwise payable only upon an act or event, uncertain as to time of occurrence, is not payable at a definite time. This instrument is not payable on demand and its payment rests upon an event that is uncertain with respect to time; therefore, it is not negotiable. Answer (b) is incorrect because it is not necessary that an instrument be dated in order to be negotiable. Answer (c) is incorrect because the payment of the instrument is not conditioned upon the two-week delivery term. Thus, the instrument does contain an unconditional promise to pay a sum certain.

E. Negotiation

9. (1182,L1,42) (d) In Olsen's hands the instrument was bearer paper since Edwards' prior indorsement was a blank indorsement. Proper negotiation of a bearer instrument merely demands delivery of the instrument. Consequently, Olsen's signature was not necessary to effectively negotiate the instrument to Maxim. Answer (a) is incorrect because Edwards' signature was necessary to negotiate the instrument. Edwards had order paper in his possession since Dawson's prior indorsement was a special indorsement and proper negotiation of an order instrument requires delivery and indorsement. Answers (b) and (c) are incorrect because a qualified indorsement (without recourse) negates contractual liability of the indorser, but not warranty liability. A qualified indorser, who receives value, warrants that s/he has no knowledge of a defense on the instrument whereas an unqualified indorser warrants there is no defense good on the instrument. The other four warranties extended by a qualified indorser are the same as those extended by an unqualified indorser.

10. (1182,L1,60) (a) If the checks are order instruments, then Apex's indorsement is necessary for proper negotiation. Theft of order paper creates the real defense of forgery, the unauthorized signing of a necessary signature. Consequently, if the checks stolen by Drummond were order instruments, he would have to forge Apex's name to properly negotiate the check, creating the real defense of forgery which would be good against all subsequent holders, including holders in due course. Answer (b) is incorrect because theft of a bearer negotiable instrument creates only a personal defense on the instrument which a holder in due course will defeat. Answer (c) would be incorrect because checks payable to cash would be bearer instruments and theft of such checks creates only a personal defense. Answer (d) is incorrect because the fact Apex was the only party that could have prevented the theft would have no bearing on Apex's right to recover the checks.

11. (582,L1,40) (d) A check must be presented for payment within seven days after indorsement to hold an indorser liable. Answer (a) is incorrect because an instrument is bearer paper if it states it is payable to a named person or bearer and there are no indorsements on the back. Answer (b) is incorrect because Maxwell's blank indorsement converts the instrument from order paper to bearer paper in Howard's possession. A blank indorsement is present when the indorser does not name a specified person in the indorsement as the indorsee. Answer (c) is incorrect because Duffy's indorsement is an example of a special indorsement which creates order paper in Maxwell's possession. Proper negotiation of order paper demands delivery and indorsement. Consequently, Maxwell's signature was necessary for negotiation of the check.

12. (582,L1,42) (b) When an order instrument is transferred for value without indorsement, the transferee has a specifically enforceable right to obtain the transferor's unqualified indorsement. Although the transferee may compel an indorsement, negotiation occurs only when the indorsement is given. Thus

Farley's rights as a holder in due course relate to the time the indorsement is made and do not relate back to the time of transfer. If Farley learns of a defense before acquiring the indorsement, she will not qualify as a holder in due course. Therefore, answer (d) is incorrect. Answers (a) and (c) are incorrect because to be a holder in due course, a person must receive the instrument by negotiation. Since this instrument was an order instrument, proper negotiation would demand delivery and indorsement. Until Farley receives Balquist's indorsement, she is unable to qualify as a holder in due course, instead she is merely an assignee with no better right to payment of the instrument than Balquist.

13. (1181,L1,39) (a) An instrument payable to order and indorsed in blank becomes payable to bearer, i.e., bearer paper. Theft of bearer paper constitutes a personal defense and a holder in due course takes free of all personal defense of any party to the instrument with whom he has not dealt. Therefore, a holder in due course will defeat Filmore's claim to the instrument. In contrast, theft of order paper would constitute a real defense, which a holder in due course would take subject to, since proper negotiation of order paper requires delivery and indorsement, which would necessitate a forgery by the thief. Answer (b) is incorrect because since the instrument is bearer paper, delivery alone would constitute proper negotiation. Answer (c) is incorrect because a holder in due course can acquire better rights than the owner. Answer (d) is incorrect because bearer paper can be converted to order paper by a special indorsement. A holder may convert a blank indorsement into a special indorsement by writing above the signature of the indorser any contract consistent with the character of the indorsement (e.g., "pay to the order of . . .").

14. (579,L1,28) (a) If an order instrument is indorsed with a restrictive indorsement, such as "for deposit only," and signed by the payee, then any transferee of the instrument must pay or apply any value given by them for the instrument consistent with the restrictive indorsement. Answer (b) is incorrect because the indorsement here is not a blank indorsement but a restrictive indorsement. Answer (c) is incorrect because restrictive indorsements that attempt to prevent further transfer or negotiation are of no effect. Answer (d) is incorrect because when a restrictive indorsement is placed on an instrument, all subsequent transferees must comply with the restriction in paying value for the instrument. Alcatraz would have notice that the indorsement was not complied with if the check was not held by a bank.

F. Holder in Due Course

15. (582,L1,36) (b) Industrial is a holder in due course to the extent they gave value for the instrument. A holder gives value to the extent he has performed the agreed upon consideration given for the instrument. If the holder performs less than the full agreed upon consideration, then the party is a holder in due course to the extent of his performance. In this question, Industrial learned of the defense before paying the balance ($2,000); consequently, Industrial only qualifies as a holder in due course to the extent of $1,000. Therefore answers (c) and (d) are incorrect. Answer (a) is incorrect because the 25% discount is not sufficient to create the presumption that Industrial did not act in good faith.

16. (1180,L1,1) (a) The correct answer is (a) since the payee is the only holder who can meet the requirements of a holder in due course. A holder in due course must be a holder who gives executed value for the instrument (cannot be a gift). The holder in due course may have no knowledge of the fact that the instrument (principal only) is overdue nor knowledge of any defense on the instrument when he or she receives it. A holder in due course must also take the instrument in good faith. Answer (b) is incorrect since a holder who does not qualify as a holder in due course cannot better his rights by transferring the instrument through a HIDC. Answer (c) is incorrect because the holder failed to give value. The holder in answer (d) cannot qualify as HIDC since he has knowledge of a defense, but the holder does receive the rights of a HIDC since he acquired the instrument through a HIDC.

17. (1180,L1,3) (d) An undated note is considered dated as of the day of issue. Thus Globe, the holder, has the authority to fill in the date with the day of issuance. After dating the instrument, Globe meets all the requirements of a HIDC. The fact that Globe received an undated instrument will not destroy its HIDC status. The time of payment is considered definite as soon as the appropriate date is entered. Answer (c) describes a personal defense (failure of consideration) which would not be good against a HIDC.

18. (580,L1,22) (b) Under the law of commercial paper to qualify as a holder in due course, the holder must have no knowledge that the instrument is overdue. A check is considered overdue if outstanding more than 30 days after issue. All other demand instruments are overdue after a reasonable time has elapsed, or if the holder is aware demand has been made for payment. Consequently, the only incorrect statement among the four answers is (b). Therefore, answers (a), (c), and (d) are incorrect.

19. (1177,L3,37) (b) In ascertaining value given by a bank, FIFO is used. In this case the bank has given value of $500. While the bank credited Ajax's account for $550, Ajax only spent $500. Answer (a) is incorrect because a $50 discount is not so great to affect good faith on a one-year note. Answer (c) is incorrect because Broadway has liability to the extent the bank is a holder in due course because nondelivery is a personal defense. Answer (d) is incorrect because as maker of a note, Broadway has primary liability.

20. (1178,L1,42) (c) A person who takes a negotiable instrument from a holder in due course acquires the rights of the holder in due course. Quirk, who knew of the prior breach, is barred as qualifying personally as a holder in due course. However, he took from a holder in due course, and thus has the rights of the holder in due course. Answer (a) is incorrect because Rose qualifies as a holder in due course and Marlin's defense is not good against Rose. Answer (b) is incorrect because as explained above, Quirk has the rights of a holder in due course. Answer (d) is incorrect because a proper stop order payment will prevent a holder in due course from collecting from the bank. The bank is not obligated to the holder in due course, who must proceed against the drawee of the check.

G. Rights of a Holder in Due Course

21. (582,L1,38) (d) Real defenses, not personal defenses, may be validly asserted against a holder in due course. Therefore, answer (d) is correct because infancy of the maker, to the extent that it is a defense to a contract, is a real defense. Failure of consideration, unauthorized completion of an incomplete instrument and nonperformance of a condition precedent are all personal defenses which may not be validly asserted against a holder in due course.

22. (1180,L1,8) (c) The only defenses good against a holder in due course are real defenses. In this case, the only defense Bristow can assert is fraud in the inducement, which is a personal defense, not good against a holder in due course. As a result, answer (c) is correct and Dunlop can recover the full $11,500 from Bristow. Bristow's only recourse will be against Harrison. Answer (a) is incorrect since the stop payment order requires the bank to refuse payment of the instrument. Oceanside's actions were proper under the circumstances making answer (b) incorrect. Answer (d) is also incorrect since Dunlop would be HIDC to the face value of the instrument since his check constitutes giving executed value for a negotiable instrument.

G.2.b. Material Alterations of Instrument

23. (1182,L1,43) (c) Bay, as a holder in due course, took the instrument free of all personal defenses but would be unable to defeat real defenses present on the instrument. Fraud in the inducement is a personal defense which would not be good against Bay. However, Dodger materially altered the check which creates a personal defense to the extent of the original tenor of the check ($900) and a real defense to the extent the instrument was altered ($1000). Consequently, Bay will prevail against Tell to the extent of $900. Answer (a) is incorrect because Dodger, being the party who materially altered the check, would have no defense to payment of this instrument. Answer (b) is incorrect because a customer (i.e., drawer) has the right to order his/her bank to stop payment of an item if the order is received at such time and in such manner as to afford the bank a reasonable opportunity to act on it prior to payment. Therefore, it would not matter that Tell's stop payment order was issued after the negotiation to Bay. Answer (d) is incorrect because normally a holder has no right to compel payment of a check by the drawee bank. This is true even though a stop payment order has not been issued by the drawer. Only when the bank has certified the check can the holder compel payment by the drawee bank.

24. (1181,L1,42) (a) Unauthorized completion of an incomplete instrument and lack of delivery are personal defenses. Thus, Good Luck, a holder in due course, takes the instrument free of these personal defenses and may enforce it as completed. Answer (b) is incorrect because a payor bank which pays an instrument which was completed in an unauthorized manner may charge the drawer's account for the face value of the instrument, except where the bank knows that the completion was improper. Answer (c) is incorrect because lack of delivery is a personal defense. Forgery, a real defense, is not present because the party who stole the instrument was Dilworth, the named payee. Answer (d) is incorrect because Excelsior will bear the loss with regard to both Good Luck and the bank, regardless of Excelsior's negligence. The loss should fall upon the party whose conduct left the instrument incomplete and made the unauthorized completion possible.

H. Liability of Parties

25. (1182,L1,38) (c) When Haskin negotiated the check with an unqualified indorsement, he extended contractual liability. Under the concept of contractual liability, the indorser guarantees payment of the instrument if the appropriate party for payment dis-

honors the instrument. Consequently, if there was proper presentment and notice given, Carlson may recover from Haskin when the bank dishonored the check. Answer (a) is incorrect because the fact that Kirk is insolvent does not create a real defense. If Kirk had been discharged from the debt in a bankruptcy proceeding, Kirk would then be able to assert a real defense that would be good against the holder in due course. The issuance of a check does not act as an assignment of the funds held in the bank, nor does it create a security interest on the part of the holder of the instrument. Therefore, answers (b) and (d) are incorrect.

26. (582,L1,39) (c) When the holder of a check procures certification of the instrument, the bank becomes primarily liable and the drawer and all prior indorsers are discharged from their secondary liability. However, if the drawer, rather than a subsequent holder, procured the certification s/he would remain secondarily liable on the instrument. Any subsequent holder, as well as the drawer, may request certification; however the bank may refuse such requests. Therefore, answers (b) and (d) are incorrect. Answer (a) is incorrect because the bank's refusal to certify does not constitute dishonor; only refusal to pay the check is dishonor.

27. (582,L1,41) (c) The instrument is a negotiable draft payable on demand and Ensign is a holder. Although Mason and Adams are the only parties to this instrument it qualifies as a draft (a three-party instrument) because Mason is both the drawer and the payee. The drawee on the instrument is Adams Wholesalers, who is primarily liable on the draft after accepting the instrument. Before acceptance, Adams had no liability on the draft. Mason, the payee and indorser, is secondarily liable on the instrument. No party would have primary liability until acceptance by the drawee. Therefore, answers (a), (b) and (d) are incorrect.

28. (1180,L1,5) (c) The correct answer is (c) since the bank is only liable to the drawer if failure to obey stop payment order caused the drawer a loss. Since Smith has no grounds for rescinding the sale, the Union Trust bank has no liability. Answer (a) is incorrect since a payee has no right to compel payment of a check by drawee bank. There is no privity of contract between the payee and drawee bank. Answer (b) is incorrect because the stop payment order can be oral or written. An oral order is effective for 14 days and a written order is effective for 6 months. A stop payment order does not destroy the drawer's liability on the instrument unless he has a valid defense, therefore, answer (d) is false.

29. (1180,L1,6) (d) An accommodating party (Hobart) is someone who lends his name to the instrument as security. Such a party is liable in the position he signs the instrument. In this case, Hobart signed as a co-maker and is therefore, primarily liable for the face value of the instrument. Micro can go against either Franks or Hobart on the due date. Hobart will be able to seek redress against Franks, the accommodated party. Therefore, answer (d) is correct. The instrument meets all the requirements of negotiability; thus, answer (a) is incorrect.

30. (580,L1,19) (a) Normally forgeries of the payee's signature would be sufficient to relieve the defrauded corporations of any liability on these instruments. However, a drawer who voluntarily transfers payment to an imposter (Gomer) must bear the loss if a holder in due course subsequently tries to collect. Therefore, answer (a) is correct. Forgery is usually a real defense that would be good against all subsequent holders in due course but the imposter exception would allow the banks, intermediate parties, and the recipients to avoid the loss. The rationale for such a result is the fact that the defrauded corporations were in the best position to keep the defense (forgery) from occurring.

H.2.c. Warranties

31. (1180,L1,9) (b) Barker, having received value for the instrument, has warranty liability to Chase, the immediate holder. Barker grants five warranties, one of which is that no defense is good on the instrument. Answer (b) is correct since this warranty was breached. If a holder performs the full agreed upon consideration or value promised for the instrument, he is a holder in due course to the face value of the instrument. This makes answer (a) incorrect. Answer (c) is incorrect because Archer's failure to endorse the instrument only extends his warranty liability (including the warranty that states all signatures are genuine) to the immediate holder, Barker. Answer (d) is incorrect since Harding is liable for the forgery he placed on the instrument.

32. (580,L1,15) (d) Corner Check Cashing Company must bear the loss because as a holder obtaining payment, it warrants that it has good title to the instrument. However, it does not have good title because the forgery prevented good title from passing. Therefore answers (a) and (c) are incorrect because of Corner Check Cashing Company's warranty of good title. Answer (b) is incorrect because Duval has a real defense in that his indorsement was forged. Corner Check Cashing Company's only recourse is to recover from Mask.

33. (580,L1,30) (b) If the drawee bank (Unity Trust Company) pays a check on which the drawer's signature (Markum) was forged, the bank is bound by the acceptance and the drawee can only recover the money paid from the forger (Robb). Normally a person who presents an instrument for payment makes three warranties. These warranties are: warranty of title; warranty of no knowledge that the signature of the drawer is unauthorized; warranty of no material alterations. However, a holder in due course or someone with the rights of a holder in due course does not warrant to the drawee bank that the drawer's signature is genuine because the drawer bank is in a better position to determine the genuineness of the drawer's signature. Therefore, the drawee bank should bear the loss.

K. Transfer of Negotiable Documents of Title

34. (1183,L1,47) (c) A document of title procured by a thief upon placing stolen goods in a warehouse confers no rights in the underlying goods. This defense is valid against a subsequent holder to whom the document of title has been duly negotiated. Therefore, Valley Instruments, the original owner of the goods, can assert better title to the goods than Reliable Finance. Accordingly, answers (a) and (d) are incorrect. Answer (b) is incorrect because Reliable Finance will be the ultimate loser, assuming Reliable is unable to collect from the thieves.

35. (583,L1,43) (b) Due negotiation of a negotiable document of title occurs when it is negotiated to a holder who takes in good faith, in the ordinary course of business, without notice of any defenses against the document, and pays value for the document. In the area of negotiable documents of title, which is governed by Article 7 of the UCC, value does not include payment of an antecedent debt. This is an important difference from the value concept required to create a holder in due course under Article 3. Answer (a) is incorrect because the transfer of a bearer contract (a document of title containing a blank endorsement is a bearer document) by delivery alone will not prevent due negotiation since a bearer document requires no endorsement for negotiation. Answer (c) is incorrect because delivery of a bearer document from one who lacks title will not prevent due negotiation. However, delivery of an order document from someone without title does prevent due negotiation. Answer (d) is incorrect because a document of title, unlike a check, is not considered overdue 30 days after issue.

36. (583,L1,44) (d) A warehouseman is a person who is in the business of storing the goods of others for compensation (a mutual benefit bailment). The warehouseman must exercise ordinary care and is liable for damages which could have been avoided through the exercise of due care. Answer (a) is incorrect because the warehouseman is not strictly liable as an insurer of the goods. Answer (b) is incorrect because a warehouseman who issues a document of title for nonexistent goods is liable for any damages that result. The warehouseman is also liable if the document of title misdescribes the goods, unless there is a conspicuous disclaimer of such liability on the document itself. Answer (c) is incorrect because a warehouseman may limit liability to a stipulated maximum. To do this, the warehouseman must offer the customer a choice of full liability at one rate and limited liability at a lower rate.

L. Transfer of Investment Securities

37. (1183,L1,48) (d) The Uniform Commercial Code defines an investment security as written evidence of debt, ownership, or other legal interest in a business which is issued in bearer or registered form and traded in markets or on securities exchanges as a medium of investment. Answer (a) is, therefore, incorrect. Answer (b) is incorrect because an investment security does not have to be of a long-term nature. Answer (c) is incorrect because an investment security may be either a secured or unsecured obligation.

38. (583,L1,46) (a) The given instrument is a debenture bond that is a negotiable investment security. Dwight, as a bona fide purchaser (received through proper negotiation, gave value, took in good faith and without notice of any adverse claim), acquires the security free of adverse title claims. Answer (b) is incorrect because the registration requirement for transfer would not affect the negotiable nature of the security, nor the rights of a bona fide purchaser. Answer (c) is incorrect because the instrument is a negotiable investment security governed by Article 8 of the UCC, not a negotiable instrument governed by Article 3. Answer (d) is incorrect because the word " assigns" is an acceptable substitute for the words of negotiability.

39. (582,L1,44) (a) An unauthorized signature placed on a stock certificate is effective in favor of a purchaser for value of the certificated security, if the purchaser is without notice of the lack of authority of the signing party and the signing has been done by an employee of the issuer entrusted with the responsible handling of the stock certificate. Therefore, the certificate is valid and the investor is entitled to a reissued certificate without having to further compensate the issuer, Sims Corporation. Answer (c) is incor-

rect because the investor is not entitled to sue the clerk for a criminal action; the criminal prosecution for the crime of forgery must be brought by the appropriate governmental state or federal authority.

40. (582,L1,45) (b) A person, by transferring a certificated security to a purchaser for value, warrants only that: (1) his transfer is effective and rightful; (2) the security is genuine and has not been materially altered; and (3) he knows of no fact which might impair the validity of the security. Therefore, since Wilberforce took the securities for value, he is entitled to assert any one of these three warranties against his transferor, Dunlop. The distinction between answer (c) and the third aforementioned warranty is that Dunlop only warrants that he has no knowledge of a defect which might impair the securities' validity, not that there is no defect.

May 1984 Answers

41. (584,L1,36) (d) A foreign draft is merely a draft which on its face is either drawn or payable outside the United States. Four types of negotiable ininstruments are included in the term "commercial paper"—drafts, checks, certificates of deposit, and notes—and are accordingly governed by Article 3 of the UCC. Answers (a) and (b) are incorrect because documents of title and investment securities, even though sometimes negotiable, do not qualify as commercial paper and are not governed by Article 3 of the UCC. Answer (c) is incorrect because foreign currency is money and, therefore, does not qualify as commercial paper. Commercial paper provides a medium of exchange in lieu of money.

42. (584,L1,37) (b) A draft is an instrument where the drawer orders the drawee to pay a stated sum of money to the payee. Thus, the draft has three parties present and contains an order. A trade acceptance is a draft drawn by the seller of goods on the buyer and is made payable to the seller. A bond is a two-party instrument that contains a promise. The same would be true of a demand promissory note. A certificate of deposit is an acknowledgement by a bank of receipt of money with a promise to repay. It is a specialized form of a note. Therefore, answers (a), (c), and (d) are incorrect.

43. (584,L1,38) (b) The requirements in order for an instrument to qualify as negotiable commercial paper permit some substitution or variance from the literal language of the UCC. Answer (a) is incorrect because the requirements in order for an instrument to qualify as negotiable commercial paper are much more extensive than the requirements for a bill of lading (Article 7 of the UCC). Answer (c) is incorrect because the face of the instrument must contain the nine requirements of negotiability as listed by Article 3 of the UCC, regardless of any provision on the instrument stating that it is to be considered negotiable. A statement to this effect has no impact whatsoever on the negotiability of the instrument. Answer (d) is incorrect because the requirements for negotiability cannot be waived by the parties to the instrument.

44. (584,L1,39) (d) The instrument meets all of the requirements needed for a negotiable instrument. It is a two-party instrument containing an unconditional promise to pay a stated sum and consequently, is a negotiable promissory note. It is a bearer note because it is payable to the order of cash. The designation of the place of payment does not affect the negotiability of an instrument. The negotiable aspect of an instrument is not affected by a provision on the face of the instrument that states security is given for the instrument. Therefore, answers (a) and (b) are incorrect. Answer (c) is incorrect because a negotiable instrument is negotiable immediately after it has been issued.

45. (584,L1,40) (a) A holder in due course takes the instrument free from all personal defenses, whereas one who takes as an assignee does not. Lack of consideration is a personal defense that would be good against the assignee but not against a holder in due course. The key difference between an assignment to a good faith purchaser and negotiation to a holder in due course is the assignee will never receive better rights than what the assignor had, where a holder in due course may receive better rights than his/her transferor. Therefore, answers (b), (c), and (d) are incorrect.

46. (584,L1,41) (c) A qualified indorsement eliminates all contractual liability of the indorsing party. Thus, since Nix & Co. indorsed the instrument in a qualified manner (without recourse), they will have no contractual liability. Answer (a) is incorrect because when an indorsement appears on a negotiable instrument without apparent reason (i.e., indorsement which is not in the chain of title), it is assumed that the indorsing party is an accommodation party. The presence of an accommodation party does not prevent further negotiation of an instrument. Answer (b) is incorrect because the blank indorsement of order paper changes the instrument from order paper to bearer paper. Answer (d) is incorrect because a restrictive indorsement does not prevent any further negotiation of the instrument.

47. (584,L1,42) (b) In order for someone in possession of a negotiable instrument to qualify as a holder, it is necessary that he receive the instrument through proper negotiation. Proper negotiation of bearer paper requires nothing more than the mere delivery of the instrument to the holder. Thus, in order to qualify as a holder of bearer paper, all that is necessary is that the transferee must have physical possession of the instrument. Answers (a), (c), and (d) are all incorrect because the requirements that the transferee give value for the instrument, take the instrument before receipt of notice of a defense, and take the instrument in good faith are all requirements in attaining holder in due course status. None of these are necessary requirements in order to be merely a holder of a bearer instrument.

48. (584,L1,43) (a) According to Article 3 of the UCC, in order for a holder to achieve holder in due course status, he must give executed value in exchange for the negotiable instrument. Future consideration is not considered to be adequate value in determining whether a person is a holder in due course. The consideration must be performed to qualify as executed value. Answer (b) is incorrect because the taking of a negotiable instrument as security for a loan will constitute executed value in determining whether a holder is a holder in due course. In this situation the holder will be deemed to have given value to the extent of the debt being secured. Answer (c) is incorrect because the exchange of one negotiable instrument for another constitutes the giving of executed value in determining whether a person is a holder in due course. Answer (d) is incorrect since the negotiable instrument is being given in exchange for services which have already been performed; thus, executed value in the form of completed services has been given in exchange for the instrument.

49. (584,L1,44) (d) A holder in due course takes a negotiable instrument subject only to the real defenses of that instrument. The assertion of any personal defense against a holder in due course will be unsuccessful. Since the discharge of the maker of an instrument in bankruptcy proceedings is a real defense, this defense can be successfully asserted against a holder in due course, thereby destroying the holder's right to collect on the instrument. The unauthorized completion of an incomplete instrument, the breach of a contractual obligation, and fraudulent misrepresentations are all merely personal defenses which could not be successfully asserted against a holder in due course. Consequently, answers (a), (b), and (c) are all incorrect.

50. (584,L1,45) (a) Certification by a bank constitutes an acceptance of the check. Upon the writing of a draft, no party to the draft has primary liability although the drawer and indorsers have secondary liability. Only after a draft has been accepted by the drawee does any party have primary liability with regard to the draft. Upon certification of a check, the bank has accepted the check and is, in effect, stating that it agrees to pay the check according to its terms. The bank's liability with regard to the check changes from no liability to primary liability upon certification. If any party other than the drawer requests certification of the check, the secondary liability of the drawer and all prior indorsers is destroyed. Therefore, answer (d) is incorrect. Answer (b) is incorrect because if certification is obtained by the drawer, the drawer's secondary liability remains intact. Only when certification is obtained by another party is the drawer's secondary liability destroyed. Answer (c) is incorrect because a bank is not obligated to certify a customer's check upon demand by the holder, even though sufficient funds are present in the drawer's account.

51. (584,L1,46) (c) Normally a warehouseman is not allowed to commingle goods of one bailor with those of another. However, in the case of fungible goods, warehousemen may commingle similar fungible goods of different bailors. Answer (a) is incorrect because a bailee may limit his liability to a stipulated maximum. To do this the warehouseman must offer the customer a choice of full liability at one rate and limited liability at a lower rate. Answer (b) is incorrect because warehousemen are not absolutely liable for any damages. The warehouseman must exercise ordinary care and is only liable for damages that could have been avoided through the exercise of due care. Answer (d) is incorrect because in the event that a bailor refuses to pay any storage charges due, a warehouseman has a lien against the goods to the extent of storage charges due and, as a result, can refuse to deliver the goods to the bailee.

Answer Outline

Problem 1 Trade Acceptance; Nonnegotiable Instrument; Holder in Due Course

Part b.

1. Instrument is a trade acceptance
    - Used in sales transactions, allowing seller to draw upon buyer for payment of goods
    - Seller is both drawer and payee
2. No, instrument lacks words of negotiability
    - Endorsement does not cure defect on face of instrument
3. No, Melba will prevail since he is a holder in due course
    - Discharging antecedent debt constitutes giving value for instrument
    - Holder in due course takes free of personal defenses
        - I.e., breach of warranty and contractual defenses

Unofficial Answer

Problem 1 Trade Acceptance; Nonnegotiable Instrument; Holder in Due Course

Part b.

1. The instrument in question is a draft and is commonly known as a trade acceptance. Such an instrument arises out of a sales transaction, whereby the seller is authorized to draw upon the purchaser for payment of the goods. Normally, as is the case here, the seller is both the drawer and the payee. The instrument is then presented for the buyer's acceptance.

2. No. The instrument lacks the magic words of negotiability on its face. That is, it is not payable to order or bearer but instead payable solely to Hardy & Company. The endorsement on the back of the instrument neither cures the defect nor provides the requisite words of negotiability. Hence, the instrument is not negotiable. The "for value received . . ." does not in any way affect negotiability.

3. No. Melba would be a holder in due course. He took in good faith and gave value even though the value in question is an antecedent indebtedness. The Uniform Commercial Code specifically provides that an antecedent indebtedness is value. Therefore, Melba as a holder in due course takes free of the so-called personal defenses. Breach of warranty and contractual defenses are personal defenses and a holder in due course such as Melba is not subject to them.

Answer Outline

Problem 2 Rights of Holder in Due Course; Unauthorized Signatures; Liability of Drawee Bank

a. Harrison will prevail against Oliver
- Harrison is a holder in due course
    - Instrument is negotiable
    - Harrison holder by negotiation
    - Harrison took in good faith and for value
    - Harrison took without notice of fraudulent procurement
- Harrison is able to recover to extent of value given ($8,500)
    - Value given to extent agreed consideration has been performed
        - Includes the $5,000 cash given
        - Includes the $3,500 check (i.e., negotiable instrument) given
    - Unperformed promise of $1,000 is executory in nature
        - Does not constitute value given

b1. Williams will not prevail against the bank
- Williams must exercise reasonable care to examine items returned by the bank
    - So as to discover unauthorized signature or alterations
- Williams must notify bank promptly after discovery thereof
- Williams must give notice within one year from the time such item is available to him
    - Or else his claim against the bank is absolutely barred
        - Regardless of negligence of either party

b2. The bank cannot collect the money paid to McCarthy
- The bank is required to know the signatures of its customers
    - Bank is in superior position to detect forgery
        - Deemed to have such knowledge of drawer's signature
- Bank is denied recovery from innocent holder, McCarthy, who has, in good faith, received proceeds of a forged instrument

b3. Answer to b1. would be changed to allow Williams to prevail over the bank
- A forged indorsement is ineffective to negotiate an order instrument
  - Bank not entitled to charge drawer's account for payment
- Williams is able to maintain claim against the bank
  - But must give notice of forged indorsement within three years from time item available to Williams
  - Williams precluded from asserting claim if his negligence contributed to the forgery
    - But bank must be free from negligence
- Answer to b2. would be changed to allow the bank to collect from McCarthy
- A forged indorsement is ineffective to negotiate an order instrument
  - Bank is permitted to recover from McCarthy who took under a forged indorsement
    - Bank is not deemed to know genuineness of indorser's signature
  - Bank is able to recover on "breach of warranty" theory
    - McCarthy breached warranty to the bank
      - That he has "good title" to the instrument.

Unofficial Answer

Problem 2 Rights of Holder in Due Course; Unauthorized Signatures; Liability of Drawee Bank

Part a.

Harrison will prevail, but only to the extent of "value," here $8,500, given for the negotiable promissory note. The primary issue in the case is the "value" requirement for holding in due course. The facts reveal that Harrison purchased the instrument in good faith, that it was not overdue, and, at the time the negotiation took place, Harrison had no knowledge of the fraudulent circumstances under which the instrument was originally obtained from Oliver. The facts indicate that the note was negotiable and that the negotiation requirement was satisfied.

The Uniform Commercial Code section dealing with "taking for value" provides that a holder, here Harrison, takes for value to the extent that the agreed consideration has been performed. Certainly the payment of the $5,000 in cash constitutes value. The code further provides that when a holder gives a negotiable instrument for the instrument received, he has given value. Although this provision is primarily concerned with the giving of one's own negotiable instrument, it is obvious that the negotiation of another's negotiable instrument as payment is value. However, the promise to pay an agreed consideration is not value even though it constitutes consideration.

Part b.

1. No. Williams will not prevail. The Uniform Commercial Code imposes upon the depositor the responsibility for reasonable care and promptness in discovering and reporting his unauthorized signature. In any case, the depositor must discover and report his unauthorized signature within one year from the time the items (checks) are made available to him. The latter rule applies irrespective of lack of care on the part of either the bank or depositor. This absolute rule is based in part upon the rationale that, after certain periods of time have elapsed in respect to commercial transactions, finality is the most important factor to be considered. Thus, after this amount of time has elapsed, existing expectations and relations are not to be altered.

2. No. The bank cannot collect from McCarthy. The Uniform Commercial Code places the burden upon the bank to know at its peril the signature of its drawer. Therefore, when the bank has paid on the forged signature of a depositor, it cannot recover the loss by seeking collection from a party who has received payment in good faith.

3. The first answer (b.1.) would be changed in that the law allows the depositor a three-year period in which to discover the forged signature of the payee or an indorser. Thus, if both the bank and depositor are not negligent (as it would appear from the excellence of the forgery), the loss rests with the bank. However, if it can be shown that the depositor was negligent (for example, he disregarded a notice from the proper party that he had not received payment), the bank will prevail if it was in no way negligent.

The restated circumstances also change the second answer (b.2.). A bank is not deemed to know the signatures of indorsers; therefore, the bank may recover its loss from McCarthy, the party collecting on the item. Section 3-417 of the Uniform Commercial Code provides that a party receiving payment on the instrument warrants to the payor that he has good title to the instrument.

Answer Outline

Problem 3 Shelter Rule; Secondary Liability

Part a.

1. Pine would recover from Beeler
   - Fraud in inducement not valid against holder who has acquired the rights of holder in due course
     - This is shelter rule
2. Pine could recover against Dunhill if he gives notice of dishonor
   - Dunhill's indorsement makes him secondarily liable
     - I.e., he promises to pay if appropriate party does not

Unofficial Answer

Problem 3 Shelter Rule; Secondary Liability

Part a.

1. Pine is not a holder in due course because he has knowledge of a defense against the note. However, Pine has the rights of a holder in due course because he acquired the note through Gordon, who was a holder in due course. The rule where a transferee not a holder in due course acquires the rights of one by taking from a holder in due course is known as the "shelter rule." Through these rights, Pine is entitled to recover the proceeds of the note from Beeler. The defense of fraud in the inducement is a personal defense and not valid against a holder in due course or one with the rights of a holder in due course.

2. As one with the rights of a holder in due course, Pine is entitled to proceed against any person whose signature appears on the note, provided he gives notice of dishonor. When Dunhill negotiated the note to Gordon, Dunhill's signature on the note made him secondarily liable. As a result, if Pine brings suit against Dunhill, Pine would prevail because of Dunhill's secondary liability.

Multiple Choice Questions (1 - 25)

1. Which of the following is included within the scope of the Secured Transactions Article of the Code?
   a. The outright sale of accounts receivable.
   b. A landlord's lien.
   c. The assignment of a claim for wages.
   d. The sale of chattel paper as a part of the sale of a business out of which it arose.

2. Donaldson, Inc., loaned Watson Enterprises $50,000 secured by a real estate mortgage which included the land, buildings, and "all other property which is added to the real property or which is considered as real property as a matter of law." Star Company also loaned Watson $25,000 and obtained a security interest in all of Watson's "inventory, accounts receivable, fixtures, and other tangible personal property." There is insufficient property to satisfy the two creditors. Consequently, Donaldson is attempting to include all property possible under the terms and scope of its real property mortgage. If Donaldson is successful in this regard, then Star will receive a lesser amount in satisfaction of its claim. What is the probable outcome of Donaldson's action?
   a. Donaldson will not prevail if the property in question is detachable trade fixtures.
   b. Donaldson will prevail if Star failed to file a financing statement.
   c. Donaldson will prevail if it was the first lender and duly filed its real property mortgage.
   d. The problem will be decided by taking all of Watson's property (real and personal) subject to the two secured creditors' claims and dividing it in proportion to the respective debts.

3. Lombard, Inc., manufactures exclusive designer apparel. It sells through franchised clothing stores on consignment, retaining a security interest in the goods. Gifford is one of Lombard's franchisees pursuant to a detailed contract signed by both Lombard and Gifford. In order for the security interest to be valid against Gifford with respect to the designer apparel in Gifford's possession, Lombard
   a. Must retain title to the goods.
   b. Does not have to do anything further.
   c. Must file a financing statement.
   d. Must perfect its security interest against Gifford's creditors.

4. Attachment and perfection will occur simultaneously when
   a. The security agreement so provides.
   b. There is a purchase money security interest taken in inventory.
   c. Attachment is by possession.
   d. The goods are sold on consignment.

5. Tawney Manufacturing approached Worldwide Lenders for a loan of $50,000 to purchase vital components it used in its manufacturing process. Worldwide decided to grant the loan but only if Tawney would agree to a field warehousing arrangement. Pursuant to their understanding, Worldwide paid for the purchase of the components, took a negotiable bill of lading for them, and surrendered the bill of lading in exchange for negotiable warehouse receipts issued by the bonded warehouse company that had established a field warehouse in Tawney's storage facility. Worldwide did not file a financing statement. Under the circumstances, Worldwide
   a. Has a security interest in the goods which has attached and is perfected.
   b. Does **not** have a security interest which has attached since Tawney has not signed a security agreement.
   c. Must file an executed financing statement in order to perfect its security interest.
   d. Must **not** relinquish control over any of the components to Tawney for whatever purpose, unless it is paid in cash for those released.

6. The Town Bank makes collateralized loans to its customers at 1% above prime on securities owned by the customer, subject to existing margin requirements. In doing so, which of the following is correct?
   a. Notification of the issuer is necessary in order to perfect a security interest.
   b. Filing is a permissible method of perfecting a security interest in the securities if the circumstances dictate.
   c. Any dividend or interest distributions during the term of the loan belong to the bank.
   d. A perfected security interest in the securities can only be obtained by possession.

7. On October 1, 1982, Winslow Corporation obtained a loan commitment of $250,000 from Liberty National Bank. Liberty filed a financing statement on October 2, 1982. On October 5, 1982, the $250,000 loan was consummated and Winslow signed a security agreement granting the bank a security interest in inventory, accounts receivable, and proceeds from the sale of the inventory and collection of the accounts receivable. Liberty's security interest was perfected

a. On October 1.
b. On October 2.
c. On October 5.
d. By attachment.

8. Vista Motor Sales, a corporation engaged in selling motor vehicles at retail, borrowed money from Sunshine Finance Company and gave Sunshine a properly executed security agreement in its present and future inventory and in the proceeds therefrom to secure the loan. Sunshine's security interest was duly perfected under the laws of the state where Vista does business and maintains its entire inventory. Thereafter, Vista sold a new pickup truck from its inventory to Archer and received Archer's certified check in payment of the full price. Under the circumstances, which of the following is correct?

a. Sunshine must file an amendment to the financing statement every time Vista receives a substantial number of additional vehicles from the manufacturer if Sunshine is to obtain a valid security interest in subsequently delivered inventory.
b. Sunshine's security interest in the certified check Vista received is perfected against Vista's other creditors.
c. Unless Sunshine specifically included proceeds in the financing statement it filed, it has no rights to them.
d. The term "proceeds" does not include used cars received by Vista since they will be resold.

9. Two Uniform Commercial Code concepts relating to secured transactions are "attachment" and "perfection." Which of the following is correct in connection with the similarities and differences between these two concepts?

a. They are mutually exclusive and wholly independent of each other.
b. Attachment relates primarily to the rights against the debtor and perfection relates primarily to the rights against third parties.
c. Satisfaction of one automatically satisfies the other.
d. It is **not** possible to have a simultaneous attachment and perfection.

10. Clearview Manufacturing, Inc., sells golf equipment to wholesale distributors, who sell to retailers, who in turn sell to golfers. In most instances, the golf equipment is sold on credit with a security interest in the goods taken by each of the respective sellers. With respect to the above described transactions

a. The only parties who qualify as purchase money secured parties are the retailers.
b. The security interests of all of the parties remain valid even against good faith purchasers despite the fact that resale was contemplated.
c. Except for the retailers, all of the sellers must file or have possession of the goods in order to perfect their security interests.
d. The golf equipment is inventory in the hands of all the parties involved.

11. Bass, an automobile dealer, had an inventory of 40 cars and ten trucks. He financed the purchase of this inventory with County Bank under an agreement dated January 5 that gave the bank a security interest in all vehicles on Bass' premises, all future acquired vehicles, and the proceeds from their sale. On January 10, County Bank properly filed a financing statement that identified the collateral in the same way that it was identified in the agreement. On April 1, Bass sold a passenger car to Dodd for family use and a truck to Diamond Company for its hardward business. Which of the following is correct?

a. The security agreement may **not** provide for a security interest in after-acquired property even if the parties so agree.
b. County Bank's security interest is perfected as of January 5.
c. The passenger car sold by Bass to Dodd continues to be subject to the security interest of County Bank.
d. The security interest of County Bank does **not** include the proceeds from the sale of the truck to Diamond Company.

12. Field warehousing is a well-established means of securing a loan. As such, it resembles a pledge in many legal respects. Which of the following is correct?

a. The field warehouseman must maintain physical control of and dominion over the property.
b. A filing is required in order to perfect such a financing arrangement.
c. Temporary relinquishment of control for any purpose will suspend the validity of the arrangement insofar as other creditors are concerned.
d. The property in question must be physically moved to a new location although it may be a part of the borrower's facilities.

13. On November 10, 1982, Cutter, a dealer, purchased 100 lawnmowers. This comprised Cutter's entire inventory and was financed under an agreement with Town Bank which gave the bank a security interest in all lawnmowers on the premises, all future acquired lawnmowers, and the proceeds of sales. On November 15, 1982, Town Bank filed a financing statement that adequately identified the collateral. On December 20, 1982, Cutter sold one lawnmower to Wills for family use and five lawnmowers to Black for its gardening business. Which of the following is correct?

a. The security interest may not cover after-acquired property even if the parties so agree.
b. The lawnmower sold to Wills would **not** ordinarily continue to be subject to the security interest.
c. The lawnmowers sold to Black would ordinarily continue to be subject to the security interest.
d. The security interest does **not** include the proceeds from the sale of the lawnmowers to Black.

14. Fogel purchased a TV set for $900 from Hamilton Appliance Store. Hamilton took a promissory note signed by Fogel and a security interest for the $800 balance due on the set. It was Hamilton's policy not to file a financing statement until the purchaser defaulted. Fogel obtained a loan of $500 from Reliable Finance which took and recorded a security interest in the set. A month later, Fogel defaulted on several loans outstanding and one of his creditors, Harp, obtained a judgment against Fogel which was properly recorded. After making several payments, Fogel defaulted on a payment due to Hamilton, who then recorded a financing statement subsequent to Reliable's filing and the entry of the Harp judgment. Subsequently, at a garage sale, Fogel sold the set for $300 to Mobray. Which of the parties has the priority claim to the set?

a. Reliable.
b. Hamilton.
c. Harp.
d. Mobray.

15. An insolvent debtor made transfers of approximately 70% of inventory to secured creditors in satisfaction of debts. The debts were secured by the inventory. Under the circumstances

a. Secured creditors must give notice to the other creditors of the debtor.
b. Transfers in settlement of the security interest are excepted from the bulk sales provisions.
c. Inventory must be held for one month to enable the creditors to file their claims for any surplus which may arise from its sale.
d. Failure of the secured creditors to demand and obtain a list of the other creditors of the debtor will invalidate the transfer.

16. Thrush, a wholesaler of television sets, contracted to sell 100 sets to Kelly, a retailer. Kelly signed a security agreement with the 100 sets as collateral. The security agreement provided that Thrush's security interest extended to the inventory, to any proceeds therefrom, and to the after-acquired inventory of Kelly. Thrush filed his security interest centrally. Later, Kelly sold one of the sets to Haynes who purchased with knowledge of Thrush's perfected security interest. Haynes gave a note for the purchase price and signed a security agreement using the set as collateral. Kelly is now in default. Thrush can

a. Not repossess the set from Haynes, but is entitled to any payments Haynes makes to Kelly on his note.
b. Repossess the set from Haynes as he has a purchase money security interest.
c. Repossess the set as his perfection is first, and first in time is first in right.
d. Repossess the set in Haynes' possession because Haynes knew of Thrush's perfected security interest at the time of purchase.

17. The Uniform Commercial Code contains numerous provisions relating to the rights and remedies of the parties upon default. With respect to a buyer, these provisions may

a. Not be varied even with the agreement of the buyer.
b. Only be varied if the buyer is apprised of the fact and initials the variances in the agreement.
c. Not be varied insofar as they require the secured party to account for any surplus realized on the disposition of collateral securing the obligation.
d. All be varied by agreement as long as the variances are not manifestly unreasonable.

18. A purchase money security interest

a. May be taken or retained only by the seller of collateral.
b. Is exempt from the Uniform Commercial Code's filing requirements.

c. Entitles the person who is the original purchase money lender to certain additional rights and advantages, which are non-transferable.
d. Entitles the purchase money lender to a priority through a ten-day grace period for filing.

19. In the course of an examination of the financial statements of Control Finance Company for the year ended September 30, 1980, the auditors learned that the company has just taken possession of certain heavy industrial equipment from Arrow Manufacturing Company, a debtor in default. Arrow had previously borrowed $60,000 from Control secured by a security interest in the heavy industrial equipment. The amount of the loan outstanding is $30,000. Which of the following is correct regarding the rights of Control and Arrow?
a. Control is **not** permitted to sell the repossessed equipment at private sale.
b. Arrow has **no** right to redeem the collateral at any time once possession has been taken.
c. Control is **not** entitled to retain the collateral it has repossessed in satisfaction of the debt even though it has given written notice to the debtor and he consents.
d. Arrow is **not** entitled to a compulsory disposition of the collateral.

20. Robert Cunningham owns a shop in which he repairs electrical appliances. Three months ago Electrical Supply Company sold Cunningham, on credit, a machine for testing electrical appliances and obtained a perfected security interest at the time as security for payment of the unpaid balance. Cunningham's creditors have now filed an involuntary petition in bankruptcy against him. What is the status of Electrical in the bankruptcy proceeding?
a. Electrical is a secured creditor and has the right against the trustee if not paid to assert a claim to the electrical testing machine it sold to Cunningham.
b. Electrical must surrender its perfected security interest to the trustee in bankruptcy and share as a general creditor of the bankrupt's estate.
c. Electrical's perfected security interest constitutes a preference and is voidable.
d. Electrical must elect to resort exclusively to its secured interest or to relinquish it and obtain the same share as a general creditor.

21. Gilbert borrowed $10,000 from Merchant National Bank and signed a negotiable promissory note which contained an acceleration clause. In addition, securities valued at $11,000 at the time of the loan were pledged as collateral. Gilbert has defaulted on the loan repayments. At the time of default, $9,250, plus interest of $450, was due, and the securities had a value of $8,000. Merchant
a. Must first proceed against the collateral before proceeding against Gilbert personally on the note.
b. Can **not** invoke the acceleration clause in the note until ten days after the notice of default is given to Gilbert.
c. Must give Gilbert 30 days after default in which to refinance the loan.
d. Is entitled to proceed against Gilbert on either the note or the collateral or both.

May 1984 Questions

22. Rich Electronics sells various brand name television and stereo sets at discount prices. Rich maintains a large inventory which it obtains from various manufacturers on credit. These manufacturer-creditors have all filed and taken security interests in the goods and proceeds therefrom which they have sold to Rich on credit. Rich in turn sells to hundreds of ultimate consumers; some pay cash but most buy on credit. Rich takes a security interest but does not file a financing statement for credit sales. Which of the following is correct?
a. Since Rich takes a purchase money security interest in the consumer goods sold, its security interest is perfected upon attachment.
b. The appliance manufacturers can enforce their security interests against the goods in the hands of the purchasers who paid cash for them.
c. A subsequent sale by one of Rich's customers to a bona fide purchaser will be subject to Rich's security interest.
d. The goods in Rich's hands are consumer goods.

23. On January 5, Wine purchased and received delivery of new machinery from Toto Corp. for $50,000. The machinery was to be used in Wine's production process. Wine paid 30% down and executed a security agreement for the balance. On January 9, Wine obtained a $150,000 loan from Safe Bank. Wine signed a security agreement which gave Safe a security interest in Wine's existing and after-acquired machinery.

The security agreement was duly filed by Safe that same day. On January 10, Toto properly filed its security agreement. If Wine defaults on both loans and there are insufficient funds to pay Toto and Safe, which party will have a superior security interest in the machinery purchased from Toto?

a. Safe, since it was the first in time to file and perfect its security interest.
b. Safe, since Toto perfected its security interest by filing after Wine took possession.
c. Toto, since it filed its security agreement within the permissible time limits.
d. Toto, since it acquired a perfected purchase money security interest without filing.

24. Under the UCC, which of the following is correct regarding the disposition of collateral by a secured creditor after the debtor's default?

a. The collateral must be disposed of at a public sale.
b. It is improper for the secured creditor to purchase the collateral at a public sale.
c. Secured creditors with subordinate claims retain the right to redeem the collateral after the disposition of the collateral to a third party.
d. A good faith purchaser for value and without knowledge of any defects in the sale takes free of any subordinate liens or security interests.

25. Which of the following is necessary in order to have a security interest attach?

a. The debtor must have rights in the collateral.
b. The creditor must take possession of the collateral.
c. There must be a proper filing.
d. The debtor must sign a security agreement which describes the collateral.

Problems

Problem 1 Purchase Money Security Interest in Consumer Goods; Equipment (1183,L2a)

(7 to 10 minutes)

Part a. Despard Finance Company is a diverse, full-line lending institution. Its "Problems & Potential Litigation" file revealed the following disputes involving loans extended during the year of examination.

- Despard loaned Fish $4,500 to purchase a $5,000 video recording system for his personal use. A note, security agreement, and financing statement, which was promptly filed, were all executed by Fish. Unknown to Despard, Fish had already purchased the system from Zeals Department Stores the previous day for $5,000. The terms were 10% down, the balance monthly, payable in three years, and a written security interest granted to Zeals. Zeals did not file a financing statement until default.
- Despard loaned Moderne Furniture Co. $13,000 to purchase certain woodworking equipment. Moderne did so. A note, security agreement, and financing statement were executed by Moderne. As a result of an oversight the financing statement was not filed until 30 days after the loan-purchase by Moderne. In the interim Moderne borrowed $11,000 from Apache National Bank using the newly purchased machinery as collateral for the loan. A financing statement was filed by Apache five days prior to Despard's filing.

Required:

Answer the following, setting forth reasons for any conclusions stated.

What are the priorities among the conflicting security interests in the same collateral claimed by Despard and the other lenders?

Problem 2 Perfection of True Consignment; Priority of Conflicting Security Interests (581,L3)

(15 to 20 minutes)

Part a. Walpole Electric Products, Inc., manufactures a wide variety of electrical applicances. Walpole uses the consignment as an integral part of its marketing plan. The consignments are "true" consignments rather than consignments intended as security interests. Unsold goods may be returned to the owner-consignor. Walpole contracted with Petty Distributors, Inc., an electrical applicance wholesaler, to market its products under this consignment arrangement. Subsequently, Petty became insolvent and made a general assignment for the benefit of creditors. Klinger, the assignee, took possession of all of Petty's inventory, including all the Walpole electrical products. Walpole has demanded return of its appliances asserting that the relationship created by the consignment between itself and Petty was one of agency and that Petty never owned the appliances. Furthermore, Walpole argues that under the consignment arrangement there is no obligation owing by Petty at any time, thus there is nothing to secure under the secured transactions provisions of the Uniform Commercial Code. Klinger has denied the validity of these assertions claiming that the consignment is subject to the Code's filing provisions unless the Code has otherwise been satisfied. Walpole sues to repossess the goods.

Required:

Answer the following, setting forth reasons for any conclusions stated.

1. What are the requirements, if any, to perfect a true consignment such as discussed above?
2. Will Walpole prevail?

Part b. Lebow Woolens, Inc., sold several thousand bolts of Australian wool on credit to Fashion Plate Exclusives, Inc., a clothing manufacturer, obtaining a duly executed security agreement and a financing statement. Fashion Plate became delinquent in meeting its payments. Lebow subsequently discovered that a miscaptioned financing statement for a $12,500 sale had been filed under the name of Fashion Styles Limited, another customer. Lebow took the following actions. First, on August 11, 1980, it repossessed the bolts of wool which were not already altered by Fashion Plate. This amounted to some 65% of the invoice in question. Next on August 20, 1980, it filed a corrected financing statement covering the sale in question. Dunbar, another creditor of Fashion Plate's, levied against Fashion Plate's inventory, work in process, and raw materials on August 13th and obtained a judgment of $14,000 against Fashion Plate, an amount in excess of the value of the Lebow bolts of wool. The judgment was obtained and entered on August 18, 1980. Dunbar asserts its rights as a lien judgment creditor.

Required:

Answer the following, setting forth reasons for any conclusions stated.

In a lawsuit to determine the rights of the parties, how should the competing claims of Lebow and Dunbar be decided?

Problem 3 Perfection and Priorities (1178,L2a)

(10 to 15 minutes)

Part a. National Finance Company engages in a wide variety of secured transactions which may be broken down into three categories.

I. Consumer loans in connection with the purchase of automobiles, appliances, and furniture. National makes these loans in two ways. First, it makes direct loans to the consumer-borrower who then makes the purchase with the proceeds. Second, it is contacted by the seller and provides the financing for the purchase by the customer. In either case National takes a security interest in the property purchased.

II. Collateralized loans to borrowers who deliver possession of property, such as diamonds, to National to secure repayment of their loans.

III. Loans to merchants to finance their inventory purchases. National takes a security interest in the inventory and proceeds.

Except for category III, National does not file a financing statement.

Required:

Answer the following, setting forth reasons for any conclusions stated.

1. When does National's security interest in the various types of property attach?

2. As a secured creditor, against what parties must National protect itself?

3. Does National have a perfected security interest in any of the above property? If so, against whom?

4. If the facts indicate that National does not have a perfected security interest against all parties, what should it do?

5. Can National fully protect itself against all subsequent parties who might claim superior rights to the property involved?

Multiple Choice Answers

1. a	6. d	11. b	16. a	21. d
2. a	7. c	12. a	17. c	22. a
3. b	8. b	13. b	18. d	23. c
4. c	9. b	14. b	19. d	24. d
5. a	10. c	15. b	20. a	25. a

Multiple Choice Answer Explanations

A. Article 9 of the UCC

1. (1180,L1,38) (a) The only item listed that is within the scope of article 9 (secured transactions) is the outright sale of accounts receivable.

B. Types of Collateral

2. (578,L1,29) (a) Detachable trade fixtures are considered personal property, not real property. Therefore, a real estate mortgagee will not obtain a security interest in property classified as a detachable trade fixture. Answer (b) is incorrect because Donaldson's mortgage does not cover any personal property which is the issue here. Answer (c) is incorrect because the mortgage attaches only to real property. Thus property which is classified as personal will not be included whether the mortgage is recorded or not. Answer (d) is incorrect because the court's job is to distinguish between real and personal property and it lacks authority to divide disputed property in proportion to respective claims.

C. Creation of Security Interest

3. (1182,L1,52) (b) Attachment relates primarily to the rights of the secured party in the collateral as against the debtor. Therefore, in order for Lombard's security interest to be valid against the debtor, Gifford, with respect to the designer apparel, only attachment of the security interest must occur. A security interest attaches when (1) the collateral is in possession of the secured party pursuant to an agreement, or the debtor has signed a security agreement which contains a description of the collateral, (2) the secured party gives value, and (3) the debtor has rights in the collateral. Since all three of these elements are present, Lombard's security interest will "attach", and Lombard does not have to perfect its security interest to protect itself against the debtor. Answer (a) is incorrect because Lombard need not retain title to the goods, since, as between the debtor and secured party, title to the goods is immaterial with regard to their respective rights and obligations. Answer (c) is incorrect because Lombard must file a financing statement only if it desired to perfect its security interest. Answer (d) is incorrect since perfection relates primarily to the rights of the secured party in the collateral against third parties. In order for the Lombard's security interest to be valid against Gifford perfection would not be necessary.

D.2.a. Possession

4. (583,L1,47) (c) Since possession is a method of perfecting a security interest, attachment and perfection will occur simultaneously when attachment is by possession. Answer (a) is incorrect because a statement in a security agreement specifying that attachment and perfection will occur simultaneously will have no legal effect. The secured party must still engage in one of the three methods of perfection before the security interest will be perfected. Answer (b) is incorrect because attachment and perfection will occur simultaneously if there is a purchase money security interest taken in consumer goods, but this does not occur when the collateral is inventory. Answer (d) is incorrect because a security interest in goods sold on consignment is not automatically perfected upon attachment. These goods qualify as inventory in the debtor's possession and, consequently, perfection would occur only when the secured party files a proper financing statement.

5. . (1182,L1,55) (a) Since documents of title, i.e., the negotiable warehouse receipts, merely represent the goods, a perfected security interest in the warehouse receipts (by taking possession of the documents) is also a perfected security interest in the goods covered by the documents. Answer (b) is incorrect because the debtor, Tawny, does not have to sign the security agreement if the collateral is in the possession of the secured party, Worldwide, pursuant to agreement. When a secured party is taking a possessory security interest, an oral security agreement is sufficient to create such an interest. Answer (c) is incorrect because Worldwide does not have to file a financing statement to perfect its security interest, since Worldwide has already perfected its security interest by taking possession of the negotiable warehouse receipts. Worldwide could have perfected its security interest by filing a financing statement, but this filing would not protect Worldwide against a good faith purchaser to whom the warehouse receipts have been duly negotiated. Answer (d) is incorrect because temporary and limited relinquishment of control of the goods to the debtor is acceptable. The Uniform Commercial Code provides for a 21 day continuation of the perfected security interest in the collateral from the date of release to the debtor.

6. (1180,L1,34) (d) A perfected security interest in securities can only be obtained by possession. An exception to this rule is when the creditor temporarily returns the security to the debtor (for sale, exchange, etc.). In such situations, the creditor's security interest remains perfected for 21 days. However, a bona fide purchaser of the security will defeat the creditor's security interest. Thus, answer (d) is correct. To perfect a security interest in securities there is no need to notify the issuer. Dividends and interest earned during the secured transaction are the property of the debtor.

D.2.b. Filing

7. (1182,L1,56) (c) Perfection of a security interest may be accomplished by the filing of a financing statement. Filing may be done anytime, even before the security agreement is made. But perfection does not occur until all the requirements for attachment of a security interest are met. The requisite acts of perfection are not a substitute for the attachment of a security interest, but are additional steps. Therefore, because a financing statement has already been filed, Liberty's security interest was perfected on October 5, when all three elements for attachment existed. Answers (a) and (b) are incorrect because attachment of the security interest has not yet occurred. Answer (d) is incorrect because a security interest will automatically be perfected upon attachment only when creditor takes a purchase money security interest in consumer goods.

8. (1179,L1,26) (b) Under the facts given, Sunshine's security interest in the certified check that Vista received is perfected against Vista's other creditors. Answer (c) is incorrect because the security interest attaches to proceeds automatically without special mention in the financing statement. Answer (d) is incorrect because the term "proceeds" is broad enough to include anything received in exchange for the collateral including used motor vehicles, i.e., "trade-ins." Answer (a) is incorrect because Sunshine covered itself in the executed security agreement by stating that the security agreement covered both present and future inventory. Therefore, an amendment is unnecessary every time Vista receives a substantial number of vehicles from the manufacturer.

D.2.c. Attachment Alone

9. (1182,L1,54) (b) The difference between the concepts of attachment and perfection is that attachment relates primarily to the rights of the secured party in the collateral against the debtor, whereas perfection relates primarily to the rights of the secured party in the collateral against third parties. Answer (a) is incorrect because attachment and perfection are not mutually exclusive and wholly independent of each other since both are required to establish an effective security interest good against third parties such as lien creditors and trustees in bankruptcy. Answer (c) is incorrect because satisfaction of one of these concepts does not automatically satisfy the other. To this extent, they are independent and the requirements of each must be satisfied. Answer (d) is incorrect because it is possible in limited circumstances to have a simultaneous attachment and perfection. This is true in the case of a purchase money security interest in consumer goods. As soon as the purchase money secured party's security interest attaches to consumer goods, the interest is also perfected.

10. (1182,L1,58) (c) Perfection of a security interest may occur in three ways: by attachment of a security interest; by possession of the collateral; or by the filing of a financing statement. When a creditor takes a purchase money security interest in consumer goods, such interest is automatically perfected upon attachment. The retailers are the only secured parties taking a security interest in collateral that would qualify as consumer goods. Therefore, all of the sellers, except for the retailers, must file or have possession of the goods in order to perfect their security interests. Answer (a) is incorrect because a security interest is a "purchase money security interest" when taken or retained by the seller of the collateral to secure all or part of the purchase price. Therefore, both the wholesalers and the retailers qualify as purchase money secured parties. Answer (b) is incorrect because a perfected security interest in inventory is defeated by a purchaser in the ordinary course of business. Also, even though the retailer's security interest was perfected upon attachment and is good against the buyer's creditors, the perfected security interest is not valid against a subsequent bona fide purchaser from the consumer. Answer (d) is incorrect because the golf equipment is consumer goods in the hands of the golfers who purchased from the retailers, since it was bought primarily for personal, family, or household purposes.

11. (1181,L1,45) (b) Even though filing did not occur until January 10, County Bank's security interest is perfected as of January 5 upon attachment of the security interest. Answer (a) is incorrect because an after-acquired property clause is very typical of a security agreement that creates a security interest (floating lien) in inventory. Answer (c) is incorrect because a purchase in the ordinary course of business

by Dodd defeats a prior perfected security interest in inventory. This is true even if Dodd had knowledge of County Bank's security interest prior to purchasing the car. Answer (d) is incorrect because proceeds include what is received upon sale of the collateral. County Bank does have a perfected security interest in the proceeds from the sale of a truck because the security agreement states proceeds are covered. The general rule states that security interest in proceeds is automatically perfected for a 10-day period if the security interest in the original collateral was perfected. However, if the security agreement states that the security interest is to cover proceeds, the perfected security interest will continue beyond the 10-day period without any additional filing.

D.3. Field Warehousing

12. (1177,L2,24) (a) A pledge is possession of the debtor's property by the creditor to secure a debt. This is the same as possessing collateral to perfect a security interest, i.e., the creditor must possess the collateral. This is done by the field warehouseman or his agent, by maintaining physical control and dominion over the property. Answer (b) is incorrect because filing is not required where there is possession. Answer (c) is incorrect because temporary relinquishment of control is acceptable to allow for an exchange of collateral, to allow the debtor to temporarily use or work on the goods. However, a holder in due course or bona fide purchaser who suffers legal detriment, i.e., purchases, lends money on, etc., during such interval will prevail. Answer (d) is incorrect because the collateral need not be moved to a new location; rather, it must be segregated and controlled.

E. Order of Priorities

13. (583,L1,49) (b) Wills is a purchaser in the ordinary course of business and, consequently, takes the goods free of Town Bank's perfected security interest in Cutter's inventory. Answer (a) is incorrect because parties may stipulate that the security interest is to cover after-acquired property. Town Bank has created a floating lien concerning Cutter's inventory. Answer (c) is incorrect because Black is also a purchaser in the ordinary course of business and will defeat Town Bank's prior perfected security interest in Cutter's inventory. The fact that Black is purchasing for business purposes would not affect its status as a purchaser in the ordinary course of business. Answer (d) is incorrect because the parties to a secured transaction may specify that the security interest include the proceeds of the sale of the collateral.

14. (583,L1,51) (b) Hamilton took a purchase money security interest in the TV set which would be considered consumer goods in Fogel's possession. Consequently, Hamilton's security interest was perfected automatically upon attachment. Therefore, Hamilton can defeat Reliable because Hamilton's security interest was perfected prior to the time Reliable perfected its security interest by filing. Hamilton can also defeat Harp because Harp's judgment was subsequent to Hamilton's perfection. Normally Mobray, as a good faith purchaser for personal use, would defeat a prior perfected secured party who gained his/her perfection through automatic perfection by attachment. However, Hamilton engaged in a second method of perfection (filing a financing statement) prior to the sale of the TV set to Mobray, allowing Hamilton to defeat the good faith purchaser for personal use. Therefore, answers (a), (c), and (d) are incorrect.

15. (1182,L1,23) (b) Transfers in settlement of a security interest are excepted from the bulk sales provisions of Article 6 of the UCC. Consequently, the secured creditors would not need to obtain a list of the debtor's other creditors, nor would they have to give notice to these creditors. Therefore, answers (a) and (d) are incorrect. Answer (c) is incorrect because there is no requirement that the inventory must be held for one month to enable the creditors to file their claims for any surplus which may arise from its sale.

16. (1182,L1,57) (a) Proceeds include whatever is received upon the sale of the collateral. The secured party, Thrush, has the ability to assert rights against the proceeds received by the debtor, Kelly, upon sale of the collateral. Thrush has a perfected security interest in the proceeds from the sale of the television sets because the security agreement states proceeds are covered. Therefore, Thrush is entitled to any payments Haynes makes to Kelly on the note. Normally, access to the proceeds upon default by the debtor is an integral part of an inventory financing agreement. Haynes, as a purchaser in the ordinary course of business, takes free of Thrush's perfected security interest in inventory. Answers (b), (c) and (d) are incorrect because since Haynes is a buyer in the ordinary course of business, he will defeat the rights of the secured creditor, Thrush, even if he were aware of Thrush's security interest at the time of purchase. Therefore, Thrush will not be able to repossess the television set. Haynes would take subject to Thrush's security interest **only** when he **knows** that the sale of the inventory is in violation of some term in the security agreement.

17. (582,L1,49) (c) The UCC gives the parties considerable latitude and wide discretion in which to fashion their own remedies by specifying them in their contractual agreement. Under these provisions, reasonable agreements which limit, add, or modify remedies will be given effect, but the parties are not free to shape their remedies in an unconscionable and unreasonable manner. However, the provision which requires the secured party to account for any surplus proceeds of collateral cannot be varied; but the parties may by agreement determine the standards by which the fulfillment of this right and duty is to be measured if such standards are not manifestly unreasonable. Answer (b) is incorrect because as long as the modifications and limitations are expressed in the agreement, the buyer does not have to initial the variances in order for them to be given effect. Answer (d) is incorrect because not all provisions may be varied by agreement, as evidenced by the above-mentioned provision concerning the secured party's duty to account for any surplus proceeds from the sale of the collateral, which cannot be varied.

18. (1181,L1,46) (d) If the secured party files with respect to a purchase money security interest before or within ten days after the debtor receives possession of the collateral, the security interest takes priority over any liens which arise between the time the security interest attaches and the time of the filing. Therefore, this provides the purchase money lender a ten-day grace period for perfection by filing. Answer (a) is incorrect because a purchase money security interest may also be taken by a person who gives value to enable the debtor to acquire the collateral. Answer (b) is incorrect because a purchase money security interest, in collateral other than consumer goods, must be perfected by filing a financing statement, unless the creditor has possession of the collateral. Only a purchase money security interest in consumer goods is automatically perfected by attachment. Answer (c) is incorrect because the additional rights can be transferred.

19. (1180,L1,31) (d) Upon default, the secured party normally has the right to retain (or sell) the collateral to satisfy the obligation. However, the secured party cannot retain the collateral if it is consumer goods and the debtor has paid 60% or more of the obligation. In such a case the debtor is entitled to a compulsory disposition of the goods. Control's security interest is in equipment not consumer goods, and Arrow has been paid only 50% of the obligation. Thus Arrow is not entitled to a compulsory disposition. Answer (d) is correct. Control can sell the possessed equipment at either a public or private sale. Either type of sale must be handled in a commercially reasonable manner. Thus answer (a) is incorrect. Arrow can redeem the collateral at any time up to when it is sold by paying the full obligation plus the expenses of the secured party. Control could retain the collateral if written notice of such was sent to the debtor and this debtor did not object within 21 days. This makes answers (b) and (c) incorrect.

20. (579,L1,22) (a) Electrical, as a secured creditor, may assert a reclamation claim against the trustee in bankruptcy for the testing mahcine. Answer (b) is incorrect because the secured party may enforce its perfected security interest and then proceed as a general creditor against the bankrupt's estate to the extent the collateral does not satisfy the debt. Electrical's perfected security interest does not constitute a voidable preference as stated in answer (c) since the simultaneous sale and creation of the security interest is considered a fair exchange. Answer (d) is incorrect because a secured party is not forced to make an exclusive choice of remedy but may proceed against the security until it is exhausted and may then proceed in the bankruptcy action as a general creditor for any deficiency.

F. Remedies on Default

21. (583,L1,52) (d) Merchant is entitled to proceed against Gilbert on either the note or the collateral or both. The reason a creditor desires collateral for an obligation is to provide another source of payment besides the debtor's personal promise. Merchant, the creditor, need not first proceed against the collateral before proceeding against Gilbert personally. Therefore, answer (a) is incorrect. Answer (b) is incorrect because Merchant is not required to wait until 10 days after notice of default is given Gilbert before invoking the acceleration clause. The clause can be invoked as stipulated on the face of the note. Answer (c) is incorrect because there is no requirement that states a debtor must be given 30 days after default in which to refinance a loan. Upon default Merchant may immediately proceed against Gilbert and the collateral.

May 1984 Answers

22. (584,L1,57) (a) A purchase money security interest in consumer goods is automatically perfected upon attachment of that interest. Because Rich holds these goods for sale in the ordinary course of his business, the goods are inventory in Rich's hands. Answer (d) is, therefore, incorrect. A purchaser who buys from a seller in the ordinary course of business takes free of a perfected security interest as long as the purchaser is without knowledge that his purchase violates the security agreement. Answer (b) is, therefore, incor-

rect. Answer (c) is incorrect because when a consumer sells consumer goods to a purchaser who buys without knowledge of a security interest, that purchaser will defeat a perfected security interest if perfection was achieved through automatic perfection by attachment and the secured party (Rich) has not also filed a financing statement.

23. (584,L1,58) (c) A purchase money security interest in collateral other than inventory has priority over all other security interests if it is perfected when the debtor receives possession of the collateral or within ten days thereafter. Because Toto perfected its purchase money security interest in equipment by filing within ten days of January 5, Toto has priority over Safe Bank. Answer (d) is incorrect because a security interest in equipment must be perfected either by possession or filing. Answer (b) is incorrect because Toto, a purchase money secured creditor with collateral other than inventory, had a ten-day grace period to perfect its interest. Answer (a) is incorrect because the "first to file or perfect" rule does not apply to purchase money security interests.

24. (584,L1,59) (d) A purchaser for value at a public sale who is without knowledge of any defects in that sale and who is not in collusion with the secured creditor will take the property free of the debtor's rights and any security interests. A purchaser for value at a private sale will take free of the debtor's rights and any security interests if he acts in good faith. The debtor's remedy for an improperly conducted sale is a cause of action for money damages against the secured party. The debtor and any secondarily secured party have an absolute right to redeem the collateral at anytime **prior** to the sale of the collateral by tendering all amounts due the secured party. Answers (a) and (b) are incorrect because a secured creditor may dispose of the collateral at either a public or private sale. The secured party may buy at any public sale and may also buy at a private sale if the collateral is either widely distributed at a standard price or is customarily sold in a recognized market. Answer(c) is incorrect because secured parties with subordinate claims do not have the right to redeem the collateral after disposition to a third party has been made. Subordinate secured parties, however, do have a right to the proceeds from the disposition after payment of the secured party's reasonable expenses and the debt secured by the collateral.

25. (584,L1,60) (a) A security interest attaches when the following occur, in any order: secured creditor gives value, debtor has rights in the collateral, and a security agreement exists. Possession of the collateral and filing a financing statement are two methods of perfecting a security interest; they are not steps essential to the creation or attachment of a security interest. Accordingly, answers (b) and (c) are incorrect. Answer (d) is incorrect because if the secured creditor takes possession of the collateral, the security agreement between the parties may be oral. In all other instances, the security agreement must be in writing, demonstrate the debtor's intent to create a security interest, describe the collateral, and be signed by the debtor.

Answer Outline

Problem 1 Purchase Money Security Interest in Consumer Goods; Equipment

Part a.

Zeals will prevail over Despard
Zeals' interest is purchase money security interest in consumer goods that is automatically perfected upon attachment
Despard's interest is not protected until filed, which is subsequent to Zeals' perfection
Filing is necessary to protect purchase money security interest in equipment
Despard as a purchase money lender has a ten-day grace period for filing
Despard did not file for 30 days
Despard's interest was not perfected until filed
Apache will prevail since the interest was perfected before Despard's

Unofficial Answer

Problem 1 Purchase Money Security Interest in Consumer Goods; Equipment

Part a.

- Zeals has priority over Despard regarding the competing security interests of the parties. Zeals is a purchase money secured party involving the sale of consumer goods. As such, the security interest is enforceable against other creditors of the buyer without the necessity of a filing. Despard would also attempt to assert a purchase money security interest in the goods, but this is questionable at best since the money advanced was obviously not used for the purchase of the goods. Even if Despard qualified as a purchase money secured party, Despard was second in point of time. The fact that it filed does not change the priority since filing was not required to perfect the interest in the consumer goods (the video system).
- Apache has priority over Despard in this instance. Although Despard was the first to advance credit and qualified as a purchase money lender, it was second in time to perfect its security interest. The subject matter of the sale was equipment and filing is required to perfect Despard's security interest. The purchase money lender has the benefit of a 10-day grace period for filing. Despard's security interest was not perfected until it filed, which was after the grace period and five days after Apache's filing.

Answer Outline

Problem 2 Perfection of True Consignment; Priority of Conflicting Security Interests

a1. A true consignment in a commercial sense implies an agency relationship
Perfection of true consignment enables consignor, Walpole, to prevail agains Petty's creditors
Walpole must comply with applicable law providing for consignor's interest to be evidenced by posted sign, or Walpole must establish that Petty is generally known by his creditors to be engaged in selling goods of others, or Walpole must comply with filing provision of Article 9 of UCC
Consignor must give written notification to Petty's creditors who have security interest in same type of goods
But only if the creditors perfected their security interest before date of filing made by Walpole
Notice must be received by creditors within five years before consignee receives possession of the goods
Notification states consignor expects to deliver goods on consignment to the consignee
Describing the goods by item or type

a2. Walpole will not prevail aginst Klinger
Walpole was unable to perfect a true consignment as outlined in a1.
Article 2 of UCC provides that where goods are delivered under a consignment agreement for sale
The goods are deemed to be on "sale or return" with respect to claims of consignee's creditors
Walpole is subject to claims of Petty's creditors

b. Conflicting security interests rank according to priority in time of filing or perfection
Lebow will prevail over Dunbar with regard to the bolts it repossessed (65% of the invoice)
Lebow's repossession of goods constituted a perfection of security interest
Security interest perfected before Dunbar's lien attaches has priority over the lien
Lebow's filing of the miscaptioned statement is ineffective to create any interests or rights in Lebow
Financing statement not relevant with regard to priority time frame
Dunbar will prevail over Lebow with regard to goods not repossessed by Lebow

Dunbar's levy and judicial lien occurs prior in time to Lebow's filing of corrected financing statement
Applies to the remaining goods

Unofficial Answer

Problem 2 Perfection of True Consignment; Priority of Conflicting Security Interests

Part a.

1. In order to prevail against the creditors of a party to whom goods have been consigned, the consignor may do one of three things according to the Uniform Commercial Code (section 2-326):

a. Comply with applicable state law providing for a consignor's interest to be evidenced by a posted sign. Most states do not have such statutes.
b. Establish that the person conducting the business is generally known by his creditors to be substantially engaged in selling the goods of others. This is either not the case or is difficult to prove.
c. Comply with the filing provisions of Article 9: Secured Transactions. From a practical standpoint, this last course of action appears to be the most logical, if not the only, choice.

Article 9 (section 9-114) requires that a consignor comply with the general filing requirements of the code (section 9-302) and also give notice in writing to the creditors of the consignee who have a perfected security interest covering the same type of goods. The written notice must be given before the date of filing by the consignor and received within five years before the consignee takes possession of the goods. The notice must state that the consignor expects to deliver goods on consignment to the consignee and must contain a description of the goods.

2. No. Walpole will not prevail. Whether a consignment is a "true" consignment (an agency relationship) or is intended as a security interest, the Uniform Commercial Code requires that notice be given to creditors of the consignee.

A consignment is governed by sections from two articles of the code: Article 2: Sales and Article 9: Secured Transactions. Section 2-326 treats a consignment as a "sale or return" because "the goods are delivered primarily for resale." Section 2-326(3) provides the following:

> Where goods are delivered to a person for sale and such person maintains a place of business at which he deals in goods of the kind involved, under a name other than the name of the person making delivery, then with respect to claims of creditors of the person conducting the business the goods are deemed to be on sale or return. The provisions of this subsection are applicable even though an agreement purports to reserve title to the person making delivery until payment or resale or uses such words as "on consignment" or "on memorandum."

It is obvious from the facts, that Walpole's marketing arrangement is covered by the above language. The code further provides that the creditors of the consignee will be able to assert claims against goods sold on a sale or return basis unless some form of notice is given.

Part b.

Lebow will prevail to the extent of the 65 percent of the bolts of wool that it repossessed on August 11, 1980. Since Lebow obtained possession of 65 percent of the shipment prior to attachment or judgment by Dunbar, Lebow's security interest with respect to those goods had been perfected as of August 11. The original erroneous filing is invalid against the creditors of Fashion Plate. Lebow's security interest was not perfected by filing initially, and, therefore, Lebow will not prevail over the rights of Dunbar, a subsequent lien creditor of Fashion Plate. The facts of the case indicate that the security interest was not perfected by filing until August 20, 1980. However, prior to that time Dunbar levied against the goods on August 13 and obtained a judgment against Fashion Plate on August 18, 1980. Both dates are prior to the August 20 filing by Lebow; thus, the lien creditor would have priority over Lebow's claim based exclusively on perfection by filing. Perfection can also be accomplished by possession, but if perfection by either method precedes the time that the lien creditor obtains rights against the property, it prevails.

Answer Outline

Problem 3 Perfection and Priorities

a1. UCC provides security interests attach when
Collateral is in possession of secured party
Or debtor signs a security agreement
Value is given by the creditor
Debtor has rights in the collateral

National transactions fulfill above criteria
Transaction types I and III require security agreements
Possession by creditor is sufficient for type II

a2. Secured creditors must protect themselves against
Debtor
Debtor's creditor
Trustee in bankruptcy
Subsequent purchasers for value

a3. National has security interest against debtor
Security agreement is sufficient
For others, creditor must have possession or file a financing statement
Except financing statement is required to protect against subsequent purchasers of consumer goods
Except subsequent purchasers of debtor's inventory take free of perfected security interest

a4. To perfect against all subsequent purchasers of consumer goods (type I), National should file a financing statement

a5. No, National may not protect itself against subsequent purchasers of goods in debtor's inventory
I.e., protection is not possible without possession

Unofficial Answer

Problem 3 Perfection and Priorities

Part a.

1. The Uniform Commercial Code provides that a security interest attaches in property when three events occur. First, collateral is in possession of the secured party pursuant to agreement, or the debtor has signed a security agreement that contains a description of the collateral. Second, value has been given by the creditor. Third, the debtor has rights in the collateral.

Insofar as National is concerned, a security interest in all three categories of secured transactions has attached. In categories I and III, there must be a security agreement signed by the debtor. Regarding the collateralized property in category II, possession pursuant to agreement without a signed writing is sufficient. In all instances, value has been given and the debtor has rights in the collateral.

2. There are four potential parties against whom National must protect itself. These are the debtor, the debtor's creditors, the trustee in bankruptcy, and subsequent purchasers for value from the debtor.

3. National's rights against the debtor are contained in the security agreement and the Uniform Commercial Code provisions relating to the agreement and the relationship between the parties. It is not necessary to file a financing statement in order to obtain these rights against the debtor; the agreement itself is sufficient.

To perfect a security interest against other parties, the creditor must either take possession (as in category II) or file a financing statement except where the creditor has taken "a purchase money security interest in consumer goods." In the latter case, perfection occurs at the time the security interest attaches, but it is only valid against the debtor's creditors and a trustee in bankruptcy and not against a bona fide purchaser unless a financing statement has been filed. Whether National uses either method described in category I to finance the purchase of the consumer goods, it will have a purchase money security interest if it gave value to enable the debtor to acquire rights in or the use of collateral if such value is in fact so used.

Where a creditor provides financing for a debtor to enable him to obtain and resell inventory items, the security interest is perfected by filing. However, since resale is clearly contemplated, purchasers for value take free of the perfected security interest.

4. The only practical suggestion would be to file a financing statement in respect to the loans described in category I, which would then provide protection against subsequent purchasers from the debtor. National already is protected against the other parties in category I upon attachment of the security interest.

5. No. As indicated above, where the goods are inventory in the hands of the debtor, a purchaser for value in the ordinary course of business takes free of the creditor's perfected security interest. In such cases, it is not possible for the lender to completely protect itself against all parties without obtaining possession.

Multiple Choice Answers (1 - 22)

1. A client has joined other creditors of the Ajax Demolition Company in a composition agreement seeking to avoid the necessity of a bankruptcy proceeding against Ajax. Which statement describes the composition agreement?
   a. It provides for the appointment of a receiver to take over and operate the debtor's business.
   b. It must be approved by all creditors.
   c. It does not discharge any of the debts included until performance by the debtor has taken place.
   d. It provides a temporary delay, not to exceed six months, insofar as the debtor's obligation to repay the debts included in the composition.

2. A voluntary bankruptcy proceeding is available to
   a. All debtors provided they are insolvent.
   b. Debtors only if the overwhelming preponderance of creditors have **not** petitioned for and obtained a receivership pursuant to state law.
   c. Corporations only if a reorganization has been attempted and failed.
   d. Most debtors even if they are **not** insolvent.

3. An involuntary petition in bankruptcy
   a. Will be denied if a majority of creditors in amount and in number have agreed to a common law composition agreement.
   b. Can be filed by creditors only once in a seven-year period.
   c. May be successfully opposed by the debtor by proof that the debtor is solvent in the bankruptcy sense.
   d. If **not** contested will result in the entry of an order for relief by the bankruptcy judge.

4. A bankrupt who has voluntarily filed for and received a discharge in bankruptcy
   a. Will receive a discharge of any and all debts owed by him as long as he has **not** committed a bankruptcy offense.
   b. Can obtain another voluntary discharge in bankruptcy after five years have elapsed from the date of the prior discharge.
   c. Must surrender for distribution to the creditors amounts received as an inheritance if the receipt occurs within 180 days after filing of the petition.
   d. Is precluded from owning or operating a similar business for two years.

5. Since the passage of the Bankruptcy Reform Act of 1978, voluntary bankruptcy proceedings have become increasingly popular with debtors. The new law
   a. Increases availability and eases filing.
   b. Increases the amount of property which is exempt.
   c. Reduces the number of creditors necessary for filing.
   d. Accepts solvency in the equity sense as the criterion for determining bankruptcy status.

6. In a bankruptcy proceeding, the trustee
   a. Must be an attorney admitted to practice in the federal district in which the bankrupt is located.
   b. Will receive a fee based upon the time and fair value of the services rendered, regardless of the size of the estate.
   c. May **not** have had any dealings with the bankrupt within the past year.
   d. Is the representative of the bankrupt's estate and as such has the capacity to sue and be sued on its behalf.

7. Haplow engaged Turnbow as his attorney when threatened by several creditors with a bankruptcy proceeding. Haplow's assets consisted of $85,000 and his debts were $125,000. A petition was subsequently filed and was uncontested. Several of the creditors are concerned that the suspected large legal fees charged by Turnbow will diminish the size of the distributable estate. What are the rules or limitations which apply to such fees?
   a. None, since it is within the attorney-client privileged relationship.
   b. The fee is presumptively valid as long as arrived at in an arm's-length negotiation.
   c. Turnbow must file with the court a statement of compensation paid or agreed to for review as to its reasonableness.
   d. The trustee must approve the fee.

8. In order to establish a preference under the federal bankruptcy act, which of the following is the trustee required to show where the preferred party is **not** an insider?
   a. That the preferred party had reasonable cause to believe that the debtor was insolvent.
   b. That the debtor committed an act of bankruptcy.

c. That the transfer was for an antecedent debt.
d. That the transfer was made within 60 days of the filing of the petition.

9. The federal bankruptcy act contains several important terms. One such term is "insider." The term is used in connection with preferences and preferential transfers. Which among the following is not an "insider?"
a. A secured creditor having a security interest in at least 25% or more of the debtor's property.
b. A partnership in which the debtor is a general partner.
c. A corporation of which the debtor is a director.
d. A close blood relative of the debtor.

10. The Bankruptcy Reform Act of 1978 provides that certain allowed expenses and claims are entitled to a priority. Which of the following is **not** entitled to such a priority?
a. Claims of governmental units for taxes.
b. Wage claims, but to a limited extent.
c. Rents payable within the four months preceding bankruptcy, but to a limited extent.
d. Unsecured claims for contributions to employee benefit plans, but to a limited extent.

11. If a secured party's claim exceeds the value of the collateral of a bankrupt, he will be paid the total amount realized from the sale of the security and will
a. Not have any claim for the balance.
b. Become a general creditor for the balance.
c. Retain a secured creditor status for the balance.
d. Be paid the balance only after all general creditors are paid.

12. Bunker Industries, Inc., ceased doing business and is in bankruptcy. Among the claimants are employees seeking unpaid wages. The following statements describe the possible status of such claims in a bankruptcy proceeding or legal limitations placed upon them. Which one is an incorrect statement?
a. They are entitled to a priority.
b. If a priority is afforded such claims, it cannot exceed $2,000 per wage earner.
c. Such claims cannot include vacation, severance, or sick-leave pay.
d. The amounts of excess wages not entitled to a priority are mere unsecured claims.

13. The Bankruptcy Reform Act of 1978 distinguishes between an exception to discharge of a debt or debts and a denial of discharge. Which of the following types of conduct will result in a denial of discharge?
a. Obtaining of money or credit by resort to actual fraud.
b. Fraud or defalcation while acting in a fiduciary capacity.
c. Transfer by the debtor, with an intent to hinder a creditor, of property within one year before the date of filing of the petition.
d. Willful and malicious injury by the debtor to another entity or its property.

14. Hapless is a bankrupt. In connection with a debt owed to the Suburban Finance Company, he used a false financial statement to induce it to loan him $500. Hapless is seeking a discharge in bankruptcy. Which of the following is a correct statement?
a. Hapless will be denied a discharge of any of his debts.
b. Even if it can be proved that Suburban did not rely upon the financial statement, Hapless will be denied a discharge either in whole or part.
c. Hapless will be denied a discharge of the Suburban debt.
d. Hapless will be totally discharged despite the false financial statement.

15. Barkam is starting a new business, Barkam Enterprises, which will be a sole proprietorship selling retail novelties. Barkam recently received a discharge in bankruptcy, but certain proved claims were unpaid because of lack of funds. Which of the following would be a claim against Barkam?
a. The unpaid amounts owed to secured creditors who received less than the full amount after resorting to their security interest and receiving their bankruptcy dividend.
b. The unpaid amounts owed to trade suppliers for goods purchased and sold by Barkam in the ordinary course of his prior business.
c. A personal loan by his father made in an attempt to stave off bankruptcy.
d. The unpaid amount of taxes due to the United States which became due and owing within three years preceding bankruptcy.

16. Hard Times, Inc., is insolvent. Its liabilities exceed its assets by $13 million. Hard Times is owned by its president, Waters, and members of his family. Waters,

whose assets are estimated at less than a million dollars, guaranteed the loans of the corporation. A consortium of banks is the principal creditor of Hard Times having loaned it $8 million, the bulk of which is unsecured. The banks decided to seek reorganization of Hard Times and Waters has agreed to cooperate. Regarding the proposed reorganization

a. Waters' cooperation is necessary since he must sign the petition for a reorganization.
b. If a petition in bankruptcy is filed against Hard Times, Waters will also have his personal bankruptcy status resolved and relief granted.
c. Only a duly constituted creditors committee may file a plan of reorganization of Hard Times.
d. Hard Times will remain in possession unless a request is made to the court for the appointment of a trustee.

17. Which of the following was a significant reform made in the reorganization provisions of the Bankruptcy Reform Act of 1978?

a. Separate treatment of publicly-held corporations under its provisions.
b. Elimination of the separate and competing procedures contained in the various chapters of the prior Bankruptcy Act.
c. Elimination of participation in bankruptcy reorganizations by the Securities and Exchange Commission.
d. The exclusion from its jurisdiction of partnerships and other noncorporate entities.

18. Skipper was for several years the principal stockholder, director, and chief executive officer of the Canarsie Grocery Corporation. Canarsie had financial difficulties and an order of relief was filed against it, and subsequently discharged. Several creditors are seeking to hold Skipper personally liable as a result of his stock ownership and as a result of his being an officer-director. Skipper in turn filed with the bankruptcy judge a claim for $1,400 salary due him. Which of the following is correct?

a. Skipper's salary claim will be allowed and he will be entitled to a priority.
b. Skipper has **no** personal liability to the creditors as long as Canarsie is recognized as a separate legal entity.
c. Skipper can **not** personally file a petition in bankruptcy for seven years.
d. Skipper is personally liable to the creditors for Canarsie's losses.

May 1984 Questions

19. A debtor will be denied a discharge in bankruptcy if the debtor

a. Failed to timely list a portion of his debts.
b. Unjustifiably failed to preserve his books and records which could have been used to ascertain the debtor's financial condition.
c. Has negligently made preferential transfers to favored creditors within 90 days of the filing of the bankruptcy petition.
d. Has committed several willful and malicious acts which resulted in bodily injury to others.

20. White is a general creditor of Ned. Ned filed a petition in bankruptcy under the liquidation provisions of the Bankruptcy Code. White wishes to have the bankruptcy court either deny Ned a general discharge or not have his debt discharged. The discharge will be granted, and it will include White's debt even if

a. Ned has unjustifiably failed to preserve the records from which Ned's financial condition might be ascertained.
b. Ned had received a previous discharge in bankruptcy under the liquidation provisions within six years.
c. White's debt is unscheduled.
d. White was a secured creditor who was **not** fully satisfied from the proceeds obtained upon disposition of the collateral.

21. Under the Bankruptcy Code, one of the elements that must be established in order for the trustee in bankruptcy to void a preferential transfer to a creditor who is not an insider is that

a. The transferee-creditor received more than he would have received in a liquidation proceeding under the Bankruptcy Code.
b. Permission was received from the bankruptcy judge prior to the trustee's signing an order avoiding the transfer.
c. The transfer was in fact a contemporaneous exchange for new value given to the debtor.
d. The transferee-creditor knew or had reason to know that the debtor was insolvent.

22. Bar, a creditor of Sy, has filed an involuntary petition in bankruptcy against Sy. Sy is indebted to six unsecured creditors including Bar for $6,000 each. If Sy opposes the petition, which of the following is correct?

a. Bar must be joined by at least two other creditors in filing the petition.
b. The court must appoint a trustee within ten days after the filing of the petition.
c. Bar may be required to file a bond indemnifying Sy for any losses which Sy may incur.
d. The court may **not** award attorney's fees to Sy due to its limited authority under the Bankruptcy Code.

Problems

Problem 1 Trustee's Avoiding Powers; Exempt Property; Priority of Secured Creditor (1183,L3a)

(7 to 10 minutes)

Part a. Skidmore, doing business as Frock & Fashions, is hopelessly insolvent. Several of his aggressive creditors are threatening to attach his property or force him to make preferential payments of their debts. In fairness to himself and to all his creditors, Skidmore has filed a voluntary petition in bankruptcy on behalf of himself and Frock & Fashions. An order for relief has been entered.

Skidmore's bankruptcy is fairly straightforward with the following exceptions:

- Skidmore claims exemptions for his summer cottage and for his home.
- Morse, a business creditor, asserts that commercial creditors have a first claim to all Skidmore's property, business and personal.
- Walton seeks a denial of Skidmore's discharge since Skidmore obtained credit from him by use of a fraudulent financial statement.
- Harper claims a priority for the amount owed him which was not satisfied as a result of his resorting to the collateral securing his loan.

Required:

Answer the following, setting forth reasons for any conclusions stated.

1. What are the principal avoiding powers of the trustee in bankruptcy?
2. Discuss in separate paragraphs each of the various claims and assertions stated above.

Problem 2 Involuntary Bankruptcy Petition (1181,L4a)

(10 to 15 minutes)

Part a. A small business client, John Barry, doing business as John Barry Fashions, is worried about an involuntary bankruptcy proceeding being filed by his creditors. His net worth using a balance-sheet approach is $8,000 ($108,000 assets – $100,000 liabilities). However, his cash flow is negative and he has been hard pressed to meet current obligations as they mature. He is, in fact, some $12,500 in arrears in payments to his creditors on bills submitted during the past two months.

Required:

Answer the following, setting forth reasons for any conclusions stated.

1. What are the current requirements for a creditor or creditors filing an involuntary petition in bankruptcy and could they be satisfied in this situation?
2. Will the fact that Barry is solvent in the bankruptcy sense result in the court's dismissing the creditors' petition if Barry contests the propriety of the filing of a petition?

Problem 3 Security Interest as a Voidable Preference (1180,L3b)

(7 to 10 minutes)

Part b. In connection with the audit of One-Up, Inc., a question has arisen regarding the validity of a $10,000 purchase money security interest in certain machinery sold to Essex Company on March 2nd. Essex was petitioned into bankruptcy on May 1st by its creditors. The trustee is seeking to avoid One-Up's security interest on the grounds that it is a preferential transfer, hence voidable. The machinery in question was sold to Essex on the following terms: $1,000 down and the balance plus interest at nine percent (9%) to be paid over a three-year period. One-Up obtained a signed security agreement which created a security interest in the property on March 2nd, the date of the sale. A financing statement was filed on March 10th.

Required:

Answer the following, setting forth reasons for any conclusions stated.

1. Would One-Up's security interest in the machinery be a voidable preference?
2. In general, what are the requirements necessary to permit the trustee to successfully assert a preferential transfer and thereby set aside a creditor's security interest?

Multiple Choice Answers

1. c	6. d	11. b	15. d	19. b
2. d	7. c	12. c	16. d	20. d
3. d	8. c	13. c	17. b	21. a
4. c	9. a	14. c	18. b	22. c
5. b	10. c			

Multiple Choice Answer Explanations

A. Alternatives to Bankruptcy Proceedings

1. (578,L1,24) (c) A composition with creditors is an agreement made between a debtor and creditors whereby the creditors agree with one another and the debtor to accept less than the full amount due. The composition does not discharge any of the debts until performance by the debtor has taken place. However, the agreement is valid from the time made. Answer (a) is incorrect because a composition does not provide for an appointment of receiver which is called a receivership. Answer (b) is incorrect because it need not be approved by all creditors, only those who wish to participate. Answer (d) is incorrect because a valid composition discharges the unpaid portion of the debts and does not merely provide a temporary delay.

B. Voluntary Bankruptcy Petitions

2. (583,L1,21) (d) A voluntary bankruptcy proceeding is available to all debtors who owe debts, irrespective of whether the debtor is insolvent, except for municipalities, railroads, banks, insurance companies, and savings and loan associations. Whether the debtor's creditors have petitioned and obtained a receivership would not effect the debtor's rights to initiate a voluntary proceeding under Chapter 7 of the Bankruptcy Reform Act. Corporations do not need to first attempt a reorganization under Chapter 11 before filing a voluntary petition. Therefore, answers (a), (b) and (c) are incorrect.

C. Involuntary Bankruptcy Petitions

3. (583,L1,22) (d) An involuntary petition in bankruptcy, if not contested will automatically result in the entry of an order for relief by the bankruptcy court. Only if the petition is contested will the creditor(s) be required to prove either that the debtor is not paying her/his debts as they mature, or that during the 120 days preceeding the filing of a petition, a custodian was appointed or took possession of the debtors property. Answer (a) is incorrect because the presence of a composition agreement will not cause denial of an involuntary petition. In many cases a creditor who is left out of such a composition agreement may wish to file an involuntary petition in order to protect her/his interest before the debtor uses a major portion of her/his assets in settling the debts owed to only the creditors involved in the composition agreement. Answer (b) is incorrect because a petition may be filed only once in a six year period, not a seven year period. Answer (c) is incorrect because a debtor need only prove that s/he is solvent in the equity sense (i.e., that s/he is paying her/his debts as they mature) and that a custodian was not appointed or did not take possession of the debtors property within 120 days before the filing of the petition. The debtor need not prove that her/his assets exceed her/his liabilities (solvency in the bankruptcy sense).

D. Bankruptcy Proceedings

4. (583,L1,23) (c) The estate which the trustee represents, consists of any property presently owned or received by the debtor within 180 days after filing of the petition by inheritance, as a result of a property settlement with a spouse, or as a beneficiary of a life insurance policy. Answer (a) is incorrect because it refers to the commission of "bankruptcy offenses" which is a term associated with the prior bankruptcy act and which is not present in the current bankruptcy law as established in the Bankruptcy Reform Act of 1978. Answer (b) is incorrect because bankruptcy can only be filed once in every 6 year period, not once in every five year period. Answer (d) is incorrect because bankruptcy law does not preclude a bankrupt who received a discharge in bankruptcy from owning or operating a similar business in the future.

5. (1182,L1,18) (b) The Bankruptcy Reform Act of 1978 includes new liberal federal exemptions for property. Such exemptions were not in existence under the old bankruptcy law. Answer (a) is incorrect because the new law did not increase the availability or ease the filing requirements for a voluntary bankruptcy proceeding. But, the new law did affect an involuntary bankruptcy by eliminating the acts of bankruptcy and the requirement of the creditors establishing insolvency in the bankruptcy sense. The new law accepted solvency in the equity sense as the standard for determining bankruptcy in an involuntary proceeding, thereby making it easier for creditor(s) to proceed against a debtor. Answer (c) is incorrect because the new law did not change the number of creditors necessary for filing under an involuntary bankruptcy proceeding. If there are twelve or more creditors, an in-

voluntary bankruptcy petition may be filed by three or more creditors having claims aggregating $5,000 more than the value of any liens securing the claims. If there are fewer than twelve creditors, the petition may be filed by one or more creditors with claims of $5,000 or more. Answer (d) is incorrect because the new law's acceptance of solvency in the equity sense as the criterion for determining bankruptcy status only applies to involuntary bankruptcy proceedings, it is not relevant to voluntary bankruptcy proceedings.

6. (581,L1,41) (d) A trustee is the representative of the estate and has the capacity to sue and be sued. Answer (a) is false since a trustee is either elected by creditors or appointed by a judge to liquidate the estate. There is no requirement that the trustee be an attorney. Answer (b) is also incorrect since a trustee is compensated using a specified percentage of the estate, not by reference to value or amount of services rendered. Answer (c) is incorrect since it is permissible for the trustee to have dealings with the debtor within the prior year.

7. (581,L1,42) (c) According to the Rules of Bankruptcy Procedure, it is necessary to file a proof of claims against the debtor's estate. The filing must be timely (within a six-month period) or the claim will be barred. A claim that is filed on time is given prima facie validity and is approved unless there is an objection by one of the creditors. Answer (a) is incorrect since all claims are subject to filing and review. Answer (b) is also false because a fee may result from an arms-length negotiation and still be disallowed by Bankruptcy Procedure. Claims for services by an attorney of the debtor, to the extent a fee exceeds a reasonable value for services rendered, are disallowed. The court must approve the reasonableness of the claim even if the transaction is an arms-length negotiation. Answer (d) is false because it is the courts, not the trustee, which approve the fees.

D.3.e.5) Preferential Transfers

8. (581,L1,44) (c) In order to establish a preference under the Bankruptcy Reform Act, the trustee is required to show that the transfer was made in payment of an antecedent debt (a debt incurred prior to the transfer as contrasted with a present transfer for value). As a result of such a transfer the preferred party receives more than he would in the bankruptcy proceedings. Answer (a) is untrue since, under the new Bankruptcy Reform Act of 1978 in order for the trustee to establish a preference, it is no longer a requirement to prove that the preferred party have reasonable cause to believe that the debtor is insolvent. Answer (b) is incorrect since, under the Act of 1978, acts of bankruptcy no longer exist. Answer (d) is incorrect since the transfer must be made within 90 days, not 60 days, of the filing of the bankruptcy petition.

9. (580,L1,3) (a) Answer (a) is correct because a secured creditor is not an "insider" for the purposes of a preferential transfer. However, a partner is an insider with regard to the partnership, a director is an insider concerning the corporation, and a close relative is an insider to the debtor.

E. Claims

10. (582,L1,20) (c) Under the Bankruptcy Reform Act of 1978 rent claims are no longer entitled to a priority concerning the distribution of the assets in the debtor's estate. Rent claims are considered claims of general creditors and these claims would be the last debts satisfied in the bankruptcy proceeding (on a pro rata basis with claims of other general creditors). Answers (a), (b), and (d) are incorrect because the new Act does retain priorities for taxes, wages earned within 90 days of the filing of the petition to a maximum of $2,000 or contributions to employee benefit plans arising from services rendered within 180 days of the filing.

11. (581,L1,43) (b) A secured creditor has a security interest in the personal property of the debtor which is acting as collateral for the debt. In a bankruptcy proceeding, there is an order of priorities concerning distribution of the debtor's estate. Secured creditors are given first priority in the sense that property subject to a valid security interest is not part of the estate for distribution purposes but belongs to the secured creditor to the extent of his security interest. The secured party can either take the property or its cash equivalent. If the value of the property is insufficient to satisfy the claim, the secured creditor becomes a general creditor for the balance. After all secured creditors and priority claims are fully satisfied, all general creditors then share in the remaining assets of the debtor's estate. Answers (a), (b), and (d) are incorrect because the secured party does have a claim for the balance, but only as an unsecured general creditor.

12. (580,L1,10) (c) Under the Bankruptcy Reform Act of 1978, a priority is given to claims of wage earners up to an amount of $2,000 per claimant, provided wages were earned within 90 days of the filing of the petition. This priority does include claims from vacation, severance, and sick leave pay; therefore, answer (c) is the correct answer. If the individual wage earner's claim exceeds $2,000, it falls to the last priority under unsecured claims (general creditors).

F. Discharge of a Bankrupt

13. (1182,L1,17) (c) A transfer of property by the debtor with the intent to hinder a creditor within one year before the date of filing of the petition (a fraudulent conveyance) will result in the debtor being denied a discharge from any of his/her debts. Obtaining credit by resort to fraud, defalcation while acting in a fiduciary capacity and willful and malicious injury by the debtor to another entity results in exception to discharge of the specific debt involved. In the three above-mentioned situations, the debtor's other obligations would be discharged unless these obligations qualify as nondischargeable debts.

14. (580,L1,35) (c) If the debtor supplies false information to obtain credit, the debt incurred will not be discharged in a bankruptcy proceedings. Answer (a) is incorrect because only the debt involving the false information will not be discharged. All other dischargeable debts will be terminated at the end of the bankruptcy proceedings. Answer (b) is incorrect because the creditor must rely on the false information before the resulting debt becomes nondischargeable. Answer (d) is incorrect because Hapless will be denied a discharge of the Suburban debt.

15. (579,L1,16) (d) Any unpaid amount of taxes due to the United States or to any state or subdivision thereof from within three years preceding bankruptcy is not discharged by the bankruptcy proceeding. The unpaid balances owed to secured creditors, as in answer (a), or unpaid amounts owed to trade suppliers for goods purchased, as in answer (b), or a personal loan from the bankrupt's father made in an attempt to stave off bankruptcy, as in answer (c), are all items which would be discharged in bankruptcy. Once these claims are discharged, the bankrupt would no longer have to pay them.

K. Business Reorganization — Chapter 11

16. (583,L1,24) (d) Under a Chapter 11 reorganization, a debtor is allowed to remain in possession of its business unless the court upon request by a party in interest appoints a trustee to take over management of the debtor's business. The court will approve such a request when it appears gross mismanagement of the business has occurred, or that the takeover by a trustee would be in the best interest of the debtor's estate. Answer (a) is incorrect because a corporate reorganization can be voluntary or involuntary. Answer (b) is incorrect because Waters, as a separate entity from Hard Times, will not have his personal bankruptcy status resolved when a petition is filed against Hard Times. Waters may be forced into bankruptcy by a separate petition, but since the corporation is a separate entity from Waters, the filing of a petition for bankruptcy against Hard Times will not automatically cause Waters' bankruptcy status to be resolved. Answer (c) is incorrect because in a Chapter 11 reorganization only the debtor may file a plan within the first 120 days after the date of the order for relief. If the debtor does not meet the 120 day deadline, any party in interest can propose a plan, but at no time is a "duly constituted creditors committee" the only party able to file a plan.

17. (582,L1,21) (b) The Bankruptcy Reform Act of 1978 eliminated the separate and competing procedures concerning reorganizations contained in Chapters 10 and 11 of the prior Bankruptcy Act. Under the new Act only one chapter (Chapter 11) concerns reorganizations. Answers (a) and (d) are incorrect because the new Bankrutpcy Reform Act does not provide separate treatment of publicly-held corporations, nor does it exclude noncorporate entities from its reorganization provisions. Answer (c) is incorrect because the Act does limit the power of the SEC concerning the Commission's participation in reorganizations, but it does not completely eliminate the SEC's participation in bankruptcy reorganizations.

Other

18. (582,L1,17) (b) A corporation is considered a separate legal entity from its owners (the shareholders). Generally, the shareholders are not personally liable for the debts of the corporation. This is normally true even concerning a principal stockholder who is a director and chief executive officer of the corporation. However, if the purpose of incorporation is to defraud the creditors, then the courts will "pierce the corporate veil" and hold the shareholders personally liable. Answer (c) is incorrect because due to the separate legal entity concept, the bankruptcy of the corporation would not affect Skipper's right to file bankruptcy in the future. Answer (a) is incorrect because claims for services rendered by insiders (a director is an insider) are only allowed to the extent the court decides the claims are reasonable. Even if the court decides the claim is reasonable, the priority given to wage claims in a bankruptcy proceeding does not include salary claims by officers of the corporation.

May 1984 Answers

19. (584,L1,16) (b) A debtor will be denied a general discharge if that debtor destroyed, falsified, concealed, or failed to keep books of account or record unless such act was justified under the circumstances. Answer (a) is incorrect because the failure to list a portion of the debts will result only in the denial of discharge of those specific debts not listed. Answer (c) is incorrect because a negligent preferential transfer to favored creditors within 90 days of the filing will merely result in the setting aside of the transfer by the trustee; a general discharge will not be denied. However, had the transfer been a fraudulent conveyance, i.e., a transfer made with the intent to hinder, delay, or defraud any creditor, the court would have sufficient grounds to deny a general discharge. Answer (d) is incorrect since only those debts which were directly caused by the commission of willful and malicious acts will be nondischargeable. A general discharge may still be granted.

20. (584,L1,17) (d) The fact that the debt of a secured party was not fully satisfied from the proceeds obtained from disposition of the collateral will not result in a denial of a general discharge, nor will the remaining portion of the secured debt be nondischargeable. In such situations the secured party has the same priority as a general unsecured creditor (lowest priority) concerning the unpaid portion of the debt. Answer (a) is incorrect because a debtor who fails to keep books will be denied a general discharge. Answer (b) is incorrect because a debtor who has received a previous discharge in bankruptcy under the liquidation provisions within six years will be denied a general discharge. Answer (c) is incorrect because unscheduled debts are not discharged in a bankruptcy proceeding.

21. (584,L1,18) (a) Under the Bankruptcy Code, one of the elements which must be established in proving that a preferential transfer was made is that the transferee-creditor received more than he would have received in a liquidation proceeding. Answer (b) is incorrect because a trustee need not obtain the permission from the bankruptcy judge prior to avoiding a preferential transfer. Answer (c) is incorrect because one of the elements which must be present to prove that a preferential transfer has been made is that the transfer involved an antecedent debt. Since the transfer described in answer (c) was a contemporaneous exchange for new value given, no antecedent debt was involved; thus, no preferential transfer can exist. Answer (d) is incorrect because the question asks what element is necessary to prove that a preferential transfer to a creditor who is not an insider exists. Although the element described in answer (d) is necessary when proving that an insider preference has occurred within one year of the filing of the bankruptcy petition, it is not a necessary element needed to prove that a general preference has occurred within 90 days of the filing of the bankruptcy petition.

22. (584,L1,19) (c) Creditors filing an involuntary petition in bankruptcy may be required to file a bond indemnifying the debtors for any losses which are incurred by the debtor in resisting the petition. This is to deter the filing of any frivolous petitions. Answer (a) is incorrect because, according to the Bankruptcy Code, when a debtor has less than 12 creditors, a petition need only be filed by one or more creditors who are owed unsecured debts of at least $5,000. Only when there are 12 or more creditors is it necessary for at least 3 creditors (whom claim agregate at least $5,000 over any security held by the creditors) to join in filing a petition. Answer (b) is incorrect because there is no requirement under the Bankruptcy Code which states that a trustee must be appointed by the court within 10 days after filing the petition. Only after an order for relief has been granted, will the court appoint an interim trustee until the permanent trustee can be elected at the first creditors' meeting. Answer (d) is incorrect since, in the event that a petition is rejected, the bankruptcy court has the authority to award the debtor attorneys' fees and other costs incurred by the debtor in refuting the petition. If the petition was filed in bad faith, punitive damages may also be awarded the debtor.

Answer Outline

Problem 1 Trustee's Avoiding Powers; Exempt Property; Priority of Secured Creditor

Part a.

1. Trustee has avoiding powers to set aside
   - Certain statutory liens
   - Preferential transfers
   - Fraudulent conveyances
   - Post-petition transfers
2. Resolution of claims and assertions
   - Claim for cottage disallowed
     - Bankruptcy Code provides one exemption on principal residence not > $7,500
       - Home qualifies
   - No rule separates business assets from personal assets
     - Skidmore and his business are one and the same
     - All assets collected and shared among creditors regardless of source
   - Bankruptcy Code states fraudulent FSs will not deny general discharge of bankrupt
     - However, Code will exempt such debt from discharge in bankruptcy
     - Walton's claim survives
   - Secured creditor entitled to collateral or equivalent
     - If collateral is insufficient, secured creditor has general creditor status for balance

Unofficial Answer

Problem 1 Trustee's Avoiding Powers; Exempt Property; Priority of Secured Creditor

Part a.

1. The principal avoiding powers of the trustee are
   - The power to set aside certain statutory liens.
   - The power to set aside preferential transfers.
   - The power to set aside fraudulent conveyances.
   - The power to set aside post-petition transfers.

2. The various claims and assertions would be resolved as follows:
   - The claim for an exemption allowance for the cottage will be disallowed. The Bankruptcy Code provides for one exemption for one's principal residence, not to exceed $7,500. The home will qualify for this exemption.
   - There is no such rule applicable to business assets as contrasted with personal assets. In fact, there is no distinction between Skidmore and his business, Frock & Fashions. They are one and the same and all assets will be collected and shared among the creditors without distinction as to the source.
   - The Bankruptcy Code makes it clear that such conduct would not result in a denial of the discharge of the bankrupt. It will, however, result in the denial of that particular debt from discharge in bankruptcy. Thus, Walton's claim will survive the bankruptcy proceeding.
   - A bona fide secured creditor is entitled to the collateral or its monetary equivalent. If this is insufficient to satisfy the loan, the secured creditor has the status of a general creditor for the balance. The priorities section of the Bankruptcy Code provides for no such priority as claimed by Harper.

Answer Outline

Problem 2 Involuntary Bankruptcy Petition

a1. Under Bankruptcy Reform Act of 1978, an involuntary petition may be filed by creditors
   - If there are 12 or more creditors
     - At least three must sign the petition
   - If there are fewer than 12 creditors
     - A single creditor may file the petition
   - The creditor(s) must have claim or claims aggregating $5,000
     - In excess of the value of any liens securing the claims
   - Involuntary petition could be validly filed by creditors

a2. Barry's defense of being solvent in the bankruptcy sense will not persuade the court to dismiss creditors' petition
   - Under the Bankruptcy Act, insolvency is measured in the equity sense
     - A debtor is deemed insolvent if not able to meet currently maturing obligations
       - Barry is unable to pay debts as they become due
     - A debtor is deemed insolvent if within 120 days preceding the filing of the petition a custodian of the debtor's property is appointed
   - Solvency in the equity sense would be a viable defense to the petition

Unofficial Answer

Problem 2 Involuntary Bankruptcy Petition

Part a.

1. Under the Bankruptcy Reform Act of 1978, an involuntary petition may be filed by three or more creditors having claims aggregating $5,000 more than the value of any liens securing the claims. In the event there are fewer than 12 creditors, one or more creditors with claims of $5,000 or more can file. The facts indicate that Barry has $12,500 in overdue debts. It would appear likely that these requirements could be met and an involuntary petition could be validly filed. The act permits the involuntary debtor to file an answer to the petition.

2. No. Under the 1978 act, the principal defense available to an involuntary debtor would still be solvency. However, the defense of solvency in the bankruptcy sense (essentially a balance sheet approach) has been rejected when an involuntary liquidation is sought. Instead, the act has adopted a modified or expanded version of insolvency in the equity sense. A debtor is insolvent if he is generally not paying debts as they become due. In addition, a debtor is insolvent if within 120 days before the date of the filing of the petition a custodian was appointed or took possession of the debtor's property. Barry, of course, appears to be squarely within the scope of the first part of this test. Realistically, he could not hope to have the petition dismissed on the grounds of solvency.

Answer Outline

Problem 3 Security Interest as a Voidable Preference

b1. No, security interest is not voidable preference
Purchase money security interest perfected within 10 days after attachment is exempted from preference states

b2. Trustee may avoid any transfer of property as preferential which is:
1. To or for benefit of a creditor
2. For antecedent debt owed by debtor before such transfer
3. Made while debtor insolvent in bankrupt sense
    a. Transfer was to "insider"
    b. Transferee had reasonable cause to believe debtor insolvent at time of transfer
4. Transfer that enables creditor to receive more than in straight liquidation proceeding

Unofficial Answer

Problem 3 Security Interest as a Voidable Preference

Part b.

1. No. The Bankruptcy Reform Act of 1978 has not only modified the requirements for establishing a voidable preference, it has also specified transactions that do not constitute preferences. One such transaction is the creditor's taking a security interest in property acquired by the debtor as a contemporaneous exchange for new value given to the debtor to enable him to acquire such property (a purchase money security interest). The security interest must be perfected (filed) within 10 days after attachment. The act is in harmony with the secured transactions provisions of the Uniform Commercial Code. Thus, One-Up has a valid security interest in the machinery it sold to Essex.

2. The Bankruptcy Reform Act of 1978 does not require that the creditor have knowledge or reasonable cause to believe the debtor is insolvent in the bankruptcy sense. Instead, under the act, where such insolvency exists on or within ninety days before the filing of the petition, knowledge of insolvency by the transferee need not be established. The act also assumes that the debtor's insolvency is presumed if the transfer alleged to be preferential is made within 90 days. Finally, the time period in which transfers may be set aside is 90 days unless the transferee is an "insider." If the transfer is to an insider, the trustee may avoid transfers made within one year prior to the filing of the petition. Thus, the trustee may avoid as preferential any transfer of property of the debtor that is

- To or for the benefit of a creditor.
- For or on account of an antecedent debt owed by the debtor before such transfer was made.
- Made while the debtor was insolvent in the bankruptcy sense (however, if the transfer is made within 90 days, the debtor's insolvency is presumed).
- Made on or within 90 days of the filing of the petition (or if made after the 90 days but within one year prior to the date of the filing of the petition and the transfer was to an "insider," it may be set aside if the transferee had reasonable cause to believe the debtor was insolvent at the time of the transfer).
- Such that it enables the creditor to receive more than he would if it were a straight liquidation proceeding.

The bankruptcy act contains a lengthy definition of the term "insider" that includes common relationships that the transferee has to the debtor, which, in case of an individual debtor, could be certain relatives, a partnership in which he is a general partner, his fellow general partners, or a corporation controlled by him.

Multiple Choice Questions (1 - 27)

1. Which of the following transactions does **not** establish Samp as a surety?

   a. Samp says: "Ship goods to my son and I will pay for them."
   b. Samp signs commercial paper as an accommodation indorser for one of his suppliers.
   c. Samp guarantees a debt of a corporation he controls.
   d. Samp sells an office building to Park, and, as a part of the consideration, Park assumes Samp's mortgage on the property.

2. Which of the following transactions does not create a surety relationship?

   a. The assumption of a mortgage by the purchaser of a parcel of real estate.
   b. The blank indorsement of a check.
   c. Signing a nonnegotiable promissory note as an accommodation maker.
   d. Obtaining professional malpractice insurance by a CPA.

3. When the debtor has defaulted on its obligation, the creditor is entitled to recover from the surety, unless which of the following is present?

   a. The surety is in the process of exercising its right of exoneration against the debtor.
   b. The debtor has died or become insolvent.
   c. The creditor could collect the entire debt from the debtor's collateral in his possession.
   d. The surety is a guarantor of collection and the creditor failed to exercise due diligence in enforcing his remedies against the debtor.

4. Knott obtained a loan of $10,000 from Charles on January 1, 1982, payable on April 15, 1982. At the time of the loan, Beck became a noncompensated surety thereon by written agreement. On April 15, 1982, Knott was unable to pay and wrote to Charles requesting an extension of time. Charles made no reply, but did not take any immediate action to recover. On May 30, 1982, Charles demanded payment from Knott and, failing to collect from him, proceeded against Beck. Based upon the facts stated

   a. Charles was obligated to obtain a judgment against Knott returned unsatisfied before he could collect from Beck.
   b. Beck is released from his surety obligation because Charles granted Knott an extension of time.
   c. Charles may recover against Beck despite the fact Beck was a noncompensated surety.
   d. Beck is released because Charles delayed in proceeding against Knott.

5. The Martin Corporation was a small family-owned corporation whose owners were also the directors and officers. The corporation's bankers insisted that if any further credit were to be extended to the corporation the owners must guarantee payment by the corporation. This guaranty was agreed to by the owners in writing, and an additional $50,000 loan was granted to Martin Corporation. Which of the following best describes the legal significance of these events?

   a. The guaranty by the owners need not have been in writing since it was primarily for their own benefit.
   b. Once the owners agreed to the undertaking they automatically assumed responsibility for all of the corporation's prior debts.
   c. In the absence of specific provisions to the contrary, the owners are immediately liable on the debt in the event of the corporation's default.
   d. Since the owners each participated equally in the guaranty, each can be held liable by the bank, but only to the extent of his proportionate share in relation to the others.

6. Park owed Collins $1,000 and $2,000, respectively, on two separate unsecured obligations. Smythe had become a surety on the $2,000 debt at the request of Park when Park became indebted to Collins. Both debts matured on June 1. Park was able to pay only $600 at that time, and he forwarded that amount to Collins without instructions. Under these circumstances

   a. Collins must apply the funds pro rata in proportion to the two debts.
   b. Collins must apply the $600 to the $2,000 debt if there is no surety on the $1,000 debt.
   c. Smythe will be discharged to the extent of $400 if Collins on request of Smythe fails to apply $400 to the $2,000 debt.
   d. Collins is free to apply the $600 to the debts as he sees fit.

7. Hargrove borrowed $40,000 as additional working capital for her business from the Old Town Bank. Old Town required that the loan be collateralized to the extent of 60%, and an acceptable surety for the entire amount be obtained. Prudent Surety Company agreed to act as surety on the loan and Hargrove pledged $24,000 of bearer negotiable bonds, which belonged to her husband, with Old Town. Hargrove has defaulted. Which of the following is correct?

a. As a result of the default, Prudent and Hargrove's husband are cosureties.
b. Old Town must first proceed against Hargrove and obtain a judgment for payment before it can proceed against the collateral.
c. Old Town must first liquidate the collateral before it can proceed against Prudent.
d. Prudent is liable in full immediately upon default by Hargrove, but will upon satisfaction of the debt be entitled to the collateral.

8. Welch is a surety on Stanton's contract to build an office building for Brent. Stanton intentionally abandoned the project after it was 85% completed because of personal animosity which developed toward Brent. Which of the following is a correct statement concerning the rights or responsibilities of the various parties?

a. Any modification of the contract, however slight and even if beneficial to Welch, will release Welch.
b. Welch would be ordered to specifically perform the completion of the building if Brent sought this remedy.
c. Neither Stanton's failure to give Welch prior notice of its intention to abandon the project **nor** its actual abandonment of the project will release Welch.
d. Welch can **not** engage a contractor to finish the job and obtain from Brent the balance due on the contract.

9. The right of subrogation

a. May permit the surety to assert rights he otherwise could **not** assert.
b. Is denied in bankruptcy.
c. Arises only to the extent that it is provided in the surety agreement.
d. Can **not** be asserted by a cosurety unless he includes all other cosureties.

10. Dependable Surety Company, Inc., issued a surety bond for value received which guaranteed: (1) completion of a construction contract Mason had made with Lund and (2) payment by Mason of his workmen. Mason defaulted and did not complete the contract. The workers were not paid for their last week's work. Mason had in fact become insolvent, and a petition in bankruptcy was filed two months after the issuance of the bond. What is the effect upon Dependable as a result of the above events?

a. If Dependable pays damages to Lund as a result of the default on the contract, Dependable is entitled to recover in the bankruptcy proceedings the entire amount it paid prior to the payment of the general creditors of Mason.
b. If Dependable pays the workers in full, it is entitled to the same priority in the bankruptcy proceedings that the workers would have had.
c. If Dependable has another separate claim against Lund, Dependable may **not** set it off against any rights Lund may have under this contract.
d. As a compensated surety, Dependable would be discharged from its surety obligation by Mason's bankruptcy.

11. Allen was the surety for the payment of rent by Lear under a lease from Rosenthal Rentals. The lease was for two years. A clause in the lease stated that at the expiration of the lease, the lessee had the privilege to renew upon thirty days' prior written notice or, if the lessee remained in possession after its expiration, it was agreed that the lease was to continue for two years more. There was a default in the payment of rent during the extended term of the lease and Rosenthal is suing Allen for the rent due based upon the guarantee. Allen contends that he is liable only for the initial term of the lease and not for the extended term. Allen is

a. Not liable since it does **not** appear that a judgment against Lear has been returned unsatisfied.
b. Not liable because there has been a material alteration of the surety undertaking.
c. Not liable because there was a binding extension of time.
d. Liable on the surety undertaking which would include the additional two years.

12. Which of the following will release a surety from liability?

a. Release of the principal debtor from liability with the consent of the surety.
b. Delegation of the debtor's obligation to another party with the acquiescence of the creditor.

c. Lack of capacity because the debtor is a minor.
d. Discharge of the debtor in bankruptcy.

13. Dinsmore & Company was a compensated surety on the construction contract between Victor (the owner) and Gilmore Construction. Gilmore has defaulted and Victor has released Dinsmore for a partial payment and other consideration. The legal effect of the release of Dinsmore is
a. To release Gilmore as well.
b. Contingent on recovery from Gilmore.
c. Binding upon Victor.
d. To partially release Gilmore to the extent that Dinsmore's right of subrogation has been diminished.

14. Dustin is a very cautious lender. When approached by Lanier regarding a $2,000 loan, he not only demanded an acceptable surety but also collateral equal to 50% of the loan. Lanier obtained King Surety Company as his surety and pledged rare coins worth $1,000 with Dustin. Dustin was assured by Lanier one week before the due date of the loan that he would have no difficulty in making payment. He persuaded Dustin to return the coins since they had increased in value and he had a prospective buyer. What is the legal effect of the release of the collateral upon King Surety?
a. It totally releases King Surety.
b. It does **not** release King Surety if the collateral was obtained after its promise.
c. It releases King Surety to the extent of the value of the security.
d. It does **not** release King Surety unless the collateral was given to Dustin with the express understanding that it was for the benefit of King Surety as well as Dustin.

15. Cornwith agreed to serve as a surety on a loan by Super Credit Corporation to Fairfax, one of Cornwith's major customers. The relationship between Fairfax and Super deteriorated to a point of hatred as a result of several late payments on the loan. On the due date of the final payment, Fairfax appeared 15 minutes before closing and tendered payment of the entire amount owing to Super. The office manager of Super told Fairfax that he was too late and would have to pay the next day with additional interest and penalties. Fairfax again tendered the payment, which was again refused. It is now several months later and Super is seeking to collect from either Cornwith or Fairfax or both. What are Super's rights under the circumstances?
a. It cannot collect anything from either party.
b. The tender of performance released Cornwith from his obligation.
c. The tender of performance was too late and rightfully refused.
d. Cornwith is released only to the extent that the refusal to accept the tender harmed him.

16. Under what conditions will both the debtor and the surety be able to avoid liability on a debt owed by the debtor to the creditor?
a. The debt exceeds $500 and the debtor's obligation is not contained in a signed writing.
b. The debtor lacks the capacity to enter into the contract with the creditor.
c. There is a tender of payment by the surety.
d. The debtor is released by the creditor.

17. Markum contacted the Variable Loan Company for a business loan. Variable refused to make the loan unless adequate security or an acceptable surety could be provided. Markum asked Duffy, one of his trade customers, to act as surety on the loan. In order to induce Duffy to sign, Markum made certain fraudulent representations and submitted a materially false financial statement. He also promised Duffy favorable treatment if Duffy would agree to act as surety for him. Markum is now insolvent and Variable seeks to hold Duffy liable. Duffy may avoid liability
a. Since the surety undertaking was void at the inception.
b. Based upon fraud if Duffy can show Variable was aware of the fraud.
c. Because Variable had a duty to warn Duffy about Markum's financial condition and did **not** do so.
d. Because the law of suretyship favors the surety where neither the surety nor the creditor is at fault.

18. Which of the following defenses by a surety will be effective to avoid liability?
a. Lack of consideration to support the surety undertaking.
b. Insolvency in the bankruptcy sense by the debtor.
c. Incompetency of the debtor to make the contract in question.
d. Fraudulent statements by the principal-debtor which induced the surety to assume the obligation and which were unknown to the creditor.

19. Don loaned $10,000 to Jon, and Robert agreed to act as surety. Robert's agreement to act as surety was induced by (1) fraudulent misrepresentations made by Don concerning Jon's financial status and (2) a bogus unaudited financial statement of which Don had no knowledge, and which was independently submitted by Jon to Robert. Which of the following is correct?

a. Don's fraudulent misrepresentations will **not** provide Robert with a valid defense unless they were contained in a signed writing.
b. Robert will be liable on his surety undertaking despite the facts since the defenses are personal defenses.
c. Robert's reliance upon Jon's financial statements makes Robert's surety undertaking voidable.
d. Don's fraudulent misrepresentations provide Robert with a defense which will prevent Don from enforcing the surety undertaking.

20. Maxwell was the head cashier of the Amalgamated Merchants Bank. The Excelsior Surety Company bonded Maxwell for $200,000. An internal audit revealed a $1,000 embezzlement by Maxwell. Maxwell persuaded the bank not to report him, and he promised to pay the money back within ten days. The bank acquiesced and neither the police nor Excelsior was informed of the theft. Maxwell shortly thereafter embezzled $75,000 and fled. Excelsior refuses to pay. Is Excelsior liable? Why?

a. Excelsior is liable since the combined total of the embezzlements is less than the face amount of the surety bond.
b. Excelsior is liable for $75,000, but not the $1,000 since a separate arrangement was agreed to by Amalgamated with Maxwell.
c. Excelsior is liable since it is a compensated surety and as such assumed the risk.
d. Excelsior is not liable since the failure to give notice of the first embezzlement is a valid defense.

21. A distinction between a surety and a co-surety is that only one is entitled to

a. Compensation.
b. Subrogation.
c. Contribution.
d. Notice upon default.

22. A release of a co-surety by the creditor

a. Will have **no** effect on the obligation of the other co-surety.
b. Will release the other co-surety entirely.
c. Will release the other co-surety to the extent that his right to contribution has been adversely affected.
d. Need **not** be a binding release in order to affect the rights of the parties.

23. Gray and Far are co-sureties on a loan of $100,000 made by the Durham Bank to Wilson Fabric, Inc. Gray guaranteed the loan in full and Far guaranteed $50,000 of the loan. Each was aware of the co-surety relationship. Gray received $50,000 of collateral from Wilson as a condition precedent to his serving as co-surety. Wilson has defaulted on the loan. With respect to their ultimate liabilities

a. Gray is liable for $50,000 but has the exclusive benefit of resort to the collateral to repay his loss.
b. Gray and Far will each be liable for $50,000.
c. Since Gray received collateral and Far did not, the relationship is actually one of subsuretyship with Gray being liable for the entire amount.
d. In the final settlement between the sureties, Far will be liable for a net amount of $16,667.

24. In order to establish a co-surety relationship the two or more sureties must

a. Be aware of each other's existence at the time of their contract.
b. Sign the same contract creating the debt and the co-surety relationship.
c. Be bound to answer for the same debt or duty of the debtor.
d. Be bound for the same amount and share equally in the obligation to satisfy the creditor.

May 1984 Questions

Items 25 and 26 are based on the following information:

Jane wishes to obtain a loan of $90,000 from Silver Corp. At the request of Silver, Jane has entered into an agreement with Bing, Piper, and Long to act as co-sureties on the loan. The agreement between Jane and the co-sureties stated that the maximum liability of each co-surety is: Bing $60,000, Piper $30,000, and

Long $90,000. Based upon the surety relationship, Silver agreed to make the loan. After paying three installments totalling $30,000, Jane defaulted.

25. Prior to making payment, the co-sureties may seek the remedy of

a. Contribution.
b. Indemnification.
c. Subrogation.
d. Exoneration.

26. If Long properly paid the entire debt outstanding of $60,000, what amount may Long recover from the co-sureties?

a. $30,000 from Bing and $30,000 from Piper.
b. $20,000 from Bing and $20,000 from Piper.
c. $20,000 from Bing and $10,000 from Piper.
d. $15,000 from Bing and $15,000 from Piper.

27. Which of the following defenses will release a surety from liability?

a. Insanity of the principal debtor at the time the contract was entered into.
b. Failure by the creditor to promptly notify the surety of the principal debtor's default.
c. Refusal by the creditor, with knowledge of the surety relationship, to accept the principal debtor's unconditional tender of payment in full.
d. Release by the creditor of the principal debtor's obligation without the surety's consent but with the creditor's reservation of his rights against the surety.

Repeat Question

(584,L1,21) Identical to item 17 above

Problems

Problem 1 Creditor Holding Collateral; Co-suretyship; Co-surety's Right of Contribution (1183,L3b)

(7 to 10 minutes)

Part b. Mars Finance Company was approached by Grant, the president of Hoover Corp., for a loan of $25,000 for Hoover. After careful evaluation of Hoover's financial condition, Mars decided it would not make the loan unless the loan was collateralized or guaranteed by one or more sureties for a total of $30,000. Hoover agreed to provide collateral in the form of a security interest in Hoover's equipment. The initial valuation of the equipment was $20,000 and Hoover obtained Victory Surety Company as a surety for the additional $10,000. Prior to the granting of the loan, the final valuation on the equipment was set at $15,000 and Mars insisted on additional surety protection of $5,000. Grant personally assumed this additional surety obligation. Hoover has defaulted and Mars first proceeded against the collateral, which was sold for $17,000. It then proceeded against Victory for the balance. Victory paid the $8,000 and now seeks a $4,000 contribution from Grant.

Grant asserts the following defenses and arguments in order to avoid or limit his liability:

- That he is not liable since Mars elected to proceed against the collateral.
- That Mars by suing Victory for the deficiency, released him.
- That he is not a cosurety because Victory did not know of his existence until after default and his surety obligation was not assumed at the same time nor was it equal in amount, hence, there is no right of contribution.
- That in no event is he liable for the full $4,000 sought by Victory.

Required:

Answer the following, setting forth reasons for any conclusions stated.

Discuss in separate paragraphs each of the above defenses asserted by Grant and indicate the amount of Grant's liability.

Problem 2 Modification of Surety's Contract; Surety's Right of Reimbursement (1179,L4)

(20 to 25 minutes)

Part a. The King Surety Company, Inc., wrote a performance bond for Allie Stores, Inc., covering the construction of a department store. Rapid Construction Company, the department store contractor, is a general contractor and is simultaneously working on several buildings. Until the entire building is completed, the bond contained a provision that obligated Allie to withhold 20% of the progress payments to be made to Rapid at various stages of completion. After approximately two-thirds of the project had been satisfactorily completed, Rapid pleaded with Allie to release the 20% withheld to date. Rapid indicated that he was having a cash flow problem and unless funds were released to satisfy the demands of suppliers, workmen, and other creditors, there would be a significant delay in the completion date of the department store. Rapid claimed that if the 20% withheld were released, the project could be completed on schedule. Allie released the amounts withheld. Two weeks later Rapid abandoned the project, citing as its reason rising cost which made the contract unprofitable. Allie has notified King of the facts and demands that either King complete the project or respond in damages. King denies liability on the surety bond.

Required:

Answer the following, setting forth reasons for any conclusions stated.

Who will prevail?

Part b. Barclay Surety, Inc., is the surety on a construction contract that the Gilmore Construction Company made with Shadow Realty, Inc. By the terms of the surety obligation, Barclay is not only bound to Shadow, but also is bound to satisfy materialmen and laborers in connection with the contract. Gilmore defaulted, and Barclay elected to complete the project and pay all claims and obligations in connection with the contract, including all unpaid materialmen and laborers' claims against Gilmore. The total cost to complete exceeded the construction contract payments Barclay received from Shadow. Some of the materialmen who were satisfied had either liens or security interests against Gilmore. Gilmore has filed a voluntary bankruptcy petition.

Required:

Answer the following setting for reasons for any conclusions stated.

What rights does Barclay have as a result of the above facts?

Problem 3 Surety's Consideration; Surety's Liability Upon Default (1180,L3a)

(7 to 10 minutes)

Part a. Hardaway Lending, Inc., had a 4-year $800,000 callable loan to Superior Metals, Inc., outstanding. The loan was callable at the end of each year upon Hardaway's giving 60 days written notice. Two and one-half years remained of the four years. Hardaway reviewed the loan and decided that Superior Metals was no longer a prime lending risk and it therefore decided to call the loan. The required written notice was sent to and received by Superior 60 days prior to the expiration of the second year. Merriweather, Superior's chief executive officer and principal shareholder, requested Hardaway to continue the loan at least for another year. Hardaway agreed, provided that an acceptable commercial surety would guarantee $400,000 of the loan and Merriweather would personally guarantee repayment in full. These conditions were satisfied and the loan was permitted to continue.

The following year the loan was called and Superior defaulted. Hardaway released the commercial surety but retained its rights against Merriweather and demanded that Merriweather pay the full amount of the loan. Merriweather refused, asserting the following:

- There was no consideration for his promise. The loan was already outstanding and he personally received nothing.
- Hardaway must first proceed against Superior before it can collect from Merriweather.
- Hardaway had released the commercial surety, thereby releasing Merriweather.

Required:

Answer the following, setting forth reasons for any conclusions stated.

Discuss the validity of each of Merriweather's assertions.

Multiple Choice Answers

1. a	7. d	13. c	18. a	23. d
2. d	8. c	14. c	19. d	24. c
3. d	9. a	15. b	20. d	25. d
4. c	10. b	16. d	21. c	26. c
5. c	11. d	17. b	22. c	27. c
6. d	12. b			

Multiple Choice Answer Explanations

A. Nature of Suretyship

1. (1182,L1,22) (a) A suretyship relationship exists where one person agrees to be answerable for the debt of another by assuring performance upon the debtor's default. A suretyship agreement involves three parties: the principal debtor, the creditor and the surety. Answer (a) is correct because it describes a third party beneficiary contract, not a suretyship arrangement. Samp is not promising to pay the debt of another, but rather engaging in an original promise, to pay for the goods the creditor delivers to Samp's son. Answer (b) is incorrect because an accommodation indorser is a surety since the indorser engages to pay if the negotiable instrument is not paid by the appropriate party after proper presentment and notice. Answer (c) is incorrect because Samp is entering into a suretyship arrangement whereby he promises to pay if the principal debtor (the corporation) does not pay. Answer (d) is incorrect because when Park, the purchaser, assumed the mortgage, a surety relationship was created in which Park, the buyer, was the principal debtor and Samp, the seller, was the surety.

2. (1177,L2,17) (d) A suretyship relationship exists when one person agrees to be answerable for the debt or default of another. Unlike a suretyship relation, insurance is the distribution of the cost of risk over a large number of individuals. Malpractice insurance is spreading the cost of possible professional liability over a large number of professionals. Answer (a) is incorrect because an assumption of a mortgage creates a suretyship relationship in which the buyer becomes the principal debtor and the seller becomes the surety. Answer (b) is incorrect because a person who endorses a check in blank is a surety in that he promises to pay if the check is dishonored (endorsement "without recourse" disclaims this liability). Answer (c) is incorrect because an accommodation maker of a nonnegotiable note is a surety in that he promises to pay if the maker does not.

E. Creditor's Rights

3. (1181,L1,25) (d) Normally, a creditor can immediately sue the surety upon the debtor's default. However, when a surety is a guarantor of collection, the creditor must exhaust his remedies against the principal debtor by reducing his claim against the debtor to judgment and showing the judgment remains unpaid before the guarantor's obligation arises. Answer (a) is incorrect because exoneration is when the surety seeks to compel the principal debtor to pay the creditor. But such relief is not available if the creditor demands prompt performance from the surety upon default. Answer (b) is incorrect because the death or insolvency of the principal debtor does not release the surety. The possibility of the debtor's insolvency is a primary reason for engaging in a surety arrangement. Answer (c) is incorrect because the creditor need not resort to the collateral pledged; instead, he may proceed immediately against the surety. But once the surety satisfies the obligation, s/he is subrogated to the creditor's rights in the collateral.

4. (1182,L1,24) (c) If the surety's undertaking arises at the time the creditor extends the loan to the principal debtor, the surety does not need to receive independent consideration to be bound. Consequently, Beck, even as a noncompensated surety, would be bound to pay Knott. Answer (a) is incorrect because since the surety is primarily liable, the creditor may proceed immediately against the surety upon debtor's default without demand first being made upon the debtor. However, when a surety is a guarantor of collection, the guarantor's liability will be conditioned on the creditor first attempting to collect from the debtor. The creditor must exhaust his remedies against the principal debtor by reducing his claim against the debtor to judgment and showing the judgment remains unpaid before the guarantor's obligation arises. Normally, an extension of time to debtor, without surety's consent, releases the surety due to a material increase in the surety's risk. However, answer (b) is incorrect because such a variance of terms must be legally enforceable and binding on the creditor in order for the surety to be released. In this case, the debtor only made a request for an extension of time, but the extension was not granted by the creditor. Answer (d) is incorrect because a delay in the creditor proceeding against the debtor does not discharge the surety, unless such time delay exceeds the statutory period within the Statute of Limitations.

5. (576,L1,11) (c) As sureties, the owners are immediately liable on the debts if the corporation defaults. No notice need be given them. If the guarantee

was primarily for the owners' benefit, the guarantee would not need to be in writing. But since the benefit only accrues to the owners indirectly (through the corporation), it is not considered to be primarily for their benefit. They only guaranteed one loan and did not assume responsibility for other debts. The bank can hold any one of them fully liable for the entire debt and the others may be required to contribute their proportionate share to the one held liable.

6. (574,L1,13) (d) When a debtor has more than one debt outstanding with the same creditor and makes a part payment, the debtor may give instructions as to which debt the part payment is to apply. If the debtor makes no instructions the creditor is free to apply the part payment to whichever debt he chooses. The fact that one debt is guaranteed by a surety makes no difference in the absence of instructions by the debtor. So Collins can apply the $600 to the debts as he sees fit.

7. (1181,L1,28) (d) The essence of a surety arrangement is that the surety promises to perform upon default of the principal debtor. Further action by the creditor versus the principal debtor is not necessary (unlike a guarantor of collection). The surety, upon satisfaction of the principal debtor's obligation to the creditor, is subrogated to the creditor's rights in the collateral. Answer (a) is incorrect because co-sureties exist when more than one surety is bound to answer for the same obligation of a debtor. Prudent is the only surety; Hargrove's husband provided only the collateral. Answer (b) is incorrect because the creditor (Old Town) is capable of resorting to the collateral pledged without reducing his claim against the debtor to judgment and execution having been returned unsatisfied. Answer (c) is incorrect because the creditor need not resort to the collateral pledged; instead, she/he may proceed against the surety as soon as the obligation is due.

8. (581,L1,37) (c) Unless the contract is a conditional guaranty, it is unnecessary for creditors to give notice of the debtor's default to the surety. With or without notice, upon default the surety is liable for the performance guaranteed under the agreement. Answer (a) is incorrect because any modifications of the contract that have the possibility of increasing the surety's risk would release the surety. Brent could sue the surety for compensatory damages, not specific performance; therefore, answer (b) is incorrect. Answer (d) is incorrect since if Welch, the surety, **did** satisfy the obligation by engaging a contractor to finish the job, Welch could collect the balance due on the agreement.

F. Surety's Rights

9. (583,L1,27) (a) The right of subrogation is where the surety pursuant to his contractual undertaking fully satisfies the obligation of the principal debtor to the creditor, and succeeds to the creditor's rights (i.e., "steps into the creditor's shoes") against the debtor. The surety acquires the identical claims or rights the creditor possessed against the principal debtor, permitting the surety to assert rights he otherwise could not assert. Answer (b) is incorrect because the right of subrogation is granted in bankruptcy. Since the surety is subrogated to the rights of the creditor, the surety is entitled to the same priority as the creditor would have in a bankruptcy proceeding. Answer (c) is incorrect because the right of subrogation exists regardless of whether it is explicitly provided for in the surety agreement. Answer (d) is incorrect because the right of subrogation can be asserted by a co-surety without including all other co-sureties. But the other co-sureties have the right to contribution.

10. (1181,L1,26) (b) When the surety pursuant to his contractual undertaking fully satisfies the obligation of the creditor, he is then subrogated to the rights of that creditor. Therefore, Dependable would be entitled to the same priority as the workers would have in the bankruptcy proceeding. Answer (a) is incorrect because since Lund is a general creditor, Dependable is subrogated to Lund's rights upon payment. Therefore, Dependable would have equal priority with other general creditors of Mason. Answer (c) is incorrect because the surety may set off any claims that s/he has against the creditor even if they do not arise out of the surety obligation. Answer (d) is incorrect because insolvency (bankruptcy) of the principal debtor does not release the surety.

G. Surety's Defenses

11. (1181,L1,29) (d) The leasing arrangement, to which Allen is a surety, remained intact with no modifications. The lease, itself, expressed a holdover clause which went into existence when Lear remained in possession after the original leasing period. The essence of a surety arrangement is that the surety promises to perform upon default of the principal debtor. Therefore, Allen becomes liable when Lear defaults during the extended term of the lease. Answer (a) is incorrect because Allen is a surety, not a guarantor of collection; therefore, the creditor need not reduce his claim against the principal debtor to judgment and have execution be unsatisfied before proceeding against the surety on his promise. Answer (b) is incorrect because there was no alteration of the contract which materially affected

the risks to the surety. Answer (c) is incorrect because a binding extension of time refers to a creditor granting additional time to the debtor to satisfy his obligation. The holdover provision was part of the original agreement and, consequently, would not be considered an alteration.

12. (1182,L1,25) (b) A material alteration of a suretyship contract by the debtor and creditor, thereby modifying the principal debtor's duty, is a defense for the surety since it changes the risk of his undertaking. A delegation of the debtor's obligation to another party is a significant variance in the surety agreement, such that the surety will be released from liability. However, if the surety had acquiesced to the alteration, then the surety would waive this defense. Answer (a) is incorrect because the surety would be released from his liability only when the debtor is released by the creditor **without** the consent of the surety. Answer (c) is incorrect because minority of the principal debtor does not release the surety from his/her obligation to pay. Answer (d) is incorrect because the discharge of the debtor in bankruptcy does not release the surety from liability. The possibility of the debtor's insolvency is a primary reason for engaging in a surety arrangement.

13. (582,L1,24) (c) Victor's release of Dinsmore, the surety, is binding because it is supported by consideration. When the debtor releases the surety, the release completely discharges the surety's obligation if the release is supported by consideration. However, a release of the surety does not also release Gilmore, the principal debtor. Gilmore's obligation would not be affected in any way by Victor's release of Dinsmore, the surety. Therefore, answers (a), (b), and (d) are incorrect.

14. (1181,L1,24) (c) Upon default, the creditor (Dustin) may resort to the collateral he holds or may proceed against the surety on his promise. But when the creditor surrenders the collateral before or after the debtor's default, the surety is released to the extent of the value of the collateral. Answers (b) and (d) are incorrect because it does not matter when the collateral was obtained by Dustin or if it was expressly understood that the collateral was to benefit King Surety. Once the collateral is returned, this reduces the surety obligation to the extent of the value of the collateral.

15. (580,L1,44) (b) The tender of performance by the principal debtor completely releases the surety from his obligation. However, such tender does not release the principal debtor if the contractual duty consists of the obligation to pay money. If the contractual duty consisted of anything but the obligation to pay money, then the tender of such performance would have also released Fairfax.

16. (1176,L2,30) (d) If a creditor releases the debtor, the surety is also released unless the creditor reserved his rights against the surety. The surety agreement must be in writing but the debt need not unless the statute of frauds applies. It does not apply here because there are many ways in which a debt may exceed $500 without there having been a single sale of goods for $500. The debtor's lack of capacity will relieve the debtor of liability, but it is not a defense for the surety. Tender of payment by the surety will relieve the surety from liability, but not the debtor.

17. (1182,L1,15) (b) Fraud by the principal debtor on the surety to induce a suretyship agreement will not release the surety if the creditor has extended credit in good faith. But if the creditor (Variable) had knowledge of the debtor's (Markum's) fraudulent representations, then the surety (Duffy) may avoid liability. Answer (a) is incorrect because the surety undertaking was not void. Fraud in the inducement would create a voidable, not void, surety agreement. If the creditor fails to notify the surety of any material facts within the creditor's knowledge concerning the debtor and his ability to perform, the surety may assert this as a defense to avoid a liability. But answer (c) is incorrect because the creditor (Variable) did not have any knowledge that the debtor, Markum, made fraudulent representations to induce the surety agreement. Answer (d) is incorrect because the law of suretyship would not favor the surety where neither party is at fault. Since the essence of a surety agreement is that the surety promises to perform upon default of the principal debtor, it is the creditor who would be favored.

18. (582,L1,23) (a) If the surety's undertaking is not supported by consideration, the surety will avoid liability. However, when the surety's and principal debtor's obligations are incurred at the same time, there is no need for any separate consideration beyond that supporting the principal debtor's contract. If the surety's undertaking is entered into subsequent to the debtor's contract, it must be supported by separate consideration. Answers (b) and (c) are incorrect because the debtor's insolvency in either sense (equity or bankruptcy) or the debtor's lack of contractual capacity will not release the surety. Answer (d) is incorrect because fraud by the principal debtor on the surety will not release the surety unless the creditor was aware of this fraud. Obviously, fraud by the creditor on the surety will release the surety.

19. (581,L1,36) (d) If the creditor obtains the surety's promise by fraud, the surety has a valid defense against the creditor. The fact that the creditor's fraud was not contained in a signed writing (answer a) will not invalidate the surety's defense. Answer (b) is incorrect because the fact that fraud in the inducement is a personal defense has relevance only under the law of negotiable instruments, not the law of suretyship. Fraud by the principal debtor on the surety will not permit the surety to avoid liability to the creditor (answer c).

20. (1178,L1,20) (d) The general rule is that a surety is released from liability for acts of the creditor which materially increase the surety's risk. In this case the failure of the creditor to give notice of the prior embezzlement materially increased the surety's risk. Answers (a) and (b) are incorrect because when the surety is released from liability it is immaterial that the embezzlements did not exceed the face value of the bond. Answer (c) is incorrect because Excelsior has not assumed the risk that the creditor would negligently and knowingly withhold material information from the surety.

H. Co-sureties

21. (583,L1,25) (c) Co-sureties exist when more than one surety is bound to answer for the same debt or duty of a debtor, and who, as between themselves, should proportionately share the loss caused by the default of the debtor. The right of contribution arises when a co-surety, in performance of the debtor's obligation, pays more than his proportionate share, and thereby entitles the co-surety to compel the other co-sureties to compensate him for the excess amount paid. Answer (a) is incorrect because neither a surety nor a co-surety need to be compensated for acting as a surety. If the surety's or co-surety's undertaking arises at the time the creditor extends the loan to the principal debtor, the surety or co-surety does not need to receive independent consideration to be bound. But, if the surety's or co-surety's undertaking is subsequent to the debtor-creditor contract, it must be supported by separate consideration. Answer (b) is incorrect because both a surety and co-surety are entitled to subrogation. When the surety or co-surety pursuant to his contractual undertaking fully satisfies the principal debtor's obligation to the creditor, he is then subrogated to the rights of the creditor and can recover from the debtor in the same manner as the creditor. Answer (d) is incorrect because unless the contract so stipulates, (i.e., a conditional guaranty) it is unnecessary for the creditor to give the surety or co-surety notice of the debtor's default. The creditor can proceed immediately against the surety or co-surety upon the default of the debtor.

22. (583,L1,26) (c) Co-sureties exist when more than one surety is bound to answer for the same obligation or duty of a debtor, and who, as between themselves, should proportionately share the loss caused by the default of the debtor. Unless the creditor specifically reserves his rights, a release of a co-surety by the creditor will release the other co-surety to the extent of the released co-surety's liability (i.e., to the extent that the remaining co-surety's right to contribution has been adversely affected). Therefore, answers (a) and (b) are incorrect. Answer (d) is incorrect because in order for a release of one co-surety to affect the rights of the other co-surety, the release by the creditor must be binding.

23. (1182,L1,20) (d) Generally, co-sureties are jointly and severally liable to the creditor; however, as between co-sureties, each is liable in proportion to the amount each has personally guaranteed. Co-sureties have the right to reimbursement upon debtor's default, and may resort to the collateral held. In the final settlement of their liability to each other, each co-surety is entitled to share in any collateral pledged to **any** of the sureties in proportion to his liability for the principal debtor's default. Since Gray guaranteed $100,000 of the debt and Far guaranteed $50,000 of the debt, then Far is only individually liable for 1/3 ($50,000/$150,000) of the debt, i.e., $33,333 (1/3 x $100,000). Also, Far can share in the collateral pledged in this same 1/3 proportion, i.e., $16,667 (1/3 x $50,000). Therefore, in the final settlement between the sureties, Far will be liable for a net amount of $16,667 (the liability of $33,333 minus the $16,667 reimbursement from collateral). Answer (a) is incorrect because Gray is individually liable for 2/3 of the debt, i.e., $66,667; and Gray would not have exclusive benefit of resort to the collateral since Far is entitled to share in the collateral pledged. Answer (b) is incorrect because Gray and Far are liable in proportion to the amount each has personally guaranteed, $66,667 and $33,333, respectively. Answer (c) is incorrect because in a subsuretyship, the principal surety is primarily liable and bears the entire burden of performance with the subsurety in effect acting as a surety for the principal surety. Whereas in a co-suretyship relationship each surety shares in the burden upon default of the debtor. The fact that Gray received collateral and Far did not, would not dictate that the relation be a subsuretyship.

24. (1176,L2,31) (c) Co-sureties are two or more sureties bound to answer for the same debt or duty of the debtor. They need not be aware of each other's existence either at the time of their contract or later. They need not sign the same contract. The only necessary connection is that they are both bound to answer for the same debt irrespective of the time they became bound. Co-sureties also need not be bound for the same amount, e.g., one could be bound for 60% and the other for 40%.

May 1984 Answers

25. (584,L1,22) (d) Before paying the debt, the surety may seek the remedy of exoneration where the surety files a suit in equity to compel the debtor to pay the creditor. Indemnification, subrogation, and contribution are all remedies available to the surety after he has paid the creditor. Specifically, indemnification is the surety's right to reimbursement from the principal debtor in the amount paid. The rule of subrogation states that the surety, to the extent he has paid, succeeds to the creditor's rights against the principal debtor, including the right to any security interests the creditor might have in the debtor's property. The right of contribution arises when a co-surety has paid more than his proportionate share of the debt and is, therefore, entitled to compensation from the other co-sureties for the excess amount paid. Answers (a), (b), and (c) are, therefore, incorrect.

26. (584,L1,23) (c) Co-sureties are jointly and severally liable to the creditor. A co-surety who is held severally liable may proceed against the other co-sureties and seek contribution for their proportionate share. To calculate the proportionate share, divide the amount each surety has individually guaranteed by the total guaranty and then multiply by the total debt paid by the co-surety seeking contribution. In the instant case, the calculation is as follows:

$$\frac{\text{Individual guaranty}}{\text{Total guaranty}} \times \text{Total debt paid by co-surety}$$

$$\text{Bing: } \frac{\$\ 60{,}000}{\$180{,}000} \times \$60{,}000 = \underline{\underline{\$20{,}000}}$$

$$\text{Piper: } \frac{\$\ 30{,}000}{\$180{,}000} \times \$60{,}000 = \underline{\underline{\$10{,}000}}$$

27. (584,L1,24) (c) The surety will be discharged by the creditor's refusal to accept the principal debtor's tender of full payment on a mature debt. However, the tender of full payment will not discharge the principal debtor but will merely stop the running of interest on the monetary obligation. Answer (a) is incorrect because a surety may not exercise the principal debtor's personal defenses (i.e., insanity). Answer (b) is incorrect because, unless the contract states otherwise, the creditor has no duty to notify the surety of the principal debtor's default. Although a release of the principal debtor without the surety's consent will usually discharge the surety, there is no discharge if the creditor expressly reserves his rights against the surety. Answer (d) is, therefore, incorrect.

Answer Outline

Problem 1 Creditor Holding Collateral; Co-suretyship; Co-surety's Right of Contribution

Part b.

Grant incorrect in first three assertions, correct in fourth because
- Resort to collateral does not affect creditor's right to proceed against surety for balance
- Creditor has option of suing one or more sureties without impairing rights against those not sued
- Grant is cosurety because
  - He is answering same debt as Victory
  - Victory has right of contribution against him
- Grant had 1/3 of total surety undertakings
  - Liable for 1/3 of $8,000 (2,666.67), not full $4,000

Unofficial Answer

Problem 1 Creditor Holding Collateral; Co-suretyship; Co-surety's Right of Contribution

Part b.

Grant is incorrect in his first three assertions and correct in connection with his fourth assertion for the following reasons:

- The law is clear regarding the right to collateral and its effect as between the creditor and the surety. The creditor has the right to resort to any available collateral. Resort to the collateral by the creditor in no way affects the creditor's right to proceed against a surety or sureties for the balance.
- A creditor may choose to sue one or more of the sureties without impairing his rights against those not sued. Similarly, he has the right to sue one surety if he wishes, and such a choice does not release the surety who was not sued insofar as the rights of his fellow surety to seek contribution. Suing one but not all of the sureties does not constitute a release by the creditor.
- All of the defenses asserted in the fact situation are invalid. Grant is a cosurety since he is answering for the same debt as Victory and there is a right of contribution which Victory may assert against Grant.
- Since Grant's surtey undertaking was one-third of the combined surety undertakings, he is liable for $2,666.67 only and not the full $4,000.

Answer Outline

Problem 2 Modification of Surety's Contract; Surety's Right of Reimbursement

a. King (Surety) will prevail
   - The creditor modified the surety contract
     - Without the surety's consent
   - Noncompensated surety is discharged on any modification
   - Compensated surety is discharged if change materially increases risk
     - If not material, surety's liability is decreased
   - Here the change materially increased the risk
     - The released monies were not committed to the project
     - The withheld monies induced builder to complete
     - The withheld monies reduced surety's exposure

b. Barclay is entitled to reimbursement from Gilmore
   - But since Gilmore is bankrupt
     - Normally Barclay would have same position as other creditors
     - Except Barclay is subrogated to materialmen and laborers' rights
       - Liens and security interests of materialmen
       - Limited priorities of wage earners

Unofficial Answer

Problem 2 Modification of Surety's Contract Surety's Right of Reimbursement

Part a.

King Surety Company will prevail. The creditor (Allie), without King's consent, has modified the surety contract. Under these circumstances, a non-compensated surety would be discharged without question; however, a compensated surety is not discharged completely unless the modification materially increases the risk. If the risk is not materially increased, the obligation is decreased to the extent of the loss. In this case, there was a material increase in the risk. First, there is nothing to indicate that the monies released by Allie were committed by Rapid to the particular project (Allie's department store) because Rapid had several simultaneous projects. Moreover, it is clear that the monies withheld provided a strong inducement for a builder such as Rapid to complete the undertaking since the expected final payment would have been large in relation to the final outlays to complete construction. Finally, the withheld payments reduced the exposure of the surety to the extent of 20 percent.

Part b.

Barclay is, of course, entitled to reimbursement from Gilmore. However, since Gilmore is bankrupt, Barclay will receive the same percentage on the dollar as will all other general creditors of Gilmore's estate. However, Barclay is subrogated to the rights of the materialmen and laborers it has satisfied. Specifically, it would have the right to assert the liens and security interests of the materialmen. Furthermore, wage earners are entitled to a limited priority in a bankruptcy proceeding, which Barclay could assert.

Answer Outline

Problem 3 Surety's Consideration; Surety's Liability Upon Default

a. Hardaway's foregoing legal right to call the loan acts as adequate consideration
   Fact that loan is already outstanding is irrelevant
   There is no requirement that creditor first proceed against debtor
   Creditor may proceed against either debtor or surety
   Release of commercial surety partially released Merriweather
   Right of contribution has been impaired to the extent contribution could have been demanded from surety

Unofficial Answer

Problem 3 Surety's Consideration; Surety's Liability Upon Default

Part a.

The first two defenses asserted by Merriweather are invalid. The third defense is partially valid.

Consideration on Hardaway's part consisted of foregoing the right to call the Superior Metals loan. The fact that the loan was already outstanding is irrelevant. By permitting the loan to remain outstanding for an additional year instead of calling it, Hardaway relinquished a legal right, which is adequate consideration for Merriweather's surety promise. Consideration need not pass to the surety; in fact, it usually primarily benefits the principal debtor.

There is no requirement that the creditor first proceed against the debtor before it can proceed against the surety, unless the surety undertaking expressly provides such a condition. Basic to the usual surety undertaking is the right of the creditor to proceed immediately against the surety. Essentially, that is the reason for the surety.

Hardaway's release of the commercial surety from its $400,000 surety undertaking partially released Merriweather. The release had the legal effect of impairing Merriweather's right of contribution against its co-surety (the commercial surety). Thus, Merriweather is released to the extent of 1/3 ($400,000 (commercial surety's guarantee)/$1,200,000 (the aggregate of the co-sureties's guarantees) of the principal amount ($800,000), or $266,667.

Multiple Choice Questions (1 - 29)

1. The key characteristic of a servant is that
   a. His physical conduct is controlled or subject to the right of control by the employer.
   b. He is paid at an hourly rate as contrasted with the payment of a salary.
   c. He is precluded from making contracts for and on behalf of his employer.
   d. He lacks apparent authority to bind his employer.

2. Winter is a sales agent for Magnum Enterprises. Winter has assumed an obligation to indemnify Magnum if any of Winter's customers fail to pay. Under these circumstances, which of the following is correct?
   a. Winter's engagement must be in writing regardless of its duration.
   b. Upon default, Magnum must first proceed against the delinquent purchaser-debtor.
   c. The above facts describe a del credere agency relationship and Winter will be liable in the event his customers fail to pay Magnum.
   d. There is no fiduciary relationship on either Winter's or Magnum's part.

3. Steel has been engaged by Lux to act as the agent for Lux, an undisclosed principal. As a result of this relationship
   a. Steel has the same implied powers as an agent engaged by a disclosed principal.
   b. Lux can **not** be held liable for any torts committed by Steel in the course of carrying out the engagement.
   c. Steel will be free from personal liability on authorized contracts for Lux when it is revealed that Steel was acting as an agent.
   d. Lux must file the appropriate form in the proper state office under the fictitious business name statute.

4. Harper Company appointed Doe as its agent. It was essential that Harper's identity be kept secret. Therefore, Doe was to act in the capacity of an agent for an undisclosed principal. The duration of the agency was for exactly one year commencing Wednesday of the following week. As a result of this agreement between Harper and Doe, Harper
   a. Is **not** liable on the agency contract unless it is in writing.
   b. Can **not** ratify the unauthorized acts of Doe.
   c. Can rely upon the parol evidence rule to avoid liability to third parties if the contract is in writing.
   d. Can **not** be held liable for torts committed by Doe while acting as an agent.

5. Which of the following is **not** an essential element of an agency relationship?
   a. It must be created by contract.
   b. The agent must be subject to the principal's control.
   c. The agent is a fiduciary in respect to the principal.
   d. The agent acts on behalf of another and **not** himself.

6. Duval Manufacturing Industries, Inc., orally engaged Harris as one of its district sales managers for an 18-month period commencing April 1, 1980. Harris commenced work on that date and performed his duties in a highly competent manner for several months. On October 1, 1980, the company gave Harris a notice of termination as of November 1, 1980, citing a downturn in the market for its products. Harris sues seeking either specific performance or damages for breach of contract. Duval pleads the Statute of Frauds and/or a justified dismissal due to the economic situation. What is the probable outcome of the lawsuit?
   a. Harris will prevail because he has partially performed under the terms of the contract.
   b. Harris will lose because his termination was caused by economic factors beyond Duval's control.
   c. Harris will lose because such a contract must be in writing and signed by a proper agent of Duval.
   d. Harris will prevail because the Statute of Frauds does **not** apply to contracts such as his.

7. A power of attorney is a useful method of creation of an agency relationship. The power of attorney
   a. Must be signed by both the principal and the agent.
   b. Exclusively determines the purpose and powers of the agent.
   c. Is the written authorization of the agent to act on the principal's behalf.
   d. Is used primarily in the creation of the attorney-client relationship.

8. Gladstone has been engaged as sales agent for the Doremus Corporation. Under which of the fol-

lowing circumstances may Gladstone delegate his duties to another?

a. Where an emergency arises and the delegation is necessary to meet the emergency.
b. Where it is convenient for Gladstone to do so.
c. Only with the express consent of Doremus.
d. If Doremus sells its business to another.

9. Wallace, an agent for Lux, made a contract with Doolittle which exceeded Wallace's authority. If Lux wishes to hold Doolittle to the contract, Lux must prove that

a. Lux ratified the contract before withdrawal from the contract by Doolittle.
b. Wallace was acting in the capacity of an agent for an undisclosed principal.
c. Wallace believed he was acting within the scope of his authority.
d. Wallace was Lux's general agent even though Wallace exceeded his authority.

10. Davidson is the agent of Myers, a fuel dealer. Myers is an undisclosed principal. Davidson contracts with Wallop to purchase 30,000 tons of coal at $20 per ton. Which of the following is correct?

a. If Davidson acts outside the scope of his authority in entering into this contract, Myers can **not** ratify the contract.
b. Wallop is bound to this contract only if Davidson acts within the scope of his authority.
c. If Davidson acts within the scope of his authority, Wallop can **not** hold Davidson personally liable on the contract.
d. Should Davidson refuse to accept delivery of the coal, Wallop will become an agent of Myers by substitution.

11. Mathews is an agent for Sears with the express authority to solicit orders from customers in a geographic area assigned by Sears. Mathews has no authority to grant discounts nor to collect payment on orders solicited. Mathews secured an order from Davidson for $1,000 less a 10% discount if Davidson makes immediate payment. Davidson had previously done business with Sears through Mathews but this was the first time that a discount-payment offer had been made. Davidson gave Mathews a check for $900 and thereafter Mathews turned in both the check and the order to Sears. The order clearly indicated that a 10% discount had been given by Mathews. Sears shipped the order and cashed the check. Later Sears attempted to collect $100 as the balance owed on the order from Davidson. Which of the following is correct?

a. Sears can collect the $100 from Davidson because Mathews contracted outside the scope of his express or implied authority.
b. Sears can **not** collect the $100 from Davidson because Mathews as an agent with express authority to solicit orders had implied authority to give discounts and collect.
c. Sears can **not** collect the $100 from Davidson as Sears has ratified the discount granted and payment made to Mathews.
d. Sears can **not** collect the $100 from Davidson because although Mathews had **no** express or implied authority to grant a discount and collect, Mathews had apparent authority to do so.

12. Moderne Fabrics, Inc., hired Franklin as an assistant vice president of sales at $2,000 a month. The employment had no fixed duration. In light of their relationship to each other, which of the following is correct?

a. Franklin has a legal duty to reveal any interest adverse to that of Moderne in matters concerning his employment.
b. If Franklin voluntarily terminates his employment with Moderne after working for it for several years, he can **not** work for a competitor for a reasonable period after termination.
c. Moderne can dismiss Franklin only for cause.
d. The employment contract between the parties must be in writing.

13. Smith has been engaged as a general sales agent for the Victory Medical Supply Company. Victory, as Smith's principal, owes Smith several duties which are implied as a matter of law. Which of the following duties is owed by Victory to Smith?

a. Not to compete.
b. To reimburse Smith for all expenditures as long as they are remotely related to Smith's employment and not specifically prohibited.
c. Not to dismiss Smith without cause for one year from the making of the contract if the duration of the contract is indefinite.
d. To indemnify Smith for liability for acts done in good faith upon Victory's orders.

14. Futterman operated a cotton factory and employed Marra as a general purchasing agent to travel through the southern states to purchase cotton. Futterman telegraphed Marra instructions from day to day as to the price to be paid for cotton. Marra entered a cotton district in which she had not previously done business and represented that she was purchasing cotton for Futterman. Although directed by Futterman to pay no more than 25 cents a pound, Marra bought cotton from Anderson at 30 cents a pound, which was the prevailing offering price at that time. Futterman refused to take the cotton. Under these circumstances, which of the following is correct?

a. The negation of actual authority to make the purchase effectively eliminates any liability for Futterman.
b. Futterman is not liable on the contract.
c. Marra has no potential liability.
d. Futterman is liable on the contract.

15. Farley Farms, Inc., shipped 100 bales of hops to Burton Brewing Corporation. The agreement specified that the hops were to be of a certain grade. Upon examining the hops, Burton claimed that they were not of that grade. Farley's general sales agent who made the sale to Burton agreed to relieve Burton of liability and to have the hops shipped elsewhere. This was done, and the hops were sold at a price less than Burton was to have paid. Farley refused to accede to the agent's acts and sued Burton for the amount of its loss. Under these circumstances

a. Farley will prevail only if the action by its agent was expressly authorized.
b. Even if Farley's agent had authority to make such an adjustment, it would not be enforceable against Farley unless ratified in writing by Farley.
c. Because the hops were sold at a loss in respect to the price Burton had agreed to pay, Burton would be liable for the loss involved.
d. Farley is bound because its agent expressly, impliedly, or apparently had the authority to make such an adjustment.

16. Ivy Corp. engaged Jones as a sales representative and assigned him to a route in southern Florida. Jones worked out of Ivy's main office and his duties, hours, and routes were carefully controlled. The employment contract contained a provision which stated: "I, *Jones*, do hereby promise to hold the corporation harmless from any and all tort liability to third parties which may arise in carrying out my duties as an employee." On a sales call, Jones negligently dropped a case of hammers on the foot of Devlin, the owner of Devlin's Hardware. Which of the following statements is correct?

a. Ivy has **no** liability to Devlin.
b. Although the exculpatory clause may be valid between Ivy and Jones, it does **not** affect Devlin's rights.
c. Ivy is **not** liable to Devlin in any event, since Jones is an independent contractor.
d. The exculpatory clause is totally invalid since it is against public policy.

17. Brian purchased an automobile from Robinson Auto Sales under a written contract by which Robinson obtained a security interest to secure payment of the purchase price. Robinson reserved the right to repossess the automobile if Brian failed to make any of the required ten payments. Ambrose, an employee of Robinson, was instructed to repossess the automobile on the ground that Brian had defaulted in making the third payment. Ambrose took possession of the automobile and delivered it to Robinson. It was then discovered that Brian was not in default. Which of the following is **incorrect**?

a. Brian has the right to regain possession of the automobile and to collect damages.
b. Brian may sue and collect from either Robinson or Ambrose.
c. If Ambrose must pay in damages, he will be entitled to indemnification from Robinson.
d. Ambrose is **not** liable for the wrongful repossession of the automobile since he was obeying the direct order of Robinson.

18. Wall & Co. hired Carr to work as an agent in its collection department, reporting to the credit manager. Which of the following is correct?

a. Carr does **not** owe a fiduciary duty to Wall since he does not compete with the company.
b. Carr will be personally liable for any torts he commits even though they are committed in the course of his employment and pursuant to Wall's directions.
c. Carr has the implied authority to engage counsel and commence legal action against Wall's debtors.
d. Carr may commingle funds collected by him if this is convenient as long as he keeps proper records.

19. The apparent authority of an agent would **not** be determined by reference to

a. Prior dealings between the parties.
b. The types of activity engaged in by the agent.
c. An undisclosed limitation on the agent's usual power.
d. Industry custom.

20. Agents sometimes have liability to third parties for their actions taken for and on behalf of the principal. An agent will **not** be personally liable in which of the following circumstances?

a. If he makes a contract which he had no authority to make but which the principal ratifies.
b. If he commits a tort while engaged in the principal's business.
c. If he acts for a principal which he knows is nonexistent and the third party is unaware of this.
d. If he acts for an undisclosed principal as long as the principal is subsequently disclosed.

21. Wanamaker, Inc., engaged Anderson as its agent to purchase original oil paintings for resale by Wanamaker. Anderson's express authority was specifically limited to a maximum purchase price of $25,000 for any collection provided it contained a minimum of five oil paintings. Anderson purchased a seven picture collection on Wanamaker's behalf for $30,000. Based upon these facts, which of the following is a correct legal conclusion?

a. The express limitation on Anderson's authority negates any apparent authority.
b. Wanamaker cannot ratify the contract since Anderson's actions were clearly in violation of his contract.
c. If Wanamaker rightfully disaffirms the unauthorized contract, Anderson is personally liable to the seller.
d. Neither Wanamaker nor Anderson is liable on the contract since the seller was obligated to ascertain Anderson's authority.

22. Wilkinson is a car salesman employed by Fantastic Motors, Inc. Fantastic instructed Wilkinson not to sell a specially equipped and modified car owned by the company. Fantastic had decided to use this car as a "super" demonstrator to impress potential purchasers. The car had just arrived from Detroit, had been serviced, and was parked alongside other similar models. Barkus "fell in love" with the car and, after some negotiation with Wilkinson, signed a contract to purchase the car. Barkus gave Wilkinson a check for 20% of the purchase price and executed a note and a purchase money security agreement. Wilkinson forged Fantastic's name on the check and disappeared. Fantastic seeks to repossess the car from Barkus. What is the probable outcome of the above facts?

a. Fantastic will be permitted to repossess the car but must compensate Barkus for any inconvenience.
b. Barkus will be permitted to keep the car if Barkus assumes the loss on the check given to Wilkinson.
c. Fantastic will be permitted to repossess the car because there was an express prohibition against the sale of this car.
d. Barkus will be permitted to keep the car because Wilkinson has the apparent authority to bind Fantastic to the contract of sale.

23. Dixon Sales, Inc., dismissed Crow as its general sales agent. Dixon notified all of Crow's known customers by letter. Hale Stores, a retail outlet located outside of Crow's previously assigned sales territory, had never dealt with Crow. However, Hale knew of Crow as a result of various business contacts. After his dismissal, Crow sold Hale goods, to be delivered by Dixon, and received from Hale a cash deposit for 20% of the purchase price. It was not unusual for an agent in Crow's previous position to receive cash deposits. In an action by Hale against Dixon on the sales contract, Hale will

a. Lose, because Crow lacked any express or implied authority to make the contract.
b. Lose, because Crow's conduct constituted a fraud for which Dixon is not liable.
c. Win, because Dixon's notice was inadequate to terminate Crow's apparent authority.
d. Win, because a principal is an insurer of an agent's acts.

24. Terrence has been Pauline's agent in the liquor business for ten years and has made numerous contracts on Pauline's behalf. Under which of the following situations could Terrence continue to have power to bind Pauline?

a. The passage of a federal constitutional amendment making the sale or purchase of alcoholic beverages illegal.
b. The death of Pauline without Terrence's knowledge.
c. The bankruptcy of Pauline with Terrence's knowledge.
d. The firing of Terrence by Pauline.

25. Downtown Disco, Inc., engaged Charleston as club manager in a written agreement providing for a $20,000 salary, plus 2% of gross revenues, and exclusive management authority including entertainment bookings. The agreement is irrevocable by Downtown for three years but terminable by Charleston upon one month's written notice. The Downtown-Charleston arrangement is

a. An agency coupled with an interest.
b. A partnership between Downtown and Charleston.
c. Terminable at any time by Downtown despite the three-year irrevocability clause.
d. Enforceable by Charleston by an action for specific performance.

May 1984 Questions

26. Dill is an agent for Mint, Inc. As such, Dill made a contract for and on behalf of Mint with Sky Co. which was not authorized and upon which Mint has disclaimed liability. Sky has sued Mint on the contract asserting that Dill had the apparent authority to make it. In considering the factors which will determine the scope of Dill's apparent authority, which of the following would **not** be important?

a. The express limitations placed upon Dill's authority which were **not** known by Sky.
b. The custom and usages of the business.
c. The status of Dill's position in Mint.
d. Previous acquiescence by the principal in similar contracts made by Dill.

27. Notice to third parties is **not** required to terminate a disclosed general agent's apparent authority when the

a. Principal has died.
b. Principal revokes the agent's authority.
c. Agent renounces the agency relationship.
d. Agency relationship terminates as a result of the fulfillment of its purpose.

28. Harp entered into a contract with Rex on behalf of Gold. By doing so, Harp acted outside the scope of his authority as Gold's agent. Gold may be held liable on the contract if

a. Gold retains the benefits of the contract.
b. Gold ratifies the entire contract after Rex withdraws from the contract.
c. Rex elects to hold Gold liable on the contract.
d. Rex was aware of the limitation on Harp's authority.

29. Jim, an undisclosed principal, authorized Rick to act as his agent in securing a contract for the purchase of some plain white paper. Rick, without informing Sam that he was acting on behalf of a principal, entered into a contract with Sam to purchase the paper. If Jim repudiates the contract with Sam, which of the following is correct?

a. Rick will be released from his contractual obligations to Sam if he discloses Jim's identity.
b. Upon learning that Jim is the principal, Sam may elect to hold either Jim or Rick liable on the contract.
c. Rick may **not** enforce the contract against Sam.
d. Sam may obtain specific performance, compelling Jim to perform on the contract.

Problems

Problem 1 Ratification; Agency Coupled With an Interest (580, L5a&b)

(10 to 15 minutes)

Part a. Vogel, an assistant buyer for the Granite City Department Store, purchased metal art objects from Duval Reproductions. Vogel was totally without express or apparent authority to do so, but believed that his purchase was a brilliant move likely to get him a promotion. The head buyer of Granite was livid when he learned of Vogel's activities. However, after examining the merchandise and listening to Vogel's pitch, he reluctantly placed the merchandise in the storeroom and put a couple of pieces on display for a few days to see whether it was a "hot item" and a "sure thing" as Vogel claimed. The item was neither "hot" nor "sure" and when it didn't move at all, the head buyer ordered the display merchandise repacked and the entire order returned to Duval with a letter that stated the merchandise had been ordered by an assistant buyer who had absolutely no authority to make the purchase. Duval countered with a lawsuit for breach of contract.

Required:

Answer the following, setting forth reasons for any conclusions stated.

Will Duval prevail?

Part b. Foremost Realty, Inc., is a real estate broker that also buys and sells real property for its own account. Hobson purchased a ranch from Foremost. The terms were 10% down with the balance payable over a 25 year period. After several years of profitable operation of the ranch, Hobson had two successive bad years. As a result, he defaulted on the mortgage. Foremost did not want to foreclose, but instead offered to allow Hobson to remain on the ranch and suspend the payment schedule until Foremost could sell the property at a reasonable price. However, Foremost insisted that it be appointed as the irrevocable and exclusive agent for the sale of the property. Although Hobson agreed, he subsequently became dissatisfied with Foremost's efforts to sell the ranch and gave Foremost notice in writing terminating the agency. Foremost has indicated to Hobson that he does not have the legal power to do so.

Required:

Answer the following, setting forth reasons for any conclusions stated.

Can Hobson terminate the agency?

Problem 2 Vicarious Liability (1178,L3a&b)

(10 to 15 minutes)

Part a. Rapid Delivery Service, Inc., hired Dolson as one of its truck drivers. Dolson was carefully selected and trained by Rapid. He was specifically instructed to obey all traffic and parking rules and regulations. One day while making a local delivery, Dolson double parked and went into a nearby customer's store. In doing so, he prevented a car legally parked at the curb from leaving. The owner of the parked car, Charles, proceeded to blow the horn of the truck repeatedly. Charles was doing this when Dolson returned from his delivery. As a result of a combination of several factors, particularly Charles' telling him to "move it" and that he was "acting very selfishly and in an unreasonable manner," Dolson punched Charles in the nose, severely fracturing it. When Charles sought to restrain him, Dolson punched Charles again, this time fracturing his jaw. Charles has commenced legal action against Rapid.

Required:

Answer the following, setting forth reasons for any conclusions stated.

1. Will Charles prevail?
2. What liability, if any, would Dolson have?

Part b. Harold Watts was employed by Superior Sporting Goods as a route salesman. His territory, route, and customers were determined by Superior. He was expected to work from 9:00 a.m. to 5:00 p.m., Monday through Friday. He received a weekly salary plus time and one-half for anything over 40 hours. He also received a small commission on sales which exceeded a stated volume. The customers consisted of sporting goods stores, department stores, athletic clubs, and large companies which had athletic programs or sponsored athletic teams. Watts used his personal car in making calls or, upon occasion, making a delivery where the customer was in a rush and the order was not large. Watts was reimbursed for the use of the car for company purposes. His instructions were to assume the customer is always right and to accommodate the customer where to do so would cost little and would build goodwill for the company and himself.

One afternoon while making a sales call and dropping off a case of softballs at the Valid Clock Company, the personnel director told Watts he was planning to watch the company's team play a game at a softball field located on the other side of town, but that his car would not start. Watts said, "Don't worry, it will be my pleasure to give you a lift and I would like to take in a few innings myself." Time was short and while on the way to the ballpark, Watts ran a light and collided with another car. The other care required $800 of repairs and the owner suffered serious bodily injury.

Required:

Answer the following, setting forth reasons for any conclusions stated.

1. What is Superior's potential liability, if any, to the owner of the other car?

2. What is Valid's potential liability, if any, to the owner of the other car?

Multiple Choice Answers

1. a	7. c	13. d	19. c	25. c
2. c	8. a	14. d	20. a	26. a
3. a	9. a	15. d	21. c	27. a
4. a/b	10. a	16. b	22. d	28. a
5. a	11. c	17. d	23. c	29. b
6. c	12. a	18. b	24. d	

Multiple Choice Answer Explanations

A. Characteristics

1. (1181,L1,15) (a) A servant is an employee whose physical conduct is controlled or subject to the right of control by the employer. In contrast, an agent is subject to a lesser and more general control, but not necessarily control of the agent's physical conduct. Answer (b) is incorrect because the manner in which a person is compensated does not distinguish between a servant and an agent. Answer (c) is incorrect because although an agent has greater authority to contract on behalf of the principal than a servant would have concerning the master, a servant is not entirely precluded from contracting on behalf of the master. Answer (d) is incorrect because a servant could have apparent authority to bind his employer, if the employer manifests such intent to another and this third party has a reasonable belief of servant's authority based upon the employer's representation.

2. (578,L1,4) (c) An agent who sells on credit and guarantees the accounts to his principal is known as a del credere agent. Answer (a) is incorrect because a del credere agent's guarantee is not a suretyship agreement and is not required to be in writing. Answer (b) is incorrect because Winter promised to indemnify Magnum if the customers failed to pay; the agreement did not require Magnum to try to collect from the customers. Answer (d) is incorrect because as an agent, Winter is a fiduciary and owes the duty of loyalty, good faith, obedience, duty to account, not to commingle, etc.

A.6. Types of Principals

3. (1183,L1,14) (a) Classification of a principal as disclosed, undisclosed, or partially disclosed affects the contractual liability of the agent toward third parties. The authority given the agent, however, is not affected. An agent representing an undisclosed principal has the same implied authority as an agent representing a disclosed principal. Answer (b) is incorrect because a principal's liability for his agent's torts is the same regardless of whether the principal is disclosed, undisclosed, or partially disclosed. Answer (c) is incorrect because once the identity of a previously undisclosed principal is known, the third party may elect to hold either the principal or the agent liable on the contract. Answer (d) is incorrect because a fictitious business name statute requires a party conducting business under an assumed name to receive the state's permission to use that name. Such a statute has no applicability to the Lux–Steel agency relationship.

4. (582,L1,6) (a/b) The AICPA accepted two answers for this question. Answer (a) is correct because contracts within the provisions of the Statute of Frauds must be in writing and signed by the party to be charged in order to be enforceable. The agency agreement between Harper and Doe is within the Statute of Frauds since the terms of their contractual agreement cannot be performed within one year from the making thereof. The agreement must be capable of being performed within one year of the date of formation of the contract, not within one year of the date of beginning of performance. Since Harper made a contract for a year's duration beginning several days after the date of agreement, the contract is unenforceable if not in writing, and Harper would not be liable on the agency contract. Answer (b) is correct because before a person can ratify the acts of another, the supposed agent must purport to act in name and on behalf of a principal. Since Harper is an undisclosed principal, he would be unable to ratify the unauthorized acts of Doe. Answer (c) is incorrect because the parol evidence rule does not apply since the extrinsic evidence, which shows that one of the signatories was acting as an agent for another, is being admitted not to contradict the writing, but merely to "explain" the capacity in which the party (agent) signed. Therefore, once the principal's identity is made known, the principal, Harper, may be held liable to third parties under the contract. Answer (d) is incorrect because under the doctrine of respondeat superior, the principal, Harper, is liable for his agent's torts if they are within the scope of the agent's employment and committed during the course of his duties.

B. Methods of Creation

5. (1181,L1,12) (a) A contract is not required to create an agency relationship. Such relationships can be created in numerous ways, including by agreement, operation of law, ratification and estoppel. Answer (b) is incorrect because an agent is subject to the continuous general control of the principal. Answer (c) is incorrect because an agent is a fiduciary; he owes the principal the obligation of faithful service. Answer (d)

is incorrect because an agent must act for the benefit of the principal; an agent acts for and in place of the principal to effect legal relations with third persons.

6. (581,L1,33) (c) The Statute of Frauds provides that contracts not performable within one year must be in writing to be enforceable. Since the Duval-Harris contract cannot be performed within one year (18 month duration), it is required to be in writing to be enforceable. Answer (a) is incorrect since Harris' past performance would allow him to recover any amount owed him from services rendered before termination. However, it will not enable him to enforce the executory portion (unperformed part) of the oral contract. Answer (b) is incorrect since the economic factors cited by Duval would not be proper grounds for avoidance of the contract. Economic factors do not qualify as an objective impossibility which would excuse Duval's duty to perform. Answer (d) is incorrect since the Statute of Frauds does apply.

7. (1180,L1,26) (c) A power of attorney is a written document authorizing another to act as one's agent. The written authorization must only be signed by the principal. Besides the express authority granted in the power of attorney, the agent can also have implied and apparent powers by which to bind the principal. Thus, answer (c) is correct.

8. (578,L1,5) (a) Generally an agency relationship involves trust and confidence and therefore cannot be delegated without consent. However, an agent would have implied authority to delegate duties in an emergency where the delegation is necessary to meet the emergency. Answer (b) is incorrect because convenience is not an adequate excuse to delegate an agent's duties. Answer (c) is incorrect because express consent is not always necessary to make a delegation, as the authority to delegate can arise from implications such as the type of business, usage, prior conduct, and the emergency doctrine as explained above. Answer (d) is incorrect because if a principal sells his business, the agency is likely to terminate rather than authorize a sales agent to delegate his duties to another.

B.5. Ratification

9. (583,L1,1) (a) If an agent acts without authority, neither the principal nor the third party is bound to perform the contract. However, if Lux ratified Wallace's unauthorized act before Doolittle withdrew from the contract, Doolittle would be bound by the agreement. Answer (b) is incorrect because the fact that Wallace was acting for an undisclosed principal would not bind Doolittle if Wallace, the agent, was acting outside his authority. Answer (c) is incorrect because Wallace's belief as to the extent of his authority has no bearing on whether Doolittle, the third party, is bound to the agreement. Answer (d) is incorrect because even though Wallace was Lux's general agent, the contract exceeded Lux's authority and therefore, Doolittle is not bound.

10. (1182,L1,7) (a) Before a person can ratify the acts of another, the supposed agent must purport to act in the name and on behalf of the ratifying party (principal). Since Myers is an undisclosed principal, he would be unable to ratify the unauthorized acts of Davidson in that Davidson never represented to Wallop that he was acting on behalf of Myers. Answer (b) is incorrect because Davidson, as an agent for an undisclosed principal, is liable on the contract whether he was acting within or outside the scope of his authority when he entered into the contract with Wallop. Answer (c) is incorrect because since Davidson acted for an undisclosed principal, Wallop can hold Davidson personally liable on the contract. However, upon learning of the existence of the undisclosed principal (Myers), Wallop can elect to hold Myers liable. Answer (d) is incorrect because the concept of agency by substitution does not exist.

11. (582,L1,7) (c) Ratification occurs when the principal, after the fact, approves an unauthorized act performed on his behalf by another individual. The essence of ratification is that the prior unauthorized act is treated as if it had been authorized by the "principal" at the outset. Ratification requires some conduct by the principal which manifests his intent to affirm the agreement. Voluntary acceptance or retention by the principal of the benefits of a transaction purportedly entered into on his behalf will generally establish ratification by the principal. Therefore, since Sears shipped the order and cashed Davidson's check, this was sufficient evidence of its intent to affirm the discount agreement, and Sears becomes bound on the contract. Answer (a) is incorrect because even though Mathews contracted outside the scope of his authority, Sears ratified the sales agreement, thereby becoming bound on the contract. Answer (b) is incorrect because Mathews' express authority consists of the duties which the principal, Sears, specifically instructed him to do, which was only to solicit orders. Implied authority normally arises to do acts reasonably necessary to accomplish an authorized act; therefore, Mathews had no implied authority to grant discounts or collect payment since this was not necessitated in Mathews carry-

ing out his function of soliciting orders for Sears. Answer (d) is incorrect because apparent authority arises when the principal's manifestations or conduct lead a third party to believe that the agent has authority beyond that to which the principal actually consented. Therefore, Mathews would not have apparent authority to grant discounts or collect payment, since Sears made no such manifestations or representations which would cause Davidson, the third party, to reasonably believe so.

E. Obligations and Rights

12. (581,L1,30) (a) An agency relationship is a fiduciary relationship which means that the agent owes great trust and loyalty to the principal while acting as an agent. An agent with interests adverse to his principal must disclose these facts to the principal. Answer (b) is incorrect since the employment contract did not contain a restrictive covenant prohibiting competition. The agent may work for a competitor, but has a duty not to disclose confidential information if detrimental to his old principal. Answer (c) is incorrect because a principal can normally dismiss the agent without cause even though the principal may be liable for breach. Answer (d) is incorrect since the contract is capable of being performed in one year; the oral contract is enforceable.

13. (578,L1,3) (d) A principal (employer) owes a duty to its agent (employee) to indemnify the agent for acts carried out in good faith upon the principal's (employer's) behalf. Answer (a) is incorrect because a principal owes no duty not to compete with its agent. It is the agent who has a duty not to compete with its principal. Answer (b) is incorrect beacuse a principal has the duty to reimburse an agent only for expenditures directly related to employment. Answer (c) is incorrect because agency agreements of an indefinite duration are generally implied to continue from pay period to pay period and may be terminated by notice of either party.

E.3. Principal's Liability to Third Parties

14. (578,L1,10) (d) The principal, Futterman, is liable for the acts of his general agent, even though the agent violated rules which were unknown to the third party. Answer (a) is incorrect because even though Marra did not have actual authority to buy at 30 cents a pound, she had apparent authority to do so (because she was a general purchasing agent). Answer (b) is incorrect because Futterman is liable on this contract. Answer (c) is incorrect because Marra has potential liability both to third parties for violating her warranty of authority and to her principal for disregarding proper instructions.

15. (1175,L1,15) (d) A general sales agent such as Farley's would have implied or apparent authority, if not express authority, to make such an adjustment and this would bind the principal, Farley. Farley will prevail only if his agent did not have any authority. Ratification is only used where the agent did not have authority in the first place, i.e., for an authorized act, and it need not be in writing. Burton would be liable for the loss only if he had breached. Since Farley arguably breached by shipping the wrong grade, and also because the parties have negotiated a modification, accord, or rescission, Burton is not liable.

E.3.g. Principal's Liability for Servant's Torts

16. (1183,L1,12) (b) Jones' activity is subject to the extensive control of Ivy Corp. Consequently, Jones must be considered Ivy Corp.'s employee and not an independent contractor. Although the exculpatory clause contained in the employment contract is valid and not against public policy, the clause only affects the rights and liabilities which Jones and Ivy Corp. owe each other. Devlin's rights are not affected by the clause and he may sue Ivy Corp., the employer, which remains liable for Jones' torts committed within the agent's scope of employment, under the doctrine of respondeat superior. Accordingly, answers (a), (c), and (d) are incorrect.

17. (1181,L1,16) (d) Ambrose's act of repossessing the car constituted the tort of conversion. An agent or employee is always liable for his own torts, even if committed in the course of discharging his duties. Answer (a) is incorrect because the injured party, Brian, has the right to regain possession of his automobile and collect money damages for the tortious act of conversion committed upon him. Answer (b) is incorrect because any third person injured by the agent's or employee's tortious act, when committed within the course of employment, can proceed against either the employee or employer—Ambrose being directly liable for his wrongful act, and Robinson being vicariously liable therefor. Brian can sue either, but can take judgment against only one. Answer (c) is incorrect because when the employee is held liable for a tortious act, which was committed upon direct instructions from the employer, he has a right of indemnification against the employer for any damages he must pay a third person.

E.4. Agent's Liability to Third Parties

18. (1183,L1,13) (b) An agent is personally liable for the torts he commits, whether inside or outside the

scope of his employment, and regardless of whether or not the principal is also liable for the tort. The principal's authorization of the tort is no defense to the agent's liability. Answer (d) is incorrect because an agent has the duty to keep the funds and property of his principal separate from his own. Maintaining proper records is no defense to the breach of this duty. Answer (a) is incorrect because every agent owes his principal a fiduciary duty of loyalty and trust. The fact that the agent does not compete with his principal does not relieve the agent of this duty. Answer (c) is incorrect because the circumstances indicate Carr's implied authority is limited. The fact that Carr must report directly to his superior, the credit manager, infers that Carr's authority does not extend to such managerial decisions as instituting legal action.

19. (1182,L1,5) (c) An agent's apparent authority is based on the principal's outward manifestations to third parties. Consequently, the apparent authority of the agent would not be determined by reference to an undisclosed limitation on the agent's usual authority since the third parties would be unaware of this limitation. The agent's apparent authority would be determined by reference to prior dealings between the parties, the types of activities engaged in by the agent and industry custom. Therefore, answers (a), (b) and (d) are incorrect.

20. (1180,L1,27) (a) The correct answer is (a) since an agent, after the principal ratifies an unauthorized act, is acting within his authority and is free of any liability on the contract. An agent is personally liable for all torts he commits; therefore, answer (b) is incorrect. An agent is liable if he acts for a principal which he knows is non-existent and knows the third party is unaware of this. Thus, answer (c) is incorrect. If an agent contracts for an undisclosed principal, the agent remains liable to the third party even though he is acting within the scope of his authority. The agent, however, has recourse against the principal. The third party can sue either the principal or agent. As a result, answer (d) is incorrect.

21. (1179,L1,33) (c) If the principal, Wanamaker, rightfully disaffirms the unauthorized contract by Anderson, the agent, Wanamaker, is personally liable to the seller on the theory of the implied warranty of authority. Anderson warranted to the seller that he had authority to bind Wanamaker to the sale contract. Answer (a) is incorrect because an express limitation on an agent's authority does not negate any apparent authority. Apparent authority is based on prior action and on what is customary in the general business community. Answer (b) is incorrect because Wanamaker, the principal, could ratify the contract made by Anderson since Anderson was purporting to act for Wanamaker. Answer (d) is incorrect because the agent is always liable on a contract that he makes on behalf of his principal on the theory that he warrants to the third party that he has authority. The seller should have ascertained Anderson's authority in order to assure that he had an enforceable contract against Wanamaker.

22. (577,L2,27) (d) Whether a contract made by an agent is binding on the principal depends on authority. While the agent, Wilkinson, lacked express or implied authority (and in fact had specific instructions not to sell this car), he nevertheless had apparent authority insofar as third persons without knowledge were concerned. A contract based on apparent authority is enforceable if it is the type usually or customarily made by similar agents in the performance of their employment relationships. In general, established business customs permit a new car salesman to bind his principal to a contract for the sale of an automobile from inventory, accept a down payment by check, and make the usual warranties and financing arrangements. The buyer can keep the car and the principal, Fantastic Motors, is deemed to have received the check when it was delivered to an agent with apparent authority.

F. Termination of Principal-Agent Relationship

23. (1183,L1,11) (c) When the agency relationship is terminated by an act of the principal and/or agent, third parties are entitled to notice of the termination from the principal. Failure of the principal to give the required notice gives the agent apparent authority to act on behalf of the principal. Specifically, the principal must give actual notice to all parties who had prior dealings with the agent or principal. Constructive or public notice must be given to parties who knew of the existence of the agency relationship, but did not actually have business dealings with the agent or principal. Since Dixon Sales, Inc. did not give proper constructive notice to Hale Stores, Crow had apparent authority to bind the principal and, therefore, Hale Stores will win. Accordingly, answer (a) is incorrect. Answer (b) is incorrect because Dixon is liable for the torts of its authorized agent under the doctrine of respondeat superior. Answer (d) is incorrect because a principal is not an absolute insurer of his agent's acts. A principal is liable for his agent's torts only if the principal expressly authorizes the conduct or the tort is committed within the scope of the agent's employment.

24. (583,L1,2) (d) An agency relationship may be terminated by operation of law or by the acts of the parties. If terminated by the acts of the parties, the agent continues to have apparent authority to bind the principal until notice is given the appropriate third parties. If the relationship is terminated by operation of law, all authority of the agent to bind the principal ends automatically upon the termination. The principal has no duty to give notice of the termination to third parties. If Pauline fired Terrence, termination would occur by acts of the parties and Terrence would continue to have apparent authority to bind Pauline until the appropriate notice was given. However, if the relationship was terminated by passage of a constitutional amendment making the subject matter of the agency illegal, death of the principal with or without knowledge by the agent, or bankruptcy of the principal with knowledge of the agent, these are terminations by operation of law and Terrence's authority to bind Pauline would end instantly. Therefore, answers (a), (b), and (c) are incorrect.

25. (1182,L1,34) (c) Since an agency is deemed to be created for the benefit of the principal, the principal has the **power** at any time to terminate (revoke) an agency relationship but not always the **right**. Where the principal's termination violates the agency agreement, as in this case, he will be subject to liability for breach of contract. However, when an agency coupled with an interest exists, the principal does not even have the power to revoke the relationship. Answer (a) is incorrect because an agency coupled with an interest is where the principal gives the agent a property or security interest in the subject matter of the agency. A percentage of gross revenue does not qualify as the requisite property or security interest. Answer (b) is incorrect because no partnership exists between Downtown and Charleston. The receipt of gross revenues does not establish a partnership. But the sharing of profits does raise a presumption that the parties are partners. However, if the receipt of profits represents payment of salary for services rendered, this presumption is overcome. Answer (d) is incorrect because specific performance is not an available remedy for breach of an agency relationship.

May 1984 Answers

26. (584,L1,1) (a) Since the limitations on Dill's authority were not known by Sky, they are not relevant to the issue of apparent authority. A third party such as Sky ordinarily has no way of learning of such limitations. The doctrine of apparent authority allows a third party to make reasonable assumptions concerning an agent's authority. Custom and useage in the business is, therefore, relevant. Likewise, the status of the agent's position with the principal is relevant. The agent's status might lead a third party to reasonably believe that the agent has a certain scope of authority. If the principal has acquiesced in similar acts by the agent and this acquiescence is known to the third party, it may also provide a basis for apparent authority. Therefore, answers (b), (c), and (d) are incorrect.

27. (584,L1,2) (a) Upon the death of either the principal or agent, the agency relationship terminates by operation of law, and there is generally no requirement that third parties be notified. If, however, the agency terminates by act of the parties, it is necessary that notice be given to third parties in order to terminate the agent's apparent authority. Answers (b), (c), and (d) state circumstances that constitute termination by act of the parties. Notice, therefore, would be required.

28. (584,L1,3) (a) Although the agent's act was outside the scope of his authority, the principal may, nevertheless, ratify the contract. Retention of the benefits of the contract constitutes implied ratification. Answer (b) is incorrect because ratification must occur before the third party withdraws from the contract. Answer (c) is incorrect because when the contract is unauthorized, the third party does not have the option of electing to hold the principal liable. The third party's awareness of the limitation on the agent's authority does not change the fact that the contract is unauthorized. Answer (d) is, therefore, also incorrect.

29. (584,L1,4) (b) Once the third party learns the identity of an undisclosed principal, the third party may elect to hold either the agent or the principal liable on the contract. Since Sam did not know that Rick was acting as an agent at the time the contract was entered into, Rick is liable as a party to the contract. The mere disclosure of the existence and identity of the principal after the parties have entered into the contract does not relieve the agent of his contractual obligations. Answer (a) is, therefore, incorrect. Answer (c) is also incorrect because an agent acting on behalf of an undisclosed principal is a party to the contract. Rick may, therefore, enforce the contract against Sam. Answer (d) is incorrect because specific performance is not an appropriate remedy when money damages will adequately compensate the plaintiff. Plain white paper is not unique; consequently, specific performance is not available.

Answer Outline

Problem 1 Ratification; Agency Coupled With an Interest

a. Yes, Duval will prevail in breach of contract action
Initially Vogel (agent) had no express or apparent authority; however, principal ratified unauthorized contract by
Retaining and displaying goods
Lack of timely notification of refusal of goods
Granite would not be liable if immediate notification had occurred

b. May Hobson terminate agency unilaterally
No, most agency-principal relationships terminable by either party
However, agency coupled with an interest is irrevocable
As mortgagee of defaulting mortgagor, creditor has interest in property

Unofficial Answer

Problem 1 Ratification; Agency Coupled With an Interest

a. Yes. Despite the stated lack of express or apparent initial authority of Vogel, Granite City Department Store's agent, there would appear to be a ratification by the principal.

It is clear from the facts stated that Granite would not have been liable on the Vogel contract if the head buyer had immediately notified Duval and returned the goods. Instead the head buyer retained the goods and placed some on display in an attempt to sell them. Had they proved to be a "hot" item, undoubtedly the art objects would have been gratefully kept by Granite. Granite wants to reject the goods if they don't sell. Such conduct is inconsistent with a repudiation based upon the agent's lack of express or apparent authority. The retention of the goods for the time indicated, the attempted sale of the goods, and a failure to notify Duval in a timely way, when taken together, constitute a ratification of the unauthorized contract.

b. No. The facts reveal an agency coupled with an interest and therefore an irrevocable agency. Most agency-principal relationships are terminable by either party. However, one clearly recognized exception to this generally prevailing rule is that the agency may not be terminated when the agent has an interest in property that is the subject of the agency. This agency, coupled with an interest rule, applies here since the creditor (Foremost Realty, Inc.) has the requisite interest in the property because it is the mortgagee-creditor of the defaulting mortgagor-debtor. Thus, the appointment by Hobson of Foremost as the irrevocable agent for the sale of the mortgaged property cannot be terminated unilaterally by Hobson.

Answer Outline

Problem 2 Vicarious Liability

a1. Yes, Rapid is probably liable for Dolson's action
Master is liable for servants' tortious conduct
Employee's conduct must be within scope of employment
Employer's lack of fault does not relieve liability

a2. Dolson is liable to Charles
For tortious injury inflicted
Rapid's liability does not relieve Dolson from liability

b1. Superior is liable to the owner of the other car
Watt's automobile trip was within scope of employment with Superior

b2. Valid has no liability to the owner of the other car
Valid's personnel director was not negligent re accident
Valid had no control or responsibility over Watts

Unofficial Answer

Problem 2 Vicarious Liability

Part a.

1. Probably yes. A master is liable for his servant's unauthorized tortious conduct within the scope of employment. This is true despite the fact that the master is in no way personally at fault or has forbidden the type of conduct engaged in by the servant. A servant is normally an employee who renders personal service to his employer and whose activities are subject to the control of the employer. A truck driver such as Dolson would clearly fall within such a description. Once this has been established, the question is whether the assaults committed upon Charles by Dolson were within the scope of his em-

ployment. When the intentional use of force is involved, the courts have taken an expansive view insofar as imposition of liability upon the employer. If the servant's actions are predictable, there is likelihood that liability will be imposed upon the master. Where the servant deals with third persons in carrying out his job, the courts ask whether the wrongful act which occurred was likely to arise out of the performance of his job. Additionally, consideration is given to whether any part of his motive was the performance of his job, or if not, whether it was a normal reaction to a situation created by the job. Truck drivers using force in situations involving parking space or after a collision resulting in a dispute are not uncommon. The courts have usually imposed liability in cases such as this unless the assault was unrelated to the job, was solely personal, or was outrageous.

2. Dolson is liable to Charles for the tortious injury inflicted. The fact that Dolson may have been acting as a servant of Rapid and may impose liability upon his employer does not relieve him from liability.

Part b.

1. Superior Sporting Goods is liable for the negligence of its servant-agent Watts. The requisite control of his activities is apparent from the facts. Furthermore, based upon the instructions Watts received, it would appear that he was acting within the scope of his employment. In fact, one could conclude from the facts that Watts had express authority to make a trip such as the one he made when the accident occurred. He specifically was told to generally accommodate the customer where to do so would cost little and would build goodwill for the company and himself. This appears to be exactly what he did. Superior will undoubtedly attempt to assert the "independent frolic" doctrine and claim that Watts had abandoned his employment in order to pursue his own interest, or pleasures. However, the deviation was not great, it took place during normal working hours, and, most importantly, was at the request of a customer and was a type of conduct Superior specifically encouraged.

2. Valid Clock Company has no liability. Its agent was not at fault, nor can it be reasonably argued that an agency relationship was created between itself and Watts because its personnel director accepted the ride offered by Watts. The requisite control of Watts' physical activities by Valid is not present.

Multiple Choice Questions (1 - 25)

1. Lamay Associates, a general partnership, and Delray Corporation are contemplating entering into a joint venture. Such a joint venture

   a. Will be treated as an association for federal income tax purposes and taxed at the prevailing corporate rates.
   b. Must incorporate in the state in which the joint venture has its principal place of business.
   c. Will be treated as a partnership in most important legal respects.
   d. Must be dissolved upon completion of a single undertaking.

2. For which of the following purposes is a general partnership recognized as an entity by the Uniform Partnership Act?

   a. Recognition of the partnership as the employer of its partners.
   b. Insulation of the partners from personal liability.
   c. Taking of title and ownership of property.
   d. Continuity of existence.

3. Many states require partnerships to file the partnership name under laws which are generally known as fictitious name statutes. These statutes

   a. Require a proper filing as a condition precedent to the valid creation of a partnership.
   b. Are designed primarily to provide registration for tax purposes.
   c. Are designed to clarify the rights and duties of the members of the partnership.
   d. Have little effect on the creation or operation of a partnership other than the imposition of a fine for noncompliance.

4. Three independent sole proprietors decided to pool their resources and form a partnership. The business assets and liabilities of each were transferred to the partnership. The partnership commenced business on September 1, 1981, but the parties did not execute a formal partnership agreement until October 15, 1981. Which of the following is correct?

   a. The existing creditors must consent to the transfer of the individual business assets to the partnership.
   b. The partnership began its existence on September 1, 1981.
   c. If the partnership's duration is indefinite, the partnership agreement must be in writing and signed.
   d. In the absence of a partnership agreement specifically covering division of losses among the partners, they will be deemed to share them in accordance with their capital contributions.

5. Daniels, Beal, and Wade agreed to form the DBW Partnership to engage in the import-export business. They had been life-long friends and had engaged in numerous business dealings with each other. It was orally agreed that Daniels would contribute $20,000, Beal $15,000 and Wade $5,000. It was also orally agreed that in the event the venture proved to be a financial disaster all losses above the amounts of capital contributed would be assumed by Daniels and that he would hold his fellow partners harmless from any additional amounts lost. The partnership was consummated with a handshake and the contribution of the agreed upon capital by the partners. There were no other express agreements.

   Under these circumstances, which of the following is correct?

   a. Profits are to be divided in accordance with the relative capital contributions of each partner.
   b. Profits are to be divided equally.
   c. The partnership is a nullity because the agreement is **not** contained in a signed writing.
   d. Profits are to be shared in accordance with the relative time each devotes to partnership business during the year.

6. One of your audit clients, Major Supply, Inc., is seeking a judgment against Danforth on the basis of a representation made by one Coleman, in Danforth's presence, that they were in partnership together doing business as the D & C Trading Partnership. Major Supply received an order from Coleman on behalf of D & C and shipped $800 worth of goods to Coleman. Coleman has defaulted on payment of the bill and is insolvent. Danforth denies he is Coleman's partner and that he has any liability for the goods. Insofar as Danforth's liability is concerned, which of the following is correct?

   a. Danforth is **not** liable if he is **not** in fact Coleman's partner.
   b. Since Danforth did **not** make the statement about being Coleman's partner, he is **not** liable.
   c. If Major Supply gave credit in reliance upon the misrepresentation made by Coleman, Danforth is a partner by estoppel.

d. Since the "partnership" is operating under a fictitious name (the D & C Partnership) a filing is required and Major Supply's failure to ascertain whether there was in fact such a partnership precludes it from recovering.

7. In the course of your audit of James Fine, doing business as Fine's Apparels, a sole proprietorship, you discovered that in the past year Fine had regularly joined with Charles Walters in the marketing of bathing suits and beach accessories. You are concerned whether Fine and Walters have created a partnership relationship. Which of the following factors is the **most** important in ascertaining this status?

a. The fact that a partnership agreement is **not** in existence.
b. The fact that each has a separate business of his own which he operates independently.
c. The fact that Fine and Walters divide the net profits equally on a quarterly basis.
d. The fact that Fine and Walters did **not** intend to be partners.

8. A general partner of a mercantile partnership

a. Can by virtue of his acts, impose tort liability upon the other partners.
b. Has **no** implied authority if the partnership agreement is contained in a formal and detailed signed writing.
c. Can have his apparent authority effectively negated by the express limitations in the partnership agreement.
d. Can **not** be sued individually for a tort he has committed in carrying on partnership business until the partnership has been sued and a judgment returned unsatisfied.

9. Which of the following is a correct statement concerning a partner's power to bind the partnership?

a. A partner has **no** authority to bind the partnership after dissolution.
b. A partner can **not** bind the partnership based upon apparent authority when the other party to the contract knows that the partner lacks actual authority.
c. A partner has **no** authority in carrying on the regular business of the partnership to convey real property held in the partnership name.
d. A partner, acting outside the scope of the partner's apparent authority, but with the express authority to act, can **not** bind the partnership unless the third party knows of the express authority.

10. In determining the liability of a partnership for the acts of a partner purporting to act for the partnership without the authorization of fellow partners, which of the following actions will bind the partnership?

a. The renewal of an existing supply contract which the other partners had decided to terminate and which they had specifically voted against.
b. An assignment of the partnership assets in trust for the benefit of creditors.
c. A written admission of liability in a lawsuit brought against the partnership.
d. Signing the partnership name as a surety on a note for the purchase of that partner's summer home.

11. A question has arisen in determining the partnership's liability for actions taken for and on behalf of a partnership, but which were in fact without express or implied authority. Which of the following actions taken by a general partner will bind the partnership?

a. Renewing an existing supply contract which had previously been negotiated, but which the partners had specifically voted **not** to renew.
b. Submitting a claim against the partnership to binding arbitration.
c. Taking an action which was known by the party with whom he dealt to be in contravention of a restriction on his authority.
d. Signing the firm name as an accommodation comaker on a promissory note not in furtherance of firm business.

12. Donaldson reached the mandatory retirement age as a partner of the Malcomb and Black partnership. Edwards was chosen by the remaining partners to succeed Donaldson. The remaining partners agreed to assume all of Donaldson's partnership liability and released Donaldson from such liability. Additionally, Edwards expressly assumed full liability for Donaldson's partnership liability incurred prior to retirement. Which of the following is correct?

a. Edward's assumption of Donaldson's liability was a matter of form since as an incoming partner he was liable as a matter of law.
b. Firm creditors are **not** precluded from asserting rights against Donaldson for debts incurred while she was a partner, the agreements of Donaldson and the remaining partners notwithstanding.

c. Donaldson has **no** continuing potential liability to firm creditors as a result of the agreements contained in the retirement plan.
d. Since Donaldson obtained a release from firm debts she has **no** liability for debts incurred while she was a partner.

13. Perone was a member of Cass, Hack & Perone, a general trading partnership. He died on August 2, 1980. The partnership is insolvent, but Perone's estate is substantial. The creditors of the partnership are seeking to collect on their claims from Perone's estate. Which of the following statements is correct insofar as their claims are concerned?
a. The death of Perone caused a dissolution of the firm, thereby freeing his estate from personal liability.
b. If the existing obligations to Perone's personal creditors are all satisfied, then the remaining estate assets are available to satisfy partnership debts.
c. The creditors must first proceed against the remaining partners before Perone's estate can be held liable for the partnership's debts.
d. The liability of Perone's estate can **not** exceed his capital contribution plus that percentage of the deficit attributable to his capital contribution.

14. A general partner will not be personally liable for which of the following acts or transactions committed or engaged in by one of the other partners or by one of the partnership's employees?
a. The gross negligence of one of the partnership's employees while carrying out the partnership business.
b. A contract entered into by the majority of the other partners but to which the general partner objects.
c. A personal mortgage loan obtained by one of the other partners on his residence to which that partner, without authority, signed the partnership name on the note.
d. A contract entered into by the partnership in which the other partners agree among themselves to hold the general partner harmless.

15. Donovan, a partner of Monroe, Lincoln, and Washington, is considering selling or pledging all or part of his interest in the partnership. The partnership agreement is silent on the matter. Donovan can
a. Sell part but not all of his partnership interest.
b. Sell or pledge his entire partnership interest without causing a dissolution.
c. Pledge his partnership interest, but only with the consent of his fellow partners.
d. Sell his entire partnership interest and confer partner status upon the purchaser.

16. The partnership agreement of one of your clients provides that upon death or withdrawal, a partner shall be entitled to the book value of his or her partnership interest as of the close of the year preceding such death or withdrawal and nothing more. It also provides that the partnership shall continue. Regarding this partnership provision, which of the following is a correct statement?
a. It is unconscionable on its face.
b. It has the legal effect of preventing a dissolution upon the death or withdrawal of a partner.
c. It effectively eliminates the legal necessity of a winding up of the partnership upon the death or withdrawal of a partner.
d. It is **not** binding upon the spouse of a deceased partner if the book value figure is less than the fair market value at the date of death.

17. King, Kline and Fox were partners in a wholesale business. Kline died and left to his wife his share of the business. Kline's wife is entitled to
a. The value of Kline's interest in the partnership.
b. Kline's share of specific property of the partnership.
c. Continue the partnership as a partner with King and Fox.
d. Kline's share of the partnership profits until her death.

18. Which of the following will not result in a dissolution of a partnership?
a. The bankruptcy of a partner as long as the partnership itself remains solvent.
b. The death of a partner as long as his will provides that his executor shall become a partner in his place.
c. The wrongful withdrawal of a partner in contravention of the agreement between the partners.
d. The assignment by a partner of his entire partnership interest.

19. Vast Ventures is a limited partnership. The partnership agreement does not contain provisions dealing with the assignment of a partnership interest. The rights of the general and limited partners regarding the assignment of their partnership interests are

a. Determined according to the common law of partnerships as articulated by the courts.
b. Basically the same with respect to both types of partners.
c. Basically the same with the exception that the limited partner must give ten days notice prior to the assignment.
d. Different in that the assignee of the general partnership interest does not become a substituted partner, whereas the assignee of a limited partnership interest automatically becomes a substituted limited partner.

20. Stanley is a well known retired movie personality who purchased a limited partnership interest in Terrific Movie Productions upon its initial syndication. Terrific has three general partners, who also purchased limited partnership interests, and 1,000 additional limited partners located throughout the United States. Which of the following is correct?

a. If Stanley permits his name to be used in connection with the business and is held out as a participant in the management of the venture, he will be liable as a general partner.
b. The sale of these limited partnership interests would **not** be subject to SEC registration.
c. This limited partnership may be created with the same informality as a general partnership.
d. The general partners are prohibited from also owning limited partnership interests.

21. Cavendish is a limited partner of Custer Venture Capital. He is extremely dissatisfied with the performance of the general partners in making investments and managing the portfolio. He is contemplating taking whatever legal action may be appropriate against the general partners. Which of the following rights would Cavendish **not** be entitled to assert as a limited partner?

a. To have a formal accounting of partnership affairs whenever the circumstances render it just and reasonable.
b. To have the same rights as a general partner to a dissolution and winding up of the partnership.
c. To have reasonable access to the partnership books and to inspect and copy them.
d. To have himself elected as a general partner by a majority vote of the limited partners in number and amount.

22. Ms. Walls is a limited partner of the Amalgamated Limited Partnership. She is insolvent and her debts exceed her assets by $28,000. Goldsmith, one of Walls' largest creditors, is resorting to legal process to obtain the payment of Walls' debt to him. Goldsmith has obtained a charging order against Walls' limited partnership interest for the unsatisfied amount of the debt. As a result of Goldsmith's action, which of the following will happen?

a. The partnership will be dissolved.
b. Walls' partnership interest must be redeemed with partnership property.
c. Goldsmith automatically becomes a substituted limited partner.
d. Goldsmith becomes in effect an assignee of Walls' partnership interest.

23. A limited partner

a. May not withdraw his capital contribution unless there is sufficient limited-partnership property to pay all general creditors.
b. Must not own limited-partnership interests in other competing limited partnerships.
c. Is automatically an agent for the partnership with apparent authority to bind the limited partnership in contract.
d. Has no liability to creditors even if he takes part in the control of the business as long as he is held out as being a limited partner.

24. Absent any contrary provisions in the agreement, under which of the following circumstances will a limited partnership be dissolved?

a. A limited partner dies and his estate is insolvent.
b. A personal creditor of a general partner obtains a judgment against the general partner's interest in the limited partnership.
c. A general partner retires and all the remaining general partners do not consent to continue.
d. A limited partner assigns his partnership interest to an outsider and the purchaser becomes a substituted limited partner.

25. A limited partner's capital contribution to the limited partnership

a. Creates an intangible personal property right of the limited partner in the limited partnership.
b. Can be withdrawn at the limited partner's option at any time prior to the filing of a petition in bankruptcy against the limited partnership.
c. Can only consist of cash or marketable securities.
d. Need not be indicated in the limited partnership's certificate.

Problems

Problem 1 Creation of Partnership; Limited Partnership (581,L5)

(15 to 20 minutes)

Part a. Davis and Clay are licensed real estate brokers. They entered into a contract with Wilkins, a licensed building contractor, to construct and market residential housing. Under the terms of the contract, Davis and Clay were to secure suitable building sites, furnish prospective purchasers with plans and specifications, pay for appliances and venetian blinds and drapes, obtain purchasers, and assist in arranging for financing. Wilkins was to furnish the labor, material, and supervision necessary to construct the houses. In accordance with the agreement, Davis and Clay were to be reimbursed for their expenditures. Net profits from the sale of each house were to be divided 80% to Wilkins, 10% to Davis, and 10% to Clay. The parties also agreed that each was to be free to carry on his own business simultaneously and that such action would not be considered a conflict of interest. In addition, the agreement provided that their relationship was as independent contractors, pooling their interests for the limited purposes described above.

Ace Lumber Company sold lumber to Wilkins on credit from mid-1980 until February 1981. Ace did not learn of the agreement between Davis, Clay and Wilkins until April 1981, when an involuntary bankruptcy petition was filed against Wilkins and an order for relief entered. Ace Lumber has demanded payment from Davis and Clay. The lumber was used in the construction of a house pursuant to the agreement between the parties.

Required:

Answer the following, setting forth reasons for any conclusions stated.

In the event Ace sues Davis and Clay as well as Wilkins, will Ace prevail? Discuss the legal basis upon which Ace will rely in asserting liability.

Part b. Lawler is a retired film producer. She had a reputation in the film industry for aggressiveness and shrewdness; she was also considered somewhat overbearing. Cyclone Artistic Film Productions, a growing independent producer, obtained the film rights to "Claws," a recent best seller. Cyclone has decided to syndicate the production of "Claws." Therefore, it created a limited partnership, Claws Productions, with Harper, Von Hinden and Graham, the three ranking executives of Cyclone, serving as general partners. The three general partners each contributed $50,000 to the partnership capital. One hundred limited partnership interests were offered to the public at $50,000 each. Lawler was offered the opportunity to invest in the venture. Intrigued by the book and restless in her retirement, she decided to purchase 10 limited partnership interests for $500,000. She was the largest purchaser of the limited partnership interests of Claws Productions. All went well initially for the venture, but midway through production, some major problems arose. Lawler, having nothing else to do and having invested a considerable amount of money in the venture, began to take an increasingly active interest in the film's production.

She began to appear frequently on the set and made numerous suggestions on handling the various problems that were encountered. When the production still seemed to be proceeding with difficulty, Lawler volunteered her services to the general partners who as a result of her reputation and financial commitment to "Claws" decided to invite her to join them in their executive deliberations. This she did and her personality insured an active participation.

"Claws" turned out to be a box office disaster and its production costs were considered to be somewhat extraordinary even by Hollywood standards. The limited partnership is bankrupt and the creditors have sued Claws Productions, Harper, Von Hinden, Graham, and Lawler.

Required:

Answer the following, setting forth reasons for any conclusions stated.

What are the legal implications and liabilities of **each** of the above parties as a result of the above facts?

Problem 2 Assumed Name Statute; Fiduciary Responsibility; Dissolution; Assignment of Partnership Interest (579,L4)

(20 to 25 minutes)

Part a. Strom, Lane, and Grundig formed a partnership on July 1, 1974, and selected "Big M Associates" as their partnership name. The partnership agreement specified a fixed duration of ten years for the partnership. Business went well for the partnership for several years and it established an excellent reputation in the business community. In 1978, Strom, much to his amazement, learned that Grundig was padding his expense accounts by substantial amounts each month and taking secret kick-backs from certain customers for price concessions and favored service. Strom informed Lane of these facts and they decided to seek an accounting of Grundig, a dissolution of the firm by ousting Grundig, and the subsequent continuation of the firm by themselves under the name, "Big M Associates."

Required:

Answer the following, setting forth reasons for any conclusions stated.

1. Were there any filing requirements to be satisfied upon the initial creation of the partnership?

2. What will be the basis for the accounting and dissolution and should such actions be successful?

3. Can Strom and Lane obtain the right to continue to use the firm name if they prevail?

Part b. Palmer is a member of a partnership. His personal finances are in a state of disarray, although he is not bankrupt. He recently defaulted on a personal loan from the Aggressive Finance Company. Aggressive indicated that if he did not pay within one month, it would obtain a judgment against him and levy against all his property including his share of partnership property and any interest he had in the partnership. Both Palmer and the partnership are concerned about the effects of this unfortunate situation upon Palmer and the partnership.

Required:

Answer the following, setting forth reasons for any conclusions stated.

1. Has a dissolution of the partnership occurred?

2. What rights will Aggressive have against the partnership or Palmer concerning Palmer's share of partnership property or his interest in the partnership?

3. Could Palmer legally assign his interest in the partnership as security for a loan with which to pay off Aggressive?

Problem 3 Partnership Property Rights of Individual Partner's Spouse and Creditors (1182,L3b)

(12 to 15 minutes)

Part b. While auditing the financial statements of Graham, Phillips, Killian, and Henderson, a real estate partnership, for the year ended December 31, 1981, a CPA uncovers a number of unrelated events which warrant closer analysis:

- Graham died and left her partnership interest to her spouse.
- Phillips owned some real estate prior to the formation of the partnership but never formally transferred legal title to the partnership. The real estate has been used for partnership business since the partnership began its existence, and the partnership has paid all taxes associated with the real estate.
- Killian owes a considerable sum of money to a creditor, Jamison. Jamison has a judgment against Killian and has begun a foreclosure action against certain land owned by the partnership in order to satisfy his claim against Killian.
- Henderson sold some of the partnership real estate for value remitted to the partnership without the approval of the other partners. This sale exceeded Henderson's actual authority but appeared to be a customary sale in the ordinary course of business.

Required:

Answer the following, setting forth reasons for any conclusions stated.

1. Graham's spouse is presently seeking to exercise his spousal rights to obtain certain specific property owned by the partnership. Discuss the likely outcome of this matter.

2. Regarding the real estate that is legally in Phillips' name, can the partnership properly reflect this as an asset in the partnership's balance sheet?

3. Will Jamison succeed in his land foreclosure action?

4. If the partnership now wishes to rescind the sale of the real estate by Henderson, can it lawfully do so?

Multiple Choice Answers

1. c	6. c	11. a	16. c	21. d
2. c	7. c	12. b	17. a	22. d
3. d	8. a	13. b	18. d	23. a
4. b	9. b	14. c	19. b	24. c
5. b	10. a	15. b	20. a	25. a

Multiple Choice Answer Explanations

A. Nature of Partnerships

1. (1183,L1,21) (c) A joint venture will be treated as a partnership in most important legal respects. Answer (a) is incorrect because a joint venture falls within the definition of a partnership by the Internal Revenue Code and, therefore, is taxed as a partnership. Answer (b) is incorrect because a joint venture is **not** a corporation and, therefore, is not required to incorporate. Answer (d) is incorrect as dissolution occurs based upon the joint venture agreement or when **all** operations cease. There is no legal requirement that a joint venture must be dissolved upon completion of a single undertaking.

2. (583,L1,3) (c) Under the Uniform Partnership Act, a partnership is recognized as a separate entity for the purposes of taking title and ownership of property. Answer (a) is incorrect because partnerships are not recognized as an entity for the purpose of being an employer of its partners. Each partner is both a principal of and an agent of the other partners. Answer (b) is incorrect because a general partnership is never formed to insulate the partners from personal liability. All general partners are personally liable to third parties for all obligations of the partnership. Answer (d) is incorrect since the partnership does not have continuity of existence. A general partnership is dissolved every time there is a change in the relationship of the partners caused by any partner ceasing to be associated with the partnership.

C. Formation of Partnership

3. (1183,L1,15) (d) The purpose of fictitious name statutes is to enable interested parties to learn the identity of the individuals who operate the business. Since the name under which the business is operating often does not include the names of the partners, these statutes provide the necessary link between the name of the business and the names of the individual partners. The typical fictitious name statute provides for the imposition of a fine in the event of noncompliance. Answer (a) is incorrect because such statutes do not affect the creation of a partnership. Answer (b) is incorrect because fictitious name statutes are not related to tax purposes. It should be kept in mind that a partnership is not a separate taxable entity. Answer (c) is incorrect because such statutes are designed for the benefit of parties outside the partnership, not for the purpose of defining the rights and duties of the partners themselves.

4. (582,L1,1) (b) The Uniform Partnership Act defines a partnership as an association of two or more persons to carry on as co-owners a business for profit. A partnership relationship can be implied by the acts of the parties, as long as it appears that the parties intended joint responsibility in the management and operation of the business, and intended to share in its profits and losses. Therefore, the partnership began its existence on September 1, 1981, when the three sole proprietors demonstrated the necessary intent to carry on a business as partners. Answer (a) is incorrect because the existing creditors do not have to consent to the transfer of the individual business assets to the partnership. However, the creditors' rights are not affected or destroyed, and the creditors can avoid the transfer of assets if proved to be a fraudulent conveyance on the part of the three sole proprietors. Answer (c) is incorrect because a written agreement is not ordinarily necessary to create a partnership, unless it falls within the provisions of the Statute of Frauds (i.e., a partnership agreement which by its terms can not be performed within a year). Therefore, this partnership agreement falls outside the Statute of Frauds, since the partnership's duration is indefinite. Answer (d) is incorrect because unless the partnership agreement provides otherwise, the law implies that profits and losses are to be shared equally by the partners.

5. (1181,L1,18) (b) Unless the partnership agreement provides otherwise, the law implies that profits are to be shared equally by the partners. The agreement to form DBW Partnership only made reference to the manner in which losses are to be handled; therefore, profits are to be divided equally. Answer (d) is incorrect because the relative time each partner devotes to the partnership business has no effect on distribution of profits. Answer (c) is incorrect because a written agreement is not ordinarily necessary to create a partnership, unless it falls within the provisions of the Statute of Frauds. This partnership agreement falls outside the requisites of the Statute of Frauds; therefore, it does not need to be evidenced by a sufficient writing in order to be effective.

6. (1180,L1,22) (c) A partnership can be created by estoppel. This occurs when a third party changes his position in reliance upon a misrepresentation of the fact that a partnership exists. Danforth is a partner by estoppel. Danforth does not need to make a statement to become a partner by estoppel; his silence would be sufficient considering he is present at the time Coleman represents that they are partners. Answer (c) is correct.

7. (1180,L1,23) (c) Two or more persons sharing profits of a business is prima facie evidence (raises a presumption) that a partnership exists. This presumption is overcome if it can be shown that the sharing of profits are for: services rendered, interest on loans, payment of debts, rent, any other reasonable explanation. The lack of intent or lack of a partnership agreement will not necessarily determine whether a partnership exists. Answer (c) is the correct answer.

E. Relationship to Third Parties

8. (1183,L1,16) (a) Partners are jointly and severally liable for torts committed by a copartner while carrying on partnership business. The partner who commits the tort can always be sued for his own actions regardless of whether the partnership has been sued. Thus, answer (d) is incorrect. Answer (b) is incorrect because the existence of implied authority is not inconsistent with a formal, detailed partnership agreement. While such an agreement may carefully spell out a partner's express authority, the partner still retains implied authority to do those things which are reasonably necessary to the exercise of his/her express authority. Answer (c) is incorrect because apparent authority is based upon the reasonable belief of a third party that the partner with whom he dealt possessed authority to represent the partnership in that matter. Since the third party is not a party to the partnership agreement and does not ordinarily have access to it, the third party is not bound by the terms of the agreement unless he has actual knowledge of its terms. The partnership agreement is, of course, binding among the partners themselves.

9. (1183,L1,17) (b) A third party, who has no notice of the dissolution of the partnership, may reasonably believe that a partner who is conducting partnership business in the usual way has authority to do so. Under such circumstances, the partner has apparent authority. Thus, answer (a) is incorrect. Likewise, if the sale of real estate is within the regular course of a partnership's business, a partner has apparent authority to convey real property held in the partnership name. Answer (c) is, therefore, incorrect. If, however, the third party knows that the partner with whom he deals lacks actual authority, there can be no apparent authority. With such knowledge, the third party can no longer reasonably believe that the partner has authority to represent the partnership. Answer (b), therefore, is correct. Answer (d) is incorrect because express authority is not based upon the knowledge of the third party. Instead it is based upon the partnership agreement itself.

10. (583,L1,5) (a) A partner has apparent authority to renew an existing supply contract which is apparently for the purpose of carrying on the partnership business in the usual way. In the absence of knowledge by a third party, that such action was unauthorized by the other partners, the contract renewal is binding on the partnership. The matters described in answers (b), (c), and (d) are actions requiring the unanimous consent of the partners: (1) assignment of partnership assets to creditors, (2) written admission of the liability of the partnership in a lawsuit, and (3) committing partnership as surety on a partner's personal debt. Therefore, a partner does not have apparent authority to bind the partnership in these matters because third parties are supposed to be aware of the requirement of unanimity.

11. (582,L1,2) (a) Every partner is an agent of the partnership for the purpose of conducting its business, and can bind the partnership to contracts with third parties. Any contracts made by a partner on behalf of the partnership and related to its business are deemed to be within the partner's apparent authority, and hence binding on the partnership, notwithstanding a limitation or agreement between the partners of which the third party had no notice. Such limitation on the partner's normal authority will only bind the third party if known to the third party before entering into the contract with the partnership. Therefore, the renewal of the supply contract would bind the partnership, regardless of the partners' vote not to renew. Answers (b) and (d) are incorrect because the Uniform Partnership Act provides certain inherent limitations on a partner's authority. Unless the partnership business has been abandoned, or all partners have expressed unanimous assent, no partner has authority to submit a partnership claim to arbitration; and no partner has authority to bind the partnership on accomodation paper unless expressly authorized, or in furtherance of firm business. Answer (c) is incorrect because when the partner is acting in excess of his authority and the person with whom he is dealing knows of that fact, the partnership is not bound.

12. (1181,L1,21) (b) A retiring partner is liable to creditors for existing debts of the partnership, but not for those incurred after retirement, so long as creditors had notice of the retirement before extending the credit. Partners may agree not to hold a retiring partner liable among themselves, but they cannot prevent him being held personally liable by third parties. Therefore, when Donaldson leaves the partnership, she is still individually liable on all past contracts and obligations, unless existing creditors agree to release her and look to the new incoming partner, Edwards (a novation). Therefore, answers (c) and (d) are incorrect. A withdrawing partner may protect herself/himself against liability upon contracts which are entered into by the firm subsequent to her/his withdrawal by giving notice that s/he is no longer a member of the firm. Otherwise, s/he is liable for the debts thus incurred and due and owing to a creditor who had no notice or knowledge of the partner having withdrawn from the firm. Answer (a) is incorrect because new partners coming into a partnership are liable for antecedent debts and obligations of the firm only to the extent of their capital contribution, unless the new partners assume personal liability for prior partnership debts.

13. (1180,L1,19) (b) In a partnership, a general partner has unlimited liability for the partnership debts. Upon the death of a partner, this liability continues and is assumed by the deceased partner's estate. Under the doctrine of marshalling of assets, personal creditors have first priority to Perone's personal assets, with any excess going to the partnership creditors. This makes answer (b) correct and answers (a) and (d) incorrect. Answer (c) is incorrect since each partner, including a deceased partner's estate, is individually liable for the entire amount of partnership debts. However, if a partner pays more than his share of the partnership debts, he can sue his co-partners to recover the excess.

14. (1177,L1,12) (c) A partner who signs the partnership name to his personal mortgage has attempted to make the partnership a guarantor or surety. Unanimous consent is needed or the other partners will not be personally liable since apparent authority is lacking. General partners are personally liable for the partnership's debts and liabilities. Answer (a) is incorrect because gross negligence of an employee may create such a liability. Answer (b) is incorrect because partnership business is carried out by majority rule and each partner will be personally liable whether he objected or not. Answer (d) is incorrect because the other partners can agree not to hold a partner liable among themselves but they cannot prevent his being held personally liable by third parties.

F. Termination of a Partnership

15. (583,L1,4) (b) A partner can sell or pledge his entire interest in a partnership without causing a dissolution of the partnership regardless of whether he has the consent of the other partners. Therefore, answers (a) and (c) are incorrect. Answer (d) is incorrect because the purchase of an interest in a partnership does not confer partner status upon the purchaser. The assignee (purchaser) receives only the right to the partner's share of the profits and upon dissolution to the value of the partner's interest, and does not receive partnership status nor the accompanying rights such as participation in management, right to an accounting, right to inspect the books, etc.

16. (1180,L1,20) (c) Such a partnership agreement does not prevent the dissolution of the partnership upon the death or withdrawal of a partner; it merely eliminates the necessity of the second step in the termination of the partnership which is the winding up process. Such an agreement is enforceable. Answer (c) is the correct answer.

17. (1179,L1,16) (a) When a partner dies, his heirs or those named in his will are entitled to the value of the deceased partner's interest in the partnership. The heirs do not become and are not entitled to become partners as in answer (c) and the survivors acquire no interest in specific property of the partnership as in (b). The heirs are only entitled to the deceased partner's interest in the partnership. Answer (d) is incorrect because the surviving wife of a deceased partner is only entitled to her husband's rights at the time of his death.

18. (1179,L1,17) (d) The assignment by a partner of his entire partnership interest does not dissolve a partnership. Answer (a) is incorrect because the bankruptcy of a partner or of the partnership itself results in dissolution. Answer (b) is incorrect because the death of a partner generally results in a court ordered dissolution even if there is a purported agreement which attempts to substitute an executor as a partner in place of the decedent. Answer (c) is incorrect because the wrongful withdrawal of a partner even though in contravention of the partnership agreement will result in a dissolution of the partnership.

G. Limited Partnerships

19. (1183,L1,18) (b) The assignment of a limited partner's interest in the partnership is treated essentially the same as the assignment of a general partner's interest. The assignee does not become a substitute partner whether the assignment is of a general or limited

partnership interest. Therefore, answer (d) is incorrect. Answer (a) is incorrect because a limited partnership can only be created if a state statute exists which would permit the creation of such an entity. Limited partnerships are governed by statute, not by common law. Answer (c) is incorrect because there is no ten-day notice requirement applicable to the assignment of a limited partnership interest.

20. (582,L1,3) (a) A limited partner will be held liable as a general partner, and therefore personally liable on partnership debts, where he takes an active part in management of the business or permits his name to be used in the firm's name. Answer (b) is incorrect because the definition of securities under the Securities Act of 1933 includes limited partnership interests. Therefore, the sale of these limited partnership interests, if interstate in character and not specifically exempted, may be covered by SEC regulations and subject to SEC registration. Answer (c) is incorrect because limited partnerships are regulated by state statutes based on the Uniform Limited Partnership Act. These statutes must be complied with when creating a limited partnership, otherwise the partners are general partners. Therefore, in contrast to the formation of a general partnership, the formation of a limited partnership must be in accordance with strict statutory requirements. Answer (d) is incorrect because a person may be both a general partner and a limited partner in the same partnership at the same time.

21. (582,L1,4) (d) The rights of a limited partner are substantially the same as those of a general partner, except that a limited partner has no rights in regard to the management responsibilities of the partnership. But a limited partner is not entitled to have himself elected as a general partner by a majority vote of the limited partners. Answers (a), (b), and (c) are incorrect because these are all rights which Cavendish is entitled to assert as a limited partner. He has rights of access to the partnership books, to an accounting as to the partnership business whenever circumstances warrant and to a dissolution and winding up by decree of court.

22. (1180,L1,24) (d) Goldsmith's charging order would in effect make him assignee of Wall's partnership interest. A limited partner may assign his partnership interest to whomever he wishes at any time. However, the assignee will not become a partner without consent of the existing partners. Goldsmith's charging order would operate as an involuntary assignment of Wall's limited partnership interest. Goldsmith would have a right to Wall's share of the profits plus Wall's capital contributions if the partnership is dissolved. Answer (a) is incorrect because an assignment of any type of partnership interest (general or limited) does not dissolve a partnership.

23. (1176,L1,11) (a) Limited partners may not withdraw their capital contributions so as to impair a creditor's status. Unless there is sufficient partnership property to pay all general creditors, withdrawal of limited partner capital impairs a creditor's status. Limited partners are not restricted in owning competing interests (but general partners are), because limited partners do not participate in management, i.e., they are merely investors. Limited partners are not agents and do not have apparent authority. General partners are agents, because they participate in management. If limited partners take part in the management of a business, they become liable as general partners.

24. (1176,L1,13) (c) If a general partner retires and the others do not consent to continue, the partnership is dissolved. Such dissolution can be avoided by a provision in the partnership agreement. If a limited partner dies (whether or not his estate is insolvent) or if he assigns his partnership interest, there is no dissolution. Remember a limited partner is similar to a stockholder of a corporation. A partnership is not dissolved if a creditor obtains a judgment against a partner's partnership interest. The creditor only has the right to income from the partnership interest; the creditor is not a substituted partner and does not have the right to manage or inspect the books.

25. (1176,L1,15) (a) A limited partner's (as does a general partner's) capital contribution creates an intangible property right in the partnership. Limited partners have no right to any specific partnership property, but rather a share of the total. The capital contribution cannot be withdrawn if it will impair a creditor's status, i.e., there must be enough partnership property to satisfy all creditors. A limited partner may contribute property just as a general partner may. A limited partner cannot contribute services if they will involve managing or operating the business. Each limited partner's capital contribution is one of the required inclusions in the limited partnership certificate (generally required to be filed).

Answer Outline

Problem 1 Creation of Partnership; Limited Partnership

a. Ace will prevail in his suit
   - Ace will rely upon the existence of a partnership relationship
     - Sharing of profits raises presumption of partnership
     - Receipt of gross returns does not itself establish a partnership
     - Joint ownership of property not prima facie evidence of partnership, but only one factor to consider
   - Objective intent of Davis, Clay and Wilkins supercedes their subjective intent
     - Parties' agreement to maintain independent contractors relationship does not contravene manifestation of partnership existence
   - Ace's lack of knowledge of partnership existence is irrelevant
     - No requirement for third party reliance on relationship
   - Partners are agents of the partnership
     - Wilkins can bind partnership to contracts with third parties
   - Partners are jointly liable for debts and obligations of the partnership

b. The limited partnership, the general partners and Lawlor are jointly liable for debts and obligations of Claws Productions
   - Limited partnership is liable to the extent of Claws Productions' assets
   - Partnership assets must be exhausted before general partners' individual assets can be reached
     - Harper, Von Hinden and Graham, as general partners, are liable for unpaid debts of Claws Productions
   - Limited partners liable for debts of partnership to extent of capital contributed
     - Lose status of limited partner where take active part in business and management functions
       - Lawlor becomes liable as general partner
         - Personally liable for partnership debts

Unofficial Answer

Problem 1 Creation of Partnership; Limited Partnership

Part a.

Yes. Ace will prevail. A partnership did exist and the parties are jointly liable. The legal basis upon which Ace will seek recovery is that a partnership exists among Wilkins, Davis, and Clay. If the parties are deemed partners among themselves, then Ace can assert liability against such partnership and against the individual partners as members thereof, since they are jointly liable for such partnership obligations.

The Uniform Partnership Act, section 7, provides rules for determining the existence of a partnership. Although it is frequently stated that the intent of the parties is important in determining the existence of a partnership relationship, this statement must be significantly qualified: it is not the subjective intent of the parties that is important when they categorically state that they do not wish to be considered as partners. If much effect were given to such statements, partnership liability could easily be shed. Further, the party dealing with the partnership need not in fact rely upon the existence of a partnership. Thus, the fact that Ace did not learn of the Davis, Clay, Wilkins agreement until after he had extended credit does not preclude him from asserting partnership liability.

The bearing of section 7 of the Uniform Partnership Act on this case can be examined as follows. First, joint, common, or part ownership of property of any type does not of itself establish a partnership. It is only one factor to be considered and was present to a limited extent in this case. Second, the sharing in gross returns does not of itself establish a partnership, but its importance is rendered moot as a result of the profit-sharing arrangement between the parties. Finally, and the key factor in partnership determination, is the receipt of profits: The act states "the receipt by a person of a share of the profits of a business is prima facie evidence that he is a partner in the business . . ."

Sharing in profits is prima facie evidence of the existence of a partnership. The defendants (Davis and Clay) must affirmatively rebut this prima facie case against them or lose. There do not appear to be facts sufficient to accomplish this.

Part b.

The limited partnership, the general partners, and Lawler are all jointly liable for the debts of Claws Productions.

Claws Productions limited partnership is liable and must satisfy the judgment to the extent it has assets. Harper, Von Hinden, and Graham are liable for the unpaid debts of the limited partnership. An interesting problem posed by the fact situation is Lawler's liability. The general rule, in fact the very basis for the existence of the limited partnership, is that the limited partner is not liable beyond its capital contribution. However, a notable exception contained in section 7 of the Uniform Limited Partnership Act applies to the facts presented here:

> A limited partner shall not become liable as a general partner unless, in addition to the exercise of his rights and powers as a limited partner, he takes part in the control of the business.

The statutory language covers the facts stated. Lawler assumed a managerial role vis à vis the partnership and in the process became liable as a general partner.

Answer Outline

Problem 2 Assumed Name Statute; Fiduciary Responsibility; Dissolution; Assignment of Partnership Interest

a1. Yes, fictitious name statute must be complied with since partnership name is not actual name of partners
- Requires recording in public records
- Purpose is to advise public who real parties are

But no filing of the partnership agreement is required

a2. Each partner is a fiduciary for all partnership related affairs per uniform partnership act (UPA)

UPA holds breach of fiduciary duty to be grounds for accounting
- Courts grant partnership dissolution when
  - Partner breaches fiduciary duty to partnership
  - Persistent breach of partnership agreement by partner makes it impractical to carry on partnership business

Dissolution and accounting should be granted
- Grundig breached fiduciary duty by
  - Dishonesty with partners
  - Stealing from partners
  - Involved partnership in illegal price discrimination

a3. Yes, continuing partners should obtain right to use firm name

UPA provides for continuation of business in same firm name when partnership has
- Fixed duration (10 years here) and
- Dissolution is a violation of the partnership agreement
  - Here, because Grundig's conduct is wrongful

b1. No, partner default on personal debt does not cause dissolution

Only bankruptcy of partner causes dissolution
- Facts state Palmer was not bankrupt
- Threats or action against partner's interest in partnership does not cause dissolution

b2. Partner creditors have no rights against partnership property
- Only partners have rights to use partnership property for partnership purposes

Aggressive has right to obtain first a judgment against Palmer and then a charging order
- Charging order entitles creditor to obtain debtor's future distributions from the partnership

b3. Yes, partner may assign his partnership interest
- Unless prohibited by partnership agreement
- Does not cause dissolution
- Does not make assignee a partner
  - Assignee only entitled to assignor's profits and capital distributions

Unofficial Answer

Problem 2 Assumed Name Statute; Fiduciary Responsibility; Dissolution; Assignment of Partnership Interest

Part a.

1. Yes. Although no filing of the partnership agreement is required, virtually all states have statutes that require registration of fictitious or assumed names used in trade or business. The purpose of such statutes is to disclose the real parties in interest to creditors and those doing business with the company. This is typically accomplished by filing in the proper office of public records the names and addresses of the parties doing business under an assumed name. The statutes vary greatly in detail (e.g., some states require newspaper publication).

2. The facts indicate a clear breach of fiduciary duty by Grundig. Section 21 of the Uniform Partnership Act holds every partner accountable as a fiduciary. It provides that "every partner must account to the

partnership for any benefit, and hold as trustee for it any profits derived by him without the consent of other partners from any transactions connected with the . . . conduct . . . of the partnership or from any use by him of its property." Grundig's conduct is squarely within the act's language. Section 22 of the act gives any partner a right to a formal accounting of partnership affairs if there is a breach of fiduciary duty by a fellow partner.

Section 32 (c) and (d) of the act provides for a dissolution by court decree upon application of a partner whenever—

- A partner has been guilty of conduct that tends to prejudicially affect the business.
- A partner willfully or persistently commits a breach of the partnership agreement or otherwise so conducts himself in matters relating to the partnership business that it is not reasonably practicable to carry on the business in partnership with him.

Certainly Grundig's conduct would appear to fall within one or both of the above categories. He breached his fiduciary duty, was dishonest with his fellow partners, was in fact stealing from his partners, and may have involved the partnership in illegal price discrimination. Thus, the grant of application for dissolution would be appropriate.

3. Probably yes. Section 38(2) (b) of the Uniform Partnership Act relating to the right to continue the business in the same firm name, under the circumstances described, is narrowly drawn. This provision was designed to cover situations where partnerships have fixed durations and one of the partners has caused a dissolution wrongfully "in contravention of the partnership agreement." The facts indicate that Big M Associates did have a fixed duration (10 years); consequently, this requirement is met. While the acts by Grundig are not in contravention of any specific express language of the partnership agreement, as would be the case where a partner wrongfully withdraws, the courts treat other types of wrongful conduct to be in contravention of the partnership agreement and thus, to be the basis for dissolution. Strom and Lane could obtain the right to continue to use the firm name for the duration of the partnership agreement if Grundig's conduct was deemed both wrongful and in contravention of the agreement.

Part b.

1. No. Since the facts clearly indicate that Palmer is not bankrupt, his financial problems will not precipitate a dissolution of the partnership. However, if Palmer were bankrupt, the Uniform Partnership Act [Sec.31(5)] specifically provides that the bankruptcy of one of the partners causes a dissolution. The fact that creditors take action against a delinquent partner's interest in the partnership, although annoying and inconvenient, does not result in a dissolution.

2. Aggressive will have no rights to the partnership property either directly or indirectly by asserting Palmer's rights. In fact, Palmer only has the right to the use of partnership property for partnership purposes. Since partnership property is insulated from attack by Aggressive, Aggressive will assert its rights against Palmer's partnership interest. The method used to reach this interest is to reduce its claim against Palmer to a judgment and then obtain from the court a "charging order" to enable Aggressive to collect on the judgment. In effect, Aggressive has obtained a right comparable to a lienholder against Palmer's interest in the partnership. The "charging order" would provide Aggressive with the right to payments (earnings or capital distributions) that would ordinarily go to Palmer, the partner-debtor.

3. Yes. There is nothing in the Uniform Partnership Act that prevents a partner from assigning all or part of his interest in a partnership. The assignment may be outright or for the more common purpose of securing a loan. If there is to be any such restriction on a partner's right to assign his partnership interest, the partnership agreement must so provide. Section 27 of the Uniform Partnership Act specifically provides that a partner's assignment of his partnership interest does not cause a dissolution. The act limits such an assignment to the partner's right to share in profits and capital distributions but does not make the assignee a partner.

Answer Outline

Problem 3 Partnership Property Rights of Individual Partner's Spouse and Creditors

Part b.

1. Graham's spouse will not be able to exercise spousal rights
   - Partners own partnership property as tenants in partnership
     - Partners have right of survivorship concerning specific pieces of property
       - A partner's right in specific partnership property vests in the surviving partners
       - Spouse has no rights in specific partnership property

2. Yes. The partnership can reflect this real estate as a partnership asset
   - Court will consider several factors in determination of whether partnership property or property of individual partner
     - How property is used
     - Source of funds to purchase property
     - Owner of record
     - Other indicia of ownership
   - Real estate has been used for partnership business
   - Partnership has paid all taxes
     - Property will be classified as partnership asset
3. No. Jamison will not succeed in land foreclosure action
   - Creditor of individual partner cannot attach partner's right in specific partnership property
   - Creditor can acquire charging order against a partner's interest in the partnership
4. No. The partnership cannot rescind the sale of real estate
   - Henderson had apparent authority to engage in sale of property
     - As long as in ordinary course of partnership business

Unofficial Answer

(Author Modified)

Problem 3 Partnership Property Rights of Individual Partner's Spouse and Creditors

Part b.

1. Graham's spouse will not be able to exercise his spousal rights to obtain specific property owned by the partnership. Individual partners own partnership property as tenants in partnership with the other partners. Under the tenancy in partnership concept, a partner's right in specific partnership property does not pass to his/her heirs in the event of death, but vests in the surviving partners. Consequently, a partner's right to specific partnership property is not subject to allowances to spouse, heirs, or next of kin. However, the remaining partners are under a duty to account to the deceased partner's estate for the value of the deceased partner's interest in the partnership.

2. Yes, the partnership can reflect real estate in question as a partnership asset. When deciding whether property is partnership property or the property of an individual partner, the courts will consider four factors:

   1. How the property is used by the partnership;
   2. The source of funds used to purchase the property;
   3. The owner of record to the property; and
   4. Other indicia of ownership, such as who pays the taxes on the property.

Consequently, even though the property is titled in Phillip's name, the real estate would be classified as a partnership asset because the property has been used for partnership purposes and the partnership has paid all taxes.

3. No, Jamison will not succeed in his land foreclosure action. A creditor of a partner cannot attach a partner's right in specific partnership property. However, a creditor may proceed by securing a charging order from the appropriate court against a partner's interest in the partnership, allowing the creditor to receive any distribution of profits or return of capital intended for the partner.

4. No, the partnership cannot rescind the sale of the real estate by Henderson. Every partner is considered an agent of the partnership for the purposes of conducting its business. Henderson had apparent authority to sell the real estate since the sale appeared to be a customary sale in the ordinary course of the partnership business. This sale is just as binding on the partnership as it would have been if Harrelson had been acting with express authority.

Multiple Choice Questions (1 - 33)

1. A court is most likely to disregard the corporate entity and hold shareholders personally liable when
   a. The owner-officers of the corporation do **not** treat it as a separate entity.
   b. A parent corporation creates a wholly owned subsidiary in order to isolate the high risk portion of its business in the subsidiary.
   c. A sole proprietor incorporates his business to limit his liability.
   d. The corporation has elected, under Subchapter S, **not** to pay any corporate tax on its income but, instead, to have the shareholders pay tax on it.

2. Golden Enterprises, Inc., entered into a contract with Hidalgo Corporation for the sale of its mineral holdings. The transaction proved to be *ultra vires.* Which of the following parties, for the reason stated, may properly assert the *ultra vires* doctrine?
   a. Golden Enterprises to avoid performance.
   b. A shareholder of Golden Enterprises to enjoin the sale.
   c. Hidalgo Corporation to avoid performance.
   d. Golden Enterprises to rescind the consummated sale.

3. Sandy McBride, president of the Cranston Corporation, inquired about the proper method of handling the expenditures incurred in connection with the recent incorporation of the business and sale of its shares to the public. In explaining the legal or tax treatment of these expenditures, which of the following is correct?
   a. The expenditures may be paid out of the consideration received in payment for the shares without rendering such shares not fully paid or assessable.
   b. The expenditures are comparable to goodwill and are treated accordingly for nontax and tax purposes.
   c. The expenditures must be capitalized and are nondeductible for federal income tax purposes since the life of the corporation is perpetual.
   d. The expenditures may be deducted for federal income tax purposes in the year incurred or amortized at the election of the corporation over a five-year period.

4. Destiny Manufacturing, Inc., is incorporated under the laws of Nevada. Its principal place of business is in California and it has permanent sales offices in several other states. Under the circumstances, which of the following is correct?
   a. California may validly demand that Destiny incorporate under the laws of the state of California.
   b. Destiny must obtain a certificate of authority to transact business in California and the other states in which it does business.
   c. Destiny is a foreign corporation in California, but not in the other states.
   d. California may prevent Destiny from operating as a corporation if the laws of California differ regarding organization and conduct of the corporation's internal affairs.

5. Hobson, Jones, Carter, and Wolff are all medical doctors who have worked together for several years. They decided to form a corporation and their attorney created a typical professional corporation for them. Which of the following is correct?
   a. Such a corporation will not be recognized for federal tax purposes if one of its goals is to save taxes.
   b. The state in which they incorporated must have enacted professional corporation statutes permitting them to do so.
   c. Upon incorporation, the doctor-shareholder is insulated from personal liability beyond his capital contribution.
   d. The majority of states prohibit the creation of professional corporations by doctors.

6. Phillips was the principal promoter of the Waterloo Corporation, a corporation which was to have been incorporated not later than July 31, 1981. Among the many things to be accomplished prior to incorporation were the obtaining of capital, the hiring of key executives and the securing of adequate office space. In this connection, Phillips obtained written subscriptions for $1.4 million of common stock from 17 individuals. He hired himself as the chief executive officer of Waterloo at $200,000 for five years and leased three floors of office space from Downtown Office Space, Inc. The contract with Downtown was made in the name of the corporation. Phillips had indicated orally that the corporation would be coming into existence shortly. The corporation did not come into existence through no fault of Phillips. Which of the following is correct?
   a. The subscribers have a recognized right to sue for and recover damages.

b. Phillips is personally liable on the lease with Downtown.
c. Phillips has the right to recover the fair value of his services rendered to the proposed corporation.
d. The subscribers were **not** bound by their subscriptions until the corporation came into existence.

7. Bixler obtained an option on a building he believed was suitable for use by a corporation he and two other men were organizing. After the corporation was sucessfully promoted, Bixler met with the Board of Directors who agreed to acquire the property for $200,000. Bixler deeded the building to the corporation and the corporation began business in it. Bixler's option contract called for the payment of only $155,000 for the building and he purchased it for that price. When the directors later learned that Bixler paid only $155,000, they demanded the return of Bixler's $45,000 profit. Bixler refused, claiming the building was worth far more than $200,000 both when he secured the option and when he deeded it to the corporation. Which of the following statements correctly applies to Bixler's conduct?
a. It was improper for Bixler to contract for the option without first having secured the assent of the Board of Directors.
b. If, as Bixler claimed, the building was fairly worth more than $200,000, Bixler is entitled to retain the entire price.
c. Even if, as Bixler claimed, the building was fairly worth more than $200,000, Bixler nevertheless must return the $45,000 to the corporation.
d. In order for Bixler to be obligated to return any amount to the corporation, the Board of Directors must establish that the building was worth less than $200,000.

8. Delta Corporation has decided to purchase $2,000,000 of its own outstanding shares. In connection with this acquisition, which of the following is a correct statement?
a. The shares may **not** be acquired out of capital surplus.
b. The share in question must be classified as treasury shares if **not** cancelled.
c. A subsequent offering of the acquired shares to the public in interstate commerce would be exempt from SEC registration.
d. If the shares are acquired at a price less than the original offering price, the corporation has realized a taxable capital gain.

9. Global Trucking Corporation has in its corporate treasury a substantial block of its own common stock, which it acquired several years previously. The stock had been publicly offered at $25 a share and had been reacquired at $15. The board is considering using it in the current year for various purposes. For which of the following purposes may it validly use the treasury stock?
a. To pay a stock dividend to its shareholders.
b. To sell it to the public without the necessity of a registration under the Securities Act of 1933, since it had been previously registered.
c. To vote it at the annual meeting of shareholders.
d. To acquire the shares of another publicly held company without the necessity of a registration under the Securities Act of 1933.

10. The Larkin Corporation is contemplating a two-for-one stock split of its common stock. Its $4 par value common stock will be reduced at $2 after the split. It has 2 million shares issued and outstanding out of a total of 3 million authorized. In considering the legal or tax consequences of such action, which of the following is a correct statement?
a. The transaction will require both authorization by the Board of Directors and approval by the shareholders.
b. The distribution of the additional shares to the shareholders will be taxed as a dividend to the recipients.
c. Surplus equal to the par value of the existing number of shares issued and outstanding must be transferred to the stated capital account.
d. The trustees of trust recipients of the additional shares must allocate them ratably between income and corpus.

11. Surplus of a corporation means
a. Net assets in excess of stated capital.
b. Liquid assets in excess of current needs.
c. Total assets in excess of total liabilities.
d. Contributed capital.

12. Ambrose purchased 400 shares of $100 par value original issue common stock from Minor Corporation for $25 a share. Ambrose subsequently sold 200 of the shares to Harris at $25 a share. Harris did not have knowledge or notice that Ambrose had not paid par. Ambrose also sold 100 shares of this stock to Gable for $25 a share. At the time of this sale, Gable knew that Ambrose had not paid par for the stock. Minor Corpora-

tion became insolvent and the creditors sought to hold all the above parties liable for the $75 unpaid on each of the 400 shares. Under these circumstances

a. The creditors can hold Ambrose liable for $30,000.
b. If $25 a share was a fair value for the stock at the time of issuance, Ambrose will have no liability to the creditors.
c. Since Harris acquired the shares by purchase, he is not liable to the creditors, and his lack of knowledge or notice that Ambrose paid less than par is immaterial.
d. Since Gable acquired the shares by purchase, he is not liable to the creditors, and the fact that he knew Ambrose paid less than par is immaterial.

13. Plimpton subscribed to 1,000 shares of $1 par value common stock of the Billiard Ball Corporation at $10 a share. Plimpton paid $1,000 upon the incorporation of Billiard and paid an additional $4,000 at a later time. The corporation subsequently became insolvent and is now in bankruptcy. The creditors of the corporation are seeking to hold Plimpton personally liable. Which of the following is a correct statement?

a. Plimpton has no liability directly or indirectly to the creditors of the corporation since he paid the corporation the full par value of the shares.
b. As a result of his failure to pay the full subscription price, Plimpton has unlimited joint and several liability for corporate debts.
c. Plimpton is liable for the remainder of the unpaid subscription price.
d. Had Plimpton transferred his shares to an innocent third party, neither he nor the third party would be liable.

14. Watson entered into an agreement to purchase 1,000 shares of the Marvel Corporation, a corporation to be organized in the near future. Watson has since had second thoughts about investing in Marvel. Under the circumstances, which of the following is correct?

a. A written notice of withdrawal of his agreement to purchase the shares will be valid as long as it is received prior to incorporation.
b. A simple transfer of the agreement to another party will entirely eliminate his liability to purchase the shares of stock.
c. Watson may not revoke the agreement for a period of six months in the absence of special circumstances.
d. Watson may avoid liability on his agreement if he can obtain the consent of the majority of other individuals committed to purchase shares to release him.

15. Which of the following statements is correct regarding the fiduciary duty?

a. A majority shareholder as such may owe a fiduciary duty to fellow shareholders.
b. A director's fiduciary duty to the corporation may be discharged by merely disclosing his self-interest.
c. A director owes a fiduciary duty to the shareholders but **not** to the corporation.
d. A promoter of a corporation to be formed owes no fiduciary duty to anyone, unless the contract engaging the promoter so provides.

16. Fairwell is executive vice president and treasurer of Wonder Corporation. He was named as a party in a shareholder derivative action in connection with certain activities he engaged in as a corporate officer. In the lawsuit, it was determined that he was liable for negligence in performance of his duties. Fairwell seeks indemnity from the corporation for his liability. The board would like to indemnify him. The articles of incorporation do not contain any provisions regarding indemnification of officers and directors. Indemnification

a. Is **not** permitted since the articles of incorporation do **not** so provide.
b. Is permitted only if he is found **not** to have been grossly negligent.
c. Can **not** include attorney's fees since he was found to have been negligent.
d. May be permitted by court order despite the fact that Fairwell was found to be negligent.

17. At their annual meeting, shareholders of the Laurelton Corporation approved several proposals made by the Board of Directors. Among them was the ratification of the salaries of the executives of the corporation. In this connection, which of the following is correct?

a. The shareholders can **not** legally ratify the compensation paid to director-officers.
b. The salaries ratified are automatically valid for federal income tax purposes.
c. Such ratification by the shareholders is required as a matter of law.
d. The action by the shareholders serves the purpose of confirming the board's action.

18. Unless otherwise provided by a corporation's articles of incorporation or by-laws, a board of directors may act without a meeting if written consent setting forth the action so taken is signed by
   a. A plurality of them.
   b. A majority of them.
   c. Two-thirds of them.
   d. All of them.

19. Derek Corporation decided to acquire certain assets belonging to the Mongol Corporation. As consideration for the assets acquired, Derek issued 20,000 shares of its no-par common stock with a stated value of $10 per share. The value of the assets acquired subsequently turned out to be much less than the $200,000 in stock issued. Under the circumstances, which of the following is correct?
   a. It is improper for the board of directors to acquire assets other than cash with no-par stock.
   b. Only the shareholders can have the right to fix the value of the shares of no-par stock exchanged for assets.
   c. In the absence of fraud in the transaction, the judgment of the board of directors as to the value of the consideration received for the shares shall be conclusive.
   d. Unless the board obtained an independent appraisal of the acquired assets' value, it is liable to the extent of the overvaluation.

20. Donald Walker is a dissident stockholder of the Meaker Corporation which is listed on a national stock exchange. Walker is seeking to oust the existing board of directors and has notified the directors that he intends to sue them for negligence. Under the circumstances, Walker
   a. Can be validly denied access to the corporate financial records.
   b. Can be legally prohibited from obtaining a copy of the stockholder list because his purpose is not bona fide.
   c. Must show personal gain on the part of the directors if he is to win his lawsuit.
   d. Can insist that the corporation mail out his proxy materials as long as he pays the cost.

21. Decanter Corporation declared a 10% stock dividend on its common stock. The dividend
   a. Must be registered with the SEC pursuant to the Securities Act of 1933.
   b. Requires a vote of the shareholders of Decanter.
   c. Has no effect on the earnings and profits for federal income tax purposes.
   d. Is includable in the gross income of the recipient taxpayers in the year of receipt.

22. The stock of Crandall Corporation is regularly traded over the counter. However, 75% is owned by the founding family and a few of the key executive officers. It has had a cash dividend record of paying out annually less than 5% of its earnings and profits over the past 10 years. It has, however, declared a 10% stock dividend during each of these years. Its accumulated earnings and profits are beyond the reasonable current and anticipated needs of the business. Which of the following is correct?
   a. The shareholders can compel the declaration of a dividend only if the directors' dividend policy is fraudulent.
   b. The Internal Revenue Service can **not** attack the accumulation of earnings and profits since the Code exempts publicly held corporations from the accumulations provisions.
   c. The fact that the corporation was paying a 10% stock dividend, apparently in lieu of a cash distribution, is irrelevant insofar as the ability of the Internal Revenue Service to successfully attack the accumulation.
   d. Either the Internal Revenue Service or the shareholders could successfully obtain a court order to compel the distribution of earnings and profits unreasonably accumulated.

23. Delray Corporation has a provision in its corporate charter as follows: "Holders of the noncumulative preferred stock shall be entitled to a fixed annual dividend of 8% before any dividend shall be paid on common stock." There are no further provisions relating to preferences or statements regarding voting rights. The preferred stock apparently
   a. Is noncumulative, but only to the extent that the 8% dividend is not earned in a given year.
   b. Is nonvoting unless dividends are in arrears.
   c. Has a preference on the distribution of the assets of the corporation upon dissolution.
   d. Is not entitled to participate with common stock in dividend distribution beyond 8%.

24. King Corp. and Queen Corp. have decided to merge pursuant to the merger provisions of the Model Business Corporation Act, which is the law of their jurisdiction. The statutory merger

a. Is one type of tax-free reorganization recognized by the Internal Revenue Code.
b. Is subject to clearly defined rules regarding the percentage and types of securities which may be used to consummate the merger.
c. May cut off the rights of creditors of the merged corporation.
d. Requires the approval of the secretary of state or the attorney general at least 90 days prior to consummation of a merger or consolidation.

25. Universal Joint Corporation has approached Minor Enterprises, Inc., about a tax-free statutory merger of Minor into Universal. The stock of both corporations is listed on the NYSE. Which of the following requirements or procedures need **not** be complied with in order to qualify as a statutory merger pursuant to state and federal law?

a. The boards of directors of both corporations must approve the plan of merger.
b. Universal, the surviving corporation, must apply for and obtain a favorable revenue ruling from the Treasury Department.
c. The boards of both corporations must submit the plan of merger to their respective shareholders for approval.
d. The securities issued and exchanged by Universal for the shares of Minor must be registered since they are considered to be "offered" and "sold" for purposes of the Securities Act of 1933.

26. Barton Corporation and Clagg Corporation have decided to combine their separate companies pursuant to the provisions of their state corporation laws. After much discussion and negotiation, they decided that a consolidation was the appropriate procedure to be followed. Which of the following is an incorrect statement with respect to the contemplated statutory consolidation?

a. A statutory consolidation pursuant to state law is recognized by the Internal Revenue Code as a type of tax-free reorganization.
b. The larger of the two corporations will emerge as the surviving corporation.
c. Creditors of Barton and Clagg will have their claims protected despite the consolidation.
d. The shareholders of both Barton and Clagg must approve the plan of consolidation.

27. Under which of the following circumstances would a corporation's existence terminate?

a. The death of its sole owner-shareholder.
b. Its becoming insolvent.
c. Its legal consolidation with another corporation.
d. Its reorganization under the federal bankruptcy laws.

May 1984 Questions

28. Which of the following statements concerning cumulative preferred stock is correct?

a. Upon the dissolution of a corporation the preferred shareholders have priority over unsecured judgment creditors.
b. Preferred stock represents a type of debt security similar to corporate debentures.
c. If dividends are **not** declared for any year, they become debts of the corporation for subsequent years.
d. Upon the declaration of a cash dividend on the preferred stock, preferred shareholders become unsecured creditors of the corporation.

29. Which of the following would be grounds for the judicial dissolution of a corporation on the petition of a shareholder?

a. Refusal of the board of directors to declare a dividend.
b. Waste of corporate assets by the board of directors.
c. Loss operations of the corporation for three years.
d. Failure by the corporation to file its federal income tax returns.

30. Able and Baker are two corporations, the shares of which are publicly traded. Baker plans to merge into Able. Which of the following is a requirement of the merger?

a. The IRS must approve the merger.
b. The common stockholders of Baker must receive common stock of Able.
c. The creditors of Baker must approve the merger.
d. The boards of directors of both Able and Baker must approve the merger.

31. For which of the following reasons would the corporate veil most likely be pierced and the shareholders held personally liable?

a. The corporation is a personal holding company.

b. The corporation was organized because the shareholders wanted to limit their personal liability.
c. The corporation and its shareholders do **not** maintain separate bank accounts and records.
d. The corporation's sole shareholder is another domestic corporation.

32. Which of the following statements concerning treasury stock is correct?
a. Cash dividends paid on treasury stock are transferred to stated capital.
b. A corporation may **not** purchase its own stock unless specifically authorized by its articles of incorporation.
c. A duly appointed trustee may vote treasury stock at a properly called shareholders' meeting.
d. Treasury stock may be resold at a price less than par value.

33. Generally, articles of incorporation must contain all of the following **except** the
a. Names of the incorporators.
b. Name of the corporation.
c. Number of shares authorized.
d. Names of initial officers and their terms of office.

Problems

Problem 1 Dividends; Contracts with Director; Director Fiduciary Responsibility (579,L3)

(25 to 30 minutes)

Part a. The Decimile Corporation is a well-established, conservatively-managed, major company. It has consistently maintained a $3 or more per share dividend since 1940 on its only class of stock, which has a $1 par value. Decimile's board of directors is determined to maintain a $3 per share annual dividend distribution to maintain the corporation's image in the financial community, to reassure its shareholders, and to prevent a decline in the price of the corporation's shares which would occur if there were a reduction in the dividend rate. Decimile's current financial position is not encouraging although the corporation is legally solvent. Its cash flow position is not good and the current year's earnings are only $0.87 per share. Retained earnings amount to $17 per share. Decimile owns a substantial block of Integrated Electronic Services stock which it purchased at $1 per share in 1950 and which has a current value of $6.50 per share. Decimile has paid dividends of $1 per share so far this year and contemplates distributing a sufficient number of shares of Integrated to provide an additional $2 per share.

Required:

Answer the following, setting forth reasons for any conclusions stated.

1. May Decimile legally pay the $2 per share dividend in the stock of Integrated?

2. As an alternative, could Decimile pay the $2 dividend in its own authorized but unissued shares of stock? What would be the **legal** effect of this action upon the corporation?

3. What are the federal income tax consequences to the noncorporate shareholders—

(a) If Decimile distributes the shares of Integrated?

(b) If Decimile distributes its own authorized but unissued stock?

Part b. Clayborn is the president and a director of Marigold Corporation. He currently owns 1,000 shares of Marigold which he purchased several years ago upon joining the company and assuming the presidency. At that time, he received a stock option for 10,000 shares of Marigold at $10 per share. The option is about to expire but Clayborn does not have the money to exercise his option. Credit is very tight at present and most of his assets have already been used to obtain loans. Clayborn spoke to the chairman of Marigold's board about his plight and told the chairman that he is going to borrow $100,000 from Marigold in order to exercise his option. The chairman was responsible for Clayborn's being hired as president of Marigold and is a close personal friend of Clayborn. Fearing that Clayborn will leave unless he is able to obtain a greater financial interest in Marigold, the chairman told Clayborn: "It is okay with me and you have a green light." Clayborn authorized the issuance of a $100,000 check payable to his order. He then negotiated the check to Marigold in payment for the shares of stock.

Required:

Answer the following, setting forth reasons for any conclusions stated.

What are the legal implications, problems, and issues raised by the above circumstances?

Part c. Towne is a prominent financier, the owner of 1% of the shares of Toy, Inc., and one of its directors. He is also the chairman of the board of Unlimited Holdings, Inc., an investment company in which he owns 80% of the stock. Toy needs land upon which to build additional warehouse facilities. Toy's president, Arthur, surveyed the land sites feasible for such a purpose. The best location in Arthur's opinion from all standpoints, including location, availability, access to transportation, and price, is an eight-acre tract of land owned by Unlimited. Neither Arthur nor Towne wish to create any legal problems in connection with the possible purchase of the land.

Required:

Answer the following, setting forth reasons for any conclusions stated.

1. What are the legal parameters within which this transaction may be safely consummated?

2. What are the legal ramifications if there were to be a $50,000 payment "on the side" to Towne in order that he use his efforts to "smooth the way" for the proposed acquisition?

Problem 2 Diversion of Corporate Opportunity; Derivative Lawsuit (1182,L3a)

(5 to 8 minutes)

Part a. William Harrelson is president of the Billings Corporation, a medium-size manufacturer of yogurt. While serving as president, Harrelson learns of an interesting new yogurt product loaded with vitamin additives and with a potentially huge market. He immediately forms another corporation, the Wexler Corporation, to produce and market the new product. In his zeal, however, Harrelson overextends his personal credit and utilized Billings' credit, along with its plant and employees, as needed, to produce the new product. The new product becomes a big success. As a result, Harrelson's Wexler stock is presently worth millions of dollars.

Required:

Answer the following, setting forth reasons for any conclusions stated.

Billings' shareholders contend that Harrelson's actions are improper and seek a remedy against him. Will they succeed and what remedies are available to them?

Problem 3 Proxy Solicitation (1182,L4b)

(8 to 12 minutes)

Part b. Powell Corporation, which owns 5% of the stock of Baron, Inc., approached the board of directors and several of the principal shareholders of Baron to see if they were willing to sell to Powell their effective controlling interest. Baron is listed on the American Stock Exchange and its management either owns or has the unquestioned support of approximately 37% of the shares outstanding. Baron's board and the shareholders who were contacted rejected Powell's overtures. Powell is now considering waging a proxy fight to obtain effective control of Baron.

Required:

Answer the following, setting forth reasons for any conclusions stated.

1. Can Baron lawfully refuse to give Powell access to the list of shareholders?

2. What rights does Powell have under the Securities Exchange Act of 1934 to have its proxy materials distributed to shareholders?

3. What major requirements under the Securities Exchange Act of 1934 must be met by both sides in a proxy fight?

Problem 4 Declaration of Dividends; Treasury Shares; Officers' Salaries; Involuntary Dissolution (583,L4)

(15 to 20 minutes)

Cox is a disgruntled shareholder of Hall, Inc. She has owned 6% of the voting stock for several years. Hall is a corporation with 425 shareholders. However, the members of the Hall family own 65% of the corporate stock, dominate the board, and are the principal officers of the corporation. There is one minority board member. Recently, there have been major changes in Hall's board and its officers as the older generation of the family has relinquished the management in favor of the next generation of Halls. It is the action of this new board and management that has caused Cox to contemplate taking drastic action against the current board and officers. Specifically, she objects to the following:

- The board has drastically cut the dividend payments on the common stock. The board's explanation is that additional funds for expansion or acquisitions are critical for the growth of the corporation. The earnings have been increasing at a rate of 10% per year during this period. Cox claims that the real reason for the dividend cut is to force minority shareholders such as herself to sell. This claim is based on conjecture on her part. Cox is considering an action against the board to compel reinstatement of the prior dividend payout.
- The board also decided to sell 5,000 shares of treasury stock at $10 a share to raise additional capital. The stock in question had originally been sold at $16 a share and had a $12 par value. It was reacquired at $13 per share. Cox first alleges that the corporation is prohibited from acquiring its own shares without specific authorization in the articles of incorporation. The articles of incorporation are silent on this matter. Cox also asserts that the corporation is prohibited from selling the shares at a price less than par.
- Substantial salaries are paid to the officers of the corporation. Salaries of the newcomers have been increased at an annual rate of 10%, which is far in excess of raises voted by the old board. Cox has evidence to show that the corporation's salary scale has risen from the top 50% to the top 33 1/3% of salaries paid by similar corporations in the industry. Cox asserts that based upon the recipients' ages, experience and contribution to the corporation, they are so grossly overpaid that the payments constitute a waste of corporate assets. Cox demands that the salary increases be repaid.
- The board has become factionalized because of hostility within the Hall family. Cox claims that this acrimony has generated useless debate and

bickering and is counterproductive to the continued success of Hall, Inc. The majority has threatened to oust the opposition at the next election of the board. Cox claims that all of these actions are seriously impairing the effective management of the corporation and she is contemplating seeking a court-ordered dissolution of Hall.

Required:

Answer the following, setting forth reasons for any conclusions stated.

Discuss the merits of each of the above claims and indicate the probable outcome of any court action taken by Cox personally or taken by her for **and** on behalf of the corporation.

Multiple Choice Answers

1. a	8. b	15. a	22. c	28. d
2. b	9. a	16. d	23. d	29. b
3. a	10. a	17. d	24. a	30. d
4. b	11. a	18. d	25. b	31. c
5. b	12. a	19. c	26. b	32. d
6. b	13. c	20. d	27. c	33. d
7. c	14. c	21. c		

Multiple Choice Answer Explanations

A. Characteristics and Advantages of Corporate Form

1. (582,L1,8) (a) Since a corporation is ordinarily treated as a legal entity distinct from its shareholders, the rights and obligations of the corporation are normally separated from those of the shareholders. Thus, when liabilities arise, the corporate entity usually shields the shareholders from the obligations of the corporation, and protects the corporation from the obligations of its shareholders. In certain cases, however, this corporate "veil" will be "pierced" to hold the shareholders personally liable for the corporation's obligations. Therefore, when the corporation is so utilized by its shareholders that in reality no separate entity is maintained (e.g., commingling of assets, lack of corporate formalities, etc.) or when the corporation's separate existence is not respected in normal business operations, the court will "pierce the corporate veil" and hold the shareholders personally liable. Answer (b) is incorrect because a parent corporation is entitled to create a subsidiary organization so as to isolate the high risk portion of its business. However, if the subsidiary is inadequately capitalized, or its activities are substantially intermingled with the parent's, or if it exists merely as an instrumentality or business conduit of the parent, then the courts will treat the two entities as one and hold the parent liable for the debts of the subsidiary. Answer (c) is incorrect because the limited liability feature, a distinct advantage of the corporate form, is a viable reason for incorporating one's business. Even where a single individual owns all the stock of the corporation, the shareholder and the corporation continue their separate and distinct existences. Answer (d) is incorrect because a subchapter S corporation is a small business corporation which, under certain conditions, may elect to have its undistributed taxable income taxed to its shareholders and thereby avoid the corporate income tax.

2. (580,L1,12) (b) An *ultra vires* doctrine applies when a corporation enters a contract outside the scope of its express or implied authority granted by its articles of incorporation. Answer (b) is correct because since the state or shareholder has the right to object to an *ultra vires* act, a competitor could not object. A shareholder can institute a derivative action against directors and officers to recover damages for such acts. Answers (a) and (c) are incorrect because when an *ultra vires* contract has been executed on one side, most state courts hold the nonperforming party may not raise the defense of *ultra vires.* Answer (d) is incorrect because when both parties have performed, neither party may sue to rescind an *ultra vires* contract.

C. Types of Corporations

3. (582,L1,11) (a) The expenditures incurred in connection with the incorporation of the business and sale of its shares to the public may be treated as an offset against the proceeds from the stock issuance and are chargeable against the paid-in capital, as long as it does not impair the amount of legal capital. This treatment is based on the premise that issue costs are unrelated to corporate operations and thus are not properly chargeable against earnings from operations; but rather viewed as a reduction of proceeds of the financing activity. Answer (b) is incorrect because goodwill is an intangible asset, which is recorded only when an entire business is purchased. Goodwill is a "going concern" valuation and cannot be separated from a business as a whole. The amount of goodwill is capitalized and amortized over the business' useful life not to exceed a period of 40 years. Answers (c) and (d) are incorrect because expenses of issuing shares of stock, such as commissions, professional fees, printing costs, and listing the stock on the exchange are not to be capitalized and amortized over the life of the corporation, and thus would not be capitalized and amortized under the organizational expenditure provision.

4. (580,L1,14) (b) A corporation "doing business" in a state other than that of incorporation must comply with that state's license requirements. This usually requires filing a certificate of authority. The concept of doing business involves something more than isolated transactions. Answer (a) is incorrect because a corporation is not required to incorporate in a state in which it does business. Answer (c) is incorrect because Destiny is a foreign corporation in any state in which it does business other than that state in which it is incorporated. Answer (d) is incorrect because Destiny needs to comply only with the incorporation laws in its state of incorporation, in this case, Nevada.

5. (1178,L1,22) (b) Professional corporations are only allowed in states which have enacted statutes permitting their incorporation. They are not normally

allowed under the general corporation statutes. Answer (a) is incorrect because such a corporation will be recognized for federal tax purposes even if its goal is to save taxes. Answer (c) is incorrect because the typical statute provides that the professional being incorporated remains personally liable for his professional acts. His liability will only be limited for ordinary business debts of the corporation. Answer (d) is incorrect because most states now permit the creation of professional corporations by doctors and similar professional persons.

D. Formation of Corporation

6. (582,L1,9) (b) A corporation is not liable on pre-incorporation contracts entered into on behalf of the corporation by the promoter unless and until the corporation approves and thereby adopts the contract of the promoter upon coming into corporate existence. However, the promoter is personally bound on these contracts. Even if the corporation adopts the contract, the promoter remains personally liable unless a novation occurs (i.e., third party agrees to look to corporation for satisfaction of the contract). However, if the promoter had clearly specified that he was contracting "in the name of the proposed corporation and not individually," the third party must rely solely on the credit of the proposed corporation and has no claim against the promoter individually. Answer (a) is incorrect because when a corporation fails to come into existence, the preincorporation stock subscribers have no legal right to sue for damages. Answer (c) is incorrect because in the absence of a statute or charter provision, the corporation is not liable for promoter's preincorporation services unless the board of directors approves payment after the corporation comes into existence. Answer (d) is incorrect because the Model Business Corporation Act provides that pre-incorporation stock subscriptions are deemed to be continuing offers which are irrevocable for a period of six months. Therefore, the subscribers are bound by their subscriptions for this six month period.

7. (581,L1,23) (c) Promoters are persons who originate and organize the formation of a corporation. They have a fiduciary duty to act for the corporation and its shareholders. For Bixler to retain the profits made from the sale of property to the corporation, he must make full disclosure to and receive approval from either the board of directors or existing shareholders. Since Bixler did not comply with these procedures, the $45,000 would be considered secret profits and must be returned to the corporation even though the building might have a market value of $200,000. Thus, answers (b) and (d) are incorrect.

Answer (a) is incorrect since the promoter may enter into preincorporation contracts (e.g., employment contracts, options on property) on behalf of the corporation. The corporation is not liable on these contracts until it adopts such agreements or enters a novation (a second agreement whereby corporation replaces the promoter under the same terms as the preincorporation contract). The corporation cannot ratify the agreement since the corporate entity was not in existence when the promoter entered the contract.

E. Corporate Financial Structure

8. (581,L1,24) (b) When a corporation purchases its own stock these shares are classified as treasury shares if not cancelled. Treasury shares are issued but not outstanding; these shares cannot be voted on and do not receive dividends. Answer (a) is incorrect because a corporation is required to purchase treasury stock with capital surplus. Capital surplus consists of earned surplus (retained earnings) and paid-in-surplus (the amount paid for stock over par or stated value). It is illegal for a corporation to buy treasury stock with legal capital (par value of issued stock). Answer (c) is untrue because the corporation would have to comply with SEC requirements when the treasury stock was resold. Answer (d) is incorrect since a corporation never recognizes gains or losses on transactions with its own stock.

9. (581,L1,26) (a) Treasury stock may be disposed of at the discretion of the board of directors through a sale or through the declaration of dividends to shareholders. Answer (b) is incorrect since the original public offering was sufficiently long ago to require the filing of a new registration statement before selling these treasury shares. Answer (c) is incorrect because treasury shares cannot be voted. Answer (d) is incorrect because treasury shares exchanged for the stock of another publicly held corporation are considered to be "offered" and "sold" for the purposes of the Securities Act of 1933. Therefore, a registration statement would have to be filed and approved before the transaction could be completed.

10. (581,L1,27) (a) Both the board of directors and the shareholders of a corporation must approve a fundamental change in the corporate structure. Examples of fundamental corporate changes would be: dissolution of corporation, amendment of corporate charter, increase of capital stock, etc. Larkin would need to amend its corporate charter to increase the number of authorized shares before engaging in the stock split. Answer (b) is incorrect because stock splits are normally exempt from income tax because

the shareholder-recipient maintains the same proportionate interest of ownership. Answer (c) is incorrect because a stock split decreases the par value in proportion to the increase in the number of shares. Therefore, total par value is unchanged. Answer (d) is incorrect because trustees are to include shares received through a stock split or stock dividend in the principal (corpus) of the trust. Cash dividends are considered income when allocating trust items between principal (corpus) and income beneficiaries.

11. (1175,L2,22) (a) Surplus of a corporation means net assets in excess of stated capital. Liquid assets in excess of current needs are net quick assets. Total assets in excess of total liabilities is net assets. Contributed capital is capital paid into the corporation not in the conduct of business, i.e., not earned surplus (retained earnings).

E.3. Marketing of Stock

12. (1183,L1,24) (a) A corporation cannot legally reduce the price of par value stock below the established par value, without amending the articles of incorporation. Since Ambrose purchased original issue stock for less than par value, he can be held liable to the creditors for the $30,000 difference between the par value of the stock and the price he actually paid. Answer (b) is, therefore, incorrect. A transferee of shares, for which full consideration has not been paid, can be held liable to the corporation or its creditors for the unpaid portion of the consideration; unless the transferee took the shares in good faith and without knowledge or notice that full consideration has not been paid. Harris is, therefore, not liable to creditors. Answer (c), however, is incorrect because it states that Harris' lack of knowledge is immaterial. Likewise, answer (d) is incorrect. Gable is liable to the creditors because of his knowledge that full consideration for the shares had not been paid.

13. (580,L1,16) (c) Plimpton has breached his subscription contract with the Billiard Ball Corporation, and is therefore liable for the remainder of the unpaid subscription price. Shares may be purchased for money, services already rendered, and property. Promissory notes are not proper consideration for the purchase of shares. Plimpton is liable to creditors for the balance due on the subscription price. This is true even if Plimpton transfers the shares to an innocent third party. The issuing corporation has a lien on those shares that have not been paid for fully. However, this lien would not be effective against an innocent third party purchaser unless the lien was conspicuously noted on the stock certificate. Plimpton's failure to pay the full purchase price of the shares would not change his limited liability concerning corporate debts.

14. (1178,L1,15) (c) The subscriber, Watson, may not revoke the agreement to purchase stock in the Marvel Corporation for a period of six months in the absence of special circumstances. Under the Model Business Corporation Act, preincorporation stock subscriptions are deemed to be continuing offers which are irrevocable for purposes of administrative convenience for a period of six months. Answer (a) is incorrect because a notice indicating withdrawal, even if written, will not be valid until the expiration of six months. Answer (b) is incorrect because a simple transfer of an agreement does not constitute a novation and thus the assigning party remains liable. Answer (d) is incorrect also because a subscriber can only avoid liability during the six-month period by obtaining the unanimous consent of the other subscribers.

H. Officers and Directors of Corporations

15. (1183,L1,23) (a) Since a majority shareholder is able to exercise substantial control over the corporation, courts have recognized that there is a fiduciary duty owed to minority shareholders. If, for instance, a majority shareholder sells controlling interest in the corporation to a party whom he should know will plunder the company, the duty owed to fellow shareholders has been breached. A director also owes a fiduciary duty to the corporation. Answer (c) is, therefore, incorrect. The duty is not discharged by disclosure alone. The director who has a conflict of interest must refrain from voting on that matter. Thus, answer (b) is incorrect. Answer (d) is incorrect because a promoter owes a fiduciary duty to subscribers, shareholders, and the corporation itself.

16. (582,L1,10) (d) Corporations have the power to properly indemnify their directors or officers for expenses incurred in defending suits against them for conduct undertaken in their official and representative capacity on behalf of the corporation. However, in shareholder derivative suits, normally no indemnification is permitted where the director or officer has been adjudged to be liable for negligence in the performance of his duty to the corporation. However, if the court in which the action or suit was brought determines that, despite the adjudication of liability, the director or officer is fairly and reasonably entitled to indemnification under the circumstances, then indeminification may be permitted regardless of the fact that the articles of incorporation do not provide therefor. Answer (c) is incorrect because under indemnification, Fairwell is

entitled to expenses, judgments, fines, and amounts actually paid and reasonably incurred by him, which include reasonable attorney's fees.

17. (581,L1,28) (d) The compensation of corporate officers is fixed by a resolution of the board of directors. If none is fixed, the law implies that the officer is paid a reasonable sum for his services. Any action by the shareholders serves merely to confirm the board's action concerning the officers' salaries. It is not needed as a matter of law, therefore, answer (c) is incorrect. Answer (a) is incorrect because the directors can confirm the officers' salaries even though not legally needed. Answer (b) is incorrect because the IRS has the power to attack any officer's salary as unreasonable. If the compensation is deemed unreasonable, the IRS treats the excessive amount as a constructive dividend.

18. (576,L2,21) (d) Normally a board of directors may only act at a meeting, and the common-law rule is that a quorum is a majority. But recently the law has developed to allow a board of directors to act more informally, i.e., without a meeting, if there is unanimous consent and if not so precluded by the articles of incorporation or the by-laws. Thus all the directors must consent.

19. (1178,L1,19) (c) The board of directors has the power and duty to determine the value of property received for stock. In the absence of fraud, such judgment shall be conclusive. Answer (a) is incorrect because cash, property, and services performed are all good consideration for both par and no-par stock. Answer (b) is incorrect because, as stated above, it is within the power and duty of the board of directors to fix the value of property received for stock. Shareholders have no right to determine the value of no-par stock. Answer (d) is not as correct because directors are merely required to exercise ordinary care and prudence in the exercise of their duties. They are not liable for honest mistakes in judgment.

I. Stockholders' Rights

20. (1174,L3,36) (d) A stockholder has a common law right to inspect the books of the corporation including the list of stockholders. This right may not be denied unless the stockholder's purpose is hostile to the corporation or the stockholder is attempting to use the corporation's books and records for unwarranted purposes. Stockholders may readily inspect the books in attempt to uncover corporate mismanagement. A dissident stockholder must also be given a list of corporation's shareholders if he is attempting to oust the management and proposes a proxy fight. Federal securities regulation requires that the corporation supply such a list and also mail the dissident's proxy material. The dissident shareholder, however, must pay the cost of the mailing. Regarding Walker's planned negligence suit, it is unnecessary that he prove personal gain on the part of the directors. Directors are liable for damages resulting from lack of reasonable care regardless of personal gain.

I.6. Right to Dividends

21. (1183,L1,25) (c) A stock dividend is not considered an "Ordinary" dividend and is, therefore, not paid out of the corporation's earnings and profits. Answer (a) is incorrect because a stock dividend is an exempt transaction under the Securities Act of 1933. Answer (b) is incorrect because a dividend payment is at the discretion of the board of directors, not the stockholders. Answer (d) is incorrect because a stock dividend is combined with the old stock to compute an adjusted basis and will affect gross income of the recipient tax payer in the year the stock is sold by the shareholder.

22. (581,L1,25) (c) The fact that the corporation was paying a 10% stock dividend instead of a cash distribution would not hinder the IRS from attacking the accumulation of earnings. Answer (a) is incorrect because stockholders can compel the declaration of a dividend when withholding dividends would be a clear abuse of the board of directors' discretion, even when such a dividend policy is not fraudulent. The Code does not exempt publicly held corporations from the accumulation provisions, therefore, answer (b) is incorrect. Answer (d) is incorrect because the IRS cannot compel the corporation to distribute earnings and profits that have unreasonably accumulated. However, the corporation is subject to an additional tax on earnings retained in excess of $150,000 if such retention is unreasonable.

23. (1174,L3,33) (d) For noncumulative preferred stock, if a dividend is not paid, the obligation to pay the dividend ceases even though it is earned, should there be a valid business reason for retention of the earnings. Usually preferred stock has no voting rights, but absent the usual provision in the certificate of incorporation which provides that preferred has no voting rights, preferred stock has the same voting rights as common stock. The preferences given preferred stock must be stated. Therefore, in this situation, the

8% noncumulative preferred has no preference in the distribution of assets nor may it participate in earnings over and above the 8% annual dividend.

K. Substantial Change in Corporate Structure

24. (1183,L1,20) (a) A statutory merger is a "type A" tax-free reorganization under the Internal Revenue Code. Answer (b) is incorrect because under the Model Business Corporations Act there are no specific requirements as to the percentage and types of securities which may be used to accomplish the merger. Under the Act, the merger can be accomplished if a plan of merger is approved by the board of directors and a majority of all shareholders of each of the merging corporations. Answer (c) is incorrect because all liabilities of the merged corporation become liabilities of the surviving corporation. Answer (d) is incorrect because there is no requirement of approval by the secretary of state or the attorney general prior to the merger.

25. (581,L1,21) (b) There is no provision requiring the surviving corporation of a tax-free statutory merger to apply for and obtain a favorable revenue ruling from the Treasury Department. Answers (a) and (c) are incorrect because the board of directors and shareholders of both corporations must approve the merger. Answer (d) is incorrect since only securities issued in conjunction with a court supervised reorganization are exempt from the registration requirements of the Securities Act of 1933. For purposes of the act, the shares exchanged between Union and Universal would be "offered" and "sold."

26. (580,L1,6) (b) A consolidation is the unifying of two or more corporations into one new corporation, extinguishing both existing corporations. Therefore, answer (b) is the correct answer since neither corporation will survive the consolidation. Answer (a) is incorrect because under the Internal Revenue Code reorganizations, including statutory mergers or consolidations, receive nonrecognition treatment for tax purposes. Answer (c) is incorrect because the rights of the creditors of the consolidating corporations are in no way impaired by the consolidation. Before a corporation can engage in a consolidation or merger, shareholder approval must be obtained. Approval by a majority is normally sufficient but some states demand approval by two-thirds of the shareholders.

L. Dissolution

27. (1174,L3,35) (c) One of the attributes of a corporation is its perpetual existence irrespective of the lives of its owners. The death of a corporation's sole shareholder would not result in the termination. Ownership would change to the deceased's heirs. The insolvency or appointment of a receiver does not terminate the existence of a corporation. Reorganization under the federal bankruptcy laws may result in the termination of the corporation, and the creation of a new corporation to conduct the business of the old corporation (this is not always the case). The best answer to this question is (c). In a consolidation with another corporation, both of the consolidating corporations are terminated and a new corporation is formed. By definition, a consolidation cannot occur without the termination of a corporation's existence.

May 1984 Answers

28. (584,L1,5) (d) Upon declaration, a cash dividend on preferred stock becomes a legal debt corporation, and the preferred shareholders become unsecured creditors of the corporation. Answer (a) is incorrect because upon the dissolution of a corporation, the preferred shareholders do not have priority over unsecured creditors. Only after all debts owing to creditors are satisfied will the remaining corporate assets be distributed among the shareholders. Preferred shareholders will have priority over common shareholders. Answer (b) is incorrect because although preferred stock does assume many characteristics of a debt security, preferred stock represents a type of ownership security and is not similar to corporate debentures which are unsecured debt securities with no such ownership rights. Answer (c) is incorrect because any dividends not paid in any year concerning cumulative preferred stock must be made up before any future distributions can be made to common shareholders. These unpaid dividends are not a liability of the corporation until they are declared.

29. (584,L1,6) (b) A judicial dissolution may be brought by a shareholder in the event that there has been a waste of the corporate assets by the board of directors. The following reasons would also constitute proper grounds for judicial dissolution:

- Directors are deadlocked in the management of the corporate affairs.
- Acts of the directors are illegal or oppressive.
- Shareholders are deadlocked and have not been able to elect directors for two consecutive annual meetings.

Answers (a), (c), and (d) are all incorrect because none of them states sufficient grounds for the judicial dissolution of a corporation on the petition of a shareholder.

30. (584,L1,7) (d) The merger of two corporations requires the approval from the boards of directors of both merging corporations. Also, normally a majority of the shareholders of each corporation must approve the merger. Answer (a) is incorrect since the merger of two corporations is not subject to the approval of the IRS. Answer (b) is incorrect because a merger can be accomplished in several different ways besides the issuance of stock to the shareholders of the merged corporation. Answer (c) is incorrect because the approval of the merging corporations' creditors is not required for a valid merger to occur. The merging corporations' creditors merely become creditors of the existing corporation upon completion of the merger.

31. (584,L1,8) (c) The court will disregard the corporate entity and hold the shareholders individually liable when the corporate form is used to perpetrate a fraud or is found to be merely an agent or instrument of its owners. An example of when the corporate veil is likely to be pierced is if the corporation and its shareholders commingle assets and financial records. In such a situation the shareholders lose their limited liability and will be personally liable for the corporation's obligations. Answer (a) is incorrect because personal holding companies are allowed to exist as corporate entities separate from the shareholders so long as the intention in forming the corporation was not to perpetrate a fraud and the assets and records of the corporation and its shareholders are maintained separately. Answer (b) is incorrect because the desire of shareholders to limit their personal liability is a valid reason to form a corporation. Limited personal liability is one advantage of the corporate entity. Answer (d) is incorrect because corporations are allowed to own 100% of another corporation as long as the owned corporation is not merely used as an instrumentality of the parent corporation.

32. (584,L1,9) (d) Treasury stock may be resold at a price less than par value. Answer (a) is incorrect because cash dividends are not paid on treasury stock. Answer (b) is incorrect because a corporation need not have specific authorization from its articles of incorporation to purchase its own stock; all corporations have the inherent authority to do so if not denied such right by state law. Answer (c) is incorrect because treasury stock cannot be voted.

33. (584,L1,10) (d) The articles of incorporation are not required to contain the names of initial officers and their terms of office. This is true because the initial officers are not elected until the first board of directors' meeting which cannot be held until after the articles of incorporation have been filed. Answers (a), (b), and (c) are all incorrect since the articles of incorporation must contain each of these items.

Answer Outline

Problem 1 Dividends; Contracts with Director; Director Fiduciary Responsibility

a1. Yes, property dividends may be paid by corporations
   With investments in stock of other companies
   Issuing company must be solvent
   Limited to unrestricted retained earnings (earned surplus)
      Decimile has retained eranings of $17/share

a2. Yes, stock dividends may be paid by corporations
   The dividends must be charged to unrestricted retained earnings
      At not less than par value
   With the amount to be credited to stated capital

a3(a) Issuance of stock of another company is a property dividend
   Recipients must report FMV as dividend income
   Dividend income is ordinary income
      Subject to $100 dividend exclusion
   Recipient's basis in property dividend is FMV when received

a3(b) If Decimile Corporation issues its own stock as dividend
   It is a non-taxable transaction
   Recipients must reallocate original cost to total shares owned after distribution

b. Loans by corporations must be for benefit of corporation
   If for corporate benefit, board of directors may approve
   Otherwise, stockholder approval is required
   Here, loan is for corporate benefit
      But chairman lacked authority and may be personally liable
      Board of directors should ratify, or recall loan

c1. To avoid contracts with interested directors being void or voidable
   The relationship of interested directors is disclosed to those approving the contracts or
   Approval by board of directors without counting votes of interested directors, or
      Interested directors may be counted to establish quorum
   Shareholders, knowing of director interest, approve the contract, or
   The transaction must be fair and reasonable to corporation

c2. Side payments to corporate directors violate fiduciary duty
   And probably constitutes a criminal act
   Towne must return money to Toy
   Toy Corporation could treat transaction as voidable

Unofficial Answer

Problem 1 Dividends; Contract with Director; Director Fiduciary Responsibility

Part a.

1. Yes. The Model Business Corporation Act authorizes the declaration and payment of dividends in cash, property, or the shares of the corporation as long as the corporation is not insolvent and would not be rendered insolvent by the dividend payment. The act limits the payment of dividends in cash or property to the unreserved and unrestricted earned surplus of the corporation. Decimile meets this requirement since it has retained earnings of $17 per share. Thus, payment of the dividend in the shares of Integrated is permitted.

2. Yes. The Model Business Corporation Act permits dividends to be declared and paid in the shares of the corporation. However, where the dividend is paid in its authorized but unissued shares, the payment must be out of unreserved and unrestricted surplus. Furthermore, when the shares paid as a dividend have a par value, they must be issued at not less than par value. Concurrent with the dividend payment, an amount of surplus equal to the aggregate par value of the shares issued as a dividend must be transferred to stated capital.

3. (a) If the shares of Integrated stock are paid as a dividend to the noncorporate shareholders, the shareholders must include the fair market value of the Integrated shares as dividend income received. Such income is ordinary income subject to a $100 dividend exclusion. The recipient taxpayer will have as a tax basis for the Integrated shares an amount equal to the fair market value of the stock received.

(b) If the shares of Decimile stock are paid as a dividend, the recipient taxpayer is not subject to tax upon receipt of the shares. Internal Revenue Code Section 305 provides that such stock dividends are not taxable. However, the recipient must allocate his basis (typically his cost) for the shares he originally owned to the total number he owned after the distribution.

Part b.
The Model Business Corporation Act specifically deals with loans to employees and directors. If the loan is not for the benefit of the corporation, then such a loan must be authorized by the shareholders. However, the board of directors may authorize loans to employees when and if the board decides that such loan or assistance may benefit the corporation. It would appear that the loan was made for the benefit of the corporation so the latter rule applies. However, the chairman's individual authorization clearly does not meet these statutory requirements and could subject him to personal liability. Therefore, a meeting of the board should be called to consider the ratification or recall of the loan.

Part c.
1. The Model Business Corporation Act allows such transactions between a corporation and one or more of its directors or another corporation in which the director has a financial interest. The transaction is neither void nor voidable even though the director is present at the board meeting which authorized the transaction or because his vote is counted for such purpose if—

- The fact of such relationship or interest is disclosed or known to the board of directors or committee that authorizes, approves, or ratifies the contract or transaction by a vote or consent sufficient for the purpose without counting the votes or consents of such interested directors; or
- The fact of such relationship or interest is disclosed or known to the shareholders entitled to vote and they authorize, approve, or ratify such contract or transaction by vote or written consent; or
- The contract or transaction is fair and reasonable to the corporation. Common or interested directors may be counted in determining the presence of a quorum at a meeting of the board of directors or a committee thereof that authorizes, approves, or ratifies such contract or transaction.

2. A $50,000 payment to Towne would be a violation of his fiduciary duty to the corporation. In addition, it might be illegal depending upon the criminal law of the jurisdiction. In any case he would be obligated to return the amount to the corporation. Furthermore, the payment would constitute grounds for permitting Toy to treat the transaction as voidable.

Answer Outline

Problem 2 Diversion of Corporate Opportunity; Derivative Lawsuit

Part a.

Yes. Billings' shareholders will succeed
Harrelson occupies a fiduciary relationship with corporation
  Must exercise good faith and act in behalf of corporation
Officer must first offer corporate opportunity to corporation
  Corporate opportunity present when
    Officer becomes aware of opportunity in his corporate capacity
    Opportunity relates to the corporation's business
    Opportunity developed with corporate capital, facilities, or personnel
  Yogurt product was corporate opportunity
    Harrelson should have offered to Billings
      Harrelson violated fiduciary duty owed corporation
Billings' shareholders could initiate derivative law suit against Harrelson
Court could hold the Wexler stock in constructive trust for Billings Corporation

Unofficial Answer

(Author Modified)

Problem 2 Diversion of Corporate Opportunity; Derivative Lawsuit

Part a.

Yes, Billings' shareholders will succeed. Harrelson, as president, occupies a fiduciary relationship with the corporation and its shareholders. Harrelson, as a fiduciary, must act in good faith and for the best interest of the corporation. An officer must first offer a corporate opportunity to the corporation before taking advantage of such opportunity for personal gain. A corporate opportunity is present when:

1. An officer becomes aware of the opportunity in his/her corporate capacity, or
2. The corporation customarily deals in such an opportunity, or
3. It is developed with corporate capital, facilities, or personnel.

The new yogurt product was obviously a corporate opportunity that Harrelson should have offered to Billings before taking advantage of it. Consequently, Billings' shareholders could initiate a derivative lawsuit in the name of Billings Corporation against Harrelson. The court would impose a constructive trust on Harrelson's Wexler stock in favor of Billings Corporation.

Answer Outline

Problem 3 Proxy Solicitation

Part b.

1. No. Baron cannot lawfully refuse to give Powell access to shareholders list
   - A shareholder has right to inspect records for any legitimate purpose
     - Obtaining stocklist in order to wage proxy fight is legitimate purpose
2. Powell has right to have Baron distribute the proxy materials
   - 1934 Act requires management to send out insurgent's proxy materials to shareholders
     - Insurgent must bear expenses
3. Proxies solicited through interstate commerce must comply with proxy solicitation provisions contained in 1934 Act
   - Proxy materials must set forth complete information
   - Proxy materials must include names and interests of all participants
     - If proxy contest involves control of management
   - Proxy materials must be filed with and approved by SEC before distribution

Unofficial Answer
(Author Modified)

Problem 3 Proxy Solicitation

Part b.

1. No, Baron cannot lawfully refuse to give Powell access to the list of shareholders. Under the Model Business Corporations Act, any person who has owned stock for at least six months immediately preceeding the demand or owns at least 5% of the outstanding shares of the corporation, upon written demand has a right to examine for any proper purpose the corporate books ,including the record of shareholders. Obtaining a list of shareholders in order to wage a proxy fight for control of the corporation is a legitimate purpose for inspecting the corporate books. Under the Model Act, Baron will be liable to Powell for 10% of the value of shares owned by Powell, if Powell is wrongfully denied access to the books.

2. Since Baron's shares fall within the provisions of the Security Exchange Act of 1934, Baron must send out Powell's proxy materials. The 1934 Act requires the management of a corporation to mail the proxy materials of the insurgents to the shareholders if the insurgents so request and pay the expenses incurred.

3. Since Baron's shares are traded on a national stock exchange, these securities must be registered under the Securities Exchange Act of 1934. All proxies solicited through interstate commerce from the holders of securities registered under the 1934 Act must comply with the proxy solicitation provisions contained in this Act. The 1934 Act requires proxy materials to set forth complete information on the matters at issue. If the proxy contest involves the control of management, the proxy materials must include names and the interest of all participants and a complete corporate financial report. These materials must be filed with and approved by the SEC before issuance to insure compliance with the above mentioned disclosure requirements.

Answer Outline

Problem 4 Declaration of Dividends; Treasury Shares; Officers' Salaries; Involuntary Dissolution

- Action to compel reinstatement of prior dividend pay-out would fail because
  - Declaration of dividends within discretion of Board of Directors (B of D)
    - In this case, Cox's only alternative would be to prove fraudulent purpose of B of D
- Action to rescind acquisition and enjoin subsequent sale of common stock would fail because
  - Corporation has right to acquire its shares with unreserved and unrestricted RE
  - Capital surplus may be used only if
    - Articles of incorporation so provide, or
    - Approved by majority of shareholders
  - TS may be sold at $<$ par
    - Requirement that shares sell $\geq$ par applies only to new issues
- Action to demand repayment of salary increases would fail because
  - B of D possesses broad discretionary power to set salaries of officers
    - Even if officers also members of B of D
    - Salary determination supported by courts unless amounts grossly unreasonable

Action for dissolution of Hall, Inc. would fail
- Courts will grant involuntary dissolution when management deadlocked and corporation suffering irreparable injury
  - However, Hall's earnings continue to increase at 10% per year making it viable economic entity

Unofficial Answer

Problem 4 Declaration of Dividends; Treasury Shares; Officers' Salaries; Involuntary Dissolution

The action to compel reinstatement of prior dividends would fail. The declaration of dividends is a matter within the discretion of the board of directors. There are very few instances in which the board's discretion will be disturbed and the facts of this problem are not within any of them unless Cox can prove the fraudulent purpose of the board which she asserts.

The predominant rule gives a corporation the right to acquire its own shares. Such purchases may be made only to the extent of unreserved and unrestricted earned surplus. Capital surplus may be used only if the articles of incorporation so provide or if there is an affirmative majority vote by shareholders. The law and the facts indicate that in all probability there was no problem from the standpoint of the proper source of funds. With respect to the sale below par value there is no requirement of selling treasury shares at par value. The corporation laws require only that newly issued shares be sold at or above par value.

Cox's action to demand repayment of the salary increases would fail. The board of directors has broad discretionary power to fix salaries of officers, even if the officers also are members of the board. The courts have supported the board's determination of salary unless the amounts are grossly unreasonable. A 10% per annum raise and the fact that the salaries are within the upper one-third of those paid by other similar corporations do not bespeak of salaries which would likely be found unreasonable and therefore a waste of corporate assets.

Cox's action for dissolution would fail. The courts have power to dissolve a corporation in an action by a shareholder when the directors are deadlocked in the management of the corporate affairs and the shareholders are unable to break the deadlock. To obtain a court-ordered dissolution Cox must also prove that irreparable injury to the corporation is being suffered or is threatened. None of these facts are present. The fact that there is bitterness and animosity does not constitute a deadlock of the management. The corporation is continuing to increase its earnings at a 10% per annum rate. Courts are loath to grant an order for an involuntary dissolution even if there is a serious deadlock provided the corporation continues to be a viable economic entity.

Multiple Choice Questions (1 - 28)

1. Loop Corp. has made a major breakthrough in the development of a micropencil. Loop has patented the product and is seeking to maximize the profit potential. In this effort, Loop can legally

a. Require its retailers to sell only Loop's products, including the micropencils, and **not** sell similar competing products.

b. Require its retailers to take stipulated quantities of its other products in addition to the micropencils.

c. Sell the product at whatever price the traffic will bear even though Loop has a monopoly.

d. Sell the product to its retailers upon condition that they do **not** sell the micropencils to the public for less than a stated price.

2. Jackson Corporation is engaging in a widespread price fixing arrangement with several of its leading competitors. Which of the following is correct?

a. Only the federal government can obtain injunctive relief.

b. The agreement will **not** be found to be illegal if the parties can show they are merely meeting competition.

c. If one of the parties to the price fixing arrangement sues Jackson for treble damages for certain breaches of the agreement, relief will be denied.

d. The officers of Jackson can **not** be prosecuted and found guilty of violating the antitrust law as long as they are acting solely for and on behalf of the corporation.

3. The four largest manufacturers in their industry have had a combined share of the market in excess of 80% each year for several years. As members of a trade association, certain officers of these corporations meet periodically to discuss various topics of mutual interest. Matters discussed include engineering design, production methods, product costs, market shares, merchandising policy, and inventory levels. Open discussion of pricing is scrupulously avoided. However, the representatives usually see each other after the association meetings and pricing is frequently discussed. These representatives have maintained prices in accordance with an informal oral agreement terminable at will by any company wishing to withdraw. They have never reduced their agreement to a written document or memorandum. The four corporations compete with each other in interstate commerce. Which of the following applies?

a. The members of the trade association may validly appoint the trade association as their representative to set minimum prices.

b. If the trade association suggested it, the distributors of the four corporations may legally enter an agreement among themselves to follow the industry leader's pricing policy.

c. The trade association could legally allocate marketing areas among its members.

d. The four corporations have illegally entered into a price maintenance agreement among themselves.

4. Grubar is a troublesome appliance price-cutter. The other retail appliance dealers dislike Grubar's price cutting and he is equally unpopular with the appliance manufacturers. Grubar's appliance sales constitute less than .001% of the market. The marketplace has an abundance of retailers, and competition is vigorous. The manufacturers and the retailers jointly decided to boycott Grubar, thereby significantly limiting the availability of appliances to him, and thus hoping to drive him out of business. Grubar has commenced legal action against the various parties based upon a violation of the Sherman Act. He is seeking injunctive relief and damages. Under the circumstances

a. Grubar is entitled to the relief requested since the facts indicate a per se violation.

b. Grubar's complaint should be dismissed since it alleges only a private wrong as contrasted with a public wrong.

c. Grubar is entitled to the relief requested against the interstate commerce manufacturers, but not the intrastate retailers.

d. Grubar is **not** entitled to injunctive relief since only the Department of Justice is entitled to obtain such relief.

5. Jay Manufacturing Company sells high quality, high-priced lawn mowers to retailers throughout the United States. Jay unilaterally announced suggested retail prices in its advertisements. Jay also informed retailers that its products would not be sold to them if the retailers used them as "loss leaders" or "come-ons." There was no requirement that any retailer agree to sell at the suggested prices or refrain from selling at whatever price they wished. Monroe Sales, Inc., a large home supply discounter, persistently engaged in loss-leader selling of the Jay mower. Jay has terminated sales to Monroe and declined to do any further business with

it. Monroe claims that Jay has violated the antitrust laws. Under the circumstances, which is a correct statement?

a. The arrangement in question is an illegal joint boycott.
b. The arrangement in question amounts to price-fixing and is illegal per se.
c. The mere unilateral refusal to deal with Monroe is not illegal under antitrust laws.
d. Even if it were found that in fact the overwhelming preponderance of retailers had willingly agreed to follow the suggested prices, Jay would not have violated antitrust laws.

6. Certain members of the Tri-State Railway Construction Association decided that something must be done about the disastrous competition, which, when coupled with the depressed status of the industry and economy, was causing financial chaos for many of its members. They met privately after one of the association meetings and decided to allocate construction projects among themselves based upon an historical share of the market. Under the arrangement, a certain designated company would submit the low bid, thereby ensuring that the company would obtain the job. Such an arrangement is

a. Illegal per se, and a criminal violation of the antitrust law.
b. Illegal under the rule of reason, but **not** a criminal violation of the antitrust law.
c. Legally justifiable due to the economic conditions in the marketplace.
d. Legal under antitrust law since it does **not** fix prices.

7. Sunrise Company has a distribution system comprised of distributors and retailers. Each distributor has a defined geographic area in which it has the exclusive right to sell to retailers and to which sales are restricted. Franchised retailers are authorized to sell Sunrise's products only within specified locations. Both distributors and retailers are forbidden to sell to nonfranchised retailers. Under present law this marketing arrangement will be

a. Judged under the rule of reason, whether or not title passes.
b. Illegal *per se* if title passes to the distributor or retailer, but judged under the rule of reason if title does **not** pass (as under an agency or consignment).
c. Illegal *per se*, whether or not title passes.
d. Illegal *per se* if title does **not** pass, but judged under the rule of reason if title passes.

8. Darby Corporation manufactures a patented and trademarked, high quality, expensive product. It has discovered that certain disreputable discount stores have been using it as a loss leader. Darby has commenced a rigorous enforcement of its suggested minimum resale price in order to protect its product. Under the circumstances, Darby is

a. Guilty of price discrimination.
b. Guilty of per se illegal price fixing.
c. Not guilty of any violation of the antitrust laws since retail price maintenance is legal.
d. Not guilty since Darby may validly set a minimum price beneath which a patented product may not be sold.

9. The Marvel Tire Company entered into agreements with its retailers whereby they agreed not to sell Marvel tires beneath the minimum prices determined by Marvel. In exchange for this agreement, Marvel promised not to sell tires at retail in the retailers' respective territories. The agreement did not preclude the retailers from selling competing brands of tires. The agreement is

a. An exception to the price fixing provision of the Sherman Act because Marvel has given up the right to sell in the various territories.
b. Illegal even though the minimum prices are reasonable.
c. Legal since the retailers are permitted to sell the competing brands at any price they choose.
d. Legal if the tires are sold under Marvel's exclusive trademark.

10. The United States Department of Justice has alleged that Variable Resources, Inc., the largest manufacturer and seller of variable speed drive motors, is a monopolist. It is seeking an injunction ordering divestiture by Variable of a significant portion of its manufacturing facilities. Variable denies it has monopolized the variable speed drive motor market. Which of the following statements is correct insofar as the government's action against Variable is concerned?

a. The government must prove that Variable is the sole source of a significant portion of the market.
b. In order to establish monopolization, the government must prove that Variable has at least 75% of the market.

c. If Variable has the power to control prices or exclude competition, it has monopoly power.

d. As long as Variable has not been a party to a contract, combination, or conspiracy in restraint of trade, it can not be found to be guilty of monopolization.

11. Wanton Corporation, its president, and several other officers of the corporation are found guilty of conspiring with its major competitor to fix prices. Which of the following sanctions would not be applicable under federal antitrust laws?

a. Suspension of corporate right to engage in interstate commerce for not more than one year.

b. Treble damages.

c. Seizure of Wanton's property illegally shipped in interstate commerce.

d. Fines against Wanton and fines and imprisonment of its president and officers.

12. Global Reproductions, Inc., makes and sells high quality, expensive lithographs of the works of famous artists. It sells to art wholesalers throughout the United States. It requires that its wholesalers not purchase lithographs of competing companies during the three-year duration of the contract. They may sell all other types of pictures, including oil, watercolor and charcoal. The Federal Trade Commission has attacked the legality of this exclusive dealing arrangement. This exclusive dealing arrangement

a. Is legal *per se* since its duration is less than five years.

b. Could be found to be illegal under the Sherman, Clayton, and Federal Trade Commission Acts.

c. Will be tested under the rule of reason, and only if found to be unreasonable, will be declared illegal.

d. Is legal since the wholesalers are permitted to sell all other types of pictures.

13. You were the auditor examining the financial statements of Mason Corporation and noted an extraordinary increase in the sales of certain items. Further inquiry revealed that Mason sold various interrelated products which it manufactured. One of the items was manufactured almost exclusively by them. This unique product was in great demand and was sold throughout the United States. Mason realized the importance of the product to its purchasers and decided to capitalize on the situation by requiring all purchasers to take at least two of its other products if they wished to obtain the item over which it had almost complete market control. At the spring sales meeting the president of Mason informed the entire sales force that they were to henceforth sell only to those customers who agreed to take the additional products. He indicated that this was a great opportunity to substantially increase sales of other items. Under the circumstances, which of the following best describes the situation?

a. The plan is both ingenious and legal and should have been resorted to long ago.

b. The arrangement is an illegal tying agreement; hence per se illegal.

c. Since Mason did not have complete market control over the unique product in question, the arrangement is legal.

d. As long as the other products which must be taken are sold at a fair price to the buyers, the arrangement is legal.

14. Over a six-year period, Yeats Corporation acquired 46% of the outstanding stock of Glick, Inc. More than 40% of the shares so acquired were purchased from Glick's past and present directors. Both Glick and Yeats have capital, surplus, and undivided profits aggregating more than $1,000,000. Yeat's current directors owned stock in both corporations and were on the board of directors of each. Yeats utilized his ownership control to elect the remaining members of the board of directors and its own slate of officers for Glick. Glick and Yeats are manufacturers of goods which are in competition with each other throughout the United States. Since Yeats acquired control of Glick, Yeats' percentage share of the nationwide market has remained relatively stable. However, Yeats and Glick each by agreement have ceased marketing in certain geographical territories where it is more advantageous for the other to sell. Which of the following statements applies to the above situation?

a. There is nothing in the facts as revealed above which would constitute a violation of the federal antitrust laws.

b. The interlocking directorate is not illegal because less than 50% of the Glick stock is owned by Yeats.

c. The interlocking directorate is a clear violation of the federal antitrust laws.

d. There is no current violation of the federal antitrust law because there has been no marked improvement in the competitive position of Yeats or Glick.

15. In a pure conglomerate merger
- a. The government must establish an actual restraint on competition in the marketplace in order to prevent the merger.
- b. The acquiring corporation **neither** competes with **nor** sells to or buys from the acquired corporation.
- c. The merger is prima facie valid unless the government can prove the acquiring corporation had an intent to monopolize.
- d. Some form of additional anticompetitive behavior must be established (e.g., price fixing) in order to provide the basis for the government's obtaining of injunctive relief.

16. Section 7 of the Clayton Act is the primary statutory provision used by the Department of Justice in controlling anticompetitive mergers and acquisitions. In general, the Clayton Act is invoked because
- a. It provides for harsher criminal penalties than does the Sherman Act.
- b. It enables the Department of Justice to proscribe mergers and acquisitions in their incipiency.
- c. It provides for exclusive jurisdiction over such activities.
- d. The Sherman Act applies to asset mergers or acquisitions only and **not** to stock mergers or acquisitions.

17. City Utility Company and Suburban Electric Company merged with the permission of the Federal Power Commission. The Department of Justice was apprised of the proposed merger from the beginning. Two years after the consummation of the merger the Department of Justice commenced an action under Section 7 of the Clayton Act and Section 1 of the Sherman Act seeking divestiture. Which of the following is correct?
- a. Public utilities are exempt from the antitrust laws.
- b. The fact that the Department of Justice was aware of the proposed merger and did nothing precludes it from obtaining an injunction at this late date.
- c. A merger can **not** be illegal under both the Sherman and Clayton Acts.
- d. Injunctive relief ordering divestiture is a proper form of relief for the Department of Justice to seek.

18. Gould Machinery builds bulldozers. Prior to 1981, it sold on credit a substantial amount of equipment to Mace Contractors. Mace went into bankruptcy in 1981. In order to protect its investment, Gould took over the business of Mace. Erhart Contractors now complains that the acquisition harms its business, on the ground that its business would have improved had not Gould entered the market as a competitor. Erhart can
- a. Not recover damages under the antitrust laws.
- b. Recover treble damages.
- c. Recover only its actual damages.
- d. Obtain injunctive relief ordering divestiture.

19. The United States Justice Department has promulgated the Merger Guidelines in order to inform the public of its views on the factors and considerations to be taken into account in ascertaining whether a merger is potentially illegal. The Merger Guidelines are
- a. Strongly influenced by the factor of size, stated in percentage shares of the market of the parties to the proposed merger.
- b. Based exclusively upon the decisions of the Supreme Court of the United States.
- c. Binding on all parties affected by them subsequent to the date of their promulgation.
- d. Not of great importance, since they are too indefinite and uncertain to have any meaning in respect to an actual merger.

20. The following facts arose during the examination of the financial statements of Western Manufacturing, Inc. Western, a large manufacturer of industrial products, is attempting to acquire a controlling block of shares of Davis, Inc., a competing manufacturer. Davis' market share is about 40% in the section of the United States in which Western and Davis compete. Western's share of this market is about 35%. Four other firms compete for the remaining 25%. Western's share of the national market is 20% and Davis' share is 8%. In the event that the Justice Department seeks to prevent the above acquisition, which of the following is the most likely result?
- a. The court would grant an injunction prohibiting the acquisition in question.
- b. The court would dismiss the Justice Department's action in that relative shares of the two corporations are less than 30% if the entire United States is taken as the geographic market.
- c. The court would permit the acquisition and agree to review the case after a year's experience under the merger to determine its actual effect upon competition.

d. The court would dismiss the Justice Department's action if Western could show that the acquisition would result in significant business efficiencies.

21. If a defendant is charged with an unfair method of competition under the Federal Trade Commission Act

a. The FTC may prevail despite the fact that the conduct alleged to be illegal did **not** violate either the Sherman or Clayton Act.
b. Criminal sanctions can generally be imposed against a defendant even though the defendant has **not** violated an FTC order to cease and desist.
c. There can be **no** violation of the Act unless one or more of the specifically enumerated unfair methods of competition are established.
d. The complaint must be based upon the purchase or sale of goods, wares, or commodities in interstate commerce.

22. Pratt Company manufactures and sells distinctive clocks. Its best selling item is a reproduction of a rare antique grandfather clock. Taylor Co. purchased 100 of the clocks from Pratt at $99 each. Much to Taylor's chagrin it discovered that Stewart, one of its competitors, had purchased the same clock from Pratt at $94 per clock. Taylor has complained and threatened legal action. In the event the issue is litigated

a. Taylor has a presumption in its favor that it has been harmed by price discrimination.
b. Pratt will prevail if it can show it did **not** intend to harm Taylor.
c. Pratt will prevail if it can show that it sold the clocks at the lower price to all customers such as Stewart who had been doing business with it continuously for ten years or more.
d. Pratt will prevail if it can establish that there were several other clock companies with which Taylor could deal if Taylor were dissatisfied.

23. Robinson's pricing policies have come under attack by several of its retailers. In fact, one of those retailers, Patman, has instigated legal action against Robinson alleging that Robinson charges other favored retailers prices for its products which are lower than those charged to it. Patman's legal action against Robinson

a. Will fail unless Patman can show that there has been an injury to competition.
b. Will be sufficient if the complaint alleges that Robinson charged different prices to different customers and there is a reasonable possibility that competition may be adversely affected.
c. Is groundless since one has the legal right to sell at whatever price one wishes as long as the price is determined unilaterally.
d. Is to be tested under the rule of reason and if the different prices charged are found to be reasonable, the complaint will be dismissed.

24. Super Sports, Inc., sells branded sporting goods and equipment throughout the United States. It sells to wholesalers, jobbers, and retailers who in turn resell the goods to their respective customers. The wholesalers and jobbers, who do not sell at retail, are charged lower prices than retailers, but are required to purchase in larger quantities than retailers with the cost savings inherent in such purchases accounting for the lower prices. The retailers are all charged the same prices but receive discounts for quantity purchases based exclusively upon the cost savings resulting from such quantity purchases. Girard, one of Super's retail customers, has demanded discounts comparable to those available to the wholesalers and jobbers in its vicinity. Super has refused to acquiesce in this demand. Therefore, Girard sues Super alleging an illegal price discrimination in violation of the Robinson-Patman Act. Which defense by Super listed below will be most likely to prevail?

a. Girard does not have the right to sue under the Robinson-Patman Act.
b. The discounts are functional, that is, Super's wholesalers and jobbers do not compete with retailers such as Girard.
c. Super does not have the requisite intent to discriminate among its purchasers.
d. The prices Super charges are reasonable, and its profit margins are low.

25. Able Corporation was charged with a violation of the Federal Trade Commission Act. Harp, a FTC examiner, concluded that Able had violated the Act and made adverse determinations on several issues. Able believes Harp has been not only arbitrary in several of the determinations, but also clearly incorrect in others. Harp has reached his decision and submitted his opinion. Able has decided not to accept the determinations in the opinion. Assuming Able's allegations are correct, Able

a. Must accept the determination unless it was denied due process.

b. Should immediately proceed in the local state court to obtain injunctive relief ordering Harp to reopen the case and redetermine his conclusions.
c. Should appeal immediately to the local federal district court to overturn the determination.
d. Must exhaust the available administrative remedies before relief in court can be sought.

26. In general, federal administrative agencies may exercise
a. Judicial power only.
b. Executive power only.
c. Both judicial and executive power, but **not** legislative power.
d. Executive, judicial, and legislative power.

May 1984 Questions

27. In general, the Truth in Lending provisions of the Consumer Credit Protection Act apply to lenders who are in the business of extending credit and imposing a finance charge where the transaction involves
a. Any real estate purchases secured by a mortgage.
b. Credit obtained primarily for personal or family purposes.
c. Credit obtained to finance the leasing of property for use in business.
d. Installment purchases of property irrespective of the purchase price.

28. As part of the administrative law process, which of the following is a major function of judicial review?
a. Providing political oversight, control, and in general shaping and influencing entire regulatory programs and their basic policies.
b. Assuring that the agency is acting in accordance with the enabling legislation.
c. Correcting the deficiencies contained in the relevant legislation.
d. Providing a re-examination of the findings of fact contained in the agency determinations.

Problems

Problem 1 Price Fixing and Discrimination (577,L6b&c)

(15 to 20 minutes)

Part b. The CPA firm of Christopher and Diana was engaged to audit the books of Starr Antenna Company. An examination of Starr's files revealed the threat of a lawsuit by Charles Grimm, the owner of Grimm's TV Sales and Service Company. An analysis of the pertinent facts revealed the following.

Grimm's complaint arose because Grimm could not obtain the quantity of television antennas ordered from Starr. The three other antenna manufacturers, who supplied the tri-state area in which Starr did business, would not sell antennas to Grimm. Grimm knows that several other retailers are encountering similar problems with Starr and the three major competitors. Diana, the partner in charge of the audit, found this to be a strange situation and talked with Baxter, Starr's Vice President of Marketing. Baxter explained that about a year ago there had been a period of "cutthroat" competition among the four major antenna manufacturers involved. In order to avoid a repetition of this disastrous situation, they had entered into an unwritten gentlemen's agreement to "limit output per manufacturer to the amount produced in the year immediately preceding that in which the cutthroat competition had occurred." They also agreed that each manufacturer would not sell to the acknowledged customers of the others. Baxter said there was still plenty of competition for new customers in the tri-state area and that they were contemplating raising the production limitation by 25%. He said that "this arrangement had made life a lot easier and profitable for all concerned." He also indicated that the prices charged were "reasonable" to the purchasers.

Required:

Answer the following, setting forth reasons for any conclusions stated.

What are the legal problems and implications of the above facts?

Part c. The General Pen Company is one of the largest manufacturers of fountain pens and does business in every state in the United States. General developed a new line of prestige pens called the "Diamond Line" which it sold at a very high price. In order to uphold its prestige and quality appeal, General decided to maintain a high resale price. Consequently, it obtained agreements from department stores, jewelers, and other outlets not to sell the pen below the $15 suggested retail price. The Double Discount Department Store refused to sign the agreement and used the pen as a sales gimmick to attract customers. Double advertised and sold Diamond Line pens for $12, to which General objected. Double threatened General with a treble damage action for price-fixing if it did not withdraw its objections.

Required:

Answer the following, setting forth reasons for any conclusions stated.

What are the legal problems and implications of the above facts?

Problem 2 Vertical Territorial Limitation (1182,L4a)

(7 to 10 minutes)

Part a. Spencer, Inc., manufactures quality stereo systems and parts. It markets these items through franchised dealers who purchase the goods, take title to them, and are granted the exclusive right to sell the product in clearly defined geographic areas. The dealers in turn are obligated not to sell in any other geographic area. The following is typical of such a territorial clause:

> Dealer is hereby granted the exclusive right as hereinafter described to sell, during the term of this agreement, in the territory described below, Spencer products purchased from the company hereunder.
>
> *(Assume geographic description of territory paragraph is included.)*
>
> Dealer agrees to develop the aforementioned territory to the satisfaction of Spencer.
>
> Dealer further agrees not to sell, nor to permit, nor to authorize any other party to sell, Spencer products in any other franchised territory.

The franchised dealers are not obligated to sell only Spencer's products, but are free to handle competing lines if they wish to do so.

Blaine Hi-Fi, Inc., applied for a franchised dealership. Spencer refused to permit Blaine to sell in the territory already granted to another dealer. Blaine claims that Spencer's franchised dealerships are illegal per se as an unreasonable restraint of trade.

Required:

Answer the following, setting forth reasons for any conclusions stated.

Are the above described franchised dealership arrangements illegal per se under the antitrust laws?

Problem 3 Price Discrimination (583,L3a)

(7 to 10 minutes)

Part a. Higgins Corporation sells coffee to chain stores and independent grocers. It offers two types of discounts. For the chain stores, Higgins offers a substantial flat discount regardless of volume purchased. For the independent grocers, Higgins grants only volume discounts, on a sliding-scale basis. Higgins received a cease and desist order from the Federal Trade Commission (FTC), and has retained Daniel Chapman, CPA, to assist Higgins in its defense. Basically, the FTC contends that Higgins' discount practices are in violation of the Robinson-Patman Act and thus must be enjoined. Higgins' management has decided not to plead possible defenses of "changed conditions" or "meeting competition" but rather focus exclusively on the "cost justification" defense. Chapman is concerned about the nature and effect of cost data he should obtain.

Required:

Answer the following, setting forth reasons for any conclusions stated.

1. Discuss the key issues and problems faced in a cost justification defense.

2. Suppose instead that Higgins had sold coffee under its own brand name to independent grocers, and under a private label to chain stores at a lower price. What ramifications, if any, would this have under a Robinson-Patman action?

Multiple Choice Answers

1. c	7. a	13. b	19. a	24. b
2. c	8. b	14. c	20. a	25. d
3. d	9. b	15. b	21. a	26. d
4. a	10. c	16. b	22. a	27. b
5. c	11. a	17. d	23. b	28. b
6. a	12. b	18. a		

Multiple Choice Answer Explanations

A.5.b. Patents

1. (1183,L1,33) (c) Government creation of monopoly status through a patent is permissible under the antitrust law as long as no other anticompetitive conduct is involved. Loop Corporation is, therefore, entitled to sell the micropencil at a price determined by the normal competitive forces of supply and demand. A patent grants the holder a 17 year exclusive right to market the product. Answer (a) is incorrect because prohibiting the retailers from selling competing products is an exclusive dealing agreement which is illegal where the effect is to substantially lessen competition in that market. Answer (b) is incorrect because tying agreements involving patented products are illegal per se if a substantial amount of business is involved. Answer (d) is incorrect because imposing a minimum resale price on the retailers is a vertical price fixing agreement which is also illegal per se.

B.1.b.1) Price Fixing

2. (582,L1,30) (c) Jackson's agreement with its competitors is an example of horizontal price fixing which is illegal per se under the Sherman Act. Any private parties who have suffered damage by reason of any violations of the Sherman Act are empowered to seek treble damages against the violators of the antitrust laws. But such a right is denied to participants in the antitrust violations (i.e., a party to the price fixing agreement). Answer (a) is incorrect because along with the federal government, state governments and private parties may seek injunctive relief to prevent continued or threatened violations of the Sherman Act. Answer (b) is incorrect because there is no legal justification (i.e., meeting the competition) for entering into such a price fixing agreement. This means that price fixing is illegal per se. Proof of engaging in this type of price-fixing activity is sufficient alone to constitute a violation of the Sherman Act. However, if this was price discrimination, under the Robinson-Patman Act, price differentials are allowed if they are instituted to meet lawful competition. Answer (d) is incorrect because a violating corporation's officers and directors are held criminally liable for violations of the Sherman Act.

3. (578,L1,8) (d) An express formal agreement is not required to constitute an illegal price maintenance agreement. The four manufacturers have, by their informal oral agreement, agreed and conspired to fix prices which is a per se violation of the federal antitrust laws. Answer (a) is incorrect because prices may not be set by a trade association any more legally than if done by the members themselves. Answer (b) is likewise incorrect because any pricing agreement is illegal even if it is to follow the industry leader's pricing, no matter who suggests it. Answer (c) is also incorrect because a trade association can no more legally allocate markets than can the members.

B.1.b.2) Joint Boycotts

4. (583,L1,31) (a) The agreement between the retailers and manufacturers to boycott Grubar constitutes a group boycott which is a per se violation of the Sherman Act. The Sherman Act's remedies include both injunctive relief and treble damages for the injured private party. Therefore, answer (b) is incorrect. Answer (c) is incorrect because the Sherman Act applies to any group boycott that affects interstate commerce. The agreement that constitutes the joint boycott obviously affects interstate commerce. Answer (d) is incorrect because private parties, as well as the Justice Department, can seek injunctive relief to prevent continued violations of the Sherman Act.

5. (580,L1,1) (c) A joint boycott requires that two or more parties agree not to deal with a third party. The mere unilateral refusal to deal with Monroe would not be a joint boycott under the provisions of the Sherman Antitrust Act. Since there is no agreement to fix prices between Monroe and Jay this activity is not a per se violation. However, if an overwhelming preponderance of the retailers had agreed to follow the price, then there would be an agreement that constituted price fixing, which is illegal per se.

B.1.c.3) Horizontal Territorial Limitations

6. (1183,L1,34) (a) Any joint action to allocate customers between competitors at the same level of distribution is illegal per se. The Association members who have entered into this horizontal market allocation agreement are subject to criminal penalties under the Sherman Antitrust Act. Answer (b) is incorrect because the Association members are at the same level of competition and have, therefore, entered into a hori-

zontal agreement which is illegal per se. A vertical market allocation would be subject to the rule of reason standard. Answer (c) is incorrect because there is no defense to per se antitrust violations. Even if the rule of reason standard applied, poor economic conditions are not a valid defense. Answer (d) is incorrect because price fixing is only one of the many possible anticompetitive agreements which violate the antitrust laws.

B.1.d. Vertical Territorial Limitations

7. (1181,L1,31) (a) Sunrise Company's distribution system engages in vertical territorial limitations in which the distributors and retailers receive an exclusive right to sell in a specific territory but are precluded from selling in any other area. The Supreme Court has ruled in Continental T.V. Inc. v. GTE Sylvania Inc. 433 U.S. 36 (1977) that such a restraint is not illegal per se, but that all such cases, regardless of whether title (of the product) passes (from the distributors to the retailers), should be judged under the rule of reason. Thus, answers (b), (c), and (d) are incorrect.

B.1.e. Vertical Resale Price Maintenance

8. (582,L1,32) (b) Darby's agreement to enforce a suggested minimum resale price is an example of vertical price fixing which is illegal per se under the Sherman Act. Answer (a) is incorrect because Darby would only be guilty of price discrimination if it were to discriminate in price between purchasers of commodities of like grade and quality, where the effect of such discrimination may be to substantially lessen competition or tend to create a monopoly. But Darby did not participate or engage in charging different prices to different purchasers. Answer (c) is incorrect because retail price maintenance agreements are illegal per se and a violation of the antitrust laws. Answer (d) is incorrect because, though Darby can sell its patented product at whatever price it desires, once Darby makes the sale, it cannot force its retail customers to sell above a certain price, since this constitutes price fixing, an illegal per se violation.

9. (582,L1,33) (b) Marvel's agreement with its retailers is an example of vertical price fixing which is illegal per se under the Sherman Act. This means there is no legal justification for entering into this type of agreement. Proof of engaging in this type of activity is sufficient to constitute a violation of the antitrust laws, even though the price charged is reasonable. Answer (a) is incorrect because there is no such exception to the price fixing provision of the Sherman Act; Marvel entered into a price fixing agreement which is illegal per se. Answer (c) is incorrect because the retailers' right to sell competing brands at any price they choose is irrelevant with regard to the illegality of the price fixing agreement concerning the sale of Marvel tires. Answer (d) is incorrect because though Marvel has the exclusive right to market the tires, by reason of its exclusive trademark, Marvel has no right to control the prices at which its retailers resell the product.

B.2. Formation of a Monopoly

10. (582,L1,27) (c) The judicial standard which the United States Department of Justice applies when determining whether a firm has monopolistic power is to look at the percentage share of the relevant market which the firm controls. If Variable's share of the market is sufficiently large to give the firm the power to control (fix) prices or to exclude competition then it is guilty of monopolization. Answer (a) is incorrect because all the government must prove is that Variable has the power to control price or to exclude competition; the government need not prove that Variable is the sole source of a significant portion of the market. Answer (b) is incorrect because though the percentage share of the market is a determining factor, there is no set minimum percentage which establishes monopolization. A much lower percentage share of the market may suffice to constitute monopolistic power. Answer (d) is incorrect because as long as it can be shown that Variable has the power to exclude competition or control prices, it does not matter that Variable was not a party to a contract, combination, or conspiracy in restraint of trade. Violations of Section One of the Sherman Act demand proof of a contract in restraint of trade, but violations of Section Two merely demand proof of creation of a monopoly or an attempt to create a monopoly.

B.3. Sanctions

11. (1179,L1,21) (a) The suspension of a corporation's right to engage in interstate commerce as a result of violations of the antitrust act is not one of the authorized sanctions under federal antitrust laws. Treble damages as in answer (b) are available to injured parties. Answer (c), seizure of property being illegally shipped in interstate commerce in violation of the antitrust laws, is also an authorized sanction. Likewise, fine and imprisonment of the corporation's officers, as in answer (d), are also authorized sanctions. Violations of the Sherman Act are felonies, subjecting individuals to a maximum sentence of three years in prison and/or a maximum fine of $100,000. Firms are subject to a maximum fine of $1,000,000.

C. Clayton Act of 1914

12. (581,L1,57) (b) The contract provision described in the question is an exclusive dealing arrangement. While the Clayton Act is usually referred to in determining the legality of such arrangements, both the Sherman and Federal Trade Commission Acts contain provisions governing exclusive dealings contracts. Basically, the criterion used to judge the legality of this type of contract is one of quantitative substantiality, i.e., the contract provision will be judged according to objective standards such as the percentage of market control gained through such restrictions or the dollar amount of transactions involved (e.g., contracts involving $500,000 are normally considered to be illegal automatically). Since these standards are objective in nature, use of the rule of reason answer (c) is normally not accepted as justification once the dollar or percentage limits are exceeded. Answer (a) is incorrect as exclusive dealings contracts are not illegal per se under the various Acts, and the duration of a contract provision will not determine whether or not an agreement is illegal per se. Answer (d) is incorrect because whether the wholesalers are allowed to sell other pictures would be irrelevant in deciding whether this exclusive dealing contract restricts competition in lithographs.

13. (1177,L3,46) (b) An arrangement requiring the buyer to take one or more other products as a condition to buying the desired product is called tying. It is illegal per se as a practical matter (because the seller will have to be in a monopolistic position to be able to force other products on a seller). Answer (c) is incorrect because even though Mason did not have total control, it did have monopolistic control. Answer (d) is incorrect because the practice is per se illegal. The price of the tied products is not considered.

14. (578,L1,7) (c) The Clayton Act prohibits interlocking directorates where either corporation has shareholders' equity (capital, surplus, and undivided profits) of more than $1 million, and competition is substantially lessened. Answer (b) is incorrect because the interlocking directorate prohibition is not dependent on ownership of 50% or more of another corporation. Answers (a) and (d) are incorrect because serious violations of the antitrust laws have occurred. Yeat's and Glick's share of the market has not changed, but competition has been substantially lessened by their division of markets which is in itself a per se violation of the federal antitrust laws.

C.1.a. Acquisitions

15. (1183,L1,35) (b) In a pure conglomerate merger the acquiring corporation neither competes with, nor sells to, nor buys from the acquired corporation. Answers (a) and (c) are incorrect because a merger may violate the Clayton Act if the effect may be to substantially lessen competition or tend to create a monopoly. Neither proof of actual restraint on competition nor intent to monopolize is required. Answer (d) is incorrect because the government may file a civil lawsuit to obtain an injunction restraining activities which violate the antitrust laws. As long as the merger itself is illegal, there are sufficient grounds to seek injunctive relief and proof of other anticompetitive behavior is not required.

16. (583,L1,33) (b) Section 7 of the Clayton Act is intended to apply to monopolistic trends in their incipiency, before the Sherman Act's restraints concerning monopolies could be applied. The basic tests applied in Section 7 of the Clayton Act is whether the merger or acquisition may "substantially lessen competition or tends to create a monopoly." Under the Sherman Act, the Justice Department must prove the merger or acquisition created, or was an attempt to create, a monopoly. Answer (a) is incorrect because there are no criminal penalties available under the Clayton Act. Answers (c) and (d) are incorrect because Section 2 of the Sherman Act applies both to asset and stock mergers or acquisitions.

17. (582,L1,29) (d) If the merger of City Utility and Suburban Electric violates Section 1 of the Sherman Act or Section 7 of the Clayton Act by creating an unreasonable restraint of trade; or by substantially lessening competition or tending to create a monopoly, the Department of Justice can seek an injunction ordering divestiture as a proper form of relief. Answer (a) is incorrect because the antitrust laws are applicable to regulated enterprises, especially when dealing with mergers. Therefore, being a member of a regulated industry, like public utilities, does not insulate the entity from application of antitrust laws. Answer (b) is incorrect because the Department of Justice may proceed against a merger any time the merger threatens to restrain commerce; the government need not act at the incipiency of the merger. Thus, there is no statute of limitations applicable to when the Department of Justice can act. Answer (c) is incorrect because if a merger creates a monopoly, it is a violation of both Section 2 of the Sherman Act and Section 7 of the Clayton Act.

18. (582,L1,31) (a) Gould did not monopolize the market, nor participate in any unfair trade practices. Erhart's claim that it was harmed, by Gould taking over Mace's business, because Erhart's business would have improved had not Gould entered the market as a competitor, is not sufficient to render Gould's actions a violation of antitrust laws. Therefore, Erhart would not be entitled to recover damages. Answers (b), (c) and (d) are incorrect because these are remedies offered Erhart if Gould would have violated the antitrust laws.

19. (1181,L1,33) (a) The Department of Justice Merger Guidelines cover horizontal, vertical and conglomerate mergers. These guidelines are essentially quantitative in nature, based on both product market and geographical market share sizes. Answer (b) is incorrect because these Merger Guidelines were promulgated solely by the Department of Justice based on market size considerations, not statutory or case law. Answers (c) and (d) are incorrect because the purpose of the guidelines is to acquaint interested parties with the standards being applied by the Department of Justice in determining whether to challenge mergers under Section 7 of the Clayton Act. Since these guidelines are quantitative in nature, they become objective and determinable and, consequently, are applicable to evaluating an actual merger. However, they are merely guidelines that do not bind unless accepted by the courts as appropriate standards in specific antitrust cases.

20. (1178,L1,5) (a) Answer (a) is the most likely result, i.e., the court would grant an injunction prohibiting Western from acquiring control of Davis. In looking at Western's percentage share of the relevant market after the acquisition, it is apparent that they would have more than 30% of the market where they compete. This creates a presumption that the merger is unlawful. Answer (b) is not so likely because share of the market analysis should be applied to the section of the country where they compete and not to the United States as a whole. Answer (c) is unlikely because the facts in this case indicate such a clear violation of the anti-merger provisions of the law. Nonetheless, it is possible for the government to review a merger after it has occurred. Answer (d) is unlikely because significant business efficiency resulting from a merger does not insulate it from attack by the Justice Department under the antitrust laws. The major exception is if the acquired company was a failing company and there was no other purchaser whose acquisition would be less anticompetitive.

D. Federal Trade Commission Act of 1914

21. (1183,L1,37) (a) Unfair methods of competition under the Federal Trade Commission Act include not only violations of the Sherman Act and Clayton Act, but conduct independent of those antitrust laws as well. Unfair methods of competition which violate neither the Sherman Act nor the Clayton Act include, for example, theft of a competitor's trade secrets and inducing customers to breach their existing contracts with a competitor. Answer (b) is incorrect because the FTC is authorized to impose civil sanctions only. Answer (c) is incorrect because the Federal Trade Commission Act only establishes a general prohibition of unfair methods of competition and does not specifically enumerate given activities. The Federal Trade Commission has authority to declare trade practices as unfair methods of competition. Answer (d) is incorrect because the Federal Trade Commission Act extends to the sale or lease of services as well as commodities.

E. Robinson-Patman Act of 1936

22. (583,L1,32) (a) Under the Robinson-Patman Act there is a presumption that competition has been harmed when the price discrimination involves competing purchasers from the same seller. Since Pratt charged Taylor more than Stewart for the same item, Taylor has a presumption in its favor that it has been harmed by Pratt's price discrimination. Answer (b) is incorrect because the fact that Pratt did not intend to harm Taylor is not a defense to the charge of price discrimination. There is no need to prove the defendant had the intent to harm competition to find a price discrimination violation. Answer (c) is incorrect because to constitute a valid defense to the charge of price discrimination, Pratt must prove that they lowered the price charged to the old customers in an attempt to retain these customers by meeting the price of lawful competition. Reducing a price merely because customers have been doing business with the company for ten years is not, in and of itself, a valid defense to charges of price discrimination. Answer (d) is incorrect because the presence of several other sellers with which the customers could deal is not a valid defense to price discrimination.

23. (1181,L1,34) (b) The Robinson-Patman Act prohibits price discrimination in interstate commerce of commodities of like grade and quality. A violation of the act exists if the effect of the price discrimination may be to substantially lessen competition or tend to create a monopoly. Therefore, all that Patman must do

to maintain a sufficient legal action is to allege that due to Robinson's pricing activities there is a reasonable possibility that competition may be adversely affected. Answer (a) is incorrect because Patman does not have to show actual injury to competition; Patman must show that such discrimination may substantially lessen competition. Answer (c) is incorrect because Congress purposely adopted the Robinson-Patman Act to prevent unilateral price determination which has the resultant effect of lessening competition or tending to create a monopoly. Answer (d) is incorrect because the reasonableness of the prices charged is irrelevant. The issue is whether the price discrimination may substantially lessen competition or tend to create a monopoly.

24. (578,L1,9) (b) Price discrimination is illegal if the effect would substantially lessen competition. In this case, the price discrimination is based on cost savings and the competition is not between competitors. The wholesalers are charging the same price and the retailers are charging the same price (except for a functional discount based on quantity cost savings). Answer (a) is incorrect because Girard has the right to sue. There has been price discrimination and it is up to the court to determine whether or not it is legal. Answer (c) is incorrect because intent to discriminate is not a factor in the legality of price discrimination. Answer (d) is incorrect because reasonable prices or low profit margins are not a justification for price discrimination. It is the competition between the buyers which is being protected and not the profits of the seller.

G. Administrative Law

25. (1183,L1,31) (d) The doctrine of exhaustion of remedies requires a party adversely affected by an administrative agency ruling to first pursue all remedies available within the administrative agency system itself. Only after exhausting these remedies may an injured party seek judicial review. Answers (b) and (c) are, therefore, incorrect. Moreover, when Able Corporation finally does seek judicial review, it will be in the federal court system. The corporation may either seek an injunction against the FTC in district court or file a petition for review in the court of appeals or U.S. Supreme Court. Answer (a) is incorrect because the Administrative Procedure Act (APA) creates a statutory right of judicial review of all actions by federal administrative agencies unless otherwise precluded by statute or the action was solely within the agency's discretion. Since neither exception is applicable here, Able Corporation is entitled to seek judicial review after exhausting its administrative remedies. The federal court may review the FTC ruling not only for a constitutional violation of due process, but also to determine whether the agency acted in an arbitrary and capricious manner and whether the agency's fact determinations are supported by substantial evidence.

26. (1183,L1,32) (d) Federal administrative agency powers parallel the executive, judicial, and legislative functions of government. Agency investigatory and prosecutorial authority is quasi-executive; the rule-making function is quasi-legislative; and the adjudicatory power is quasi-judicial. Answers (a), (b), and (c) are, therefore, incorrect.

May 1984 Answers

27. (584,L1,25) (b) The Truth in Lending provisions apply to consumer credit transactions where credit is given to a natural person for personal, family, or household purposes. Truth in Lending does not apply to transactions extending credit for business or government purposes or to transactions involving more than $25,000 of credit. Also exempt from coverage are any consumer credit transactions involving real property (i.e., real estate mortgage) and secured transactions involving personal property to be used as a consumer's principal residence. Answers (a), (c), and (d) are, therefore, incorrect.

28. (584,L1,26) (b) Generally, a federal court reviewing an administrative agency's action will review only questions of law. One such question of law is whether the agency acted within the scope of its authority as delegated by Congress in the enabling statute. Unless Congress states otherwise in the enabling legislation, reviewing courts do not conduct a new trial (trial de novo) or make their own independent findings of fact. The agency's findings of fact are binding on the reviewing court unless there is no substantial evidence to support those findings. Answer (d) is, therefore, incorrect. Answer (c) is incorrect because the scope of judicial review does not permit courts to take affirmative steps to amend legislation. Answer (a) is incorrect because reviewing courts are not given any broad political authority. Instead, the courts must review only the agency decision and issues presented by the specific case.

Answer Outline

Problem 1 Price Fixing and Discrimination

b. There is a possible violation of the Sherman Act
  The manufacturers conspired to restrain interstate commerce
  I.e., they agreed to limit output and allocate customers
  This is similar to price-fixing and is per se illegal
    The specific circumstances do not affect the illegality
    Oral understanding
    To eliminate destructive price cutting
    To charge reasonable prices

c. General Pen's price-fixing arrangement is illegal
    I.e., Double Discount has a valid cause of action
  Price-fixing used to be legal if per state price maintenance law
  General Pen comes within these "fair trade laws"
  In 1975 Congress removed this exception which was previously permitted
  Thus Pen's arrangement is not legal.

Unofficial Answer

Problem 1 Price Fixing and Discrimination

Part b.

The fact situation described poses obvious violations of the Sherman Act. First, the four competing antenna manufacturers entered into an illegal "contract, combination, or conspiracy" in restraint of interstate commerce when they agreed to limit their output. This is akin to price fixing and is, per se, illegal. The fact that the understanding was oral does not matter, nor does it matter that their goal was to eliminate destructive price cutting or charge reasonable prices. Additionally, the agreement among the four antenna manufacturers to allocate customers among themselves is another clearly anticompetitive device which has been placed in the, per se, illegal category. The anticompetitive effects are so obvious that this kind of conduct has been held to be without legal justification.

Part c.

The problem raised by the facts is whether the price-fixing arrangement engaged in by General Pen Company is illegal. Normally, price fixing is, per se, illegal. However, Congress originally permitted an exception to this blanket prohibition. In effect the price-fixing agreement was legal if there was (1) a state law permitting resale price maintenance (a manufacturer fixing the minimum price at which purchasers could sell); (2) free and open competition among other makers of the product; and (3) one or more retail sellers agreeing to retail price maintenance. The facts of the case indicate that General Pen comes within the scope of the prior "fair trade" laws. However, in 1975, Congress amended the law concerning resale price maintenance and removed the exception previously permitted under the Sherman Act. Consequently, resale price maintenance (vertical price fixing) is now illegal. Thus, Double Discount has a valid cause of action against General Pen based upon the amended statute.

Answer Outline

Problem 2 Vertical Territorial Limitation

Part a.

No. The franchised dealership arrangements are not illegal per se
These franchised dealerships are examples of vertical territorial limitations
  Vertical territorial limitations are not illegal per se
    But judged by rule of reason
      Violate antitrust laws if unreasonable restraint of trade

Unofficial Answer
(Author Modified)

Problem 2 Vertical Territorial Limitation

Part a.

No, the franchised dealership arrangements are not illegal per se under the antitrust laws. A recent Supreme Court decision stated that the described franchise dealerships, which are examples of vertical territorial limitations, are no longer illegal per se, but are to be tested under the rule of reason. Presently, such limitations only violate the antitrust laws if they unreasonably restrain trade.

Answer Outline

Problem 3 Price Discrimination

Part a.

1. Defense of cost justification
   - Higgins must prove cost difference between supplying two different classes
     - Proof requires looking to manufacturing, sales, delivery, collection, and accounting costs
     - Cost justification defense usually not successful
2. Fact some sales under Higgins' brand name and some under private label not successful defense to price discrimination
   - Issue whether coffee of like grade and quality irrespective of difference in labels

Unofficial Answer

Problem 3 Price Discrimination

Part a.

1. Since Higgins has two different discount structures, there is a prima facie price discrimination case. In order to prevail in such a case the seller may affirmatively prove cost justification as a defense as provided in the Robinson-Patman Act. Although, in general, quantity discounts may be granted based on amounts purchased, a manufacturer must grant these discounts on the basis of reasonably-drawn classes. The company need not prove actual cost savings resulting from purchases made by each member of the class. However, the costs of the sales to the buyers must be of sufficient homogeneity. This means that the costs incurred in selling to members of a particular class must be very similar, i.e., there must be a rational and persuasive basis for the determination of the class. Higgins has established two classes, chain stores and independent grocers. In order for Higgins to establish the cost reductions, it might look to manufacturing, sales, delivery, collection, and accounting costs. The defense of cost justification requires precise accounting data and historically has not met with much success in the courts.

2. One of the elements set forth in this action is that the sales relate to commodities of "like grade and quality." The test here is that the commodities affected must either be physically identical or so physically similar that the commercial value of the commodities is not significantly different. Thus, the phrase "like grade and quality" relates exclusively to the physical characteristics of the commodity. In this case, the fact that some of the sales were under Higgins' brand name and some under a "private label" would not affect the outcome.

Multiple Choice Questions (1 - 30)

1. Under the Securities Act of 1933, an accountant may be held liable for any materially false or misleading financial statements, including an omission of a material fact therefrom, provided the purchaser
   a. Proves reliance on the registration statement or prospectus.
   b. Proves negligence or fraud on the part of the accountant.
   c. Brings suit within four years after the security is offered to the public.
   d. Proves a false statement or omission existed and the specific securities were the ones offered through the registration statement.

2. Under the Securities Act of 1933, subject to some exceptions and limitations, it is unlawful to use the mails or instruments of interstate commerce to sell or offer to sell a security to the public unless
   a. A surety bond sufficient to cover potential liability to investors is obtained and filed with the Securities and Exchange Commission.
   b. The offer is made through underwriters qualified to offer the securities on a nationwide basis.
   c. A registration statement has been properly filed with the Securities and Exchange Commission, has been found to be acceptable, and is in effect.
   d. The Securities and Exchange Commission approves of the financial merit of the offering.

3. Mr. Jackson owns approximately 40% of the shares of common stock of Triad Corporation. The rest of the shares are widely distributed among 2,000 shareholders. Jackson needs funds for other business ventures and would like to raise about $2,000,000 through the sale of some of his Triad shares. He accordingly approached Underwood & Sons, an investment banking house in which he knew one of the principals, to purchase his Triad shares and distribute the shares to the public at a reasonable price through its offices in the United States. Any profit on the sales could be retained by Underwood pursuant to an agreement reached between Jackson and Underwood. In this situation
   a. The securities to be sold probably do not need to be registered with the Securities and Exchange Commission.
   b. Underwood & Sons probably is not an underwriter as defined in the federal securities law.
   c. Jackson probably is considered an issuer under federal securities law.
   d. Under federal securities law, no prospectus is required to be filed in connection with this contemplated transaction.

4. Tweed Manufacturing, Inc., plans to issue $5 million of common stock to the public in interstate commerce after its registration statement with the SEC becomes effective. What, if anything, must Tweed do in respect to those states in which the securities are to be sold?
   a. Nothing, since approval by the SEC automatically constitutes satisfaction of any state requirements.
   b. Make a filing in those states which have laws governing such offerings and obtain their approval.
   c. Simultaneously apply to the SEC for permission to market the securities in the various states without further clearance.
   d. File in the appropriate state office of the state in which it maintains its principal office of business, obtain clearance, and forward a certified copy of that state's clearance to all other states.

5. Harvey Wilson is a senior vice president, 15% shareholder and a member of the Board of Directors of Winslow, Inc. Wilson has decided to sell 10% of his stock in the company. Which of the following methods of disposition would subject him to SEC registration requirements?
   a. A redemption of the stock by the corporation.
   b. The sale by several brokerage houses of the stock in the ordinary course of business.
   c. The sale of the stock to an insurance company which will hold the stock for long-term investment purposes.
   d. The sale to a corporate officer who currently owns 5% of the stock of Winslow and who will hold the purchased stock for long-term investment.

6. Which of the following securities or security transactions is automatically exempt under the Securities Act of 1933 from the Act's registration requirements?

a. An offering of $3,000,000 or less of stock to 25 or fewer persons.
b. A $10 million offering of first mortgage bonds to the public.
c. An exchange by a corporation of its own securities with existing shareholders without payment of brokerage commissions.
d. Sale by a director of her shares of stock providing that she owns less than 10% of the corporation's stock and that the sale is on a registered stock exchange.

7. Theobold Construction Company, Inc., is considering a public stock offering for the first time. It wishes to raise $1.2 million by a common stock offering and do this in the least expensive manner. In this connection, it is considering making an offering pursuant to Regulation A. Which of the following statements is correct regarding such an offering?

a. Such an offering can **not** be made to more than 250 people.
b. The maximum amount of securities permitted to be offered under Regulation A is $1 million.
c. Only those corporations which have had an initial registration under the Securities Act of 1933 are eligible.
d. Even if Regulation A applies, Theobold is required to distribute an offering circular.

8. Which of the following is exempt from registration under the Securities Act of 1933?

a. First mortgage bonds.
b. The usual annuity contract issued by an insurer.
c. Convertible preferred stock.
d. Limited partnership interests.

9. Under which of the following circumstances is a public offering of securities exempt from the registration requirements of the Securities Act of 1933?

a. There was a prior registration within one year.
b. The corporation is a public utility subject to regulation by the Federal Power Commission.
c. The corporation was closely held prior to the offering.
d. The issuing corporation and all prospective security owners are located within one state, and the entire offering, sale, and distribution is made within that state.

10. The Securities Act of 1933 specifically exempts from registration, securities offered by any person

a. Other than an issuer, underwriter, or dealer.
b. Who is an issuer of a public offering.
c. If the securities in question have previously been registered.
d. In a small company.

11. Although the Securities and Exchange Commission has broad powers in conducting a formal investigative proceeding, the SEC can **not**

a. Impose monetary penalties without court proceedings.
b. Compel a witness to appear.
c. Subpoena records.
d. Conduct its investigations secretly.

12. The president of XK Corporation has been charged by the Securities and Exchange Commission with a criminal violation of the Securities Exchange Act of 1934. Under these circumstances

a. The SEC may elect to prosecute the case itself or turn the case over to the Justice Department.
b. It is irrelevant whether the president had knowledge of his wrongdoing in determining whether to impose a fine or prison term.
c. The SEC must elect between civil and criminal action but may **not** pursue both.
d. A fine or prison term or both may be imposed.

13. Which of the following is required under the Securities Exchange Act of 1934 or the SEC's reporting requirements issued pursuant thereto?

a. Current reporting by issuers of registered securities of certain specified corporate and financial events within ten days after the close of the month in which they occur.
b. Quarterly audited financial reports and statements by those corporations listed on a national exchange.
c. Reporting by issuers of securities which are traded over-the-counter, but only if the securities are actively traded.
d. Annual filing of audited financial reports by all corporations engaged in interstate commerce.

14. Insofar as the Securities Act of 1933 and the Securities Exchange Act of 1934 are concerned with fraud

a. The Acts are identical with respect to proscribing fraudulent transactions.
b. The anti-fraud provisions are contained exclusively in the 1934 Act.
c. The 1933 act does not require proof of scienter in all circumstances whereas the 1934 Act does.
d. Only the 1933 Act contains criminal sanctions against those found to be guilty of fraud.

15. The Securities Exchange Act of 1934 requires that certain persons register and that the securities of certain issuers be registered. In respect to such registration under the 1934 Act, which of the following statements is **incorrect?**

a. All securities offered under the Securities Act of 1933 also must be registered under the 1934 Act.
b. National securities exchanges must register.
c. The equity securities of issuers, which are traded on a national securities exchange, must be registered.
d. The equity securities of issuers having in excess of $1 million in assets and 500 or more stockholders which are traded in interstate commerce must be registered.

16. Shariff is a citizen of a foreign country. He has just purchased six percent (6%) of the outstanding common shares of Stratosphere Metals, Inc., a company listed on a national stock exchange. He has instructed the brokerage firm that quietly and efficiently handled the execution of the purchase order that he wants the securities to be held in street name. What are the legal implications of the above transactions? Shariff must

a. Immediately have the securities registered in his own name and take delivery of them.
b. Sell the securities because he has violated the anti-fraud provisions of the Securities Exchange Act of 1934.
c. Notify Stratosphere Metals, Inc., of his acquisition and file certain information as to his identity and background with the SEC.
d. Notify the SEC and Stratosphere Metals, Inc., only if he acquires ten percent (10%) or more of Stratosphere's common shares.

17. Which of the following statements concerning the scope of Section 10(b) of the Securities Exchange Act of 1934 is correct?

a. In order to come within its scope, a transaction must have taken place on a national stock exchange.
b. It applies exclusively to securities of corporations registered under the Securities Exchange Act of 1934.
c. There is an exemption from its application for securities registered under the Securities Act of 1933.
d. It applies to purchases as well as sales of securities in interstate commerce.

18. The Securities and Exchange Commission is not empowered to

a. Obtain an injunction which will suspend trading in a given security.
b. Sue for treble damages.
c. Institute criminal proceedings against accountants.
d. Suspend a broker-dealer.

19. The Securities Exchange Act of 1934 holds certain insiders liable for short-swing profits under section 16(b) of the act. Which of the following classes of people would not be insiders in relation to the corporation in which they own securities?

a. An executive vice president.
b. A major debenture holder.
c. An 11% owner, 8% of which he owns in his or her own name and 3% in an irrevocable trust for his or her benefit for life.
d. A director who owns less than 10% of the shares of stock of the corporation.

20. Whitworth has been charged by Bonanza Corporation with violating the Securities Exchange Act of 1934. Whitworth was formerly the president of Bonanza, but he was ousted as a result of a proxy battle. Bonanza seeks to recover from Whitworth any and all of his short-swing profits. Which of the following would be a valid defense to the charges?

a. Whitworth is a New York resident, Bonanza was incorporated in New York, and the transactions were all made through the New York Stock Exchange; therefore, an interstate commerce was not involved.
b. Whitworth did not actually make use of any insider information in connection with the various stock transactions in question.

c. All the transactions alleged to be in violation of the 1934 act were purchases made during February 1979 with the corresponding sales made in September 1979.

d. Whitworth's motivation in selling the stock was solely a result of the likelihood that he would be ousted as president of Bonanza.

21. Young owns 200 shares of stock of Victory Manufacturing Company. Victory is listed on a national stock exchange and has in excess of one million shares outstanding. Young claims that Truegood, a Victory director, has purchased and sold shares in violation of the insider trading provisions of the Securities Exchange Act of 1934. Young has threatened legal action. Which of the following statements is correct?

a. Truegood will have a valid defense if he can show he did not have any insider information which influenced his purchases or sales.

b. Young can sue Truegood personally, but his recovery will be limited to his proportionate share of Truegood's profits plus legal expenses.

c. In order to prevail, Young must sue for and on behalf of the corporation and establish that the transactions in question occurred within less than six months of each other and at a profit to Truegood.

d. Since Young's stock ownership is less than 1%, his only recourse is to file a complaint with the SEC or obtain a sufficient number of other shareholders to join him so that the 1% requirement is met.

22. Which of the following corporations are subject to the accounting requirements of the Foreign Corrupt Practices Act?

a. All corporations engaged in interstate commerce.

b. All domestic corporations engaged in international trade.

c. All corporations which have made a public offering under the Securities Act of 1933.

d. All corporations whose securities are registered pursuant to the Securities Exchange Act of 1934.

23. Under the Foreign Corrupt Practices Act, an action may be brought which seeks

a. Treble damages by a private party.

b. Injunctive relief by a private party.

c. Criminal sanctions against both the corporation and its officers by the Department of Justice.

d. Damages and injunctive relief by the Securities and Exchange Commission.

May 1984 Questions

24. A requirement of a private action to recover damages for violation of the registration requirements of the Securities Act of 1933 is that

a. The plaintiff has acquired the securities in question.

b. The issuer or other defendants commit either negligence or fraud in the sale of the securities.

c. A registration statement has been filed.

d. The securities be purchased from an underwriter.

25. Which of the following financing methods will be exempt from the registration requirements of the Securities Act of 1933?

a. Direct public offering of stock to potential investors without the use of an underwriter.

b. Interstate marketing of securites by a subsidiary which is engaged in intra-state commerce.

c. Sale of long-term notes to a consortium of local banks.

d. Public sale of nonconvertible bonds to investors.

26. The provisions of the Securities Exchange Act of 1934

a. Do **not** require distribution of an annual report unless proxies are solicited.

b. Require the distribution of financial statements prior to or concurrent with a proxy solicitation.

c. Apply only to those corporations engaged in interstate commerce where there is a significant dispute between management and dissenting shareholders.

d. Apply only to those corporations that have securities traded on a national securities exchange.

27. The Foreign Corrupt Practices Act provisions relating to the maintaining of a system of internal accounting controls apply to

a. All domestic corporations that do an annual foreign trade business in excess of $1 million.
b. All corporations that are registered or reporting corporations under the Securities Exchange Act of 1934.
c. Only those corporations engaged in foreign commerce.
d. All corporations engaged in interstate or foreign commerce.

28. Which of the following statements is correct with respect to criminal prosecution under the Securities Acts?

a. Reckless disregard for the truth is a sufficient basis for a criminal conviction.
b. Personal monetary gain from the alleged criminal conduct is required in order to be convicted.
c. The anti-fraud provisions of the Securities Acts are the only basis upon which a person can be indicted and convicted.
d. Corporations are **not** subject to criminal prosecution.

29. The anti-fraud provisions of the Securities Act of 1933 and the Securities Exchange Act of 1934

a. Are the same insofar as the transactions to which they apply.
b. Are unavailable to plaintiffs who are unable to establish diversity of citizenship and a minimum of $10,000 monetary damages.
c. Contain criminal sanctions against those who engage in fraudulent activities.
d. Contain remedies which are mutually exclusive of each other.

30. For the purpose of liability under the short swing profit provisions of the Securities Exchange Act of 1934, a person is deemed to be an "insider" if the person

a. Received inside information from one who is an insider.
b. Owns 11% of the voting stock outstanding.
c. Is an employee of the corporation.
d. Has access to and uses insider information.

Problems

Problem 1 Legal Implications of Merger; Securities Implications in Employee Stock Purchase Plan (1181,L2)

(15 to 20 minutes)

Part a. Diversified Enterprises, Inc., and Cardinal Manufacturing Corporation have each appointed a committee to discuss Diversified's proposed acquisition of Cardinal. After protracted bargaining, the two committees have agreed to the following terms: Diversified would acquire Cardinal in exchange for 500,000 shares of Diversified's voting common stock and 250,000 shares of its 11% noncumulative, nonvoting preferred. The committees have submitted a proposal incorporating the above to their respective boards of directors. Both corporations are incorporated in the same state and this state has adopted the Model Business Corporation Act. Cardinal has only one class of stock outstanding, 250,000 shares of common. Diversified has 2,000,000 shares of $1 par value common stock authorized of which 700,000 shares are outstanding. The preferred stock would be a new class of stock with a $5 par value. Diversified is in the lower 20th percentile of the Fortune 500 companies and is listed on the New York Stock Exchange. Cardinal is considerably smaller with assets of $11 million and sales of $4 million. It is traded in the over-the-counter market. Diversified does not compete with, nor does it buy from or sell to, Cardinal. The form of the acquisition is to be a statutory merger.

You have been assigned to an accounting team to provide assistance to Diversified in this undertaking.

Required:

Answer the following, setting forth reasons for any conclusions stated.

1. In separate paragraphs, discuss the requirements of the Securities Act of 1933 arising out of the above facts as well as federal antitrust implications.

2. From a corporate law standpoint, what must be done to validly consummate the proposed merger?

Part b. During the initial audit of Haskell Corporation, a medium-sized company engaged in interstate commerce, the CPA discovers that Haskell has recently instituted a generous and broadly-based employees' stock purchase plan. Haskell's philosophy is based upon maximum participation by all employees. This philosophy is generally stated in Haskell's employment brochures and has been fully implemented. Haskell employs approximately 13,000 people in plants located in several states. Approximately 95% of the employees are participating in the plan.

Required:

Answer the following, setting forth reasons for any conclusions stated.

Does the Securities Act of 1933 pose any problems to Haskell in connection with its employees' stock purchase plan or can it claim an exemption as a private placement?

Problem 2 Registration Requirements Under 1933 Act (582,L2)

(15 to 20 minutes)

Various Enterprises Corporation is a medium sized conglomerate listed on the American Stock Exchange. It is constantly in the process of acquiring smaller corporations and is invariably in need of additional money. Among its diversified holdings is a citrus grove which it purchased eight years ago as an investment. The grove's current fair market value is in excess of $2 million. Various also owns 800,000 shares of Resistance Corporation which it acquired in the open market over a period of years. These shares represent a 17% minority interest in Resistance and are worth approximately $2½ million. Various does its short-term financing with a consortium of banking institutions. Several of these loans are maturing; in addition to renewing these loans, it wishes to increase its short-term debt from $3 to $4 million.

In light of the above, Various is considering resorting to one or all of the following alternatives in order to raise additional working capital.

- An offering of 500 citrus grove units at $5,000 per unit. Each unit would give the purchaser a 0.2% ownership interest in the citrus grove development. Various would furnish management and operation services for a fee under a management contract and net proceeds would be paid to the unit purchasers. The offering would be confined almost exclusively to the state in which the groves are located or in the adjacent state in which Various is incorporated.
- An increase in the short-term borrowing by $1 million from the banking institution which currently provides short-term funds. The existing debt would be consolidated, extended, and increased to $4 million and would mature over a nine-month period. This would be evidenced by a short-term note.

- Sale of the 17% minority interest in Resistance Corporation in the open market through its brokers over a period of time and in such a way as to minimize decreasing the value of the stock. The stock is to be sold in an orderly manner in the ordinary course of the broker's business.

Required:

Answer the following, setting forth reasons for any conclusions stated.

In separate paragraphs discuss the impact of the registration requirements of the Securities Act of 1933 on each of the above proposed alternatives.

Multiple Choice Answers

1.	d	7.	d	13.	a	19.	b	25.	c
2.	c	8.	b	14.	c	20.	c	26.	b
3.	c	9.	d	15.	a	21.	c	27.	b
4.	b	10.	a	16.	c	22.	d	28.	a
5.	b	11.	a	17.	d	23.	c	29.	c
6.	c	12.	d	18.	b	24.	a	30.	b

Multiple Choice Answer Explanations

A. Securities Act of 1933

1. (1179,L1,29) (d) Under the Securities Act of 1933, an accountant is liable to a purchaser of securities if the purchaser proves a false financial statement (including statements with a material omission), and the specific securities were ones offered through a registration statement. Answer (a) is incorrect because the purchaser need not prove reliance on the registration statement or prospectus. Instead, the burden is shifted from the plaintiff to the defendant accountant to show that he is not responsible for the investment loss by the purchaser, i.e., accountant must prove due diligence. Answer (b) is incorrect because the purchaser need not prove negligence or fraud on the part of the accountant. Again, all that need be proven is the misstatement or omission. Answer (c) is incorrect because the maximum time limitation for bringing such an action is 3 years after the security is offered to the public.

2. (577,L1,3) (c) Unless a registration statement has been filed with the SEC and accepted, it is generally unlawful under the 1933 Act to offer or sell securities to the public using instruments of interstate commerce. There is no exception to registration by obtaining a surety bond. Nor does it matter who makes the offer; qualified underwriters are subject to the same rules. The SEC never evaluates the financial merit of an offering. Instead, the SEC requires full and fair disclosure so that investors can make their own determination. Registration statements are the vehicles of full and fair disclosures.

3. (578,L1,6) (c) Jackson is considered to be an issuer under the Securities Act of 1933. The definition of issuer includes a controlling person. Jackson is a controlling person because as substantial holder (40%), he has the power to influence the management and policies of the corporation. This transaction does not come within any exception and, therefore, is required to be registered with the SEC. Thus, answer (a) is incorrect since a registration is required. Answer (b) is incorrect because Underwood & Sons is an underwriter. It has purchased securities from an issuer for public distribution. Answer (d) is incorrect since this is a public sale of securities under the provisions of the Securities Act of 1933, i.e., all registration requirements including the filing of a prospectus are necessary.

4. (579,L1,43) (b) Anyone planning to issue common stock must make a filing in those states that have laws governing such offerings and obtain their approval in addition to meeting the registration requirements of the SEC. Answer (a) is incorrect since approval by the SEC does not automatically constitute satisfaction of state "blue-sky" laws. Answer (c) is incorrect because the issuer must apply to each state for permission to market the securities in addition to the SEC. Answer (d) is incorrect because each state makes its own approval of the stock issue; it cannot be done by one state for the other states.

5. (579,L1,48) (b) Wilson, the officer and stockholder of Winslow, Inc., will be required to comply with SEC registration requirements if he chooses to dispose of his 15% stock in the corporation by having it sold by several brokerage houses in the ordinary course of business. Wilson is deemed to be a controlling person, i.e., one who has the power to influence management and policies of the issuer, and thus his stock would be considered to be restricted stock. Sale by a controlling person through a broker is not exempted from SEC registration if more than 1% of the outstanding stock is sold. Answer (a) is incorrect because a redemption of stock is not an offering to the public and therefore not covered by the 1933 Act. Answers (c) and (d) are not subject to the SEC registration requirements because they are private placements of securities to sophisticated investors.

A.5. Exempt Transactions

6. (1182,L1,31) (c) An exchange of securities by an issuer exclusively with its existing shareholders without payment of brokerage commissions or solicitation fees automatically qualifies as an exempt security under the 1933 Act. There is no registration requirement for the sale of securities up to 35 sophisticated purchasers. Regulation A (small issues) provides an exemption for certain issuances up to $1.5 million. Thus, answer (a) is incorrect because the $3 million amount exceeds that of Regulation A ($1.5 million), and there is no indication the 25 purchasers were "sophisticated." Answer (b) is incorrect because first mortgage bonds are securities under the Act and the sale of such instruments must meet the Act's registra-

tion requirements. Answer (d) is incorrect because a director owning less than 10% of the corporation's stock would be a controlling person. When a controlling person sells significant amounts of stock through a broker, the controlling person is considered an issuer and the broker is viewed as an underwriter. Consequently, such sales must comply with the Act's registration requirements.

7. (1180,L1,40) (d) The correct answer is (d). Small issues (up to $1,500,000) may be exempt from the full registration requirements of the SEC Act of 1933 if there is a notification filing with the SEC and an offering circular under Regulation A. A Regulation A offering can be made to any number of people as long as issuance does not exceed $1,500,000. A corporate issuer need not show an initial registration under the Securities Act of 1933 before being eligible to make a Regulation A offering.

8. (1179,L1,18) (b) Usual insurance and annuity contracts (including variable annuities) issued by an insurance company are exempt from the Securities Act of 1933. Answers (a), (c), and (d) are incorrect because each is regulated: first mortgage bonds, convertible preferred stock, and limited partnership interests.

9. (577,L1,4) (d) There is an exemption from the registration requirements for transactions which take place wholly within one state. It is called an intrastate offering. No purchaser or offeree can reside in another state, nor can any offer, sale, or distribution be made in another state. Each new offering of the issuer corporation's securities must be registered. Public utilities are not exempt, nor does it matter whether the issuing corporation was closely held or publicly held prior to the offering.

10. (576,L2,30) (a) There is a broad specific exemption for securities offered by any person other than an issuer, underwriter, or dealer. Thus under the Act public offerings of securities are regulated, but private offerings are exempted. This exemption permits most investors to sell their own securities without registration, prospectus, or other regulations except the antifraud provisions. To avoid circumvention of the Act, the SEC has promulgated a number of complicated provisions dealing with this exemption when the security sold is "restricted" or the seller is a "controlling person."

B. Securities Exchange Act of 1934

11. (1183,L1,43) (a) The Securities and Exchange Commission's powers include the authority to conduct investigations secretly and subpoena witnesses and records. The Commission does not, however, have the **authority** to assess monetary penalties without court proceedings. Answers (b), (c), and (d) are, therefore, incorrect.

12. (1183,L1,44) (d) An individual who commits a criminal violation of the Securities Exchange Act of 1934 is subject to a maximum fine of $10,000 and/or a maximum sentence of five years in prison. Corporations are subject to fines not to exceed $1,000,000. Answer (a) is incorrect because the SEC has no power to prosecute criminal cases. Criminal cases must be referred to the Justice Department. Answer (b) is incorrect because only willful violations of the securities laws are criminal offenses. It is, therefore, essential that the president had the requisite knowledge or intent to commit the act. Answer (c) is incorrect because both civil and criminal remedies are available for violations of the 1934 Act. The SEC is not required to make an election, but may pursue both avenues.

13. (1182,L1,32) (a) Under the Securities Exchange Act of 1934, current reports of certain specified corporate and financial items such as a change in corporate control, revaluation of assets, or a change in the amount of issued securities must be filed within ten days of the close of the month in which the events took place. Answer (b) is incorrect because although quarterly financial reports must be filed, they are not required to be audited. Answer (c) is incorrect because issuers of securities which are traded over-the-counter must report only when they have in excess of $3 million in total assets and more than 500 holders of record (stockholders) as of the last day of the issuer's fiscal year. Answer (d) is incorrect because only those issuers registered under the Securities Exchange Act of 1934 must file annual audited financial reports; and not all corporations engaged in interstate commerce fall within the jurisdiction and scope of the registration requirements under the 1934 Act.

14. (1182,L1,33) (c) Both the 1933 Act and the 1934 Act contain antifraud provisions. However, the 1933 Act does not require proof of scienter (knowledge of the falsity of the statement) in all circumstances whereas the 1934 Act does. Both Acts contain criminal sanctions against those found guilty of fraud. Those convicted under either Act are subject to a fine of up to $10,000 and/or imprisonment of up to five years. Therefore answers (a), (b) and (d) are incorrect.

15. (1180,L1,39) (a) The correct answer is (a). The Securities Act of 1933 applies to the initial issuance of securities and has the purpose of providing investors with full and fair disclosure concerning these securities. The Securities Exchange Act of 1934 generally applies to the subsequent trading of securities but not necessarily all securities required to register under the 1933 Act. Each of the following are required to register under the 1934 Act: (1) national securities exchange; (2) brokers and dealers, (3) dealers in municipal securities, (4) securities that are traded on any national exchange, (5) equity securities traded in interstate commerce having in excess of $1 million in assets and 500 or more shareholders.

16. (1180,L1,41) (c) According to the tender offer provisions of the Securities Exchange Act of 1934, anyone who acquired more than 5% of a company's equity securities must notify the issuer and disclose his/her identity and other relevant facts to SEC. If a tender offer is involved (in this question it was not present), the purchaser must give this information to the SEC and shareholders before making the offer. Thus, answer (c) is correct.

17. (1180,L1,42) (d) Answer (d) is correct because under Rule 10b-5 (Securities Exchange Act of 1934) it is unlawful to use any manipulative or deceptive devices in the purchase or sale of securities if the mail, interstate commerce, or a national stock exchange is used. Answer (a) is incorrect because it is unlawful to use the mail or any instrumentality of interstate commerce in addition to a national stock exchange. The rule is not limited to securities subject to the 1934 Act but applies to any sale of a security if interstate commerce is used. Therefore, answers (b) and (c) are incorrect.

18. (577,L1,1) (b) The SEC is not empowered to sue for treble damages. Treble damages are a civil remedy for those injured by an antitrust violation. The SEC may take administrative action to suspend a broker-dealer when there has been a violation of the federal securities laws. The SEC also may institute criminal proceedings against accountants or others for willful violations of the Securities Act. Also, the SEC may seek and obtain preliminary and final injunctions to prevent trading which is in violation of the Act.

19. (579,L1,49) (b) A major debenture holder is not considered an insider. Insiders are defined as officers, directors, and owners of greater than 10% of any class of the issuer's securities. Therefore answers (a) and (d) are incorrect. Answer (c) is incorrect because beneficial ownership will satisfy the over 10% ownership requirement. Stock held by an irrevocable trust is beneficially owned by the beneficiary.

B.6. Regulation of Insiders and Insiders' Profits

20. (1179,L1,32) (c) Transactions in excess of 6 months are not short-swing profits since the statute defines short-swing as 6 months or less. Purchase of the stock in February and sale in September is more than 6 months. Answer (a) is incorrect because the securities were traded on the New York Stock Exchange. Thus, Bonanza stock was offered, if not sold, to persons in very many states. Answer (b) is not a good defense because the 1934 statute provides that all short-swing profits by an insider belong to the corporation, i.e., proving that insider information was used is not necessary. Answer (d) is not a good defense because the motivation in selling the stock is not relevant. The issue is whether or not the stock was sold in less than a 6 month period. The insider's motive and intent are irrelevant.

21. (1178,L1,33) (c) A stockholder of a corporation whose stock is traded on an exchange may sue for and on behalf of the corporation for profits on insider purchases and sales of company stock occurring within less than six months of each other. Insiders are corporate directors and officers; also stockholders owning more than 10% of any class of stock are insiders. Answer (a) is incorrect because insiders are liable for any profit from the purchase and sale of securities held for less than six months whether or not they have insider information. Answer (b) is incorrect because Young cannot sue Truegood personally, but instead must do so for and on behalf of the corporation. Answer (d) is incorrect because no rule requires a stockholder to own 1% or more of the stock of the corporation if the stockholder is seeking enforcement of the insider trading provisions of the Securities Act of 1934.

D. Foreign Corrupt Practices Act of 1977

22. (1183,L1,45) (d) All corporations whose securities are registered pursuant to the Securities Exchange Act of 1934 are subject to the **accounting requirements** of the Foreign Corrupt Practices Act. The Act prohibits foreign bribery, illegal foreign payments, and political contributions to foreign candidates by all domestic corporations engaged in interstate commerce. Therefore, answers (a), (b), and (c) are incorrect.

23. (1182,L1,30) (c) Under the Foreign Corrupt Practices Act, an action may be brought which seeks fines (up to $10,000) and imprisonment (up to 5 years) against the corporate officers and fines (up to $1,000,000) against the corporation. The Foreign Corrupt Practices Act has no provision allowing private parties or the SEC to seek treble damages or injunctive relief. Therefore, answers (a), (b) and (d) are incorrect.

May 1984 Answers

24. (584,L1,29) (a) In order to establish damages under the Securities Act of 1933, the plaintiff must establish that he has acquired the securities in question. There is no requirement under the Act that fraud or negligence be proven so long as there is a misstatement of a material fact or the omission of a material fact is present in the registration statement. Answer (c) is incorrect since the anti-fraud section of the Act applies to the sale of all securities in interstate commerce regardless of whether filing of a registration statement was required. Answer (d) is incorrect because the Act does not require that the securities be purchased from an underwriter in order for the purchaser to maintain an action for damages.

25. (584,L1,30) (c) A nonpublic offering to sophisticated investors who have access to the type of information required in a registration statement is exempt under the 1933 Act. Answer (a) is incorrect because a direct public offering by the issuer is not exempt. Answer (b) is incorrect because to qualify for the intrastate exemption the offering must be completely intrastate. Answer (d) is incorrect because nonconvertible bonds are considered securities. A public sale of such bonds is not exempt.

26. (584,L1,31) (b) Any person requested to sign a proxy must be furnished with a proxy statement disclosing material financial information as well as other information. Answer (a) is incorrect because the duty to distribute an annual report is not tied to proxy solicitations. The 1934 Act applies not only to securities traded on a national securities exchange, but also applies if there are 500 or more owners of the security and the issuer has more than $3,000,000 in assets. Answers (c) and (d) are, therefore, incorrect.

27. (584,L1,32) (b) The Foreign Corrupt Practices Act's internal accounting controls provisions apply only to corporations which are registered or reporting corporations under the 1934 Act, while the Foreign Corrupt Practices Act's provisions outlawing the payment of overseas bribes applies to all domestic corporations involved in interstate commerce. Therefore, answers (a), (c), and (d) are incorrect.

28. (584,L1,33) (a) Proof of criminal intent is not required in criminal prosecutions under the Securities Acts. Any person who willfully violates any provision of the federal securities statutes may be criminally prosecuted. A reckless disregard for the truth provides a basis for such criminal conviction. Answer (b) is incorrect because it is not necessary to prove that the party charged with the crime made a monetary gain. Answer (c) is incorrect because the registration provisions as well as the anti-fraud provisions of the Acts can provide the basis for criminal convictions. Answer (d) is incorrect because corporations can be convicted of crimes under the Securities Acts.

29. (584,L1,34) (c) The anti-fraud provisions of both the 1933 and 1934 Acts contain criminal sanctions which apply when there is proof of fraudulent activities. Section 10b of the 1934 Act is broader in its coverage than the anti-fraud provisions of the 1933 Act in that it provides protection to a defrauded seller, whereas the 1933 Act's provisions protected only the buyer. Answer (a), therefore, is incorrect. Answer (b) is incorrect because diversity of citizenship is not required since both the 1933 and 1934 Acts are federal statutes and thus provide an independent basis for federal jurisdiction. Answer (d) is incorrect because a plaintiff could conceivably obtain remedies under both Acts.

30. (584,L1,35) (b) The short-swing profit provision of the Securities Exchange Act of 1934 applies to directors, officers, and owners of more than 10% of the outstanding stock of a registered security. Answers (a) and (d) are incorrect because a person who has received inside information from one who is an insider or who has access to and uses insider information is not deemed an insider under the short-swing profit provisions. Answer (c) is incorrect because one may be an employee of the corporation without being a director, officer, or owner of more than 10% of the outstanding stock.

Answer Outline

Problem 1 Legal Implications of Merger; Securities Implications in Employee Stock Purchase Plan

Part a1.

SEC ruled that merger constitutes a sale
The securities must be registered pursuant to Securities Act of 1933
- A registration statement must be filed with the SEC
- A prospectus must be distributed to Cardinal's shareholders

Congress has required all mergers to be scrutinized under the provisions of Section 7 of the Clayton Act
- Applies to vertical, horizontal, and conglomerate mergers
- Violation of Clayton Act if merger substantially lessens competition or tends to create a monopoly
  - Must apply judicial standards
  - Department of Justice Merger Guidelines should be examined

Part a2.

Form of acquisition is a statutory merger
- Must comply with applicable state laws and Model Business Corporation Act

Diversified's and Cardinal's boards must approve formal plan of merger
Majority of shareholders of each corporation must approve the proposed merger
Articles of merger are executed and filed with Secretary of State
Diversified need not amend its corporate charter to reflect new class of preferred stock
- Model Business Corporation Act provides articles of surviving corporation (Diversified) are automatically amended
  - So as to reflect the formal plan of merger

Part b.

Employees' stock purchase plan is subject to provisions of Securities Act of 1933
- Haskell engaged in the offering and sale of its securities in interstate commerce
  - A registration statement must be filed with the SEC
  - A prospectus must be distributed to the employees

Stock purchase plan does not qualify for a private placement exemption
- Employees are neither sophisticated nor sufficiently informed about the issuer
- Number of employees involved is too large

Haskell subject to sanctions for noncompliance with registration requirements
- SEC could obtain injunction prohibiting sale of stock
- Damages could be awarded
- Employees could seek legal remedy of rescission

Unofficial Answer

Problem 1 Legal Implications of Merger; Securities Implications in Employee Stock Purchase Plan

Part a.

1. The Securities and Exchange Commission has ruled that a merger such as this one constitutes a "sale." Therefore, this merger must satisfy the requirements of the Securities Act of 1933. Accordingly, absent some possible exemption or exclusion, the securities must be registered and a prospectus must be distributed by Diversified to the Cardinal shareholders.

Also a possible danger, albeit a remote one, is that the merger may violate the provisions of section 7 of the Clayton Act. Although the two corporations do not compete and Cardinal is not a customer of Diversified's, the act applies not only to vertical or horizontal mergers but also to conglomerate mergers such as this one. The Justice Department's guidelines should be examined, and if there is any doubt about the validity of the acquisition from an antitrust standpoint, a ruling from the Justice Department should be sought.

2. Since this is to be a statutory merger pursuant to state law, the provisions of the appropriate statute, the Model Business Corporation Act, must be strictly complied with as well as any additional state law requirements. The steps to be followed by Diversified and Cardinal are as follows:

- The representatives of the two corporations must agree on a formal plan of merger. The plan containing the details of the merger must then be submitted to the board of directors in the form of a resolution and be approved by both boards.
- After approval of the plan of merger, the board, by resolution, directs that the plan be submitted to a vote at a meeting of shareholders.
- Due notice of the meeting, including a copy or summary of the plan, should be given to the shareholders. At each corporation's meeting, a vote of

the shareholders must be taken on the proposed plan. The plan or merger must be approved upon the affirmative vote of a majority of the shareholders of each corporation.

- Upon such approval by the respective shareholders, articles of merger are executed by the president or a vice president and the secretary of each corporation and then verified by one of the officers signing. The articles, along with the appropriate fees and taxes, must then be filed with the secretary of state, who will then issue a certificate of merger if the articles conform to law.

- Diversified need not amend its corporate charter to reflect the new class of preferred stock to be used in the merger. The act provides that, "In the case of a merger, the articles of the surviving corporation shall be deemed to be amended to the extent, if any, that changes in the articles of incorporation are stated in the plan of merger."

Part b.

Yes. Problems are posed for Haskell Corporation because it is engaged in the offering and sale of its securities in interstate commerce. Therefore, under the Securities Act of 1933, it must file a registration statement, have it become effective, and supply a prospectus to the employees to whom stock is offered.

A claim of exemption as a private placement would fail for several reasons. First, among a great number of the employees, the quality of the investor's financial knowledge would undoubtedly be quite low, and their employee relationship to Haskell would likely be such that they would not have access to the kind of information a registration would disclose. These are the very individuals that the act seeks to protect. Second, the number of individuals involved is so large that the offering cannot be considered nonpublic.

If Haskell does not comply with the registration and prospectus requirements, the SEC could obtain an injunction prohibiting such offers and sales. The possibility of damages is also present. In addition, purchasers of the Haskell stock could later seek rescission or damages based on noncompliance with the act's requirements.

Answer Outline

Problem 2 Registration Requirements Under 1933 Act

Since sale of interest in citrus groves meets definition of security, must comply with registration requirement of 1933 Act
- Unless one of the three exemptions are present
  - Small offering exemption
  - Intrastate offering exemption
  - Private offering exemption
- None met; therefore, Various must comply

Short-term note qualifies as exempt security under 1933 Act
- Since it is commercial paper with maturity of nine months or less
  - And proceeds to be used for current operations
- Also qualifies as exempt transaction as private offering

Issue is whether Various is a controlling person of Resistance Corporation
- If not controlling person, sale of these shares exempted from registration requirements
  - Under casual sales exemption
- If controlling person, Various must meet registration requirements of 1933 Act
  - Unless sale of shares meets requirements of Rule 144

Unofficial Answer
(Author Modified)

Problem 2 Registration Requirements Under 1933 Act

- The sale of the ownership interests in the citrus groves qualifies as a security under the 1933 Act. A security is the sale of any interest in a scheme where a person invests money in a common enterprise and is led to expect profits solely from the endeavors of others. The purchasers of the citrus grove units would be expecting profits from the operation and management of these units by Various. Consequently, unless an exemption can be found under the 1933 Act, Various must file a registration statement with the SEC, and such statement must be approved before the issuance of these interests. The only possible exemptions would be an intrastate offering, a small offering and a private offering. The sale of citrus grove interests would not constitute an intrastate offering because interests are offered to persons residing in more than one state. This offering would not qualify as a small offering in that the aggregate value would exceed $1,500,000. Also, it does not appear that it is a private offering, since the offering is not limited to a small number of sophisticated investors.

• The issuance of a short-term note by Various would not require the filing of a registration statement with the SEC. Commercial paper having a maturity date not exceeding nine months is exempt from the registration requirements of the 1933 Act. This is only true if the proceeds gained from the issuance of this paper have been or are to be used for current operations. However, if the proceeds are to be used for long-term capital investments, this exemption would not apply. Since the problem states the instrument would be used to finance current operations, it appears that the note would qualify as an exemption to the 1933 Securities Act requirement for filing. It appears that the requirements for a private placement would be met in this situation. The offering is limited to one sophisticated investor, since institutional investors such as banks and insurance companies are considered to be sophisticated in nature.

• Concerning Various' sale of the Resistance shares, the important fact is to determine whether Various qualifies as a controlling person of Resistance Corporation. If Various does not qualify as a controlling person, the sale of these shares would be exempted from the registration requirements of the 1933 Act under the casual sales exemption. The casual sales exemption states that a transaction by any person other than an issuer, underwriter or dealer is exempt from registration. A controlling person in a corporation has been construed to mean anyone with direct or indirect power to determine the policies of the business. Obviously, ownership of a majority share of existing stock in a company would constitute control. However, in past court decisions, as little as 10% ownership of outstanding shares has been determined to constitute control when combined with such other factors as being a member of the board of directors; an officer of the corporation; or the fact that the remaining shares are distributed over a large number of shareholders. Thus, the fact that Various only owns 17% would not keep it from being a controlling person. If held to be a controlling person, Various' sale of shares would not fall within the casual sales exemption of the 1933 Act. Since this exemption is not met, Various would have to file a registration statement when selling these shares even though the sale is accomplished through a broker. However, the SEC does permit controlling persons to sell limited quantities of their securities without registration of their security if their sale complies with requirements of Rule 144. Rule 144 requires: adequate information concerning the company be publicly available; sale of no more than 1% of all outstanding shares of that class during any three month period; that all sales take place in broker's transactions, with the broker receiving only the ordinary brokerage commission and the broker not engaging in any solicitations of offers to buy from prospective purchasers. Thus, even if Various was considered to be a controlling person, upon compliance with the above requirements, Various would still be able to sell a limited number of its shares without registration.

Multiple Choice Questions (1 - 19)

1. In an action for negligence against a CPA, "the custom of the profession" standard is used at least to some extent in determining whether the CPA is negligent. Which of the following statements describes how this standard is applied?

   a. If the CPA proves he literally followed GAAP and GAAS, it will be conclusively presumed that the CPA was **not** negligent.
   b. The custom of the profession argument may only be raised by the defendant.
   c. Despite a CPA's adherence to the custom of the profession, negligence may nevertheless be present.
   d. Failure to satisfy the custom of the profession is equivalent to gross negligence.

2. Magnus Enterprises engaged a CPA firm to perform the annual examination of its financial statements. Which of the following is a correct statement with respect to the CPA firm's liability to Magnus for negligence?

   a. Such liability can not be varied by agreement of the parties.
   b. The CPA firm will be liable for any fraudulent scheme it does not detect.
   c. The CPA firm will not be liable if it can show that it exercised the ordinary care and skill of a reasonable man in the conduct of his own affairs.
   d. The CPA firm must not only exercise reasonable care in what it does, but also must possess at least that degree of accounting knowledge and skill expected of a CPA.

3. With respect to privileged communications of accountants, which of the following is correct?

   a. A state statutory privilege will be recognized in a case being tried in a federal court involving a federal question.
   b. Most courts recognize a common-law privilege between an accountant and the client.
   c. As a result of legislative enactment and court adoption, the client–accountant privilege is recognized in the majority of jurisdictions.
   d. The privilege will be lost if the party asserting the privilege voluntarily submits part of the privileged communications into evidence.

4. Working papers prepared by a CPA in connection with an audit engagement are owned by the CPA, subject to certain limitations. The rationale for this rule is to

   a. Protect the working papers from being subpoenaed.
   b. Provide the basis for excluding admission of the working papers as evidence because of the privileged communication rule.
   c. Provide the CPA with evidence and documentation which may be helpful in the event of a lawsuit.
   d. Establish a continuity of relationship with the client whereby indiscriminate replacement of CPAs is discouraged.

5. In which of the following statements concerning a CPA firm's action is scienter or its equivalent absent?

   a. Reckless disregard for the truth.
   b. Actual knowledge of fraud.
   c. Intent to gain monetarily by concealing fraud.
   d. Performance of substandard auditing procedures.

6. Gleam is contemplating a common law action against Moore & Co., CPAs, based upon fraud. Gleam loaned money to Lilly & Company relying upon Lilly's financial statements which were audited by Moore. Gleam's action will fail if

   a. Gleam shows only that Moore failed to meticulously follow GAAP.
   b. Moore can establish that they fully complied with the statute of frauds.
   c. The alleged fraud was in part committed by oral misrepresentations and Moore pleads the parol evidence rule.
   d. Gleam is **not** a third party beneficiary in light of the absence of privity.

7. Lewis & Clark, CPAs, rendered an unqualified opinion on the financial statements of a company that sold common stock in a public offering subject to the Securities Act of 1933. Based on a false statement in the financial statements, Lewis & Clark are being sued by an investor who purchased shares of this public offering. Which of the following represents a viable defense?

   a. The investor has **not** met the burden of proving fraud or negligence by Lewis & Clark.
   b. The investor did **not** actually rely upon the false statement.

c. Detection of the false statement by Lewis & Clark occurred after their examination date.
d. The false statement is immaterial in the overall context of the financial statements.

8. Major, Major & Sharpe, CPAs, are the auditors of MacLain Industries. In connection with the public offering of $10 million of MacLain securities, Major expressed an unqualified opinion as to the financial statements. Subsequent to the offering, certain misstatements and omissions were revealed. Major has been sued by the purchasers of the stock offered pursuant to the registration statement which included the financial statements audited by Major. In the ensuing lawsuit by the MacLain investors, Major will be able to avoid liability if
a. The errors and omissions were caused primarily by MacLain.
b. It can be shown that at least some of the investors did **not** actually read the audited financial statements.
c. It can prove due diligence in the audit of the financial statements of MacLain.
d. MacLain had expressly assumed any liability in connection with the public offering.

9. A CPA is subject to criminal liability if the CPA
a. Refuses to turn over the working papers to the client.
b. Performs an audit in a negligent manner.
c. Willfully omits a material fact required to be stated in a registration statement.
d. Willfully breaches the contract with the client.

10. Josephs & Paul is a growing medium-sized partnership of CPAs. One of the firm's major clients is considering offering its stock to the public. This will be the firm's first client to go public. Which of the following is true with respect to this engagement?
a. If the client is a service corporation, the Securities Act of 1933 will not apply.
b. If the client is not going to be listed on an organized exchange, the Securities Exchange Act of 1934 will not apply.
c. The Securities Act of 1933 imposes important additional potential liability on Josephs & Paul.
d. As long as Josephs & Paul engages exclusively in intrastate business, the federal securities laws will not apply.

11. A CPA firm is being sued by a third-party purchaser of securities sold in interstate commerce to the public. The third party is relying upon the Securities Act of 1933. The CPA firm had issued an unqualified opinion on incorrect financial statements. Which of the following represents the best defense available to the CPA firm?
a. The securities sold had not been registered with the SEC.
b. The CPA firm had returned the entire fee it charged for the engagement to the corporation.
c. The third party was not in privity of contract with the CPA firm.
d. The action had not been commenced within one year after the discovery of the material misrepresentation.

12. Donalds & Company, CPAs, audited the financial statements included in the annual report submitted by Markum Securities, Inc., to the Securities and Exchange Commission. The audit was improper in several resepcts. Markum is now insolvent and unable to satisfy the claims of its customers. The customers have instituted legal action against Donalds based upon section 10b and rule 10b-5 of the Securities Exchange Act of 1934. Which of the following is likely to be Donalds' best defense?
a. They did **not** intentionally certify false financial statements.
b. Section 10b does **not** apply to them.
c. They were **not** in privity of contract with the creditors.
d. Their engagement letter specifically disclaimed any liability to any party which resulted from Markum's fradulent conduct.

13. Locke, CPA, was engaged by Hall, Inc., to audit Willow Company. Hall purchased Willow after receiving Willow's audited financial statements, which included Locke's unqualified auditor's opinion. Locke was negligent in the performance of the Willow audit engagement. As a result of Locke's negligence, Hall suffered damages of $75,000. Hall appears to have grounds to sue Locke for

	Breach of contract	*Negligence*
a.	Yes	Yes
b.	Yes	No
c.	No	Yes
d.	No	No

14. A CPA was engaged by Jackson & Wilcox, a small retail partnership, to examine its financial statements. The CPA discovered that due to other commitments, the engagement could not be completed on time. The CPA, therefore, unilaterally delegated the duty to Vincent, an equally competent CPA. Under these circumstances, which of the following is true?

a. The duty to perform the audit engagement is delegable in that it is determined by an objective standard.
b. If Jackson & Wilcox refuses to accept Vincent because of a personal dislike of Vincent by one of the partners, Jackson & Wilcox will be liable for breach of contract.
c. Jackson & Wilcox must accept the delegation in that Vincent is equally competent.
d. The duty to perform the audit engagement is nondelegable and Jackson & Wilcox need not accept Vincent as a substitute if they do not wish to do so.

15. Sharp, CPA, was engaged by Peters & Sons, a partnership, to give an opinion on the financial statements which were to be submitted to several prospective partners as part of a planned expansion of the firm. Sharp's fee was fixed on a per diem basis. After a period of intensive work, Sharp completed about half of the necessary field work. Then due to unanticipated demands upon his time by other clients, Sharp was forced to abandon the work. The planned expansion of the firm failed to materialize because the prospective partners lost interest when the audit report was not promptly available. Sharp offers to complete the task at a later date. This offer was refused. Peters & Sons suffered damages of $4,000 as a result. Under the circumstances, what is the probable outcome of a lawsuit between Sharp and Peters & Sons?

a. Sharp will be compensated for the reasonable value of the services actually performed.
b. Peters & Sons will recover damages for breach of contract.
c. Peters & Sons will recover both punitive damages and damages for breach of contract.
d. Neither Sharp nor Peters & Sons will recover against the other.

16. On July 25, 1978, Archer, the president of Post Corporation, with the approval of the board of directors, engaged Biggs, a CPA, to examine Post's July 31, 1978, financial statements and to issue a report in time for the annual stockholders' meeting to be held on September 5, 1978. Notwithstanding Biggs' reasonable efforts, the report was not ready until September 7 because of delays by Post's staff. Archer, acting on behalf of Post, refused to accept or to pay for the report since it no longer served its intended purpose. In the event Biggs brings a legal action against Post, what is the probable outcome?

a. The case would be dismissed because it is unethical for a CPA to sue for his fee.
b. Biggs will be entitled to recover only in quasi contract for the value of the services to the client.
c. Biggs will not recover since the completion by September 5th was a condition precedent to his recovery.
d. Biggs will recover because the delay by Post's staff prevented Biggs from performing on time and thereby eliminated the timely performance condition.

17. The Internal Revenue Code provisions dealing with tax return preparation

a. Require tax return preparers who are neither attorneys nor CPAs to pass a basic qualifying examination.
b. Apply to all tax return preparers whether they are compensated or uncompensated.
c. Apply to a CPA who prepares the tax returns of the president of a corporation the CPA audits, without charging the president.
d. Only apply to preparers of individual tax returns.

18. Gaspard & Devlin, a medium-sized CPA firm, employed Marshall as a staff accountant. Marshall was negligent in auditing several of the firm's clients. Under these circumstances which of the following statements is true?

a. Gaspard & Devlin is not liable for Marshall's negligence because CPAs are generally considered to be independent contractors.
b. Gaspard & Devlin would not be liable for Marshall's negligence if Marshall disobeyed specific instructions in the performance of the audits.
c. Gaspard & Devlin can recover against its insurer on its malpractice policy even if one of the partners was also negligent in reviewing Marshall's work.
d. Marshall would have no personal liability for negligence.

19. Georges, a CPA, has prepared a tax return for his client, Arbor. The return was prepared in a fraudulent manner. Regarding Georges' potential liability to various parties, which of the following would be dismissed?

a. A federal criminal action.
b. A federal action for civil penalties.
c. A federal action to revoke Georges' CPA certificate.
d. A malpractice action by the client.

Problems

Problem 1 Accountant's Criminal Liability Under 1934 Act; Negligence (1182,L2)

(15 to 20 minutes)

The following information applies to both Parts a and b.

James Danforth, CPA, audited the financial statements of the Blair Corporation for the year ended December 31, 1981. Danforth rendered an unqualified opinion on February 6, 1982. The financial statements were incorporated into Form 10-K and filed with the Securities and Exchange Commission. Blair's financial statements included as an asset a previously sold certificate of deposit (CD) in the amount of $250,000. Blair had purchased the CD on December 29, 1981, and sold it on December 30, 1981, to a third party who paid Blair that day. Blair did not deliver the CD to the buyer until January 8, 1982. Blair deliberately recorded the sale as an increase in cash and other revenue thereby significantly overstating working capital, stockholders' equity, and net income. Danforth confirmed Blair's purchase of the CD with the seller and physically observed the CD on January 5, 1982.

Part a. Assume that on January 18, 1982, while auditing other revenue, Danforth discovered that the CD had been sold. Further assume that Danforth agreed that in exchange for an additional audit fee of $20,000, he would render an unqualified opinion on Blair's financial statements (including the previously sold CD).

Required:

Answer the following, setting forth reasons for any conclusions stated.

1. The SEC charges Danforth with criminal violations of the Securities Exchange Act of 1934. Will the SEC prevail? Include in your discussion what the SEC must establish in this action.

2. Assume the SEC discovers and makes immediate public disclosure of Blair's action with the result that no one relies to his detriment upon the audit report and financial statements. Under these circumstances, will the SEC prevail in its criminal action against Danforth?

Part b. Assume that Danforth performed his audit in accordance with generally accepted auditing standards (GAAS) and exercised due professional care, but did not discover Blair's sale of the CD. Two weeks after issuing the unqualified opinion, Danforth discovered that the CD had been sold. The day following this discovery, at Blair's request, Danforth delivered a copy of the audit report, along with the financial statements, to a bank which in reliance thereon made a loan to Blair that ultimately proved uncollectible. Danforth did not advise the bank of his discovery.

Required:

Answer the following, setting forth reasons for any conclusions stated.

If the bank sues Danforth for the losses it sustains in connection with the loan, will it prevail?

Problem 2 Anti-fraud Section of Security Act of 1934; Liability and Defenses Under Sec. 11(A) of 1933 Act (1180,L4)

(15 to 20 minutes)

Part a. Whitlow & Company is a brokerage firm registered under the Securities Exchange Act of 1934. The Act requires such a brokerage firm to file audited financial statements with the SEC annually. Mitchell & Moss, Whitlow's CPAs, performed the annual audit for the year ended December 31, 1979, and rendered an unqualified opinion, which was filed with the SEC along with Whitlow's financial statements. During 1979 Charles, the president of Whitlow & Company, engaged in a huge embezzlement scheme that eventually bankrupted the firm. As a result substantial losses were suffered by customers and shareholders of Whitlow & Company, including Thaxton who had recently purchased several shares of stock of Whitlow & Company after reviewing the company's 1979 audit report. Mitchell & Moss' audit was deficient; if they had complied with generally accepted auditing standards, the embezzlement would have been discovered. However, Mitchell & Moss had no knowledge of the embezzlement nor could their conduct be categorized as reckless.

Required:

Answer the following, setting forth reasons for any conclusions stated.

1. What liability to Thaxton, if any, does Mitchell & Moss have under the Securities Exchange Act of 1934?

2. What theory or theories of liability, if any, are available to Whitlow & Company's customers and shareholders under the common law?

Part b. Jackson is a sophisticated investor. As such, she was initially a member of a small group who was going to participate in a private placement of $1 million of common stock of Clarion Corporation. Numerous meetings were held among management and the investor group. Detailed financial and other information was supplied to the participants. Upon the eve of completion of the placement, it was aborted when one major investor withdrew. Clarion then decided to offer $2.5 million of Clarion common stock to the public pursuant to the registration requirements of the Securities Act of 1933. Jackson subscribed to $300,000 of the Clarion public stock offering. Nine months later, Clarion's earnings dropped significantly and as a result the stock dropped 20% beneath the offering price. In addition, the Dow Jones Industrial Average was down 10% from the time of the offering.

Jackson has sold her shares at a loss of $60,000 and seeks to hold all parties liable who participated in the public offering including Allen, Dunn, and Rose, Clarion's CPA firm. Although the audit was performed in conformity with generally accepted auditing standards, there were some relatively minor irregularities. The financial statements of Clarion Corporation, which were part of the registration statement, contained minor misleading facts. It is believed by Clarion and Allen, Dunn, and Rose that Jackson's asserted claim is without merit.

Required:

Answer the following, setting forth reasons for any conclusions stated.

1. Assuming Jackson sues under the Securities Act of 1933, what will be the basis of her claim?

2. What are the probable defenses which might be asserted by Allen, Dunn, and Rose in light of these facts?

Problem 3 Accountant—Client Privilege; Accountants' Liability for Compilation of Financial Statements (582,L3)

(15 to 20 minutes)

Part a. Ralph Sharp, CPA, has audited the Fargo Corporation for the last ten years. It was recently discovered that Fargo's top management has been engaged in some questionable financial activities since the last audited financial statements were issued.

Subsequently, Fargo was sued in state court by its major competitor, Nuggett, Inc. In addition, the SEC commenced an investigation against Fargo for possible violations of the federal securities laws.

Both Nuggett and the SEC have subpoenaed all of Sharp's workpapers relating to his audits of Fargo for the last ten years. There is no evidence either that Sharp did anything improper or that any questionable financial activities by Fargo occurred prior to this year.

Sharp estimates that the cost for his duplicate photocopying of all of the workpapers would be $25,000 (approximately one year's audit fee). Fargo has instructed Sharp not to turn over the workpapers to anyone.

Required:

Answer the following, setting forth reasons for any conclusions stated.

1. If Sharp practices in a state which has a statutory accountant—client privilege, may the state's accountant—client privilege be successfully asserted to avoid turning over the workpapers to the SEC?

2. Assuming Sharp, with Fargo's permission, turns over to Nuggett workpapers for the last two audit years, may the state's accountant—client privilege be successfully asserted to avoid producing the workpapers for the first eight years?

3. Other than asserting an accountant—client privilege, what major defenses might Sharp raise against the SEC and Nuggett in order to resist turning over the subpoenaed workpapers?

Part b. Pelham & James, CPAs, were retained by Tom Stone, sole proprietor of Stone Housebuilders, to compile Stone's financial statements. Stone advised Pelham & James that the financial statements would be used in connection with a possible incorporation of the business and sale of stock to friends. Prior to undertaking the engagement, Pelham & James were also advised to pay particular attention to the trade accounts payable. They agreed to use every reasonable means to determine the correct amount.

At the time Pelham & James were engaged, the books and records were in total disarray. Pelham & James proceeded with the engagement applying all applicable procedures for compiling financial statements. They failed, however, to detect and disclose in the financial statements Stone's liability for certain unpaid bills. Documentation concerning those bills was available for Pelham & James' inspection had they looked. This omission led to a material understatement ($60,000) of the trade accounts payable.

Pelham & James delivered the compiled financial statements to Tom Stone with their compilation report which indicated that they did not express an opinion or any other assurance regarding the financial statements. Tom Stone met with two prospective investors, Dickerson and Nichols. At the meeting, Pelham & James stated that they were confident that the trade accounts payable balance was accurate to within $8,000.

Stone Housebuilders was incorporated. Dickerson and Nichols, relying on the financial statements, became stockholders along with Tom Stone. Shortly thereafter, the understatement of trade accounts payable was detected. As a result, Dickerson and Nichols discovered that they had paid substantially more for the stock than it was worth at the time of purchase.

Required:

Answer the following, setting forth reasons for any conclusions stated.

Will Pelham & James be found liable to Dickerson and Nichols in a common law action for their damages?

Multiple Choice Answers

1.	c	5.	d	9.	c	13.	a	17.	c
2.	d	6.	a	10.	c	14.	d	18.	c
3.	d	7.	d	11.	d	15.	b	19.	c
4.	c	8.	c	12.	a	16.	d		

Multiple Choice Answer Explanations

A. Common Law Liability to Clients

1. (1183,L1,4) (c) Despite a CPA's adherence to custom of the profession, negligence may nevertheless be present. In certain cases the SEC and the courts have held that even though the CPA adhered to GAAP and GAAS, negligence was present when misleading financial statements resulted. Answer (a) is incorrect because literal adherence to GAAP and GAAS will be persuasive, but not conclusive, in proving that the CPA was not negligent. Answer (b) is incorrect because the custom of the profession argument may be raised by the plaintiff—client to prove that the CPA's deviation from that standard constituted negligence. Answer (d) is incorrect because failure to satisfy the custom of the profession constitutes negligence, but not gross negligence. To prove gross negligence, the client would have to show a reckless disregard for the truth by the CPA.

2. (1178,L1,2) (d) A CPA firm must exercise reasonable care and also must possess that degree of accounting knowledge and skill expected of an average CPA. Answer (a) is incorrect because a CPA's liability can be varied by agreement between the CPA and the client. Answer (b) is incorrect because a CPA firm is not liable for failing to detect fraudulent schemes provided their negligence did not prevent discovery. Answer (c) is incorrect because a CPA firm must exercise the care and skill of an average CPA rather than that of a reasonable person who is not trained as a CPA.

A.1.f. Privileged Communications

3. (1183,L1,9) (d) Privileged communications between accountants and their clients do not exist under common law; they exist only if created by statute in a given jurisdiction. Privileged communications statutes were created for the benefit of the accountant's clients; thus, the client is the only party who may waive the privilege and voluntarily submit the communication. However, once there is partial voluntary submission of privileged communication, the entire privilege is lost. Answer (a) is incorrect because federal courts do not recognize a state statute when deciding federal questions. Answer (b) is incorrect because privileged communications do not exist at common law. Answer (c) is incorrect because relatively few jurisdictions have enacted privileged communications statutes.

4. (1183,L1,10) (c) The rationale behind granting ownership of the working papers to the CPA who prepared them is twofold. First, the working papers are documentation of the nature and extent of the services rendered by the CPA. They are also the evidence to support the conclusions reached by the CPA. As such, they are invaluable evidence when preparing a defense in the event of a lawsuit against the CPA. Answer (a) is incorrect because even though working papers are owned by the CPA, they may be subpoenaed by a court or government agency. Answer (b) is incorrect because ownership of the working papers by the accountant is not a valid ground for refusing to produce them in evidence when required by legal process. Answer (d) is incorrect because preventing the indiscriminate replacement of CPAs is not a rationale behind granting ownership to the CPA.

B. Common Law Liability to Third Parties (Nonclients)

5. (1183,L1,2) (d) Scienter is the intent to deceive, manipulate, or defraud. Scienter is present when there is a reckless disregard for the truth, actual knowledge of fraud, or intent to gain monetarily by concealing fraud. The intent to deceive is not present in the performance of substandard auditing procedures; however, such performance would constitute negligence which does not require scienter. Thus, answers (a), (b), and (c) are incorrect.

6. (1183,L1,3) (a) To prevail in a common law action based upon fraud, either actual fraud or constructive fraud must be proven. Actual fraud is an intentional act of deceit. Constructive fraud is gross negligence showing a reckless disregard for the truth. Failure to meticulously follow GAAP constitutes neither actual nor constructive fraud; however, it may provide for a successful common law action based upon negligence. Answer (b) is incorrect because the Statute of Frauds requires that certain agreements must be in writing to be enforceable. This Statute is irrelevant in determining whether fraud is present. Answer (c) is incorrect because the parol evidence rule concerns prior or contemporaneous oral evidence which contradicts a written agreement intended by the parties to be the final and complete agreement. This rule is irrelevant in determining whether Moore & Co. have committed actual or constructive fraud, and whether Gleam will

prevail in a common law action based on fraud. Answer (d) is incorrect because even if Gleam is not a third party beneficiary (i.e., identified third party for whose express benefit the audit is undertaken), Gleam may sue because even an unforeseen third party may institute a common law action based upon fraud.

C. Statutory Liability to Third Parties – Securities Act of 1933

7. (1183,L1,5) (d) Section II of the Securities Act of 1933 makes it unlawful for a registration statement to contain an untrue material fact or to omit a material fact. Under the 1933 Act, the plaintiff must prove damages were incurred and that there was a **material** misstatement or omission in the financials included in the registration statement. Thus, proving that the false statement is **immaterial** is a viable defense. Other viable defenses are the due diligence defense, proving that the plaintiff knew the financials were incorrect when the investment was made, and proving the loss was caused by factors other than the misstatement or omission. Answer (a) is incorrect because the plaintiff need not prove fraud or negligence. Answer (b) is incorrect because the plaintiff need not prove reliance on the financials (unless the securities were purchased after the CPA firm issued an income statement covering at least 12 months subsequent to the effective date of the registration statement). Answer (c) is incorrect because Lewis & Clark's unqualified opinion, included in the registration statement, is a certification of the financials as of the time the registration statement becomes effective. Thus, it extends Lewis & Clark's legal liability from the examination date to the effective date. They would have a duty to disclose the detection of the false statement.

8. (581,L1,3) (c) The SEC Act of 1933 concerns the regulation of initial public offerings of stock. The Act requires the filing of a registration statement including a certified financial statement. Any person acquiring a security covered by the registration can sue the accountant, if the certified financial statements contained false statements or omitted material facts. The presence of such misstatements and omissions is prima facie evidence that the accountant is liable. This means that plaintiff-purchaser does not have the burden of proving the accountant's negligence; the accountant must prove he was not negligent and that he acted with due diligence (skill and care of the average accountant). Answer (a) is incorrect since the auditor's certification of the financial statements covers management's representations. The fact that the errors were caused by MacLain's actions will not relieve the auditor of liability. Answer (b) is also incorrect since the plaintiff does not have to prove reliance on the financial statements or that the loss was suffered from the misstatement. Answer (d) is incorrect since MacLain's express assumption of liability will not relieve the auditor.

9. (1177,L1,1) (c) Criminal liability is only incurred by violating a statute. A CPA who willfully omits a material fact required to be stated in a registration statement is in violation of the Securities Acts and is subject to criminal liability. Civil liability is incurred by violating a legal duty owed to another. Answers (b) and (d) are incorrect because performing an audit in a negligent manner and willfully breaching a contract are violations of a legal duty owed to another and give rise to civil liability. Answer (a) is incorrect because a CPA owns his workpapers and has no duty to turn them over to a client.

10. (1177,L1,9) (c) Before the client goes public, Josephs & Paul is only liable to the client and known intended third-party beneficiaries (i.e., users) of the financial statements, absent fraud or constructive fraud. After the client "goes public" and becomes subject to the 1933 Act, Josephs & Paul may be held liable by any purchaser of the securities for any misleading statement in addition to incurring criminal liability. Answer (a) is incorrect because the Securities Act of 1933 covers the initial sales of securities regardless of the seller's form of organization. Answer (b) is incorrect because the Securities Exchange Act of 1934 applies to over-the-counter stocks in addition to securities listed on organized exchanges. Answer (d) is incorrect because the securities acts apply to securities sold in interstate commerce or through the mails even if the seller or its CPAs conduct business wholly intrastate.

11. (1178,L1,11) (d) The best defense for the CPA firm is that the third-party purchaser failed to commence his action within one year after discovery of the untrue statement or omission, or after such discovery should have been made by the exercise of reasonable diligence. This is the statute of limitations under the Securities Act of 1933. Answer (a) is not the best defense, because these securities should have been registered with the SEC and therefore the CPA firm can be held liable under the 1933 Act whether or not the securities were registered. Answer (b) is not the best defense because an accountant can be held liable whether or not he was paid. Answer (c) is not the best defense because the Securities Act of 1933 eliminates the necessity for privity of contract.

D. Statutory Liability to Third Parties – Securities Exchange Act of 1934

12. (581,L1,4) (a) The SEC Act of 1934 has antifraud provisions. These provisions apply to all transactions involving interstate commerce, mail, or transactions on the national exchange involving the purchase or sale of securities. Rule 10b-5 makes it unlawful for any person to defraud, make untrue statements of material facts or omit material facts on the financial statements or engage in a business which operates as a fraud on persons involved in the purchase or sale of the securities. The correct answer is (a) since this would be the best defense. Scienter by the auditor must be established to hold them liable. This means that the defendant had knowledge of false statements or that the statement was made with a reckless disregard of the truth. Answer (b) is incorrect because Rule 10b-5 applies to the accountants. Answer (c) is incorrect because privity (a contract between the creditors and the accountants) is not required to hold accountants liable. Answer (d) is incorrect since the auditor cannot disclaim liability in this manner.

G.1. Engagement Contracts

13. (1183,L1,1) (a) Breach of contract and negligence are two potential common law grounds upon which Hall, Inc. may sue Locke. Hall may sue for negligence if Locke fails to exercise due care in the performance of the audit. Due care, in this case, means that degree of care which the reasonable CPA would exercise in this circumstance. Also, Hall may sue for breach of contract if Locke contracts to perform an audit and issues a standard report, but does not make an examination of the financials in accordance with GAAS. Locke did not discharge his contractual obligation. Since the facts indicate that Locke was negligent in his/her performance of the audit, it appears that Hall, Inc. has grounds to sue Locke under both breach of contract and negligence.

14. (1177,L1,3) (d) The duty to perform the audit is not delegable, because the audit is a contract for personal services based on personal trust or character. Only in certain cases, i.e., where services are mechanical and only the end result is desired, can personal services be delegated, e.g., moving goods, but never an audit. Jackson and Wilcox need not accept Vincent as a substitute, but they may if they wish. Thus answers (a) and (c) are incorrect. Answer (b) is incorrect because since Jackson and Wilcox have no duty to accept Vincent, they may refuse him for any reason, even personal dislike.

15. (1177,L1,5) (b) The probable outcome is that Peters & Sons will recover their damages, because Sharp knew the purpose of the audit and it was Sharp's fault that the audit was not finished. Answer (a) is incorrect because Sharp will not be compensated, since he breached the contract and Peters & Sons realized no value from his work. Answer (c) is incorrect because punitive damages are not usually allowed for breach of contract. Punitive damages are allowed for fraud, gross negligence, and intentionally inflicted wrongs.

16. (1178,L1,32) (d) Accountants are responsible for performing contracts with their clients in accordance with the contractual terms. Additionally the rules of contracts also apply, and since Biggs was prevented from performing timely due to the client's delays, Biggs will recover his fees. Answer (a) is incorrect because a suit by an accountant to collect his fee would be handled as would any other contract for personal services. Similarly, answer (b) is incorrect because Biggs may recover in full under the contract. Answer (c) is incorrect because the the client prevented Biggs from meeting the deadline.

H. Liability of Income Tax Return Preparers

17. (1183,L1,6) (c) The Internal Revenue Code provisions dealing with tax return preparation apply to preparers. A preparer is defined as an individual or firm who prepares returns for compensation. The compensation can be implied or explicit. This is an example of implied compensation. Answer (a) is incorrect because anyone may prepare a return; passage of an exam is only necessary to practice before the IRS. Answer (b) is incorrect as the Code applies to compensated preparers. Answer (d) is incorrect as the Code applies to preparers of all returns or claims for refund.

18. (1177, L1,4) (c) Gaspard & Devlin can recover on its malpractice insurance no matter who in the firm was negligent, i.e., a malpractice policy insures negligence. Although CPA firms and individual practitioners are independent contractors, the firm independently contracted with the client. Answer (a) is incorrect because the firm as employer is liable for the negligence of its employees acting within the course and scope of their employment. Answer (b) is incorrect because Marshall's disobeyance of instructions would not matter because the firm is responsible for the actions of its employees. Answer (d) is incorrect because Marshall may be held personally liable either by the client, or by the firm if it is held liable by the client.

Other

19. (1183,L1,7) (c) The CPA certificate is issued by a state licensing board and, therefore, could not be revoked by a federal action. Answers (a) and (b) are incorrect because the Internal Revenue Code provisions on tax return preparation provide for both civil and criminal penalties regarding fraudulent returns. Answer (d) is incorrect because malpractice suits by a client may be predicated on the basis of negligence (or fraud).

Answer Outline

Problem 1 Accountant's Criminal Liability Under 1934 Act; Negligence

Part a.

1. Yes. SEC will prevail against Danforth
   Section 32(a) of Securities Exchange Act of 1934 provides criminal sanctions
      For a person who "willfully and knowingly" makes a statement which is false or misleading
         With respect to a material fact
            In reports filed under the 1934 Act
      SEC must establish
         The falsity of the information in financial statements
         Falsehood concerned a material fact
         Danforth's criminal intent
      Danforth's criminal intent inferred from his rendering unqualified opinion
         Knowing that the financial statements were false
2. Yes. SEC will prevail against Danforth
      SEC need not prove reliance by third parties
         To impose criminal liability upon Danforth
      SEC need only prove what was stated above in part a.1.

Part b.

Yes. The bank will prevail against Danforth
Subsequent discovery of a fact existing at date of Danforth's audit report
   Which would have affected his report had he been aware of such fact
      Auditor should take action to prevent future reliance on audit report
   Danforth had knowledge that bank was to rely on financial statements
      Danforth should have notified bank to no longer rely on audit report
   Danforth guilty of common law fraud for failure to notify bank
      Of subsequently discovered information
   Bank must prove
      Material misstatement of financial statements
      Reasonably believed statements to be true
      Relied on statements to its detriment

Unofficial Answer
(Author Modified)

Problem 1 Accountant's Criminal Liability Under 1934 Act; Negligence

Part a.

1. Yes, the SEC will prevail in its criminal action against Danforth. Section 32(a) of the Securities Exchange Act of 1934 provides criminal sanctions for a person who willfully violates the Act or who "willfully and knowingly" makes, or causes to be made, a statement which is false or misleading with respect to any material fact in reports required to be filed under the Securities Exchange Act of 1934. Danforth's source of liability under the Act results from the required filing of certified financial statements that must accompany the annual report to the SEC.

The SEC must establish:

- The falsity of the information in the financial statements contained in Form 10-K filed with the SEC.
- That the falsehood contained in the financial statements concerned a material fact.
- Danforth's criminal intent.

The SEC could establish the first two elements by proving the significant overstatement of working capital, stockholders' equity and net income. The third element of criminal intent (scienter) can be inferred from Danforth's act of issuing an unqualified opinion while knowing that the financial statements were false in return for $20,000.

2. Yes, the SEC will prevail in its criminal action against Danforth. The SEC need not prove reliance by third parties to impose criminal liability upon Danforth. Therefore, the fact that Danforth can establish that no one relied to his/her detriment upon the audit report will not be a valid defense to the criminal action. The SEC need only prove what was stated above in part a.1. But, a third party would have to prove reliance upon the financial statements to his/her detriment in order to impose civil liability on Danforth.

Part b.

Yes, the bank will prevail against Danforth. After issuing the unqualified opinion, Danforth discovered the CD had been sold. Therefore, there was a subsequent discovery of a fact existing at date of auditor's report which would have affected Danforth's report had he been aware of such fact, since the financial statements would now be misleading. Upon such subsequent discovery, the auditor should take appropriate action to prevent future reliance on his/her report. Danforth has a duty to anyone still relying on his audit report to disclose subsequently discovered error(s) in the report. Since Danforth had knowledge that the bank was to rely on the financial statements, he should have notified the bank that his report should no longer be relied upon.

Danforth's performance of the audit in accordance with generally accepted auditing standards (GAAS) does not relieve him of his duty to disclose the subsequently discovered falsity of the financial statements. The law imposes upon the auditor the profession's generally accepted standards of competence and due care. When there is a duty to speak, the concealment of a material fact is equivalent to a fraudulent misrepresentation. Such fraudulent intent can be inferred from the auditor's conduct. Danforth was guilty of common law fraud for failure to notify the bank of the subsequently discovered information.

The bank must prove:

- There was a material misstatement of the financial statements.
- It reasonably believed the statements to be true.
- It relied on such statements.
- Damages or losses resulted from such reliance.

These elements are established since the bank made a loan to Blair in reliance upon the auditor's report, and such loan proved to be uncollectible resulting in a loss to the bank.

Answer Outline

Problem 2 Anti-fraud Section of Security Act of 1934; Liability and Defenses Under Sec. 11(A) of 1933 Act

a1. Under antifraud provision in section 10(b) of SEC Act of 1934, Thaxton is required to show
  Misstatement or omission of material fact in financials utilized in purchasing Whitlow & Co. stock
  Loss resulted from purchase of stock
  Loss resulted from reliance on misleading financials
  Auditors acted with knowledge (scienter)
Facts indicated that proof of first three requirements by Thaxton is probable; however, facts show that auditors did not have knowledge

a2. Negligence as evidenced by failure to comply with GAAS; if auditors were negligent, customers and shareholders must show
  They had third party beneficiary status relative to auditor's contract to audit Whitlow & Co., or
  A legal duty to act without negligence was due to them

b1. Basis of claim is that loss was sustained from using misleading statements; section 11(a) of 1933 SEC Act applies
  Potential liability arises if minor irregularities result in certification of materially false or misleading financials
  Jackson's case asserts that financials contain false statement and that damages were sustained
  Jackson does not have to prove reliance of negligence (company or auditor)
  To avoid liability defendant must supply acceptable defenses

b2. Probable defenses which Allen, Dunn and Rose might assert are
  Jackson knew of false statement or omission in audited financials included in registration statement
    Jackson (plaintiff) may not recover if proof exists that she had knowledge of "untruth or omission"
    Facts indicate Jackson may have had adequate knowledge
  False statement or omission was not material; test is whether investor would have been influenced not to purchase stock if right information had been disclosed
  Loss did not result from false statement or omission
    Portion of loss probably resulted from stock market decline
    Lack of evidence linking earnings decline to false statement or omission would give auditors defense
  Departure from GAAS did not represent noncompliance with due diligence standard

Unofficial Answer

Problem 2 Anti-fraud Section of Security Act of 1934; Liability and Defenses Under Sec. 11(A) of 1933 Act

Part a.

1. In order for Thaxton to hold Mitchell & Moss liable for his losses under the Securities Exchange Act

of 1934, he must rely upon the antifraud provisions of section 10(b) of the act. In order to prevail Thaxton must establish that

- There was an omission or misstatement of a material fact in the financial statements used in connection with his purchase of the Whitlow & Company shares of stock.
- He sustained a loss as a result of his purchase of the shares of stock.
- His loss was caused by reliance on the misleading financial statements.
- Mitchell & Moss acted with scienter.

Based on the stated facts, Thaxton can probably prove the first three requirements cited above. To prove the fourth requirement, Thaxton must show that Mitchell & Moss had knowledge (scienter) of the fraud or recklessly disregarded the truth. The facts clearly indicate that Mitchell & Moss did not have knowledge of the fraud and did not recklessly disregard the truth.

2. The customers and shareholders of Whitlow & Company would attempt to recover on a negligence theory based on Mitchell & Moss' failure to comply with GAAS. Even if Mitchell & Moss were negligent, Whitlow & Company's customers and shareholders must also establish either that —

- They were third party beneficiaries of Mitchell & Moss' contract to audit Whitlow & Company, *or*
- Mitchell & Moss owed the customers and shareholders a legal duty to act without negligence.

Although recent cases have expanded a CPA's legal responsibilities to a third party for negligence, the facts of this case may fall within the traditional rationale limiting a CPA's liability for negligence; that is, the unfairness of imputing an indeterminate amount of liability to unknown or unforeseen parties as a result of mere negligence on the auditor's part. Accordingly, Whitlow & Company's customers and shareholders will prevail only if (1) the courts rule that they are either third-party beneficiaries or are owed a legal duty and (2) they establish that Mitchell & Moss was negligent in failing to comply with generally accepted auditing standards.

Part b.

1. The basis of Jackson's claim will be that she sustained a loss based upon misleading financial statements. Specifically, she will rely upon section 11(a) of the Securities Act of 1933, which provides the following:

> In case any part of the registration statement, when such part became effective, contained an untrue statement of a material fact or omitted to state a material fact required to be stated therein or necessary to make the statements therein not misleading, any person acquiring such security (unless it is proved that at the time of such acquisition he knew of such untruth or omission) may, either at law or in equity, in any court of competent jurisdiction, sue . . . every accountant . . . who has with his consent been named as having prepared or certified any part of the registration statement . . .

To the extent that the relatively minor irregularities resulted in the certification of materially false or misleading financial statements, there is potential liability. Jackson's case is based on the assertion of such an untrue statement or omission coupled with an allegation of damages. Jackson does not have to prove reliance on the statements nor the company's or auditor's negligence in order to recover the damages. The burden is placed on the defendant to provide defenses that will enable it to avoid liability.

2. The first defense that could be asserted is that Jackson knew of the untruth or omission in audited financial statements included in the registration statement. The act provides that the plaintiff may not recover if it can be proved that at the time of such acquisition she knew of such "untruth or omission."

Since Jackson was a member of the private placement group and presumably privy to the type of information that would be contained in a registration statement, plus any other information requested by the group, she may have had sufficient knowledge of the facts claimed to be untrue or omitted. If this be the case, then she would not be relying on the certified financial statements but upon her own knowledge.

The next defense assertable would be that the untrue statement or omission was not material. The SEC has defined the term as meaning matters about which an average prudent investor ought to be reasonably informed before purchasing the registered security. For section 11 purposes, this has been construed as meaning a fact that, had it been correctly stated or disclosed, would have deterred or tended to deter the average prudent investor from purchasing the security in question.

Allen, Dunn, and Rose would also assert that the loss in question was not due to the false statement or omission; this is, that the false statement was not the cause of the price drop. It would appear that the general decline in the stock market would account for at least a part of the loss. Additionally, if the decline in earnings was not factually connected with the false statement or omission, the defendants have another basis for refuting the causal connection between their wrongdoing and the resultant drop in the stock's price.

Finally, the accountants will claim that their departure from generally accepted auditing standards was too minor to be considered a violation of the standard of due diligence required by the act.

Answer Outline

Problem 3 Accountant–Client Privilege; Accountants' Liability for Compilation of Financial Statements

Part a.

1. Common law does not recognize accountant-client privilege
   Privilege can be created by statute to be adopted by state
   No such privilege exists under federal law
   Subpoena issued by SEC falls within federal law
   State statute creating privilege is not applicable
   Sharp must produce workpapers
2. Accountant-client privilege preserves confidentiality of communications between client and accountant
   Privilege can only be claimed by the client
   Client may waive the statutory privilege
   Fargo's waiver for two years of workpapers constitutes waiver of privilege for remaining years
3. SEC has power to subpoena relevant material
   Subpoena must be limited in scope
   Subpoena must be relevant in purpose
   Such that compliance will not be unreasonably burdensome
   Sharp could contend subpoena unreasonably burdensome
   Sharp did nothing improper
   Cost of duplicating workpapers is excessive

Part b.

Compilation of financial statements is representation of management's information
Accountants must still exercise ordinary and reasonable care
In accordance with professional standards of competence
Failure to meet these standards is negligence
Accountant liable to third party for negligence
If accountant knows services are primarily for third party
Accountant liable for constructive fraud
If shows reckless disregard for truth
Accountant had duty to all third parties to prepare reports without fraud
Third party can recover if reasonably relied on accountant's work
Pelham & James oral representation was reckless disregard for truth
Pelham & James foresaw Dickerson's and Nichols' reliance on financial representations

Unofficial Answer
(Author Modified)

Problem 3 Accountant–Client Privilege; Accountants' Liability for Compilation of Financial Statements

Part a.

1. No. In the absence of statute or agreement to the contrary, workpapers are generally owned by the accountant. But ownership of the workpapers is not a valid ground for refusing to produce them in evidence when such production is required by legal process. The common law recognizes no accountant–client privilege, but such privilege can be created by statute. Several states have adopted such statutes, but Congress has not. Due to the fact that the federal government has not yet granted such privilege, and this case applies federal law (i.e., federal securities laws), the accountant must produce the workpapers for the federal government or for a federal agency (i.e., SEC, IRS) if served with an enforceable subpoena. Since the matters before these agencies are based on federal law, state statutes creating the accountant–client privilege are not applicable, and no privilege exists on behalf of accountants in these proceedings. Therefore, since Sharp was served with an enforceable subpoena by the SEC, a federal agency, he must turn over the workpapers.

Also, Rule 301 of the AICPA Professional Code of Ethics, dealing with the accountant's duty not to disclose any confidential information obtained in the course of a professional audit, states that such Rule is not to be construed to affect the accountant's compliance with a validly issued subpoena.

2. No. To properly perform an audit, the accountant should have access to the details of his client's operations, many of which the client may consider confidential. The accountant–client privilege enables the accountant to obtain more complete information, by preserving the confidentiality of communications between the client and the accountant, thus promoting increased financial disclosure and greater accuracy. But where this privilege does exist, it can only be claimed by the client. This privilege belonging to the

client is consistent with the AICPA Code of Professional Ethics provisions which prohibit disclosure of confidential information attained in the course of a professional engagement except with the consent of the client. Therefore, the client may waive this privilege, resulting in the accountant being required to comply with Nuggett's request. By Fargo giving permission for the introduction of two years of workpapers, this constitutes waiver of the accountant—client privilege and Sharp must comply by producing the previous eight years as well as the last two audit years.

3. Congress has endowed the SEC with power to conduct investigations. This power allows the SEC to issue subpoenaes for the production of relevant documents concerning a matter under investigation. However, this investigatory power does not provide the SEC with a "blank check." The investigation must not be of such a sweeping and broad nature and so unrelated to matters properly under inquiry as to exceed this granted investigatory power. Therefore, the subpoena issued by the SEC is required to be sufficiently limited in scope, relevant in purpose and specific so that compliance will not be unreasonably burdensome.

Because there is no evidence that Sharp did anything improper during the last ten years, Sharp could contend that a subpoena calling for the production of all his workpapers would be unreasonably burdensome and too broad in nature, thereby exceeding the SEC's investigatory power.

Although a subpoenaed party can legitimately be required to absorb reasonable expenses of compliance with administrative subpoenas, Sharp could assert that the subpoena is unduly burdensome due to the fact that the cost of producing (i.e., photocopying) all the workpapers exceeds that which a party ought reasonably be expected to bear.

Part b.

Yes. A compilation of statements is the presentation in the form of financial statements consisting of information that is the representation of management (owners), without the accountants undertaking to express any assurances on the statements. The accountants engaged for such a procedure are normally not required to make inquiries or to perform any procedures to validate or verify the information provided to them. However, Pelham & James must still exercise ordinary and reasonable care in accordance with the special skills and training of reasonably prudent auditors.

The law imposes upon the accountants the profession's generally accepted standards of competence and due care. Failure to meet these professional standards constitutes negligence. In order to have an action for negligence, the injured party does not have to be in privity of contract with the accountants, but must be a person whose reliance on the financial representations was actually foreseen by the accountant. An accountant may be held liable by third parties for ordinary negligence when the accountant knows that the services for a client are primarily for a third party. Pelham & James knew that Dickerson and Nichols were intended beneficiaries of both the compilation report and the oral statements concerning the accuracy of payables. Therefore, Pelham & James had a duty to perform with due care which appears to have been breached.

In addition, Pelham & James may be found liable for constructive fraud. The court will find constructive fraud where the performing party, based on gross negligence or willful indifference, shows a reckless disregard for the truth. Accountants owe a duty to all third parties to prepare their reports without fraud. This third party liability for fraud exists regardless of whether the accountant's services were intended primarily for the benefit of the client or primarily for the benefit of third parties. Therefore, in constructive fraud there need not be actual intent to deceive. In order for a third party to recover damages from an accountant for constructive fraud, the third party must show that s/he reasonably relied on the accountant's work.

Pelham & James were advised to pay particular attention to the trade accounts payable. They did not engage in audit verification procedures to determine the accuracy of these payables. Yet, they informed Dickerson and Nichols that the accounts payable balance was accurate to within $8,000, when in fact it was materially understated by $60,000. Such an understatement could have been discovered had the compilation been made with average professional skill and related reasonable care by inspecting Stone's unpaid bills. This indicates a reckless disregard for the truth and gross negligence. Dickerson and Nichols reasonably relied on both the financial statements and Pelham & James' oral representations. Therefore, regardless of Pelham & James' disclaimer of opinion in the compilation report concerning the financial statements, they will be found liable to Dickerson and Nichols in a common law action for damages.

Multiple Choice Questions (1 - 23)

1. Which of the following employees are exempt from the minimum and maximum hour provisions of the Fair Labor Standards Act?

   a. Children.
   b. Railroad and airline employees.
   c. Members of a union recognized as the bargaining agent by the National Labor Relations Board.
   d. Office workers.

2. Under the Fair Labor Standards Act the Secretary of Labor does **not** have the power to

   a. Issue subpoenas compelling attendance by a witness and the production of records by an employer.
   b. Conduct investigations regarding practices subject to the Act.
   c. Issue a wage order which requires an employer to pay wages found to be due and owing under the Act.
   d. Issue injunctions to restrain obvious violations of the Act.

3. Under the Fair Labor Standards Act, certain employment of children is considered oppressive and is prohibited. Which of the following is **not** a legal exception to the Act?

   a. Employment in agriculture outside of school hours.
   b. Employment of children under sixteen by a parent.
   c. Newspaper delivery.
   d. After school part-time work in the fast-food industry.

4. Stephens is an employee of the Jensen Manufacturing Company, a multi-state manufacturer of roller-skates. The plant in which he works is unionized and Stephens is a dues paying union member. Which statement is correct insofar as the Federal Fair Labor Standards Act is concerned?

   a. The Act allows a piece-rate method to be employed in lieu of the hourly-rate method where appropriate.
   b. Jensen is permitted to pay less than the minimum wage to employees since they are represented by a bona fide union.
   c. The Act sets the maximum number of hours that an employee can work in a given day or week.
   d. The Act excludes from its coverage the employees of a labor union.

5. Ichi Ban Mopeds, Inc., is a Japanese manufacturer which has a manufacturing facility in the United States. United States business comprises ten percent (10%) of the sales of Ichi Ban of which four percent (4%) is manufactured at its United States facility. Under these circumstances

   a. Ichi Ban is exempt from state workmen's compensation laws.
   b. Ichi Ban is exempt from the Fair Labor Standards Act provided it is governed by comparable Japanese law.
   c. Ichi Ban is subject to generally prevailing federal and state laws applicable to American employees with respect to its employees at the United States facility.
   d. Ichi Ban could legally institute a policy which limited promotions to Japanese-Americans.

6. The Federal Fair Labor Standards Act

   a. Prohibits any employment of a person under 16 years of age.
   b. Requires payment of time-and-one-half for overtime to actors engaged in making television productions.
   c. Contains an exemption from the minimum-wage provision for manufacturing plants located in areas of high unemployment.
   d. Prohibits the delivery by a wholesaler to a dealer in another state of any goods where the wholesaler knew that oppressive child labor was used in the manufacture of the goods.

7. Which of the following classes of employees is exempt from both the minimum wage and maximum hours provisions of the Federal Fair Labor Standards Act?

   a. Members of a labor union.
   b. Administrative personnel.
   c. Hospital workers.
   d. No class of employees is exempt.

8. Hicks is employed as executive sales manager by Foster Fabrics. She received a salary of $30,000 in 1982. In addition, she earned $15,000 net in 1982 as a free lance photographer. As a result of the above earnings for 1982 and the application of the provisions of the Federal Insurance Contributions Act, Hicks

   a. Owed nothing since her salary was fully subjected to withholding of FICA tax by Foster.
   b. Was required to pay a self-employment tax on the difference between the FICA tax base amount and $30,000.

c. Was required to pay both an employer and employee FICA tax on the $15,000.
d. Was required to ascertain the gross amount of income from the free lance photography and compute the FICA tax owed on that amount.

9. There are federal and state unemployment taxes. Regarding the Federal Unemployment Tax Act
a. Payment of the tax is shared equally by the employer and the employee.
b. Employees who earn less than $7,000 are exempt from coverage.
c. Benefits to an employee can **not** exceed the amount contributed to his account.
d. A credit is generally available for contributions made by the employer to state unemployment funds.

10. The social security tax does **not** apply to which of the following?
a. Payments on account of sickness including medical and hospital expenses paid by the employer.
b. Compensation paid in forms other than cash.
c. Self-employment income of $1,000.
d. Bonuses and vacation time pay.

11. The Social Security Act provides for the imposition of taxes and the disbursement of benefits. Which of the following is a correct statement regarding these taxes and disbursements?
a. Only those who have contributed to Social Security are eligible for benefits.
b. As between an employer and its employee, the tax rates are the same.
c. A deduction for federal income tax purposes is allowed the employee for Social Security taxes paid.
d. Social Security payments are includable in gross income for federal income tax purposes unless they are paid for disability.

12. Which of the following is a correct statement regarding the federal income tax treatment of social security tax payments and retirement benefits?
a. The employer's social security tax payments are **not** deductible from its gross income.
b. Social security retirement benefits are fully includable in the gross income of the retiree if he earns an amount in excess of certain established ceilings.
c. Social security retirement benefits are excludable from the retiree's gross income even if the retiree has recouped all he has contributed.
d. The employee's social security tax payments are deductible from the employee's gross income.

13. At age 66, Jonstone retired as a general partner of Gordon & Co. He no longer participates in the affairs of the partnership but does receive a distributive share of the partnership profits as a result of becoming a limited partner upon retirement. Jonstone has accepted a part-time consulting position with a corporation near his retirement home. Which of the following is correct regarding Jonstone's Social Security situation?
a. Jonstone's limited partner distributive share will be considered self-employment income for Social Security purposes up to a maximum of $10,000.
b. There is no limitation on the amount Jonstone may earn in the first year of retirement.
c. Jonstone will lose $1 of Social Security benefits for each $1 earnings in excess of a statutorily permitted amount.
d. Jonstone will be subject to an annual earnings limitation until he attains a stated age which, if exceeded, will reduce the amount of Social Security benefits.

14. During the 1976 examination of the financial statements of Viscount Manufacturing Corporation, the CPAs noted that although Viscount had 860 full-time and part-time employees, it had completely overlooked its responsibilities under the Federal Insurance Contributions Act (FICA). Under these circumstances, which of the following is true?
a. No liability under the act will attach if the employees voluntarily relinquish their rights under the act in exchange for a cash equivalent paid directly to them.
b. If the union which represents the employees has a vested pension plan covering the employees which is equal to or exceeds the benefits available under the act, Viscount has no liability.
c. Since employers and employees owe FICA taxes at the same rate and since the employer must withhold the employees' tax from their wages as paid, Viscount

must remit to the government a tax double the amount assessed directly against the employer.

d. The act does not apply to the part-time employees.

15. Jane Sabine was doing business as Sabine Fashions, a sole proprietorship. Sabine suffered financial reverses and began to use social security and income taxes withheld from her employees to finance the business. Sabine finally filed a voluntary petition in bankruptcy. Which of the following would not apply to her as a result of her actions?

a. She would remain liable for the taxes due.

b. She is personally liable for fines and imprisonment.

c. She could justify her actions by showing that the use of the tax money was vital to continuation of the business.

d. She may be assessed penalties up to the amount of taxes due.

16. Fairfax was employed by Wexford Manufacturing Company as a salaried salesman. While Fairfax was driving a company car on a sales call, a truck owned and operated by Red Van Lines ran a stop light and collided with Fairfax's car. Fairfax applied for and received worker's compensation for the injuries sustained. As a result of receiving worker's compensation, Fairfax

a. Must assign any negligence cause of action to Wexford pursuant to the doctrine of respondeat superior.

b. Is precluded from suing Red for negligence because of the worker's compensation award.

c. Can recover in full against Red for negligence, but must return any duplication of the worker's compensation award.

d. Can recover in full against Red for negligence and retain the full amounts awarded under worker's compensation.

17. Which of the following would be the employer's best defense to a claim for workers' compensation by an injured route salesman?

a. A route salesman is automatically deemed to be an independent contractor, and therefore excluded from workers' compensation coverage.

b. The salesman was grossly negligent in carrying out the employment.

c. The salesman's injury was caused primarily by the negligence of an employee.

d. The salesman's injury did **not** arise out of and in the course of employment.

18. Musgrove Manufacturing Enterprises is subject to compulsory worker's compensation laws in the state in which it does business. It has complied with the state's worker's compensation provisions. State law provides that where there has been compliance, worker's compensation is normally an exclusive remedy. However, the remedy will **not** be exclusive if

a. The employee has been intentionally injured by the employer personally.

b. The employee dies as a result of his injuries.

c. The accident was entirely the fault of a fellow-servant of the employee.

d. The employer was only slightly negligent and the employee's conduct was grossly negligent.

19. Harris was engaged as a crane operator by the Wilcox Manufacturing Corporation, a company complying with state worker's compensation laws. Harris suffered injuries during regular working hours as a result of carelessly climbing out on the arm of the crane to make an adjustment. While doing so, he lost his balance, fell off the arm of the crane and fractured his leg. Wilcox's safety manual for the operation of the crane strictly forbids such conduct by an operator. Wilcox denies any liability, based upon Harris' gross negligence, his disobedience and a waiver of all liability signed by Harris shortly after the accident. Wilcox further asserts that Harris is **not** entitled to worker's compensation because he is a skilled worker and is on a guaranteed biweekly salary. Which of the following is a correct statement insofar as Harris' rights are concerned?

a. If he elects to sue under common law for negligence, his own negligence will result in a denial of recovery.

b. Harris is **not** entitled to worker's compensation because he is **not** an "employee."

c. Harris is **not** entitled to recovery because his conduct was a clear violation of the safety manual.

d. Harris waived his rights by signing a waiver of liability.

20. Yeats Manufacturing is engaged in the manufacture and sale of convertible furniture in interstate commerce. Yeats' manufacturing facilities are located in a jurisdiction which has a compulsory workmen's

compensation act. Hardwood, Yeats' president, decided that the company should, in light of its safety record, choose to ignore the requirement of providing workmen's compensation insurance. Instead, Hardwood indicated that a special account should be created to provide for such contingencies. Basset was severely injured as a result of his negligent operation of a lathe which accelerated and cut off his right arm. In assessing the potential liability of Yeats, which of the following is a correct answer?

a. Federal law applies since Yeats is engaged in interstate commerce.
b. Yeats has no liability, since Basset negligently operated the lathe.
c. Since Yeats did not provide workmen's compensation insurance, it can be sued by Basset and cannot resort to the usual common law defenses.
d. Yeats is a self-insurer, hence it has no liability beyond the amount of the money in the insurance fund.

21. The Equal Employment Opportunity Commission

a. Has authority to impose criminal penalties under the Equal Employment Opportunity Act.
b. Has the power to file a civil suit in federal district court and to represent a person charging a violation of the act.
c. Has **no** jurisdiction over the Civil Rights Act.
d. Has authority to issue cease and desist orders in those cases where there have been repeated violations.

May 1984 Questions

22. Which of the following statements is correct regarding social security benefits?

a. Retirement benefits are fully includable in the determination of the recipient's federal taxable income if his gross income exceeds certain maximum limitations.
b. Retirement benefits paid in excess of the recipient's contributions will be included in the determination of the recipient's federal taxable income regardless of his gross income.
c. Individuals who have made **no** contributions may be eligible for some benefits.
d. Upon the death of the recipient, immediate family members within certain age limits are entitled to a death benefit equal to the unpaid portion of the deceased recipient's contributions.

23. Wilk, an employee of Young Corp., was injured by the negligence of Quick, an independent contractor. The accident occurred during regular working hours and in the course of employment. If Young has complied with the state's workers' compensation laws, which of the following is correct?

a. Wilk is barred from suing Young or Quick for negligence.
b. Wilk will be denied workers' compensation if he was negligent in failing to adhere to the written safety procedures.
c. The amount of damages Wilk will be allowed to recover from Young will be based on comparative fault.
d. Wilk may obtain workers' compensation benefits and also properly maintain an action against Quick.

Problems

Problem 1 Workmen's Compensation (1178,L3c)

(5 to 10 minutes)

Part c. Eureka Enterprises, Inc., started doing business in July 1977. It manufactures electronic components and currently employs 35 individuals. In anticipation of future financing needs, Eureka has engaged a CPA firm to audit its financial statements. During the course of the examination, the CPA firm discovers that Eureka has no workmen's compensation insurance, which is in violation of state law, and so informs the president of Eureka.

Required:

Answer the following, setting forth reasons for any conclusion stated.

1. What is the purpose of a state workmen's compensation law?
2. What are the legal implications of not having workmen's compensation insurance?

Multiple Choice Answers

1.	b	6.	d	11.	b	16.	c	20.	c
2.	d	7.	b	12.	c	17.	d	21.	b
3.	d	8.	b	13.	d	18.	a	22.	c
4.	a	9.	d	14.	c	19.	a	23.	d
5.	c	10.	a	15.	c				

Multiple Choice Answer Explanations

A. Fair Labor Standards Act

1. (1182,L1,28) (b) Special exemptions from both the minimum wage and maximum hour provisions of the Fair Labor Standards Act are granted to several classes of employees. These include employees of the railroad and air carriers. Answers (a), (c) and (d) are incorrect because the provisions of the Act provide protection for each of these types of employees.

2. (1182,L1,29) (d) Only the courts have the power to issue injunctions to restrain obvious violations of the Fair Labor Standards Act. Answers (a), (b) and (c) are incorrect because these are all powers which the Secretary of Labor possesses in the regulation and enforcement of the Act's provisions.

3. (582,L1,34) (d) The child labor provisions of the Fair Labor Standards Act prohibit the employment of "oppressive child labor." Employment of children in after school part-time work in the fast-food industry falls within the child labor provisions as one of the employment situations which the Fair Labor Standards Act seeks to prevent if deemed to be oppressive in nature. Answers (a), (b), and (c) are incorrect because they are occupations and employment situations which are exempted from the child labor provisions.

4. (581,L1,58) (a) Under the Fair Labor Standards Act an employer can substitute a piece-rate method of payment for the hourly rate. Answers (b) and (d) are incorrect since the fact that the employees are represented by a union would be irrelevant when applying this act. Union members are covered by the act and must be paid at least the statutory minimum wage. Answer (c) is incorrect since the act does not specify the maximum number of hours an employee can work in a given day. The act does stipulate that an employee is to be paid time and a half for hours worked in excess of 40 hours per week.

5. (1180,L1,58) (c) Since Ichi Ban Mopeds, Inc., is doing business in the United States, it is subject to applicable federal and state laws concerning the employees at the United States facility. This includes state workmen's compensation laws, the Fair Labor Standards Act, and many other regulatory statutes. Answer (d) is incorrect because Title VII of Civil Rights Act of 1964 states that employers cannot discriminate on the basis of religion, sex or national origin unless the above categories are bona fide occupational qualifications reasonably necessary to normal business operation. National origin would not be a bona fide occupational qualification for promotion.

6. (574,L3,42) (d) The Fair Labor Standards Act (FLSA) prohibits the shipment or sale of goods in interstate commerce when the seller knows such goods were produced in violation of the Act (e.g., where oppressive child labor was used in the manufacture of the goods). Answer (a) is incorrect because the FLSA provides child labor exemptions for employment in agriculture outside school hours, employment of child actors, employment by a parent in a nonhazardous occupation, and employment to deliver newspapers. Answer (b) is incorrect because professionals, such as actors, are exempt from the FLSA provision for overtime payment. Answer (c) is incorrect because the FLSA does not provide an exemption from the minimum wage provision for manufacturing plants in areas of high unemployment.

7. (577,L1,13) (b) Administrative personnel are exempt from the minimum wage and maximum hours provisions of the FLSA as are executive and professional employees. Labor union members and hospital workers are covered by the FLSA.

B. Federal Social Security Act

8. (1183,L1,39) (b) In 1982 only the first $32,400 of wages were taxable under FICA. Thus, Hicks was required to pay the self-employment FICA tax rate on $2,400 of her earnings as a free-lance photographer which is the difference between the FICA tax base amount and $30,000 (her salary from Foster). Answer (a) is incorrect because a self-employed individual must pay FICA tax if they have not already paid such taxes on a salary equal to the base amount. Answer (c) is incorrect because Hicks would only pay the self-employment tax rate (9.35%) on her self-employed income, which is less than the sum of the employer's and employee's tax rates (13.4%). Answer (d) is incorrect because the FICA tax would not be computed on Hicks' gross income from the photography, but the net income.

9. (1183,L1,41) (d) Employers are entitled to a credit against their federal unemployment tax for con-

tributions made to state unemployment funds. Answer (a) is incorrect because the federal unemployment tax is only paid by the employers. Answer (b) is incorrect because an employer, when covered by the Federal Unemployment Act, must pay a federal unemployment tax of 3.4% on the first $6,000 wages of every employee. Answer (c) is incorrect because benefits to an employee can exceed the amount contributed to his/her account by the employer.

10. (1181,L1,30) (a) The social security tax within the Federal Social Security Act applies to compensation received which is considered to be "wages." Answers (b), (c), and (d) are incorrect because under the Act wages include compensation paid in forms other than cash, such as bonuses and vacation time, and self-employment income. But hospitalization and medical expenses paid by the employer are not considered wages.

11. (581,L1,59) (b) An employer is required to match contributions of employees to the Social Security System on a dollar-for-dollar basis. Answer (a) is incorrect since benefits may be paid to the surviving spouse or other dependents of a deceased individual who was covered under the Social Security System. Answer (c) is incorrect since the amount of Social Security taxes paid is not an allowable deduction on an individual's tax return. Payments to the system are taxed in full when made, and are recovered on a tax-free basis when received by the individual in the form of benefits. Answer (d) is incorrect because Social Security payments are not included in the gross income of a taxpayer.

12. (1180,L1,60) (c) Out of social concern for the well-being of the elderly, social security income may be excluded from gross income, when filing a federal tax return. Therefore answer (b) is incorrect. Answer (a) is false since the employer may deduct all ordinary and necessary business expense including social security tax. Answer (d) is incorrect because federal tax laws provide that since social security benefits are not included in gross income, social security payments cannot be deducted from gross income during the taxpayer's working years.

13. (580,L1,18) (d) Answer (d) is correct because there is no limit on earnings after age 72 under the Social Security laws. Answer (a) is incorrect because under Social Security law an individual's wages normally shall be computed without regard to any maximum limitations and a partner's distributive share will be excluded entirely if certain requirements are met. Answer (b) is incorrect because the limitation on Jonstone's earnings may occur in the first year if he had excess earnings above the statutorily permitted amount. Answer (c) is incorrect because Social Security law does reduce benefits on the basis of a complicated statutory formula that would not result in a loss of $1 of Social Security benefits for each $1 of earnings in excess of a statutorily permitted amount.

14. (1177,L1,13) (c) It is the employer's duty to withhold FICA taxes from the employee and remit both these and the employer's share to the government. If the employer neglects to withhold, the employer is liable for both the employer and employee taxes, i.e., to pay double. Answer (a) is incorrect because FICA is mandatory and employees may not relinquish their rights. Answer (b) is incorrect because pension plans and other benefits are no substitute for FICA. Answer (d) is incorrect because FICA applies to all employees whether part-time or full-time.

15. (579,L1,50) (c) The requirement is the statement that would not apply to Jane Sabine's actions. An employer who withholds social security and income taxes from employees may not justify using such funds to finance her business even if such action were vital to continuation of the business. Such action is a criminal act and would subject the perpetrator to absolute liability. Even should she be adjudicated a bankrupt, she would, as in answer (a), remain personally liable for taxes due. As in answer (b), she would be personally liable for fines and imprisonment. Also in answer (d), she may be assessed penalties up to the amount of the taxes due (100%).

C. Workmen's Compensation Acts

16. (583,L1,34) (c) Workmen's compensation laws provide coverage for employee's injuries which occur on the job or in the course of employment. The employee's acceptance of workmen's compensation benefits does not bar a suit against a third party whose negligence caused the injury. However, if the employee recovers from the third party, his employer is entitled to compensation for the benefits he paid to the employee. If the employee's recovery exceeds the benefits paid to him by his employer, the employee may keep the excess. Therefore, answers (b) and (d) are incorrect. Answer (a) is incorrect because the employee (Fairfax) can maintain his own cause of action for negligence; he does not have to assign the cause of action to his employer (Wexford). But an employer is subrogated to the employee's claim against a third party if the employee accepts workmen's compensation benefits. Therefore, the employer could

maintain a cause of action against the third party if the employee did not. The doctrine of respondent superior has no relevance to the situation in question since it refers to the employer being held liable for employee's torts if they are within the scope of his employment and committed during the course of his duties.

17. (1182,L1,27) (d) Workmen's compensation laws provide coverage for employees' injuries which occur on the job or in the course of employment. Answer (a) is incorrect because although an independent contractor is not entitled to workmen's compensation coverage, a route salesman would be considered an employee, since his work is subject to the control and supervision of the employer, and thus be extended workmen's compensation coverage. Answers (b) and (c) are incorrect because the liability of an employer is a form of strict liability, whereby an employee is entitled to workmen's compensation for an injury related to employment without regard to fault. Negligence, or even gross negligence, on the part of the employee is not a bar to such recovery. The only injuries which are generally not covered are those which are intentionally self-inflicted, and those which result from the employee's intoxication.

18. (581,L1,60) (a) If the employer intentionally injures the employee, the employee would not only have a right to proceed under worker's compensation, but could sue the employer in a civil court of law on the basis of an intentional tort. Answers (b), (c) and (d) are incorrect because they do not state grounds that would allow the injured employee to sue in a civil court of law if covered by a proper worker's compensation plan. Even though the injury was caused by contributory negligence of the employee or the act of a fellow servant, the injured employee could still recover, but recovery under worker's compensation would be the exclusive remedy.

19. (1180,L1,59) (a) The correct answer is (a) since if Harris elects to sue under common law for negligence, the employer can use the defense of contributory negligence which will prevent Harris from recovering. Since the purpose of the workmen's compensation laws is to give employees certainty of benefits for job-related injuries and diseases, most state statutes prohibit waiver of these benefits by employees. Thus answer (d) is wrong. Workmen's compensation laws destroy the employer's common law defenses of: assumption of risk; negligence of a fellow employee; contributory negligence. Even though the employee's conduct that caused the injury was a violation of prescribed safety rules, the employee will recover under workmen's compensation laws if the injury occurred on the job. Thus answer (d) is incorrect. Answer (b) is incorrect because a skilled worker on a guaranteed biweekly salary is not exempted from the provisions of workmen's compensation laws. However, workmen's compensation laws do not cover all employees; some exemptions are: agricultural workers; domestic workers; causal employees; employers who employ below a fixed number of employees.

20. (1179,L1,48) (c) The usual result when the employer fails to provide workmen's compensation insurance is that the injured employee may sue in a common law action, and the employer cannot resort to the usual common law defenses (such as contributory negligence, assumption of risk, or fellow servant rule). Answer (a) is incorrect because there is no federal law applying to workmen's compensation. Workmen's compensation is regulated by state statutes, which are only affected by federal guidelines. Answer (b) is incorrect because the employer does have liability for job-related injuries even if the injured employee was negligent. Answer (d) is incorrect in that Yeats is not a self-insurer because the problem indicates that he is doing business in a state that has a compulsory workmen's compensation act, i.e., does not recognize self-insurance plans.

D. Equal Employment Opportunity Laws

21. (1183,L1,40) (b) The Equal Employment Opportunity Commission (EEOC) is the federal agency responsible for administering and enforcing Title VII of the Civil Rights Act of 1964. To assist in carrying out this mandate, the Civil Rights Act of 1964 was amended in 1972 by the Equal Employment Opportunity Act, which authorizes the EEOC to file civil lawsuits in federal district court on behalf of individuals who have been discriminated against in violation of the Act. Although the EEOC may award back pay and seek injunctions in federal court, the EEOC has no authority to either impose criminal sanctions or issue cease and desist orders. Accordingly, answers (a), (c), and (d) are incorrect.

May 1984 Answers

22. (584,L1,27) (c) Since children may receive death benefits because of the death of a parent, it is possible for some individuals who have made no contributions to be eligible to receive social security benefits. Answers (a) and (b) are incorrect because social security benefits are not taxable. Answer (d) is incorrect because upon the death of a recipient, immediate family members within certain age limits are not en-

titled to a death benefit equal to the unpaid portion of the deceased recipient's contributions. The amount of survivor's benefits are not dependent upon the amount of contributions made by the deceased. Rather, the amount received by the beneficiary is dependent on both the average monthly earnings and the relationship of the beneficiary to the deceased worker.

23. (584,L1,28) (d) Wilk may obtain worker's compensation benefits and also maintain an action against Quick (third party that caused injury). If Wilk recovers against third party (Quick) after obtaining worker's compensation benefits, a part of the recovery equal to the benefits received belong to the employer (Young Corp.). Answer (a) is incorrect because although Wilk is barred from suing the employer for negligence, he can sue Quick. Answer (b) is incorrect because worker's compensation laws eliminate the employer's defense of contributory negligence. Consequently, Wilk will recover because the injury occurred in the course of employment. Answer (c) is incorrect because the amount of damages Wilk will be allowed is not based on comparative fault but on a scheme proscribed by state statute, usually a percentage of the injured employee's wages.

Answer Outline

Problem 1 Workmen's Compensation

c1. Workmen's comp compensates employees injured at work
   Benefits available to injured, survivors, or dependents

c2. Workmen's comp is generally mandatory by statute
   Employers with no workmen's comp have liability
   Also precludes common-law defenses of
      Fellow-servant
      Assumption of risk
      Contributory negligence
   Employer may also be liable for workmen's comp benefits, also fines and possibly imprisonment

Unofficial Answer

Problem 1 Workmen's Compensation

Part c.

1. Workmen's compensation laws provide a system of compensation for employees who are injured, disabled, or killed as a result of accidents or occupational diseases in the course of their employment. Benefits also extend to survivors or dependents of these employees.

2. In all but a distinct minority of jurisdictions, workmen's compensation coverage is mandatory. In those few jurisdictions that have elective workmen's compensation, employers who reject workmen's compensation coverage are subject to common law actions by injured employees and are precluded from asserting the defenses of fellow-servant, assumption of risk, and contributory negligence. The number of such jurisdictions having elective compensation coverage has been constantly diminishing. The penalty in these jurisdictions is the loss of the foregoing defenses.

The more common problem occurs in connection with the failure of an employer to secure compensation coverage even though he is obligated to do so in the majority of jurisdictions. The one uniform effect of such unwise conduct on the part of the employer is to deny him the use of the common law defenses mentioned above.

In addition to the foregoing, an increasing number of states have provided for the payment of workmen's compensation by the state to the injured employee of the uninsured employer. The state in turn proceeds against the employer to recover the compensation cost and to imposé penalties that include fines and imprisonment. Other jurisdictions provide for a penalty in the form of additional compensation payments over and above the basic amounts, or they require an immediate lump-sum payment.

Multiple Choice Questions (1 - 20)

1. Wilmont owned a tract of waterfront property on Big Lake. During Wilmont's ownership of the land, several frame bungalows were placed on the land by tenants who rented the land from Wilmont. In addition to paying rent, the tenants paid for the maintenance and insurance of the bungalows, repaired, altered and sold them, without permission or hindrance from Wilmont. The bungalows rested on surface cinderblock and were not bolted to the ground. The buildings could be removed without injury to either the buildings or the land. Wilmont sold the land to Marsh. The deed to Marsh recited that Wilmont sold the land, with buildings thereon, "subject to the rights of tenants, if any, . . ." When the tenants attempted to remove the bungalows, Marsh claimed ownership of them. In deciding who owns the bungalows, which of the following is **least** significant?
   a. The leasehold agreement itself, to the extent it manifested the intent of the parties.
   b. The mode and degree of annexation of the buildings to the land.
   c. The degree to which removal would cause injury to the buildings or the land.
   d. The fact that the deed included a general clause relating to the buildings.

2. Franklin's will left his ranch "to his wife, Joan, for her life, and upon her death to his sons, George and Harry, as joint tenants." Because of the provisions in Franklin's will
   a. Joan cannot convey her interest in the ranch except to George and Harry.
   b. The ranch must be included in Joan's estate for federal estate tax purposes upon her death.
   c. If George predeceases Harry, Harry will obtain all right, title, and interest in the ranch.
   d. Joan holds the ranch in trust for the benefit of George and Harry.

3. Dombres is considering purchasing Blackacre. The title search revealed that the property was willed by Adams jointly to his children, Donald and Martha. The language contained in the will is unclear as to whether a joint tenancy or a tenancy in common was intended. Donald is dead and Martha has agreed to convey her entire interest by quitclaim deed to Dombres. The purchase price is equal to the full fair market price of the property. Dombres is not interested in anything less than the entire title to the tract. Under the circumstances, which of the following is correct?
   a. There is a statutory preference which favors the finding of a joint tenancy.
   b. Whether the will created a joint tenancy or a tenancy in common is irrelevant since Martha is the only survivor.
   c. Dombres will not obtain title to the entire tract of land by Martha's conveyance.
   d. There is no way or means whereby Dombres may obtain a clear title under the circumstances.

4. Marcross and two business associates own real property as tenants in common that they have invested in as a speculation. The speculation proved to be highly successful, and the land is now worth substantially more than their investment. Which of the following is a correct legal incident of ownership of the property?
   a. Upon the death of any of the other tenants, the deceased's interest passes to the survivor(s) unless there is a will.
   b. Each of the co-tenants owns an undivided interest in the whole.
   c. A co-tenant cannot sell his interest in the property without the consent of the other tenants.
   d. Upon the death of a co-tenant, his estate is entitled to the amount of the original investment, but not the appreciation.

5. Fosdick's land adjoins Tracy's land and Tracy has been using a trail across Fosdick's land for a number of years. The trail is the shortest route to a roadway which leads into town. Tracy is asserting a right to continue to use the trail despite Fosdick's objections. In order to establish an easement by prescription, Tracy must show
   a. Implied consent by Fosdick.
   b. Use of the trail for the applicable statutory period.
   c. His use of the trail with an intent to assert ownership to the underlying land.
   d. Prompt recordation of the easement upon its coming into existence.

6. Which of the following is true with respect to an easement created by an express grant?
   a. The easement will be extinguished upon the death of the grantee.
   b. The easement cannot be sold or transferred by the owner of the easement.
   c. The easement gives the owner of the easement the right to the physical possession of the property subject to the easement.
   d. The easement must be in writing to be valid.

7. Dunbar Dairy Farms, Inc., pursuant to an expansion of its operations in Tuberville, purchased from Moncrief a 140-acre farm strategically located in the general area in which Dunbar wishes to expand. Unknown to Dunbar, Cranston, an adjoining landowner, had fenced off approximately five acres of the land in question. Cranston installed a well, constructed a storage shed and garage on the fenced-off land, and continuously farmed and occupied the five acres for approximately 22 years prior to Dunbar's purchase. Cranston did this under the mistaken belief that the five acres of land belonged to him. Which of the following is a correct answer in regard to the five acres occupied by Cranston?

a. Under the circumstances Cranston has title to the five acres.
b. As long as Moncrief had properly recorded a deed which includes the five acres in dispute, Moncrief had good title to the five acres.
c. At best, the only right that Cranston could obtain is an easement.
d. If Dunbar is unaware of Cranston's presence and Cranston has failed to record, Dunbar can oust him as a trespasser.

8. A condition in a contract for the purchase of real property which makes the purchaser's obligation dependent upon his obtaining a given dollar amount of conventional mortgage financing

a. Can be satisfied by the seller if the seller offers the buyer a demand loan for the amount.
b. Is a condition subsequent.
c. Is implied as a matter of law.
d. Requires the purchaser to use reasonable efforts to obtain the financing.

9. Fulcrum Enterprises, Inc., contracted to purchase a four acre tract of land from Devlin as a site for its proposed factory. The contract of sale is silent on the type of deed to be received by Fulcrum and does not contain any title exceptions. The title search revealed that there are 51 zoning laws which affect Fulcrum's use of the land and that back taxes are due. A survey revealed a stone wall encroaching upon a portion of the land Devlin is purporting to convey. A survey made 23 years ago also had revealed the wall. Regarding the rights and duties of Fulcrum, which of the following is correct?

a. Fulcrum is entitled to a warranty deed with full covenants from Devlin at the closing.
b. The existence of the zoning laws above will permit Fulcrum to avoid the contract.
c. Fulcrum must take the land subject to the back taxes.
d. The wall results in a potential breach of the implied warranty of marketability.

10. Purdy purchased real property from Hart and received a warranty deed with full covenants. Recordation of this deed is

a. Not necessary if the deed provides that recordation is **not** required.
b. Necessary to vest the purchaser's legal title to the property conveyed.
c. Required primarily for the purpose of providing the local taxing authorities with the information necessary to assess taxes.
d. Irrelevant if the subsequent party claiming superior title had actual notice of the unrecorded deed.

11. Your client, Albert Fall, purchased a prominent industrial park from Josh Barton. At the closing, Barton offered a quitclaim deed. The contract of sale called for a warranty deed with full covenants.

a. Fall should accept the quitclaim deed since there is no important difference between a quitclaim deed and a warranty deed.
b. An undisclosed mortgage which was subsequently discovered would violate one of the covenants of a warranty deed.
c. Fall cannot validly refuse to accept Barton's quitclaim deed.
d. The only difference between a warranty deed with full covenants and a quitclaim deed is that the grantor of a quitclaim does not warrant against defects past his assumption of title.

12. Smith purchased a tract of land. To protect himself, he ordered title insurance from Valor Title Insurance Company. The policy was the usual one issued by title companies. Accordingly

a. Valor will **not** be permitted to take exceptions to its coverage if it agreed to insure and prepared the title abstract.
b. The title policy is assignable in the event Smith subsequently sells the property.
c. The title policy provides protection against defects in record title only.
d. Valor will be liable for any title defect which arises, even though the defect could **not** have been discovered through the exercise of reasonable care.

13. Which of the following is an **incorrect** statement regarding a real property mortgage?

a. It transfers title to the real property to the mortgagee.
b. It is invariably accompanied by a negotiable promissory note which refers to the mortgage.
c. It creates an interest in real property and is therefore subject to the Statute of Frauds.
d. It creates a nonpossessory security interest in the mortgagee.

14. Moch sold her farm to Watkins and took back a purchase money mortgage on the farm. Moch failed to record the mortgage. Moch's mortgage will be valid against all of the following parties **except**

a. The heirs or estate of Watkins.
b. A subsequent mortgagee who took a second mortgage since he had heard there was a prior mortgage.
c. A subsequent bona fide purchaser from Watkins.
d. A friend of Watkins to whom the farm was given as a gift and who took without knowledge of the mortgage.

15. Peters defaulted on a purchase money mortgage held by Fairmont Realty. Fairmont's attempts to obtain payment have been futile and the mortgage payments are several months in arrears. Consequently, Fairmont decided to resort to its rights against the property. Fairmont foreclosed on the mortgage. Peters has all of the following rights **except**

a. To remain in possession as long as his equity in the property exceeds the amount of debt.
b. An equity of redemption.
c. To refinance the mortgage with another lender and repay the original mortgage.
d. A statutory right of redemption.

16. Golden sold his moving and warehouse business, including all the personal and real property used therein, to Clark Van Lines, Inc. The real property was encumbered by a duly-recorded $300,000 first mortgage upon which Golden was personally liable. Clark acquired the property subject to the mortgage but did not assume the mortgage. Two years later, when the outstanding mortgage was $260,000, Clark decided to abandon the business location because it had become unprofitable and the value of the real property was less than the outstanding mortgage. Clark moved to another location and refused to pay the installments due on the mortgage. What is the legal status of the parties in regard to the mortgage?

a. Clark took the real property free of the mortgage.
b. Clark breached its contract with Golden when it abandoned the location and defaulted on the mortgage.
c. Golden must satisfy the mortgage debt in the event that foreclosure yields an amount less than the unpaid balance.
d. If Golden pays off the mortgage, he will be able to successfully sue Clark because Golden is subrogated to the mortgagee's rights against Clark.

17. Tremont Enterprises, Inc., needed some additional working capital to develop a new product line. It decided to obtain intermediate term financing by giving a second mortgage on its plant and warehouse. Which of the following is true with respect to the mortgages?

a. If Tremont defaults on both mortgages and a bankruptcy proceeding is initiated, the second mortgagee has the status of general creditor.
b. If the second mortgagee proceeds to foreclose on its mortgage, the first mortgagee must be satisfied completely before the second mortgagee is entitled to repayment.
c. Default on payment to the second mortgagee will constitute default on the first mortgage.
d. Tremont can **not** prepay the second mortgage prior to its maturity without the consent of the first mortgagee.

18. Farber sold his house to Ronald. Ronald agreed among other things to pay the existing mortgage on the house. The Safety Bank, which held the mortgage, released Farber from liability on the debt. The above described transaction (relating to the mortgage debt) is

a. Invalid in that the bank did not receive any additional consideration from Farber.
b. Not a release of Farber if Ronald defaults, and the proceeds from the sale of the mortgaged house are insufficient to satisfy the debt.
c. A novation.
d. A delegation.

19. Marks is a commercial tenant of Tudor Buildings, Inc. The term of the lease is five years and two years have elapsed. The lease prohibits subletting, but does **not** contain any provision relating to assignment.

Marks approached Tudor and asked whether Tudor could release him from the balance of the term of the lease for $500. Tudor refused unless Marks would agree to pay $2,000. Marks located Flint who was interested in renting in Tudor's building and transferred the entire balance of the lease to Flint in consideration of his promise to pay Tudor the monthly rental and otherwise perform Marks' obligations under the lease. Tudor objects. Which of the following statements is correct?

a. A prohibition of the right to sublet contained in the lease completely prohibits an assignment.
b. The assignment need **not** be in writing.
c. The assignment does **not** extinguish Marks' obligation to pay the rent if Flint defaults.
d. The assignment is invalid without Tudor's consent.

20. Vance obtained a 25-year leasehold interest in an office building from the owner, Stanfield.

a. Vance's interest is nonassignable.
b. The conveyance of the ownership of the building by Stanfield to Wax will terminate Vance's leasehold interest.
c. Stanfield's death will not terminate Vance's leasehold interest.
d. Vance's death will terminate the leasehold interest.

Problems

Problem 1 Easement by Prescription (1183,L5a)

(7 to 10 minutes)

Part a. Dogwood Construction Company purchased from Acorn a tract of land for use in its business. There was a secondary roadway in the rear of the tract. At the closing of the sale, Dogwood received a deed with a description which was based on a 20-year old survey. The survey showed the secondary road to be entirely included within the tract purchased. The survey was in error by approximately nine feet and therefore did not reveal that the roadway was encroaching upon an adjoining tract of land by six feet. Acorn was the only prior owner of the property, which included both tracts of land. He had owned both tracts for 11 years, and had continuously used the back road. Dogwood took possession and used the back road for five years until Maple purchased the adjoining tract. Maple's survey accurately indicated the exact location of the boundary lines in relation to the road. Consequently, Maple informed Dogwood that unless it ceased using the road, that he, Maple, would bring an action for trespass. Dogwood claims an easement right to continue to use the road.

Required:

Answer the following, setting forth reasons for any conclusions stated.

1. What kind of an easement is Dogwood claiming?

2. In general, what are the requirements that must be satisfied by Dogwood to establish such an easement?

3. In the event Maple brought a lawsuit for trespass against Dogwood, who would likely prevail?

Problem 2 Trade Fixtures (1182,L5b)

(7 to 10 minutes)

Part b. Darby Corporation, a manufacturer of power tools, leased a building for 20 years from Grayson Corporation commencing January 1, 1981. During January 1981, Darby affixed to the building a central air conditioning system and certain heavy manufacturing machinery, each with an estimated useful life of 30 years.

While auditing Darby's financial statements for the year ended December 31, 1981, the auditor noted that Darby was depreciating the air conditioning equipment and machinery, for financial accounting purposes, over their estimated useful lives of 30 years. In reading the lease, the auditor further noted that there was no provision with respect to the removal by the lessee of the central air conditioning system or machinery upon expiration of the lease. To verify that the appropriate estimated useful lives are being utilized for recording depreciation, the auditor is interested in establishing the rightful ownership of these assets upon the expiration of the lease. The auditor knows that in order to determine ownership of the assets at the expiration of the lease, one must first determine whether the assets would be considered personalty or realty.

Required:

Answer the following, setting forth reasons for any conclusions stated.

What major factors would likely be considered by a court in determining whether the air conditioning system and the machinery are to be regarded as personalty or realty, and what would be the likely determination with respect to each?

Problem 3 Purchase of Property with Existing Mortgage (1181,L4b)

(10 to 15 minutes)

Vance Manufacturing, Inc., needed an additional plant location. The executive committee of Vance made a survey to determine what property was available and to select the most desirable location. After much deliberation, Vance decided to purchase a four-acre tract of land belonging to Dave Lauer. Lauer was in financial difficulty and desperately needed to raise money. Vance felt that the asking price of $70,000 was too high and that Lauer would come down to $60,000 in light of his financial difficulties. After much negotiation, Lauer agreed to sell for $61,000. Vance's attorney promptly examined Lauer's title to the property and found that a $40,000 mortgage had recently been filed by Second Bank & Trust Company. Lauer had mentioned this and indicated that the mortgage would be satisfied out of the $61,000 sale price. The title search, completed on February 2, 1981, revealed that Lauer's title was otherwise clear. Closing was scheduled for March 1.

Meanwhile, desperate for additional financing, Lauer had been negotiating a second mortgage with Adventure Mortgage Company. Lauer did not reveal to Adventure that he was in the process of selling the property to Vance, nor did he tell Vance about the second mortgage. Adventure loaned Lauer $10,000 on February 20 and took a second mortgage on the property. This mortgage was filed by Adventure on February 22. Vance's attorney made a cursory final examination of the title on February 20, and the parties proceeded to close on March 1 as scheduled. Lauer promptly cashed his check for $21,000 and disappeared. Adventure is demanding that it be paid by Vance and threatens foreclosure of its second mortgage.

Required:

Answer the following, setting forth reasons for any conclusions stated.

Discuss the legal rights and liabilities of each of the parties involved in the above situation.

Problem 4 Assignment of Lease (579,L5a)

(8 to 12 minutes)

Part a. Hammar Hardware Company, Inc., purchased all the assets and assumed all the liabilities of JoMar Hardware for $60,000. Among the assets and liabilities included in the sale was a lease of the building in which the business was located. The lessor-owner was Marathon Realty, Inc., and the remaining unexpired term of the lease was nine years. The lease did not contain a provision dealing with the assignment of the leasehold. Incidental to the purchase, Hammar expressly promised JoMar that it would pay the rental due Marathon over the life of the lease and would hold JoMar harmless from any future liability thereon.

When Marathon learned of the proposed transaction, it strenuously objected to the assignment of the lease and to the occupancy by Hammar. Later, after this dispute was resolved and prior to expiration of the lease, Hammar abandoned the building and ceased doing business in that area. Marathon has demanded payment by JoMar of the rent as it matures over the balance of the term of the lease.

Required:

Answer the following, setting forth reasons for any conclusions stated.

1. Was the consent of Marathon necessary in order to assign the lease?

2. Is JoMar liable on the lease?

3. If Marathon were to proceed against Hammar, would Hammar be liable under the lease?

Multiple Choice Answers

1.	d	5.	b	9.	d	13.	a	17.	b
2.	c	6.	d	10.	d	14.	c	18.	c
3.	c	7.	a	11.	b	15.	a	19.	c
4.	b	8.	d	12.	d	16.	c	20.	c

Multiple Choice Answer Explanations

A.4. Fixtures

1. (583,L1,53) (d) In order to establish the rightful ownership of the bungalows, it must be determined whether these bungalows would be considered personalty or realty. If these assets are considered personalty, then upon expiration of the lease, the tenants retain ownership and the right of removal. But if these assets are considered realty, then they remain with the land and Marsh retains ownership of the bungalows. Therefore, the issue is whether the bungalows become realty, as a result of being fixtures. A fixture is an item that was originally personal property, but which is affixed in a relatively permanent fashion such that it is considered to be part of the real property. There are several factors which must be applied in determining whether personal property (bungalows) which has been attached to real property is a fixture (realty).

1. The leasehold agreement itself, to the extent it manifested the intent of the parties (i.e., objective intent as to whether property is to be regarded as personalty or realty).
2. The mode and degree of annexation of the buildings to the land (i.e., the method and permanence to which the bungalow is physically attached to the real property).
3. The degree to which removal of the bungalows would cause injury to the buildings or the land.

The fact that the deed included a general clause relating to the bungalows is the least significant factor with regard to the determination of rightful ownership.

B. Interests in Real Property

2. (575,L1,8) (c) Joan has a life estate and may convey it to anyone. Upon Joan's death the ranch becomes the estate of George and Harry and will not be included in Joan's estate. George and Harry have joint tenancy so if George dies first, Harry obtains all rights, title, and interest in the ranch. The holder of a life estate does not hold it in trust for the future interests.

B.3. Concurrent Interest

3. (580,L1,26) (c) When the deed is unclear as to whether a joint tenancy or tenancy in common was intended, there is a statutory presumption in favor of tenancy in common. Thus, Donald and Martha were tenants in common and when Donald died his interest passed to his heirs. Thus, if Dombres wanted to obtain the entire title, he would have to purchase the interest of Donald's heirs, as well as Martha's interest.

4. (1179,L1,10) (b) The correct legal incident of ownership of property as tenants in common is that each of the co-tenants owns an undivided interest in the whole. Answer (a) is incorrect because upon the death of any of the other tenants in common, the deceased tenant's interest will pass to his heirs and not to the surviving co-tenants. Answer (c) is incorrect because a co-tenant in common can sell his interest in the property without the consent of the other co-tenants. Answer (d) is incorrect because upon the death of a co-tenant, his estate owns the same interest as the decedent.

B.5. Easement

5. (583,L1,54) (b) An easement is a nonpossessory interest in land consisting of a right of use over the property of another. In order to establish an easement by prescription, there must be shown:

1. Open and notorious use of trail (i.e., the use must be made without any attempt at concealment).
2. The use must be under an adverse claim of right. The use must be "hostile," without permission or consent from the owner (Fosdick).
3. Continuous and uninterrupted use of trail for the applicable statutory period.

Answer (a) is incorrect because implied consent by Fosdick, the owner, would be contradictory and in violation of the prescription requirement for adverse claim of right or hostile, nonpermissive use of trail by Tracy. Answer (c) is incorrect because since an easement is simply the right to use the land of another, Tracy need not show an intent to assert ownership to the underlying land. Although this would be a necessary element for a claim under adverse possession where the person must indicate intentions of property ownership. Answer (d) is incorrect because the recording statutes and the satisfaction thereof have no application or relevance to an easement being created by prescription.

6. (577,L3,36) (d) An easement is the right to make use of another's land. This right, if established by an express grant, is an "interest in land," which under the Statute of Frauds requires a writing to be valid. The owner of an easement does not have the right to possess the land; he can only use it. In most cases, an easement will not terminate upon the death of the grantee unless specifically stated in the grant, or if the easement is personal, such as an easement in gross. As a general rule, only certain types of easements are not assignable; even these can be made assignable by proper wording and intent in the grant.

C. Adverse Possession

7. (1179,L1,41) (a) Cranston has acquired title to the 5 acres by adverse possession. Even though by mistake, Cranston did occupy the property under the claim of right doctrine, hostile to the actual owner in an open, notorious, and exclusive manner for a continuous period which would be sufficient under common law and most jurisdictions. Answer (b) is incorrect because an actual owner of rural property can lose title by adverse possession as described above. Answer (c) is incorrect because at best, Cranston could, and apparently did, obtain full ownership of the property by adverse possession. Note that "at worst," Cranston could only obtain an easement but answer (c) said "at best." Answer (d) is incorrect because a purchaser of real property is deemed to have constructive notice of the presence of all persons located on the property that he is buying. Thus, in law, Dunbar is on notice of Cranston's presence.

D. Contracts for Sale of Land

8. (582,L1,51) (d) When a "subject to financing" clause is in a contract for the purchase of real property, there must be good faith on the part of the buyer to use reasonable efforts to search out and obtain the requisite financing amount. Answer (a) is incorrect because a demand loan offered by the seller is inconsistent with the parties' intent of obtaining conventional mortgage financing and therefore does not satisfy the financing condition of the sales contract. Answer (b) is incorrect because a "subject to financing" clause is a condition precedent to the buyer's performance of the contract. Answer (c) is incorrect because a "subject to financing" clause is not implied as a matter of law, but must appear as part of the contract for purchase of real property. The rule in construing a "subject to financing" clause is that the court will infer the intent of the parties in light of the contract and all the circumstances surrounding the making of the contract, including customary community practices in financing of similar transactions. Unless the "subject to financing" clause is definite enough so as to determine the necessary financing requirements, the contract may become illusory in nature and not be enforceable.

9. (582,L1,53) (d) Unless there is a provision in the contract to the contrary, it is implied in a contract of sale that the seller must furnish the buyer with good and marketable title at closing (implied warranty of marketability). Marketable title is title which is reasonably free from doubt, one which a prudent purchaser would accept. The title should be free from all encumbrances, encroachments and other such defects. Therefore, the stone wall encroaching upon the land results in a potential breach of the implied warranty of marketability. Answer (a) is incorrect because when the contract is silent on the type of deed to be given, the buyer is not entitled to a warranty deed with full covenants, but rather a special warranty deed which does not contain full covenants. Answer (b) is incorrect because zoning law restrictions will not render a title unmarketable. Therefore, Fulcrum would not be permitted to avoid the contract. Answer (c) is incorrect because Fulcrum does not have to take the land subject to back taxes unless it appears as a reservation on the face of the deed.

E. Conveyance by Deed

10. (583,L1,56) (d) Recordation of a deed gives constructive notice "to the world" that title to the property has been conveyed. Therefore, the primary purpose of recording is to protect the grantee against subsequent purchasers, by putting subsequent purchasers "on notice." If the subsequent party claiming superior title had actual notice of the unrecorded deed, then the recordation objective has been met and recordation of the deed is irrelevant with regard to this particular party. An unrecorded deed is binding upon all persons having actual notice of its existence. Answer (a) is incorrect because recording of a deed is necessary to protect the grantee against subsequent purchasers even though the deed provides that recordation is not required. Answer (b) is incorrect because recordation is not essential to the validity of the deed, as between the grantor (Hart) and grantee (Purdy). A deed is effective when delivered and vests the purchaser's legal title to the property conveyed without recording. Answer (c) is incorrect because the primary purpose of recording a deed is to protect grantee against subsequent purchasers, not to provide local taxing authorities with information necessary to assess taxes.

11. (1173,L3,40) (b) There is an important difference between a quitclaim deed and a warranty deed in that the quitclaim deed does not contain any of the warranties of a warranty deed. An undisclosed mortgage violates a covenant that the deed is free from encumbrances. If the deed does not comply with the contract of sale, Fall does not have to accept it.

E.7. Title Insurance

12. (583,L1,55) (d) Title insurance is insurance against loss or damage resulting from defects in the title for a particular parcel of realty. Standard title insurance policies insure the buyer against title defects, such that the title insurance company is liable for any damages or expenses for a defect which is later discovered that is insured against. The maximum liability of the insurance company is the amount set in the policy. The company is generally liable for the difference in value of the property with and without the defect, up to the maximum set by the policy. The title insurance company (Valor) will be liable for title defects which arise, even though the defect could not have been discovered through the exercise of reasonable care. Therefore, answer (c) is incorrect because the title policy also provides protection against defects which are not shown on the public record. Answer (a) is incorrect because the title insurance company (Valor) is permitted to take exceptions to its insurance coverage, even if it agreed to insure and prepare the title abstract. Certain defects may not be insured against (i.e., "excepted") by the title policy. But such exceptions must be present on the face of the policy. A standard title insurance policy normally does not insure against losses arising from the following defects (i.e., exceptions which are stated on face of policy): liens imposed by law but not shown on the public record; claims of parties in possession not shown on the public record; zoning and building ordinances. Answer (b) is incorrect because Smith, the purchaser of a title insurance policy, is insured, but the policy does not run with the land. A subsequent purchaser of the land must procure his/her own title policy.

F. Mortgages

13. (583,L1,57) (a) Answer (a) is an incorrect statement because under the "lien theory," a mortgage does not transfer title to the real property to the mortgagee. The mortgagor (borrower) gives the mortgagee (lender) a nonpossessory lien to secure the debt, and therefore, legal title remains with the mortgagor. Answer (b) is a true statement because a mortgage is usually accompanied by a negotiable promissory note which is incorporated in or refers to the mortgage. Answer (c) is a true statement because since a mortgage is an interest in real property, it is subject to the Statute of Frauds and, therefore, must be in writing and signed by the party to be charged (mortgagor). Answer (d) is a true statement because a mortgage provides a nonpossessory security interest in the mortgagee, with the mortgagor retaining possession of the real property used as the collateral.

14. (583,L1,59) (c) A purchase money mortgage is created when a mortgage is given concurrently with a sale of property by the buyer to the seller to secure the unpaid balance of the purchase price. A purchase money mortgage creates a nonpossessory lien that attaches to the land purchased. The purpose for recordation of a real property mortgage is to give constructive notice of the mortgage, such that all persons who subsequently acquire an interest in the mortgaged property will take subject to it. Therefore, if a mortgage is not duly recorded, a subsequent purchaser from Watkins will take property free of mortgage as long as purchaser had no knowledge of prior, unrecorded mortgage (i.e., a subsequent bona fide purchaser). Answer (a) is incorrect because an unrecorded mortgage is binding and valid against the mortgagor (Watkins) and his heirs or estate. Answer (b) is incorrect because an unrecorded mortgage is binding upon all persons having actual notice of its existence. For a subsequent mortgagee to have priority, or take free of the mortgage, s/he must have no knowledge of the prior, unrecorded mortgage. Therefore, Moch's mortgage will be valid against a subsequent mortgagee who had actual notice of the prior mortgage. Answer (d) is incorrect because donees do not come within the protection of the recording system since they do not give valuable consideration and therefore do not qualify as a bona fide purchaser for value. Thusly, Moch's mortgage will be valid against Watkin's friend who was given the farm as a gift, regardless if the friend took without notice of the mortgage.

15. (583,L1,60) (a) If the mortgagor (Peters) defaults on payment of the note which refers to the mortgage, the mortgagee (Fairmont) may resort to the land for payment. Fairmont may foreclose his mortgage upon Peters' default. If the foreclosure is successful, the court will direct that the property be sold at a foreclosure sale. The mortgagor, Peters, has several rights upon the foreclosure on the mortgage. The mortgagor has an equity of redemption. This right entitles the mortgagor to redeem the property even after foreclosure, but before the foreclosure sale, by paying the amount due plus interest and any other costs. When a mortgage foreclosure sale is held the

equity of redemption ends. But the mortgagor has a statutory right of redemption which commences when the equity of redemption ends. The right of redemption affords the mortgagor one last chance to redeem the property. This right is strictly statutory in nature and the period of redemption after foreclosure sale varies from state to state. The mortgagor also has the right to refinance the loan with another lender and repay the original mortgage to Fairmont. The fact that the mortgagor's (Peters') equity in the property exceeds the amount of debt does not give Peters the right to remain in possession upon the mortgage foreclosure. However, Peters does have a right to the proceeds of the foreclosure sale to the extent the proceeds exceed the outstanding balance plus interest and any other costs the mortgagee has incurred.

16. (581,L1,53) (c) Golden, the original debtor, must satisfy the mortgage debt in the event that the foreclosure yields an amount less than the unpaid balance. Golden was originally liable on the mortgage, and no novation or release was granted by the mortgagor when Golden sold the warehouse to Clark. Answer (a) is incorrect because Clark did not take the property free of the mortgage. The property was subject to the mortgage at all times, but Clark was not personally liable as he did not **assume** the mortgage. Answer (b) is incorrect because Clark bought the property only **subject** to the mortgage and therefore, did not breach his agreement with Golden when he abandoned the location and stopped making the mortgage payments. Answer (d) is incorrect because Golden will not be able to sue Clark because Clark did not contract to be liable on the mortgage debt. Thus, there is no one for Golden to be subrogated to.

17. (581,L1,54) (b) Upon foreclosure, the first mortgagee has priority and must be paid in full before any payment is made to a subsequent mortgagee (second or third mortgagees). Answer (a) is incorrect because a second mortgagee remains a secured creditor in the bankruptcy proceedings although his interest is inferior to a first mortgagee. The doctrine of marshalling of assets may help a second mortgagee since it allows him to compel a first mortgagee to foreclose on other property available to the first mortgagee as security before foreclosing on property which a second mortgagee has a claim on. Answer (c) is incorrect because default of the second mortgage does not constitute a default of the first mortgage. Answer (d) is incorrect since second mortgages are sometimes obtained for a short period of time and can be paid off before maturity without consent of first mortgagee.

18. (1176,L3,40) (c) A novation (a substituted contract) in a mortgage transaction occurs when the purchaser agrees to assume the mortgage and the mortgagee agrees to release the original mortgagor with the purchaser as replacement. It is not invalid. In consideration for releasing Farber, the bank got Ronald to be personally liable on the debt. After the novation Farber has no liability even if Ronald defaults and the proceeds from the sale of the house are insufficient to satisfy the debt. A delegation is when a party to a contract turns over his duties to another party. Duties are delegated and rights are assigned. A delegant is still liable if the delegatee defaults, but Farber (as delegant) had no liability because of the novation.

G. Landlord Tenant

19. (1180,L1,48) (c) A tenant may engage in an assignment or a sublease unless expressly prohibited by the lease. An assignment of the lease is the transfer by the lessee of his entire interest without reserving any right of re-entry. The assignor remains liable on the lease despite the assignment. Answer (c) is correct. Answer (a) is incorrect because a clause in the lease prohibiting a sublease does not prohibit an assignment. Since there were 3 years left on the lease when assigned, it was not capable of being performed within one year and consequently the agreement to transfer such an interest must be in writing [answer (b)]. There is no need for the landlord to consent to the assignment unless the lease expressly prohibited assignment.

20. (1176,L3,41) (c) A lease is not terminated by the death of either the lessor or the lessee. Thus, neither Stanfield's death nor Vance's death will terminate the lease. Transfer of ownership of leased property also does not terminate a lease. Therefore, if Stanfield conveys to Wax, Wax will take subject to the lease. As a general rule a lessee may assign or sublet a leasehold interest in accordance with reasonable restrictions in the lease; thus, Vance's interest is assignable.

Answer Outline

Problem 1 Easement by Prescription

Part a.

1. Easement by prescription
   Also easement appurtenant
2. Requirements needed to establish such easements are
   Continuous, exclusive, open, notorious, and adverse use of land for statutory period (normally 15 to 20 years)
3. Maple would prevail
   Dogwood used land adversely for only five years (not 15-20 years)
   Cannot tack Elkhart's use because it was not adverse

Unofficial Answer

Problem 1 Easement by Prescription

Part a.

1. Dogwood is claiming an easement by prescription resulting from adverse usage.

2. The easement by prescription is the counterpart of obtaining ownership of land by adverse possession. The requirements to establish such an easement are

- Adverse use as distinguished from a permissive usage.
- An open and notorious use.
- Continuous and exclusive use for the time required for the acquisition of title to real property by adverse possession, typically 15-20 years.

3. Maple would prevail. Although tacking (adding on) of a prior owner's use is permitted where there is privity, such tacking will not satisfy the first requirement since the use by Acorn of his own land cannot be adverse. Furthermore, the use by Dogwood for five years will not satisfy the statutory time period required for the acquisition of an easement by prescription, typically 15-20 years.

Answer Outline

Problem 2 Trade Fixtures

Part b.

To establish rightful ownership of air conditioning and machinery
 Auditor must determine whether these items are personalty or realty
  If personalty, then Darby has ownership rights
  If realty, then Grayson has ownership rights
Issue is whether these items have become realty by virtue of being fixtures
 Several factors must be considered in determining whether personal property attached to real property is a fixture
  Affixer's objective intent as to whether property is to be regarded as personalty or realty
  Method and permanence of physical attachment
  Adaptability of personal property use for the purpose for which real property is used
Personal property affixed by tenant for purpose of conducting business is a trade fixture
 Trade fixtures remain personal property
  Tenant has right to remove upon expiration of lease
Manufacturing machinery is a trade fixture
 Since integral part of Darby's business
Darby has right to remove upon expiration of lease
 Therefore, should be depreciated over machinery's useful life, i.e., 30 years
Air conditioning system is a fixture
 Does not appear to be used by Darby for conducting business
 Would result in material damage to realty if removed
Darby does not have right to remove upon expiration of lease
 Therefore, should be depreciated over life of lease, i.e., 20 years

Unofficial Answer
(Author Modified)

Problem 2 Trade Fixtures

Part b.

In order for the auditor to establish the rightful ownership of the central air conditioning system and the manufacturing machinery upon the expiration of the lease, s/he must determine whether these items would be considered personalty or realty. If these assets are considered **personalty,** then upon expiration of the lease Darby Corporation retains ownership. But if these assets are considered **realty**, then upon expiration of the lease they remain with the leased building (real property) and Grayson Corporation has ownership rights. Therefore, the issue is whether the air conditioning system and the machinery have become realty, as a result of being fixtures.

A fixture is an item that was originally personal property, but which is affixed to real property in a relatively permanent fashion such that it is considered to be part of the real property. There are several factors which must be applied in determining whether personal property which has been attached to real property is a fixture (realty).

1. **Affixer's objective intent as to whether property is to be regarded as personalty or realty.** In general, a court will hold that an item is a fixture if it were the intention of the parties that it becomes part of the real property. If the intent is clear, then this becomes the controlling factor in the determination of whether an item is a fixture or not.

This intent can be determined from various factors:

- The intention of the parties as expressed in the agreement.
- The nature of the article affixed.
- The relationship of the parties (i.e., the affixer and the owner of the real property).

2. **The method and permanence with which the item is physically attached (annexed) to the real property.** If the item cannot be removed without material injury to the real property, it is generally held that the item has become part of the realty (i.e., a fixture).

3. **Adaptability of use of the personal property for the purpose for which the real property is used.** If the personal property is necessary or beneficial to the use of the real property, the more likely the item is a fixture. But if the use or purpose of the item is unusual for the type of realty involved, it might be reasonable to conclude that it is personalty, and the affixer intends to remove the item when s/he leaves.

4. **The property interest of that person in the real property at the time of the attachment of the item.**

An item installed (affixed) by a tenant in connection with a business s/he is conducting on the leased premises is called a trade fixture. The personal property must be brought onto the leased business premises for the purpose of conducting and engaging in the trade or business for which the tenant occupies the premises.

Trade fixtures remain personal property, giving the tenant the right to remove these items upon expiration of the lease. But the tenant's right is limited to the extent that his/her action of removing the fixture may not materially damage the realty. If the item is so affixed onto the real property that removing it would cause substantial damage, then it is considered part of the realty.

Based upon the aforementioned analysis, the manufacturing machinery qualifies as a trade fixture. Since Darby Corporation is a manufacturer, this asset is integral to the conduct of business for which Darby occupies the premises. As a trade fixture, Darby retains rightful ownership of the machinery, giving Darby the right to remove the machinery upon expiration of the lease. However, Darby would be required to compensate Grayson for any damage caused by removal of the machinery. Therefore, Darby was correct to depreciate the machinery over its estimated useful life (i.e., 30 years).

However, the air conditioning system would not appear to qualify as a trade fixture. It does not appear to be employed by Darby in the furtherance of business operations for which the premises are leased. The air conditioning system would also be considered part of the realty, since it is probably so attached to the building that it would result in permanent structural damage to the building upon removal. Therefore, the air conditioning system would be considered a fixture (realty). As such, Darby would not have the right to remove it upon expiration of the lease. Thus, Darby should depreciate the air conditioning system over the life of the lease, (i.e. 20 years).

Answer Outline

Problem 3 Purchase of Property with Existing Mortgage

Adventure will prevail over Vance
- Adventure's mortgage valid against Vance
  - Properly filed and recorded prior to closing of title
  - Adventure had no notice of Lauer's fraudulent activity
- Vance had constructive notice of second mortgage
  - Vance took title subject to Adventure's mortgage

Vance has cause of action against Lauer based upon fraud

Vance has cause of action against attorney based upon negligence
- Attorney's examination of title was improper and inadequate
  - Attorney would be subrogated to Vance's rights against Lauer

Unofficial Answer

Problem 3 Purchase of Property with Existing Mortgage

Adventure Mortgage Company is correct in its assertion. Adventure had no actual or constructive notice of the fraud. It has a valid second mortgage that was properly filed and recorded prior to the closing. Vance Manufacturing, Inc., had constructive notice of the mortgage as a result of the filing and took title to the property subject to the Adventure mortgage. Vance must either pay Adventure or be subject to a foreclosure action.

Although Vance stands to lose $10,000 with respect to Adventure's claim, it is likely that Vance can recover the loss from its attorney, based on an action for negligence. The attorney's final examination of the title prior to closing was clearly inadequate. It was made at a time that was too far in advance of the closing to provide the protection needed. Final examination of title is generally made immediately prior to closing.

Of course, Vance would have a cause of action against Lauer based on deceit (fraud), although recovery seems unlikely. Vance's attorney, assuming he is liable as a result of a finding that he was negligent, would be subrogated to the rights of his client and entitled to recover from Lauer for deceit.

Answer Outline

Problem 4 Assignment of Lease

a1. No, lessor's consent is not necessary to assign a lease unless lease prohibits assignment
  Rare for court to prohibit assignment
    Exception might be lease involving personal trust

a2. Yes, assignor of a contract remains liable unless
    Novation granted i.e., creditor released assignor
  JoMar has only delegated the duty to pay to Marathon
  JoMar becomes a surety as part of the transaction

a3. Yes, Hammar is liable to Marathon
    Marathon is a third party creditor beneficiary
      Hammar promised JoMar he would pay Marathon
      Privity and consideration requirements do not apply

Unofficial Answer

Problem 4 Assignment of Lease

Part a.

1. No. In the absence of a restriction on the right to assign specifically stated in the lease, a lessee may assign his leasehold interest to another. Only in unusual circumstances, where the lease involves special elements of personal trust and confidence as contrasted with mere payment for occupancy, will the courts limit the right to assign.

2. Yes. Although JoMar may effectively assign the lease, which in effect is an assignment of the right to occupy the leasehold premises and a delegation of its duty to pay Marathon, it cannot shed its liability to Marathon for the rental payments. In the absence of a release, JoMar remains liable. The transaction described in the fact situation is in the nature of a surety relationship.

3. Yes. Marathon is a third-party creditor beneficiary of Hammar's promise to JoMar. As such, Marathon can assert rights on the promise even though it was not a party to the contract. Marathon is not barred by lack of privity or the fact that it gave no consideration to Hammar for the promise.

Multiple Choice Questions (1 - 13)

1. Fuller Corporation insured its factory and warehouse against fire with the Safety First Insurance Company. As a part of the bargaining process, in connection with obtaining the policy Fuller was required by Safety First to give in writing certain warranties regarding the insured risk. Fuller did so and they were incorporated into the policy. Which of the following correctly describes the law applicable to such warranties?
   a. The warranties given by Fuller will be treated as representations.
   b. It was **not** necessary that the warranties given by Fuller be in writing to be effective.
   c. In the event that Fuller does **not** strictly comply with the warranties it has given, it will be denied recovery in a substantial number of states.
   d. In deciding whether the language contained in a policy constitutes a warranty, the courts usually construe ambiguous language in a way which favors the insurance company.

2. The insurable interest in property
   a. Can be waived by consent of the parties.
   b. Is subject to the incontestability clause.
   c. Must be present at the time the loss occurs.
   d. Is only available to owners, occupiers, or users of the property.

3. A fire insurance policy is one common type of contract. As such it must meet the general requirements necessary to establish a binding contract. In a dispute between the insured and the insurance company, which of the following is correct?
   a. The contract is always unilateral.
   b. Insurance contracts are specifically included within the general Statute of Frauds.
   c. The insured must satisfy the insurable interest requirement.
   d. The actual delivery of the policy to the insured is a prerequisite to the creation of the insurance contract.

4. Burt owns an office building which is leased to Hansen Corporation under the terms of a long-term lease. Both Burt and Hansen have procured fire insurance covering the building. Which of the following is correct?
   a. Both Burt and Hansen have separate insurable interests.
   b. Burt's insurable interest is limited to the book value of the property.
   c. Hansen has an insurable interest in the building, but only to the extent of the value of any additions or modifications it has made.
   d. Since Burt has legal title to the building, he is the only party who can insure the building.

5. Peters leased a restaurant from Brady with all furnishings and fixtures for a period of five years with an option to renew for two additional years. Peters made several structural improvements and modifications to the interior of the building. He obtained a fire insurance policy for his own benefit insuring his interest in the property for $25,000. The restaurant was totally destroyed by an accidental fire. Peters seeks recovery from his insurer. Subject to policy limits, which of the following is correct?
   a. Peters is entitled to recover damages to the extent of the value of his leasehold interest.
   b. Peters is entitled to recover for lost profits due to the fire even though the policy is silent on the point.
   c. Peters must first seek redress from the owner before he is entitled to recover.
   d. Peters will not recover because he lacks the requisite insurable interest in the property.

6. Bernard Manufacturing, Inc., owns a three-story building which it recently purchased. The purchase price was $200,000 of which $160,000 was financed by the proceeds of a mortgage loan from the Cattleman Savings and Loan Association. Bernard immediately procured a standard fire insurance policy on the premises for $200,000 from the Magnificent Insurance Company. Cattleman also took out fire insurance of $160,000 on the property from the Reliable Insurance Company of America. The property was subsequently totally destroyed as a result of a fire which started in an adjacent loft and spread to Bernard's building. Insofar as the rights and duties of Bernard, Cattleman, and the insurers are concerned, which of the following is a correct statement?
   a. Cattleman Savings and Loan lacks the requisite insurable interest to collect on its policy.
   b. Bernard Manufacturing can only collect $40,000.

c. Reliable Insurance Company is subrogated to Cattleman's rights against Bernard upon payment of Cattleman's insurance claim.
d. The maximum amount that Bernard Manufacturing can collect from Magnificent is $40,000, the value of its insurable interest.

7. Alphonse, a sole CPA practitioner, obtained a malpractice insurance policy from the Friendly Casualty Company. In regard to this coverage
a. Issuance of an unqualified opinion by Alphonse when he knows the statements are false does not give Friendly a defense.
b. The policy would automatically cover the work of a new partnership formed by Alphonse and Borne.
c. Friendly will not be subrogated to rights against Alphonse for his negligent conduct of an audit.
d. Coverage includes injury to a client resulting from a slip on a rug negligently left loose in Alphonse's office.

8. Tedland Trading Corporation insured its 17 automobiles for both liability and collision. Milsap, one of its salesmen, was in an automobile accident while driving a company car on a sales trip. The facts clearly reveal that the accident was solely the fault of Williams, the driver of the other car. Milsap was seriously injured, and the automobile was declared a total loss. The value of the auto was $3,000. Which of the following is an **incorrect** statement regarding the rights and liabilities of Tedland, its insurer, Milsap and Williams?
a. Tedland's insurer must defend Tedland against any claims by Milsap or Williams.
b. Tedland's insurer has **no** liability whatsoever since the accident was the result of Williams' negligence.
c. Milsap has an independent action against Williams for the injuries caused by Williams' negligence.
d. Tedland's insurer is liable for $3,000, less any deductible, on the collision policy, but will be subrogated to Tedland's rights.

9. Adams Company purchased a factory and warehouse from Martinson for $150,000. Adams obtained a $100,000 real estate mortgage loan from a local bank and was required by the lender to pay for the cost of title insurance covering the bank's interest in the property. In addition, Adams was required to obtain fire insurance sufficient to protect the bank against loss due to fire. The co-insurance factor has been satisfied. Under these circumstances, which of the following is correct?
a. Adams can purchase only $50,000 of title insurance since it already obtained a $100,000 title policy for the bank equal to the bank loan.
b. The bank could not have independently obtained a fire insurance policy on the property because Adams has legal title.
c. If Adams obtained a $150,000 fire insurance policy which covered its interest and the bank's interest in the property and there is an estimated $50,000 of fire loss, the insurer will typically be obligated to pay the owner and the bank the amounts equal to their respective interests as they may appear.
d. If Adams obtained a $100,000 fire insurance policy covering the bank's interest and $150,000 covering his own interest, each would obtain these amounts upon total destruction of the property.

10. Margo, Inc., insured its property against fire with two separate insurance companies, Excelsior and Wilberforce. Each carrier insured the property for its full value, and neither insurer was aware that the other had also insured the property. The policies were the standard fire insurance policies used throughout the United States. If the property is totally destroyed by fire, how much will Margo recover?
a. Nothing because Margo has engaged in an illegal gambling venture.
b. The full amount from both insurers.
c. A ratable or pro rata share from each insurer, not to exceed the value of the property insured.
d. Only 80% of the value of the property from each insurer because of the standard coinsurance clause.

11. The underlying rationale which justifies the use of the coinsurance clause in fire insurance is
a. It provides an insurable interest in the insured if this is **not** already present.
b. To require certain minimum coverage in order to obtain full recovery on losses.
c. It prevents arson by the owner.
d. It makes the insured more careful in preventing fires since the insured is partially at risk in the event of loss.

12. Carter, Wallace, and Jones are partners. Title to the partnership's office building was in Carter's name. The Carter, Wallace, and Jones partnership procured a $150,000 fire insurance policy on the building from the Amalgamated Insurance Company. The policy contained an 80% coinsurance clause. Subsequently, the building was totally destroyed by fire. The value of the building was $200,000 at the time the policy was issued, and $160,000 at the time of the fire. Under the fire insurance policy, how much can the partnership recover?

a. Nothing, since it did **not** have legal title to the building.
b. The face value of the policy ($150,000).
c. Eighty percent of the loss ($128,000).
d. The value at the time of the loss ($160,000).

13. Hazard & Company was the owner of a building valued at $100,000. Since Hazard did not believe that a fire would result in a total loss, it procured two standard fire insurance policies on the property. One was for $24,000 with the Asbestos Fire Insurance Company and the other was for $16,000 with the Safety Fire Insurance Company. Both policies contained standard pro rata and 80% coinsurance clauses. Six months later, at which time the building was still valued at $100,000, a fire occurred which resulted in a loss of $40,000. What is the total amount Hazard can recover on both policies and the respective amount to be paid by Asbestos?

a. $0 and $0.
b. $20,000 and $10,000.
c. $20,000 and $12,000.
d. $40,000 and $20,000.

Problems

Problem 1 Coinsurance, Standard Mortgagee, and Pro Rata Clauses (1182,L5a)

(10 to 15 minutes)

Part a. While auditing the financial statements of Jackson Corporation for the year ended December 31, 1981, Harvey Draper, CPA, desired to verify the balance in the insurance claims receivable account. Draper obtained the following information:

- On November 4, 1981, Jackson's Parksdale plant was damaged by fire. The fire caused $200,000 damage to the plant, which was purchased in 1970 for $600,000. When the plant was purchased, Jackson obtained a loan secured by a mortgage from Second National Bank of Parksdale. At the time of the fire the loan balance, including accrued interest, was $106,000. The plant was insured against fire with Eagle Insurance Company. The policy contained a "standard mortgagee" clause and an 80% coinsurance clause. The face value of the policy was $600,000 and the value of the plant was $1,000,000 at the time of the fire.
- On December 10, 1981, Jackson's Yuma warehouse was totally destroyed by fire. The warehouse was acquired in 1960 for $300,000. At the time of the fire, the warehouse was unencumbered by any mortgage; it was insured against fire with Eagle for $300,000; and it had a value of $500,000. The policy contained an 80% coinsurance clause.
- On December 26, 1981, Jackson's Rye City garage was damaged by fire. At the time of the fire, the garage had a value of $250,000 and was unencumbered by any mortgage. The fire caused $60,000 damage to the garage, which was constructed in 1965 at a cost of $50,000. In 1975 Jackson expanded the capacity of the garage at an additional cost of $50,000. When the garage was constructed in 1965, Jackson insured the garage against fire for $50,000 with Eagle, and this policy was still in force on the date of the fire. When the garage was expanded in 1975, Jackson obtained $100,000 of additional fire insurance coverage from Queen Insurance Company. Each policy contains an 80% coinsurance clause and a standard pro-rata clause.

Required:

Answer the following, setting forth reasons for any conclusions stated.

1. How much of the fire loss relating to the Parksdale plant will be recovered from Eagle?
2. How will such recovery be distributed between Second National and Jackson?
3. How much of the fire loss relating to the Yuma warehouse will be recovered from Eagle?
4. How much of the fire loss relating to the Rye City garage will be recovered from the insurance companies?
5. What portion of the amount recoverable in connection with the Rye City garage loss will Queen be obligated to pay?

Problem 2 Insurable Interests (1176,L6b&c)

(15 to 20 minutes)

Part b. Balsam was a partner in the firm Wilkenson, Potter & Parker. The firm had a buy-out arrangement whereby the partnership funded the buy-out agreement with insurance on the lives of the partners payable to the partnership. When the insurance policies were obtained by the partnership, Balsam understated his age by three years. Eight years later, Balsam decided to sell his partnership interest to Gideon. The sale was consummated and the other partners admitted Gideon as a partner in Balsam's place. The partnership nevertheless retained ownership in the policy on the life of Balsam and continued to pay the premiums thereon. Balsam died one year later. The insurance company refuses to pay the face value of the policy claiming that the partnership is only entitled to the amount of the premiums paid. As a basis for this position, the insurance company asserts lack of an insurable interest and material misrepresentation.

Required:

Answer the following, setting forth reasons for any conclusions stated.

Will Wilkenson, Potter & Parker prevail in an action against the insurance company? Give specific attention to the assertions of the insurance company.

Part c. Anderson loaned the Drum Corporation $60,000. The loan was secured by a first mortgage on Drum's land and the plant thereon. Anderson independently procured a fire insurance policy for $60,000 on the mortgaged property from the Victory Insurance Company. Six years later when the mortgage had been amortized down to $52,000, the plant was totally destroyed by a fire caused by faulty electrical wiring in the rear storage area.

Required:

Answer the following, setting forth reasons for any conclusions stated.

1. Anderson seeks recovery of $60,000 from the Victory Insurance Company. How much will it collect?
2. Upon payment by Victory Insurance Company, what rights does Victory have?

Multiple Choice Answers

1.	c	4.	a	7.	c	10.	c	12.	b
2.	c	5.	a	8.	b	11.	b	13.	c
3.	c	6.	c	9.	c				

Multiple Choice Answer Explanations

B. Insurance Contract

1. (1181,L1,60) (c) A warranty is a statement of fact by the insured which materially relates to the insurer's risk and must be incorporated into the policy to qualify as a warranty. The warranties given by Fuller constitute condition precedents to the liability of the insurer. Therefore, if Fuller fails to comply with these warranties, the policy is voidable at the option of the insurer and Fuller will be denied recovery. Answer (a) is incorrect because representations are statements not inserted in the policy. By statute, most warranties in life insurance policies are representations but this is not true of warranties in property insurance policies. Answer (b) is incorrect because a warranty must appear on the face of, be embodied in, or be attached to the policy itself to be effective. Therefore, the warranties given by Fuller must be in writing. Answer (d) is incorrect because the courts will construe ambiguous language based upon the mutual intent of the parties.

B.6.b. Insurable Interest – Property

2. (583,L1,36) (c) The essence of the insurable interest concept is to prevent recovery by those who have no economic interest in the property. Therefore, there must be a relationship (i.e., an insurable interest) between the insured and the insured event such that the occurrence of the event will cause the insured to suffer substantial loss. The insurable interest in property need not necessarily be present at the inception of the policy but it must be present at the time of the loss. Answer (a) is incorrect because the insurable interest requirement cannot be waived by the parties to an insurance contract. Answer (b) is incorrect because an incontestability clause relates to life insurance, whereby upon expiration of a certain time period (usually 2 years), the insurer is estopped from contesting the insurance policy based on misstatements or concealments. Answer (d) is incorrect because an insurable interest is also available to others who have a legal or economic interest and a possibility of pecuniary loss in property such as: a secured creditor who has an insurable interest in specific property that secures the debt or against which the judgment attaches; a stockholder who has an insurable interest in property owned by corporation; a bailee who has insurable interest in property held in his possession.

3. (1181,L1,59) (c) An essential element of an insurance contract is the existence of an insurable interest. There must be a relationship between the insured and the insured event such that, if the event occurs, the insured will suffer substantial loss. An insurable interest in property exists when there is both a legal interest in the property and a possibility of pecuniary loss if the property is destroyed. Answer (a) is incorrect because an insurance contract often is unilateral in nature, but there is no requirement that it must be. Answer (b) is incorrect because the Statute of Frauds does not require a written contract because the event insured against may occur within one year from the issuance of the insurance policy. Answer (d) is incorrect because physical delivery of the policy is not a requisite for validity. An act or words by the insurer that clearly manifests an intent to be bound will constitute constructive delivery. The insurance contract is generally binding at the time of unconditional acceptance of the application by the insurer and communication of such acceptance to the insured.

4. (581,L1,48) (a) A person has an insurable interest in property if he will benefit by its continued existence or suffer from its destruction and has a legal or equitable interest in the property (e.g., a mortgagee, mortgagor, tenant in rented property, or partner in partnership property). Both Burt (owner of legal title) and Hansen (tenant in leased property) have an insurable interest; therefore, answer (a) is true. Answer (b) is incorrect because Burt has an insurable interest to the extent of any economic loss he might suffer. Such a loss would normally be measured by market value of the property, not book value. Answer (c) is also false because the tenant has an insurable interest for the amount of economic loss he will suffer in the event the property is destroyed. This amount may be greater or less than the value of the additions or modifications. The tenants would measure their economic loss in reference to items such as the expense of finding a new office building or new business space.

5. (578,L1,20) (a) A lessee has an insurable interest to the extent of the value of his leasehold interest. Therefore Peters is entitled to recover damages to the extent of the value of his leasehold interest, not to exceed the $25,000 policy limit. Answer (b) is incorrect because lost profits are not recoverable unless specifically included in the policy. Answer (c) is incorrect because an insured party may recover upon loss and need not seek redress from any other party first. Peters' insurance carrier would obtain by right of subrogation, how-

ever, any potential claim he has against the owner. Answer (d) is incorrect because a lessee has an insurable interest in leased property.

C. Subrogation

6. (1180,L1,53) (c) Answer (c) is correct because under a fire insurance policy, an insurer who pays a claim is subrogated (succeeds to the rights of the insured) to any rights that the insured had against a third party. Answer (a) is incorrect since Cattleman, as mortgagee, has an insurable interest to the extent of the outstanding debt ($160,000). If the policy is a valued policy, then Bernard will collect $200,000. If it is an open policy, then Bernard will collect the market value of the building at the time of destruction up to a maximum of $200,000. Thus, answers (b) and (d) are incorrect.

7. (574,L3,53) (c) The insurance company would not be subrogated to the rights against its insured who holds a malpractice policy for negligence. The reason for a malpractice insurance policy is to protect the insured against this type of action. Malpractice insurance would not cover intentional wrongs such as fraud. A malpractice policy would not automatically cover the new partnership, because the character of the new partner is crucial to the risk that the insurance company takes. Injuries such as a slip on a rug are not covered under malpractice insurance, but under personal liability.

E. Automobile Insurance

8. (582,L1,59) (b) Tedland's insurer has liability even though the accident was the result of William's negligence. Tedland had collision coverage under the insurance policy, therefore the insurer is liable for any damage to Tedland's car, irrespective of whose negligence caused the damage. Answer (a) is incorrect because one of the insurer's obligations under an auto insurance policy is to defend the insured against any lawsuits arising from operation of the vehicle covered by the policy. Answer (c) is incorrect because Milsap does possess a cause of action against Williams for the injuries sustained due to William's negligence. Answer (d) is incorrect because the insurance company is liable for damages to Tedland's automobile caused by the collision, less the amount of deductible (which the insured must pay). The insurance company is also subrogated to Tedland's rights and is able to recover from any person legally liable for the loss.

I. Fire Insurance

9. (578,L1,17) (c) Where both the owner and a mortgagee are insured under a policy, typically a loss payable clause will allow the mortgagee to collect to the extent of his loss. Answer (d) is incorrect because the policy is probably open or unvalued rather than a stated value policy. Unless it is a stated value policy, the insurance company will only be liable for the smaller of the policy face value or the FMV of the loss at the time of the loss. Answer (b) is incorrect because a mortgagee has an insurable interest and can independently obtain a fire insurance policy on mortgaged property. Answer (a) is incorrect because an owner of property can purchase any amount of title insurance that the insurance company agrees to sell.

10. (1175,L3,38) (c) A person who insures with multiple policies can only collect the proportionate amount of the loss from each insurer. The limit of recovery is the value of the loss. There is nothing illegal about insuring with more than one policy or to insure for more than the value of the property. A coinsurance clause must be stated in the policy and does not affect recovery if insurance is carried for full value.

I.5. Coinsurance Clause

11. (583,L1,37) (b) The coinsurance requirement provides that if the property is insured for less than a certain percent (usually 80%) of its fair market value at the time of the loss, the insurance company will be liable for only a portion of any loss, i.e., the owner becomes a coinsurer with the insurance company and must proportionately bear the loss. Therefore, if the owner insures his/her property at this stated minimum percentage, s/he will recover any loss in full up to the face amount of the policy. Answer (a) is incorrect because the insurable interest requirement is distinct and separate from the coinsurance feature of property insurance. Answers (c) and (d) are incorrect because the underlying rationale of the coinsurance clause is not to prevent arson by the owner nor to increase the care of the insured; the coinsurance provision only relates to the amount of insurance recovery in the event of loss.

12. (1181,L1,56) (b) The coinsurance clause would only apply if there had been partial destruction of the property insured. Since there was total destruction with the property being valued at $160,000 ($10,000 above the face value of the policy), the partnership would recover the face value ($150,000). Thus, answers (c) and (d) are incorrect. Answer (a) is

incorrect because for the partnership to recover, it must have an insurable interest in the property which is satisfied by both a legal interest in the property and a possibility of pecuniary loss if the property is destroyed. The Carter, Wallace, and Jones partnership meets the requisite criteria for possessing an insurable interest in the office building without the necessity of having legal title in the partnership's name.

13. (580,L1,48) (c) When there is a partial loss for property covered under a policy with a co-insurance clause, the following formula is applied to determine the recovery:

$$\frac{\text{Face value of policy}}{\text{Fair value of property x co-insurance \%}} \times \text{Loss} = \text{Recovery}$$

$$\frac{\$16{,}000}{\$100{,}000 \times 80\%} \times \$40{,}000 = \$8{,}000$$

$$\frac{\$24{,}000}{\$100{,}000 \times 80\%} \times \$40{,}000 = \underline{\$12{,}000}$$

$$\$20{,}000$$

Thus answer (c) is the correct answer.

Answer Outline

Problem 1 Coinsurance, Standard Mortgagee, and Pro Rata Clauses

Part a.

1. Jackson will recover $150,000 from Eagle
   Fire insurance policy contains 80% coinsurance clause
      Jackson must carry an amount of insurance equal to 80% of FMV of Parksdale plant
         In order to recover full amount of loss
      Jackson did not insure property to required 80% of its value
         Becomes a coinsurer and must proportionally share with Eagle the loss suffered

$$\frac{\text{Amount of insurance}}{\left(\begin{array}{c}\text{Coinsurance}\\ \text{percentage x FMV}\\ \text{of property}\end{array}\right)} \times \begin{array}{c}\text{Amount}\\ \text{of loss}\end{array} = \text{Recovery}$$

2. Second National Bank will receive $106,000 and Jackson will receive $44,000
   Insurance policy contains "standard mortgagee clause"
      Proceeds applied first to mortgagee
         In satisfaction of mortgage debt
      Any surplus paid to mortgagor
3. Jackson will recover $300,000 from Eagle
   Yuma warehouse was totally destroyed
      Coinsurance provision only applies to partial destruction of insured property
   Amount of recovery limited to face value of insurance policy
4. Jackson will recover $45,000 from the insurance companies
   Fire insurance policies contain 80% coinsurance clause
      Jackson must carry an amount of insurance equal to 80% of FMV of Rye City garage
         In order to recover full amount of loss
      Jackson did not insure property to required 80% of its value
         Becomes coinsurer and must proportionally share with the insurance companies the loss suffered

$$\frac{\begin{array}{c}\text{Amount of}\\ \text{insurance policies}\end{array}}{\left(\begin{array}{c}\text{Coinsurance}\\ \text{percentage x FMV}\\ \text{of property}\end{array}\right)} \times \begin{array}{c}\text{Amount}\\ \text{of loss}\end{array} = \text{Recovery}$$

5. Queen will be obligated to pay $30,000
   Insurance policies contain a pro rata clause
      If insured has multiple insurance policies covering same property
         Loss must be apportioned among the insurers
      Each insurer is liable for its pro rata share of loss

$$\frac{\begin{array}{c}\text{Amount of}\\ \text{insurance coverage}\\ \text{from Queen}\end{array}}{\begin{array}{c}\text{Total amount}\\ \text{of insurance}\\ \text{coverage}\end{array}} \times \begin{array}{c}\text{Liability}\\ \text{due to}\\ \text{fire}\end{array} = \begin{array}{c}\text{Pro rata}\\ \text{share}\end{array}$$

Unofficial Answer

(Author Modified)

Problem 1 Coinsurance, Standard Mortgagee, and Pro Rata Clauses

Part a.

1. Under a fire insurance policy that contains an 80% coinsurance clause, the insured must carry an amount of insurance equal to 80% of the value of the property insured in order to recover any loss in full up to the face amount of the policy, but if the insured carries an amount of insurance less than the 80%, s/he becomes a coinsurer and must proportionally bear with the insurance company any loss suffered due to partial destruction of the property.

Jackson did not insure its property to the required 80% of its value, therefore its recovery would be computed on the following basis:

$$\frac{\text{Amount of insurance}}{\left(\begin{array}{c}\text{Coinsurance percentage x}\\ \text{FMV of property}\end{array}\right)} \times \begin{array}{c}\text{Amount}\\ \text{of loss}\end{array} = \textbf{Recovery}$$

$$\frac{\$600{,}000}{80\% \times \$1{,}000{,}000} \times \$200{,}000 = \mathbf{\$150{,}000}$$

2. The total amount of recovery from the fire loss was $150,000. Second National Bank will receive $106,000 and Jackson will receive $44,000. The insurance policy contained a "standard mortgagee clause" which provides that in the event of loss, the proceeds will be applied first to the mortgagee (Second National Bank) in satisfaction of the mortgage debt (including accrued interest) and any surplus will be paid to the owner of the property, i.e., mortgagor (Jackson).

3. Jackson will recover the face value of the insurance policy from Eagle. The application of a coinsurance provision contained in a fire insurance policy is limited to partial destruction of the insured property.

When the property is totally destroyed, as was the Yuma warehouse, the coinsurance provision has no relevance. Since the value of Jackson's Yuma warehouse, at the time of total destruction, exceeded the policy coverage, Jackson's recovery will be limited to the face value of the insurance policy ($300,000).

4. Since the insurance policy contained an 80% coinsurance clause, the insured (Jackson) must carry an amount of insurance equal to 80% of the value of the property insured in order to recover any loss in full. Jackson did not insure its property to the required 80% of its value, therefore it becomes a coinsurer and must proportionally bear with the insurance companies any loss suffered due to partial destruction of the property.

Jackson's recovery from the insurance companies would be computed on the following basis:

$$\left(\frac{\text{Amount of ins. policies}}{\text{Coinsurance percentage} \times \text{FMV of property}}\right) \times \text{Amount of loss} = \textbf{Recovery}$$

$$\frac{\$50,000 + \$100,000}{80\% \times \$250,000} \times \$60,000 = \mathbf{\$45,000}$$

5. A pro rata clause provides that if the insured has multiple fire insurance policies covering the same property, any loss must be apportioned among the insurers in the ratio that the amount of insurance issued by each insurer bears to the total amount of the insurance procured, and each insurer is liable to the insured for its pro rata share of such loss.

Consequently, since the total insurance coverage on the garage was $150,000, with Queen providing $100,000 of this, Queen must pay two-thirds of the liability due to the fire loss.

$$\frac{\text{Amount of insurance issued by Queen}}{\text{Total amount of insurance coverage}} \times \text{Liability due to fire} = \textbf{Queen's pro rata share}$$

$$\frac{\$100,000}{\$50,000 + \$100,000} \times \$45,000 = \mathbf{\$30,000}$$

Answer Outline

Problem 2 Insurable Interests

b. The insurance company must pay
   An insurable interest in Balsom existed
      I.e., there was an economic interest
   Insurable interest only required at policy inception
   Age misrepresentation does not void policy
      But does reduce amount recoverable
      To the insurance purchasable with premiums paid

c1. Anderson's recovery (insurable interest) is principal plus
      Interest at time of the fire
      Limited to policy face value

c2. Victory is subrogated to Anderson's rights
      I.e., to receive mortgage payments

Unofficial Answer

Problem 2 Insurable Interests

b. Yes. An insurable interest in the life of another is present here since the firm has a substantial economic interest in the life of Balsam at the time the policy was procured. It is well recognized that an entity has the requisite standing to procure insurance on its key participants. Certainly a general partner qualifies as a key participant. In addition, the funding of buy-out agreements is essential in many instances, and insurance law recognizes this economic necessity. The insurable interest required for a life insurance policy need only exist at the inception of the policy. Balsam's subsequent retirement does not invalidate it.

The fact that Balsam misrepresented his age will not cause the loss of the entire insurance proceeds. The general rule provides that such a misrepresentation merely reduces the amount recoverable to that which the premiums would purchase if the correct age had been stated.

c. 1. Anderson's insurable interest equals the extent of the mortgage debt outstanding. Thus, his recovery is limited to the $52,000 debt outstanding plus accrued interest on the debt, but the total recovery cannot exceed $60,000, the maximum coverage under the policy.

2. Upon payment, Victory is subrogated to the rights of Anderson and will succeed to Anderson's rights to receive payments under the terms of the mortgage and mortgage bond. If Drum Corporation fails to continue the payments, Victory may foreclose on the mortgage.

Multiple Choice Questions (1 - 21)

1. The last will and testament of Jean Bond left various specific property and sums of money to relatives and friends. She left the residue of her estate equally to her favorite niece and nephew. Which of the various properties described below will become a part of Bond's estate and be distributed in accordance with her last will and testament?

   a. A joint savings account which listed her sister, who is still living, as the joint tenant.
   b. The entire family homestead which she had owned in joint tenancy with her older brother who predeceased her and which was still recorded as jointly owned.
   c. Several substantial gifts that she made in contemplation of death to various charities.
   d. A life insurance policy which designated a former partner as the beneficiary.

2. Paul Good's will left all of his commercial real property to his wife Dorothy for life and the remainder to his two daughters, Joan and Doris, as tenants in common. All beneficiaries are alive and over 21 years of age. Regarding the rights of the parties, which of the following is a correct statement?

   a. Dorothy may **not** elect to take against the will and receive a statutory share instead.
   b. The daughters **must** survive Dorothy in order to receive any interest in the property.
   c. Either of the daughters may sell her interest in the property without the consent of their mother or the other daughter.
   d. If only one daughter is alive upon the death of Dorothy, she is entitled to the entire property.

3. The intestate succession distribution rules

   a. Do not apply to property held in joint tenancy.
   b. Do not apply to real property.
   c. Effectively prevent a decedent from totally disinheriting his wife and children.
   d. Apply to situations where the decedent failed to name an executor.

4. An executor named in the decedent's will

   a. Must consent to serve, have read the will, and be present at the execution of the will.
   b. Need **not** serve if he does **not** wish to do so.
   c. Must serve without compensation unless the will provides otherwise.
   d. Can **not** be the principal beneficiary of the will.

5. Madison died 15 years after executing a valid will. He named his son, Walker, as the executor of his will. He left two-thirds of his estate to his wife and the balance equally to his children. Which of the following is a right or duty of Walker as executor?

   a. Walker must post a surety bond even if a provision in the will attempts to exempt him from this responsibility.
   b. Walker has an affirmative duty to discover, collect, and distribute all the decedent's assets.
   c. If the will is silent on the point, Walker has complete discretion insofar as investing the estate's assets during the term of his administration.
   d. Walker can sell real property without a court order, even though he has not been expressly authorized to do so.

6. Assuming that a given trust indenture is silent on the point, the trustee has certain rights and duties as a matter of law. The trustee

   a. Has a fiduciary duty to the trust but **not** to the beneficiaries.
   b. Is **not** entitled to commissions unless so provided.
   c. Can elect to terminate the trust as long as the beneficiaries unanimously concur.
   d. Must act in a competent, nonnegligent manner, or he may face removal.

7. Martins created an irrevocable fifteen-year trust for the benefit of his minor children. At the end of the fifteen years, the principal reverts to Martins. Martins named the Bloom Trust Company as trustee and provided that Bloom would serve without the necessity of posting a bond. In understanding the trust and rules applicable to it, which of the following is correct?

   a. If Martins dies ten years after creation of the trust, it is automatically revoked and the property is distributed to the beneficiaries of his trust upon their attaining age 21.
   b. Martins may revoke the trust after eleven years, since he created it, and the principal reverts to him at the expiration of the fifteen years.

c. The facts indicate that the trust is a separate legal entity for both tax and non-tax purposes.
d. The trust is **not** a separate legal entity for federal tax purposes.

8. With respect to trusts, which of the following states an **invalid** legal conclusion?
a. The trustee must obtain the consent of the majority of the beneficiaries if a major change in the investment portfolio of the trust is to be made.
b. For federal income tax purposes, a trust is entitled to an exemption similar to that of an individual although **not** equal in amount.
c. Both the life beneficiaries of a trust and the ultimate takers have rights against the trustee, and the trustee is accountable to them.
d. A trust is a separate taxable entity for federal income tax purposes.

9. Larson is considering the creation of either a lifetime (inter vivos) or testamentary (by his will) trust. In deciding what to do, which of the following statements is correct?
a. If the trust is an inter vivos trust, the trustee must file papers in the appropriate state office roughly similar to those required to be filed by a corporation to qualify.
b. An inter vivos trust must meet the same legal requirements as one created by a will.
c. Property transferred to a testamentary trust upon the grantor's (creator's) death is **not** included in the decedent's gross estate for federal tax purposes.
d. Larson can retain the power to revoke an inter vivos trust.

10. James Gordon decided to create an inter vivos trust for the benefit of his grandchildren. He wished to bypass his own children, and to provide an independent income for his grandchildren. He did not, however, wish to completely part with the assets he would transfer to the trust. Therefore, he transferred the assets to the York Trust Company, in trust for the benefit of his grandchildren irrevocably for a period of 12 years. Which of the following is correct regarding the trust?
a. The trust will fail for want of a proper purpose.
b. The trust income will not be taxable to Gordon during its existence.
c. Gordon retains beneficial title to the property transferred to the trust.
d. If Gordon demands the return of the trust assets prior to the 12 years, York must return them to him since he created the trust and the assets will eventually be his again.

11. Wayne & Company, CPAs, was engaged by Harding, the trustee of the Timmons Testamentary Trust. The will creating the Timmons Trust gave Harding wide discretion with respect to the investment of the trust principal but was silent on the question of the allocation of receipts and charges to principal or income. Among the assets invested in by Harding is a $500,000 annuity and a $50,000 limited partnership interest in an offshore investment limited partnership. The partnership has reported a $40,000 loss for the year. Regarding the trust in general and the limited partnership loss allocation in particular, which of the following is correct?
a. It is against public policy to permit the investment by the trustee in the offshore investment limited partnership.
b. Since the trust is silent on the allocation question, Harding has wide discretion in making allocations.
c. The loss attributable to the offshore partnership is allocable equally to principal and income.
d. The receipts from the $500,000 annuity must be apportioned between principal and income.

12. The Martin Trust consisted primarily of various income-producing real estate properties. During the year, the trustee incurred various charges. Among the charges were the following: depreciation, principal payments on various mortgages, and a street assessment. Which of the following would be a proper allocation of these items?
a. All to income, except the street assessment.
b. All are to be allocated equally between principal and income.
c. All to principal.
d. All to principal, except depreciation.

13. Shepard created an inter vivos trust for the benefit of his children with the remainder to his grandchildren upon the death of his last surviving child. The trust consists of both real and personal property. One of the assets is an apartment building. In administer-

ing the trust and allocating the receipts and disbursements, which of the following would be **improper**?

a. The allocation of forfeited rental security deposits to income.
b. The allocation to principal of the annual service fee of the rental collection agency.
c. The allocation to income of the interest on the mortgage on the apartment building.
d. The allocation to income of the payment of the insurance premiums on the apartment building.

14. The Astor Bank and Trust Company is the trustee of the Wayne Trust. A significant portion of the trust principal has been invested in AAA rated public utility bonds. Some of the bonds have been purchased at face value, some at a discount, and others at a premium. Which of the following is a proper allocation of the various items to income?

a. The income beneficiary is entitled to the entire interest without dilution for the premium paid but is not entitled to the proceeds attributable to the discount upon collection.
b. The income beneficiary is entitled to the entire interest without dilution and to the proceeds attributable to the discount.
c. The income beneficiary is only entitled to the interest less the amount of the premium amortized over the life of the bond.
d. The income beneficiary is entitled to the full interest and to an allocable share of the gain resulting from the discount.

Items 15 and 16 are based on the following information:

Martin is the trustee of the Baker Trust which has assets in excess of $1 million. Martin has engaged the CPA firm of Hardy & Fox to prepare the annual accounting statement for the allocation of receipts and expenditures between income and principal. The trust indenture provides that "receipts and expenses are to be allocated to income or principal according to law."

15. Which of the following receipts should be allocated to income?

a. Rights to subscribe to shares of the distributing corporation.
b. Sale of rights to subscribe to shares of the distributing corporation.
c. A 2% stock dividend.
d. Rights to subscribe to shares of another corporation.

16. Which of the following receipts from real property should be allocated to principal?

a. An unexpected payment of nine months' arrears in rental payments.
b. A six-month prepayment of rent.
c. Insurance proceeds for the destruction of a garage on one of the properties.
d. Interest on a purchase money mortgage arising from the sale of a parcel of the trust's real property.

17. Which of the following receipts should be allocated by a trustee exclusively to income?

a. A stock dividend.
b. An extraordinary year-end cash dividend.
c. A liquidating dividend whether in complete or partial liquidation.
d. A stock split.

18. Which of the following receipts or disbursements by a trustee should be credited to or charged against income?

a. Amortization payment on real property subject to a mortgage.
b. Capital gain distributions received from a mutual fund.
c. Stock rights received from the distributing corporation.
d. The discount portion received on redemption of treasury bills.

19. Madison died 15 years after executing a valid will. In it she named her daughter, Janet, as the executix of the will and bequeathed two-thirds of her estate to her husband after all taxes, expenses, and fees were paid, and the balance equally to her children. The approximate size of Madison's estate is $1 million. Which of the following is correct?

a. Immediately upon Madison's death, Janet has the legal right to act for and on behalf of the estate even though the will has not been admitted to probate and she has not yet been appointed as executrix.
b. All the property bequeathed to Madison's husband will be excluded from her estate for federal estate tax purposes.
c. Upon execution of her will, Madison's beneficiaries had a vested interest in her property.
d. Had Madison died without making a will, her husband would have received everything.

20. Annette's will provides for a trust upon her death. York Trust Company is named as the trustee and the trust's terms provide for the payment of income to Annette's husband for life and the remainder to her children. The Annette Trust

a Is **not** recognized as a taxable entity for income tax purposes.

b. Does qualify for the estate tax marital deduction if Annette's husband's rights represent a qualified terminable interest.

c. Is subject to an implied restriction which obligates York to obtain the beneficiaries' consent if it wishes to dispose of trust assets.

d. Vests legal and equitable title in York.

21. The Marquis Trust has been properly created and it qualifies as a real estate investment trust (REIT) for federal income tax purposes. As such, it will

a. Be taxedas any other trust for income tax purposes.

b. Have been created under the Federal Trust Indenture Act.

c. Provide limited liability for the parties investing in the trust.

d. Be exempt from the Securities Act of 1933.

Problems

Problem 1 Creation of Trust; Clifford Trust (1183,L5b)

(7 to 10 minutes)

Part b. Mr. & Mrs. Charles Crawford were in the 50% income tax bracket for federal income tax purposes. The Crawfords had two children, June and Virgil, ages 16 and 15. The Crawfords decided that they would like to shift some of their income to the children, but were unwilling to make outright gifts. They consulted with their CPA, banker and attorney and, after considerable discussion, decided to create a short-term irrevocable trust for the benefit of the children with Clearview Trust Company as trustee. The duration of the trust was, as stated in the trust agreement, ten years plus one day from the execution of the trust agreement. The trust agreement was dated August 1, 1982, and the intent of the parties was to convey the Sunnydale property to the trustee after the mortgage on the property had been satisfied. The mortgage was satisfied on November 15, 1982, and the property conveyed in trust to the trustee on December 1, 1982. Net rental income from the Sunnydale property for the period from December 1, 1982, to December 31, 1982, the end of the tax year chosen for the trust, was $14,000. This amount was paid to the children in 1982 and $7,000 of trust income was reported for income tax purposes by each of the children. Mr. & Mrs. Crawford excluded the $14,000 from their income tax return.

As a result of a routine audit of the Crawford family returns for 1982, the Internal Revenue Service refused to accept the income as being properly includable in the children's returns and reallocated it to Mr. & Mrs. Crawford.

Required:

Answer the following, setting forth reasons for any conclusions stated.

1. What are the basic elements for the creation of a valid trust?

2. At what point in time was the trust created in this case?

3. Is the Internal Revenue Service's denial of the shifting of the $14,000 income to the children proper?

4. Can Mr. & Mrs. Crawford, without the consent of the beneficiaries revoke the trust, assuming the Internal Revenue Service is correct?

Multiple Choice Answers

1. b	6. d	10. b	14. a	18. d
2. c	7. c	11. d	15. d	19. b
3. a	8. a	12. d	16. c	20. b
4. b	9. d	13. b	17. b	21. c
5. b				

Multiple Choice Answer Explanations

A. Estates

1. (581,L1,50) (b) A joint tenancy is a form of concurrent property ownership in which the joint tenants have a right of survivorship in the property concurrently held. Thus, if a joint tenant dies, that tenant's interest in the property is divided equally among the surviving joint tenants. The deceased tenant's interest in the property will not pass to his heirs. Since Jean had full ownership of the property upon her brother's death and on her death, such property is properly included in her estate. Answer (a) is incorrect because, upon Jean's death, her sister will receive full ownership of the savings account regardless of any provision to the contrary in a will. Answer (c) is incorrect since gifts made in contemplation of death are irrevocable once made. Answer (d) is incorrect since a life insurance policy will pass to the named beneficiary without regard to the will of the deceased.

2. (1180,L1,50) (c) The will created a life estate in Dorothy, the wife, and a vested remainder in fee simple that the daughters owned as tenants in common. This means that the daughters' ownership rights to the property came into existence when Paul, the decedent, died, even though their right of possession does not occur until Dorothy dies, and her life estate terminates. One daughter could sell her interest without the consent of either of the other two parties. Answer (c) is correct. Answer (a) is incorrect because a spouse under the concept of statutory share has the right to denounce the will and elect to take stated share (normally 1/3) of the dead spouse's estate. Answer (d) is incorrect because the daughters received the remainder as tenants in common, not as joint tenants. Tenancy in common does not have the right of survivorship thus, if one of the daughters predeceased Dorothy, the interest of the dead daughter would pass by the deceased daughter's estate.

3. (1178,L1,34) (a) Property held in joint tenancy passes to the survivor whether or not there is a will. The intestate succession rules apply to persons who die intestate, i.e., without a will. Answer (b) is incorrect because intestate succession applies to all property of a decedent dying without a will. Answer (c) is incorrect because the intestate succession rules do not effectively prevent a decedent from totally disinheriting his wife and children because such effect might be accomplished by other estate planning devises such as a will. Answer (d) is incorrect because the failure to name an executor would not have the effect of converting a decedent from the status of testate to intestate. An administrator would be appointed by the court in place of an executor.

B. Administration of Estates

4. (1180,L1,52) (b) An executor is the personal representative of the decedent that is named in a will. If the decedent died intestate, then, the court would appoint an administrator as the personal representative. The person named as executor can decline to serve; in which case, the court will then appoint an executor. If the will does not provide compensation for the services of an executor, the court will order that the person serving in this capacity receive a reasonable fee for services rendered. The executor can be the principal beneficiary of the will, but need not have read the will nor be present at the signing of the will.

5. (577,L3,41) (b) As executor of his father's will, Walker has the affirmative duty to carry out the wishes of his father. He must collect all debts, pay all expenses, and carry out the distribution of the assets to those specified. The will may provide that a surety bond is not necessary for the executor but the probate court in its discretion may not comply with this provision. An executor may not sell real property without the court's approval unless the will specifically grants this power. Unless the will grants unlimited discretion, Walker must conform to various prudent investment guidelines in the management of the estate's assets during administration.

C. Trusts

6. (582,L1,55) (d) The trustee must act in a competent, nonnegligent manner. The trustee faces possible removal unless he exercises that degree of care and skill which a reasonably prudent person would in the administration of the trust. Answer (a) is incorrect because the trustee owes a fiduciary duty to the beneficiaries. A trustee holds the legal title to the trust property for the benefit of the beneficiaries. Answer (b) is incorrect because the trustee is entitled to compensation for duties performed in managing the trust property and distributing the trust income to the beneficiaries as directed by the trust instrument. Answer (c) is incorrect because the trustee does not have the

power to make such an election for termination. However, if all the parties join in a suit to terminate a trust, the trust may be terminated, with agreement of settlor, if termination would not defeat a material trust purpose.

7. (582,L1,57) (c) The trust created by Martins is a legal entity for both tax and nontax purposes even though the settlor is also the remainderman (the person who receives the trust corpus at the termination of the trust). When the grantor retains a reversionary interest in the trust property such that the corpus or income is to revert to him within ten years after the transfer into trust (this qualifies as a Grantor Trust), the trust is not considered a separate legal entity for tax purposes. The income from such trust is then taxable as personal income to the grantor. Since Martins' trust is for fifteen years, it falls outside the scope of a Grantor Trust, and consequently will be a separate legal entity for tax purposes. Answer (a) is incorrect because Martins' death does not terminate the trust since he is not the measuring life for the trust's duration. If Martins dies after ten years, the trust will continue for the remaining five years for the benefit of the children and will then pass to his heirs or devisees. Answer (b) is incorrect because the trust is irrevocable for a fifteen-year period, and Martins can revoke only if he reserved a power of revocation in the trust agreement or if all the beneficiaries agree and the termination would not defeat a material trust purpose.

8. (581,L1,49) (a) A trust is a fiduciary relationship wherein one person (trustee) holds legal title to property for the benefit of another (beneficiary). A trustee has the power to do what is necessary to fulfill the terms of the trust. A trustee cannot speculate, must diversify and can make major changes in an investment portfolio without the consent of beneficiaries. Answer (b) is not incorrect because a simple trust is entitled to a $300 per year exemption for federal tax purposes which is similar to an individual's exemption. Answer (c) is not incorrect because a trustee is a fiduciary to the beneficiaries and can take no personal advantage from his position. All beneficiaries can sue for mismanagement, conversion or waste by the trustee. A trustee must also keep trust assets separate from his personal assets and be accountable for both trust assets and his actions. Answer (d) is not an incorrect statement since a trust is a separate taxable entity for federal income tax purposes although it may not be subject to any tax.

9. (1180,L1,51) (d) A settlor may revoke a trust if the trust instrument reserves this right. Thus, answer (d) is correct. Creation of an inter vivos (living) trust only need be in writing when the trust involves real property, or where performance is not capable of being completed in one year from the date of creation. Inter vivos trusts involving personal property can be oral. Testamentary trusts must meet the same legal requirements for a valid will (i.e., in writing, signed, witnessed, etc.). Thus, answers (a) and (b) are incorrect. Answer (c) is incorrect because property in a testamentary trust is considered to have been transferred at the decedent's death and is therefore part of the decedent's gross estate for federal estate tax purposes.

10. (1179,L1,44) (b) In a properly drafted inter vivos trust, irrevocable for a period of 12 years, the trust income will not be taxable to the donor (settlor) during its existence but will be taxable to the beneficiaries. Answer (a) is incorrect because the trust as described will not fail for lack of a proper purpose. The property that has been transferred to the trust must be managed; thus the trust is an active one with a proper purpose since the trustee must actually perform these duties. Answer (c) is incorrect because the settlor, Gordon, does not retain the beneficial title to the trust since the duration of the trust is sufficiently long. The beneficiary holds the beneficial title to the property. Answer (d) is incorrect because under the facts as stated, Gordon has created an irrevocable trust. Thus, he may not demand return of the trust assets prior to the expiration of the 12 years. The only possibility of this occuring is if the settlor and all beneficiaries agree to a termination prior to the expiration of the 12 years.

D. Allocation of Principal and Income

11. (582,L1,56) (d) The allocation of principal and income is governed by the provisions of the Uniform Principal and Income Act. The receipts from the annuity are equitably apportioned between principal and income. Answer (a) is incorrect because it is not against public policy for the trustee to invest in the offshore investment limited partnership. The trustee has a duty to preserve the trust assets and to make the trust property productive. The trustee must invest the trust assets as a reasonably prudent person. The limited partnership can be construed to be a prudent investment due to its limited liability aspect, unlike investment in a general partnership where there is unlimited liability. Answer (b) is incorrect because the trustee, Harding, has no discretion in making allocations since the Uniform Principal and Income Act governs. Answer (c) is incorrect because the loss attributable to the partnership is chargeable to trust principal.

12. (1181,L1,51) (d) The Uniform Principal and Income Act governs the allocation of Principal and Income. Items allocated to income include ordinary operating expenses such as depreciation. This is further supported by Internal Revenue Code § 167 permitting a deduction of a reasonable allowance for exhaustion, or wear and tear (i.e., depreciation of property held for the production of income). On the other hand, principal paid on the mortgage and permanent improvements to the trust property (e.g., a street assessment) are expenses incurred in preserving the trust corpus (the income-producing real estate). They are, therefore, allocated to principal.

13. (581,L1,51) (b) An inter vivos trust comes into existence while the settlor (grantor) is living. The allocation of trust items to principal and income is governed by the Uniform Principal and Income Act (adopted by most states). Allocations made to trust principal include: original trust property, proceeds and gains from sale of trust property, insurance received on destruction of property, new property purchased with principal or proceeds from the principal, stock dividends and splits and a reserve for depreciation. Disbursements from trust principal are for reduction of indebtedness, litigation over trust property, permanent improvements and costs related to purchase/sale of trust property. Income includes profits from trust principal, e.g., rent, interest, cash dividends and royalties. Expenses from income include interest, insurance premiums, taxes, repairs, and depreciation. The annual service fee should be allocated to income because it is an expense associated with administration and management of trust property. It should not be allocated to principal. Answers (a), (c), and (d) are all proper allocations to income.

14. (580,L1,28) (a) Normally the income beneficiary is entitled to all interest earned by the items making up the corpus of the trust and the principal beneficiary is charged with any loss or gain relevant to the value of the corpus of the trust. Thus, answer (a) is correct.

15. (1179,L1,46) (d) Rights to subscribe to shares of another corporation should be allocated to income. Answers (a), subscription rights to the distributing corporation, (b) sale of subscription rights to the distributing corporation, and (c), a stock dividend, are examples of items that should be allocated to principal.

16. (1179,L1,47) (c) Insurance proceeds for the destruction of a garage located on the trust property should be allocated to principal since the insurance proceeds represent a change in the form of principal. The rental payments in answer (a), the prepayment of rent in answer (b), and the interest on a purchased money mortgage in answer (d) are all items that should be allocated to income.

17. (1178,L1,37) (b) Under the Uniform Principal and Income Act a year-end cash dividend, whether regular or extraordinary, should be allocated by a trustee exclusively to income. Stock dividends, liquidating dividends, and stock splits are all examples of receipts which should be allocated to principal.

18. (1178,L1,40) (d) In allocating between income and principal of a trust, the trustee should credit the discount portion received on redemption of treasury bills to income. This is essentially interest, which is an income item. The mortgage payments in answer (a), the capital gains distribution in answer (b), and the stock rights received from a distributing corporation in answer (c) are all examples of receipts or disbursements which a trustee should allocate to principal.

E. Federal Estate Tax

19. (1181,L1,52) (b) Under the Economic Recovery Tax Act of 1981 (which applies to decedents dying after December 31, 1981), there is an unlimited marital deduction for the fair market value of the property passing to a surviving spouse. Therefore, all the property bequeathed to Madison's husband will qualify for the marital deduction, and thereby be excluded from Madison's estate for federal estate tax purposes. Answer (a) is incorrect because an executrix is appointed by and under the control of the probate court. Hence, the executrix, Janet, does not have the legal right to act for and on behalf of the estate until she has been duly appointed in a probate proceeding. Answer (c) is incorrect because execution of a will does not vest ownership rights in the named beneficiaries. The testator is free to dispose of the property if he/she wishes after execution of the will. Answer (d) is incorrect because no state would allow a decedent's spouse to receive everything when there are surviving children.

20. (1181,L1,53) (b) A terminable interest granted to a surviving spouse will **not** generally qualify for the marital deduction. However, the Economic Recovery Tax Act of 1981 (which applies to decedents dying after December 31, 1981) stipulates that if certain conditions are met, a life interest granted to a surviving spouse (i.e., Annette's husband's life estate) will not be treated as a terminable interest, but rather as a **qualified terminable interest.** If decedent's executor elects, a transfer of **qualified terminable interest**

property (i.e., property placed in trust with income to surviving spouse for life and remainder to someone else at surviving spouse's death) will qualify for the unlimited marital estate deduction, provided that income from the property is paid at least annually to the surviving spouse and the property is not subject to transfer during the surviving spouse's lifetime. Therefore, Annette's husband's rights would qualify for the estate tax marital deduction, assuming it meets the aforementioned criteria for qualified terminable interest property. Answer (a) is incorrect because a trust is recognized as a taxable entity for income tax purposes. Answer (c) is incorrect because although the trustee is a fiduciary with respect to the beneficiaries and must act with their interest in mind, in the absence of an explicit restriction, there is no implied restriction which obligates the trustee, York, to obtain the beneficiaries' consent if he wishes to dispose of the trust assets. Answer (d) is incorrect because the trustee, York, holds only legal title, not equitable title. The beneficiaries of the trust hold equitable title.

F. Real Estate Investment Trusts (REITS)

21. (1180,L1,45) (c) The certificateholders (owners) of a real estate investment trust have limited liability. Their liability is limited to their investment in the trust similar to the limited liability of a shareholder in a corporation and a limited partner. Thus answer (c) is correct. Answer (d) is incorrect because the sale of an interest in a real estate investment trust is the sale of a security under the Securities Act of 1933. Consequently, the seller of these interests would have to comply with the registration requirements of this act. A real estate investment trust does not fall within the provisions of the Federal Trust Indenture Act. This makes answer (b) incorrect. The normal trust, as distinguished from a real estate investment trust, is a taxable entity for income tax purposes, while a real estate investment trust is not a taxable entity. Ordinary income passes through to the investors and each investor pays income tax on his/her share.

Answer Outline

Problem 1 Creation of Trust; Clifford Trust

Part b.

1. Trust must have
   - Creator
   - Trust property
   - Trustee
   - Beneficiary

   If trust property is real property, there must be a writing
2. Trust was created on December 1, 1982, when Crawfords conveyed land to trustee in writing
   - *Inter vivos* trust begins when title to real property vests in trustee
3. Yes, duration of trust is less than 10 years
   - Thus, does not qualify as a Clifford trust, which would have properly shifted income to children
4. No, normally once irrevocable trust is created, state law prohibits termination until expiration of stated term

Unofficial Answer

Problem 1 Creation of Trust; Clifford Trust

Part b.

1. A trust must have a creator (settlor or grantor), trust property, (principal, corpus, or res), a trustee, and a beneficiary. There must be a writing if the subject matter of the trust is real property.

2. The Crawfords' trust was not created until December 1, 1982, when the land (the res) was conveyed to the trustee in writing. In the case of an intervivos trust of real property with an independent trustee, the settlor (here the Crawfords) must go through whatever formalities (here a conveyance) are required to vest title in the trustee.

3. Yes. Although a trust having a duration of 10 years or more will qualify as a bona fide transferee of property for the purposes of shifting income to the trust or its beneficiaries, a transfer to a trust for a lesser duration will not qualify according to the Internal Revenue Code and Regulations. This trust was intended to be what is popularly known as a "Clifford Trust."

4. No. State law precludes, except in rare circumstances, the termination of an irrevocable trust once created. Hence, the Crawfords are stuck with a useless trust for the balance of its term.

CHAPTER FOUR

FINANCIAL ACCOUNTING PROBLEMS AND SOLUTIONS

Financial accounting is the most extensively tested topic on both the accounting theory and accounting practice sections of the examination.

Theory, tested from 1:30 to 5:00 Friday afternoon, consists of 60 multiple choice questions (60% of the theory grade) and 4 essay questions (40% of the theory grade). Generally 40 to 50 of the multiple choice questions concern financial accounting topics along with 2 or 3 of the essay questions. The remaining questions cover cost, managerial, and governmental accounting.

Practice, tested from 1:30 to 6:00 on Wednesday and Thursday afternoons, consists of 120 multiple choice questions (60% of the practice grade) in six problem "sets" of 20 multiple choice questions each. The practice sections also contain 4 practice problems (40% of the practice grade). The coverage of financial topics on the May 1984 examination (typical of recent exams) consisted of 60 multiple choice questions and 2½ practice problems. The remaining items cover federal taxation as well as cost, managerial, and governmental accounting. A complete analysis of recent examinations and the *AICPA Content Specification Outlines* appear in Volume I, *Outlines and Study Guides*.

Each question is coded as to month, year, section, problem number, and multiple choice question number. For example, (1183,P2,31) indicates November 1983, problem 2 of the Practice I section, multiple choice question number 31. Note that P = Practice I, Q = Practice II, and T = Theory. Some questions were altered to make them applicable due to changes in GAAP.

FINANCIAL PROBLEMS INDEX

	Exam reference	No. of minutes	Problem page no.	Answer page no.
Module 26/Fixed Assets (FA)				
50 Multiple Choice			579	589
3 Essay Questions and				
2 Practice Problems:				
1. Accounting for R&D	578,T5	20–25	586	597
2. Property, Plant, and Equipment	1180,T2	15–25	586	598
3. Property, Plant, and Equipment	576,T3	20–25	586	599
4. Comprehensive Schedules: Fixed Assets	1182,P5	40–50	587	601
5. Plant Asset Transactions	582,P5a	20–30	588	603
Module 27/Deferred Tax (DETX)				
31 Multiple Choice			606	612
2 Essay Questions and				
1 Practice Problem:				
1. Recording and Classifying Deferred Taxes	582,T4	15–25	611	617
2. Gross vs. Net Change Method	1179,T4a	5–10	611	618
3. Calculation of Deferred Taxes	1182,Q4	45–55	611	618
Module 28/Stockholders' Equity (STK)				
56 Multiple Choice			622	635
6 Essay Questions and				
4 Practice Problems:				
1. Primary vs. Fully Diluted EPS	580,T2b	10–15	630	645
2. Stock Option Plans	580,T4b	10–15	630	645
3. Treasury Stock	1179,T2b	10–15	630	646
4. Common Stock Equivalents	1178,T2	15–20	630	647
5. Categories of Stockholders' Equity	576,T7	20–25	630	648
6. Earnings Per Share	574,T6	25–30	631	650
7. Stock Appreciation Rights	Kieso & Weygandt, 4th Ed., p. 777–adapted	15–25	631	651
8. Retained Earnings Statement and Stockholders' Equity Section of Balance Sheet	1183,P4	45–55	631	653
9. Stock Options and EPS	1181,P5	40–50	632	655
10. Stockholders' Equity Transactions	578,P3	50–60	633	658
Module 29/Present Value Applications (PV)				
Fundamental Concepts				
19 Multiple Choice			663	667
1 Essay Question and				
1 Practice Problem:				
1. Valuation of Notes	1172,T3	25–30	666	670
2. Noninterest Bearing Note	579,P4c	15–20	666	671

	Exam reference	No. of minutes	Problem page no.	Answer page no.
Bonds				
21 Multiple Choice			673	678
2 Essay Questions and				
3 Practice Problems:				
1. Bond Investments	581,P4a	25–30	676	682
2. Conversion of Bonds into Common Stock; Issuance of Bonds	1182,T3	15–25	676	683
3. Accounting for Bonds	1180,T4	15–25	676	684
4. Issuance and Extinguishment	1179,P5	40–50	676	685
5. Discount Calculation	1178,P3a	15–20	677	686
Debt Restructure				
4 Multiple Choice			689	691
1 Practice Problem:				
1. Entries for Modification of Terms	Kieso & Weygandt, 4th Ed., p. 650–adapted	40–50	690	692
Pensions				
16 Multiple Choice			694	698
1 Essay Question and				
1 Practice Problem:				
1. Definitions	578,T4	20–25	697	701
2. Pension Calculations	582,P5b	20–30	697	703
Leases				
33 Multiple Choice			706	713
2 Essay Questions and				
1 Practice Problem:				
1. Description of Lease Accounting	580,T3	15–25	711	718
2. Lease Classification and Accounting	1183,T5	15–25	711	719
3. Lessor and Lessee Accounting	581,P5	40–50	711	719
Module 30/Inflation Accounting (INFL)				
42 Multiple Choice			722	733
4 Essay Questions and				
3 Practice Problems				
1. SFAS 33	CMA,681,PRS 5	30	728	739
2. SFAS 33	Author constructed	25–30	728	740
3. Constant Dollar Accounting	CMA,1281,PRS 3	30	728	740
4. Current Valuation of Assets	578,T6	25–30	729	742
5. Constant Dollar Theory	575,T7	25–30	730	743
6. Constant Dollar and Current Cost	Kieso & Weygandt, 4th Ed., p. 1195	60–75	731	745
7. Foreign Currency Translation	1177,P4c	15–20	732	747
Module 31/Ratio Analysis (RATO)				
32 Multiple Choice			749	755
1 Essay Question:				
1. Corporation Solvency Ratios	1173,T7	25–30	754	759

BASIC CONCEPTS

Multiple Choice Questions (1 - 38)

1. Weaver Company sells magazine subscriptions for a one-year, two-year, or three-year period. Cash receipts from subscribers are credited to magazine subscriptions collected in advance, and this account had a balance of $1,700,000 at December 31, 1981. Information for the year ended December 31, 1982, is as follows:

Cash receipts from subscribers	$2,100,000
Magazine subscriptions revenue (credited at 12/31/82)	1,500,000

In its December 31, 1982, balance sheet, what amount should Weaver report as the balance for magazine subscriptions collected in advance?

a. $1,400,000
b. $1,900,000
c. $2,100,000
d. $2,300,000

2. Under Gerber Company's accounting system, all insurance premiums paid are debited to prepaid insurance. For interim financial statements, Gerber makes monthly estimated charges to insurance expense with an offset to prepaid insurance. Additional information for the year ended December 31, 1982, is as follows:

Prepaid insurance at December 31, 1981	$150,000
Charges to insurance expense during 1982 (including a year-end adjustment of $25,000)	625,000
Unexpired insurance premiums at December 31, 1982	175,000

What was the total amount of insurance premiums paid by Gerber during 1982?

a. $475,000
b. $600,000
c. $625,000
d. $650,000

3. Kipling Company does not carry insurance on its office typewriters. On December 28, 1980, one of its typewriters was stolen. The book value of the typewriter at the date of the burglary was $500. On January 15, 1981, another typewriter was vandalized. The book value of that typewriter, depreciated to the date of the vandalism, was $600. On February 1, 1981, before the issuance of the 1980 financial statements, the vandalized typewriter was repaired for $120. The total amount of losses that should be charged to income in 1980 is

a. $0
b. $ 500
c. $ 620
d. $1,100

4. Empire Corporation owns an office building and leases the offices under a variety of rental agreements involving rent paid monthly in advance and rent paid annually in advance. Not all tenants make timely payments of their rent. Empire's balance sheets contained the following information:

	1982	*1981*
Rentals receivable	$3,100	$2,400
Unearned rentals	6,000	8,000

During 1982, Empire received $20,000 cash from tenants. How much rental revenue should Empire record for 1982?

a. $17,300
b. $18,700
c. $21,300
d. $22,700

5. Under Statement of Financial Accounting Concepts No. 3, comprehensive income includes which of the following?

	Losses	*Contribution margin*
a.	No	No
b.	No	Yes
c.	Yes	Yes
d.	Yes	No

6. Under Statement of Financial Accounting Concepts No. 3, the term recognized is synonymous with the term

a. Recorded.
b. Realized.
c. Matched.
d. Allocated.

7. Some costs cannot be directly related to particular revenues but are incurred to obtain benefits in the period in which the costs are incurred. An example of such a cost is

a. Electricity used to light offices.
b. Transportation to customers.
c. Cost of merchandise sold.
d. Sales commissions.

8. Under Statement of Financial Accounting Concepts No. 2, feedback value is an ingredient of the primary quality of

	Relevance	*Reliability*
a.	No	No
b.	No	Yes

c.	Yes	Yes
d.	Yes	No

9. Under Statement of Financial Accounting Concepts No. 2, which of the following interacts with both relevance and reliability to contribute to the usefulness of information?
   a. Comparability.
   b. Timeliness.
   c. Neutrality.
   d. Predictive value.

10. Under Statement of Financial Accounting Concepts No. 3, interrelated elements that are directly related to measuring performance and status of an enterprise include

	Distribution to owners	*Notes to financial statements*
a.	Yes	Yes
b.	Yes	No
c.	No	Yes
d.	No	No

11. Under Statement of Financial Accounting Concepts No. 3, gains on assets unsold are identified, in a precise sense, by the term
   a. Unrecorded.
   b. Unrealized.
   c. Unrecognized.
   d. Unallocated.

12. Which of the following is expensed under the principle of systematic and rational allocation?
   a. Salesmen's monthly salaries.
   b. Insurance premiums.
   c. Transportation to customers.
   d. Electricity to light office building.

13. The premium on a three-year insurance policy expiring on December 31, 1982 was paid in total on January 1, 1980. Assuming that the original payment was recorded as a prepaid asset, how would each of the following be affected in 1982?

	Prepaid assets	*Expenses*
a.	No change	Increase
b.	No change	No change
c.	Decrease	No change
d.	Decrease	Increase

14. According to Statement of Financial Accounting Concepts No. 2, an interim earnings report is expected to have which of the following?

	Predictive value	*Feedback value*
a.	No	No
b.	Yes	Yes
c.	Yes	No
d.	No	Yes

15. Uncertainty and risks inherent in business situations should be adequately considered in financial reporting. This statement is an example of the concept of
   a. Conservatism.
   b. Completeness.
   c. Neutrality.
   d. Representational faithfulness.

16. The information provided by financial reporting pertains to
   a. Individual business enterprises, rather than to industries or an economy as a whole or to members of society as consumers.
   b. Individual business enterprises and industries, rather than to an economy as a whole or to members of society as consumers.
   c. Individual business enterprises and an economy as a whole, rather than to industries or to members of society as consumers.
   d. Individual business enterprises, industries, and an economy as a whole, rather than to members of society as consumers.

17. A patent, purchased in 1978 and being amortized over a ten-year life, was determined to be worthless in 1981. The write-off of the asset in 1981 is an example of which of the following principles?
   a. Associating cause and effect.
   b. Immediate recognition.
   c. Systematic and rational allocation.
   d. Objectivity.

18. The valuation of a promise to receive cash in the future as present value on the financial statements of a business entity is valid because of the accounting concept of
   a. Entity.
   b. Materiality.
   c. Going concern.
   d. Neutrality.

19. Which of the following is an example of the expense recognition principle of associating cause and effect?
   a. Allocation of insurance cost.
   b. Sales commissions.

c. Depreciation of fixed assets.
d. Officers' salaries.

20. Accruing net losses on firm purchase commitments for inventory is an example of the accounting concept of
  a. Conservatism.
  b. Realization.
  c. Consistency.
  d. Materiality.

21. When a specific customer's account receivable is written off as uncollectible, what will be the effect on net income under each of the following methods of recognizing bad debt expense?

	Allowance	*Direct Write Off*
a.	None	Decreased
b.	Decreased	None
c.	Decreased	Decreased
d.	None	None

22. Which of the following is an accrued liability?
  a. Cash dividends payable.
  b. Wages payable.
  c. Rent revenue collected one month in advance.
  d. Portion of long-term debt payable in current year.

23. The concept of consistency is sacrificed in the accounting for which of the following income statement items?
  a. Discontinued operations.
  b. Loss on disposal of a segment of a business.
  c. Extraordinary items.
  d. Cumulative effect of change in accounting principle.

24. When bad debt expense is estimated on the basis of the percentage of past actual losses from bad debts to past net credit sales, and this percentage is adjusted for anticipated conditions, the accounting concept of
  a. Matching is being followed.
  b. Matching is **not** being followed.
  c. Substance over form is being followed.
  d. Going concern is **not** being followed.

25. The principle of objectivity includes the concept of
  a. Summarization.
  b. Classification.
  c. Conservatism.
  d. Verifiability.

26. Under what condition is it proper to recognize revenues prior to the sale of merchandise?
  a. When the ultimate sale of the goods is at an assured sales price.
  b. When the revenue is to be reported as an installment sale.
  c. When the concept of internal consistency (of amounts of revenue) must be complied with.
  d. When management has a long-established policy to do so.

27. What accounting concept justifies the usage of accruals and deferrals?
  a. Going concern.
  b. Materiality.
  c. Consistency.
  d. Stable monetary unit.

28. What theory of ownership equity is enumerated by the following equation: assets minus liabilities minus preferred stock equity equals common stock equity?
  a. Fund.
  b. Enterprise.
  c. Entity.
  d. Residual equity.

29. The computation of the current value of an asset using the present value of future cash flows method does *not* include the
  a. Cost of alternate uses of funds given up.
  b. Productive life of the asset.
  c. Applicable interest rate.
  d. Future amounts of cash receipts or cash savings.

30. Historical cost is a measurement base currently used in financial accounting. Which of the following measurement bases is (are) also currently used in financial accounting?

	Current selling price	*Discounted cash flow*	*Replacement cost*
a.	Yes	No	Yes
b.	Yes	Yes	Yes
c.	Yes	No	No
d.	No	Yes	Yes

31. Bucca Warehousing Corporation bought a building at auction on June 30, 1980, for $1,000,000. On July 2, 1980, before occupying the building, Bucca sold it to a triple-A rated company for $1,200,000.

proceed	1050	
bookvalue	735	
	315	
	180	
	135	

$$\frac{315}{1050)\,315.0}\quad 3 \qquad 3150$$

Paid Cash	150	
note	900	
	1050	

150
3
450

300			
90	Gross on sale	315	
~~45~~	Applied on instal	135	
135	Balance	180	

Deferred Gross Profit

		315 Total Gross
Recognized 1982	45	
Recognized 1983	90	
	135	180 Balance 12/31/83

Bucca received a cash down payment of $300,000 and a first mortgage note at the market rate of interest, for the balance. No additional payments were required until 1981. On September 1, 1980, an independent appraiser valued the property at $1,500,000. On its 1980 income tax return, Bucca reported the sale on the installment basis. How much gain should Bucca recognize in its income statement for the year ended December 31, 1980?

a. $0
b. $ 50,000
c. $200,000
d. $300,000

32. On December 31, 1982, Tower Pizza, Inc., signed an agreement authorizing Greene Company to operate as a franchisee for an initial franchise fee of $50,000. Of this amount, $20,000 was received upon signing of the agreement and the balance is due in three annual payments of $10,000 each beginning December 31, 1983. The agreement provides that the down payment (representing a fair measure of the services already performed by Tower) is not refundable and substantial future services are required of Tower. Greene's credit rating is such that collection of the note is reasonably certain. The present value at December 31, 1982, of the three annual payments discounted at 14% (the implicit rate for a loan of this type) is $23,220. On December 31, 1982, Tower should record unearned franchise fees in respect of the Greene franchise of

a. $23,220
b. $30,000
c. $43,220
d. $50,000

May 1984 Questions

33. Greene Company sells office equipment service contracts agreeing to service equipment for a two-year period. Cash receipts from contracts are credited to unearned service contract revenue, and service contract costs are charged to service contract expense as incurred. Revenue from service contracts is recognized as earned over the lives of the contracts. Additional information for the year ended December 31, 1983, is as follows:

Unearned service contract revenue at January 1, 1983	$600,000
Cash receipts from service contracts sold	980,000
Service contract revenue recognized	860,000
Service contract expense	520,000

What amount should Greene report as unearned service contract revenue at December 31, 1983?

a. $460,000
b. $480,000
c. $490,000
d. $720,000

34. On January 1, 1982, Bartell Company sold its idle plant facility to Cooper, Inc., for $1,050,000. On this date the plant had a depreciated cost of $735,000. Cooper paid $150,000 cash on January 1, 1982, and signed a $900,000 note bearing interest at 10%. The note was payable in three annual installments of $300,000 beginning January 1, 1983. Bartell appropriately accounted for the sale under the installment method. Cooper made a timely payment of the first installment on January 1, 1983, of $390,000, which included interest of $90,000 to date of payment. At December 31, 1983, Bartell has deferred gross profit of

a. $153,000
b. $180,000
c. $225,000
d. $270,000

35. Decker Company assigns some of its patents to other enterprises under a variety of licensing agreements. In some instances advance royalties are received when the agreements are signed and, in others, royalties are remitted within 60 days after each license year end. The following data are included in Decker's December 31 balance sheets:

	1982	*1983*
Royalties receivable	$90,000	$85,000
Unearned royalties	60,000	40,000

During 1983 Decker received royalty remittances of $200,000. In its income statement for the year ended December 31, 1983, Decker should report royalty income of

a. $195,000
b. $215,000
c. $220,000
d. $225,000

36. On January 3, 1983, Paterson Services, Inc., signed an agreement authorizing Cobb Company to operate as a franchisee over a 20-year period for an initial franchise fee of $50,000 received when the agreement was signed. Cobb commenced operations on July 1, 1983, at which date all of the initial services required of Paterson had been performed. The agreement also provides that Cobb must pay a continuing franchise fee equal to 5% of the revenue from the franchise annually to Paterson. Cobb's franchise revenue for 1983 was $400,000. For the year ended Decem-

ber 31, 1983, how much should Paterson record as revenue from franchise fees in respect of the Cobb franchise?

a. $70,000
b. $50,000
c. $45,000
d. $22,500

37. Under Statement of Financial Accounting Concepts No. 2, timeliness is an ingredient of the primary quality of

a. Reliability.
b. Relevance.
c. Verifiability.
d. Representational faithfulness.

38. Under Statement of Financial Accounting Concepts No. 3, comprehensive income includes changes in equity resulting from

	Investments by owners	*Distributions to owners*
a.	No	No
b.	No	Yes
c.	Yes	No
d.	Yes	Yes

Repeat Questions

(584,T1,3) Identical to item 17 above

(584,T1,14) Identical to item 13 above

BASIC CONCEPTS

Problems

Problem 1 SFAC 2 (CMA, 681, PRS 7)

(30 minutes)

The Financial Accounting Standards Board (FASB) has been working on a conceptual framework for financial accounting and reporting. The FASB has issued four Statements of Financial Accounting Concepts. These statements are intended to set forth objectives and fundamentals that will be the basis for developing financial accounting and reporting standards. The objectives identify the goals and purposes of financial reporting. The fundamentals are the underlying concepts of financial accounting—concepts that guide the selection of transactions, events, and circumstances to be accounted for; their recognition and measurement; and the means of summarizing and communicating them to interested parties.

The purpose of Statement of Financial Accounting Concepts No. 2, "Qualitative Characteristics of Accounting Information," is to examine the characteristics that make accounting information useful. The characteristics or qualities of information discussed in Concepts No. 2 are the ingredients that make information useful and are the qualities to be sought when accounting choices are made.

Required:

a. Identify and discuss the benefits which can be expected to be derived from the FASB's conceptual framework study.

b. What is the most important quality for accounting information as identified in Statement of Financial Accounting Concepts No. 2 and explain why it is the most important.

c. Statement of Financial Accounting Concepts No. 2 describes a number of key characteristics or qualities for accounting information. Briefly discuss the importance of any three of these qualities for financial reporting purposes.

Problem 2 Revenue Recognition (1174,T4)

(25 to 30 minutes)

Part a. The earning of revenue by a business enterprise is recognized for accounting purposes when the transaction is recorded. In some situations, revenue is recognized approximately as it is earned in the economic sense. In other situations, however, accountants have developed guidelines for recognizing revenue by other criteria; such as, at the point of sale.

Required (ignore income taxes):

1. Explain and justify why revenue is often recognized as earned at time of sale.

2. Explain in what situations it would be appropriate to recognize revenue as the productive activity takes place.

3. At what times, other than those included in 1. and 2. above, may it be appropriate to recognize revenue? Explain.

Part b. Income measurement can be divided into different income concepts classified by income recipients. The following income concepts are tailored to the listed categories of income recipients.

	Income concepts	*Income recipients*
1.	Net income to residual equity holders.	Common stockholders.
2.	Net income to investors.	Stockholders and long-term debt holders.
3.	Value-added income.	All employees, stockholders, governments, and some creditors.

Required:

For each of the concepts listed above, explain in separately numbered paragraphs what major categories of revenue, expense, and other items would be included in the determination of income.

Problem 3 Accounting Entity (572,T5)

(25 to 30 minutes)

The concept of the accounting entity often is considered to be the most fundamental of accounting concepts, one that pervades all of accounting.

Required:

a. 1. What is an accounting entity? Explain.
   2. Explain why the accounting entity concept is so fundamental that it pervades all of accounting.

b. For each of the following indicate whether an accounting concept of entity is applicable; discuss and give illustrations.
   1. A unit created by or under law.
   2. The product-line segment of an enterprise.

3. A combination of legal units and/or product-line segments.
4. All of the activities of an owner or a group of owners.
5. An industry.
6. The economy of the United States.

Problem 4 Fictitious Statements About GAAP (577,T5)

(20 to 30 minutes)

Three independent, unrelated statements follow regarding financial accounting. Each statement contains some unsound reasoning.

Statement I

One function of financial accounting is to measure a company's net earnings for a given period of time. An earnings statement will measure a company's true net earnings if it is prepared in accordance with generally accepted accounting principles. Other financial statements are basically unrelated to the earnings statement. Net earnings would be measured as the difference between revenues and expenses. Revenues are an inflow of cash to the enterprise and should be realized when recognized. This may be accomplished by using the sales basis or the production basis. Expenses should be matched with revenues to measure net earnings. Usually, variable expenses are assigned to the product, and fixed expenses are assigned to the period.

Statement II

One function of financial accounting is to accurately present a company's financial position at a given point in time. This is done with a statement of financial position, which is prepared using historical-cost valuations for all assets and liabilities except inventories. Inventories are stated at first-in, first-out (FIFO), last-in, first-out (LIFO), or average valuations. The statement of financial position must be prepared on a consistent basis with prior years' statements.

In addition to reflecting assets, liabilities, and stockholders' equity, a statement of financial position should, in a separate section, reflect a company's reserves. The section should include three different types of reserves: depreciation reserves, product warranty reserves, and retained earnings reserves. All three of these types of reserves are established by a credit to the reserve account.

Statement III

Financial statement analysis involves using ratios to test past performance of a given company. Past performance is compared to a predetermined standard, and the company is evaluated accordingly. One such ratio is the current ratio, which is computed as current assets divided by current liabilities, or as monetary assets divided by monetary liabilities. A current ratio of 2 to 1 is considered good for companies; but the higher the ratio, the better the company's financial position is assumed to be. The current ratio is dynamic because it helps to measure fund flows.

Required:

Identify the areas that are not in accordance with generally accepted accounting principles or are untrue with respect to the financial statement analysis discussed in each of the statements and explain why the reasoning is incorrect. Complete your identification and explanation of each statement before proceeding to the next statement.

Problem 5 Accrual vs. Cash Basis (1179,T3)

(15 to 20 minutes)

Generally accepted accounting principles require the use of accruals and deferrals in the determination of income.

Required:

a. How does accrual accounting affect the determination of income? Include in your discussion what constitutes an accrual and a deferral, and give appropriate examples of each.

b. Contrast accrual accounting with cash accounting.

Multiple Choice Answers

1. d	9. a	17. b	25. d	32. a
2. d	10. b	18. c	26. a	33. d
3. b	11. b	19. b	27. a	34. b
4. d	12. b	20. a	28. d	35. b
5. c	13. d	21. a	29. a	36. a
6. a	14. b	22. b	30. b	37. b
7. a	15. a	23. d	31. c	38. a
8. d	16. a	24. a		

Multiple Choice Answer Explanations

A.1.–4. Basic Concepts

1. (1183,P1,4) (d) The requirement is to determine the December 31, 1982, balance for magazine subscriptions collected in advance. The solutions approach is to set up a T-account for the liability.

Subscriptions Collected in Advance

Revenue		1,700,000	12/31/81 bal.
earned	1,500,000	2,100,000	Cash receipts
		2,300,000	12/31/82 bal.

As receipts are collected, cash is debited and the liability account is credited because the company owes customers subscriptions valued at that amount. At year end, the liability is debited and a revenue account credited to reflect the revenue earned on magazines delivered.

2. (583,P1,6) (d) The requirement is the total amount of insurance premiums paid by Gerber during 1982. The solutions approach is to set up a prepaid insurance T-account, since all applicable transactions flow through that account.

Prepaid Insurance

12/31/81	150,000		To insurance
Premiums paid	?	625,000	expense
12/31/82	175,000		

The amount of premiums paid and debited to prepaid insurance, therefore, must be $650,000.

3. (1181,P1,7) (b) The requirement is the total amount of losses Kipling should charge to income in 1980. Losses should be recognized in the period when the cause of the loss occurs. The loss on the typewriter stolen in 1980 should be recognized in 1980. The loss on the typewriter vandalized in 1981 should be recognized in 1981. Therefore the 1980 loss is the book value of the stolen typewriter, $500.

4. (583,Q1,9) (d) Rental revenue recorded in 1982 will consist of the current recognition of previously deferred rental revenues (unearned rentals) plus any increase in rentals receivable. The solutions approach is to use journal entries and T-account analysis to derive the correct answer. The problem states that all rents are paid in advance; we will assume all $20,000 was recorded as unearned rentals.

Cash	20,000	
Unearned rentals		20,000

Although part of the $20,000 may have been for collection of rental receivables, any combination of collection of rental receivables or prepayment of rent will result in the correct answer.

Unearned Rentals

Revenue		8,000	1/1/82
recognized	?	20,000	Cash collections
		6,000	12/31/82

The journal entry to balance the T-account is

Unearned rentals	22,000	
Rental revenue		22,000

Since not all tenants made timely payments of their rent, the increase in rentals receivable constitutes accrued rental revenue.

Rentals Receivable

1/1/82	2,400	
Accrual	?	
12/31/82	3,100	

The journal entry to balance the T-account is

Rentals receivable	700	
Rental revenue		700

Therefore, the total rental revenue recorded in 1982 is $22,700 ($22,000 + $700).

5. (1183,T1,1) (c) SFAC 3, para 62 states that comprehensive income consists of not only its basic components (revenues, expenses, gains, and losses) but also various intermediate components or measures that result from combining the basic components. Examples of such components or measures which are, in effect, subtotals of comprehensive income are gross margin, contribution margin, income from continuing operations before taxes, income from continuing operations, and operating income.

6. (1183,T1,2) (a) The requirement is to determine the term that is synonymous with the term "recognized." Per SFAC 3, para 83, recognition is the process of formally recording [answer (a)] or incorporating an item in the financial statements of an entity. The term "realized" [answer (b)] identifies revenues or gains (losses) on assets sold. Realization and recognition are not used as synonyms in SFAC 3, as they some-

times are in accounting and financial literature. Answer (c), matched, refers to the simultaneous recognition of revenues and expenses which are related directly or jointly to the same transactions or events. Answer (d), allocated, refers to the process of how an amount is assigned or distributed according to a plan or formula.

7. (1183,T1,3) (a) When an expenditure lacks direct association with revenue (i.e., a cause and effect relationship) and provides no discernable future benefits so no systematic and rational allocation can be made, then such a cost should be recognized as an expense in the period it is incurred. Electricity used to light offices [answer (a)] fits this description as it cannot be directly related to particular revenues, nor does it provide any discernable future benefits (SFAC 3, para 88). Answers (b), (c), and (d) represent costs that have a direct association with revenue generated by them and require expense recognition at the same time the revenue is recognized.

8. (583,T1,1) (d) Per SFAC 2, para 33, the two primary decision-specific qualities are relevance and reliability. These qualities each have three ingredients. The three ingredients of relevance are feedback value, predictive value, and timeliness. Feedback value is the concept that information can affect a decision by confirming or correcting an earlier expectation (SFAC 2, para 51). The other primary decision-specific quality, reliability, is composed of verifiability, neutrality, and representational faithfulness. Thus answer (d) is correct.

9. (583,T1,2) (a) Comparability interacts with both relevance and reliability. "Comparability is not a quality of information in the same sense as relevance and reliability are, but is rather a quality of the relationship between two or more pieces of information. Improving comparability may destroy or weaken relevance or reliability if, to secure comparability between two measures, one of them has to be obtained by a method yielding less relevant or less reliable information (SFAC 2, para 116)." Timeliness and predictive value [answers (b) and (d)] are ingredients of relevance. Neutrality [answer (c)] is an ingredient of reliability.

10. (583,T1,3) (b) SFAC 3 defines 10 interrelated elements of financial statements that are directly related to measuring the performance and status of an enterprise. Included among the elements (per para 52) are distributions to owners because these transactions decrease ownership interests in an enterprise. Per para 5, notes to financial statements are not considered elements. Although notes are an integral part of financial statements, they serve different functions, including amplifying or complementing information about items contained in the financial statements.

11. (583,T1,4) (b) SFAC 3, para 83 states that realization in the most precise sense involves the process of converting noncash resources and rights into money. Realization is used most precisely in accounting and financial reporting to refer to sales of assets for cash or claims of cash. The term "unrealized" [answer (b)] identifies gains or losses on unsold assets. Answers (a) and (c) are incorrect because per para 83, recognition involves the process of formally recording or incorporating an item in the financial statements of an entity. Answer (d) is a nonsensical answer.

12. (583,T1,5) (b) When an expenditure lacks direct association with revenue (i.e., a cause and effect relationship) but benefits more than one accounting period, the expenditure is to be allocated to the periods benefited in a systematic and rational manner. If, however, no future benefit results from the expenditure, it should be expensed immediately. Answer (b) is correct because the advance payment of insurance premiums benefits future periods. However a cause and effect relationship, as a basis for expensing the premiums, would be virtually impossible to establish. These premiums would be amortized to expense using the straight-line method. Answers (a), (c), and (d) represent expenditures which do not have future benefit and therefore should be expensed immediately.

13. (583,T1,19) (d) When the premium on a three-year insurance policy is paid in total at the beginning of the first year, a prepaid asset results. At the end of each of the next three years, one third of the premium should be amortized to expense using the following journal entry:

Insurance expense	XXX	
Prepaid insurance (asset)		XXX

The effect of this amortization is to increase expenses for the year and decrease prepaid assets [answer (d)].

14. (582,T1,15) (b) SFAC 2, para 52 states that interim earnings reports provide both feedback on past performance and a basis for prediction of annual earnings before year end. Feedback value and predictive value are both components of relevance.

15. (582,T1,16) (a) SFAC 2, para 95 states that conservatism is a prudent reaction to uncertainty, an attempt to ensure that uncertainties and risks inherent in business situations are adequately considered. Com-

pleteness [answer (b)] is the inclusion of all material items. Neutrality [answer (c)] refers to absence of bias. Representational faithfulness [answer (d)] is correspondence or agreement between a measure or description and the phenomenon that it purports to represent (also called validity).

16. (1181,T1,2) (a) Para 19, SFAC 1, states that information provided by financial reporting pertains to individual business enterprises rather than to industries or an economy as a whole or to members of society as consumers.

17. (1181,T1,4) (b) APB Statement 4, para 160, states that the principle of immediate recognition requires that items carried as assets in prior periods that are discovered to have no discernible future benefit be charged to expense (e.g., a patent that is determined to be worthless). Associating cause and effect [answer (a)] and systematic and rational allocation [answer (c)] are the other two pervasive expense recognition principles discussed in APB Statement 4. Objectivity [answer (d)] is an underlying accounting principle but is not a logical answer for this question.

18. (581,T1,2) (c) The requirement is the concept that establishes the validity of presenting a promise to receive cash in the future at its present value on the financial statements. The going concern principle implies that a firm will remain in existence long enough to collect the receivable, justifying its recording. Answer (a) is incorrect because the entity concept means that the activity of a business enterprise can be kept separate and distinct from its owners. Answer (b), materiality, applies to information which is significant enough to affect evaluations of investment decisions. Neutrality, (answer d), is defined as freedom from bias.

19. (581,T1,3) (b) The requirement is for an example of the "associating cause and effect expense recognition principle". Cause and effect presumes that some costs are recognized as expenses on the basis of a presumed direct association with specific revenue (APB Statement 9, para 21); sales commissions (answer b) fits this category. Answers (a) and (c) are incorrect because these costs are expensed using the "systematic" and "rational" allocation expense principle. Answer (d) is an example of the "immediate recognition" expense principle.

20. (581,T1,4) (a) The requirement is the accounting concept which supports the accrual of net losses on a firm's purchase commitments. Conservatism refers to a preference on the part of accountants for understating rather than overstating when doubt exists (e.g., the salability of inventory). Accruing these losses is preferable to waiting until the firm purchase commitments are consummated. Realization (answer b) specifies when revenue should be recognized. Consistency (answer c) refers to achieving comparability overtime by using the same accounting methods, etc. Materiality (answer d) refers to information which is significant enough to affect investor evaluations of investment alteratives.

21. (1180,T1,1) (a) The requirement is the effect, on net income, of writing off a specific customer's account receivable under both the allowance and direct write-off methods. The solutions approach is to prepare journal entries for both methods.

Allowance:		
Allowance for doubtful accounts	XXX	
Accounts receivable		XXX
Direct write-off:		
Bad debt expense	XXX	
Accounts receivable		XXX

In the Allowance method, the journal entry does not include any income statement accounts, so there is no effect on net income. In the Direct Write-Off method, the journal entry includes a debit to an expense account, indicating decreased net income.

22. (1180,T1,3) (b) An accrued liability results from recording an expense which has been incurred but not paid. Wages payable is an example of an expense incurred but not paid. The other choices are liabilities, but not accrued liabilities. Cash dividends payable and the current portion of long-term debt do not result from expenses. Rent revenue collected in advance is an example of an unearned revenue.

23. (1180,T1,6) (d) The concept of consistency is sacrificed in accounting for the cumulative effect of a change in accounting principle. The principle of consistency requires that similar events be accounted for in a similar fashion from year to year. Discontinued operations (a), losses on disposal (b), and extraordinary items (c), while they may not occur every year, are accounted for consistently when they do occur. However, by definition, a change in accounting principle indicates that a different principle or method has been used for the same type of transactions.

24. (1180,T1,12) (a) When bad debt expense is estimated based on a percentage of credit sales, the matching principle is being followed. The entity is attempting to estimate what part of this year's sales will

not be collected, thereby matching this year's expense with this year's sales. It is important to note that either choice (a) or (b) must be correct. One states that matching is followed, the other that matching is not followed. Obviously either matching is or is not followed; there is no other alternative.

25. (580,T1,26) (d) Objectivity and verifiability both refer to the adequacy of evidence concerning the validity of accounting data. Summarization refers to the compilation of numerical data, classification to the categorization of financial data, and conservatism to the avoidance of overstating assets and income.

26. (1179,T1,5) (a) The requirement is the condition permitting revenue recognition prior to the sale of merchandise. Per para 1 of Chapter 1A of ARB 43, profit is to be considered realized when a sale in the ordinary course of business is effected. Statement 9 (para 16) of Chapter 4 of ARB 43 indicates that inventory valuation above cost can only be jusitifed by the following: an inability to determine approximate costs, immediate marketability at a quoted price, and the characteristic of unit interchangeability. Thus, a condition permitting recognition of revenue prior to sale would be an assured sales price. Answer (b) is incorrect because, with the installment sales method, revenue recognition is deferred until cash is collected (as a result of the questionability of collection of the sales price). Answer (c) is incorrect because the concept of internal consistency of amounts of revenue is a nonsense term. Answer (d) is incorrect because a long established management policy of noncompliance with GAAP does not justify noncompliance.

27. (578,T1,7) (a) The going concern concept or postulate means that an enterprise is going to continue in the future in the absence of information to the contrary. Thus accruals and deferrals may be used to allocate the effects of multi-period transactions to the period in which they belong. For example, revenues and expenses may be deferred to future periods if revenue or expense is to be recognized in the future. Conversely, revenue or expense can be recognized in the current period even though the cash flow will occur in future periods (para 117 of Statement 4). The principle of materiality [answer (b)] simply means that only material items need be of concern in financial reporting decisions. Answer (c) is incorrect because consistency is an objective of financial accounting which enhances comparability across time by requiring the use of the same accounting procedures, methods, etc., period after period. Answer (d), stable monetary unit, refers to the implicit assumption in financial statements that the purchasing power of the monetary unit (dollar) is stable enough not to warrant the use of price-level adjusted statements.

28. (1176,T1,8) (d) Residual interest is the interest in the economic resources of an enterprise remaining after economic obligations, i.e., A – L = SE (para 59 APB Statement 4). The fund theory is based on the equation, assets equals liabilities or sources of assets. The emphasis is on the assets, the credit side of the balance sheet just indicates the sources of the assets. The enterprise theory of ownership, like the entity theory, is concerned with the ownership of the assets or the credit side of the balance sheet in contrast to the fund theory. The enterprise theory considers the corporation to be a social enterprise for the benefit of many parties including creditors, employees, customers, etc. The entity theory emphasizes the business as a separate legal entity apart from the personal affairs and interests of the owners.

A.5. Asset Valuation

29. (1180,T1,7) (a) When computing the current value of an asset using the present value method, the future amounts of cash receipts or cash savings (d) over the productive life of the asset (b) are discounted at the applicable interest rate (c). The cost of alternate uses of funds given up (a) is not considered in the computation.

30. (580,T1,28) (b) Current selling price is used as a measurement base, for example, in the case of precious metals having a fixed selling price with no substantial cost of marketing (ARB 43, Chapter 4, para 16). Discounted cash flow is used as a measurement base for assets capitalized under long-term leases (SFAS 13, para 10). Replacement cost is used as a measurement base for inventories when the replacement cost has fallen below historical cost (ARB 43, Chapter 4, para 9).

A.6. Installment Sales

31. (1181,Q2,40) (c) The requirement is the gain to be recognized on the 1980 income statement. APB 10, para 12, states that the installment method of recognizing revenue is not acceptable unless the circumstances are such that the collection of the sales price is not reasonably assured. Since the property was sold to a Triple-A rated company and the value of the property is appreciating, collection can be as-

sumed to be reasonably assured. Therefore, the entire gain should be recognized for financial statement purposes at the date of sale.

Sales price	–	Cost of building	=	Gain recognized
$1,200,000		$1,000,000		$200,000

A.10. Franchise Agreements

32. (583,P1,16) (a) The requirement is the amount to be recorded as unearned franchise fees at 12/31/82. Per SFAS 45, para 5 franchise fee revenue shall be recognized when all material services have been substantially performed by the franchisor; i.e., the franchisor has no remaining obligation to refund any cash received and substantially all of the **initial services** of the franchisor have been performed. Of the initial fee of $50,000, apparently the $20,000 applies to the **initial services** already performed by Tower. Additionally, this amount is not refundable. Therefore, the $20,000 may be recognized as revenue in 1982. The three remaining $10,000 installment payments relate to substantial future services to be performed by the franchisor (Tower). The present value of these payments, $23,220, is recorded as unearned fees and would be recognized as revenue once substantial performance has occurred.

Cash	20,000	
Notes receivable	30,000	
Discounts on N/R		6,780
Unearned franchise fees		23,220
Franchise revenue		20,000

May 1984 Answers

33. (584,P2,21) (d) The requirement is the amount to be reported as unearned service contract revenue at 12/31/83. The solutions approach is to set up a T-account for the liability.

Unearned Service Contract Revenue

		600,000	1/1/83
Revenue earned	860,000	980,000	Cash receipts
		720,000	12/31/83

Cash receipts are credited to the liability account because Greene Co. owes its customers services worth that amount. As the services are performed, the liability is reduced and the revenue is recognized. Note that the service contract expense ($520,000) does not affect the liability account.

34. (584,P2,28) (b) The requirement is the amount of deferred gross profit at 12/31/83 using the installment method. The total gross profit on the sale is $315,000 (selling price of $1,050,000 less depreciated cost of $735,000), and the gross profit rate is 30% ($315,000 ÷ $1,050,000). Gross profit recognized in 1982 is $45,000 (30% x $150,000 down payment), and gross profit recognized in 1983 is $90,000 (30% x $300,000 installment). This leaves a balance of $180,000 in the deferred gross profit account.

Deferred Gross Profit

Recognized—1982	45,000	315,000	Total gross profit
Recognized—1983	90,000		
		180,000	12/31/83

Gross profit is recognized only on the portion of the sales price collected, not on the interest collected ($90,000). A short-cut approach is to take the remaining balance in installment notes receivable and multiply by the gross profit rate ($600,000 x 30% = $180,000).

35. (584,P2,32) (b) The requirement is the amount of royalty income to be recognized in 1983. Cash collected for royalties totalled $200,000 in 1983. However, this amount must be adjusted for changes in the related accounts, as follows:

$200,000
(90,000)
85,000
60,000
(40,000)
$215,000

The beginning receivable balance ($90,000) is subtracted because that portion of the cash collected was recognized as revenue last year. The ending receivable balance ($85,000) is added because that amount is 1983 revenue, even though it has not yet been collected. The beginning balance of unearned royalties ($60,000) is added because that amount is assumed to be earned during the year. Finally, the ending balance of unearned royalties ($40,000) is subtracted since this amount was collected, but not earned as revenue, by 12/31/83.

36. (584,P3,54) (a) The requirement is the amount of 1983 revenue from franchise fees. Per SFAS 45, initial franchise fees are recognized as revenue when substantially all the initial services required of the franchisor have been performed. Continuing franchise fees are reported as revenue as the fees are earned and become receivable. In this case, since all the initial services were performed by 7/1/83, the ini-

tial fee ($50,000) is recognized as revenue in 1983. Also, continuing fees of $20,000 (5% x $400,000) should be recognized. Therefore, the total franchise fee revenue to be recognized in 1983 is $70,000 ($50,000 + $20,000).

37. (584,T1,1) (b) Per SFAC 2, para 56 timeliness is an ingredient of the primary quality of relevance. Answer (a), reliability, is the other primary quality of information which is useful for decision making. Answers (c) and (d) are ingredients of reliability.

38. (584,T1,2) (a) SFAC 3, para 56 states that comprehensive income includes all changes in equity during a period **except** those resulting from investments by owners and distributions to owners; therefore, answer (a) is correct.

BASIC CONCEPTS

Unofficial Answer*

Problem 1 SFAC 2

a. FASB's conceptual framework study should provide benefits to the accounting community such as

- guiding the FASB in establishing accounting standards on a consistent basis.
- determining bounds for judgment in preparing financial statements by prescribing the nature, functions, and limits of financial accounting and reporting.
- increasing users' understanding of and confidence in financial reporting.

b. Statement of Financial Accounting Standards No. 2 identifies the most important quality for accounting information as usefulness for decision-making. Relevance and reliability are the primary qualities leading to this decision usefulness. Usefulness is the most important quality because, without usefulness, there would be no benefits from information to set against its costs.

c. A number of key characteristics or qualities that make accounting information desirable are described in the Statement of Financial Accounting Concepts No. 2. The importance of three of these characteristics or qualities are discussed below.

- Understandability—information provided by financial reporting should be comprehensible to those who have a reasonable understanding of business and economic activities and are willing to study the information with reasonable diligence. Financial information is a tool and, like most tools, cannot be of much direct help to those who are unable or unwilling to use it or who misuse it.
- Relevance—the accounting information is capable of making a difference in a decision by helping users to form predictions about the outcomes of past, present, and future events or to confirm or correct expectations.
- Reliability—the reliability of a measure rests on the faithfulness with which it represents what it purports to represent, coupled with an assurance for the user, which comes through verification, that it has representational quality.

**The format of the Unofficial Answer precludes the need for an Answer Outline.*

Answer Outline

Problem 2 Revenue Recognition

1. Part a requires justification for revenue recognition at the point of sale, situations where revenue is recognized as it is produced, and other revenue recognition points. Part b. requires delineation of revenue, expense, and other income determination items for three concepts of income: net income to common stockholders, net income to investors, and net income to all participants in the business enterprise.

2. You should organize your solution in the outline format of the requirements. Each of the three requirements under both a and b should contain two short paragraphs of discussion.

3. Revenue is recognized at the point of sale out of convention and also is the "best" of the alternative recognition points. If output is sold as it is produced, e.g., service industries, newspapers, etc., revenue is recognized as production takes place. Alternatives to point of sale are cash collection, e.g., the installment method of accounting for receivables, and production, e.g, mining of valuable minerals or meat packing.

4. Net income to common stockholders is the residual after payment of all other production costs, e.g., labor, interest, raw materials, etc. Net income to investors would be the residual income plus interest paid on long-term debt. The value added concept of income is the value of the output less the value of all inputs.

Unofficial Answer

Problem 2 Revenue Recognition

a. 1. Most merchandising concerns deal in finished products and would recognize revenue at the point of sale. This is often identified as the moment when title legally passes from seller to purchaser. At the point of sale there is an arm's-length transaction to objectively measure the amount of revenue to be recognized. With accounting theory based heavily on objective measurement, it is logical that point-of-sale transaction revenue recc_ tion would be used by many firms, especially merchandising concerns.

Other advantages of point-of-sale timing for revenue recognition include the following:

- It is a discernible event (as contrasted to the accretion concept).
- The seller has completed his part of the bargain—that is, the revenue has been earned with the passage of title when the goods are delivered.
- Realization has occurred in the sense that cash or near-cash assets have been received—there is some merit in holding that it is not earned revenue until cash or near-cash assets have been received.
- The seller's costs have been incurred with the result that net income can be measured.

2. For service-type firms, accounting recognition of revenue approximates the earning process. The recognition of revenue for accounting purposes takes place (is recorded) during the period the services are rendered. Although it is theoretically possible to continuously accrue revenue as the services are rendered, for practical reasons revenue is usually accrued periodically with emphasis on the appropriate period of recognition. Theoretically, the revenue is properly recognized in the accounting period in which the revenue-generating activity takes place.

   In some nonservice firms, revenue can be recognized as the productive activity takes place instead of at a later period (as at point of sale). The most common situation where revenue is recognized as production takes place has been through the application of percentage-of-completion accounting to long-term construction contracts. Under this procedure revenue is approximated, based on degree of contract performance to date, and recorded as earned in the period in which the productive activity takes place.

   A similar situation is present where, applying the accretion concept, the recognition of revenue takes place when increased values arise from natural growth or an aging process. In an economic sense, increases in the value of inventory give rise to revenue.

   Revenue recognition by the accretion concept is not the result of recorded transactions, but is accomplished by the process of making comparative inventory valuations. Examples of applying the accretion concept would include the aging of certain liquors and wines, growing timber, and raising livestock.

3. Revenue is sometimes recognized at completion of the production activity, or after the point of sale. The recognition of revenue at completion of production is justified only if certain conditions are present. The necessary conditions are that there must be a relatively stable market for the product, marketing costs must be nominal, and the units must be homogeneous. The three necessary conditions are not often present except in the case of certain precious metals and agricultural products. In these situations it has been considered appropriate to recognize revenue at the completion of production.

   In rare situations it may be necessary to postpone the recognition of revenue until after the point of sale. The circumstances would have to be unusual to postpone revenue recognition beyond the point of sale because of the theoretical desirability to recognize revenue as early in the earning process as possible. A situation where it would be justified to postpone revenue recognition until a time after the point of sale would be where there is substantial doubt as to the ultimate collectibility of the receivable.

b. 1. Net income to the residual equity holders would be determined by including all revenues, expenses, gains, and losses in the computation of net income. The net income would include all extraordinary gains and losses, and gains and losses from discontinued operations of a segment of a business, but would exclude any prior period adjustments. The net income determined in accordance with these limitations (as discussed in Accounting Principles Board Opinion, Numbers 9 and 30) must be reduced by any current period claim the preferred equity holders have on net income.

   The resulting amount is the amount of net income available to the residual equity holders. Accordingly, the amount of income accruing to the residual equity holders would be the reported net income of the corporation reduced by the amount of prior claim of any preferential class(es) of stock.

2. The net income to investors would be the amount of net income normally reported on the income statement plus the interest (net of income tax effect) on long-term debt. Thus, net income to investors includes all revenues, expenses, gains, losses, extraordinary items, and gains and losses from discontinued operations of a segment of a business, but excludes financing charges for long-term debt.

3. The value-added concept of income is the broadest of the operational-approach concepts to income determination. The value-added concept is a special net-income concept closely akin to the gross-national-product (GNP) determination.

   The value added is the value of the output of the firm less the value of supplies, goods, fuels, electrical energy, and similar items (often called transfers in GNP determination) acquired from other firms and individuals. Thus, all employees, governments, and owners, and many creditors are recipients of the income when following this concept.

   The value-added concept requires the recognition of income during production because all values are expressed in terms of the product selling price.

Answer Outline

Problem 3 Accounting Entity

a1. Accounting entity is a specific firm or enterprise
    Apart from owners
    And other separate legal enterprises
  Can also be a unit controlling resources
    Individual
    Profit-seeking company
    Not-for-profit enterprise
  Alternatively in terms of an economic interest group
    E.g., owners
    Approach used for financial reports

a2. Accounting entity defines boundaries of accounting information system
    Determines data to be included in system
    E.g., transaction between entity and third parties
  All other accounting concepts are in reference to the entity
    It is the most basic premise of the accounting model

b1. Legal units are the most common accounting entities
    Corporations, partnerships, and proprietorships

b2. Product lines are also entities

b3. A group of legal entities may be an accounting entity
    E.g., consolidated statements
    Combination of product-line segments

b4. Accounting entities can be in terms of owners
    E.g., personal financial statements
    Estate reporting

b5. Accounting entity could embrace an industry
    E.g., industry financial data

b6. USA economy is entity for GNP data

Unofficial Answer

Problem 3 Accounting Entity

a. 1. The conventional or traditional approach has been to define the accounting entity in terms of a specific firm or enterprise unit that is separate and apart from the owner or owners and from other enterprises having separate legal and accounting frames of reference. For example, partnerships and sole proprietorships were accounted for separately from the owners although such a distinction might not exist legally. Thus it was recognized that the transactions of the enterprise should be accounted for and reported upon separately from those of the owners.

   An extension of this approach is to define the accounting entity in terms of an economic unit that controls resources, makes and carries out commitments and conducts economic activity. In the broadest sense an accounting entity could embrace any object, event, or attribute of an object or event for which there is an input-output relationship. Such an accounting entity may be an individual, a profit-seeking or not-for-profit enterprise, or any subdivision or attribute thereof for which a system of accounts is maintained. Thus this approach is oriented toward the unit for which financial reports are prepared.

   An alternative approach is to define the accounting entity in terms of an area of economic interest to a particular individual, group, or institution. The boundaries of such an economic entity would be identified by determining (1) the interested individual, group, or institution and (2) the nature of that individual's, group's, or institution's interest. Thus this approach is oriented to the users of financial reports.

2. The accounting entity concept defines the area of interest and thus narrows the range and establishes the boundaries of the possible objects, activities, or attributes of objects or activities that may be selected for inclusion in accounting records and reports. Further, postulates as to the nature of the entity also may aid in determining (1) what information to include in reports of the entity and (2) how to best present information of the entity so that relevant features are disclosed and irrelevant features do not cloud the presentation.

   The applicability of all the other generally accepted concepts (or principles or postulates) of accounting (e.g., continuity, money measurement, and time periods) depends upon the established boundaries and the nature of the accounting entity. The other accounting concepts lack significance without reference to an entity. The entity must be defined before the balance of the accounting model can be applied and the accounting can begin. Thus the accounting entity concept is so fundamental that it pervades all of accounting.

b. 1. Yes, units created by or under law would include corporations, partnerships, and occasionally sole proprietorships. Thus, legal units probably are the most common types of accounting entities.

2. Yes, a product line or other segment of an enterprise, such as a division, department, profit center, branch, or cost center, could be an accounting entity. The stimuli for financial reporting by segment include investors, the Securities and Exchange Commission, financial executives, and the accounting profession.

3. Yes, most large corporations issue consolidated financial reports for two or more legal entities that constitute a controlled economic entity. Accounting for investments in subsidiary companies by the equity method also is an example of an accounting unit that extends beyond the legal entity. The financial reports for a business enterprise that includes two or more product-line segments would also be a form of a consolidated report that most commonly would be considered to be the report of a single legal entity.

4. Yes, although the accounting entity often is defined in terms of a business enterprise that is separate and distinct from other activities of the owner or owners, it also is possible for an accounting entity to embrace all of the activities of an owner or a group of owners. Examples include financial statements for an individual (personal financial statements) and the financial report of a person's estate.

5. Yes, the accounting entity could embrace an industry. Examples include financial data compiled for an industry by a trade association (industry averages) or by the federal government. Probably the best examples of an industry being the accounting entity are in the accounting systems prescribed by the Federal Power Commission and the Federal Communications Commission which define the original cost of an asset in terms of the cost to the person first devoting it to public service.

6. Yes, the accounting entity concept can embrace the economy of the United States. An example is the national income accounts compiled by the U.S. Department of Commerce. Another area where the entity concept is applicable is in the yet to be developed area of socio-economic accounting.

Answer Outline

Problem 4 Fictitious Statements About GAAP

Statement I
- "True" earnings not determinable due to estimates
- GAAP is to fairly present
- All statements related to income statement
- Revenues are more than cash inflow
- Revenues recognized when realized
- Sales revenues recognized when realized
  - Production revenues recognized when earned
- Production basis justifiable if reasonably estimable and realization is reasonably assured
- Some expenses cannot be matched with revenues
- Period vs. product (manufacturing) expenses

Statement II
- "Fairly" rather than "accurately"
- Various valuation methods are in balance sheet
- Inventories are at lower of cost or market
- Consistency is important
- A separate "reserve" section is unacceptable
- Reserve not proper terminology, instead
  - Accumulated depreciation
  - Warranty liability
  - Retained earnings appropriations

Statement III
- Statement analysis involves future estimates
- Involves application of analytic tools for decision making
- Current ratio is not monetary assets ÷ monetary liabilities
- Current ratio must be in context of type of company
- High ratio does not automatically mean better
  - E.g., high ratio may indicate idle assets
- Current ratio is not dynamic, i.e., measured at a point in time

Unofficial Answer

Problem 4 Fictitious Statements About GAAP

Statement I

The function of financial accounting is to provide quantitative financial information intended to help make economic decisions about a business enterprise. Measurement of net earnings is certainly one aspect of the above generalization. Nonetheless, it is not possible to measure true net earnings because of the flexibility permitted by generally accepted accounting principles and because of the estimates and judgment factors inherent in the financial accounting process. The intent behind generally accepted accounting principles is to fairly present net earnings. Other financial statements, the statement of financial position and the statement of changes in financial position, are definitely related to the earnings statement of a company. Although each financial statement discloses a different aspect of the company, all of these financial statements are based on the same underlying data. These financial statements, therefore, inherently articulate with each other.

Revenues are gross increases in assets or gross decreases in liabilities resulting from an enterprise's earnings-directed activities that can change owners' equity. In other words, revenues are more than just an inflow of cash; not all cash inflows are revenues, for example, borrowing money or issuing capital stock. It is incorrect to state that revenues are realized when they are recognized. These concepts should be distinguished. Revenues are theoretically earned throughout the entire production and distribution process, although the recognition or recording is generally based on more practical considerations. Revenues are realized when evidenced by other new liquid assets. Revenue recognition refers to recording revenues in the accounts.

The general procedure followed in the sales basis of revenue recognition clearly recognizes revenues when they are realized. The production basis of revenue recognition is a variation from the sales basis because the former tends to recognize revenues when they are earned, as opposed to realized. The production basis, for example, percentage-of-completion contracts, is justifiable if total profit can be reasonably estimated and ultimate realization is reasonably assured.

To the extent possible, expenses should be matched with revenues; nevertheless, such cause and effect association is not always possible. Some expenses are recognized by systematic and rational allocation to periods. Other expenses are recognized because their incurrence provides no discernible future benefits.

Product expenses (manufacturing expenses), whether variable or fixed, should be assigned to the product. Period expenses, whether variable or fixed, are generally those that are far removed from production, for example, marketing, general, and administrative expenses, and are, therefore, assigned to the period.

Statement II

Measurement of financial position is one aspect of the function of financial accounting; nonetheless, financial accounting strives for fair presentation rather than "accurate" presentation. The term "accurate" is invalid because of the flexibility permitted by generally accepted accounting principles and because of the estimates and judgment factors inherent in the accounting process.

A statement of financial position is actually a mixture of various valuations for assets and liabilities. For example, monetary assets, such as cash and accounts receivable, are generally reflected at net realizable value; fixed assets are generally reflected at historical cost; long-term liabilities are generally reflected at present value at inception; and leases are also generally reflected at present value. Deferred taxes are reflected at a nondiscounted amount.

Inventories should be reflected at lower-of-cost-or-market valuation. FIFO, LIFO, and average cost are not methods of inventory valuation. They are assumptions regarding the flow of units or costs and are all based on historical costs. Consistency is a vital part of the financial accounting process; but consistency does not preclude an accounting change if such a change is warranted. Therefore, there will be circumstances in which the need for consistency will be superseded by other needs such as preferred methods of accounting or economic reality.

A statement of financial position should not have a separate section for reserves. The three types of reserves cited (depreciation, product warranty, and retained earnings) should be classified among the assets, liabilities, and stockholders' equity sections as explained below. The use of the term "reserve" in these cases is not proper. The generally accepted meaning of reserve indicates that an amount of retained earnings has been appropriated for a specific purpose.

A depreciation reserve should be called "allowance for depreciation" or "accumulated depreciation." It is established by charging an expense and should be classified as a contra-asset account.

A reserve for product warranty is established by charging an expense and should be classified as a liability. It should be considered current or noncurrent depending on the amounts estimated to be liquidated each future period.

A retained earnings reserve is established by charging retained earnings. It does not affect net earnings. It is merely an appropriation of retained earnings and should be so reflected on a statement of financial position as part of stockholders' equity.

Statement III

Financial statement analysis is the judgmental process which aims to evaluate the current and past financial positions and results of operations of a company with the primary objective of determining the best possible estimates and predictions about future conditions and performance. The process of financial statement analysis consists of applying analytical tools and techniques to financial statements in order to derive from them measurements and relationships that are significant and useful for decision making. This definition stresses two aspects. First, financial statement analysis is intended to aid decision making which is usually future oriented. The past is used as a guide to the future. Second, while ratios are an important tool for the analyst, they are not the only such tool. Other tools and techniques of financial statement analysis include comparative financial statements showing year-to-year amount changes, index number trend series showing year-to-year percentage changes, and common-size financial statements showing percentage relationships within a given statement. Other tools also include cash forecasts, analysis of changes in financial position, analysis of variation in gross margin, and analysis of cost-volume-earnings (profit) relationships.

The use of financial ratios involves more than merely comparing the results to a predetermined standard. Other sources of comparison are industry averages and trends within the company.

The current ratio cannot be computed as monetary assets divided by monetary liabilities because "monetary" is not synonymous with "current." A monetary asset or liability is an account that will be received or paid in a predetermined fixed amount of dollars regardless of the effect of inflation or deflation. Examples of monetary assets and liabilities include cash, accounts receivable (current and noncurrent) in stated amounts of cash, and accounts payable and other debt (current and noncurrent) in stated amounts of cash. A nonmonetary asset or liability is an account that is not stated in a fixed amount of dollars, and can be adjusted subsequent to its creation to reflect the effects of inflation or deflation. An example of a nonmonetary asset is inventory. In the event that prices increase, the sales price of that inventory can be adjusted accordingly. The elements of the current ratio, therefore, contain both monetary and nonmonetary components and cannot be defined as monetary assets divided by monetary liabilities. A current ratio of 2:1 is considered good for many companies, but such an evaluation is a function of the type of company and industry. Therefore, a blanket standard is misleading. It is better to view standard performance in terms of ranges rather than single amounts. In other words, a predetermined standard range may be from 1.8:1 to 2.2:1. A company's ratio that falls outside this range, either below or above, should be carefully analyzed. In other words, a higher ratio is not necessarily advantageous. For example, too high a current ratio may indicate excessive idle funds which should be put to better use.

The current ratio is not dynamic and does not measure fund flows. It is a static concept which compares certain elements at a point in time. It measures the ability of present current assets to cover existing liabilities. It is probably more a test of liquidation than of a going concern because current assets and current liabilities are, in reality, revolving, that is, being continuously replaced with new current assets and new current liabilities. This replacement is better evaluated by future activity, such as sales, earnings, or working-capital flow, than by a static measure.

Answer Outline

Problem 5 Accrual vs. Cash Basis

a. Accrual accounting recognizes asset and liability effects of transactions in periods to which they relate
  - To match revenues and expenses
  - I.e., revenue and expense are not only recognized when received or paid
  - Revenues are recognized and recorded when earned
  - Expenses are recognized and recorded as follows:
    - Associating cause and effect
      - Direct association of expense with specific revenue
    - Systematic and rational allocation
      - Allocation among periods benefited
    - Immediate recognition
      - No future benefit from costs incurred this period
      - No future benefit from costs incurred in prior period
      - Allocation serves no useful purposes

Accrual
  - Transaction affecting income but is not reflected in cash
    - Accrued revenue is revenue earned, but not collected
      - E.g., interest revenue earned but not collected
    - Accrued expense is expense incurred but not paid
      - E.g., salaries incurred but not paid by year-end

Deferral
  - Transaction reflected in cash, but not in income
    - Deferred revenue is revenue collected, but not yet earned
      - E.g., rent collected in advance for future periods
    - Deferred expense is expense paid, but not yet incurred
      - E.g., insurance premiums paid for future periods

b. Cash basis accounting reflects effects on assets and liabilities only when cash is paid or collected

Accrual accounting reflects these effects in periods to which they relate

Thus, cash basis does not properly match revenue and expense and is not per GAAP

Unofficial Answer

Problem 5 Accrual vs. Cash Basis

a. Accrual accounting recognizes and reports the effects of transactions and other events on the assets and liabilities of a business enterprise in the time periods to which they relate rather than only when cash is received or paid. Accrual accounting attempts to match revenues and the expenses associated with those revenues in order to determine net income for an accounting period. Revenues are recognized and recorded as earned. Expenses are recognized and recorded as follows:

- Associating Cause and Effect. Some expenses are recognized and recorded on a presumed direct association with specific revenue.
- Systematic and Rational Allocation. In the absence of a direct association with specific revenue, some expenses are recognized and recorded by attempting to allocate expenses in a systematic and rational manner among the periods in which benefits are provided.
- Immediate Recognition. Some costs are associated with the current accounting period as expenses because (1) costs incurred during the period provide no discernible future benefits, (2) costs recorded as assets in prior periods no long provide discernible benefits, or (3) allocating costs either on the basis of association with revenues or among several accounting periods is considered to serve no useful purpose.

An accrual represents a transaction that affects the determination of income for the period but has not yet been reflected in the cash accounts of that period. Accrued revenue is revenue earned but not yet collected in cash. An example of accrued revenue is accrued interest revenue earned on bonds from the last interest payment date to the end of the accounting period. An accrued expense is an expense incurred but not yet paid in cash. An example of an accrued expense is salaries incurred for the last week of the accounting period that are not payable until the subsequent accounting period.

A deferral represents a transaction that has been reflected in the cash accounts of the period but has not yet affected the determination of income for that period. Deferred (prepaid) revenue is revenue collected or collectible in cash but not yet earned. An example of deferred (prepaid) revenue is rent collected in advance by a lessor in the last month of the accounting period, which represents the rent for the first month of the subsequent accounting period. A deferred (prepaid) expense is an expense paid or payable in cash but not yet incurred. An example of a deferred (prepaid) expense is an insurance premium paid in advance in the current accounting period, which represents insurance coverage for the subsequent accounting period.

b. In cash accounting, the effects of transactions and other events on the assets and liabilities of a business enterprise are recognized and reported only when cash is received or paid; while in accrual accounting, these effects are recognized and reported in the time periods to which they relate. Because cash accounting does not attempt to match revenues and the expenses associated with those revenues, cash accounting is not in conformity with generally accepted accounting principles.

ERROR CORRECTION

Multiple Choice Questions (1 – 7)

Items 1, 2, and 3 are based on the following information:

Declaration, Inc., is a calendar-year corporation. Its financial statements for the years 1974 and 1973 contained errors as follows:

	1974	*1973*
Ending inventory	$1,000 understated	$3,000 overstated
Depreciation expense	$ 800 understated	$2,500 overstated

1. Assume that the proper correcting entries were made at December 31, 1973. By how much will 1974 income before income taxes be overstated or understated?
   a. $ 200 understated.
   b. $ 500 overstated.
   c. $2,700 understated.
   d. $3,200 understated.

2. Assume that no correcting entries were made at December 31, 1973. Ignoring income taxes, by how much will retained earnings at December 31, 1974, be overstated or understated?
   a. $200 understated.
   b. $500 overstated.
   c. $2,700 understated.
   d. $3,200 understated.

3. Assume that no correcting entries were made at December 31, 1973, or December 31, 1974, and that no additional errors occurred in 1975. Ignoring income taxes, by how much will working capital at December 31, 1975, be overstated or understated?
   a. $0.
   b. $1,000 overstated.
   c. $1,000 understated.
   d. $1,700 understated.

4. During the course of your examination of the financial statements of H Co., a new client, for the year ended December 31, 1972, you discover the following:

- Inventory at January 1, 1972, had been overstated by $3,000.
- Inventory at December 31, 1972, was understated by $5,000.
- An insurance policy covering three years had been purchased on January 2, 1971, for $1,500. The entire amount was charged as an expense in 1971.

During 1972 the company received a $1,000 cash advance from a customer for merchandise to be manufactured and shipped during 1973. The $1,000 had been credited to sales revenue. The company's gross profit on sales is 50%.

Net income reported on the 1972 income statement (before reflecting any adjustments for the above items) is $20,000.

The proper net income for 1972 is
   a. $26,500
   b. $23,500
   c. $16,500
   d. $20,500

5. During 1983, Olsen Company discovered that the ending inventories reported on its financial statements were understated as follows:

Year	*Understatement*
1980	$50,000
1981	$60,000
1982	$0

Olsen ascertains year-end quantities on a periodic inventory system. These quantities are converted to dollar amounts using the FIFO cost flow method. Assuming no other accounting errors, Olsen's retained earnings at December 31, 1982, will be
   a. Correct.
   b. $ 60,000 understated.
   c. $ 60,000 overstated.
   d. $110,000 understated.

Items 6 and 7 are based on the following information:

The Shannon Corporation began operations on January 1, 1978. Financial statements for the years ended December 31, 1978, and 1979, contained the following errors:

	December 31,	
	1978	*1979*
Ending inventory	$16,000 understated	$15,000 overstated
Depreciation expense	$ 6,000 understated	–
Insurance expense	$10,000 overstated	$10,000 understated
Prepaid insurance	$10,000 understated	–

In addition, on December 31, 1979, fully depreciated machinery was sold for $10,800 cash, but the sale was not recorded until 1980. There were no other errors during 1978 or 1979 and no corrections have been made for any of the errors.

6. Ignoring income taxes, what is the total effect of the errors on 1979 net income?

a. Net income overstated by $30,200.
b. Net income overstated by $11,000.
c. Net income overstated by $5,800.
d. Net income understated by $1,800.

7. Ignoring income taxes, what is the total effect of the errors on the amount of working capital at December 31, 1979?

a. Working capital overstated by $4,200.
b. Working capital understated by $5,800.
c. Working capital understated by $6,000.
d. Working capital understated by $9,800.

ERROR CORRECTION

Problem

Problem 1 Worksheet to Prepare Corrected Financial Statements (583,P5)

(40 to 50 minutes)

Bryant Corporation was incorporated on December 1, 1981, and began operations one week later. Bryant is a nonpublic enterprise. Before closing the books for the fiscal year ended November 30, 1982, Bryant's controller prepared the following financial statements:

Bryant Corporation
Balance Sheet
November 30, 1982

Assets:	
Current assets	
Cash	$ 150,000
Marketable securities, at cost	60,000
Accounts receivable	450,000
Less allowance for doubtful accounts	(59,000)
Inventories	430,000
Prepaid insurance	15,000
Total current assets	1,046,000
Property, plant & equipment	426,000
Less accumulated depreciation	(40,000)
Research & development costs	120,000
Total assets	$1,552,000
Liabilities & Stockholders' Equity:	
Current liabilities	
Accounts payable & accrued expenses	$ 592,000
Income taxes payable	224,000
Total current liabilities	816,000
Stockholders' equity	
Common stock, $10 par value	400,000
Retained earnings	336,000
Total stockholders' equity	736,000
Total liabilities & stockholders' equity	$1,552,000

Bryant Corporation
Statement of Income
For the Year Ended November 30, 1982

Net sales	$2,950,000
Operating expenses	
Cost of sales	1,670,000
Selling & administrative	650,000
Depreciation	40,000
Research & development	30,000
	2,390,000
Income before income taxes	560,000
Provision for income taxes	224,000
Net income	$ 336,000

Bryant is in the process of negotiating a loan for expansion purposes and the bank has requested audited financial statements. During the course of the audit, the following additional information was obtained:

1. The investment portfolio consists of short-term investments in marketable equity securities with a total market valuation of $55,000 as of November 30, 1982.
2. Based on an aging of the accounts receivable as of November 30, 1982, it was estimated that $36,000 of the receivables will be uncollectible.
3. Inventories at November 30, 1982, did not include work-in-process inventory costing $12,000 sent to an outside processor on November 29, 1982.
4. A $3,000 insurance premium paid on November 30, 1982, on a policy expiring one year later was charged to insurance expense.
5. Bryant adopted a pension plan on June 1, 1982, for eligible employees to be administered by a trustee. Based upon actuarial computations, the first 12 months' normal pension plan cost was estimated at $45,000.
6. On June 1, 1982, a production machine purchased for $24,000 was charged to repairs and maintenance. Bryant depreciates machines of this type on the straight-line method over a five-year life, with no salvage value, for financial and tax purposes.
7. Research and development costs of $150,000 were incurred in the development of a patent which Bryant expects to be granted during the fiscal year ending November 30, 1983. Bryant initiated a five-year amortization of the $150,000 total cost during the fiscal year ended November 30, 1982.
8. During December 1982 a competitor company filed suit against Bryant for patent infringement claiming $200,000 in damages. Bryant's legal counsel believes that an unfavorable outcome is probable. A reasonable estimate of the court's award to the plaintiff is $50,000.
9. The 40% effective tax rate was determined to be appropriate for calculating the provision for income taxes for the fiscal year ended November 30, 1982. Ignore computation of deferred portion of income taxes.

Required:

Complete the tear-out worksheet to prepare a corrected balance sheet of Bryant Corporation as of November 30, 1982, and a corrected statement of income for the year ended November 30, 1982. Formal statements and journal entries are not required. Supporting computations should be in good form. Include the completed tear-out worksheet in the proper sequence and turn in with other answer sheets.

Bryant Corporation
Worksheet for Balance Sheet
and Income Statement
November 30, 1982

Balance Sheet	*Unadjusted balance*	*Adjustments Debit*	*Adjustments Credit*	*Adjusted balance*
Assets:				
Cash	$ 150,000			
Marketable securities, at cost	60,000			
Accounts receivable	450,000			
Allowance for doubtful accounts	(59,000)			
Inventories	430,000			
Prepaid insurance	15,000			
Property, plant & equipment	426,000			
Accumulated depreciation	(40,000)			
Research & development costs	120,000			
	$1,552,000			
Liabilities & stockholders' equity:				
Accounts payable & accrued expenses	$ (592,000)			
Income taxes payable	(224,000)			
Common stock	(400,000)			
Retained earnings	(336,000)			
	$(1,552,000)			
Statement of Income				
Net sales	$(2,950,000)			
Cost of sales	1,670,000			
Selling & administrative expenses	650,000			
Depreciation expense	40,000			
Research & development expense	30,000			
Provision for income taxes	224,000			
Net income	$ (336,000)			

Multiple Choice Answers

1. a	3. a	5. a	6. a	7. a
2. c	4. a			

Multiple Choice Answer Explanations

B. Error Correction

1. (576,P1,3) (a) If the accounts are correct at the beginning of 1974, the only errors are an understatement of ending inventory of $1,000 which results in an overstatement of cost of goods sold, and an understatement of depreciation expense. The $1,000 overstatement of cost of goods sold is offset by the $800 understatement of depreciation expense, resulting in an understatement of income of $200.

2. (576,P1,4) (c) The requirement is the effect of the 1973 and 1974 errors on 1974 ending retained earnings. It is useful to note that the inventory errors are counterbalancing, in that the $3,000 overstatement of inventory at the end of 1973 overstates retained earnings at the end of 1973 but understates income in 1974. Thus the $3,000 inventory error is nullified in 1974 ending retained earnings. The depreciation errors, however, are not counterbalancing until the assets have been sold. In this case the $2,500 overstatement in 1973 is offset by the $800 understatement in 1974, to give a net overstatement of depreciation expense of $1,700. This $1,700 coupled with the overstatement of cost of sales during 1974 of $1,000 results in a $2,700 understatement of retained earnings at the end of 1974.

3. (576,P1,5) (a) The requirement is to compute the error in working capital at the end of 1975 assuming no errors occuring in 1975. Since ending inventory at the end of 1975 will be presumably correct, and the depreciation expense, accumulated depreciation, etc. do not affect working capital, there should be no overstatement or understatement of working capital. It is important for you to recognize the need for a time diagram and care in reading dates, as many of you have missed this problem because you did not realize that the requirement was with respect to 1975 rather than 1974.

4. (1173,P1,12) (a) The effect of beginning inventory overstatement is understatement of the current years income, because cost of goods sold is overstated. The effect of understatement of ending inventory will be understatement of current income, because cost of goods sold will be overstated. The three year insurance policy was expensed in 1971, and $500 should have been expensed in 1972. All of the $1,000 should be adjusted out of 1972 income (no costs of sales was expensed this period). The adjustments are summarized below.

Reported income	20,000
B. I. overstatement	+ 3,000
E. I. understatement	+5,000
1972 insurance	– 500
Deferred revenue	–1,000
	$26,500

5. (583,Q1,5) (a) The requirement is to determine the effect on the December 31, 1982 retained earnings balance from the understatement of ending inventories in 1980 and 1981. If ending inventories are understated, cost of goods sold is overstated, and net income is, therefore, understated. The opposite is true if ending inventory is overstated. Since ending inventory of one period is the beginning inventory of the next period, errors in inventory determination affect income of two consecutive periods. Since the effects will be in opposite directions they will offset one another, and therefore the retained earnings balance will be correct (assuming no additional errors) at the end of the second period even though income amounts of both periods will be incorrect. Although net income is affected in each year, as shown below, retained earnings at the end of 1982 is correctly stated due to the offsetting nature of the errors.

	1980	*1981*	*1982*
Beg. inventory		$(50,000)	$(60,000)
+ Purchases			
Goods avail. for sale		(50,000)	(60,000)
–End inventory	$(50,000)	(60,000)	
Cost of goods sold	50,000	10,000	(60,000)
Net income	(50,000)	(10,000)	(60,000)
Retained earnings balance	$(50,000)	$(60,000)	$ –0–

6. (1180,Q1,7) (a) The requirement is the total effect of several errors on 1979 net income. The requirement for the second problem in this set is the total effect of the same errors on the amount of working capital at 12/31/79. The overstatement or understatement of a year-end current asset or liability affects the amount of working capital. The solutions approach is to identify the effect of each error separately:

Error	Effect on 1979 income	Effect on 12/31/79 WC
Beginning inventory understated	$16,000 over	–
Ending inventory overstated	15,000 over	$15,000 over
1978 depreciation understated	–	–
1978 insurance expense overstated	–	–
1979 insurance expense understated	10,000 over	–
Prepaid insurance understated at 12/31/78	–	–
Sale of machinery	10,800 under	10,800 under
Total effect	$30,200 over	$ 4,200 over

The understatement of 1979 beginning inventory means cost of goods sold is also understated; therefore, net income is overstated. The overstatement of ending inventory means less cost assigned to cost of goods sold which also results in an overstatement of income. Only the overstatement of inventory and understatement of cash affected working capital.

7. (1180,Q1,8) (a) See explanation for (1180,Q1,7).

ERROR CORRECTION

Solution Guide

Problem 1 Worksheet to Prepare Corrected Financial Statements

1. In number five a worksheet to prepare a corrected balance sheet and income statement must be completed for the first accounting (fiscal) year of an enterprise's operations. Formal statements and journal entries are not required. The given information includes tentative year-end financial statements, nine items of additional information, and the worksheet to be completed.

2. The solutions approach is to first skim through the problem, then go through the additional data in detail, preparing necessary supporting schedules and filling in the worksheet as you proceed. [Note where possible that debits and credits should be made to the line items (classifications) given in the worksheet.]

2.1 The short-term investment portfolio of marketable equity securities (MES) has an aggregate market value of $55,000 at year end. Since aggregate cost is $60,000, an unrealized loss of $5,000 must be recorded.

Unrealized loss on MES	5,000	
Allowance to reduce MES to market		5,000

2.2 Bryant estimates uncollectible accounts using an aging of accounts receivable to determine the necessary balance in the allowance account. Based on a year-end aging of accounts receivable, an allowance of $36,000 is deemed adequate. Since the allowance account is currently stated at $59,000, the account must be reduced by $23,000 with an accompanying reduction in selling and administrative expenses. The expense reduction is necessary because the expense was overstated in the year in which the allowance balance was overestimated. Per APB 20 para 10 this is a change in estimate that is handled as an adjustment of income in the current year.

Allowance for doubtful accounts	23,000	
Sell. and admin. expenses		23,000

2.3 The ending inventory balance did not include work-in-process inventory held by an outside processor. This $12,000 of inventory should be included in Bryant's inventory balance since Bryant retains ownership while the goods are in the hands of the outside processor. The processor is merely performing a service for Bryant; it is not purchasing the goods. Therefore, the inventory account must be increased and cost of sales (where goods not included in ending inventories are reflected) decreased.

Inventories	12,000	
Cost of sales		12,000

2.4 The $3,000 insurance premium paid on 11/30/82 should not have been expensed in the current year since it pertains, in total, to insurance coverage during the next accounting year. Therefore, this amount must be removed from expenses and capitalized as prepaid insurance.

Prepaid insurance	3,000	
Sell. and admin. expenses		3,000

2.5 Normal cost relating to the pension plan must be accrued. The cost for the first twelve months of the plan is $45,000. The plan was in existence for only six months (June 1 – November 30) during the current accounting year, so 6/12 of $45,000, or $22,500, must be recorded as an expense and liability.

Sell. and admin. expenses	22,500	
Accrued pension expense		22,500

Note that generally a portion of past service cost (PSC) would be amortized; however, PSC is not mentioned in the problem. The most likely reason is that since the corporation was just organized, no provision was necessary for credits for past service.

2.6 The $24,000 cost of the production machine must be removed from cost of sales and capitalized as property, plant, and equipment.

Prop., plant, and equip.	24,000	
Cost of sales		24,000

In addition, depreciation expense must be recorded for the period from June 1 through November 30 ($24,000 x 1/5 x 6/12 = $2,400).

Depreciation expense	2,400	
Accumulated depreciation		2,400

Since this is depreciation of a **production** machine, theoretically the $2,400 should be debited proportionately to inventories and cost of sales. However, note that the unadjusted balances of both depreciation expense and accumulated depreciation are $40,000. This indicates that all depreciation is charged to the depreciation expense accounts.

2.7 Research and development (R & D) costs of $150,000 were incurred while working on a potential patent. Bryant expensed $30,000 and capitalized the remaining $120,000. Per SFAS 2, all R & D costs of this nature must be expensed as incurred. Therefore, the $120,000 deferred by Bryant must be expensed.

R & D expense	120,000	
R & D costs		120,000

2.8 During December of 1982, a competitor company filed a patent infringement suit against Bryant. Per SFAS 5, para 8 a contingent liability must be accrued if information available prior to the issuance of the financial statements indicates that it is **probable** a liability existed at the balance sheet date (11/30/82 in this case), and if the amount of the liability is **reasonably estimable.** The problem states that an unfavorable outcome is probable and a reasonable estimate of the liability is $50,000. Even though the suit was not filed until December, it appears that the infringement must have occurred prior to 11/30/82. Therefore, the liability existed at the balance sheet date and meets both the probable and reasonably estimable criteria, and must, therefore, be accrued.

Estimated loss due to lawsuit	50,000	
Estimated liability due to lawsuit		50,000

2.9 The adjustment to the income tax provision and liability is determined by multiplying the effective tax rate (40%) times the net change in income before taxes ($137,900 decrease) resulting from the previous adjustments. This results in a credit adjustment to income tax expense of $55,160. The $137,900 decrease is computed by netting all the debit and credit adjustments to income from the worksheet.

3. The final step is to total the columns and rows in the completed worksheet. Note that retained earnings must be adjusted by a debit of $82,740, the net amount of all other debit and credit adjustments to the balance sheet.

Unofficial Answer

Problem 1 Worksheet to Prepare Corrected Financial Statements

Bryant Corporation
Worksheet for Balance Sheet
and Statement of Income
November 30, 1982

Balance Sheet	*Unadjusted balance*	*Adjustments* Debit	Credit	*Adjusted balance*
Assets:				
Cash	$ 150,000			$ 150,000
Marketable securities, at cost	60,000			60,000
Allowance for reduction to market			5,000 (1)	(5,000)
Accounts receivable	450,000			450,000
Allowance for doubtful accounts	(59,000)	23,000 (2)		(36,000)
Inventories	430,000	12,000 (3)		442,000
Prepaid insurance	15,000	3,000 (4)		18,000
Property, plant, & equipment	426,000	24,000 (6)		450,000
Accumulated depreciation	(40,000)		2,400 (6)	(42,400)
Research & development costs	120,000		120,000 (7)	–
	$ 1,552,000			$ 1,486,600

Balance Sheet	Unadjusted balance	Adjustments Debit	Adjustments Credit	Adjusted balance
Liabilities & stockholders' equity:				
Accounts payable & accrued expenses	$ (592,000)		22,500 (5)	(614,500)
Estimated liability from lawsuit			50,000 (8)	(50,000)
Income taxes payable	(224,000)	55,160 (9)		(168,840)
Common stock	(400,000)			(400,000)
Retained earnings	(336,000)	82,740 (x)		(253,260)
	$(1,552,000)			$(1,486,600)
Statement of Income				
Net sales	$(2,950,000)			$(2,950,000)
Cost of sales	1,670,000		12,000 (3) 24,000 (6)	1,634,000
Selling & administrative expenses	650,000	22,500 (5)	23,000 (2) 3,000 (4)	646,500
Depreciation expense	40,000	2,400 (6)		42,400
Research & development expense	30,000	120,000 (7)		150,000
Unrealized loss on marketable securities		5,000 (1)		5,000
Estimated loss from lawsuit		50,000 (8)		50,000
Provision for income taxes	224,000		55,160 (9)	168,840
Net income	$ (336,000)	82,740 (x)		$ (253,260)

Bryant Corporation
Adjusting Journal Entries
November 30, 1982
(Not required)

	Debit	Credit
(1)		
Unrealized loss on marketable securities	$ 5,000	
Allowance to reduce marketable securities to market		$ 5,000
To reduce short-term investments to market valuation ($60,000 – $55,000)		
(2)		
Allowance for doubtful accounts	23,000	
Selling and administrative expenses (bad debts)		23,000
To reduce allowance account to balance determined by aging of receivables ($59,000 – $36,000)		
(3)		
Inventories	12,000	
Cost of sales		12,000
To adjust for work-in-process inventory held by outside processor		
(4)		
Prepaid insurance	3,000	
Selling and administrative expenses (insurance)		3,000
To adjust for nonrecognition of prepaid expense		
(5)		
Selling and administrative expenses (pension)	22,500	
Accounts payable and accrued expenses		22,500
To accrue normal pension cost (45,000 x 6/12)		
(6)		
Property, plant, and equipment	24,000	
Depreciation	2,400	
Cost of sales (repairs and maintenance)		24,000
Accumulated depreciation		2,400
To adjust for charge to repairs and maintenance of machine purchased on 6/1/82, and to record depreciation to 11/30/82 (24,000 x 20% x 6/12)		

	Debit	Credit
(7)		
Research and development expense	120,000	
Research and development costs		120,000
To write off research and development costs in accordance with GAAP		
(8)		
Estimated loss from lawsuit	50,000	
Estimated liability from lawsuit		50,000
To record probable damages payable re: Lawsuit for patent infringement		
(9)		
Income taxes payable	55,160	
Provision for income taxes		55,160
To adjust provision for year ended 11/30/82 (Schedule 1)		

Schedule 1

Adjustment to Income Tax Provision
Year Ended November 30, 1982

Unadjusted income before income taxes		$560,000
Add adjustments increasing income		
Reduction in allowance for doubtful accounts	$ 23,000	
Work-in-process inventory at outside processor	12,000	
Recognition of prepaid insurance	3,000	
Reversal of 6/1/82 charge to repairs & maintenance	24,000	62,000
		622,000
Deduct adjustments decreasing income		
Unrealized loss on marketable securities	$ 5,000	
Pension expense	22,500	
Depreciation on machine purchased 6/1/82	2,400	
Research & development expense	120,000	
Estimated loss from lawsuit	50,000	199,900
Adjusted income before income taxes		422,100
Effective income tax rate		x 40%
Adjusted provision for income taxes		168,840
Provision for income taxes per books		$224,000
Adjusted provision for income taxes		168,840
Adjustment to reduce provision (J.E. #9)		$ 55,160

ACCOUNTING CHANGES

Multiple Choice Questions (1 - 18)

1. On January 1, 1979, Miller Company purchased for $275,000 a machine with an estimated useful life of 10 years and no salvage value. The machine was depreciated using the sum-of-the-years'-digits method. On January 1, 1980, Miller changed to the straight-line method of depreciation. Miller can justify the change. What should be the depreciation expense on this machine for the year ended December 31, 1981?

a. $18,000
b. $22,500
c. $25,000
d. $27,500

2. On January 1, 1980, Belmont Company changed its inventory cost flow method to the FIFO cost method from the LIFO cost method. Belmont can justify the change, which was made for both financial statement and income tax reporting purposes. Belmont's inventories aggregated $4,000,000 on the LIFO basis at December 31, 1979. Supplementary records maintained by Belmont showed that the inventories would have totaled $4,800,000 at December 31, 1979, on the FIFO basis. Ignoring income taxes, the adjustment for the effect of changing to the FIFO method from the LIFO method should be reported by Belmont in the 1980

a. Income statement as an $800,000 debit.
b. Retained earnings statement as an $800,000 debit adjustment to the beginning balance.
c. Income statement as an $800,000 credit.
d. Retained earnings statement as an $800,000 credit adjustment to the beginning balance.

3. From inception of operations, Essex Corporation recognized income in its financial statements and for income tax reporting under the completed-contract method of reporting income from long-term construction contracts. On January 1, 1979, Essex changed to the percentage-of-completion method of income recognition for financial statement reporting but not for income tax reporting. Essex can justify the change.

As of December 31, 1978, Essex compiled data showing that income under the completed-contract method aggregated $350,000. If the percentage-of-completion method had been used, the accumulated income for these contracts through December 31, 1978, would have been $440,000. Assume that the income tax rate for all years is 50%. The cumulative effect of changing from the completed-contract method to the percentage-of-completion method must be reported by Essex in the 1979

a. Retained earnings statement as a $45,000 credit adjustment to the beginning balance.
b. Income statement as a $45,000 credit.
c. Retained earnings statement as a $90,000 credit adjustment to the beginning balance.
d. Income statement as a $90,000 credit.

4. A company has included in its consolidated financial statements this year a subsidiary acquired several years ago that was appropriately excluded from consolidation last year. This results in

a. An accounting change that should be reported prospectively.
b. An accounting change that should be reported by restating the financial statements of all prior periods presented.
c. A correction of an error.
d. Neither an accounting change nor a correction of an error.

5. When a cumulative effect type change in accounting principle is made during the year, the cumulative effect on retained earnings is determined

a. During the year using the weighted-average method.
b. As of the date of the change.
c. As of the beginning of the year in which the change is made.
d. As of the end of the year in which the change is made.

6. Pro forma effects of retroactive application would usually be reported on the face of the income statement for a

a. Correction of error.
b. Change in entity.
c. Change in accounting estimate.
d. Change in accounting principle.

7. When a company makes a change in accounting principle, prior year financial statements are not generally restated to reflect the change. The Accounting Principles Board decided that this procedure would prevent a dilution of public confidence in financial statements but recognized that this procedure conflicts with the accounting concept of

a. Materiality.
b. Conservatism.
c. Objectivity.
d. Comparability.

8. Which of the following describes a change in reporting entity?

a. A company acquires a subsidiary that is to be accounted for as a purchase.
b. A manufacturing company expands its market from regional to nationwide.
c. A company acquires additional shares of an investee and changes from the equity method of accounting to consolidation of the subsidiary.
d. A business combination is made using the pooling of interests method.

9. Effective January 1, 1981, Younger Company adopted the accounting principle of expensing as incurred advertising and promotion costs. Previously, advertising and promotion costs applicable to future periods were recorded in prepaid expenses. Younger can justify the change, which was made for both financial statement and income tax reporting purposes. Younger's prepaid advertising and promotion costs totaled $500,000 at December 31, 1980. Assume that the income tax rate is 40% for 1980 and 1981. The adjustment for the effect of this change in accounting principle should result in a net charge against income in the 1981 income statement of

a. $0
b. $200,000
c. $300,000
d. $500,000

10. Evergreen Company purchased a patent on January 1, 1977, for $178,500. The patent was being amortized over its remaining legal life of 15 years expiring on January 1, 1992. During 1980 Evergreen determined that the economic benefits of the patent would not last longer than ten years from the date of acquisition. What amount should be charged to patent amortization expense for the year ended December 31, 1980?

a. $10,500
b. $17,850
c. $20,400
d. $35,700

Items 11 and 12 are based on the following information:

Bond Company purchased a machine on January 1, 1975, for $3,000,000. At the date of acquisition, the machine had an estimated useful life of six years with no salvage. The machine is being depreciated on a straight-line basis. On January 1, 1978, Bond determined, as a result of additional information, that the machine had an estimated useful life of eight years from the date of acquisition with no salvage. An accounting change was made in 1978 to reflect this additional information.

11. Assuming that the direct effects of this change are limited to the effect on depreciation and the related tax provision, and that the income tax rate was 50% in 1975, 1976, 1977 and 1978, what should be reported in Bond's income statement for the year ended December 31, 1978, as the cumulative effect on prior years of changing the estimated useful life of the machine?

a. $0
b. $187,500
c. $250,000
d. $375,000

12. What is the amount of depreciation expense on this machine that should be charged in Bond's income statement for the year ended December 31, 1978?

a. $100,000
b. $300,000
c. $375,000
d. $500,000

13. A change in the salvage value of an asset depreciated on a straight-line basis and arising because additional information has been obtained is

a. An accounting change that should be reported in the period of change and future periods if the change affects both.
b. An accounting change that should be reported by restating the financial statements of all prior periods presented.
c. A correction of an error.
d. Not an accounting change.

14. On January 1, 1975, an intangible asset with a thirty-five year estimated useful life was acquired. On January 1, 1980, a review was made of the estimated useful life, and it was determined that the intangible asset had an estimated useful life of forty-five more years. As a result of the review

a. The original cost at January 1, 1975, should be amortized over a fifty-year life.
b. The original cost at January 1, 1975, should be amortized over the remaining thirty-year life.
c. The unamortized cost at January 1, 1980, should be amortized over a forty-year life.
d. The unamortized cost at January 1, 1980, should be amortized over a thirty-five year life.

15. How should a change in accounting estimate that is recognized by a change in accounting principle be reported?

	Change in accounting estimate	*Change in accounting principle*
a.	No	No
b.	Yes	Yes
c.	No	Yes
d.	Yes	No

May 1984 Questions

16. During 1983 White Company determined that machinery previously depreciated over a seven-year life had a total estimated useful life of only five years. An accounting change was made in 1983 to reflect the change in estimate. If the change had been made in 1982, accumulated depreciation would have been $1,600,000 at December 31, 1982, instead of $1,200,000. As a result of this change, the 1983 depreciation expense was $100,000 greater. The income tax rate was 40% in both years. What should be reported in White's income statement for the year ended December 31, 1983, as the cumulative effect on prior years of changing the estimated useful life of the machinery?

a. $0
b. $240,000
c. $300,000
d. $400,000

17. On December 31, 1983, Foster, Inc., appropriately changed to the FIFO cost method from the weighted-average cost method for financial statement and income tax purposes. The change will result in a $150,000 increase in the beginning inventory at January 1, 1983. Assuming a 40% income tax rate, the cumulative effect of this accounting change for the year ended December 31, 1983, is

a. $0
b. $ 60,000
c. $ 90,000
d. $150,000

18. The cumulative effect of an accounting change, on the amount of retained earnings at the beginning of the period in which the change is made, should generally be included in net income for the period of the change for a

	Change in accounting principle	*Change in accounting entity*
a.	Yes	Yes
b.	Yes	No
c.	No	Yes
d.	No	No

ACCOUNTING CHANGES

Problem

Problem 1 Types of Accounting Changes (1181,T2)

(15 to 25 minutes)

It is important in accounting theory to be able to distinguish the types of accounting changes.

Required:

a. If a public company desires to change from the sum-of-the-years-digits depreciation method to the straight-line method for its fixed assets, what type of accounting change would this be? Discuss the permissibility of this change.

b. When pro forma disclosure is required for an accounting change, how are these pro forma amounts determined?

c. If a public company obtained additional information about the service lives of some of its fixed assets which showed that the service lives previously used should be shortened, what type of accounting change would this be? Include in your discussion how the change should be reported in the income statement of the year of the change, and what disclosures should be made in the financial statements or notes.

d. Changing specific subsidiaries comprising the group of companies for which consolidated financial statments are presented is an example of what type of accounting change, and what effect does it have on the consolidated income statements?

Multiple Choice Answers

1. d	5. c	9. c	13. a	16. a
2. d	6. d	10. c	14. d	17. c
3. a	7. d	11. a	15. d	18. b
4. b	8. d	12. b		

Multiple Choice Answer Explanations

C. Accounting Changes

1. (582,P1,1) (d) The requirement is the depreciation expense for 1981, after an accounting change has been made in 1980. Per APB 20, the cumulative effect on beginning retained earnings in the year of change (1980) is included in that year's income statement, as a special item (net of tax) after extraordinary items. The new accounting principle is used in the year of change and thereafter. In this problem, the new principle is straight-line depreciation, and it would be used in 1980 and later years. 1981 depreciation expense is $275,000 cost less $-0- salvage value, divided by 10-year useful life, or $27,500.

2. (581,P1,13) (d) The requirement is to determine whether the cumulative effect of changing from LIFO to FIFO is a debit or credit as well as to indicate the appropriate location of the cumulative effect in Belmont's 1980 financial statements. The solutions approach is to prepare the journal entry to restate the inventory from $4,000,000 up to $4,800,000. Since the inventory account must be debited, the cumulative effect is a credit.

Inventory	$800,000	
?		$800,000

Generally, the cumulative effect of any accounting change should be shown in the income statement between extraordinary items and net income. However, one of the exceptions to this general rule per APB 20 is a change from LIFO to any other inventory valuation method. These exceptions require an adjustment to beginning retained earnings and retroactive restatement of prior years' financial statements.

3. (580,P1,1) (a) The requirement is to compute the cumulative effect of a change in accounting principle from the completed-contract method to the percentage-of-completion method as well as to indicate the appropriate location of the cumulative effect in Essex's 1979 financial statements. Per para 27 of APB 20, a change in method of accounting for long-term contracts is one of three changes requiring retroactive restatement of all prior periods presented. The cumulative effect at the beginning of each period to be added or subraacted from the opening balance of retained earnings is the difference between the $440,000 of income which would have resulted from using the percentage-of-completion method had Essex used this method since its inception and the $350,000 of income since inception under the completed-contract method. The cumulative effect of $90,000 must be reduced by the income tax effect at the 50% tax rate resulting in a net cumulative effect of $45,000. Answers (b) and (d) are incorrect because this type of accounting change is one of the special changes requiring restatement of all prior periods presented. Answer (c) is incorrect because it does not reflect the related tax effect.

4. (1183,T1,32) (b) The requirement is the determination of the consequences of including a subsidiary in the current year's statements when it was appropriately excluded in last year's. Per APB 20, para 12, when (1) consolidated or combined statements are presented in place of individual statements; (2) there is a change in the group of subsidiaries for which consolidated statements are prepared [answer (b)]; (3) there is a change in companies included in combined statements; or (4) there is a business combination accounted for as a pooling of interests, then a change in the reporting entity has occurred. Such changes should be reported by restating the financial statements of all prior periods presented in order to show financial information for the new reporting entity for all periods (APB 20, para 34). Answer (a) is incorrect because retroactive restatement is required. Answer (c) is incorrect since errors consist of correcting mathematical mistakes, mistakes in applying principles, oversights or misuse of avoidable facts, and changes from unacceptable to acceptable GAAP. Answer (d) is incorrect since a change in reporting entity is an accounting change.

5. (583,T1,36) (c) When a cumulative effect type change in accounting principle is made during the year, the cumulative effect on retained earnings is determined as of the beginning of the year in which the change is made (APB 20, para 19b). It is determined at the beginning of the year because the new principle is used throughout the current year. Answer (a) is nonsensical and answers (b) and (d) are incorrect because the effect of the change is determined at the **beginning** of the year.

6. (583,T1,40) (d) Per APB 20, para 19d, the pro forma effects of a cumulative effect type change in accounting principle should be shown on

the face of the income statements for all periods presented. A correction of an error [answer (a)] is a prior period adjustment (SFAS 16, para 11), the effects of which may be disclosed in the notes to the financial statements. Answer (b) is incorrect because the financial statements of prior periods are **restated** when a change in entity occurs (APB 20, para 34). A change in accounting estimate [answer (c)] is accounted for currently, and prospectively (APB 20, para 31), the effects of which may also be disclosed in the notes to the financial statements.

7. (1178,T1,5) (d) When changes in accounting principle are made, statements of prior years are restated only in four special cases (changing from LIFO, changing method of accounting for long-term contracts, changing to or from full cost method in extractive industries, and changes made by a company for its first issuance of statements). All other changes are given "cumulative effect" treatment. The rationale for generally not restating prior financial statements is to prevent a weakening of investor confidence in previously determined accounting numbers. Therefore, "cumulative effect" treatment is used even though prior year statements will not be comparable with current year statements, which use the new principle. Materiality [answer (a)] is a constraint which states that information need not be disclosed if it is not significant enough to influence users (see SFAC 2). Conservatism [answer (b)] is a modifying convention which calls for understatement rather than overstatement of income and assets when uncertainty is present (APB Statement 4). Objectivity [answer (c)], referred to as a reliability in SFAC 2, is a qualitative characteristic of accounting information. Objectivity consists of verifiability, representational faithfulness, and neutrality.

8. (578,T1,6) (d) Para 34 of APB 20 indicates the accounting changes which produce a different reporting entity, i.e., a new reporting entity, are changes in an accounting entity which should be presented by restating the financial statements of all prior periods presented. Examples are poolings, presenting consolidated statements in the place of previously issued individual statements of related companies, changing specific subsidiaries comprising a consolidated group, and changing companies which have previously been reported as a combined group. Answers (a) and (c) do not indicate changed conditions due to economic events, i.e., purchase of a subsidiary. Answer (b) is incorrect because the change in reporting is based upon a change in markets.

C.1. Changes in Accounting Estimates

9. (1182,P1,15) (c) The requirement is the net charge against 1981 income as the result of an accounting change. The change from deferring marketing costs to expensing these costs as incurred is a "change in estimate effected by a change in accounting principle." This type of change is treated as a change in estimate for financial reporting purposes (ABP 20, para 32). However, note that regardless of whether this item is treated as a change in estimate or in principle, the **net** charge against 1981 earnings is the same. Income is reduced by the $500,000 write-off and increased by 40% tax benefit ($200,000) which results. Therefore, the net charge against income is $500,000 less $200,000, or $300,000.

10. (1181,P1,19) (c) The requirement is the amount of patent amortization expense to be recorded in 1980 when the estimate of useful life is adjusted from 15 years to 10 years. Per para 31 of APB 20, changes in accounting estimates are reflected prospectively. The solutions approach is to determine the yearly amortization for 1977-79, the book value of the patent at 1/1/80, and finally, the 1980 amortization expense.

Yearly amortization, 1977–79:	
$178,500 ÷ 15 years =	$11,900
Book value at 1/1/80:	
$178,500 – (3 x $11,900)=	$142,800
1980 amortization:	
$142,800/7 years =	$20,400

The remaining useful life of 7 years is the total useful life of 10 years less 3 years already amortized.

	Patent		Amortization for
Balance 1/1/77	$178,500	$11,900	1977
		11,900	1978
		11,900	1979
Book Value 1/1/80	$142,800		

11. (1179,P1,1) (a) The requirement is the cumulative effect of a change in the estimated life of a machine from 6 years to 8 years at the beginning of the fourth year. Para 31 of APB 20 requires that changes in accounting estimates, e.g., useful life of an asset, should be reflected in the period of change and

in future periods. Also, there should be no restatement of amounts recorded in prior statements (para 19). Thus, the cumulative effect on previous periods resulting from a change in the estimated useful life of the asset is zero.

12. (1179,P1,2) (b) The requirement is the amount of depreciation expense for the year in which the remaining useful life is revised from three to five years. Per para 31 of APB 20, changes in accounting estimates are reflected prospectively, i.e., no retroactive adjustment. Accordingly, the solutions approach is to determine the amount of depreciation to date, subtract it from the depreciation base (here, cost because there is no salvage value), and divide by the remaining 5-year useful life. As computed below, the depreciation base beginning in 1978 is $1,500,000. The depreciation taken in 1975-1977 was $1,500,000 ($3,000,000 ÷ 6 years x 3 years). The remaining depreciation base of $1,500,000 ($3,000,000 – $1,500,000) is divided by 5 years, resulting in $300,000 per year depreciation.

$3,000,000	Cost (no salvage)
1,500,000	1975, 1976, 1977 depreciation
$1,500,000	to be depreciated in 1978-1982

$1,500,000 ÷ 5 years = $300,000

13. (1182,T1,28) (a) This situation is covered in APB 20. A change in the salvage value of an asset is a change in accounting estimate (para 32). Para 31 states that a change in accounting estimate should be accounted for in the period of change and future periods if the change affects both. Answer (b) is incorrect because per para 27, only changes from LIFO to another inventory pricing method, changes in accounting for long-term construction contracts, and changes to or from the "full cost" method of accounting in extractive industries should be reported by restating the financial statements of all prior periods presented. A change in accounting estimate is not a correction of an error [answer (c)] because the change arose from new information (para 10). Answer (d) is incorrect because para 32 states that changes in estimates are accounting changes.

14. (582,T1,3) (d) If the estimated useful life of an intangible asset is revised, the unamortized cost should be allocated over the remaining periods of the new useful life. The remaining periods cannot exceed forty years reduced by the number of years of amortization taken previously (APB 17, para 31). In this case, five years have passed since acquisition on 1/1/75. Thus, the maximum period for amortization of the unamortized cost at 1/1/80 is 35 years. Answers (a) and (c) are incorrect because the period of amortization would exceed the 40 year maximum. Answer (b) is incorrect because it does not reflect the revised useful life.

15. (581,T1,29) (d) The requirement is how a change in accounting estimate that is recognized by a change in accounting principle is reported. Per para 31 of APB 20, the effect of a change in accounting estimate should be handled prospectively; that is, no attempt should be made to go back and restate prior years financial statements. Changes in accounting principles are handled by a cumulative effect type adjustment in the income statement. APB 20, para 32 states that a change in accounting estimate that is recognized in whole or in part by a change in accounting principle should be reported as a change in an estimate because the cumulative effect attributable to the change in accounting principle usually cannot be separated from the current or future effects of the change in estimate.

May 1984 Answers

16. (584,P3,43) (a) The requirement is the amount to be reported in the income statement as the cumulative effect on prior years of changing the estimated useful life of machinery. Per APB Opinion 20, changes in estimate are handled prospectively. No cumulative effect on prior years is reported; the effect is spread out over the current and future periods through a revised depreciation rate. Therefore, the cumulative effect is $0.

17. (584,P3,60) (c) The requirement is the cumulative effect of an accounting change from weighted-average to FIFO. The change results in a $150,000 increase in the inventory valuation, which means the **before-tax** effect on income is also $150,000. Since a cumulative effect must be reported net of tax effects, the tax effect of $60,000 (40% x $150,000) must be subtracted to leave a cumulative effect of $90,000 which should be added to income before the cumulative effect of a change in accounting principle.

18. (584,T1,32) (b) The requirement is to determine when an accounting change results in a cumulative effect which is included in net income for the period of the change. APB 20, para 19b states that a change in an accounting principle requires a cumulative effect to be shown on the income statement. Para 34 states that a change in an accounting entity should be reported by restating the financial statements of prior periods; therefore, answer (b) is correct.

ACCOUNTING CHANGES

Answer Outline

Problem 1 Types of Accounting Changes

a. Change from sum-of-the-years-digits depreciation to straight-line is a change in accounting principle
   - Consistency concept presumes accounting principle, once adopted, should not be changed
     - Applies when accounting for similar transactions
     - Change permitted only if enterprise justifies use of alternative acceptable principles on basis of preferability

b. When an accounting change requires pro forma disclosure, pro forma amounts required are
   - Direct effects of the change,
   - Nondiscretionary adjustments in items based on income before taxes or net income and
     - E.g., profit sharing and certain royalties
   - Income tax effects for direct effects and nondiscretionary adjustments

c. Information indicating service lives previously used should be shortened is a change in accounting estimate
   - Account for in year of change and future years
   - Depreciation expense (an operating item) would be increased
   - Disclose effect for current period on
     - Income before extraordinary items,
     - Net income, and
     - Related per share amounts

d. Changing specific subsidiaries comprising group of companies for which consolidated statements are presented is example of change in reporting entity
   - This is a special type of change in accounting principle
   - Restate prior periods' consolidated income statements to reflect different reporting entity

Unofficial Answer

Problem 1 Types of Accounting Changes

a. A change from the sum-of-the-years-digits depreciation method to the straight-line method for fixed assets is a change in accounting principle. The concept of consistency presumes that an accounting principle, once adopted, should not be changed in accounting for events and transactions of a similar type. A change is permissible only if the enterprise justifies the preferability of an alternative acceptable accounting principle.

b. When pro forma disclosure is required for an accounting change, the pro forma amounts will include both the direct effects of the change and the nondiscretionary adjustments in items based on income before taxes or net income, such as profit-sharing expense and certain royalties, that would have been recognized if the newly adopted accounting principle had been followed in prior periods. Related income tax effects should be recognized for both direct effects of the change and nondiscretionary adjustments.

c. If a public company obtained additional information about the service lives of some of its fixed assets showing that the service lives previously used should be shortened, such a change would be a change in accounting estimate. The change in accounting estimate should be accounted for in the year of change and future years since the change affects both. Specifically, the operating item, depreciation expense, would be increased. In addition, the effect on income before extraordinary items, net income, and related per-share amounts of the current period should be disclosed.

d. Changing specific subsidiaries comprising the group of companies for which consolidated financial statements are presented is an example of a change in the reporting entity (a special type of change in accounting principle). Such a change requires that the consolidated income statments be restated to reflect the different reporting entity.

FINANCIAL STATEMENTS

Multiple Choice Questions (1 - 25)

1. On July 1, 1981, an erupting volcano destroyed Coastal Corporation's operating plant, resulting in a loss of $1,500,000, of which only $500,000 was covered by insurance. Coastal's income tax rate is 46%. How should this event be shown in Coastal's income statement for the year ended December 31, 1981?

   a. As an operating loss of $540,000, net of $460,000 income tax.
   b. As an extraordinary loss of $540,000, net of $460,000 income tax.
   c. As an operating loss of $1,000,000.
   d. As an extraordinary loss of $1,000,000.

2. A review of the December 31, 1978, financial statements of Rhur Corporation revealed that under the caption "extraordinary losses," Rhur reported a total of $260,000. Further analysis revealed that the $260,000 in losses was comprised of the following items:

   1. Rhur recorded a loss of $50,000 incurred in the abandonment of equipment formerly used in the business.
   2. In an unusual and infrequent occurrence, a loss of $75,000 was sustained as a result of hurricane damage to a warehouse.
   3. During 1978, several factories were shut down during a major strike by employees. Shutdown expenses totaled $120,000.
   4. Uncollectible accounts receivable of $15,000 were written off as uncollectible.

Ignoring income taxes, what amount of loss should Rhur report as extraordinary on its 1978 Statement of Income?

   a. $50,000
   b. $75,000
   c. $135,000
   d. $260,000

3. Which of the following should be disclosed in the Summary of Significant Accounting Policies?

   a. Composition of plant assets.
   b. Pro forma effect of retroactive application of an accounting change.
   c. Basis of consolidation.
   d. Maturity dates of long-term debt.

4. Which of the following facts concerning plant assets should be disclosed in the Summary of Significant Accounting Policies?

	Composition	Depreciation expense amount
a.	No	Yes
b.	No	No
c.	Yes	No
d.	Yes	Yes

5. A transaction that is material in amount, unusual in nature, but **not** infrequent in occurrence, should be presented separately as a (an)

   a. Component of income from continuing operations, but **not** net of applicable income taxes.
   b. Component of income from continuing operations, net of applicable income taxes.
   c. Extraordinary item, net of applicable income taxes.
   d. Prior period adjustment, but **not** net of applicable income taxes.

6. Which of the following should be disclosed in the Summary of Significant Accounting Policies?

   a. Rent expense amount.
   b. Maturity dates of long-term debt.
   c. Methods of amortizing intangibles.
   d. Composition of plant assets.

7. APB Opinion No. 22, "Disclosure of Accounting Policies,"

   a. Requires description of every accounting policy followed by a reporting entity.
   b. Provides a specific listing of all types of accounting policies which must be disclosed.
   c. Requires disclosure of the format for the statement of changes in financial position.
   d. Requires description of all significant accounting policies to be included as an integral part of the financial statements.

8. Each of the following areas must always have a footnote included in the financial statements commenting on normal transactions within that area except

   a. Assets acquired by lease.
   b. Trade accounts receivable.
   c. Pension plans.
   d. Employee stock options.

9. Which of the following items, if material in amount, would normally be considered an extraordinary item for reporting results of operations?

a. Utilization of a net operating loss carry-forward.
b. Gains or losses on disposal of a segment of a business.
c. Adjustments of accruals on long-term contracts.
d. Gains or losses from a fire.

10. Palo Corporation incurred the following losses, net of applicable taxes, for the year ended December 31, 1982:

• Loss on disposal of a segment of Palo's business	$400,000
• Loss on translation of foreign currency due to major devaluation	500,000

How much should Palo report as extraordinary losses on its 1982 income statement?
a. $0
b. $400,000
c. $500,000
d. $900,000

11. A loss from early extinguishment of debt, if material, should be reported as a component of income
a. After cumulative effect of accounting changes and after discontinued operations of a segment of a business.
b. After cumulative effect of accounting changes and before discontinued operations of a segment of a business.
c. Before cumulative effect of accounting changes and after discontinued operations of a segment of a business.
d. Before cumulative effect of accounting changes and before discontinued operations of a segment of a business.

12. The correction of an error in the financial statements of a prior period should be reflected, net of applicable income taxes, in the current
a. Income statement after income from continuing operations and before extraordinary items.
b. Income statement after income from continuing operations and after extraordinary items.
c. Retained earnings statement as an adjustment of the opening balance.
d. Retained earnings statement after net income but before dividends.

13. An example of an item which should be reported as a prior period adjustment is the
a. Collection of previously written-off accounts receivable.
b. Payment of taxes resulting from examination of prior year income tax returns.
c. Correction of error in financial statements of a prior year.
d. Receipt of insurance proceeds for damage to building sustained in a prior year.

14. On May 1, 1982, the board of directors of Edgewood, Inc., approved a formal plan to sell its electronics division. The division is considered a segment of the business. It is expected that the actual sale will occur in the first three months of 1983. During 1982 the electronics division had a loss from operations of $1,200,000 which was incurred evenly during the year. Edgewood's effective tax rate for 1982 is 40%. For the year ended December 31, 1982, Edgewood should report a loss from operations of discontinued electronics division of
a. $240,000
b. $400,000
c. $480,000
d. $720,000

15. Gulliver Company is disposing of a segment of its business. At the measurement date the net loss from the disposal is estimated to be $475,000. Included in this $475,000 are severance pay of $50,000 and employee relocation costs of $25,000, both of which are directly associated with the decision to dispose of the segment, and estimated net operating losses of the segment from the measurement date to the disposal date of $100,000. Net losses of $75,000 from operations from the beginning of the year to the measurement date are not included in the $475,000 estimated disposal loss. Ignoring income taxes, how much should be reported on Gulliver's income statement as the total loss under the heading "Discontinued operations"?
a. $175,000
b. $425,000
c. $450,000
d. $550,000

16. On April 30, 1980, Empire Corporation, whose fiscal year-end is September 30, adopted a plan to discontinue the operations of Bello Division on November 30, 1980. Bello contributed a major portion of Empire's sales volume. Empire estimated that Bello would sustain a loss of $460,000 from May 1, 1980, through September 30, 1980, and would sustain an additional loss of $220,000 from October 1, 1980, to November 30, 1980. Empire also estimated that it would realize a gain of $600,000 on the sale of Bello's

assets. At September 30, 1980, Empire determined that Bello had actually lost $1,120,000 for the fiscal year, of which $420,000 represented the loss from May 1 to September 30, 1980.

Ignoring income tax effects, how much should Empire report in its September 30, 1980, financial statements as gain or loss on disposal of Bello?

a. $ 40,000 loss.
b. $ 80,000 loss.
c. $180,000 gain.
d. $600,000 gain.

Items 17 and 18 are based on the following information:

The following condensed statement of income of Helen Corporation, a diversified company, is presented for the two years ended December 31, 1979 and 1978:

	1979	*1978*
Net sales	$10,000,000	$9,600,000
Cost of sales	6,200,000	6,000,000
Gross profit	3,800,000	3,600,000
Operating expenses	2,200,000	2,400,000
Operating income	1,600,000	1,200,000
Gain on sale of division	900,000	–
	2,500,000	1,200,000
Provision for income taxes	1,250,000	600,000
Net income	$ 1,250,000	$ 600,000

On January 1, 1979, Helen entered into an agreement to sell for $3,200,000 the assets and product line of one of its separate operating divisions. The sale was consummated on December 31, 1979, and resulted in a gain on disposition of $900,000. This division's contribution to Helen's reported income before income taxes for each year was as follows:

1979 $(640,000) loss
1978 $(500,000) loss

Assume an income tax rate of 50%.

17. In the preparation of a revised comparative statement of income, Helen should report income from continuing operations after income taxes for 1979 and 1978, respectively, amounting to

a. $1,120,000 and $600,000.
b. $1,120,000 and $850,000.
c. $1,250,000 and $600,000.
d. $1,250,000 and $850,000.

18. In the preparation of a revised comparative statement of income, Helen should report under the caption "Discontinued Operations" for 1979 and 1978, respectively

a. Income of $130,000 and a loss of $250,000.
b. Income of $130,000 and $0.
c. Income of $260,000 and a loss of $500,000.
d. A loss of $640,000 and a loss of $500,000.

19. When a segment of a business has been discontinued during the year, the loss on disposal should

a. Be an extraordinary item.
b. Be an operating item.
c. Exclude operating losses of the current period up to the measurement date.
d. Exclude operating losses during the phase-out period.

20. When reporting the loss on disposal of a segment of a business which is to be abandoned, an estimated amount for operating losses during the phase-out period should

a. Be included in the income statement as part of the loss on disposal of the discontinued segment.
b. Be included in the income statement as part of the income (loss) from operations of the discontinued segment.
c. Be included in the income statement as part of the income (loss) from continuing operations.
d. Not be included in the income statement.

May 1984 Questions

21. The following expenses were among those incurred by Sayre Company during 1983:

Accounting and legal fees	$160,000
Interest	60,000
Loss on sale of office equipment	25,000
Rent for office space	200,000

One-quarter of the rented premises is occupied by the sales department. How much of the expenses listed above should be included in Sayre's general and administrative expenses for 1983?

a. $310,000
b. $335,000
c. $360,000
d. $370,000

22. Martin Company had the following account balances for the year ended December 31, 1983:

Interest expense	$120,000
Loss on disposal of noncurrent investment	80,000
Write-down of plant and equipment to estimated realizable value	60,000

In its income statement for 1983, how much should Martin report as total extraordinary items?

a. $0
b. $140,000
c. $180,000
d. $200,000

23. On July 1, 1983, Tyler Corporation approved a formal plan to sell its plastics division, considered a segment of the business. The sale will occur in the first three months of 1984. The division had an operating loss of $400,000 for the six months ended December 31, 1983, and expects to incur a loss of $200,000 for the first quarter of 1984. The sales price is $22,000,000 and the carrying value at the date of sale should be $20,000,000. Tyler's effective tax rate for 1983 is 40%. For the year ended December 31, 1983, how much gain should Tyler report on disposal of the plastics division?

a. $0
b. $ 840,000
c. $1,080,000
d. $1,200,000

24. Which of the following should be reflected, net of applicable income taxes, in the statement of stockholders' equity as an adjustment of the opening balance in retained earnings?

a. Correction of an error in previously issued financial statements.
b. Cumulative effect of a change in depreciation method.
c. Loss on disposal of a segment of a business.
d. Extraordinary item.

25. A material loss should be presented separately as a component of income from continuing operations when it is

a. An extraordinary item.
b. A cumulative effect type change in accounting principle.
c. Infrequent in occurrence but **not** unusual in nature.
d. Infrequent in occurrence and unusual in nature.

FINANCIAL STATEMENTS

Problems

Problem 1 Evaluation of Presentation of Current Assets and Income Statement (1183,T4)

(15 to 25 minutes)

Selected information from the financial statements of the Pace Company follows:

Pace Company
Current Assets Section of
Balance Sheets

	December 31, 1982	December 31, 1981
	(000 omitted)	
Cash	$ 7,000	$ 7,200
Marketable securities, at cost which approximates market	26,000	22,000
Accounts receivable, net of allowance for doubtful accounts	210,000	190,000
Inventories	252,000	308,000
Prepaid expenses	5,000	4,800
Total current assets	$500,000	$532,000

Pace Company
Statements of Income

	Year ended December 31, 1982	Year ended December 31, 1981
	(000 omitted)	
Net sales	$1,200,000	$1,000,000
Costs and expenses:		
Cost of goods sold	960,000	800,000
Selling, general and administrative expenses	147,000	120,000
Other, net	24,000	18,300
Total costs and expenses	1,131,000	938,300
Income from continuing operations before income taxes	69,000	61,700
Income taxes	26,900	25,300
Income from continuing operations	42,100	36,400
Cumulative effect of change in estimates of salvage values of property, plant, and equipment, less applicable income taxes of $1,500,000	–	3,000
Net income	$ 42,100	$ 33,400
Earnings per share of common stock:		
Income from continuing operations	$ 4.21	$ 3.64
Cumulative effect of change in estimates of salvage values of property, plant, and equipment, less applicable income taxes	–	.30
Net income	$ 4.21	$ 3.34

Selected information from the notes to the financial statements of the Pace Company is as follows:

[From Summary of Significant Accounting Policies]

Inventories – Inventories are stated at the lower of cost (first-in, first-out) or market.

Deferred Income Taxes – Deferred income taxes arise from timing differences when profits or expenses are included in taxable income on the income tax return later or earlier than they are included in the statement of income. Such timing differences principally relate to depreciation.

A provision for deferred income taxes of $6,700,000 in 1982 and $6,300,000 in 1981 is included in the statements of income in "other, net."

[From Notes to Financial Statements]

Inventories – Inventories are comprised of the following:

	December 31, 1982	December 31, 1981
	(000 omitted)	
Finished goods	$176,000	$215,000
Goods in process	13,000	14,000
Raw materials	63,000	79,000
	$252,000	$308,000

Inventories at December 31, 1982, were reduced from a cost of $292,000,000 to a market value of $252,000,000 using the direct inventory reduction method. The cost of inventories at December 31, 1981, approximated their market value.

Accounting change – During the third quarter of 1981, Pace Company revised earlier estimates of salvage values for its property, plant, and equipment. This change in accounting reduced the 1981 net income by $3,000,000 ($0.30 per share).

Required:

a. Are inventories and the related cost of goods sold presented appropriately? Explain why or why not. If the presentation is not appropriate, specify the appropriate presentation and explain why.

b. 1. What are the components of the quick (acid-test) ratio?

2. How should the quick (acid-test) ratio be used?

c. Is the provision for deferred income taxes presented appropriately? Explain why or why not. If the presentation is not appropriate, specify the appropriate presentation and explain why.

d. Is the accounting change presented appropriately? Explain why or why not. If the presentation is not appropriate, specify the appropriate presentation and explain why. Assume that the accounting change did not involve deferred income taxes.

Problem 2 Income Statement Preparation (582,Q4)

(45 to 55 minutes)

The following information pertains to Woodbine Circle Corporation:

Adjusted Trial Balance
December 31, 1981

	Dr.	*Cr.*
Cash	$ 500,000	
Accounts receivable, net	1,500,000	
Inventory	2,500,000	
Property, plant, and equipment	15,100,000	
Accumulated depreciation		$ 4,900,000
Accounts payable		1,400,000
Income taxes payable		100,000
Notes payable		1,000,000
Common stock ($1 par value)		1,100,000
Additional paid-in capital		6,100,000
Retained earnings, 1/1/81		3,000,000
Sales – regular		10,000,000
Sales – AL Division		2,000,000
Interest on municipal bonds		100,000
Cost of sales – regular	6,200,000	
Cost of sales – AL Division	900,000	
Administrative expenses – regular	2,000,000	
Administrative expenses – AL Division	300,000	
Interest expense – regular	210,000	
Interest expense – AL Division	140,000	
Loss on disposal of AL Division	250,000	
Gain on repurchase of bonds payable		300,000
Income tax expense	400,000	
	$30,000,000	$30,000,000

Other financial data for the year ended December 31, 1981:

Federal income taxes

Paid on Federal Tax Deposit Forms 503	$ 300,000
Accrued	100,000
Total charged to income tax expense (estimated)	$ 400,000*

*Does not properly reflect current or deferred income tax expense or intraperiod income tax allocation for income statement purposes

Income per tax return	$2,150,000
Tax rate on all types of taxable income	40%

Timing difference

Depreciation, per financial statements	$ 600,000
Depreciation, per tax return	750,000

Permanent difference

Interest on municipal bonds	100,000

Discontinued operations

On September 30, 1981, Woodbine sold its Auto Leasing (AL) Division for $4,000,000. Book value of this business segment was $4,250,000 at that date. For financial statement purposes, this sale was considered as discontinued operations of a segment of a business. Since there was no phase-out period, the measurement date was September 30, 1981.

Liabilities

On June 30, 1981, Woodbine repurchased $1,000,000 carrying value of its long-term bonds for $700,000. All other liabilities mature in 1982.

Capital structure

Common stock, par value $1 per share, traded on the New York Stock Exchange:

Number of shares outstanding at 1/1/81	900,000
Number of shares sold for $8 per share on 6/30/81	200,000
Number of shares outstanding at 12/31/81	1,100,000

Required:

Using the multiple-step format, prepare a formal income statement for Woodbine for the year ended December 31, 1981, together with the appropriate supporting schedules. Recurring and nonrecurring items in the income statement should be properly separated. All income taxes should be appropriately shown.

Problem 3 Evaluation of Income Statement Presentation (1182,T5)

(15 to 25 minutes)

David Company's Statements of Income for the year ended December 31, 1981, and December 31, 1980 are presented below:

David Company
Statement of Income

	Year ended December 31,	
	1981	*1980*
	(000 omitted)	
Net sales	$900,000	$750,000
Costs and expenses:		
Cost of goods sold	720,000	600,000
Selling, general and administrative expenses	112,000	90,000
Other, net	11,000	9,000
Total costs and expenses	843,000	699,000
Income from continuing operations before income taxes	57,000	51,000
Income taxes	23,000	24,000
Income from continuing operations	34,000	27,000
Loss on disposal of Dex Division, including provision of $1,500,000 for operating losses during phase-out period, less applicable income taxes of $8,000,000	8,000	–
Cumulative effect on prior years of change in depreciation method, less applicable income taxes of $1,500,000	–	3,000
Net income	$ 26,000	$ 30,000
Earnings per share of common stock:		
Income before cumulative effect of change in depreciation method	$ 2.60	$ 2.70
Cumulative effect on prior years of change in depreciation method, less applicable income taxes	–	.30
Net income	$ 2.60	$ 3.00

Additional facts are as follows:

- On January 1, 1980, David Company changed its depreciation method for previously recorded plant machinery from the double-declining-balance method to the straight-line method. The effect of applying the straight-line method for the year of and the year after the change is included in David Company's Statements of Income for the year ended December 31, 1981, and December 31, 1980, in "cost of goods sold."
- The loss from operations of the discontinued Dex Division from January 1, 1981, to September 30, 1981, (the portion of the year prior to the measurement date) and from January 1, 1980, to December 31, 1980, is included in David Company's Statements of Income for the year ended December 31, 1981, and December 31, 1980, respectively, in "other, net."
- David Company has a simple capital structure with only common stock outstanding and the net income per share of common stock was based on the weighted average number of common shares outstanding during each year.
- David Company common stock is listed on the New York Stock Exchange and closed at $13 per share on December 31, 1981, and $15 per share on December 31, 1980.

Required:

a. Determine from the additional facts above whether the presentation of those facts in David Company's Statements of Income is appropriate. If the presentation is appropriate, discuss the theoretical rationale for the presentation. If the presentation is not appropriate, specify the appropriate presentation and discuss its theoretical rationale.

Do not discuss disclosure requirements for the Notes to the Financial Statements.

b. Describe the general significance of the price-earnings ratio. Based on David Company's Statements of Income, and the additional facts above, describe how to determine the price-earnings ratio for 1981 only.

Multiple Choice Answers

1. b	6. c	11. c	16. a	21. a
2. b	7. d	12. c	17. b	22. a
3. c	8. b	13. c	18. a	23. a
4. b	9. a	14. a	19. c	24. a
5. a	10. a	15. d	20. a	25. c

Multiple Choice Answer Explanations

D. Financial Statements

1. (1181,Q2,39) (b) The requirement is the presentation of an extraordinary item on the income statement. To qualify as an extraordinary item an event must be both unusual and infrequent. A volcanic eruption would generally meet these criteria (APB 30, para 19-24). In APB 30, para 10-11, the Board states that extraordinary items should be shown net of taxes in a separate section in the income statement.

Loss from volcano	
($1,500,000 – 500,000)	$1,000,000
Less: Tax effect (46% tax rate)	– 460,000
Net loss after tax effect	$ 540,000

2. (579,Q1,13) (b) The requirement is the amount of extraordinary losses which should be reported by Rhur Corporation. Extraordinary losses are those that are both unusual and infrequent per para 20 of APB 30. Only the $75,000 hurricane damage is unusual and infrequent. The $50,000 equipment abandonment loss, the $120,000 strike loss and the $15,000 writeoff of accounts receivable are all prohibited by para 23 of APB 30.

3. (1182,T1,36) (c) APB 22, para 12 states that the Summary of Significant Accounting Policies should encompass those accounting principles and methods that involve a selection from existing acceptable alternatives (or are peculiar to the industry in which the entity operates). Of the answers listed, only basis of consolidation [answer (c)] involves a choice among acceptable methods.

4. (582,T1,37) (b) APB 22, para 12 states that disclosure of accounting policies should identify and describe the accounting principles and the methods of applying them. Information and details presented elsewhere as a part of the financial statements should not be repeated (para 14). Thus, the depreciation expense amount should not be disclosed in the Summary of Significant Accounting Policies. Para 14 specifically states that composition of plant assets should not be presented.

5. (581,T1,21) (a) The requirement is the presentation on the income statement of a transaction that is material in amount, unusual in nature, but not infrequent in occurrence. To be classified as an extraordinary item net of applicable taxes on the income statement, a material item must be both unusual in nature **and** infrequent in occurrence (APB 30, para 20). If an item does not meet the criteria above, it is shown with the normal, recurring revenues, costs, and expenses from continuing operations before taxes. Answer (b) is incorrect because these items are not shown net of tax. Answer (c) is incorrect because the "infrequent occurrence" criterion is not met. Answer (d) is incorrect because the transaction does not represent the correction of an error on a prior years' financial statements.

6. (581,T1,28) (c) The requirement is an example of an item that should be disclosed in the Summary of Significant Accounting Policies. APB 22 recommends that when financial statements are issued, a statement identifying the accounting policies adopted and followed by the reporting entity should be presented as an integral part of the financial statements. The accounting policies are the specific accounting principles and the methods of applying the principles that have been adopted for preparing the financial statements. Answers (a), (b) and (d) are incorrect because these items are not accounting principles and methods for applying the adopted principles; these items would, however, be disclosed in footnotes in other parts of the financial statements.

7. (580,T1,23) (d) Para 8 of APB 22 requires a description of all significant accounting policies to be included as an integral part of the financial statements. It does not require a description of every policy nor does it list which types of policies need to be disclosed.

8. (1178,T1,44) (b) The requirement is a type of transaction that does not require special footnote disclosures. As trade accounts receivable arise in the normal course of business, no special disclosures are necessary. In contrast, assets acquired by lease (SFAS 13, para 16), pension plans (APB 8, para 46), and employee stock option plans are more unusual (ARB 43, Chapter 13B, para 15). These specific type transactions require extended disclosure in financial statements.

9. (578,T1,24) (a) Accounting for extraordinary items is specified in APB 30. Extraordinary items are those which are both unusual and infrequent. Unusual means possessing a high degree of abnormality and being clearly unrelated to the ordinary activities of

an entity. Infrequency indicates no reasonable expectation of reoccurrence in the foreseeable future. Thus, very few items are extraordinary. Answer (c) is incorrect because adjustments of accrual for long-term contracts are usual rather than unusual. Answer (d) is incorrect because gains or losses from a fire are not infrequent because they can be reasonably expected to recur. Answer (b) is incorrect because gains or losses on disposal of a segment are to be accounted for separately in the income statement and specifically not as an extraordinary item per para 8 of APB 30. Answer (a), utilization of an operating loss carry-forward, is specifically deemed to be an extraordinary item per para 45 of APB 11.

D.1. Income and Retained Earnings Statement Format

10. (583,Q1,18) (a) The requirement is to determine how much should be reported as extraordinary losses on Palo's 1982 income statement. Neither of the losses indicated in the problem should be recorded as an extraordinary item, therefore, the correct answer is $0. APB 30, para 8 prescribes reporting for discontinued operations (and extraordinary items). Gains (losses) on the sale of a segment should be shown after income from continuing operations but before extraordinary items or cumulative effects of accounting changes under the heading: "Discontinued Operation." The loss on translation of foreign currency due to a major devaluation does not meet the criteria for an extraordinary item either (SFAS 30, para 23b). The translation loss should be classified as other revenues/gains (expenses/losses) which together with income from operations comprise income from continuing operations.

11. (1183,T1,29) (c) The requirement is to determine where a loss from early extinguishment of debt (extraordinary item) is to be reported on the income statement in relation to a cumulative effect of accounting changes and a provision for gain (loss) on discontinued operations of a segment of a business. APB 30, para 8 requires that a discontinued segment be shown separately as a component of income before extraordinary items. APB 20, para 20 requires that the cumulative effect of changing to a new accounting principle be reported between extraordinary items and net income. Therefore, the correct order on the income statement is as follows:

- Income from continuing operations.
- Discontinued operations.
- Extraordinary items.
- Cumulative effect of accounting changes.
- Net income.

12. (1182,T1,13) (c) APB 20, para 36 requires that correction of an error in the financial statements of a prior period be reported as a prior period adjustment, and APB 9, para 18 states that prior period adjustments should be reflected as adjustments of the opening balance of retained earnings.

13. (581,T1,13) (c) The requirement is an example of an item which should be reported as a prior period adjustment. The correction of an accounting error in prior years financial statements is one of the items that should be reported as a prior period adjustment. Answer (a) is an example of an accounting estimate, which means that at the time of the write-off, the best available information was used for the determination of the uncollectibility. Answer (b) is incorrect only in the context that the examination was performed by the Internal Revenue Service and not by the company. If the latter, payment of additional taxes would have been an error to be accounted for as a prior period adjustment. Answer (d) is incorrect because it assumes that the collection of insurance proceeds was not anticipated in the previous year.

D.2. Discontinued Operations

14. (1183,P1,13) (a) The requirement is to determine the amount of loss from the operations of the discontinued electronics division to be recognized in 1982. Per APB 30, discontinued operations consist of two components: the income (loss) from operating the discontinued segment, and the gain (loss) on disposal of the discontinued segment. The first component (loss from operating the discontinued segment) consists of the income (loss) resulting from operating the discontinued segment before the measurement date. The measurement date is the date upon which management commits itself to a formal plan of disposal. In this case the measurement date is May 1. Since the segment's loss was incurred evenly throughout the year, the operating loss prior to May 1 is 4/12 of $1,200,000 or $400,000. In accordance with APB 30, this loss is reported net of tax [$400,000 – (40% x $400,000) or $240,000].

15. (1182,Q1,19) (d) The requirement is the amount of total loss to appear under the heading "Discontinued operations." APB 30, para 8 states that the results of discontinued operations should be reported separately from continuing operations and that both the "Gain (Loss) from Disposal of a Segment of a Business" and the related "Income (Loss) From Operations of Discontinued Operations" should be reported under the heading "Discontinued operations." APB 30,

para 15 states that the determination of a gain (loss) resulting from the disposal of a business segment should be made at the measurement date based on estimates at that date. The amount of gain (loss) should include an estimate of income (loss) from operations between the measurement date and the disposal date if the disposal plan is to be carried out over a period of time. In this case, the estimated net operating losses from the measurement date to disposal date, $100,000, are already included in the $475,000 estimated disposal loss at the measurement date. Also, inclusion of the $50,000 of severance pay and the $75,000 of employee relocation costs is appropriate because APB 30, paras 16 and 17 state that costs directly associated with the decision to dispose, including items such as severance pay and employee relocation expenses, should be included in determining the gain (loss) on disposal. The amount of net operating loss from the beginning of the year to the measurement date, $75,000, should be disclosed as a separate component under the heading "Discontinued operations." Therefore, the total loss to be reported is $475,000 + $75,000 or $550,000. Note that in this case, since a net loss on disposal results it is not necessary to know if the phase out period (measurement date to disposal date) overlaps accounting periods.

16. (1181,Q2,35) (a) The requirement is the gain (loss) to be reported on the 9/30/80 financial statements resulting from the disposal of a segment. Per APB 30, the determination of whether a gain or loss results from the disposal of a segment should be made at the "measurement" date based on estimates of the net realizable value of the segment after giving consideration to any estimated income or losses from operations during the phase-out period. Any differences between the estimated and actual amounts are treated as changes in estimates. In this case the $600,000 gain expected to be realized on the disposal date would be netted against the operating losses expected during the phase-out period [$420,000 actual (5/1 to 9/30) + $220,000 estimated (10/1 to 11/30)]. Since this results in a combined loss from disposal of $40,000, this loss would be provided for in the fiscal period of the measurement date. Estimated amounts of income or loss from operations of a segment after 9/30/80 ($220,000) are accrued and recorded in the current year because the cause of the loss is the decision to dispose, which was made on 4/30/80. Results of Bello Division's operations before the measurement date (not given) should not be included in the gain or loss on disposal, but in a separate section of the discontinued operations section of the income statement entitled "Income (Loss) from Operations of Discontinued Division."

17. (1180,Q1,2) (b) The requirement is the amount of income from continuing operations after income taxes for 1979 and 1978 to be reported on a revised comparative income statement. Helen discontinued a segment in 1979. APB Opinion 30 requires that "financial statements of **current** and **prior** periods . . . should disclose the results of operations of the disposed segment, less applicable taxes, as a separate component of income . . ." Therefore, the discontinued operations should be reported separately, net of taxes, for both 1979 and 1978. Income from continuing operations must be adjusted so the effect of the discontinued segment is taken out:

	1979	1978
Operating income, as reported	$1,600,000	$1,200,000
Add back loss from discontinued operations	640,000	500,000
Income from continuing operations, before taxes	2,240,000	1,700,000
Less 50% income taxes	(1,120,000)	(850,000)
Income from continuing operations	$1,120,000	$ 850,000

Under the caption "Discontinued Operations", Helen should report:

	1979	1978
Loss from operations	$(640,000)	$(500,000)
Gain on sale	900,000	–
	260,000	(500,000)
50% tax effect	(130,000)	250,000
Discontinued operations	$ 130,000	$(250,000)

18. (1180,Q1,3) (a) See explanation for (1180, Q1,2).

19. (1183,T1,28) (c) Per APB 30, para 16, results of operations before the measurement date should not be included in the gain (loss) on disposal of a discontinued segment. Operating losses of the current period up to the measurement date should, therefore, be excluded [answer (c)]. Answer (d) is incorrect because any operating losses incurred during the phase-out period (the time between the measurement date and the disposal date) are included in the gain (loss) on disposal (APB 30, para 15). Answer (a) is incorrect because gains (losses) on a disposal of a segment of a business are specifically excluded from being reported as extraordinary items (APB 30, para 23). Answer (b) is incorrect since the results of continuing operations should be reported separately from discontinued operations (APB 30, para 8); thus, a loss on disposal cannot be considered an operating item.

20. (582,T1,2) (a) An estimated amount for operating losses during the phase-out period should be included in the income statement as part of the loss on disposal of the discontinued segment (APB 30, para 8). Recall that the phase-out period is the period between the date a formal plan of disposal is adopted (measurement date) and the date of sale or abandonment (disposal date). Answer (b) is incorrect because the income (loss) from operations of the discontinued segment includes only the results of operations up to the measurement date. Answer (c) is incorrect because APB 30 specifically states that the results of discontinued operations should be reported separately from continuing operations.

May 1984 Answers

21. (584,P2,35) (a) The requirement is the amount of expense to be included in general and administrative expenses. The accounting and legal fees ($160,000) and the portion of office rent not allocable to sales (¾ x $200,000 = $150,000) are all considered general and administrative expenses. The total amount is $310,000 ($160,000 + $150,000). The interest expense ($60,000) would be included with financial expense or other expenses. The $25,000 loss on the sale of office equipment should be included in other expenses and losses. The office rent for the sales department (¼ x $200,000 = $50,000) is an operating expense and included in selling expenses rather than general and administrative expenses.

22. (584,P3,41) (a) The requirement is the total amount of extraordinary items in the 1983 income statement. To qualify as extraordinary, an item must be both **unusual in nature** and **infrequent in occurrence.** Interest expense ($120,000) is a normal, recurring expense. A loss on the disposal of a noncurrent investment ($80,000), while possibly occurring infrequently, is not unusual in a business environment. A write-down of plant and equipment ($60,000) is specifically excluded from the extraordinary category by APB 30, unless it is the direct result of a major casualty, an expropriation, or a prohibition under a newly enacted law. None of these exceptions is specified in the problem. Therefore, answer (a) is correct.

23. (584,P3,44) (a) The requirement is the reported gain on the disposal of a discontinued segment for the year ended 12/31/83. The problem can be diagrammed as follows:

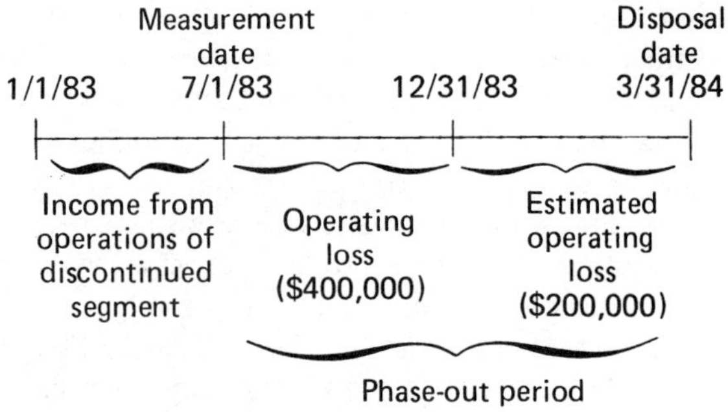

Per APB 30, the gain (loss) on the disposal of a segment is composed of two parts: (1) the income (loss) from operations during the phase-out period and (2) the gain (loss) from the disposal of segment assets. If the phase-out period extends over more than one reporting period, APB 30 requires that the realized loss from operations of the discontinued segment during the phase-out period included in the current reporting period be reduced by any combined gain on disposal (from both operations and the sale of the assets) estimated for the following period. Thus, the $400,000 loss from operations in 1983 would be reduced to $0 by the net gain of $1,800,000 estimated for 1984 ($2,000,000 gain from the sale of assets less $200,000 expected loss from operations). Since APB 30 also requires that any estimated net gain which is not used to offset the loss from operations incurred during the current period ($1,800,000 - $400,000 = $1,400,000 gain not used to offset losses) not be recognized until they are realized, the gain on disposal to be reported by Tyler for the year ended 12/31/83 should be $0.

24. (584,T1,22) (a) The requirement is to determine the item which would be reflected in the statement of stockholders' equity, net of taxes, as an adjustment to the opening balance in retained earnings. This describes the treatment of a prior period adjustment. SFAS 16, para 11 states that corrections of errors in previously issued financial statements are prior period adjustments; thus, answer (a) is correct. Answers (b), (c), and (d) are shown net of taxes on the income statement after income from continuing operations.

25. (584,T1,28) (c) Per APB 30, para 26 a material loss that is unusual in nature **or** infrequent in occurrence, but not both, should be reported as a separate component of income from continuing operations. Answers (a) and (d) are incorrect because an extraordinary item must be **both** unusual in nature and infrequent in occurrence. Answer (b) is incorrect because material losses do not result from a change in an accounting principle.

FINANCIAL STATEMENTS

Answer Outline

Problem 1 Evaluation of Presentation of Current Assets and Income Statement

a. Inventories
- Appropriately presented on balance sheet
  - Presented as current asset
- Appropriately presented in summary of significant accounting policies
  - Lower of cost (FIFO) or market disclosed
- Appropriately presented in notes to financial statements
  - Composition of inventories disclosed
  - Significant reduction of inventories to market on December 31, 1982, adequately disclosed
  - Cost of inventories on December 31, 1982, approximated market

Cost of Goods Sold
- Appropriately presented in statements of income
  - Component of continuing operations presented as separate item of costs and expenses to arrive at income from continuing operations

b1. Components of quick (acid-test) ratio
- Numerator
  - Quick assets include
    - Cash, short-term marketable securities, short-term notes receivable, and accounts receivable
  - For Pace Company, components would be cash, marketable securities, accounts receivable
- Denominator
  - Total current liabilities

b2. Quick (acid-test) ratio tests
- Ability to meet sudden demands upon liquid current assets
- Immediate liquidity by short-term creditors and others

c. Provision for deferred taxes presented inappropriately
- Deferred income taxes part of income taxes
  - Should be presented in statements of income in "income taxes," not "other-net"
- Presentation of breakdown between current and deferred income taxes
  - Include in statements of income , or
  - Disclose in notes to financial statements
    - Include in note on deferred income taxes, not in summary of significant accounting policies

d. Accounting change presented inappropriately
- Change in estimate, not a change in principle
  - Should not be included in statements of income separately as "cumulative effect"
- Effect should be reflected in depreciation expense for current and future years
  - Present as separate component of income from continuing operations before income taxes
    - Material event, usual but infrequent
  - "Income taxes" adjusted each year
  - Separate per share amount should not be presented

Unofficial Answer

Problem 1 Evaluation of Presentation of Current Assets and Income Statement

a. Inventories are presented appropriately as a current asset in the current assets section of the balance sheets.

Cost of goods sold is presented appropriately in the statements of income as a separate item of costs and expenses to arrive at income from continuing operations because it is part of the continuing operations.

Inventories are presented appropriately in the summary of significant accounting policies because the accounting policy regarding inventories, lower of cost (first-in, first-out) or market is disclosed.

Inventories are presented appropriately in the note to financial statements on inventories because the following items are disclosed:

- The composition of the inventories.
- The reduction of inventories from cost to market at December 31, 1982, which is an adjustment that, due to its significance, should be adequately disclosed in the notes to the financial statements.
- The fact that the cost of inventories at December 31, 1981, approximated their market value.

b. 1. The components of the quick (acid-test) ratio are as follows:
- The quick assets that comprise the numerator are cash, short-term marketable securities, short-term notes receivable, and accounts receivable. In the Pace Company current assets section of balance sheets it would be the cash, the marketable securities, and the accounts receivable.
- Total current liabilities is the denominator.

2. The quick (acid-test) ratio tests the ability to meet sudden demands upon liquid current assets. It is used as a test of immediate liquidity by short-term creditors and others.

c. The provision for deferred income taxes should not be included in the statements of income in "other-net." Deferred income taxes are part of income taxes and should be presented in the statements of income in "income taxes."

The breakdown between current income taxes and deferred income taxes should be presented in the statements of income or disclosed in the notes to the financial statements. If the breakdown between current income taxes and deferred income taxes is disclosed in the notes to the financial statements, it should be disclosed in the note on deferred income taxes, not in summary of significant accounting policies.

d. The accounting change is a change in estimate, not a change in principle, and should not be included in the statements of income separately as "cumulative effect, less applicable income taxes of $1,500,000." The effect of the change should be reflected in depreciation expense in the current and future years as a separate component of income from continuing operations before income taxes because it is a material event that is usual but infrequently occurring. "Income taxes" should be adjusted each year. A separate per share amount for this change should not be presented in the statements of income under "earnings per share of common stock."

Solution Guide

Problem 2 Income Statement Preparation

1. The requirement is to prepare a multiple-step income statement separating the recurring and nonrecurring items and supporting schedules. Also, the income taxes should be appropriately presented.

2. The basic outline for a formal multiple-step income statement is presented below:

Sales
– Cost of sales
Gross Profit
– Less operating expenses
Income from operations
± Other income or expense
Income from Continuing Operations before taxes
– Income taxes
Income from continuing operations
± Discontinued operations (net of tax)
Income before extraordinary items
± Extraordinary items (net of tax)
± Cumulative effect of change in accounting principle (net of tax)
Net Income

Per share data

3. APB 30 states that income (loss) from the operations of a discontinued division and the gain (loss) from the disposal of a division should be reported as a separate item, net of the applicable tax effect. It should be placed on the income statement after income from continuing operations and before extraordinary items.

3.1 The income from the operations of the discontinued division is found by subtracting the divisions expenses from its revenues (Schedule 2).

3.2 The loss on disposal of the discontinued division is computed by comparing the book value of the division with its sales price (Schedule 3).

4. SFAS 4 specifically includes a gain (loss) on the early extinguishment of debt as an extraordinary item. The $300,000 gain ($1,000,000 – $700,000) on the repurchase of long-term bonds should be classified as an extraordinary item and shown net of the tax effect (Schedule 4).

5. Once the special items have been identified, the top half of income statement can be prepared.

5.1 The sales, cost of sales and expense figures are given in the problem. Remember, however, that these figures for the Auto Leasing division should not be included with figures denoted as "regular".

5.2 The interest on municipal bonds should be listed as "other income" and the interest expense—regular should be shown as "other expense".

5.3 The income tax expense deducted from "income from continuing operations before taxes" should be 40% of that income amount after deducting the municipal interest (Schedule 1). The interest from municipal bonds is a permanent difference and, therefore, does not require interperiod tax allocation. Notice that the information under the heading **Federal income taxes** (except the 40% tax rate) is extraneous, since it deals with taxable income, tax payments and expense estimates. The information under the heading **Timing difference** is needed to determine the deferred portion of the income tax expense applicable to income from continuing operations. The deferred income tax amount is computed by multiplying the timing difference $150,000 ($750,000 – $600,000) by the applicable tax rate of 40%.

6. Earnings per share data must be presented on the face of the income statement because Woodbine Circle Corporation is publicly held as evidenced by the fact that their stock is traded on the New York Stock Exchange.

6.1 Because stock was sold on June 30, 1981, a weighted average number of shares needs to be calculated for use in computing the per share data. 900,000 shares were outstanding all year, while 200,000 shares were outstanding for only six months (Schedule 5).

6.2 Recall that earnings per share information must be shown on the face of the income statement for the following items:

- income from continuing operations,
- income before extraordinary item and/or cumulative effect of an accounting change,
- cumulative effect of change in accounting principle, and
- net income.

Three of these items apply in this problem: income from continuing operations, income before extraordinary item, and net income. These earnings amounts are simply divided by the 1,000,000 weighted average number of shares outstanding (Schedule 6). As noted in the solutions, EPS accounts **may** be shown for the discontinued operations and extraordinary item.

Unofficial Answer

(Author Modified)

Problem 2 Income Statement Preparation

Woodbine Circle Corporation
Income Statement
For the Year Ended December 31, 1981

Sales		$10,000,000
Cost of sales		6,200,000
Gross profit		$ 3,800,000
Less operating expenses:		
Administrative expense		2,000,000
Income from operations		$ 1,800,000
Other income:		
Interest income	100,000	
Other expense:		
Interest expense	(210,000)	(110,000)
Income from continuing operations before taxes		$ 1,690,000
Income taxes (Schedule 1)		
Current	576,000	
Deferred	60,000	636,000
Income from continuing operations		$ 1,054,000
Discontinued operations: (Schedules 2 and 3)		
Income from operations of Auto Leasing Division, less applicable income taxes of 264,000	396,000	
Loss on disposal of Auto Leasing Division, less applicable income of 100,000	(150,000)	246,000
Income before extraordinary item		$1,300,000
Extraordinary item:		
Gain on the redemption of bonds, net of income taxes of $120,000 (Schedule 4)		180,000
Net income		$1,480,000

Earnings per share of common stock (Schedules 5 and 6)

Income from continuing operations	$1.05
*Discontinued operations	.25
Income before extraordinary item	1.30
*Extraordinary item, net of tax	.18
Net Income	$1.48

*Not required by APBs 9, 15 or 30.

Schedule 1

Income Tax Expense on Continuing Operations

Income from continuing operations, before taxes	$1,690,000
Less interest on municipal bonds	100,000
Adjusted income figured	$1,590,000
Tax rate	x 40%
Total income taxes on continuing operations	$ 636,000
Depreciation timing difference	$ 150,000
Tax rate	x 40%
Deferred portion	$ 60,000

Schedule 2

Income from Discontinued AL Division

Sales	$2,000,000
Cost of Sales	900,000
Gross Profit	$1,100,000
Less operating expenses:	
Administrative expense	300,000
Operating income	$ 800,000
Other expense:	
Interest expense	140,000
Income from AL Division before taxes	$ 660,000
Income taxes ($660,000 x 40%)	264,000
Income from discontinued AL Division	$ 396,000

Schedule 3

Loss on Disposal of Discontinued AL Division

Sales price of AL Division	$4,000,000
Book value of AL Division	4,250,000
Loss on sale of AL Division before tax benefit	($ 250,000)
Tax effect of loss ($250,000 x 40%)	100,000
Loss on disposal of discontinued AL Division (net of tax)	($ 150,000)

Schedule 4

Extraordinary Gain

Book value of bonds redeemed	$1,000,000
Repurchase cost	700,000
Gain on redemption of bonds	$ 300,000
Less income taxes ($300,000 x 40%)	(120,000)
Gain on redemption of bonds (net of tax)	$ 180,000

Schedule 5

Weighted Average Number of Shares Outstanding

Number of Shares outstanding, 1/1/81		900,000
Issued on 6/30/81	200,000	
x 6 months/year	x 6/12	100,000
Weighted average number of shares		1,000,000

Schedule 6

Per Share Data

	Income figure		*Weighted average*		*Per share*
Income from cont. ops.	$1,054,000	÷	1,000,000	=	$1.05
Discontinued operations	246,000	÷	1,000,000	=	.25
Income before X/O item	$1,300,000	÷	1,000,000	=	$1.30
Extraordinary item	180,000	÷	1,000,000	=	.18
Net income	$1,480,000	÷	1,000,000	=	$1.48

Answer Outline

Problem 3 Evaluation of Income Statement Presentation

a. Change in accounting principle
- Appropriately presented, except for lack of adequate caption preceding disclosure of cumulative effect
- Rationale for appropriately presented elements
  - Change from DDB to SL depreciation is cumulative effect type change in principle
  - Depreciation on SL basis properly reflected in CGS for 1980 and 1981
    - Comparability achieved by consistent treatment
  - Cumulative effect appropriately presented net-of-tax after "income from continuing operations"
    - Effects of such changes not part of continuing operations
    - Restatement of prior years' statements may dilute public confidence
  - No pro forma information disclosed; however, none required
    - Income data prior to year of change (1980) are not disclosed (APB 20, para 2)
- Rationale for missing caption
  - Adequate disclosure requires caption: "Income before cumulative effect of change in accounting principle"

Discontinued operations

- Caption entitled "Discontinued Operations" needed to show its two components (operations and disposal)
  - Loss from operations component of Dex Division not disclosed properly for 1980 and 1981
    - Should be shown net-of-tax after income from continuing operations
    - Would include amount incurred to September 30 (measurement date)
  - Loss on disposal of Dex Division presented appropriately because it:
    - Includes provision for operating losses during phase-out period
    - Is presented net-of-tax
- Corrections needed to increase "income from operations" (both before and after income taxes)
  - Reduce "other, net" and "total costs and expenses" by amount of the loss reclassified under discontinued operations
  - Increase "income taxes" to reflect moving loss to discontinued operations
- Rationale
  - Loss from operations of Dex should be shown after income from continuing operations to enhance comparability of financial reports

EPS information

- EPS appropriately computed using weighted-average number of common shares outstanding
- EPS of common stock needed for income from continuing operations
- EPS data not required for discontinued operations

b. PE ratio useful in assessing whether to purchase, hold, or sell common stock by relating firm's earnings to market price of its common stock

- Measures stock market's perception of factors such as relative risk, stability of earnings, etc.
- Generally, higher PE ratio means high investor confidence in stock under study
- PE ratio calculated as:

$$\frac{\text{Market price per share of common}}{\text{EPS of common stock}}$$

- EPS used should be from continuing operations
  - For David Company, necessary to compute new EPS of common stock based on corrected income from continuing operations

Unofficial Answer

Problem 3 Evaluation of Income Statement Presentation

a. Change in accounting principle

The change in accounting principle is appropriately presented except for the lack of an adequate caption preceding disclosure of the cumulative effect. The change from the double-declining balance method to the straight-line method of depreciation is properly treated as a cumulative effect type change in principle. Depreciation for 1980 and 1981 is computed using the straight-line method and is properly reflected in cost of goods sold. This promotes comparability for the periods subsequent to the change in principle.

The cumulative effect of the change is appropriately presented as a separate component of income because it is not part of continuing operations. The cumulative effect is presented net-of-tax to comply with the requirement of intraperiod tax allocation.

Generally, a change in accounting principle should be treated as a cumulative effect type change because it is felt that restatement of the prior periods' financial statements may dilute public confidence and confuse those who use them. Although APB 20 requires that in comparative statements, the pro forma effects of retroactive application of the newly adopted principle be shown on the face of the income statement, this information is not required in this situation because income data prior to the year of change (1980) are not disclosed.

Discontinued operations

The loss on disposal, including the operating loss during the phase-out period, is presented appropriately; however, for financial statements to have predictive value and comparability, all elements related to disposed segments should be segregated from continuing operations. Therefore, a caption entitled "discontinued operations" is needed that shows both the "operations" and "disposal" subcaptions.

The first subcaption, "loss **from operations** of the discontinued Dex Division, net of applicable taxes," consists of the operating losses prior to the measurement date (9/30/81) which are presently included in "other, net." The other subcaption is "loss **on disposal** of Dex Division" which includes the operating loss during phase-out period which is already broken out from continuing operations.

The loss from operations of the segment being discontinued needs to be moved from the continuing operations section to the discontinued operations section. This will reduce "other, net," and "total costs and expenses." "Income from continuing operations before income taxes," "income taxes," and "income from continuing operations" will increase. "Income taxes" increase because intraperiod tax allocation requires that the tax effect related to the loss from operations of the discontinued Dex Division be netted against the loss.

EPS information

Earnings per share is presented on the face of the income statement and is appropriately computed using weighted-average number of common shares outstanding. The presentation is inappropriate in that "income from continuing operations" should be reported as the first item in the EPS section. EPS data for discontinued operations are not required; however, such data may be reported (on the face of the income statement or in the notes) if desired.

b. A firm's price earnings (PE) ratio is a measure of the stock market's perception of factors such as relative risk, stability of earnings, trend in earnings, and growth potential. The PE ratio is used in assessing whether to purchase, hold, or sell common stock by relating the firm's earnings to the market price of its common stock. A high PE ratio indicates high investor confidence and vice versa.

The price earnings ratio is calculated by dividing the market price of stock by earnings per share. Because the PE ratio is an indicator of future operating results, EPS from continuing operations should be used. For David Company, income from continuing operations, as presented, should be adjusted for the loss from operations of the discontinued Dex Division which has been included in "other, net."

INTERIM FINANCIAL REPORTING

Multiple Choice Questions (1 - 12)

1. On January 15, 1980, Forrester Company paid property taxes on its factory building for the calendar year 1980 in the amount of $60,000. The first week of April 1980 Forrester made unanticipated major repairs to its plant equipment at a cost of $240,000. These repairs will benefit operations for the remainder of the calendar year. How should these expenses be reflected in Forrester's quarterly income statements?

	Three months ended			
	March 31, 1980	*June 30, 1980*	*September 30, 1980*	*December 31, 1980*
a.	$15,000	$ 95,000	$95,000	$95,000
b.	$15,000	$255,000	$15,000	$15,000
c.	$60,000	$240,000	$0	$0
d.	$75,000	$ 75,000	$75,000	$75,000

2. Bailey Company, a calendar year corporation, has the following income before income tax provision and estimated effective annual income tax rates for the first three quarters of 1979:

Quarter	*Income before income tax provision*	*Estimated effective annual tax rate at end of quarter*
First	$60,000	40%
Second	70,000	40%
Third	40,000	45%

Bailey's income tax provision in its interim income statement for the third quarter should be

a. $18,000
b. $24,500
c. $25,500
d. $76,500

3. On January 1, 1979, Builder Associates entered into a $1,000,000 long-term, fixed-price contract to construct a factory building for Manufacturing Company. Builder accounts for this contract under the percentage-of-completion and estimated costs at completion at the end of each quarter for 1979 were as follows:

Quarter	*Estimated percentage of completion*	*Estimated costs at completion*
1	10%	$750,000
2*	10%	$750,000
3	25%	$960,000
4*	25%	$960,000

*No work performed in the 2nd and 4th quarters.

What amounts should be reported by Builder as "Income on Construction Contract" in its quarterly income statements based on the above information?

	Gain (Loss) for the three months ended			
	March 31, 1979	*June 30, 1979*	*September 30, 1979*	*December 31, 1979*
a.	$ 0	$0	$ 0	$10,000
b.	$25,000	$0	$(15,000)	$ 0
c.	$25,000	$0	$ 0	$ 0
d.	$25,000	$0	$ 6,000	$ 0

4. In August 1978 Ella Company spent $150,000 on an advertising campaign for subscriptions to the magazine it sells on getting ready for the skiing season. There are only two issues; one in October and one in November. The magazine is only sold on a subscription basis and the subscriptions started in October 1978. Assuming Ella's fiscal year ends on March 31, 1979, what amount of expense should be included in Ella's quarterly income statement for the three months ended December 31, 1978, as a result of this expenditure?

a. $ 37,500
b. $ 50,000
c. $ 75,000
d. $150,000

5. Ross Corporation expects to sustain an operating loss of $100,000 for the full year ending December 31, 1983. Ross operates entirely in one jurisdiction where the tax rate is 40%. Anticipated tax credits for 1983 total $10,000. No permanent differences are expected. Realization of the full tax benefit of the expected operating loss and realization of anticipated tax credits are assured beyond any reasonable doubt because they will be carried back. For the first quarter ended March 31, 1983, Ross reported an operating loss of $20,000. How much of a tax benefit should Ross report for the interim period ended March 31, 1983?

a. $0
b. $ 8,000
c. $10,000
d. $12,500

6. For external reporting purposes, it is appropriate to use estimated gross profit rates to determine the cost of goods sold for

	Interim financial reporting	*Year-end financial reporting*
a.	Yes	Yes
b.	Yes	No
c.	No	Yes
d.	No	No

7. An inventory loss from a market decline occurred in the first quarter that was not expected to be restored in the fiscal year. For interim financial reporting purposes, how would the dollar amount of inventory in the balance sheet be affected in the first and fourth quarters?

	First quarter	*Fourth quarter*
a.	Decrease	No effect
b.	Decrease	Increase
c.	No effect	Decrease
d.	No effect	No effect

8. Which of the following is an inherent difficulty in the determination of the results of operations on an interim basis?

a. Cost of sales reflects only the amount of product expense allocable to revenue recognized as of the interim date.
b. Depreciation on an interim basis is a partial estimate of the actual annual amount.
c. Costs expensed in one interim period may benefit other periods.
d. Revenues from long-term construction contracts accounted for by the percentage-of-completion method are based on annual completion and interim estimates may be incorrect.

9. If annual major repairs made in the first quarter and paid for in the second quarter clearly benefit the entire year, when should they be expensed?

a. An allocated portion in each of the last three quarters.
b. An allocated portion in each quarter of the year.
c. In full in the first quarter.
d. In full in the second quarter.

10. For interim financial reporting, an inventory loss from a temporary market decline in the first quarter which can reasonably be expected to be restored in the fourth quarter

a. Should be recognized as a loss proportionately in each of the first, second, third, and fourth quarters.
b. Should be recognized as a loss proportionately in each of the first, second, and third quarters.
c. Need **not** be recognized as a loss in the first quarter.
d. Should be recognized as a loss in the first quarter.

11. The computation of a company's third quarter provision for income taxes should be based upon earnings

a. For the quarter at an expected annual effective income tax rate.
b. For the quarter at the statutory rate.
c. To date at an expected annual effective income tax rate less prior quarters' provisions.
d. To date at the statutory rate less prior quarters' provisions.

12. In considering interim financial reporting, how did the Accounting Principles Board conclude that such reporting should be viewed?

a. As a "special" type of reporting that need not follow generally accepted accounting principles.
b. As useful only if activity is evenly spread throughout the year so that estimates are unnecessary.
c. As reporting for a basic accounting period.
d. As reporting for an integral part of an annual period.

INTERIM FINANCIAL REPORTING

Problem

Problem 1 Treatment of Selected Items (1178,T6)

(15 to 20 minutes)

Interim financial reporting has become an important topic in accounting. There has been considerable discussion as to the proper method of reflecting results of operations at interim dates. Accordingly, the Accounting Principles Board issued an opinion clarifying some aspects of interim financial reporting.

Required:

a. Discuss generally how revenue should be recognized at interim dates and specifically how revenue should be recognized for industries subject to large seasonal fluctuations in revenue and for long-term contracts using the percentage-of-completion method at annual reporting dates.

b. Discuss generally how product and period costs should be recognized at interim dates. Also discuss how inventory and cost of goods sold may be afforded special accounting treatment at interim dates.

c. Discuss how the provision for income taxes is computed and reflected in interim financial statements.

Multiple Choice Answers

1. a	4. d	7. a	9. b	11. c
2. b	5. c	8. c	10. c	12. d
3. b	6. b			

Multiple Choice Answer Explanations

E. Interim Reporting

1. (1181,P1,15) (a) The requirement is the treatment of annual property taxes and unanticipated major repairs to plant equipment in Forrester's quarterly income statements. Per APB 28, a cost charged to expense in an annual period should be allocated among the interim periods clearly benefitted through the use of accruals and/or deferrals. Annual property taxes clearly benefit all four quarters, so the $60,000 cost should be reflected as $15,000 expense in each of the four quarters. The repairs in April of 1980 will benefit operations for the remainder of the calendar year, so the $240,000 cost should be reflected as $80,000 expense in each of the second, third, and fourth quarters.

	Q1	Q2	Q3	Q4
Taxes	$15,000	$15,000	$15,000	$15,000
Repairs	0	80,000	80,000	80,000
Total	$15,000	$95,000	$95,000	$95,000

Para 14 of APB 28 states that unanticipated manufacturing variances should be recognized in the interim period in which they occur. This would support recognizing the total $240,000 unanticipated factory repairs in the second quarter. However, the problem does not say that Forrester uses a standard cost accounting system.

2. (1180,P1,9) (b) The requirement is Bailey's income tax provision (expense) in its interim income statement for the third quarter. FASB Interpretation 18 states that the tax provision for an interim period is the tax for the year to date (estimated annual rate times year-to-date income) less the total tax provisions reported for previous interim periods.

Year to date tax (45%)($170,000)	$76,500
Previously reported tax (40% x $130,000)	52,000
Third quarter tax provision	$24,500

3. (580,P1,8) (b) The requirement is to compute the income to be recognized in quarterly (interim) financial statements on a construction contract using the percentage-of-completion method. The solutions approach is to compute the income on the contract at the end of each quarter by (1) applying the estimated percentage of completion to the total estimated income to be recognized on the contract, and (2) subtracting the income recognized in preceding quarters to arrive at the income for the latest quarter. In the second and fourth quarters there was no work done on the contract and no change in the total estimated cost of completion. In quarter three the estimated costs of completion are revised upward. Since the cumulative income to date is less than income recognized in the first quarter, it is necessary to recognize a loss in the second quarter. The loss is handled as a change in accounting estimate rather than restating the first quarter.

Quarter 1:
10% ($1,000,000 – $750,000) = $25,000 income recognized

Quarter 2:
-0-

Quarter 3:
25% ($1,000,000 – $960,000) = $10,000 income earned to date

$10,000 income to date – $25,000 income recognized in previous periods = $(15,000) loss for quarter

Quarter 4:
-0-

4. (1179,P1,11) (d) The requirement is the amount of advertising expense to be included in a quarterly statement when the advertising relates only to revenue productivity of that particular quarter. Since the advertising relates only to the quarter ended 12/31/78, all the advertising should be expensed in that quarter. Per para 15a of APB 28, expenses other than product costs should be allocated among interim periods based on an estimate of the benefit received or activity associated with the period. Since the advertising will only benefit the quarter in which the magazines are sold, all of the expense should be allocated to the interim period ending 12/31/78.

5. (583,Q1,17) (c) At the end of each interim period, Ross Corporation should make its best estimate of the effective tax rate expected to be applicable for the full fiscal year. This rate should reflect anticipated tax credits and should be used to provide for taxes on a current year-to-date basis (APB 28, para 19). The computation of the rate (FASB Interpretation 18, para 49) is:

Tax benefit at statutory rate ($100,000 x 40%)	$(40,000)
Tax credits	(10,000)
Net tax benefit	$(50,000)
Annual effective tax rate (50,000 ÷ 100,000)	50%

To be recognized in the loss period, realization of the full tax benefit **must be assured beyond any reasonable doubt.** Since realization is assured when tax effects are carried back, as in this problem, the tax benefits are appropriately recognized in the loss period (APB 11, para 44). Therefore the tax benefit for the quarter ending March 31, 1983, is $10,000 ($20,000 x 50%).

6. (1183,T1,35) (b) The requirement is the appropriateness of estimated gross profit rates in determining the cost of goods sold for interim and year-end external financial reporting purposes. The use of estimated gross profit rates to determine the cost of goods sold for an interim period is appropriate per APB 28, para 14. The method of estimation used and any significant adjustments that result from reconciliations with the annual physical inventory should be disclosed. An estimation of cost of goods sold is not allowable for year-end financial reporting per APB 43, para 4. (The actual cost of the goods sold must be determined by the use of a cost flow assumption which most clearly reflects periodic income.) Thus, an estimated cost of goods sold figure may be used for interim but not year-end statements [answer (b)].

7. (1182,T1,32) (a) Per APB 28, para 14c inventory losses from market declines that are considered permanent should be recognized in the interim period in which the decline occurs. Since inventory was written down in the first quarter, there is no effect on the fourth quarter inventory valuation [answer (a)]. Answer (b) is incorrect because losses from permanent market declines are not subject to subsequent recovery. Answers (c) and (d) are incorrect because a write down must be taken in this situation.

8. (1177,T1,13) (c) The requirement is specification of a major problem in measuring income in interim periods. The most serious problem specified is dealing with costs that are expensed in one interim period but may provide benefits to other interim periods. See para 4, 15, and 16 of APB 28. Answer (a) is incorrect because cost of sales consists of product expenses which are relatively easy to define. Once the sale has been recorded, the cost of sales is determinable. Answer (b) is incorrect because depreciation in an interim period can be based upon a proportionate amount of the annual rate, i.e., the estimates have been made on an annual basis and only have to be broken down as to the interim periods. Answer (d) is incorrect because revenue from percentage of completion estimates of long-term construction contracts is as accurate for interim periods as it is for annual periods.

9. (1181,T1,36) (b) Para 16 of APB 28 states that when a cost which must be expensed for annual reporting purposes clearly benefits two or more interim periods (e.g., major repairs), each interim period benefited should be charged for an appropriate portion of the cost incurred.

10. (581,T1,32) (c) The requirement is the proper treatment in interim financial reporting of an inventory loss from a temporary market decline in the first quarter which can reasonably be expected to be restored in the fourth quarter. Per APB 28, para 14, companies that prepare interim financial statements should generally use the same inventory pricing methods (FIFO, LIFO, average, etc.) and make provisions for write-downs to market at interim dates on the same basis as used at annual inventory dates. Inventory losses from market declines should not be deferred beyond the interim period in which the decline occurs. Subsequent recoveries from increases in market prices in the same fiscal year on the same inventory should be recognized as gains in the interim period of the market increase. However, APB 28, para 14(c) allows for not recognizing a loss in interim periods from a decline in market prices of inventory if these declines are temporary and can reasonably be expected to be restored in the fiscal year.

11. (1180,T1,16) (c) FASB Interpretation 18 requires computation of quarterly income tax provisions by applying the estimated annual effective tax rate to year-to-date ordinary income to obtain the year-to-date tax. From this amount is subtracted prior quarters' provisions applicable to ordinary income to obtain the current quarter's tax. In other words, the "change in estimate" approach is used. The income tax effects of capital gains are assigned to the quarter in which the related item occurred.

12. (1176,T1,18) (d) The basic premise of APB 28 is that each interim period is an integral part of an annual period (para 9). Thus, interim reporting is not a special type reporting and must follow GAAP. The major issues concerning interim reporting are situations where activity is not evenly spread, i.e., is seasonal. The costs of seasonal activities require estimates, e.g., annual rate of federal income tax. As an integral part of an annual period, an interim period is not a basic accounting period.

INTERIM FINANCIAL REPORTING

Answer Outline

Problem 1 Treatment of Selected Items

a. Recognition of revenue in interim statements
 - Recognize revenue as is recognized for annual statements
   - I.e., normally point of sale or performance of service
 - Seasonal variations should be disclosed by footnote
 - Long-term contract recognized same as for annual statements

b. Recognition of costs in interim statement
 - Also the same as in annual statements
 - Product cost should be matched with associated revenues
 - Period costs should be expensed as incurred
   - Or allocated to interim periods based on time expired, etc.
 - Recognize gains or losses in full when incurred
   - Unless type to be deferred at year-end
 - Cost allocation among interim periods must be reasonable
 - Interim inventory valuation exceptions
   - Gross profit method may be used to estimate inventory and cost of goods sold
   - Temporary liquidation of LIFO inventory tiers may be ignored
     - Difference in carrying value and replacement cost is a current liability
 - Inventory market value declines are recognized as they occur
 - Standard cost variances are treated as for annual statements

c. Recognition of income taxes in interim statements
 - Expense is based upon the expected annual rate
 - Rate based on income for book purposes rather than tax purposes
 - Compute expected annual rate based on expected
   - Annual earnings
   - Investment tax credits
   - Foreign tax rates
   - Percentage depletion, capital gains rates
   - And other tax-planning alternatives
 - Calculation excludes
   - Extraordinary items
   - Discontinued operations
   - Cumulative effect of changes
   - These items are reported net of tax effect
 - Compute provision for interim taxes on a cumulative basis
   - E.g., compute tax to date and adjust for taxes recognized in previous interim periods
   - No retroactive adjustments for changes in expected rate

Unofficial Answer

Problem 1 Treatment of Selected Items

a. Sales and other revenues should be recognized for interim financial statement purposes in the same manner as revenues are recognized for annual reporting purposes. This means normally at the point of sale or, in the case of services, at completion of the earnings process.

In the case of industries whose sales vary greatly due to the seasonal nature of business, revenues should still be recognized as earned, but a disclosure should be made of the seasonal nature of the business in the notes.

In the case of long-term contracts recognizing earnings on the percentage-of-completion basis, the current state of completion of the contract should be estimated and revenue recognized at interim dates in the same manner as at the normal year end.

b. For interim reporting purposes, product costs (costs directly attributable to the production of goods or services) should be matched with the product and associated revenues in the same manner as for annual reporting purposes.

Period costs (costs not directly associated with the production of a particular good or service) should be charged to earnings as incurred or allocated among interim periods based on an estimate of time expired, benefit received, or other activity associated with the particular interim period(s). Also, if a gain or loss occurs during an interim period and is a type that would not be deferred at year end, the gain or loss should be recognized in full in the interim period in which it occurs. Finally, in allocating period costs among interim periods, the basis for allocation must be supportable and may not be based on merely an arbitrary assignment of costs between interim periods.

The AICPA Accounting Principles Board allowed for some variances from the normal method of determining cost of goods sold and valuation of inventories at interim dates in Opinion no. 28, but these methods are allowable only at interim dates and must be fully disclosed in a footnote to the financial statements. Some companies use the gross profit method of estimating cost of goods sold and ending inventory at interim dates instead of taking a complete physical inventory. This is an allowable procedure at interim dates, but the company must disclose the method used and any significant variances that subsequently result from reconciliation of the results obtained using the gross profit method and the results obtained after taking the annual physical inventory.

At interim dates, companies using the LIFO cost-flow assumption may temporarily have a reduction in inventory level that results in a liquidation of base period tiers of inventory. If this liquidation is considered temporary and is expected to be replaced prior to year end, the company should charge cost of goods sold at current prices. The difference between the carrying value of the inventory and the current replacement cost of the inventory is a current liability for replacement of LIFO base inventory temporarily depleted. When the temporary liquidation is replaced, inventory is debited for the original LIFO value and the liability is removed.

Inventory losses from a decline in market value at interim dates should not be deferred but should be recognized in the period in which they occur. However, if in a subsequent interim period the market price of the written-down inventory increases, a gain should be recognized for the recovery up to the amount of the loss previously recognized. If a temporary decline in market value below cost can reasonably be expected to be recovered prior to year end, no loss should be recognized.

Finally, if a company uses a standard costing system to compute cost of goods sold and to value inventories, variances from the standard should be deferred instead of being immediately recognized.

c. The AICPA Accounting Principles Board stated that the provision for income taxes shown in interim financial statements must be based upon the effective tax rate expected for the entire annual period for ordinary earnings. The effective tax rate is, in accordance with previous APB opinions, based on earnings for financial statement purposes as opposed to taxable income which may consider timing differences. This effective tax rate is the combined federal and state(s) income tax rate applied to expected annual earnings, taking into consideration all anticipated investment tax credits, foreign tax rates, percentage depletion capital gains rates, and other available tax planning alternatives. Ordinary earnings do not include unusual or extraordinary items, discontinued operations, or cumulative effects of changes in accounting principles, all of which will be separately reported or reported net of their related tax effect in reports for the interim period or for the fiscal year. The amount shown as the provision for income taxes at interim dates should be computed on a year-to-date basis. For example, the provision for income taxes for the second quarter of a company's fiscal year is the result of applying the expected rate to year-to-date earnings and subtracting the provision recorded for the first quarter. There are several variables in this computation (expected earnings may change, tax rates may change), and the year-to-date method of computation provides the only continuous method of approximating the provision for income taxes at interim dates. However, if the effective rate or expected annual earnings change between interim periods, the change is not reflected retroactively but the effect of the change is absorbed in the current interim period.

SEGMENT REPORTING

Multiple Choice Questions (1 - 9)

1. Hines Corporation reports operating profit as to industry segments in its supplementary financial information annually. The following information is available for 1981:

	Sales	*Traceable costs*
Segment A	$ 750,000	$450,000
Segment B	500,000	225,000
Segment C	250,000	125,000
	$1,500,000	$800,000

Additional expenses not included above are as follows:

Indirect operating expenses	$240,000
General corporate expenses	180,000
Interest expense	96,000

Hines allocates common costs based on the ratio of a segment's sales to total sales. What should be the operating profit for segment B for 1981?

a. $103,000
b. $135,000
c. $163,000
d. $195,000

2. Plains, Inc., engages in three lines of business, each of which is considered to be a significant industry segment. Company sales aggregated $1,800,000 in 1980, of which Segment No. 3 contributed 60%. Traceable costs were $600,000 for Segment No. 3 out of a total of $1,200,000 for the company as a whole. In addition $350,000 of common costs are allocated based on the ratio of a segment's income before common costs to the total income before common costs. What should Plains report as operating profit for Segment No. 3 in 1980?

a. $200,000
b. $270,000
c. $280,000
d. $480,000

3. Kee Co. has five manufacturing divisions, each of which has been determined to be a reportable segment. Common costs are appropriately allocated on the basis of each division's sales in relation to Kee's aggregate sales. Kee's Sigma division comprised 40% of Kee's total sales in 1982. For the year ended December 31, 1982, Sigma had sales of $1,000,000 and traceable costs of $600,000. In 1982 Kee incurred operating expenses of $100,000 that were not directly traceable to any of the five divisions. In addition, Kee incurred interest expense of $80,000 in 1982. In reporting supplementary segment information, how much should be shown as Sigma's operating income for 1982?

a. $300,000
b. $328,000
c. $360,000
d. $400,000

4. Kaycee Corporation's revenues for the year ended December 31, 1981, were as follows:

Consolidated revenue per income statement	$1,200,000
Intersegment sales	180,000
Intersegment transfers	60,000
Combined revenues of all industry segments	$1,440,000

Kaycee has a reportable segment if that segment's revenues exceed

a. $ 6,000
b. $ 24,000
c. $120,000
d. $144,000

5. In financial reporting for segments of a business enterprise, which of the following assets should be included as an identifiable asset of industry segment A?

a. An intangible asset used by industry segment A.
b. An advance from nonfinancial industry segment A to another industry segment.
c. An allocation of a tangible asset used for general corporate purposes, and **not** used in the operations of any particular industry segment.
d. An allocation of a tangible asset used by another industry segment which transfers products to industry segment A.

6. In financial reporting for segments of a business enterprise, the operating profit or loss of a segment should include among other items

a. Traceable costs.
b. Foreign income taxes.
c. Extraordinary items.
d. Loss on discontinued operations.

7. In financial reporting for segments of a business enterprise, the operating profit or loss of a segment should include

a. Federal income taxes.
b. Interest expense even though segment's operations are not principally of a financial nature.
c. Revenue earned at the corporate level.
d. Common costs allocated on a reasonable basis.

May 1984 Questions

8. Eller Company discloses supplemental industry segment information. The following data are available for 1983:

Segment	*Sales*	*Traceable costs*	*Allocable costs*
R	$300,000	$240,000	?
S	400,000	220,000	?
T	200,000	140,000	?
	$900,000	$600,000	$120,000

Costs are appropriately allocated based on the ratio of a segment's income before allocable costs to total income before allocable costs. What is the operating profit for segment R for 1983?

a. $20,000
b. $24,000
c. $36,000
d. $48,000

9. In financial reporting for segments of a business enterprise, the operating profit or loss of a segment should include

a. Income taxes.
b. Expenses that relate to revenue from intersegment transfers.
c. Equity in income from unconsolidated subsidiaries.
d. General corporate expenses.

SEGMENT REPORTING

Problem

Problem 1 Definitions and Tests (579,T5)

(15 to 20 minutes)

Part a. In order to properly understand current generally accepted accounting principles with respect to accounting for and reporting upon segments of a business enterprise, as stated by the Financial Accounting Standards Board in its Statement 14, it is necessary to be familiar with certain unique terminology.

Required:

With respect to segments of a business enterprise, explain the following terms:

1. Industry segment.
2. Revenue.
3. Operating profit and loss.
4. Identifiable assets.

Part b. A central issue in reporting on industry segments of a business enterprise is the determination of which segments are reportable.

Required:

1. What are the tests to determine whether or not an industry segment is reportable?
2. What is the test to determine if enough industry segments have been separately reported upon and what is the guideline on the maximum number of industry segments to be shown?

Multiple Choice Answers

1. d	3. c	5. a	7. d	9. b
2. a	4. d	6. a	8. c	

Multiple Choice Answer Explanations

F. Segment Reporting

1. (1182,P1,20) (d) The requirement is the operating profit for segment B in 1981. In SFAS 14, operating profit for a segment is defined as that segment's total revenue less all **operating** expenses, including both traceable costs and common costs. Items which would have to be allocated on an arbitrary basis, such as general corporate expenses and interest expense, are **not** used in the computation of operating profit or loss. Therefore segment B's operating profit would be $195,000 as computed below:

Sales	$500,000
Traceable costs	(225,000)
Common costs [indirect operating expenses ($240,000 x 1/3)]	(80,000)
Operating profit	$195,000

Segment B is allocated 1/3 of common costs based on the ratio of B's sales to total sales ($500,000/ $1,500,000).

2. (581,P1,4) (a) The requirement is the amount reported as operating profit for Segment No. 3 in 1980. The solutions approach is to first visualize Segment 3's income statement. Then write in the headings and information given. The common costs and operating profit are filled in after they are determined.

Sales	$1,080,000	(60%)($1,800,000)
Traceable Costs	(600,000)	(given)
Common Costs	(280,000)	(80%)($ 350,000)
Operating Profit	$ 200,000	

Common costs are allocated based on the ratio of a segment's income before common costs to the company's total income before common costs. Segment 3 has income before common costs of $480,000 ($1,080,000 – $600,000). The company's total income before common costs is $600,000 ($1,800,000 – $1,200,000). Therefore, Segment No. 3's share of the common costs is 80% ($480,000 ÷ $600,000).

3. (1183,Q1,4) (c) The requirement is the operating income for the Sigma division, a reportable segment, in 1982. In SFAS 14, operating income for a segment is defined as that segment's total revenue less all operating expenses, including both traceable costs and common costs. Items which would have to be allocated on an arbitrary basis, such as interest expense, are not used in the computation of operating income (loss) of a segment. The common costs were allocated on the basis of division sales to total sales. Therefore, the Sigma division's operating income would be $360,000 as computed below:

Sales	$1,000,000
Traceable costs	(600,000)
Common costs [indirect operating expenses ($100,000 x 40%)]	(40,000)
Operating income	$ 360,000

4. (582,Q1,16) (d) The requirement is to determine the amount of revenue that would cause a segment to be a reportable segment. SFAS 14 requires that selected data for a segment be reported separately if one of three criteria are met. One of these criteria is met when a segment's revenue is 10% or more of the combined revenues of all industry segments. Para 10 (c) of SFAS 14 defines revenue to include both sales to unaffiliated customers and intersegment sales or transfers. Thus, Kaycee would have a reportable segment if that segment's revenues exceed $144,000 (10% of $1,440,000).

5. (1181,T1,40) (a) Identifiable assets of an industry segment are defined in para 10(e), SFAS 14 as tangible and intangible enterprise assets that are used by the industry segment including assets that are used exclusively by that industry segment and an allocated portion of assets used jointly by two or more industry segments. Answers (b), (c), and (d) are mentioned in para 10(e) as not being identifiable assets under this definition.

6. (581,T1,39) (a) The requirement is to identify an item that should be included in the calculation of the operating profit or loss of a segment. Per para 10(d) of SFAS 14, the operating profit or loss of an industry segment is its revenue minus all operating expenses. As used therein, operating expenses include those expenses that relate to both sales to unaffiliated customers and revenue from intersegment sales. Costs that are not traceable to segments shall be allocated on a reasonable basis among those industry segments for whose benefit the expenses were incurred. The items listed in answers (b) and (c) are explicitly excluded from the calculation of segmental operating profit and loss and answer (d) is implicitly excluded because a loss from discontinued operations relates to a particular segment.

7. (580,T1,38) (d) SFAS 14, para 10d, describes which elements are to be included in and excluded from the operating profit and loss of a segment. Answers (a), (b), and (c) are specifically excluded. Costs incurred by the enterprise that are not directly traceable to an industry segment (common costs) are to be allocated on a reasonable basis to those segments for whose benefit the expenses were incurred.

May 1984 Answers

8. (584,P3,53) (c) The requirement is the operating profit for segment R. The first step is to compute the segment's income before allocable costs.

Sales	$300,000
Less traceable costs	(240,000)
Income before allocable costs	$ 60,000

Allocable costs are allocated based on segment income before allocable costs to total income before allocable costs. Total income before allocable costs is $300,000 (sales of $900,000 less traceable costs of $600,000). Therefore, segment R's share of allocable costs is $24,000 [($60,000/$300,000) x $120,000], and segment R's operating profit is $36,000.

Sales	$300,000
Less traceable costs	(240,000)
Income before allocable costs	60,000
Less allocable costs	(24,000)
Operating profit	$ 36,000

9. (584,T1,33) (b) Per SFAS 14, para 10d the operating profit or loss of a segment should include operating expenses that relate to both revenue from sales to unaffiliated customers and revenue from intersegment transfers. Answers (a), (c), and (d) are incorrect because para 10d also states that income taxes, equity in income from unconsolidated subsidiaries, and general corporate expenses shall not be added or deducted in computing the operating profit or loss of a segment.

SEGMENT REPORTING

Answer Outline

Problem 1 Definitions and Tests

a1. Industry segment – Enterprise component providing products or services to unaffiliated customers
 Specification of unaffiliated customers precludes reporting vertically integrated operations as segments

a2. Segment revenue – Sales revenues from all unaffiliated and intersegment sales (or transfers)
 Intersegment sales accounted for at internal transfer prices
 Interest is included if receivables are segment identifiable assets
  Except interest on loans to other segments

a3. Segment operating profit – Revenue minus all operating expenses
 Operating expenses include those for unaffiliated and intersegment sales
 Nondirect operating expenses should be allocated to segments on a reasonable basis
 Intersegment purchases accounted at internal transfer price
 Items not included in determining operating profit
 Revenue earned at the corporate level and not derived from the operations of any industry segment
  General corporate expenses
  Interest expense
  Domestic and foreign income taxes
  Income or loss of unconsolidated subsidiaries
  Discontinued operations gains or losses
  Extraordinary items
  Minority interest
  Cumulative affect of an accounting principle change

a4. Identifiable assets – Assets used by industry segment
 Including allocated portion of jointly used assets
 And adjusted for appropriate valuation allowance e.g., goodwill allocable to a particular segment
 But no general corporate assets
 And not intersegment loans (unless a financing segment)

b1. Segments are reportable
 If segment revenue is 10% or more of total revenue
 If operating profit (or loss) is 10% or more of operating profits for all segments reporting profits or operating losses for all segments reporting losses
 If assets are 10% or more of all segment assets
 Other segments may be required for interperiod comparability

b2. Separately reported segments must account for 75% of revenues to unaffiliated customers
 If not, additional segments must be reported to meet the criteria
 Separately reported segments should not exceed 10

Unofficial Answer

Problem 1 Definitions and Tests

Part a.

1. An industry segment is a component of an enterprise engaged in providing a product or service or group of related services primarily to unaffiliated customers for a profit. By defining an industry segment in terms of products and services sold primarily to unaffiliated customers, it can be seen that vertically integrated operations of an enterprise are not segments.

2. The revenue of an industry segment includes revenue both from sales to unaffiliated customers and from intersegment sales or transfers, if any, of products and services similar to those sold to unaffiliated customers. Interest earned from sources outside the enterprise and from intersegment trade receivables is included in revenue if the asset on which the interest is earned is included among the industry segment's identifiable assets, but interest earned on advances or loans to other industry segments is not included unless the primary function of the segment is financial in nature. Also, revenue from intersegment sales or transfers is accounted for on the basis used by the enterprise to price the intersegment sales or transfers.

3. The operating profit or loss of an industry segment is its revenue minus all operating expenses. Operating expenses inlcude expenses that relate to both revenue from sales to unaffiliated customers and revenue from intersegment sales or transfers. An enterprise's operating expenses that are not directly traceable to an industry segment should be allocated on a reasonable basis among those segments for whose benefit the ex-

penses were incurred. Intersegment purchases should be accounted for on the same basis as intersegment sales or transfers. Statement of Financial Accounting Standards No. 14 does, however, specify certain items of revenue and expense that should not be considered in determining operating profit or loss for an industry segment:

a. Revenue earned at the corporate level and not derived from the operations of any industry segment.
b. General corporate expenses.
c. Interest expense (unless the segment's principal purpose is of a financial nature).
d. Domestic and foreign income taxes.
e. Equity in the earnings or losses of unconsolidated subsidiaries.
f. Gains or losses on discontinued operations.
g. Extraordinary items.
h. Minority interest.
i. Cumulative effect of a change in accounting principles.

4. The identifiable assets of an industry segment are those tangible and intangible enterprise assets that are used exclusively by that segment and an allocated portion of assets used jointly by two or more segments. Goodwill allocable to a particular industry segment is a part of that segment's identifiable assets. However, assets maintained for general corporate purposes (i.e., those not used in the operations of any industry segment) should not be allocated to industry segments. Identifiable assets of industry segments should not include loans or transfers to other segments unless the primary business of the segment is financial in nature. The identifiable assets of an industry segment also include the appropriate valuation allowances, such as allowance for doubtful accounts, accumulated depreciation, and marketable securities valuation allowance.

Part b.

1. There are three basic tests to be applied to segments of an industry to see if they are significant enough to be separately reportable. If a segment meets any one of the tests it is deemed significant and reportable.

The first test is based upon revenue. If a segment's revenue from sales to unaffiliated customers and intersegment sales and transfers is equal to 10 percent or more of the enterprise's combined revenues, the segment is reportable.

The second test is based upon operating profits or losses. There are two subtests in this category based upon absolute amounts of operating profits or losses. A segment is deemed reportable if the operating profit or loss shown by the segment is equal to or greater than 10 percent of the higher of the following two absolute amounts:

- Sum of all operating profits or all segments reporting operating profits.
- Sum of all operating losses for all segments reporting operating losses.

Third, a segment is significant and reportable if the identifiable assets of the segment equal or exceed 10 percent of the combined identifiable assets of all of the industry segments within the enterprise.

Finally, all segments, whether deemed reportable or not, must be reviewed from the standpoint of interperiod comparability, because the primary purpose of presenting segment information is to aid the financial statement reader.

2. Statement of Financial Accounting Standards no. 14 states that enough industry segments must be separately reported so that the total of revenues from sales to unaffiliated customers for the reportable segments equals or exceeds 75 percent of the combined revenues from sales to unaffiliated customers for the entire enterprise. If applying the prescribed tests does not yield the required percentage of revenues described above, additional segments must be reported on until the 75 percent test is met.

The Financial Accounting Standards Board has stated that if an enterprise has many reportable segments, benefit to the reader may be lost if more than 10 segments are reported. In such a situation, the board suggests combining related reportable segments until the total is ten or fewer.

PERSONAL FINANCIAL STATEMENTS

Multiple Choice Question

May 1984 Question

1. Mr. & Mrs. Carson are applying for a bank loan and the bank has requested a personal statement of financial condition as of December 31, 1983. Included in their assets at this date are the following:

- 1,000 shares of Alden Corporation common stock purchased in 1980 at a cost of $50,000. The quoted market value of the stock was $75 per share on December 31, 1983.
- A residence purchased in 1981 at a cost of $120,000. Improvements costing $15,000 were made in 1982. Unimproved similar homes in the area are currently selling at approximately the same price levels as in 1981.

In the Carsons' December 31, 1983, personal statement of financial condition, the above assets should be reported at a total amount of

a. $170,000
b. $185,000
c. $195,000
d. $210,000

Multiple Choice Answer

1. d

Multiple Choice Answer Explanation

May 1984 Answer

1. (584,P3,57) (d) The requirement is the total amount at which two assets should be reported in a personal statement of financial condition. Per SOP 82-1, assets are to be reported at estimated current values in such statements. The current value of the investment in stock is $75,000 (1,000 shares x $75 per share). The current value of the residence can be estimated at $135,000. This consists of the cost of $120,000 (since similar unimproved homes are selling at the same price level which they were selling at in 1981) and the cost of improvements ($15,000). It can be assumed that the improvements will increase the value of the house by at least their cost. Therefore, the total amount is $210,000 (investment of $75,000 plus the house worth $135,000).

Multiple Choice Questions (1 - 64)

1. Greenfield Company had the following cash balances at December 31, 1982:

Cash in banks	$1,500,000
Petty cash funds (all funds were reimbursed on December 31, 1982)	20,000
Cash legally restricted for additions to plant (expected to be disbursed in 1984)	2,000,000

Cash in banks includes $500,000 of compensating balances against short-term borrowing arrangements at December 31, 1982. The compensating balances are not legally restricted as to withdrawal by Greenfield. In the current assets section of Greenfield's December 31, 1982, balance sheet, what total amount should be reported as cash?

a. $1,020,000
b. $1,520,000
c. $3,020,000
d. $3,520,000

2. In preparing its bank reconciliation for the month of March 1982, Derby Company has available the following information:

Balance per bank statement, 3/31/82	$36,050
Deposit in transit, 3/31/82	6,250
Outstanding checks, 3/31/82	5,750
Credit erroneously recorded by bank in Derby's account, 3/12/82	250
Bank service charges for March	50

What should be the correct balance of cash at March 31, 1982?

a. $35,250
b. $36,250
c. $36,300
d. $36,550

3. Lee Corporation's checkbook balance on December 31, 1980, was $4,000. In addition, Lee held the following items in its safe on December 31:

Check payable to Lee Corporation, dated January 2, 1981, not included in December 31 checkbook balance	$1,000
Check payable to Lee Corporation, deposited December 20, and included in December 31 checkbook balance, but returned by bank on December 30, stamped "NSF." The check was redeposited January 2, 1981, and cleared January 7	200
Postage stamps received from mail-order customers	75
Check drawn on Lee Corporation's account, payable to a vendor, dated and recorded December 31, but not mailed until January 15, 1981	500

The proper amount to be shown as Cash on Lee's balance sheet at December 31, 1980, is

a. $3,800
b. $4,000
c. $4,300
d. $4,875

4. Barrett Company's account balances at December 31, 1982, for accounts receivable and the related allowance for doubtful accounts were $1,200,000 and $60,000, respectively. An aging of accounts receivable indicated that $106,000 of the December 31, 1982, receivables may be uncollectible. The net realizable value of accounts receivable was

a. $1,034,000
b. $1,094,000
c. $1,140,000
d. $1,154,000

5. On July 1 of this year a company received a one-year note receivable bearing interest at the market rate. The face amount of the note receivable and the entire amount of the interest are due on June 30 of next year. At December 31 of this year, the company should report in its balance sheet

a. A deferred credit for interest applicable to next year.
b. No interest receivable.
c. Interest receivable for the entire amount of the interest due on June 30 of next year.
d. Interest receivable for the interest accruing this year.

6. Alden Corporation provides an allowance for its doubtful accounts receivable. At December 31, 1980, the allowance account had a credit balance of $8,000. Each month Alden accrues bad debt expense in an amount equal to 2% of credit sales. Total credit sales during 1981 amounted to $2,000,000. During 1981 uncollectible accounts receivable totaling $22,000 were written off against the allowance account. An aging of accounts receivable at December 31, 1981, indicates that an allowance of $42,000 should be provided for doubtful accounts as of that date. Accordingly, bad debt expense previously accrued during 1981 should be increased by

a. $62,000
b. $42,000
c. $26,000
d. $16,000

7. For the month of December 1975, the records of Ranger Corporation show the following information:

Cash received on accounts receivable	$35,000
Cash sales	30,000
Accounts receivable, December 1, 1975	80,000
Accounts receivable, December 31, 1975	74,000
Accounts receivable written off as uncollectible	1,000

The corporation uses the direct write-off method in accounting for uncollectible accounts receivable. What are the gross sales for the month of December 1975?

a. $59,000
b. $60,000
c. $65,000
d. $72,000

8. A method of estimating bad debts that focuses on the income statement rather than the balance sheet is the allowance method based on

a. Direct write off.
b. Aging the trade receivable accounts.
c. Credit sales.
d. The balance in the trade receivable accounts.

9. Anderson Company accepted a $20,000, 90-day, 12% interest-bearing note dated September 15, 1982, from a customer. On October 15, 1982, Anderson discounted the note at Provident National Bank at a 15% discount rate. The customer paid the note at maturity. Based on a 360-day year, what amount should Anderson report as net interest revenue from the note transaction?

a. $ 85
b. $100
c. $150
d. $200

10. On January 7, 1983, Dean Company discounted its own $100,000, 180-day note at United National Bank at a discount rate of 20%. Dean repaid the note on the July 6, 1983, due date. Based on a 360-day year, the effective rate of interest on the borrowing was

a. 18.2%
b. 20.0%
c. 22.2%
d. 25.0%

11. After being held for 30 days, a 90-day 15% interest-bearing note receivable was discounted at a bank at 18%. The proceeds received from the bank upon discounting would be the

a. Maturity value less the discount at 18%.
b. Maturity value plus the discount at 18%.
c. Face value less the discount at 18%.
d. Face value plus the discount at 18%.

12. On January 10, 1979, Wayne, Inc., purchased 5,000 shares of Jason Corporation's common stock at $60 per share. The purchase is a long-term investment and is less than 20% of Jason's outstanding shares. This investment is appropriately reflected in Wayne's balance sheet as a noncurrent marketable equity security at December 31, 1979. The market value of Wayne's investment in Jason's common stock was as follows:

	Market Value	
Date	*Per share*	*Total*
December 15, 1979	$47	$235,000
December 31, 1979	46	230,000

On December 15, 1979, Wayne determined that there had been an other than temporary decline in the market value. What amount should Wayne record as a loss in its income statement for the year ended December 31, 1979?

a. $0
b. $ 5,000
c. $65,000
d. $70,000

13. Which of the following conditions generally exists before market value can be used as the basis for valuation of a company's marketable equity securities?

a. Management's intention must be to dispose of the securities within one year.
b. Market value must be less than cost for each security held in the company's marketable equity security portfolio.
c. Market value must approximate historical cost.
d. The aggregate market value of a company's marketable equity security portfolio must be less than the aggregate cost of the portfolio.

14. During 1982 Anthony Company purchased marketable equity securities as a long-term investment. Pertinent data are as follows:

Security	Cost	Market value at 12/31/82
A	$ 20,000	$ 18,000
B	40,000	30,000
C	90,000	93,000
	$150,000	$141,000

Anthony appropriately carries these securities at the lower of aggregate cost or market value. The amount of unrealized loss on these securities to flow through Anthony's income statement for 1982 should be

a. $0
b. $ 3,000
c. $ 9,000
d. $12,000

15. Denso Corporation reports on a calendar-year basis. Its December 31, 1982, financial statements were issued on February 3, 1983. The auditor's report was dated January 22, 1983. The following information pertains to Denso's aggregate marketable equity securities portfolio:

Cost	$500,000
Market value, 12/31/82	400,000
Market value, 1/22/83	350,000
Market value, 2/3/83	300,000

How much should be reported on Denso's balance sheet at December 31, 1982, for marketable equity securities?

a. $500,000
b. $400,000
c. $350,000
d. $300,000

16. A security in a current marketable equity securities portfolio is transferred to a noncurrent marketable equity securities portfolio. The security should be transferred between the corresponding portfolios at

a. The book value at date of transfer if higher than the market value at date of transfer.
b. The market value at date of transfer, regardless of its cost.
c. Its cost, regardless of the market value at date of transfer.
d. The lower of its cost or market value at date of transfer.

17. Accumulated changes in the valuation allowance for a long-term marketable equity securities portfolio should be a component of

a. Current assets.
b. Noncurrent assets.
c. Noncurrent liabilities.
d. Net income.

18. A truck owned and operated by Ward Company was involved in an accident with an auto driven by Stillman on January 12, 1981. Ward received notice on April 24, 1981, of a lawsuit for $800,000 damages for a personal injury suffered by Stillman. Ward's counsel believes it is reasonably possible that Stillman will be successful against the company for an estimated amount in the range between $100,000 and $400,000. No amount within this range is a better estimate of potential damages than any other amount. It is expected that the lawsuit will be adjudicated in the latter part of 1982. What amount of loss should Ward accrue at December 31, 1981?

a. $0
b. $100,000
c. $250,000
d. $400,000

19. On March 1, 1982, a suit was filed against Dean Company for patent infringement. Dean's legal counsel believes an unfavorable outcome is probable, and estimates that Dean will have to pay between $500,000 and $900,000 in damages. However, Dean's legal counsel is of the opinion that $600,000 is a better estimate than any other amount in the range. The situation was unchanged when the December 31, 1982, financial statements were released on February 24, 1983. How much of a liability should Dean report on its balance sheet at December 31, 1982, in connection with this suit?

a. $0
b. $500,000
c. $600,000
d. $900,000

20. Warren Waste Products Company carries a $5,000,000 comprehensive public liability policy which contains a $50,000 deductible clause. A personal injury liability suit was brought against Warren in 1981, which probably will be settled for $75,000. How much should appear on Warren's December 31, 1981, balance sheet for contingent liabilities?

a. $0
b. $25,000
c. $50,000
d. $75,000

21. On December 20, 1982, an uninsured property damage loss was caused by a company car being driven on company business by a company salesman. The company did not become aware of the loss until January 25, 1983. The amount of the loss was reasonably estimable before the company's 1982 financial statements were issued. The company's December 31, 1982, financial statements should report an estimated loss as

a. A disclosure, but **not** an accrual.
b. An accrual.
c. Neither an accrual nor a disclosure.
d. An appropriation of retained earnings.

22. A loss contingency for which the amount of loss can be reasonably estimated should be accrued when the occurrence of the loss is

	Reasonably possible	*Remote*
a.	Yes	No
b.	Yes	Yes
c.	No	No
d.	No	Yes

23. Gain contingencies are usually recognized in the income statement when
a. Realized.
b. Occurrence is reasonably possible and the amount can be reasonably estimated.
c. Occurrence is probable and the amount can be reasonably estimated.
d. The amount can be reasonably estimated.

24. Marsh, Inc., has an incentive compensation plan under which the president is paid a bonus of 10% of corporate income in excess of $100,000 before income tax but after deducting the bonus. The 1982 income before income tax and bonus is $430,000. The bonus should be
a. $39,091
b. $36,667
c. $33,000
d. $30,000

25. Morgan Company determined that: (1) it has a material obligation relating to employees' rights to receive compensation for future absences attributable to employees' services already rendered, (2) the obligation relates to rights that vest, and (3) payment of the compensation is probable. The amount of Morgan's obligation as of December 31, 1982, is reasonably estimated for the following employee benefits:

Vacation pay	$100,000
Holiday pay	25,000

What total amount should Morgan report as its liability for compensated absences in its December 31, 1982, balance sheet?
a. $0
b. $ 25,000
c. $100,000
d. $125,000

26. Starr Trading Stamp Company records stamp service revenue and provides for the cost of redemptions in the year stamps are furnished to licensees. Starr's past experience indicates that only 90% of the stamps sold to licensees will be redeemed. Starr's liability for stamp redemptions was $18,000,000 at December 31, 1981. Additional information for 1982 is as follows:

Stamp service revenue from stamps furnished to licensees	$10,000,000
Cost of redemptions	$ 8,500,000
Estimated cost of future redemptions as a percentage of stamps redeemable	60%

What amount should Starr report as a liability for stamp redemptions at December 31, 1982?
a. $ 9,500,000
b. $14,900,000
c. $18,500,000
d. $19,500,000

27. In an effort to increase sales, Mills Company inaugurated a sales promotional campaign on June 30, 1981. Mills placed a coupon redeemable for a premium in each package of cereal sold. Each premium costs Mills $1 and five coupons must be presented by a customer to receive a premium. Mills estimated that only 60% of the coupons issued will be redeemed. For the six months ended December 31, 1981, the following information is available:

Packages of cereal sold	*Premiums purchased*	*Coupons redeemed*
1,600,000	120,000	400,000

What is the estimated liability for premium claims outstanding at December 31, 1981?
a. $ 80,000
b. $112,000
c. $144,000
d. $192,000

28. During 1978 Lawton Company introduced a new line of machines that carry a three-year warranty against manufacturer's defects. Based on industry experience, warranty costs are estimated at 2% of sales in the year of sale, 4% in the year after sale, and 6% in the second year after sale. Sales and actual warranty expenditures for the first three-year period were as follows:

	Sales	*Actual warranty expenditures*
1978	$ 200,000	$ 3,000
1979	500,000	15,000
1980	700,000	45,000
	$1,400,000	$63,000

What amount should Lawton report as a liability at December 31, 1980?

a. $0
b. $ 5,000
c. $ 68,000
d. $105,000

Items 29 and 30 pertain to classification of short-term obligations expected to be refinanced, and are based on the following data:

Royal Corporation's liabilities at December 31, 1980, were as follows:

Trade accounts payable	$100,000
16% notes payable issued November 1, 1980, maturing July 1, 1981	30,000
14% debentures payable issued February 1, 1980; final installment due February 1, 1985; balance at December 31, 1980, including annual installment of $50,000 due February 1, 1981	300,000
	$430,000

Royal's December 31, 1980, financial statements were issued on March 31, 1981. On January 5, 1981, the entire $300,000 balance of the 14% debentures was refinanced by issuance of a long-term obligation. In addition, on March 1, 1981, Royal consummated a noncancelable agreement with the lender to refinance the 16% note payable on a long-term basis, on readily determinable terms that have not yet been implemented. Both parties are financially capable of honoring the agreement, and there have been no violations of any of the agreement's provisions.

29. The total amount of Royal's short-term obligations that may properly be excluded from current liabilities at December 31, 1980, is

a. $0
b. $30,000
c. $50,000
d. $80,000

30. Assume the same facts for Royal Corporation's liabilities, except that the agreement with the lender to refinance the 16% note payable on a long-term basis is cancelable at any time upon ten days' notice by the lender. The total amount of Royal's short-term obligations that may properly be excluded from current liabilities at December 31, 1980, is

a. $0
b. $30,000
c. $50,000
d. $80,000

31. In determining whether to accrue employees' compensation for future absences, one of the conditions that must be met is that the employer has an obligation to make payment even if an employee terminates. This is an example of a (an)

a. Vested right.
b. Accumulated right.
c. Contingent right.
d. Estimable right.

32. When a company receives a deposit from a customer to protect itself against nonpayment for future services, the deposit should be classified by the company as

a. Revenue.
b. A liability.
c. Part of the allowance for doubtful accounts.
d. A deferred credit deducted from accounts receivable.

33. Selected information from Brook Corporation's accounting records and financial statements for 1980 is as follows:

Working capital provided by operations	$1,500,000
Mortgage payable issued to acquire land and building	1,800,000
Common stock issued to retire preferred stock	500,000
Proceeds from sale of equipment	400,000
Cost of office equipment purchased	200,000

On the statement of changes in financial position for the year ended December 31, 1980, Brook should disclose total sources of funds in the amount of

a. $1,700,000
b. $2,400,000
c. $3,700,000
d. $4,200,000

34. The net income for Mountain Corporation was $4,000,000 for the year ended December 31, 1980. Additional information is as follows:

Depreciation on fixed assets	$2,000,000
Provision for doubtful accounts on short-term receivables	200,000
Provision for doubtful accounts on long-term receivables	300,000
Dividends on preferred stock	400,000

The working capital provided from operations in the statement of changes in financial position for the year ended December 31, 1980, should be

a. $4,900,000
b. $6,000,000
c. $6,300,000
d. $6,500,000

35. The working capital of Rogers Company at December 31, 1979, was $10,000,000. Selected information for the year 1980 for Rogers is as follows:

Working capital provided from operations	$1,700,000
Capital expenditures	3,000,000
Proceeds from short-term borrowings	1,000,000
Proceeds from long-term borrowings	2,000,000
Payments on short-term borrowings	500,000
Payments on long-term borrowings	600,000
Proceeds from issuance of common stock	1,400,000
Dividends paid on common stock	800,000

What is Rogers' working capital at December 31, 1980?
a. $10,700,000
b. $11,200,000
c. $11,500,000
d. $12,000,000

36. George Corporation declared a cash dividend of $10,000 on January 17, 1981. This dividend was payable to stockholders of record on February 10, 1981, and payment was made on March 2, 1981. As a result of this cash dividend, working capital will increase (decrease) on

	January 17	*February 10*
a.	$ 0	$0
b.	$ 10,000	$0
c.	$(10,000)	$0
d.	$(10,000)	$10,000

Items 37 and 38 are based on the following information:

Magnolia, Inc.
Balance Sheets

	December 31, 1980	*December 31, 1979*
Current assets	$ 474,000	$ 320,000
Equipment	1,230,000	1,200,000
Accumulated depreciation	(436,000)	(420,000)
Goodwill	480,000	500,000
Total assets	$1,748,000	$1,600,000
Current liabilities	$ 360,000	$ 160,000
Bonds payable	400,000	600,000
Discount on bonds	(12,000)	(20,000)
Common stock	1,112,000	1,112,000
Retained earnings (deficit)	(112,000)	(252,000)
Total liabilities and stockholders' equity	$1,748,000	$1,600,000

You have discovered the following facts:

- During 1980, Magnolia sold at no gain or loss equipment with a book value of $76,000 and purchased new equipment costing $150,000.
- During 1980, bonds with a face and book value of $200,000 were extinguished, with no gain or loss. They were not current liabilities prior to their extinguishment.
- Retained earnings was affected only by the 1980 net income or loss.

37. How much working capital was provided by operations during 1980?
a. $208,000
b. $212,000
c. $220,000
d. $228,000

38. Assume that $200,000 face value of bonds became current at December 31, 1980, to be repaid in early 1981. What should be the change in working capital under this assumption after considering all changes in financial position?
a. $ 46,000 increase.
b. $ 46,000 decrease.
c. $246,000 increase.
d. $246,000 decrease.

39. The conversion of nonparticipating preferred stock into common stock should be presented in a statement of changes in financial position as a

	Source of funds	*Use of funds*
a.	Yes	Yes
b.	Yes	No
c.	No	No
d.	No	Yes

40. A gain on the sale of a long-term investment should be presented in a statement of changes in financial position of a company with substantial operating profits as a (an)

a. Deduction from income from continuing operations.
b. Addition to income from continuing operations.
c. Source and use of funds.
d. Use of funds.

41. The retirement of long-term debt by the issuance of common stock should be presented in a statement of changes in financial position as a

	Source of funds	*Use of funds*
a.	No	No
b.	No	Yes
c.	Yes	No
d.	Yes	Yes

42. If a company issues both a balance sheet and an income statement with comparative figures from last year, a statement of changes in financial position
a. Is no longer necessary; but may be issued at the company's option.
b. Should not be issued.
c. Should be issued for each period for which an income statement is presented.
d. Should be issued for the current year only.

43. The working capital format is an acceptable format for presenting a statement of changes in financial position. Which of the following formats is (are) also acceptable?

	Cash	*Quick assets*
a.	Acceptable	Not acceptable
b.	Not acceptable	Not acceptable
c.	Not acceptable	Acceptable
d.	Acceptable	Acceptable

44. Which of the following must be disclosed in a statement of changes in financial position or in a related tabulation for at least the current period?
a. Net change in each balance sheet account.
b. Net change in each element of working capital.
c. Gross changes in depreciable assets.
d. Earnings per share.

Items 45 and 46 are based on the following information:

Patsy Corp., has estimated its activity for December 1976. Selected data from these estimated amounts are as follows:

• Sales	$350,000
Gross profit (based on sales)	30%
Increase in trade accounts receivable during month	$10,000
Change in accounts payable during month	$0
Increase in inventory during month	$5,000

• Variable selling, general and administrative expenses (S,G&A) includes a charge for uncollectible accounts of 1% of sales.

• Total S,G&A is $35,500 per month plus 15% of sales.

• Depreciation expense of $20,000 per month is included in fixed S,G&A.

45. On the basis of the above data, what are the estimated cash receipts from operations for December?
a. $336,500
b. $340,000
c. $346,500
d. $350,000

46. On the basis of the above data, what are the estimated cash disbursements from operations for December?
a. $309,500
b. $313,000
c. $314,500
d. $318,000

Items 47 through 50 relate to data to be reported in the Statement of Changes in Financial Position of Debbie Dress Shops, Inc., based on the following information:

Debbie Dress Shops, Inc.
Balance Sheets

	December 31, 1980	December 31, 1979
Assets:		
Current assets:		
Cash	$ 300,000	$ 200,000
Accounts receivable — net	840,000	580,000
Merchandise inventory	660,000	420,000
Prepaid expenses	100,000	50,000
Total current assets	1,900,000	1,250,000
Long-term investments	80,000	—
Land, buildings and fixtures	1,130,000	600,000
Less accumulated depreciation	110,000	50,000
	1,020,000	550,000
Total assets	$3,000,000	$1,800,000
Equities:		
Current liabilities:		
Accounts payable	$ 530,000	$ 440,000
Accrued expenses	140,000	130,000
Dividends payable	70,000	—
Total current liabilities	740,000	570,000
Note payable — due 1983	500,000	—
Stockholders' equity:		
Common stock	1,200,000	900,000
Retained earnings	560,000	330,000
	1,760,000	1,230,000
Total liabilities and stockholders' equity	$3,000,000	$1,800,000

Debbie Dress Shops, Inc.
Income Statements

	Year ended December 31, 1980	Year ended December 31, 1979
Net credit sales	$6,400,000	$4,000,000
Cost of goods sold	5,000,000	3,200,000
Gross profit	1,400,000	800,000
Expenses (including income taxes)	1,000,000	520,000
Net income	$ 400,000	$ 280,000

Additional information available included the following:

- Although the Corporation will report all changes in financial position, management has adopted a format emphasizing the flow of cash.
- All accounts receivable and accounts payable related to trade merchandise. Accounts payable are recorded net and always are paid to take all of the discount allowed. The Allowance for Doubtful Accounts at the end of 1980 was the same as at the end of 1979; no receivables were charged against the Allowance during 1980.
- The proceeds from the note payable were used to finance a new store building. Capital stock was sold to provide additional working capital.

47. Cash collected during 1980 from accounts receivable amounted to
    a. $5,560,000
    b. $5,840,000
    c. $6,140,000
    d. $6,400,000

48. Cash payments during 1980 on accounts payable to suppliers amounted to
    a. $4,670,000
    b. $4,910,000
    c. $5,000,000
    d. $5,150,000

49. Cash receipts during 1980 which were not provided by operations totaled
    a. $140,000
    b. $300,000
    c. $500,000
    d. $800,000

50. Cash payments for non-current assets purchased during 1980 were
    a. $ 80,000
    b. $530,000

c. $610,000
d. $660,000

51. The following information on selected cash transactions for 1978 has been provided by the Smith Company:

Proceeds from short-term borrowings	$1,200,000
Proceeds from long-term borrowings	4,000,000
Purchases of fixed assets	3,200,000
Purchases of inventories	8,000,000
Proceeds from sale of Smith's common stock	2,000,000

What is the increase in working capital for the year ended December 31, 1978, as a result of the above information?

a. $ 800,000
b. $2,000,000
c. $2,800,000
d. $4,000,000

52. The Hutch Company sells household furniture. Customers who purchase furniture on the installment basis make payments in equal monthly installments over a two-year period, with no down payment required. Hutch's gross profit on installment sales equals 60% of the selling price of the furniture.

For financial accounting purposes, sales revenue is recognized at the time the sale is made. For income tax purposes, however, the installment method is used. There are no other book and income tax accounting differences, and Hutch's income tax rate is 50%.

If Hutch's December 31, 1976, balance sheet includes a deferred tax credit of $30,000 arising from the difference between book and tax treatment of the installment sales, it should also include installment accounts receivable of

a. $ 30,000
b. $ 50,000
c. $ 60,000
d. $100,000

May 1984 Questions

53. On December 31, 1982, Clark Company purchased marketable equity securities as a temporary investment. Pertinent data are as follows:

Security	Cost	Market value at 12/31/83
W	$24,000	$26,000
X	36,000	33,000
Y	72,000	65,000

On December 31, 1983, Clark reclassified its investment in security Y from current to noncurrent because Clark intends to retain security Y as a long-term investment. What total amount of loss on these securities should be included in Clark's income statement for the year ended December 31, 1983?

a. $0
b. $1,000
c. $7,000
d. $8,000

54. Tallent Corporation had the following account balances at December 31, 1983:

Cash on hand and in banks	$975,000
Cash legally restricted for additions to plant (expected to be disbursed in 1985)	600,000
Bank certificates of deposit (due February 1, 1984)	250,000

In the current assets section of Tallent's December 31, 1983, balance sheet, what total amount should be reported under the caption "cash and cash equivalents"?

a. $ 975,000
b. $1,225,000
c. $1,575,000
d. $1,825,000

55. Farr Company pays its outside salespersons fixed monthly salaries and commissions on net sales. Sales commissions are computed and paid on a monthly basis (in the month following the month of sale), and the fixed salaries are treated as advances against commissions for this purpose. However, if the fixed salaries for salespersons exceed their sales commissions earned for a month, such excess is not charged back to them. Pertinent data for the month of March 1984 for the three salespersons in sales region 101 are as follows:

Salesperson	*Fixed salary*	*Net sales*	*Commission rate*
A	$ 2,500	$100,000	2%
B	3,500	200,000	3%
C	4,500	300,000	3%
	$10,500	$600,000	

In respect of sales region 101, what total amount should Farr accrue for sales commissions payable at March 31, 1984?

a. $ 6,500
b. $ 7,000
c. $17,000
d. $17,500

56. On December 31, 1983, Jordan Company was involved in a tax dispute with the IRS. Jordan's tax counsel believed that an unfavorable outcome was

probable and a reasonable estimate of additional taxes was $400,000, with a chance that the additional taxes could be as much as $650,000. After the 1983 financial statements were issued, Jordan accepted an IRS settlement offer of $450,000. What amount of additional taxes should have been charged to income in 1983?

a. $0
b. $400,000
c. $450,000
d. $650,000

57. Based on the aging of its accounts receivable at December 31, 1983, Drury Company determined that the net realizable value of the receivables at that date is $95,000. Additional information is as follows:

Accounts receivable at 12/31/83	$110,000
Allowance for doubtful accounts at 1/1/83—credit balance	16,000
Accounts written off as uncollectible at 9/30/83	12,000

Drury's bad debt expense for the year ended December 31, 1983, was

a. $11,000
b. $13,000
c. $15,000
d. $19,000

58. Lenox Company has a retirement savings plan which provides that: (1) eligible employees may deposit up to 5% of their salaries through payroll deduction, and (2) the company is required to make an annual contribution of an amount equal to 50% of the participants' deposits. Data for the year ended December 31, 1983, relating to eligible employees are as follows:

Total salaries	$750,000
Total employee deposits made	25,000

What amount should Lenox report as retirement savings plan expense for 1983?

a. $0
b. $12,500
c. $18,750
d. $25,000

59. In May 1980 Tooker Company filed suit against Rogers Corporation seeking to recover $1,000,000 for copyright infringement. A court verdict rendered in September 1983 awarded Tooker $700,000 in damages. Rogers appealed the verdict but a final decision is not expected before October 1984. Tooker's counsel believes it is probable that Tooker will be successful against Rogers for an estimated amount of $500,000. What amount should Tooker accrue by a credit to income in the year ended December 31, 1983?

a. $0
b. $500,000
c. $600,000
d. $700,000

60. A 90-day 15% interest-bearing note receivable is sold to a bank after being held for 30 days. The proceeds are calculated using an 18% interest rate. The note receivable has been

	Discounted	Pledged
a.	No	Yes
b.	No	No
c.	Yes	No
d.	Yes	Yes

61. A company is in its first year of operations and has never written off any accounts receivable as uncollectible. When the allowance method of recognizing bad debt expense is used, the entry to recognize that expense

a. Increases net income.
b. Decreases current assets.
c. Has **no** effect on current assets.
d. Has **no** effect on net income.

62. Which of the following contingencies should generally be recognized on the balance sheet when the occurrence of the contingent event is probable and its amount can be reasonably estimated?

	Gain contingency	Loss contingency
a.	Yes	Yes
b.	Yes	No
c.	No	Yes
d.	No	No

63. A loss on the sale of machinery in the ordinary course of business should be presented in a statement of changes in financial position as a(an)

a. Deduction from income from continuing operations.
b. Additions to income from continuing operations.
c. Source and a use of funds.
d. Use of funds.

64. The purchase for cash of treasury stock should be presented in a statement of changes in financial position as a

	Source of funds	Use of funds
a.	No	No
b.	No	Yes
c.	Yes	No
d.	Yes	Yes

Repeat Question

(584,P1,20) Identical to item 28 above

Problems

Problem 1 Bad Debts (1179,T2a)

(10 to 15 minutes)

When a company has a policy of making sales for which credit is extended, it is reasonable to expect a portion of those sales to be uncollectible. As a result of this, a company must recognize bad debt expense. There are basically two methods of recognizing bad debt expense: (1) direct write-off method, and (2) allowance method.

Required:

1. Describe fully both the direct write-off method and the allowance method of recognizing bad debt expense.

2. Discuss the reasons why one of the above methods is preferable to the other and the reason why the other method is not usually in accordance with generally accepted accounting principles.

Problem 2 Discounting Notes Receivable and Estimating Bad Debts (1182,T2)

(15 to 25 minutes)

Part a. On July 1, 1981, Carme Company, a calendar-year company, sold special-order merchandise on credit and received in return an interest-bearing note receivable from the customer. Carme Company will receive interest at the prevailing rate for a note of this type. Both the principal and interest are due in one lump sum on June 30, 1982.

Required:

1. When should Carme Company report interest income from the note receivable? Discuss the rationale for your answer.

2. Assume that the note receivable was discounted without recourse at a bank on December 31, 1981. How would Carme Company determine the amount of the discount and what is the appropriate accounting for the discounting transaction?

Part b. On December 31, 1981, Carme Company had significant amounts of accounts receivable as a result of credit sales to its customers. Carme Company uses the allowance method based on credit sales to estimate bad debts. Based on past experience, 1% of credit sales normally will not be collected. This pattern is expected to continue.

Required:

1. Discuss the rationale for using the allowance method based on credit sales to estimate bad debts. Contrast this method with the allowance method based on the balance in the trade receivables accounts.

2. How should Carme Company report the allowance for bad debts account on its balance sheet at December 31, 1981? Also, describe the alternatives, if any, for presentation of bad debt expense in Carme Company's 1981 income statement.

Problem 3 Marketable Equity Securities (SFAS 12) (1177,T4)

(20 to 25 minutes)

Part a. The Financial Accounting Standards Board issued its Statement Number 12 to clarify accounting methods and procedures with respect to certain marketable securities. An important part of the statement concerns the distinction between noncurrent and current classification of marketable securities.

Required:

1. Why does a company maintain an investment portfolio of current and noncurrent securities?

2. What factors should be considered in determining whether investments in marketable equity securities should be classified as current or noncurrent, and how do these factors affect the accounting treatment for unrealized losses?

Part b. Presented below are four unrelated situations involving marketable equity securities:

Situation I

A noncurrent portfolio with an aggregate market value in excess of cost includes one particular security whose market value has declined to less than one-half of the original cost. The decline in value is considered to be other than temporary.

Situation II

The statement of financial position of a company does not classify assets and liabilities as current and noncurrent. The portfolio of marketable equity securities includes securities normally considered current that have a net cost in excess of market value of $2,000. The remainder of the portfolio has a net market value in excess of cost of $5,000.

Situation III

A marketable equity security, whose market value is currently less than cost, is classified as noncurrent but is to be reclassified as current.

Situation IV

A company's noncurrent portfolio of marketable equity securities consists of the common stock of one company. At the end of the prior year the market value of the security was fifty percent of original cost, and this effect was properly reflected in a valuation allowance account. However, at the end of the current year the market value of the security had appreciated to twice the original cost. The security is still considered noncurrent at year end.

Required:

What is the effect upon classification, carrying value, and earnings for each of the above situations. Complete your response to each situation before proceeding to the next situation.

Problem 4 Loss Contingencies (SFAS 5) (1177,T6)

(25 to 30 minutes)

Part a. The two basic requirements for the accrual of a loss contingency are supported by several basic concepts of accounting. Three of these concepts are: periodicity (time periods), measurement, and objectivity.

Required:

Discuss how the two basic requirements for the accrual of a loss contingency relate to the three concepts listed above.

Part b. The following three independent sets of facts relate to (1) the possible accrual or (2) the possible disclosure by other means of a loss contingency.

Situation I

A company offers a one-year warranty for the product that it manufactures. A history of warranty claims has been compiled and the probable amount of claims related to sales for a given period can be determined.

Situation II

Subsequent to the date of a set of financial statements, but prior to the issuance of the financial statements, a company enters into a contract which will probably result in a significant loss to the company. The amount of the loss can be reasonably estimated.

Situation III

A company has adopted a policy of recording self-insurance for any possible losses resulting from injury to others by the company's vehicles. The premium for an insurance policy for the same risk from an independent insurance company would have an annual cost of $2,000. During the period covered by the financial statements, there were no accidents involving the company's vehicles which resulted in injury to others.

Required:

Discuss the accrual and/or type of disclosure necessary (if any) and the reason(s) why such disclosure is appropriate for each of the three independent sets of facts above. Complete your response before proceeding to the next situation.

Problem 5 Contingencies: Conditions and Disclosures (1180,T3a)

(10 to 15 minutes)

Part a. Loss contingencies may exist for companies.

Required:

1. What conditions should be met for an estimated loss from a contingency to be accrued by a charge to income?

2. When is disclosure required, and what disclosure should be made for an estimated loss from a loss contingency that need not be accrued by a charge to income?

Problem 6 Statement of Changes (1177,T5)

(20 to 25 minutes)

The statement of changes in financial position is normally a required basic financial statement for each period for which an earnings statement is presented. The reporting entity has flexibility in form, content, and terminology of this statement to meet the objectives of differing circumstances. For example, the concept of "funds" may be interpreted to mean, among other things, cash or working capital. However, the statement should be prepared based on the "all financial resources" concept.

Required:

a. What is the "all financial resources" concept?

b. What are two types of financial transactions which would be disclosed under the "all financial resources" concept that would not be disclosed without this concept?

c. What effect, if any, would each of the following seven items have upon the preparation of a statement of changes in financial position prepared in accordance with generally accepted accounting principles using the cash concept of funds?

1. Accounts receivable—trade.
2. Inventory.
3. Depreciation.
4. Deferred income tax credit from interperiod allocation.
5. Issuance of long-term debt in payment for a building.
6. Payoff of current portion of debt.
7. Sale of a fixed asset resulting in a loss.

Problem 7 Statement of Changes—Cash Basis (1182,P4)

(45 to 55 minutes)

Author's note: In view of the increasing preference for the cash versus the working capital basis for preparing statements of changes in financial position now appearing in the literature and the recent switch by many companies to a "cash basis" you are strongly urged to work this problem during your review.

Presented below are the balance sheets of Farrell Corporation as of December 31, 1981 and 1980, and the statement of income and retained earnings for the year ended December 31, 1981.

Farrell Corporation
Balance Sheets
December 31, 1981 and 1980

	1981	1980	Increase (decrease)
Assets:			
Cash	$ 275,000	$ 180,000	$ 95,000
Accounts receivable, net	295,000	305,000	(10,000)
Inventories	549,000	431,000	118,000
Investment in Hall, Inc., at equity	73,000	60,000	13,000
Land	350,000	200,000	150,000
Plant and equipment	624,000	606,000	18,000
Less accumulated depreciation	(139,000)	(107,000)	(32,000)
Goodwill	16,000	20,000	(4,000)
Total assets	$2,043,000	$1,695,000	$348,000
Liabilities and stockholders' equity:			
Accounts payable and accrued expenses	$ 604,000	$ 563,000	$ 41,000
Note payable, long-term	150,000	—	150,000
Bonds payable	160,000	210,000	(50,000)
Deferred income taxes	41,000	30,000	11,000
Common stock, par value $10	430,000	400,000	30,000
Additional paid-in capital	226,000	175,000	51,000
Retained earnings	432,000	334,000	98,000
Treasury stock, at cost	—	(17,000)	17,000
Total liabilities and stockholders' equity	$2,043,000	$1,695,000	$348,000

Farrell Corporation
Statement of Income
and Retained Earnings
For the Year Ended December 31, 1981

Net sales		$1,950,000
Operating expenses:		
	Cost of sales	1,150,000
	Selling and administrative expenses	505,000
	Depreciation	53,000
		1,708,000
Operating income		242,000
Other (income) expense:		
	Interest expense	15,000
	Equity in net income of Hall, Inc.	(13,000)
	Loss on sale of equipment	5,000
	Amortization of goodwill	4,000
		11,000
Income before income taxes		231,000
Income taxes:		
	Current	79,000
	Deferred	11,000
Provision for income taxes		90,000
Net income		141,000
Retained earnings, January 1, 1981		334,000
		475,000
Cash dividends, paid August 14, 1981		43,000
Retained earnings, December 31, 1981		$ 432,000

Additional information:

- On January 2, 1981, Farrell sold equipment costing $45,000, with a book value of $24,000, for $19,000 cash.
- On April 1, 1981, Farrell issued 1,000 shares of common stock for $23,000 cash.
- On May 15, 1981, Farrell sold all of its treasury stock for $25,000 cash.
- On June 1, 1981, individuals holding $50,000 face value of Farrell's bonds exercised their conversion privilege. Each of the 50 bonds was converted into 40 shares of Farrell's common stock.
- On July 1, 1981, Farrell purchased equipment for $63,000 cash.
- On December 31, 1981, land with a fair market value of $150,000 was purchased through the issuance of a long-term note in the amount of $150,000. The note bears interest at the rate of 15% and is due on December 31, 1986.
- Deferred income taxes represent timing differences relating to the use of accelerated depreciation methods for income tax reporting and the straight-line method for financial statement reporting.

Required:

Using the cash basis approach (funds defined as cash), prepare a statement of changes in financial position of Farrell Corporation for the year ended December 31, 1981.

Problem 8 Statement of Changes (1180,Q4)

(45 to 55 minutes)

Presented below are comparative statements of financial position of Kenwood Corporation as of December 31, 1979, and December 31, 1978, respectively.

Kenwood Corporation
Statement of Financial Position

	December 31, 1979	December 31, 1978	Increase (decrease)
Assets:			
Current assets:			
Cash	$ 100,000	$ 90,000	$ 10,000
Accounts receivable (net of allowance for uncollectible accounts of $10,000 and $8,000, respectively)	210,000	140,000	70,000
Inventories	260,000	220,000	40,000
Total current assets	570,000	450,000	120,000
Land	325,000	200,000	125,000
Plant and equipment	580,000	633,000	(53,000)
Less: accumulated depreciation	(90,000)	(100,000)	10,000
Patents	30,000	33,000	(3,000)
Total assets	$1,415,000	$1,216,000	$199,000

	December 31, 1979	December 31, 1978	Increase (decrease)
Liabilities and shareholders' equity:			
Liabilities:			
Current liabilities:			
Accounts payable	$ 260,000	$ 200,000	$ 60,000
Accrued expenses	200,000	210,000	(10,000)
Total current liabilities	460,000	410,000	50,000
Deferred income taxes	140,000	100,000	40,000
Long-term bonds (due December 15, 1990)	130,000	180,000	(50,000)
Total liabilities	730,000	690,000	40,000
Shareholders' equity:			
Common stock, par value $5, authorized 100,000 shares, issued and outstanding 50,000 and 42,000 shares, respectively	250,000	210,000	40,000
Additional paid-in capital	233,000	170,000	63,000
Retained earnings	202,000	146,000	56,000
Total shareholders' equity	685,000	526,000	159,000
Total liabilities and shareholders' equity	$1,415,000	$1,216,000	$199,000

Presented below is the income statement of Kenwood Corporation for the year ended December 31, 1979.

Kenwood Corporation
Income Statement
For the Year Ended December 31, 1979

Sales	$1,000,000
Expenses:	
Cost of sales	560,000
Salary and wages	190,000
Depreciation	20,000
Amortization	3,000
Loss on sale of equipment	4,000
Interest	16,000
Miscellaneous	8,000
Total expenses	801,000
Income before income taxes and extraordinary item	199,000
Income taxes	
Current	50,000
Deferred	40,000
Provision for income taxes	90,000
Income before extraordinary item	109,000
Extraordinary item—gain on repurchase of long-term bonds (net of $10,000 income tax)	12,000
Net income	$ 121,000
Earnings per share:	
Income before extraordinary item	$2.21
Extraordinary item	.24
Net income	$2.45

Additional information:

- On February 2, 1979, Kenwood issued a 10% stock dividend to shareholders of record on January 15, 1979. The market price per share of the common stock on February 2, 1979, was $15.
- On March 1, 1979, Kenwood issued 3,800 shares of common stock for land. The common stock and land had current market values of approximately $40,000 on March 1, 1979.
- On April 15, 1979, Kenwood repurchased long-term bonds with a face value of $50,000. The gain of $22,000 was reported as an extraordinary item on the income statement.
- On June 30, 1979, Kenwood sold equipment costing $53,000, with a book value of $23,000, for $19,000 cash.
- On September 30, 1979, Kenwood declared and paid a $0.04 per share cash dividend to shareholders of record August 1, 1979.
- On October 10, 1979, Kenwood purchased land for $85,000 cash.
- Deferred income taxes represent timing differences relating to the use of accelerated depreciation methods for income tax reporting and straight-line depreciation methods for financial statement reporting.

Required:

Using the working-capital concept of funds, prepare a statement of changes in financial position of Kenwood Corporation for the year ended December 31, 1979. (Do not prepare a schedule of changes in working capital.)

Problem 9 Allowance for Doubtful Accounts (583,P4a)

(25 to 30 minutes)

Part a. From inception of operations to December 31, 1981, Harris Corporation provided for uncollectible accounts receivable under the allowance method: provisions were made monthly at 2% of credit sales; bad debts written off were charged to the allowance account; recoveries of bad debts previously written off were credited to the allowance account; and, no year-end adjustments to the allowance account were made. Harris's usual credit terms are net 30 days.

The balance in the allowance for doubtful accounts was $130,000 at January 1, 1982. During 1982 credit sales totaled $9,000,000, interim provisions for doubtful accounts were made at 2% of credit sales, $90,000 of bad debts were written off, and recoveries of accounts previously written off amounted to $15,000. Harris installed a computer facility in November 1982 and an aging of accounts receivable was prepared for the first time as of December 31, 1982. A summary of the aging is as follows:

Classification by month of sale	*Balance in each category*	*Estimated % uncollectible*
Nov-Dec 1982	$1,140,000	2%
Jul-Oct	600,000	10
Jan-June	400,000	25
Prior to 1/1/82	130,000	75
	$2,270,000	

Based on the review of collectibility of the account balances in the "prior to 1/1/82" aging category, additional receivables totaling $60,000 were written off as of December 31, 1982. Effective with the year ended December 31, 1982, Harris adopted a new accounting method for estimating the allowance for doubtful accounts at the amount indicated by the year-end aging analysis of accounts receivable.

Required:

1. Prepare a schedule analyzing the changes in the allowance for doubtful accounts for the year ended December 31, 1982. Show supporting computations in good form.

2. Prepare the journal entry for the year-end adjustment to the allowance for doubtful accounts balance as of December 31, 1982.

Multiple Choice Answers

1. b	14. a	27. b	40. a	53. d
2. c	15. b	28. d	41. d	54. b
3. c	16. d	29. d	42. c	55. b
4. b	17. b	30. c	43. d	56. b
5. d	18. a	31. a	44. b	57. a
6. d	19. c	32. b	45. a	58. b
7. b	20. c	33. d	46. c	59. a
8. c	21. b	34. c	47. c	60. c
9. a	22. c	35. a	48. d	61. b
10. c	23. a	36. c	49. d	62. c
11. a	24. d	37. d	50. c	63. b
12. d	25. d	38. d	51. c	64. b
13. d	26. b	39. a	52. d	

Multiple Choice Answer Explanations

A. Bank Reconciliations

1. (583,P1,20) (b) The requirement is the total amount to be reported as cash in the 12/31/82 balance sheet. To be reported as cash, a cash item must be readily available for current needs, with no legal restrictions limiting its use. Cash in banks ($1,500,000) and petty cash ($20,000) both qualify as cash. The compensating balances ($500,000) included in cash in banks are not legally restricted, so inclusion of these amounts in cash is appropriate. The cash legally restricted for additions to plant ($2,000,000) would be classified as an investment on the 12/31/82 balance sheet.

2. (582,P1,6) (c) The requirement is the correct balance of cash at 3/31/82. The balance per bank statement ($36,050) must be adjusted to reflect corrections as of 3/31/82 not yet recorded by the bank and the items which have not reached the bank.

Balance per bank		$36,050
Add: Deposit in transit		6,250
		42,300
Deduct: Outstanding checks	$5,750	
Bank error	250	(6,000)
Correct balance		$36,300

The bank service charges ($50) would be an adjustment to balance per **books**; it has already been recorded in the bank's records.

3. (1181,Q1,2) (c) The requirement is the proper amount to be shown as cash at year end. To be classified as cash, resources must be readily available for the payment of current obligations and must be free from any restrictions that limit its use in satisfying debts. In this situation the $1,000 postdated check should be classified as a receivable. The $200 NSF check should be subtracted from the checkbook balance and classified as a receivable. The $75 of postage stamps should be included in office supplies inventory. Since the company still maintains physical control of the $500 drawn against the checking account it should be added back to the cash balance.

Checkbook balance	$4,000
Add: Check drawn but not mailed	+ 500
Less: NSF check	− 200
Corrected cash balance	$4,300

D. Receivables

4. (1183,P2,21) (b) The requirement is the net realizable value (NRV) of accounts receivable. The NRV of accounts receivable is the gross amount of receivables less the estimated uncollectible accounts. In this case, the accounts receivable balance ($1,200,000) must be reduced by the estimated uncollectible accounts ($106,000), leaving a NRV of $1,094,000.

5. (583,T1,11) (d) The requirement is the account to be reported on the balance sheet in connection with interest on a note receivable. Under the accrual basis of accounting, revenues should be recognized when earned, regardless of when the cash is received. The portion of interest earned from July 1 to December 31 should be accrued at the end of the year. The journal entry to be made on December 31 is:

Interest receivable	XXX	
Interest revenue		XXX

Answer (a) is incorrect because the portion of the interest pertaining to next year has not yet been received, thus no deferral is possible. Answer (b) is incorrect because interest earned this year is owed to the company; therefore, a receivable is reported. Since the interest applicable from January 1 to June 30 has not yet been earned [answer (c)], no revenue may be recognized.

F. Bad Debts Expense

6. (1182,P1,3) (d) The requirement is the amount by which previously accrued bad debt expense should be increased at year-end. The solutions approach is to prepare a T-account for the allowance for doubtful accounts.

	Allowance for D.A.		
Accounts written off	$22,000	$ 8,000	12/31/80 balance
		40,000	BD exp. accrued (2,000,000 x 2%)
		26,000	12/31/81 bal. before adjustment
		16,000	Adjustment at year end
		$42,000	Required year-end balance

The allowance account must be increased by $16,000, from $26,000 to $42,000.

7. (1176,Q1,8) (b) The requirement is gross sales. Add cash sales of $30,000, credit sales of $35,000, the accounts written off of $1,000 and subtract the decrease in receivables of $6,000. The decrease in receivables must be considered a reduction in sales, because $6,000 of the $35,000 were not sales of this period but rather collections of sales of a previous period. The $1,000 written off was sold and is part of gross sales even though not collectible.

Cash sales	$30,000
Charge sales	+35,000
AR decrease	– 6,000
AR writeoff	+ 1,000
Gross sales	$60,000

8. (583,T1,12) (c) The requirement is the method of estimating bad debts under the allowance method which focuses on the income statement. Estimating bad debts based on credit sales of the period is the income statement approach in that bad debts are treated as a function of sales. Estimating bad debts on the basis of accounts receivable [answers (b) and (d)] focuses on the balance sheet by treating bad debts as a function of the age of or balance in accounts receivable at year end. Answer (a) is not a method which estimates bad debts but rather an alternative to the estimation methods. Under the direct write-off method, bad debts are considered an expense in the period in which they are written off. This method is not in accordance with GAAP.

H. Discounting Notes Receivable

9. (1183,P2,22) (a) The requirement is the net amount of interest revenue to be recognized from a discounted note receivable. The $20,000 note has a maturity value of $20,600 [$20,000 + ($20,000 x 12% x 90/360)]. When Anderson discounts the note at the bank, they will receive the maturity value less a $515 discount ($20,600 x 15% x 60/360). Therefore, Anderson's proceeds from the transaction are $20,085 ($20,600 – $515). The net interest revenue from the note is the excess of the proceeds ($20,085) over the face value ($20,000), or $85.

10. (1183,P2,24) (c) The requirement is the effective rate of interest on a discounted note payable. The discount rate is 20% on a 180 day, $100,000 note. This results in a $10,000 discount ($100,000 x 20% x 180/360) and $90,000 proceeds ($100,000 – $10,000) for Dean Company. Since Dean must repay the face amount of $100,000, they are effectively borrowing $90,000 and paying $10,000 interest. The effective interest rate can be computed as follows:

$90,000 x I x 180/360 = $10,000

Solving for I, the equation becomes:

I = $10,000/$90,000 x 360/180,
I = 11.1% x 2,
I = 22.2%.

11. (1183,T1,7) (a) The requirement is to determine cash proceeds. The maturity value (face value plus interest due at maturity) of the note less the bank's discount yields the cash proceeds of the note. Answer (b) is incorrect by definition. Answers (c) and (d) are incorrect because they attempt a solution using the face value of the note and ignore the interest due on the note at maturity.

I. Short-Term Investments

12. (1180,P1,13) (d) The requirement is the amount which should be recorded as a loss in Wayne, Inc.'s income statement from an other than temporary decline in the market value of a noncurrent marketable equity security. Per para 21 of SFAS 12, the loss realized in this situation is measured as the difference between their cost and market value on the balance sheet date.

1/10/79	Cost 5,000 shares x $60 =	$300,000
12/31/79	Market value 5,000 shares x $46 =	230,000
Realized loss to be recognized		$ 70,000

13. (1181,T1,16) (d) Investments in marketable equity securities are typically carried on the balance sheet at lower of aggregate cost or market (LCM). Answer (a) is incorrect because both long term and short term portfolios are carried at LCM. Answer (b) is wrong because the aggregate cost of the portfolios is

compared to the aggregate market as if all the securities were one unit. Answer (c) is incorrect because the market value must be less than historical cost for the portfolios to be written down to market value.

J. Marketable Equity Securities

14. (583,P1,2) (a) The requirement is the amount of unrealized loss on a long-term investment in marketable equity securities (MES) to be reported in income statement. The amount of the unrealized loss is the deficiency of portfolio market value below portfolio cost ($150,000 – $141,000, or $9,000). However, per para 11 of SFAS 12, unrealized losses on **long-term** investments in MES are subtracted separately in the equity section of the balance sheet; such losses do not flow through the income statement. Unrealized losses on **short-term** investments in MES are included in the determination of net income.

15. (583,Q1,10) (b) The requirement is to determine how much should be reported on the December 31, 1982, balance sheet for marketable equity securities. SFAS 12, para 13 indicates that an enterprise's financial statements shall not be adjusted for changes in market prices with respect to marketable equity securities when such changes occur after the date of the financial statements but prior to their issuance. Thus, the market value at 12/31/82 of $400,000 is reported for marketable equity securities because it is lower than the $500,000 cost of the marketable equity securities.

16. (1183,T1,5) (d) The requirement is the proper valuation of a marketable security transferred between current and noncurrent portfolios. When there is a change in the classification of a marketable equity security between current and noncurrent, the security should be transferred between the corresponding portfolios at the lower of its cost or market value at the date of the transfer. If the market value is lower than cost, the market value becomes the new cost basis, and the difference is accounted for in the current year's determination of net income as a realized loss (SFAS 12, para 10). Answer (a) is incorrect because it does not properly employ the lower of cost or market concept. Answers (b) and (c) are incorrect because they ignore the lower of cost or market concept.

17. (583,T1,8) (b) The requirement is the classification of the allowance account for a long-term marketable equity securities portfolio. The accounting for marketable equity securities depends upon the securities' balance sheet classification. Classification as a current or noncurrent asset is based upon management's intent for holding the securities. SFAS 12, para 8 requires that the amount by which the aggregate cost of the noncurrent portfolio exceeds the market value should be carried in a valuation allowance account. The entry to record the decline in market value would be as follows:

Net unrealized loss on noncurrent market equity securities	XXX	
Allowance for excess of cost of long-term equity securities over market value		XXX

When the securities are classified as **long-term**, the debit is a separate reduction of stockholders' equity in the equity section of the balance sheet. The credit is recorded as a contra asset account to long-term investments in marketable equity securities, which is carried in the noncurrent asset section of the balance sheet [answer (b)]. Answer (d) is incorrect because only changes in the valuation account for **current** marketable equity securities are carried to the income statement.

L. Current Liabilities

18. (1182,P1,19) (a) The requirement is the amount of loss to be accrued in 1981 as the result of a contingent lawsuit. SFAS 5 states that an estimated loss from a loss contingency should be accrued only if it is probable that a liability exists at the balance sheet date and if the loss is reasonably estimable. According to guidelines set forth in FASB Interpretation 14, an estimate of the range of the loss meets the "reasonably estimable" criteria. Therefore, this contingency is reasonably estimable. However, this item does not meet the "probable" criteria since it is only reasonably possible that Stillman will win the lawsuit. SFAS 5 indicates that a future event is reasonably possible if it is more than remote but **less than probable**. However, since the reasonably possible criterion is met, footnote disclosure is required. Note that if this contingency was probable, a loss of $100,000 would be accrued, and the range of $100,000 to $400,000 would be disclosed.

19. (583,Q1,8) (c) The requirement is to determine the contingent liability, if any, which Dean should report on its 12/31/82 balance sheet. The criteria for accruing a loss contingency are met; it is probable that a liability has been incurred and the amount of the loss can be reasonably estimated (SFAS 5, para 8). A range of the amount of the loss is sufficient to meet the "subject to reasonable estimation" criteria of SFAS 5, and when one amount in the range is a better estimate, use it (FASB Interpretation 14, para 3). Since $600,000

is the best estimate, a contingent liability in that amount should be reported on its 12/31/82 balance sheet.

20. (1182,Q1,15) (c) The requirement is to determine the amount that should appear on the balance sheet as a contingent liability. SFAS 5, para 8 states that an estimated loss from a contingency should be accrued by charging income and crediting a liability only if it is probable (future event likely to occur) that a liability had been incurred at the date of the financial statements **and** the amount of the loss can be reasonably estimated. This problem indicates the liability suit will probably be settled for $75,000. However, the contingent liability is limited to the $50,000 deductible that the company must pay.

21. (1183,T1,18) (b) A loss contingency must be accrued when the event occurred on or before the date of the financial statements and the amount of the loss can be reasonably estimated. It does not matter that the company did not become aware of the existence or possibility of the contingency until after the date of the financial statements (SFAS 5, para 8). Answer (a) is incorrect because disclosure, as opposed to accrual, is required for events occurring **subsequent** to the financial statement date. Answer (c) is incorrect because a contingency must be either accrued or disclosed, depending upon the time frame, when an event is both probable and reasonably estimable. Answer (d) is incorrect because losses shall not be charged to an appropriation of retained earnings.

22. (582,T1,40) (c) SFAS 5, para 8 requires accrual of a loss contingency only if **both** of the following conditions are met: (1) the future losses are probable and (2) the loss amount can be reasonably estimated. Loss contingencies that do not meet one or both of these criteria, but that are at least reasonably possible should be disclosed, but not accrued. Loss contingencies that have only a remote possibility of occurrence are generally not disclosed.

23. (581,T1,36) (a) The requirement is to identify the point at which gain contingencies are usually recognized in the income statement. "Contingency" designates a claim or right whose existence is uncertain but which may become valid property rights eventually. Accountants have adopted a conservative policy in the area of gain contingencies. Accordingly, the following provision of para 3 of ARB 50 shall be applicable. It states that gain contingencies are not reflected in the accounts since to do so might be to recognize revenue prior to its realization.

M. Examples of Current Liabilities

24. (1183,P2,39) (d) The requirement is the president's bonus under an incentive compensation plan. The bonus is equal to 10% of income in excess of $100,000 after deducting the bonus. Since income was $430,000, income in excess of $100,000 is $330,000. The solutions approach is to set up and solve an equation.

$$
\begin{aligned}
B &= .10\ (\$430{,}000 - \$100{,}000 - B) \\
B &= .10\ (\$330{,}000 - B) \\
B &= \$33{,}000 - .10B \\
1.10B &= \$33{,}000 \\
B &= \$30{,}000
\end{aligned}
$$

25. (583,P1,7) (d) The requirement is the total amount to be reported as the liability for compensated absences at 12/31/82. Per para 6 of SFAS 43, a liability for compensated absences should be accrued if the obligation is attributable to employees' services already rendered, the obligation relates to rights which vest or accumulate, payment is probable, and the amount is reasonably estimable. All four conditions are met. Since the definition of compensated absences in para 1 of SFAS 43 includes vacation, illness, and holidays, both the vacation pay ($100,000) and holiday pay ($25,000) should be accrued.

26. (583,P1,10) (b) The requirement is the amount to be reported as the liability for stamp redemptions at 12/31/82. The solutions approach is to set up a T-account for this liability. The increase in the liability is based on the amount of trading stamps sold during the year. $10,000,000 of stamps were sold, but only 90% are expected to be redeemed, bringing the expected redemptions at sales prices down to $9,000,000. This amount must be converted to the estimated cost of future redemption by multiplying by the cost percentage of 60%. Therefore, the credit to the liability account is 60% of $9,000,000, or $5,400,000.

	Liability		
		18,000,000	12/31/81
Redemptions	8,500,000	5,400,000	Increase
		14,900,000	12/31/82

27. (1182,P1,7) (b) The requirement is the estimated liability for premium claims outstanding at 12/31/81. Only 60% of the 1,600,000 coupons, or 960,000 coupons, are expected to be redeemed. Since 400,000 coupons have already been redeemed, a liability exists for 560,000 more coupons. Five coupons are required per premium, so 112,000 premiums

(560,000 ÷ 5) are expected to be used at a cost of $1 each. This results in a liability of $112,000.

28. (581,P1,3) (d) The requirement is the amount to be reported as a warranty liability at 12/31/80. The solutions approach is to prepare a T-account for the liability. The liability is credited for total estimated warranty expense, which is 12% of 1978-80 sales. The liability is debited when actual warranty expenditures are made. Since the expenditures made are less than the total estimated expense to date, a credit balance of $105,000 results.

Warranty Liability	
	(12%)($1,400,000)
Expenditures $ 63,000	$168,000 Estimated expense
	$105,000 End. bal.

29. (581,Q2,31) (d) The requirement is the total amount of Royal's short-term obligations that may properly be excluded from current liabilities at 12/31/80. Per SFAS 6, an enterprise may exclude a short-term obligation from current liabilities only if (1) it **intends** to refinance the obligation on a long-term basis and (2) it demonstrates an **ability** to consummate the refinancing. The $50,000 current installment of the 14% debentures qualify for exclusion because those debentures were actually refinanced on a long-term basis. When a financing agreement is used to provide evidence of ability to consummate, the agreement must: be noncancellable; be long-term; and, possess readily determinable terms. In addition, the company must not be in violation of the agreement, and both the lender and investor must be financially capable of honoring the agreement. Since all these requirements are met by the described financing agreement, the $30,000 note payable may also be excluded from current liabilities.

30. (581,Q2,32) (c) Refer to the discussion of the previous question. Since the financing agreement is no longer noncancellable, the $30,000 note payable may not be excluded from current liabilities. However, the $50,000 current installment of the 14% debentures may be excluded as discussed in the previous question.

31. (1183,T1,26) (a) Vested rights are those which are not contingent on an employee's future service; the employer has an obligation to make payment even if an employee terminates (SFAS 43, footnote 1). Thus, answer (a) is correct. Accumulated rights, answer (b), are **earned** but unused rights which may be carried forward to future periods, but are contingent upon the employee's future service. Answer (c), contingent rights, is incorrect because such rights are totally dependent on the future actions of the parties involved and are not the result of past service. Answer (d), estimable rights, is a nonsensical term.

32. (583,T1,21) (b) The requirement is the classification of a deposit received from a customer. The revenue realization principle provides that revenue is realized when the earnings process is virtually complete and an exchange has occurred. Although an exchange has occurred, the earnings process has not been completed since the deposit relates to future services. The deposit is, therefore, unearned and considered a liability because it represents an obligation to perform services in the future. Answer (a) is incorrect because revenue may not be recognized until the earnings process has been completed. Answer (c) is incorrect because the allowance for doubtful accounts is used to estimate uncollectible amounts for performed services. Answer (d) is incorrect because the net realizable value of accounts receivable would be understated, and the obligation to perform future services would not be disclosed.

N. Statement of Changes in Financial Position (APB 19), and Section O.–Q.

33. (1181,P1,18) (d) The requirement is total sources of funds to be disclosed on the statement of changes in financial position. It must be assumed that the statement is prepared on a working capital basis since the information given includes working capital provided by operations. Both working capital provided by operations ($1,500,000) and proceeds from sale of equipment ($400,000) are sources of working capital. Also, under the all-financial-resources concept, issuance of mortgage payable to acquire land and building ($1,800,000) and issuance of common stock to retire preferred stock ($500,000) are reported as both sources and uses on the statement. Thus, total sources of funds on the statement of changes in financial position is $4,200,000 ($1,500,000 + 400,000 + 1,800,000 + 500,000).

The "Sources" section of a Statement of Changes in Financial Position would appear as follows:

Sources	
From operations	$1,500,000
Proceeds from sale of equipment	400,000
Issuance of mortgage payable	1,800,000
Common stock issued	500,000
Total sources	$4,200,000

34. (1181,P1,20) (c) The requirement is to compute the amount of working capital provided from operations for 1980. The solutions approach is to begin with net income ($4,000,000) and adjust for those items which affected net income but did not affect working capital. Both depreciation on fixed assets and the provision for doubtful accounts on **long-term** receivables are expenses which decrease net income, but do not involve a decrease or outflow of working capital. The provision for doubtful accounts on short-term receivables decrease net income, but also decreases working capital in the form of net accounts receivable. Therefore, it should not be added back to net income. Dividends on preferred stock do not affect reported net income at all. Dividends are a distribution of income which is reported as a use of funds on the statement of changes in financial position. Therefore, working capital provided by operations is $6,300,000.

Net income		$4,000,000
Add:		
Depreciation	$2,000,000	
Provision for doubtful accounts on long-term receivables	300,000	2,300,000
		$6,300,000

35. (581,P1,10) (a) The requirement is Roger's working capital at 12/31/80. The solutions approach is to visualize a working capital T-account.

Working Capital	
Beginning balance + Sources	– Uses
Ending balance	

Note that the proceeds from and payments on **short-term** borrowings do not affect the amount of working capital because in both transactions, only current accounts (cash and short-term debt) are involved. The remaining items must be identified as sources or uses and placed in the T-account described above.

	Working Capital		
Beginning balance	$10,000,000		
Sources:			Uses:
From operations	1,700,000	$3,000,000	Cap. expenditures
From LT borrowing	2,000,000	600,000	LT debt payments
From iss. C.S.	1,400,000	800,000	Dividends
Ending balance	$10,700,000		

36. (1181,Q1,18) (c) The requirement is the date when the declaration of a cash dividend affects working capital. The solutions approach is to make the journal entry to record the cash dividend

1/17/81	Dividends declared (Retained earnings)	10,000	
	Dividends payable		10,000

Note that dividends first become liabilities when they are declared by the Board of Directors. Therefore, working capital would decrease $10,000 on January 17 when the liability is established.

37. (581,Q2,29) (d) The requirement is the amount of working capital provided by operations in 1980. Working capital provided by operations is net income adjusted for any revenues or expenses which do not provide or use working capital. Since the deficit was affected only by net income, the $140,000 decrease in the retained earnings deficit is the 1980 net income. The next step is to examine the comparative balance sheets and additional information to locate any net income adjustments. There are three such items: depreciation expense (computed below), goodwill amortization ($500,000 – $480,000 = $20,000) and bond discount amortization ($20,000 – $12,000 = $8,000). Note that no part of the $8,000 reduction in the bond discount account relates to the bonds extinguished, since the face and book value of these bonds were the same.

In order to determine the amount of depreciation expense, both the equipment and accumulated depreciation accounts have to be analyzed. The equipment T-account analysis reveals that the cost of equipment sold was $120,000.

	Equipment		
12/31/79	$1,200,000		
Purchase	$ 150,000	?	Sale
12/31/80	$1,230,000		

The equipment sold had a book value of $76,000; if it originally cost $120,000, the accumulated depreciation at the time of sale was $44,000. The accumulated depreciation T-account below indicates that 1980 depreciation expense is $60,000.

	Accumulated Deprec.		
		$420,000	12/31/79
Sale	$44,000	?	Deprec. exp.
		$436,000	12/31/80

The working capital provided by operations is computed below. Because all three adjustments are expenses which do not involve an outflow of working capital, they are added back to net income.

Net income	$140,000
Add back:	
Deprec. exp.	60,000
Goodwill amort.	20,000
Bond discount amort.	8,000
Working capital provided by operations	$228,000

38. (581,Q2,30) (d) The requirement is the change in working capital, assuming that $200,000 face value of bonds became current at 12/31/80. The solutions approach is to prepare a schedule of changes in working capital based on the balance sheets given, and subtract the decrease in working capital caused by reclassification of the bonds payable as a current liability.

	12/31/80	*12/31/79*	*Change in working capital*
Current Assets	$ 474,000	$ 320,000	$ 154,000
Current Liab.	$(360,000)	$(160,000)	$(200,000)
	$ 114,000	$ 160,000	

Change in WC before bond reclassification	$(46,000)
Bond reclassification	$(200,000)
Decrease in working capital	$(246,000)

Note that it must be assumed that none of the unamortized bond discount relates to the bonds reclassified, or the answer would not match any of the four choices given.

39. (1183,T1,30) (a) The requirement is the effect of converting nonparticipating preferred stock into common stock on the statement of changes in financial position. This statement, per APB 19, para 6, should disclose separately the financing and investing aspects of all significant transactions that affect financial position during a period. These transactions include certain financing and investing activities which do not affect either cash or working capital. Converting preferred stock into common stock, answer (a), is an example of such a transaction mentioned in APB 19, para 14C, which should be clearly disclosed. In this case, the redemption of the preferred stock would be considered a use of funds and the issuance of the common stock would be a source of funds. Note the net effect is zero, as the source and use offset each other.

40. (583,T1,38) (a) The requirement is the treatment of a gain on a sale of a long-term investment on the statement of changes in financial position. The statement begins with income (loss) from operations in the financial resources provided section of the statement. Deducted from this figure are items which increase income but do not increase working capital (APB 19, para 10). Gains on sales of assets increase net income, but do not measure the total amount of cash or working capital provided by the sale. The gain is subtracted (eliminated) from income from operations with the entire proceeds from the sale shown as a separate source of cash or working capital. Answer (b) is incorrect as this is the required treatment for a **loss** on the sale of an asset. Answers (c) and (d) are incorrect as the sale of long-term investments is strictly a source of funds; it does not use or apply funds.

41. (583,T1,39) (d) The requirement is for the proper presentation of the retirement of long-term debt by issuance of common stock in a statement of changes in financial position. Per APB 19, para 14, other significant financing and investing activities which have no effect on working capital should be clearly disclosed; this is known as the all financial resources concept. One of these activities is the conversion of long-term debt to common stock. Such issuance and retirement can be viewed as two separate, concurrent transactions. First, the common stock is treated as if it were sold for cash (i.e., a source of funds). Next, the proceeds from the above "sale" are immediately used to repurchase the outstanding bonds (i.e., a use of funds). These items would be disclosed as "other financing/investing activities having no effect on working capital (cash)" in a special section after the other sources/uses of working capital (cash) section.

42. (580,T1,16) (c) Para 7, APB 19, requires that when a balance sheet, income statement and statement of retained earnings are issued, a statement of changes in financial position must be presented for each period for which an income statement is presented. Answers (a), (b), and (d) all contradict the requirement of APB 19.

43. (580,T1,18) (d) The requirement is whether or not cash and/or quick assets are/is an acceptable format for the statement of changes in financial position. Para 11 of APB 19 permits both of these formats.

44. (580,T1,20) (b) Para 12 of APB 19 requires the disclosure of net changes in each element of working capital for at least the current period either in the statement of changes in financial position or in a related tabulation.

R. Cash Format

45. (1176,P2,35) (a) Estimated cash receipts for December are the sales figure of $350,000 less bad debts of $3,500 less the $10,000 increase in accounts receivable.

CR	
$350,000	Sales
– 3,500	Bad debts
– 10,000	Increase in AR
$336,500	

46. (1176,P2,36) (c) The estimated cash disbursements for December are 70% (1.00 – GP%) of the $350,000 of sales, plus $5,000 of inventory increase, plus SG&A of $64,500. The $64,500 of SG&A consists of $35,500 plus 15% of sales, totalling $88,000 adjusted for noncash items of $20,000 depreciation and $3,500 of bad debts.

CD		*SG&A*	
$350,000		$35,500	Fixed
70%		52,500	Variable
$245,000		– 20,000	Depreciation
+ 5,000	Inventory incr.	– 3,500	Bad debts
+ 64,500	SG&A	$64,500	
$314,500			

47. (581,Q2,25) (c) The requirement is cash collected during 1980 from accounts receivable. The solutions approach is to prepare a T-account for accounts receivable. The allowance account has no effect on this analysis, because the problem states that the balance in this account has not changed and no accounts receivable were written off. Net credit sales are the only debit to accounts receivable because all accounts receivable relate to trade merchandise. In the T-account below, you must solve for the missing credit to determine that $6,140,000 was collected on account during 1980.

	AR—Net		
12/31/79 balance	$ 580,000		1980
1980 Net Credit Sales	6,400,000	?	Collections
12/31/80 balance	$ 840,000		

Author's Note: Based on the information given in this problem, no bad debt expense was recorded during 1980. However, unrealistic as this assumption might be, it is important to simply work with the information as given.

48. (581,Q2,26) (d) The requirement is cash payments during 1980 on accounts payable. The solutions approach is to visualize the accounts payable T-account.

	Accounts Payable		
		$440,000	12/31/79
Payments	?	?	Purchases
		$530,000	12/31/80

It is apparent that in order to determine payments to suppliers, purchases of trade merchandise must first be computed. The cost of goods sold statement can be used to compute purchases.

Beginning Inventory		$ 420,000
+ Purchases	+	?
– Ending Inventory	–	660,000
Cost of Goods Sold		$5,000,000

Purchases = $5,000,000 – ($420,000 – $660,000)
= $5,240,000

Finally, the purchases are entered into the accounts payable T-account, and payments to suppliers of $5,150,000 can be plugged in.

	Accounts Payable		
		$ 440,000	12/31/79
Payments	5,150,000	5,240,000	Purchases
		$ 530,000	12/31/80

49. (581,Q2,27) (d) The requirement is cash receipts during 1980 which were not provided by operations. In solving the 2 remaining items, the solutions approach is to work through the comparative balance sheets noting increases and decreases; the additional information given must be considered in connection with these changes. These cash receipts include proceeds from long-term borrowing, and issuance of capital stock.

Proceeds from long-term note	$500,000
Proceeds from issuance of common stock	$300,000
	$800,000

50. (581,Q2,28) (c) The requirement is cash payments for noncurrent assets purchased during 1980. The two noncurrent assets shown on the balance sheet (long-term investments and land, building, and fixtures) have increased from 12/31/79 to 12/31/80, indicating cash purchases since the additional information does not suggest any other means of acquisition. Therefore, cash payments include $80,000 for long-term investments and $530,000 ($1,130,000 – $600,000) for land, building and fixtures.

Other

51. (1179,P1,18) (c) The requirement is the increase in working capital as a result of a series of transactions. The solutions approach is to identify the transactions affecting working capital. Proceeds from short-term borrowings do not affect working capital because both current assets and current liabilities are increased. Proceeds from long-term borrowings increase working capital because current assets are increased. Noncurrent liabilities are also increased but do not affect working capital. Purchases of fixed assets decrease working capital as current liabilities are increased or current assets are decreased. Purchases of inventories do not affect working capital because inventory is increased by decreasing current assets and/or increasing current liabilities. Proceeds from sale of common stock increase current assets (stockholders' equity is also increased). Thus, the long-term borrowing, fixed asset purchases, and stock sale transactions affect working capital as detailed below.

1978 Working Capital Changes	
Long-term borrowings	$4,000,000
FA purchases	(3,200,000)
Stock sale	2,000,000
	$2,800,000 increase

52. (577,Q1,12) (d) The requirement is the amount of installment accounts receivable at the end of 1976. The deferred tax credit of the $30,000 exists because installment profit has been reported per books, but not on the tax return. Thus for every dollar of gross profit receivable, there should be $.50 in the deferred tax credit account. Thus the $30,000 credit indicates that there is $60,000 of gross profit in the receivable. Given a 60% gross profit rate, the receivable must equal $100,000.

May 1984 Answers

53. (584,P1,1) (d) The requirement is the amount of loss on marketable equity securities to be included in the income statement. Per SFAS 12, para 11 unrealized losses on **temporary** investments in marketable equity securities are reported in the income statement. The amount of the unrealized loss at 12/31/83 is determined by comparing the total cost and the total market value of the current portfolio which consists of securities W and X. The cost is $60,000 ($24,000 + $36,000) and the market value is $59,000 ($26,000 + $33,000). Therefore, the unrealized loss is $1,000 ($60,000 - $59,000). Additionally, a loss must be recognized on security Y. Para 10 states that when there is reclassification of a marketable equity security between current and noncurrent, the excess of cost over market value is recognized as a realized loss. When Y was reclassified, its cost ($72,000) exceeded its market value ($65,000) by $7,000. This $7,000 loss plus the unrealized loss of $1,000 is reported in the income statement. Therefore, answer (d) is correct.

54. (584,P1,2) (b) The requirement is the amount to be reported as "cash and cash equivalents" on the December 31, 1984, balance sheet. Cash on hand and in banks ($975,000) is included in this amount because it is both unrestricted and readily available. Bank certificates of deposit ($250,000 due on February 1, 1984) are also included even though a possibility exists that redemption prior to maturity may result in some type of penalty, e.g., a reduction of the interest rate. However, this possibility is not sufficient to exclude it. Cash legally restricted for plant additions should be shown in the long-term assets section as an investment. Therefore, answer (b) is correct.

55. (584,P1,19) (b) The requirement is the total amount of sales commissions payable to be accrued on 3/31/84. No sales commissions are due salesperson A because his commissions earned (2% x $100,000 = $2,000) are less than his fixed salary ($2,500). Note that this deficit is not charged against A. Commissions totalling $7,000 are due to salespersons B and C as computed below:

	Commissions earned		*Salary paid*	*Commissions payable*
B	$6,000($200,000 x 3%)	-	3,500	2,500
C	$9,000($300,000 x 3%)	-	4,500	4,500
				$7,000

56. (584,P2,26) (b) The requirement is the amount of additional taxes that should have been charged to income in 1983. As a loss contingency, additional taxes must be accrued when an unfavorable outcome is **probable** and the amount is **reasonably estimable**. Per FASB Interpretation 14, when a range of possible losses exists, the best estimate in the range (in this case, $400,000) is accrued. Since the $450,000 settlement occurred after the statements were issued, this information was not available when the estimate was made.

57. (584,P2,37) (a) The requirement is the amount of 1983 bad debt expense. At 12/31/83, the total accounts receivable is $110,000. Since the net realizable value of the receivables is estimated to be $95,000, the balance in the allowance account must be adjusted to $15,000 (110,000 – $95,000) at year end.

The solutions approach is to set up a T-account for the allowance account.

Allowance for Doubtful Accounts

		16,000	1/1/83
Write-offs	12,000		
		4,000	Balance before adjustment
		11,000	Bad debt expense
		15,000	12/31/83

The account had a balance of $16,000 at 1/1/83 but was reduced to $4,000 when $12,000 of accounts were written off on 9/30/83. Since a year-end balance of $15,000 is required, bad debt expense of $11,000 must be recorded to increase the balance from $4,000 to $15,000.

58. (584,P3,55) (b) The requirement is the amount to be reported as retirement savings plan expense for 1983. The savings plan requires the company to contribute $.50 for every dollar employees deposit up to 5% of their salary. Total employee deposits during 1983 equal $25,000. Total company expense equals $12,500 ($25,000 x .50).

59. (584,P3,58) (a) The requirement is the amount of a contingent gain from a lawsuit to be accrued in 1983. Per SFAS 5, para 17 gain contingencies are not reflected in the accounts since to do so might be to recognize revenue before its realization. Therefore, the amount accrued is $0. Note that even though there was a decision in September of 1983 awarding the company $700,000, the appeal has caused the situation to remain a contingency due to the continued uncertainty.

60. (584,T1,7) (c) The requirement is to determine the correct term for the sale of a note receivable. Discounting occurs when notes receivable are sold to a third party (usually a bank) prior to maturity. Pledging is a term used when one party uses a receivable to act as security for a loan. The receivable pledged serves as collateral in case of default. Thus, answer (c) is correct.

61. (584,T1,8) (b) When the allowance method of recognizing bad debt expense is used, the journal entry is:

Bad debt expense	XXX	
Allowance for bad debts		XXX

The allowance account is a contra account to accounts receivable. Since accounts receivable is a current asset, current assets will be decreased by the contra asset [answer (b)]. Net income is decreased by the bad debt expense; therefore, answers (a) and (d) are incorrect. Answer (c) is incorrect because the allowance account decreases current assets.

62. (584,T1,19) (c) The requirement is to determine when to recognize the occurrence of a contingent gain or loss which is both probable and reasonably estimable on the balance sheet. Per SFAS 5, para 8 a loss contingency is generally recognized on the financial statements when the occurrence of the event giving rise to the contingency is probable and the amount is reasonably estimable. Per para 17, a conservative approach is taken with regard to gain contingencies; generally, they are not recognized until realized. Therefore, answer (c) is the correct answer.

63. (584,T1,30) (b) The requirement is to determine the proper treatment of a loss on the sale of machinery in the statement of changes in financial position. A loss on the sale of machinery is a noncash deduction which reduces income from continuing operations but does not result in a decrease in funds. APB 19, para 10 states that noncash deductions for income from continuing operations should be added back to determine funds provided from operations. Since the loss did not use funds but was subtracted in determining income from operations, it is proper to add it back to income from continuing operations in determining funds from operations. Answer (a) is incorrect because gains are deducted from income from operations. The total proceeds from the sale were a source of funds; the gain that was added to income did not provide any additional funds and, therefore, must be eliminated. Answers (c) and (d) are incorrect because a loss on the sale of an asset is neither a source nor a use of funds.

64. (584,T1,31) (b) The requirement is to determine the appropriate method of presenting a purchase of treasury stock for cash on the statement of changes in financial position. Per APB 19, para 14 transactions which involve an outlay of cash or working capital, such as the purchase of treasury stock, should be reported as a use of funds. The purchase of treasury stock would not be considered source of funds since no funds are provided by the transaction and since it is not considered a significant financing or investing activity under the all financial resources concept.

Answer Outline

Problem 1   Bad Debts

a1. Direct write-off method requires identification of specific uncollectible balances before expense recognition, then

Bad debt expense	XXX	
Accounts receivable		XXX

Allowance method requires estimate of bad debt expense prior to identification of specific bad debts, then

Record estimated bad debts at year end as expense

Bad debt expense	XXX	
Allowance for doubtful accounts		XXX

When specific bad debts are identified, then

Allowance for doubtful accounts	XXX	
Accounts receivable		XXX

No expense recognized when accounts are written off

Two methods of estimating bad debts expense
- As a percentage of accounts receivable at year-end
- As a percentage of sales of the period

a2. Allowance method is preferable
- Credit sale costs are matched with revenue
- Gives proper carrying value of accounts receivable

Direct write-off method is inferior and generally not per GAAP
- May be written off in a period subsequent to sale
- I.e., does not comply with matching concept
- Proper carrying value for accounts receivable not achieved

Unofficial Answer

Problem 1   Bad Debts

1. There are basically two methods of recognizing bad debt expense: (1) direct write-off and (2) allowance.

The direct write-off method requires the identification of specific balances that are deemed to be uncollectible before any bad debt expense is recognized. At the time that a specific account is deemed uncollectible, the account is removed from accounts receivable and a corresponding amount of bad debt expense is recognized. The allowance method requires an estimate of bad debt expense for a period of time by reference to the composition of the accounts receivable balance at a specific point in time (aging) or to the overall experience with credit sales over a period of time. Thus, total bad debt expense expected to arise as a result of operations for a specific period is estimated, the valuation account (allowance for doubtful accounts) is appropriately adjusted, and a corresponding amount of bad debt expense is recognized. As specific accounts are identified as uncollectible, the account is written off; that is, it is removed from accounts receivable and a corresponding amount is removed from the valuation account (allowance for doubtful accounts). Net accounts receivable do not change, and there is no charge to bad debt expense when specific accounts are identified as uncollectible and written off using the allowance method.

2. The allowance method is preferable because it matches the cost of making a credit sale with the revenues generated by the sale in the same period and achieves a proper carrying value for accounts receivable at the end of a period. Since the direct write-off method does not recognize the bad debt expense until a specific amount is deemed uncollectible, which may be in a subsequent period, it does no comply with the matching concept and does not achieve a proper carrying value for accounts receivable at the end of a period.

Answer Outline

Problem 2   Discounting Notes Receivable and Estimating Bad Debts

Part a.

1. Report interest income in periods earned
   - 1981: 6-month accrual, 12/31/81
   - 1982: Cash received for interest on 6/30/82 minus 12/31/81 accrual

   Rationale
   - Accrual basis provides more useful information than cash basis
   - Interest accrues with passage of time
   - Recognize revenue when earned regardless of cash inflow

2. Amount of discount found by
   - First computing maturity value (principal + stated interest) of note and
   - Then computing discount (maturity value x bank discount rate x length of time bank holds note)
   - Accounting would include debit to cash and credit to N/R
     - Debit interest expense or credit interest income for difference between cash proceeds and face value
   - No contingent liability because discount "without recourse"

Part b.

1. Rationale for using allowance method based on credit sales versus using allowance method based on trade A/R balance
   - Allowance method based on credit sales to estimate bad debts rests on matching principle
     - Bad debts result from making credit sales
     - Method emphasizes income statement
   - Allowance method based on balance in trade A/R typically does not associate bad debts expense with period of sale
     - Method emphasizes balance sheet
   - Both methods in accordance with GAAP
2. FS presentation of allowance for bad debts
   - Balance sheet: deduction from trade accounts receivable
   - Income statement: either as operating (selling/general and administrative) expense, financial expense, or deduction from sales

Unofficial Answer

Problem 2 Discounting Notes Receivable and Estimating Bad Debts

Part a.

1. Since Carme is a calendar-year company, six months of interest should be accrued on 12/31/81. The remaining interest income should be recognized on 6/30/81 when the note is collected. The rationale for this treatment is: the accrual basis of accounting provides more useful information than does the cash basis. Therefore, since interest accrues with the passage of time, interest earned on Carme's note receivable should be recognized over the life of the note, regardless of when the cash is received.

2. The amount of the discount is calculated in a two-step process. First, the maturity value of the note is derived by adding the interest to be earned until maturity to the principal. Then, the discount is calculated by multiplying the maturity value times the bank discount rate times the length of time the bank will hold the note (December 31, 1981—June 30, 1982).

The appropriate accounting (by Carme) for the discounting transaction will include a debit to cash for the proceeds from the bank and a credit to notes receivable for the face value of the note. In addition, there will be either a debit to interest expense or a credit to interest income. When the proceeds are less than the face of the note, interest expense is debited, and when the proceeds are greater than the face of the note, interest income is credited. Since this note was discounted "without recourse," the transaction does **not** result in a contingent liability to Carme.

Part b.

1. The use of the allowance method based on credit sales to estimate bad debts is consistent with the matching principle because bad debts arise from and are a function of making credit sales. Therefore, bad debt expense for the current period should be matched with current credit sales. This is an income statement approach because the balance in the allowance for bad debts account is ignored when computing bad debt expense.

The allowance method based on the balance in accounts receivable is not consistent with the matching principle. This method attempts to value accounts receivable at the amount expected to be collected. The method is facilitated by preparing an aging schedule of accounts receivable and plugging bad debt expense with the adjustment necessary to bring the allowance account to the required balance. Alternatively, the ending balance in accounts receivable can be used to determine the required balance in the allowance account without preparing an aging schedule by using a composite percentage. Bad debt expense is then determined in the same manner as when an aging schedule is used. However, neither of these approaches associates bad debt expense with the period of sale, especially for sales made in the last month or two of the period.

2. On the balance sheet, the allowance for bad debts is presented as a contra asset account to accounts receivable with the resulting difference representing the accounts receivable net (i.e., their net realizable value). Bad debt expense would generally be included on Carme's income statement with the other operating (selling/general and administrative) expenses for the period. However, theoretical arguments can be made for (1) reducing sales revenue by the bad debts adjustment in the same manner that sales returns and allowances and trade discounts are considered reductions of the amount to be received from sales of products or (2) classifying the bad debts expense as a financial expense.

Answer Outline

Problem 3 Marketable Equity Securities (SFAS 12)

a1. Current marketable securities
- Provide a return on liquid investments
- Are an investment of idle excess funds

Noncurrent marketable investments
- Provide dividend or interest earnings
- Can provide appreciation of market value
- Can create desirable relationships with suppliers, etc.

a2. Current assets are resources to be converted into cash or sold or consumed
- During the operating cycle, or one year, whichever is longer
- Current securities are readily marketable
  - And intended to be liquidated

Noncurrent securities must also be marketable
- Intended to be held for more than one year

Feasibility of disposal must also be considered

Write-downs to market are
- Recognized in earnings for current marketable securities
- Deferred as part of shareholder's equity for noncurrent securities
  - Unless permanent decline, then recognize loss

b1. Permanent decline in market value of noncurrent security
- Write security down
- Recognize loss in current period
- No write-up for subsequent market value recovery

b2. Nonclassified balance sheet
- All equity securities are considered noncurrent
- Use cost, because aggregate market exceeds cost by $3,000
- Thus, no effect on earnings

b3. Reclassification of noncurrent marketable equity security with market below cost
- Transfer from noncurrent to current
  - Market is new basis if less than cost
  - Difference is loss in current period

b4. Noncurrent marketable equity securities below cost and then above cost
- For noncurrent, market below cost results in debit valuation account in shareholder's equity
- When market increases over cost
  - Valuation account reduced to zero
  - Carrying value cannot exceed cost
  - Thus no effect on earnings

Unofficial Answer

Problem 3 Marketable Equity Securities (SFAS 12)

a. 1. A company invests in marketable equity securities that are classified as current assets primarily to earn interest or dividends on cash used as emergency funds and excess cash being held by the company. Easy and quick access to these funds is a primary requirement for this type of investment, and as a result, these investments must be considered nearly as liquid as cash.

Investments in marketable equity securities that are classified as noncurrent assets are made by a company with the intent to hold them for a period in excess of one operating cycle (or one year if the normal operating cycle is less than one year). While the ultimate reason for a company's investing in noncurrent securities of another company is to improve earnings, this may be accomplished by investing for several specific reasons. The first reason might be for dividends (or interest) paid on the investment. Second, a company may feel that the security will appreciate in market value. Third, the company may desire to assure itself of a satisfactory operating relationship with another company in terms of supply or distribution. None of these reasons requires the immediate liquidity of the investment.

2. The general classification of any asset as being current in nature is that the asset will be converted to cash, sold, or consumed during the normal operating cycle of the business or within one year, if the operating cycle is less than one year. In the case of marketable equity securities classified as current, the above general rule is complied with by meeting the following two requirements: (1) the security must be readily marketable; (2) it must be the intention of management to dispose of the investment within the next succeeding operating cycle or fiscal year if the normal operating cycle is less than one year. Because of this assumed liquidity, it follows that any reduction in market value below original cost should be immediately reflected in earnings, since the original intent was to use the funds as cash within the current operating cycle (or year if the normal operating cycle is less than one year).

Noncurrent assets represent amounts that are not expected to be converted to cash, sold, or consumed within the normal operating cycle of the business (or within one year if the operating cycle is less than one year). While noncurrent marketable equity securities have a ready market, the central point to be considered in classification is the intent of management. Management must have determined that the security is to be held for greater than one cycle (or year, as the case may be) in order for the security to be classified as noncurrent. Because of the intent of management to retain the investment regardless of the current market situation, any reduction in market value below cost, other than a permanent decline, should properly be deferred until such time as management's intent is to liquidate the investment in the current operating cycle (or year, if the normal operating cycle is less than one year).

It can be seen from the foregoing discussion that any given security, if it initially meets the requirements of being readily marketable, can be classified either as current or noncurrent depending on the intent of management. However, the intent of management (presumably related to the company's investment objectives) must be mitigated by the additional factor of feasibility. Management must consider such factors as cash flow or asset stewardship in determining whether or not its intent is feasible under prevailing business conditions.

b. Situation I

If the market value of an equity security declines in value below cost and the decline in value is considered to be other than temporary, a realized loss should be recognized and reflected in the determination of net earnings for the current period. A transaction of this nature reduces the cost basis of the security, and the new cost basis should not be adjusted for subsequent recoveries in market value.

Situation II

In the case of a statement of financial position that does not classify assets and liabilities between current and noncurrent, the entire portfolio of marketable equity securities should be treated as if it were noncurrent in nature. The carrying value of marketable equity securities should be the lower of cost or market value at the date of the statement of financial position. From the facts given, it can be determined that the aggregate market valuation exceeds cost; thus, the carrying value of the portfolio would be at cost. Therefore, there would be no effect on earnings.

Situation III

If there is a change in the classification of a marketable equity security between current and noncurrent, the security shall be transferred between the corresponding portfolios at the lower of its cost or market value at the date of transfer. If the market value is less than cost, the market value shall become the new cost basis, and the difference shall be accounted for as if it were a realized loss and included in the determination of net earnings.

Situation IV

A valuation allowance is created to reflect a net unrealized loss in the aggregate for a given portfolio of securities. In the facts given, the portfolio in question consists of one security that had decreased in value in a prior year and had appreciated to a value in excess of cost in the current period. Since the carrying value of the security is the lower of cost or market, the valuation allowance established in the prior year must be adjusted to zero, resulting in carrying the security at original cost at the end of the current period. Since this is a noncurrent security, the adjustment of the valuation allowance will affect the equity section of the statement of financial position and have no effect on current earnings.

Answer Outline

Problem 4 Loss Contingencies (SFAS 5)

a. Accrual of loss contingency—SFAS 5
 Recognize loss if asset impairment, viability, etc., is probable
  And subject to estimate
 Periodicity
  Write down asset or reflect liability in period event occurs
  Failure to accrue loss will overstate income
 Measurement
  Since timing and magnitude are not exactly known
  Make reasonable estimate of loss contingency
 Objectivity
  Loss estimate by independent parties should be similar
  Loss must be probable before accrual
  Future should confirm existence of the loss

b1. Warranty
 Liability is probable
 Amount is estimable
  Based upon past experience
 Thus the liability and expense should be accrued
  Further disclosure may be necessary

b2. Subsequent event
 No liability incurred during period
 Thus the event should not be accrued
 Use footnote disclosure
 Should include nature and estimate of loss

b3. Self-insurance
 No loss contingency occurred during current period
 Thus no loss should be recorded
 Cannot record amount not paid to insurance company
 Footnote should disclose self-insurance policies

Unofficial Answer

Problem 4 Loss Contingencies (SFAS 5)

a. The two basic requisites for the accrual of a loss contingency (probability of loss and reasonable estimation) are the results of the interaction of several concepts of accounting theory. Three of these concepts are (1) periodicity (time periods), (2) measurement, and (3) objectivity. The first of these concepts relates to the first characteristic of an event necessary before accruing a loss contingency, and the second and third concepts listed relate to the second necessary requirement for the accrual of a loss contingency.

The first requirement that must be satisfied for the accrual of a loss contingency is that at a time prior to the issuance of the financial statements there is an indication that it is probable that an asset has been impaired or a liability has been incurred at the date of the financial statements. A basic objective in the recognition of losses is to record them in the particular period in which they are incurred. With respect to the accrual of a loss contingency, a probable loss should be recognized in the same period in which it resulted in the probable impairment of an asset or the probable incurrence of a liability. The failure to accrue the loss contingency in the period of occurrence will generally overstate earnings initially and understate earnings in future periods.

The second requirement for the accrual of a loss contingency states that the amount of the loss must be reasonably estimable. The concept of measurement requires that the event must be quantifiable in terms of a standard unit of measure (dollars). In the case of a loss contingency related to the period covered in the current financial statements, the exact timing and magnitude of the loss may not be known in advance, but based on past experience or other methods of analysis, a reasonable estimate of the loss contingency can be made. In making the estimate, the probability that a reasonable amount will be determined statistically is enhanced by a large population of accounts from which the probable loss will occur (law of large numbers).

Also related to the reasonable estimation of the probable future loss, the concept of objectivity requires that the estimate be supported by quantitative data. The basis for the estimate must yield essentially the same estimate when computed by different individuals using the available supporting data. The concept of objectivity is supportive of the contention that future events will confirm the occurrence of a loss at the date of the financial statements. Of course the loss must be probable as well as estimable and justified in light of future events.

b. Situation I

When a company sells a product subject to a warranty, it is probable that there will be expenses incurred in future accounting periods relating to revenues recognized in the current period. As such, a liability has been incurred to honor the warranty at the same date as the recognition of the revenue. Based on prior experience or technical analysis, the occurrence of warranty claims can be reasonably estimated and a probable dollar estimate of the liability can be made. The contingent liability for warranties meets both of the requirements for the accrual of a loss contingency, and the estimated amount of the loss should be reflected in the financial statements. In addition to recording the accrual, it may be advisable to disclose the factors used in arriving at the estimate by means of a footnote especially when there is a possibility of a greater loss than was accrued.

Situation II

Even though (1) there is a probable loss on the contract, (2) the amount of the loss can be reasonably estimated and (3) the likelihood of the loss was discovered prior to the issuance of the financial statements, the fact that the contract was entered into subsequent to the date of the financial statements precludes accrual of the loss contingency in financial statements for periods prior to the incurrence of the loss. However, the fact that a material loss has been incurred subsequent to the date of the financial statements but prior to their issuance should be disclosed by means of a footnote in the financial statements. The disclosure should contain the nature of the contingency and an estimate of the amount of the probable loss or a range into which the loss will probably fall.

Situation III

The fact that a company chooses to self-insure the contingency of injury to others caused by its vehicles is not basis enough to accrue a loss contingency that has not occurred at the date of the financial statements. An accrual or "reserve" cannot be made for the amount of insurance premium that would have been paid had a policy been obtained to insure the company against this particular risk. A loss contingency may only be accrued if prior to the date of the financial statements a specific event has occurred that will impair an asset or create a liability and an amount related to that specific occurrence can be reasonably estimated. The fact that the company is self-insuring this risk should be disclosed by means of a footnote to alert the financial statement reader to the exposure created by the lack of insurance.

Answer Outline

Problem 5 Contingencies: Conditions and Disclosures

a1. Conditions necessary to accrue an estimated loss contingency are
 It is probable that an asset has been impaired or a liability incurred at financial statement date, and amount of loss can be reasonably estimated

a2. Disclose unaccrued loss contingencies if reasonable possibility exists that loss may have been incurred
 Disclose loss contingency involving unasserted claim when it is probable that the claim will be asserted, and reasonably possible that the outcome will be unfavorable
 Disclosure should indicate:
  Nature of contingency, and
  Estimate of possible loss, range of loss, or that an estimate connot be made

Unofficial Answer

Problem 5 Contingencies: Conditions and Disclosures

Part a.

1. An estimated loss from a loss contingency shall be accrued by a charge to income if both of the following conditions are met:

- Information available prior to issuance of the financial statements indicates that it is probable that an asset had been impaired or a liability had been incurred at the date of the financial statements. It is implicit in this condition that it must be probable that one or more future events will occur confirming the fact of the loss.
- The amount of loss can be reasonably estimated.

2. Disclosure should be made for an estimated loss from a contingency that need not be accrued by a charge to income when there is at least a reasonable possibility that a loss may have been incurred. The disclosure should indicate the nature of the contingency and should estimate the possible loss or range of loss or state that such an estimate cannot be made.

Disclosure of a loss contingency involving an unasserted claim is required when it is probable that the claim will be asserted and there is a reasonable possibility that the outcome will be unfavorable.

Answer Outline

Problem 6 Statement of Changes

a. All financial resources concept
 Discloses all material financing transactions
 Even those not affecting funds

b. Item disclosed per all financial resources concept
  Acquisition of noncurrent assets with
    Noncurrent debt
    Other noncurrent assets
    Equity securities
  Reduction of long-term debt by
    Other long-term debt
    Issuance of noncurrent assets
    Issuance of equity

c. Treatment per cash concept of funds
  1. Change in accounts receivable is source or use of cash
  2. Change in inventory represents source or use of cash
  3. Depreciation is noncash expense
     Add back to operating earnings
  4. Change in deferred tax credits is source or use of cash
  5. Long-term debt issued for building does not affect cash
     A financing and investing transaction per all financial resources concept
  6. Reduction of current debt is use of cash
  7. Loss on fixed asset sale is added back to income
     Proceeds are a source of cash

Unofficial Answer

Problem 6   Statement of Changes

a. The "all financial resources" concept requires that all material financial transactions be disclosed in the statement of changes in financial position. Transactions that technically do not increase or decrease funds (regardless of the concept of funds employed) but that represent significant financing and investing activities entered into by an entity must also be disclosed within this statement. Disclosure of a significant transaction that does not increase or decrease "funds" is made by showing one side of the transaction as a source of funds and the other side of the transaction as a corresponding use of funds.

b. Opinion 19 of the Accounting Principles Board states that all important changes in financial position should be disclosed. Inasmuch as all changes in financial position with respect to "funds" (i.e., cash, working capital, quick assets, etc.) are disclosed in the normal preparation of the statement, the "all financial resources" concept refers to those transactions that affect financial position but do not increase or decrease "funds." These transactions would include the following:

1. Purchase of noncurrent assets by the issuance of capital stock or long-term debt, or a reduction in another noncurrent asset.
2. Reduction of a long-term liability by the issuance of capital stock or the incurrence of another long-term liability, or a reduction in a noncurrent asset.

c. The effects and procedural considerations required by Opinion 19 of the Accounting Principles Board of the seven account balances (transactions) upon the preparation of a statement of changes in financial position using the cash concept of funds are as follows.

1. Accounts receivable—trade are generated as a result of credit sales. A balance in accounts receivable—trade represents sales (a part of operating earnings) not represented by cash. An increase in the accounts receivable—trade balance indicates that the actual cash generated is equal to sales as reported on the earnings statement less the increase in accounts receivable—trade balance. Conversely, a net decréase in the accounts receivable—trade balance would have to be added to sales as reported on the earnings statement to arrive at cash generated from sales. In the preparation of a statement of changes in financial position the increase (decrease) in this account balance between two periods represents a use (source) of funds.
2. Inventory is a component part of cost-of-goods-sold. The net change in inventory balances affects the cash used for cost-of-goods-sold. An increase in ending inventory over beginning inventory reduces the cost-of-goods-sold. However, cash was presumed to be used to increase the inventory balance. An increase in the inventory balance represents a "use" of cash. When there is an increase in inventory balances, the cash used for cost-of-goods-sold is the cost-of-goods-sold as shown in the current earnings statement plus the increase in inventory balance.

   A similar analysis leads to the conclusion that a decrease in ending inventory balance with respect to beginning inventory balance gives rise to a net increase in cost-of-goods-sold as shown in the current earnings statement but a reduction in the cash so used.

3. Depreciation represents a systematic allocation of the cost of a fixed asset to the accounting periods benefited by the asset. The process of recognizing depreciation does not affect cash. Operating earnings is determined using depreciation as an expense, so in determining cash generated from operations, depreciation must be added back to operating earnings.
4. Deferred income taxes are the difference between income taxes matched against earnings and the actual amount paid or payable for the period. If the balance of deferred income tax credits, for example, increases between two periods, the amount of income taxes paid was less than the indicated income tax expense. Therefore, an increase in deferred income tax credits represents an expense not requiring cash and thus must be added back to net earnings in a manner similar to depreciation. Conversely, if deferred income tax credits decrease, the amount "paid" was greater than the current income tax expense and represents a "use" of funds.
5. The purchase of a building by issuing long-term debt obviously does not require the use of funds using the cash concept. However, APB Opinion 19 requires that all important changes in financial position be disclosed. The purchase of the building must be shown as a "use" of funds and the issuance of long-term debt must be shown as a "source" of funds.
6. The payment of the current portion of debt using the cash concept of funds represents a use of funds.
7. In the sale of a fixed asset there are two component parts to be considered in the transaction: (1) recovery of book value and (2) resultant gain or loss on the transaction. Only the resultant gain or loss is reflected in net earnings, and the gain or loss is not the result of ordinary operations for statement of changes in financial position purposes (although it is part of ordinary operations for earnings statement purposes). The gain (loss) should be deducted from (added to) net earnings, and the total proceeds from the sale of the fixed asset should be shown as a source of cash. In general practice, the earnings effect is left in the net earnings (loss) figure and only the book value is added back as a source of funds.

Solution Guide

Problem 7 Statement of Changes—Cash Basis

Author's note: We have provided two alternatives for preparing this solution. One is the direct approach described below prior to the unofficial answer. The other is the "T-account approach" which is illustrated after the unofficial answer. Both alternatives yield the same result; therefore, only one unofficial answer is presented.

1. This problem requires a statement of changes in financial position, cash basis. Note that the requirement does not mention the need for any supporting schedules. All of the necessary numbers are given in the problem.

2. The solutions approach is to directly analyze the increases or decreases in the balance sheet accounts by relating them to the additional text information. The increase (decrease) column shown in the problem reflects the effect on total assets or total liabilities resulting from the change in each specific account balance. Supporting schedules, journal entries, and T-accounts can be used as necessary.

   Author's note: The AICPA solution to this problem includes a worksheet (not required). We (the authors) believe that such an approach is too time consuming because of the necessity to copy the accounts and numbers (increases and decreases) from the exam booklet onto a worksheet, identify (write) the source and use items on the worksheet, and finally transfer the information to the required statement. We believe use of the direct approach enables candidates to analyze carefully the more complex transactions but avoids wasting valuable time transferring information on and off of a worksheet.

3. As each item is analyzed it can be entered into a "skeleton" statement. This statement can be prepared first by listing the heading and main categories, such as cash provided from operations, cash provided by other sources, and cash applied. Then the numbers are filled in as you go through the problem.

3.1 Cash increased by $95,000. This should be the final result in the SCFP.

3.2 Accounts receivable decreased by $10,000. This is **added** as an adjustment to net income in the computation of cash provided by operations. The decrease of $10,000 means that an additional $10,000 cash was collected on account above and beyond the sales reported in the income statement.

3.3 Inventories increased by $118,000. This is **subtracted** as an adjustment to net income in the computation of cash provided by operations. The increase of $118,000 means that additional cash was spent to increase inventories; this expenditure is not reflected in cost of goods sold.

3.4 Investment in Hall increased by $13,000. Note that the equity method is used, and the income statement lists $13,000 as Farrell's equity in the net income of Hall. This item is **subtracted** as an adjustment to net income in computing cash provided by operations, because it increases income while not representing a cash inflow (see entry below).

Investment in Hall	$13,000	
Equity in income of Hall		$13,000

3.5 Land increased by $150,000. The additional information states that land was purchased through issuance of a long-term interest-bearing note. The entry to record this transaction is:

Land	$150,000	
Long-term note payable		$150,000

Although cash is not affected by this transaction, it is included on the statement of changes as both a resource provided and applied under the all-financial-resources concept. The reasoning is that this is a significant financing (issuance of note payable) and investing (purchase of land) activity, which should be pointed out to financial statement users.

3.6 Plant and equipment increased by $18,000. This is the result of two transactions described in the additional information. Equipment (cost, $45,000) with a book value of $24,000 was sold for $19,000 cash:

Cash	$19,000	
Loss on sale ($19,000 – $24,000)	5,000	
Accumulated depreciation ($45,000 – $24,000)	21,000	
Equipment		$45,000

The $19,000 cash received is a source (sale of equipment). The $5,000 loss is **added** as an adjustment to net income in computing cash provided by operations because it decreases net income but does not involve an outflow of cash. The other transaction is a purchase of equipment, $63,000, which is a use of cash. These two transactions explain the $18,000 net change in the plant and equipment account.

	Plant and Equipment		
Purchase of equip.	$63,000	$45,000	Sale of equip.
	$18,000		

3.7 Accumulated depreciation increased by $32,000. This net change is the result of the sale of equipment (discussed in 3.6) and depreciation expense of $53,000 listed in the income statement.

	Accumulated Depreciation		
Sale of equip.	$21,000	$53,000	Depr. exp.
		$32,000	

Depreciation expense is **added** as an adjustment to net income in computing cash provided by operations because it decreased net income but did not use cash.

3.8 Goodwill decreased by $4,000 as a result of goodwill amortization shown in the income statement. This is **added** as an adjustment to net income in computing cash provided by operations. Similar to depreciation, amortization decreases income but does not use cash.

3.9 Accounts payable and accrued expenses increased by $41,000. This is **added** as an adjustment to net income in computing cash provided by operations. The increase of $41,000 means that $41,000 of expenses and purchases were not paid in cash; therefore, income was decreased but cash was not affected.

3.10 The $150,000 increase in note payable (long-term) was discussed in 3.5.

3.11 Bonds payable decreased by $50,000. This is the result of the conversion into common stock described in the additional information. The bonds were converted into 2,000 (50 x 40) shares of stock. Since no extraordinary items are shown in the income statement, the book value method of recording the conversion (no gain or loss) must have been used.

Bonds payable	$50,000	
Common stock (2,000 x $10)		$20,000
Additional paid-in capital ($50,000 – $20,000)		30,000

Although cash is not affected by this transaction, it is included on the statement of changes as both a resource provided and applied under the all-financial-resources concept. Issuing stock is a significant **financing** activity while retiring bonds is a significant **investing** activity. Therefore, both of these transactions will be reported on the SCFP, even though they do not directly affect the cash account.

3.12 Deferred income taxes increased by $11,000. This is **added** as an adjustment to net income in the computation of cash provided by operations. This increase means that $11,000 of income tax expense reduced net income, but was not currently payable in cash.

3.13 Common stock increased by $30,000. $20,000 of this change was the result of the conversion of bonds payable (item 3.11). The other $10,000 was due to the issuance of stock for cash described in the additional information.

Cash	$23,000	
Common stock (1,000 x $10)		$10,000
Additional paid-in capital		13,000

The $23,000 inflow is a source of cash.

3.14 The change in additional paid-in capital ($51,000 increase) is explained in items 3.11 ($30,000), 3.13 ($13,000), and 3.16 ($8,000).

3.15 Retained earnings increased by $98,000. Examination of the statement of income and retained earnings reveals that the change consists of $141,000 net income (source of cash, subject to net income adjustments) and $43,000 of cash dividends (use of cash).

3.16 Treasury stock decreased by $17,000. The additional information indicates that this stock was sold for $25,000. Per the balance sheet, the cost method is used, resulting in the following entry:

Cash	$25,000	
Treasury stock		$17,000
Additional paid-in capital		8,000

The $25,000 inflow is a source of cash.

Unofficial Answer

Problem 7 Statement of Changes—Cash Basis

Farrell Corporation
Statement of Changes in Financial Position
(Cash Basis)
For the Year Ended December 31, 1981

Financial resources provided:		
Cash provided:		
Net income		$141,000
Add (or deduct) items not affecting cash:		
Loss on sale of equipment	$ 5,000	
Depreciation expense	53,000	
Goodwill amortization	4,000	
Decrease in accounts receivable	10,000	
Increase in accounts payable/accrued expenses	41,000	
Increase in deferred income taxes	11,000	
Equity in earnings of Hall, Inc.	(13,000)	
Increase in inventories	(118,000)	(7,000)
Cash provided from operations		$134,000
Other sources:		
Sale of equipment		19,000
Issuance of common stock		23,000
Sale of treasury stock		25,000
Financial resources provided not affecting cash:		
Issuance of common stock to convert bonds payable		50,000
Issuance of note payable to purchase land		150,000
Total resources provided		$401,000
Financial resources applied to:		
Purchase of equipment	$ 63,000	
Payment of dividends	43,000	
Financial resources used not requiring cash:		
Convert bonds payable to common stock	50,000	
Purchase of land through issuance of note payable	150,000	
Total resources applied		306,000
Increase in cash		$ 95,000

Alternate Solution Guide

Problem 7 Statement of Changes—Cash Basis

The problem may also be solved using the **"T-account approach."** This method provides a systematic way to accumulate the information necessary to prepare the statement.

1. The first step would be to calculate the change in cash; however, this is given as a $95,000 increase. This change is used as the "bottom line" figure in the Statement of Changes in Financial Position (SCFP).

2. Next, set up T-accounts for each of the accounts and enter the beginning and ending balances. Also set up two different T-accounts for cash, one for cash (including the beginning and ending balance) and another for cash provided by operations.

3. After this is done, analyze the events that affect cash, distinguishing between items that affect cash provided by operations and other items that affect cash but are not part of normal operations (i.e., sale of stock, redemption of bonds, etc.). Begin with the effects of the additional information and then consider the Statement of Income and Retained Earnings. Lastly, examine the Balance Sheet to ascertain that all changes have been explained.

Additional information:

(a) Using the T-account approach, the journal entry would be:

Cash	19,000	
Cash—operations	5,000	
Accum. depreciation	21,000	
Plant and equipment		45,000

The cash proceeds would be considered a source and is, therefore, debited to cash. The loss is debited to cash provided by operations since the loss reduced net income without affecting cash. The debit to accumulated depreciation and the credit to equipment remove the asset from the books.

(b) The $23,000 proceeds would be considered a source of cash. The remaining credits would be to common stock for the par value ($10,000) of the stock and additional paid-in capital (APIC) for the amount received in excess of par ($13,000).

(c) The proceeds ($25,000) would be considered a source of cash and debited to cash. The credits would be to treasury stock for the original purchase price ($17,000) and to APIC for the proceeds in excess of cost ($8,000). The change in the treasury stock account is now explained.

(d) The journal entry to record the conversion of the bonds into common stock would be recorded as:

Bonds payable	50,000	
Common stock		20,000
APIC		30,000

Although this entry does not affect cash, it would be reported on the SCFP under an "all financial resources" concept. The information contained in this and the previous two adjustments explains the net increase of $51,000 in additional paid-in capital. Also, the information in (b) and the current adjustment (d) explain the $30,000 increase in common stock.

(e) The purchase of equipment used cash of $63,000, while increasing plant and equipment by the same amount. Additionally, once this information and the entry made in (a) are entered, the entire increase ($18,000) in the plant and equipment account is reconciled.

(f) Land was purchased through the issuance of notes payable, thereby increasing both the land and notes payable accounts and accounting for their changes. This transaction, although not affecting cash, would be reported on the SCFP under the "all financial resources" concept.

(g) Deferred taxes increased by $11,000 and was recognized as an expense of the period, arriving at net income. Since this expense did not require the outlay of cash during the current period, it is added back to net income. The entry would debit cash provided by operations and credit deferred taxes, thus reconciling this latter account.

Statement of Income and Retained Earnings:

(h) Net income of $141,000 was reported for the year. It is treated as a source of cash and adjusted for items that do not affect cash flow. Net income is credited to retained earnings since it increases retained earnings for the year.

(i) Depreciation, although recognized as an expense, does not require the outlay of cash. Therefore, depreciation expense is added back to cash provided by operations. The credit to accumulated depreciation provides the necessary credit to explain the $32,000 increase in accumulated depreciation after the sale of the asset in (a).

(j) The equity in net income of Hall, Inc., is a reconciling item since the equity method is being used to account for this investment. The entry made to record the accrual of Hall's income is:

Investment in Hall	13,000	
Equity in income of Hall		13,000

This does not represent a cash inflow; therefore, it must be deducted from net income in order to compute cash provided by operations. The debit to the investment account explains its $13,000 increase for the year.

(k) The next reconciling item is the amortization of goodwill. Like depreciation expense, amortization reduces net income without affecting cash flows. Therefore, it is added back to net income to arrive at cash provided by operations. The corresponding credit to goodwill explains the $4,000 decrease in the account.

(l) The payment of a cash dividend ($43,000) was a use of cash during the period and reduces retained earnings. This entry along with the net income for the period explains the net increase of $98,000 in retained earnings.

Balance Sheet:

(m) The $10,000 decrease in accounts receivable must be added to cash provided by operations. The decrease means that an additional $10,000 was collected on account above and beyond the sales reported in the income statement. With this entry the change in accounts receivable is explained.

(n) The increase in inventory indicates that an additional $118,000 was spent to increase inventories but was not included in cost of goods sold. Therefore, $118,000 should be subtracted from net income to arrive at cash provided by operations.

The increases (decreases) in the asset accounts are now reconciled.

(o) Accounts payable and accrued expenses increased by $41,000. This amount is added to cash provided by operations. The increase indicates $41,000 of expenses and purchases were not paid in cash; therefore, income was decreased due to accrued expenses without affecting cash provided by operations. The accounts payable account is now reconciled.

The increases (decreases) have now been explained for all of the liability and stockholders' equity accounts.

(p) The final adjustment is to transfer the cash provided by operations into the cash account. Once the cash is transferred, the net increase in cash is reconciled ($95,000) and the SCFP can be prepared.

4. The final step is the preparation of the statement. Both the postings into the cash accounts and the postings resulting from the application of the "all financial resources" concept make up the line items of the statement. The unofficial answer of the SCFP would appear the same as presented earlier.

Cash	
	180,000	
(a)	19,000	63,000 (e)
(b)	23,000	43,000 (l)
(c)	25,000	
(p)	134,000	
	275,000	

	Cash—Operations	
(a)	5,000	13,000 (j)
(g)	11,000	118,000 (n)
(h)	141,000	134,000 (p)
(i)	53,000	
(k)	4,000	
(m)	10,000	
(o)	41,000	
	265,000	265,000

Accounts Receivable	
305,000	
	10,000 (m)
295,000	

Inventories	
431,000	
(n) 118,000	
549,000	

Investment in Hall	
60,000	
(j) 13,000	
73,000	

Land	
200,000	
(f) 150,000	
350,000	

Plant & Equipment	
606,000	
	45,000 (a)
(e) 63,000	
624,000	

Accum. Depreciation	
	107,000
(a) 21,000	53,000 (i)
	139,000

Goodwill	
20,000	
	4,000 (k)
16,000	

Accounts Payable	
	563,000
	41,000 (o)
	604,000

Notes Payable	
	-0-
	150,000 (f)
	150,000

Bonds Payable	
	210,000
(d) 50,000	
	160,000

Deferred Inc. Taxes	
	30,000
	11,000 (g)
	41,000

Common Stock	
	400,000
	10,000 (b)
	20,000 (d)
	430,000

APIC	
	175,000
	13,000 (b)
	8,000 (c)
	30,000 (d)
	226,000

Retained Earnings	
	334,000
	141,000 (h)
(l) 43,000	
	432,000

Treasury Stock	
17,000	
	17,000 (c)
-0-

Solution Guide

Problem 8 Statement of Changes

1. The requirement is to prepare a statement of changes in financial position using the working capital concept of funds; a schedule of changes in working capital is **not** required.

2. This solution guide uses the "direct" approach to preparing the statement of changes in financial position. Under this approach the increases or decreases in the non-current accounts are analyzed by relating them to the additional text information; supporting schedules, including journal entries and "T" accounts are used, as necessary, in arriving at the sources and uses. Some of the sources and uses are identified directly in the additional information, e.g., a statement that $XXXX of cash dividends were declared. These can be entered directly in the sources or uses section of the statement (uses in the case of dividends); no further analysis is necessary. Once the increases, decreases and additional information have been analyzed, there may still be some unexplained increases and/or decreases; e.g., if an increase in equipment is unexplained, assume working capital was used to acquire equipment.

   Author's note: The AICPA solution to this problem includes a work sheet (not required). We (the authors) believe that such an approach is too time consuming because of the necessity to copy the accounts and numbers (increases and decreases) from the exam booklet onto a worksheet, identify (write) the source and use items on the worksheet, and finally transfer the information to the required statement. We believe use of the direct approach enables candidates to analyze carefully the more complex transactions but avoids wasting valuable time transferring information on and off of a worksheet.

3. The solutions approach is to set up a skeleton statement entering the company title, etc. and the main headings.

   Financial Resources Provided
   Working Capital from Operations
   Working Capital from Other Sources
   Financial Resources not Affecting Working Capital

   Financial Resources Used
   Working Capital Uses
   Financial Resources not Affecting Working Capital

3.1 Begin by entering the income before extraordinary item in the operations section; as explained below, per APB 19, the extraordinary item must be separately reported in a statement of changes in financial position.

3.2 The next step is to analyze the additional information given in the problem which is marked with a bullet. As the total amount of each change (increase or decrease) in the "noncurrent accounts" is explained, make a mark next to the dollar amount of the increase or decrease. If only part of a change is explained, note the amount explained next to the total amount of the increase or decrease. As noted above, it may be necessary to use journal entries and or "T" accounts for analyzing some of the changes.

3.3 The first item of additional information is not used in the required statement of changes in financial position because stock dividends are not shown in this statement per APB 19; however, it is necessary to analyze this change in the accounts affected to ensure that all changes are explained. Enter (4,200 shares x $ 5 par value) or $21,000 next to the $40,000 increase in the common stock account. Also note the ($63,000 market value of stock – $21,000 par value) $42,000 next to the $63,000 increase in additional paid-in capital.

3.4 The issuance of common stock for land is shown under both the sources and uses section as "financial resources not affecting working capital" at $40,000. Note the $40,000 next to the $125,000 increase in land, (3,800 shares x $5) or $19,000 next to the common stock account, and ($40,000 fair value – $19,000 par value) or $21,000 next to additional paid-in capital. The changes in common stock and additional paid-in capital have now been explained. Note that the constructor of this problem intentionally made the total change in the common stock account ($40,000) the same as the fair value of that transaction and the total change in the additional paid-in capital account ($63,000) the same as the total amount of retained earnings to be capitalized. A more systematic approach for the first two transactions is to enter these transactions into "T" accounts. Use abbreviations liberally in these "T" accounts.

CS		
	$210,000	Beg. bal.
	21,000	Stock dividend
	19,000	Issued for land
	$250,000	End. bal.

APIC		
	$170,000	Beg. bal.
	42,000	Stock dividend
	21,000	Issued for land
	$233,000	End. bal.

	R.E.		
		$146,000	Beg. bal.
Stock dividend	$63,000		
Cash dividend (see 3.7 below)	2,000	121,000	Net income
		202,000	End. bal.

3.5 Per APB 19, working capital effect of the extraordinary item of $12,000 ($22,000 gain net of $10,000 of income taxes) must be reported separately from working capital from operations in the statement of changes. The journal entry to record the bond reacquisition was

Bonds payable	50,000	
Gain		22,000
Cash		28,000

The income tax effect can also be reflected in an entry:

Income tax expense—extraordinary item	$10,000	
Income tax payable		$10,000

The working capital effect of the above entries is a decrease of ($28,000 decrease in cash + $10,000 increase in income taxes payable). This amount ($38,000) can also be obtained by deducting the net gain of $12,000 from the $50,000 par value of the bonds reacquired. Although APB 19 is not specific on the treatment of the book value portion of these transactions, there is a preference in practice for combining the two components (see AICPA solution). Place a mark beside the $50,000 increase in bonds payable and enter the $38,000 extraordinary item under the uses section of the statement.

3.6 The $4,000 loss on sale of equipment did not require the use of working capital; therefore, $4,000 is added to income before extraordinary item. The $19,000 realized on the sale of equipment is shown under working capital from "other source." The $53,000 decrease in equipment has been explained. The accumulated depreciation is analyzed as follows:

	Accum. Deprec.		
Deprec.	$30,000	$100,000	Beg. bal.
		20,000	Equip. sold
		$ 90,000	End. bal.

The $20,000 of depreciation must be added back since it was deducted in arriving at net income, the starting point in computing funds from operations, but did not require working capital.

3.7 The cash dividends of $2,000 (50,000 shares x $.04) are a use of working capital.

3.8 The purchase of land for $85,000 is a use of working capital. The total change of $125,000 in the land account has now been explained.

3.9 The $40,000 increase in deferred income taxes must be added to the income from operations section, because although the $40,000 was deducted (income tax expense) in determining income before extraordinary items, it did not require the use of working capital because a current liability was not credited for the $40,000.

3.10 The only change in a noncurrent account which has not been dealt with is the $3,000 decrease in patents. The $3,000 is an addition to net income for the same reason cited above for depreciation.

3.11 In solving these problems, valuable time should not be spent trying to reconcile the change in working capital derived from the change in the current assets and current liabilities with the change reflected in the required statement of changes in financial position. The target amount is:

Increase in current assets	$120,000
Less: increase in current liabilities	50,000
Net increase in working capital	$ 70,000

Unofficial Answer

Problem 8 Statement of Changes

Kenwood Corporation
Statement of Changes in
Financial Position
For the Year Ended December 31, 1979

Financial Resources Provided		
Working capital provided from operations:		
Income before extraordinary item		$109,000
Add items not affecting working capital in the current period		
Depreciation	$20,000	
Amortization	3,000	
Loss on sale of equipment	4,000	
Deferred income taxes	40,000	67,000
Working capital provided from operations		176,000
Working capital from other sources		
Proceeds from sale of equipment		19,000
Financial resources not affecting working capital		
Issuance of common stock to purchase land		40,000
Total financial resources provided		$235,000
Financial Resources Used		
Working capital used		
Extraordinary item—repurchase of long-term bonds (including income tax of $10,000 on the gain) (50,000 - 12,000)		$ 38,000
Cash dividends (50,000 shs. x $0.04)		2,000
Purchase of land		85,000
Financial resources not affecting working capital		
Purchase of land by issuance of common stock		40,000
Total financial resources used		165,000
Increase in working capital		$ 70,000

Solution Guide

Problem 9 Allowance for Doubtful Accounts

Part a.

1. The first requirement is an analysis of the changes in the allowance for doubtful accounts where the method used to estimate uncollectible accounts was changed from the percentage of credit sales method to the aging method for the year ended December 31, 1982.

1.1 The 1/1/82 balance is given as $130,000.

1.2 Interim provisions made during the year were 2% of credit sales ($9,000,000), or $180,000. These provisions increased the allowance account:

Bad debt expense (provision for doubtful accounts)	180,000	
Allowance for doubtful accounts		180,000

1.3 Accounts in the amount of $15,000 previously written off were recovered. This amount would also increase the allowance account:

Accounts receivable	15,000	
Allowance for doubtful accounts		15,000
Cash	15,000	
Accounts receivable		15,000

1.4 During 1982, $90,000 of bad debts were written off. At 12/31/82, additional receivables totaling $60,000 were written off. These amounts would decrease the allowance account:

Allowance for doubtful accounts	150,000	
Accounts receivable		150,000

1.5 These changes result in a balance in the account of $175,000 before the year-end adjustment.

1.6 At year end, an aging analysis of accounts receivable was prepared. The required balance in the allowance account is computed to be $235,300 by taking the amount in each category and multiplying by the percentage estimated to be uncollectible, and adding the four products. In the "prior to 1/1/82" category, it is necessary to multiply the 75% expected uncollectible rate times $70,000 because $60,000 of these were written off the same day. This is the correct amount ($70,000) because the wording of the problem implies that the $60,000 was written off subsequent to the preparation of the aging schedule but before the determination of the provision for doubtful accounts for 1982.

1.7 The allowance account is increased by $60,300 (from $175,000 to $235,300) as a result of the aging.

2. The second requirement is the journal entry for the year-end adjustment to the allowance for doubtful accounts. The accounting change is a change in estimate, which is handled currently and prospectively. Therefore, the entry is to debit bad debt expense and credit the allowance account.

Unofficial Answer

Problem 9 Allowance for Doubtful Accounts

Part a.

1. **Harris Corporation**
Analysis of Changes in the
Allowance for Doubtful Accounts
For the Year Ended December 31, 1982

Balance at January 1, 1982	$130,000
Provision for doubtful accounts ($9,000,000 x 2%)	180,000
Recovery in 1982 of bad debts written off previously	15,000
	325,000
Deduct write-offs for 1982 ($90,000 + $60,000)	150,000
Balance at December 31, 1982, before change in accounting estimate	175,000
Increase due to change in accounting estimate during 1982 ($235,300 – $175,000)	60,300
Balance at December 31, 1982, adjusted (Schedule 1)	$235,300

Schedule 1

Computation of Allowance for Doubtful Accounts at December 31, 1982

Aging category	*Balance*	*%*	*Doubtful accounts*
Nov–Dec 1982	$1,140,000	2	$ 22,800
Jul–Oct	600,000	10	60,000
Jan–Jun	400,000	25	100,000
Prior to 1/1/82	70,000 [a]	75	52,500
			$235,300

[a] $130,000 – $60,000

2. **Harris Corporation**
Journal Entry
December 31, 1982

Account	*Dr.*	*Cr.*
Provision for doubtful accounts	$60,300	
Allowance for doubtful accounts		$60,300
To increase the allowance for doubtful accounts at December 31, 1982, resulting from a change in accounting estimate.		

Multiple Choice Questions (1- 51)

1. Dixon Menswear Shop regularly buys shirts from Colt Company and is allowed trade discounts of 20% and 10% from the list price. Dixon purchased shirts from Colt on May 27, 1983, and received an invoice with a list price amount of $5,000, and payment terms of 2/10, n/30. Dixon uses the net method to record purchases. Dixon should record the purchase at

   a. $3,600
   b. $3,528
   c. $3,500
   d. $3,430

2. From a theoretical viewpoint, which of the following costs would be considered inventoriable?

	Freight	Warehousing
a.	No	No
b.	No	Yes
c.	Yes	No
d.	Yes	Yes

3. The following costs were among those incurred by Woodcroft Corporation during 1981:

Merchandise purchased for resale	$500,000
Salesmen's commissions	40,000
Interest on notes payable to vendors	5,000

How much should be charged to the cost of the merchandise purchases?

   a. $500,000
   b. $505,000
   c. $540,000
   d. $545,000

4. The following information is available for The Gant Company for 1976:

Freight-in	$ 20,000
Purchase returns	80,000
Selling expenses	200,000
Ending inventory	90,000

The cost of goods sold is equal to 700% of selling expenses.

What is the cost of goods available for sale?

   a. $1,390,000
   b. $1,490,000
   c. $1,500,000
   d. $1,590,000

5. For the year 1975, the gross profit of Dumas Company was $96,000; the cost of goods manufactured was $340,000; the beginning inventories of goods in process and finished goods were $28,000 and $45,000, respectively; and the ending inventories of goods in process and finished goods were $38,000 and $52,000, respectively. The sales of Dumas Company for 1975 must have been

   a. $419,000
   b. $429,000
   c. $434,000
   d. $436,000

6. A company using a periodic inventory system neglected to record a purchase of merchandise on account at year end. This merchandise was omitted from the year-end physical count. How will these errors affect assets, liabilities, and stockholders' equity at year end and net earnings for the year?

	Assets	Liabilities	Stock-holders' equity	Net earnings
a.	No effect	understate	overstate	overstate.
b.	No effect	overstate	understate	understate.
c.	Understate	understate	no effect	no effect.
d.	Understate	no effect	understate	understate.

7. When using the periodic-inventory method, which of the following generally would not be separately accounted for in the computation of cost of goods sold?

   a. Trade discounts applicable to purchases during the period.
   b. Cash (purchase) discounts taken during the period.
   c. Purchase returns and allowances of merchandise during the period.
   d. Cost of transportation-in for merchandise purchased during the period.

8. An example of an inventory accounting policy that should be disclosed is the

   a. Effect of inventory profits caused by inflation.
   b. Composition of inventory into raw materials, work-in-process, and finished goods.
   c. Identification of major suppliers.
   d. Method used for inventory pricing.

9. Which method of inventory pricing best approximates specific identification of the actual flow of costs and units in most manufacturing situations?

a. Average cost.
b. First-in, first-out.
c. Last-in, first-out.
d. Base stock.

10. In a periodic inventory system which uses the weighted average cost flow method, the beginning inventory is the
a. Net purchases minus the cost of goods sold.
b. Net purchases minus the ending inventory.
c. Total goods available for sale minus the net purchases.
d. Total goods available for sale minus the cost of goods sold.

Items 11 and 12 are based on the following information:

The following information was available from the inventory records of the Alexander Company for January 1977:

	Units	Unit cost	Total cost
Balance at January 1, 1977	2,000	$ 9.775	$19,550
Purchases:			
January 6, 1977	1,500	10.300	15,450
January 26, 1977	3,400	10.750	36,550
Sales:			
January 7, 1977	1,800		
January 31, 1977	3,200		
Balance at January 31, 1977	1,900		

11. Assuming that Alexander maintains perpetual inventory records, what should be the inventory at January 31, 1977 using the weighted moving average inventory method rounded to the nearest dollar?
a. $19,523
b. $19,703
c. $19,950
d. $19,998

12. Assuming that Alexander does not maintain perpetual inventory records, what should be the inventory at January 31, 1977, using the weighted average inventory method rounded to the nearest dollar?
a. $19,523
b. $19,703
c. $19,950
d. $19,998

13. The moving average inventory cost flow method is applicable to which of the following inventory systems?

	Periodic	*Perpetual*
a.	Yes	Yes
b.	Yes	No
c.	No	No
d.	No	Yes

14. Moore Company carries product A in inventory on December 31, 1982, at its unit cost of $7.50. Because of a sharp decline in demand for the product, the selling price was reduced to $8.00 per unit. Moore's normal profit margin on product A is $1.60, disposal costs are $1.00 per unit, and the replacement cost is $5.30. Under the rule of cost or market, whichever is lower, Moore's December 31, 1982, inventory of product A should be valued at a unit cost of
a. $5.30
b. $5.40
c. $7.00
d. $7.50

15. The replacement cost of an inventory item is below the net realizable value and above the net realizable value less the normal profit margin. The original cost of the inventory item is above the replacement cost and below the net realizable value. As a result, under the lower of cost or market method, the inventory item should be valued at the
a. Replacement cost.
b. Original cost.
c. Net realizable value.
d. Net realizable value less the normal profit margin.

16. Moore Corporation has two products in its ending inventory, each accounted for at the lower of cost or market. A profit margin of 30% on selling price is considered normal for each product. Specific data with respect to each product follows:

	Product #1	Product #2
Historical cost	$17.00	$ 45.00
Replacement cost	15.00	46.00
Estimated cost to dispose	5.00	26.00
Estimated selling price	30.00	100.00

In pricing its ending inventory using the lower of cost or market, what unit values should Moore use for products #1 and #2 respectively?

a. $15.00 and $44.00.
b. $16.00 and $44.00.
c. $16.00 and $45.00.
d. $17.00 and $46.00.

17. When inventory declines in value below original (historical) cost, and this decline is considered other than temporary, what is the maximum amount that the inventory can be valued at?

a. Sales price net of conversion costs.
b. Net realizable value.
c. Historic cost.
d. Net realizable value reduced by a normal profit margin.

18. Q Co. prepares monthly income statements. A physical inventory is taken only at year end; hence, month-end inventories must be estimated. All sales are made on account. The rate of mark-up on cost is 50%. The following information relates to the month of June 1973.

Accounts receivable, June 1, 1973	$10,000
Accounts receivable, June 30, 1973	15,000
Collection of accounts receivable during June 1973	25,000
Inventory, June 1, 1973	18,000
Purchases of inventory during June 1973	16,000

The estimated cost of the June 30, 1973, inventory would be

a. $12,000
b. $14,000
c. $19,000
d. $22,000

19. Hestor Company's records indicate the following information:

Merchandise inventory, January 1, 1980	$ 550,000
Purchases, January 1 through December 31, 1980	2,250,000
Sales, January 1 through December 31, 1980	3,000,000

On December 31, 1980, a physical inventory determined that ending inventory of $600,000 was in the warehouse. Hestor's gross profit on sales has remained constant at 30%. Hestor suspects some of the inventory may have been taken by some new employees. At December 31, 1980, what is the estimated cost of missing inventory?

a. $100,000
b. $200,000
c. $300,000
d. $700,000

20. At December 31, 1981, the following information was available from Crisford Company's books:

	Cost	*Retail*
Inventory, 1/1/81	$14,700	$ 20,300
Purchases	83,300	115,500
Additional markups	–	4,200
Available for sale	$98,000	$140,000

Sales for the year totaled $110,600; markdowns amounted to $1,400. Under the approximate lower of average cost or market retail method, Crisford's inventory at December 31, 1981, was

a. $19,600
b. $21,560
c. $28,000
d. $30,800

21. The Good Trader Company values its inventory by using the retail method (FIFO basis, lower of cost or market). The following information is available for the year 1978.

	Cost	*Retail*
Beginning inventory	$ 80,000	$140,000
Purchases	297,000	420,000
Freight-in	4,000	
Shortages	--	8,000
Markups (net)	--	10,000
Markdowns (net)	--	2,000
Sales	--	400,000

At what amount would The Good Trader Company report its ending inventory?

a. $112,000
b. $113,400
c. $117,600
d. $119,000

22. Under the retail inventory method, freight-in would be included in the calculation of the goods available for sale for which of the following?

	Cost	*Retail*
a.	No	No
b.	No	Yes
c.	Yes	No
d.	Yes	Yes

23. The retail inventory method would include which of the following in the calculation of the goods available for sale at both cost and retail?

a. Freight-in.
b. Purchase returns.
c. Markups.
d. Markdowns.

24. On January 1, 1979, Jay Company changed to the weighted-average cost method from the first-in, first-out (FIFO) cost method for inventory cost flow purposes. Jay can justify the change, which was made for both financial statement and income tax reporting purposes. The change will result in a $120,000 decrease in the beginning inventory at January 1, 1979. Ignoring income taxes, the cumulative effect of changing to the weighted-average method from the FIFO method must be reported by Jay in the 1979

a. Income statement as a $120,000 debit.
b. Retained earnings statement as a $120,000 debit adjustment to the beginning balance.
c. Income statement as a $120,000 credit.
d. Retained earnings statement as a $120,000 credit adjustment to the beginning balance.

25. The Hastings Company began operations on January 1, 1976, and uses the FIFO method in costing its raw material inventory. Management is contemplating a change to the LIFO method and is interested in determining what effect such a change will have on net income. Accordingly, the following information has been developed:

	1976	1977
Final Inventory		
FIFO	$240,000	$270,000
LIFO	200,000	210,000
Net Income		
(computed under the FIFO method)	120,000	170,000

Based upon the above information, a change to the LIFO method in 1977 would result in net income for 1977 of

a. $110,000
b. $150,000
c. $170,000
d. $230,000

26. The LIFO inventory cost flow method may be applied to which of the following inventory systems?

	Periodic	Perpetual
a.	No	No
b.	No	Yes
c.	Yes	Yes
d.	Yes	No

27. In a period of rising prices, the use of which of the following inventory cost flow methods would result in the highest cost of goods sold?

a. FIFO.
b. LIFO.
c. Weighted average cost.
d. Moving average cost.

28. In a periodic inventory system which uses the LIFO inventory cost flow method, the cost of goods sold is the total cost of goods available for sale

a. Plus the ending inventory.
b. Minus the ending inventory.
c. Plus the beginning inventory.
d. Minus the beginning inventory.

29. Which of the following statements is not valid as it applies to inventory costing methods?

a. If inventory quantities are to be maintained, part of the earnings must be invested (plowed back) in inventories when FIFO is used during a period of rising prices.
b. LIFO tends to smooth out the net income patterns since it matches current cost of goods sold with current revenue, when inventories remain at constant quantities.
c. When a firm using the LIFO method fails to maintain its usual inventory position (reduces stock on hand below customary levels) there may be a matching of old costs with current revenue.
d. The use of FIFO permits some control by management over the amount of net income for a period through controlled purchases, which is not true with LIFO.

30. On December 31, 1981, Kern Company adopted the dollar value LIFO inventory method. All of Kern's inventories constitute a single pool. The inventory on December 31, 1981, using the dollar value LIFO inventory method was $600,000. Inventory data for 1982 are as follows:

12/31/82 inventory at year-end prices	$780,000
Relevant price index at year-end (base year 1981)	120

Under the dollar value LIFO inventory method, Kern's inventory at December 31, 1982, would be

a. $650,000
b. $655,000
c. $660,000
d. $720,000

31. The double extension method and the link-chain method are two variations of which of the following inventory cost flow methods?

a. Moving average.
b. FIFO.
c. Dollar value LIFO.
d. Conventional (lower of cost or market) retail.

32. Which of the following inventory cost flow methods could use dollar-value pools?

a. Conventional (lower of cost or market) retail.
b. Weighted average.
c. FIFO.
d. LIFO.

33. Adams Construction Co. uses the percentage-of-completion method of accounting. During 1982, Adams contracted to build an apartment house for Roper for $10,000,000. Adams estimated that total costs would amount to $8,000,000 over the period of construction. In connection with this contract, Adams incurred $1,000,000 of construction costs during 1982. Adams billed and collected $1,500,000 from Roper in 1982. How much gross profit should Adams recognize in 1982?

a. $300,000
b. $250,000
c. $187,500
d. $125,000

34. In accounting for a long-term construction contract for which there is a projected profit, the balance in the appropriate asset accounts at the end of the first year of work using the completed-contract method would be

a. Zero.
b. The same as the percentage-of-completion method.
c. Higher than the percentage-of-completion method.
d. Lower than the percentage-of-completion method.

35. On April 1, 1980, Pine Construction Company entered into a fixed-price contract to construct an apartment building for $6,000,000. Pine appropriately accounts for this contract under the percentage-of-completion method. Information relating to the contract is as follows:

	At December 31, 1980	*At December 31, 1981*
Percentage of completion	20%	60%
Estimated costs at completion	$4,500,000	$4,800,000
Income recognized (cumulative)	$ 300,000	$ 720,000

What is the amount of contract costs incurred during the year ended December 31, 1981?

a. $1,200,000
b. $1,920,000
c. $1,980,000
d. $2,880,000

36. Mercer Construction Company recognizes income under the percentage-of-completion method of reporting income from long-term construction contracts. During 1978 Mercer entered into a fixed-price contract to construct a bridge for $15,000,000. Contract costs incurred and estimated costs to complete the bridge were as follows:

	Cumulative contract costs incurred	*Estimated costs to complete*
At December 31, 1978	$ 1,000,000	$8,000,000
At December 31, 1979	5,500,000	5,500,000
At December 31, 1980	10,000,000	2,000,000

How much income should Mercer recognize on the above contract for the year ended December 31, 1980?

a. $ 500,000
b. $ 833,333
c. $1,350,000
d. $2,500,000

37. For annual reporting purposes, Storrar Co. appropriately accounts for revenues from long-term construction-type contracts under the precentage-of-completion method. In December 1975, for budgeting purposes, Storrar estimated that these revenues would be $1,600,000 for 1976. Favorable business conditions occurred in October 1976 and, as a result, Storrar recognized revenues of $2,000,000 for the year ended December 31, 1976. If the percentage-of-completion method had been used for the quarterly income statements on the same basis followed for the year-end income statement, revenues would have been as follows:

Three months ended March 31, 1976	$ 300,000
Three months ended June 30, 1976	400,000
Three months ended September 30, 1976	200,000
Three months ended December 31, 1976	1,100,000
Total	$2,000,000

What amount of revenues from long-term construction-type contracts should be reflected in Storrar's quarterly income statement for the three months ended December 31, 1976?

a. $ 500,000
b. $ 800,000
c. $1,100,000
d. $2,000,000

Items 38 and 39 are based on the following information:

In 1974, Long Corporation began construction work under a three-year contract. The contract price is $800,000. Long uses the percentage-of-cost-completion method for financial accounting purposes. The income to be recognized each year is based on the proportion of cost incurred to total estimated costs for completing the contract. The financial statement presentations relating to this contract at December 31, 1974, follow:

Balance Sheet

Accounts receivable—construction contract billings		$15,000
Construction in progress	$50,000	
Less contract billings	47,000	
Cost-of-uncompleted contract in excess of billings		3,000

Income Statement

Income (before tax) on the contract recognized in 1974	$10,000

38. How much cash was collected in 1974 on this contract?

a. $15,000
b. $32,000
c. $35,000
d. $47,000

39. What was the initial estimated total income before tax on this contract?

a. $10,000
b. $30,000
c. $160,000
d. $200,000

40. Which of the following would be used in the calculation of the income recognized in the third and final year of a construction contract which is accounted for using the percentage-of-completion method?

	Contract price	Actual total costs	Income previously recognized
a.	Yes	Yes	No
b.	Yes	Yes	Yes
c.	Yes	No	Yes
d.	No	No	Yes

41. When should an indicated loss on a long-term contract be recognized under the completed-contract method and the percentage-of-completion method, respectively?

	Completed-contract	Percentage-of-completion
a.	Immediately	Immediately
b.	Immediately	Over the life of the project
c.	Completion of contract	Over the life of the project
d.	Completion of contract	Immediately

42. During 1972 R Corp., a manufacturer of chocolate candies, contracted to purchase 100,000 pounds of cocoa beans at $1.00 per pound, delivery to be made in the spring of 1973. Because a record harvest is predicted for 1973, the price per pound for cocoa beans had fallen to $.80 by December 31, 1972.

Of the following journal entries, the one which would properly reflect in 1972 the effect of the commitment of R Corp. to purchase the 100,000 pounds of cocoa is

		Debit	Credit
a.	Cocoa inventory	100,000	
	Accounts payable		100,000
b.	Cocoa inventory	80,000	
	Loss on purchase commitments (an expense account)	20,000	
	Accounts payable		100,000
c.	Loss on purchase commitments (an expense account)	20,000	
	Accrued loss on purchase commitments (a liability account)		20,000
d.	No entry would be necessary in 1972.		

43. The balance in Ashwood Company's accounts payable account at December 31, 1982, was $900,000 before any necessary year-end adjustment relating to the following:

- Goods were in transit from a vendor to Ashwood on December 31, 1982. The invoice cost was $50,000, and the goods were shipped F.O.B. shipping point on December 29, 1982. The goods were received on January 4, 1983.
- Goods shipped F.O.B. shipping point on December 20, 1982, from a vendor to Ashwood were lost in transit. The invoice cost was $25,000. On January 5, 1983, Ashwood filed a $25,000 claim against the common carrier.
- Goods shipped F.O.B. destination on December 21, 1982, from a vendor to Ashwood were received on January 6, 1983. The invoice cost was $15,000.

What amount should Ashwood report as accounts payable on its December 31, 1982, balance sheet?

a. $925,000
b. $940,000
c. $950,000
d. $975,000

44. Wildwood Company's usual sales terms are net 60 days, F.O.B. shipping point. Sales, net of returns and allowances, totaled $2,000,000 for the year ended December 31, 1982, before year-end adjustment. Additional information is as follows:

- Goods with an invoice amount of $40,000 were billed to a customer on January 3, 1983. The goods were shipped on December 31, 1982.
- On January 5, 1983, a customer notified Wildwood that goods billed and shipped to it on December 21, 1982, were lost in transit. The invoice amount was $50,000.
- On December 27, 1982, Wildwood authorized a customer to return, for full credit, goods shipped and billed at $25,000 on December 15, 1982. The returned goods were received by Wildwood on January 4, 1983, and a $25,000 credit memo was issued on the same date.

Wildwood's adjusted net sales for 1982 should be

a. $1,965,000
b. $1,975,000
c. $1,990,000
d. $2,015,000

45. The following items were included in Venicio Corporation's inventory account at December 31, 1981:

• Merchandise out on consignment, at sales price, including 40% markup on selling price	$14,000
• Goods purchased, in transit, shipped f.o.b. shipping point	12,000
• Goods held on consignment by Venicio	9,000

Venicio's inventory account at December 31, 1981, should be reduced by

a. $14,600
b. $17,400
c. $23,000
d. $35,000

May 1984 Questions

46. Shunpike Company's inventory records for product Y provide the following data for 1983:

	Units	*Unit cost*
Inventory, 1/1/83	12,000	$ 9.00
Purchases:		
April 8	20,000	9.50
October 25	8,000	10.00

A physical inventory on December 31, 1983, shows 10,000 units on hand. Under the FIFO cost flow method, the December 31, 1983, inventory should be

a. $100,000
b. $ 99,000
c. $ 95,000
d. $ 90,000

47. Hadley Construction Company has consistently used the percentage-of-completion method of recognizing income. During 1982 Hadley started work on a $3,000,000 construction contract which was completed in 1983. The accounting records provided the following data:

	1982	*1983*
Progress billings	$1,100,000	$1,900,000
Costs incurred	900,000	1,800,000
Collections	700,000	2,300,000
Estimated cost to complete	1,800,000	—

How much income should Hadley have recognized in 1982?

a. $100,000
b. $110,000
c. $150,000
d. $200,000

48. On September 30, 1983, a fire at Brock Company's only warehouse caused severe damage to its entire inventory. Based on recent history, Brock has a gross profit of 30% of net sales. The following information is available from Brock's records for the nine months ended September 30, 1983:

Inventory at 1/1/83	$ 550,000
Purchases	3,000,000
Net sales	4,000,000

A physical inventory disclosed usable damaged goods which Brock estimates can be sold to a jobber for $50,000. Using the gross profit method, the estimated cost of goods sold for the nine months ended September 30, 1983, should be

a. $2,050,000
b. $2,485,000
c. $2,750,000
d. $2,800,000

49. Richland Company uses the retail inventory method to estimate its inventory for interim statement purposes. Data relating to the computation of the inventory at July 31, 1983, are as follows:

	Cost	*Retail*
Inventory, 2/1/83	$ 70,000	$110,000
Purchases	350,000	500,000
Additional markups		90,000
Sales		600,000
Estimated normal shoplifting losses		10,000

Under the approximate lower of average cost or market retail method, Richland's estimated inventory at July 31, 1983, is

a. $90,000
b. $63,000
c. $60,000
d. $54,000

50. Office supplies were ordered by Dwyer Company from Orcutt Company on December 15, 1983. The terms of sale were FOB destination. Orcutt shipped the office supplies on December 28, 1983, and Dwyer received them on January 3, 1984. When should Dwyer record the account payable?

a. December 15, 1983.
b. December 28, 1983.
c. December 31, 1983.
d. January 3, 1984.

51. At the time progress billings are sent on a long-term contract, income is recognized under the

	Completed-contract method	*Percentage-of-completion method*
a.	Yes	Yes
b.	Yes	No
c.	No	No
d.	No	Yes

Repeat Question

(584,P1,7) Identical to item 14 above

Problems

Problem 1 LIFO and Inventory Cut-off (1181,P4)

(45 to 55 minutes)

Part a. On January 1, 1976, Grover Company changed its inventory cost flow method to the LIFO cost method from the FIFO cost method for its raw materials inventory. The change was made for both financial statement and income tax reporting purposes. Grover uses the multiple-pools approach under which substantially identical raw materials are grouped into LIFO inventory pools; weighted average costs are used in valuing annual incremental layers. The composition of the December 31, 1978, inventory for the Class F inventory pool is as follows:

	Units	*Weighted average unit cost*	*Total cost*
Base year inventory—1976	9,000	$10.00	$ 90,000
Incremental layer—1977	3,000	11.00	33,000
Incremental layer—1978	2,000	12.50	25,000
Inventory, December 31, 1978	14,000		$148,000

Inventory transactions for the Class F inventory pool during 1979 were as follows:

- On March 1, 1979, 4,800 units were purchased at a unit cost of $13.50 for $64,800.
- On September 1, 1979, 7,200 units were purchased at a unit cost of $14.00 for $100,800.
- A total of 15,000 units were used for production during 1979.

The following transactions for the Class F inventory pool took place during 1980:

- On January 10, 1980, 7,500 units were purchased at a unit cost of $14.50 for $108,750.
- On May 15, 1980, 5,500 units were purchased at a unit cost of $15.50 for $85,250.
- On December 29, 1980, 7,000 units were purchased at a unit cost of $16.00 for $112,000.
- A total of 16,000 units were used for production during 1980.

Required:

1. Prepare a schedule to compute the inventory (units and dollar amounts) of the Class F inventory pool at December 31, 1979. Show supporting computations in good form.

2. Prepare a schedule to compute the cost of Class F raw materials used in production for the year ended December 31, 1979.

3. Prepare a schedule to compute the inventory (units and dollar amounts) of the Class F inventory pool at December 31, 1980. Show supporting computations in good form.

Part b. Layne Corporation, a manufacturer of small tools, provided the following information from its accounting records for the year ended December 31, 1980:

Inventory at December 31, 1980 (based on physical count of goods in Layne's plant at cost on December 31, 1980)	$1,750,000
Accounts payable at December 31, 1980	1,200,000
Net sales (sales less sales returns)	8,500,000

Additional information is as follows:

1. Included in the physical count were tools billed to a customer F.O.B. shipping point on December 31, 1980. These tools had a cost of $28,000 and were billed at $35,000. The shipment was on Layne's loading dock waiting to be picked up by the common carrier.

2. Goods were in transit from a vendor to Layne on December 31, 1980. The invoice cost was $50,000, and the goods were shipped F.O.B. shipping point on December 29, 1980.

3. Work-in-process inventory costing $20,000 was sent to an outside processor for plating on December 30, 1980.

4. Tools returned by customers and held pending inspection in the returned goods area on December 31, 1980, were not included in the physical count. On January 8, 1981, the tools costing $26,000 were inspected and returned to inventory. Credit memos totaling $40,000 were issued to the customers on the same date.

5. Tools shipped to a customer F.O.B. destination on December 26, 1980, were in transit at December 31, 1980, and had a cost of $25,000. Upon notification of receipt by the customer on January 2, 1981, Layne issued a sales invoice for $42,000.

6. Goods, with an invoice cost of $30,000, received from a vendor at 5:00 p.m. on December 31, 1980, were recorded on a receiving report dated January 2, 1981. The goods were not included in the physical count, but the invoice was included in accounts payable at December 31, 1980.

7. Goods received from a vendor on December 26, 1980, were included in the physical count. However, the related $60,000 vendor invoice was not included in accounts payable at December 31, 1980,

because the accounts payable copy of the receiving report was lost.

8. On January 3, 1981, a monthly freight bill in the amount of $4,000 was received. The bill specifically related to merchandise purchased in December 1980, one-half of which was still in the inventory at December 31, 1980. The freight charges were not included in either the inventory or in accounts payable at December 31, 1980.

Required:

Using the format shown below, prepare a schedule of adjustments as of December 31, 1980, to the initial amounts per Layne's accounting records. Show separately the effect, if any, of each of the eight transactions on the December 31, 1980 amounts. If the transactions would have no effect on the initial amount shown, state NONE.

	Inventory	*Accounts payable*	*Net sales*
Initial amounts	$1,750,000	$1,200,000	$8,500,000
Adjustments—increase (decrease)			
1			
2			
3			
4			
5			
6			
7			
8			
Total adjustments			
Adjusted amounts	$	$	$

Problem 2 Change to LIFO (1176,T5)

(20 to 25 minutes)

Part a. Inventory may be computed under one of various cost-flow assumptions. Among these assumptions are first-in, first-out (FIFO) and last-in, first-out (LIFO). In the past, some companies have changed from FIFO to LIFO for computing portions or all of their inventory.

Required:

1. Ignoring income tax, what effect does a change from FIFO to LIFO have on net earnings and working capital? Explain.

2. Explain the difference between the FIFO assumption of earnings and operating cycle and the LIFO assumption of earnings and operating cycle.

Part b. Companies using LIFO inventory sometimes establish a "Reserve for the Replacement of LIFO Inventory" account.

Required:

Explain why and how this "Reserve" account is established and where it should be shown on the statement of financial position.

Problem 3 LIFO Problem (576,P4)

(40 to 50 minutes)

Number 3 consists of three unrelated parts.

Part a. The Topanga Manufacturing Company manufactures two products: Mult and Tran. At December 31, 1974, Topanga used the first-in, first-out (FIFO) inventory method. Effective January 1, 1975, Topanga changed to the last-in, first-out (LIFO) inventory method. The cumulative effect of this change is not determinable and, as a result, the ending inventory of 1974 for which the FIFO method was used, is also the beginning inventory for 1975 for the LIFO method. Any layers added during 1975 should be costed by reference to the first acquisitions of 1975 and any layers liquidated during 1975 should be considered a permanent liquidation.

The following information was available from Topanga's inventory records for the two most recent years:

	Mult		*Tran*	
	Units	*Unit cost*	*Units*	*Unit cost*
1974 purchases:				
January 7	5,000	$4.00	22,000	$2.00
April 16	12,000	4.50		
November 8	17,000	5.00	18,500	2.50
December 13	10,000	6.00		
1975 purchases:				
February 11	3,000	7.00	23,000	3.00
May 20	8,000	7.50		
October 15	20,000	8.00		
December 23			15,500	3.50

Units on hand:		
December 31, 1974	15,000	14,500
December 31, 1975	16,000	13,000

Required:

Compute the effect on income before income taxes for the year ended December 31, 1975, resulting from the change from the FIFO to the LIFO method.

Part b. The Barometer Company manufactures one product. On December 31, 1972, Barometer adopted the dollar-value LIFO inventory method. The inventory on that date using the dollar-value LIFO method was $200,000.

Inventory data are as follows:

Year	*Inventory at respective year-end prices*	*Price index (base year 1972)*
1973	$231,000	1.05
1974	299,000	1.15
1975	300,000	1.20

Required:

Compute the inventory at December 31, 1973, 1974, and 1975, using the dollar-value LIFO method for each year.

Part c. The Jericho Variety Store uses the LIFO retail inventory method. Information relating to the computation of the inventory at December 31, 1975, follows:

	Cost	*Retail*
Inventory, January 1, 1975	$ 29,000	$ 45,000
Purchases	120,000	172,000
Freight-in	20,000	
Sales		190,000
Net markups		40,000
Net markdowns		12,000

Required:

Assuming that there was no change in the price index during the year, compute the inventory at December 31, 1975 using the LIFO retail inventory method.

Problem 4 Long-Term Contracts (1183,T3)

(15 to 25 minutes)

The Michael Company is accounting for a long-term construction contract using the percentage-of-completion method. It is a four-year contract that is presently in its second year. The latest estimates of total contract costs indicate that the contract will be completed at a profit to Michael Company.

Required:

a. What theoretical justification is there for Michael Company's use of the percentage-of-completion method?

b. How would progress billings be accounted for? Include in your discussion the classification of progress billings in the Michael Company financial statements.

c. How would the income recognized in the second year of the four-year contract be determined using the cost-to-cost method of determining percentage of completion?

d. What would be the effect on earnings per share in the second year of the four-year contract of using the percentage-of-completion method instead of the completed-contract method? Discuss.

Problem 5 Long-Term Contracts (1180,P4)

(45 to 55 minutes)

Problem 5 consists of two unrelated parts.

Part a. Curtiss Construction Company, Inc., entered into a firm fixed-price contract with Axelrod Associates on July 1, 1977, to construct a four-story office building. At that time, Curtiss estimated that it would take between two and three years to complete the project. The total contract price for construction of the building is $4,000,000. Curtiss appropriately accounts for this contract under the completed-contract method in its financial statements and for income tax reporting. The building was deemed substantially completed on December 31, 1979. Estimated percentage-of-completion, accumulated contract costs incurred, estimated costs to complete the contract, and accumulated billings to Axelrod under the contract were as follows:

	At December 31, 1977	At December 31, 1978	At December 31, 1979
Percentage-of-completion	10%	60%	100%
Contract costs incurred	$ 350,000	$2,500,000	$4,250,000
Estimated costs to complete the contract	$3,150,000	$1,700,000	–
Billings to Axelrod	$ 720,000	$2,160,000	$3,600,000

Required:

1. Prepare schedules to compute the amount to be shown as "cost of uncompleted contract in excess of related billings" or "billings on uncompleted contract in excess of related costs" at December 31, 1977, 1978, and 1979. Ignore income taxes. Show supporting computations in good form.

2. Prepare schedules to compute the profit or loss to be recognized as a result of this contract for the years ended December 31, 1977, 1978, and 1979. Ignore income taxes. Show supporting computations in good form.

Part b. On April 1, 1979, Butler, Inc., entered into a cost-plus-fixed-fee contract to construct an electric generator for Dalton Corporation. At the contract date, Butler estimated that it would take two years to complete the project at a cost of $2,000,000. The fixed fee stipulated in the contract is $300,000. Butler appropriately accounts for this contract under the percentage-of-completion method. During 1979 Butler incurred costs of $700,000 related to the project, and the estimated cost at December 31, 1979, to complete the contract is $1,400,000. Dalton was billed $500,000 under the contract.

Required:

Prepare a schedule to compute the amount of gross profit to be recognized by Butler under the contract for the year ended December 31, 1979. Show supporting computations in good form.

Problem 6 Dollar-Value LIFO (583,P4b)

(20 to 25 minutes)

Part b. On January 1, 1981, Lucas Distributors, Inc., adopted the dollar value LIFO inventory method for income tax and external financial statements reporting purposes. However, Lucas continued to use the FIFO inventory method for internal accounting and management purposes. In applying the LIFO method Lucas uses internal conversion price indexes and the multiple-pools approach under which substantially identical inventory items are grouped into LIFO inventory pools. The following data were available for Inventory Pool No. 1, which is comprised of products A and B, for the two years following the adoption of LIFO:

	FIFO basis per records		
	Units	*Unit cost*	*Total cost*
Inventory, 1/1/81			
Product A	12,000	$30	$360,000
Product B	8,000	25	200,000
			$560,000
Inventory, 12/31/81			
Product A	17,000	35	$595,000
Product B	9,000	28	252,000
			$847,000
Inventory, 12/31/82			
Product A	13,000	40	$520,000
Product B	10,000	32	320,000
			$840,000

Required:

1. Prepare a schedule to compute the internal conversion price indexes for 1981 and 1982. Round indexes to two decimal places.

2. Prepare a schedule to compute the inventory amounts at December 31, 1981 and 1982, using the dollar value LIFO inventory method.

Problem 7 Inventory: Theoretical Issues (583,T2)

(15 to 25 minutes)

Taylor Company, a household appliances dealer, purchases its inventories from various suppliers. Taylor has consistently stated its inventories at the lower of cost (FIFO) or market.

Required:

a. Taylor is considering alternate methods of accounting for the cash discounts it takes when paying its suppliers promptly. From a theoretical standpoint, discuss the acceptability of each of the following methods:

1. Financial income when payments are made.
2. Reduction of cost of goods sold for period when payments are made.
3. Direct reduction of purchase cost.

b. Identify the effects on both the balance sheet and the income statement of using the LIFO inventory method instead of the FIFO method over a substantial time period when purchase prices of household appliances are rising. State why these effects take place.

c. Why is the lower of cost or market rule used for valuing inventories when the FIFO method is used?

Multiple Choice Answers

1.	b	12.	b	22.	c	32.	d	42.	c
2.	d	13.	d	23.	b	33.	b	43.	d
3.	a	14.	b	24.	a	34.	d	44.	d
4.	b	15.	a	25.	a	35.	c	45.	a
5.	b	16.	c	26.	c	36.	a	46.	b
6.	c	17.	b	27.	b	37.	c	47.	a
7.	a	18.	b	28.	b	38.	b	48.	d
8.	d	19.	a	29.	d	39.	c	49.	d
9.	b	20.	a	30.	c	40.	b	50.	d
10.	c	21.	a	31.	c	41.	a	51.	c
11.	c								

Multiple Choice Answer Explanations

A. Determining Inventory and Cost of Goods Sold

1. (1183,P1,1) (b) The requirement is the amount at which a purchase should be recorded using the net method. Purchases are always recorded net of trade discounts; when using the net method, purchases are also recorded net of cash discounts. When more than one trade discount is applied to a list price, it is called a chain discount. Chain discounts are applied in steps, i.e., each discount applies to the previously discounted price.

List price	$5,000
20% discount	(1,000)
Discounted list price	4,000
10% discount	(400)
Gross billing price	$3,600

The cash discount of 2% (from 2/10, n/30) is then applied to the gross billing price computed above.

Gross billing price	$3,600
2% discount	72
Net purchase price	$3,528

Using the net method, the purchase is, therefore, recorded at $3,528.

2. (1183,T1,9) (d) From a theoretical viewpoint all costs incurred to acquire goods or to prepare them for market are inventoriable. Freight is a cost incurred to acquire goods; warehousing is a cost incurred to store purchased goods (merchandising firm) or component parts and raw materials (manufacturing firm). (See ARB 43, Ch. 4, para 3.)

3. (582,Q1,14) (a) The requirement is the amount of the costs to be included in merchandise purchases. The salesmen's commissions are a selling expense not related to the aquisition of the merchandise and are, therefore, treated as a period cost rather than as a product cost. Further, interest costs incurred in acquiring inventory are expensed as incurred. They are financing expenses. Per para 10 of SFAS 34, interest costs are not capitalized for assets that are in use or ready for their intended use (e.g., merchandise held for resale). Thus, only the $500,000 should be included in the cost of the purchases.

4. (577,Q1,13) (b) The requirement is goods available for sale. Goods available for sale are equal to ending inventory plus cost of sales or beginning inventory plus purchases. Cost of goods sold is 7 times the selling expense of $200,000, or $1,400,000. Add the $90,000 of ending inventory to the $1,400,000 to obtain goods available for sale of $1,490,000.

5. (576,Q1,15) (b) The solutions approach is to set up the T account for the finished goods inventory so that you can determine the cost of sales. Cost of sales plus gross profit of $96,000 will equal sales. Notice that the problem gives you beginning and ending inventory for the work-in-process account which are not relevant to the problem. The beginning finished goods inventory of $45,000 plus the cost of goods manufactured of $340,000 provides $385,000 available for sale. The $52,000 of ending inventory is subtracted to obtain $333,000 for cost of sales. Add the $333,000 of cost of sales to gross profit of $96,000 to obtain $429,000 for sales.

	FG Inventory		
BI	$ 45,000	$333,000	C of S
CGM	340,000	52,000	
	$385,000	$385,000	

6. (577,T2,25) (c) When inventory is excluded from both purchases and ending inventory, there is no effect on net income or shareholders' equity, because ending inventory is subtracted from the sum of purchases plus beginning inventory to determine cost of sales. Failure to record inventory, however, does understate the inventory and the liability accounts. Thus answer (c) is correct.

7. (1175,T1,1) (a) Traditionally, purchases are recorded net of trade discounts. Thus if something were selling with a 30% trade discount, one would record it at the net amount rather than the gross amount. Purchase discounts are usually recorded separately, i.e., purchases are recorded at gross and purchase discounts are recorded when taken. Purchase returns and allowances are generally accounted for separately as is transportation-in.

B. Inventory Valuation and Cost Flow Methods

8. (580,T1,24) (d) Para 6 of APB Opinion No. 22 defines the accounting policies of a reporting entity as the specific accounting principles and the methods of applying those principles that have been adapted for preparing the financial statements. Using this definition, the only accounting policy listed among the answers is the method used for inventory pricing.

B.1. Specific Identification

9. (1177,T1,19) (b) Most manufacturing operations process and sell inventory in the order it is received, i.e., the first items in are the first to be sold, which is FIFO. LIFO and base stock would mean that inventory that is originally purchased would be kept on hand and never sold. An example of a base stock situation might be a sand and gravel storage area. Average cost would imply that inventories were continually mixed and there was always some of the original inventory on hand.

B.2. Weighted Average

10. (1182,T1,21) (c) In a periodic inventory system (regardless of the cost flow method assumed) beginning inventory equals net goods available for sale minus net purchases. Answers (a) and (b) are nonsensical answers and answer (d) is incorrect because it is the formula for determining ending inventory.

B.4. Moving Average

11. (1177,P1,12) (c) The requirement is the ending inventory using the moving average inventory method. The moving average inventory method requires that a new unit cost be computed each time new goods are purchased. A computation is not needed when goods are sold, because the inventory account is credited at the average price. The computations below result in an ending inventory quantity of 1,900 units, to be priced at $10.50 each, resulting in an ending inventory quantity of $19,950. Note that no calculation is needed after computing the unit price for the last purchase.

2,000	$19,550
+1,500	15,450
3,500	$35,000 = $10.00
−1,800	18,000
1,700	$17,000 = $10.00
+3,400	36,550
5,100	$53,550 = $10.50
−3,200	
1,900	

1,900 x $10.50 = $19,950

12. (1177,P1,13) (b) The requirement is the ending inventory based upon the weighted average (not moving average) method. The weighted average method is simply a weighted average unit cost of inventory throughout the period. Thus the total number of units available for sale is divided into their total cost (here $71,550 ÷ 6,900 units). The ending inventory of 1,900 units times the average unit cost of $10.37 is $19,703.

2,000	$19,550
1,500	15,450
3,400	36,550
6,900	71,550 = $10.37

1,900 x $10.37 = $19,703

13. (1181,T1,10) (d) The **moving average** method is used with perpetual records. A new average unit cost is computed each time a purchase is made and this unit cost is used in costing withdrawals of inventory until another purchase is made. The **weighted-average** method is used with periodic records.

B.5. Lower of Cost or Market

14. (1183,P1,3) (b) The requirement is to determine the valuation of product A using the lower of cost or market (LCM) rule (ARB 43, Ch. 4, para 9). The rule is applied by valuing the inventory at the lower of its cost or market value. Cost is historical cost ($7.50 in this case). Market value is the replacement cost subject to an upper limit (ceiling) and a lower limit (floor). The ceiling is the net realizable value, which is the selling price less disposal costs. The floor is the net realizable value less a normal profit margin. The ceiling is $7.00 ($8.00 – $1.00) and the floor is $5.40 ($7.00 – $1.60). Since the replacement cost of $5.30 is below the floor, the floor ($5.40) represents market value to be compared with cost. Since market ($5.40) is less than cost ($7.50), the proper valuation is $5.40.

15. (1183,T1,11) (a) The requirement is proper valuation of an inventory item under lower of cost or market. Under lower of cost or market, market is replacement cost provided that replacement cost is lower than net realizable value (ceiling) and higher than the net realizable value less the normal profit margin (floor). This is the situation in this question; therefore, replacement cost is market, and the valuation should be at market because it is lower than original cost (ARB 43, Ch. 4, para 8 and 9). Answer (b) is incorrect because the market value is lower than the original cost. Answers (c) and (d) are incorrect as they represent the ceiling [answer (c)] and the floor [answer (d)] which the replacement cost falls between.

16. (577,Q1,14) (c) The requirement is to price products 1 and 2 at the lower of cost or market. See Chapter 4 of ARB 43, para 9. The lower of cost or market rule is applied by selecting the lower of cost or market. Cost is historical cost. Market is replacement cost subject to a ceiling and a floor, i.e., maximum and minimum. The maximum (ceiling) is net realizable value which is selling price less disposal costs, and the minimum (floor) is the net realizable value less normal profit, i.e., the ceiling less normal profit. To recap, first compute market and then compare it with cost. As computed below, the net realizable value (ceiling) is the selling price less the cost of disposal, or $25 and $74 respectively. The net realizable value minus profit (floor) is $16 and $44 respectively. Since the replacement cost for product 1 of $15 is below the floor, market is the floor, or $16. The replacement cost of $46 for product 2 is within the floor-ceiling range, and thus market for product 2 is $46. The lower of cost or market is $16 (market) for product 1, and $45 (cost) for product 2.

	1	2
NRV	$30 - $5	$100 - $26
NRV - profit	25 - 9	74 - 30
Replacement	15	46
Market	16	46
Cost	17	45
Lower	16	45

17. (1178,T1,12) (b) The requirement is the maximum amount at which inventory can be valued provided that market is less than historical cost. Per para 9 of Chapter 4 of ARB 43, market cannot exceed net realizeable value (nor can it be less than net realizable value reduced by normal profit margins). Net realizable value is selling price less estimated completion and disposal costs. Note that whether the decline is considered temporary or other than temporary has no effect on inventory valuation.

B.6. Gross Profit

18. (1173,P1,10) (b) The ending inventory is determined by T-account analysis of accounts receivable and cost of goods sold. Sales at retail are $30,000 as evidenced by the T-account analysis of AR below. Markup of 50% of cost is a markup of 1/3 on retail and thus sales at cost are $20,000. The T-account analysis of C of GS indicates ending inventory of $14,000.

	A/R		
6/1/73 bal.	$10,000		
Sales	30,000	$25,000	Collections
6/30/73 bal.	$15,000		

	C of GS		
Beg. inventory	$18,000		
Purchases	16,000	$20,000	C of GS
End. inventory	$14,000		

19. (581,Q1,14) (a) The requirement of this problem is to find the cost of missing inventory at the end of the year. The solutions approach to this problem is to calculate the estimated amount of inventory and compare this amount to the actual inventory on hand to determine the loss.
Set up a schedule using the format of the income statement.

Cost of G.S.		
Beg. Inv.	$ 550,000	
+ Purchases	2,250,000	
Goods avail.	$2,800,000	
– End Inv.	?	
(70% x $3,000,000)		$2,100,000
		$ 900,000

*The cost of goods sold as a percentage of sales is 100% minus the 30% gross profit rate. The estimated ending inventory is $2,800,000 goods available less $2,100,000 cost of G.S. or $700,000. The estimated cost of the missing inventory is $700,000 – $600,000 = $100,000.

B.7. Retail Method

20. (582,Q1,19) (a) The requirement is the lower of average cost or market amount of the 12/31/81 inventory using the retail method. The first step is to review the fundamentals of solving these problems. Recall that to approximate lower of cost or market, markups are included in the denominator of the ratio, but markdowns are not. The effect is to make the denominator larger which results in a lower, more conservative, inventory valuation. The ratio would be computed as follows:

Cost/Retail Ratio = $98,000/$140,000 = 70%

The ending inventory at retail is

	Cost	*Retail*
Available for sale	$98,000	$140,000
Markdowns		(1,400)
Sales		(110,600)
		$ 28,000

The final step is to multiply the cost-to-retail ratio by the ending inventory at retail to find the ending inventory at cost.

$28,000 x 70% = $19,600

21. (1179,Q1,9) (a) The requirement is the ending inventory for Good Trader Company based on the retail method (FIFO basis, lower of cost or market). The solutions approach is to set up a cost to retail schedule as illustrated below. The first step is to determine the ending inventory at retail which is $160,000. Note that the inventory flow is FIFO. Thus, ending inventory will be made up of this period's purchases. The cost/retail ratio to be applied to the ending inventory is 301/430, which is 70%. Note that the freight-in applies to this year's purchases, and an assumption is usually made that markups apply only to purchases. Thus, 70% of $160,000 is $112,000, which is ending inventory.

	Cost	Retail
BI	$ 80,000	$140,000
Purchases	+297,000	+420,000
Freight-in	+4,000	
Markups (net)		+10,000
Goods available	$381,000	$570,000
Shortages		−8,000
Markdowns (net)		−2,000
Sales		−400,000
EI		$160,000

301 ÷ 430 = 70%
$160,000 x 70% = $112,000

22. (1182,T1,7) (c) The requirement is to determine whether, under the retail inventory method, freight-in is included in the cost and/or retail calculation of the cost of goods available for sale. For the retail inventory method, total cost of goods available for sale includes freight-in costs. The amounts in the retail column are the result of applying a markup percentage to the cost of the goods and the result of making certain adjustments to the selling price (e.g., net markups and net markdowns).

23. (1181,T1,11) (b) The requirement is the item which would be included in cost of goods available for sale at both cost and retail in the retail inventory method. Purchase returns and allowances are ordinarily considered both as an adjustment of the cost price and the retail price. Freight charges [answer (a)] are typically an additional cost of purchasing and markups [answer (c)] and markdowns [answer (d)] are adjustments to the retail (selling) price.

B.8. & B.9. First-In, First-Out (FIFO), and Last-In, First-Out (LIFO)

24. (1180,P1,3) (a) The requirement is to compute the cumulative effect of a change in accounting principle from the weighted-average method to the FIFO method for inventory cost flow purposes, as well as to indicate its appropriate placement in the 1979 financial statements. Except for specific exceptions, APB No. 20 requires that changes in accounting principle be reported in the income statement rather than as an adjustment in the retained earnings statement. To determine whether the cumulative effect is a debit or credit, it is helpful to visualize the journal entry to record this change. The decrease in the inventory would be recorded as a credit; therefore, the income statement effect would be a debit.

Cumulative effect of accounting change	120,000	
Inventory		120,000

25. (578,Q1,7) (a) The requirement is 1977 net income if a change is made to LIFO in 1977. Usually, a change to LIFO does not result in a cumulative effect because of the impracticality of determining LIFO cost in past years. The beginning inventory in the year of change under FIFO ($240,000) becomes the beginning inventory under LIFO. The ending LIFO inventory of $210,000 is subtracted from goods available for sale. Since purchases are the same under both LIFO and FIFO, cost of goods sold is $60,000 greater than if FIFO has been used in 1977. This causes the income under FIFO, which was $170,000, to fall to $110,000 under LIFO.

Note, the data in this problem allow for the calculation of the cumulative effect because data are given for 1976 under LIFO. However, the answer does not change because the cumulative effect is part of net income. Since the question asks for net income, you do not have to be concerned about the calculation of the cumulative effect in this case.

26. (1182,T1,6) (c) The requirement is to determine the inventory system(s) to which the LIFO cost flow method is applicable. The LIFO method is applicable to both periodic and perpetual inventory systems. The LIFO method may be applied at the end of the period (periodic), or continuously throughout the period as sales and purchases occur (perpetual).

27. (582,T1,21) (b) Under the LIFO cost flow assumption, cost of goods sold consists of the most recent purchases which were made at prices higher than existed earlier in the period. Accordingly, cost of

goods sold will be the highest under LIFO when prices are rising. Answer (a) is incorrect because under the FIFO cost flow assumption, cost of goods sold is made up of purchases made earlier in the period which were at lower deflated prices. Answers (c) and (d) are incorrect because under both methods the various prices are averaged in determining cost of goods sold.

28. (1181,T1,21) (b) In a periodic inventory system (regardless of the cost flow method assumed) cost of goods sold is measured as a residual amount determined by subtracting ending inventory, which is determined by a physical inventory count, from goods available for sale (beginning inventory plus purchases during the period).

29. (1174,T2,22) (d) Under FIFO, current purchases usually become part of ending inventory rather than cost of goods sold and thus do not affect current income. Under LIFO, however, current purchases are normally included in cost of goods sold and thus net income could be affected by controlled purchases.

B.11. Dollar-Value LIFO

30. (1183,P1,20) (c) The requirement is Kern's December 31, 1982, inventory under the dollar value LIFO inventory method. First, the December 31, 1982, inventory at year-end prices ($780,000) must be restated back to base-year prices ($780,000 ÷ 1.20 = $650,000). Thus, the ending inventory consists of the base-year layer of $600,000 (December 31, 1981, inventory) and an incremental layer of $50,000 added in 1982 ($650,000 – $600,000). The base-year layer is left at base-year prices, but the 1982 layer must be expressed in terms of 1982 prices.

Base-year layer	$600,000
1982 layer ($50,000 x 1.20)	60,000
12/31/82 inventory	$660,000

31. (582,T1,7) (c) Dollar value LIFO bases inventory on "dollars" in inventory rather than "units" in inventory. Inventory layers are identified with the price index in the year in which the layer was added. "Double extension" and "link-chain" are two variations of dollar value LIFO. Link-chain differs from double extension in that inventory values are extended at beginning of the year prices for link-chain and at base year prices for double extension. Because of this difference, link-chain is more appropriate for situations in which inventory is going through rapid technological changes. The two variations are not alternatives and use of the link-chain method should be restricted to situations in which the double extension method is impractical.

32. (1180,T1,18) (d) A variation of LIFO, dollar-value LIFO, uses dollar-value pools; to qualify for inclusion in a dollar-value LIFO pool the items must be "similar" rather than "identical" as is the case under unit LIFO. No other inventory methods utilize dollar-value pools.

B.17. Long-Term Construction Contracts

33. (1183,Q1,2) (b) The requirement is the amount of gross profit for 1982 using the percentage-of-completion method. The solutions approach is to first determine the expected total income on the contract, which is the contract price of $10,000,000 less the estimated contract costs of $8,000,000, or $2,000,000 estimated income. (Note that had Roper revised estimated costs at the end of 1982, the estimated income would have also changed.) The formula for recognizing profit under the percentage-of-completion method is

$$\frac{\text{Costs to date}}{\text{Total expected costs}} \times \text{Expected profit} = \text{Profit recognized to date}$$

The percentage of the job completed ($1,000,000 costs incurred to date ÷ $8,000,000 estimated costs) is multiplied by the expected profits of $2,000,000 to yield gross profit to be recognized in 1982 of $250,000. Note that the amount billed and collected ($1,500,000) does not affect the computation of the gross profit.

34. (583,T1,43) (d) Both the percentage-of-completion and the completed-contract method accumulate, in appropriate asset accounts, the costs of contracts in progress and the amount receivable from current billings. Under the percentage-of-completion method, income is to be recognized as work progresses on a contract, thereby increasing the construction in progress account (ARB 45, para 4). Under the completed-contract method, income is recognized only when the contract is complete or substantially complete (ARB 45, para 9). Accordingly, the appropriate asset accounts under the completed-contract method will be lower than under the percentage-of-completion method because no income will be recognized until the contract is substantially complete. Answer (a) is incorrect because costs incurred during the first year are recorded in appropriate asset accounts. In order for construction in process to have the same balance under both methods [answer (b)], zero profits must be projected for the contract.

35. (1182,P1,14) (c) The requirement is the amount of contract costs incurred during 1981. Based on the information given, it must be assumed that costs incurred are used to measure the extent of progress to-

ward project completion. At 12/31/80, the project is 20% complete and total estimated costs are $4,500,000. Therefore, costs incurred as of 12/31/80 are 20% of $4,500,000, or $900,000. At 12/31/81, the project is 60% complete and total estimated costs are $4,800,000. Therefore, costs incurred as of 12/31/81 are 60% of $4,800,000, or $2,880,000. The costs incurred during 1981 are $2,880,000 less $900,000, or $1,980,000.

36. (581,P1,5) (a) The requirement is the amount of income Mercer should recognize in 1980 on a long term contract, using the percentage-of-completion method. The income to be recognized in 1980 will be the difference between total income earned in 1978-1980 less the amount of income recognized in 1978-79. At 12/31/79, the contract was 50% complete ($5,500,000 ÷ $11,000,000) based on estimates available then. At that time, the total expected income was $4,000,000 ($15,000,000 contract price – $11,000,000 estimated total costs). Therefore, the income recognized as of 12/31/79 was 50% of $4,000,000, or $2,000,000. At 12/31/80, the contract is 5/6 complete ($10,000,000 ÷ $12,000,000), and the total expected income is $3,000,000 ($15,000,000 contract price – $12,000,000 estimated total costs). Therefore, the income earned as of 12/31/80 is 5/6 of $3,000,000, or $2,500,000. Income to be recognized in 1980 is $500,000 as illustrated below:

Income earned as of 12/31/80	–	Income previously recognized	=	Income to be recognized in 1980
$2,500,000	–	$2,000,000	=	$500,000

37. (1177,P1,10) (c) The requirement is the amount of revenue to be recognized on the interim income statement for the last three months of the year. Since $1,100,000 would have been recognized in the last three months based upon the method to determine annual income, it is the amount of revenue to be recognized in the interim period. In other words, the same accounting principles are used in the preparation of interim statements as for annual statements. See para 10 of APB 28. Para 11 specifically states that revenues should be recognized during an interim period on the same basis as followed for the annual period.

38. (575,P1,13) (b) In long-term construction accounting, the account "construction in progress" is a deferred debit: it consists of all of the costs to date (and profits recognized to date under the percentage-of-completion method). "Contract billings" is a deferred credit: as the customer is billed, receivables is debited and contract billings is credited. In this problem contract billings totaled $47,000. Thus $47,000 has been billed and $15,000 is still outstanding, which means $32,000 has been collected.

39. (575,P1,14) (c) To date $10,000 has been recognized on a total of cost plus profits in the "construction in progress account" of $50,000. Thus the ratio of profit to cost plus profit is 20%. The contract price is $800,000 and the estimated total income is $160,000.

40. (1181,T1,34) (b) Income recognized in the final year of construction using the percentage-of-completion method is measured by subtracting the income recognized in previous periods from total income earned on the project, which is equal to the contract price less the total actual costs incurred.

41. (1180,T1,2) (a) The requirement is when to recognize an indicated loss on a long-term contract under both the completed-contract and percentage-of-completion methods. ARB 45 requires that expected losses should be recognized immediately under both methods.

C. Losses on Purchase Commitments

42. (1173,P1,11) (c) Losses on purchase commitments, if material, should be recognized in the accounts. See statement number 10 (Paragraph 17) of Chapter 4 of ARB 43. In this question there is a purchase commitment loss of $.20 per pound on 100,000 lbs. of cocoa beans. The loss should be accrued by debiting a loss account and crediting a liability or deferred revenue account. Next period when the cocoa beans are purchased at $.80, purchases will be debited at $.80, and accrued loss on purchase commitments will be debited for $.20 per pound.

D. & E. Items to Include in Inventory and Consignments

43. (583,P1,1) (d) The requirement is the amount reported as accounts payable on the 12/31/82 balance sheet. The balance before adjustment is $900,000. The $50,000 of goods in transit from a vendor to Ashwood were shipped FOB shipping point. Therefore, title passes to Ashwood when the goods are delivered to the carrier, and the purchase and payable should be recorded in 1982. Similarly, the goods lost in transit ($25,000) should be recorded as a purchase and payable in 1982 since the terms are also FOB shipping point. Ashwood, not the vendor, is

ultimately responsible for the lost goods; note that Ashwood is suing the common carrier, not the vendor. The goods shipped FOB destination ($15,000) remain the property of the vendor until Ashwood receives these goods from the carrier, so the payable should not be recorded until 1983. Therefore, the corrected accounts payable balance is $900,000 + $50,000 + $25,000, or $975,000.

44. (583,P1,17) (d) The requirement is the amount of adjusted net sales for 1982. Net sales total $2,000,000, subject to three possible adjustments. Since sales terms are FOB shipping point, title passes when the seller (Wildwood) delivers the goods to the common carrier. Therefore, the goods shipped on 12/31/82 ($40,000) should be added to the sales amount given, since the sale was not recorded until 1983. The goods lost in transit ($50,000) were correctly recorded as a sale in 1982. Even though the goods were lost, the seller has a valid receivable, and legally the buyer must proceed against the common carrier since the terms were FOB shipping point. The goods returned ($25,000) should be recorded as a return in 1982, when Wildwood authorized the return. Since the return was not recorded until 1983, 1982 net sales must be adjusted downward. Therefore, adjusted net sales is $2,015,000 ($2,000,000 + $40,000 – $25,000).

45. (582,Q1,3) (a) The requirement is the amount by which the inventory account should be reduced as the result of improperly included or overstated items. The merchandise out on consignment should be priced at cost, not retail, by reducing the account for the $5,600 markup above cost ($14,000 x 40%). The goods purchased FOB shipping point are appropriately included in the inventory account as the title has transferred to Venicio; no adjustment is necessary. Finally, the inventory account should be reduced for the goods held on consignment by Venicio. These goods are owned by the consignor, not Venicio.

Consignment inventory markup	$ (5,600)
Goods held on consignment	(9,000)
	$(14,600)

May 1984 Answers

46. (584,P1,6) (b) The requirement is the ending inventory using the FIFO cost flow method. Under the FIFO method, it is assumed that the first goods in are the first sold. Therefore, the last goods purchased remain in ending inventory. The 10,000 units in ending inventory consist of the 8,000 units purchased on October 25 and 2,000 of the units purchased on April 8. The dollar value of the ending inventory is $99,000, as computed below:

8,000 x $10.00 =	$80,000
2,000 x $ 9.50 =	19,000
	$99,000

47. (584,P2,22) (a) The requirement is the amount of income to be recognized in 1982 on a construction contract using the percentage-of-completion method. Under this method, income is recognized based on the progress the company has made toward completion of the project. Generally, such progress is measured by comparing costs incurred with the total estimated costs of the project. In 1982 costs incurred were $900,000, and the total costs were estimated at $2,700,000 ($900,000 + $1,800,000). Therefore, the project was 1/3 ($900,000 ÷ $2,700,000) completed at 12/31/82. Since the estimated total income from the project is $300,000 (contract price of $3,000,000 less total estimated cost of $2,700,000), income of $100,000 (1/3 x $300,000) should have been recognized in 1982.

48. (584,P2,34) (d) The requirement is the estimated cost of goods sold using the gross profit method. Since net sales are $4,000,000 and the estimated gross profit rate is 30% of net sales, gross profit can be estimated at $1,200,000. The estimated cost of goods sold is net sales ($4,000,000) less estimated gross profit ($1,200,000), or $2,800,000. A short cut is to realize that if the gross profit rate is 30%, cost of goods sold must be 70% of sales; therefore, COGS is $2,800,000 (4,000,000 x 70%).

49. (584,P2,47) (d) The requirement is the estimated ending inventory using the approximate lower of average cost or market retail (conventional retail) method. To approximate lower of cost or market, markups are included in the cost/retail ratio but markdowns are not. Also, for **average** cost, the beginning inventory is included in the ratio. The **first** step is to compute the ending inventory at retail.

	Cost	*Retail*
Beg. inventory	$ 70,000	$110,000
Purchases	350,000	500,000
Markups		90,000
Available for sale	$420,000	$700,000
Sales		(600,000)
Normal shoplifting losses		(10,000)
End. inventory		$ 90,000

The **second** step is to compute the cost/retail ratio.

$420,000/$700,000 = 60%

Note that **normal** shoplifting losses do not affect the cost/retail ratio since normal losses are reflected in the company's selling prices. **Abnormal** shoplifting losses would be subtracted from both cost and retail so as to not distort the cost/retail ratio. The **third** and final step is to multiply the ending inventory at retail by the cost/retail ratio to find the ending inventory at cost.

$90,000 x 60% = $54,000

50. (584,T1,16) (d) The requirement is to determine the date Dwyer should record the account payable arising from the purchase of office supplies. When goods are shipped FOB destination, title does not pass to the buyer until the goods have been delivered. The purchase and related liability will not be recorded by Dwyer until title passes, which is on the date the supplies are received—January 3, 1984 [answer (d)].

51. (584,T1,34) (c) The requirement is the determination of income recognition at the time progress billings are sent on a long-term contract under completed-contract and percentage-of-completion methods. The measurement of income should not be based on progress billings (ARB 45, para 2). The amount billed on a project during a period is determined by contract terms that do not necessarily measure performance on a project. Under the percentage-of-completion method, income should be recognized as work progresses on a contract (ARB 45, para 4). Under the completed-contract method, income is recognized only when the contract is completed or substantially completed (ARB 45, para 9).

Solution Guide

Problem 1 LIFO and Inventory Cut-off

1. This problem consists of two unrelated parts. Part a requires several computations for a company using the multiple-pools approach of LIFO inventory costing. Part b requires an analysis of the year-end inventory, purchase cutoff and sales cutoff for another company.

2. The inventory method (LIFO with layers valued at weighted average prices in the year of origin) used in part a may be somewhat unfamiliar to the CPA candidate. It is important to notice, however, that the method is fully described in the given information. A last-in-first-out cost flow assumption is used. If there are less units in ending inventory than there were in beginning inventory, the most recently added inventory layers are eliminated first. If there are more units in ending inventory, the incremental layer is valued at the weighted average cost of units purchased (total dollars spent for purchases ÷ number of units purchased) during the year.

2.1 The first requirement is a computation of the 12/31/79 ending inventory. First, determine how many units remain in the ending inventory.

Beginning inventory	14,000
Units purchased (4,800 + 7,200)	12,000
Units available	26,000
Units used for production	(15,000)
Ending inventory	11,000

Since the number of units in inventory decreased, some of the more recent layers were eliminated. Start with the base year layer and work forward to get 11,000 units. Remember, the oldest purchases remain in ending inventory under a LIFO assumption. Therefore, the ending inventory consists of 9,000 units from the 1976 base year layer and 2,000 units from the 1977 incremental layer. The rest of the 1977 layer and all of the 1978 layer have been eliminated.

2.2 The second requirement is a computation of the cost of raw materials used in production (i.e., charged to work-in-process) in 1979. The most recent purchases are assumed to be used first in a LIFO cost flow assumption. Therefore, start with the 1979 purchases and work backwards to get 15,000 units used; the 12,000 units purchased in 1979, the 2,000 units in the 1978 layer, and 1,000 of the units in the 1977 layer were used during 1979. Of course, any units not included in ending inventory in the first requirement must be included in materials used in the second requirement.

2.3 The third requirement is a computation of the 12/31/80 ending inventory. First, determine how many units remain in the ending inventory.

Beginning inventory	11,000
Units purchased (7,500 + 5,500 + 7,000)	20,000
Units available	31,000
Units used for production	(16,000)
Ending inventory	15,000

During 1980, an incremental layer of 4,000 units was added to the Class F pool inventory [15,000 units in ending inventory less 11,000 units in beginning inventory (see 2.1 above)]. This incremental layer must be valued at the weighted average cost of 1980 purchases, as computed below:

$$\frac{\text{1980 total purchases cost}}{\text{1980 total units purchased}} =$$

$$\frac{\$108,750 + \$85,250 + 112,000}{7,500 + 5,500 + 7,000} = \$15.30$$

The 12/31/80 ending inventory consists of the base year layer (9,000 units), the remaining 1977 incremental layer (2,000 units per 2.1 above), and the new 1980 layer (4,000 units at $15.30 each). Note that layers eliminated in 1979 cannot be "recreated"; they are permanently eliminated.

3. Part b requires a schedule listing the effects of eight situations on inventory, accounts payable, and net sales. The format of the schedule to be used in the solution is provided in the problem. The "solutions approach" is to study the requirement and preliminary data first, then to analyze each of the situations individually.

3.1 The $28,000 of tools on the loading dock were properly included in the physical count. The sale should not be recorded until the goods are picked up by the common carrier. Therefore, no adjustment is made to inventory, but sales must be reduced by the $35,000 billing price.

3.2 The $50,000 of goods in transit from a vendor to Layne were shipped FOB shipping point on 12/29/80. Title passes to the buyer as soon as goods are delivered to the common carrier when sold FOB shipping point. Therefore, these goods are properly includable in Layne's inventory and accounts payable at 12/31/80. Both inventory and accounts payable must be increased by $50,000.

3.3 The work-in-process inventory sent to an outside processor is Layne's property and should be included in ending inventory. Since this inventory was not in the plant at the time of the physical count, the inventory column must be increased by $20,000.

3.4 The tools costing $26,000 were recorded as sales ($40,000) in 1980. However, these items were returned by customers on December 31, so 1980 net sales should be reduced by the $40,000 return. Also, $26,000 has to be added to the inventory column since these goods were not included in the physical count.

3.5 The $25,000 of tools shipped to a customer FOB destination are still owned by Layne while in transit because title does not pass on these goods until they are received by the buyer. Therefore, $25,000 must be added to the inventory column. No adjustment is necessary in the sales column because the sale was properly recorded in 1981 when the customer received the goods.

3.6 The goods received from a vendor at 5:00 p.m. on 12/31/80 should be included in ending inventory, but were not included in the physical count. Therefore, $30,000 must be added to the inventory column. No adjustement is made to accounts payable, since the invoice was included in 12/31/80 accounts payable.

3.7 The $60,000 of goods received on 12/26/80 were properly included in the physical count of inventory. $60,000 must be added to accounts payable since the invoice was not included in the 12/31/80 accounts payable balance.

3.8 Since one-half of the freight-in cost ($4,000) pertains to merchandise properly included in inventory as of 12/31, $2,000 should be added to the inventory column. The full $4,000 must be added to accounts payable since the liability was not recorded.

Author's Note: The supporting schedules in the preceding Solution Guide to this problem would be an integral part of the candidate's solution as follows:

Part a.1. (See 2.1 for schedule of 12/31/79 inventory)
Part a.2. (See 2.3 for schedule of 12/31/80 inventory)
Part a.3. (See 2.3 for schedule of weighted average cost of purchases)

Unofficial Answer

Problem 1 LIFO and Inventory Cut-off

Part a.

1.

Grover Company
Computation of Inventory Amounts
for Class F Pool
12/31/79

	Units	Weighted Average Unit Cost	Total Cost
Base year inventory (1976)	9,000	$10.00	$ 90,000
Incremental layer (1977)	2,000	11.00	22,000
Inventory (12/31/79)	11,000		$112,000

2.

Grover Company
Computation of Cost of Class F
Raw Materials Used During 1979

	Units	Unit Cost	Total Cost
9/1/79 purchase	7,200	$14.00	$100,800
3/1/79 purchase	4,800	13.50	64,800
1978 incremental layer	2,000	12.50	25,000
1977 incremental layer	1,000	11.00	11,000
Raw Materials Used	15,000		$201,600

3. **Grover Company**
Computation of Inventory Amounts
for the Class F Pool
12/31/80

	Units	*Weighted average unit cost*	*Total cost*
Base year inventory (1976)	9,000	$10.00	$ 90,000
Incremental layer (1977)	2,000	11.00	22,000
Incremental layer (1980)	4,000	15.30[a]	61,200
Inventory (12/31/80)	15,000		$173,200

[a] $306,000/20,000

Part b.

Layne Corporation
Schedule of Adjustments
December 31, 1980

	Inventory	*Accounts payable*	*Sales*
Initial amounts	$1,750,000	$1,200,000	$8,500,000
Adjustments			
1	NONE	NONE	(35,000)
2	50,000	50,000	NONE
3	20,000	NONE	NONE
4	26,000	NONE	(40,000)
5	25,000	NONE	NONE
6	30,000	NONE	NONE
7	NONE	60,000	NONE
8	2,000	4,000	NONE
Total adjustments	153,000	114,000	(75,000)
Adjusted amounts	$1,903,000	$1,314,000	$8,425,000

Answer Outline

Problem 2 Change to LIFO

a1. LIFO matches most recent costs with revenues
LIFO inventory is priced at earliest costs
In rising prices, LIFO reports less income
(Assuming stable or increasing inventory)
In falling prices, LIFO reports more income
(Assuming stable or increasing inventory)
Decreasing inventories tend to have the opposite effect

a2. FIFO combines operating and holding gains
Operating cycle is cash-inventory-cash
Earnings are net of actual goods sold
LIFO profits provide for inventory replacement
In contrast, LIFO excludes holdings gains
Operating cycle is inventory-cash-inventory

b. Reserve account is used when LIFO inventory decreases
Otherwise early inventory costs are matched with current revenues
Cost temporary inventory decrease at current prices
Reserve account set up for excess of replacement cost over LIFO carrying cost
Reserve account is a current liability

Unofficial Answer

Problem 2 Change to LIFO

a. 1. When using LIFO, the most recently incurred costs are included in cost of goods sold on the earnings statement, and the earlier costs are included in the inventory reported on the statement of financial position. When using FIFO, the earlier costs are included in cost of goods sold on the earnings statement, and the later, more current costs are included in the inventory on the statement of financial position.

If all prices remain constant and inventory quantities remain constant, there will be no effect upon net earnings or working capital resulting from the use of LIFO rather than FIFO.

If prices are rising and inventory quantities remain constant or increase, LIFO will produce a larger cost of goods sold and a smaller net earnings. The change from FIFO to LIFO would, thus, reduce net earnings. Likewise, rising prices yield a lower LIFO inventory cost on the statement of financial position than the corresponding FIFO inventory cost. Therefore, the change to LIFO would reduce working capital.

If prices are falling and inventory quantities remain constant or increase, LIFO would produce a smaller cost of goods sold and, therefore, a larger net earnings than FIFO. The change to LIFO would, thus, increase net earnings. Likewise, falling prices yield a higher LIFO inventory cost on the statement of financial position than the corresponding FIFO inventory cost. Therefore, the change to LIFO would increase working capital.

If inventory quantities decrease, the relative effects of using LIFO rather than FIFO cannot be determined without giving consideration to the direction of price changes and the magnitude of the inventory change.

2. The use of FIFO as an inventory method results in recognizing all elements of earnings at the time of sale. Holding gains (or losses) are combined with the operating (trading) earnings and are not separately identified. Holding gains arise from holding inventory during periods of rising prices. Operating earnings result from selling a product at a price above current cost.

Under FIFO, the operating cycle is viewed as cash to merchandise and back to cash again; therefore, reported earnings should be net of goods (actually) sold. An assumed FIFO cost flow generally is a good approximation of specific identification for most goods in most industries. According to FIFO proponents, FIFO generally matches the actual cost of the (actual) goods sold with the revenue produced.

Because FIFO ignores the cost of the replacement of the inventory at possible higher prices (in a period of rising prices), it includes a "paper" profit that is not really available for distribution to owners because it is needed to replace inventory.

The use of LIFO as an inventory method matches the most recently incurred costs with the revenue produced. It, therefore, largely excludes holding gains from the reported earnings if inventory quantity remains constant or increases. Reported earnings from the period are more likely to include a deduction for goods sold in an amount that approximates more closely the higher cost required to replace inventory (during periods of rising prices) and, thereby, represent the distributable earnings accruing to the owners under the going-concern concept. The operating cycle is viewed as merchandise to cash and back to merchandise. In other words, LIFO proponents claim that the actual flow of goods should not be a determinant of net earnings.

b. The account "Reserve for Replacement of LIFO Inventory" may also be called "Excess of Replacement Cost over LIFO Cost of Basic Inventory Temporarily Liquidated." The use of this account arises when there are less units in ending inventory than in beginning inventory for a company using LIFO. This sale of part of the inventory results in matching some older, lower costs (assuming rising prices) with current revenues. Furthermore, if the inventory is replaced, the new inventory cost would exceed the prior, basic inventory cost, because replacement would be at higher prices. In other words, this decline in inventory would lead to the reporting of an amount of net earnings that is distorted simply because replacement did not occur prior to the end of the accounting period.

Assuming that the inventory decline is temporary, LIFO proponents would suggest avoiding this potential distortion by charging cost of goods sold with current costs even though some of the goods sold may have been carried at older, lower costs. The reserve account is then credited for the excess of the current replacement cost over the LIFO carrying cost for the inventory temporarily liquidated, as the alternative account title implies. When this inventory is replenished, the temporary reserve (credit) is removed, and the goods acquired are placed in inventory at their old LIFO costs. While it exists, the reserve account should be shown among the current liabilities on the statement of financial position to currently reflect the expected reduction of reported working capital of this amount when the goods are replaced.

Under the dollar-value LIFO method, changes in actual units are ignored, and the concern shifts to dollars invested in inventories. This often permits rather drastic shifts in inventory mix without causing a recovery of any of the older LIFO costs. This may be affected by the number of inventory pools a firm establishes; the fewer the inventory pools, the less likelihood of any invasion of LIFO base costs.

Solution Guide

Problem 3 LIFO Problem

1. The requirement in part a is to determine the effect on 1975 income of changing from FIFO to LIFO at the beginning of 1975.

1.1 Use a Time Diagram to determine that the difference in income is due to the difference in ending 1975 inventory.

1974	1975
Change occurs, inventory per LIFO and FIFO are the same.	Inventory per LIFO and FIFO are different.

1.2 Calculate FIFO for 1975 ending inventories, i.e., ending inventory priced at latest costs.

Mult	16,000 @ $8.00 =	$128,000
Tran	13,000 @ 3.50 =	45,500
	Ending 1975 FIFO	$173,500

1.3 Calculate LIFO inventories, i.e., ending inventory is beginning inventory adjusted for change during 1975. Beginning inventory is ending 1974 inventory at LIFO.

Mult		
Beginning		
10,000 @ $6.00 =	$60,000	
5,000 @ 5.00 =	25,000	
		$85,000
Increase of 1,000 @ $7.00		7,000
		$92,000
Tran		
Beginning		
14,500 @ $2.50 =	$36,250	
Decrease of 1,500 @ $2.50 =	3,750	
		$ 32,500
Ending 1975 LIFO		$124,500

1.4 Since LIFO of $124,500 is used instead of FIFO of $173,500, income is $49,000 less than if FIFO had been used. Note this same approach could be used on cost of sales.

2. The requirement is to calculate the dollar LIFO inventory value at the end of 1973, 1974, 1975.

2.1 Reduce the year-end inventory values to base year dollars.

2.2 Multiply the base year and subsequent layers times their respective price levels.

3. The requirement is ending inventory per LIFO retail.

3.1 Compute the cost to retail ratio for 1975 purchases.

3.2 Determine ending inventory at retail.

3.3 Multiply the cost to retail ratio times the increase in retail inventory during the year.

3.4 Add the cost of the increase in inventory to the cost of beginning inventory.

Unofficial Answer

Problem 3 LIFO Problem

a. **The Topanga Manufacturing Company**
Effect on Income Before Income Taxes – Change From FIFO to LIFO Inventory Method
For the Year Ended December 31, 1975

Inventory at December 31, 1975 if on FIFO Inventory Method:		
Mult–16,000 units x $8.00 (10/15/75 unit cost)	$128,000	
Tran–13,000 units x $3.50 (12/23/75 unit cost)	45,500	$173,500
Inventory at December 31, 1975 on LIFO Inventory Method:		
Mult		
Beginning inventory:		
5,000 units x $5.00 (11/8/74 unit cost)	25,000	
10,000 units x $6.00 (12/13/74 unit cost)	60,000	
	85,000	
Layer added in 1975:		
1,000 units x $7.00 (2/11/75 unit cost)	7,000	
		92,000
Tran		
Beginning inventory:		
14,500 units x $2.50 (11/8/74 unit cost)	36,250	
Layer liquidated in 1975:		
1,500 units x $2.50 (11/8/74 unit cost)	(3,750)	
		32,500
		124,500
Decrease in income before income taxes–change from FIFO to LIFO inventory method		$ 49,000

b.

The Barometer Company
Dollar-Value LIFO Computations

Year	Inventory at respective year-end prices	Price index (base year 1972)	Inventory at base year (1972) prices
1973	$231,000	1.05	$220,000
1974	299,000	1.15	260,000
1975	300,000	1.20	250,000

December 31, 1973:

Base	$200,000
1973 layer at 1973 cost ($220,000 – $200,000 = $20,000) x 1.05	21,000
	$221,000

December 31, 1974:

Base	$200,000
1973 layer at 1973 cost	21,000
1974 layer at 1974 cost ($260,000 – $220,000 = $40,000) x 1.15	46,000
	$267,000

December 31, 1975:

Base	$200,000
1973 layer at 1973 cost	21,000
1974 layer at 1974 cost [$250,000 – $260,000 = ($10,000) + $40,000 = $30,000] x 1.15	34,500
	$255,500

c.

The Jericho Variety Store
LIFO Retail Computation
December 31, 1975

	Cost	Retail
Purchases	$120,000	$172,000
Freight-in	20,000	
Net markups		40,000
Net markdowns		(12,000)
	$140,000	200,000
Cost ratio (140,000 ÷ $200,000)	70%	
Sales		190,000
1975 layer:		
At retail		10,000
At cost ($10,000 x 70%)	$ 7,000	
Inventory, 1/1/75 (base)	$ 29,000	$ 45,000
Inventory, 12/31/75	$ 36,000	$ 55,000

Answer Outline

Problem 4 Long-Term Contracts

a. Percentage-of-completion method
  - Revenue should be earned as work is performed
    - Right to revenue is established
    - Collectibility is reasonably assured
  - Provides best matching of revenue and expense
  - Eliminates interperiod distortion

b. Entry to record progress billings

  A/R XXX
    Progress billings XXX

  Progress billings is contra-asset offset against construction in progress for each contract account
  - Total of contracts having net debits shown as current assets
  - Total of contracts having net credits shown as current liabilities

c. Cost-to-cost method of percentage of completion
  - First, determine estimated total income
    - Contract price minus estimated total costs
      - Estimated total costs equal actual costs to date plus estimated costs to complete
  - Second, determine percentage completed to date
    - Actual costs to date divided by estimated total costs
  - Percentage completed to date used to determine total income recognized to date
    - Estimated total income times percentage completed
  - Third, determine income recognized in second year of contract
    - Total income recognized to date minus income recognized in first year of contract

d. Completed contract method recognizes income only in period contract is completed
  - No income recognized in second year of contract
  - Percentage-of-completion method recognizes income ratably over contract period
    - Some income recognized in second year of contract
      - Greater EPS in second year using percentage-of-completion

Unofficial Answer

Problem 4 Long-Term Contracts

a. Michael Company should earn revenue as it performs the work on the contract (the percentage-of-completion method) because the right to revenue is established and collectibility is reasonably assured. Furthermore, the use of the percentage-of-completion method avoids distortion of income from period to period and provides for better matching of revenues with the related expenses.

b. Progress billings would be accounted for by increasing accounts receivable and increasing progress billings on contract, a contra-asset account which is offset against the construction costs in progress account. If the construction costs in progress account exceeds the progress billings on contract account, the two accounts would be shown in the current asset section of the balance sheet. If the progress billings on contract account exceeds the construction costs in progress account, the two accounts would be shown, in most cases, in the current liability section of the balance sheet.

c. The income recognized in the second year of the four-year contract would be determined using the cost-to-cost method of determining percentage of completion as follows:

- First, the estimated total income from the contract would be determined by deducting the estimated total costs of the contract (the actual costs to date plus the estimated cost to complete) from the contract price.
- Second, the actual costs to date would be divided by the estimated total costs of the contract to arrive at a percentage completed which would be multiplied by the estimated total income from the contract to arrive at the total income recognized to date.
- Third, the total income recognized in the second year of the contract would be determined by deducting the income recognized in the first year of the contract from the total income recognized to date.

d. Earnings per share in the second year of the four-year contract would be higher using the percentage-of-completion method instead of the completed-contract method because income would be recognized in the second year of the contract using the percentage-of-completion method, whereas no income would be recognized in the second year of the contract using the completed-contract method.

Solution Guide

Problem 5 Long-Term Contracts

1. Problem 5 consists of two unrelated parts consisting of preparing schedules for a "firm fixed-price contract" accounted for under the completed-contract method and a cost-plus-fixed-fee contract accounted for by the percentage-of-completion method.

2. Part A has two requirements. The first requirement is to prepare a schedule to show the "cost of uncompleted contract in excess of related billings" or "billings on uncompleted contract in excess of related costs" at 12-31-77, 78 and 79.

2.1 The first requirement can be mapped onto a schedule as follows:

Curtiss Construction Company
"Costs in Excess of Related Billings" or
"Billings in Excess of Related Costs"
at December 31,

	1977	*1978*	*1979*
Contract costs incurred to date			
Billings to Axelrod to date			

Note that we have started to prepare a single schedule whereas the AICPA solution (shown in the unofficial answer following this solution guide) has a separate schedule for each year.

2.2 The next step is to use the data given to complete the above schedule. The first line in the table of information (percentage-of-completion) is not needed since the fourth sentence indicated that "Curtiss appropriately uses the completed-contract method . . ." The second and third lines, contract costs incurred and billings to Axelrod are cumulative numbers so they can be entered directly into the skeleton schedule above.

Curtiss Construction Company
"Costs in Excess of Billings" of
"Billings in Excess of Related Costs"
at December 31,

	1977	*1978*	*1979*
Contract costs incurred to date	$350,000	$2,500,000	$4,250,000
Billings to Axelrod to date	720,000	2,160,000	3,600,000
Costs in excess of billing:		$ 340,000	$ 650,000
Billings in Excess of Costs	$370,000		

3. The second requirement of Part A is to prepare a schedule of profit or loss for the years 1977, 1978, and 1979.

3.1 Remember that Curtiss uses the completed-contract method for this project; therefore, (para 11, ARB 45) no income should be recognized until the project is completed. However, if a loss is expected from the contract, the entire estimated amount of the loss from the contract should be recognized in the year it is determined that a loss will result on the contract.

3.2 As in the first requirement, a more efficient approach than the use of single year schedules shown in the AICPA solution is to prepare one schedule for the three years.

(3.2 continued)

Curtiss Construction Co.
Profit or Loss Recognized on Contract
For the Year Ended December 31

	1977	*1978*	*1979*
Contract Price:	$4,000,000	$4,000,000	$4,000,000
Estimated Total Costs:			
Costs incurred to date	$ 350,000	$2,500,000	$4,250,000
Estimated costs to complete	3,150,000	1,700,000	–0–
Estimated total costs for the three year period, actual for 1979	$3,500,000	$4,200,000	$4,250,000
Estimated total income (loss) for three year period, actual for 1979	500,000	(200,000)	(250,000)
Loss previously recognized			(200,000)
Estimated amount of income (loss) recognized in the current period, actual for 1979	$ 0	$ (200,000)	$ (50,000)

3.3 Journal entries (not required) to record the loss are

1978 Loss on L-T Construction Contract	200,000	
Construction in Progress		200,000

To record estimated loss on L-T contract

1979 Loss on L-T Construction Contract	50,000	
Construction in Progress		50,000

To record additional loss on L-T Contract

4. Part b. requires the computation of the amount of gross profit to be recognized by Butler Corp. for the year ended December 31, 1979 on a cost-plus-fixed-fee contract. Butler appropriately uses the percentage-of-completion method for this contract.

4.1 Butler will earn $300,000 in total income from this project, regardless of the actual costs incurred, since it is a cost-plus-fixed-fee contract. The amount to be recognized in 1979 is computed as follows:

$$\frac{\text{Costs incurred to date}}{{}^{*}\text{Total estimated costs}} \times \text{Fixed Fee} = \text{Income recognized for 1979}$$

$$\frac{\$700{,}000}{{}^{*}\$700{,}000 + \$1{,}400{,}000} \times \$300{,}000 =$$

$100,000 Income recognized for 1979

* Costs incurred to date plus estimated costs to complete the project.

Note that the $500,000 billed under the contract is not relevant in determining the amount of gross profit to be recognized.

Unofficial Answer

Problem 5 Long-Term Contracts

Part a.

1. **Curtiss Construction Company, Inc.**
Computation of Billings on Uncompleted Contract in Excess of Related Costs
December 31, 1977

Partial billings on contract during 1977	$720,000
Deduct construction costs incurred during 1977	350,000
Balance, December 31, 1977	$370,000

Curtiss Construction Company, Inc.
Computation of Costs of Uncompleted Contract in Excess of Related Billings
December 31, 1978

Balance, December 31, 1977—excess of billings over costs	$ (370,000)
Add construction costs incurred during 1978 ($2,500,000 – $350,000)	2,150,000
	1,780,000
Deduct provision for loss on contract recognized during 1978 ($2,500,000 + $1,700,000 – $4,000,000)	200,000
	1,580,000
Deduct partial billings during 1978 ($2,160,000 – $720,000)	1,440,000
Balance, December 31, 1978	$ 140,000

Curtiss Construction Company, Inc.
Computation of Costs Relating to Substantially Completed Contract In Excess of Billings
December 31, 1979

Balance, December 31, 1978—excess of costs over billings	$ 140,000
Add construction costs incurred during 1979 ($4,250,000 – $2,500,000)	1,750,000
	1,890,000
Deduct loss on contract recognized during 1979 ($4,250,000 – $4,000,000 – $200,000)	50,000
	1,840,000
Deduct partial billings during 1979 ($3,600,000 – $2,160,000)	1,440,000
Balance, December 31, 1979	$ 400,000

2. **Curtiss Construction Company, Inc.**
Computation of Profit or Loss to be Recognized on Uncompleted Contract
Year Ended December 31, 1977

Contract price	$4,000,000
Deduct contract costs	
Incurred to December 31, 1977	$ 350,000
Estimated costs to complete	3,150,000
Total estimated contract cost	$3,500,000
Estimated gross profit on contract at completion	$ 500,000
Profit to be recognized	$ –

(The completed-contract method recognizes income only when the contract is completed, or substantially so.)

Curtiss Construction Company, Inc.
Computation of Loss to be Recognized On Uncompleted Contract
Year Ended December 31, 1978

Contract price	$4,000,000
Deduct contract costs	
Incurred to December 31, 1978	2,500,000
Estimated costs to complete	1,700,000
Total estimated contract cost	4,200,000
Loss to be recognized	$ (200,000)

(The completed-contract method requires that provision should be made for an expected loss.)

Curtiss Construction Company, Inc.
Computation of Loss to be Recognized
On Substantially Completed Contract
Year Ended December 31, 1979

Contract price	$4,000,000
Deduct contract costs incurred	4,250,000
Loss on contract	(250,000)
Deduct provision for loss booked at December 31, 1978	200,000
Loss to be recognized	$ (50,000)

Part b.

Butler, Inc.
Computation of Gross Profit to be
Recognized on Uncompleted Contract
Year Ended December 31, 1979

Total contract price	
Estimated contract cost at completion ($700,000 + $1,400,000)	$2,100,000
Fixed fee	300,000
Total	2,400,000
Total estimated cost	2,100,000
Gross profit	$ 300,000
Percentage-of-completion ($700,000 ÷ $2,100,000)	33-1/3%
Gross profit to be recognized ($300,000 x 33-1/3%)	$ 100,000

Solution Guide

Problem 6 Dollar-Value LIFO

Part b.

1. The first requirement is a schedule to compute the internal conversion price indexes for Inventory Pool No. 1 using the dollar-value LIFO inventory method.

1.1 These indexes are computed by dividing ending inventory quantities at year-end prices by ending inventory quantities at base-year prices.

1.2 Ending inventory quantities at year-end prices are given at $847,000 and $840,000 at December 31, 1981 and 1982, respectively.

1.3 Ending inventory dollar amounts at base-year prices are computed by multiplying the given quantities by the base-year prices of $30 for product A and $25 for product B.

2. The second requirement is the inventory amounts at end of 1981 and 1982 using the dollar-value LIFO method.

2.1 At 12/31/81, the ending inventory in base-year prices (computed earlier) is $735,000. Since the beginning inventory (FIFO inventory on date of adoption of the dollar-value LIFO method) was $560,000, the ending inventory consists of a base layer of $560,000 and an incremental layer of $175,000 (735,000 – 560,000). The incremental layer, added during 1981, is priced at the 1981 index by multiplying $175,000 by 1.15 (computed earlier).

2.2 At 12/31/82, the ending inventory in base-year prices (computed earlier) is $640,000. This is a decrease from 12/31/81, when the inventory at base-year prices was $735,000. Therefore, some of the 1981 incremental layer of $175,000 has been depleted, and there is no incremental layer added in 1982. The 1982 ending inventory consists of the base layer of $560,000 and the remaining 1981 layer of $80,000 ($640,000 – $560,000). This layer must again be priced at the 1981 index by multiplying $80,000 by 1.15.

Unofficial Answer

Problem 6 Dollar-Value LIFO

Part b.

1.

Lucas Distributors, Inc.
Computation of Internal Conversion Price Index
for Inventory Pool No. 1
Double Extension Method

	December 31, 1981	*December 31, 1982*
Current inventory at current year cost		
Product A	17,000 x $35 = $595,000	13,000 x $40 = $520,000
Product B	9,000 x $28 = 252,000	10,000 x $32 = 320,000
	$847,000	$840,000
Current inventory at base cost		
Product A	17,000 x $30 = $510,000	13,000 x $30 = $390,000
Product B	9,000 x $25 = 225,000	10,000 x $25 = 250,000
	$735,000	$640,000
Conversion price index	$847,000 ÷ $735,000 = 1.15	$840,000 ÷ $640,000 = 1.31

2.

Lucas Distributors, Inc.
Computation of Inventory Amounts
under Dollar-Value LIFO Method
for Inventory Pool No. 1
at December 31, 1981 and 1982

	Current inventory at base cost	*Conversion price index*	*Inventory at LIFO cost*
December 31, 1981			
Base inventory	$560,000	1.00	$560,000
1981 layer ($735,000 – $560,000)	175,000	1.15 (a)	201,250
Total	$735,000 (a)		$761,250
December 31, 1982			
Base inventory	$560,000	1.00	$560,000
1981 layer (remaining)	80,000 (b)	1.15 (a)	92,000
1982 layer	0	1.31 (a)	0
Total	$640,000 (a)		$652,000

(a) Per schedule for Required No. 1.
(b) After liquidation of $95,000 at base cost:

Product A (4,000 x $30)	$120,000
Product B (1,000 x $25)	(25,000)
Net	$95,000

Answer Outline

Problem 7 Inventory: Theoretical Issues

Part a.

1. Financial income when payments made
   - Cash discounts **should not be**
     - Recorded as income
       - Recognize income as inventories sold
     - Recorded when payments made
       - Record discount when related purchase recorded
2. Reduction of period's CGS when payments made
   - Cash discounts **should not be**
     - Accounted as reduction of CGS when payments made
       - CGS reduced as inventories are sold
     - Recorded when payments made
       - Discount recorded when purchase recorded for proper matching
3. Direct reduction of purchase cost
   - Cash discounts should be accounted for as direct reduction of purchase price
     - Reduce cost of inventories
     - Purchases recorded net of discount reflect net cash paid
     - Basis of accounting for inventories is cost
     - Price paid to acquire inventory

Part b.

Effects of using LIFO during a period of rising prices
- I/S
  - CGS higher and net income lower
    - Goods sold at most recent (higher) prices
- B/S
  - Inventories and R/E lower
    - Goods at oldest (lower) purchase prices
- Greater cash flow
  - Lower taxable income decreases income taxes

Part c.

LCM rule used with FIFO because of
- Matching principle
  - Recognize decline in utility of inventories currently as loss
- Balance sheet conservatism

Unofficial Answer

Problem 7 Inventory: Theoretical Issues

a. 1. Cash discounts should not be accounted for as financial income when payments are made. Income should be recognized when the earning process is complete (when Taylor sells the inventory). Furthermore, cash discounts should not be recorded when the payments are made because in order to properly match a cash discount with the related purchase, the cash discount should be recorded when the related purchase is recorded.

2. Cash discounts should not be accounted for as a reduction of cost of goods sold for period when payments are made. Cost of goods sold should be reduced when the earning process is complete (when Taylor sells the inventory which has been reduced by the cash discounts). Furthermore, cash discounts should not be recorded when the payments are made because in order to properly match a cash discount with the related purchase, the cash discount should be recorded when the related purchase is recorded.

3. Cash discounts should be accounted for as a direct reduction of purchase cost because they reduce the cost of the inventories. Purchases should be recorded net of cash discount to reflect the net cash to be paid. The primary basis of accounting for inventories is cost, which represents the price paid or consideration given to acquire an asset.

b. Inventories would be lower using the LIFO inventory method instead of the FIFO method over a substantial time period when purchase prices of household appliances are rising because the inventories are at the oldest (lower) purchase prices instead of the most recent (higher) purchase prices. Correspondingly, cost of goods sold would be higher because the cost of goods sold is at more recent (higher) purchase prices instead of older (lower) purchase prices. Consequently, net income and retained earnings would be lower.

More cash flow would generally be available using the LIFO inventory method instead of the FIFO method because taxable income is decreased, resulting generally in accrual and payment of lower income taxes. Correspondingly, income tax expense would generally be lower.

c. The lower of cost or market rule is used for valuing inventories when the FIFO method is used because of (a) the matching principle, that is, the decline in the utility of the household appliances inventories below its cost should be recognized as a loss in the current period, and (b) the concept of balance sheet conservatism.

Multiple Choice Questions (1 - 50)

1. Herr, Inc., has a fiscal year ending April 30. On May 1, 1982, Herr borrowed $10,000,000 at 15% to finance construction of its own building. Repayments of the loan are to commence the month following completion of the building. During the year ended April 30, 1983, expenditures for the partially completed structure totaled $6,000,000. These expenditures were incurred evenly throughout the year. Interest earned on the unexpended portion of the loan amounted to $400,000 for the year. How much should be shown as capitalized interest on Herr's financial statements at April 30, 1983?
   a. $0
   b. $ 50,000
   c. $ 450,000
   d. $1,100,000

2. During 1980, Belardo Corporation constructed and manufactured certain assets, and incurred the following interest costs in connection with those activities:

	Interest costs incurred
Warehouse constructed for Belardo's own use	$20,000
Special-order machine for sale to unrelated customer, produced according to customer's specifications	9,000
Inventories routinely manufactured, produced on a repetitive basis	7,000

All of these assets required an extended period of time for completion. Assuming the effect of interest capitalization is material, what is the total amount of interest costs to be capitalized?
   a. $0
   b. $20,000
   c. $29,000
   d. $36,000

3. In October 1982 Ewing Company exchanged an old packaging machine, which cost $120,000 and was 50% depreciated, for a dissimilar used machine and paid a cash difference of $16,000. The market value of the old packaging machine was determined to be $70,000. For the year ended December 31, 1982, what amount of gain or loss should Ewing recognize on this exchange?
   a. $0.
   b. $ 6,000 loss.
   c. $10,000 loss.
   d. $10,000 gain.

4. Madden Company owns a tract of land which it purchased in 1980 for $100,000. The land is held as a future plant site and has a fair market value of $140,000 on July 1, 1983. Hall Company also owns a tract of land held as a future plant site. Hall paid $180,000 for the land in 1982 and the land has a fair market value of $200,000 on July 1, 1983. On this date Madden exchanged its land and paid $50,000 cash for the land owned by Hall. At what amount should Madden record the land acquired in the exchange?
   a. $150,000
   b. $160,000
   c. $190,000
   d. $200,000

5. On September 1, 1982, Sol, Inc., exchanged 2,000 shares of its $25 par value common stock held in treasury, for a parcel of land to be held for a future plant site. The treasury shares were acquired by Sol at a cost of $60 per share. Sol's common stock had a fair market value of $80 per share on September 1, 1982. Sol received $9,000 from the sale of scrap when an existing building on the site was razed. The land should be carried at
   a. $111,000
   b. $120,000
   c. $151,000
   d. $160,000

6. On September 1, 1982, Bertz, Inc., exchanged a delivery truck for a parcel of land. Bertz bought this truck in 1980 for $10,000. At September 1, 1982, the truck had a book value of $6,500 and a fair market value of $5,000. Bertz gave $6,000 in cash in addition to the truck as part of this transaction. The previous owner of the land had listed the land for sale at $12,000. At what amount should Bertz record the land?
   a. $11,000
   b. $11,500
   c. $12,000
   d. $12,500

7. In December 1980 Belmont Company exchanged an old bottling machine, which cost $60,000 and was two-thirds depreciated, for a similar used machine having a current fair value of $24,000, and received a cash difference of $8,000. What is the amount of gain that Belmont should recognize on this exchange in the year ended December 31, 1980?
   a. $0
   b. $3,000
   c. $5,000
   d. $8,000

8. Minor Baseball Company had a player contract with Doe that was recorded in its accounting records at $145,000. Better Baseball Company had a player contract with Smith that was recorded in its accounting records at $140,000. Minor traded Doe to Better for Smith by exchanging each player's contract. The fair value of each contract was $150,000. What amount should be shown in the accounting records after the exchange of player contracts?

	Minor	*Better*
a.	$140,000	$140,000
b.	$140,000	$145,000
c.	$145,000	$140,000
d.	$150,000	$150,000

9. Bicar Corporation owns 10% of the outstanding capital stock of Kopel, Inc. On December 31, 1981, when Kopel's retained earnings was $50,000, Bicar received a plot of land from Kopel in a nonreciprocal transfer. Kopel's cost of the land was $7,000 and its fair market value at December 31, 1981, was $15,000. At what amount should this land be recorded on Bicar's books?

a. $0
b. $ 5,000
c. $ 7,000
d. $15,000

10. On July 14, 1981, JX Corporation exchanged 1,000 shares of its $8 par value common stock for a plot of land. JX's common stock is listed on the NYSE and traded at an average price of $21 per share on July 14. The land was appraised by independent real estate appraisers on July 14 at $23,000. As a result of this exchange, JX's additional paid-in capital will increase by

a. $0
b. $ 8,000
c. $13,000
d. $15,000

11. A donated fixed asset for which the fair value has been determined should be recorded as a debit to fixed assets and a credit to

a. Additional paid-in capital.
b. Retained earnings.
c. Deferred income.
d. Other income.

12. During 1979, the Commander Corporation acquired 3 pieces of machinery at an auction for a lump sum price of $240,000. In addition, Commander paid $12,000 to have the machines installed. An appraisal disclosed the following values:

Machine A	$ 50,000
Machine B	$150,000
Machine C	$100,000

What costs should be assigned to Machines A, B, and C, respectively?

a. $40,000, $120,000, and $ 80,000.
b. $42,000, $126,000, and $ 84,000.
c. $50,000, $150,000, and $100,000.
d. $84,000, $ 84,000, and $ 84,000.

13. On June 18, 1982, Paul Printing Company incurred the following costs for one of its printing presses:

Purchase of collating and stapling attachment	$42,000
Installation of attachment	18,000
Replacement parts for overhaul of press	13,000
Labor and overhead in connection with overhaul	7,000
Total	$80,000

The overhaul resulted in a significant increase in production. Neither the attachment nor the overhaul increased the estimated useful life of the press. How much of the above costs should be capitalized?

a. $42,000
b. $55,000
c. $60,000
d. $80,000

14. When a company replaces an old asphalt roof on its plant with a new fiberglass insulated roof, which of the following types of expenditure occurs?

a. Ordinary repair and maintenance.
b. Addition.
c. Rearrangement
d. Betterment.

Items 15 through 17 are based on the following information:

Vorst Corporation's schedule of depreciable assets at December 31, 1981, was as follows:

Asset	*Cost*	*Accumulated depreciation*	*Acquisition date*	*Salvage value*
A	$100,000	$ 64,000	1980	$20,000
B	55,000	36,000	1979	10,000
C	70,000	33,600	1979	14,000
	$225,000	$133,600		$44,000

Vorst takes a full year's depreciation expense in the year of an asset's acquisition, and no depreciation expense in the year of an asset's disposition. The estimated useful life of each depreciable asset is five years.

15. Vorst depreciates asset A on the double-declining-balance method. How much depreciation expense should Vorst record in 1982 for asset A?

a. $32,000
b. $25,600
c. $14,400
d. $ 6,400

16. Using the same depreciation method as used in 1979, 1980, and 1981, how much depreciation expense should Vorst record in 1982 for asset B?

a. $ 6,000
b. $ 9,000
c. $11,000
d. $12,000

17. Vorst depreciates asset C by the straight-line method. On June 30, 1982, Vorst sold asset C for $28,000 cash. How much gain or (loss) should Vorst record in 1982 on the disposal of asset C?

a. $2,800
b. ($2,800)
c. ($5,600)
d. ($8,400)

18. When one machine is retired, the accumulated depreciation account is debited for the original cost of that machine less any residual recovery under which of the following depreciation methods?

	Composite	*Group*
a.	No	No
b.	No	Yes
c.	Yes	No
d.	Yes	Yes

19. On January 2, 1979, Luco Manufacturing Company bought a new machine for $1,000,000. The machine has an estimated useful life of eight years and a salvage value of $100,000. Depreciation was computed by the sum-of-the-years-digits method. What amount should appear for this machine on Luco's balance sheet at December 31, 1980, net of accumulated depreciation?

a. $525,000
b. $625,000
c. $787,500
d. $825,000

20. On July 1, 1980, Mundo Corporation purchased factory equipment for $50,000. Salvage value was estimated at $2,000. The equipment will be depreciated over ten years using the double-declining-balance method. Counting the year of acquisition as one-half year, Mundo should record 1981 depreciation expense of

a. $ 7,680
b. $ 9,000
c. $ 9,600
d. $10,000

21. On January 1, 1976, Kent Corporation purchased a machine for $50,000. Kent paid shipping expenses of $500 as well as installation costs of $1,200. The machine was estimated to have a useful life of ten years and an estimated salvage value of $3,000. In January 1977, additions costing $3,600 were made to the machine in order to comply with pollution control ordinances. These additions neither prolonged the life of the machine nor did they have any salvage value. If Kent records depreciation under the straight-line method, depreciation expense for 1977 is

a. $4,870
b. $5,170
c. $5,270
d. $5,570

22. On January 2, 1975, Mogul Company acquired equipment to be used in its manufacturing operations. The equipment has an estimated useful life of 10 years and an estimated salvage value of $5,000. The depreciation applicable to this equipment was $24,000 for 1977, computed under the sum-of-the-years-digits method. What was the acquisition cost of the equipment?

a. $165,000
b. $170,000
c. $240,000
d. $245,000

23. A schedule of machinery owned by Lester Manufacturing Company is presented below:

	Total cost	*Estimated salvage value*	*Estimated life in years*
Machine A	$550,000	$50,000	20
Machine B	200,000	20,000	15
Machine C	40,000	—	5

Lester computes depreciation on the straight-line method. Based upon the information presented, the composite life of these assets (in years) should be

a. 13.3
b. 16.0
c. 18.0
d. 19.8

24. On January 1, 1978, Walton Company purchased a machine for $200,000 and established an annual straight-line depreciation rate of 10%, with no salvage value. During 1982 Walton determined that the machine will not be economically useful in its production process after December 31, 1982. Walton estimated that the machine had no scrap value at December 31, 1982, and would be disposed of in early 1983 at a cost of $5,000. In its income statement for the year ended December 31, 1982, what amount(s) and type of charge(s) should Walton report for the machine?

	Depreciation expense	*Loss on abandonment*
a.	$0	$125,000
b.	$ 20,000	$100,000
c.	$ 20,000	$105,000
d.	$120,000	$ 5,000

25. On July 1, 1981, Stone Corporation received a condemnation award of $300,000 as compensation for the forced sale of a plant located on company property which stood in the path of a new highway. On this date the plant building had a depreciated cost of $150,000 and the land cost was $50,000. On October 1, 1981, Stone purchased a parcel of land for a new plant site at a cost of $125,000. Ignoring income taxes, Stone should report on its income statement for the year ended December 31, 1981, a gain of

a. $0
b. $ 25,000
c. $ 75,000
d. $100,000

26. Crowder Company acquired a tract of land containing an extractable natural resource. Crowder is required by the purchase contract to restore the land to a condition suitable for recreational use after it has extracted the natural resource. Geological surveys estimate that the recoverable reserves will be 5,000,000 tons, and that the land will have a value of $1,000,000 after restoration. Relevant cost information follows:

Land	$9,000,000
Estimated restoration costs	1,500,000

If Crowder maintains no inventories of extracted material, what should be the charge to depletion expense per ton of extracted material?

a. $2.10
b. $1.90
c. $1.80
d. $1.60

27. In January 1978, the Under Mine Corporation purchased a mineral mine for $3,400,000 with removable ore estimated by geological surveys at 4,000,000 tons. The property has an estimated value of $200,000 after the ore has been extracted. The company incurred $800,000 of development costs preparing the mine for production. During 1978, 400,000 tons were removed and 375,000 tons were sold. What is the amount of depletion that Under Mine should record for 1978?

a. $375,000
b. $393,750
c. $400,000
d. $420,000

28. On July 1, 1982, a fire destroyed $100,000 of Brody Company's $300,000 inventory (fair market values). Brody carried a $120,000 fire insurance policy with an 80% coinsurance clause. What is the maximum amount of insurance that Brody can collect as a result of this loss?

a. $ 50,000
b. $ 80,000
c. $ 96,000
d. $100,000

29. A purchased patent has a remaining legal life of 15 years. It should be

a. Expensed in the year of acquisition.
b. Amortized over 15 years regardless of its useful life.
c. Amortized over its useful life if less than 15 years.
d. Amortized over 40 years.

30. Should the following fees associated with the registration of an internally developed patent be capitalized?

	Legal fees	*Registration fees*
a.	Yes	Yes
b.	Yes	No
c.	No	Yes
d.	No	No

31. During 1975, Traco Machine Company spent $176,000 on research and development costs for an invention. This invention was patented on January 2, 1976, at a nominal cost that was expensed in 1976. The patent had a legal life of 17 years and an estimated useful life of 8 years. In January 1980, Traco paid $16,000 for legal fees in a successful defense of the patent. Amortization for 1980 should be

a. $0
b. $ 1,231
c. $ 4,000
d. $26,000

32. In January 1975 Tracy Corporation purchased a patent for a new consumer product for $180,000. At the time of purchase, the patent was valid for fifteen years. Due to the competitive nature of the product however, the patent was estimated to have a useful life of only ten years. During 1978 the product was permanently removed from the market under governmental order because of a potential health hazard present in the product. What amount should Tracy charge to expense during 1978, assuming amortization is recorded at the end of each year?

a. $12,000
b. $18,000
c. $126,000
d. $144,000

33. The general ledger of the Flint Corporation as of December 31, 1976, includes the following accounts:

Organization costs	$ 5,000
Deposits with advertising agency (will be used to promote goodwill)	8,000
Discount on bonds payable	15,000
Excess of cost over book value of net assets of acquired subsidiary	70,000
Trademarks	12,000

In the preparation of Flint's balance sheet as of December 31, 1976, what should be reported as total intangible assets?

a. $ 87,000
b. $ 92,000
c. $ 95,000
d. $110,000

34. Which of the following should be expensed as incurred by the franchisee for a franchise with an estimated useful life of ten years?

a. Amount paid to the franchisor for the franchise.
b. Periodic payments to a company, other than the franchisor, for that company's franchise.
c. Legal fees paid to the franchisee's lawyers to obtain the franchise.
d. Periodic payments to the franchisor based on the franchisee's revenues.

35. On January 1, 1980, Ulmer Corporation incurred organization costs of $12,000. For financial accounting purposes, Ulmer is amortizing these costs on the same basis as the maximum allowable for Federal income tax purposes. What portion of the organization costs will Ulmer defer to years subsequent to 1980?

a. $0
b. $ 2,400
c. $ 9,600
d. $12,000

36. The Plaza Company was organized late in 1978 and began operations on January 1, 1979. Plaza is engaged in conducting market research studies on behalf of manufacturers. Prior to the start of operations, the following costs were incurred:

Attorney's fees in connection with organization of Plaza	$ 4,000
Improvements to leased offices prior to occupancy	7,000
Meetings of incorporators, state filing fees and other organization expenses	5,000
	$16,000

Plaza has elected to record amortization of organization costs over the maximum period allowable under generally accepted accounting principles. What is the amount of organization costs amortized for 1979?

a. $ 225
b. $ 400
c. $1,800
d. $3,200

37. Frye Company incurred research and development costs in 1982 as follows:

Equipment acquired for use in research and development projects	$1,000,000
Depreciation on the above equipment	150,000
Materials used	200,000
Compensation costs of personnel	500,000
Outside consulting fees	100,000
Indirect costs appropriately allocated	250,000

The total research and development costs charged in Frye's 1982 income statement should be

a. $ 650,000
b. $ 900,000
c. $1,200,000
d. $1,800,000

38. Tech Products, Inc., incurred the following costs during the year ended December 31, 1980:

Laboratory research aimed at discovery of new knowledge	$ 7,000
Design, construction, and testing of pre-production prototypes	9,000
Design of tools, jigs, molds, and dies involving new technology	15,000
Quality control during commercial production, including routine testing of products	18,000

The total amount to be classified and expensed as research and development is

a. $ 7,000
b. $22,000
c. $31,000
d. $49,000

39. An activity that would be expensed currently as research and development costs is the

a. Adaptation of an existing capability to a particular requirement or customer's need as a part of continuing commercial activity.
b. Legal work in connection with patent applications or litigation, and the sale or licensing of patents.
c. Engineering follow-through in an early phase of commercial production.
d. Testing in search for or evaluation of product or process alternatives.

40. Which of the following principles best describes the current method of accounting for research and development costs?

a. Associating cause and effect.
b. Systematic and rational allocation.
c. Income tax minimization.
d. Immediate recognition as an expense.

May 1984 Questions

41. During 1983 Cooke Company made the following expenditures relating to plant machinery and equipment:

Continuing, frequent, and low cost repairs	$36,000
Special long-term protection devices were attached to ten machines	11,000
A broken gear on a machine was replaced	2,000

How much should be charged to repairs and maintenance in 1983?

a. $36,000
b. $38,000
c. $47,000
d. $49,000

42. On November 1, 1983, Rice Company purchased for $200,000 a tract of land as a factory site. The old building on the property was razed and salvaged materials resulting from demolition were sold. Additional costs incurred and salvage proceeds realized during November 1983 were as follows:

Demolition of old building	$25,000
Legal fees for purchase contract and recording ownership	5,000
Title guarantee insurance	6,000
Proceeds from sale of salvaged materials	4,000

In its November 30, 1983, balance sheet, Rice should report a balance in the land account of

a. $211,000
b. $221,000
c. $230,000
d. $232,000

43. Grey Company purchased a machine on January 2, 1982, for $500,000. The machine has an estimated useful life of five years and a salvage value of $50,000. Depreciation was computed by the 150% declining balance method. The accumulated depreciation balance at December 31, 1983, should be

a. $180,000
b. $229,500
c. $245,000
d. $255,000

44. The following expenditures relating to the plant building were made by Pine Company during the year ended December 31, 1983:

Replacement of the old shingle roof with a fireproof tile roof	$75,000
Repainted the plant building	5,000
Major improvements to the electrical wiring system	35,000

How much should be capitalized in 1983?

a. $ 35,000
b. $ 75,000
c. $110,000
d. $115,000

45. On December 31, 1983, Marsh Company completed the rearrangement of a group of factory machines to secure greater efficiency in production and incurred the following costs:

Moving costs	$20,000
Reinstallation costs	40,000
Total	$60,000

Marsh estimated that the benefits resulting from the rearrangement would extend over the remaining five-year useful lives of the machines. How much of the rearrangement costs should be capitalized at December 31, 1983?

a. $0
b. $20,000
c. $40,000
d. $60,000

46. During 1983 Mann Company developed a new product to be marketed beginning January 1, 1984. The following costs, incurred during 1983 in the development of this product, are expected to be recovered by December 31, 1985:

Research and development departmental costs	$365,000
Materials and supplies consumed	110,000
Compensation paid to research consultants	200,000
	$675,000

How much of the costs incurred should Mann charge to expense in 1983?

a. $675,000
b. $475,000
c. $225,000
d. $0

47. On December 30, 1983, Diamond Company traded in an old machine with a book value of $10,000 for a similar new machine having a list price of $32,000, and paid a cash difference of $19,000. Diamond should record the new machine at

a. $32,000
b. $29,000
c. $22,000
d. $19,000

48. On October 10, 1983, Girard, Inc., exchanged 2,000 shares of its $50 par value common stock held in treasury for a patent owned by Waxman Company. The treasury shares were acquired in 1982 at a cost of $80,000. At the exchange date Girard's common stock was quoted at $55 per share and the patent had a net carrying value on Waxman's books of $90,000. Girard should record the patent at

a. $ 80,000
b. $ 90,000
c. $100,000
d. $110,000

49. A machine with a four-year estimated useful life and an estimated 15% salvage value was acquired on January 1. Would depreciation expense using the sum-of-the-years'-digits method of depreciation be higher or lower than depreciation expense using the double-declining-balance method of depreciation in the first and second years?

	First year	*Second year*
a.	Higher	Higher
b.	Higher	Lower
c.	Lower	Higher
d.	Lower	Lower

50. A machine with an original estimated useful life of ten years was moved to another location in the factory after it had been in service for three years. The efficiency of the machine is increased for its remaining useful life. The reinstallation costs should be capitalized if the remaining useful life of the machine is

	Five years	*Ten years*
a.	No	No
b.	No	Yes
c.	Yes	No
d.	Yes	Yes

Repeat Questions

(584,P1,15) Identical to item 32 above

(584,T1,9) Identical to item 11 above

Problems

Problem 1 Accounting for R&D (578,T5)

(20 to 25 minutes)

The Thomas Company is in the process of developing a revolutionary new product. A new division of the company was formed to develop, manufacture, and market this new product. As of year end (December 31, 1977) the new product has not been manufactured for resale; however, a prototype unit was built and is in operation.

Throughout 1977 the new division incurred certain costs. These costs include design and engineering studies, prototype manufacturing costs, administrative expenses (including salaries of administrative personnel), and market research costs. In addition, approximately $500,000 in equipment (estimated useful life—10 years) was purchased for use in developing and manufacturing the new product. Approximately $200,000 of this equipment was built specifically for the design development of the new product; the remaining $300,000 of equipment was used to manufacture the pre-production prototype and will be used to manufacture the new product once it is in commercial production.

Required:

a. What is the definition of "research" and of "development" as defined in Statement of Financial Accounting Standards No. 2?

b. Briefly indicate the practical and conceptual reasons for the conclusion reached by the Financial Accounting Standards Board on accounting and reporting practices for research and development costs.

c. In accordance with Statement of Financial Accounting Standards No. 2, how should the various costs of Thomas described above be recorded on the financial statements for the year ended December 31, 1977?

Problem 2 Property, Plant, and Equipment (1180,T2)

(15 to 25 minutes)

Among the principal topics related to the accounting for the property, plant, and equipment of a company are acquisition and retirement.

Required:

a. What expenditures should be capitalized when equipment is acquired for cash?

b. Assume that the market value of equipment acquired is not determinable by reference to a similar purchase for cash. Describe how the acquiring company should determine the capitalizable cost of equipment purchased by exchanging it for each of the following:

1. Bonds having an established market price.
2. Common stock not having an established market price.
3. Similar equipment having a determinable market value.

c. Describe the factors that determine whether expenditures relating to property, plant, and equipment already in use should be capitalized.

d. Describe how to account for the gain or loss on the sale of property, plant, and equipment for cash.

Problem 3 Property, Plant and Equipment (576,T3)

(20 to 25 minutes)

Part a. Property, plant, and equipment (plant assets) generally represent a material portion of the total assets of most companies. Accounting for the acquisition and usage of such assets is, therefore, an important part of the financial reporting process.

Required:

1. Distinguish between revenue and capital expenditures and explain why this distinction is important.

2. Briefly define depreciation as used in accounting.

3. Identify the factors that are relevant in determining the annual depreciation and explain whether these factors are determined objectively or whether they are based on judgment.

4. Explain why depreciation is usually shown in the sources of funds section of the statement of changes in financial position.

Part b. A company may acquire plant assets (among other ways) for cash, on a deferred-payment plan, by exchanging other assets, or by a combination of these ways.

Required:

1. Identify six costs that should be capitalized as the cost of land. For your answer, assume that land with an existing building is acquired for cash and that the existing building is to be removed

in the immediate future in order that a new building can be constructed on that site.

2. At what amount should a company record a plant asset acquired on a deferred-payment plan?

3. In general, at what amount should plant assets received in exchange for other nonmonetary assets be recorded? Specifically, at what amount should a company record a new machine acquired by exchanging an older, similar machine and paying cash?

Problem 4 Comprehensive Schedules: Fixed Assets (1182,P5)

(40 to 50 minutes)

This problem consists of two unrelated parts.

Part a. Information concerning Tully Corporation's intangible assets is as follows:

- On January 1, 1981, Tully signed an agreement to operate as a franchisee of Rapid Copy Service, Inc., for an initial franchise fee of $85,000. Of this amount, $25,000 was paid when the agreement was signed and the balance is payable in four annual payments of $15,000 each beginning January 1, 1982. The agreement provides that the down payment is not refundable and no future services are required of the franchisor. The present value at January 1, 1981, of the four annual payments discounted at 14% (the implicit rate for a loan of this type) is $43,700. The agreement also provides that 5% of the revenue from the franchise must be paid to the franchisor annually. Tully's revenue from the franchise for 1981 was $900,000. Tully estimates the useful life of the franchise to be ten years.
- Tully incurred $78,000 of experimental and development costs in its laboratory to develop a patent which was granted on January 2, 1981. Legal fees and other costs associated with registration of the patent totaled $16,400. Tully estimates that the useful life of the patent will be eight years.
- A trademark was purchased from Walton Company for $40,000 on July 1, 1978. Expenditures for successful litigation in defense of the trademark totaling $10,000 were paid on July 1, 1981. Tully estimates that the useful life of the trademark will be 20 years from the date of acquisition.

Required:

1. Prepare a schedule showing the intangibles section of Tully's balance sheet at December 31, 1981. Show supporting computations in good form.

2. Prepare a schedule showing all expenses resulting from the transactions that would appear on Tully's income statement for the year ended December 31, 1981. Show supporting computations in good form.

Part b. On January 1, 1980, Brock Corporation purchased a tract of land (site number 101) with a building for $600,000. Additionally, Brock paid a real estate broker's commission of $36,000, legal fees of $6,000, and title guarantee insurance of $18,000. The closing statement indicated that the land value was $500,000 and the building value was $100,000. Shortly after acquisition, the building was razed at a cost of $75,000.

Brock entered into a $3,000,000 fixed-price contract with Barnett Builders, Inc., on March 1, 1980, for the construction of an office building on land site number 101. The building was completed and occupied on September 30, 1981. Additional construction costs were incurred as follows:

Plans, specifications and blueprints	$12,000
Architects' fees for design and supervision	95,000

The building is estimated to have a forty-year life from date of completion and will be depreciated using the 150% declining balance method.

To finance the construction cost, Brock borrowed $3,000,000 on March 1, 1980. The loan is payable in ten annual installments of $300,000 plus interest at the rate of 14%. Brock's average amounts of accumulated building construction expenditures were as follows:

For the period March 1 to December 31, 1980	$ 900,000
For the period January 1 to September 30, 1981	2,300,000

Required:

1. Prepare a schedule which discloses the individual costs making up the balance in the land account in respect of land site number 101 as of September 30, 1981.

2. Prepare a schedule which discloses the individual costs that should be capitalized in the office building account as of September 30, 1981. Show supporting computations in good form.

3. Prepare a schedule showing the depreciation expense computation of the office building for the year ended December 31, 1981.

Problem 5 Plant Asset Transactions (582,P5a)

(20 to 30 minutes)

Part a. After a two-year search for a buyer, Hobson, Inc., sold its idle plant facility to Jackson Company for $700,000 on January 1, 1977. On this date the plant had a depreciated cost on Hobson's books of $500,000. Under the agreement Jackson paid $100,000 cash on January 1, 1977, and signed a $600,000 note bearing interest at 10%. The note was payable in installments of $100,000, $200,000, and $300,000 on January 1, 1978, 1979 and 1980, respectively. The note was secured by a mortgage on the property sold. Hobson appropriately accounted for the sale under the cost recovery method since there was no reasonable basis for estimating the degree of collectibility of the note receivable. Jackson repaid the note with three late installment payments, which were accepted by Hobson, as follows:

Date of payment	*Principal*	*Interest*
July 1, 1978	$100,000	$90,000
December 31, 1979	200,000	75,000
February 1, 1981	300,000	32,500

On April 1, 1981, Hobson exchanged a tract of land, which it had acquired for $105,000 as a potential future building site, for a used printing press of Tyler Company, and paid a cash difference of $30,000. The fair value of the land was $190,000 on the exchange date based on a recent appraisal. The fair value of the printing press was not reasonably determinable, but it had a depreciated cost of $210,000 on Tyler's books at April 1, 1981.

Required:

1. Prepare a schedule (using the format shown below) to record the initial transaction for the sale of the idle plant facility, the application of subsequent cash collections on the note, and the necessary journal entry on the date the transaction is complete.

Date	*Cash received*	*Note receivable*	*Idle plant (net)*	*Deferred income*	*Income recognized*
	Debit	*Dr. (Cr.)*	*(Credit)*	*Dr. (Cr.)*	*(Credit)*
1/1/77	$100,000				
7/1/78	190,000				
12/31/79	275,000				
2/1/81	332,500				
2/1/81					

2. Prepare the journal entry on Hobson's books to record the exchange transaction with Tyler. Show supporting computations in good form.

Multiple Choice Answers

1.	c	11.	a	21.	c	31.	c	41.	b
2.	c	12.	b	22.	b	32.	c	42.	d
3.	d	13.	d	23.	b	33.	a	43.	d
4.	a	14.	d	24.	c	34.	d	44.	c
5.	c	15.	c	25.	d	35.	c	45.	d
6.	a	16.	a	26.	b	36.	a	46.	a
7.	b	17.	d	27.	c	37.	c	47.	b
8.	c	18.	d	28.	a	38.	c	48.	d
9.	d	19.	b	29.	c	39.	d	49.	c
10.	c	20.	b	30.	a	40.	d	50.	d

Multiple Choice Answer Explanations

A. Capitalization of Interest

1. (583,Q1,14) (c) The requirement is to determine the amount of interest to be capitalized on Herr's financial statements at April 30, 1983. The requirements of SFAS 34, para 17 are met: (1) expenditures for the asset have been made, (2) activities that are necessary to get the asset ready for its intended use are in progress, and (3) interest cost is being incurred. The amount to be capitalized is determined by applying an interest rate to the average amount of accumulated expenditures for the asset during the period (SFAS 34, para 13). Because the $6,000,000 of expenditures incurred for the year ended April 30, 1983, were incurred evenly throughout the year, the average amount of expenditures for the year is $3,000,000 ($6,000,000 ÷ 2). Therefore, the amount of interest to be capitalized is $450,000 ($3,000,000 x 15%). In any period the total amount of interest cost to be capitalized shall not exceed the total amount of interest cost incurred by the enterprise. Finally, per FASB Technical Bulletin 81-5, para 8, the interest earned of $400,000 is irrelevant to the question addressed in this problem because such interest earned on the unexpended portion of the loan is not to be offset against the amount eligible for capitalization.

2. (1181,Q1,14) (c) The requirement is total interest costs to be capitalized. Para 9-10 of SFAS 34 identify assets which qualify for interest capitalization: assets constructed for an enterprise's own use; and assets intended for sale or lease that are produced as discrete projects. Inventories that are routinely produced in large quantities on a repetitive basis do not qualify for interest capitalization.

C. Nonmonetary Exchanges

3. (1183,P1,9) (d) The requirement is the amount of gain (loss) to be recognized on an exchange of dissimilar assets. Per APB 29, nonmonetary exchanges of **dissimilar** assets are accounted for on the basis of fair values. In this transaction, an asset with a book value of $60,000 (50% x $120,000) is exchanged when it has a fair market value of $70,000. Therefore, a $10,000 gain ($70,000 – $60,000) is recognized. The new asset acquired is recorded at the fair value of the assets surrendered ($16,000 cash and $70,000 machine, or $86,000).

New machine	86,000		(70,000 + 16,000)
Accum. depr.	60,000		(50% x 120,000)
Old machine		120,000	
Cash		16,000	
Gain on exchange		10,000	(70,000 – 60,000)

4. (1183,P1,16) (a) The requirement is the amount at which Madden should record land acquired in a nonmonetary exchange of similar assets. Per APB 29, such exchanges are recorded on the basis of book value since the earnings process has not culminated. Therefore, the land acquired is recorded at total of the cash paid ($50,000) and the book value of the land surrendered ($100,000), or $150,000. The economic gain of $40,000 ($140,000 market value less $100,000 book value) is not recognized. The journal entry is:

Land	150,000	
Land		100,000
Cash		50,000

5. (583,Q1,1) (c) The requirement is to determine the cost of a future plant site. APB 29, para 18 indicates that nonmonetary transactions should be based on fair market values. The land was acquired in exchange for treasury stock that had a fair market value of $160,000 (2,000 shares at $80). Also, $9,000 was received from the sale of scrap, resulting from the razing of a building existing on the site when it was purchased. This $9,000 is treated as a reduction of the cost of the plant site, resulting in a capitalized value of $151,000 ($160,000 – $9,000).

6. (583,Q1,2) (a) The requirement is the amount at which to record land acquired in exchange for a delivery truck. Per APB 29, para 18 both gains and losses are recognized in exchanges involving dissimilar assets and fair values reasonably determinable. The solutions approach is to prepare the journal entry to record the trade of the delivery truck for the land.

Land	11,000	
Accumulated deprec.	3,500	
Loss on exchange	1,500	
Delivery truck		10,000
Cash		6,000

The loss on the exchange of the delivery truck for the land is $1,500 ($6,500 book value – $5,000 fair market value). The value assigned to the land is the fair value of the asset(s) given up, i.e., the delivery truck ($5,000) plus cash paid ($6,000), or $11,000.

7. (1181,P1,5) (b) The requirement is the amount of gain to be recognized by Belmont on an exchange of similar assets. According to APB 29, an exchange of similar productive assets does **not** result in the culmination of an earnings process. A gain on such an exchange is recognized only to the extent that monetary consideration (boot) is received. See para 22 of APB 29. The logic involved is that a gain is only recognized on the portion of the asset sold (for cash), not on the portion of the asset exchanged (for a similar asset).The solutions approach is to first compute the total gain **realized** on the sale, then compute the portion of the gain **recognized.** The gain realized is the difference between the fair value of the assets received ($24,000 + $8,000) and the book value of asset relinquished ($60,000 – $40,000). The portion of the total $12,000 which is recognized is that portion relating to the boot received:

$$\left(\frac{\text{Boot}}{\text{Boot + FV of asset received}}\right) \times \left(\begin{matrix}\text{Total}\\ \text{gain}\end{matrix}\right) = \begin{matrix}\text{Gain}\\ \text{recognized}\end{matrix}$$

$$\left(\frac{\$8{,}000}{\$8{,}000 + \$24{,}000}\right) \times \$12{,}000 = \underline{\underline{\$3{,}000}}$$

8. (1178,P1,17) (c) The requirement is the asset carrying values on the books of two baseball companies after exchanging player contracts. Generally, nonmonetary exchanges are recorded at fair market value per APB 29. The exception (for which the nonmonetary exchange is recorded on a cost basis) is when the exchange is not the culmination of an earnings process per para 21. More specifically, an exchange of a productive asset not held for sale in the ordinary course of business for a similar productive asset is not the culmination of an earnings process. Accordingly the exchange of player contracts should be accounted for at cost. Thus, Minor exchanged a player contract that had a cost of $145,000 for another contract which will now be valued at $145,000. Better Company exchanged a contract that had a cost of $140,000 for another contract. Thus the other contract will be valued by Better at $140,000.

9. (582,Q1,6) (d) The requirement is the amount at which land received in a nonreciprocal transfer from an investee company should be recorded. Per para 23 of APB 29, nonreciprocal transfers of nonmonetary assets to owners should be accounted for at the fair value of the assets distributed unless fair value is not determinable within reasonable limits, in which case the book value should be used.

10. (1181,Q2,22) (c) The requirement is the increase in additional paid-in capital resulting from a noncash stock transaction. Generally, property acquired in a noncash transaction should be recorded at the FMV of the consideration given (common stock), unless the FMV of the property acquired (land) is more clearly determinable. Since the common stock is listed on the NYSE, its valuation appears to be more clearly determinable than the appraised valuation of the land. Therefore, the value of the common stock (1,000 shares x $21 = $21,000) should be used to measure the transaction. The increase in additional paid-in capital is $21,000 less $8,000 par value of stock, or $13,000. Note that if the FMVs of the stock and land are considered equally determinable, the FMV of the stock is still used as the measurement basis because it is the consideration given in the transaction.

11. (1181,T1,13) (a) Donated capital results from donations to an enterprise from stockholders and other outside parties and should be reported in stockholder's equity as additional paid-in capital. Retained earnings [answer (b)] is earned capital and credits to this account are typically limited to net income from operations and prior period adjustments. Deferred or unearned income [answer (c)] implies that donated capital represents a liability that will be recognized in the future on the income statement which is incorrect. Answer (d) is incorrect because contributed capital is not incurred as a result of an earnings process and, therefore, should not be included on an income statement as revenue.

D. Purchase of Groups of Fixed Assets

12. (1180,Q1,9) (b) The requirement is the costs to be assigned to Machines A, B and C in a lump sum purchase. Note that the 4 choices show 4 different values for both machine A and machine B; therefore, to answer this problem, only the cost assigned to A or B need be computed. The total cost to be allocated among the three machines is the cost to acquire ($240,000) and prepare for use ($12,000), a total of $252,000. $300,000 is the total appraised value of the three machines. This total cost is allocated on the basis of relative appraised value:

Machine A
($ 50,000/$300,000) ($252,000) = $ 42,000

Machine B
($150,000/$300,000) ($252,000) = $126,000

Machine C
($100,000/$300,000) ($252,000) = $ 84,000

E. Capital Versus Revenue Expenditures

13. (583,Q2,23) (d) The requirement is to determine whether expenditures on a printing press should be expensed immediately or capitalized and depreciated over the remaining useful life. The cost of the attachment would be capitalized since it probably has an estimated life that exceeds one year. The costs incurred to install the attachment would also be capitalized because these expenditures were required to get the attachment in condition and ready for use. Also, the overhaul costs (parts, labor, and overhead) should be capitalized, even though the useful life was not extended, because productive capacity has increased as a result of the overhaul.

14. (1182,T1,8) (d) The requirement is to determine the type of expenditure which has occurred when a company replaces an asphalt roof with a new fiberglass insulated roof. This expenditure is a betterment because the roof replacement increases the future service potential of the building by making it more energy and maintenance efficient. Ordinary repair and maintenance [answer (a)] would occur if the company replaced the roof with another asphalt roof. An addition [answer (b)] is an increase or extension of existing assets. Rearrangement [answer (c)] is incorrect because it deals with moving existing assets (i.e. machinery rearranged to facilitate future production).

F. Depreciation

15. (583,Q2,31) (c) The requirement is the 1982 depreciation expense on asset A using the double-declining balance (DDB) method. Salvage value is ignored in the calculation of DDB depreciation. The formula for DDB depreciation is twice the straight-line rate times the asset's book value at the beginning of the year. Since the information given indicates that Vorst takes a full year's depreciation in the year of acquisition and no depreciation in the year of disposal, the computation in the third year will not involve two computations as is necessary when a partial year's depreciation is taken in the first year. In this problem, the depreciation expense for 1982 would be determined as follows:

$$\frac{100\%}{5 \text{ years}} \times 2 = 40\%$$

40% x Book value, 12/31/81 ($100,000–$64,000) = $14,400.

16. (583,Q2,32) (a) The requirement is to determine depreciation expense for 1982 based on the unspecified method used in 1979, 1980, and 1981. The logical choices are the straight-line (SL), declining balance (DB), and sum-of-the-years'-digits (SYD) methods. By trial and error, the balance in the December 31, 1981, accumulated depreciation account for asset B corresponds to SYD depreciation.

$$\text{SYD} = \frac{n(n+1)}{2} = \frac{5(5+1)}{2} = 15$$

1979	5/15	x	($55,000 – $10,000)	=	$15,000
1980	4/15	x	($55,000 – $10,000)	=	12,000
1981	3/15	x	($55,000 – $10,000)	=	9,000
	Accumulated depreciation 12/31/81				$36,000

Note that this result can also be obtained by applying the SYD formula on a cumulative basis as follows:

$$\frac{5+4+3}{15} \times (\$55{,}000 - \$10{,}000) = \$36{,}000$$

Depreciation expense for 1982 is 2/15 x ($55,000 – $10,000) = $6,000.

17. (583,Q2,33) (d) The requirement is the amount of gain (loss) to be recognized on the sale of asset C. Vorst's depreciation policy is to take a full year's depreciation expense in the year of acquisition and no depreciation expense in the year of disposition. Thus, for purposes of computing gain (loss) the book value on asset C would be $36,400 ($70,000 cost – $33,600 accumulated depreciation). The asset was sold for $28,000, resulting in a loss of $8,400 ($28,000 cash proceeds – $36,400 book value). The entry to record the sale would be:

Cash	28,000	
Accumulated deprec.	33,600	
Loss on sale	8,400	
Asset C		70,000

18. (583,T1,14) (d) The composite and group methods of depreciation compute the average service life of a number of property units and depreciate the group as a single unit. Since both methods treat multiple assets as one, no gain or loss is recognized on an asset's retirement because some assets will be retired before and some will be retired after the average service life. Any gain (loss) on retirement is, in effect, credited (debited) to accumulated depreciation.

Cash	(Amt. received)	
Accumulated deprec.	(Difference)	
Machine		(Cost)

19. (1181,Q1,4) (b) The requirement is the net book value of an asset at the end of its second year in operation if the SYD method of depreciation is used.

$$SYD = \frac{n(n+1)}{2} = \frac{8(8+1)}{2} = 36$$

Depreciation for year 1		
8/36($1,000,000 – $100,000)	=	$200,000
Depreciation for year 2		
7/36($1,000,000 – $100,000)	=	175,000
Accumulated depreciation at 12/31/80	=	375,000

The net book value of the asset at 12/31/80 is

$1,000,000 – $375,000 = $625,000

Alternatively:

Portion of asset not depreciated	x	Depreciable base	+
[36 – (8 + 7)] / 36	x	$1,000,000 – $100,000	+

Salvage value	=	Net book value
$100,000	=	$625,000

20. (1181,Q2,23) (b) The requirement is double-declining balance (DDB) depreciation expense to be recorded in 1981. It should be remembered that salvage value is not considered in the calculation of DDB depreciation. Also, in computing depreciation expense for partial periods, the depreciation for a whole year should be determined and pro-rated between the two periods involved. The DDB rate is twice the straight-line rate (1/10), or 20%.

Depreciation for first year	
(20%)($50,000)	= $10,000
Depreciation for second year	
(20%)($50,000 – 10,000)	= $ 8,000
1981 Depreciation	
Last half of first year (½)($10,000)	= $ 5,000
First half of second year (½)($8,000)	= 4,000
	$ 9,000

21. (1178,Q1,11) (c) The requirement is depreciation expense for 1977 based on the straight-line method for a machine purchased in the beginning of 1976. The machine cost is $51,700 ($50,000 cost plus shipping cost of $500 and installation cost of $1,200). The depreciation base is $48,700 (cost of $51,700 less salvage value of $3,000) resulting in an annual depreciation cost of $4,870 ($48,700 ÷ 10 yr.). The pollution control additions of $3,600 made at the beginning of 1977 are to be amortized over the remaining nine years with no salvage value, resulting in a $400 per year cost. Thus the depreciation for 1977 is $5,270 ($4,870 + $400).

22. (578,Q1,15) (b) The requirement is the acquisition cost of the equipment given SYD, 10-year life, salvage value of $5,000, and 1977 depreciation of $24,000. The denominator of the SYD fraction is 55, as computed below. In 1977 the SYD fraction becomes 8/55. Set up an equation as below indicating 8/55 of the cost minus salvage value is equal to 1977 depreciation of $24,000. Solve for cost by multiplying both sides by 55/8, as illustrated below.

$$\frac{n(n+1)}{2} = 55, \quad 1975 = 10/55$$
$$1976 = 9/55$$
$$1977 = 8/55$$
$$8/55\,(\text{cost} - \$5{,}000) = \$24{,}000$$
$$\text{cost} - \$5{,}000 = \$24{,}000 \times 55/8$$
$$\text{cost} - \$5{,}000 = \$165{,}000$$
$$\text{cost} = \$170{,}000$$

23. (1177,Q1,5) (b) The requirement is the composite life of the asset. The solutions approach is to determine the annual straight-line depreciation and divide the annual depreciation into the total amount to be depreciated. Per the schedule below, the annual depreciation is $45,000, which when divided into the total depreciation base of $720,000, indicates a composite life of 16 years.

Machine A	$500 dep. base ÷ 20 yrs.	=	$25 dep.
Machine B	180 dep. base ÷ 15 yrs.	=	12 dep.
Machine C	40 dep. base ÷ 5 yrs.	=	8 dep.
	$720 total dep. base		$45 total dep.

$720 ÷ $45 = 16 years

Composite depreciation permits assets to be grouped for depreciation purposes precluding individual records for each asset. When applied to similar assets, the method is sometimes called group depreciation. Generally major repair and replacement expenditures are charged to the accumulated depreciation account. Relatedly, gains and losses on disposal of individual assets are usually not recognized, i.e., they are charged to the accumulated depreciation account.

G. Other Disposals

24. (1183,P2,27) (c) The requirement is the amounts of depreciation expense and loss to be recorded on a machine abandoned at year end. Since the machine was used until 12/31/82, a full year's depreciation (10% x $200,000, or $20,000) should be recorded in 1982. A loss should also be recognized (in 1982 when the decision to abandon was made), even though the actual disposal will not take place until 1983. The amount of the loss is the sum of the book value of the machine [$200,000 – (5 x $20,000), or $100,000] and the estimated disposal cost ($5,000), for a total of $105,000. The 12/31/82 entries would be:

Depreciation expense	20,000	
Accumulated depreciation		20,000
Loss on disposal	105,000	
Accumulated depreciation	100,000	
Machine		200,000
Accrued disposal costs		5,000

25. (582,P1,12) (d) The requirement is the amount of gain to be recognized on the condemnation of a plant. FASB Interpretation 30 requires that "gain (loss) be recognized when a nonmonetary asset is involuntarily converted into monetary assets even though an enterprise reinvests the monetary assets in replacement nonmonetary assets." The land and building have a book value of $200,000 ($150,000 + $50,000). The condemnation award received was $300,000, resulting in a gain of $100,000 ($300,000 – $200,000).

H. Depletion

26. (1183,P2,35) (b) The requirement is the amount of depletion cost per ton. The depletion computation is:

$$\frac{\text{Net cost of resource}}{\text{Units of resource}} = \text{Depletion charge per unit}$$

The estimated net cost is the cost of the land ($9,000,000) and the related restoration costs ($1,500,000), less the salvage value of the land ($1,000,000). This results in a net cost of $9,500,000. The estimated recoverable reserves total 5,000,000 tons. Therefore, the depletion charge is $1.90 per ton.

$$\frac{\$9{,}500{,}000}{5{,}000{,}000 \text{ tons}} = \underline{\underline{\$1.90 \text{ per ton}}}$$

27. (1179,Q1,16) (c) The requirement is the 1978 depletion for Under Mine. The solutions approach is to determine the depletion expense per ton as illustrated below. The $4,000,000 estimated net cost of the mine divided by the 4,000,000 estimated removable tons results in a depletion rate of $1 per ton. Since 400,000 tons were removed, the depletion expense would be $400,000. Since 375,000 tons were sold, there would be an inventory of $25,000 at $1 per ton.

Mine cost	$3,400,000
Development cost	+800,000
Salvage value	–200,000
Cost to be depreciated	$4,000,000
÷ est. recover.	4,000,000 tons
	= $1/ton

I. Insurance

28. (1182,Q1,6) (a) The requirement is for the amount of insurance that will be collected from the insurance company. Since there is an 80% coinsurance clause, Brody Company and the insurance company are co-insurers. The amount recoverable from the insurance company is the lowest of the following three amounts:

1. Fair market value of the loss ($100,000)
2. Face value of the policy ($120,000)
3. Amount calculated by the coinsurance formula

$$\frac{\text{Face of policy}}{\text{coinsurance \% x value of total property}} \times \text{Actual Loss} = \text{Amount Recoverable}$$

$$\frac{\$120{,}000}{80\%\ (\$300{,}000)} \times \$100{,}000 = \$50{,}000$$

J. Intangible Assets (APB 17)

29. (1183,T1,12) (c) Intangible assets, in general, are to be amortized over their useful lives which may not exceed 40 years. The maximum useful life of a patent, however, is limited to its legal life of 17 years or useful life (15 years in this case), whichever is less. In addition, other factors such as changes in demand or technological changes resulting in obsolescence of the patentable process may further reduce its useful life (APB 17, para 27). Answer (a) is incorrect because APB 17, para 28 states that intangible assets shall not be written off in the period of acquisition. Answer (b) is incorrect because it disregards other factors which may limit the patent's useful life. Answer (d) is incorrect because it ignores the legal life of the patent.

30. (583,T1,17) (a) APB 17, para 9 states that intangible assets should be recorded at cost. Legal and registration fees must, however, be differentiated from any research and development costs incurred in connection with the internally developed patent. SFAS 2, para 12 generally requires R&D costs to be expensed immediately, but lists these fees as costs that should be capitalized.

31. (1181,Q1,5) (c) The requirement is the amortization for 1980. Two different costs are involved in this problem; research and development costs of $176,000 and legal fees of $16,000. SFAS 2 requires that research and development costs be charged to expense as incurred. The unrecovered cost of a successful legal suit can be capitalized as part of the patent's cost. In this case the cost of patenting the invention was nominal and expensed when incurred which means the $16,000 of legal fees should be the only costs capitalized and subsequently amortized. Per APB 17 these costs should be amortized on a straight-line basis over the remaining useful life or the remaining legal life whichever is shorter. At the time these costs are capitalized there are 13 years of legal life remaining and 4 years of remaining useful life. Therefore, amortization would be $16,000 ÷ 4 = $4,000.

32. (579,Q1,14) (c) The requirement is the amount of expense that should be recorded as a result of owning a patent that was purchased for $180,000 4 years ago that is now worthless. In 1975, 1976, and 1977, the patent was amortized $18,000 per year or a total of $54,000. Since the patent was deemed to be worthless in 1978, the remaining book value of $126,000 should be expensed in 1978. Note that the capitalization and amortization of a patent (R&D) purchased from others is not a violation of para 11 of SFAS 2. Intangibles purchased from others having alternative future uses, e.g., potential sale, are to be capitalized and amortized.

33. (1177,Q1,4) (a) APB 17 requires the cost of intangible assets acquired from others (including goodwill acquired in a business combination) to be recorded as assets (para 24). These assets should be amortized to income over the period to be benefited (not to exceed 40 years). See para 29 of APB 17. Here total intangible assets are $87,000 ($5,000 of organization costs, $70,000 of goodwill, and $12,000 in trademarks). The deposits with the advertising agency are a prepaid expense. When the advertising agency performs the services contracted, the $8,000 will be expensed. The $15,000 of discount on bonds payable is a deferred charge which is considered a contra long-term liability.

34. (581,T1,7) (d) The requirement is the item which should be expensed as incurred by a franchisee. Answers (a), (b) and (c) all represent payments by the franchise as part of the purchase of the franchise. These payments relate to the future right to use the asset and are, therefore, capitalized and amortized over the estimated useful life of the franchise or 40 years, whichever is shorter, as an operating expense. In this case, the payments in items (a), (b), and (c) would be amortized over the ten-year estimated useful life. Item (d) represents annual payments made under the franchise agreement and should be entered as operating expenses in the period in which they were incurred. They do not represent an asset to the franchise since they do not relate to future rights to use the franchise.

K. Deferred Charges

35. (1181,Q2,30) (c) The requirement is the amount of organization costs to be deferred to years subsequent to 1980. For financial accounting, Ulmer reports amortization equal to the maximum allowed under tax law (federal income tax regulations permit the amortization of organization costs over a period of 5 years or more). Accordingly, 1/5 of the costs or $2,400 would be expensed in 1980, and 4/5 or $9,600 would be deferred to subsequent years.

36. (580,Q1,2) (a) Organizational costs that are amortizable include the attorney's fees and meetings of incorporators, state filing fees, and other organizational expenses. Leasehold improvements are assets to amortize but not as organization costs. For financial accounting, intangible assets are generally amortized over a 40-year period.

Attorney's fees	$4,000	
Meetings, etc.	5,000	
	$9,000	÷ 40 yrs. = $225/year

L. Research and Development Costs (SFAS 2)

37. (1183,P1,10) (c) The requirement is the total research and development (R&D) expense in Frye Company's 1982 income statement. Per SFAS 2, all R&D costs are to be charged to expense when incurred. R&D expenditures for items such as materials, equipment, and purchased intangibles may be capitalized if they have alternative future uses in R&D projects or other areas. Therefore, the full cost ($1,000,000) of the equipment acquired for use in R&D projects is not expensed; rather, the depreciation ($150,000) on the equipment would be expensed along with the other R&D costs incurred (SFAS 2, para 11).

Depreciation	$150,000
Materials	200,000
Compensation	500,000
Consulting fees	100,000
Indirect costs	250,000
R&D expense	$1,200,000

38. (1181,Q1,10) (c) Research and development are defined in SFAS 2, para 8. The first three costs listed in the problem are identified in para 9 of SFAS 2 as being activities which are typically included in research and development costs. The fourth cost is identified in para 10 of SFAS 2 as being a cost which is typically excluded from research and development.

39. (1182,T1,25) (d) SFAS 2 requires that all research and development costs be charged to expense as incurred. Paras 9-10 of that statement provide guidelines by listing examples of activities that are and are not considered R&D. Testing in search for or evaluation of product or process alternatives is an example given of R&D, while the other choices are not considered R&D.

40. (1179,T1,9) (d) Research and development costs are expensed when incurred per para 12 of SFAS 2. Answer (a) is incorrect because if R&D were accounted for by associating cause and effect, R&D would be capitalized and amortized to the periods in which the R&D produced revenue. Answer (b) is incorrect because systematic and rational allocation implies capitalization and amortization. Answer (c) is incorrect because the method of accounting for R&D for financial reporting purposes does not determine the method to be used for income tax purposes. Thus, R&D may be expensed for tax purposes regardless of what is done for financial reporting purposes.

May 1984 Answers

41. (584,P1,5) (b) The requirement is the amount to be charged to repairs and maintenance expense in 1983. Continuing, frequent, and low-cost repairs ($36,000) should be expensed. These expenditures merely maintain existing assets in the condition necessary for future operations. Special long-term protection devices attached to machines ($11,000) should be capitalized as an asset. This expenditure was for a distinct addition which improved the existing assets. The replacement of the broken gear on a machine ($2,000) should be expensed since it merely maintains the machine at its current operating level. Therefore, the total amount to be expensed is $38,000 ($36,000 + $2,000).

42. (584,P1,8) (d) The requirement is the 11/30/83 balance in the land account. The amount reported as land should include the purchase price and the net cost to prepare the land for its intended use. The purchase price of the land is $200,000. Legal fees associated with the purchase total $5,000 and title guarantee insurance cost $6,000. Also, the land account is capitalized for the cost of demolishing the old building, $21,000 (cost of $25,000 less proceeds from sale of salvaged materials of $4,000). Therefore, the total balance in the land account should be $232,000 ($200,000 + $5,000 + $6,000 + $21,000).

43. (584,P1,9) (d) The requirement is the accumulated depreciation balance at 12/31/83, using the 150% declining balance (DB) method. Salvage value is ignored when using a DB approach. The formula for 150% DB depreciation is 150% x the straight-line rate multiplied by the beginning-of-the-year book value. Since the straight-line rate is 20% (100% ÷ 5 years), the DB rate is 30%. The book value for the first year is $500,000 (original cost). Therefore, 1982 depreciation is $150,000.

$500,000 x 30% = $150,000

The book value for the second year is $350,000 (original cost of $500,000 less accumulated depreciation of $150,000). Therefore, 1983 depreciation is $105,000.

$350,000 x 30% = $105,000

The total accumulated depreciation at 12/31/83 is $255,000 ($150,000 + $105,000).

44. (584,P1,10) (c) The requirement is the amount of plant expenditures to be capitalized in 1983. Generally, a cost should be capitalized if it improves the asset or expensed if it merely maintains the asset at its current level. The old shingle roof was replaced with a fireproof tile roof; thus, the $75,000 should be capitalized. Similarly, the $35,000 cost of major improvements to the electrical wiring system should be capitalized. However, the cost of repainting the plant building ($5,000) should be expensed since it is an ordinary, regularly occurring expenditure which maintains, rather than improves, the plant. Therefore, the total cost capitalized is $110,000 ($75,000 + $35,000).

45. (584,P1,11) (d) The requirement is the amount of rearrangement costs to be capitalized at 12/31/83. The rearrangement costs, consisting of moving costs of $20,000 and reinstallation costs of $40,000, were incurred to secure greater efficiency in production. Since the benefits of the rearrangement will extend for five years, the total cost of $60,000 should be capitalized and charged to expense over the five-year period.

46. (584,P2,38) (a) The requirement is the amount of research and development (R&D) costs to be expensed in 1983. Generally, SFAS 2 requires that

all R&D costs be expensed as incurred. While there are some exceptions (primarily when an R&D expenditure is for an item with alternative future uses), none of them apply here. Therefore, the entire cost of $675,000 is expensed. The fact that the company expects to recover these costs through the sale of a new product is irrelevant to the solution. Due to the uncertainties of associating costs with specific projects and determining the amount and life span of future benefits, SFAS 2 requires that most R&D costs be expensed when incurred.

47. (584,P3,50) (b) The requirement is the amount at which to record a new machine obtained in a nonmonetary exchange of **similar** productive assets. Per APB 29, para 21 such exchanges do not result in the culmination of an earnings process. Gains on these exchanges are recognized only to the extent that boot is received. Since boot is not received by Diamond, no gain is recognized and the basis of the asset received is recorded at the book value of the asset(s) surrendered, or $29,000 [book value of the asset exchanged ($10,000) plus the cash ($19,000)]. Note that the list price of an asset is not always representative of the fair market value of the asset. An asset can often be purchased for less than its list price.

48. (584,P3,51) (d) The requirement is the amount at which a patent should be recorded. The patent was acquired through the issuance of treasury stock. Generally, assets acquired in a noncash transaction should be recorded at the FMV of the consideration given (treasury stock) unless the FMV of the property acquired (patent) is more clearly determinable. Since no FMV is given for the patent, the quoted value of the stock should be used to determine the cost of the patent. Therefore, the patent is recorded at $110,000 (2,000 shares x $55 per share). The cost of the patent ($90,000) on Waxman's books is irrelevant.

49. (584,T1,10) (c) The equation for calculating sum-of-the-years' digits (SYD) depreciation is:

$$\frac{\text{Years remaining}}{\text{SYD}} \times \begin{array}{c}\text{Cost minus}\\ \text{salvage value}\end{array}$$

Year 1: 4/10(1.00 - .15) = 34.0%
Year 2: 3/10(1.00 - .15) = 25.5%

The equation for calculating double-declining-balance (DDB) depreciation is:

$$\frac{200\%}{\text{Useful life}} \times \begin{array}{c}\text{Book}\\ \text{value}\end{array}$$

Year 1: 200%/4(1.00) = 50.0%
Year 2: 200%/4(1.00 - .50) = 25.0%

Therefore:

Year 1: SYD is lower than DDB (i.e., 34.0% < 50.0%)

Year 2: SYD is higher than DDB (i.e., 25.5% > 25.0%)

Recall that salvage value is included in the SYD calculation and not in the DDB calculation. Regardless of the cost of the asset, answer (c) will be correct.

50. (584,T1,11) (d) The requirement is to determine the proper accounting treatment for reinstallation costs which increase the efficiency of a machine over its remaining useful life. Reinstallation or rearrangement costs which are material, provide greater efficiency in production, and benefit future accounting periods should be capitalized. The exact number of years of useful life in excess of the current period is irrelevant to the decision to capitalize the expenditures.

Answer Outline

Problem 1 Accounting for R&D

a. Research – planned search or critical investigation
   - Aimed at discovery of new knowledge to produce
     - New products and significant benefit to existing products
   - Development – translation of research findings
     - Into new product or product betterment designs

b. SFAS 2 reduced the alternatives of accounting for R&D
   - Practice alternatives were
     - Expense as incurred
     - Capitalize when incurred with subsequent amortization
     - Selective capitalization
     - Capitalize until future benefits determined
   - Alternative rationale were
     - Associating cause and effect
     - Systematic and rational allocation
     - Immediate recognition
   - FASB determined the "immediate recognition" principle applied
     - Uncertainties of future R&D benefits and lack of objective criteria undermined the capitalization method

c. Expense as R&D
   - Design and engineering studies
   - Prototype manufacturing costs
   - R&D administrative costs
   - Cost of R&D equipment to be used only for one product
   - Capitalize and depreciate remaining $300,000 of equipment
     - Such depreciation is R&D cost
   - Market research and related costs are not R&D
     - Are period costs appearing separately from R&D

Unofficial Answer

Problem 1 Accounting for R&D

a. Research, as defined in Statement of Financial Accounting Standards no. 2, is "planned search or critical investigation aimed at discovery of new knowledge with the hope that such knowledge will be useful in developing a new product or service . . . or a new process or technique . . . or in bringing about a significant improvement to an existing product or process."

Development, as defined in Statement of Financial Accounting Standards no. 2, is "the translation of research findings or other knowledge into a plan or design for a new product or process or for a significant improvement to an existing product or process whether intended for sale or use."

b. The current accounting and reporting practices for research and development costs were promulgated by the Financial Accounting Standards Board (FASB) in order to reduce the number of alternatives that previously existed and to provide useful financial information about research and development costs. The FASB considered four alternative methods of accounting: (1) charge all costs to expense when incurred; (2) capitalize all costs when incurred; (3) selective capitalization; and (4) accumulate all costs in a special category until the existence of future benefits can be determined. The FASB concluded that all research and development costs should be charged to expense as incurred. (Statement of Financial Accounting Standards no. 2 does not apply to activities that are unique to enterprises in the extractive industries, and accounting for the costs of research and development activities conducted for others under a contractual arrangement is a part of accounting for contracts in general and is beyond the scope of that statement.)

In reaching this decision, the FASB considered the three pervasive principles of expense recognition: (1) associating cause and effect; (2) systematic and rational allocation, and (3) immediate recognition. The FASB found little or no evidence of a direct causal relationship between current research and development expenditures and subsequent future benefits. The high degree of uncertainty surrounding future benefits, if any, of individual research and development projects makes it doubtful that there is any useful purpose to be served by capitalizing the costs and allocating them over future periods. In view of the above, the FASB concluded that the first two principles of expense recognition do not apply, but rather that the "immediate recognition" principle of expense recognition should apply.

The high degree of uncertainty about whether research and development expenditures will provide any future benefits, the lack of objectivity in setting criteria, and the lack of usefulness of the resulting information led the FASB to reject the alternatives of capitalization, selective capitalization, and accumulation of costs in a special category.

c. In accordance with Statement no. 2 of the Financial Accounting Standards Board, the following costs attributable only to research and development should be expensed as incurred:

- Design and engineering studies.
- Prototype manufacturing costs.
- Administrative costs related solely to research and development.
- The cost of equipment produced solely for development of the product ($200,000).

The remaining $300,000 of equipment should be capitalized and shown on the statement of financial position at cost. The depreciation expense resulting from the current year is a part of research and development expense for the year. The market research direct costs and related administrative expenses are not research and development costs. These costs are treated as period costs and are shown as expense items in the current earnings statement.

Answer Outline

Problem 2 Property, Plant, and Equipment

a. Expenditures to be capitalized in cash acquisition of equipment include
   Invoice price (net of discounts, even if not taken), plus
   All costs incurred in acquiring equipment and preparing it for use
      E.g., freight, installation, breaking-in costs, etc.

b. Capitalizable cost of equipment having no "cash equivalent price" is determined as follows:

b1. If equipment is acquired by giving bonds with an established market price, capitalize equipment at market value of consideration given up, which is market value of bonds

b2. If equipment is acquired by giving common stock, capitalize equipment at market value given or received whichever is more evident (independent appraisal may be used)

b3. If equipment is acquired by giving similar equipment, capitalize acquired equipment at lower of recorded amount of equipment relinquished or market value of equipment received

c. Factors which determine whether expenditures relating to property, plant, and equipment in use should be capitalized
   Amount is relatively large
   Nonrecurring in nature
   Extend useful life of the property, plant, and equipment
   Increase the usefulness of the property, plant, and equipment

d. Accounting for gain or loss on sale of property, plant, and equipment
   Remove net book value (cost less accumulated depreciation) from accounts
   Gain = excess of cash received over net book value
   Loss = excess of net book value over cash received

Unofficial Answer

Problem 2 Property, Plant, and Equipment

a. The expenditures that should be capitalized when equipment is acquired for cash should include the invoice price of the equipment (net of discounts) plus all incidental outlays relating to its purchase or preparation for use, such as insurance during transit, freight, duties, ownership search, ownership registration, installation, and breaking-in costs. Any available discounts, whether taken or not, should be deducted from the capitalizable cost of the equipment.

b. 1. When the market value of the equipment is not determinable by reference to a similar cash purchase, the capitalizable cost of equipment purchased with bonds having an established market price should be the market value of the bonds.

2. When the market value of the equipment is not determinable by reference to a similar cash purchase, and the common stock used in the exchange does not have an established market price, the capitalizable cost of equipment should be the equipment's estimated fair value if that is more clearly evident than the fair value of the common stock. Independent appraisals may be used to determine the fair values of the assets involved.

3. When the market value of equipment acquired is not determinable by reference to a similar cash purchase, the capitalizable cost of equipment purchased by exchanging similar equipment having a determinable market value should be the lower of the recorded amount of the equipment relinquished or the market value of the equipment exchanged.

c. The factors that determine whether expenditures relating to property, plant, and equipment already in use should be capitalized are as follows:

- Expenditures are relatively large in amount.
- They are nonrecurring in nature.
- They extend the useful life of the property, plant, and equipment.
- They increase the usefulness of the property, plant, and equipment.

d. The net book value at the date of the sale (cost of the property, plant, and equipment less the accumulated depreciation) should be removed from the accounts. The excess of cash from the sale over the net book value removed is accounted for as a gain on the sale, while the excess of net book value removed over cash from the sale is accounted for as a loss on the sale.

Answer Outline

Problem 3 Property, Plant and Equipment

a1. Revenue expenditures benefit only current period
  Are expensed in the period incurred
 Capital expenditures benefit several periods
  Are expensed in periods benefitted
 Distinction determines timing of expense recognition
  Affects periodic earnings
  And reported assets
 When revenue expenditures are capitalized
  Current earnings are overstated
  Assets are overstated
  Future earnings are understated
 The reverse is true if a capital item is expensed.

a2. Depreciation allocates historical cost to periods benefited
  Process of cost allocation, not valuation
  Not intended to provide replacement funds
  Application of matching concept

a3. Factors in determining annual depreciation
  Original cost
  Estimated salvage value
  Estimated useful life
  Depreciation method

a4. Depreciation reduces net earnings
  Does not require an outflow of funds
  Add back to earnings to calculate funds provided by operations
 Depreciation is not a direct source of funds
  Thus, indirect source through tax savings

b1. Costs of land are listed in the Unofficial Answer below, items (a) through (k)

b2. Record deferred-payment plan cost at equivalent cash price
  Impute interest rate if necessary
  To determine present value
   Interest portion of contract is interest expense

b3. Generally value asset acquisitions at fair value
  Of asset given or received
  Whichever is more clearly evident
 No gain recognized on exchange of productive assets
  New cost is undepreciated cost of old assets plus cash paid

Unofficial Answer

Problem 3 Property, Plant and Equipment

a. 1. Relative to plant assets, a cost incurred or an expenditure made, that is assumed to benefit only the current accounting period is called a revenue expenditure and is charged to expense in the period believed to benefit. A capital expenditure is similarly a cost incurred or an expenditure made but is expected to yield benefits either in all future accounting periods (acquisition of land) or in a limited number of accounting periods. Capital expenditures (if material in amount) are capitalized, that is, recorded as assets, and, if related to assets of limited life, amortized over the periods believed to benefit.

The distinction between capital and revenue expenditures is of significance because it involves the timing of the recognition of expense, and consequently, the determination of periodic earnings. It also affects the amounts reported as assets whose costs generally have to be recouped from future periods' revenues.

If a revenue expenditure is improperly capitalized, current earnings are overstated, assets are overstated, and future earnings are understated for all the periods to which the improperly capitalized cost is amortized. If the cost is not amortized, future earnings will not be affected but assets and retained earnings will continue to be overstated for as long as the cost remains on the books. If a nonamortizable capital expenditure is improperly expensed, current earnings are understated and assets and retained earnings are understated for all foreseeable periods in the future. If an amortizable capital expenditure is improperly expensed, current earnings are understated, assets and retained earnings are understated, and future earnings are overstated for all periods to which the cost should have been amortized.

2. Depreciation is the accounting process of allocating an asset's historical cost (recorded amount) to the accounting periods benefitted by the use of the asset. It is a process of cost allocation, not valuation. Depreciation is not intended to provide funds for an asset's replacement; it is merely an application of the matching concept.

3. The factors relevant in determining the annual depreciation for a depreciable asset are the initial recorded amount (cost), estimated salvage value, estimated useful life, and depreciation method.

   Assets are typically recorded at their acquisition cost, which is in most cases objectively determinable. But cost assignments in other cases—"basket purchases" and the selection of an implicit interest rate in asset acquisition under deferred-payment plans—may be quite subjective involving considerable judgment.

   The salvage value is an estimate of an amount potentially realizable when the asset is retired from service. It is initially a judgment factor and is affected by the length of its useful life to the enterprise.

   The useful life is also a judgment factor. It involves selecting the "unit" of measure of service life and estimating the number of such units embodied in the asset. Such units may be measured in terms of time periods or in terms of activity (for example, years or machine hours). When selecting the life, one should select the lower (shorter) of the physical life or the economic life to this user. Physical life involves wear and tear and casualties; economic life involves such things as technological obsolescence and inadequacy.

   Selecting the depreciation method is generally a judgment decision; but, a method may be inherent in the definition adopted for the units of service life, as discussed earlier. For example, if such units are machine hours, the method is a function of the number of machine hours used during each period. A method should be selected that will best measure the portion of services expiring each period. Once a method is selected, it may be objectively applied by using a predetermined, objectively derived formula.

4. Because revenue usually represents an inflow of funds, and expense usually represents an outflow of funds, net earnings represent a net inflow of funds. Depreciation reduces reported net earnings but does not involve an outflow of funds. Therefore, it is added back to reported net earnings to calculate funds provided by operations. On a statement of changes in financial position, depreciation should be clearly shown as an adjustment to net earnings not requiring a use of funds rather than be shown as a source of funds. Depreciation is not a direct source of funds. It can be considered an indirect source only through income tax savings.

b. 1. The following costs, if applicable, should be capitalized as a cost of land:

   (a) Negotiated purchase price
   (b) Brokers' commission
   (c) Legal fees
   (d) Title fee
   (e) Recording fee
   (f) Escrow fees
   (g) Surveying fees
   (h) Existing unpaid taxes, interest, or liens assumed by the buyer
   (i) Clearing, grading, landscaping, and subdividing

(j) Cost of removing old building (less salvage)
(k) Special assessments such as lighting or sewers if they are permanent in nature.

2. A plant asset acquired on a deferred-payment plan should be recorded at an equivalent cash price excluding interest. If interest is not stated in the sales contract, an imputed interest should be determined. The asset should then be recorded at its present value, which is computed by discounting the payments at the stated or imputed interest rate. The interest portion (stated or imputed) of the contract price should be charged to interest expense over the life of the contract.

3. In general, plant assets should be recorded at the fair value of the consideration given or the fair value of the asset received, whichever is more clearly evident. This general theoretical preference is somewhat constrained by the requirements of APB Opinion No. 29.

   Specifically when exchanging an old machine and paying cash for a new machine, the new machine should be recorded at the amount of monetary consideration (cash) paid plus the undepreciated cost of the nonmonetary asset (old machine) surrendered if there is no indicated loss. An indicated loss should be recognized; this would reduce the recorded amount of the new machine. No indicated gain, however, should be recognized by the party paying monetary consideration.

Solution Guide

Problem 4 Comprehensive Schedules: Fixed Assets

1. This problem consists of two unrelated parts. Part a. requires computations concerning intangible assets, while part b. requires computations involving land and a building.

2. Part a. requires a schedule listing the intangible assets at 12/31/81, as well as a schedule showing all 1981 expenses resulting from various transactions related to the intangibles.

2.1 The cost of the franchise on 1/1/81 is the cash paid ($25,000) and the present value of the future cash payments ($43,700). During 1981 franchise amortization should be recorded based on the ten-year useful life (1/10 x $68,700 = $6,870). On the 12/31/81 balance sheet, the franchise would be reported at a net amount of $61,830 ($68,700 – $6,870).

2.2 The cost of the patent on 1/2/81 is the registration cost of $16,400. Per SFAS 2, the research and development costs ($78,000) are expensed as incurred. Since the patent has a useful life of eight years, 1981 amortization is 1/8 of $16,400, or $2,050. On the 12/31/81 balance sheet, the patent would be reported at a net amount of $14,350 ($16,400 – $2,050).

2.3 The cost of the trademark on 7/1/78 is $40,000. Through 7/1/81, amortization totals $6,000 ($40,000 x 3/20). On 7/1/81, the $10,000 paid to successfully defend the trademark is properly capitalized in the trademark account. The new net balance ($40,000 – $6,000 + $10,000) of $44,000 should be amortized over the remaining 17 years (20–3) of the useful life. Amortization for the last six months of 1981 is $1,294 ($44,000 x 1/17 x 6/12). On the 12/31/81 balance sheet, the trademark is reported at a net amount of $42,706 ($44,000 – $1,294).

2.4 1981 expenses relating to the franchise include the amortization of $6,870, interest expense on the loan, and the continuing franchise fee. Interest expense is $6,118, obtained by multiplying the present value of the note ($43,700) by the effective interest rate (14%). The continuing franchise fee is 5% of franchise revenue ($900,000), or $45,000.

2.5 The only 1981 expense relative to the patent is the amortization of $2,050. Note that the $78,000 R&D costs incurred in developing the patent would have been expensed prior to 1981 since the patent was granted on 1/2/81.

2.6 The only 1981 expense relative to the trademark is the amortization of $2,294 which consists of a full year's amortization on the original $40,000 cost ($40,000 x 1/20 = $2,000) and a half-year's amortization on the additional $10,000 cost ($10,000 x 1/17 x 6/12 = $294).

3. Part b. requires schedules computing the cost of land, the cost of the building, and the 1981 depreciation expense on the building.

3.1 All the costs of the land and the old building are considered to be costs of the land, since the site was purchased with removal of the old building in mind (management intent). Similarly, the cost of removing the old building is capitalized to the land account because this is a necessary cost of getting the land ready for its intended use. Therefore, the total cost of the land includes purchase price ($600,000), broker's commission ($36,000), legal fees ($6,000), title insurance ($18,000), and removal of the old building ($75,000). The information concerning the separation of the $600,000 into $500,000 for the land and $100,000 for the building is extraneous because the old building was not acquired for use in Brock's operations.

3.2 The cost of the new building includes the construction contract price of $3,000,000; the cost of plans and blueprints, $12,000; architects' fees of $95,000; and capitalized interest cost.

3.3 The amount of interest to be capitalized in this problem is based only on the average amounts of accumulated building construction expenditures. It would be necessary to capitalize (as part of the cost of the building) interest related to the cost of acquiring the land and preparing it for its intended use if the information given would have indicated that a borrowing had been incurred specifically to finance the land acquisition or that there were other interest bearing debt outstanding during the period.

3.4 For 1980 interest capitalized is computed by multiplying the average amount of accumulated building expenditures ($900,000) times the annual interest rate on the $3,000,000 loan (14%) weighted 10/12 for the ten months in 1980 during which both: (1) construction was in progress and (2) interest cost was being incurred.

3.5 For 1981, it is necessary to assume that the $105,000 of interest capitalized in 1980 is included in the $2,300,000 of accumulated expenditures because SFAS 34 requires compounding of interest in applying its provisions. The interest capitalized is computed by multiplying the $2,300,000 of accumulated expenditures times the 14% weighted for 9/12 of a year giving $241,500.

3.6 The last requirement is to compute the 1981 depreciation expense on the building, using the 150% declining balance method. The rate used is 150% times the straight-line rate of 1/40. Because the building was not completed until 9/30/81, depreciation is computed for only the last three months of 1981.

Unofficial Answer

Problem 4 Comprehensive Schedules: Fixed Assets

Part a.

1.

Tully Corporation
Intangible Assets
December 31, 1981

Franchise, net of accumulated amortization of $6,870 (Schedule 1)	$ 61,830
Patent, net of accumulated amortization of $2,050 (Schedule 2)	14,350
Trademark, net of accumulated amortization of $7,294 (Schedule 3)	42,706
Total intangible assets	$118,886

Schedule 1

Franchise

Cost of franchise on 1/1/81 ($25,000 + $43,700)	$68,700
1981 amortization ($68,700 x 1/10)	(6,870)
Cost of franchise, net of amortization	$61,830

Schedule 2

Patent

Cost of securing patent on 1/2/81	$16,400
1981 amortization ($16,400 x 1/8)	(2,050)
Cost of patent, net of amortization	$14,350

Schedule 3

Trademark

Cost of trademark on 7/1/78	$40,000
Amortization, 7/1/78 to 12/31/80 ($40,000 x 5/40)	(5,000)
Amortization, 1/1/81 to 7/1/81 (40,000 x 1/40)	(1,000)
Book value on 7/1/81	$34,000
Cost of successful legal defense on 7/1/81	10,000
Book value after legal defense	$44,000
Amortization, 7/1/81 to 12/31/81 ($44,000 x 1/17 x 6/12)	(1,294)
Cost of trademark, net of amortization	$42,706

2. **Tully Corporation**
Expense Resulting from Selected Intangibles Transactions
For the Year Ended December 31, 1981

Interest expense ($43,700 x 14%)	$ 6,118
Franchise amortization (Schedule 1)	6,870
Franchise fee ($900,000 x 5%)	45,000
Patent amortization (Schedule 2)	2,050
Trademark amortization (Schedule 4)	2,294
Total expenses	$62,332

Note: The $78,000 of research and development costs incurred in developing the patent would have been expensed per SFAS 2 prior to 1981.

Schedule 4

Trademark Amortization

Amortization of original cost ($40,000 x 1/20)	$ 2,000
Amortization of legal fees ($10,000 x 1/17 x 6/12)	294
Total trademark amortization	$ 2,294

Part b.

1. **Brock Corporation**
Cost of Land (Site #101)
As of September 30, 1981

Cost of land and old building	$600,000
Real estate broker's commission	36,000
Legal fees	6,000
Title insurance	18,000
Removal of old building	75,000
Cost of land	$735,000

2. **Brock Corporation**
Cost of Building
As of September 30, 1981

Fixed construction contract price	$3,000,000
Plans, specifications, and blueprints	12,000
Architects' fees	95,000
Interest capitalized during 1980 (Schedule 1)	105,000
Interest capitalized during 1981 (Schedule 1)	241,500
Cost of building	$3,453,500

Schedule 1

Interest Capitalized During 1980

Avg. accumulated construction expenditures	x	Interest rate for portion of year	=	Interest to be capitalized
1980:				
$900,000	x	(14% x 10/12)	=	$105,000
1981:				
$2,300,000	x	(14% x 9/12)	=	$241,500

3. **Brock Corporation**
Depreciation Expense on Office Building
For Year Ended December 31, 1981

Cost	$3,453,500
150% declining balance rate [(100% ÷ 40 years) x 1.5 = 3.75%]	x 3.75%
First full year's depreciation	$ 129,506
1981 (10/1 to 12/31) depreciation ($129,506 x 3/12)	$ 32,377

Solution Guide

Problem 5 Plant Asset Transactions

1. Part a. requires a schedule recording the disposition of property and a journal entry recording an exchange of dissimilar assets.

2. Part a1. requires a schedule incorporating entries to record the sale of an idle plant facility, subsequent cash collection, and to record income recognized. Note that the cost recovery method is used to account for the sale. You should briefly review the cost recovery method before

proceeding, neither the gain on sale nor the interest on the note is recognized until the cost of the plant has been collected. Finally, note that the format for the schedule is given in the problem.

2.1 On 1/1/77, the idle plant facility is sold. Hobson receives $100,000 cash (debit) and a $600,000 note receivable (debit). The idle plant facility is credited for its cost of $500,000. The remaining $200,000 credit is **not** recognized as a gain on sale because the cost recovery method is used. Therefore, the $200,000 will be credited to deferred income. This income and the interest income on the note will not be recognized until the $500,000 cost has been recovered. Since $100,000 cash has already been collected, $400,000 of principal and interest on the note must also be collected before any income is recognized. The 1/1/77 entry in general journal form appears below:

Cash	$100,000	
Note receivable	600,000	
Idle plant (net)		$500,000
Deferred income		200,000

2.2 On 7/1/78, $190,000 cash is received, $100,000 principal and $90,000 interest.

Cash	$190,000	
Note receivable		$100,000
Deferred income		90,000

Additional deferred income of $90,000 is recorded, because to date, $290,000 of the cost has been collected ($100,000 + $190,000).

2.3 On 12/31/79, $275,000 cash is collected, $200,000 principal and $75,000 interest.

Cash	$275,000	
Note receivable		$200,000
Income recognized		65,000
Deferred income		10,000

To date, $565,000 or $65,000 more than the cost has been collected.

2.4 Finally, on 2/1/81, $332,500 cash is received, $300,000 principal and $32,500 interest.

Cash	$332,500	
Note receivable		$300,000
Income recognized		32,500

The $32,500 is recognized as income, since total collections on 12/31/79 exceed the idle plant cost of $500,000. Finally, since the entire note has now been paid, the $300,000 of deferred income may be recognized as income.

The journal entry is:

Deferred income	$300,000	
Income recognized		$300,000

3. Part a2. requires the journal entry Hobson, Inc. should prepare to record the exchange transaction with Tyler Company. Note that this is an exchange of dissimilar assets. The cost of a nonmonetary asset acquired in exchange for a dissimilar nonmonetary asset is the fair value of the assets surrendered, and a gain (loss) is recognized on the exchange.

3.1 First, determine the fair market value of the assets given up to obtain the printing press. The fair market value of the land is $190,000 and the cash given is $30,000. Thus, the total fair market value of the assets given up is $220,000 ($190,000 + $30,000). This is the cost at which the printing press should be recorded.

3.2 To remove the land from Hobson's books, the Land account must be credited for its cost, $105,000, since this is the amount at which it is carried on Hobson's books. Cash would be credited for $30,000.

3.3 Finally, the gain on the exchange can be determined by computing the difference between the fair market value and the book value of the land given up.

FMV of land	$190,000
BV of land	105,000
Gain on exchange	$85,000

Unofficial Answer

(Author Modified)

Problem 5 Plant Asset Transactions

Part a.

1.

Hobson, Inc.
Disposition of Idle Plant
1977–81

Date	Cash received Debit	Note receivable Dr. (Cr.)	Idle plant (net) (Credit)	Deferred income Dr. (Cr.)	Income recognized (Credit)
January 1, 1977	$100,000	$600,000	($500,000)	($200,000)	
July 1, 1978	190,000	(100,000)		(90,000)	
December 31, 1979	275,000	(200,000)		(10,000)	(65,000)*
February 1, 1981	332,500	(300,000)			(32,500)
February 1, 1981				300,000	(300,000)

*($100,000 + $190,000 + $275,000) – $500,000 = $65,000

2.

Hobson, Inc.
Journal Entry-Exchange of Assets
April 1, 1981

	Debit	Credit
Printing press (Schedule 1)	$220,000	
Land-future building site		$105,000
Cash		30,000
Gain on exchange (Schedule 2)		85,000

To record the exchange of land for a printing press.

Schedule 1

Cost of Printing Press

Fair market value of land exchanged	$190,000
Cash paid	30,000
Fair market value of assets given up	$220,000

Schedule 2

Gain on Exchange

Fair market value of land exchanged	$190,000
Cost of land	105,000
Gain on exchange	$85,000

Multiple Choice Questions (1 – 31)

1. The Carine Company, which was formed on January 1, 1975, adopted a policy of deferring investment tax credits for accounting purposes. Investment tax credits of $100,000 were available in 1975 on equipment that was purchased on January 1, 1975. The equipment has an estimated ten-year life. What is the amount of investment tax credit that should be credited to income in 1975?

a. $ 10,000
b. $ 14,286
c. $ 90,000
d. $100,000

2. Andan Corp. purchased machinery in 1982 that qualified for an investment tax credit of $10,000. This machinery is being depreciated over a five-year period. Andan's 1982 taxable income and book income before income taxes, was $250,000. Andan's effective income tax rate for 1982 was 40%. If Andan accounts for the investment tax credit by the flow-through method, how much should Andan report in its 1982 income statement for income tax expense?

a. $ 90,000
b. $ 96,000
c. $ 98,000
d. $100,000

3. The amount of income tax applicable to transactions that must be reported using intraperiod income tax allocation is computed

a. By multiplying the item by the effective income tax rate.
b. As the difference between the tax computed based on taxable income without including the item and the tax computed based on taxable income including the item.
c. As the difference between the tax computed on the item based on the amount used for financial reporting and the amount used in computing taxable income.
d. By multiplying the item by the difference between the effective income tax rate and the statutory income tax rate.

4. Assuming **no** prior period adjustments, would the following affect net income?

	Interperiod income tax allocation	*Intraperiod income tax allocation*
a.	Yes	Yes
b.	Yes	No
c.	No	Yes
d.	No	No

5. On December 20, 1982, Sussex Corporation received a condemnation award of $300,000 as compensation for the forced sale of a company plant with a book value of $200,000. In its income tax return for the year ended December 31, 1982, Sussex elected to replace the condemned plant within the allowed replacement period. Accordingly, the $100,000 gain was not reported as taxable income for 1982. Sussex has an effective income tax rate of 40% for 1982. In its December 31, 1982, balance sheet, what amount should Sussex report as a liability for deferred taxes on the above gain?

a. $60,000
b. $40,000
c. $20,000
d. $0

6. Martin Company began operations on January 1, 1981, and a substantial part of its sales are made on an installment basis. For financial reporting Martin recognizes revenues from all sales under the accrual method. However, on its income tax returns, Martin reports revenues from installment sales under the installment method. Information concerning gross profit from installment sales under each method is as follows:

Year	*Accrual method*	*Installment method*
1981	$400,000	$150,000
1982	650,000	350,000

For both years, assume the effective income tax rate is 40% and there are no other timing differences. In its December 31, 1982, balance sheet, Martin should report a liability for deferred taxes of

a. $220,000
b. $200,000
c. $180,000
d. $120,000

7. The books of Curtis Company for the year ended December 31, 1982, showed income of $360,000 before provision for income tax. In computing the taxable income for federal income tax purposes, the following differences were taken into account:

Depreciation deducted for tax purposes in excess of depreciation recorded on the books	$16,000
Income from installment sale reportable for tax purposes in excess of income recognized on the books	12,000

Assuming a corporate income tax rate of 40%, what should Curtis record as its current federal income tax liability at December 31, 1982?

a. $137,600
b. $142,400

c. $144,000
d. $145,600

8. In 1978, West Company accrued, for financial statement reporting, estimated losses on disposal of unused plant facilities of $800,000. The facilities were sold in March 1979. Also, in 1978 West paid $100,000 of premiums on officers' life insurance. Assuming that the effective income tax rate was 40%, the amount reported in the provision for deferred income taxes in West's income statement for the year ended December 31, 1978, should be a

a. $320,000 credit.
b. $320,000 debit.
c. $360,000 credit.
d. $360,000 debit.

9. Agard Company's effective income tax rate is 40%. For the year ended December 31, 1982, Agard's income statement reflected depletion expense of $1,000,000 based on the cost of assets being depleted. However, Agard properly deducted $4,000,000 for percentage depletion on its 1982 tax return. How much should be reported as provision for deferred income taxes in Agard's 1982 financial statements?

a. $1,600,000
b. $1,200,000
c. $ 400,000
d. $0

Items 10 and 11 are based on the following information:

Bee Corp. prepared the following reconciliation between book income and taxable income for the year ended December 31, 1982:

Income before income taxes, per books	$500,000
Taxable income, per Form 1120	300,000
Difference	$200,000
Permanent difference—	
interest on municipal bonds	$ 50,000
Timing difference—	
lower depreciation per books	150,000
Total differences	$200,000

Bee's effective income tax rate for 1982 is 40%. Bee reported the following information in its annual report:

Income before income taxes		$500,000
Provision for income taxes:		
Current	$?	
Deferred	?	
Net income		$

10. What amount should Bee report as the current portion of its provision for income taxes?

a. $120,000
b. $140,000
c. $180,000
d. $200,000

11. What amount should Bee report as the deferred portion of its provision for income taxes?

a. $ 20,000
b. $ 60,000
c. $ 80,000
d. $120,000

12. Reynella Corporation commenced operations on January 1, 1981. For the year ended December 31, 1981, Reynella had pretax income of $1,500,000, after accruing estimated warranty expense of $570,000. Reynella's effective income tax rate was 40%, resulting in income tax payable of $624,000 and deferred income tax of $24,000 at December 31, 1981. What was the amount of actual warranty payments in 1981?

a. $0
b. $510,000
c. $570,000
d. $630,000

13. Burns Co., an installment seller of furniture, records sales on the accrual basis for financial reporting purposes but on the installment method for tax purposes. As a result, $50,000 of deferred income taxes have been accrued at December 31, 1974. In accordance with trade practice, installment accounts receivable from customers are shown as current assets, although the average collection period is approximately three years.

At December 31, 1974, Burns Co. has recorded a $20,000 deferred income tax debit arising from a book accrual of noncurrent deferred compensation expense which is not presently tax deductible.

Also, at December 31, 1974, Burns has accrued $15,000 of deferred income taxes resulting from the use of accelerated depreciation for tax purposes and straight-line depreciation for financial-reporting purposes.

How should the deferred income taxes be shown on Burns' December 31, 1974 balance sheet?

a. Current deferred income tax debit of $50,000; noncurrent deferred income tax debit of $20,000; and noncurrent deferred income tax credit of $15,000.

b. Current deferred income tax credit of $50,000; current deferred income tax debit of $20,000; and noncurrent deferred income tax credit of $15,000.

c. Noncurrent deferred income tax debit of $20,000; and noncurrent deferred income tax credit of $65,000.
d. Current deferred income tax credit of $50,000; and noncurrent deferred income tax debit of $5,000.

14. A machine with a ten-year useful life is being depreciated on a straight-line basis for financial statement purposes, and over five years for income tax purposes under the accelerated cost recovery system. Assuming that the company is profitable and that there are and have been **no** other timing differences, the related deferred income taxes would be reported in the balance sheet at the end of the first year of the estimated useful life as a

a. Current liability.
b. Current asset.
c. Noncurrent liability.
d. Noncurrent asset.

15. Which of the following could require interperiod tax allocation?

a. Premiums paid on officers' life insurance.
b. Unearned service contract revenue.
c. Interest received on municipal obligations.
d. Dividends received exclusion.

16. Interperiod income tax allocation is justified by the basic theory that income taxes should be treated as which of the following?

a. An expense for the current portion and a distribution of earnings for the deferred portion.
b. An expense.
c. A distribution of earnings for the current portion and an expense for the deferred portion.
d. A distribution of earnings.

17. Which of the following interperiod tax allocation methods uses the tax rates in effect at the origination of the timing differences and does not adjust for subsequent changes in tax rates?

a. Deferred method.
b. Liability method.
c. Net of tax method.
d. Net present value method.

18. A company has four "deferred income tax" accounts arising from timing differences involving: (1) current assets, (2) noncurrent assets, (3) current liabilities, and (4) noncurrent liabilities. The presentation of these four "deferred income tax" accounts in the statement of financial position should be shown as

a. A single net amount.
b. A net current and a net noncurrent amount.
c. Four accounts with no netting permitted.
d. Valuation adjustments of the related assets and liabilities that gave rise to the deferred tax.

19. Interperiod income tax allocation in corporate financial statements can best be justified by which of the following accounting concepts or principles?

a. Conservatism.
b. Matching.
c. Realization.
d. Objectivity.

20. Tramway Corporation is a stable, going concern which each year invests about $25,000 in new plant and equipment as an equal amount of older equipment is retired. It has been reporting income for both tax and financial-statement purposes by using straight-line depreciation, but it has now changed to accelerated depreciation for tax purposes. This difference in depreciation methods will cause a deferred tax credit which over the years will build up

a. And then remain relatively constant.
b. Rapidly and then slowly increase.
c. Indefinitely.
d. Rapidly and then slowly decline.

21. Boa Constructors, Inc., had an operating loss carryforward of $100,000 at December 31, 1979, for which the tax benefit was fully realized at the end of 1980, when the income tax rate was 40%. For the year ended December 31, 1980, the tax benefit should be reported in the income statement as

a. A $40,000 reduction in income tax expense.
b. An extraordinary item of $40,000.
c. An operating gain of $40,000.
d. An extraordinary item of $100,000.

22. Gomer Corporation reported the following results for its first three years of operations:

1974 - Operating income (before income taxes)	$ 10,000
1975 - Operating loss (before income taxes)	(200,000)
1976 - Operating income (before income taxes)	350,000

There were no permanent or timing differences during these years. For the year ended December 31, 1976, what should Gomer record as its current income tax liability, assuming a corporate income tax rate of 45% for all years?

a. $ 67,500
b. $ 72,000
c. $ 90,000
d. $157,500

23. Pacter Co., an installment seller, earns a $300 pretax gross profit on each installment sale. For financial reporting purposes the entire $300 is recognized at the time of sale, but for income tax purposes the installment method of accounting is used.

Assume Pacter makes one sale in 1978, another sale in 1979, and a third sale in 1980. In each case, one-third of the gross sales price is collected in the year of sale, one-third in the next year, and the final installment in the next year.

Assume that on January 1, 1980, the tax rate increased to 60% from 50%. The appropriate amount to report as "deferred income taxes" under the "gross change method" on Pacter's December 31, 1980, balance sheet is

a. $120
b. $170
c. $270
d. $300

24. Saratoga, Inc., owns 75% of the voting common stock of its domestic subsidiary, Bell Corporation. During 1982 Bell reported earnings of $150,000 and paid dividends of $50,000. Saratoga assumes that all of the undistributed earnings of Bell will be distributed as dividends in future periods. Assuming that Saratoga's income tax rate is 40%, the amount of deferred tax to be reported for 1982 is

a. $ 4,500
b. $ 6,750
c. $30,000
d. $40,000

25. In 1975, The Chrol Company formed a foreign subsidiary. Income before United States and foreign income taxes for this wholly-owned subsidiary was $500,000 in 1975. The income tax rate in the country of the foreign subsidiary was 40%. None of the earnings of the foreign subsidiary have been remitted to Chrol; however, there is nothing to indicate that these earnings will not be remitted to Chrol in the future.

The country of the foreign subsidiary does not impose a tax on remittances to the United States. A tax credit is allowed in the United States for taxes payable in the country of the foreign subsidiary.

Assuming the income tax rate in the United States is 48%, what is the total amount of income taxes relating to the foreign subsidiary that should be shown in the income statement of Chrol in 1975?

a. $0
b. $ 40,000
c. $200,000
d. $240,000

May 1984 Questions

26. In 1983 Stone Corporation received interest income of $50,000 on U.S. Government obligations and $300,000 in royalties under a licensing agreement. Royalties are reported as taxable income in the year received, but in the financial statements, royalties are recognized as income in the year earned and amounted to $200,000 for the year ended December 31, 1983. Stone's effective income tax rate is 40%. By what amount would the deferred income tax asset account balance increase for 1983?

a. $20,000
b. $40,000
c. $60,000
d. $80,000

27. On January 1, 1983, Wolfe Company purchased a building for $1,500,000. The building will be depreciated $50,000 per year by the straight-line method for financial statement reporting. For income tax reporting, Wolfe uses the ACRS and will be allowed a cost recovery deduction of $180,000 for 1983. Assuming an income tax rate of 40%, what amount of deferred income taxes should be added to Wolfe's deferred income tax liability at December 31, 1983?

a. $ 52,000
b. $ 72,000
c. $ 78,000
d. $130,000

Items 28 and 29 are based on the following information:

Hanson Corporation's income statement for the year ended December 31, 1983, shows pretax book income of $400,000. The following items for 1983 are treated differently on the tax return and on the books:

	Per tax return	Per books
Royalty income	$ 20,000	$ 40,000
Depreciation expense	125,000	100,000
Amortization of goodwill	None	15,000

Assume that Hanson's effective tax rate for 1983 is 40%.

28. Of Hanson's total income tax expense, how much should be reported as current portion of income taxes in Hanson's 1983 income statement?
    a. $142,000
    b. $148,000
    c. $160,000
    d. $166,000

29. Of Hanson's total income tax expense, how much should be reported as deferred income taxes in Hanson's 1983 income statement?
    a. $ 8,000
    b. $10,000
    c. $12,000
    d. $18,000

30. At the most recent year end, a company's deferred income tax charge related to a noncurrent liability exceeded a deferred income tax credit related to a current asset. Which of the following should be reported in the company's most recent year-end balance sheet?
    a. The deferred income tax charge as a current asset.
    b. The excess of the deferred income tax charge over the deferred income tax credit as a current asset.
    c. The deferred income tax charge as a noncurrent asset.
    d. The excess of the deferred income tax charge over the deferred income tax credit as a noncurrent asset.

31. Royalties are recognized when received in 1983 for income tax purposes and recognized when earned in 1984 for financial statement purposes. This is an example of a
    a. Permanent difference that gives rise to interperiod tax allocation.
    b. Permanent difference that does **not** give rise to interperiod tax allocation.
    c. Timing difference that gives rise to interperiod tax allocation.
    d. Timing difference that does **not** give rise to interperiod tax allocation.

Repeat Question

(584,T1,20) Identical to item 14 above

Problems

Problem 1 Recording and Classifying Deferred Taxes (582,T4)

(15 to 25 minutes)

Part a. This year Lorac Company has each of the following items in its income statement:

- Gross profits on installment sales.
- Revenues on long-term construction contracts.
- Estimated costs of product warranty contracts.
- Premiums on officers' life insurance with Lorac as beneficiary.

Required:

1. Under what conditions would deferred income taxes need to be reported in the financial statements?
2. Specify when deferred income taxes would need to be recognized for each of the items above, and indicate the rationale for such recognition.

Part b. Eneri Company's president has heard that deferred income taxes can be variously classified in the balance sheet.

Required:

Identify the conditions under which deferred income taxes would be classified as a noncurrent item in the balance sheet. What justification exists for such classification?

Problem 2 Gross vs. Net Change Method (1179,T4a)

(5 to 10 minutes)

Part a. Deferred income taxes are required under generally accepted accounting principles. Accounting Principles Board Opinion No. 11 requires the use of the deferred method of comprehensive interperiod tax allocation. Two ways to account for timing differences under the deferred method are: (1) gross change method, and (2) net change method.

Required:

1. Describe the gross change method.
2. Describe the net change method.

Problem 3 Calculation of Deferred Taxes (1182,Q4)

(45 to 55 minutes)

In January 1982, you began the examination of the financial statements for the year ended December 31, 1981, of Howe Corporation, a new audit client. During your examination the following information was disclosed:

- On January 2, 1979, packaging equipment was purchased at a cost of $450,000. The equipment had an estimated useful life of five years and a salvage value of $60,000. Howe was entitled to and claimed an investment credit of $30,000 on its 1979 income tax return. For financial reporting purposes, the investment credit was treated as an offset against the cost of the equipment. The sum-of-the-years' digits method of depreciation was used for income tax reporting and the straight-line method was used on the financial statements.
- On January 3, 1980, $120,000 was collected in advance rental of a building for a three-year period. The $120,000 was reported as taxable income in 1980, but $80,000 was reported as deferred revenue in 1980 in the financial statements. The building will continue to be rented for the foreseeable future.
- On February 9, 1981, Howe sold land with a book and tax basis of $300,000 for $400,000. The gain, reported in full in 1981 on the financial statements, was reported by the installment method on the income tax return equally over a period of ten years and is taxable at the capital gains rate.
- On March 10, 1981, a patent was purchased at a cost of $68,000. Howe is amortizing the patent over a period of four years on the financial statements and over 17 years on its income tax return. Howe elected to record a full year's amortization in 1981 on both its financial statements and income tax return.

Based on effective income tax rates of 40% on ordinary income and 28% on long-term capital gains, the following federal income tax liabilities were reported on Howe's income tax returns:

1979	$ 50,000
1980	142,400
1981	101,280

Required:

Prepare schedules computing

1. Net deductions for tax reporting purposes, giving rise to interperiod tax allocation on ordinary income for each year ended December 31, 1979, 1980, and 1981.
2. Net deductions for financial statements adjusted for applicable permanent differences, giving rise to interperiod tax allocation on ordinary income for each year ended December 31, 1979, 1980, and 1981.
3. Deferred tax credit at the capital gains rate at December 31, 1981.
4. Total net deferred tax credits and debits at December 31, 1979, 1980, and 1981.
5. Total income tax expense for financial statement purposes for each year ended December 31, 1979, 1980, and 1981.

Multiple Choice Answers

1.	a	8.	a	14.	c	20.	a	26.	b
2.	a	9.	d	15.	b	21.	b	27.	a
3.	b	10.	a	16.	b	22.	b	28.	b
4.	b	11.	b	17.	a	23.	b	29.	d
5.	b	12.	b	18.	b	24.	a	30.	c
6.	a	13.	d	19.	b	25.	d	31.	c
7.	b								

Multiple Choice Answer Explanations

A. Investment Tax Credit

1. (576,P1,6) (a) There are two methods of accounting for the investment credit, the deferred method and the flow-through method. The flow-through method recognizes investment credits as a reduction in tax expense in the year that they become available. The deferred method considers investment tax credits as a reduction in the cost of assets, and the credits are amortized over the useful life of the assets. Thus with a 10 year life, the $100,000 should be amortized 10% per year or $10,000.

2. (1183,Q1,9) (a) The requirement is the 1982 income tax expense when the investment tax credit is accounted for using the flow-through (immediate recognition) method. Although the deferral method is the preferred method (APB 4), the flow-through method is also acceptable. The flow-through method reduces tax expense and the tax liability by the amount of the credit in the year of purchase. Andan's 1982 income tax expense is $90,000.

Taxable income	$250,000
Effective tax rate	x .40
Tax before credits	100,000
Investment tax credit	10,000
Income tax expense	$ 90,000

B. Intraperiod Tax Allocation

3. (579,T1,9) (b) Intraperiod income tax allocation of annual tax expense must be made to income from ordinary operations, discontinued operations, extraordinary items, cumulative effect of an accounting change, and prior period adjustments. The tax effect to be associated with any of the special items (other than income from ordinary operations) is computed by determining the income tax on overall taxable income and comparing it with the income tax on ordinary operations. If more than one special item exists, the difference between tax on ordinary operations and tax on overall taxable income must be allocated among the special items. See para 52 of APB 11 and Interpretation No. 19 of APB 11.

4. (583,T1,35) (b) Interperiod income tax allocation is a **measurement** problem which deals with the effects of recording some revenue and expense items in a different period for financial reporting purposes than they are recognized for tax purposes. Intraperiod income tax allocation is a **disclosure** problem. The total amount of income taxes for financial reporting must be allocated to income from continuing operations, discontinued operations, extraordinary items, the cumulative effects of a change in accounting principle, prior period adjustments, and certain other direct entries to stockholders' equity accounts.

C. Interperiod Tax Allocation

5. (1183,P2,29) (b) The requirement is the amount of liability for deferred taxes on a gain from the condemnation of a plant. Per FASB Interpretation 30, such gains on involuntary conversions are to be recognized in the financial statements in the year they occur. Furthermore, the interpretation specifies that such a gain, which is not recognized for tax purposes in the same year as for financial accounting purposes, is a timing difference for which interperiod tax allocation is required. Therefore, a deferred tax credit of $40,000 (40% x $100,000) is necessary, since accounting income exceeds taxable income by $100,000.

6. (1183,P2,31) (a) The requirement is the liability for deferred taxes at 12/31/82. Martin Company recognizes sales revenue on the accrual basis for financial reporting purposes, but uses the installment method for tax purposes. This results in a timing difference which gives rise to deferred taxes. Martin's cumulative accounting income before taxes ($400,000 + $650,000 = $1,050,000) exceeds its cumulative taxable income ($150,000 + $350,000 = $500,000) by $550,000 ($1,050,000 – $500,000). This excess results in a credit to deferred taxes of $220,000 (40% x $550,000).

7. (583,P1,9) (b) The requirement is the amount to be recorded as the current federal income tax liability at 12/31/82. The current income tax payable is based on taxable income, while income tax expense is based on pretax accounting income ($360,000 in this case). This amount must be adjusted for the two timing differences listed. Tax depreciation is $16,000 larger than accounting depreciation; this would reduce taxable income. Installment sales income was $12,000 higher for tax purposes; this would increase taxable income. Taxable income therefore is $356,000 ($360,000 – $16,000 + $12,000), and taxes currently payable are $142,400 ($356,000 x 40%). The journal entry to record tax expense and taxes payable is:

Income tax expense	144,000		($360,000 x 40%)
Income tax payable		142,400	($356,000 x 40%)
Deferred income taxes		1,600	

8. (1179,P1,12) (a) The requirement is the deferred portion of income tax expense on the income statement resulting from an accrual of an estimated $800,000 loss on disposal of unused plant facilities given a tax rate of 40%. The accrual of $800,000 of estimated losses (1978) is a timing difference because it will not be deductible for tax purposes until the loss is incurred (1979). As a result of this transaction, 1978 income tax expense will be $320,000 less than income taxes payable. In the income statement, the deferred income tax effect is subtracted from the current portion of income tax expense to arrive at income tax expense. The solutions approach is to make two entries to record income tax expense.

Income tax expense	xxxxxx	
Income taxes payable		xxxxxx
Deferred income taxes	320,000	
Income tax expense		320,000

Using this approach, the $320,000 credit effect is easily identified. Note that the Institute refers to "provision for deferred taxes" as the tax expense effect of the adjustment to the deferred tax account. Also note that the $100,000 premium on officers' life insurance is not a timing difference. It is either an expense for both tax and book purposes or it is a permanent difference depending on who is named as beneficiary. It is a permanent difference only if the corporation is named as the beneficiary.

9. (1183,Q1,8) (d) The requirement is the amount of the provision for deferred income taxes to be reported in the 1982 financial statements. A common mistake when solving this problem would be to treat the depletion difference between book and tax income as a timing difference, similar to using an accelerated depreciation method for tax and the straight-line method for book purposes. But, using percentage depletion for tax, which means taking depletion in excess of cost, creates a permanent difference which does not affect the deferred income tax provision (APB 11, para 33). Therefore, the correct answer would be $0.

10. (583,Q2,36) (a) The requirement is the current portion of the provision for income taxes. The current portion of taxes is the tax liability shown on Bee Corporation's income tax return, per Form 1120. Bee Corporation shows taxable income of $300,000 on its tax return, which, when multiplied by Bee's 1982 effective income tax rate of 40% results in the current provision for income taxes of $120,000. See solution to next problem for further discussion.

11. (583,Q2,37) (b) The requirement is the deferred portion of the provision for income taxes. The deferred tax account is only affected by timing differences; thus, since the municipal bond interest income is a permanent difference, it will have no effect on deferred taxes. The data in the problem can be reformatted in the following manner:

Book income before taxes	$500,000
Permanent difference: municipal bond interest	(50,000)
	450,000
Timing difference: depreciation	(150,000)
Taxable income, per Form 1120	$300,000

Income tax expense	180,000	
Deferred income taxes		60,000
Income taxes payable		120,000

The income tax expense on the books is $180,000 (40% x $450,000) and the tax liability is $120,000 (40% x $300,000). Therefore, the credit to deferred income taxes results from the $150,000 timing difference (40% x $150,000 = $60,000).

12. (582,Q1,20) (b) The requirement is the amount of actual warranty payments in 1981. The first step is to calculate the amount of the timing difference in 1981. Visualize the journal entry to record the current year's taxes.

*Tax expense	$600,000	
Deferred taxes	24,000	
Tax liability		$624,000

*$1,500,000 x 40%

The amount of taxable income in 1981 must have been $1,560,000 ($624,000 ÷ .40 = $1,560,000). Thus, the amount of the timing difference is $60,000 ($1,560,000 – $1,500,000). This is the amount by which the accrual of estimated warranty expenses exceeded actual warranty payments in 1981. The amount of actual warranty payments is thus $510,000 ($570,000 – $60,000).

Warranty Liability

1981 actual payments	$510,000	$0	Balance 1/1/81
		$570,000	1981 estimated expense
		$ 60,000	Balance 12/31/81

13. (575,Q1,4) (d) APB 11, para 57 requires that deferred taxes be classified into two categories, current and noncurrent. The classification should parallel the classification of the accounts that gave rise to the deferred taxes. In the current problem, the $50,000 of deferred taxes resulting from the accrual method of financial reporting and installment method for tax reporting results in a $50,000 deferred credit. It is current because the installment receivables are classified as current. It is a credit balance because the installment method defers the recognition of revenue and payment of taxes. The $20,000 deferred debit is noncurrent because the deferred compensation expense is noncurrent. The $15,000 of deferred taxes resulting from the use of accelerated depreciation for tax purposes and straight-line for financial reporting has a credit balance, because the accelerated depreciation for tax purposes defers payment of taxes. It is noncurrent because the assets are not current assets. Thus on the balance sheet the current deferred taxes will have a $50,000 credit balance. The noncurrent deferred taxes will have a $5,000 debit balance ($20,000 debit less $15,000 credit).

14. (583,T1,20) (c) Deferred tax charges and credits arising from timing differences should be classified in the same manner as the related asset or liability which created it (SFAS 37, para 4). In the first year of an asset's life, a deferred credit (liability) arises when the asset is being depreciated over a shorter period for tax purposes than for financial reporting purposes as in this problem. Since the asset is a machine with a useful life of 10 years, the deferred tax credit (a liability) would be classified as a noncurrent item, consistent with classification of the machine. Answers (a) and (b) are incorrect because the deferred credit is related to a noncurrent asset. Answer (d) is incorrect because income taxes payable is less than the income tax expense when an asset is depreciated over a shorter period for tax purposes; thus, a deferred credit (liability) arises, not a deferred charge (asset).

15. (1182,T1,14) (b) Interperiod tax allocation is the adjustment process that reflects tax expense based on pretax accounting income where the tax expense is different from taxes paid. Unearned service contract revenue [answer (b)] is the only item listed that would create a timing difference. The unearned revenue would be included in income for tax purposes but would not be recognized on the books as revenue until it is earned. The other answers are incorrect because they result in permanent differences.

16. (1181,T1,35) (b) Under interperiod tax allocation, income tax expense is based on pretax accounting income and this expense is different from the actual liability to be paid because of timing differences. Income tax expense includes both the current portion and deferred portion resulting from differences between pretax accounting income and taxable income. Income tax is considered to be an expense deducted to arrive at net income and, therefore, is not a distribution of earnings which eliminates answers (a), (c), and (d).

17. (580,T1,12) (a) Under the deferred method, adjustments are not made for subsequent changes in the tax rate. The liability method does require adjustment and the net of tax method allows for either rates when the timing difference originated or expected rates when reversal is scheduled to occur. The net present value method is a capital budgeting technique, not an interperiod tax allocation method. See APB 11, para 19-21.

18. (1176,T1,6) (b) Deferred taxes rising from timing differences should be classified in two categories on the balance sheet. The first category is the net current amount and the second is the net noncurrent amount. See para 57 of APB 11. Answer (d), "valuation adjustments of the related assets and liabilities" is a net of tax method which in addition to being a nonacceptable disclosure procedure, is unacceptable as a method of interperiod tax allocation (para 21).

19. (575,T1,9) (b) Interperiod income tax allocation is based upon the matching principle. In tax allocation, federal tax expense is reported in the year in which income is reported for financial reporting purposes. It is the application of accrual accounting to federal income tax expense. See para 36 of APB 11.

20. (575,T1,17) (a) The deferred credit will build up in the first few years and then remain relatively constant because a constant amount of equipment will be purchased and retired each year. Thus in every year approximately the same amount of equipment will be depreciated at accelerated rates and approximately the same amount of equipment will be depreciated at decelerated rates, e.g., every year $25,000 will be depreciated at the first year's depreciation rate and $25,000 will be depreciated at the last year's depreciation rate.

D. Loss Carryforwards and Carrybacks

21. (581,Q2,36) (b) The requirement of this problem is to calculate the tax benefit arising from a net operating loss carryforward and indicate how this benefit is reported on the income statement. According to APB 11, the tax benefit should be reported as an extraordinary item. The amount reported is the amount of the loss ($100,000) multiplied by the tax

rate (40%), or $40,000. Note that if in 1979, realization of the carryforward was assured beyond any reasonable doubt, the tax benefit of the loss carryforward would be recognized as an operating item in 1979.

22. (1177,Q1,13) (b) The requirement is the income tax liability in the third year of operations. Since the respective operating results were a $10,000 profit, $200,000 loss, and $350,000 profit, the operating loss in the second year of $200,000 will be carried back $10,000 to the first year and $190,000 will offset income in the third year. Thus the income tax liability in the third year will be $350,000 less $190,000, or $160,000 times 45% which is $72,000. Note that the requirement is the current tax liability.

The effect of the operating loss carryforward is $190,000 times 45%, or $85,500, which would be reported as an extraordinary item on the income statement (para 61, APB 11). The expense associated with operating income would be 45% of the $350,000 of operating income (i.e., $157,500) which is required by para 52 of APB 11 (intraperiod tax allocation). To recap:

1976 tax expense	
(45% of $350,000)	$157,500
Operating loss carryforward	
Extraordinary item	
(45% of $190,000)	85,500
1976 taxes payable	$ 72,000

E. Complicating Factors in Tax Allocation

23. (574,Q1,8) (b) Under the "gross change method" the amount of deferred income taxes is found by multiplying an originating timing difference by the tax rate in effect in the year in which the timing difference originates. When the timing difference reverses, the deferred income tax account is reduced by the amount originally recorded for the specific timing difference. A direct solutions approach is to calculate the balance in deferred income taxes at December 31, 1980, based on the deferred gross margin.

1979 sale: $100 deferred gross margin x 50% =	$ 50
1980 sale: $200 deferred gross margin x 60% =	120
	$170

An alternative approach is a "T-account" analysis.

Deferred Income Taxes	
(Reversing differences)	(Originating differences)
	$100 ($200 x 50%) :1978
1979: ($100 x 50%) $ 50	100 ($200 x 50%) :1979
1980: ($200 x 50%) 100	120 ($200 x 60%) :1980
	$170 Balance 12/31/80

Note that if the "net change method" were used, the balance would be $150 because the net timing difference in 1980 would be zero ($200 originating – $200 reversing). Recall that the "net change method" uses the current year's tax rate for both originating and reversing timing differences.

F. & G. Income Tax Effects from Investee Co. and Subsidiary Co.

24. (583,P1,12) (a) The requirement is the amount of deferred tax to be recorded by a parent corporation as a result of transactions with a subsidiary. Subsidiary earnings not distributed as dividends cause a timing difference. For accounting purposes, the parent recognizes its share of subsidiary earnings (75% of $150,000, or $112,500) as income. For tax purposes, dividends received (75% of $50,000, or $37,500) are recognized as income. This results in a $75,000 difference (a shortcut approach is to take 75% of undistributed earnings of $100,000). This $75,000 difference is partially a permanent difference and partially a timing difference. The permanent difference results because dividends received by one corporation from another domestic corporation are subject to an 85% dividends received deduction. Therefore, 85% of such dividends are permanently removed from taxable income. The permanent difference in this case is 85% of $75,000, or $63,750. The timing difference is 15% of $75,000, or $11,250. With a tax rate of 40%, the deferred tax to be recorded is $4,500 (40% x $11,250).

25. (576,P1,11) (d) APB 23 (para 10) requires that parent companies consider undistributed earnings of a subsidiary as a timing difference unless there is definite evidence that the subsidiary's earnings will be remitted in a tax free liquidation or will not be remitted in the future. Thus the taxes on the $500,000 of income will be 48%. Foreign taxes will be 40% and domestic taxes will be 8% (48% less the 40% credit for foreign taxes per the problem).

May 1984 Answers

26. (584,P1,17) (b) The requirement is the increase in the deferred income tax asset account for 1983. The interest income ($50,000) on U.S. government obligations does **not** affect deferred taxes because such income is included in both accounting income and taxable income in the same year. The royalty revenue is a timing difference which will affect deferred taxes. It is a timing difference because revenue is recognized in different years for accounting purposes (when earned) and tax purposes (when received). Income tax

expense is based on accounting income ($200,000 x 40% = $80,000), while income taxes **payable** is based on taxable income ($300,000 x 40% = $120,000). The difference ($120,000 - $80,000 = $40,000) is debited to the deferred income tax asset account.

27. (584,P2,23) (a) The requirement is the increase in the deferred income tax liability account in 1983. The deferred tax account is affected by timing differences, in this case, depreciation expense. Accounting income is reduced by $50,000 for straight-line depreciation, while taxable income is reduced by $180,000 for ACRS depreciation. Therefore, accounting income exceeds taxable income by $130,000 ($180,000 - $50,000). This will increase the deferred tax liability by $52,000 ($130,000 x 40%).

28. (584,P3,45) (b) The requirement is the amount to be reported as the current portion of the 1983 income taxes on the income statement. According to the AICPA Accounting Interpretation of APB 11, para 20, the components of income tax expense must be allocated as to the amount currently payable (current portion) and the tax effects of timing differences (deferred portion). The current portion is computed based on taxable income. The pretax book income must be adjusted as follows to arrive at taxable income:

Pretax book income	$400,000
Book deductions (income):	
Royalty income	(40,000)
Depreciation expense	100,000
Amortization of goodwill	15,000
Tax (deductions) income:	
Royalty income	20,000
Depreciation expense	(125,000)
Amortization of goodwill	–
Taxable income	$370,000

The taxes currently payable are 40% of taxable income or $148,000.

29. (584,P3,46) (d) The requirement is the amount of deferred taxes to be disclosed on the income statement in 1983. The deferred tax is the difference between the tax based on taxable income computed "with" timing differences and taxable income computed "without" timing differences.

	Taxable income	
	"With"	*"Without"*
Pretax book income	$400,000	$400,000
Permanent difference:		
Amortization of goodwill	15,000	15,000
Timing differences:		
Royalty income ($40,000 - $20,000)	(20,000)	–
Depreciation expense ($125,000 - $100,000)	(25,000)	–
	$370,000	$415,000
Income tax rate	40%	40%
Income tax	$148,000	$166,000

The amount of deferred tax is $18,000 ($166,000 - $148,000). Notice that the goodwill amortization has no effect on the deferred tax computation since it is a permanent difference.

30. (584,T1,15) (c) The requirement is to determine the proper balance sheet classification of deferred income taxes. Per APB 11, para 57 deferred taxes should be separated and classified into two components: one for net current amounts and one for net noncurrent amounts. Therefore, the company's balance sheet should report the deferred income charge as a noncurrent asset [answer (c)] and the deferred income tax credit as a current liability. Answer (a) is incorrect because the deferred tax amount relating to the current asset is a credit and should be classified as a current liability, not a current asset. Current and noncurrent components should not be netted; thus, answers (b) and (d) are incorrect.

31. (584,T1,21) (c) The requirement is to determine the correct accounting treatment for royalties recognized when received for income tax purposes and when earned for financial statement purposes. Per APB 11, para 34 timing differences arise when revenue or expense transactions are included in the computation of income for financial statement purposes in one period and taxable income in a different period. Interperiod income tax allocation arises because timing differences cause income tax expense based on pretax accounting income to be different than the actual tax liability based on taxable income. Since permanent differences do not affect other periods, interperiod tax allocation is not appropriate for such differences. Answers (a) and (b) are incorrect because they are examples of timing differences, not a permanent difference. Answer (d) is incorrect because the timing difference described would give rise to interperiod tax allocation.

Answer Outline

Problem 1 Recording and Classifying Deferred Taxes

Part a.

1. GAAP and tax law may measure income differently
   - Permanent difference—no need for deferred income taxes
   - Timing difference—need for deferred income taxes
2. First three items may involve deferred taxes if timing difference occurs
   - Gross profits on installment sales (timing)
     - Generally, GAAP recognizes gross profit at time of sale
     - Generally, for tax purposes gross profit recognized when cash is collected
     - Originating vs. reversing
   - Revenues on long-term construction contracts (timing)
     - Generally, GAAP prescribes percentage of completion method
     - Generally, for tax purposes completed contract method is used
     - Originating vs. reversing
   - Estimated costs of product warranty contracts (timing)
     - GAAP—related warranty expense is accrued in year of sale
     - Income tax—expense recognized when paid
     - Originating vs. reversing
   - Rationale:
     - Matching costs and revenues
     - Going concern
   - Premium on officer's life insurance with Lorac as beneficiary (permanent)
     - For GAAP, expensed as paid
     - For tax purposes, not deductible

Part b.

Classification of deferred income taxes (DIT) as noncurrent
- Depends on classification of related asset or liability
- If no related asset or liability classification, depends on expected reversal date

Rationale:
- Future payment or use of DIT depends on payment date

Unofficial Answer
(Author Modified)

Problem 1 Recording and Classifying Deferred Taxes

Part a.

1. Generally accepted accounting principles (GAAP) and federal income tax law (Internal Revenue Code) may measure income differently. If a difference between pretax accounting income and taxable income is permanent, there is no need to provide for deferred taxes. A permanent difference occurs when an item is used to compute pretax accounting income but is never used to compute taxable income; or when an item is used to compute taxable income but is never used to compute pretax accounting income. However, if a difference between taxable income and pretax accounting income is temporary (timing difference), deferred income taxes need to be recorded and reported in the financial statements. A timing difference occurs when an item of revenue or expense enters into the calculation of pretax accounting income and taxable income in different periods.

2. Gross profits on installment sales would result in deferred income taxes being reported in the financial statements if these gross profits are recognized in full at the time of sale for accounting purposes, but are recognized as cash is collected for tax purposes. In this case, a timing difference would originate and deferred income taxes would be credited in the year of sale. In future years, as gross profit is recognized for tax purposes, the timing difference reverses and deferred income taxes would be debited.

Revenues on long-term construction contracts would result in deferred income taxes being reported in the financial statements if the conditions of ARB 45 are met for use of the percentage-of-completion method for recognizing such revenues, while for tax purposes the completed-contract method is used. This would result in higher revenues under GAAP in the early years, but higher tax revenues in the year the contract is completed. In the early (originating) years, deferred income taxes would be credited. When the timing difference reverses in the final year (year of completion), deferred taxes would be debited.

Accounting for the estimated costs of product warranty contracts would ordinarily result in a timing difference. Per SFAS 5, warranty expenses are accrued in the year of sale and matched with the related revenue recognized. For tax purposes, warranty expense is recognized as incurred. Therefore, the financial statements would show a higher level of expense and a lower income than is computed for tax purposes. This would result in a debit to deferred taxes. When the timing difference reverses, deferred taxes would be credited. The rationale for recognizing and reporting deferred income taxes is based on the going concern and matching concepts.

Deferred income taxes would not be reported in connection with the premium on officer's life insurance on which Lorac is the beneficiary. The portion of the premium which does not increase the cash surrender value of the policy would be expensed in determining pretax accounting income, while no part of the premium is deductible for tax purposes. Therefore, deferred income taxes would not result from this permanent difference.

Part b.

The classification of deferred income taxes as a noncurrent or current item in the balance sheet depends on the classification of the related asset or liability (APB 11, para 57). An asset or liability is considered to be related to a deferred income tax charge or credit if its reduction will cause the original timing difference to reverse. For example, a deferred income tax credit related to property, plant, and equipment (use of different depreciation methods for financial and tax income) would be classified as noncurrent. On the other hand, a deferred income tax credit related to installment accounts receivable would be classified as current if collection of the receivable falls within the firm's operating cycle.

If a specific timing difference is not related to an asset or liability, the deferred income taxes are classified as current or noncurrent based on the expected reversal date of the timing difference (SFAS 37, para 4). This treatment is justified by the fact that the ultimate use of or payment of deferred income taxes is dependent on the reversal date.

Answer Outline

Problem 2 Gross vs. Net Change Method

a1. Gross change method
    Timing differences originating in current period are reflected at current tax rates
    Timing differences reversing in current period are reflected at tax rates existing in the deferred taxes account

a2. Net change method applies the current rate to the net change in originating and reversing timing differences

Unofficial Answer

Problem 2 Gross vs. Net Change Method

a. 1. Under the gross change method, the tax effects of timing differences originating in the current period are determined at the current income tax rates. The tax effects of timing differences originating in prior periods and reversing in the current period are determined at the applicable income tax rates reflected in the accounts as of the beginning of the current period.

2. Under the net change method, the tax effects of the net change in the originating and reversing timing differences are determined at the current income tax rates.

Solution Guide

Problem 3 Calculation of Deferred Taxes

1. This problem requires five schedules involving deferred taxes and income tax expense. Recall the treatment of deferred taxes. When tax expense (book income) is in excess of the tax liability (taxable income) the deferred tax account is credited. Conversely, when the tax liability is in excess of tax expense the deferred tax account is debited.

2. Part one requires a schedule computing net deductions for tax reporting purposes, giving rise to interperiod tax allocation on ordinary income for 1979, 1980, and 1981. This would include the timing differences on equipment depreciation, rental income, and patent amortization. The investment credit is not included because it is a credit, not a deduction. The gain on sale of land is not included because it is capital gains income, not ordinary income.

2.1 The problem states that for financial reporting purposes the investment credit was treated as an offset against the cost of the equipment. This statement refers to the balance sheet presentation of the investment credit only, and would not affect the computations of depreciation, the amount of any timing differences, and income tax expense.

2.2 Sum-of-the-years' digits depreciation is used for tax purposes. The cost less salvage value

($390,000) is depreciated 5/15, 4/15, 3/15, 2/15, 1/15 over the five-year life. The denominator is computed by the formula n(n + 1)/2, which is (5 x 6)/2, or 15.

2.3 The $120,000 rent collected in advance is all taxable in the year collected (1980).

2.4 A full year's patent amortization ($68,000 ÷ 17) is deducted in the year of purchase (1981).

3. Part two requires the same computation as part one, except for financial reporting, rather than tax reporting purposes.

3.1 Straight-line depreciation is used for financial purposes. The cost less salvage ($390,000) is depreciated 1/5 per year over the five-year period.

3.2 The $120,000 rent collected in advance in 1980 is recognized ratably ($40,000 per year) over a three-year period.

3.3 A full year's patent amortization ($68,000 ÷ 4) is deducted in the year of purchase (1981).

4. Part three requires the computation of the deferred tax credit at 12/31/81, arising from the capital gains transaction.

4.1 The gain on the sale of land ($400,000 – $300,000 = $100,000) is recognized in full in the year of sale (1981) for financial reporting purposes.

4.2 For tax purposes, this gain is recognized equally over a ten-year period ($100,000 ÷ 10 = $10,000) using the installment method.

4.3 At 12/31/81, a gain of $100,000 had been recognized for financial purposes but only a $10,000 gain for tax purposes. This $90,000 timing difference results in a deferred tax credit of $25,200 ($90,000 x 28%).

5. Part four requires the computation of total net deferred tax credits or debits at 12/31/79, 80, and 81.

5.1 The beginning balance in deferred taxes for 1979 is assumed to be zero.

5.2 The debit or credit to deferred taxes resulting from ordinary income is calculated by comparing tax deductions (part one) and financial deductions (part two). In 1979, net tax deductions related to timing differences totaled $130,000, while the net financial deductions totaled $78,000. This means taxable income was $52,000 lower ($130,000 – $78,000) than financial income, resulting in a credit of $20,800 to deferred taxes ($52,000 x 40%). Similar computations are performed for 1980 and 1981, taking the difference between net tax deductions and net financial deductions and multiplying by 40%.

5.3 In 1981, there is also a credit to deferred taxes of $25,200 from capital gains income (as computed in part three).

5.4 The beginning balance in deferred taxes for 1980 and 1981 are the ending balances at 12/31/79 and 12/31/80, respectively.

6. Part five requires the total income tax expense for the years 1979, 1980, and 1981.

6.1 The income tax expense each year is computed by taking the income taxes currently payable and adjusting for deferred taxes and the investment credit.

6.2 The adjustment for deferred taxes on ordinary income each year is the debit or credit to deferred taxes that year as computed in part four.

6.3 The adjustment for deferred taxes on capital gains income in 1981 is the credit to deferred taxes computed in part three and reflected in part four.

6.4 The investment credit in 1979 of $30,000 is accounted for using the deferred method. Thus, the investment credit is reflected in net income as a reduction of income tax expense over the useful life of the acquired asset rather than as a $30,000 reduction of income tax expense in the year of purchase. However, since the $30,000 credit was deducted in determining the income tax liability, it must be added back to the income tax liability in order to find income tax expense for financial statement purposes. The credit is then recognized as a reduction of income tax expense over the five-year life of the asset ($6,000 per year).

Unofficial Answer

Problem 3 Calculation of Deferred Taxes

1.

Howe Corporation
Net Tax Deductions for Tax Reporting Purposes
Giving Rise to Interperiod Tax Allocation
1979, 1980, and 1981

	1979	*1980*	*1981*
Depreciation on equipment:			
($450,000 – $60,000) x 5/15	$130,000		
($450,000 – $60,000) x 4/15		$104,000	
($450,000 – $60,000) x 3/15			$78,000
Rental income		(120,000)	
Patent amortization			
$68,000 ÷ 17			4,000
	$130,000	$(16,000)	$82,000

2.

Howe Corporation
Net Financial Statement Deductions
Giving Rise to Interperiod Tax Allocation
1979, 1980, and 1981

	1979	*1980*	*1981*
Depreciation on equipment:			
($450,000 – $60,000) x 1/5	$78,000	$78,000	$78,000
Rental income ($120,000/3)		(40,000)	(40,000)
Patent amortization			
$68,000 ÷ 4			17,000
	$78,000	$38,000	$55,000

3.

Howe Corporation
Deferred Tax Credit at the Capital Gains Rate
12/31/81

Gain on sale of land ($400,000 – $300,000)	$100,000
Gain reported on tax return ($100,000 x 1/10)	(10,000)
Timing difference	$ 90,000
Deferred tax credit ($90,000 x 28%)	$ 25,200

4.

Howe Corporation
Total Net Deferred Tax Credits and Debits
at 12/31/79, 80, and 81

	12/31/79	*12/31/80*	*12/31/81*
Beginning balance	$ –0–	$(20,800)	$ 800
Debit (credit) to deferred taxes from ordinary income			
[$130,000 – $78,000] x 40%	(20,800)		
[($16,000) – $38,000] x 40%		21,600	
[$ 82,000 – $55,000] x 40%			(10,800)
Credit to deferred taxes from capital gains income			(25,200)
Ending balance, debit (credit)	$(20,800)	$ 800	$(35,200)

5.

Howe Corporation
Income Tax Expense
1979, 1980, and 1981

	1979	*1980*	*1981*
Current portion	$50,000	$142,400	$101,280
Adjustment for deferred taxes on ordinary income	20,800	(21,600)	10,800
Adjustment for deferred taxes on capital gains income			25,200
Investment credit on tax return	30,000		
Investment credit amortization (30,000 ÷ 5)	(6,000)	(6,000)	(6,000)
Income tax expense	$94,800	$114,800	$131,280

Multiple Choice Questions (1–56)

1. Following is the condensed balance sheet of Fine Products, an individual proprietorship, at December 31, 1982:

Current assets	$100,000
Equipment	200,000
Accumulated depreciation	(120,000)
	$180,000
Liabilities	$ 40,000
Silvia Fine, Capital	140,000
	$180,000

Fair market values of assets at December 31, 1982, were as follows:

Current assets	$110,000
Equipment	290,000

The liabilities were fairly stated at book values. On January 2, 1983, the proprietorship was incorporated, with 2,000 shares of $20 par value common stock issued. How much should be credited to additional paid-in capital?

a. $100,000
b. $140,000
c. $320,000
d. $360,000

2. The excess of the fair value of the consideration received over the stated value of no par common stock should be credited to

a. A liability account.
b. Common stock.
c. Additional paid-in capital.
d. Retained earnings.

3. During 1980 Bradley Corporation issued for $110 per share, 5,000 shares of $100 par value convertible preferred stock. One share of preferred stock can be converted into three shares of Bradley's $25 par value common stock at the option of the preferred shareholder. On December 31, 1981, all of the preferred stock was converted into common stock. The market value of the common stock at the conversion date was $40 per share. What amount should be credited to the common stock account on December 31, 1981?

a. $375,000
b. $500,000
c. $550,000
d. $600,000

Items 4 and 5 are based on the following information:

A company wishes to raise funds by issuing either bonds or cumulative preferred stock.

4. How will the annual interest or dividend affect total liabilities each year?

a. Interest is a current liability each year (until paid).
b. Cumulative preferred dividends are a current liability each year (until paid).
c. Both interest and cumulative preferred dividends are current liabilities each year (until paid).
d. Interest and cumulative preferred dividends in arrears are current liabilities each year (until paid).

5. How will the annual interest or dividend affect annual net earnings available to common stockholders each year?

a. Annual net earnings available to common stockholders are reduced by annual interest but not by preferred dividends.
b. Annual net earnings available to common stockholders are reduced by preferred dividends but not by annual interest.
c. Annual net earnings available to common stockholders are reduced by annual interest and preferred dividends.
d. Annual net earnings available to common stockholders are not reduced by annual interest or preferred dividends.

6. How should cumulative preferred dividends in arrears be shown in a corporation's statement of financial position?

a. Footnote.
b. Increase in stockholders' equity.
c. Increase in current liabilities.
d. Increase in current liabilities for the amount expected to be declared within the year or operating cycle, and increase in long-term liabilities for the balance.

7. The Amlin Corporation was incorporated on January 1, 1977, with the following authorized capitalization:

20,000 shares of common stock, no par value, stated value $40 per share.
5,000 shares of 5% cumulative preferred stock, par value $10 per share.

During 1977 Amlin issued 12,000 shares of common stock for a total of $600,000 and 3,000 shares of preferred stock at $16 per share. In addition, on December 20, 1977, subscriptions for 1,000 shares of preferred stock were taken at a purchase price of $17. These subscribed shares were paid for on January 2, 1978. What should Amlin report as total contributed capital on its December 31, 1977, balance sheet?

a. $520,000
b. $648,000
c. $665,000
d. $850,000

8. The excess of the subscription price over the par value of nonredeemable preferred stock subscribed should be recorded as

a. A liability.
b. Additional paid-in capital.
c. Retained earnings.
d. Revenue.

9. Authorized common stock is sold on a subscription basis at a price in excess of par value. Additional paid-in capital should be recorded when the subscribed stock is

a. Contracted for.
b. Paid for.
c. Issued.
d. Authorized.

10. Victor Corporation was organized on January 2, 1982, with 100,000 authorized shares of $10 par value common stock. During 1982 Victor had the following capital transactions:

- January 5—issued 75,000 shares at $14 per share.
- December 27—purchased 5,000 shares at $11 per share.

Victor used the par value method to record the purchase of the treasury shares. What would be the balance in the paid-in capital from treasury stock account at December 31, 1982?

a. $0
b. $ 5,000
c. $15,000
d. $20,000

11. The stockholders' equity account balances of Rice Corporation as of December 31, 1981, are as follows:

Common stock, $10 par; 50,000 shares authorized; 25,000 shares issued	$250,000
Paid-in capital in excess of par	50,000
Retained earnings	100,000
Less treasury stock, 2,000 shares at cost	(32,000)
Total stockholders' equity	$368,000

On January 4, 1982, Rice sold the treasury shares on the open market at $20 per share. The entry to record this sale on Rice's books should include a credit to

a. Gain from sale of treasury stock of $8,000.
b. Paid-in capital from treasury stock of $8,000.
c. Retained earnings of $8,000.
d. Paid-in capital from treasury stock of $12,000.

12. Newton Corporation was organized on January 1, 1977. On that date it issued 200,000 shares of its $10 par value common stock at $15 per share (400,000 shares were authorized). During the period January 1, 1977, through December 31, 1979, Newton reported net income of $750,000 and paid cash dividends of $380,000. On January 5, 1979, Newton purchased 12,000 shares of its common stock at $12 per share. On December 31, 1979, 8,000 treasury shares were sold at $8 per share. Newton used the cost method of accounting for treasury shares. What is the total stockholders' equity of Newton as of December 31, 1979?

a. $3,290,000
b. $3,306,000
c. $3,338,000
d. $3,370,000

13. Jordon Corporation has 80,000 shares of $50 par value common stock authorized, issued and outstanding. All 80,000 shares were issued at $55 per share. Retained earnings of the company amounts to $160,000. If 1,000 shares of Jordon common stock are reacquired at $62 and the par value method of accounting for treasury stock is used, stockholders' equity would decrease by

a. $0
b. $50,000
c. $55,000
d. $62,000

14. When treasury stock is purchased for cash at more than its par value, what is the effect on total stockholders' equity under each of the following methods?

	Cost method	Par value method
a.	Increase	Increase
b.	Decrease	Decrease

c.	No effect	Decrease
d.	No effect	No effect

15. When treasury stock accounted for by the cost method is subsequently sold for more than its purchase price, the excess of the cash proceeds over the carrying value of the treasury stock should be recognized as
   a. Extraordinary gain.
   b. Income from continuing operations.
   c. Increase in additional paid-in capital.
   d. Increase in retained earnings.

16. When treasury stock is purchased for more than its par value, treasury stock is debited for the purchase price under which of the following methods?

	Cost method	*Par value method*
a.	No	No
b.	No	Yes
c.	Yes	No
d.	Yes	Yes

17. The stockholders' equity section of Peter Corporation's balance sheet at December 31, 1982, was as follows:

Common stock ($10 par value, authorized 1,000,000 shares, issued and outstanding 900,000 shares)	$9,000,000
Additional paid-in capital	2,700,000
Retained earnings	1,300,000
Total stockholders' equity	$13,000,000

On January 2, 1983, Peter purchased and retired 100,000 shares of its stock for $1,800,000. Immediately after retirement of these 100,000 shares, the balances in the additional paid-in capital and retained earnings accounts should be

	Additional paid-in capital	*Retained earnings*
a.	$ 900,000	$1,300,000
b.	$1,400,000	$ 800,000
c.	$1,900,000	$1,300,000
d.	$2,400,000	$ 800,000

18. On September 30, 1982, Grey Company issued 3,000 shares of its $10 par common stock in connection with a stock dividend. No entry was made on the stock dividend declaration date. The market value per share immediately after issuance was $15. Grey's stockholders' equity accounts immediately before issuance of the stock dividend shares were as follows:

Common stock, $10 par; 50,000 shares authorized; 20,000 shares outstanding	$200,000
Additional paid-in capital	300,000
Retained earnings	350,000

What should be the retained earnings balance immediately after the stock dividend?
   a. $305,000
   b. $320,000
   c. $327,500
   d. $350,000

19. The following information pertains to a property dividend of marketable securities, declared by Tyson Corp.:

	Fair value
Declaration date—December 20, 1982	$300,000
Record date—January 10, 1983	310,000
Distribution date—January 28, 1983	305,000

Carrying value of the securities on Tyson's books was $200,000. How much gain should Tyson recognize in 1982 as a result of this property dividend?
   a. $0
   b. $100,000
   c. $105,000
   d. $110,000

20. The following changes in account balances of the Marvel Corporation during 1979 are presented below:

	Increase
Assets	$356,000
Liabilities	108,000
Capital stock	240,000
Additional paid-in capital	24,000

Assuming there were no charges to retained earnings other than for a dividend payment of $52,000, the net income for 1979 should be
   a. $16,000
   b. $36,000
   c. $52,000
   d. $68,000

21. The Culture Corporation had the following classes of stock outstanding as of December 31, 1979:

Common stock, $20 par value, 20,000 shares outstanding.
Preferred stock, 6%, $100 par value, cumulative and fully participating, 1,000 shares outstanding.

Dividends on preferred stock have been in arrears for 1977 and 1978. On December 31, 1979, a total cash dividend of $90,000 was declared. What are the amounts of dividends payable on both the common and preferred stock, respectively?

a. $57,600 and $32,400.
b. $62,400 and $27,600.
c. $67,200 and $22,800.
d. $72,000 and $18,000.

22. A property dividend should be debited to retained earnings at the property's

a. Market value at date of declaration.
b. Market value at date of issuance (payment).
c. Book value at date of declaration.
d. Book value at date of issuance (payment).

23. The dollar amount of total stockholders' equity remains the same when there is a(an)

a. Issuance of preferred stock in exchange for convertible debentures.
b. Issuance of nonconvertible bonds with detachable stock purchase warrants.
c. Declaration of a stock dividend.
d. Declaration of a cash dividend.

24. The issuer should directly charge retained earnings for the market value of the shares issued in a (an)

a. Pooling of interests.
b. 2 for 1 stock split.
c. Employee stock bonus.
d. 10 percent stock dividend.

25. Effective April 27, 1981, the stockholders of Bennett Corporation approved a two-for-one split of the company's common stock, and an increase in authorized common shares from 100,000 shares (par value $20 per share) to 200,000 shares (par value $10 per share). Bennett's stockholders' equity accounts immediately before issuance of the stock split shares were as follows:

Common stock, par value $20; 100,000 shares authorized; 50,000 shares outstanding	$1,000,000
Additional paid-in capital (premium of $3 per share on issuance of common stock)	150,000
Retained earnings	1,350,000

What should be the balances in Bennett's additional paid-in capital and retained earnings accounts immediately after the stock split is effected?

	Additional paid-in capital	*Retained earnings*
a.	$0	$ 500,000
b.	$ 150,000	$ 350,000
c.	$ 150,000	$1,350,000
d.	$1,150,000	$ 350,000

26. On July 1, 1981, Boulevard Corporation split its common stock 4 for 1, when the market value was $80 per share. Prior to the split, Boulevard had 50,000 shares of $12 par value common stock issued and outstanding. After the split, the par value of the stock

a. Remained the same.
b. Was reduced by $3 per share.
c. Was reduced to $3 per share.
d. Was reduced by $4 per share.

27. What is the most likely effect of a stock split on the par value per share and the number of shares outstanding?

	Par value per share	*Number of shares outstanding*
a.	Decrease	Increase
b.	Decrease	No effect
c.	Increase	Increase
d.	No effect	No effect

28. A clearly identified appropriation of retained earnings for reasonably possible loss contingencies should be

a. Charged with all losses related to that contingency.
b. Transferred to income as losses are realized.
c. Classified in the liability section of the balance sheet.
d. Shown within the stockholders' equity section of the balance sheet.

29. On January 1, 1981, Stoner Corporation granted stock options to key employees for the purchase of 10,000 shares of the company's common stock at $25 per share. The options are intended to compensate employees for the next two years. The options are exercisable within a four-year period beginning January 1, 1983, by grantees still in the employ of the company. The market price of Stoner's common stock was $32 per share at the date of grant. Stoner plans to distribute up to 10,000 shares of treasury stock when options are exercised. The treasury stock was acquired by Stoner during 1980 at a cost of $28 per share and was recorded under the cost method. Assume that no stock options were terminated during the year. How much should Stoner charge to compensation expense for the year ended December 31, 1981?

a. $70,000
b. $35,000

c. $30,000
d. $15,000

Items 30 and 31 are based on the following information:

On January 1, 1980, Karva Company granted James Dean, the president, an option to purchase 1,000 shares of Karva's $30 par value common stock at $40 per share. The option becomes exercisable on January 1, 1982, after Dean has completed two years of service.

30. Assume that the quoted market prices of Karva's $30 par value common stock were as follows:

January 1, 1980	$40
December 31, 1980	55

As a result of the option granted to Dean, Karva should recognize compensation expense in 1980 of

a. $0.
b. $ 5,000.
c. $ 7,500.
d. $15,000.

31. Assume that the quoted market prices of Karva's $30 par value common stock were as follows:

January 1, 1980	$45
December 31, 1980	55

As a result of the option granted to Dean, Karva should recognize compensation expense in 1980 of

a. $0
b. $2,500
c. $5,000
d. $7,500

32. Compensation cost should be recognized in the income statement of each period in which services are rendered for a compensatory stock option plan for which the date of grant and the measurement date are

	Different	*Identical*
a.	No	No
b.	No	Yes
c.	Yes	Yes
d.	Yes	No

33. If the stock for a compensatory stock option plan is issued before some or all of the services are performed, a part of the consideration recorded for the stock issued is unearned compensation and should be shown in the balance sheet as a line item in

a. Noncurrent liabilities.
b. Stockholders' equity.
c. Current assets.
d. Noncurrent assets.

34. At December 31, 1979, Sonic Company had 20,000 shares of common stock issued and outstanding and 5,000 shares of nonconvertible preferred stock issued and outstanding. Sonic's net income for the year ended December 31, 1980, was $120,000. During 1980 Sonic declared and paid $50,000 cash dividends on common stock and $8,000 cash dividends on the nonconvertible preferred stock. There were no common stock or preferred stock transactions during the year. The earnings per common share for the year ended December 31, 1980, should be

a. $3.50
b. $4.80
c. $5.60
d. $6.00

35. For purposes of computing the weighted-average number of shares outstanding during the year, a midyear event that must be treated as occurring at the beginning of the year is the

a. Declaration and payment of stock dividend.
b. Purchase of treasury stock.
c. Sale of additional common stock.
d. Issuance of stock warrants.

36. Information relating to the capital structure of Vauxhall Corporation is as follows:

	December 31	
	1978	*1979*
Outstanding shares of:		
Common stock	200,000	200,000
Preferred 6% stock, $100 par, convertible into 3 shares of common stock for each share of preferred	10,000	10,000

The preferred stock was issued at par on July 1, 1978, when the average Aa corporate bond yield was 9.5%. During 1979, Vauxhall paid dividends of $6 per share on its preferred stock. The net income for the year ended December 31, 1979, is $860,000. The primary earnings per common share, rounded to the nearest penny, for the year ended December 31, 1979, should be

a. $3.74
b. $4.00
c. $4.10
d. $4.30

37. Weaver Company had 100,000 shares of common stock issued and outstanding at December 31, 1978. On July 1, 1979, Weaver issued a 10% stock dividend.

Unexercised stock options to purchase 20,000 shares of common stock (adjusted for the 1979 stock dividend) at $20 per share were outstanding at the beginning and end of 1979. The average market price of Weaver's common stock (which was not affected by the stock dividend) was $25 per share during 1979. Net income for the year ended December 31, 1979, was $550,000. What should be Weaver's 1979 primary earnings per common share, rounded to the nearest penny?

a. $4.82
b. $5.00
c. $5.05
d. $5.24

Items 38 and 39 are based on the following data:

At December 31, 1981 and 1980, Gravin Corporation had 90,000 shares of common stock and 20,000 shares of convertible preferred stock outstanding, in addition to 9% convertible bonds payable in the face amount of $2,000,000. During 1981, Gravin paid dividends of $2.50 per share on the preferred stock. The preferred stock is convertible into 20,000 shares of common stock, and is considered a common stock equivalent. The 9% convertible bonds are convertible into 30,000 shares of common stock, but are not considered common stock equivalents. Net income for 1981 was $970,000. Assume an income tax rate of 40%.

38. How much is the primary earnings per share for the year ended December 31, 1981?

a. $ 7.70
b. $ 8.36
c. $ 8.82
d. $10.78

39. How much is the fully diluted earnings per share for the year ended December 31, 1981?

a. $ 7.70
b. $ 8.21
c. $ 9.35
d. $10.22

40. Antidilutive common stock equivalents would generally be used in the calculation of

	Primary earnings per share	*Fully diluted earnings per share*
a.	Yes	Yes
b.	No	Yes
c.	No	No
d.	Yes	No

41. In determining earnings per share, interest expense, net of applicable income taxes, on convertible debt which is both a common stock equivalent and dilutive should be

a. Added back to net income for primary earnings per share, and ignored for fully diluted earnings per share.
b. Added back to net income for both primary earnings per share and fully diluted earnings per share.
c. Deducted from net income for primary earnings per share and ignored for fully diluted earnings per share.
d. Deducted from net income for both primary earnings per share and fully diluted earnings per share.

42. In determining primary earnings per share, dividends on nonconvertible cumulative preferred stock should be

a. Deducted from net income whether declared or not.
b. Deducted from net income only if declared.
c. Added back to net income whether declared or not.
d. Disregarded.

43. When computing fully diluted earnings per share, convertible securities that are **not** common stock equivalents are

a. Ignored.
b. Recognized whether they are dilutive or anti-dilutive.
c. Recognized only if they are dilutive.
d. Recognized only if they are anti-dilutive.

44. In applying the treasury stock method of computing the dilutive effect of outstanding options or warrants, for quarterly fully diluted earnings per share, when is it appropriate to use the ending market price of common stock as the assumed repurchase price?

a. Always.
b. Never.
c. When the ending market price is higher than the average market price and the exercise price.
d. When the ending market price is lower than the average market price and higher than the exercise price.

45. Scott Company filed a voluntary bankruptcy petition on June 25, 1982, and the statement of affairs reflects the following amounts:

	Book carrying amount	Estimated current value
Assets:		
Assets pledged with fully secured creditors	$160,000	$190,000
Assets pledged with partially secured creditors	90,000	60,000
Free assets	200,000	140,000
	$450,000	$390,000
Liabilities:		
Liabilities with priority	$ 20,000	
Fully secured creditors	130,000	
Partially secured creditors	100,000	
Unsecured creditors	260,000	
	$510,000	

Assume that the assets are converted into cash at the estimated current values and the business is liquidated. What total amount of cash should the partially secured creditors receive?

a. $ 60,000
b. $ 84,000
c. $ 90,000
d. $100,000

46. Livingston Corporation has incurred losses from operations for several years. At the recommendation of the newly hired president, the board of directors voted to implement a quasi-reorganization, subject to stockholder approval. Immediately prior to the restatement, on June 30, 1980, Livingston's balance sheet was as follows:

Current assets	$ 550,000
Property, plant, and equipment (net)	1,350,000
Other assets	200,000
	$2,100,000
Total liabilities	$ 600,000
Common stock	1,600,000
Additional paid-in capital	300,000
Retained earnings (deficit)	(400,000)
	$2,100,000

The stockholders approved the quasi-reorganization effective July 1, 1980, to be accomplished by a reduction in other assets of $150,000, a reduction in property, plant, and equipment (net) of $350,000, and appropriate adjustment to the capital structure. To implement the quasi-reorganization, Livingston should reduce the common stock account in the amount of

a. $0
b. $100,000
c. $400,000
d. $600,000

47. A company with a substantial deficit undertakes a quasi-reorganization. Certain assets will be written down to their present fair market value. Liabilities will remain the same. How would the entries to record the quasi-reorganization affect each of the following?

	Contributed capital	Retained earnings
a.	Increase	Decrease
b.	Decrease	No effect
c.	Decrease	Increase
d.	No effect	Increase

48. On July 1, 1977, Round Company issued for $525,000 a total of 5,000 shares of $100 par value, 7% noncumulative preferred stock along with one detachable warrant for each share issued. Each warrant contains a right to purchase one share of Round's $10 par value common stock for $15 a share. The market price of the rights on July 1, 1977, was $2.25 per right. On October 31, 1977, when the market price of the common stock was $19 per share and the market value of the rights was $3.00 per right, 4,000 rights were exercised. As a result of the exercise of the 4,000 rights and the issuance of the related common stock, what journal entry would Round make?

		Debit	Credit
a.	Cash	$60,000	
	Common stock		$40,000
	Additional paid-in capital		20,000
b.	Cash	$60,000	
	Common stock rights outstanding	9,000	
	Common stock		$40,000
	Additional paid-in capital		29,000
c.	Cash	60,000	
	Common stock rights outstanding	12,000	
	Common stock		40,000
	Additional paid-in capital		32,000

d.	Cash	60,000	
	Common stock rights outstanding	16,000	
	Common stock		40,000
	Additional paid-in capital		36,000

49. On July 1, 1980, Metaro Corporation purchased for $108,000, 2,000 shares of Jean Corporation's newly issued 6% cumulative $20 par value preferred stock. Each share also had one stock warrant attached, which entitled the holder to acquire, at $19, one share of Jean $10 par value common stock for each two warrants held. On July 2, 1980, the market price of the preferred stock (without warrants) was $50 per share and the market price of the stock warrants was $10 per warrant. On September 1, 1980, Metaro sold all the stock warrants for $19,800.

What should be the gain on the sale of the stock warrants?

a. $0
b. $ 800
c. $1,800
d. $9,800

50. A company issued rights to its existing shareholders to purchase 5,000 unissued shares of common stock with a par value of $10 per share for $25 per share. Additional paid-in capital would be recorded when the rights

a. Expire.
b. Are exercised.
c. Become exercisable.
d. Are issued.

51. Which of the following is issued to shareholders by a corporation as evidence of the ownership of rights to acquire its unissued or treasury stock?

a. Stock options.
b. Stock warrants.
c. Stock dividends.
d. Stock subscriptions.

May 1984 Questions

52. On January 1, 1983, Whalen, Inc., had 120,000 shares of common stock outstanding. A 10% stock dividend was issued on April 1, 1983. Whalen issued 40,000 shares of common stock for cash on July 1, 1983. What is the number of shares that should be used in computing earnings per share for the year ended December 31, 1983?

a. 146,000
b. 149,000
c. 152,000
d. 172,000

53. Cox Corporation had 1,200,000 shares of common stock outstanding on January 1 and December 31, 1983. In connection with the acquisition of a subsidiary company in June 1982, Cox is required to issue 50,000 additional shares of its common stock on July 1, 1984, to the former owners of the subsidiary. Cox paid $200,000 in preferred stock dividends in 1983, and reported net income of $3,400,000 for the year. Cox's fully diluted earnings per share for 1983 should be

a. $2.83
b. $2.72
c. $2.67
d. $2.56

54. How would the declaration of a 10% stock dividend by a corporation affect each of the following on its books?

	Retained earnings	*Total stockholders' equity*
a.	Decrease	Decrease
b.	Decrease	No effect
c.	No effect	Decrease
d.	No effect	No effect

55. A company issued rights to its existing shareholders to purchase for $15 per share, 5,000 unissued shares of common stock with a par value of $10 per share. Common stock will be credited at

a. $15 per share when the rights are exercised.
b. $15 per share when the rights are issued.
c. $10 per share when the rights are exercised.
d. $10 per share when the rights are issued.

56. Treasury stock was acquired for cash at more than its par value, and then subsequently sold for cash at more than its acquisition price. Assuming that the cost method of accounting for treasury stock transactions is used, what is the effect on additional paid-in capital from treasury stock transactions?

	Purchase of treasury stock	*Sale of treasury stock*
a.	No effect	No effect
b.	No effect	Increase
c.	Decrease	Increase
d.	Decrease	No effect

Repeat Question

(584,T1,29) Identical to item 42 above

Problems

Problem 1 Primary vs. Fully Diluted EPS (580,T2b)

(10 to 15 minutes)

Part b. Public enterprises are required to present earnings per share data on the face of the income statement.

Required:

Compare and contrast primary earnings per share with fully diluted earnings per share for each of the following:

1. The effect of common stock equivalents on the number of shares used in the computation of earnings per share data.
2. The effect of convertible securities that are **not** common stock equivalents on the number of shares used in the computation of earnings per share data.
3. The effect of antidilutive securities.

Problem 2 Stock Option Plans (580,T4b)

(10 to 15 minutes)

Part b. A corporation has a noncompensatory stock purchase plan for all of its employees and a compensatory stock option plan for some of its corporate officers.

Required:

1. Compare and contrast the accounting at the date the stock is issued for the noncompensatory stock purchase plan and the compensatory stock option plan.
2. What entry should be made for the compensatory stock option plan at the date of the grant?

Problem 3 Treasury Stock (1179,T2b)

(10 to 15 minutes)

For numerous reasons a corporation may reacquire shares of its own capital stock. When a company purchases treasury stock, it has two options as to how to account for the shares: (1) cost method, and (2) par value method.

Required:

Compare and contrast the cost method with the par value method for each of the following:

1. Purchase of shares at a price less than par value.
2. Purchase of shares at a price greater than par value.
3. Subsequent resale of treasury shares at a price less than purchase price, but more than par value.
4. Subsequent resale of treasury shares at a price greater than both purchase price and par value.
5. Effect on net income.

Problem 4 Common Stock Equivalents (1178,T2)

(15 to 20 minutes)

The earnings per share data required of a company depend on the nature of its capital structure. A corporation may have a simple capital structure and only compute "earnings per common share" or may have a complex capital structure and have to compute "primary earnings per share" and "fully diluted earnings per share."

Required:

a. Define the term "common stock equivalent" and describe what securities would be considered common stock equivalents in the computation of earnings per share.

b. Define the term "complex capital structure" and discuss the disclosures (both financial and explanatory) necessary for earnings per share when a corporation has a complex capital structure.

Problem 5 Categories of Stockholders' Equity (576,T7)

(20 to 25 minutes)

Part a. A corporation's capital (stockholders' equity) is a very important part of its statement of financial position.

Required:

Identify and discuss the general categories of capital (stockholders' equity) for a corporation. Be sure to enumerate specific sources included in each general category.

Part b. Stock splits and stock dividends may be used by a corporation to change the number of shares outstanding.

Required:

1. What is meant by a stock split effected in the form of a dividend?
2. From an accounting viewpoint, explain how the stock split effected in the form of a dividend differs from an ordinary stock dividend.
3. How should a stock dividend which has been declared but not yet issued be classified in a statement of financial position? Why?

Part c. Jones Company has adopted a traditional stock option plan for its officers and other employees. This plan is properly considered a compensatory plan.

Required:

Discuss how accounting for this plan will affect net earnings and earnings per share. Ignore income tax considerations and accounting for income tax benefits.

Problem 6 Earnings Per Share (574,T6)

(25 to 30 minutes)

"Earnings per share" (EPS) is the most featured single financial statistic about modern corporations. Daily published quotations of stock prices have recently been expanded to include a "times earnings" figure for many securities which is based on EPS. Often the focus of analysts' discussions will be on the EPS of the corporations receiving their attention.

Required:

a. Explain how dividends or dividend requirements on any class of preferred stock that may be outstanding affect the computation of EPS.

b. One of the technical procedures applicable in EPS computations is the "treasury-stock method."

1. Briefly describe the circumstances under which it might be appropriate to apply the treasury-stock method.
2. There is a limit to the extent to which the treasury-stock method is applicable. Indicate what this limit is and give a succinct indication of the procedures that should be followed beyond the treasury-stock limits.

c. Under some circumstances convertible debentures would be considered "common stock equivalents" while under other circumstances they would not.

1. When is it proper to treat convertible debentures as common stock equivalents? What is the effect on computation of EPS in such cases?
2. In case convertible debentures are not considered as common stock equivalents, explain how they are handled for purposes of EPS computations.

Problem 7 Stock Appreciation Rights (Adapted from Kieso and Weygandt, *Intermediate Accounting*, 4th edition, p. 777)

(15 to 25 minutes)

Futuristic Products Company establishes a stock appreciation rights program which entitles its new president, Jill Castleberry, to receive cash for the difference between the market price of the stock and a preestablished price of $30 (also market price) on December 31, 1980 on 20,000 SARs. The date of grant is December 31, 1980 and the required employment (service) period is three years. President Castleberry exercises all of the SARs in 1986. The market value of the stock fluctuates as follows: 12/31/81–$36; 12/31/82–$39; 12/31/83–$45; 12/31/84–$36; 12/31/85–$48.

Required:

1. Prepare a five-year (1981-1985) schedule of compensation expense pertaining to the 20,000 SARs granted President Castleberry.
2. Prepare the journal entry for compensation expense in 1981, 1984, and 1985 relative to the 20,000 SARs.

Problem 8 Retained Earnings Statement and Stockholders' Equity Section of Balance Sheet (1183,P4)

(45 to 55 minutes)

Ashwood, Inc., is a public enterprise whose shares are traded in the over-the-counter market. At December 31, 1981, Ashwood had 6,000,000 authorized shares of $10 par value common stock, of which 2,000,000 shares were issued and outstanding. The stockholders' equity accounts at December 31, 1981, had the following balances:

Common stock	$20,000,000
Additional paid-in capital	7,500,000
Retained earnings	6,500,000

Transactions during 1982 and other information relating to the stockholders' equity accounts were as follows:

- On January 5, 1982, Ashwood issued at $54 per share, 100,000 shares of $50 par value, 9% cumulative convertible preferred stock. Each share of preferred stock is convertible, at the option of the holder, into two shares of common stock. Ashwood had 600,000 authorized shares of preferred stock. The preferred stock has a liquidation value equal to its par value.
- On February 1, 1982, Ashwood reacquired 20,000 shares of its common stock for $16 per share. Ashwood uses the cost method to account for treasury stock.
- On April 30, 1982, Ashwood sold 500,000 shares (previously unissued) of $10 par value common stock to the public at $17 per share.
- On June 18, 1982, Ashwood declared a cash dividend of $1 per share of common stock, payable on July 12, 1982, to stockholders of record on July 1, 1982.
- On November 10, 1982, Ashwood sold 10,000 shares of treasury stock for $21 per share.
- On December 14, 1982, Ashwood declared the yearly cash dividend on preferred stock, payable on January 14, 1983, to stockholders of record on December 31, 1982.
- On January 20, 1983, before the books were closed for 1982, Ashwood became aware that the ending inventories at December 31, 1981, were understated by $300,000 (after tax effect on 1981 net income was $180,000). The appropriate correction entry was recorded the same day.
- After correcting the beginning inventory, net income for 1982 was $4,500,000.

Required:

1. Prepare a statement of retained earnings for the year ended December 31, 1982. Assume that only single-period financial statements for 1982 are presented.
2. Prepare the stockholders' equity section of Ashwood's balance sheet at December 31, 1982.
3. Compute the book value per share of common stock at December 31, 1982.

Problem 9 Stock Options and EPS (1181,P5)

(40 to 50 minutes)

This problem consists of two unrelated parts.

Part a. On January 1, 1978, Holt, Inc., granted stock options to officers and key employees for the purchase of 20,000 shares of the company's $10 par common stock at $25 per share. The options were exercisable within a four-year period beginning January 1, 1980, by grantees still in the employ of the company, and expiring December 31, 1984. The market price of Holt's common stock was $33 per share at the date of grant. Holt prepares a formal journal entry to record this award.

On April 1, 1979, 2,000 option shares were terminated when the employees resigned from the company. The market value of the common stock was $35 per share on this date.

On March 31, 1980, 12,000 option shares were exercised when the market value of the common stock was $40 per share.

Required:

Prepare journal entries to record issuance of the stock options, termination of the stock options, exercise of the stock options, and charges to compensation expense, for the years ended December 31, 1978, 1979 and 1980. Show supporting computations in good form.

Part b. Mason Corporation's capital structure is as follows:

	December 31	
	1980	1979
Outstanding shares of:		
Common stock	336,000	300,000
Nonconvertible preferred stock	10,000	10,000
8% convertible bonds	$1,000,000	$1,000,000

The following additional information is available:

- On September 1, 1980, Mason sold 36,000 additional shares of common stock.
- Net income for the year ended December 31, 1980, was $750,000.
- During 1980 Mason paid dividends of $3.00 per share on its nonconvertible preferred stock.
- The 8% convertible bonds are convertible into 40 shares of common stock for each $1,000 bond, and were not considered common stock equivalents at the date of issuance.
- Unexercised stock options to purchase 30,000 shares of common stock at $22.50 per share were outstanding at the beginning and end of 1980. The average market price of Mason's common stock was $36 per share during 1980. The market price was $33 per share at December 31, 1980.
- Warrants to purchase 20,000 shares of common stock at $38 per share were attached to the preferred stock at the time of issuance. The warrants, which expire on December 31, 1985, were outstanding at December 31, 1980.

• Mason's effective income tax rate was 40% for 1979 and 1980.

Required (show supporting computations in good form, and round earnings per share to the nearest penny):

1. Compute the number of shares which should be used for the computation of primary earnings per common share for the year ended December 31, 1980.
2. Compute the primary earnings per common share for the year ended December 31, 1980.
3. Compute the number of shares which should be used for the computation of fully diluted earnings per common share for the year ended December 31, 1980.
4. Compute the fully diluted earnings per common share for the year ended December 31, 1980.

Problem 10 Stockholders' Equity Transactions (578,P3)

(50 to 60 minutes)

This problem consists of two unrelated parts.

Part a. Howard Corporation is a publicly-owned company whose shares are traded on a national stock exchange. At December 31, 1976, Howard had 25,000,000 shares of $10 par value common stock authorized, of which 15,000,000 shares were issued and 14,000,000 shares were outstanding.

The stockholders' equity accounts at December 31, 1976, had the following balances:

Common stock	$150,000,000
Additional paid-in capital	80,000,000
Retained earnings	50,000,000
Treasury stock	18,000,000

During 1977, Howard had the following transactions:

• On February 1, 1977, a secondary distribution of 2,000,000 shares of $10 par value common stock was completed. The stock was sold to the public at $18 per share, net of offering costs.

• On February 15, 1977, Howard issued at $110 per share, 100,000 shares of $100 par value, 8% cumulative preferred stock with 100,000 detachable warrants. Each warrant contained one right which with $20 could be exchanged for one share of $10 par value common stock. On February 15, 1977, the market price for one stock right was $1.

• On March 1, 1977, Howard reacquired 20,000 shares of its common stock for $18.50 per share. Howard uses the cost method to account for treasury stock.

• On March 15, 1977, when the common stock was trading for $21 per share, a major stockholder donated 10,000 shares which are appropriately recorded as treasury stock.

• On March 31, 1977, Howard declared a semiannual cash dividend on common stock of $0.10 per share, payable on April 30, 1977, to stockholders of record on April 10, 1977. The appropriate state law prohibits cash dividends on treasury stock.

• On April 15, 1977, when the market price of the stock rights was $2 each and the market price of the common stock was $22 per share, 30,000 stock rights were exercised. Howard issued new shares to settle the transaction.

• On April 30, 1977, employees exercised 100,000 options that were granted in 1975 under a noncompensatory stock option plan. When the options were granted, each option had a preemptive right and entitled the employee to purchase one share of common stock for $20 per share. On April 30, 1977, the market price of the common stock was $23 per share. Howard issued new shares to settle the transaction.

• On May 31, 1977, when the market price of the common stock was $20 per share, Howard declared a 5% stock dividend distributable on July 1, 1977, to stockholders of record on June 1, 1977. The appropriate state law prohibits stock dividends on treasury stock.

• On June 30, 1977, Howard sold the 20,000 treasury shares reacquired on March 1, 1977, and an additional 280,000 treasury shares costing $5,600,000 that were on hand at the beginning of the year. The selling price was $25 per share.

• On September 30, 1977, Howard declared a semiannual cash dividend on common stock of $0.10 per share and the yearly dividend on preferred stock, both payable on October 30, 1977, to stockholders of record on October 10, 1977. The appropriate state law prohibits cash dividends on treasury stock.

• On December 31, 1977, the remaining outstanding rights expired.

• Net income for 1977 was $25,000,000.

Required:

Prepare a worksheet to be used to summarize, for each transaction, the changes in Howard's stockholders' equity accounts for 1977. The columns on this worksheet should have the following headings:

Date of transaction (or beginning date)
Common stock—number of shares
Common stock—amount
Preferred stock—number of shares

Preferred stock—amount
Common stock warrants—number of rights
Common stock warrants—amount
Additional paid-in capital
Retained earnings
Treasury stock—number of shares
Treasury stock—amount

Show supporting computations in good form.

Part b. Tomasco, Inc., began operations in January 1973 and had the following reported net income or loss for each of its five years of operations:

1973	$ 150,000 loss
1974	130,000 loss
1975	120,000 loss
1976	250,000 income
1977	1,000,000 income

At December 31, 1977, the Tomasco capital accounts were as follows:

Common stock, par value $10 per share; authorized 100,000 shares; issued and outstanding 50,000 shares	$ 500,000
4% nonparticipating noncumulative preferred stock, par value $100 per share; authorized, issued and outstanding 1,000 shares	100,000
8% fully participating cumulative preferred stock, par value $100 per share; authorized, issued and outstanding 10,000 shares	1,000,000

Tomasco has never paid a cash or stock dividend. There has been no change in the capital accounts since Tomasco began operations. The appropriate state law permits dividends only from retained earnings.

Required:

Prepare a work sheet showing the maximum amount available for cash dividends on December 31, 1977, and how it would be distributable to the holders of the common shares and each of the preferred shares. Show supporting computations in good form.

Multiple Choice Answers

1.	c	13.	d	24.	d	35.	a	46.	d
2.	c	14.	b	25.	c	36.	a	47.	c
3.	a	15.	c	26.	c	37.	a	48.	b
4.	a	16.	c	27.	a	38.	c	49.	c
5.	c	17.	d	28.	d	39.	a	50.	b
6.	a	18.	a	29.	b	40.	c	51.	b
7.	c	19.	b	30.	a	41.	b	52.	c
8.	b	20.	b	31.	b	42.	a	53.	d
9.	a	21.	b	32.	c	43.	c	54.	b
10.	c	22.	a	33.	b	44.	c	55.	c
11.	b	23.	c	34.	c	45.	b	56.	b
12.	a								

Multiple Choice Answer Explanations

A. Common Stock

1. (583,Q1,12) (c) The requirement is to determine the proper amount that should be credited to additional paid-in capital when the proprietorship incorporated. The basis for determining value of the stock should be the fair value of the net assets contributed to the corporation.

Current assets	$110,000
Equipment	290,000
Liabilities	(40,000)
Fair value of net assets	$360,000

The par value of the stock issued is $40,000 (2,000 shares at $20 par value per share). Thus, the credit to additional paid-in capital should be $320,000 ($360,000 – $40,000).

2. (582,T1,9) (c) Laws of some states require issuances of no par common stock to have a **stated value** which establishes a minimum amount that the stock may be issued for. If this is the case, the stock is treated, for all practical purposes, in the same manner as par value stock. The entry to record an issuance of no par stock with a stated value is:

Cash	XXX	
Common stock (stated value)		XX
Paid-in capital		XX

True no par stock does not have a **stated value** and is carried in the common stock account at issue price [answer (b)]. Answers (a) and (d) are inappropriate in all situations.

B. Preferred Stock

3. (1182,P1,4) (a) The requirement is the amount to be credited to the common stock account as a result of the conversion of preferred stock. All 5,000 shares of the convertible preferred stock were converted to common stock at the rate of 3 shares of common for every share of preferred. Therefore, 15,000 shares of common stock were issued (5,000 x 3). The common stock account is credited for the par value of these shares: 15,000 x $25 or $375,000. Although not necessary, the journal entry to record the conversion can be prepared:

Preferred stock	500,000		5,000 x $100
Paid-in capital, PS	50,000		5,000 x $ 10
Common stock		375,000	15,000 x $ 25
Paid-in capital, CS		175,000	plugged in

Note that the $40 market value of the common stock is ignored. Gains and/or losses are not recognized on the conversion of preferred stock. The book value method is used and the paid-in capital, common stock account is credited for the amount necessary to balance the entry.

4. (577,T2,32) (a) Only bond interest is a current liability. Cumulative preferred dividends may carry restrictions on financing or investing activities of the corporation, but are not liabilities until declared by the board of directors.

5. (577,T2,33) (c) Annual net earnings available to common stockholders, e.g., the numerator in EPS calculations, are reduced by both bond interest and preferred dividends. The interest reduces income in the income statement (and also reduces tax expense). The preferred dividends are subtracted from net income in computing net earnings available to common stockholders.

6. (1176,T1,12) (a) Cumulative preferred dividends in arrears should be disclosed in aggregate and on a per share basis. See footnote 16 to para 50 of APB 15. Cumulative preferred dividends are those which must be paid in subsequent years if not declared in any one year; they have a cumulative preference prior to the payment of common stock dividends. There is no entry to record a liability, because a liability to pay dividends does not exist until they have been declared. Cumulative dividends in arrears are not an increase in stockholders' equity. If anything, preferred dividends in arrears increase the equity of preferred stockholders and reduce the equity of common stockholders.

C. Stock Subscriptions

7. (1178,Q1,5) (c) The requirement is the total contributed capital as of 12/31/77. Total contributed capital is total legal capital plus other paid-in amounts.

Thus the $600,000 received for common and the $48,000 received for preferred are part of contributed capital. Also, when the 1,000 shares of preferred were subscribed for $17 in December, the following entry was made:

Stock subscriptions receivable	$17,000	
Pref. stock subscribed		$10,000
Paid-in on preferred		7,000

Both the preferred stock subscribed and the paid-in capital on preferred are considered contributed capital. Thus, the contributed capital consists of:

Common	$600,000
Preferred	48,000
Preferred subscribed	17,000
	$665,000

8. (1182,T1,9) (b) When preferred stock is sold on a subscription basis, preferred stock subscribed is recorded at its par value, and a subscription receivable is set up for the balance of cash to be collected. Any difference between the amount to be received and the par value of the preferred stock is charged to additional paid-in capital. The journal entry would be

Cash	(if any received)	
Subscription receivable	(balance)	
Preferred stock subscribed		(par value)
Additional paid-in capital		(forced)

Answer (a) is incorrect because a liability is not credited with the excess when a company deals with its own capital stock. Answer (c) is incorrect because the transaction is related to the contributed capital of the company; retained earnings is not affected. Answer (d) is incorrect because revenue is never recognized from a transaction in a company's own capital stock (APB 9, para 28).

9. (1181,T1,20) (a) When stock is sold on a subscription basis, the full price of the stock is not received initially, and the stock is not issued until the full subscription price is received. At the subscription contract date

Cash	(any cash received)	
Subscriptions receivable	(balance)	
Common stock subscribed		(par)
Paid-in excess		(forced)

Answer (b) is incorrect because subscribed stock is typically paid for subsequent to the subscription contract date. Answer (c) is incorrect because subscribed stock is not typically issued until it has been fully paid for. Answer (d) is incorrect because the stock would have been authorized in the charter of incorporation when the corporation was organized.

D. Treasury Stock Transactions

10. (583,P1,15) (c) The requirement is the balance in the paid-in capital from treasury stock account at 12/31/82. Using the par value method, treasury stock is debited for par value (5,000 x $10, or $50,000) when purchased. Any excess over par from the original issuance (5,000 x $4, or $20,000) is removed from the appropriate paid-in capital account. In effect, the total original issuance price (5,000 x $14, or $70,000) is charged to the two accounts. Any difference between the original issuance price ($70,000) and the cost of the treasury stock (5,000 x $11, or $55,000) is credited to paid-in capital from treasury stock, as illustrated below.

Treasury stock	50,000		(5,000 x $10)
P-I cap. in X of par	20,000		(5,000 x $ 4)
Cash		55,000	(5,000 x $11)
P-I cap. from TS		15,000	($70,000 – $55,000)

11. (1182,P1,10) (b) The requirement is the account and amount credited upon the sale of treasury stock. Since the treasury shares are subtracted from stockholders' equity at cost, the cost method is being used. Under the cost method, treasury stock is recorded at cost. When sold for more than cost, the excess is credited to paid-in capital from treasury stock. The solutions approach is to prepare the journal entry to record the sale.

Cash	40,000		2,000 x $20
Treasury stock		32,000	Cost
PI Cap. from TS		8,000	Excess

12. (1180,Q1,4) (a) The requirement is the total stockholders'equity at 12/31/79. The cost method of accounting for treasury shares is used. The solutions approach is to identify the effect of each transaction on stockholders' equity.

		Effect
1/1/77	200,000 shares issued for $15	$3,000,000
77-79	Net income	750,000
77-79	Dividends	(380,000)
1/5/79	Purchased 12,000 treasury shares at $12	(144,000)
12/31/79	Sold 8,000 treasury shares at $8	64,000
	12/31/79 Stockholders' equity	$3,290,000

When treasury shares were purchased on 1/5/79, the transaction is recorded at cost. When resold, the following entry would be made:

Cash	$64,000	
* Retained Earnings	$32,000	
Treasury stock		$96,000

*8,000($12 cost – $8 reissue price)

The debit to Retained Earnings decreases stockholders' equity, while the credit to Treasury Stock increases stockholders' equity. The net effect is an increase of $64,000.

13. (580,Q1,19) (d) When using the par value method of recording acquisitions of treasury stock, the Treasury Stock account is debited for the par value of the stock. The additional paid-in capital account should be reduced for the amount originally credited for the number of shares involved. Any further reductions must reduce the Retained Earnings account. All of the debits reduce stockholders' equity.

Treasury Stock	$50,000	
Add'l. Pd.-in Cap.	5,000	
R.E.	7,000	
Cash		$62,000

14. (1183,T1,22) (b) The requirement is to determine the effect on stockholders' equity of a purchase of treasury stock at a price above par under both the par value and cost methods. When treasury stock is repurchased under the cost method, the entry to record the purchase is:

Treasury stock	(cost)	
Cash		(cost)

The entry to record the purchase of treasury stock under par value method is:

Treasury stock	(par)	
Additional paid-in capital	*	
Retained earnings	(plug)	
Cash		(cost)

*Amount of excess over par when stock was originally issued.

The treasury stock account reduces total stockholders' equity. Therefore, stockholders' equity is reduced under both methods and answer (b) is correct.

15. (583,T1,27) (c) When treasury stock is accounted for by the cost method, it is carried on the books at its purchase price regardless of its par value or original issue price.

Treasury stock	XX	
Cash		XX

When the treasury stock is subsequently sold for more than its purchase price, the excess of the cash proceeds over cost (carrying value) is recognized as an increase in additional paid-in capital (APIC) from treasury stock transactions.

Cash	(proceeds)	
Treasury stock		(carrying value)
APIC—treasury stk		(excess)

Answers (a) and (b) are incorrect because an enterprise does not record income (expense) or gain (loss) on transactions in its own stock. Answer (d) is incorrect because retained earnings may, in some cases, be reduced as a result of treasury stock transactions, but it may never be increased.

16. (582,T1,11) (c) When treasury stock is purchased for more than its par value, treasury stock is debited for the purchase price (cost) if the cost method is used. The entry using the par value method is typically more complex. Treasury stock is always debited for the par value of the shares, with a pro rata amount of any excess over par on original issuance being charged to the appropriate Paid-in Capital account and any excess of the purchase price over the original issue price being charged to Retained Earnings.

E. Retirement of Stock

17. (583,Q2,34) (d) The requirements are the balances in additional paid-in capital and retained earnings accounts after the purchase and retirement of common stock. Per APB 6, para 12, an excess of the purchase price over par value shall be allocated between additional paid-in capital and retained earnings. The portion charged to additional paid-in capital should be limited to the sum of (a) all capital surplus arising from previous retirements and net "gains" on sales of treasury stock of the same issue and (b) the pro rata portion of capital surplus paid in, arising from declaration of stock dividends etc., on the same issue. The solutions approach is to make the journal entry to record the retirement.

Common stock	1,000,000	
Additional paid-in capital	300,000	
Retained earnings	500,000	
Cash		1,800,000

Common stock is debited for $1,000,000 par value ($10 per share x 100,000 shares). For each share of stock issued, there is $3 of additional paid-in capital ($2,700,000 ÷ 900,000 shares). Thus, the pro rata share of the excess of purchase price over par, $800,000, is allocated by a $300,000 debit to additional paid-in capital and a $500,000 debit to retained earnings. Therefore, the balances of additional paid-in capital and retained earnings after retirement of 100,000 shares are $2,400,000 ($2,700,000 – $300,000) and $800,000 ($1,300,000 – $500,000) respectively. Even though a corporation may have additional paid-in capital from stock transactions, APB 6, para 12a(i), states that alternatively the entire excess of purchase price over par value may be charged entirely to retained earnings.

F. Dividends

18. (1182,P1,9) (a) The requirement is the retained earnings balance immediately after the issuance of a stock dividend. The stock dividend is a 15% dividend (3,000/20,000). ARB 43, Chapter 7 requires that a stock dividend of less than 20-25% be recorded at the FMV, on the date of declaration, of the shares to be issued. This amount is charged to retained earnings and credited to the stock dividend distributable and paid-in capital accounts. The FMV of the stock on the date of declaration is not indicated in the problem; however, the FMV immediately after issuance of the stock dividend is $15. This is the best choice based on the information available. Therefore, retained earnings would be charged for $45,000 (3,000 x $15). The retained earnings balance would then be $305,000 ($350,000 – $45,000).

19. (1183,Q1,6) (b) The requirement is the amount of gain to be recognized as a result of a property dividend. A property dividend is a nonreciprocal transfer of nonmonetary assets between an enterprise and its owners. Per APB 29 a transfer of a nonmonetary asset to a stockholder or to another entity in a nonreciprocal transfer should be recorded at the fair value of the asset transferred, and a gain (loss) should be recognized on the disposition of the asset. The fair value of the property on the declaration date is used to calculate the gain (loss). (The declaration date is the date that the dividend becomes a liability to the corporation.) Therefore, the amount of gain to be recognized is $300,000 – $200,000 = $100,000.

20. (1180,Q1,12) (b) The requirement is the net income for 1979. First the change in owners' equity can be determined:

$$\Delta A - \Delta L = \Delta OE$$
$$\$356,000 - \$108,000 = \Delta OE$$
$$\$248,000 = \Delta OE$$

Three items caused this change in owners' equity: a change in contributed capital (+$240,000 + $24,000), dividends (–52,000), and net income. The net income, then can be isolated in the following equation:

$$\Delta OE = \Delta \text{ Contributed capital} + NI - \text{Dividends}$$
$$\$248,000 = \$264,000 + NI - \$52,000$$
$$NI = \$36,000.$$

21. (580,Q1,13) (b) The requirement is to allocate the $90,000 cash dividends between preferred and common stockholders. Cumulative preferred stock requires the years in arrearage to be paid first. This amount [(6%)($100)(1,000 shares)(2 yrs)] is $12,000. The $12,000 in arrears plus the current year's $6,000 for preferred is to be deducted from the $90,000 total cash dividend. Common stock is then given 6%. This amounts to (6% x $20 x 20,000) = $24,000. The remaining $48,000 ($90,000 – $18,000 – $24,000) is allocated among the classes of stock in proportion to their relative shares of total stockholders' equity. Preferred shareholders have equity of $100,000 over the total equity of $500,000; this, multiplied by $48,000, is the participating portion for preferred stockholders. The common stockholders' share of the $48,000 is $400,000 ÷ $500,000, or 80%.

	Preferred	*Common*	*Total*
6% '77-'78 arrearage	$12,000	–	$12,000
1979 current	6,000	$24,000	30,000
	$18,000	$24,000	$42,000
Participating	9,600	38,400	48,000
	$27,600	$62,400	$90,000

22. (1183,T1,20) (a) The requirement is the determination of the appropriate amount to be debited to retained earnings for a property dividend. APB 29, para 18 requires that nonmonetary assets distributed in nonreciprocal transfers (dividends-in-kind) be recorded at the fair value of the assets transferred. Therefore, answers (c) and (d) are incorrect. Because the liability for dividends arises when dividends are declared, not when issued, the appropriate debit to retained earnings is the market value at date of declaration, answer (a).

23. (582,T1,10) (c) Stock dividends are distributed by management as a method of capitalizing retained earnings. The entry is:

Retained earnings	(Mkt. value)	
Common stock		(Par value)
Paid-in capital		(Plug)

The effect is a reduction of retained earnings and an increase in contributed capital, both owners' equity accounts. Therefore, total stockholders' equity remains the same. Issuance of preferred stock in exchange for convertible debentures [answer (a)] and issuance of nonconvertible bonds with detachable warrants [answer (b)] both increase stockholders' equity. Declaration of a cash dividend [answer (d)] reduces stockholders' equity.

24. (580,T1,39) (d) Issuance of a stock dividend of less than 20-25% is accounted for by transferring from retained earnings to paid-in capital an amount equal to the fair value of the stock issued, as explained in ARB 43, Chapter 7B, para 10-13. In a pooling of interests, the book value of assets received is used to record the transaction. Pure stock splits result in no accounting entries. An employee stock bonus would result in a charge to an expense account.

G. Stock Splits

25. (1181,P1,11) (c) The requirement is the balances in Bennett's additional paid-in capital and retained earnings accounts immediately after a two-for-one stock split is effected. A stock split results in a decrease in par value per share and an increase in the number of shares outstanding. The total par value of shares outstanding remains unchanged, as does the balances of additional paid-in capital and retained earnings. No journal entries are recorded for a stock split.

26. (1181,Q2,38) (c) The requirement is the par value of common stock after a 4 for 1 stock split. A stock split results in an increase or decrease in the number of shares outstanding and a corresponding decrease or increase in the par value per share. A 4 for 1 split in this case would increase the shares outstanding to 200,000 and decrease the par value per share to $3 ($12/4). Total par value is not affected by a stock split (50,000 x $12 before split; 200,000 x $3 after split).

27. (581,T1,1) (a) The requirement is the most likely effect of a stock split on the par value per share and the number of shares outstanding. A stock split results in a decrease in the par value per share and a corresponding increase in the number of shares outstanding.

H. Appropriation of Retained Earnings

28. (1182,T1,37) (d) An amount that is clearly identified as an appropriation of retained earnings should be shown within the stockholders' equity section of the balance sheet (SFAS 5, para 15). Answer (a) is incorrect because such appropriations should not be debited to record the occurrence of a loss. Answer (b) is incorrect because no part of the appropriation shall be transferred to income. Answer (c) is incorrect because an appropriation of retained earnings should be classified within the stockholders' equity section.

I. Stock Options

29. (1182,P1,17) (b) The requirement is the amount to be charged to 1981 compensation expense as the result of a stock option plan. Per APB 25, total compensation is computed as the difference between the option price and the market price on the measurement date, which generally is the date the option is granted. These options were granted on 1/1/81 when the market price is $32 per share. Since the option price is $25 per share, total compensation cost is $70,000 (10,000 shares x $32 – $25). This total compensation cost is allocated to the periods benefited. Since these options are intended to compensate employees for the next two years, $35,000 expense ($70,000/2) would be recognized in each of the years 1981 and 1982.

30. (581,Q1,10) (a) The requirement is to determine the appropriate compensation expense for 1980. The future compensation expense is calculated as the difference between the option price and the market price of the stock on the date the option was granted times the number of shares which can be purchased under the option. On the date of grant, the option price was $40 per share and the market price was $40 per share, therefore, the difference is zero and the compensation expense is zero.

31. (581,Q1,11) (b) The requirement is the same as for the above item. If the market price is $45 per share on the grant date and the option price is $40 per share, the total compensation expense is $5 x 1,000 shares or $5,000. However, this total compensation should be allocated over the number of periods the employee is required to provide service in order to be able to exercise the option. In this problem, two years of service are required; therefore, the compensation expense is $5,000 ÷2, or $2,500 per year.

32. (583,T1,32) (c) The requirement is the recognition of compensation cost in the income statement under a compensatory stock option when either (1) the date of grant and measurement date are different or (2) when they are identical. Compensation is measured on the measurement date, the date on which **both** the number of shares the employee is entitled to and the option or purchase price are known. When the date of grant and measurement date are identical, the compensation amount is the excess of the market price over the option price multiplied by the number of shares under option. The entry to be recorded is:

Deferred compensation expense	XX	
Stock options outstanding		XX

Per APB 25, para 12, compensation cost should be recognized as an expense over the employee's period of service by making the following entry:

Compensation expense	XX	
Deferred compensation expense		XX

In cases where the measurement date follows the grant date, the compensation expense is also measured, but such measurement (estimate) is based on the market values existing at the end of each period until the measurement date is reached. The journal entry each period is:

Compensation expense	XX	
Accrued compensation expense		XX

(Note that the accrued compensation expense is not a liability; it would be shown as an element of stockholders' equity).

When the measurement date is reached, the accrued compensation is cancelled, and the remaining actual compensation (now measurable) is recorded and amortized over future periods still to be benefited by the employees' services. The entry at the measurement date is:

Accrued comp. exp.	XX (previously accrued)	
Deferred comp. exp.	XX (currently accrued)	
Stock options O/S		XX (market-option value)

33. (582,T1,35) (b) When stock options are granted before some or all of the services are performed the following entry **may** be made:

Deferred compensation expense	XX	
Paid-in capital-stock options		XX

The deferred compensation expense is a contra stockholders' equity account which is amortized to income over the periods in which the service is performed (APB 25, para 14). If an entry is **not** made at the date of grant, compensation is accrued as follows:

Compensation expense	XX	
Paid-in capital-stock options		XX

When an entry is not made and stock is issued before all of the services are rendered, a debit to deferred compensation will arise as follows:

Cash	XX	
Paid-in capital-stock options	XX	
Deferred compensation expense	XX	
Paid-in capital in excess of par		XX

In summary, when an entry is made at the date of grant, the deferred (unearned) compensation is recorded at that point. However, if entries are made only as compensation is accrued, a debit to deferred (unearned) compensation is created if stock is issued before all of the related compensation is earned. In both cases the deferred compensation is shown as a contra account to owners' equity.

K. Earnings Per Share for Simple Capital Structures

34. (581,P1,18) (c) The requirement is to compute the earnings per common share for Sonic Company. Since Sonic Company has no potentially dilutive securities, the specific requirement is to find EPS for a simple capital structure. The formula is

$$\text{EPS} = (\text{Net income} - \text{Pref. dividends}) \div \begin{array}{l}\text{weighted}\\\text{average}\\\text{number of}\\\text{shares}\end{array}$$

The numerator in this problem is $112,000 ($120,000 net income – $8,000 preferred dividends). Recall that preferred dividends are always deducted for **cumulative** preferred stock and for **noncumulative** only if declared. Although this problem does not indicate whether the preferred stock is cumulative, the fact that dividends were declared is a sufficient indication that they should be deducted. Since no common stock transactions occurred during the period, the denominator for the EPS computation is simply the 20,000 shares of common stock outstanding. The EPS is computed as $112,000 ÷ 20,000 = $5.60.

35. (581,T1,25) (a) The requirement is the midyear event that must be treated as ocurring at the beginning of the year for the purposes of computing the weighted average number of shares outstanding during the year. The computation of earnings per share data should be based on the weighted average number of common shares and common share equivalents outstanding during each period presented. Per para 3A of APB 15, if the number of common shares outstanding increases as a result of a stock dividend or stock split, the computation should give retroactive recognition to the beginning of the period in which they were declared or issued.

L. Earnings Per Share for Complex Capital Structures

36. (1180,P1,4) (a) The requirement is to compute primary earnings per share (PEPS). The solutions approach is to first determine EPS based only on common stock outstanding to use as a "benchmark" against which to measure potential dilution:

$$\frac{\underset{\text{Net income}}{\$860{,}000} - \underset{\text{Preferred dividend}}{\$60{,}000}}{200{,}000 \text{ shares}} = \$4.00$$

The next step is to find EPS assuming conversion

$$\frac{\$860{,}000 \text{ net income}}{200{,}000 \text{ shares} + 30{,}000 \text{ shares}} = \$3.74$$

Since $3.74 is less than $4.00, the preferred stock is dilutive. Finally, it is necessary to determine if the preferred stock is a common stock equivalent (CSE). The

6% dividend rate is less than 2/3 of 9.5% average Aa corporate bond yield; therefore, this security is a CSE, and PEPS is $3.74. Fully diluted earnings per share (FDEPS) is also $3.74. (Note that if the preferred stock had not been a CSE, PEPS and FDEPS would have been $4.00 and $3.74 respectively.)

37. (1180,P1,10) (a) The requirement is Weaver's 1979 primary earnings per share (PEPS). Common shares outstanding at the beginning of the year were 100,000, and 10,000 shares were issued as a stock dividend. The stock dividend is a retroactive adjustment for EPS calculations, all 110,000 shares are treated as being outstanding for the entire year. Stock options are always common stock equivalents, and the treasury stock method is used to determine the number of incremental shares in computing PEPS.

Proceeds from exercise (20,000 shares x $20)	$400,000
Shares issued upon exercise	20,000
Treasury shares purchasable ($400,000 ÷ $25)	16,000
Incremental shares	4,000

Primary earnings per share is the net income of $550,000 divided by 114,000 shares, or $4.82.

38. (1182,Q1,17) (c) The requirement is to calculate primary earnings per share (PEPS). The solutions approach is to first determine EPS based only on common stock outstanding to use as a "benchmark" against which to measure potential dilution:

$$\frac{\underset{\text{\$970,000}}{\text{Net income}} - \underset{\text{\$50,000}}{\text{Preferred dividend}}}{\underset{\text{90,000 shares}}{\text{Weighted avg. no. of shares outstan.}}} = \$10.22$$

The problem states that the convertible preferred stock is a common stock equivalent (CSE) and the convertible bonds are not a CSE. Therefore, only the convertible preferred will be considered in computing PEPS. Additionally, since only dilutive CSEs are used in computing PEPS, the next step is to determine if the preferred stock would dilute the benchmark EPS. The incremental effects of the preferred stock are calculated assuming conversion at the beginning of the year:

$$\frac{\text{\$50,000 preferred dividends not paid}}{\text{20,000 incremental shares of common stock}} = \$2.50$$

Since $2.50 is less than benchmark EPS of $10.22, the preferred stock is a dilutive security. PEPS including conversion of the preferred stock is:

$$\frac{\overset{\text{\$970,000}}{\text{Income available for C.S.}}}{\text{90,000 shares + 20,000 shares}} = \$8.82 \text{ per share}$$

39. (1182,Q1,18) (a) The requirement is to calculate fully diluted earnings per share (FDEPS). FDEPS should reflect the dilution of EPS that would have occurred if **all** contingent issuances of common stock that would have reduced earnings per share had taken place. The preceding answer shows the preferred stock is dilutive. The convertible bonds will be dilutive if the computation using the if converted method gives an amount less than the PEPS of $8.82. The if converted method which assumes that the preferred stock and bonds are converted to common shares at the beginning of the year is:

$$\frac{\underset{\text{Net income}}{\text{\$970,000}} + \underset{\text{Interest exp., net of tax}}{(\text{\$2,000,000} \times 9\% \times 60\%)}}{\text{90,000 shares + 20,000 shares + 30,000 shares}} = \$7.70$$

Since $7.70 is less than $8.82, FDEPS is $7.70.

40. (583,T1,37) (c) The requirement is to determine the use of antidilutive common stock equivalents in the calculation of either primary and/or fully diluted earnings per share. Per APB 15, paras 30 and 40, computation of these EPS figures should **exclude** those securities where conversion, exercise, or contingent issuance would have the effect of increasing the EPS figures for the period (i.e., they are antidilutive).

41. (1182,T1,24) (b) If the convertible debt is considered a common stock equivalent and dilutive, then the debt is treated as common stock by the "if converted" method; and interest expense is added back to net income for **both** primary earnings per share and fully diluted earnings per share per APB 15, para 5. Answer (a) is incorrect because common stock equivalents that are dilutive cannot be ignored in computing fully dilutive earnings per share. Answer (c) is incorrect because the debt is assumed to be converted at the beginning of the period, and interest must be added to net income. Answer (d) is incorrect for the same reasons that answers (a) and (c) are incorrect.

42. (582,T1,20) (a) Dividends on nonconvertible cumulative preferred stock must be considered in EPS calculations whether or not declared. Although no actual liability exists, the cumulative preferred stock owners must receive their dividends before any distributions are made to common stockholders when they are eventually declared in the future. Answer (b) is incorrect because it describes the treatment of dividends for **noncumulative** preferred stock. Answer (c) is incorrect because cumulative preferred stock dividends are deducted, not added, to net income in EPS calculations. Answer (d) is incorrect because dividends on nonconvertible cumulative preferred stock are never disregarded in computing EPS.

43. (581,T1,24) (c) The requirement is the treatment of convertible securities that are not common stock equivalents in computing fully diluted earnings per share. Convertible securities which are not common stock equivalents enter into the computation of fully diluted earnings per share only if they are dilutive. The if-converted method is used to determine the incremental effect of the conversion assumption.

44. (1180,T1,11) (c) The treasury stock method is used to measure the extent of dilution in terms of the number of incremental shares issued for which no proceeds from any assumed conversion are added to the firm's assets. It is used only when the exercise price is below the market price for all of three consecutive months with the most recent month being the last month of the period. APB 15 states that when applying the treasury stock method to compute fully diluted EPS, the ending market price of common stock should be used as the assumed purchase price when it is higher than average market price. AICPA Interpretation 60 of APB 15 reasserts that this rule should also be followed for quarterly computations.

M. Corporate Bankruptcy

45. (1183,P1,8) (b) The requirement is the total amount of cash received by the partially secured creditors. Partially secured creditors receive the proceeds of the collateral and become unsecured (general) creditors for any unpaid balance. In this case, these creditors will receive the $60,000 proceeds from their pledged assets, and they will also receive a portion of their remaining $40,000 claim ($100,000 – $60,000) as an unsecured creditor. The assets available for unsecured creditors and priority creditors include the free assets of $140,000 and the excess proceeds from the assets pledged with fully secured creditors ($190,000 less $130,000, or $60,000). This total amount ($140,000 + $60,000, or $200,000) would be used first to satisfy the priority liabilities of $20,000. The remaining $180,000 would be used to pay partially secured creditors ($40,000 remaining balance) and unsecured creditors ($260,000 balance). The partially secured creditors claim represents 13 1/3% [$40,000 ÷ ($260,000 + $40,000)] of the total amount owed. Therefore, partially secured creditors would receive $60,000 plus 13 1/3% of $180,000 ($24,000), or a total of $84,000.

N. Quasi-Reorganization

46. (581,P1,20) (d) The requirement is to compute the amount of the reduction in common stock as a result of a quasi-reorganization. The solutions approach is to prepare the journal entries to give effect to the quasi-reorganization.

Step 1: Revalue all assets to their current values by adjusting the deficit in retained earnings.

RE	500,000	
P, P & E		350,000
OA		150,000

Step 2: Create enough paid-in-capital to eliminate the $900,000 deficit in retained earnings, which results after the above entry is posted. Since a $300,000 balance already exists in paid-in-capital, the additional amount needed is $600,000.

CS	600,000	
Paid-in-capital		600,000

Step 3: Eliminate the deficit in Retained Earnings.

Paid-in-capital	900,000	
RE		900,000

The answer ($600,000) is derived in the second entry; the third entry is not necessary if you remembered that common stock would not be further affected.

47. (1182,T1,16) (c) Many states prohibit a company from declaring dividends when it has a deficit retained earnings balance. A quasi-reorganization eliminates an accumulated deficit and permits the company to continue as if it were legally reorganized without the additional expense of legal reorganization. In a quasi-reorganization, assets are revalued to their fair market value, and retained earnings is charged against additional paid-in capital to eliminate the deficit. In this question, the assets were written down which means the deficit balance in retained earnings will increase. However, when the deficit is eliminated, retained earnings will increase and additional paid-in capital is decreased as shown by the entry below

Paid-in capital	(Deficit amount)	
Retained earnings		(Deficit amount)

Note that retained earnings will have increased from its negative balance to zero.

O. Stock Rights

48. (1178,P1,19) (b) The requirement is the journal entry to reflect the exercise of 4,000 common stock rights that were previously issued with preferred stock. The solutions approach is to prepare the journal entry to reflect the original issuance of the preferred stock.

Cash	$525,000	
Preferred stock		$500,000
Com. stock rights		11,250
Paid in on pref.		13,750

When the 5,000 shares of preferred were issued, $525,000 was received which is a debit to cash. The credit is to $500,000 of preferred stock (5,000 shares at $100 par). The allocation to the stock rights is $11,250 (5,000 rights at $2.25 per right). Since only the market value of the rights at the date of issuance is given, the assumption is made that the value of each preferred stock is $102.75 (each unit of 1 preferred share and 1 common stock right has a value of $105).

When the rights are exercised, cash of $60,000 (4,000 rights at $15) and the stock rights of $9,000 (4,000 rights at $2.25) are debited. Common stock is credited for par (4,000 shares at $10) and the difference of $29,000 ($60,000 + $9,000 – $40,000) is paid in excess of common par.

Cash	$60,000	
Com. stock rights	9,000	
Common stock		$40,000
Paid in on com.		29,000

49. (581,Q1,12) (c) The requirement is to determine the gain on the sale of stock warrants. The solutions approach is to calculate the amount of purchase price allocated to the stock and the amount allocated to the warrants. This allocation is made on the basis of the ratios of the relative fair market values of the stock and warrants over the total fair market value of stock and warrants. The combined fair market value is $60 ($50 stock + $10 warrants). The allocation is:

Warrants: $10/$60 x $108,000 = $18,000
Stock: $50/$60 x $108,000 = $90,000

The final step is to compute the gain or loss on the sale of warrants by comparing the purchase price allocated to the warrants with the selling price of the warrants. The selling price was $19,800 and the allocation of purchase price to the warrants was $18,000; therefore, the gain on the sale of warrants was $1,800.

50. (1182,T1,15) (b) A stock right gives present stockholders the opportunity to purchase additional shares of new stock issues before they are offered to the general public. When the rights are exercised, the company receives the cash for the stock, and makes the appropriate journal entry which in this case is

Cash (5,000 x $25)	$125,000	
Common stock (5,000 x $10)		$50,000
Paid-in capital (5,000 x $15)		$75,000

Paid-in capital is recorded at this time because this is when additional funds are invested in the enterprise. Answer (a) is incorrect because the expiration date signifies the rights offer is terminated, and no cash related to the rights offer has been or will be received by the company. Answer (c) is incorrect because the date the rights become exercisable is the beginning of the period of time in which the stockholder may exercise the right, and no cash is transferred until exercised. Answer (d) is incorrect because the issue of rights requires only a memorandum entry.

51. (582,T1,13) (b) Stock warrants are certificates issued by a corporation giving the holder evidence of a stock right. This stock right entitles the holder to acquire a specified number of shares at a fixed price (normally somewhat below the anticipated market price) within a stated period of time, so as to allow the existing shareholders to maintain their percentage ownership through the preemptive right. Answer (a) is incorrect because a stock option is the right to purchase a specified number of shares of stock for a specified price within a specific time period, normally granted to officers and key employees as a form of additional compensation. The term stock option is used when the rights are issued other than pro rata to all existing shareholders. Answer (c) is incorrect because stock dividends are pro rata distributions of the corporation's own shares to existing shareholders based on their stock ownership. The effect is to increase the number of shares outstanding and to capitalize retained earnings (i.e., increase the legal capital of the corporation). Answer (d) is incorrect because a stock subscription is an offer to purchase a number of shares of corporate stock. This offer is not binding upon the subscriber until accepted by the corporation through the issuance of the shares. Consequently, the subscribers have no ownership rights.

May 1984 Answers

52. (584,P3,48) (c) The requirement is the number of shares to be used in computing 1983 earnings per share. APB 15, para 48 states that for EPS purposes, shares of stock issued as a result of stock dividends or splits should be considered outstanding for the entire period in which they were issued. Therefore, both the original 120,000 shares and the additional 12,000 shares (10% x 120,000) are treated as outstanding for the entire year. The July 1 issuance of 40,000 shares results in a weighted average of 20,000 shares (6/12 x 40,000) because the shares were outstanding for six

months during 1983. Thus, the total number of shares for EPS computations is 152,000.

Outstanding 1/1/83	120,000
Stock dividend (10% x 120,000)	12,000
July 1 issuance (6/12 x 40,000)	20,000
	152,000

53. (584,P3,49) (d) The requirement is to compute the fully diluted earnings per share (FDEPS) for 1983. The purpose of FDEPS is to show the maximum potential dilution of current earnings per share (EPS) on a prospective basis (APB 15, para 40). Therefore, **all** contingent issuances of common stock that **reduce** current EPS must be included in the computation. The formula for FDEPS is

$$\frac{\text{Net income available to common shareholders}}{\text{Weighted-average common shares outstanding}}$$

The net income available to common shareholders is \$3,200,000. This is the net income of \$3,400,000 less the preferred stock dividend of \$200,000. The weighted-average common shares outstanding is 1,250,000. This is computed as the actual common shares outstanding for the full year of 1,200,000 plus the contingent common shares of 50,000 which were outstanding for the full year because the contingency was incurred in 1982. Thus,

$$\text{FDEPS} = \frac{\$3,200,000}{1,250,000} = \$2.56$$

54. (584,T1,23) (b) The requirement is to determine the effect of a 10% stock dividend on retained earnings and total stockholders' equity. Per ARB 43, Chapter 7, para 10, a stock dividend that is less than 20-25% of the outstanding shares is accounted for on the books of the issuer by capitalizing retained earnings in an amount equal to the fair value of the stock dividend issued. An appropriate journal entry would be

Retained earnings	(FMV)	
Common stock		(par value)
Add'l paid-in capital		(plug)

Accordingly, retained earnings will decrease and total stockholders' equity will not change; therefore, answer (b) is correct.

55. (584,T1,24) (c) The requirement is to determine the proper amount and the appropriate point in time common stock should be credited when stock rights are issued to shareholders. At issuance, the issuer makes only a memorandum entry indicating the number and price at which the shares may be purchased. Upon **exercise**, the company receives the cash and makes the following entry:

Cash	(proceeds)	
Common stock		(par value)
Paid-in capital		(plug)

Answer (c) is correct because upon exercise, common stock is credited for the par value of the stock issued, \$10 per share in this problem.

56. (584,T1,25) (b) The requirement is to determine the effect of treasury stock transactions recorded under the cost method on additional paid-in capital. When capital stock is repurchased, treasury stock is debited for the acquisition price (cost) under the cost method. The purchase has no effect on paid-in capital.

Treasury stock	(cost)	
Cash		(cost)

When the shares are later resold for an amount greater than cost, the excess is credited to additional paid-in capital.

Cash	(proceeds)	
Treasury stock		(cost)
APIC–TS		(excess)

Answer (b) is correct because under the cost method the purchase of treasury stock has no effect on additional paid-in capital; whereas, the subsequent sale increases paid-in capital.

Answer Outline

Problem 1 Primary vs. Fully Diluted EPS

b. Primary earnings per share computation versus fully diluted earnings per share computation

b1. Common stock equivalents, if dilutive, increase number of shares for both

b2. Convertible securities not common stock equivalents, if dilutive, increase number of shares for fully diluted

b3. Antidilutive securities are not included in either earnings per share figures

Unofficial Answer

Problem 1 Primary vs. Fully Diluted EPS

Part b.

1. Common stock equivalents are included in the computation of the number of shares for both primary earnings per share and fully diluted earnings per share as long as the common stock equivalents have a dilutive effect.

2. Convertible securities that are not common stock equivalents are excluded from the computation of the number of shares for primary earnings per share; however, they are included in the computation of the number of shares for fully diluted earnings per share as long as they have a dilutive effect.

3. Antidilutive securities are excluded from both primary earnings per share and fully diluted earnings per share.

Answer Outline

Problem 2 Stock Option Plans

b1. Accounting for stock purchase (option) plans at stock issue date

Noncompensatory Plan

Cash	XXX	
Capital stock (par value)		XXX
Additional paid-in capital		XXX

Compensatory Plan

Cash	XXX	
Compensation expense[(1)]	XXX	
Capital stock (par value)		XXX
Additional paid-in capital[(2)]		XXX

(1) Dr. stock options outstanding if expense recorded previously

(2) Credit = (debit to cash + debit to options outstanding or compensation expense) – credit to capital stock

b2. Accounting for compensatory stock option plan at date of grant

When Date of Grant and Measurement Date Coincide

Compensation expense or deferred compensation	XXX[(1)]	
Stock options outstanding		XXX

(1) Amount = Market price of stock – option price

When Date of Grant and Measurement Date Do Not Coincide

No entry is made

Unofficial Answer

Problem 2 Stock Option Plans

Part b.

1. For the noncompensatory stock purchase plan, the entry at the date the stock is issued is as follows:

- Debit to cash (or appropriate liability account if amounts were previously withheld through payroll deductions) for the cash price
- Credit to capital stock for the par value of the stock
- Credit to additional paid-in-capital for the excess of the cash price over the par value

For the compensatory stock option plan, the entry at the date the stock is issued is as follows:

- Debit to cash for the cash price
- Debit to stock options outstanding (when the compensation expense has already been recognized) or debit to compensation expense

- Credit to capital stock for the par value of the stock
- Credit to additional paid-in-capital for the excess of (a) the debit to cash (cash price) and (b) the debit to stock options outstanding, over the par value

2. If the date of the grant and the measurement date are the same, the entry for the compensatory stock option plan at the date of the grant is to debit compensation or deferred compensation expense and credit stock options outstanding for the excess of the market price of the stock over the option price.

If the date of the grant and the measurement date are different, no entry is made for the compensatory stock option plan at the date of the grant.

Answer Outline

Problem 3 Treasury Stock

1. Accounting for treasury stock when purchase price is less than par value

Cost method — Debit treasury stock for purchase price
Par method — Debit treasury stock for par value of shares
Credit paid-in capital for excess

2. Treasury stock when purchase price is greater than par value

Cost method — Debit treasury stock for purchase price
Par method — Debit treasury stock for par value of shares
Debit excess to paid-in capital and/or retained earnings

3. Treasury stock when sold at less than purchase price, but more than par value

Cost method — Credit treasury stock for cost
Debit excess first to paid-in capital from prior treasury stock transactions and then to retained earnings
Par method — Credit treasury stock for par
Credit excess to paid-in capital

4. Treasury stock when sold at more than purchase price and par

Cost method — Credit treasury stock for cost
Credit excess to paid-in capital
Par method — Credit treasury for par
Credit excess to paid-in capital

5. Treasury stock transactions do not affect net income.

Unofficial Answer

Problem 3 Treasury Stock

1. Under the cost method, treasury stock is debited for the purchase price of the shares even though the purchase price is less than the par value.

Under the par value method, treasury stock is debited for the par value of the shares, and a separate paid-in capital account is credited for the excess of the par value over the purchase price.

2. Under the cost method, treasury stock is debited for the purchase price of the shares.

Under the par value method, treasury stock is debited for the par value of the shares, and the debit for the excess of the purchase price over the par value is assigned to additional paid-in capital arising from past transactions in the same class of stock and/or retained earnings.

3. Under the cost method, treasury stock is credited for the original cost (purchase price) of the shares, and the excess of the original cost (purchase price) over the sales price first is debited to additional paid-in capital from earlier sales or retirements of treasury stock, and any remainder then is debited to retained earnings.

Under the par value method, treasury stock is credited for the par value of the shares, and the excess of the sales price over the par value is credited to additional paid-in capital from sale of treasury stock.

4. Under the cost method, treasury stock is credited for the original cost (purchase price) of the shares, and the excess of the sales price over the original cost (purcahse price) is credited to additional paid-in capital from sale of treasury stock.

Under the par value method, treasury stock is credited for the par value of the shares, and the excess of the sales price over the par value is credited to additional paid-in capital from sale of treasury stock.

5. There is no effect on net income as a result of treasury stock transactions.

Answer Outline

Problem 4 Common Stock Equivalents

a. Common stock equivalents (CSE) are equivalent to common stock
    - But are not in the form of common stock
    - E.g., CSE values are determined by common stock characteristics or conversion features
  - CSEs are reflected in both primary and fully diluted EPS
    - If their effect is dilutive
  - Convertible securities are CSE if
    - They yield less than 2/3 of the average Aa corporate bond yield at issuance
    - Or have same terms as other outstanding CSE
    - Or another convertible CSE is issued with same terms
  - Options, warrants, etc., are always CSE
    - Including convertible securities requiring cash payments
  - Participating securities with common stock features are CSE
  - Contingent issuances, based only on passage of time, are CSE

b. Complex captial structure has potentially dilutive convertible securities, options, etc., which could dilute EPS
    - A complex capital structure requires dual EPS presentation
      - Primary earnings per share (PEPS)
        - Based on outstanding stock and CSE
      - Fully diluted earnings per share (FDEPS)
        - Based on all contingent issuances of common stock
    - Required disclosures for complex capital structure
      - Summary descriptions of outstanding securities
      - Schedule explaining computation of PEPS and FDEPS
      - Number of shares issued upon conversion, etc.
      - The effect on EPS of conversion as if they had taken place at the beginning of the period
      - Effect on EPS of intended use of stock sale proceeds to retire debt

Unofficial Answer

Problem 4 Common Stock Equivalents

a. A common stock equivalent is a security which, because of the terms and the circumstances under which it was issued, is in substance equivalent to common stock. The securities are not common stock in form, but a characteristic of a common stock equivalent is that a large part of its value is derived from its common stock characteristics or conversion privileges. Common stock equivalents are included in both primary and fully diluted earnings-per-share computations only when their effect is dilutive.

Convertible securities that yield less than two-thirds of the average Aa corporate bond yield at the time of issuance are considered common stock equivalents. Also, convertible securities issued with the same terms as those of an outstanding common stock equivalent, regardless of their yield, are considered common stock equivalents. Outstanding convertible securities that were not originally a common stock equivalent become a common stock equivalent if another convertible security with the same terms is issued and classified as a common stock equivalent.

Options and warrants, stock purchase contracts, and certain agreements to issue common stock in the future are considered to be common stock equivalents. Convertible securities that allow or require the payment of cash at the exercise date are considered to be equivalent to warrants.

Some participating securities and two-class common stock are considered to be common stock equivalents if their participation features enable the holders to share in the earnings potential on the same basis as that of common stockholders.

Finally, contingent shares are common stock equivalents if they are to be issued in the future upon the mere passage of time.

b. A capital structure is regarded as complex when it includes potentially dilutive convertible securities, options, warrants, or other rights that upon conversion or exercise could, in the aggregate, dilute earnings per common share.

When a corporation has a complex capital structure, there should be a dual presentation with equal prominence on the face of the earnings statement. This presentation is to include a primary earnings per share that is based on outstanding common shares and securities equivalent to common shares that have a dilutive effect divided into net earnings adjusted for any interest or dividends paid on the common stock equivalents. Also included in this presentation is the calculation of the fully diluted earnings per share. This is a pro forma presentation which reflects dilution of earnings per share that would have occurred if all contingent issues of common stocks that would individually reduce earnings per share had taken place at the beginning of the year.

Additional disclosures when a complex structure exists include (1) a summary description explaining pertinent rights and privileges of the various outstanding securities, (2) a schedule or note explaining the basis upon which primary and fully diluted earnings per share are calculated, (3) a disclosure of the numbers of shares issued upon conversion, exercise, or satisfaction of required conditions during at least the most recent fiscal period and any other subsequent period presented. If conversion during the current period would have affected primary earnings per share if they had taken place at the beginning of the period, then supplementary information should be furnished for the latest period showing what primary earnings per share would have been if such conversion had taken place at the beginning of that period. If the proceeds from a sale of common stock or common stock equivalents are used to retire or there is the intent to retire preferred stock or debt, then disclosure should be made of what the earnings per share would have been if the retirement had taken place at the beginning of the period.

Answer Outline

Problem 5 Categories of Stockholders' Equity

a. Contributed capital is amount paid in for all stock and amounts capitalized by board of directors, including
   - Legal capital
   - Premiums over par
   - Donations of assets
   - Assessments on stockholders
   - Stock subscription forfeitures
   - Gains on treasury stock
   - Excess on common par issued for convertibles
   - Acquisition of TS below par
   - Tax benefits on certain stock options

   Retained earnings are net earnings less
   - Net losses from operations
   - Dividends (cash or stock)
   - Net effects of prior period adjustments
   - Retained earnings may be appropriated or unappropriated

   Appraisal capital is the recognized revaluation of assets
   - Not a conventional accounting procedure

b1. A stock split is a proportional distribution of stock to stockholders
   - In excess of 20%-25% of the outstanding shares
   - Causes material decrease in market value
   - May be called a stock split "effected as a dividend"

b2. Stock dividend: Dr retained earnings for dividend market value

   Stock split: no change in shareholders' equity accounts
   - Just a change in par or stated value

b3. Unissued stock dividends are disclosed in shareholders' equity
   - Not a liability, as they may be rescinded
   - Do not require the use of corporate assets
   - Disclose number of shares to be issued

c. Reduce net income of compensation expense is recognized
   - By amount market price exceeds option price
     - At measurement date
   - Expense recognized in periods earned by employee
   - EPS reduced by reduced income
     - Number of shares outstanding increased

Unofficial Answer

Problem 5 Categories of Stockholders' Equity

a. The general categories of a corporation's capital are contributed (invested) capital, earned capital (retained earnings), and appraisal capital.

Contributed capital represents the amounts paid in for all classes of shares of stock and the amounts capitalized by order of the corporation's board of directors. Included in contributed capital is legal capital, which is usually the aggregate par value or stated value of the shares issued. Legal capital is usually not subject to withdrawal; it is intended to protect corporate creditors. Contributed capital also includes other amounts in addition to the legal capital. These amounts are generaly referred to as additional paid-in capital and include the following:

- Premiums over the par (stated) value of the stock issued (including stock dividends).

- Donations of assets to the corporation by stockholders or others.
- Assessments on stockholders.
- Forfeitures of stock subscriptions.
- Excess of proceeds from reissuing treasury stock over its cost.
- Conversion of convertible bonds or preferred stock.
- Reacquisition of outstanding shares at an amount below par (stated) value.
- Tax benefits from certain stock options.

Retained earnings are the accumulated net earnings of a corporation in excess of any net losses from operations and dividends (cash or stock). Total retained earnings should also include prior-period adjustments as direct increases or decreases and may include certain reserves. These reserves are appropriations of retained earnings as unavailable for dividends. These reserves and related restrictions may arise as a result of a restriction in a bond indenture or other formal agreement or they may be created at the discretion of the board of directors.

Appraisal capital represents the recognized upward revaluation of net assets. This capital is unrealized from a conventional accounting point of view and should, therefore, be segregated from contributed capital and retained earnings. Because such write-ups are a departure from generally accepted accounting principles, their use is usually restricted to situations where state law provides for the creation of appraisal surplus and the payment of dividends therefrom. Even if legally acceptable, the creation of appraisal surplus can present some significant reporting problems.

b. 1. A stock split effected in the form of a dividend is a distribution of corporate stock to present stockholders in proportion to each stockholder's current holdings and can be expected to cause a material decrease in the market value per share of the stock. Accounting Research Bulletin No. 43 specifies that a distribution in excess of 20% to 25% of the number of shares previously outstanding would cause a material decrease in the market value. This is a characteristic of a stock split as opposed to a stock dividend, but, for legal reasons, the term "dividend" must be used for this distribution. From an accounting viewpoint, it should be disclosed as a stock split effected in the form of a dividend because it meets the accounting definition of a stock split as explained above.

2. The stock split effected in the form of a dividend differs from an ordinary stock dividend in the amount of other paid-in capital or retained eranings to be capitalized. An ordinary stock dividend involves capitalizing (charging) retained eranings equal to the market value of the stock distributed. A stock split effected in the form of a dividend involves no charge to retained eranings or other paid-in capital if the par (stated) value of the stock is reduced in inverse proportion to the distribution. If the stock's par (stated) value is not reduced in inverse proportion to the distribution of stock, other paid-in capital or retained eranings would be charged for the par (stated) value of the additional shares issued.

Another distinction between a stock dividend and a stock split is that a stock dividend usually involves distributing additional shares of the same class of stock with the same par or stated value. A stock split usually involves distributing additional shares of the same class of stock but with a proportionate reduction in par or stated value. The aggregate par or stated value would then be the same before and after the stock split.

3. A declared but unissued stock dividend should be classified as part of corporate capital rather than as a liability in a statement of financial position. A stock dividend affects only capital accounts; that is, retained earnings are decreased and contributed capital is increased. Thus, there is no debt to be paid, and, consequently, there is no severance of corporate assets when a stock dividend is issued. Furthermore, stock dividends declared can be revoked by a corporation's board of directors any time prior to issuance. Finally, the corporation usually will formally announce its intent to issue a specific number of additional shares, and these shares must be reserved for this purpose.

c. Accounting for this stock option plan will reduce net earnings if compensation expense is to be recognized. If the option price equals or exceeds the stock's market price at the measurement date, which is the date of grant for a traditional stock option plan, no compensation is recognized, and, accordingly, there is no effect on net earnings.

If the option price is less than the stock's market price at the measurement date, the difference is considered compensation. This compensation should be recognized as an expense of one or more periods in which an employee performs services. The period or periods benefitted may be specified in the plan or may be inferred from the terms or from the past pattern of such plans. Compensation expense would, of course, reduce net earnings each period.

Earnings per share computations are based on adjusted net earnings divided by adjusted number of shares. The adjusted net earnings are affected as discussed above. The adjusted number of shares may include potential common stock represented by these options, thereby diluting the earnings per share because the options are common stock equivalents.

Answer Outline

Problem 6 Earnings Per Share

a. For EPS, subtract preferred dividends from net income
   - For noncumulative, only when declared
   - Always if dividend is cumulative
   - Except when assuming conversion
     - Must be common stock equivalents for PEPS
       - Determined at time of issuance
       - (2/3 of prime interest rate)
     - Or if included in FDEPS

b1. TS method used when option price less than market price
   - Usually for substantially all of the three months preceding year-end
   - If option price exceeded market price, options are antidilutive
     - Not included in EPS calculations

b2. TS method limited to reacquisition of 20% of outstanding
   - Any remaining funds are considered to reduce debt
     - Any further remaining funds assumed invested in securities
   - All net of tax effects

c1. Convertible bonds are CSE if they yield less than 2/3 of prime rate
   - Determined at issuance
   - Are included in both PEPS and FDEPS if dilutive
   - Interest saving less tax effect added to EPS numerator
   - Shares from conversion added to EPS denominator

c2. Convertible bonds, not CSE, are included in FDEPS
   - If dilutive
   - Interest saving less tax effect added to EPS numerator
   - Shares from conversion added to EPS denominator

Unofficial Answer

Problem 6 Earnings Per Share

a. Dividends on outstanding preferred stock must be subtracted from net income or added to net loss for the period before computing EPS on the common shares. This generalization will be modified by the various features and different requirements preferred stock may have with respect to dividends. Thus, if preferred stock is cumulative, it is necessary to subtract its current dividend requirements from net income (or to add them to net loss) in order to arrive at the amount into which to divide outstanding common shares to compute EPS on the latter. This must be done regardless of whether or not the preferred dividends were actually declared. Where the preferred shares are noncumulative, only preferred dividends actually declared during the current period need be subtracted from net income (or added to net loss) to arrive at the amount to be used in EPS calculations.

In case the preferred shares are convertible into common stock, when assuming conversion, dividend requirements on the preferred shares are not deducted from net income. This applies when testing for potential dilution to determine whether or not the diluted EPS figures for the period are lower than primary EPS figures. Diluted EPS figures are reported if they are lower by 3% or more than the primary EPS figure; if the degree of dilution is less than 3%, diluted figures are not reported.

It is possible for preferred stock to be a common stock equivalent. A common stock equivalent is a security which is not, in form, a common stock but which contains provision to enable its holder to become a common stockholder and which, because of the terms and circumstances under which it was issued, is in substance equivalent to a common stock. The basic test for convertible preferred shares is applied when the shares are first issued. If at that time the cash yield (dividend rate) of the convertible preferred shares is less than two-thirds of the then-current average Aa corporate bond yield, they should be considered common stock equivalents. Common stock equivalents are added to common shares outstanding to determine primary EPS. If preferred shares are accorded this treatment, their dividends are not subtracted from income for EPS calculation purposes.

b. 1. When options and warrants to buy common stock are outstanding and their exercise price (i.e., proceeds the corporation would derive from issuance of common stock pursuant to the warrants and options) is less than the average price at which the company could acquire its outstanding shares as treasury stock, the treasury stock method is generally applicable. In these circumstances, existence of the options and warrants would be dilutive. However, if the exercise price of options and warrants exceeded the average price of common stock, the cash proceeds from their assumed exercise would provide for repurchasing more common shares than were issued when the warrants were exercised, thereby reducing the number of shares outstanding. In these circumstances assumed exercise of the warrants would be antidilutive, so exercise would not be presumed for purposes of computing primary EPS.

2. The application of the treasury-stock method is modified if the number of common shares issuable upon the exercise of warrants and options exceeds 20% of the number of common shares outstanding at the end of the period. The applicable procedure in such event is to assume that all warrants and options have been exercised and the aggregate proceeds therefrom are applied in two steps. First, funds are applied to repurchase outstanding common shares at the average market price during the period (treasury-stock method) but not to exceed 20% of the outstanding shares. Next, the balance of funds are applied to reduce any short-term or long-term borrowings and any remaining funds are assumed to be invested in United States government securities or commercial paper, withappproriate recognition of any income tax effects.

c. 1. Convertible debentures are common stock equivalents when at the time of their issuance their cash yield rate of interest (or lowest scheduled rate in the first five years thereafter) is less than two-thirds of the then-current average Aa corporate bond yield. If their conversion would have a dilutive effect, then for purposes of calculating primary EPS, their interest (less tax effect) is added to net income as the numerator of the EPS calculation while the number of shares resulting from their assumed conversion is added to the denominator portion of the EPS calculation.

2. In case convertible debentures are not treated as common stock equivalents (therefore, are not treated as having been converted for purposes of calculating primary EPS) they might still be accorded the treatment of conversion for purposes of calculating fully diluted EPS figures. For this to happen, other elements would also have to enter into the fully diluted EPS calculations in conjunction with convertible debentures and the convertible debentures would have had to be issued at an original interest rate of more than two-thirds the average Aa corporate bond yield. In arriving at the calculation of fully diluted EPS figures where convertible debentures are assumed to be converted, their interest (less tax effect) is added back to net income as the numerator element of the EPS calculation while the number of shares of common stock into which they would be convertible is added to the shares outstanding to arrive at the denominator element of the calculation.

Solution Guide

Problem 7 Stock Appreciation Rights

1. The requirements are to prepare a five year schedule of compensation expense related to SAR's and to prepare journal entries for three of those years. Before attempting the schedule, refresh your memory concerning what SAR's are and the way in which we account for them under FASB Interpretation No. 28.

2. Recall that SAR's entitle the holder to receive share appreciation, i.e., the excess of the stock's market price at the date of exercise over a pre-established price. The appreciation may be paid in cash (as in this problem), shares of stock; or a combination of both. This means that unlike stock compensation plans, in which the expense of the plan to the company can generally be

measured at the date of grant, the compensation expense for SAR's cannot be accurately measured until they are exercised.

3. Until that date, however, the matching principle indicates that compensation expense must be recorded. This is accomplished by establishing an accrued liability during the service period on the basis of the difference between the market price for the period and the pre-established price, i.e., what could be called an "esti-measurable" expense at any given point. Using the data from the problem this means:

3.1 With a three year service period, year one must accrue a liability of 1/3 of the appreciation esti-measurable **at that point.** Year two must have accrued 2/3 of the appreciation esti-measurable, and at year three, 100% of appreciation esti-measurable must be accrued. After that the accrued liability at the end of each period should equal what the **total** expense to the company **would be** if the holder exercised the SAR's at that point.

3.2 This means that compensation expense will be charged or credited each year until exercise with the amount needed to maintain the accrued liability balance at 33-1/3%, 66-2/3%, 100%, 100% . . . esti-measurable compensation. Note that compensation expense recorded **to date** must equal the balance of the esti-measurable liability accrued to date. It should be obvious that if at any time the market price of the stock is below the pre-established price, the company does not in fact have a liability and therefore the compensation expense recognized to date would be zero.

Unofficial Answer

Problem 7 Stock Appreciation Rights

(a)

Solution
Schedule of Compensation Expense
Stock Appreciation Rights (20,000)

Date	*Market price*	*Pre-established price*	*Esti-measurable compensation*	*% to be accrued*	*Esti-measurable liability accrued to date*	*Period's compensation expense*	*Comp. exp. to date*
12/31/81	$36	$30	$120,000	33-1/3%	$ 40,000	$ 40,000	$ 40,000
12/31/82	39	30	180,000	66-2/3%	120,000	80,000	120,000
12/31/83	45	30	300,000	100%	300,000	180,000	300,000
12/31/84	36	30	120,000	100%	120,000	(180,000)	120,000
12/31/85	48	30	360,000	100%	360,000	240,000	360,000

(b)

1981	Compensation Expense - SAR's	40,000	
	Liability under Stock Appreciation Plan		40,000
1984	Liability under Stock Appreciation Plan	180,000	
	Compensation Expense - SAR's		180,000
1985	Compensation Expense - SAR's	240,000	
	Liability under Stock Appreciation Plan		240,000

Solution Guide

Problem 8 Retained Earnings Statement and Stockholders' Equity Section of Balance Sheet

1. This problem consists of three related requirements. For the same company, the candidate must prepare a statement of retained earnings in part one; prepare the stockholders' equity section in part two; and compute the book value per share of common stock in part three. Only single-period (1982) financial statements are presented.

2. The requirement in part one is a statement of retained earnings. The 12/31/81 balance was reported at \$6,500,000. The solutions approach is to then go through the other information and determine which items affect retained earnings.

2.1 The issuance of preferred stock, purchase and sale of treasury stock, and issuance of common stock do **not** affect retained earnings. The treasury stock transactions do not affect retained earnings because: 1) the cost method is used, and 2) the treasury stock is resold for more than its original cost.

2.2 The common stock dividend is a subtraction in the RE statement. Remember that dividends are paid only on outstanding stock. Therefore, the 2,000,000 shares outstanding on 1/1/82 must be adjusted for treasury shares purchased and the shares issued on 4/30/82, both of which occurred before the 7/1/82 date of record.

2.3 The preferred stock dividend is also a subtraction in the RE statement. The computation is the preferred dividend rate (9%) times the par value of preferred stock outstanding (\$5,000,000).

2.4 The correction of the understatement of 12/31/81 inventories is a prior period adjustment to retained earnings. The RE statement should start with the 1/1/82 balance as previously reported (to enable users to correlate this amount with prior years). Then the prior period adjustment is added or subtracted to result in the adjusted 1/1/82 balance. In this case, the net-of-tax adjustment (\$180,000) is added because the prior period (1981) income was understated. (If ending inventory is understated, cost of goods sold is overstated, and net income is understated.)

2.5 The corrected 1982 net income of \$4,500,000 is an addition in the RE statement.

2.6 The proper RE statement format includes a heading.

3. The requirement in part two is the 12/31/82 stockholders' equity section. The solutions approach is to take each equity item and determine any changes from the other information.

3.1 There was no preferred stock outstanding until \$5,000,000 was issued in 1982.

3.2 \$20,000,000 of common stock was outstanding at 12/31/81. An additional \$5,000,000 was issued in 1982. This brings the balance in the common stock account to \$25,000,000. Note that the treasury stock transactions are recorded in a separate treasury stock account and do not affect the common stock account, the balance of which equals the par value of shares **issued** (not outstanding).

3.3 The additional paid-in capital at 12/31/81 was \$7,500,000, pertaining entirely to common stock. The additional paid-in capital from common stock increased when common stock was issued above par (500,000 x \$7 = \$3,500,000) and when treasury stock was sold above cost (10,000 x \$5 = \$50,000). This brings the balance to \$11,050,000. The balance in additional paid-in capital stock was created when preferred stock was issued above par (100,000 x \$4 = \$400,000).

3.4 The ending retained earnings balance from the RE statement is \$8,250,000.

3.5 Using the **cost** method, the cost of any stock held in treasury is subtracted from total paid-in capital and retained earnings. Treasury stock was purchased at a cost of \$320,000 on 2/1/82, but half of this stock was resold on 11/10/82, leaving a balance of \$160,000.

3.6 When preparing the stockholders' equity section, pertinent information such as par value, shares issued, etc., must be included.

4. The requirement in part three is the computation of book value per common share at 12/31/82. This is computed by dividing **common** stockholders' equity by the common shares outstanding.

4.1 Common stockholders' equity is total stockholders' equity ($49,540,000) less the liquidation value of preferred stock (in this case, its par value of $5,000,000) and any dividends in arrears (none, in this case).

4.2 At 12/31/81, there were 2,000,000 common shares outstanding. On 2/1/82, 20,000 treasury shares were purchased. On 4/30/82, 500,000 shares were issued, and on 11/10/82, 10,000 of the treasury shares were resold. Thus, shares outstanding at year end totalled 2,490,000.

4.3 The book value per share is approximately $17.89 ($44,540,000 ÷ 2,490,000).

Unofficial Answer

Problem 8 Retained Earnings Statement and Stockholders' Equity Section of Balance Sheet

1. **Ashwood, Inc.**
Statement of Retained Earnings
For the Year Ended December 31, 1982

Retained earnings, 1/1/82, as previously reported		$6,500,000
Correction of an understatement of 12/31/81 inventories (net of $120,000 tax effect)		180,000
Adjusted balance of retained earnings at 1/1/82		6,680,000
Add: 1982 net income		4,500,000
Total before deducting dividends		11,180,000
Deduct 1982 dividends declared on:		
Preferred stock (Schedule 1)	$450,000	
Common stock (Schedule 2)	2,480,000	(2,930,000)
Retained earnings, 12/31/82		$8,250,000

2. **Ashwood, Inc.**
Stockholders' Equity Section of Balance Sheet
December 31, 1982

Preferred stock, $50 par value, 9% cumulative, convertible; 600,000 shares authorized; 100,000 shares issued and outstanding	$ 5,000,000
Common stock, $10 par value; 6,000,000 shares authorized; 2,500,000 shares issued (2,000,000 + 500,000), of which 10,000 shares are held in treasury	25,000,000
Additional paid-in capital from preferred stock [100,000 x $4 ($54 – $50)]	400,000
Additional paid-in capital from common stock (Schedule 3)	11,050,000
Retained earnings	8,250,000
	49,700,000
Less common stock in treasury, 10,000 shares at cost [$16 x 10,000 (20,000 – 10,000)]	(160,000)
Total stockholders' equity	$49,540,000

3. **Ashwood, Inc.**
Book Value Per Share of Common Stock
December 31, 1982

Total stockholders' equity	$49,540,000
Less liquidation value of preferred stock	(5,000,000)
Common stockholders' equity	$44,540,000
Common shares outstanding	2,490,000
Book value per share ($44,540,000 ÷ 2,490,000)	$17.89

Schedule 1*

Preferred Stock Dividend

Par value of preferred stock (100,000 x $50)	$5,000,000
Preferred dividend rate	x 9%
Preferred stock dividend	$450,000

Schedule 2*

Common Stock Dividend

Common shares outstanding 1/1/82	2,000,000
Less treasury shares purchased, 2/1/82	(20,000)
Plus shares issued, 4/30/82	500,000
Common shares outstanding	2,480,000
Cash dividend per common share	x $1
Common stock dividend	$2,480,000

Schedule 3

Additional Paid-In Capital from Common Stock

Balance, December 31, 1981	$ 7,500,000
From issuance of 500,000 shares on April 30, 1982 [500,000 x $7 ($17 – $10)]	3,500,000
From sale of 10,000 shares treasury stock on November 10, 1982 [10,000 x $5 ($21 – $16)]	50,000
Balance, December 31, 1982	$11,050,000

*The authors believe that inclusion of these schedules would allow the graders to follow your work if your answers do not agree with those of the AICPA.

Solution Guide

Problem 9 Stock Options and Earnings Per Share

1. Number nine consists of two unrelated parts. Part a. requires journal entries for a stock option plan. Part b. requires several computations for an earnings per share (EPS) presentation for another company with a complex capital structure.

2. The information given in part a describes the activities of a stock option compensation plan for a three-year period. The "solutions approach" is to first quickly review mentally the basic concepts of accounting for stock option plans; second, read through the information given; and third, make the necessary computations and prepare journal entries chronologically. The following journal entries must be prepared:

1/1/78	Grant of stock options
12/31/78	Charge to compensation expense
4/1/79	Termination of stock options
12/31/79	Possible charge to compensation expense
3/31/80	Exercise of stock options
12/31/80	Possible charge to compensation expense

2.1 The first entry is to record the grant of the options on 1/1/78. The value assigned to the options is the difference between the market value of the option shares at the date of grant (measurement date) and the option price (see Schedule 1 for computations). This amount will be recognized as compensation expense over the period being benefited, but is initially debited to a deferred compensation account. The credit is to a stockholders' equity account indicating paid-in capital from stock options.

2.2 At the end of 1978, an entry must be prepared to record compensation expense attributable to that year. In order to determine the amount of expense to record, the length of the period benefited by the stock option plan must be estimated. The given information does not specify a period of benefit, so a logical assumption must be made. The plan does benefit Holt from the date of grant (1/1/78) until the date the options become exercisable (1/1/80), a period of two years. The benefit after 1/1/80 is less definite. After 1/1/80, employees can exercise their options anytime as long as they remain in the employ of the company. Based on a two-year period of benefit, one-half of the $160,000 deferred compensation cost is recognized as expense in 1978.

2.3 On 4/1/79, an entry is made to record the termination of 2,000 option shares held by resigned employees. Per APB 25, a termination of this type is handled as a change in estimate. In other words, the original estimate of the amount of deferred compensation was incorrect. Therefore, 1978 expense is not restated. In 1979, the amount of deferred compensation attributable to the terminated options is removed from the books and 1979 expense is adjusted downward using the "current and prospective" approach. On 4/1/79, the entry is to remove the amount (see computations in Schedule 2) of deferred compensation attributable to the terminated options from both the deferred compensation account and the paid-in capital from stock options account.

2.4 At the end of 1979, an entry must be made to record the expense attributable to that year, less the "current and prospective" adjustment for terminated options. The amount of expense attributable to 1979 is $72,000 (18,000 option shares x $8 value per option share x ½). However,

$8,000 of expense was recognized in 1978 on the options terminated in 1979 (2,000 option shares x $8 value per option share x ½). Therefore, the adjusted amount of expense to be recorded in 1979 is $72,000 – $8,000 or $64,000. A simpler solutions approach is to recall that 1979 is the last year of the period benefited. Therefore, any balance remaining in the Deferred Compensation account (see T-account below) must be charged to expense at the end of 1979.

Deferred Compensation Cost			
1/1/78	$160,000		
		$80,000	12/31/78
		16,000	4/1/79
Balance	$ 64,000		

2.5 On 3/31/80, an entry must be prepared to record the exercise of 12,000 option shares. Upon exercise of options, the sum of cash received ($25 per share) and the value assigned to the options ($8 per share) is accounted for as consideration received for the shares issued. Therefore, a total of $33 per share is credited to the contributed capital accounts ($10/share par value to common stock, and the remaining $23 per share to paid-in capital in excess of par).

3. There are four requirements in part b: number of shares and EPS computations for both primary earnings per share (PEPS) and fully diluted earnings per share (FDEPS). Before immersing yourself in the details of the problem, quickly review mentally the basic EPS rules of APB 15. Then read through the given information, making notes as you proceed.

3.1 The first step is to compute the "benchmark" EPS (the first two columns of the second table in the solution). Benchmark EPS is the EPS which would be reported if Mason had a simple capital structure. The "benchmark" EPS of $2.31 will be used to determine which of the potentially dilutive securities are dilutive. Note that supporting Schedule 1 is needed before the "benchmark" can be computed.

3.2 The options are dilutive because application of the treasury stock method results in an increase in the denominator of 11,250 shares. Options and warrants are always considered CSEs if exercisable within 5 years. Note that the ending market price of Mason's common stock is less than the average market price; therefore, the average price is used in both PEPS and FDEPS computations. If the ending market price were higher, it would have been used in the treasury stock computation for FDEPS.

3.3 The bonds are dilutive because EPS is reduced from $2.23 to $2.11.

3.4 The warrants are antidilutive because the option price is greater than the market price. Application of the treasury stock method would result in a **decrease** in the denominator, which is antidilutive.

4. After the securities are analyzed, the last four columns of the second table in the solution can be completed. The incremental effect of the convertible bonds is shown only in the FDEPS columns, since the bonds are not CSEs. The incremental effect of the stock options appears in both the PEPS and FDEPS columns; the options are CSEs. The FDEPS of $2.11 is less than 97% of $2.31, the "benchmark EPS". Therefore, a dual presentation is required. The answers to the specific problem requirements are identified at the bottom of the columns.

Unofficial Answer

Problem 9 Stock Options and Earnings Per Share

Part a.

Holt, Inc.
Journal Entries
1978-80

Date	*Accounts*	*Debit*	*Credit*
1/1/78	Deferred compensation cost	$160,000	
	Paid-in capital–stock options (see Schedule 1)		$160,000
	To record the grant of stock options to officers and key employees.		
12/31/78	Compensation expense	$ 80,000	
	Deferred compensation cost ($160,000 x ½)		$ 80,000
	To recognize compensation expense attributable to first year of stock option plan.		

Date	*Accounts*	*Debit*	*Credit*
4/1/79	Paid-in capital–stock options	$ 16,000	
	Deferred compensation cost (see Schedule 2)		$ 16,000
	To record termination of stock options held by resigned employees.		
12/31/79	Compensation expense	$ 64,000	
	Deferred compensation cost [$160,000 – ($80,000 + $16,000)]		$ 64,000
	To recognize compensation expense attributable to second year of stock option plan, less adjustment for terminated options.		
3/31/80	Cash	$300,000	
	Paid-in capital--stock options	96,000	
	Common stock		$120,000
	Paid-in capital in excess of par (see Schedule 3)		276,000
	To record exercise of stock options.		

Schedule 1

Deferred Compensation Cost to be Recorded at Date of Stock Option Grant

Market value of shares at date of grant	$33
Option price of shares	25
Value assigned each option share (to Schedule 2)	$ 8
Number of option shares	x 20,000
Deferred compensation cost	$160,000

Schedule 2

Deferred Compensation Cost Attributable to Options Terminated at 4/1/79

Value assigned each option share (from Schedule 1)	$ 8
Number of option shares terminated	x 2,000
Deferred compensation cost	$16,000

Schedule 3

Amounts to be Recorded Upon Exercise of Stock Options on 3/31/80

Cash received upon exercise (12,000 x $25)	$300,000
Value originally assigned to options (12,000 x $8)	96,000
Total amount assigned to common shares issued	$396,000
Par value of shares issued (12,000 x $10)	120,000
Paid-in capital in excess of par	$276,000

Part b.

Mason Corporation
Computations of Earnings Per Share
1980

Items	*Benchmark EPS* Numerator (Dollars)	Denominator (Shares)	*Primary EPS* Numerator (Dollars)	Denominator (Shares)	*Fully diluted EPS* Numerator (Dollars)	Denominator (Shares)
Net Income	$750,000		$750,000		$750,000	
Preferred Dividends (10,000 x $3)	(30,000)		(30,000)		(30,000)	
Convertible bonds (schedule 2)					48,000	40,000
Stock options (schedule 3)				11,250		11,250
Common shares (schedule 1)		312,000		312,000		312,000
Totals	$720,000 ÷	312,000	$720,000 ÷	323,250	$768,000 ÷	363,250
EPS	$2.31		$2.23 (2)	(1)	$2.11 (4)	(3)

Key to problem requirements

Schedule 1

Weighted Average Common Shares Outstanding

Shares outstanding 1/1/80	300,000
Shares issued on 9/1/80 (36,000 x 4/12)	12,000
Weighted average number of shares	312,000

Schedule 2

Convertible Bonds Computations

Interest on bonds ($1,000,000 x 8%)	$80,000
Income tax effect ($80,000 x 40%)	32,000
Numerator effect	$48,000
Number of $1,000 bonds ($1,000,000/$1,000)	1,000
Conversion factor	x 40
Denominator effect	40,000 shares

Schedule 3

Stock Options Computations

Shares issuable under options		30,000
Proceeds if options exercised (30,000 x $22.50)	$675,000	
Average market price	÷ 36	
Treasury shares obtainable		18,750
Denominator effect		11,250

Note: Average market price used for both PEPS and FDEPS since it is greater than year end market price.

Solution Guide

Problem 10 Stockholders' Equity Transactions

1. Part a. requires a worksheet to summarize stockholder equity transactions in 1977. The column headings are provided. Note that the beginning balances are indicated and should be put at the top of the worksheet including number of shares data.

2. Since 12 transactions are indicated for 1977, the solutions approach is to analyze each transaction in terms if its journal entry.

2.1 February 1

Cash	$36,000,000	
Common stock		$20,000,000
Paid-in capital		16,000,000

[Sale of 2,000,000 shares common stock ($10 par) at $18/share]

2.2 February 15

Cash	$11,000,000	
Preferred stock		$10,000,000
Paid-in capital		900,000
Common stock warrants		100,000

[Sale of 100,000 shares of preferred stock ($100 par) and detachable common stock warrants at $110/share; allocate $1 to each warrant]

2.3 March 1

Treasury stock—common	$ 370,000	
Cash		$ 370,000

(Reacquisition of 20,000 shares treasury stock—common at $18.50/share)

2.4 March 15

Treasury stock—common	$ 210,000	
Donated capital		$ 210,000

(Donation of 10,000 shares of treasury stock—common when market was $21/share)

2.5 March 31

Retained earnings	$ 1,597,000	
Cash		$ 1,597,000

($.10/share cash dividend on common)

Beginning O/S	15,000,000 shares
Less beginning T/S	(1,000,000)
Sale	2,000,000
TS purchase	(20,000)
TS donation	(10,000)
	15,970,000 shares @ $.10 = $1,597,000 dividend

2.6 April 15

Common stock warrants	$ 30,000	
Cash	600,000	
Common stock		$ 300,000
Paid-in capital		330,000

(Exercise of 30,000 of the outstanding common stock warrants; exercise price $20/share)

2.7 April 30

Cash	$ 2,000,000	
Common stock		$ 1,000,000
Paid-in-capital		1,000,000

(Sale of 100,000 common shares to employees at $20/share per noncompensatory stock options—no value was attributed to the options when granted)

2.8 May 31

Retained earnings	$16,100,000	
Common stock		$ 8,050,000
Paid-in capital		8,050,000

(5% common stock dividend, $10 par and $20 market)

Beginning O/S	15,000,000 shares
Less beginning TS	(1,000,000)
Sale	2,000,000
TS purchase	(20,000)
TS donation	(10,000)
Exercise warrants	30,000
Sale to employees	100,000
	16,100,000 x 5% = 805,000 shares

2.9 June 30

Cash	$ 7,500,000	
Treasury stock—common		$ 5,970,000
Paid-in capital		1,530,000

(Sale of 300,000 treasury shares at $25; 20,000 shares acquired on March 1 cost $370,000, and the 280,000 other shares cost $5,600,000)

2.10 September 30

Retained earnings	$ 2,520,500	
Common stock dividend payable		$ 1,720,500
Preferred stock dividend payable		800,000

(Preferred stock of $10,000,000 at 8% equals $800,000. Common stock shares outstanding are 17,205,000 – 16,100,000 in 2.8 above plus 805,000 stock dividend plus 300,000 TS sale – at $.10 is $1,720,500)

2.11 December 31

Common stock warrants	$ 70,000	
Paid-in capital		$ 70,000

(Expiration of 70,000 warrants at $1—of the 100,000 issued, only 30,000 were exercised)

2.12 December 31

P&L account	$25,000,000	
Retained earnings		$25,000,000

(net income for 1977)

3. Based on the analysis of each of the transactions, record the amounts in the summary worksheet previously prepared (note that the number of shares and rights is also required). This could have been done simultaneously with the analysis of each transaction.

4. Part b. requires a worksheet showing the maximum amount available for cash dividends at 12/31/77 for Tomasco and how it would be distributed to common and preferred stockholders.

4.1 The solutions approach is to understand the capital structure which consists of a common stock, a 4% nonparticipating noncumulative preferred stock, and an 8% fully participating cumulative preferred stock. Also the business has operated for five years and no dividends have been paid. Dividends are payable only from retained earnings.

4.2 Retained earnings at the end of 1977 are $850,000:

1973	$ (150,000)
1974	(130,000)
1975	(120,000)
1976	250,000
1977	1,000,000
	$ 850,000

4.3 The 4% nonparticipating noncumulative preferred will receive only $4,000 (4% of $100,000). Since this preferred stock is noncumulative there are no dividends in arrears.

4.4 The 8% fully participating cumulative preferred will receive $400,000 as a result of the cumulative preferred status, i.e., 5 years at 8% of $1,000,000. The remaining retained earnings would be prorated between the 8% participating preferred and the common after $40,000 of dividends are allocated to common to compensate for the 8% allocated to the preferred in 1977.

Retained earnings available	$850,000
4% nonparticipating noncumulative preferred 1977 payment	(4,000)
8% participating cumulative preferred 1973–77 payment	(400,000)
8% of $500,000 of common to offset 1977 8% dividend for participating preferred	(40,000)
To be prorated between participating, preferred, and common	$406,000

Common $\frac{\$500,000}{\$1,000,000 + \$500,000^*} \times \$406,000$
$= \$135,333$

Preferred $\frac{\$1,000,000}{\$1,000,000 + \$500,000^*} \times \$406,000$
$= \$270,667$

*$1,000,000 of preferred O/S and $500,000 of common O/S

4.5 Recap:

4% nonparticipating noncumulative preferred	$ 4,000
8% participating cumulative preferred	670,667
Common	175,333
	$850,000

Unofficial Answer

Problem 10 Stockholders' Equity Transactions

Part a. appears on the following page.

Part b.

Tomasco, Inc.
Maximum Cash Dividend Distribution
December 31, 1977

	Common stock	*4% Preferred stock*	*8% Preferred stock*	*Total*
8% preferred stock, dividends in arrears for 1973–1976 ($1,000,000 x 8% x 4 years)			$320,000	$320,000
4% preferred stock dividends for 1977 ($100,000 x 4%)		$4,000		4,000
8% preferred stock dividends for 1977 ($1,000,000 x 8%)			80,000	80,000
Distribution of remaining retained earnings *(Schedule 1)*	$175,333	—	270,667	446,000
	$175,333	$4,000	$670,667	$850,000

Schedule 1

Distribution of Remaining Retained Earnings

	Common stock	*8% Preferred stock*	*Total*
Dividends on common stock at preferred rate ($500,000 x 8%)	$ 40,000		$ 40,000
Distribution of remaining retained earnings of $406,000* based on the ratio of par values:			
Common stock $\left(\frac{\$\ 500{,}000}{\$1{,}500{,}000} \times \$406{,}000\right)$	135,333		406,000
8% preferred stock $\left(\frac{\$1{,}000{,}000}{\$1{,}500{,}000} \times \$406{,}000\right)$		$270,667	
	$175,333	$270,667	$446,000

*$850,000 – $320,000 – $4,000 – $80,000 – $40,000

Schedules from Unofficial Answers were not used because they duplicate our Solution Guide.

Part a.

Howard Corporation
Summary of Stockholders' Equity Accounts Transactions
For 1977

Date of transaction	Common stock: Number of shares	Common stock: Amount	Preferred stock: Number of shares	Preferred stock: Amount	Common stock warrants: Number of rights	Common stock warrants: Amount	Retained earnings	Additional Paid-in capital	Treasury stock: Number of shares	Treasury stock: Amount
Beginning	15,000,000	$150,000,000					$ 80,000,000	$50,000,000	1,000,000	$18,000,000
2/1/77 (See SG 2.1*)	2,000,000	20,000,000					16,000,000			
2/15/77 (See SG 2.2)			100,000	$10,000,000	100,000	$100,000	900,000			
3/1/77 (See SG 2.3)									20,000	370,000
3/15/77 (See SG 2.4)							210,000		10,000	210,000
3/31/77 (See SG 2.5)								(1,597,000)		
4/15/77 (See SG 2.6)	30,000	300,000			(30,000)	(30,000)	330,000			
4/30/77 (See SG 2.7)	100,000	1,000,000					1,000,000			
5/31/77 (See SG 2.8)	805,000	8,050,000					8,050,000	(16,100,000)		
6/30/77 (See SG 2.9)							1,530,000		(300,000)	(5,970,000)
9/30/77 (See SG 2.10)								(2,520,500)		
12/31/77 (See SG 2.11)					(70,000)	(70,000)	70,000			
12/31/77 (See SG 2.12)								25,000,000		
	17,935,000	$179,350,000	100,000	$10,000,000	-0-	$ -0-	$108,090,000	$54,782,500	730,000	$12,610,000

*SG = Solution Guide

FUNDAMENTAL CONCEPTS

Multiple Choice Questions (1 - 19)

1. White Airlines sold a used jet aircraft to Brown Company for $800,000, accepting a five-year 6% note for the entire amount. Brown's incremental borrowing rate was 14%. The annual payment of principal and interest on the note was to be $189,930. The aircraft could have been sold at an established cash price of $651,460. The present value of an ordinary annuity of $1 at 8% for five periods is 3.99. The aircraft should be capitalized on Brown's books at

   a. $651,460
   b. $757,820
   c. $800,000
   d. $949,650

2. On January 1, 1982, Robert Harrison signed an agreement to operate as a franchisee of Perfect Pizza, Inc., for an initial franchise fee of $40,000. Of this amount, $15,000 was paid when the agreement was signed and the balance is payable in five annual payments of $5,000 each beginning January 1, 1983. The agreement provides that the down payment is not refundable and no future services are required of the franchisor. Harrison's credit rating indicates that he can borrow money at 12% for a loan of this type. Information on present and future value factors is as follows:

Present value of $1 at 12% for 5 periods	.567
Future amount of $1 at 12% for 5 periods	1.762
Present value of an ordinary annuity of $1 at 12% for 5 periods	3.605

Harrison should record the acquisition cost of the franchise on January 1, 1982, at

   a. $29,175
   b. $33,025
   c. $40,000
   d. $44,050

3. On January 1, 1981, Dorr Company borrowed $200,000 from its major customer, Pine Corporation, evidenced by a note payable in three years. The promissory note did not bear interest. Dorr agreed to supply Pine's inventory needs for the loan period at favorable prices. The going rate of interest for this type of loan is 14%. Assume that the present value (at the going rate of interest) of the $200,000 note is $135,000 at January 1, 1981. What amount of interest expense should be included in Dorr's 1981 income statement?

   a. $0
   b. $18,900
   c. $21,667
   d. $28,000

4. On January 1, 1981, Gray Company sold a building which cost $190,000 and had accumulated depreciation of $80,000 on the date of sale. Gray received as consideration a $200,000 noninterest bearing note due on January 1, 1984. There was no established exchange price for the building, and the note had no ready market. The prevailing rate of interest for a note of this type at January 1, 1981, was 10%. The present value of $1 at 10% for three periods is 0.75. What amount of interest income should be included in Gray's 1981 income statement?

   a. $ 6,750
   b. $15,000
   c. $16,667
   d. $20,000

5. On January 1, 1980, Derby Company lent $20,000 cash to Elliott Company. The promissory note made by Elliott did not bear interest and was due on December 31, 1981. No other rights or privileges were exchanged. The prevailing interest for a loan of this type was 12%. The present value of $1 for two periods at 12% is 0.797. Derby should recognize interest income in 1980 of

   a. $0
   b. $1,913
   c. $2,030
   d. $2,400

6. The Mitchell Company received a seven-year noninterest bearing note on February 22, 1974, in exchange for property it sold to the Grispin Company. There was no established exchange price for this property and the note has no ready market. The prevailing rate of interest for a note of this type was 10% on February 22, 1974, 10.2% on December 31, 1974, 10.3% on February 22, 1975, and 10.4% on December 31, 1975. What interest rate should be used to calculate the interest revenue from this transaction for the year ended December 31, 1975 and 1974, respectively?

   a. 0% and 0%.
   b. 10% and 10%.
   c. 10% and 10.3%.
   d. 10.2% and 10.4%.

7. Tollner Company sold a machine to Snead Corporation on January 1, 1980, for which the cash sales price was $379,100. Snead entered into an installment sales contract with Tollner, calling for annual payments of $100,000 for five years, including interest at 10%. The first payment was due on December 31, 1980. How much interest income should be recorded by Tollner in 1981?

a. $27,910
b. $31,701
c. $37,910
d. $50,000

8. For which of the following transactions would the use of the present value of an annuity due concept be appropriate in calculating the present value of the asset obtained or liability owed at the date of incurrence?

a. A capital lease is entered into with the initial lease payment due one month subsequent to the signing of the lease agreement.
b. A capital lease is entered into with the initial lease payment due upon the signing of the lease agreement.
c. A ten-year 8% bond is issued on January 2 with interest payable semi-annually on July 1 and January 1 yielding 7%.
d. A ten-year 8% bond is issued on January 2 with interest payable semi-annually on July 1 and January 1 yielding 9%.

9. Glen, Inc., purchased certain plant assets under a deferred payment contract on December 31, 1980. The agreement was to pay $10,000 at the time of purchase and $10,000 at the end of each of the next five years. The plant assets should be valued at

a. The present value of a $10,000 ordinary annuity for five years.
b. $60,000.
c. $60,000 plus imputed interest.
d. $60,000 less imputed interest.

10. On May 1, 1980, a company purchased a new machine which it does not have to pay for until May 1, 1982. The total payment on May 1, 1982, will include both principal and interest. Assuming interest at a 10% rate, the cost of the machine would be the total payment multiplied by what time value of money concept?

a. Future amount of annuity of 1.
b. Future amount of 1.
c. Present value of annuity of 1.
d. Present value of 1.

11. At the beginning of 1973, Garmar Company received a three-year noninterest-bearing $1,000 trade note. The market rate for equivalent notes was 8% at that time. Garmar reported this note as $1,000 trade notes receivable on its 1973 year-end statement of financial position and $1,000 as sales revenue for 1973. What effect did this accounting for the note have on Garmar's net earnings for 1973, 1974, and 1975, and its retained earnings at the end of 1975, respectively?

a. Overstate, understate, understate, zero.
b. Overstate, understate, understate, understate.
c. Overstate, overstate, understate, zero.
d. No effect on any of these.

12. An accountant wishes to find the present value of an annuity of $1 payable at the beginning of each period at 10% for eight periods. He has only one present-value table which shows the present value of an annuity of $1 payable at the end of each period. To compute the present-value factor he needs, the accountant would use the present-value factor in the 10% column for

a. Seven periods.
b. Seven periods and add $1.
c. Eight periods.
d. Nine periods and subtract $1.

Items 13 through 16 apply to the appropriate use of present-value tables. Given below are the present-value factors for $1.00 discounted at 8% for one to five periods. Each of the following items is based on 8% interest compounded annually from day of deposit to day of withdrawal.

Periods	*Present value of $1 discounted at 8% per period*
1	0.926
2	0.857
3	0.794
4	0.735
5	0.681

13. What amount should be deposited in a bank today to grow to $1,000 three years from today?

a. $\frac{\$1,000}{0.794}$
b. $1,000 x 0.926 x 3
c. ($1,000 x 0.926) + ($1,000 x 0.857) + ($1,000 x 0.794)
d. $1,000 x 0.794

14. What amount should an individual have in his bank account today before withdrawal if he needs $2,000 each year for four years with the first withdrawal to be made today and each subsequent withdrawal at one-year intervals? (He is to have exactly a zero balance in his bank account after the fourth withdrawal.)

a. $2,000 + ($2,000 x 0.926) + ($2,000 x 0.857) + ($2,000 x 0.794)

b. $\frac{\$2,000}{0.735} \times 4$

c. ($2,000 x 0.926) + ($2,000 x 0.857) + ($2,000 x 0.794) + ($2,000 x 0.735)

d. $\frac{\$2,000}{0.926} \times 4$

15. If an individual put $3,000 in a savings account today, what amount of cash would be available two years from today?

a. $3,000 x 0.857

b. $3,000 x 0.857 x 2

c. $\frac{\$3,000}{0.857}$

d. $\frac{\$3,000}{0.926} \times 2$

16. What is the present value today of $4,000 to be received six years from today?

a. $4,000 x 0.926 x 6

b. $4,000 x 0.794 x 2

c. $4,000 x 0.681 x 0.926

d. Cannot be determined from the information given.

17. On December 27, 1982, Holden Company sold a building, receiving as consideration a $400,000 non-interest bearing note due in three years. The building cost $380,000 and the accumulated depreciation was $160,000 at the date of sale. The prevailing rate of interest for a note of this type was 12%. The present value of $1 for three periods at 12% is 0.71. In its 1982 income statement, how much gain or loss should Holden report on the sale?

a. $ 20,000 gain.

b. $ 64,000 gain.

c. $ 96,000 loss.

d. $180,000 gain.

18. On July 1, 1983, a company received a one-year note receivable bearing interest at the market rate. The face amount of the note receivable and the entire amount of the interest are due on June 30, 1984. When the note receivable was recorded on July 1, 1983, which of the following were debited?

	Interest receivable	*Unearned discount on note receivable*
a.	Yes	No
b.	Yes	Yes
c.	No	No
d.	No	Yes

May 1984 Question

19. On September 1, 1982, a company borrowed cash and signed a two-year interest-bearing note on which both the principal and interest are payable on September 1, 1984. At December 31, 1983, the liability for accrued interest should be

a. Zero.

b. For 4 months of interest.

c. For 12 months of interest.

d. For 16 months of interest.

FUNDAMENTAL CONCEPTS

Problems

Problem 1 Valuation of Notes (1172,T3)

(25 to 30 minutes)

Business transactions often involve the exchange of property, goods, or services for notes or similar instruments that may stipulate no interest rate or an interest rate that varies from prevailing rates.

Required:

a. When a note is exchanged for property, goods, or services, what value should be placed upon the note:

1. If it bears interest at a reasonable rate and is issued in a bargained transaction entered into at arm's length? Explain.
2. If it bears no interest and/or is not issued in a bargained transaction entered into at arm's length? Explain.

b. If the recorded value of a note differs from the face value:

1. How should the difference be accounted for? Explain.
2. How should this difference be presented in the financial statements? Explain.

Problem 2 Noninterest Bearing Note (579,P4c)

(15 to 20 minutes)

On January 1, 1977, the Lock Company sold property to the Key Company which originally cost Lock $600,000. Key gave Lock a $900,000 noninterest bearing note payable in six equal annual installments of $150,000, with the first payment due and paid on January 1, 1977. There was no established exchange price for the property and the note has no ready market. The prevailing rate of interest for a note of this type is 12%. The present value of an annuity of $1 in advance for six periods at 12% is 4.605.

Required:

1. Prepare a schedule computing the balance in Lock's net receivables from Key at December 31, 1978, based on the above facts. Show supporting computations in good form.
2. Prepare a schedule showing the income or loss before income taxes for the years ended December 31, 1977, and 1978, that Lock should record as a result of the above facts.

Multiple Choice Answers

1. a	5. a	9. d	13. d	17. b
2. b	6. b	10. d	14. a	18. c
3. b	7. b	11. a	15. c	19. d
4. b	8. b	12. b	16. c	

Multiple Choice Answer Explanations

A.1. Time Value of Money Formulas

1. (1182,P1,13) (a) The requirement is the amount at which Brown should capitalize an aircraft purchased using a note bearing an unreasonably low stated rate of interest. Brown's incremental borrowing rate is 14%, which is significantly higher than the stated rate of 6%. Therefore, the acquisition should not be recorded at the face value ($800,000) of the note. The cost of the aircraft is the present value of the note and stated interest payments discounted at 14% or the fair market value of the aircraft, whichever is more clearly evident. Since the aircraft has an established cash price of $651,460 that amount is an appropriate basis for recording the transaction.

2. (582,P1,10) (b) The requirement is the acquisition cost of a franchise to the franchisee. The acquisition cost is equal to the $15,000 down payment plus the present value of the $25,000 loan. The loan is payable in 5 equal installments of $5,000 at the end of each year (ordinary annuity).

Down payment on 1/1/82	$15,000
Present value of ordinary annuity ($5,000 x 3.605)	18,025
Total acquisition cost	$33,025

3. (582,P1,14) (b) The requirement is the amount of interest expense to be included in Dorr's 1981 income statement. Dorr Company borrowed $200,000 cash by signing a noninterest-bearing note. However, Dorr agreed to supply the lender with inventory at favorable prices over the loan period. APB 21 requires that in these circumstances, the liability should be recorded at its present value by establishing a discount account. The difference between cash proceeds and the present value of the note is credited to an unearned income account, which is recognized as revenue as the agreement is fulfilled.

Cash	200,000	
Discount on N/P	65,000	
Note payable		200,000
Unearned income		65,000

Interest expense is then recognized using the effective interest method. For 1981, interest expense is equal to the present value of the note ($135,000) times the effective interest rate (14%), or $18,900.

4. (582,P1,18) (b) The requirement is the amount of interest income to be recognized in 1981 on a noninterest-bearing note. The note receivable should be recorded at its present value of $150,000 ($200,000 x .75), by recording a discount of $50,000. In the first year (1981), interest income of $15,000 would be recognized using the effective interest method. The present value of the note ($150,000) is multiplied by the effective interest rate (10%).

5. (1181,P1,2) (a) The requirement is the amount of interest income Derby should recognize in 1980 on a noninterest-bearing promissory note. Per APB 21, when a note is received or issued solely for cash and no other right or privilege is exchanged, interest is measured by the difference between the actual amount of cash received by the borrower and the total amount agreed to be repaid to the lender. Since the promissory note does not bear interest, the total amount to be repaid to the lender is the face value of the note. The face value of the promissory note is not given, but the problem states that the note did not bear interest; therefore a face value of $20,000 is assumed. This results in $0 interest income in both 1980 and 1981.

6. (1176,P1,11) (b) The determination of an interest rate to value a note should be made at the time the note is issued and not changed thereafter. See the last sentence in para 12 of APB 21. Thus, interest revenue would be calculated at 10% throughout the life of the note.

7. (1182,Q1,13) (b) The requirement is to calculate the amount of interest income to be recorded from an installment sales contract. It is important to remember that installment payments are set up incorporating the interest charges; that is, each installment payment consists of interest and principal. The solutions approach is to set up a partial amortization table to compute the interest income for 1981:

Date	*Cash (debit)*	*Interest earned (credit)*	*Installment receivable (credit)*	*Unpaid balance*
1/1/80	—	—	—	$379,100
12/31/80	$100,000	$37,910*	$62,090	317,010
12/31/81	100,000	31,701**		

*$379,100 x 10% **$317,010 x 10%

8. (582,T1,4) (b) The requirement is the situation which illustrates an annuity due. An annuity due (annuity in advance) is a series of payments where the first payment is made at the beginning of the first period, in contrast to an ordinary annuity (annuity in arrears), in which the first payment is made at the end of the first period. Answer (b) is correct because the initial lease payment is due immediately (at the beginning of the first period). Answers (a), (c), and (d) all illustrate situations in which the first lease or interest payment occurs at the end of the first period. Note that in answers (c) and (d), the stated rate and yield rate of the bonds differ; while this would effect the present value of the bonds, it has no effect on the classification as an annuity due or an ordinary annuity.

9. (581,T1,6) (d) The requirement is the amount that plant assets should be valued at when such assets are purchased under a deferred payment contract. Assets purchased on a deferred payment contract should be accounted for at the present value of the consideration to be exchanged between the contracting parties at the date of the transaction; this is necessary in order to properly reflect cost. The asset should not, therefore, be valued at $60,000, but at the present value of the total $60,000 in payments. To estimate the present value of these payments under these circumstances, an appropriate interest rate must be imputed. Answer (a) is incorrect because it does not take into consideration the $10,000 down payment. Answer (b) is incorrect because it does not take into consideration imputed interest on the obligation. Answer (c) is incorrect because imputed interest is **deducted** from the face of the obligation.

10. (580,T1,48) (d) The cost of the machine is the present value of the one lump-sum payment being made two years from the purchase date. The present value of an annuity of 1 is not used because a series of payments is not involved.

11. (1176,T1,15) (a) The requirement is to determine the effect of errors on 1973, 1974, 1975 income and ending 1975 retained earnings. The solutions approach is to draw a time diagram as illustrated below. In 1973, sales will be overstated because the note and sales were recorded at the gross rather than the net present value (as required per para 12, APB 21). In 1974, interest income from the note will not be recorded, thus understating income. The same will be true in 1975. The end of 1975 retained earnings will be the same. The effect of the error is to overstate 1973 income by the understatement of interest income in 1974 and 1975.

1973	1974	1975
over	under	under

12. (576,T2,29) (b) The solutions approach to time value of money problems is a time diagram as illustrated below. As the problem indicates, it is an annuity in advance of eight payments, i.e., payments are made at the beginning of the period in contrast with an ordinary annuity wherein payments are made at the end of each period. Given a table for an ordinary annuity (or an annuity in arrears), simply note that it is an annuity of 7 payments plus the present value of the first payment. The present value of the first payment is 1, i.e., there is no discount. Thus the present value of an annuity in advance of 8 payments is the present value of an ordinary annuity for 7 payments plus 1.

PERIODS		1	2	3	4	5	6	7	8
Annuity in Advance	1	2	3	4	5	6	7	8	
Annuity in Arrears			1	2	3	4	5	6	7

13. (1174,T2,23) (d) The question asks for the present value of $1,000 to be received 3 years from today. The table presented is the present value of an amount. Simply take the present value factor of .794 times $1,000. Answer (a) is incorrect because it is the future value of $1,000 deposited today, i.e., if you deposit $1,000 today earning interest at 8% per year, the future value will be $1,000 divided by .794. Answers (b) and (c) imply annuities which are incorrect for this question.

14. (1174,T2,24) (a) This question involves an annuity, because there are to be annual payments of the same amount. The question asks for the present value of a $2,000 payment today and every year thereafter for a total of 4 payments. Thus, one must compute the present value of the four payments. The present value of $2,000 today is $2,000. The present value of $2,000 one year from now is .926 x $2,000. The present value of $2,000 two years from now is $2,000 x .857. Answer (c) would have been correct if the first of the four payments were to be received at the end of the first year instead of the beginning of the first year. When the first payment of an annuity is received at the end of the first year, it is called an ordinary annuity. When the first payment of an annuity is received at the

beginning of the first year, it is called an annuity due. Present value of an annuity tables are usually presented assuming an ordinary annuity, i.e., the first payment comes at the end of the first period.

15. (1174,T2,25) (c) The question calls for the future value of an amount rather than a present value of an amount. Present value of an amount is the reciprocal of the future value of an amount. For example, the present value of $10 to be received one year from now is $10/1 + i and the value of $10 in one year is simply 1 + i x $10. In this case we wish to find the future value of $3,000 two years from now so we divide $3,000 by the present value factor for n = 2 and i = 8%.

16. (1174,T2,26) (c) The present value of $4,000 six years from today would be the present value of $4,000 one year from today discounted back an additional five years, i.e., to find the present value factors for 6 years multiply the present value factor for 1 year times the present value factor for 5 years.

A.11. Notes Receivable and Payable

17. (1183,P2,32) (b) The requirement is the amount of gain (loss) on the sale of a building. The gain (loss) is the difference between the value of the consideration received and the book value of the building sold. The consideration received is a three-year, noninterest-bearing, $400,000 note. Per APB 21, such receivables are to be recorded at present value. The present value of this note is $284,000 (.71 x $400,000). The book value of the building sold is $380,000 less $160,000, or $220,000. Therefore, a $64,000 gain ($284,000 – $220,000) is recognized.

Note receivable	400,000	
Accum. depr.	160,000	
Discount on N/R		116,000
Building		380,000
Gain		64,000

18. (1183,T1,8) (c) The requirement is to determine the account which is debited when a note receivable bearing interest at the market date is received. The journal entry to record the receipt is:

Notes receivable	XXX	
Sales (or cash, etc.)		XXX

Answers (a) and (b) are incorrect because no interest has been earned on the note and, therefore, no receivable is accrued. Answer (d) is incorrect because no discount is recorded on a note bearing interest at the market rate.

May 1984 Answer

19. (584,T1,17) (d) The requirement is the number of months of interest accrued as of December 31, 1983, for a note on which the interest is payable at maturity. In this situation an adjusting entry would have to be made at the end of both 1982 (4 months' interest) and 1983 (12 months' interest). The entries would be as follows:

Interest expense	XXX	
Accrued interest payable		XXX

Thus, the balance in the liability account would contain 16 months' interest on December 31, 1983.

FUNDAMENTAL CONCEPTS

Answer Outline

Problem 1 Valuation of Notes

a1. Notes should be valued at present value
  Also should be FMV of property exchanged
  At face if at a reasonable interest rate
 Notes consist of two elements
  Principal for property received
  Interest to compensate for use of funds
a2. Value noninterest-bearing notes at FMV of property
  Or FMV of note, whichever is clearer
 If FMV of note cannot be established, impute interest rate
  Establish when note is issued based on
   Credit standing of issuer
   Restrictive covenants
   Collateral
   Payment and other terms
   Tax consequences to buyer and seller
   No subsequent change for changed interest rate
 Should not be less than debtor would pay elsewhere
 Objective is to approximate reasonable rate
b1. Difference between FMV and face value is discount or premium
  Amortize as interest
  To result in a constant rate of interest
  I.e., the interest method
 May use other methods if not materially different
b2. Discount or premium is offset to note
  I.e., not separate asset or liability
  Not deferred charge or deferred credit
 Disclose effective interest rate
  Amortization is interest in income statement

Unofficial Answer

Problem 1 Valuation of Notes

a. 1. A note received in exchange for property, goods, or services should be recorded at its present value which is presumably the value of the property exchanged. In the case of a note bearing interest at a reasonable rate and issued in an arm's-length transaction, the face value of the note should be used, as explained below.

A note received for property, goods, or services represents two elements, which may or may not be stipulated in the note: (1) the principal amount, equivalent to the bargained exchange price of the property, goods, or services as established between the seller and the buyer and (2) an interest factor to compensate the seller over the life of the note for the use of funds he would have received in a cash transaction at the time of the exchange. Notes so exchanged are accordingly valued and accounted for at the present value of the consideration exchanged between the contracting parties at the date of the transaction in a manner similar to that followed for a cash transaction.

When a note is exchanged for property, goods, or services in a bargained transaction entered into at arm's-length, there is a presumption that the rate of interest stipulated by the parties to the transaction represents fair and adequate compensation to the seller for the use of the related funds. In these circumstances the note's present value is identical with its face value. Furthermore, where the rate of interest is reasonable and separately stated, the face value of the note is equal to the bargained exchange price for the property.

2. When a note bears no interest (or has a stated interest rate that differs sharply from the prevailing rate) and/or is not issued in an arm's-length transaction, the present value must be determined through consideration of the economic substance of the transaction.

The note and the sales price of the property, goods, or services exchanged for the note should be recorded at the fair value of the property, goods, or services or at an amount that reasonably approximates the market value of the note, whichever is the more clearly determinable. That amount may or may not be the same as the face amount; any resulting discount or premium should be accounted for as an element of interest over the life of the note.

In the absence of established exchange prices for the related property, goods, or services or evidence of the market value of the note, the present value of a note that stipulates no interest (or a rate of interest that differs sharply from the prevailing rate) should be determined by discounting all future payments on the note, using an imputed rate of interest as described below. This determination should be made at the time the note is issued; any subsequent changes in prevailing interest rates should be ignored.

The variety of transactions encountered precludes any specific interest rate from being applicable in all circumstances. However, some general guides may be stated. The choice of a rate may be affected by the credit standing of the issuer, restrictive covenants, the collateral, payment, other terms pertaining to the debt, and the tax consequences to the buyer and seller. The prevailing rates for similar instruments of issuers with similar credit ratings will normally help determine the appropriate interest rate. In any event, the rate used for valuation purposes will normally be at least equal to the rate at which the debtor can obtain financing of a similar nature from other sources at the date of the transaction. The objective is to approximate the rate that would have resulted if an independent borrower and an independent lender had negotiated a similar transaction under comparable terms and conditions with the option to pay the cash price upon purchase or to give a note for the amount of the purchase that bears the prevailing rate of interest to maturity.

b. 1. If the recorded value of a note differs from its face value, the difference should be treated as discount or premium and amortized as interest over the life of the note in such a way as to result in a constant rate of interest when applied to the amount outstanding at the beginning of any given period. This is the "interest" method. Other methods of amortization may be used if the results obtained are not materially different from those which would result from the "interest" method.

2. The discount or premium is not an asset or liability separable from the note that gives rise to it. Therefore, the discount or premium should be reported in the balance sheet as a direct deduction from or addition to the face amount of the note. It should not be classified as a deferred charge or deferred credit. The description of the note should include the effective interest rate. A valid alternative would be to report the note at its net value, disclosing the face amount of the note and the effective rate of interest on the face of the financial statements or in the notes to the statements. Amortization of discount or premium should be reported as interest in the income statement.

Solution Guide

Problem 2 Noninterest Bearing Note

This problem requires (1) the net receivable from Key at 12/31/78 and (2) the related income or loss before taxes for 1977 and 1978. The receivable is noninterest bearing and was received by Lock Company upon sale of property.

1. The solutions approach is to determine the present value of the note at the beginning of 1977, and then to compute the interest income on the note in 1977 and 1978.

2. Since there was no established exchange for the property, the present value of the note should be determined using the prevailing market interest rate for the type of note being discounted per paras 12-14 of APB 21. Thus the note should have been discounted at the prevailing interest rate of 12%. The time value of money factor for the present value of an annuity in advance (i = 12%, n = 6 where the first payment is made at the beginning of the first period) is 4.605. The present value of the note at the beginning of 1979 was $690,750 ($150,000 x 4.605).

3. The interest for 1977 is $64,890 which is computed as 12% of the net receivable during 1977. The net receivable during 1977 was the present value of the future payments at 1/1/77 of $690,750 minus the $150,000 initial payment. Thus 1977 interest income should have been $64,890 ($540,750 x 12%).

4. The interest income in the second year should be $54,677 which is 12% of the net receivable during 1978 of $455,640 ($690,750 original present value minus 1/1/77 payment of $150,000 plus 1977 interest of $64,890 minus 1/1/78 payment of $150,000).

5. Finally, note that profit on sale on the property in 1977 was $90,750 (the sales price of $690,750 minus $600,000 original cost).

Unofficial Answer

Problem 2 Noninterest Bearing Note

1.

Lock Company
Computation of Balance in Net Receivables from Key
December 31, 1978

	Principal	*Unearned interest*	*Net receivable*
Sales price ($150,000 X 4.605)	$900,000	$209,250	$690,750
Payment made on January 1, 1977	150,000	—	150,000
	750,000	209,250	540,750
Interest income for 1977 (Schedule 1)	—	64,890	64,890
Balance at December 31, 1977	750,000	144,360	605,640
Payment made on January 1, 1978	150,000	—	150,000
	600,000	144,360	455,640
Interest income for 1978 (Schedule 2)	—	54,677	54,677
Balance at December 31, 1978	$600,000	$ 89,683	$510,317

2.

Lock Company
Income Before Income Taxes
For the Years Ended December 31, 1977 and 1978

		1977	*1978*
Profit on sale:			
Sales price ($150,000 X 4.605)	$690,750		
Cost of property	600,000	$ 90,750	—
Interest income (Schedules 1 and 2)		64,890	$54,677
Income before income taxes		$155,640	$54,677

Schedule 1

Computation of Interest Income for 1977

Sales price	$690,750
Payment made on January 1, 1977	150,000
	540,750
Interest rate	12%
Interest income	$ 64,890

Schedule 2

Computation of Interest Income for 1978

Balance at December 31, 1977 ($540,750 + $64,890)	$605,640
Payment made on January 1, 1978	150,000
	455,640
Interest rate	12%
Interest income	$ 54,677

BONDS

Multiple Choice Questions (1 - 21)

1. On January 1, 1982, Hansen, Inc., issued for $939,000, one thousand of its 9%, $1,000 bonds. The bonds were issued to yield 10%. The bonds are dated January 1, 1982, and mature on December 31, 1991. Interest is payable annually on December 31. Hansen uses the interest method of amortizing bond discount. In its December 31, 1982, balance sheet, Hansen should report unamortized bond discount of

a. $57,100
b. $54,900
c. $51,610
d. $51,000

2. On January 1, 1982, Weaver Company purchased as a long-term investment $500,000 face value of Park Corporation's 8% bonds for $456,200. The bonds were purchased to yield 10% interest. The bonds mature on January 1, 1988, and pay interest annually on January 1. Weaver uses the interest method of amortization. What amount should Weaver report on its December 31, 1982, balance sheet as long-term investment?

a. $450,580
b. $456,200
c. $461,820
d. $466,200

3. On January 1, 1982, Jaffe Corporation issued at 95, five hundred of its 9%, $1,000 bonds. Interest is payable semiannually on July 1 and January 1, and the bonds mature on January 1, 1992. Jaffe paid bond issue costs of $20,000 which are appropriately recorded as a deferred charge. Jaffe uses the straight-line method of amortizing bond discount and bond issue costs. On Jaffe's December 31, 1982, balance sheet, the bonds payable should be reported at their carrying value of

a. $459,500
b. $477,500
c. $495,500
d. $522,500

4. On January 1, 1981, Welling Company purchased 100 of the $1,000 face value, 8%, ten-year bonds of Mann, Inc. The bonds mature on January 1, 1991, and pay interest annually on January 1. Welling purchased the bonds to yield 10% interest. Information on present value factors is as follows:

Present value of $1 at 8% for 10 periods	0.4632
Present value of $1 at 10% for 10 periods	0.3855
Present value of an annuity of $1 at 8% for 10 periods	6.7101
Present value of an annuity of $1 at 10% for 10 periods	6.1446

How much did Welling pay for the bonds?

a. $ 87,707
b. $ 92,230
c. $ 95,477
d. $100,000

5. The issuer of a 10-year term bond sold at par three years ago with interest payable May 1 and November 1 each year, should report on its December 31 balance sheet a (an)

a. Liability for accrued interest.
b. Addition to bonds payable.
c. Increase in deferred charges.
d. Contingent liability.

6. How would the amortization of premium on bonds payable affect each of the following?

	Carrying value of bond	*Net income*
a.	Increase	Decrease
b.	Increase	Increase
c.	Decrease	Decrease
d.	Decrease	Increase

7. An investor purchased a bond as a long-term investment on January 1. Annual interest was received on December 31. The investor's interest income for the year would be lowest if the bond was purchased at

a. A discount.
b. A premium.
c. Par.
d. Face value.

8. Should the following bond issue costs be expensed as incurred?

	Legal fees	*Underwriting costs*
a.	No	No
b.	No	Yes
c.	Yes	No
d.	Yes	Yes

9. For the issuer of a ten-year term bond, the amount of amortization using the interest method would increase each year if the bond was sold at a

	Discount	*Premium*
a.	No	No
b.	Yes	Yes
c.	No	Yes
d.	Yes	No

10. A gain on the conversion of outstanding bonds into common stock would be recognized when using the

	Book value method	Market value method
a.	Yes	No
b.	Yes	Yes
c.	No	No
d.	No	Yes

11. On December 31, 1981, Dumont Corporation had outstanding 8%, $2,000,000 face value convertible bonds maturing on December 31, 1985. Interest is payable annually on December 31. Each $1,000 bond is convertible into 60 shares of Dumont's $10 par value common stock. The unamortized balance on December 31, 1982, in the premium on bonds payable account was $45,000. On December 31, 1982, an individual holding 200 of the bonds exercised the conversion privilege when the market value of Dumont's common stock was $18 per share. Using the book value method, Dumont's entry to record the conversion should include a credit to additional paid-in capital of

a. $ 80,000
b. $ 84,500
c. $ 96,000
d. $125,000

12. On June 4, 1982, Xmar Corporation sold $200,000 face amount of 12% bonds for $198,000, with interest payable semiannually beginning December 3, 1982. Each $1,000 bond had ten detachable warrants entitling the holder to buy one share of Xmar's common stock for each warrant surrendered, plus $20 cash. Shortly after the bonds were sold, each bond was selling for $1,000 without the warrants, while the warrants were selling for $10 each. What portion of the $198,000 proceeds should be credited to "Additional paid-in capital—warrants"?

a. $0
b. $ 2,000
c. $18,000
d. $20,000

13. On April 7, 1975, the Script Corporation sold a $1,000,000 twenty-year, 8 percent bond issue for $1,030,000. Each $1,000 bond has a detachable warrant that permits the purchase of one share of the corporation's common stock for $30. The stock has a par value of $25 per share. Immediately after the sale of the bonds, the corporation's securities had the following market values:

8% bond without warrants	$1,020
Warrants	10
Common stock	28

What accounts should the corporation credit to record the sale of the bonds?

a.	Bonds payable	$1,000,000
	Premium on bonds payable	2,000
	Common stock warrants outstanding	28,000
b.	Bonds payable	1,000,000
	Premium on bonds payable	5,000
	Common stock warrants outstanding	25,000
c.	Bonds payable	1,000,000
	Premium on bonds payable	20,000
	Common stock warrants outstanding	10,000
d.	Bonds payable	1,000,000
	Premium on bonds payable	30,000

14. A portion of the proceeds should be allocated to paid-in capital for bonds issued with

	Detachable stock purchase warrants	Nondetachable stock purchase warrants
a.	No	No
b.	No	Yes
c.	Yes	No
d.	Yes	Yes

15. On July 1, 1982, Chatham, Inc., called for redemption all of its $1,000,000 face amount bonds payable outstanding at the call price of 105. As of June 30, 1982, the unamortized discount was $50,000 and the unamortized bond issue costs were $30,000. The market value of the bonds was $1,060,000 on July 1, 1982. Chatham's effective income tax rate was 40% for 1982. In its income statement for the year ended December 31, 1982, what amount should Chatham report as extraordinary gain or loss from bond redemption?

a. $0.
b. $30,000 gain.
c. $60,000 loss.
d. $78,000 loss.

16. Which of the following material gains on refunding of bonds payable should be recognized separately as an extraordinary gain?

	Direct exchange of old bonds for new bonds	Issuance of new bonds proceeds used to retire old bonds
a.	Yes	No
b.	Yes	Yes

c.	No	Yes
d.	No	No

17. When the issuer of bonds exercises the call provision to retire the bonds, the excess of the cash paid over the carrying amount of the bonds should be recognized separately as a (an)
   a. Extraordinary loss.
   b. Extraordinary gain.
   c. Loss from continuing operations.
   d. Loss from discontinued operations.

May 1984 Questions

18. On January 1, 1983, Wright Company purchased Keeler Corporation 9% bonds with a face value of $200,000, for $187,800. The bonds were purchased to yield 10%. The bonds are dated January 1, 1983, mature on December 31, 1992, and pay interest annually on December 31. Wright uses the interest method of amortizing bond discount. In its income statement for the year ended December 31, 1983, what total amount should Wright report as interest income from the long-term bond investment?
   a. $17,220
   b. $18,000
   c. $18,780
   d. $20,000

19. On June 30, 1983, Dean Company had outstanding 8%, $1,000,000 face value, 15-year bonds maturing on June 30, 1993. Interest is payable on June 30 and December 31. The unamortized balances on June 30, 1983, in the bond discount and deferred bond issue costs accounts were $45,000 and $15,000, respectively. Dean reacquired all of these bonds at 93 on June 30, 1983, and retired them. Ignoring income taxes, how much gain should Dean report on this early extinguishment of debt?
   a. $10,000
   b. $25,000
   c. $40,000
   d. $70,000

20. On March 1, 1984, Riley Corporation issued $1,000,000 of 10% nonconvertible bonds at 103 which are due on February 28, 1999. In addition, each $1,000 bond was issued with 30 detachable stock warrants, each of which entitled the bondholder to purchase, for $50, one share of Riley common stock, par value $25. On March 1, 1984, the quoted market value of Riley's common stock was $40 per share and the quoted market value of each warrant was $4. What amount of the proceeds from the bond issue should Riley record as an increase in stockholders' equity?
   a. $0
   b. $ 30,000
   c. $120,000
   d. $750,000

21. An investor purchased a bond classified as a long-term investment between interest dates at a premium. At the purchase date, the carrying value of the bond is more than the

	Cash paid to seller	*Face value of bond*
a.	Yes	Yes
b.	Yes	No
c.	No	Yes
d.	No	No

Repeat Question

(584,P2,40) Identical to item 11 above

BONDS

Problems

Problem 1 Bond Investments (581,P4a)

(25 to 30 minutes)

Part a. On June 1, 1979, Warner, Inc., purchased as a long-term investment 800 of the $1,000 face value, 8% bonds of Universal Corporation for $738,300. The bonds were purchased to yield 10% interest. Interest is payable semiannually on December 1 and June 1. The bonds mature on June 1, 1984. Warner uses the effective interest method of amortization. On November 1, 1980, Warner sold the bonds for $785,000. This amount includes the appropriate accrued interest.

Required:

Prepare a schedule showing the income or loss before income taxes from the bond investment that Warner should record for the years ended December 31, 1979, and 1980. Show supporting computations in good form.

Problem 2 Conversion of Bonds into Common Stock; Issuance of Bonds (1182,T3)

(15 to 25 minutes)

On February 1, 1979, Aubrey Company sold its 5-year, $1,000 par value, 8% bonds which were convertible at the option of the investor into Aubrey Company common stock at a ratio of 10 shares of common stock for each bond. The convertible bonds were sold by Aubrey Company at a discount. Interest is payable annually each February 1. On February 1, 1982, Mel Company, an investor in the Aubrey Company convertible bonds, tendered 1,000 bonds for conversion into 10,000 shares of Aubrey Company common stock which had a market value of $110 per share at the date of the conversion.

On May 1, 1982, Aubrey Company sold its 10-year, $1,000 par value, 14% nonconvertible term bonds dated April 1, 1982. Interest is payable semiannually and the first interest payment date is October 1, 1982. Due to market conditions, the bonds were sold at an effective interest rate (yield) of 16%.

Required:

a. How should Aubrey Company account for the conversion of the convertible bonds into common stock under both the book value and market value methods? Discuss the rationale for each method.

b. Were the nonconvertible term bonds sold at par, at a discount, or at a premium? Discuss the rationale for your answer.

c. Identify and discuss the effects on Aubrey Company's 1982 income statement associated with the nonconvertible term bonds.

Problem 3 Accounting for Bonds (1180,T4)

(15 to 25 minutes)

One way for a corporation to accomplish long-term financing is through the issuance of long-term debt instruments in the form of bonds.

Required:

a. Describe how to account for the proceeds from bonds issued with detachable stock purchase warrants.

b. Contrast a serial bond with a term (straight) bond.

c. For a five-year term bond issued at a premium, why would the amortization in the first year of the life of the bond differ using the interest method of amortization instead of the straight-line method? Include in your discussion whether the amount of amortization in the first year of the life of the bond would be higher or lower using the interest method instead of the straight-line method.

d. When a bond issue is sold between interest dates at a discount, what journal entry is made and how is the subsequent amortization of bond discount affected? Include in your discussion an explanation of how the amounts of each debit and credit are determined.

e. Describe how to account for and classify the gain or loss from the reacquisition of a long-term bond prior to its maturity.

Problem 4 Issuance and Extinguishment (1179,P5)

(40 to 50 minutes)

a. On January 1, 1979, the Hopewell Company sold its 8% bonds that had a face value of $1,000,000. Interest is payable at December 31, each year. The bonds mature on January 1, 1989. The bonds were sold to yield a rate of 10%. The present value of an ordinary annuity of $1 for 10 periods at 10% is 6.1446. The present value of $1 for 10 periods at 10% is 0.3855.

Required:

Prepare a schedule to compute the total amount received from the sale of the bonds. Show supporting computations in good form.

b. On September 1, 1978, the Junction Company sold at 104, (plus accrued interest) four thousand of its 9%, ten-year, $1,000 face value, nonconvertible bonds with detachable stock warrants. Each bond carried two detachable warrants; each warrant was for one share of common stock, at a specified option price of $15 per share. Shortly after issuance, the warrants were quoted on the market for $3 each. No market value can be determined for the bonds above. Interest is payable on December 1, and June 1. Bond issue costs of $40,000 were incurred.

Required:

Prepare in general journal format the entry to record the issuance of the bonds. Show supporting computations in good form.

c. On December 1, 1976, the Cone Company issued its 7%, $2,000,000 face value bonds for $2,200,000, plus accrued interest. Interest is payable on November 1 and May 1. On December 31, 1978, the book value of the bonds, inclusive of the unamortized premium, was $2,100,000. On July 1, 1979, Cone reacquired the bonds at 98, plus accrued interest. Cone appropriately uses the straight-line method for the amortization of bond premium because the results do not materially differ from using the interest method.

Required:

Prepare a schedule to compute the gain or loss on this early extinguishment of debt. Show supporting computations in good form.

Problem 5 Discount Calculation (1178,P3a)

(15 to 20 minutes)

On January 1, 1978, MyKoo Corporation issued $1,000,000 in five-year, 5% serial bonds to be repaid in the amount of $200,000 on January 1, of 1979, 1980, 1981, 1982, and 1983. Interest is payable at the end of each year. The bonds were sold to yield a rate of 6%. Information on present value and future amount factors is as follows:

Present value of an ordinary annuity of $1 for 5 years		*Future amount of an ordinary annuity of $1 for 5 years*	
5%	*6%*	*5%*	*6%*
4.3295	4.2124	5.5256	5.6371

	Present value of $1		*Future amount of $1*	
Number of years	*5%*	*6%*	*5%*	*6%*
1	.9524	.9434	1.0500	1.0600
2	.9070	.8900	1.1025	1.1236
3	.8638	.8396	1.1576	1.1910
4	.8227	.7921	1.2155	1.2625
5	.7835	.7473	1.2763	1.3382

Required:

1. Prepare a schedule showing the computation of the total amount received from the issuance of the serial bonds. Show supporting computations in good form.

2. Assume the bonds were originally sold at a discount of $26,247. Prepare a schedule of amortization of the bond discount for the first two years after issuance, using the interest (effective rate) method. Show supporting computations in good form.

Multiple Choice Answers

1.	a	6.	d	10.	d	14.	c	18.	c
2.	c	7.	b	11.	b	15.	d	19.	a
3.	b	8.	a	12.	c	16.	b	20.	c
4.	a	9.	b	13.	c	17.	a	21.	c
5.	a								

Multiple Choice Answer Explanations

B.1.– 3. Bonds

1. (1183,P1,2) (a) The requirement is the amount of unamortized bond discount to be reported on the 12/31/82 balance sheet. The solutions approach is to prepare the 12/31/82 interest entry.

Interest expense	93,900	
Cash		90,000
Discount on bonds payable		3,900

Using the interest method, interest expense is the book (carrying) value of the bonds outstanding during the year ($939,000) times the yield rate of 10%. The cash interest paid was the face amount of the bonds ($1,000,000) times the stated rate of 9%. The difference of $3,900 is the bond discount amortization. Since the original discount was $61,000 ($1,000,000 less $939,000), the unamortized discount at 12/31/82 is $57,100 ($61,000 less $3,900).

2. (583,P1,3) (c) The requirement is the amount to be reported on the 12/31/82 balance sheet as a long-term investment in bonds. $500,000 of bonds were purchased on 1/1/82 for $456,200, and the interest method is used to amortize the discount. Using the interest method, interest revenue is equal to the book (carrying) value of the bonds times the yield rate of interest. Discount or premium amortization is the difference between interest revenue and interest receivable. Therefore, on 12/31/82, Weaver prepares the following adjusting entry:

Int. rec.	40,000		($500,000 x 8%)
Inv. in bonds	5,620		
Int. income		45,620	($456,200 x 10%)

The carrying amount of the bonds on 12/31/82 is $456,200 plus $5,620, or $461,820.

3. (583,P1,19) (b) The requirement is the carrying value of bonds payable to be reported on the 12/31/82 balance sheet. The carrying value of the bonds is their face amount ($500,000) less the unamortized discount. Since the bonds were issued at 95 ($475,000), the original discount was $25,000. Using the straight-line method of amortization, 1/10 of the discount would be amortized during the first year (1/10 x $25,000 = $2,500). Therefore, the unamortized discount at 12/31/82 is $22,500 ($25,000 – $2,500), and the carrying value is $477,500 ($500,000 – $22,500). The bond issue costs of $20,000 can be disregarded, since these are appropriately recorded as a deferred charge and reported in the asset section of the balance sheet.

4. (581,P2,31) (a) The requirement is to compute how much Welling paid for the $100,000 bonds of Mann, Inc. The solutions approach is to recall that the market price of a bond is equal to the present value of the (1) maturity value and (2) future cash interest receipts. The present value of the maturity value and interest receipts is computed using the yield or market rate, not the nominal rate. Thus, the amount paid for the bonds is:

amount		*factor*		
100,000	x	.3855	=	$38,550
8,000	x	6.1446	=	49,157
				$87,707

5. (1183,T1,13) (a) The requirement is to determine the correct manner of reporting accrued interest payable on the balance sheet. At December 31 two months' interest (for November and December) has accrued. The required year-end adjusting entry would be:

Bond interest expense	XXX	
Bond interest payable		XXX

Bond interest payable is reported on the balance sheet as a current liability. Answer (b) is incorrect because only unamortized premium on bonds payable is reported as an addition to bonds payable on the balance sheet. Answer (c) is incorrect because deferred charges are assets from expenditures for expense prepayments. Answer (d) is incorrect because a contingent liability by definition is dependent upon the occurrence or nonoccurrence of some future event whereas accrued bond interest payable arises with the passage of time.

6. (1183,T1,15) (d) The requirement is to determine the effect of amortizing a premium on the carrying value of bonds payable and on net income. The entry to record the amortization of a premium is:

Premium on bonds payable	XXX	
Interest expense		XXX

The effect is to reduce both the carrying value of bonds payable and interest expense by the amount of amortization; a decrease in interest expense would cause net income to increase. Therefore, answer (d) is correct.

7. (583,T1,9) (b) The purchase price of a bond is its market value on the date of acquisition. If the market rate of interest is lower than the stated rate on the date of purchase the bond would sell at a premium, and the purchase price would exceed the face value. The premium is recognized over the life of the investment as a reduction of interest income. Yearly interest income for a bond purchased at a premium would equal the cash interest received **less** the premium amortization for the year. Answer (a) is incorrect because interest income for a bond purchased at a discount would equal the cash interest received **plus** the discount amortization for the year. Answers (c) and (d) are incorrect because if the bonds sold at par (face value), the interest income would be the amount stated on the face of the bonds.

8. (583,T1,23) (a) The requirement is whether either or both of two types of bond issue costs, legal fees and underwriting costs, should be expensed as incurred. APB 21, para 16 states that such issue costs should be reported in the balance sheet as a deferred charge. Both the legal fees and underwriting costs would be debited to a deferred charge account, unamortized expenses of bond issue, and amortized over the life of the issue. These issue costs should **not** be combined with any discount or premium that resulted from the issuance of the bonds.

9. (583,T1,24) (b) The requirement is to determine whether the amount of amortization increases each year using the interest method when a bond is sold either at a discount or premium or both. Using the interest method, interest expense for the period is based on the carrying value of the bond multiplied by the effective rate of interest. Cash interest paid for the period equals the face value of the bond multiplied by the stated rate of interest. The difference between these two resulting figures is the amortization of the discount or premium each period. The solutions approach is to prepare a table for a bond issued at a discount and at a premium and examine the direction of the successive amortization amounts. Consider $100,000 of 8% bonds issued on January 1, 1983, due on January 1, 1988, with interest payable each July 1 and January 1. Investors wish to obtain a yield of 10% on the issue. The amortization for the first two periods is as follows:

Date	*Credit cash*	*Debit interest expense*	*Credit bond discount*	*Carrying value of bonds*
1/1/83				$92,278
7/1/83	$4,000	$4,614	$614	92,892
1/1/84	4,000	4,645	645	93,537

Assume the same facts, except the investors wish to obtain a yield of only 6% on the issue:

Date	*Credit cash*	*Debit interest expense*	*Debit bond premium*	*Carrying value of bonds*
1/1/83				$108,530
7/1/83	$4,000	$3,256	$744	107,786
1/1/84	4,000	3,234	766	107,020

The above tables show that when bonds are sold at either a discount or a premium, the amount of amortization using the interest method will increase each year.

B.5. Convertible Bonds

10. (1183,T1,16) (d) The requirement is to determine which method of accounting for conversion of bonds would require recognition of a gain. When bonds are converted using the book value method, common stock and additional paid-in capital are credited for the carrying value of the bonds and no gain (loss) is recognized. When bonds are converted using the market value method, common stock and additional paid-in capital are credited for either the market value of the common stock or the market value of the bond, whichever is more reliably determinable. The difference between the carrying value of the bonds and the market value is recognized as a gain (loss). Therefore, answer (d) is correct.

11. (583,P1,8) (b) The requirement is the amount of the credit to additional paid-in capital when recording a conversion of bonds into common stock under the **book value method.** Following this method, the common stock is recorded at the carrying amount of the converted bonds, and no gain or loss is recognized. The bonds converted ($200,000) are 1/10 of the total $2,000,000 issued; therefore, 1/10 of the $45,000 premium, or $4,500, relates to the converted bonds. The common stock and additional paid-in capital are recorded at the carrying value ($204,500) of the bonds. Since 12,000 shares of stock (200 bonds x 60 shares of stock) were issued, the credit to common stock is for $120,000 (12,000 shares x $10 par value per share). The difference of $84,500 ($204,500 less $120,000) is credited to additional paid-in capital.

Bonds pay.	200,000		(200 x $1,000)
Prem. on B.P.	4,500		($45,000 x 1/10)
Com. stk.		120,000	(12,000 x $10)
Addl. P-I cap.		84,500	($204,500–$120,000)

B.6. Debt Issued with Detachable Purchase Warrants

12. (583,Q1,20) (c) The requirement is to determine what portion of the proceeds of a bond issue with detachable warrants should be credited to "additional paid-in capital—warrants." The allocation of the proceeds is made on the basis of the ratios of the relative fair market values of the bonds and warrants to the total fair market value of bonds and warrants (APB 14, para 16). The combined fair market value is $1,100 ($1,000 bond + $100 warrants). The allocation of the proceeds to "additional paid-in capital—warrants" is

$$\frac{\$100}{\$1,100} \times \$198,000 = \$18,000.$$

13. (1176,Q1,3) (c) The proceeds of bonds issued with detachable purchase warrants should be allocated based upon fair market values at the time of issuance and accounted for separately. See para 16 of APB 14. In this instance, the portion attributed to warrants is 10 over 1,030 and the portion attributable to bonds is 1,020 over 1,030. Since the $1,030 was received for each bond, $10 would be credited to warrants and $1,020 credited to bonds payable ($1,000 to the liability and $20 to the premium account). The solutions approach is to journalize the entry.

Cash	$1,030	
Stk. warrants		$ 10
Bonds payable		1,000
Bond prem.		20

14. (583,T1,25) (c) Bonds issued with either detachable or nondetachable stock purchase warrants are, in substance, composed of two elements, a debt element and a stockholders' equity element. Per APB 14, para 15, proceeds from bonds issued with **detachable** stock purchase warrants should be allocated between the bonds and the warrants on the basis of their relative fair market values. Detachable warrants trade separately from the debt; thus, a market value is available. The amount allocated to the warrants should be accounted for as paid-in capital. Bonds issued with **nondetachable** stock purchase warrants must be surrendered in order to exercise the warrants. Since this inseparability prevents the determination of individual market values, no allocation is permitted under APB 14.

B.7. Refunding of Bonds

15. (1183,P1,14) (d) The requirement is the amount to be reported as an extraordinary gain (loss) from bond redemption. Per SFAS 4, all gains (losses) from extinguishment of debt (except those which result from a conversion agreement), if material, are classified as extraordinary items. The solutions approach is to prepare the journal entry to record the extinguishment. The bonds payable, unamortized discount, and unamortized bond issue costs must be removed from the books. The loss on extinguishment is the excess of the cash paid ($1,000,000 x 105% = $1,050,000) over the net carrying amount of the liability ($1,000,000 – $50,000 – $30,000 = $920,000).

Bonds payable	1,000,000	
Loss on redemption	130,000*	
Discount on B.P.		50,000
Bond issue costs		30,000
Cash		1,050,000

*($920,000 – $1,050,000)

Since the loss is extraordinary, it is reported net of $52,000 tax (40% x $130,000), at $78,000 ($130,000 – $52,000).

16. (1183,T1,17) (b) The requirement is to determine whether or not material gains on refunding of debt by either direct exchange of bonds or issuance of new bonds and use of the proceeds to retire old bonds should be recognized separately as an extraordinary item. SFAS 4, as amended by SFAS 64, requires that all early extinguishments of debt prior to one year before maturity, except cash purchases to satisfy present or future sinking fund requirements, are to be separately recognized as extraordinary items, if material. Therefore, answer (b) is correct.

17. (583,T1,30) (a) Gain (loss) on the early extinguishment of debt should be classified on the income statement as an extraordinary item, net of the related income tax effect (SFAS 4, para 8). Answer (b) is incorrect because when the reacquisition price exceeds the carrying amount, a loss results, not a gain. Answer (c) is incorrect because an extraordinary item is a separate component of net income reported below income (loss) from operations on the income statement. Answer (d) is incorrect because the retirement of bonds is not a disposal of a segment.

May 1984 Answers

18. (584,P1,3) (c) The requirement is the interest income to be reported from a long-term bond investment using the interest method of amortization. Under this method, interest revenue is computed using the following formula:

(Book value of bonds) x (Yield rate) = Interest revenue

The book value of the bonds when purchased on 1/1/83 is equal to the purchase price ($187,800). Therefore, the interest revenue recognized in 1983 is

$187,800 x 10%, or $18,780. It may be helpful to visualize the journal entry for interest.

Cash (9% x $200,000)	18,000	
Investment in bonds (plug)	780	
Interest revenue (10% x $187,800)		18,780

19. (584,P2,25) (a) The requirement is the gain (ignoring income taxes) to be reported on an early extinguishment of debt. When the bonds are retired, the bonds payable, the unamortized discount, and the unamortized bond issue costs must be taken off the books. Cash is credited for the amount paid (93% x $1,000,000 = $930,000), and the difference is the gain or loss on retirement.

Bonds payable	1,000,000	
Bond discount		45,000
Bond issue costs		15,000
Cash		930,000
Gain		10,000

The gain can also be computed as follows:

Net carrying amount of bonds ($1,000,000 - $45,000 - 15,000)	$940,000
Cash paid (93% x $1,000,000)	(930,000)
Gain	$ 10,000

20. (584,P2,30) (c) The requirement is the amount of proceeds to be recorded as an increase in stockholders' equity. The proceeds are from the issuance of bonds with detachable stock warrants. APB 14, para 13 states that the proceeds from the sale of debt with **detachable** stock warrants should be allocated between the separate debt and equity elements. 1,000 bonds ($1,000,000 ÷ $1,000) are issued with 30 detachable stock warrants each, for a total of 30,000 warrants. Paid-in capital from stock warrants is credited for the FMV of the warrants issued (30,000 x $4 = $120,000). Note that if a FMV is available for the bonds **without** the warrants, APB 14 states that the proceeds should be allocated to the bonds and warrants based upon the relative FMVs at the time of issuance.

21. (584,T1,6) (c) The requirement is to compare the carrying value of a bond purchased between interest dates to both the cash paid to the seller and the face value of the bond. The solutions approach is to prepare the appropriate journal entry:

Investment in bonds	XXX	
Interest receivable (or revenue)	XXX	
Cash		XXX

The investment in bonds account is debited for the market value of the bond (price paid to seller) while the interest receivable account is debited for the amount of interest accrued from the previous interest payment date to the purchase date. The cash paid is the sum of the bond's market value plus the accrued interest. Thus, the carrying value, which is represented by the amount in the investment account, **is not** greater than the cash paid. The fact that the bond was purchased at a premium, by definition, means that the market value (i.e., carrying value) **is** greater than the face value of the bond. Therefore, answer (c) is correct.

BONDS

Solution Guide

Problem 1 Bond Investments

1. Part a requires a schedule showing the income or loss before income taxes from $800,000 of 8% bonds that were purchased at a discount to yield 10% to the purchaser. Interest is received semi-annually; the bonds mature in five years, and the purchaser uses the effective interest method of amortization.

1.1 The solutions approach is to set up a bond amortization schedule using the effective interest method. Under the effective interest (vs. straight line) method of amortizing the bond discount, a varying amount will be recorded as interest income from period to period. In cases where bonds are purchased at a discount the interest income will increase as the carrying amount increases through amortization of the discount.

1.2 The effective interest rate is applied to the beginning book (carrying) value of the bonds for each interest period. In this problem, there are two interest periods per year; therefore, the effective interest rate is one half of 10%, or 5%.

1.3 The amount of cash to be received is equal to the interest rate stated on the face of the bonds times the face value of the bonds (8% x $800,000). Again, because the payment periods are semi-annual, the interest to be received each period is one half of the yearly amount.

1.4 The difference between the cash proceeds and the amount recorded as interest income is amortization of bond discount and is added to the beginning book (carrying) value of the bonds.

1.5 The gain or loss that will be recognized in 1980 when the bonds are sold will be determined by comparing the book (carrying) value at the date of sale (with all amortization to date taken) and the proceeds from the sale (excluding that amount attributable to accrued interest).

Unofficial Answer

Problem 1 Bond Investments

Part a.

Warner, Inc.
Schedule of Income or Loss from Bond Investment
For Years Ending December 31, 1980 and 1979

	1980	1979
Interest income (Schedule 1)	$62,149	$43,109
Gain on sale of bonds (Schedule 2)	5,442	–
Total income	$67,591	$43,109

Schedule 1

Interest Income

	1980	1979
6/1/79–12/1/79 (Schedule 3)		$36,915
12/1/79– 6/1/80 (Schedule 3)		
1/6 ($37,161)		6,194
5/6 ($37,161)	$30,967	
6/2/80–11/1/80 (Schedule 3)	31,182	
Totals	$62,149	$43,109

Schedule 2

Gain on Sale of Bonds

Proceeds from sale attributable to bonds ($785,000 total – $26,667 accrued interest)	$758,333
Book value of bonds at date of sale (Schedule 3)	752,891
Gain on Sale	$ 5,442

Schedule 3

orization of Bond Discount
Effective Interest Method

Interest date	(A) 4% cash interest	(B) 5% Interest income (B x D)	(C) Increase in bond investment (B – A)	(D) Book value of bonds (D + C)
6/1/79				$738,300
12/1/79	32,000	36,915	4,915	743,215
6/1/80	32,000	37,161	5,161	748,376
11/1/80	26,667[a]	31,182[b]	4,515	752,891

[a]800,000 x 8% x 5/12

[b]748,376 x 10% x 5/12

Answer Outline

Problem 2 Conversion of Bonds into Common Stock; Issuance of Bonds

a. Under both methods, bonds payable is debited at par, unamortized discount is credited and common stock is credited at par

Book value method

Paid-in capital in excess of par credited for difference between book (carrying) value of bonds and par value of stock issued

Rationale

Conversion simply completes transaction initiated when bonds issued

Gain (loss) should not result from equity investment

Market value method

Gain (loss) recognized for difference between market value of bonds or stock (whichever is more reliable) and book value of bonds

Paid-in capital in excess of par credited for difference between market value of bonds or market value of stock (use same value as used for gain/loss) and par value of stock issued

Rationale

Convertibles are debt not stockholders' equity

Conversion is significant event

Earnings process culminated and gain (loss) results

b. Nonconvertible bonds were sold at discount because effective (yield/market) interest rate exceeds stated rate

Rationale

Purchase at discount increases investors' rates of return from stated rate to yield rate

Price investors pay is amount such that future cash interest receipts plus excess of par (received at maturity) over price paid will provide yield of 16%

c. Aubrey Company's Income Statement would include eight months of interest expense consisting of:

Cash interest paid 10/1 minus one month's interest received from investors on 5/1

Discount amortization under "interest method" on 10/1 and 12/31

May use SL amortization if results not affected materially

Accrued interest from 10/1 to 12/31

Unofficial Answer

Problem 2 Conversion of Bonds into Common Stock; Issuance of Bonds

a. To account for the conversion of bonds (under either the book value or market value method), bonds payable would be debited at par for the amount converted, unamortized discount would be credited and common stock would be credited at par for the amount issued. The primary difference between the two methods involves the recognition or nonrecognition of the gain (loss). Using the book value method, no gain (loss) on the conversion would be recorded. The amount to be recorded for the stock is equal to the book (carrying) value (par value less unamortized discount) of the bonds on the conversion date. Paid-in capital in excess of par would be credited for the difference between the book value of the bonds and the par value of the stock issued. The rationale for the book value method is that the conversion is simply the completion of the transaction initiated when the bonds were issued. Since this is viewed as a transaction with stockholders no gain (loss) should result.

Using the market value method, any difference between the market value of the bonds or the stock (whichever is more reliable) and the carrying value of the bonds on the conversion date will result in a gain (loss). Paid-in capital in excess of par should be credited for the difference between the market value (of either the bonds or stock) used in determining the gain or loss and the par value of the stock issued. The rationale is that the convertibles are debt, not stockholders' equity, and the conversion is, therefore, a significant event representing the culmination of the earnings process resulting in a gain (loss).

b. The nonconvertible bonds were sold at a discount because the effective (market/yield) interest rate (16%) exceeds the stated rate (14%). Buying bonds at a discount increases the investors' rates of return on their investments from the stated rate to the rate demanded by the market (effective rate). The price investors pay is an amount such that the future cash interest receipts plus the excess of par (received at maturity) over the price paid (at issuance) will provide a yield of 16%.

c. The 1982 income statement would include eight months of interest expense including:

- Cash interest paid October 1 less the one month's (April's) interest received at issuance on May 1.

• Discount amortization on October 1 and December 31 using the "interest" method.

• Accrued interest from October 1 to December 31.

Aubrey Company may use the straight-line method of amortization if the results are not materially different than those obtained using the "interest" method.

Answer Outline

Problem 3 Accounting for Bonds

a. Accounting for proceeds from bonds issued with detachable stock purchase warrants
   Portion of proceeds allocable to warrants should be accounted for as paid-in capital
   Remainder of proceeds should be allocated to the debt security
      Discount (or, infrequently, a decreased premium) usually results

b. Serial bond matures at a series of installment dates; term bond matures entirely on a single date

c. Difference between interest method and straight-line method of bond premium amortization
   Interest method uses constant interest rate applied to changing balance (carrying value)
   Use of straight-line method results in recognition of equal amount of premium amortization each period
   Amount of amortization in year 1 would be lower using interest method than if straight-line method were used

d. Entry to record bonds issued between interest dates is

Cash (amount = bond price + accrued interest)	XXX	
Discount on bonds payable	XXX	
Bonds payable (par)		XXX
Accrued interest payable (or interest expense)		XXX

   Amortization is affected because discount should be amortized over the period from date of sale (not date of bond) to the maturity date

e. Gain (loss) on reacquisition of long-term bond prior to maturity; classify by purpose of reacquisition
   To meet sinking fund requirements – ordinary income
   All other reacquisitions – if material, extraordinary item (net of tax)

Unofficial Answer

Problem 3 Accounting for Bonds

a. Because detachable stock purchase warrants are equity instruments that have a separate fair value at the issue date, the portion of the proceeds from bonds issued with detachable stock purchase warrants allocable to the warrants should be accounted for as paid-in capital. The remainder of the proceeds should be allocated to the debt security portion of the transaction. This usually results in issuing the debt security at a discount (or, occasionally, a reduced premium).

b. A serial bond progressively matures at a series of stated installment dates, for example, one-fifth each year. A term (straight) bond completely matures on a single date.

c. The amortization in the first year of the life of a five-year term bond issued at a premium would differ using the interest method instead of the straight-line method because the interest method employs a uniform interest rate based upon a changing balance, whereas the straight-line method provides for the recognition of an equal amount of premium amortization each period. Because the interest method provides for an increasing premium amortization each period, the amount of amortization in the first year of the life of the bond would be lower.

d. The journal entry to record a bond issue sold between interest dates is as follows:

• Debit cash for the price of the bond plus the accrued interest from the last interest date.

• Debit discount on bonds payable for the amount of discount to be amortized over the remaining life of the issue.

• Credit bonds payable for the par value of the bonds.

• Credit accrued interest payable (or interest expense) for the accrued interest from the last interest date.

The subsequent amortization of bond discount is affected when a bond issue is sold between interest dates because the discount should be amortized over the period from the date of sale (not the date of the bond) to the maturity date.

e. The gain or loss from the reacquisition of a long-term bond prior to its maturity should be included in the determination of net income for the period reacquired and, if material, classified as an extraordinary item, net of related income taxes.

Solution Guide

Problem 4 Issuance and Extinguishment

1. This problem consists of 3 unrelated parts concerning bonds payable.

2. Part a. requires a schedule computing the total amount received from the sale of $1,000,000 of 8% bonds. The bonds mature ten years after the date of sale, and interest is paid at the end of each year. The bonds were sold to yield a 10% return to the purchaser.

2.1 The solutions approach is to compute the present value of the $1,000,000 maturity value, and the present value of the annuity of the ten $80,000 (8% of $1,000,000) interest payments.

2.2 The present value of $1,000,000 ten years in the future is $1,000,000 times .3855 (the present value of $1 for 10 periods at 10%).

2.3 The present value of 10 annual payments of $80,000 is $80,000 times 6.1446 (the present value of an ordinary annuity of $1 for 10 periods).

3. Part b. requires the general journal entry to record the issuance of 4,000 bonds with detachable stock purchase warrants. Each bond carried two warrants and the warrants had a quoted market price of $3 shortly after issuance.

3.1 The $100,000 bonds were sold for 104 or $4,160,000 plus accrued interest less issue costs. The accrued interest is for 3 months (June–August) which is 25% of the annual interest cost of $360,000 (4,000,000 @ 9%) or $90,000. The bond issue costs were $40,000. Thus cash is to be debited for $4,210,000 ($4,160,000 + $90,000 – $40,000).

3.2 The bond issue costs of $40,000 are debited as a deferred charge per para 16 of APB 21.

3.3 The credits are to bonds payable $4,000,000 interest expense or payable $90,000, stock warrants $24,000, and bond premium $136,000. The stock warrants are credited for $6 (2 warrants per bond @ $3) times 4,000 bonds. No allocation of the net proceeds is made between the bonds and the warrants, because no market value was established for the bonds. The $136,000 credit to bond premium is the $160,000 (4% of $4,000,000) less the $24,000 assigned to stock warrants.

4. Part c. requires a schedule to compute the gain or loss on the reacquisition of $2,000,000 of 7% bonds. The bonds were issued on 1/1/76 for $2,200,000. Interest is payable on November 1 and May 1. Note that the premium has been amortized on a straight-line basis.

4.1 The solutions approach is to determine the book value of the bonds at the date of sale (7/1/79) and compare it with the reacquisition price.

4.2 If the book value of the bonds was $2,200,000 on 12/1/76 and $2,100,000 on 12/31/78, 25 months have results in $100,000 of amortization, i.e., $4,000/month.

4.3 Thus the book value of the bonds will be $2,076,000 (2,100,000 less 6 months at $4,000) on 7/1/79. The bonds were repurchased for $1,960,000 (2,000 bonds @ $980). Thus the gain is $116,000 ($2,076,000 liability extinguished for $1,960,000). Note that the accrued interest on the bonds at issuance or reacquisition has no effect on the bond book value, reacquisition cost, or gain or loss.

Unofficial Answer

Problem 4 Issuance and Extinguishment

Part a.

Hopewell Company
Computation of Total Amount Received
From Sale of Bonds
January 1, 1979

Present value of the future principle ($1,000,000 X 0.3855)	$385,500
Present value of future annual interest payments ($80,000 ($1,000,000 X 8%) X 6.1446)	491,568
Amount received from sale of bonds	$877,068

Part b.

Junction Company
Journal Entry
September 1, 1978

	Debit	Credit
Cash	$4,210,000	
Bond issue costs deferred	40,000	
Bonds payable (4,000 X $1,000)		$4,000,000
Premium on bonds payable (Schedule 1)		136,000
Detachable stock warrants (Schedule 1)		24,000
Bond interest expense (Schedule 2)		90,000
To record the issuance of the bonds.		

Schedule 1

Premium on Bonds Payable and Value of Stock Warrants

Sales price (4,000 X $1,040)	$4,160,000
Face value of bonds	4,000,000
	160,000
Deduct value assigned to stock warrants (4,000 X 2 = 8,000 warrants X $3)	24,000
Premium on bonds payable	$ 136,000

Schedule 2

Accrued Bond Interest to Date of Sale

Face value of bonds	$4,000,000
Interest rate	9%
Annual interest	$ 360,000
Accrued interest (3 months) – ($360,000 X 3/12)	$ 90,000

Part c.

Cone Company
Computation of Gain on Early Extinguishment of Debt
July 1, 1979

Book value of bonds on December 1, 1976	$2,200,000
Book value of bonds on December 31, 1978	2,100,000
Amortization for 25 months	$ 100,000
Monthly amortization ($100,000 ÷ 25)	$ 4,000
Book value of bonds on December 31, 1978	$2,100,000
Amortization for 1979 to July 1, 1979 ($4,000 x 6 months)	24,000
Book value of bonds on July 1, 1979	2,076,000
Cost of reacquisition (2,000 x $980)	1,960,000
Gain on early extinguishment of debt	$ 116,000

Solution Guide

Problem 5 Discount Calculation

1. Part a. requires (1) the total amount received from the issuance of $1,000,000 of serial bonds, and (2) an amortization schedule of bond discount assuming the bonds were sold at a $26,247 discount.

2. The amount to be received from the issuance of serial bonds is the present value of the principal and interest payments to be made on the bonds. Interest is to be paid annually at the end of each year. Thus the solutions approach is to determine the cash flow at the beginning of years 1979 through 1983 and then compute the present value of each cash flow at a discount rate of 6% as illustrated below. Note that the principal payment for each of the years 1979 through 1983 is $200,000.

Year	*Interest payment**	*Total payment*	*TVMF (6%)*	*Present value*
1/1/79	$50,000	$250,000	.9434	$235,850
1/1/80	40,000	240,000	.8900	213,600
1/1/81	30,000	230,000	.8396	193,108
1/1/82	20,000	220,000	.7921	174,262
1/1/83	10,000	210,000	.7473	156,933
	Net cash proceeds of bond issue			$973,753

*5% of $1,000,000 for 1978, 5% of $800,000 for 1979, etc.

2.1 An alternative solution would be to compute the present value of each interest payment separately and then compute the present value of the principal repayments as the present value of an annuity of $200,000 for five years.

3. The second requirement of part a. is to prepare a bond discount amortization schedule for the first two years if the bonds were sold at a $26,247 discount.

4. Recall that under the interest method, interest income or interest expense is the effective rate times the outstanding book value of the receivable or payable. The cash payment is the contract rate times the maturity or face value. The difference between the interest income or expense and the cash receipt or cash payment is the amortization of discount or premium.

4.1 If the discount is $26,247, the net book value during 1978 is $973,753 ($1,000,000 – $26,247). The interest expense for MyKoo Corporation in 1978 would be $58,425 ($973,753 x 6%). Since the cash payment is $50,000 ($1,000,000 x 5%), the amortization is $8,425 ($58,425 – $50,000). The entry is:

Bond interest expense	$58,425	
Cash		$50,000
Bond discount		8,425

4.2 During 1979 the carrying value of the bonds is $782,178 ($1,000,000 maturity value minus $200,000 principal payment minus $17,822 bond discount). Recall that the original discount of $26,247 was amortized by $8,425 during 1978. Thus the interest expense in 1979, the second year of the issue, is $46,930 ($782,178 x 6%), and the interest payment is $40,000 ($800,000 x 5%). The resulting amortization is $6,930. The entry is:

Bond interest expense	$46,930	
Cash		$40,000
Bond discount		6,930

Unofficial Answer

Problem 5 Discount Calculation

1.

MyKoo Corporation
Schedule of Total Amount Received for Serial Bond

Present value of amount to be paid on January 1 each year for 5 years at an annual yield of 6% ($200,000 x 4.2124) — $842,480

Present value of interest to be paid at the end of each year for 5 years at an annual yield of 6% computed as follows:

Date	Bonds Outstanding	Interest at 5%	Present value factor at 6%	Present value of interest payments	
12/31/78	$1,000,000	$50,000	.9434	$47,170	
12/31/79	800,000	40,000	.8900	35,600	
12/31/80	600,000	30,000	.8396	25,188	
12/31/81	400,000	20,000	.7921	15,842	
12/31/82	200,000	10,000	.7473	7,473	
			Total present value of interest payments		131,273
					$973,753

2.

MyKoo Corporation
Amortization of Bond Discount
Interest (Effective Rate) Method

Year	(A) *Carrying value of bonds ($1,000,000 – E – F)*	(B) *Effective interest expense (6% x A)*	(C) *Interest payments*	(D) *Amortization of bond discount (B – C)*	(E) *Bond discount balance (E – D)*	(F) *Cumulative principal payments*
Issue	$973,753				$26,247	
1	782,178	$ 58,425	$ 50,000	$ 8,425	17,822	$ 200,000
2	589,108	46,930	40,000	6,930	10,892	400,000
3	394,454	35,346	30,000	5,346	5,546	600,000
4	198,121	23,667	20,000	3,667	1,879	800,000
5	–	11,879*	10,000	1,879	–	1,000,000
		$176,247	$150,000	$26,247		

*Rounding differences ignored.

Note: Computations for years 3, 4, and 5 are not part of requirement but are included in answer so that complete schedule can be presented.

DEBT RESTRUCTURE

Multiple Choice Questions (1 - 4)

1. Bricker Company is indebted to Springburn Bank under a $200,000, 16%, three-year note dated January 1, 1981. Interest, payable annually on December 31, was paid on the December 31, 1981, due date. During 1982 Bricker experienced severe financial difficulties and is likely to default on the note and interest unless a concession is made by the bank. On December 31, 1982, the bank agreed to settle the note and interest for 1982 for $10,000 cash and a tract of land having a current market value of $140,000. Bricker's acquisition cost of the land is $100,000. Ignoring income taxes, what amount should Bricker report as extraordinary gain on the debt restructure in its income statement for the year ended December 31, 1982?

a. $0
b. $ 50,000
c. $ 82,000
d. $122,000

2. On December 31, 1979, Marsh Company entered into a debt restructuring agreement with Saxe Company, which was experiencing financial difficulties. Marsh restructured a $100,000 note receivable as follows:

- Reduced the principal obligation to $70,000.
- Forgave $12,000 of accrued interest.
- Extended the maturity date from December 31, 1979 to December 31, 1981.
- Reduced the interest rate from 12% to 8%.

Interest was payable annually on December 31, 1980, and 1981.

In accordance with the agreement, Saxe made payments to Marsh on December 31, 1980 and 1981. How much interest income should Marsh report for the year ended December 31, 1981?

a. $0
b. $ 5,600
c. $ 8,400
d. $11,200

3. Tapscott, Inc., is indebted to Bush Finance Company under a $600,000, 10%, five-year note dated January 1, 1978. Interest, payable annually on December 31, was paid on the December 31, 1978, and 1979 due dates. However, during 1980 Tapscott experienced severe financial difficulties and is likely to default on the note and interest unless some concessions are made. On December 31, 1980, Tapscott and Bush signed an agreement restructuring the debt as follows:

- Interest for 1980 was reduced to $30,000 payable March 31, 1981.
- Interest payments each year were reduced to $40,000 per year for 1981 and 1982.
- The principal amount was reduced to $400,000.

What is the amount of gain that Tapscott should report on the debt restructure in its income statement for the year ended December 31, 1980?

a. $120,000
b $150,000
c. $200,000
d. $230,000

4. For a troubled debt restructuring involving only modification of terms, it is appropriate for a debtor to recognize a gain when the carrying amount of the debt

a. Exceeds the total future cash payments specified by the new terms.
b. Is less than the total future cash payments specified by the new terms.
c. Exceeds the present value specified by the new terms.
d. Is less than the present value specified by the new terms.

May 1984 Question

Repeat Question

(584,P3,42) Identical to item 3 above

DEBT RESTRUCTURE

Problem

Problem 1 Entries for Modification of Terms (Adapted from Kieso and Weygandt, *Intermediate Accounting,* 4th edition, p. 650)

(40 to 50 minutes)

Irish, Inc. owes English Bank a 10-year, 19% note in the amount of $110,000 plus $11,000 of accrued interest. The note is due today, 12/31/78. Because Irish, Inc. is in financial trouble, English agrees to accept 40,000 shares of Irish's $1.00 par value common stock which is selling for $1.25, forgive the accrued interest, reduce the face amount of the note to $60,000, extend the maturity date to 12/31/81, and reduce the interest rate to 5%. Interest will continue to be due on 12/31 each year.

Required:

a. Prepare all the necessary journal entries on the books of Irish, Inc. from restructure through maturity.

b. Prepare all the necessary journal entries on the books of English Bank from restructure through maturity.

c. Assume that instead of Irish, Inc. giving English Bank the 40,000 shares of common stock, a piece of land with a book value of $50,000 and a fair value of $55,000 is given as part of the restructure arrangement. All other facts remain unchanged.

1. Prepare the entries on the books of both entities on 12/31/78.
2. Describe verbally how the interest revenue (English Bank) and interest expense (Irish, Inc.) for 1979, 1980, and 1981 would be determined.

Multiple Choice Answers

1. c 2. a 3. b 4. a

Multiple Choice Answer Explanations

C. Debt Restructure

1. (583,P1,14) (c) The requirement is the amount to be reported as an extraordinary gain as the result of a troubled debt restructure. In this restructure, the debt is retired by transferring cash and land to the creditor. The extraordinary gain, per para 13 of SFAS 15, is the excess of the carrying amount of the debt over the fair value of the assets transferred. The carrying amount of the debt is its book value ($200,000) plus any accrued interest ($200,000x16%, or $32,000). The extraordinary gain is, therefore, $82,000.

Carrying amount of debt ($200,000 + $32,000)	$232,000
FV of assets transferred ($10,000 + $140,000)	150,000
X/O gain on restructure	$ 82,000

The difference between the market value ($140,000) and cost ($100,000) of the land is treated as a $40,000 gain on the transfer of the asset, which is included in income before taxes.

2. (1182,P1,18) (a) The requirement is the amount of interest income to be recorded by Marsh in 1981 after a modification of terms type of troubled debt restructure on 12/31/79. Per SFAS 15, when a troubled debt restructure involves modification of terms, the creditor recognizes a loss (and **no** interest income in the future) if the carrying amount (principal + accrued interest) exceeds all cash payments to be received in the future. In this instance, the carrying amount is $112,000 ($100,000 note receivable plus accrued interest of $12,000). The future payments total $81,200 (principal of $70,000 plus two annual 8% interest payments of $5,600 each). The difference of $30,800 ($112,000 less $81,200) is recognized as a loss by Marsh in 1979 and no interest income is recognized in 1980 or 1981.

3. (1181,P1,14) (b) The requirement is the amount of gain that Tapscott should report in 1980 on the debt restructure. According to SFAS 15, if the debt is continued with a modification of terms, an extraordinary gain is recognized by the debtor if the future cash payments on the debt are less than the carrying value of the debt. For troubled debt restructures, carrying value is defined as the principal amount plus accrued interest. In this case, the carrying value is $660,000 ($600,000 principal plus $60,000 accrued interest). The future cash payments total $510,000 ($400,000 reduced principal plus $110,000 adjusted interest payments). The $150,000 difference ($660,000 – $510,000) is recognized as an extraordinary gain. It might be helpful to visualize the journal entry to be recorded by Tapscott on the debt restructure:

Note payable	600,000		Carrying amount
Interest payable	60,000		
Note pay. (restruc. amt.)		510,000	Future payments
X/O gain		150,000	

4. (1181,T1,29) (a) SFAS 15 states that the debtor records a gain and the creditor records a loss at the date of a restructure involving only a modification of terms when the pre-restructure carrying amount exceeds the total future cash flows per the modification. The gain recognized is the difference between the pre-restructure carrying amount and the future cash flows. No gain or loss is recorded if the carrying amount is less than total future cash flows [answer (b)]. Present values of future cash flows are not considered in determining whether a gain or loss is recognized on a restructuring of troubled debt [answers (c) and (d)].

DEBT RESTRUCTURE

Solution Guide

Problem 1 Entries for Modification of Terms

1. SFAS No. 15 prescribed the accounting treatment for "troubled" debt which is either satisfied by the exchange of an asset or equity interest, is extended with a modification of terms, or a combination of the two. This problem deals with a combination situation whereby the debt is partially satisfied by English Bank accepting shares of Irish, Inc.'s stock (requirements a and b) or land (requirement c) and then extending the debt and modifying its terms.

2. A quick review of the steps to take in debt restructuring problems should make this problem straight-forward.

2.1 If the debt is forgiven entirely by an asset or equity interest transferred, the difference between the book value of the debt including accrued interest and the FMV of the transfer is a "gain" to the debtor and a "loss" to the creditor.

2.2 If the debt is only partially satisfied by the transfer of an asset or equity interest (the situation in this problem), the debt is first reduced by the FMV of the transfer.

2.3 The difference between the pre-restructure debt amount and the FMV is treated as modification of terms. The steps to take are:
Calculate the total future cash flows under the new terms.
Compare the total future cash flows to the loan payable or loan receivable balance on each set of books.

2.4 If the total future cash flows are less than the debt, write the debt down to equal the future cash flows recognizing a gain (debtor) and loss (creditor). In this case the remaining debt is equal to the PV of future cash flows. Consequently, there is no future interest to be recognized, i.e., each cash payment is applied totally against the debt.

2.5 If the future cash flows are greater than the debt, there is no gain or loss recognized. In this situation the debt on the books is the PV of the future cash flows, i.e., the cash flows discounted at some effective interest rate have a PV equal to the debt before restructure. The rate which will equate the future cash flow and debt must be determined and interest expense and revenue will be recognized for each cash payment using the effective interest method.

Unofficial Answer

Problem 1 Entries for Modification of Terms

Debt on books at restructure	$110,000 + $11,000 =	$121,000
FMV of stock transferred	40,000 x $1.25 =	50,000
Debt after transfer of stock		$ 71,000
Cash flow under new terms	$60,000 + ($60,000 x .05 x 3) =	$ 69,000
Excess of debt over total cash flow		($ 2,000)

Since the total future cash flow is less than the debt on the books at restructure recognize gain or loss and apply each future cash payment totally against debt.

a. Entries by Irish, Inc.:

1978		
Accrued interest payable	$11,000	
Notes payable ($110,000 – $69,000)	41,000	
Common stock		$40,000
Additional paid-in capital		10,000
Gain on restructure (extraordinary)		2,000
1979, 1980, and 1981		
Notes payable	$ 3,000	
Cash		$ 3,000
Also in 1981		
Notes payable	$60,000	
Cash		$60,000

b. Entries by English Bank:

1978		
Allowance for doubtful accounts (or loss on restructure	$ 2,000	
Investments: Irish, Inc. CS	50,000	
Notes receivable ($110,000 – $69,000)		$41,000
Accrued interest receivable		11,000
1979, 1980, and 1981		
Cash	$ 3,000	
Notes receivable		$ 3,000
Also in 1981		
Cash	$60,000	
Notes receivable		$60,000

c. 1.

Pre-restructure amount	$121,000
Fair value of land transferred	55,000
Unrecovered pre-restructure amount	66,000
Total future cost flows [$60,000 + (60,000 x .05 x 3)]	69,000
Excess of future cash flows over pre-structure amount	3,000

Therefore no gain or loss is recognized on modification of terms.

Irish, Inc. – 1978		
Land	$ 5,000	
Gain on transfer		$ 5,000
Accrued interest payable	11,000	
Notes payable	44,000	
Land		55,000
English Bank – 1978		
Investments – land	$55,000	
Notes receivable		$44,000
Accrued interest rec.		11,000

2. Since the total future cash flows after the restructure exceed the pre-restructure amount and no gain or loss is recognized, a new effective interest rate must be determined. (Computation under "c.1." above.) The difference between the annual $3,000 of stated interest per the restructure agreement and the interest based on the effective rate is a reduction of note receivable (English Bank) and notes payable (Irish, Inc.). The amount of "stated interest dollars" that are used to reduce the pre-restructure debt remaining is:

Unrecovered pre-restructure amount	$66,000
New face amount of note	60,000
	6,000

As a result over the remaining three years $6,000 of the $9,000 specified as interest is used to reduce the principal of the note per books.

PENSIONS

Multiple Choice Questions (1 - 16)

1. Lee Corporation has a noncontributory pension plan covering substantially all of its employees. Lee's policy is to fund pension costs as accured. At December 31, 1981, the actuarially computed value of vested benefits equalled the cash on deposit with the trustee. The total pension expense for 1981 was $900,000, which included normal cost of $700,000 and amortization of past service cost of $200,000. The unamortized balance of past service cost at December 31, 1981, was $600,000. How much should appear on Lee's balance sheet at December 31, 1981, for pension liability?
   a. $0
   b. $200,000
   c. $600,000
   d. $900,000

Items 2 and 3 are based on the following information:

The Johnson Corporation adopted a pension plan in 1976 on a funded, noncontributory basis. Johnson elected to amortize past service costs over twelve years and to fund past service costs over ten years. Normal costs are to be funded as incurred each year. The following schedule reflects both amortization of the past service cost and funding for the years 1976 and 1977.

	1976	*1977*
12-year accrual	$100,000	$100,000
Reduction for interest	–	835
Past service pension cost	100,000	99,165
10-year funding	113,909	113,909
Balance sheet—deferred charge:		
Balance	13,909	28,653
Increase	13,909	14,744

2. If normal cost for 1976 was $70,000, Johnson should record pension expense in 1976 of
   a. $70,000
   b. $113,909
   c. $170,000
   d. $183,909

3. If normal cost in 1977 was $75,000, the entry that Johnson should make in 1977 to record pension expense and funding is

		Debit	*Credit*
a.	Pension expense	$100,000	
	Deferred charge – funding in excess of costs	13,909	
	Cash		$113,909
b.	Pension expense (normal cost)	$ 75,000	
	Pension expense (past service)	99,165	
	Deferred charge – funding in excess of costs	14,744	
	Cash		$188,909
c.	Pension expense	$175,000	
	Deferred charge – funding in excess of costs	13,909	
	Cash		$188,909
d.	Pension expense (normal cost)	$ 75,000	
	Pension expense (past service)	100,000	
	Deferred charge – funding in excess of costs	14,744	
	Cash		$189,744

4. The pension expense accrued by a company will be increased by interest equivalents when
   a. The plan is fully vested.
   b. The plan is fully funded.
   c. Amounts funded are less than pension cost accrued.
   d. Amounts funded are greater than pension cost accrued.

5. In which of the following pension instances would the accrual of past service costs have to be reduced for interest presumed earned?
   a. When past service costs have been fully accrued prior to funding.
   b. When pension expense exceeds the maximum allowable accrual.
   c. When past service costs have been fully funded prior to accrual.
   d. When interest presumed earned on previously accrued past service cost exceeds interest presumed earned on unaccrued past service cost.

6. What is the difference between the terms past service costs and prior service costs?

a. Past service costs refer to costs applicable to periods prior to a particular date of actuarial valuation, and prior service costs refer to costs applicable to employee service prior to the inception of a pension plan.
b. Past service costs refer to costs applicable to employee service prior to the inception of a pension plan, and prior service costs refer to costs applicable to periods prior to a particular date of actuarial valuation.
c. Past service costs refer to costs applicable to a pension plan for an employee who enters the plan after the inception of the plan in order to bring the employee's benefits into line with the other participants in the plan, and prior service costs refer to changes in prior period pension costs that are caused by a change in actuarial valuation.
d. There is no difference between the two terms, and they may be used interchangeably.

7. On January 1, 1982, Chestnut Corporation adopted a noncontributory pension plan. The actuarial consultant recommended a 7% interest rate, and applying an acceptable actuarial method, determined that the past service cost is $500,000 at January 1, 1982. The normal cost will be funded fully each year and the past service cost will be amortized and funded over 20 years. Information relating to the plan for 1982 is as follows:

Normal pension cost	$100,000
Past service cost amortized and funded	47,200

In its income statement for the year ended December 31, 1982, Chestnut should report pension expense of

a. $100,000
b. $135,000
c. $147,200
d. $150,000

8. On January 1, 1980, Pierce, Inc., adopted a noncontributory pension plan for all of its eligible employees. The plan requires Pierce to make annual payments to the designated trustee three months after the end of each year. The first payment was due on March 31, 1981. Information relating to the plan is as follows:

Normal cost for 1980	$ 200,000
Past service cost at January 1, 1980 (unfunded)	1,000,000
Funds held by the trustee are expected to earn an 8% return.	

Assuming that Pierce elects to maximize its pension expense in accordance with GAAP, what would be the amount of accrued pension expense at December 31, 1980?

a. $216,000
b. $280,000
c. $300,000
d. $380,000

9. In the calculation of the annual provision for pension cost, 10 percent of past service cost (until fully amortized) would be included in the

	Minimum limit	*Maximum limit*
a.	Yes	Yes
b.	Yes	No
c.	No	No
d.	No	Yes

10. The maximum annual provision for pension cost permitted is normal cost, plus

a. 10 percent of past service cost (until fully amortized).
b. 10 percent of past service cost (until fully amortized), plus 10 percent of any increases or decreases in prior service cost arising on amendments of the plan, plus interest equivalents on the difference between provisions and amounts funded.
c. Interest equivalents on any unfunded prior service cost, plus a provision for the excess of the actuarially computed value of vested benefits over the total of the pension fund if such excess is **not** at least 5 percent less than the comparable excess at the beginning of the year.
d. A provision for vested benefits.

11. In accounting for the cost of pension plans, an acceptable actuarial cost method for financial reporting purposes is

a. Pay-as-you-go.
b. Unit credit.
c. Turnover.
d. Terminal funding.

12. For its defined benefit pension plans, an employer should disclose for each complete set of financial statements, as of the most recent benefit information date for which the data are available, the actuarial present value of accumulated plan benefits that are

	Vested	*Nonvested*
a.	Yes	Yes
b.	Yes	No
c.	No	Yes
d.	No	No

13. Actuarial gains or losses directly related to the operation of a pension plan should be

a. Allocated to current and future periods.
b. Deferred until pension plan investments give rise to actuarial gains or losses.
c. Offset against pension expense in year of occurrence.
d. Disclosed in a note to the financial statements only.

14. Which of the following disclosures concerning pension plans should be made in a company's financial statements or their notes?

a. A statement of a company's accounting and funding policies.
b. The amount of retirement benefits paid during the year.
c. A description of the actuarial assumptions made.
d. The amount of unfunded past service costs.

May 1984 Questions

15. On January 1, 1983, Trapp Company adopted a noncontributory pension plan which requires Trapp to make annual payments to an independent trustee two months after the end of each year. The first payment was due on February 29, 1984. Information relating to the pension plan is as follows:

Past service cost at 1/1/83 (unfunded)	$500,000
Normal cost for 1983	150,000
Funds held by the trustee are expected to earn a 6% return	

Trapp elects to minimize its annual pension cost. At December 31, 1983, how much should Trapp accrue for pension expense?

a. $150,000
b. $159,000
c. $180,000
d. $200,000

16. Brown Company adopted a noncontributory pension plan on January 1, 1983. Brown decided to amortize the past service cost over 15 years and to fund this cost by making equal payments to the fund trustee at the end of each of the first ten years. The normal pension cost is also funded fully at the end of each year. The following pension plan data are available for 1983:

Normal pension cost	$80,000
Past service cost:	
Amortized	46,700
Funded	59,600

In its December 31, 1983, balance sheet, Brown should report deferred pension cost at

a. $12,900
b. $20,400
c. $46,700
d. $59,600

PENSIONS

Problems

Problem 1 Definitions (578,T4)

(20 to 25 minutes)

Part a. Generally accepted accounting principles require that pension costs be accounted for on the accrual basis. The various components of pension expense include (but are not limited to):

1. Normal cost
2. Past service cost
3. Prior service cost
4. Interest

Required:

Define each of the four terms designated above and discuss how each of the costs is accounted for under generally accepted accounting principles.

Part b. The accounting for past service cost has been a controversial issue. Some members of the profession advocate the accrual of past service cost only to the extent funded, and others advocate the accrual of past service cost regardless of the amount funded.

Required:

1. What are the arguments in favor of accruing past service cost only to the extent funded?
2. What are the arguments in favor of accruing past service cost regardless of the amount funded?

Problem 2 Pension Calculations (582,P5b)

(20 to 30 minutes)

Part b. Foster Corporation, a calendar-year company, adopted a noncontributory defined benefit pension plan on January 1, 1980. Foster's actuarial consulting firm recommended a 6% interest rate as appropriate and, applying an acceptable actuarial method, determined that the past service cost at the date of adoption of the plan is $300,000. Management decided to amortize the past service cost over 16 years and to fund the past service cost by making equal payments to the pension fund trustee at the end of each of the first 20 years. As of December 31, 1981, no benefits have vested. The normal (current) pension cost is to be funded fully each year. Information provided by the actuarial consultant relating to the pension plan for the years 1980 and 1981 is as follows:

	1980	*1981*
Amortization of past service cost	$29,685	$29,685
Funding of past service cost	26,155	26,155
Normal pension cost	60,000	65,000

Required:

1. Prepare schedules to compute the amounts relating to the pension plan that Foster should report on its income statement and balance sheet for 1980 and 1981. Show supporting computations in good form.
2. Compute the minimum and maximum pension cost limits allowable under generally accepted accounting principles for 1980. Show supporting computations in good form.

Multiple Choice Answers

1. a	5. c	8. c	11. b	14. a
2. c	6. b	9. d	12. a	15. c
3. b	7. c	10. b	13. a	16. a
4. c				

Multiple Choice Answer Explanations

D.1.–3. Pensions

1. (1182,Q1,12) (a) The requirement is to determine the amount of pension liability to appear on the balance sheet. If the recorded pension expense exceeds the cash contributions to the pension fund, the excess would be reported as a pension liability on the balance sheet. Since Lee Corporation funds pension costs as accrued, no pension liability would appear on the balance sheet. Past service cost, the pension cost associated with the years prior to the date of adoption of the plan, does not represent a liability under current GAAP (APB 8).

2. (1178,Q1,14) (c) The requirement is pension expense for 1976 which consists of past cost and normal cost. In 1976, the normal costs are given as $70,000. While only $100,000 of past costs are going to be expensed in 1976, $113,909 is going to be funded. The result is a debit to deferred charges. The solutions approach is to record the entry for past pension cost in 1976 as illustrated below. Thus the $100,000 of past costs plus $70,000 normal costs results in pension expense of $170,000.

Pension expense	$100,000	
Deferred pension costs	13,909	
Cash		$113,909

3. (1178,Q1,15) (b) The requirement is the entry to record 1977 pension expense. Since the $75,000 normal cost was funded, and $113,909 of past cost is funded, the credit to cash is $188,909. Normal cost is given as $75,000. The problem indicates deferred charges increased by $14,744. Thus the past cost is a plug figure of $99,165 which consists of past costs amortization of $100,000 less $835 of interest equivalents. The $835 of interest equivalent is the interest earned on the amount that had been funded in 1976 in excess of the 12-year accrual.

Pension expense (normal)	$75,000	
Pension expense (past)	99,165	
Deferred pension costs	14,744	
Cash		$188,909

4. (1182,T1,18) (c) The pension expense accrued by a company will be increased by interest equivalents when "amounts funded are less than pension costs accrued." When a pension plan is underfunded, the amount of earnings actuarily assumed to accumulate will not exist. Therefore, expense is increased by the amount of missing earnings (interest equivalents). Vesting [answer (a)] is not directly related to interest equivalents. If the plan is fully funded [answer (b)] there would not be an increase for interest equivalents. Answer (d), "funding greater than pension cost accrued," would result in a decrease in pension expense for interest equivalents.

5. (579,T1,8) (c) The requirement is the situation in which amortization of past service costs would have to be reduced for interest presumed earned. Pension actuarial methods assume interest is being earned on funds assumed to be deposited. A typical assumption is that deposits are made as expense is accrued. When past service costs have been funded prior to accrual, there would be interest earned that was not expected in the actuarial assumptions. Para 17, APB8, requires that interest adjustments be made when amounts deposited vary from actuarial assumptions. Answer (a) is incorrect because if past service costs have been accrued, but not funded, an additional pension cost provision would have to be made for the interest that was not earned on the unfunded amounts. Answer (b) is incorrect because the interest equivalents are determined by the relationship of pension cost accruals to pension funding, rather than between the amount of expense recorded and the maximum amount that could be recorded per APB 8. Answer (d) is incorrect because no interest is presumed earned on unaccrued costs.

6. (1177,T1,15) (b) Past service costs are the costs attributable to years of service prior to the inception of a pension plan. Prior service costs are those costs attributable to prior service as of a certain valuation date. Prior costs also include any remaining past service costs. Other prior costs arise from amendments to the plan, i.e., retroactive increases in benefits. See Appendix B – Glossary of APB 8. Answer (a) is incorrect because the definitions of past service costs and prior costs are interchanged.

D.4. Minimum and Maximum

7. (1183,P2,38) (c) The requirement is the amount of 1982 pension expense. The pension expense reported includes the normal cost ($100,000) and past service cost amortization ($47,200), for a total of

$147,200. This amount is acceptable because it falls between the defined minimum and maximum amounts per APB 8. The **minimum** pension expense is $135,000 [$100,000 + (7% x $500,000)], while the **maximum** pension expense is $150,000 [$100,000 + (10% x $500,000)].

8. (581,P1,7) (c) The requirement is to compute the **maximum** amount that Pierce can record as pension expense. The solutions approach is to remember that the maximum pension expense recorded in any one year should not be more than the total of

1. Normal Cost
2. 10% of past service cost
3. 10% of prior costs arising from amendments
4. Interest equivalent on any difference between amounts funded and amounts expensed.

Thus, the maximum pension expense allowed under APB 8 is $200,000 normal cost + $100,000 ($1,000,000 x .10) PSC amortization = $300,000.

9. (1183,T1,27) (d) The requirement is to determine whether or not 10% of the unamortized past service cost is to be included in the calculation of either the minimum or maximum limits applicable to the annual provision for pension costs. APB 8, para 17 states that 10% of the unamortized past service cost shall be included in the calculation of the maximum limit, but is not included in the calculation of the minimum limit. Therefore, answer (d) is correct.

10. (580,T1,34) (b) APB 8, para 17 permits a maximum annual provision for pension cost which includes normal cost plus the three other elements identified in answer (b). Answer (a) is incorrect because this is only one of the four costs considered in the maximum provision. Answers (c) and (d) are incorrect because these are elements used to calculate the **minimum** provision.

11. (583,T1,42) (b) The five acceptable actuarial cost methods listed in APB 8, para 20 are the unit credit or accrued benefit cost method, the projected benefit cost method, the entry age normal method, the individual level premium method, and the aggregate method. Under the unit credit method, the pension cost for the current year is the present value of the units of future benefit credited to employees for service in the current year. The pay-as-you-go method [answer (a)] and the terminal funding method [answer (d)] are unacceptable methods because they do not recognize pension costs prior to retirement of employees as required per APB 8, para 24. Answer (c) is incorrect because turnover is not an actuarial cost method but a term which means termination of employment other than by death or retirement.

Other

12. (1182,T1,39) (a) Per SFAS 36, para 8, a defined benefit pension plan must disclose for each complete set of financial statements, as of the most recent benefit information date, the actuarial present value of **both** vested and nonvested accumulated plan benefits. The required disclosures should be determined in accordance with SFAS 35.

13. (1181,T1,25) (a) Para 30 of APB 8 states that actuarial gains and losses, including realized investment gains and losses, should be spread or averaged over current and future periods. Answer (c), immediate recognition, would be appropriate for gains or losses that arise from a single occurrence not directly related to the operation of the pension plan and not in the ordinary course of the employer's business [e.g., a plant closing in which case the actuarial gain (loss) should be treated as an adjustment of the gain or loss from that occurrence and not as an adjustment of pension expense]. Answers (b) and (d) are inappropriate in all cases.

14. (580,T1,21) (a) Para 46 of APB 8 lists five items which should be disclosed concerning pension plans. These items are a statement identifying employee groups covered, a statement of accounting and funding policies [answer (a)], the provision for pension cost for the period, the excess of vested benefits over the amount funded or accrued, and the nature and effect of significant matters affecting comparability for all periods presented.

May 1984 Answers

15. (584,P1,16) (c) The requirement is the minimum amount which can be recorded as pension expense. Per APB 8, para 17a the minimum allowable pension expense equals the sum of

1. Normal costs.
2. Interest on unfunded past service costs.
3. A provision for vested benefits (if necessary).

Normal cost is given as $150,000. Interest on unfunded past service cost is $30,000 (6% x 500,000). Vested benefits are not mentioned. Therefore, the minimum allowable expense is $180,000 which is computed below.

Normal cost	$150,000
Int. on unfunded PSC (6% x $500,000)	30,000
Provision for vested benefits	—
Minimum	$180,000

16. (584,P1,18) (a) The requirement is the amount of deferred pension cost at 12/31/83. Normal cost generally has no effect on deferred pension cost or liability because, as in this problem, it is funded and expensed in the same year. However, past service cost may give rise to deferred pension cost or liability if the amount amortized does not equal the amount funded. In this case, funding ($59,600) exceeds amortization ($46,700) by $12,900, which is the amount debited to deferred pension cost. The journal entry, excluding normal cost, is as follows:

Pension expense	46,700	
Deferred pension cost	12,900	
Cash		59,600

PENSIONS

Answer Outline

Problem 1 Definitions

a1. Normal cost is pension cost attributable to specific years subsequent to the inception of a pension plan
- I.e., actuarially determined cost of an additional year of employee service
- To be accrued annually

a2. Past service cost represents cost attributable to employee service prior to the inception of the pension plan
- Incurred at the adoption of a plan
- Not set up as a liability unless the benefits are vested
- Expensed over future years to income
  - Minimum is assumed interest on unfunded amounts
  - Maximum is 10% amortization per year (straight-line)
  - Independent of funding

a3. Prior service cost is attributable to years prior to a date when the plan is actuarially evaluated
- I.e., similar in nature to past service costs
  - And by definition includes past service costs
- Typically due to a retroactive amendment
- Expensed as are past costs (see a2. above)

a4. Pension "interest" refers to the actual or anticipated return on amounts funded or amounts expected to be funded
- To be obtained on pension fund investment portfolio
  - Includes interest, dividends, gains, losses, etc.
  - Accounted for per the accrual basis
- Accrue interest on unfunded prior service costs annually

b1. Arguments in favor of accruing past service costs as funded
- Past service cost may never be funded except as to interest
  - I.e., may be indefinitely deferred
- Past service cost is an intangible not diminishing value
- Actuarial assumptions do not apply to individuals
- Accrual may create misconception concerning pension accounting
  - And may result in a drop in expense when totally amortized
    - And does not extinguish the liability for nonaccrued and nonfunded past service cost
    - Pension costs are expensed without regard to any particular period of time (and employee benefit)
    - Other employment costs are discretionary, e.g., bonuses

b2. Arguments for accruing past service cost irrespective of funding
- Past service cost is an employment cost and should be expensed over a reasonable period
- Funding interest only is subjective and if underfunded may increase past service costs
- While actuarial assumptions are invalid for individuals, they do apply to groups of people
- The matching concept is a pervasive argument
- Pension liabilities do not require immediate payment and thus should be done on the accrual basis
- Conservatism dictates expensing over a reasonable period rather than deferral

Unofficial Answer

Problem 1 Definitions

Part a.

1. Normal cost. Normal cost represents the annual cost assigned, under the actuarial cost method in use, to years subsequent to the inception of a pension plan or to a particular valuation date. Depending on the actuarial method adopted, this cost may represent (1) the present value of an annuity, to be paid at a future date, in an amount equal to the benefits earned by the employee(s) during the year (unit credit) or (2) the incremental cost of an annuity in a projected amount representing the total benefits expected to be paid to an employee or group of employees at a future date (entry age normal). Generally accepted accounting principles require that normal cost be accrued annually.

2. Past service cost. Past service cost represents pension cost assigned to years prior to the inception of a pension plan. This cost arises when a company chooses to recognize (at the date of the adoption of a formal pension plan) the past service of employees as a credit towards their eventual retirement.

Generally accepted accounting principles provide some latitude in the accrual of past service cost. At minimum, the interest presumed to be earned on the unfunded past service cost must be accrued. The minimum accrual reflects the theory held by some actuaries that, because of the nature of a large pool of employees covered by a pension plan, it is highly probable that the actual amounts representing past service cost need never be funded in order to pay benefits as employees retire. Under this theory it is only necessary to accrue the assumed interest earned to avoid increasing the total amount attendant to past service cost.

Presently the maximum accrual of past service cost is 10 percent per year (straight-line basis) until fully accrued. The maximum accrual was determined to prevent arbitrary and excessive write-offs of past service cost and to recognize that the past service cost has a finite life with respect to the benefits provided to the company by their incurrence. It must be stressed, however, that the accrual of past service cost is to be accomplished in the current and future periods (if done at all) and not as some type of prior-period adjusting. The accrual of past service cost is usually independent (with the exception of interest accrual for unfunded amounts) of the actual funding of the cost.

3. Prior service cost. Prior service cost represents pension cost assigned, under the actuarial cost method in use, to years prior to the date of a particular actuarial valuation. Past service cost (cost that represents the amount of benefits earned by existing employees prior to the adoption of a specific pension plan) is classified as prior service cost, and costs attributable to prior service resulting from the amendment of an existing pension plan are also classified as prior service cost.

Prior service cost resulting from amendment of an existing pension plan is accounted for in the same manner as past service cost. At a minimum, the interest presumed earned on the amount of unfunded prior service cost must be accrued on an annual basis, and the maximum accrual (amortization) of prior service cost is 10 percent per year (straight-line basis). As with past service cost, prior service cost is to be accrued (if done at all) in the current and future periods and not as some type of prior-period adjustment. The accrual of prior service cost is completely independent (with the exception of interest accrual for unfunded amounts) of the actual funding of the cost.

4. Interest. In actuarial terminology, the term interest connotes the return earned or assumed to be earned on funds invested or to be invested to provide for future pension benefits. In calling the return "interest," it is recognized that, in addition to interest on debt securities, the earnings of a pension fund may include dividends on equity securities, rentals on real estate, and gains or (as offsets) losses on fund investments.

Interest earned (or assumed to be earned on unfunded prior cost) is recognized on the accrual basis.

Part b.

1. Proponents of accruing past service cost only to the extent funded list the following arguments for doing so:

- Many employers believe that past service cost will never be funded except with regard to interest. If this is true it would be improper to make accounting provision for amounts that will never be paid.
- In granting past service credits under a pension plan, an employer obtains diverse advantages of indefinite duration. Past service cost is thus in the nature of an intangible that does not diminish in value and need not be amortized (accrued).
- To require an annual provision for past service cost (in excess of payments) is to espouse the erroneous concept that pension accounting can be based on particular people at a particular time. Actuarial assumptions are not valid for individuals.
- The credit balance from accrued but not funded past service cost, if a liability, is a curious one, since it is not payable to anyone in particular.
- If the objective of accruing past service cost over a period of years is to provide a level charge to earnings, it must be considered that a sharp drop in annual pension expense may occur when the accrual (amortization) of past service cost has been completed.
- Accruing pension cost in excess of amounts funded does not effectively extinguish the liability for pensions in that the unfunded portion remains at risk as though no accrual had been made.
- Pension cost is a loading on employment cost, but without regard to the way employee benefits are measured and without regard to any particular period of time, either before or after the adoption of a pension plan. The key requirement is that the annual pension charge be a reasonable measurement of the annual amount required to balance the benefits to be paid in the future. For a relatively mature employee group, the amount of such an annuity would be approximately the same as an annual contribution of normal cost plus interest on past service cost for present employees.
- Many companies, in successful years, pay discretionary additional compensation (bonuses). Other companies have deferred profit-sharing arrangements. The cost of both bonuses and profit-sharing plans varies from year to year. Consequently, employers should have flexibility in deciding when (if at all) to charge past service cost to expense.

2. Proponents of the accrual of past service cost whether or not funded cite the following arguments in favor of their position:

- Past service cost is a cost of providing pensions for the employees initially covered and so should be charged to expense over a reasonable period following the inception of a plan.
- Funding interest alone on past service cost is subjective regarding the rate of interest the funds will earn. In fact, if the interest rate factor is too low, past service costs may grow because too little interest is accrued (funded) during a period.
- Even though actuarial assumptions are invalid for individuals, the facts concerning individuals are the raw materials for making the pension cost calculation. Since the purpose of pension cost is to estimate the cost of providing pensions for a specific groups of individuals, the entire cost (including past service costs) must be considered based on the individuals that compose the group.
- The matching concept is a pervasive argument in accounting for past service cost. Matching expenses and revenues for a given period of time is essentially independent of funding the expenses. Further, a desire for levelness in charges to expense is not an adequate reason for failing to record an element of cost.
- The commitment to pay pensions to employees is long term and is not motivated by the immediate availability of earnings and cash as may be the case for bonuses and profit sharing. As such, the cost of the pension plan should be recorded in accordance with the matching and accrual concept without direct regard to earnings and availability of cash.
- The accounting concept of conservatism would appear to require that these costs, when their existence is known, be charged to earnings in a manner that does not defer a charge against earnings to a future period when a cause-and-effect relationship cannot be clearly established. If this concept were not adhered to, the effect would be to overstate earnings in the current period and understate earnings in future periods.

Solution Guide

Problem 2 Pension Calculations

1. The first requirement of part b. is to prepare schedules computing the amounts relating to Foster's pension plan which should be reported on its income statement and balance sheet for 1980 and 1981. The "solutions approach" is to first study the requirements; second, quickly review mentally the basic concepts of accounting for pension costs; third, read through the information given; and fourth, make the necessary computations and prepare the schedules.

1.1 The first step is to calculate the amount of pension expense for 1980. The normal pension cost for 1980 is $60,000. The amount of past service cost to be included as pension expense for 1980 is $29,685, the annual amortization of past service cost. The total of these two items, $89,685 ($60,000 + $29,685), is the amount of pension expense for 1980.

1.2 Next, determine the amount relating to the pension plan which would appear on the balance sheet for 1980. Because the past service cost is being funded over more years than it is being amortized, Foster has an excess of pension expense over the amount funded. This excess must be reported on Foster's balance sheet as a liability. The amount of this liability is the difference between the total amount expensed and the total amount funded. At 12/31/80, this difference is $3,530 ($89,685 – $86,155).

1.3 Now compute the pension expense for 1981. As in 1980, this will include the normal pension cost ($65,000 in 1981) and the annual amortization of past service cost ($29,685). Additionally, pension expense must be increased by 6% interest on the 1/1/81 balance in the liability account ($3,530). This amount was not available in the pension fund during the year to earn interest. The amount of interest lost is $211.80 ($3,530 x 6%). Thus, the total amount of pension expense for 1981 is $94,896.80 ($65,000 + $29,685 + $211.80).

1.4 The last requirement of part one is to compute the pension amount which should appear on the balance sheet for 1981. As in 1980, this is a liability since the total amounts expensed are greater than the amounts funded. To compute the increase in pension liability for 1981, take the difference between the amounts expensed and funded in 1981. This increase is $3,741.80 ($94,896.80 – $91,155). The total pension liability at 12/31/81 would then be $7,271.80, which is the balance in the account at the beginning of 1981 ($3,530) plus the increase in 1981 ($3,741.80).

2. Part b. 2 requires the computation of the minimum and maximum pension cost limits allowable under generally accepted accounting principles for 1980.

2.1 Recall that per APB 8, the minimum pension cost limit includes:

- normal cost,
- interest on unfunded amounts, and
- a provision for vested benefits.

2.2 Normal cost for 1980 is $60,000.

2.3 Since 1980 is the first year of the plan, the entire past service cost ($300,000) was unfunded during the year. The interest on this amount is $18,000 ($300,000 x 6%).

2.4 There were no vested benefits at the end of 1980; the provision for vested benefits can thus be ignored in this problem.

2.5 Therefore, the minimum pension cost limit for 1980 would be:

Normal Cost	$60,000
Interest on unfunded amount	18,000
Minimum pension cost limit	$78,000

2.6 Recall that per APB 8, the maximum pension cost limit includes:

- normal cost,
- 10% of past service costs,
- 10% of prior service costs, and
- interest equivalents on the difference between the amounts expensed and funded in prior years.

2.7 Normal cost is $60,000.

2.8 Past service cost is $300,000. 10% of $300,000 is $30,000.

2.9 There is no prior service cost; thus, this item can be ignored in this problem. Furthermore, since this is the first year of the plan, there is no difference between the amounts expensed and funded in prior years. Thus, the calculation of interest equivalents can also be ignored.

3. The maximum pension cost limit for 1980 is:

Normal cost	$60,000
10% of past service cost	30,000
Maximum pension cost limit	$90,000

3.1 Since the pension expense of $89,685 computed for 1980 in 4.1 above falls between $78,000 (minimum) and $90,000 (maximum) it is an acceptable amount to record.

Unofficial Answer
(Author Modified)

Problem 2 Pension Calculations

Part b.

1.

Foster Corporation
Pension Expense
For the years ended December 31, 1980 and 1981

	1980		*1981*	
Normal cost		$60,000		$65,000
Past service cost:				
16-year amortization	$29,685		$29,685	
Interest on 1/1 balance in pension liability account:				
1980:	–	29,685		
1981: ($29,685 – $26,155) x 6%			212	29,897
Pension expense		$89,685		$94,897

Foster Corporation
Pension liability
December 31, 1980 and 1981

	1980		*1981*	
Pension expense (per preceeding schedule)		$89,685		$94,897
Amount funded:				
Normal cost	($60,000)		($65,000)	
Past service cost (20-year amortization)	(26,155)	(86,155)	(26,155)	(91,155)
Increase in pension liability		3,530		3,742
Previous balance		–		3,530
Pension liability		$ 3,530		$ 7,272

2.

Foster Corporation
Pension Expense: Minimum Cost Limit
For the Year Ended December 31, 1980

Normal cost	$60,000
Interest on unfunded amounts ($300,000 x 6%)	18,000
Provision for vested benefits	–
Minimum pension cost	$78,000

Foster Corporation
Pension Expense: Maximum Cost Limit
For the Year Ended December 31, 1980

Normal cost	$60,000
10% of past service costs ($300,000 x 10%)	30,000
10% of prior service costs	– 0 –
Interest equivalent	– 0 –
Maximum pension cost	$90,000

LEASES

Multiple Choice Questions (1 - 33)

1. Arrow Company purchased a machine on January 1 1979, for $1,440,000 for the purpose of leasing it. The machine is expected to have an eight-year life from date of purchase, no residual value, and be depreciated on the straight-line basis. On February 1, 1979, the machine was leased to Baxter Company for a three-year period ending January 31, 1982, at a monthly rental of $30,000. Additionally, Baxter paid $72,000 to Arrow on February 1, 1979, as a lease bonus. What is the amount of income before income taxes that Arrow should report on this leased asset for the year ended December 31, 1979?

   a. $172,000
   b. $187,000
   c. $222,000
   d. $237,000

Items 2 and 3 are based on the following information:

The Morn Company leased equipment to the Lizard Company on May 1, 1978. At that time the collectibility of the minimum lease payments was not reasonably predictable. The lease expires on May 1, 1980. Lizard could have bought the equipment from Morn for $900,000 instead of leasing it. Morn's accounting records showed a book value for the equipment on May 1, 1978, of $800,000. Morn's depreciation on the equipment in 1978 was $200,000. During 1978 Lizard paid $240,000 in rentals to Morn. Morn incurred maintenance and other related costs under the terms of the lease of $18,000 in 1978. After the lease with Lizard expires, Morn will lease the equipment to the Cold Company for another two years.

2. The income before income taxes derived by Morn from this lease for the year ended December 31, 1978, should be

   a. $ 22,000
   b. $100,000
   c. $122,000
   d. $240,000

3. Ignoring income taxes, the amount of expense incurred by Lizard from this lease for the year ended December 31, 1978, should be

   a. $ 22,000
   b. $200,000
   c. $218,000
   d. $240,000

4. The Standard Company leased a piece of equipment to the Piping Company on July 1, 1977, for a one-year period expiring June 30, 1978, for $90,000 a month. On July 1, 1978, Standard leased this piece of equipment to the Tacking Company for a three-year period expiring June 30, 1981, for $100,000 a month. The original cost of the piece of equipment was $6,000,000. The piece of equipment which has been continually on lease since July 1, 1973, is being depreciated on a straight-line basis over an eight-year period with no salvage value. Assuming that both the lease to Piping and the lease to Tacking are appropriately recorded as operating leases for accounting purposes, what is the amount of income (expense) before income taxes that each would record as a result of the above facts for the year ended December 31, 1978?

	Standard	*Piping*	*Tacking*
a.	$ 390,000	($540,000)	($600,000)
b.	$ 390,000	($540,000)	($975,000)
c.	$1,140,000	($165,000)	($225,000)
d.	$1,140,000	($915,000)	($600,000)

5. On December 31, 1981, Paulison Corporation signed an operating lease for a warehouse with Outwater Company for ten years, at $12,000 per year. Upon execution of the lease, Outwater paid Paulison $24,000, covering rent for the first two years. Paulison closed its books on December 31, and correctly reported $24,000 as gross rental income on its 1981 federal income tax return. How much should be shown in Paulison's 1981 income statement as gross rental income?

   a. $0
   b. $ 1,000
   c. $12,000
   d. $24,000

6. Howard Company sublet a portion of its warehouse for five years at an annual rental of $18,000, beginning on May 1, 1980. The tenant paid one year's rent in advance, which Howard recorded as a credit to unearned rental income. Howard reports on a calendar-year basis. The adjustment on December 31, 1980, should be

		Dr.	*Cr.*
a.	No Entry		
b.	Unearned rental income	$ 6,000	
	Rental income		$ 6,000
c.	Rental income	$ 6,000	
	Unearned rental income		$ 6,000
d.	Unearned rental income	$12,000	
	Rental income		$12,000

7. Rent received in advance by the lessor for an operating lease should be recognized as revenue

a. When received.
b. At the lease's inception.
c. In the period specified by the lease.
d. At the lease's expiration.

8. When equipment held under an operating lease is subleased by the original lessee, the original lessee would account for the sublease as a (an)

a. Operating lease.
b. Sales-type lease.
c. Direct financing lease.
d. Capital lease.

Items 9 and 10 are based on the following information:

Fox Company, a dealer in machinery and equipment, leased equipment to Tiger, Inc., on July 1, 1979. The lease is appropriately accounted for as a sale by Fox and as a purchase by Tiger. The lease is for a 10-year period (the useful life of the asset) expiring June 30, 1989. The first of 10 equal annual payments of $500,000 was made on July 1, 1979. Fox had purchased the equipment for $2,675,000 on January 1, 1979, and established a list selling price of $3,375,000 on the equipment. Assume that the present value at July 1, 1979, of the rent payments over the lease term discounted at 12% (the appropriate interest rate) was $3,165,000.

9. What is the amount of profit on the sale and the amount of interest income that Fox should record for the year ended December 31, 1979?

a. $0 and $159,900.
b. $490,000 and $159,900.
c. $490,000 and $189,900.
d. $700,000 and $189,900.

10. Assuming that Tiger uses straight-line depreciation, what is the amount of depreciation and interest expense that Tiger should record for the year ended December 31, 1979?

a. $158,250 and $159,900.
b. $158,250 and $189,900.
c. $168,750 and $159,900.
d. $168,750 and $189,900.

11. In a lease that is recorded as a sales-type lease by the lessor, the difference between the gross investment in the lease and the sum of the present values of the components of the gross investment should be recognized as income

a. In full at the lease's expiration.
b. In full at the lease's inception.
c. Over the period of the lease using the interest method of amortization.
d. Over the period of the lease using the straight-line method of amortization.

12. The excess of the fair value of leased property at the inception of the lease over its cost or carrying amount should be classified by the lessor as

a. Unearned income from a sales-type lease.
b. Unearned income from a direct-financing lease.
c. Manufacturer's or dealer's profit from a sales-type lease.
d. Manufacturer's or dealer's profit from a direct-financing lease.

13. On December 31, 1982, Jackson Company leased a new machine from Nash Corporation. The following information relates to the lease transaction:

- The machine has an estimated useful life of seven years which coincides with the lease term.
- Lease rentals consist of seven equal annual payments of $100,000, the first of which was paid on December 31, 1982.
- Nash's implicit interest rate is 12%, which is known by Jackson.
- Jackson's incremental borrowing rate is 14% at December 31, 1982.
- Present value of an annuity of $1 in advance for seven periods at 12% is 5.11.
- Present value of an annuity of $1 in advance for seven periods at 14% is 4.89.

At the inception of the lease, Jackson should record a capitalized lease liability of

a. $389,000
b. $489,000
c. $500,000
d. $511,000

14. On January 4, 1982, Hadley Company signed a 10-year nonrenewable lease for a building to be used in its manufacturing operations. During January 1982 Hadley incurred the following costs:

- $64,000 for general improvements to the leased premises with an estimated useful life of eight years.
- $32,000 for a movable assembly line equipment installation with an estimated useful life of eight years.

A full year's amortization is taken for the calendar year 1982. What amount should Hadley record as amortization of leasehold improvements for 1982?

a. $ 6,400
b. $ 8,000
c. $ 9,600
d. $12,000

15. Star Company leased a new machine from Fox Company on December 31, 1981, under a lease with the following pertinent information:

Lease term	10 years
Annual rental payable at the beginning of each year	$200,000
Useful life of the machine	15 years
Implicit interest rate	10%
Present value of an annuity of $1 in advance for 10 periods at 10%	6.76
Present value of $1 for 10 periods at 10%	0.39

Star has the option to purchase the machine on December 31, 1991, by paying $250,000, which is significantly less than the $500,000 expected fair market value of the machine on the option exercise date. Assume that, at the inception of the lease, the exercise of the option appears to be reasonably assured. At the inception of the lease, Star should record a capitalized lease liability of

a. $1,254,500
b. $1,352,000
c. $1,449,500
d. $1,547,000

16. Harris, Inc., leased equipment under a capital lease for a period of seven years, contracting to pay $100,000 rent in advance at the start of the lease term on December 31, 1980, and $100,000 annually on December 31 of each of the next six years. The present value at December 31, 1980, of the seven rent payments over the lease term discounted at 10% (the implicit interest rate) was $535,000. Harris amortizes its liability under capital lease using the effective interest method. In its December 31, 1981, balance sheet, Harris should report a liability under capital lease of

a. $378,500
b. $391,500
c. $437,350
d. $500,000

17. An office equipment representative has a machine for sale or lease. If you buy the machine, the cost is $7,596. If you lease the machine, you will have to sign a noncancellable lease and make 5 payments of $2,000 each. The first payment will be paid on the first day of the lease. At the time of the last payment you will receive title to the machine. The present value of an ordinary annuity of $1 is as follows:

Number of periods	*Present value 10%*	*12%*	*16%*
1	0.909	0.893	0.862
2	1.736	1.690	1.605
3	2.487	2.402	2.246
4	3.170	3.037	2.798
5	3.791	3.605	3.274

The interest rate implicit in this lease is approximately

a. 10%.
b. 12%.
c. Between 10% and 12%.
d. 16%.

Items 18 and 19 are based on the following information:

On January 2, 1982, Doe Company leased a new crane from Leasement Corp. under the following terms:

- Noncancellable for eight years
- Annual lease payments of $10,000 beginning Jaunary 2, 1982, through January 2, 1989
- Nonrenewable

Crane to be returned to Leasement on January 2, 1990

Doe properly recorded the crane as a "Leased asset—crane" in the amount of $52,880, based on a 14% interest rate implicit in the lease. Leasement paid $56,000 for the crane on December 31, 1981. The crane has an estimated useful life of ten years, with no salvage value. Both Doe and Leasement use the straight-line method of depreciation.

18. How much depreciation expense should Doe record in 1982 for "Leased asset—crane"?

a. $0
b. $ 6,610
c. $ 7,000
d. $10,000

19. How much interest income should Leasement recognize in 1982?

a. $10,000
b. $ 7,403
c. $ 6,003
d. $0

20. On January 2, 1980, Lafayette Machine Shops, Inc., signed a ten-year noncancellable lease for a heavy duty drill press, stipulating annual payments of $15,000 starting at the end of the first year, with title passing to Lafayette at the expiration of the lease.

Lafayette treated this transaction as a capital lease. The drill press has an estimated useful life of 15 years, with no salvage value. Lafayette uses straight-line depreciation for all of its fixed assets. Aggregate lease payments were determined to have a present value of $92,170, based on implicit interest of 10%. For 1980, Lafayette should record

	Interest expense	*Depreciation expense*
a.	$0	$0
b.	$7,717	$6,145
c.	$9,217	$6,145
d.	$9,217	$9,217

21. For a capital lease, an amount equal to the present value at the beginning of the lease term of minimum lease payments during the lease term, excluding that portion of the payments representing executory costs such as insurance, maintenance, and property taxes to be paid by the lessor, together with any profit thereon, should be recorded by the lessee as a (an)
    a. Expense.
    b. Liability but **not** an asset.
    c. Asset but **not** a liability.
    d. Asset and a liability.

22. For a six-year capital lease, the portion of the minimum lease payment in the third year applicable to the reduction of the obligation should be
    a. Less than in the second year.
    b. More than in the second year.
    c. The same as in the fourth year.
    d. More than in the fourth year.

23. What is the cost basis of an asset acquired by a lease which is in substance an installment purchase?
    a. The net realizable value of the asset determined at the date of the lease agreement plus the sum of the future minimum lease payments under the lease.
    b. The sum of the future minimum lease payments under the lease.
    c. The present value of the amount of future minimum lease payments under the lease (exclusive of executory costs and any profit thereon) discounted at an appropriate rate.
    d. The present value of the market price of the asset discounted at an appropriate rate as an amount to be received at the end of the lease.

24. On January 1, 1980, Cardow Corporation sold a machine to Simpson Corporation, and simultaneously leased it back for three years. Pertinent data are:

Estimated remaining useful life at December 31, 1979	10 years
Sales price	$120,000
Carrying value at December 31, 1979	$ 20,000
Monthly rental under leaseback	$ 1,266
Interest rate implicit in lease	12%
Present value of lease rentals ($1,266 for 36 months @ 12%)	$ 38,116

How much profit should Cardow recognize on January 1, 1980, on the sale of the machine?
    a. $0
    b. $ 33,333
    c. $ 61,884
    d. $100,000

25. On June 30, 1977, Gulch Corporation sold equipment to an unaffiliated company for $550,000. The equipment had a book value of $500,000 and a remaining useful life of 10 years. That same day, Gulch leased back the equipment at $1,500 per month for 5 years with no option to renew the lease or repurchase the equipment. Gulch's equipment rent expense for this equipment for the year ended December 31, 1977, should be
    a. $ 4,000
    b. $ 5,000
    c. $ 9,000
    d. $11,000

May 1984 Questions

26. On January 2, 1983, Evans Company signed an eight-year lease for office space. Evans has the option to renew the lease for an additional four-year period on or before January 2, 1990. During January 1983 Evans incurred the following costs:

- $120,000 for general improvements to the leased premises with an estimated useful life of ten years.
- $160,000 for office furniture and equipment with an estimated useful life of ten years.

At December 31, 1983, Evans' intentions as to exercise of the renewal option are uncertain since they depend upon future office space requirements. Assuming that a full year's amortization of leasehold improvements is taken for calendar year 1983, Evans should record amortization expense of
    a. $10,000
    b. $12,000

c. $15,000
d. $28,000

27. Hines Company leased a new machine from Ashwood Company on December 31, 1982, under a lease with the following pertinent information:

Lease term	8 years
Annual rental payable at the beginning of each lease year	$ 50,000
Useful life of the machine	10 years
Present value of the 8 lease payments at 12/31/82	$258,000
Machine reverts to Ashwood at lease expiration date	

The machine has a fair value of $280,000 at the inception of the lease. Hines uses the straight-line method of depreciation. For the year ended December 31, 1983, how much depreciation (amortization) should Hines record for the capitalized leased machine?

a. $35,000
b. $32,250
c. $28,000
d. $25,800

28. On December 31, 1982, Kern Company leased a machine from Woods Company for a ten-year period expiring December 30, 1992. Equal annual payments under the lease are $50,000 and are due on December 31 of each year. The first payment was made on December 31, 1982, and the second payment was made on December 31, 1983. The present value at December 31, 1982, of the ten lease payments over the lease term discounted at 10% was $338,000. The lease is appropriately accounted for as a capital lease by Kern. In its December 31, 1983, balance sheet Kern should report the capitalized lease liability at

a. $243,000
b. $259,200
c. $266,800
d. $400,000

29. Hiller Company manufactures equipment which is sold or leased. On December 31, 1983, Hiller leased equipment to Drake Company for a five-year period expiring December 31, 1988, at which date ownership of the leased asset is transferred to Drake. Equal payments under the lease are $20,000 and are due on December 31 of each year. The first payment was made on December 31, 1983. Collectibility of the remaining lease payments is reasonably assured, and Hiller has no material cost uncertainties. The normal sales price of the equipment is $77,000 and Hiller's cost is $60,000. For the year ended December 31, 1983, how much income should Hiller recognize from the lease transaction?

a. $0
b. $17,000
c. $20,000
d. $23,000

30. On January 1, 1983, Kipling Company paid $12,000 to White Properties as a lease bonus to obtain a four-year nonrenewable lease on premises beginning on that date. Additionally, Kipling will pay $14,000 annual rent on each December 31 throughout the term of the lease. For the year ended December 31, 1983, Kipling should report rent expense at

a. $12,000
b. $14,000
c. $17,000
d. $26,000

31. A lease contains a bargain purchase option. In determining the lessee's capitalizable cost at the beginning of the lease term, the payment called for by the bargain purchase option would

a. Not be capitalized.
b. Be subtracted at its present value.
c. Be added at its exercise price.
d. Be added at its present value.

32. The lessee's net carrying value of an asset arising from the capitalization of a lease would be periodically reduced by the

a. Total minimum lease payment.
b. Portion of minimum lease payment allocable to interest.
c. Portion of minimum lease payment allocable to reduction of principal.
d. Amortization of the asset.

33. The present value of the minimum lease payments should be used by the lessee in the determination of a(an)

	Capital lease liability	*Operating lease liability*
a.	Yes	No
b.	Yes	Yes
c.	No	Yes
d.	No	No

Repeat Questions

(584,P2,33) Identical to item 1 above

(584,P2,39) Identical to item 20 above

LEASES

Problems

Problem 1 Description of Lease Accounting (580,T3)

(15 to 25 minutes)

Part a. Capital leases and operating leases are the two classifications of leases described in FASB pronouncements, from the standpoint of the **lessee.**

Required:

1. Describe how a capital lease would be accounted for by the lessee both at the inception of the lease and during the first year of the lease, assuming the lease transfers ownership of the property to the lessee by the end of the lease.
2. Describe how an operating lease would be accounted for by the lessee both at the inception of the lease and during the first year of the lease, assuming equal monthly payments are made by the lessee at the beginning of each month of the lease. Describe the change in accounting, if any, when rental payments are not made on a straight-line basis.

Do **not** discuss the criteria for distinguishing between capital leases and operating leases.

Part b. Sales-type leases and direct financing leases are two of the classifications of leases described in FASB pronouncements, from the standpoint of the **lessor.**

Required:

Compare and contrast a sales-type lease with a direct financing lease as follows:

1. Gross investment in the lease.
2. Amortization of unearned interest income.
3. Manufacturer's or dealer's profit.

Do **not** discuss the criteria for distinguishing between the leases described above and operating leases.

Problem 2 Lease Classification and Accounting (1183,T5)

(15 to 25 minutes)

On January 1, Borman Company, a lessee, entered into three noncancelable leases for brand new equipment, Lease J, Lease K, and Lease L. None of the three leases transfers ownership of the equipment to Borman at the end of the lease term. For each of the three leases, the present value at the beginning of the lease term of the minimum lease payments, excluding that portion of the payments representing executory costs such as insurance, maintenance, and taxes to be paid by the lessor, including any profit thereon, is 75% of the excess of the fair value of the equipment to the lessor at the inception of the lease over any related investment tax credit retained by the lessor and expected to be realized by the lessor.

The following information is peculiar to each lease:

- Lease J does not contain a bargain purchase option; the lease term is equal to 80% of the estimated economic life of the equipment.
- Lease K contains a bargain purchase option; the lease term is equal to 50% of the estimated economic life of the equipment.
- Lease L does not contain a bargain purchase option; the lease term is equal to 50% of the estimated economic life of the equipment.

Required:

a. How should Borman Company classify each of the three leases above, and why? Discuss the rationale for your answer.

b. What amount, if any, should Borman record as a liability at the inception of the lease for each of the three leases above?

c. Assuming that the minimum lease payments are made on a straight-line basis, how should Borman record each minimum lease payment for each of the three leases above?

Problem 3 Lessor and Lessee Accounting (581,P5)

(40 to 50 minutes)

Part a. On February 20, 1980, Riley, Inc., purchased a machine for $1,200,000 for the purpose of leasing it. The machine is expected to have a ten-year life, no residual value, and will be depreciated on the straight-line basis. The machine was leased to Sutter Company on March 1, 1980, for a four-year period at a monthly rental of $18,000. There is no provision for the renewal of the lease or purchase of the machine by the lessee at the expiration of the lease term. Riley paid $60,000 of commissions associated with negotiating the lease in February 1980.

Required:

1. What expense should Sutter record as a result of the above facts for the year ended December 31, 1980? Show supporting computations in good form.

2. What income or loss before income taxes should Riley record as a result of the above facts for the year ended December 31, 1980? Show supporting computations in good form.

Part b. Dumont Corporation, a lessor of office machines, purchased a new machine for $500,000 on December 31, 1979, which was delivered the same day (by prior arrangement) to Finley Company, the lessee.

The following information relating to the lease transaction is available:

- The leased asset has an estimated useful life of seven years which coincides with the lease term.
- At the end of the lease term, the machine will revert to Dumont, at which time it is expected to have a residual value of $60,000 (none of which is guaranteed by Finley).
- The 10% investment tax credit on the asset cost is retained by Dumont and is expected to be realized in its 1979 income tax return.
- Dumont's implict interest rate (on its net investment) is 12%, which is known by Finley.
- Finley's incremental borrowing rate is 14% at December 31, 1979.
- Lease rental consists of seven equal annual payments, the first of which was paid on December 31, 1979.
- The lease is appropriately accounted for as a direct financing lease by Dumont and as a capital lease by Finley. Both lessor and lessee are calendar-year corporations and depreciate all fixed assets on the straight-line basis.

Information on present value factors is as follows:

Present value of $1 for seven periods at 12%	0.452
Present value of $1 for seven periods at 14%	0.400
Present value of an annuity of $1 in advance for seven periods at 12%	5.111
Present value of an annuity of $1 in advance for seven periods at 14%	4.889

Required (round all amounts to the nearest dollar):

1. Compute the annual rental under the lease. Show all computations in good form.

2. Compute the amounts of the gross lease rentals receivable and the unearned interest revenue that Dumont should disclose at the inception of the lease on December 31, 1979. Show all computations in good form.

3. What expense should Finley record for the year ended December 31, 1980? Show supporting computations in good form.

Multiple Choice Answers

1. a	8. a	15. c	22. b	28. c
2. a	9. b	16. a	23. c	29. b
3. d	10. a	17. d	24. c	30. c
4. a	11. c	18. b	25. a	31. d
5. a	12. c	19. c	26. c	32. d
6. d	13. d	20. c	27. b	33. a
7. c	14. b	21. d		

Multiple Choice Answer Explanations

E.1.a. & b. Operating and Direct Financing Leases, Lessor and Lessee

1. (1180,P1,16) (a) The requirement is the amount of income Arrow should report on the leased asset for 1979. Income from the lease is the monthly rental plus a proportionate fraction of the lease bonus less any depreciation expense.

Rental income	= 11 months x $30,000 =	$330,000
Lease bonus income	= $72,000 x 11/36 =	$ 22,000
Depreciation expense	= $1,440,000 / 8 years =	($180,000)
Income from leased asset		$172,000

Note that the lease bonus is recognized as income proprotionately over the 36 month lease period. The leased asset is depreciated for a full year since it has an 8-year life from the *date of purchase* (January 1).

2. (1179,P1,14) (a) The requirement is the amount of 1978 income before taxes for a lessor. First, note that the lease shall be accounted for as an operating lease, because the collectibility of the minimum lease payments are not reasonably predictable (para 8 of SFAS 13). The lessor's income per the operating method is the $240,000 rental income less the 1978 depreciation of $200,000 and maintenance and related costs of $18,000, which results in a $22,000 income for 1978.

3. (1179,P1,15) (d) The requirement is the amount of lease expense for the lessee under an operating lease. The operating method is appropriate because none of the four criteria which would require Lizard to capitalize the lease are met. The lease expense to Lizard (lessee) is the lease payment of $240,000.

4. (579,P1,11) (a) The requirement is the income (expense) for a lessor and two lessees regarding a piece of equipment on lease during 1978. Since it is an operating lease, the lessor (Standard) will recognize a total of $1,140,000 rental income (6 months' rent at $90,000 and 6 months' rent at $100,000). The lessor's depreciation will be $750,000 ($6,000,000 asset costs ÷ 8 yr.). Note that the requirement is for income (not total revenue), which is $390,000 ($1,140,000 – $750,000).

The first lessee (Piping) will incur lease expense of $540,000 ($90,000 for 6 months). The second lessee (Tacking) will incur lease expense of $600,000 ($100,000 for 6 months).

5. (582,Q1,11) (a) The requirement is the amount of gross rental income to be recognized in 1981 on an operating lease signed on December 31, 1981. Per para 19 (b) of SFAS 13, income from operating leases should ordinarily be recognized on a straight-line basis even if the rental-payments vary from a straight-line basis. The entire $24,000 payment by the lessee is unearned at the end of 1981 because it relates to use of the warehouse for the next two years. Thus, no rental income should be recognized in 1981. Rather, the revenue should be deferred and allocated to the proper periods.

6. (581,Q2,38) (d) The requirement of this problem is to make the necessary adjusting entry on December 31 to record the appropriate rental income. The solutions approach is to determine how much of the annual rental payment is earned income and how much should be deferred to the next period. The amount earned this period is calculated by multiplying the annual payment by the number of months this year used up over the total 12 months which is $18,000 x 8/12 or $12,000. The adjusting entry is:

Unearned rental income	12,000	
Rental income		12,000

7. (583,T1,29) (c) The requirement is to determine when rent, received in advance by the lessor for an operating lease, should be recognized as revenue. Per the revenue recognition principle, under an operating lease rental revenue is to be recognized in each accounting period on a straight-line basis unless another systematic and rational basis is more representative of the decline in the asset's service potential. Answer (a) is incorrect because when the cash is received is irrelevant since revenue recognition is on the accrual basis. Answer (b) is incorrect because the earnings process is not complete at the lease's inception. Answer (d) is incorrect because rental revenue is earned daily by the lessor as the property is being leased; therefore, deferring revenue recognition until the lease's expiration would violate the revenue recognition principle.

8. (583,T1,34) (a) The requirement is the treatment of a sublease of equipment held under an operating lease by the original lessee. A sublease arises when the lease agreement between the two original parties remain in effect, and the leased property is released to a third party by the original lessee. Consequently, if the original lease is an operating lease, the original lessee shall account for the sublease as an operating lease (SFAS 13, para 39).

E.1.c. Sales-Type Lease, Lessor

9. (580,P1,10) (b) The requirement is to compute the gross profit and interest income of Fox. The situation is a sales-type lease for Fox and a capital lease for Tiger. Fox's gross profit is the difference between the present value of the lease payments (sales) and the cost of goods sold ($3,165,000 – $2,675,000 = $490,000 gross profit). Interest income for Fox is found by subtracting the first lease payment ($500,000) from the present value of the lease payments ($3,165,000). The difference is the outstanding balance for the first year ($2,665,000). Interest under the effective method is 12% (effective rate) x ½ year x $2,665,000 outstanding balance = $159,900 interest income in 1979.

10. (580,P1,11) (a) Tiger's interest expense is equal to the interest income recorded by Fox because Tiger capitalizes on an amount equal to the sales price. Straight-line depreciation is $3,165,000 ÷ 10 x ½ year = $158,250.

11. (1182,T1,10) (c) For a sales-type lease, the difference between the gross investment in the lease and the sum of the present values of the components of the gross investment is, by definition, unearned interest income. Per para 17 of SFAS 13, the unearned interest income is amortized to income over the lease term using the effective interest method. Other methods of amortization are allowed by SFAS 13 providing the results are not materially different from those obtained by applying the prescribed method. Because no information is given concerning such materiality, answer (c) is clearly the best answer.

12. (1182,T1,17) (c) Per SFAS 13, para 17, the excess of the fair value of leased property at the inception of the lease over the lessor's cost is defined as the manufacturer's or dealer's profit. Answer (a) is incorrect because the unearned income from a sales-type lease is defined as the difference between the gross investment in the lease and the sum of the present values of the components of the gross investment. Answer (b) is incorrect because the unearned income from a direct-financing lease is defined as the excess of the gross investment over the cost (also the PV of lease payments) of the leased property. Answer (d) is incorrect because a sales-type lease involves a manufacturer's or dealer's profit while a direct-financing lease does not.

E.1.a. & c. Operating and Capital Leases, Lessee

13. (1183,P2,33) (d) The requirement is the amount of capitalized lease liability to be recorded. This lease qualifies as a capital lease because the lease term is equal to the useful life (7 years) of the leased machine. In a capital lease, the lessee records as a liability the lower of (1) the present value (PV) of the minimum lease payments, and (2) the FMV of the leased asset. Since the FMV is not given, we must assume that the liability is to be recorded at the PV of the minimum lease payments. Also, no information is given concerning any residual value, bargain purchase option, etc. Therefore, the liability is recorded at present value of the $100,000 annuity in advance. Per SFAS 13, the rate implicit in the lease (12%) is to be used by the lessee to discount the minimum lease payments if that rate is known by the lessee and it is less than the lessee's incremental borrowing rate. Since both conditions are met, the 12% implicit rate is used. Thus, the liability is recorded at $511,000 ($100,000 x 5.11).

14. (583,P1,5) (b) The requirement is the amount of amortization of leasehold improvements to be recorded in 1982. General improvements to leased property are capitalized as leasehold improvements and amortized over their useful life on the remaining life of the lease, whichever is shorter. Therefore, the improvements are capitalized at $64,000 and amortized over their 8-year useful life ($64,000 ÷ 8 = $8,000). Since the assembly line equipment is movable, it should be recorded as equipment and depreciated over its useful life using Hadley's normal depreciation methods.

15. (1182,P1,1) (c) The requirement is the amount of capitalized lease liability Star should record at the inception of the lease. Per SFAS 13 (comprehensive restatement), the lessee records as a liability the lower of the present value of the minimum lease payments (excluding executory costs), or the fair market value of the leased asset. Minimum lease payments for the lessee include the minimum rental payments and the amount of any bargain purchase option if exercise of the option appears reasonably assured. Since the fair market value of the leased asset is not given, the leased asset and lease obligation are recorded

as the present value of the minimum lease payments, as computed below.

Present value of annual rental	
$200,000 x 6.76	$1,352,000
Present value of bargain purchase option	
$250,000 x .39	97,500
Present value of minimum lease payments	$1,449,500

16. (1182,P1,8) (a) The requirement is the amount Harris should report as a liability under capital lease at 12/31/81. The solutions approach is to set up a partial amortization table. The first payment (made on the day the lease is signed) contains no interest and is, therefore, entirely a reduction of principal. The second payment includes both interest (10% x $435,000) and principal ($100,000 – $43,500) elements.

Date	*Cash payment*	*10% interest*	*Reduction of principal*	*Lease liability*
12/31/80				$535,000
12/31/80	$100,000	–0–	$100,000	435,000
12/31/81	100,000	43,500	56,500	378,500

17. (1178,P2,39) (d) The requirement is the implicit rate of interest in the lease given that $7,596 is the cash price or present value. The lease payments are an annuity in advance (note the table is given for an ordinary annuity, or annuity in arrears) of $2,000 each. The solutions approach is to compute the present value at 10%, 12%, and 16% of the annuity. The time value of money factor for an ordinary annuity of 4 years is multiplied times $2,000 to obtain the present value of the payments for the beginning of the years 2 through 5. The present value of the $2,000 paid at the beginning of the year 1 is $2,000 which must be added to the present value of the annuity. As the table below indicates, the present value of the annuity in advance at 16% is $7,596.

	10%	*12%*	*16%*
TVMF			
(n = 4)	3.170	3.037	2.798
x $2,000	$6,340	$6,074	$5,596
+ $2,000	$8,340	$8,074	$7,596

18. (583,Q2,21) (b) The leasing agreement is classified as a capital lease because the lease term (8 years) is greater than 75% of the crane's economic life (10 years). Also, the present value of the minimum lease payments ($52,880) is greater than 90% of the fair value of the crane ($56,000). Since the lease agreement does not transfer ownership nor contain a bargain purchase option, Doe should depreciate the crane over the eight-year lease term, rather than the ten-year life of the crane. Therefore, depreciation expense to be recognized in 1982 is $6,610 ($52,880 ÷ 8 years).

19. (583,Q2,22) (c) The requirement is the amount of interest income to be recognized by the lessor in 1982. The present value of the minimum lease payments, based on the lessor's 14% implicit interest rate is the lessor's net investment in the capital lease. The effective interest method, applied to the lease's net investment, allocates each lease payment between a reduction of the lease receivable and interest income (SFAS 13, para 12). Note that the first lease payment takes place at the inception of the lease (i.e., the stream of receipts is an annuity due). Therefore, during 1982, interest is earned on $42,880 because the first lease payment of $10,000 is exclusively a reduction of the lease receivable. In 1982, the interest income recognized by the lessor is $6,003 [($52,880 – $10,000) 14%].

20. (1181,Q1,9) (c) The requirement is interest expense and depreciation expense related to a capital lease. Per SFAS 13, the amortization of the leased asset and discharge of the obligation are independent accounting processes. Since the lease agreement transfers ownership of the asset, it should be amortized over its economic useful life in accordance with lessees normal depreciation policy, SFAS 13, para 11a. The effective interest method is used to allocate each lease payment between a reduction of the lease obligation and interest expense. The discount rate (10% in this case) used to determine the present value of the minimum lease payments is used in applying the effective interest method to capital leases.

Depreciation = $92,170 ÷ 15 years = $6,145

Interest = $92,170 x 10% = $9,217

Journal entries resulting from this lease would be:

Depreciation expense –		
Capital leases	$6,145	
Accumulated depreciation –		
Capital leases		$ 6,145
Interest expense	$9,217	
Obligations under capital leases	5,783	
Cash		$15,000

21. (583,T1,16) (d) Per SFAS 13, para 10, the lessee should record a capital lease at an amount equal to the present value (at the beginning of the lease term) of the minimum lease payments during the lease term as both an asset and an obligation (liability). This

amount should exclude that portion of the payments representing executory costs. Therefore, answers (a), (b), and (c) are incorrect.

22. (583,T1,22) (b) The requirement is to determine how the amount of reduction in a lease obligation during the third year compares with other years. During the lease term, each minimum lease payment is allocated between a reduction in the lease obligation and interest expense. The reduction in the lease obligation is the difference between the minimum lease payment and the amount of interest expense determined by using the effective interest method. Under this method, the effective interest rate is applied to the obligation's outstanding balance to obtain interest expense, which would decrease each period due to the decrease in the carrying value of the lease obligation. Consequently, since the minimum lease payments are constant and interest expense decreases each period, the difference between the two (the reduction in the lease obligation) would increase each period. During the third year, the reduction in the obligation would, therefore, be more than in the second year. Answers (c) and (d) are incorrect because the reduction in the obligation during the third year is less than in the fourth year.

23. (1177,T1,5) (c) Lessees record leased assets which are in substance an installment purchase by debiting the asset and crediting a liability for the present value of the future minimum lease payments (para 10 of SFAS 13). Also see para 5j for the definition of minimum lease payments. The other answers are incorrect because the asset and liability are simply recorded at the present value of all future payments that have to be made for the asset.

E.2.d. Sales — Leaseback

24. (1181,Q2,33) (c) The requirement is the profit to be recognized on the date of sale of a machine if the machine is to be leased back for a three-year period. SFAS 13, para 33, generally treats a sale-leaseback as a single financing transaction in which any profit or loss on the sale is deferred and amortized by the seller. SFAS 28 amends this general rule in three specific situations. Per the guidelines established in SFAS 28, the seller in this problem is retaining more than a "minor" portion but less than "substantially all" of the use of the property through the leaseback and the profit on the sale exceeds the present value of the minimum lease payments under the operating lease. When this is the case, the difference between the total profit on the sale and present value of the lease payments should be recognized as profit at the date of sale.

Sales price of machine		$120,000
Less: carrying value at 12/31/79	–	20,000
Profit from sale		100,000
Less: present value of lease rentals	–	38,116
Profit recognized on 1/1/80		$ 61,884

"Minor" and "substantially all" are defined in the footnotes to SFAS 28. Essentially, "minor" means the present value of the lease payments is 10% or less of FMV of the sales-leaseback property and "substantially all" means that a leaseback of **the entire property sold** meets the criteria of SFAS 13 for classification as a capital lease.

The journal entry to record the sale-leaseback would be:

Cash	$120,000	
Machinery (carrying value)		$20,000
Unearned profit on sale-leaseback		38,116
Revenue (earned)		61,884

25. (578,Q1,14) (a) The requirement is six months' rent expense resulting from an equipment sale on 6/30/77 and leaseback. Para 33 of SFAS 13 requires that profit or loss on the sale of assets which are leased back be deferred and amortized in proportion to rental payments over the lease if it is an operating lease. Accordingly the $50,000 of gain on sale of the equipment must be amortized over the remaining lease life of five years. Thus, for the last six months of 1977, $5,000 of the gain will be recognized, reducing the lease expense from $9,000 to $4,000.

May 1984 Answers

26. (584,P1,13) (c) The requirement is the **amortization** expense on leasehold improvements for 1983. The $160,000 spent for office furniture and equipment is not considered a leasehold improvement; it would be a fixed asset and depreciated. The remaining $120,000 is charged to the leasehold improvements account and amortized. The amortization period is the shorter of (1) the lease term or (2) the useful life of the improvements. In this case, the lease term is eight years, and the useful life is ten years; therefore, the improvements are amortized over eight years. Amortization expense is $15,000 per year ($120,000 ÷ 8 years). Note the option to renew the lease for four years is not included in the lease term because the likelihood of renewal is uncertain.

27. (584,P1,14) (b) The requirement is the 1983 depreciation on a capitalized leased asset. Per SFAS 13, para 10, the lessee records the asset at the lower of (1) the present value of the minimum lease payments or (2) the fair market value of the leased asset. In this case, the present value ($258,000) is less than the fair market value ($280,000); therefore, $258,000 is capitalized. Since the machine reverts to the lessor at the end of the lease, the lessee should depreciate it over the lease term (8 years) even though it is less than the useful life (10 years). Depreciation expense is $32,250 ($258,000 ÷ 8 years).

28. (584,P1,24) (c) The requirement is the capitalized lease liability at 12/31/83. The initial liability at 12/31/82 was $338,000. On the same date, a payment of $50,000 reduced the principal portion of the liability to $288,000 ($338,000 – $50,000). On 12/31/83, another payment of $50,000 was made; this payment included both interest (10% x $228,000 = $28,800) and principal ($50,000 – $28,000 = $21,200). Therefore, the lease liability is reduced to $266,800 at 12/31/83 ($288,000 – $21,200).

29. (584,P2,27) (b) The requirement is the amount of income to be recognized by a lessor in 1983. The lease is a sales-type lease because title to the leased asset transfers, collectibility is reasonably assured, there are no material cost uncertainties, and a manufacturer's profit exists. Therefore, the lessor would recognize sales of $77,000 and cost of sales of $60,000, resulting in a profit of $17,000. There is no interest income in 1983 since the sale occurs on the last day of the year.

30. (584,P3,52) (c) The requirement is the amount to be recorded as 1983 rent expense on an operating lease. Per SFAS 13, para 15, when rental payments are **not** made on a straight-line basis, rental expense is nevertheless recognized on a straight-line basis unless another systematic and rational basis is more appropriate. The bonus paid to obtain the lease, considered a component of rental expense, would receive such treatment. Therefore, the 1983 rent expense is the 1983 rental ($14,000) plus a proportionate fraction of the lease bonus ($12,000 ÷ 4 years = $3,000 per year), or $17,000.

31. (584,T1,12) (d) The requirement is to determine whether or not a bargain purchase option should be capitalized as part of the minimum lease payments. Per SFAS 13, para 5j, minimum lease payments include the rental payments plus the amount of the bargain purchase option if it exists. Per para 10, the amount to be capitalized is the present value of the minimum lease payments. Therefore, the present value of the bargain purchase option would be added to the present value of the rental payments (assumed to be previously calculated) in determining the lessee's capitalizable cost [answer (d)].

32. (584,T1,13) (d) The requirement is to determine what will reduce the carrying value of an asset arising from the capitalization of a lease. The solutions approach is to prepare the journal entry for the lease payment

Capital lease obligation (principal)	XXX	
Interest expense	XXX	
Cash		XXX

and the journal entry for the lease amortization

Amortization of capital lease	XXX	
Leased asset		XXX

Only the amortization of the leased asset, in accordance with SFAS 13, para 11, results in a reduction of the carrying value of the asset. Therefore, answer (d) is correct.

33. (584,T1,18) (a) The requirement is to determine whether or not the present value of the minimum lease payments is used to determine the lease liability under an operating and/or a capital lease. Per SFAS 13, para 10, the present value of the minimum lease payments should be used to determine the liability under a capital lease. Under an operating lease, a liability arises when rent expense is recorded but has not been paid. Furthermore, it is recorded at the actual amount of cash to be paid, not its present value. Therefore, answer (a) is correct.

LEASES

Answer Outline

Problem 1 Description of Lease Accounting

a1. Accounting for lessee's capital lease which transfers title to leased property
 Inception of lease
  Record asset and obligation
 During first year
  Apply lease payments to reduction of principal and interest expense
 Depreciate leased asset using lessee's normal depreciation policy
  Use life of asset in this case because title will pass to lessee

a2. Accounting for lessee's operating lease
 Inception of lease
  No asset or liability recorded
 During first year
  Recognize rent expense on a straight-line basis
   Use other basis only if more representative of benefit receipt pattern (i.e., more rational)

b1. Sales-type leases versus direct financing leases
 For both gross investment in lease is
 Minimum lease payments + unguaranteed residual value
  Minimum lease payments include guaranteed residual value but exclude executory costs

b2. Amortization of unearned interest (lease) income for both utilizes the effective interest method
 Results in a constant rate of return per period
 Other methods of amortization acceptable if amounts obtained not materially different

b3. Manufacturer's or dealer's profit
 Sales-type
  Profit = sales price – carrying amount
 Direct financing
  No dealer's profit
   Only income is from interest

Unofficial Answer

Problem 1 Description of Lease Accounting

Part a.

1. A lessee would account for a capital lease as an asset and an obligation at the inception of the lease. Rental payments during the year would be allocated between a reduction in the obligation and interest expense. The asset would be amortized in a manner consistent with the lessee's normal depreciation policy for owned assets, except that in some circumstances, the period of amortization would be the lease term.

2. No asset or obligation would be recorded at the inception of the lease. Normally, rental on an operating lease would be charged to expense over the lease term as it becomes payable. If rental payments are not made on a straight-line basis, rental expense nevertheless would be recognized on a straight-line basis unless another systematic or rational basis is more representative of the time pattern in which use benefit is derived from the leased property, in which case that basis would be used.

Part b.

1. The gross investment in the lease is the same for both a sales-type lease and a direct-financing lease. The gross investment in the lease is the minimum lease payments (net of amounts, if any, included therein for executory costs such as maintenance, taxes, and insurance to be paid by the lessor, together with any profit thereon) plus the unguaranteed residual value accruing to the benefit of the lessor.

2. For both a sales-type lease and a direct-financing lease, the unearned interest income would be amortized to income over the lease term by use of the interest method to produce a constant periodic rate of return on the net investment in the lease. However, other methods of income recognition may be used if the results obtained are not materially different from the interest method.

3. In a sales-type lease, the excess of the sales price over the carrying amount of the leased equipment is considered manufacturer's or dealer's profit and would be included in income in the period when the lease transaction is recorded.

In a direct-financing lease, there is no manufacturer's or dealer's profit. The income on the lease transaction is composed solely of interest.

Answer Outline

Problem 2 Lease Classification and Accounting

a. Lease should be classified as capital when:
  Substantially all benefits and risks inherent to ownership are transferred
  Any of four criteria per SFAS 13 must be met
 Lease J
  Classify as capital lease
   Lease term of 80% of estimated economic life $\geq$ 75%
 Lease K
  Classify as capital lease
   Contains bargain purchase option
 Lease L
  Classify as operating lease
   Criteria for capital lease not met

b. Lease J
  At inception, lessee records liability equal to present value of minimum lease payments
   Exclude portion relating to executory costs to be paid by lessor, including any profit thereon
   Record liability at fair value, if lower
 Lease K
  Lessee records in same manner as Lease J, and additionally
   Includes payment for bargain purchase option in minimum lease payments
 Lease L
  Lessee records no liability at inception

c. Lease J
  Allocate each minimum lease payment between reduction of liability and interest expense using "interest method"
   Interest expense is constant percentage of remaining liability
 Lease K
  Allocate minimum lease payments in same manner as Lease J
 Lease L
  Charge minimum lease (rental) payments to rental expense when due

Unofficial Answer

Problem 2 Lease Classification and Accounting

a. A lease should be classified as a capital lease when it transfers substantially all of the benefits and risks inherent to the ownership of property by meeting any one of the four criteria established by FAS No. 13 for classifying a lease as a capital lease.

Lease J should be classified as a capital lease because the lease term is equal to 80% of the estimated economic life of the equipment, which exceeds the 75% or more criterion.

Lease K should be classified as a capital lease because the lease contains a bargain purchase option.

Lease L should be classified as an operating lease because it does not meet any of the four criteria for classifying a lease as a capital lease.

b. For Lease J, Borman Company should record as a liability at the inception of the lease an amount equal to the present value at the beginning of the lease term of minimum lease payments during the lease term, excluding that portion of the payments representing executory costs such as insurance, maintenance, and taxes to be paid by the lessor, including any profit thereon. However, if the amount so determined exceeds the fair value of the equipment at the inception of the lease, the amount recorded as a liability should be the fair value.

For Lease K, Borman Company should record as a liability at the inception of the lease an amount determined in the same manner as for Lease J plus the payment called for in the bargain purchase option should be included in the minimum lease payments.

For Lease L, Borman Company should not record a liability at the inception of the lease.

c. For Lease J, Borman Company should allocate each minimum lease payment between a reduction of the liability and interest expense so as to produce a constant periodic rate of interest on the remaining balance of the liability.

For Lease K, Borman Company should allocate each minimum lease payment in the same manner as for Lease J.

For Lease L, Borman Company should charge minimum lease (rental) payments to rental expense as they become payable.

Solution Guide

Problem 3 Lessor and Lessee Accounting

1. This problem consists of two unrelated parts. Part a. involves an operating lease; part b. deals with a lease classified as a direct financing lease by the lessor and as a capital lease by the lessee.

2. The first requirement of part a. is the amount of expense to be recorded by Sutter (lessee) for 1980.

2.1 This lease does not meet any of the four criteria listed in SFAS 13, so it is accounted for as an operating lease by both the lessee and the lessor.

2.2 For the lessee, rent expense accrues as the machine is used under an operating lease. The machine was used for 10 months (March through December) during 1980. At $18,000 per month, the total expense is $180,000.

3. The second requirement of part a. is the income or loss before income taxes to be recorded by Riley (lessor) during 1980.

3.1 Under an operating lease, the lessor records rental revenue as the machine is used by the lessee. Again, the machine was used for 10 months at $18,000/month, resulting in rental revenue of $180,000. The lessor must also depreciate the leased asset, resulting in depreciation expense of $100,000 for 1980 [($1,200,000 cost/10 years) x 10/12]. Note that the asset is not depreciated until the lease term begins. Per SFAS 13 initial direct costs of $60,000 must be deferred and allocated over the lease term in proportion to the recognition of rental revenue. Therefore, 10/48 of this cost, or $12,500, is expensed in 1980; the remaining $47,500 is deferred and recognized as expense over the remaining 38 months of the lease term.

4. The first requirement of part b. is to compute the annual rental under the lease.

4.1 The lease will provide Dumont (lessor) a return of 12% on its net investment. The solutions approach is to treat this as a time adjusted rate of return problem. Therefore, the present value of the future cash inflows (rentals), discounted at 12%, must equal the net cost of the machine.

4.2 Dumont's net cost (investment) in the machine is the purchase price of $500,000 less the $50,000 investment credit realized (10% of $500,000). This results in a net cost of $450,000.

4.3 The future cash inflows consist of seven equal annual lease rentals (amount unknown) and the unguaranteed residual value of the machine (a single inflow of $60,000 at the end of seven years).

4.4 Using the 12% present value factors given, the annual rental can be computed.

Net cost (see 4.2)	=	PV of rentals + PV of residual value
$450,000	=	(5.111)(rental) + (.452)($60,000)
$422,880	=	(5.111)(rental)
$ 82,739	=	rental

5. The second requirement of part b. is the amounts of gross lease rentals receivable and the unearned interest revenue that Dumont should disclose at the inception of the lease, 12/31/79.

5.1 The "amount to be disclosed as gross lease rentals receivable" is not clear in this case because the first lease payment is due on the same date as the inception of the lease. The best approach in this situation is to show the seven payments of $82,739 less the initial payment made 12/31/79.

5.2 The unearned interest revenue is the gross lease rentals receivable (7 x $82,739 = $579,173) plus the unguaranteed residual value ($60,000) less the net cost of the machine ($450,000).

6. The third requirement of part b. is the amount of expense Finley (lessee) should record for 1980 under the capital lease.

6.1 The lessee's costs under a capital lease will normally consist of depreciation, interest and executory costs (none in this problem).

6.2 The lessee records the leased asset at the present value of the gross (minimum) lease payments (5.111 x $82,739 = $422,880). Finley would record a full year's depreciation in 1980, which is $422,880 divided by 7 years, or $60,441.

6.3 The amount of interest to be recorded by Finley for 1980 is equal to the present value of the lease payments at 1/1/80 multiplied by 12%. The present value of lease payments at 12/31/79 was $422,880 **before** the 12/31/79 rental payment ($82,739). This payment is subtracted from $422,880 to leave $340,041 as the outstanding balance for 1980. This amount multiplied by 12% results in interest of $40,817. The amortization table below is a useful tool in solving these problems; it would serve as schedule 1 in the solution which follows.

Date	Rental payment	Interest expense	Reduction in lease oblig.	Balance of lease oblig.
12/31/79				422,880
12/31/79	82,739		82,739	340,041
12/31/80	82,739	40,817	*	*

*not needed

Unofficial Answer

Problem 3 Lessor and Lessee Accounting

Part a.

1.

Sutter Corporation
Rental Expense
For the Year Ended December 31, 1980

Monthly rental	$ 18,000
Lease period in 1980 (Mar. – Dec.)	x 10 months
	$180,000

2.

Riley, Inc.
Income or Loss from Lease before Taxes
For the Year Ended December 31, 1980

Rental revenue ($18,000 x 10 months)		$180,000
Less expenses:		
Depreciation	$100,000*	
Commission ($60,000 x 10/48)	12,500	– 112,500
Income from lease, before taxes		$ 67,500

*$1,200,000 cost ÷ 10 years = $120,000/year
$120,000 x 10/12 = $100,000

Part b.

1.

Dumont Corporation
Amount of Lease Rental
December 31, 1979

Cost of machine		$500,000
Less investment tax credit		50,000
Net cost of machine		$450,000
Less present value of	$60,000	
unguaranteed residual value	x .452	27,120
Present value of rentals		$422,880
PV factor, 7-year annuity in advance, 12%		÷ 5.111
Annual lease rental		$ 82,739

2.

Dumont Corporation
Gross Lease Rentals Receivable
and Unearned Interest Revenue
December 31, 1979

Gross (minimum) lease rentals receivable at inception of lease (7 x $82,739)		$579,173
Less: 12/31/79 rental received		82,739
Gross lease rentals receivable after receipt of first rental		$496,434
Gross lease rentals at inception of lease		$579,173
Add unguaranteed residual value		60,000
Gross investment in lease*		$639,173
Less net cost of machine		
Purchase price	$500,000	
less 10% investment credit	50,000	450,000
Unearned interest revenue, 12/31/79		$189,173

*This is the term used in SFAS 13 (para 17a & 18a) when the residual value is unguaranteed. Note, however, that the lessor treats an "unguaranteed" residual value in the same manner as a "guaranteed" residual value. In most cases, lessees do not need to consider "unguaranteed residual values" (in applying the 90% test and in booking the lease).

3.

Finley Company
Lease Expense
For the Year Ended December 31, 1979

Depreciation ($422,880 capitalized amount* ÷ 7 years)	$ 60,411
Interest expense (Schedule 1)	40,817
Total expense	$101,228

*Present value of 7 rental payments of $82,739 (b1. above)

Schedule 1

Interest Expense

PV of lease payments before 12/31/79 payment	$422,880
12/31/79 payment	– 82,739
PV of lease payments at 1/1/80	$340,141
Implicit interest rate	x 12%
1980 interest expense	$ 40,817

Multiple Choice Questions (1 - 42)

1. On January 1, 1982, Nutley Corporation had monetary assets of $2,000,000 and monetary liabilities of $1,000,000. During 1982 Nutley's monetary inflows and outflows were relatively constant and equal so that it ended the year with net monetary assets of $1,000,000. Assume that the Consumer Price Index was 200 on January 1, 1982, and 220 on December 31, 1982. In end-of-year constant dollars, what is Nutley's purchasing power gain or loss on net monetary items for 1982?

a. $0.
b. $ 50,000 gain.
c. $100,000 gain.
d. $100,000 loss.

2. Level, Inc., was formed on January 1, 1977, when common stock of $200,000 was issued for cash of $50,000 and land valued at $150,000. Level did not begin operations until 1978, and no transactions occurred in 1977 except the recording of the issuance of the common stock. If the consumer price index was 100 at December 31, 1976, and averaged 110 during 1977, what would the purchasing power gain or loss be for Level in 1977?

a. $0.
b. $5,000 loss.
c. $5,000 gain.
d. $15,000 gain.

3. Index Co. was formed on January 1, 1977. Selected balances from the historical-dollar balance sheet at December 31, 1977, were as follows:

Cash	$60,000
Marketable securities, stocks (purchased January 1, 1977)	70,000
Marketable securities, bonds, (purchased January 1, 1977 and held for price speculation)	80,000
Long-term receivables	90,000

If the consumer price index was 100 at December 31, 1976, and averaged 110 during 1977, these selected accounts should be shown in a comprehensive historical cost/constant dollar balance sheet at December 31, 1977, at

	Cash	*Marketable securities, stocks*	*Marketable securities, bonds*	*Long-term receivables*
a.	$60,000	$70,000	$80,000	$90,000
b.	$60,000	$70,000	$80,000	$99,000
c.	$60,000	$77,000	$88,000	$90,000
d.	$60,000	$77,000	$88,000	$99,000

4. Loy Corp. purchased a machine in 1980 when the average Consumer Price Index (CPI) was 180. The average CPI was 190 for 1981, and 200 for 1982. Loy prepares supplementary constant dollar statements (adjusted for changing prices). Depreciation on this machine is $200,000 a year. In Loy's supplementary constant dollar statement for 1982, the amount of depreciation expense should be stated as

a. $180,000
b. $190,000
c. $210,526
d. $222,222

5. The following schedule lists the average consumer price index (all urban consumers) of the indicated year:

1978	100
1979	125
1980	150

Carl Corporation's plant and equipment at December 31, 1980, are as follows:

Date acquired	*Percent depreciated*	*Historical cost*
1978	30	$30,000
1979	20	20,000
1980	10	10,000
		$60,000

Depreciation is calculated at 10% per annum, straight-line. A full year's depreciation is charged in the year of acquisition. There were no disposals in 1980.

What amount of depreciation expense would be included in the income statement adjusted for general inflation (historical cost/constant dollar accounting)?

a. $6,000
b. $7,200
c. $7,900
d. $9,000

Items 6 and 7 are based on the following information:

The following schedule lists the following consumer price indices:

12/31/71	100
12/31/72	110
12/31/73	115
12/31/74	120
12/31/75	140
Average 1975	130

6. In December 1974, the Meetu Corporation purchased land for $300,000. The land was held until December 1975, when it was sold for $400,000. If a

comprehensive historical cost/constant dollar income statement is prepared using end of year 1975 dollars, how much gain or loss would be reported from this sale?

a. $20,000 loss.
b. $20,000 general price-level loss.
c. $50,000 gain.
d. $100,000 gain.

7. On January 1, 1972, the Silver Company purchased equipment for $300,000. The equipment was being depreciated over an estimated life of 10 years on the straight-line method, with no estimated salvage value. On December 31, 1975, the equipment was sold for $200,000. If a comprehensive historical cost/constant dollar income statement is prepared using end of year 1975 dollars, how much gain or loss would be reported from this sale?

a. $10,600 loss.
b. $16,000 gain.
c. $20,000 gain.
d. $52,000 loss.

8. In preparing constant dollar financial statements, monetary items consist of

a. Cash items plus all receivables with a fixed maturity date.
b. Cash, other assets expected to be converted into cash and current liabilities.
c. Assets and liabilities whose amounts are fixed by contract or otherwise in terms of dollars regardless of price-level changes.
d. Assets and liabilities which are classified as current on the balance sheet.

9. When computing information on a historical cost/constant dollar basis, which of the following is classified as monetary?

a. Equity investment in unconsolidated subsidiaries.
b. Obligations under warranties.
c. Unamortized discount on bonds payable.
d. Deferred investment tax credits.

10. When computing information on a historical cost/constant dollar basis, which of the following is classified as nonmonetary?

a. Allowance for doubtful accounts.
b. Accumulated depreciation of equipment.
c. Unamortized premium on bonds payable.
d. Advances to unconsolidated subsidiaries.

11. In accordance with FASB Statement No. 33, the Consumer Price Index for All Urban Consumers is used to compute information on a

a. Historical cost basis.
b. Current cost basis.
c. Constant dollar basis.
d. Nominal dollar basis.

12. In accordance with FASB Statement No. 33, purchasing power gain or loss results from which of the following?

	Monetary assets and liabilities	*Nonmonetary assets and liabilities*
a.	Yes	Yes
b.	Yes	No
c.	No	Yes
d.	No	No

13. Constant dollar financial statements have been a controversial issue in accounting. Which of the following arguments in favor of such financial statements is not valid?

a. Constant dollar financial statements use historical cost.
b. Constant dollar financial statements compare uniform purchasing power among various periods.
c. Constant dollar financial statements measure current value.
d. Constant dollar financial statements measure earnings in terms of a common dollar.

14. Information with respect to Roundtree Company's cost of goods sold for 1980 is as follows:

	Units	*Historical cost*
Inventory, January 1, 1980	10,000	$ 530,000
Production during 1980	45,000	2,790,000
	55,000	3,320,000
Inventory, December 31, 1980	15,000	945,000
Cost of goods sold	40,000	$2,375,000

Roundtree estimates that the current cost per unit of inventory was $58 at January 1, 1980, and $72 at December 31, 1980. In Roundtree's supplementary information restated into average current cost, the cost of goods sold for the year ended December 31, 1980, should be

a. $2,290,000
b. $2,520,000
c. $2,600,000
d. $2,880,000

15. Details of Monmouth Corporation's fixed assets at December 31, 1980, are as follows:

Year acquired	Percent depreciated	Historical cost	Estimated current cost
1978	30	$50,000	$70,000
1979	20	15,000	19,000
1980	10	20,000	22,000

Monmouth calculates depreciation at 10% per annum, using the straight-line method. A full year's depreciation is charged in the year of acquisition. There were no disposals of fixed assets. Monmouth prepares supplementary information for inclusion in its 1980 annual report as required by the Financial Accounting Standards Board. In Monmouth's supplementary information restated into current cost, the net current cost (after accumulated depreciation) of the fixed assets should be stated as

a. $58,000
b. $65,000
c. $84,000
d. $91,000

16. Victor Company purchased a machine on December 31, 1977, for $100,000. The machine is being depreciated on the straight-line basis with no salvage value and a five-year life. Assume that there was a rise in current (replacement) cost of the machine of 10% during 1978, and of 10% during 1979 (based on the December 31, 1978, current cost). In a supplementary current cost statement at December 31, 1979, Victor would report accumulated depreciation for the above machine of

a. $42,000
b. $44,000
c. $46,200
d. $48,400

17. On December 30, 1976, Future, Incorporated, paid $2,000,000 for land. At December 31, 1977, the current value of the land was $2,200,000. In January 1978, the land was sold for $2,250,000. Ignoring income taxes, by what amount should stockholders' equity be increased for 1977 and 1978 as a result of the above facts in current value financial statements?

	1977	1978
a.	$0	$ 50,000
b.	$0	$250,000
c.	$200,000	$0
d.	$200,000	$ 50,000

18. Coleman, Incorporated, purchased a machine on January 1, 1970, for $100,000. Coleman is depreciating the machine on a straight-line basis with no salvage and a ten-year life. At December 31, 1976, the current cost of the machine was $32,000. On January 1, 1977, the machine was sold for $35,000. Ignoring income taxes, what amount should be shown as the gain or loss on the sale of the machine in a current cost income statement for 1977?

a. $2,000 gain.
b. $3,000 loss.
c. $3,000 gain.
d. $5,000 gain.

19. Essex Corporation bought a machine for $105,000 on January 3, 1981. The machine has an estimated useful life of ten years, with no salvage value. The current cost of this machine at December 31, 1981, was $135,000. Using straight-line depreciation on an average current cost basis, how much depreciation should be charged to current cost income from continuing operations for 1981?

a. $10,500
b. $12,000
c. $13,500
d. $24,000

20. A method of accounting based on measures of current cost or lower recoverable amount, without restatement into units having the same general purchasing power, is

a. Historical cost/constant dollar accounting.
b. Historical cost/nominal dollar accounting.
c. Current cost/constant dollar accounting.
d. Current cost/nominal dollar accounting.

21. When measuring the current cost of inventories in accordance with FASB Statement No. 33, the "entry" date can mean which of the following?

	Beginning of year	Date of sale
a.	Yes	No
b.	Yes	Yes
c.	No	Yes
d.	No	No

22. FASB Statement No. 33 requires that the current cost for inventories be measured as the

a. Recoverable amount regardless of the current cost.
b. Current cost regardless of the recoverable amount.
c. Higher of current cost or recoverable amount.
d. Lower of current cost or recoverable amount.

23. In current cost financial statements
    a. Purchasing power gains or losses are recognized on net monetary items.
    b. Amounts are always stated in common purchasing power units of measurements.
    c. All balance sheet items are different in amount than they would be in a historical-cost balance sheet.
    d. Holding gains are recognized.

24. Which of the following is not a method of determining the current value of an asset?
    a. Replacement cost.
    b. Market value.
    c. Restatement of cost for changes in general price level.
    d. Net present value of expected future cash flows.

25. On January 1, 1982, Kiner Company formed a foreign branch. The branch purchased merchandise at a cost of 720,000 local currency units (LCU) on February 15, 1982. The purchase price was equivalent to $180,000 on this date. The branch's inventory at December 31, 1982, consisted solely of merchandise purchased on February 15, 1982, and amounted to 240,000 LCU. The exchange rate was 6 LCU to $1 on December 31, 1982, and the average rate of exchange was 5 LCU to $1 for 1982. Assume that the LCU is the functional currency of the branch. In Kiner's December 31, 1982, balance sheet, the branch inventory balance of 240,000 LCU should be translated into United States dollars at
    a. $40,000
    b. $48,000
    c. $60,000
    d. $84,000

26. Certain balance sheet accounts in a foreign subsidiary of Rose Company at December 31, 1980, have been translated into United States dollars as follows:

	Translated at	
	Current rates	*Historical rates*
Accounts receivable, current	$200,000	$220,000
Accounts receivable, long-term	100,000	110,000
Prepaid insurance	50,000	55,000
Goodwill	80,000	85,000
	$430,000	$470,000

What total should be included in Rose's balance sheet at December 31, 1980, for the above items? Assume the U.S. dollar currency is the functional currency.
    a. $430,000
    b. $435,000
    c. $440,000
    d. $450,000

27. A wholly owned foreign subsidiary of Union Corporation has certain expense accounts for the year ended December 31, 1979, stated in local currency units (LCU) as follows:

	LCU
Amortization of patent (related patent was acquired January 1, 1977)	40,000
Provision for doubtful accounts	60,000
Rent	100,000

The exchange rates at various dates are as follows:

	Dollar equivalent of 1 LCU
December 31, 1979	$.20
Average for the year ended December 31, 1979	.22
January 1, 1977	.25

What total dollar amount should be included in Union's income statement to reflect the above expenses for the year ended December 31, 1979? Assume the U.S. dollar is the functional currency.
    a. $40,000
    b. $42,000
    c. $44,000
    d. $45,200

28. The France Company owns a foreign subsidiary with 2,400,000 local currency units (LCU) of property, plant, and equipment before accumulated depreciation at December 31, 1978. Of this amount, 1,500,000 LCU were acquired in 1976 when the rate of exchange was 1.5 LCU to $1, and 900,000 LCU were acquired in 1977 when the rate of exchange was 1.6 LCU to $1. The rate of exchange in effect at December 31, 1978, was 1.9 LCU to $1. The weighted average of exchange rates which were in effect during 1978 was 1.8 LCU to $1. Assuming that the property, plant, and equipment are depreciated using the straight-line method over a ten-year period with no salvage value, how much depreciation expense relating to the foreign subsidiary's property, plant, and equipment should be charged in France's income statement for 1978? Assume the U.S. dollar is the functional currency.

a. $126,316
b. $133,333
c. $150,000
d. $156,250

29. Dale, Inc., a U.S. corporation, bought machine parts from Kluger Company of West Germany on March 1, 1981, for 30,000 marks, when the spot rate for marks was $.4895. Dale's year-end was March 31, 1981, when the spot rate for marks was $.4845. Dale bought 30,000 marks and paid the invoice on April 20, 1981, when the spot rate was $.4945. How much should be shown in Dale's income statements as foreign exchange gain or loss for the years ended March 31, 1981 and 1982?

	1981	*1982*
a.	$0	$0
b.	$0	$150 loss
c.	$150 loss	$0
d.	$150 gain	$300 loss

30. At what translation rates should the following balance sheet accounts in foreign statements be translated into United States dollars? Assume the functional currency is the U.S. dollar.

	Equipment	*Accumulated depreciation of equipment*
a.	Current	Current
b.	Current	Average for year
c.	Historical	Current
d.	Historical	Historical

31. When translating foreign currency financial statements, which of the following items would be translated using historical exchange rates? Assume the foreign currency is the functional currency.

a. Notes payable.
b. Long-term debt.
c. Capital stock.
d. Accrued expenses payable.

32. The year-end balance of accounts receivable on the books of a foreign subsidiary should be translated by the parent company for consolidation purposes at the

a. Historical rate.
b. Current rate.
c. Negotiated rate.
d. Spot rate.

33. A change in the foreign currency exchange rate between the date a transaction occurred and the date of the current financial statements would give rise to an exchange gain or loss if

a. The asset or liability being translated is carried at a price in a current purchase or sale exchange.
b. The asset or liability being translated is carried at a price in a past purchase or sale exchange.
c. The revenue or expense item relates to an asset or liability that is translated at historical rates.
d. The revenue or expense item relates to a deferred asset or liability shown on a previous statement of financial position.

34. On July 1, 1981, Stone Company lent $120,000 to a foreign supplier, evidenced by an interest bearing note due on July 1, 1982. The note is denominated in the currency of the borrower and was equivalent to 840,000 local currency units (LCU) on the loan date. The note principal was appropriately included at $140,000 in the receivables section of Stone's December 31, 1981, balance sheet. The note principal was repaid to Stone on the July 1, 1982, due date when the exchange rate was 8 LCU to $1. In its income statement for the year ended December 31, 1982, what amount should Stone include as a foreign currency transaction gain or loss?

a. $0.
b. $15,000 loss.
c. $15,000 gain.
d. $35,000 loss.

35. The Marvin Company has a receivable from a foreign customer which is payable in the local currency of the foreign customer. The amount receivable for 900,000 local currency units (LCU), has been translated into $315,000 on Marvin's December 31, 1975, balance sheet. On January 15, 1976, the receivable was collected in full when the exchange rate was 3 LCU to $1. What journal entry should Marvin make to record the collection of this receivable?

		Debit	*Credit*
a.	Cash	$300,000	
	Accounts receivable		$300,000
b.	Cash	300,000	
	Exchange loss	15,000	
	Accounts receivable		315,000
c.	Cash	300,000	
	Deferred exchange loss	15,000	
	Accounts receivable		315,000
d.	Cash	315,000	
	Accounts receivable		315,000

36. On November 30, 1980, Tyrola Publishing Company, located in Colorado, executed a contract with Ernest Blyton, an author from Canada, providing for payment of 10% royalties on Canadian sales of Blyton's book. Payment is to be made in Canadian dollars each January 10 for the previous year's sales. Canadian sales of the book for the year ended December 31, 1981, totaled $50,000 Canadian. Tyrola paid Blyton his 1981 royalties on January 10, 1982. Tyrola's 1981 financial statements were issued on February 1, 1982. Spot rates for Canadian dollars were as follows:

November 30, 1980	$.87
January 1, 1981	$.88
December 31, 1981	$.89
January 10, 1982	$.90

How much should Tyrola accrue for royalties payable at December 31, 1981?

a. $4,350
b. $4,425
c. $4,450
d. $4,500

37. U.S. Importers, Inc., bought 5,000 dolls from Latin American Exporters, S.A., at 12.5 pesos each, when the rate of exchange was $.08 per peso. How much should U.S. Importers record on its books as the total dollar cost for the merchandise purchased?

a. $ 400
b. $ 625
c. $5,000
d. $6,250

38. A sale of goods, denominated in a currency other than the entity's functional currency, resulted in a receivable that was fixed in terms of the amount of foreign currency that would be received. Exchange rates between the functional currency and the currency in which the transaction was denominated changed. The resulting gain should be included as a (an)

a. Separate component of stockholders' equity.
b. Deferred credit.
c. Component of income from continuing operations.
d. Extraordinary item.

May 1984 Questions

39. Blackwood Corporation had a $20,000 translation loss adjustment resulting from the translation of the accounts of its wholly owned foreign subsidiary for the year ended December 31, 1983. Blackwood also had a receivable from a foreign customer which was payable in the local currency of the foreign customer. On December 31, 1982, this receivable for 100,000 local currency units (LCU) was appropriately included in Blackwood's balance sheet at $55,000. When the receivable was collected on February 10, 1983, the exchange rate was 2 LCU to $1. In Blackwood's 1983 consolidated income statement, what amount should be included as foreign exchange loss?

a. $0
b. $ 5,000
c. $20,000
d. $25,000

40. When measuring the current cost of inventories in accordance with FASB Statement No. 33, the "exit" date can mean the

	End of year	*Date of sale*
a.	Yes	Yes
b.	Yes	No
c.	No	No
d.	No	Yes

41. When computing information on a historical cost/constant dollar basis, which of the following is classified as nonmonetary?

a. Deferred income tax credits.
b. Long-term receivables.
c. Goodwill.
d. Unamortized premium on bonds payable.

42. Losses resulting from the process of translating a foreign entity's financial statements from the functional currency, which is experiencing a 3% inflation rate, to U.S. dollars should be included as a(an)

a. Deferred charge.
b. Separate component of stockholders' equity.
c. Component of income from continuing operations.
d. Extraordinary item.

Repeat Question

(584,P3,59) Identical to item 15 above

CHANGING PRICES

Problems

Problem 1 SFAS 33 (CMA,681,PRS 5)

(30 minutes)

In September 1979 Statement of Financial Accounting Standards No. 33, "Financial Reporting and Changing Prices," (SFAS 33) was released. This statement applies to public enterprises that have either (1) inventories and property, plant, and equipment (before deducting accumulated depreciation) of more than $125 million or (2) total assets amounting to more than $1 billion (after deducting accumulated depreciation). No changes are required in the basic financial statements, but information required by SFAS No. 33 is to be presented in supplementary statements, schedules or notes in the financial reports.

Required:

a. A number of terms are defined and used in SFAS 33.
   1. Differentiate between the terms *constant dollar* and *current cost*.
   2. Explain what is meant by *current cost/constant dollar accounting* and how it differs from *historical cost/nominal dollar acting.*

b. Identify the accounts for which an enterprise must measure the effects of changing prices in order to present the supplementary information required by SFAS No. 33.

c. SFAS No. 33 is based upon FASB Concepts Statement No. 1, "Objectives of Financial Reporting by Business Enterprises," which concludes that financial reporting should provide information to help investors, creditors, and other financial statement users assess the amounts, timing and uncertainty of prospective net cash inflows to the enterprise.
   1. Explain how SFAS No. 33 may help in attaining this objective.
   2. Identify and discuss two ways in which the information required by SFAS No. 33 may be useful for internal management decisions.

Problem 2 SFAS 33*

(25 to 30 minutes)

In 1979, SFAS 33 was issued in response to the changing price dilemma. The following questions address the issue of changing prices.

a. Marketable equity securities are presently accounted for on the lower of cost or market basis. Compare this basis with accounting for such securities on a current cost basis in regards to asset valuation and income recognition.

b. Explain briefly the theory of capital maintenance and how it relates to:
   1. Constant dollar accounting
   2. Current cost accounting

**Prepared by John C. Borke, University of Wisconsin—Platteville*

Problem 3 Constant Dollar Accounting (CMA, 1281,PRS 3)

(20 to 25 minutes)

Retail Showcase Mart was organized on December 15, 1980. The company's initial Statement of Financial Position is presented below.

Retail Showcase Mart
Statement of Financial Position
December 31, 1980

Assets:	
Cash	$200,000
Inventory (at historical cost which equals market value; FIFO; periodic)	400,000
Furniture & fixtures	200,000
Land (held for future store site)	100,000
Total assets	$900,000
Liabilities and stockholders' equity:	
Accounts payable	$300,000
Capital stock ($5 par, 200,000 shares authorized; 120,000 issued and outstanding	600,000
Total liabilities and stockholders' equity	$900,000

The Statement of Income and the Statement of Financial Position prepared at the close of business on December 31, 1981, are presented below.

Retail Showcase Mart
Statement of Income
For the Year Ended December 31, 1981

Sales		$1,100,000
Cost of goods sold:		
Inventory 1/1/81	$ 400,000	
Purchases	1,000,000	
Goods available	$1,400,000	
Inventory 12/31/81	600,000	800,000
Gross profit		$ 300,000
Operating expenses		
Rent	$ 36,000	
Depreciation	20,000	
Other (all required cash expenditures)	44,000	100,000
Income before taxes		$ 200,000
Income tax expense		80,000
Net income		$ 120,000
Earnings per share		$1.00

Retail Showcase Mart
Statement of Financial Position
December 31, 1981

Assets:	
Cash	$ 240,000
Accounts receivable	400,000
Inventory (at historical cost, FIFO, periodic)	600,000
Furniture and fixtures (net)	180,000
Land (held for future store site)	100,000
Total assets	$1,520,000
Liabilities and stockholders' equity:	
Accounts payable	$ 800,000
Capital stock ($5 par, 200,000 shares authorized; 120,000 issued and outstanding)	600,000
Retained earnings	120,000
Total liabilities and stockholders' equity	$1,520,000

Retail Showcase Mart rents its showroom facilities on an operating lease basis at a cost of $3,000 per month. The rent would be $5,000 per month if it were based on the current cost of the facility. All sales and cash outlays for costs and expenses occur uniformly throughout the year.

The following information is indicative of the changing prices since Retail Showcase Mart began its operations.

- The Consumer Price Index for All Urban Consumers for the following times is:

December 31, 1980	200
October 1, 1981	216
December 31, 1981	220
Average for 1981	212

- The ending inventory was acquired on October 1, 1981.
- Inventory at current cost on December 31, 1981, is $700,000.
- Cost of goods sold at current cost as of date of sale is $875,000.
- Current cost of the land on December 31, 1981, is $150,000.
- The sales and purchases occurred uniformly throughout 1981.
- The "net recoverable amounts" for inventories and fixed assets have been determined by management to be in excess of the net current costs.

The accounting manager of Retail Showcase Mart has decided to comply voluntarily with the reporting requirements presented in the Statement of Financial Accounting Standards No. 33, "Financial Reporting and Changing Prices."

Required:

a. Calculate Retail Showcase Mart's purchasing power gain or loss for 1981 in terms of December 31, 1981, dollars. Round all computations to the nearest $100.

b. Prepare a constant dollar income statement for 1981 for Retail Showcase Mart in terms of December 31, 1981, dollars. Round all computations to the nearest $100.

Problem 4 Current Valuation of Assets (578,T6b)

(15 to 20 minutes)

Part b. The financial statements of a business entity could be prepared by using historical cost or current value as a basis. In addition, the basis could be stated in terms of unadjusted dollars or dollars restated for changes in purchasing power. The various permutations of these two separate and distinct areas are shown in the following matrix:

	Unadjusted dollars	Dollars restated for changes in purchasing power
Historical cost	1	2
Current value	3	4

Block number 1 of the matrix represents the traditional method of accounting for transactions in accounting today, wherein the absolute (unadjusted) amount of dollars given up or received is recorded for the asset or liability obtained (relationship between resources). Amounts recorded in the method described in block number 1 reflect the original cost of the asset or liability and do not give effect to any change in value of the unit of measure (standard of comparison). This method assumes the validity of the accounting concepts of going concern and stable monetary unit. Any gain or loss (including holding and purchasing power gains or losses) resulting from the sale or satisfaction of amounts recorded under this method is deferred in its entirety until sale or satisfaction.

Required:

For each of the remaining matrix blocks (2, 3 and 4) respond to the following questions. Limit your discussion to nonmonetary assets only.

- How will this method of recording assets affect the relationship between resources and the standard of comparison?
- What is the theoretic justification for using each method?
- How will each method of asset valuation affect the recognition of gain or loss during the life of the asset and ultimately from the sale or abandonment of the asset? Your response should include a discussion of the timing and magnitude of the gain or loss and conceptual reasons for any difference from the gain or loss computed using the traditional method.

Complete your discussion for each matrix block before proceeding to the discussion of the next matrix block.

Problem 5 Constant Dollar Theory (575,T7)

(25 to 30 minutes)

Published financial statements of United States companies are currently prepared on a stable-dollar assumption even though the general purchasing power of the dollar has declined considerably because of inflation in recent years. To account for this changing value of the dollar, many accountants suggest that financial statements should be adjusted for general price-level changes. Three independent unrelated statements regarding constant dollar financial statements follow. Each statement contains some fallacious reasoning.

Statement I

The accounting profession has not seriously considered constant dollar financial statements before because the rate of inflation usually has been so small from year-to-year that the adjustments would have been immaterial in amount. Constant dollar financial statements represent a departure from the historical-cost basis of accounting. Financial statements should be prepared from facts, not estimates.

Statement II

If financial statements were adjusted for general price-level changes, depreciation charges in the earnings statement would permit the recovery of dollars of current purchasing power and, thereby, equal the cost of new assets to replace the old ones. Constant dollar adjusted data would yield statement-of-financial-position amounts closely approximating current values. Furthermore, management can make better decisions if constant dollar financial statements are published.

Statement III

When adjusting financial data for general price-level changes, a distinction must be made between monetary and nonmonetary assets and liabilities, which, under the historical-cost basis of accounting, have been identified as "current" and "non-current." When using the historical-cost basis of accounting, no purchasing-power gain or loss is recognized in the accounting process, but when financial statements are adjusted for general price-level changes, a purchasing-power gain or loss will be recognized on monetary and nonmonetary items.

Required:

Evaluate each of the independent statements and identify the areas of fallacious reasoning in each and explain why the reasoning is incorrect. Complete your discussion of each statement before proceeding to the next statement.

Problem 6 Constant Dollar and Current Cost (Adapted from Kieso and Weygandt, *Intermediate Accounting,* 4th edition, p. 1195)

(60 to 75 minutes)

Presented below is information related to Hood, Inc.

1978 Purchased land for $40,000 cash on December 31. Current cost at year end was $40,000.
1979 Held this land all year. Current cost at year end was $52,000.
1980 October 31--sold this land for $68,000. Current cost of land at date of sale is $65,000.

General price-level index:

December 31, 1978	100
December 31, 1979	110
October 31, 1980	120
December 31, 1980	120

Required:

a. Determine the amount at which the land would be stated on a balance sheet at December 31, 1978 and 1979 under the following assumptions (end-of-year dollars):

1. Constant dollar accounting
2. Current cost accounting
3. Current cost/constant dollar accounting

b. Determine the following items (end-of-year dollars):

1. Constant dollar income for 1978, 1979, and 1980.
2. Unrealized holding gain (loss) on current cost basis for 1979.
3. Income from continuing operations on a current cost basis for 1980.
4. Realized holding gain (loss) on current cost basis in 1980.
5. The total holding gain recognized on a current cost/constant dollar basis for 1980.

c. Indicate the amount of income from continuing operations that would be reported under FASB Statement No. 33 for 1978, 1979, and 1980. Assume that the general indexes presented above also reflect the average index for the year; that is, 1978 average index equals 100; 1979 average index equals 110; 1980 average index equals 120.

FOREIGN CURRENCY

Problems

Problem 7 Foreign Currency Translation (1177, P4c)

(15 to 20 minutes)

Part c. On January 1, 1975, the Franklin Company formed a foreign subsidiary which issued all of its currently outstanding common stock on that date. Selected captions from the balance sheets, all of which are shown in local currency units (LCU), are as follows:

	December 31, 1976	December 31, 1975
	(All amounts given in LCU)	
Accounts receivable (net of allowance for uncollectible accounts of 2,200 LCU at December 31, 1976, and 2,000 LCU at December 31, 1975)	40,000	35,000
Inventories, at cost	80,000	75,000
Property, plant and equipment (net of allowance for accumulated depreciation of 31,000 LCU at December 31, 1976, and 14,000 LCU at December 31, 1975)	163,000	150,000
Long-term debt	100,000	120,000
Common stock, authorized 10,000 shares, par value 10 LCU per share, issued and outstanding 5,000 shares at December 31, 1976, and December 31, 1975	50,000	50,000

Additional information is as follows:

- Exchange rates are as follows:

January 1, 1975–July 31, 1975	2 LCU to \$1
August 1, 1975–October 31, 1975	1.8 LCU to \$1
November 1, 1975–June 30, 1976	1.7 LCU to \$1
July 1, 1976–December 31, 1976	1.5 LCU to \$1
Average monthly rate for 1975	1.9 LCU to \$1
Average monthly rate for 1976	1.6 LCU to \$1

- An analysis of the accounts receivable balance is as follows:

Accounts receivable:	1976	1975
	(All amounts given in LCU)	
Balance at beginning of year	37,000	–
Sales (36,000 LCU per month in 1976 and 31,000 LCU per month in 1975)	432,000	372,000
Collections	423,600	334,000
Write-offs (May 1976 and December 1975)	3,200	1,000
Balance at end of year	42,200	37,000

Allowance for uncollectible accounts:	1976	1975
	(All amounts given in LCU)	
Balance at beginning of year	2,000	–
Provision for uncollectible accounts	3,400	3,000
Write-offs (May 1976 and December 1975)	3,200	1,000
Balance at end of year	2,200	2,000

- An analysis of inventories, for which the first-in, first-out (FIFO) inventory method is used, is as follows:

	1976	1975
	(All amounts given in LCU)	
Inventory at beginning of year	75,000	–
Purchases (June 1976 and June 1975)	335,000	375,000
Goods available for sale	410,000	375,000
Inventory at end of year	80,000	75,000
Cost of goods sold	330,000	300,000

- On January 1, 1975, Franklin's foreign subsidiary purchased land for 24,000 LCU and plant and equipment for 140,000 LCU. On July 4, 1976, additional equipment was purchased for 30,000 LCU. Plant and equipment is being depreciated on a straight-line basis over a ten-year period with no salvage value. A full year's depreciation is taken in the year of purchase.

- On January 15, 1975, 7% bonds with a face value of 120,000 LCU were sold. These bonds mature on January 15, 1981, and interest is paid semi-annually on July 15 and January 15. The first payment was made on January 15, 1976.

Required:

Prepare a schedule translating the selected captions above into United States dollars at December 31, 1976, and December 31, 1975, respectively. Show supporting computations in good form.

Multiple Choice Answers

1. d	10. b	19. b	27. d	35. b
2. b	11. c	20. d	28. d	36. c
3. c	12. b	21. a	29. d	37. c
4. d	13. c	22. d	30. d	38. c
5. c	14. c	23. d	31. c	39. b
6. c	15. c	24. c	32. b	40. a
7. d	16. d	25. a	33. a	41. c
8. c	17. d	26. c	34. d	42. b
9. c	18. c			

Multiple Choice Answer Explanations

A. Constant Dollar Accounting

1. (1183,P1,17) (d) The requirement is Nutley's purchasing power gain (loss) on net monetary items in end-of-year dollars. At 1/1/82, Nutley's net monetary assets are $1,000,000 ($2,000,000 – $1,000,000). During 1982, there was no net change and net monetary assets remained at $1,000,000 at 12/31/82. In order to keep up with inflation, net monetary assets would have to be $1,100,000 ($1,000,000 x 220/200) at year end. Therefore, Nutley has suffered a purchasing power loss of $100,000 ($1,100,000 – $1,000,000).

2. (1178,P1,13) (b) The requirement is the purchasing power gain or loss for 1977. Per SFAS 33, purchasing power gains and losses arise on monetary items during changes in the general price level. Essentially a purchasing power gain or loss is computed as the difference between 1) the net monetary items on hand at the end of the year, and 2) the amount of the net monetary items as they would have been if they were nonmonetary items. In other words, adjust all monetary items to reflect changes in purchasing power.

In this case, cash is the monetary item, and if it had been a nonmonetary item it would have been restated to $55,000 ($50,000 x 110/100) at the end of the year. Since cash is a monetary item, it is only worth $50,000 and not $55,000. Thus there was a purchasing power loss of $5,000 on the cash which was held during the year. The price-level adjusted balance sheet appears below in the T-account. Both land and common stock (nonmonetary items) are adjusted upward by the 10% increase in the price level. Also the $5,000 general price-level loss is included in retained earnings.

Price Level Statement
12/31/77

Cash	$ 50,000		
Land	165,000		
		Stock	$220,000
		RE	(5,000)
	$215,000		$215,000

3. (578,P1,12) (c) The requirement is the constant dollar adjusted amounts to be shown at the end of 1977. Only nonmonetary items are adjusted for changes in the price level. Cash and long-term receivables are monetary items. The marketable securities are nonmonetary items (even the bonds, because they were purchased for price speculation). Accordingly, cash and long-term receivables are not adjusted. The marketable securities (both stocks and bonds) are increased by 10% as the price level increases by 10% during 1977.

4. (583,Q1,15) (d) The requirement is the amount of depreciation expense for a constant dollar supplementary statement in 1982. Depreciation is a nonmonetary item. Therefore, it must be adjusted to current year dollars. The $200,000 of historical cost depreciation is converted into 1982 dollars by multiplying it by the To/From ratio of 200/180.

$$\$200{,}000 \times \frac{200}{180} = \$222{,}222$$

5. (581,Q1,1) (c) The requirement of this problem is to calculate depreciation expense on an income statement adjusted for general inflation using constant dollar accounting. It is necessary to calculate the amount for each asset in terms of constant dollars by multiplying the historical cost by the current year's price index over the price index that was in effect when the asset was purchased. These amounts are then used for calculating depreciation expense. The cost of each asset adjusted for inflation is:

1978	30,000 x 150/100	=	$45,000
1979	20,000 x 150/125	=	24,000
1980	10,000 x 150/150	=	10,000
	Total		$79,000

Since depreciation expense is 10% per year, straight-line, and a full year's depreciation is charged in the year of acquisition, total depreciation can be calculated by multiplying 10% by the total cost of the assets adjusted for inflation ($79,000). Depreciation expense is $7,900.

6. (1176,Q1,5) (c) Land is a nonmonetary item and therefore is adjusted by changes in the purchasing

power of the dollar. The $300,000 is adjusted by the TO/FROM ratio (price-level-adjusting-to divided by price-level-adjusting-from) of 140/120. Thus, the land cost on 12-31-75 dollars is $350,000 resulting in a $50,000 gain (400–350).

7. (1176,Q1,6) (d) In 1975 dollars, the cost of the equipment was $420,000 ($300,000 x 140/100); the equipment was purchased at the beginning of 1972 which is the end of 1971. The equipment was depreciated for four of the ten-year useful life, resulting in a book value of $252,000 ($420,000 x 60%). Since the equipment was sold for $200,000, there was a $52,000 loss.

8. (1171,Q2,23) (c) Answer (c) is the definition of monetary items. Receivables and payables may be monetary items without a fixed maturity date. In addition to current liabilities, long-term liabilities are often monetary items, e.g., bonds payable. See SFAS 33.

9. (1183,T1,4) (c) SFAS 33, para 47 defines a monetary item as an amount which is fixed in amount by contract or otherwise. An unamortized discount on bonds payable is inseparable from the debt to which it relates—a monetary item. Therefore, the discount is a monetary item. Answers (a), (b), and (d) are nonmonetary items since they are not fixed in amount.

10. (583,T1,6) (b) Monetary (nonmonetary) items are assets and liabilities whose amounts are fixed (may change over time) in terms of a monetary unit (e.g., the U.S. dollar). Examples of monetary and nonmonetary items are identified in SFAS 33, Appendix D. Accumulated depreciation on equipment is listed as a nonmonetary item. The other three items [answers (a), (c), and (d)] are all monetary items.

11. (1182,T1,3) (c) In accordance with SFAS 33, the Consumer Price Index is used to compute information on a "constant dollar" basis. The index is used to restate financial statement elements to dollars which have the same purchasing power. Historical cost or nominal dollar information [answers (a) and (d)] requires no restatement. Information on a current cost basis [answer (b)] would be restated using a specific, rather than a general price index.

12. (582,T1,39) (b) According to SFAS 33, the dollar amounts of monetary assets and liabilities are fixed by contract or statute. If the general price level changes a purchasing power gain (loss) on net monetary items occurs. Since the dollar amount of nonmonetary items is not fixed, a change in the general price level does not result in a purchasing power gain or loss.

13. (577,T1,7) (c) Answers (a), (b) and (d) are descriptive of constant dollar statements. Since constant dollar statements only account for inflation, i.e., changes in the purchasing power of the dollar, they usually do not measure current value. Historical costs can be converted into current values with very specific, not general, price-level indexes. There are many components of differences between historical costs and current costs, e.g., inflation, market factors, etc.

B. Current Cost Accounting

14. (1181,P1,17) (c) The requirement is the 1980 cost of goods sold in Roundtree's supplementary information restated into average current cost. Per appendix E of SFAS 33, average current cost of goods sold is computed by multiplying units sold (40,000) by the average current cost during the year. Average current cost is current cost at the beginning of the year plus current cost at the end of the year, divided by 2:

$$(\$58 + \$72) \div 2 = \$65$$

Average current cost of goods sold is 40,000 units x $65, or $2,600,000.

15. (581,P1,1) (c) The requirement is to compute the net current cost of the fixed assets at December 31, 1980. The solutions approach is to realize that the net current cost is the estimated current cost less the percentage of the asset depreciated to date. Thus, the net current cost is computed as follows:

1978	70,000	–	.30 (70,000)	=	$49,000
1979	19,000	–	.20 (19,000)	=	15,200
1980	22,000	–	.10 (22,000)	=	19,800
			Net current cost		$84,000

16. (1180,P1,18) (d) The requirement is the accumulated depreciation to be reported by Victor in a supplementary current cost statement at 12/31/79. The current cost of the machine at the end of each year is:

12/31/77		$100,000
12/31/78	($100,000)(110%)	$110,000
12/31/79	($110,000)(110%)	$121,000

Note that the 10% increase in 1979 current cost is based on 1978 current cost, not the 1977 cost. After two years of the five-year life, accumulated depreciation should be 2/5 of the current cost:

$$(\$121{,}000)(2/5) = \underline{\underline{\$48{,}400}}$$

17. (579,P1,20) (d) In current value accounting, stockholders' equity is adjusted each period as a result of the assets and liabilities being recorded at current cost. During 1977, the land increased from $2,000,000 to $2,200,000 (a $200,000 increase in

stockholders' equity), and in 1978 the land was sold for $2,250,000 resulting in an additional $50,000 increase in stockholders' equity.

18. (1178,P1,15) (c) The requirement is the gain on the sale of a machine per current value accounting. Since the current cost of the machine was $32,000, and it was sold for $35,000, there would be a $3,000 gain. Note the sale took place on January 1, 1977, and thus no depreciation would be recorded. The depreciation under current value accounting is the decrease (increase) in the replacement cost from the beginning to the end of the year. Therefore the book value on December 31, 1976 would have to be $32,000.

19. (582,Q1,8) (b) The requirement is the amount of current cost depreciation expense for 1981 using the straight-line method. Per para 52(b) of SFAS 33, depreciation is to be measured based on the average current cost of the asset during the period of use. The first step is to calculate the average current cost of the machine during 1981.

$$\frac{\$105,000 + \$135,000}{2} = \$120,000$$

Depreciation expense for 1981 is $12,000 ($120,000 ÷ 10 years).

20. (583,T1,7) (d) Current cost/nominal dollar accounting is a method of accounting based on measures of current cost or lower recoverable amount without restatement into units, each of which has the same general purchasing power (SFAS 33, para 22). Answers (a) and (b) are incorrect because historical cost is an alternative to current cost in which items are measured and reported at their historical prices. Answer (c) is incorrect because under constant dollar accounting, dollars are restated into units having the same general purchasing power.

21. (1182,T1,34) (a) SFAS 33, para 55 states that when measuring the current cost of inventories or property, plant and equipment the "entry" date means the beginning of the year or the date of acquisition, whichever is applicable. The "exit" date means the end of the year or the date of sale.

22. (1181,T1,6) (d) Para 51 of SFAS 33 requires that the current cost for inventories be measured at the lower of current cost or recoverable amount at the measurement date.

23. (1179,T1,24) (d) In current value accounting, holding gains are recognized when asset values are revised upward to current values. As assets are revalued (debited), holding gains are credited. Answers (a) and (b) are incorrect because current value financial statements reflect asset values adjusted for specific changes in value and make no separate distinction as to changes in the purchasing power of the dollar. Answer (c) is incorrect because if the current value and the historical cost were equal, there would be no difference no matter whether historical cost or current value accounting was used.

24. (1178,T1,22) (c) The requirement is the method which does not determine the current value of an asset. Current values of assets are determined by a number of factors in addition to changes in the purchasing power of the dollar. Answer (c), restatement of costs for changes in the general price level, is only concerned with the changing purchasing power of the dollar and not the other factors, e.g., changes in supply and demand for the asset. Replacement cost [answer (a)], market value [answer (b)], and present value of future cash flows [answer (d)], all are "current values."

F. Translation of Foreign Currency Statements

25. (1183,P2,37) (a) The requirement is the amount of branch inventory after translation into U.S. dollars. Per SFAS 52, if the functional currency is that of the foreign branch or subsidiary, assets and liabilities are translated using the exchange rate at the balance sheet date. This exchange rate is 6 LCU to $1. Therefore, the inventory balance of 240,000 LCU is translated to $40,000 (240,000 ÷ 6).

26. (581,P1,17) (c) The requirement is to compute the total dollar amount translated for the assets presented in Rose Company's balance sheet. According to SFAS 52, when the U.S. dollar is the functional currency, account balances which are the result of past exchanges are translated using historical exchange rates while account balances which are the result of current exchanges are translated using current exchange rates. Furthermore, monetary assets and monetary liabilities are translated using the current rate. Accounts receivable are carried in terms of current prices and, therefore, are translated at current rates. Goodwill and prepaid insurance are carried at historical prices and are translated at historical rates. Thus, the total translated dollar amount is computed as

A/R, current	$200,000
A/R, long-term	100,000
Prepaid insurance	55,000
Goodwill	85,000
	$440,000

27. (1180,P1,11) (d) The requirement is the dollar amount of expense to be included in Union's consolidated income statement for three of the subsidiary's expense items stated in local currency units. When the U.S. dollar is the functional currency, SFAS 52 requires remeasurement into U.S. dollars, i.e., each foreign currency balance is translated at the exchange rate(s) in effect when the foreign transaction(s) occurred. Therefore, historical exchange rates are used for historical balances and current rates are used for balances which are current. Average exchange rates are used for balances that result from several transactions during a period. Patent amortization relates to a cost incurred on 1/1/77, so the exchange rate on that date (.25) should be used. The other two expenses (bad debts and rent) were incurred evenly throughout the year; the average-for-the-year rate (.22) would be used for their translation.

Amortization	(.25)	(40,000)	$10,000
Bad debts	(.22)	(60,000)	13,200
Rent	(.22)	(100,000)	22,000
			$45,200

28. (579,P1,10) (d) The requirement is the amount of depreciation expense relating to a foreign subsidiary's fixed assets for 1978. SFAS 52 requires remeasurement when the U.S. dollar is the functional currency. Remeasurement means that all assets and liabilities on the balance sheet and revenues and expenses on the income statement are translated at the rates in effect when the transactions originally occurred, e.g., depreciation is translated at the exchange rate in effect at the original transaction date (i.e., the historical rate). Since the useful life of the fixed assets is 10 years with no salvage value, depreciation will be 150,000 LCU for the equipment acquired in 1976 and 90,000 LCU for the equipment acquired in 1977. These are converted to dollars at their respective historical rates of 1.5 and 1.6 LCU.

$1,500,000 x 10% ÷ 1.5 = $100,000
$900,000 x 10% ÷ 1.6 = 56,250
$156,250

29. (582,Q1,7) (d) The requirement is the amount of foreign exchange gain (loss) shown in Dale's income statement for the fiscal years ending 3/31/81 and 3/31/82. In this case, a transaction has occured in which settlement will be made in German marks. Since the functional currency of the purchaser (Dale, Inc.) is the U.S. dollar, not the German mark, a transaction (gain) loss will result if the spot rate on the settlement date is different than the rate existing on the transaction date (SFAS 52, para 15). Additionally, a provision must be made at any intervening year-end date for such rate changes (para 15). At 3/31/81 a $150 gain [30,000 x ($.4895 – $.4845)] would be recognized. On the date of settlement (4/20/81), a $300 loss [30,000 x (.4945 – .4845] would be recognized. Therefore, Dale's income statements would show a $150 transaction gain in F/Y 81 and in F/Y 82 a $300 loss. Note: Candidates who noticed that only one of the answers had $150 for F/Y 81 could have saved some time on this question.

30. (1181,T1,27) (d) When the functional currency is the U.S. dollar, SFAS 52 requires monetary assets and monetary liabilities be translated to U.S. dollars by using the current rate. Nonmonetary assets and liabilities are translated by using the exchange rates in effect when the transactions occurred which gave rise to the foreign currency balances. Historical exchange rates would be used to translate historical cost balances. Consequently, both property, plant, and equipment and accumulated depreciation should be translated by using historical rates.

31. (580,T1,32) (c) When the functional currency is the foreign currency, SFAS 52 requires that the current rate be applied to all assets and liabilities listed on the foreign currency financial statements. This rule means that responses (a), (b), and (d) are incorrect. SFAS 52 requires that historical rates be applied to the capital section of the foreign currency financial statements. This means response (c) is correct.

32. (579,T1,2) (b) The balance of accounts receivable is translated by using the current rate at the balance sheet date. Note that this is the procedure regardless of whether the U.S. dollar or the foreign currency is the functional currency.

33. (1178,T1,25) (a) The requirement is the type of transaction that would give rise to an exchange gain or loss if there is a change in the foreign currency exchange rate. An exchange gain or loss is recognized if an asset or liability is being translated at the current rate when there is a change in the foreign currency exchange rate. Conversely, if a historical translation rate is used, changes in the foreign current exchange rate do not affect the evaluation of assets or liabilities and will not result in an exchange gain or loss. Thus assets and liabilities carried at the same price of a current purchase or sale are being carried at the current rate and will produce exchange gains and losses if foreign currency exchange rates change. Answers (b), (c), and (d) are incorrect because assets and liabilities translated at the historical rate do not produce exchange gains or losses.

G. Translation of Foreign Currency Transactions

34. (1183,P1,11) (d) The requirement is the foreign currency transaction gain (loss) in Stone's 1982 income statement. Since the rate is denominated in a foreign currency at a fixed 840,000 (LCU), fluctuations in the exchange rates will produce foreign currency gains (losses). Per SFAS 52, the increase (decrease) in expected functional currency cash flows is a foreign currency transaction gain (loss) to be included in income in the period during which the exchange rate changes. At December 31, 1981 changes in the exchange rates produced a recognized gain of $20,000. At the repayment date (July 1, 1982) changes in the exchange rate resulted in a realized loss of $35,000 computed as follows:

$$\frac{\text{Received from borrower 840,000 LCU}}{\text{8 LCU for each \$1}} = \$105,000$$

Note carrying value	$140,000
Cash received	– 105,000
Translation loss	$ 35,000

35. (577,P1,4) (b) The requirement is the journal entry to record the collection of a receivable. The receivable was $315,000 when 900,000 LCU were received at an exchange rate of 3 LCU to $1. Thus $300,000 was received to settle a $315,000 receivable resulting in a $15,000 exchange loss. Note that exchange gains and losses from foreign currency transactions, which are of an import/export nature, are reported on the income statement for the period in which the rate changes.

36. (582,Q1,1) (c) The requirement is the amount which Tyrola should accrue for royalties payable, 12/31/81. This situation is a foreign currency transaction in which settlement is denominated in other than a company's functional currency (SFAS 52, paras 5 and 15). In this case the functional currency is the U.S. dollar because it is the currency of the primary economic environment in which the Colorado firm operates. Note that in this royalty agreement, 12/31/81 is the point at which the amount due to the author (50,000 Canadian dollars x 10% = 5,000 Canadian dollars) is determined. Royalty expense is measured and the related liability is denominated at 12/31/81. The year-end accrual would be:

.89 (10% x 50,000 Canadian dollars) = $4,450.

On January 10, 1982, Tyrola will have to purchase 5,000 Canadian dollars for payment to the Canadian author. The amount of U.S. dollars required to accomplish this will depend on the spot rate on January 10th ($.90 in this case). The number of U.S. dollars required to satisfy the obligation will be $50 greater [($.90 – .89) x 5,000 Canadian dollars]. This will result in a $50 transaction loss which would be included in 1982 net income.

37. (1181,Q2,32) (c) The requirement is the dollar cost of merchandise purchased with foreign currency. Each doll cost 12.5 pesos which is equivalent to $1(12.5 x $.08). Therefore, the cost of 5,000 dolls would be $5,000.

38. (1183,T1,25) (c) SFAS 52, para 15 states that the increase (decrease) in expected functional currency cash flows is a foreign currency transaction gain (loss) that generally shall be included in determining net income for the period in which the exchange rate changes. The gain (loss) is then shown on the income statement under other income as part of income from continuing operations. Answers (a) and (b) are incorrect because the item is not a balance sheet component. Answer (d) is incorrect because the gain is not considered both unusual and infrequent in nature and is, therefore, not an extraordinary item.

May 1984 Answers

39. (584,P1,36) (b) The requirement is the amount that should be included as a foreign exchange loss on Blackwood's 1983 consolidated income statement. Per SFAS 52, para 13, **translation adjustments** result from translating an entity's financial statements into the reporting currency. Such adjustments, which result when the entity's functional currency is the foreign currency, should **not** be included in the determination of net income. Rather, such adjustments should be reported in stockholders' equity. Note that if the functional currency was the reporting currency, a **remeasurement** process would have been used, with the resulting gain (loss) reported on the income statement. Conversely, gains and losses which result from foreign exchange transactions **are** reported on the income statement. At 12/31/82, the receivable was translated at $55,000 (representing 100,000 LCU). When the 100,000 LCU were collected, they were worth $50,000 (100,000 ÷ 2). Therefore, an exchange loss of $5,000 should be reported on the income statement.

40. (584,T1,4) (a) The requirement is to determine the proper meaning of the term "exit date" when measuring the current cost of inventories. Per SFAS 33, para 55 increases or decreases in the current cost amounts of inventory represent the difference between the measures of the assets at their "entry dates" for the

year and measures of the assets at their "exit dates" for the year. The "entry date" is either the beginning of the year or, if purchased during the year, the acquisition date. The "exit date" is the date of sale, the end of the year, or the date the inventory is committed to a specific use, whichever is most applicable. Therefore, answer (a) is correct.

41. (584,T1,5) (c) The requirement is to determine which item is classified as nonmonetary on a historical cost/constant dollar basis. SFAS 33, para 47 defines a monetary item as an amount which is fixed or determinable without reference to future prices. Para 48 defines a nonmonetary item as anything that is not considered a monetary item. Goodwill is a nonmonetary asset because it does not represent a claim to a fixed amount. Monetary and nonmonetary items are identified in SFAS 33, Appendix D. Answers (a), (b), and (c) are all listed as monetary items because they represent a claim to a fixed amount or require payment of a fixed amount.

42. (584,T1,27) (b) The requirement is to determine the proper classification of foreign currency translation losses. Per SFAS 52, para 13, when an entity's functional currency is the foreign currency, that entity's financial statements are to be translated into the reporting currency using the current rate. Gains and losses from the translation process are known as **translation adjustments** and are **not** to be included in the computation of net income. Such adjustments are to be reported as a separate component of stockholders' equity. Note that when the foreign entity is in a highly inflationary economy, one with a cumulative inflation rate of 100% or more over a three-year period, the foreign entity's financial statements would be **re-measured** into the reporting currency, with the gains and losses from the remeasurement process included in the determination of net income.

CHANGING PRICES

Answer Outline

Problem 1 SFAS 33

a1. Constant dollar refers to adjusting dollar amounts by an index to reflect purchasing power.
Constant dollar accounting adjusts for general price level changes only.
Current cost refers to adjusting accounts to reflect current value or replacement cost.
Current cost accounting adjusts for specific price changes only.

a2. Current cost/constant dollar accounting restates accounts to current value.
Current cost/constant dollar adjusts for changes in general purchasing power and specific price changes.
Historical cost/nominal dollar makes no adjustments for changes in general or specific price levels.

b. Major nonmonetary assets requiring restatement include: inventory; property, plant, and equipment; cost of goods sold; depreciation, depletion, and amortization expenses.

c1. SFAS 33 may help external users assess financial performance, capital maintenance, dividend policy and overall effect of inflation.

c2. SFAS 33 may help internal users in capital budgeting, pricing, performance evaluation, liquidating and financing policy as well as the items in c1. above.

Unofficial Answer

Problem 1 SFAS 33

a. 1. *Constant dollar accounting* is a method of reporting financial statement elements in dollars, each of which has the same general purchasing power. This method of accounting is often described as accounting in units of general (usually current) purchasing power or as price level accounting. Because it uses an index of general purchasing power, constant dollar accounting adjusts for and measures general inflation.

Current cost accounting is a method of measuring and reporting assets and expenses associated with the use or sale of assets, at their current replacement cost or lower recoverable amount at the balance sheet date or at the date of use or sale. This method adjusts for price changes in specific items or classes of items.

The basic difference between these methods is that constant dollar accounting adjusts amounts to the same general price level while current cost accounting represents the current value of amounts without necessary reference to general price level changes.

2. *Current cost/constant dollar accounting* is a method of accounting based on measures of current cost or lower recoverable amount in terms of dollars, each of which has the same general purchasing power. The method adjusts current costs of all years reported on a comparative basis to reflect constant purchasing power.

Historical cost/nominal dollar accounting is the generally accepted method of accounting, used in the primary financial stat statements, based on measures of historical prices in dollars without restatement for changed replacement costs or changes in the purchasing power of the dollar.

b. Accounts for which an enterprise must measure the effects of changing prices in order to present the supplementary information required by SFAS No. 33 are inventory; property, plant and equipment; cost of goods sold; and depreciation, depletion, and amortization expense.

c. 1. SFAS No. 33 may help in attaining the objective of providing information to help investors, creditors, and other financial statement users assess the amounts, timing and uncertainty of prospective net cash inflows to the enterprise by analyzing information related to:

- the maintenance of the firm's productive capital through the replacement of inventory to support future sales, or the replacement of existing fixed assets as they wear out to maintain operating capability.
- assessment of financial performance in relation to price structure of products sold.
- the general effect of inflation and the resulting problems on specific categories of assets and expenses.

2. Information required by SFAS No. 33 may be useful for internal management decisions for:
   - capital budgeting analyses and to plan for assets replacements to be sure the firm's productive capacity is maintained.
   - decision-making situations such as pricing, make or buy, standard costing, and special orders.
   - a more accurate evaluation of performance from one period to the next.
   - evaluation of inventory valuation policy, monetary asset and liability policy, and dividend policy.

Answer Outline

Problem 2 SFAS 33

a. Lower of cost or market
   Changes in market value below cost recorded
   Unrealized holding losses recognized
   Unrealized holding gains above cost ignored
   Current cost
   All changes in asset value recorded
   All changes in market value affect earnings
   Unrealized holding losses and gains

b. Capital maintenance theory
   Capital must be maintained before income is recognized
   Well-offness
   Constant dollar
   Maintain purchasing power
   Current cost
   Maintain operating capacity

Unofficial Answer

Problem 2 SFAS 33

a. Short-term investments in marketable equity securities are accounted for on a lower-of-cost-or-market basis. The asset is reported on the balance sheet at cost, unless market value falls below cost. Then the asset valuation becomes market value. Therefore unrealized holding losses (and recoveries of those losses up to cost) are recognized, while unrealized holding gains above cost are not recognized until the asset is sold.

If accounted for on a current cost basis, the marketable equity securities would be recorded at cost when acquired. Subsequent asset valuation would be based on market value, whether above or below cost. All changes in market value would be reflected in earnings, i.e., both unrealized holding losses and gains are recognized.

b. Capital maintenance theory holds that a company's capital must be maintained before any income can be recognized. In other words, earnings is the amount an entity can distribute to its owners and be as well off at year-end as at the beginning of the year.

Constant dollar accounting measures well-offness in terms of purchasing power. An entity must maintain its purchasing power before income is recognized.

Current cost accounting measures well-offness in terms of operating capacity. An entity must maintain its operating capacity before income is recognized.

Solution Guide

Problem 3 Constant Dollar Accounting

1. Part a. requires calculation of the purchasing power gain (loss).

1.1 Purchasing power gain (loss) is the net gain (loss) from **restating** net balances (opening and closing) of, and transactions in, monetary items.

1.2 Monetary items are those items with amounts fixed by contract or statute.

1.3 Restate items by the TO/FROM ratio:

$$\text{Historical Cost} \times \frac{\text{Price level adjusting TO}}{\text{Price level adjusting FROM}} = \text{Restated Cost}$$

1.4 SFAS 33 requires use of average-for-the-year index for firms **not** presenting comprehensive supplementary financial statements.

2. Part b. requires a constant dollar income statement (note that the current cost information given is superfluous).

2.1 Restate transactions occurring uniformly throughout the year using average-for-the-year index.

2.2 Restate beginning inventory by using

$$\frac{\text{End-of-year index}}{\text{Beginning-of-year index}}$$

2.3 Restate nonmonetary items (e.g., ending inventory and depreciation) using appropriate index at time of purchase.

2.4 Include the purchasing power gain as an element of constant dollar net income.

Unofficial Answer

Problem 3 Constant Dollar Accounting

a.

	Nominal value	*Restatement ratio*	*Adjusted to constant 12/31/81 dollars*
Monetary Assets 12/31/80:			
Cash	$ 200,000		
Accounts receivable	– 0 –		
Accounts payable	(300,000)		
	$ (100,000)	220/200	$ (110,000)
Add: Increases in monetary assets			
Sales	$1,100,000	220/212	$1,141,500
	$1,100,000		$1,031,500
Less: Decreases in monetary assets			
Purchases	$1,000,000	220/212	$1,037,700
Rent	36,000	220/212	37,400
Other cash expenditures	44,000	220/212	45,700
Income taxes	80,000	220/212	83,000
	$1,160,000		$1,203,800
Net monetary assets at 12/31/81 – restated			$ (172,300)
Net monetary assets at 12/31/81 – not restated			
Cash	$ 240,000		
Accounts receivable	400,000		
Accounts payable	(800,000)		$ (160,000)
Purchasing power gain			$ 12,300

b.

Retail Showcase Mart
Statement of Earnings
For the Year Ended December 31, 1983
Adjusted to Constant Dollars, 12/31/81

	Nominal dollars	*Restatement ratio*	*Constant dollars Dec. 31, 1981*	
Sales	$1,100,000	220/212		$1,141,500
Cost of goods sold:				
Inventory 1/1/81	$ 400,000	220/200	$ 440,000	
Purchases in 1981	1,000,000	220/212	1,037,700	
Goods available	$1,400,000		$1,477,700	
Inventory 12/31/81	600,000	220/216	611,100	866,600
Gross Profit				274,900
Operating Expenses				
Rent expense	36,000	220/212	37,400	
Depreciation expense	20,000	220/200	22,000	
Other cash expenses	44,000	220/212	45,700	105,100
Income before taxes				169,800
Income tax expense	80,000	220/212		83,000
Net income before purchasing power gain				86,800
Purchasing power gain				12,300
Constant dollar net income				$ 99,100

Answer Outline

Problem 4 Current Valuation of Assets

b1. Matrix block 2
- Retains historical cost relationships between assets
- Compares units of purchasing power rather than monetary units
- Changes asset dollar amounts in periods of inflation or deflation
  - Compensates for a change in the value of the dollar
- All gain and loss is deferred until ultimate disposition
  - Gains and losses are reported in current purchasing power
  - Purchasing power gains and losses are eliminated
  - Gain or loss is different from historical cost amount

b2. Matrix block 3
- Asset current value relationships differ from historical cost
- No restatement due to changes in purchasing power
- Outside market forces determine asset values
- Change in current values represents "holding" gains
  - Recognized currently in income statements
  - Theoretically no gain or loss at disposition
- Total gain or loss is the same as historical cost

b3. Matrix block 4
- Historical cost is simultaneously modified by current values, e.g.,
  - Replacement cost
  - Market value
  - Net present value
  - Changes in purchasing power of the dollar
- Corrects for changes in market values and purchasing power
- Annual recognition of changes in market value
  - But adjusted for changes in purchasing power
  - Theoretically no gain or loss at disposition
- Total gain or loss varies from historical cost

Unofficial Answer

Problem 4 Current Valuation of Assets

b1. Matrix block 2. Nonmonetary assets recorded under the method described in block 2 will retain the historical cost basis, but the standard of comparison has been changed from units of money to units of general purchasing power. This method of reflecting nonmonetary assets will cause the amount shown as an asset to differ from the traditional method in periods of inflation or deflation.

This notion is supported by the argument that the unit of measure is not a stable monetary unit, and, by stating assets in terms of a "constant dollar", the assets are stated in terms of a stable unit of measure.

All holding gains or losses not recognized during the life of the nonmonetary asset will be deferred until the ultimate disposal of the asset because the basis of the asset has not been altered during the life of the asset. This deferral of gain or loss is the same as occurs using the traditional method discussed in matrix block 1. However, the amount of gain or loss recognized upon sale or abandonment of the nonmonetary asset may be different from the amount computed using the traditional method. This difference results from the restatement of the original cost basis in terms of the constant dollar. In effect, gains or losses from the changing value of the dollar are eliminated and the gain or loss on disposal or abandonment is limited to holding gains or losses and any residual excess over or under current value stated in terms of the common dollar.

b2. Matrix block 3. The relationship of assets recorded under the method described in block 3 has been changed from historical cost to current value, although the standard of comparison is still units of money. Under this method there is no attempt to restate the original dollars expended in terms of a "common dollar." However, it may be argued that, implicit in any current valuation method (replacement value, market value, or net present value), there is an element of current value compensating for the changing value of the dollar. This method of asset valuation does not recognize any implicit change in the unit of measure. Therefore, any difference in amounts recorded using this method and the traditional method is due to a change in the current value of the asset.

The justification for such an adjustment is based on the assumption that the value of an asset is affected by outside market factors.

The change in current value of assets throughout the life of the assets (commonly referred to as "holding" gains and losses) are recognized as gains or losses periodically during the productive life of the asset resulting in annual earnings statement recognition of holding gains or losses. Upon disposal of the asset, there theoretically will be no gain or loss because the asset is shown at current value. The sum of the holding gains or losses recognized in prior periods will comprise the total gain or loss, and any recognized gain or loss on disposal merely results in a correction of the current estimate of current value. While the timing of the gain or loss recognition under this method differs from the traditional method, the magnitude of the total gain or loss recognized will be the same under both methods. This is because the purchasing power of the dollar is assumed to remain unchanged throughout the life of the asset, and the amount of the gain or loss is computed as the difference between the dollars given up and current value of the asset (dollars received).

b3. Matrix block 4. The relationship of assets recorded under the method described in block 4 has been changed from historic cost to current value determined by one of several methods, that is, replacement value, market value, or net present value. Further, the standard of comparison has changed in that the current value amount is restated in terms of a common dollar. For these two reasons, the amount shown for assets will differ from the amount shown using the traditional method.

This method draws its support from the justification for the methods depicted in matrix blocks 2 and 3, namely, compensating for the unstable dollar and recognition that market forces affect the value of an asset over a period of time.

Using this method of asset valuation, the earnings statement will periodically reflect holding gains or losses, but these gains or losses will be restated in terms of a common dollar. As in block 3, gains or losses will be recognized over the life of the asset due to the recognition of holding gains or losses, and at the date of sale or abandonment any remaining gain or loss recognized is merely a recognition of the error in estimating true current value. Because the current value is restated in terms of a common dollar, the total gain or loss will be different from the amount computed using the traditional method.

Answer Outline

Problem 5 Constant Dollar Theory

Statement I

- Constant dollar statements are not required
  - Some disclosures required by SFAS 33
- Inflation may be immaterial for one year but material for a series of years
- LIFO inventories, fixed assets, etc., are more relevant when adjusted for price-level changes
- Constant dollar statements are an extension of historical cost
  - I.e., historical costs adjusted by the consumer price index
- Price indices are objectively derived

Statement II

- Constant dollar costs are unrelated to replacement costs
  - Constant dollar amounts equal current value only by coincidence
- Historical depreciation is not concerned with asset replacement
  - Depreciation is historical cost
  - Depreciation is concerned with cost allocation, not replacement
- Indices are based upon average change in prices
  - Current values are based upon specific asset prices
- Constant dollar data may improve management decisions

Statement III

- Current-noncurrent and monetary-nonmonetary are different
  - Current is based on 12 months
  - Or operating cycle, whichever is longer
  - Monetary is cash or other fixed-dollar contract
- Purchasing power G&L only occur on monetary items
  - Based on net monetary position
  - And direction of price-level change
  - Nonmonetary item restatement has no effect on purchasing power G&L
    - Converts historical cost to current dollar purchasing power

Unofficial Answer

Problem 5 Constant Dollar Theory

Statement I

The accounting profession has never required that published financial statements be adjusted for general price-level changes, but it has seriously discussed, considered, and recommended such adjustments. SFAS 33 requires some constant dollar and current cost disclosures for certain companies, and both SFAS 33 and APB statement 3 recommend that general price-level adjusted financial statements should be presented as a supplement to the basic historical-dollar financial statements.

The rate of inflation may be immaterial for any given year. However, the rate has been considered material in recent years and it certainly has been material when considering a period of years. Because corporations generally publish financial statements for a series of years, the cumulative effect of constant dollar adjustments on these statements would be material. Furthermore, financial statements often contain LIFO inventories, long-lived assets, and other amounts incurred two or more years earlier that should be adjusted for general price-level changes to make the amounts more relevant and more easily understood.

Constant dollar financial statements are not a departure from, but an extension of, historical-cost financial statements. The historical-cost amounts are adjusted for changes in the general price level by use of the consumer price index. Thus, the dollar amounts contained in general price-level adjusted financial statements are historical-cost amounts adjusted for the change in the purchasing power of the dollar.

The argument for the use of facts, not estimates, should have no bearing on thisdiscussion. Accounting is replete with estimates, such as estimates of asset lives for depreciation purposes, uncollectible accounts, income taxes expense, and many others. The average change in price levels is objectively determined (not a simple estimate) and could be used to present the facts in a more useful form.

Statement II

Constant dollar adjusted costs have no direct relationship to replacement costs. Depreciation is historical in nature and is not concerned with asset replacements; it is a process of cost allocation, not funding for asset replacements. Depreciation and constant dollar adjustments could be considered remotely related if, for example, net earnings were reduced by price-level adjustments, which in turn caused management to reduce dividends and thereby retain some assets that would otherwise have been paid out as dividends.

Constant dollar adjusted data would approximate current values only by coincidence. General price-level indexes are based on the average change in prices in the economy, not on changes in specific asset costs or industry prices. Current values are usually based on specific asset prices or asset appraisal values. These are usually a function of technology and supply and demand for these particular assets, rather than the general effect of inflation or deflation.

Management could probably make better decisions with constant dollar adjusted data than with unadjusted data, but there is a difference in purpose between internal and external reporting. Internal financial information for management decisions can be in any form that management desires. Internal financial reports are not bound by generally accepted accounting principles; they are prepared with the objective of maximum benefit to management and may be in any form or style management feels is the most useful. Thus, whether constant dollar adjusted financial statements are published or not, management should make decisions on what it believes is relevant information.

Statement III

There is a difference between classifying assets and liabilities as (1) current and noncurrent and (2) monetary and nonmonetary. Some current assets and current liabilities are monetary and some are nonmonetary, while some monetary assets and liabilities are current and some are noncurrent. The classification of an asset or liability as current is based on a period of 12 months or the operating cycle, whichever is longer. The classification of an asset or liability as monetary is based on whether it is cash or some other asset or liability whose amount is fixed by contract or otherwise in terms of numbers of dollars regardless of changes in specific prices or in the general price level.

With adjustments for general price-level changes, purchasing-power gains and losses are recognized on the holding of monetary items, but not on nonmonetary items. If monetary assets exceed monetary liabilities, the company is said to be a net monetary creditor. When the monetary assets are less than monetary liabilities, the company is said to be a net monetary debtor. The net monetary position and the amount and the direction of the change in the general price level will determine the price-level gain or loss. For example, if the company is a net monetary debtor, it will show a purchasing-power gain during an inflationary period and would show a purchasing-power loss during a deflationary period.

Restatement of nonmonetary items for changes in the general level of prices will have no effect on the amount of the purchasing-power gain or loss. It will simply cause historical-dollar amounts to be stated in current-dollar amounts of equal purchasing power.

Solution Guide

Problem 6 Constant Dollar and Current Cost

1. Part a. requires the balance sheet amount for three reporting models.

1.1 Constant dollar balance sheet would show the historical cost of the land adjusted by the TO/FROM ratio:

$$\text{Historical cost} \times \frac{\text{Price level adjusting to}}{\text{Price level adjusting from}} = \text{Restated cost}$$

1.2 Current cost balance sheet would show the current cost of replacing the land.

1.3 Current cost/constant dollar balance sheet would show the same amount as current cost balance sheet because current cost is stated in terms of current purchasing power.

2. Part b. requires the computations of several income statement items.

2.1 Constant dollar income does not result until a sale has occurred; the conventional realization concept still applies.

2.2 Unrealized holding gain (loss) in a current cost system is the difference between the historical cost and current cost of assets held at year end.

2.3 Income from continuing operations is the difference between sales revenue less the current cost of inputs. Sales revenue is different from the current cost of the land because sales revenue is the amount we can sell the land for (exit value), while current cost is the amount we would pay today to acquire the land (entry value). Assets more likely to have different entry and exit values would include inventory and buildings.

2.4 Realized holding gain (loss) is the difference between the current cost and historical cost of an asset sold or consumed.

2.5 The total holding gain *recognized* on a current cost/constant dollar basis is the sum of: the holding gains and losses realized during the year, and the *change* in the unrealized holding gain or loss during the year. Only the change in unrealized items is included so as to avoid "double counting" of these gains or losses. For example, the realized holding gain ($17,000) in this problem includes the unrealized holding gain ($8,000) recognized last year. If no adjustment were made, the $8,000 would be included in both 1979 and 1980 income.

3. Part c. requires the amount of income from continuing operations as required by FASB Statement No. 33 for 1978, 1979 and 1980.

3.1 Income from continuing operations must be presented on both a constant dollar basis and a current cost basis.

3.2 See 2.1 and 2.3 above for further explanations.

Unofficial Answer

Problem 6 Constant Dollar and Current Cost

Part a.

Valuation of land	*Constant dollar*	*Current cost*	*Current cost/ constant dollar*
12/31/78	$40,000	$40,000	$40,000
12/31/79	44,000[a]	52,000	52,000

[a]$40,000 x 110/100 = $44,000

Part b.

1. Constant dollar income

1978	–
1979	–
1980	$20,000[a]

[a]$40,000 x 120/100 = $48,000 constant dollar basis

$68,000 – $48,000 = $20,000 income

2. Current cost of land $52,000
 Historical cost of land 40,000
 Unrealized holding gain $12,000

3. Sales $68,000
 Current cost of land 65,000
 Income from continuing
 operations (current cost) $ 3,000

4. Current cost of land $65,000
 Historical cost of land 40,000
 Realized holding gain $25,000

5. Realized holding gain:
 Current cost of land $65,000
 Cost of land on constant
 dollar basis ($40,000
 x 120/100) 48,000
 Realized holding gain $17,000

Unrealized holding gain:	1/1/80	10/31/80
Current cost of land	$52,000	—
Cost of land on constant dollar basis	44,000	—
Unrealized holding gain	$ 8,000	—
	x120/110	
Unrealized holding gain in constant dollars 10/31/80	$ 8,727	

Total holding gain recognized:

Realized holding gain $17,000
Change in unrealized holding gains ($0 − $8,727) (8,727)
 Total holding gain
 recognized $ 8,273

Part c.

Income from continuing operations

Year	Constant dollar	Current cost
1978	—	—
1979	—	—
1980	$20,000[a]	$3,000[b]

[a]$40,000 x 120/100 = $48,000 constant dollar basis
 $68,000 − $48,000 = $20,000 income
[b]$68,000 − $65,000 = $3,000

FOREIGN CURRENCY
Solution Guide

Problem 7 Foreign Currency Translation

1. Translation of selected accounts from a foreign balance sheet into United States dollars at 12/31/76 is required. The solutions approach is to determine the proper exchange rate for each balance sheet item at December 31 of both 1975 and 1976. When the U.S. dollar is the functional currency, SFAS 52 requires the following rules be followed in the translation process:

1a. Monetary assets and monetary liabilities are translated at the current rate at the balance sheet date, and

1b. Nonmonetary assets, nonmonetary liabilities, and stockholders' equity balances are translated at exchange rates in existence when the balances originated.

1.1 Accounts receivable is a monetary item and accordingly is translated at the current rate. The allowance for bad debts is also translated at the current rate. Thus, the analysis of the accounts receivable and allowance accounts is not relevant to the solution. The current rate at the end of 1976 was 1.5 and the current rate at the end of 1975 was 1.7.

1.2 Inventories carried at cost are translated at the historical rate, and inventories carried at the current market price are translated at the current rate. In this problem, inventory is carried at FIFO cost. Since the inventories are based on FIFO, ending inventory consists of purchases of the current year. The 1976 purchases were made in June at which time the exchange rate was 1.7. The 1975 purchases were also made in June when the exchange rate was 2.0.

1.3 Property, plant, and equipment and the related accumulated depreciation are translated at the historical rate. Begin your analysis with 1975 as the balance in the fixed asset account is cumulative, i.e., the assets on hand at the end of 1975 continue to be on hand at the end of 1976. The $150,000 of net assets was all purchased when the exchange rate was 2.0 (before July 31, 1975). Thus the $150,000 of 1975 P,P&E is translated at the 2.0 exchange rate.

Note that there is no need to be concerned with the depreciation as it is to be translated at the same rate as the related fixed assets. The $150,000 of 12/31/75 fixed assets resulted from the 1975 acquisitions of 24,000 LCU and 140,000 LCU, less the 14,000 LCU of 1975 depreciation.

The 12/31/76 net fixed assets consisted of the 1975 ending balance of 150,000 LCU less another 14,000 LCU of depreciation which is to be translated at 2.0. Additionally 30,000 LCU of equipment was purchased in 1976 and 3,000 LCU thereof depreciated. The net 1976 addition is 27,000 units to be translated at 1.5 (the exchange rate of July 1976 when the 1976 acquisitions were made).

1.4 Long-term debt is a monetary item and accordingly is translated at the current rate. The current rate at the end of 1976 was 1.5 and the current rate at the end of 1975 was 1.7.

1.5 Since the ending balance of long-term debt is translated at the current rate, the information provided on additional issuances of debt is irrelevant to the solution. Common stock is a nonmonetary item and is translated at the historical rate. The stock was issued at the beginning of 1975 when the exchange rate was 2.0. Since there were no additional issuances of stock in 1976, the capital stock account is translated at the historical rate of 2.0 at both the end of 1975 and the end of 1976.

Unofficial Answer

Problem 7 Foreign Currency Translation

Franklin Company's Foreign Subsidiary
Translation of Selected Captions Into United States Dollars
December 31, 1976 and December 31, 1975

	LCU	Translation rate	United States dollars
December 31, 1976			
Accounts receivable (net)	40,000 LCU	1.5 LCU to $1	$26,667
Inventories, at cost	80,000	1.7 LCU to $1	47,059
Property, plant, and equipment (net)	163,000	Schedule 1	86,000
Long-term debt	100,000	1.5 LCU to $1	66,667
Common stock	50,000	2 LCU to $1	25,000
December 31, 1975			
Accounts receivable (net)	35,000	1.7 LCU to $1	20,588
Inventories, at cost	75,000	2 LCU to $1	37,500
Property, plant, and equipment (net)	150,000	2 LCU to $1	75,000
Long-term debt	120,000	1.7 LCU to $1	70,588
Common stock	50,000	2 LCU to $1	25,000

Schedule 1

Computation of Translation of Property, Plant and Equipment (Net) into United States Dollars at December 31, 1976

	LCU	Translation rate	United States dollars
Land purchased on January 1, 1975	24,000 LCU	2 LCU to $1	$12,000
Plant and equipment purchased on January 1, 1975:			
Original cost	140,000	2 LCU to $1	70,000
Depreciation for 1975	(14,000)	2 LCU to $1	(7,000)
Depreciation for 1976	(14,000)	2 LCU to $1	(7,000)
	112,000	2 LCU to $1	56,000
Plant and equipment purchased on July 4, 1976:			
Original cost	30,000	1.5 LCU to $1	20,000
Depreciation for 1976	(3,000)	1.5 LCU to $1	(2,000)
	27,000	1.5 LCU to $1	18,000
	163,000 LCU		$86,000

Multiple Choice Questions (1 - 32)

1. Information from Greg Company's balance sheet is as follows:

Current assets:	
Cash	$ 2,400,000
Marketable securities	7,500,000
Accounts receivable	57,600,000
Inventories	66,300,000
Prepaid expenses	1,200,000
Total current assets	$135,000,000
Current liabilities:	
Notes payable	$ 1,500,000
Accounts payable	19,500,000
Accrued expenses	12,500,000
Income taxes payable	500,000
Payments due within one year on long-term debt	3,500,000
Total current liabilities	$ 37,500,000

What is the quick (acid test) ratio?

a. 1.60 to 1.
b. 1.80 to 1.
c. 1.99 to 1.
d. 3.60 to 1.

2. Inventories would be included in the calculation of which of the following?

	Acid test (quick) ratio	*Working capital (current) ratio*
a.	Yes	Yes
b.	Yes	No
c.	No	Yes
d.	No	No

3. If current assets exceed current liabilities, payments to creditors made on the last day of the month will

a. Decrease current ratio.
b. Increase current ratio.
c. Decrease net working capital.
d. Increase net working capital.

4. Which of the following ratios measures short-term solvency?

a. Current ratio.
b. Age of receivables.
c. Creditors' equity to total assets.
d. Return on investment.

5. A company has a current ratio of 2 to 1. This ratio will decrease if the company

a. Receives a 5% stock dividend on one of its marketable securities.
b. Pays a large account payable which had been a current liability.
c. Borrows cash on a six-month note.
d. Sells merchandise for more than cost and records the sale using the perpetual-inventory method.

6. Selected information from the accounting records of Dalton Manufacturing Company is as follows:

Net sales for 1982	$1,800,000
Cost of goods sold for 1982	1,200,000
Inventories at December 31, 1981	336,000
Inventories at December 31, 1982	288,000

Assuming there are 300 working days per year, what is the number of days' sales in average inventories for 1982?

a. 78
b. 72
c. 52
d. 48

7. Utica Company's net accounts receivable were $250,000 at December 31, 1978, and $300,000 at December 31, 1979. Net cash sales for 1979 were $100,000. The accounts receivable turnover for 1979 was 5.0. What were Utica's total net sales for 1979?

a. $1,475,000
b. $1,500,000
c. $1,600,000
d. $2,750,000

8. Bretton Corporation's books disclosed the following information as of and for the year ended December 31, 1981:

Net credit sales	$2,000,000
Net cash sales	500,000
Merchandise purchases	1,000,000
Inventory at beginning	600,000
Inventory at end	200,000
Accounts receivable at beginning	300,000
Accounts receivable at end	700,000
Net income	100,000

Bretton's accounts receivable turnover is

a. 2.9 times.
b. 3.6 times.
c. 4.0 times.
d. 5.0 times.

9. Georgia, Inc., has an authorized capital of 1,000 shares of $100 par, 8% cumulative preferred stock and 100,000 shares of $10 par common stock. The equity account balances at December 31, 1981, are as follows:

Cumulative preferred stock	$ 50,000
Common stock	90,000
Additional paid-in capital	9,000
Retained earnings	13,000
Treasury stock, common—100 shares at cost	(2,000)
	$160,000

Dividends on preferred stock are in arrears for the year 1981. The book value of a share of common stock, at December 31, 1981, should be

a. $11.78
b. $11.91
c. $12.22
d. $12.36

10. Ventura Corporation was organized on January 1, 1981, with the following capital structure:

10% cumulative preferred stock, par and liquidation value $100; authorized, issued, and outstanding 1,000 shares	$100,000
Common stock, par value $5; authorized 20,000 shares; issued and outstanding 10,000 shares	50,000

Ventura's net income for the year ended December 31, 1981, was $450,000, but no dividends were declared. How much was Ventura's book value per common share at December 31, 1981?

a. $44
b. $45
c. $49
d. $50

11. Bretton Corporation's books disclosed the following information as of and for the year ended December 31, 1981:

Net credit sales	$2,000,000
Net cash sales	500,000
Merchandise purchases	1,000,000
Inventory at beginning	600,000
Inventory at end	200,000
Accounts receivable at beginning	300,000
Accounts receivable at end	700,000
Net income	100,000

Bretton's percent of net income on sales is

a. 4%
b. 9%
c. 44%
d. 56%

12. For a company that has only common stock outstanding, total shareholders' equity divided by the number of shares outstanding represents the

a. Return on equity.
b. Stated value per share.
c. Book value per share.
d. Price-earnings ratio.

13. Selected information for Irvington Company is as follows:

	December 31	
	1978	*1979*
Preferred stock, 8%, par $100, nonconvertible, noncumulative	$125,000	$125,000
Common stock	300,000	400,000
Retained earnings	75,000	185,000
Dividends paid on preferred stock for year ended	10,000	10,000
Net income for year ended	60,000	120,000

Irvington's return on common stockholders' equity, rounded to the nearest percentage point, for 1979 is

a. 17%
b. 19%
c. 23%
d. 25%

14. Barr Corporation's capital stock at December 31, 1982, consisted of the following:

- Common stock, $2 par value; 100,000 shares authorized, issued, and outstanding
- 10% noncumulative, nonconvertible preferred stock, $100 par value; 1,000 shares authorized, issued, and outstanding

Barr's common stock, which is listed on a major stock exchange, was quoted at $4 per share on December 31, 1982. Barr's net income for the year ended December 31, 1982, was $50,000. The 1982 preferred dividend was declared. No capital stock transactions occurred during 1982. What was the price-earnings ratio on Barr's common stock at December 31, 1982?

a. 8 to 1.
b. 10 to 1.
c. 16 to 1.
d. 20 to 1.

15. The following common size income statements are available for Sparky Corporation for the two years ended December 31, 1975, and 1974:

	1975	1974
Sales	100%	100%
Cost of sales	55	70
Gross profit on sales	45	30
Operating expenses (including income tax expense)	20	18
Net income	25%	12%

The trend percentages for sales are as follows:

1975	130%
1974	100%

What should be the trend percentage for gross profit on sales for 1975?

a. 58.5%
b. 130%
c. 150%
d. 195%

16. How are the following used in the calculation of the dividend payout ratio for a company with only common stock outstanding?

	Dividends per share	Earnings per share	Book value per share
a.	Denominator	Numerator	Not used
b.	Denominator	Not used	Numerator
c.	Numerator	Denominator	Not used
d.	Numerator	Not used	Denominator

17. Which of the following is an appropriate computation for return on investment?

a. Income dividend by total assets.
b. Income divided by sales.
c. Sales divided by total assets.
d. Sales divided by stockholders' equity.

Items 18, 19, and 20 are based on the following information:

The December 31, 1975, balance sheet of Ratio, Inc., is presented below. These are the only accounts in Ratio's balance sheet. Amounts indicated by a question mark (?) can be calculated from the additional information given.

Assets:	
Cash	$ 25,000
Accounts receivable (net)	?
Inventory	?
Property, plant and equipment (net)	294,000
	$432,000
Liabilities and stockholders' equity:	
Accounts payable (trade)	?
Income taxes payable (current)	25,000
Long-term debt	?
Common stock	300,000
Retained earnings	?
	?

Additional information:

Current ratio (at year end)	1.5 to 1
Total liabilities divided by total stockholders' equity	.8
Inventory turnover based on sales and ending inventory	15 times
Inventory turnover based on cost of goods sold and ending inventory	10.5 times
Gross margin for 1975	$315,000

18. What was Ratio's December 31, 1975, balance in trade accounts payable?

a. $ 67,000
b. $ 92,000
c. $182,000
d. $207,000

19. What was Ratio's December 31, 1975, balance in retained earnings?

a. $60,000 deficit.
b. $60,000.
c. $132,000 deficit.
d. $132,000.

20. What was Ratio's December 31, 1975, balance in the inventory account?

a. $ 21,000
b. $ 30,000
c. $ 70,000
d. $135,000

Items 21 through 24 are based on the following instructions:

Each item describes an independent situation. For each situation, one factor is denoted X and the other factor is denoted Y. For each situation, compare the two factors to determine whether X is greater than, equal to, or less than Y.

21. Delta Corporation wrote off a $100 uncollectible account receivable against the $1,200 balance in its allowance account. Compare the current ratio before the write off (X) with the current ratio after the write off (Y).

a. X greater than Y.
b. X equals Y.
c. X less than Y.
d. Cannot be determined.

22. Kappa, Inc., neglected to amortize the premium on its bonds payable. Compare the company's net earnings without this premium amortization (X) and the company's net earnings with such amortization (Y).
a. X greater than Y.
b. X equals Y.
c. X less than Y.
d. Cannot be determined.

23. Aaron, Inc., owns 80% of the outstanding stock of Belle, Inc. Compare the consolidated net earnings of Aaron and Belle (X) and Aaron's net earnings if it does not consolidate with Belle (Y).
a. X greater than Y.
b. X equals Y.
c. X less than Y.
d. Cannot be determined.

24. Epsilon Company has a current ratio of 2 to 1. A transaction reduces the current ratio. Compare the working capital before this transaction (X) and the working capital after this transaction (Y).
a. X greater than Y.
b. X equals Y.
c. X less than Y.
d. Cannot be determined.

Items 25 through 30 deal with the calculations of ratios and the determination of other factors considered important in analysis of financial statements. Prior to the occurrence of the independent events described below the corporation concerned had current and quick ratios in excess of one to one and reported a net income (as opposed to a loss) for the period just ended. Income tax effects of the events are to be ignored. The corporation had only one class of shares outstanding.

25. The effect of recording a 100% stock dividend would be to
a. Decrease the current ratio, decrease working capital, and decrease book value per share.
b. Leave inventory turnover unaffected, decrease working capital, and decrease book value per share.
c. Leave working capital unaffected, decrease earnings per share, and decrease book value per share.
d. Leave working capital unaffected, decrease earnings per share, and decrease the debt to equity ratio.

26. Recording the payment (as distinguished from the declaration) of a cash dividend whose declaration was already recorded will
a. Increase the current ratio but have no effect on working capital.
b. Decrease both the current ratio and working capital.
c. Increase both the current ratio and working capital.
d. Have no effect on the current ratio or earnings per share.

27. What would be the effect on book value per share and earnings per share if the corporation purchased its own shares in the open market at a price greater than book value per share?
a. No effect on book value per share but increase earnings per share.
b. Increase both book value per share and earnings per share.
c. Decrease both book value per share and earnings per share.
d. Decrease book value per share and increase earnings per share.

28. If the corporation were to increase the extent to which it successfully "traded on the equity" this fact would likely be manifested in a combination of facts that its
a. Ratio of owner's equity to total assets decreased while its ratio of net income to owners' equity increased.
b. Book value and earnings per share decreased.
c. Working capital decreased while its current ratio increased.
d. Asset turnover and return on sales both decreased.

29. The corporation exercises control over an affiliate in which it holds a 40% common stock interest. If its affiliate completed a fiscal year profitably but paid no dividends, how would this affect the investor corporation?
a. Result in an increased current ratio.
b. Result in increased earnings per share.
c. Increase several turnover ratios.
d. Decrease book value per share.

30. What would be the most probable cause of an increase in the rate of inventory turnover while the rate of receivables turnover decreased when compared with the prior period?

a. Sales volume has changed markedly.

b. Investment in inventory has decreased while investment in receivables has increased.

c. Investment in inventory has increased while investment in receivables has decreased.

d. The corporation has shortened the credit period for customers (tightened credit terms).

May 1984 Questions

31. Selected information for Moore Corporation is as follows:

	December 31	
	1982	*1983*
Preferred stock	$180,000	$180,000
Common stock	648,000	840,000
Retained earnings	192,000	360,000
Net income for year ended	144,000	240,000

What is Moore's rate of return on average stockholders' equity for 1983?

a. 16.0%

b. 20.0%

c. 23.5%

d. 26.0%

32. How is the average inventory used in the calculation of each of the following?

	Acid test (quick ratio)	*Inventory turnover rate*
a.	Numerator	Numerator
b.	Numerator	Denominator
c.	Not used	Denominator
d.	Not used	Numerator

Problem

Problem 1 Corporation Solvency Ratios (1173,T7)

(25 to 30 minutes)

As the CPA responsible for an "opinion" audit engagement, you are requested by the client to organize the work to provide him at the earliest possible date with some key ratios based on the final figures appearing on the comparative financial statements. This information is to be used to convince creditors that the client business is solvent and to support the use of going-concern valuation procedures in the financial statements. The client wishes to save time by concentrating on only these key data.

The data requested and the computations taken from the financial statements follow:

	Last year	*This year*
Current ratio	2.0:1	2.5:1
Quick (acid test) ratio	1.2:1	.7:1
Property, plant, and equipment to owners' equity	2.3:1	2.6:1
Sales to owners' equity	2.8:1	2.5:1
Net income	Down 10%	Up 30%
Earnings per common share	$2.40	$3.12
Book value per common share	Up 8%	Up 5%

Required:

a. The client asks that you prepare a list of brief comments stating how each of these items supports the solvency and going-concern potential of his business. He wishes to use these comments to support his presentation of data to his creditors. You are to prepare the comments as requested, giving the implications and the limitations of each item separately and then the collective inference one may draw from them about the client's solvency and going-concern potential.

b. Having done as the client requested in part a., prepare a brief listing of additional ratio-analysis-type data for this client which you think his creditors are going to ask for to supplement the data provided in part a. Explain why you think the additional data will be helpful to these creditors in evaluating this client's solvency.

c. What warnings should you offer these creditors about the limitations of ratio analysis for the purpose stated here?

Multiple Choice Answers

1. b	8. c	15. d	21. b	27. d
2. c	9. b	16. c	22. c	28. a
3. b	10. c	17. a	23. b	29. b
4. a	11. a	18. a	24. d	30. b
5. c	12. c	19. a	25. c	31. b
6. a	13. c	20. c	26. a	32. c
7. a	14. b			

Multiple Choice Answer Explanations

A. Solvency

1. (1181,P1,4) (b) The requirement is the quick (acid-test) ratio. The quick ratio is quick assets (cash, temporary investments in marketable securities, accounts receivable, and notes receivable) divided by current liabilities. The quick ratio measures the ability to pay current liabilities from cash and near-cash items. In this case, quick assets total $67,500,000, and current liabilities total $37,500,000, resulting in a quick ratio of 1.80 to 1.

2. (583,T1,45) (c) The requirement is the inclusion or exclusion of inventories in the calculation of the acid test (quick) and working capital (current) ratios. The acid test ratio is defined as the sum of cash, net receivables, and marketable securities divided by total current liabilities. Inventories and prepaid items should be excluded from this ratio. The working capital ratio is defined as total current assets (including inventory and prepaid expenses) divided by total current liabilities.

3. (580,T1,1) (b) Payments to creditors will decrease both cash (current asset) and payables (current liability). Therefore, both answers (c) and (d) are incorrect because there is no effect on net working capital. If current assets exceed current liabilities prior to this payment, the current ratio is greater than one. Subtracting equal amounts from both the numerator and the denominator of a fraction which is greater than one will increase the fraction. Note that such a payment in cases where the current ratio is less than one will decrease the ratio.

4. (580,T1,50) (a) Age of receivables is an activity ratio (measures how effectively assets are used). Return on investment is a profitability ratio. Both the current ratio and creditors' equity to total assets measure solvency, but the latter is geared more to long-term creditors.

5. (576,T1,12) (c) A solutions approach is to begin with the ratio of current asset to current liabilities of 2:1 as illustrated below. In answer (a) the 5% stock dividend on a marketable security will not affect the numerator or denominator, because receipt of stock dividends just changes the cost per share of stock and not the overall cost of the investment in marketable securities. Answer (b) is incorrect because the payment of an account payable would reduce both the numerator and denominator an equal amount, e.g., would bring it to 1.5/.5, which is an increase in the current ratio. Answer (c) is correct because both the numerator and denominator would increase by an equal amount, in this case 1, bringing it to a current ratio of 1.5 rather than 2. In the last case selling merchandise for more than cost would result in an increase in current assets with no change in current liabilities. Once again the solutions approach is to jot down a revised current ratio for each answer.

2/1 2/1 1.5/.5 3/2 2.5/1

B. Operational Efficiency

6. (1183,P1,18) (a) The requirement is the number of days' sales in average inventories during 1982. The average sales per day, at cost, is computed below.

$$\frac{\text{Cost of goods sold}}{\text{Working days}} = \frac{\$1{,}200{,}000}{300} = \underline{\underline{\$4{,}000}}$$

The average inventories (also at cost) are computed by averaging beginning and ending inventories.

$$\frac{BI + EI}{2} = \frac{\$336{,}000 + \$288{,}000}{2} = \underline{\underline{\$312{,}000}}$$

Therefore, the number of days' sales in average inventories is 78 days, as computed below.

$$\frac{\text{Avg. inv. at cost}}{\text{Avg. sales per day at cost}} = \frac{\$312{,}000}{\$4{,}000} = \underline{\underline{78 \text{ days}}}$$

7. (1180,P1,5) (a) The requirement is Utica's total net sales for 1979. The amount of cash sales ($100,000) was given, so only credit sales must be computed using the information given on accounts receivable turnover.

$$\text{A/R turnover} = \frac{\text{Credit Sales}}{\text{Average A/R}}$$

The information given can be inserted into the above equation:

$$5.0 = \frac{\text{Credit Sales}}{(250{,}000 + 300{,}000)/2}$$

Therefore, credit sales are $1,375,000. Total sales are $100,000 higher, or $1,475,000.

8. (1182,Q1,9) (c) The requirement is to calculate the accounts receivable turnover. This turnover is calculated by dividing the credit sales for the year by the average accounts receivable balance. The average balance is used because credit sales, which increase the accounts receivable balance, take place throughout the year. The average accounts receivable balance is calculated by adding the accounts receivable balance at the beginning and end of the year together and dividing by 2: ($300,000 + $700,000) ÷ 2 = $500,000, and the accounts receivable turnover is $2,000,000 ÷ 500,000 = 4 times.

D. Profitability

9. (582,P1,5) (b) The requirement is the book value of a share of common stock at 12/31/81. The book value per share of common stock is the amount each share would receive if the company was liquidated at the net book value of all amounts reported as assets and liabilities on the balance sheet. The owners' equity must first be allocated to the preferred stock, then to the common stock. The amount allocated to the preferred stock is equal to its par value (or liquidation value, if stated) plus any dividends in arrears.

Par value of preferred stock outstanding	+	1981 dividends in arrears	=	Amount allocated to preferred
$50,000	+	(8%)($50,000)	=	$54,000

The remaining unallocated owners' equity is $106,000 (total owners' equity of $160,000 less preferred's share of $54,000). This amount must be divided by outstanding common shares. 9,000 shares have been issued ($90,000 total par value ÷ $10 par per share), and 100 are held in treasury, leaving 8,900 shares outstanding. The book value per share, then, is $11.91 ($106,000 ÷ 8,900 shares). Note that treasury shares are deducted since these shares will receive nothing in the event of liquidation. Essentially, they represent previous disinvestment by the entity.

10. (1182,Q1,5) (c) The requirement is to calculate the book value per share of common stock. The book value per share of common stock is the amount each share would receive if the company were liquidated based on amounts reported on the balance sheet. Owners' equity must be allocated first to the preferred stockholders then to the common stockholders. The amount of owners' equity allocated to the preferred stockholders is equal to the sum of the liquidation value of the preferred stock (if such a value exists) plus any dividends in arrears on cumulative preferred stock. If a liquidation value is not given, the par value for preferred stock is used instead. In this problem, the liquidation value is the par value. The par value multiplied by the 1,000 preferred shares outstanding gives $100,000. Dividends are in arrears for the current year in the amount of $10,000 (10% x $100,000). Therefore, the total amount of owners' equity allocated to common stock is the residual amount of capital or $490,000 ($600,000 total owners' equity – $110,000 owners' equity allocated to preferred stockholders). Book value per common share is $490,000 ÷ 10,000 common shares outstanding or $49.

11. (1182,Q1,10) (a) The requirement is to calculate net income as a percentage of sales. Both credit and cash sales contributed to the net income figure. The calculation is net income divided by total net sales:

$$\frac{\$100{,}000}{(\$2{,}000{,}000 + \$500{,}000)} = 4\%$$

12. (1181,T1,19) (c) Book value per common share is defined as total common equity less the portion allocable to preferred stock, if any, divided by number of common shares and measures the amount of common stockholders' equity in each share of stock. Answer (a), return on equity is found by dividing net income by average common stockholders' equity as a measure of the rate of return earned by owners on their investment. Answer (b), stated value per share, like par value, is an arbitrary value assigned to common stock, typically to indicate the minimum amount at which the stock can be issued. The price-earnings ratio, answer (d), is the price per share of common stock divided by earnings per share of common stock and indicates how much investors are paying to obtain their return on investment.

F. Other

13. (1180,P1,7) (c) The requirement is Irvington's return on common stockholders' equity for 1979, which is computed by dividing net income available to common stockholders (net income less preferred dividends) by average common stockholders' equity:

$$\frac{\$120{,}000 - \$10{,}000}{(\$375{,}000 + \$585{,}000)/2} = 23\%$$

14. (1183,Q1,19) (b) The requirement is the price-earnings ratio. The price-earnings ratio is equal to the market price of common stock divided by the earnings per share. This ratio is used to measure a firm's profitability relative to the selling price of its common stock. The price-earnings ratio in this problem is 10 to 1 calculated as follows:

$$P/E = \frac{\text{Market price per share}}{\text{Earnings per share}} = \frac{\$4 \text{ (given)}}{\$.40 \text{ (calculated below)}} = \underline{\underline{10}}$$

The earnings per share is calculated as follows:

$$EPS = \frac{\underset{\text{(net income)}}{\$50,000} - \underset{\text{(preferred dividends)}}{\$10,000}}{\underset{\text{(common shares outstanding)}}{100,000}} = \underline{\underline{\$.40}}$$

The $10,000 preferred dividends (10% x $100 par value x 1,000 shares) were declared and therefore, are subtracted from net income in the EPS calculation as this amount is not available to the common shareholders.

15. (1176,Q1,1) (d) The requirement is the trend percentage for gross profit in 1975. In percentage analysis of financial statements, vertical analysis presents each item in a financial statement as a percentage of some other item, e.g., sales. Note that both the 1975 and 1974 income statements are presented as percentages of sales for their respective years. These are known as common size statements. Horizontal analysis constitutes percentages reflecting the change from one period to the next period on an item by item basis, e.g., the trend percentages in this problem.

The solutions approach to this problem is to recognize that 1975 sales are 130% of 1974 sales. In the absence of other information the gross profit rate continues to be 45% resulting in a 58.5% gross profit rate in 1975 relative to the gross profit rate of 30% in 1974. Thus the gross profit and percentage for 1975 is 195%.

1975	
130%	Sales
x45%	GP rate
58.5%	GP on sales
÷30%	1974 GP on sales
195%	1975 trend %

16. (1182,T1, 40) (c) The requirement is to determine the dividend payout ratio.

$$\text{Payout ratio} = \frac{\text{Dividends per share}}{\text{Earnings per share}}$$

Answer (c) is correct.

17. (581,T1,30) (a) The requirement is the appropriate computation for return on investment. The return on investment is the product of two components: net income as a percentage of sales and capital turnover as shown below:

$$ROI = \frac{\text{Net income}}{\text{Sales}} \times \frac{\text{Sales}}{\text{Total assets}}$$

Through a simple algebraic manipulation, the "sales" in both ratios cancel each other out, leaving ROI equal to income divided by total assets. Answer (b) is incorrect because it only takes into consideration the first component of the return on investment calculation. Answer (c) is incorrect because it only takes into consideration the second component of the return on investment calculation. Answer (d) is incorrect because stockholders' equity is equivalent to total assets only if the company has incurred no liabilities (a highly unlikely situation), and also because sales do not appear in the numerator of the ROI computation.

Multiple Problems

18. (576,P1,7) (a) This and the following two questions are a good example of the need for working some related multiple choice questions simultaneously. As noted elsewhere, you should be in the habit of studying the requirements of all related objective questions before beginning to work them. This is parallel to the suggestion that you study all of the requirements of practice problems before attempting to continue with the solutions approach. In this particular case the first step is to compute the ending inventory with the gross margin and turnover data. As illustrated below, the sales less cost of sales equals $315,000. Sales divided by the inventory is 15, and cost of sales divided by inventory is 10.5. This is solved below by determining that sales are equal to 15 I, cost of sales equal to 10.5 I, and then subtracting the CS equation from the S equation and obtaining S – CS equals 4.5 I. You already know that S – CS equals $315,000, which we substitute in the next to the last equation on the right and thus determine inventory equal to 70,000.

$$S - CS = 315{,}000 \qquad\qquad S = 15\ I$$

$$\frac{S}{I} = 15 \qquad\qquad CS = 10.5\ I$$

$$\frac{CS}{I} = 10.5 \qquad\qquad S - CS = 4.5\ I$$

$$315{,}000 = 4.5\ I$$

$$I = 70{,}000$$

Once you have computed inventory to be 70,000, you can compute accounts receivable to be $43,000 as illustrated below. When you have the accounts receivable, you can compute total current assets to be $138,000, which is equal to 1½ times the current liability. The current liabilities consist of $25,000 of taxes payable plus accounts payable. This is solvable to determine accounts payable equal to $67,000.

95,000 + 294,000 + AR = 432,000
AR = 43,000

(95,000 + 43,000) = 1.5(25,000 + AP)
138,000 = 37,500 + 1.5 AP
100,500 = 1.5 AP
AP = 67,000

After you have computed payables to be $67,000, you can compute debt plus retained earnings equal to $40,000. You have also been told that the total liabilities equals 80% of the stockholders' equity, which means that the $92,000 of current liabilities plus debt equals 80% of $300,000 of common stock plus retained earnings. Substituting in $40,000 minus retained earnings for D, you can solve retained earnings to be a deficit $60,000, as computed below.

D + RE = 432,000 – 67,000 – 25,000 – 300,000
D + RE = 40,000 or
D = 40,000 – RE
92,000 + D = .8(300,000 + RE)
92,000 + 40,000 – RE = 240,000 + .8 RE
–108,000 = 1.8 RE
RE = –60,000

It may be advisable to pass over a problem this lengthy until later on in the exam when you find yourself with spare time. Note that these multiple choice questions are budgeted approximately three minutes each. Could you work these three problems in nine minutes?

19. (576,P1,8) (a) See the preceding explanation.

20. (576,P1,9) (c) See the preceding explanation.

21. (1176,T1,19) (b) The requirement is to compare the current ratio before and after the transaction. Next, explicitly note the composition of the current ratio: current assets over current liabilities. Next, note the effect of the transaction on both current assets and current liabilities. The writing off of accounts receivable against an allowance account decreases both a current asset and a contra current asset account, thus, no effect on current assets. Likewise the transaction does not affect current liabilities. Thus, the current ratio remains the same.

22. (1176,T1,20) (c) The requirement is to compare earnings without bond premium amortization (X) to earnings with bond premium amortization (Y). The entry to record bond premium amortization is to debit the premium and credit interest expense, i.e., reduce expense or increase income. Thus, the income without amortization (X) is less than income with amortization (Y).

23. (1176,T1,21) (b) Are the consolidated earnings of Aaron and Belle greater than Aaron's earnings alone? They are the same, because the equity method is applied in consolidation. The equity method is also required for unconsolidated subsidiaries (para 14, APB 18).

24. (1176,T1,22) (d) The requirement is the change in working capital resulting from a decrease in the current ratio. As illustrated below, the current ratio of 2/1 can be reduced by adding the same amount to both numerator and denominator or it can be reduced by increasing the denominator or reducing the numerator. If the same amount is added to both numerator and denominator, working capital remains the same. If the numerator is reduced or the denominator increased, working capital would decrease. Thus, we cannot determine whether working capital will remain the same or decrease.

$$\frac{2}{1} \qquad \frac{3}{2} \qquad \frac{1.5}{1}$$

25. (1174,T1,4) (c) Remember in ratio analysis that you have to evaluate the numerator and the denominator as well as know whether the ratio is less than one, equal to one, or greater than one before considering the effect of some transaction on the ratio. A 100% stock dividend simply doubles the amount of stock outstanding and transfers retained earnings to paid in capital. Thus, it does not affect the current ratio or working capital nor does it affect the debt to equity ratio, because total shareholders' equity remains the same. It does decrease earnings per share and book value per share because there are more shares outstanding.

26. (1174,T1,5) (a) Payment of a dividend results in a reduction of cash and a current liability. When the dividend was declared, dividends payable, a current liability, was credited. The effect is to increase the current ratio but have no effect on working capital. Working capital remains the same because both current assets and current liabilities are decreased by the same amount, thus the difference remains constant. The current ratio increases because the current ratio was in excess of one, e.g., 4 to 3, and equal amounts are removed from the numerator and denominator, e.g., 3 to 2.

27. (1174,T1,6) (d) When a corporation purchases its own shares at a price greater than book value, the book value is decreased and the earnings per share is increased. The earnings per share increases because there are a smaller number of shares outstanding. The book value per share decreased because while the denominator, number of shares, decreased, the numerator, net assets, decreased by more than a proportionate amount.

28. (1174,T1,7) (a) Increasing leverage or trading on the equity results in more debt relative to owners' equity. If it is done successfully the income available to owners' equity should increase also. The concept does not affect return on sales, but rather return on shareholders' equity. Likewise, leverage does not affect the concept of working capital.

29. (1174,T1,8) (b) A 40% common stock interest is accounted for in an investment account which is noncurrent on the books of the investor. The investor must also use the equity method to account for the investee's earnings, i.e., accrue its share of undistributed earnings. In this question, earnings per share increase because the investee operated profitably. Instead of decreasing the book value per share, book value would be increased because of the increase in the investment account. The fact that the investment is accounted for in a noncurrent investment account precludes answers (a) and (c).

30. (1174,T1,9) (b) The solutions approach would be to jot down both ratios. The inventory turnover ratio is cost of sales over inventory, and the receivable turnover is sales over accounts receivable. Inventory turnover would decrease if the denominator inventory were increased. Receivable turnover would decrease if the denominator of accounts receivable were increased.

May 1984 Answers

31. (584,P3,56) (b) The requirement is the rate of return on average stockholders' equity. The formula for this ratio is:

$$\frac{\text{Net income}}{\text{Average stockholders' equity}}$$

1983 net income is $240,000. Average stockholders' equity for 1983 is computed by adding 12/31/82 and 12/31/83 stockholders' equity and dividing by 2. Stockholders' equity is computed below.

	12/31/82	12/31/83
Preferred stock	$ 180,000	$ 180,000
Common stock	648,000	840,000
Retained earnings	192,000	360,000
Total	$1,020,000	$1,380,000

Average stockholders' equity is $1,200,000 [($1,020,000 + $1,380,000) ÷ 2]. Therefore, the rate of return on average stockholders' equity is 20%.

$$\frac{\$240{,}000}{\$1{,}200{,}000} = 20\%$$

32. (584,T1,35) (c) The requirement is to determine whether average inventory is used in the calculation of the acid test (quick) ratio and the inventory turnover rate. The formula for the acid test ratio is:

$$\frac{\text{Cash + Net receivables + Marketable securities}}{\text{Current liabilities}}$$

The formula for the inventory turnover rate is:

$$\frac{\text{Cost of goods sold}}{\text{Average inventory}}$$

Therefore, answer (c) is correct.

Answer Outline

Problem 1 Corporation Solvency Ratios

1. This question asks you to evaluate how the change in 7 ratios affects the solvency and going concern of the subject company. Also required are additional ratios relevant to the analysis and limitations of ratio analysis.

2. With all three requirements in mind, you should write out all of the ratios in the margin, e.g., current assets/current liabilities. This exercise will enable you to interrelate the ratios and provide more complete answers.

3. Write up a 2 to 3 sentence paragraph for each ratio.

4. Other ratios not listed include changes in current items other than quick assets, inventory and receivable turnover, and debt to equity.

5. The unofficial answer also contains three multiple sentence paragraphs describing the limitations of ratio analysis.

Unofficial Answer

Problem 1 Corporation Solvency Ratios

a. The current-ratio increase is a favorable indication as to solvency, but alone tells little about the going-concern potential of the client. From this ratio change alone, it is impossible to know the amount and direction of the changes in individual accounts, total current assets, and total current liabilities. Also unknown are the reasons for the changes.

The quick-ratio decline is an unfavorable indication as to solvency, especially when the current-ratio increase is also considered. This decline is also unfavorable to the going-concern prospects of the client because it reflects a declining cash position and raises questions as to reasons for the increases in other current assets, such as inventories.

The increase in the ratio of property, plant, and equipment to owners' equity cannot alone tell anything about either solvency or going concern prospects. There is no way to know the amount and direction of the changes in the two items. If assets increased, one must know whether the new assets are immediately productive or need further development. A reduction in owners' equity at this point would cause much concern for the creditors of this client.

The decrease in the ratio of sales to owners' equity is in itself an unfavorable indicator because the most likely reason is a sales decline. However, this decline, which is more relevant to going-concern prospects than to solvency, is largely offset by the fact that net income has significantly increased.

The increase in net income is a favorable indicator for both solvency and going-concern prospects although much depends on the quality of receivables generated from sales and how quickly they can be converted into cash. A significant factor here may be that despite a decline in sales, the client's management has been able to reduce costs to produce this increase. Indirectly, the improved income picture may have a favorable impact on solvency and going-concern potential by enabling the client to borrow currently to meet cash requirements.

The 30% increase in earnings per common share, which is identical to the percentage increase in net income, is an indication that there has probably been no change in the number of shares of common stock outstanding. This in turn indicates that financing was not obtained through the issuance of common stock. It is not possible to reach conclusions about solvency and going-concern prospects without additional information about the nature and extent of financing.

The percentage increases in book values per common share demonstrate nothing so far as solvency and going-concern potential are concerned. It is probable that the smaller percentage increase in the current year only reflects the larger base value created in the preceding year. It is not possible to tell from these figures what the dividend policy of the client is or whether there is an increase in net assets which is capable of generating future earnings, thus making it possible to raise capital for current needs by the issue of additional common stock.

The collective implications of these data alone are that the client entity is about as solvent and as viable as a going-concern at the end of the current year as it was at the beginning although there may be a need for short-term operating cash.

b. The creditors will probably ask for the information listed below to overcome the limitations inherent in the ratios discussed in part a. and to obtain more evidence to support the conclusions drawn from them.

1. Additional ratios and other comparative data may be requested. They are likely to include such items as the following:
   (a) Changes in current assets other than quick assets.
   (b) Receivables turnover, inventory turnover, and the number of days it takes to complete the cycle from cash to inventories to receivables to cash.
   (c) Liabilities to owners' equity.
2. The creditors will probably want explanations for the changes in ratios during the current year. The client should be prepared to respond to questions about the age and collectibility of the receivables, the condition and salability of the inventories, the cause of the quick-asset position in the current year, the nature of increases in property, plant and equipment and their potential for providing greater sales or cost reductions in the future, the presence of long-term debt and the dates when it must be repaid, and the manner of controlling costs so that a larger net income was shown in the current year. (The comparative financial statements themselves will answer many of these questions and will provide insight into the client's capability of meeting current obligations as well as continuing profitable operations.) The client may also be expected to provide information about future plans and projections.
3. The creditors may also ask for ratios and related information for several recent years. These data may demonstrate trends and can be compared to data for other companies and for the industry.

c. Although a quick evaluation of a reporting entity can be made using only a few ratios and comparing these with past ratios and industry statistics, the creditors should realize the limitations of such analysis even from the best prepared statements carrying a CPA's unqualified opinion.

A limitation on comparisons with industry statistics or other companies within the industry exists because material differences can be created through the use of alternative (but acceptable) accounting methods. Further, when evaluating changes in ratios or percentages, the evaluation should be directed to the nature of the item being evaluated because very small differences in ratios or percentages can represent significant changes in dollar amounts or trends.

The creditors should evaluate conclusions drawn from ratio analysis in the light of the current status of, and expected changes in, such things as general economic conditions, the client's competitive position, the public's demand (for the product itself, increased quality of the product, control of noise and pollution, etc.), and the client's specific plans.

Multiple Choice Questions (1 - 13)

1. Luca and Mira formed a partnership on July 1, 1982, and contributed the following assets:

	Luca	*Mira*
Cash	$65,000	$100,000
Realty		300,000

The realty was subject to a mortgage of $25,000, which was assumed by the partnership. The partnership agreement provides that Luca and Mira will share profits and losses in the ratio of one-third and two-thirds respectively. Mira's capital account at July 1, 1982, should be

a. $400,000
b. $391,667
c. $375,000
d. $310,000

2. On July 1, 1981, Motta and Puleo formed a partnership, agreeing to share profits and losses in the ratio of 4:6, respectively. Motta contributed a parcel of land that cost him $25,000. Puleo contributed $50,000 cash. The land was sold for $50,000 on July 1, 1981, four hours after formation of the partnership. How much should be recorded in Motta's capital account on formation of the partnership?

a. $10,000
b. $20,000
c. $25,000
d. $50,000

3. Arthur Plack, a partner in the Brite Partnership, has a 30% participation in partnership profits and losses. Plack's capital account had a net decrease of $60,000 during the calendar year 1974. During 1974, Plack withdrew $130,000 (charged against his capital account) and contributed property valued at $25,000 to the partnership. What was the net income of the Brite Partnership for 1974?

a. $150,000
b. $233,333
c. $350,000
d. $550,000

4. Geller and Harden formed a partnership on January 2, 1974, and agreed to share profits 90%, 10%, respectively. Geller contributed capital of $25,000. Harden contributed no capital but has a specialized expertise and manages the firm full time. There were no withdrawals during the year. The partnership agreement provides for the following:

Capital accounts are to be credited annually with interest at 5% of beginning capital.

Harden is to be paid a salary of $1,000 a month.

Harden is to receive a bonus of 20% of income calculated before deducting his salary and interest on both capital accounts.

Bonus, interest, and Harden's salary are to be considered partnership expenses.

The partnership 1974 income statement follows:

Revenues	$96,450
Expenses (including salary, interest, and bonus)	49,700
Net income	$46,750

What is Harden's 1974 bonus?

a. $11,688
b. $12,000
c. $15,000
d. $15,738

5. Partners C and K share profits and losses equally after each has been credited in all circumstances with annual salary allowances of $15,000 and $12,000, respectively. Under this arrangement, C will benefit by $3,000 more than K in which of the following circumstances?

a. Only if the partnership has earnings of $27,000 or more for the year.
b. Only if the partnership does not incur a loss for the year.
c. In all earnings or loss situations.
d. Only if the partnership has earnings of at least $3,000 for the year.

6. Cicci and Arias are partners who share profits and losses in the ratio of 7:3, respectively. On October 5, 1980, their respective capital accounts were as follows:

Cicci	$35,000
Arias	30,000
Total	$65,000

On that date they agreed to admit Soto as a partner with a one-third interest in the capital and profits and losses, upon his investment of $25,000. The new partnership will begin with a total capital of $90,000. Immediately after Soto's admission, what are the capital balances of Cicci, Arias, and Soto, respectively?

a. $30,000; $30,000; $30,000
b. $31,500; $28,500; $30,000
c. $31,667; $28,333; $30,000
d. $35,000; $30,000; $25,000

Items 7 and 8 are based on the following information:

Presented below is the condensed balance sheet of the partnership of Kane, Clark and Lane who share profits and losses in the ratio of 6:3:1, respectively:

Cash	$ 85,000
Other assets	415,000
	$500,000
Liabilities	$ 80,000
Kane, capital	252,000
Clark, capital	126,000
Lane, capital	42,000
	$500,000

7. The assets and liabilities on the above balance sheet are fairly valued and the partnership wishes to admit Bayer with a 25% interest in the capital and profits/losses without recording goodwill or bonus. How much should Bayer contribute in cash or other assets?

a. $ 70,000
b. $105,000
c. $125,000
d. $140,000

8. Assume that the partners agree instead to sell Bayer 20% of their respective capital and profit and loss interests for a total payment of $90,000. The payment by Bayer is to be made directly to the individual partners. The partners agree that implied goodwill is to be recorded prior to the acquisition by Bayer. What are the capital balances of Kane, Clark, and Lane, respectively, after the acquisition by Bayer?

a. $198,000; $ 99,000; $33,000.
b. $201,600; $100,800; $33,600.
c. $216,000; $108,000; $36,000.
d. $255,600; $127,800; $42,600.

9. Pat, Helma, and Diane are partners with capital balances of $50,000, $30,000, and $20,000, respectively. The partners share profits and losses equally. For an investment of $50,000 cash, MaryAnn is to be admitted as a partner with a one-fourth interest in capital and profits. Based on this information, the amount of MaryAnn's investment can best be justified by which of the following?

a. MaryAnn will receive a bonus from the other partners upon her admission to the partnership.
b. Assets of the partnership were overvalued immediately prior to MaryAnn's investment.
c. The book value of the partnership's net assets was less than their fair value immediately prior to MaryAnn's investment.
d. MaryAnn is apparently bringing goodwill into the partnership and her capital account will be credited for the appropriate amount.

10. On June 30, 1981, the balance sheet for the partnership of Coll, Maduro, and Prieto, together with their respective profit and loss ratios, were as follows:

Assets, at cost	$180,000
Coll, loan	$ 9,000
Coll, capital (20%)	42,000
Maduro, capital (20%)	39,000
Prieto, capital (60%)	90,000
Total	$180,000

Coll has decided to retire from the partnership. By mutual agreement, the assets are to be adjusted to their fair value of $216,000 at June 30, 1981. It was agreed that the partnership would pay Coll $61,200 cash for Coll's partnership interest, including Coll's loan which is to be repaid in full. No goodwill is to be recorded. After Coll's retirement, what is the balance of Maduro's capital account?

a. $36,450
b. $39,000
c. $45,450
d. $46,200

11. James Dixon, a partner in an accounting firm, decided to withdraw from the partnership. Dixon's share of the partnership profits and losses was 20%. Upon withdrawing from the partnership he was paid $74,000 in final settlement for his interest. The total of the partners' capital accounts before recognition of partnership goodwill prior to Dixon's withdrawal was $210,000. After his withdrawal the remaining partners' capital accounts, excluding their share of goodwill, totaled $160,000. The total agreed upon goodwill of the firm was

a. $120,000
b. $140,000
c. $160,000
d. $250,000

12. The following condensed balance sheet is presented for the partnership of Alexander, Bell and Graham, who share profits and losses in the ratio of 6:2:2, respectively:

Cash	$ 80,000
Other assets	280,000
Total	$360,000
Liabilities	$140,000
Alexander, capital	100,000
Bell, capital	100,000
Graham, capital	20,000
Total	$360,000

The partners agreed to liquidate the partnership after selling the other assets. If the other assets are sold for $160,000, how much should Alexander receive upon liquidation?

a. $ 25,000
b. $ 26,000
c. $ 28,000
d. $100,000

May 1984 Question

13. The partnership agreement for the partnership of Mayo and Pack provided for salary allowances of $45,000 to Mayo and $35,000 to Pack, and the residual profit was allocated equally. During 1983, Mayo and Pack each withdrew cash equal to 80 percent of their salary allowances. If during 1983 the partnership had profits in excess of $100,000 without regard to salary allowances and withdrawals, Mayo's equity in the partnership would

a. Increase more than Pack's.
b. Decrease more than Pack's.
c. Increase the same as Pack's.
d. Decrease the same as Pack's.

Problem

Problem 1 Partnership Liquidation (582,P4a)

(35 to 40 minutes)

Part a. On January 1, 1982, the partners of Allen, Brown, and Cox, who share profits and losses in the ratio of 5:3:2, respectively, decide to liquidate their partnership. The partnership trial balance at this date is as follows:

	Debit	Credit
Cash	$ 18,000	
Accounts receivable	66,000	
Inventory	52,000	
Machinery and equipment, net	189,000	
Allen, loan	30,000	
Accounts payable		$ 53,000
Brown, loan		20,000
Allen, capital		118,000
Brown, capital		90,000
Cox, capital		74,000
	$355,000	$355,000

The partners plan a program of piecemeal conversion of assets in order to minimize liquidation losses. All available cash, less an amount retained to provide for future expenses, is to be distributed to the partners at the end of each month. A summary of the liquidation transactions is as follows:

January 1982:

a. $51,000 was collected on accounts receivable; the balance is uncollectible.

b. $38,000 was received for the entire inventory.

c. $2,000 liquidation expenses were paid.

d. $50,000 was paid to outside creditors, after offset of a $3,000 credit memorandum received on January 11, 1982.

e. $10,000 cash was retained in the business at the end of the month for potential unrecorded liabilities and anticipated expenses.

February 1982:

f. $4,000 liquidation expenses were paid.

g. $6,000 cash was retained in the business at the end of the month for potential unrecorded liabilities and anticipated expenses.

March 1982:

h. $146,000 was received on sale of all items of machinery and equipment.

i. $5,000 liquidation expenses were paid.

j. No cash was retained in the business.

Required:

Prepare a schedule to compute safe installment payments to the partners as of January 31, 1982. Show supporting computations in good form.

Multiple Choice Answers

1. c	4. c	7. d	10. c	12. a
2. d	5. c	8. c	11. a	13. a
3. a	6. b	9. c		

Multiple Choice Answer Explanations

A. Partnership Formation

1. (583,Q1,11) (c) The requirement is to determine Mira's capital account balance at July 1, 1982. Mira's capital balance is the fair value of his equity in the assets contributed: cash of $100,000 and realty of $275,000, or a total of $375,000. Mira's equity in the realty contributed to the partnership is $300,000 less the existing mortgage of $25,000 assumed by the partnership.

2. (1181,Q2,27) (d) The requirement is Motta's capital account balance upon formation of the partnership. As is the case with all entities, investments in the capital of a partnership should be measured at the fair market value of the assets contributed. In this case, the FMV of the land would be measured by its sales price on the date of sale ($50,000) which is also the date of the partnership formation. Recording the land at Motta's cost would result in the partners sharing the gain from the sale in accordance with their profit and loss ratio. This is not equitable since the gain accrued while the land was held by Motta.

B. Distribution of Income and Loss

3. (575,P1,9) (a) The solutions approach is to construct a ledger account for Plack's investment in the partnership as is illustrated below. Given the net decrease of $60,000 during the year, a $130,000 withdrawal and a $25,000 capital contribution, the net income allocable to Plack was $45,000. Since Plack owns 30% of the partnership, the entire partnership income was $150,000.

	Debit	Credit	
Withdrawal		130,000	
Contribution	25,000		
Net income	45,000		.30NI = $45,000
Net change	60,000		NI = $150,000

4. (575,P1,11) (c) The requirement is a calculation of Harden's 1974 bonus. You are given net income after deducting salary, interest, and bonus. The bonus is 20% of income before deducting salary, interest and bonus. Thus as calculated below, you must add back the salary and interest to obtain $60,000, which is the income after the bonus. If the bonus is 20%, the income after the bonus will be 80% of the income before the bonus. The income before the bonus is $75,000 and the bonus is therefore $15,000.

NI	$46,750	
Salary	12,000	
Interest	1,250	
	$60,000	income after bonus
	60,000	= .80 NI before bonus
	$75,000	= NI before bonus

5. (575,T1,4) (c) Since the salary allowances are credited to the partners accounts before sharing the profits and losses, C will always benefit by $3,000. One solutions approach is to go through and distribute salary and P&L for each of the other answers (a), (b), and (d) as below. Assuming $30,000 income, $10,000 loss and $4,000 income, the P&L after salary distributions would be $3,000 of income, a $37,000 loss, and a $23,000 loss respectively. These gains or losses are allocated equally between C and K. As you can see in each case, C is $3,000 better off than K.

	30,000 inc.	*10,000 loss*	*4,000 inc.*
C salary	15,000	15,000	15,000
C P&L	1,500	(18,500)	(11,500)
	16,500	(3,500)	3,500
K salary	12,000	12,000	12,000
K P&L	1,500	(18,500)	(11,500)
	13,500	(6,500)	500

C. Changes in Ownership

6. (1181,Q2,24) (b) The requirement is the balances in the capital accounts of a partnership after the admission of a new partner. In this case the new partner is investing $25,000 for a one-third interest in the new total capital of $90,000. This means that a bonus of $5,000 [(1/3)($90,000) – $25,000] is being credited to the new partner for contribution of some intangible element in addition to his tangible contribution. The bonus to the new partner is charged to the old partners in their profit and loss ratio.

Cicci [$35,000 – 7/10 ($5,000)]	= $31,500
Arias [$30,000 – 3/10 ($5,000)]	= 28,500
Soto [$90,000 ÷ 3)	= 30,000
Total capital	$90,000

7. (580,Q1,8) (d) The requirement is the amount to be paid by a new partner (Bayer) for a 25% interest with no bonus or goodwill to be recorded. The current net capital of $420,000 [($252,000 + $126,000 + $42,000) or ($500,000 – $80,000)] will be 75% of the total capital after Bayer is admitted. Thus, $420,000 ÷ 75% is $560,000, which will be the new partnership capital. Accordingly, Bayer will have to contribute $140,000 [($560,000 – $420,000) or (25% x $560,000)].

8. (580,Q1,9) (c) The requirement is the capital balances of the partners after recording goodwill and selling 20% of their interest. If 20% of the partnership is worth $90,000, the entire partnership is worth $450,000. Thus, goodwill of $30,000 needs to be recorded and allocated to the old partners in their P & L ratio. The sale is recorded by crediting Bayer's account for $90,000 and debiting the old partners' accounts for one-fifth of the respective balances.

	Capital		*GW*		*Sale*		*New capital*
Kane	$252,000	+	18,000	–	54,000	=	$216,000
Clark	126,000	+	9,000	–	27,000	=	108,000
Lane	42,000	+	3,000	–	9,000	=	36,000
Bayer				+	90,000	=	90,000

9. (575,T1,5) (c) The net assets of the partnership prior to admission of MaryAnn is $100,000. If 1/4 of the partnership is worth $50,000, the partnership assets prior to the infusion of the $50,000 would appear to be worth $150,000 ($200,000 – $50,000 cash infusion). Thus, answer (c), the book value of the partnership's net assets was less than their fair value prior to the admission of MaryAnn, was the correct answer. Answer (b) is incorrect as it indicates that partnership book value was greater than the fair value. Answer (a) is incorrect because if the excess of fair value over book value were accounted for as a bonus, MaryAnn would give a bonus to the other partners. If the admission were to be recorded under the bonus method (see the first journal entry below), MaryAnn's capital would be credited for $37,500 (1/4 of the $100,000 of book value plus the $50,000 cash contribution). The remaining $12,500 would be divided equally between Pat, Helma, and Diane as their P&L ratios are equal. The second entry reflects the requirements of the problem: goodwill to the new partners.

Cash	$50,000	
MaryAnn capital		$37,500
Pat capital		4,166
Helma capital		4,167
Diane capital		4,167

Cash	$50,000	
Goodwill	50,000	
MaryAnn capital		$50,000
Pat capital		16,666
Helma capital		16,667
Diane capital		16,667

Answer (d) is incorrect because if goodwill were recorded (the second journal entry) the capital accounts of the old partners would be credited. The unrecorded goodwill would be $50,000 (the difference between the book value and the fair value of the assets of $150,000).

D. Partner Deaths and Withdrawals

10. (1181,Q2,25) (c) The requirement is the balance in Maduro's capital account after Coll's retirement. When a partner withdraws from a partnership a determination of the fair market value of the entity must be made. Since it is stated in the problem that the withdrawing partner is selling his interest to the partnership and that no goodwill is to be recorded, the bonus method must be employed after restatement of assets to FMV. The capital accounts after restatement to FMV would be:

Coll
[$42,000 + 20%($216,000 – $180,000)] = $49,200
Maduro
[$39,000 + 20%($216,000 – $180,000)] = $46,200
Prieto
[$90,000 + 60%($216,000 – $180,000)] = $111,600

The bonus paid to Coll is the difference between the cash paid to him for his partnership interest and the balance of that interest plus his loan balance:

Bonus = [$61,200 – ($49,200 + $9,000)] = $ 3,000

Maduro's capital account would be reduced by his proportionate share of the bonus, based on the profit and loss ratio of the remaining partners [20%/(20% + 60%) = 25%].

Maduro's capital [$46,000 – 25% ($3,000)] = $45,450

11. (580,Q1,4) (a) The requirement is the total agreed-upon goodwill of a firm from which a partner is withdrawing. The partner is being paid $74,000 for his interest. His capital account balance is $50,000 ($210,000 – $160,000). Thus an additional $24,000 was paid to him for his share of goodwill. The with-

drawing partner shares in profits and losses at a 20% rate, so the $24,000 is 20% of total goodwill, which therefore must be $120,000.

F. Partnership Liquidation

12. (1181,Q2, 26) (a) The requirement is the amount Alexander will receive upon liquidation of the partnership. The first step is to allocate the loss from the sale of assets to the three capital accounts according to the profit and loss ratio. Since the loss on the sale of the assets causes a $4,000 debit balance in Graham's capital account, this must be allocated among the remaining partners according to their profit and loss ratio. Collection of this amount by the other partners will depend on the personal wealth of Graham and legal considerations. Following is a summary of the distribution (amounts in thousands). Note that the first distribution is to outside creditors.

	Cash	*O.A.*	*Liab.*
Beginning	$ 80	$280	$140
Sale of assets	+ 160	– 280	
	240	0	140
Alloc. of deficit	0	0	0
	240	0	140
Dist. to creditors	– 140	0	– 140
	100	0	0
Dist. to partners	100	0	0

	Capital		
	A	*B*	*G*
Beginning	$100	$100	$20
Sale of assets	– 72	– 24	– 24
	28	76	(4)
Alloc. of deficit	– 3	– 1	+ 4
	25	75	0
Dist. to creditors	0	0	0
	25	75	0
Dist. to partners	– 25	– 75	0

May 1984 Answer

13. (584,T1,26) (a) The requirement is to determine how Mayo's equity interest in the partnership will change in relation to Pack's during 1983. Each partner withdrew 80% of his/her salary during the year, leaving his/her equity interest to increase by the remaining 20% plus half of the net profit after salaries. Because Mayo's salary is $10,000 greater than Pack's, Mayo's equity interest will increase by $2,000 (20% of $10,000) more than Pack's [answer (a)].

Solution Guide

Problem 1 Partnership Liquidation

1. Part a. requires a schedule computing safe installment payments to partners liquidating their partnership.

2. The information given in part a. describes the activities of a partnership in liquidation over a three-month period. The "solutions approach" is to first quickly review mentally the basic accounting concepts for partnership liquidations; second, read through the information; third, make the necessary computations and prepare the schedule of safe installment payments as of **January 31, 1982.** The additional information given for Febuary and March is extraneous and can be ignored.

2.1 Before the schedule of safe installment payments can be prepared, the effect of partnership transactions in January must be determined in order to compute the account balances as of January 31. This is done in the top half of the schedule.

2.2 Recall that, in partnership liquidations, any loans to (receivables) or from (payables) partners are offset against or added to each partner's capital balance. Thus, the $30,000 loan to Allen would be deducted from his capital balance and the $20,000 loan from Brown would be added to his capital balance. The balances to be used in the liquidation schedule for the net investment of Allen, Brown and Cox would then be $88,000, $110,000, and $74,000, respectively.

3. Begin analyzing each transaction during the month of January by determining the effect of each on the columns in the schedule.

3.1 In transaction (a), the collection of accounts receivable, $51,000 was collected. The balance of $15,000 ($66,000 – $51,000) is uncollectible and must be written off as a loss. Recall that, unless stated otherwise, partners share profits and losses equally. In this problem, however, the profit and loss ratio is stated; the ratio of 5:3:2 must therefore be used to allocate the $15,000 loss. Before entering this transaction in the schedule, visualize how it would appear in general journal form:

Cash	51,000	
Allen, Capital		
($15,000 x .5)	7,500	
Brown, Capital		
($15,000 x .3)	4,500	
Cox, Capital		
($15,000 x .2)	3,000	
Accounts Receivable		66,000

3.2 In transaction (b), $38,000 was received for the entire inventory. Since the book value of the inventory was $52,000, this transaction resulted in a $14,000 loss ($52,000 – $38,000). This loss must be allocated among the partners in the stated profit and loss ratio. In general journal form, this transaction would appear as:

Cash	38,000	
Allen, Capital		
($14,000 x .5)	7,000	
Brown, Capital		
($14,000 x .3)	4,200	
Cox, Capital		
($14,000 x .2)	2,800	
Inventory		52,000

3.3 In transaction (c), the partnership paid $2,000 in liquidation expenses. These expenses must be allocated among the partners as a reduction of capital. The general journal entry would be:

Allen, Capital		
($2,000 x .5)	1,000	
Brown, Capital		
($2,000 x .3)	600	
Cox, Capital		
($2,000 x .2)	400	
Cash		2,000

3.4 In transaction (d), the balance in accounts payable was paid after the receipt of a $3,000 credit memorandum. The credit memo was either an adjustment for goods purchased or returned. Since the entire inventory has already been sold, if the credit memorandum was for goods returned, it is necessary to assume the goods were recorded as purchases and closed to Income Summary. To record the credit memo, the following entry is prepared:

Accounts Payable	$3,000	
Allen, Capital ($3,000 x .5)		$1,500
Brown, Capital ($3,000 x .3)		900
Cox, Capital ($3,000 x .2)		600

The entry to record the payment of the balance in accounts payable would then be:

Accounts Payable	$50,000	
Cash		$50,000

3.5 Transaction (e) states that $10,000 cash is being retained in the business for potential liabilities and anticipated expenses. There are a number of alternative treatments possible for this fact. One treatment is to remove the $10,000 from cash and include it in other assets. This cash is restricted in use and is not available for distribution.

4. After the 1/31/82 balances have been totaled, the schedule of safe payments can be prepared.

4.1 To prepare the schedule of safe installment payments, first recall that the largest potential loss must be allocated among the partners. In this problem the largest potential loss is $199,000, the book value of the machinery and equipment ($189,000) and the amount of cash retained ($10,000). This is the loss which would result if the partnership realized $0 on the disposal of the machinery and equipment, and incurred additional liablities of $10,000.

4.2 Next, calculate each partner's share of the loss in the profit and loss ratio of 5:3:2 as follows:

Partner	Potential loss	% share =	$ allocation
Allen	$199,000	50%	$ 99,500
Brown	199,000	30%	59,700
Cox	199,000	20%	39,800
			$199,000

4.3 Now the new potential balance in each partner's capital account can be computed. Allen would have a deficit of $25,500 ($74,000 – $99,500); Brown would have a credit of $41,900 ($101,600 – $59,700); Cox would have a credit of $28,600 ($68,400 – $39,800).

4.4 The next step is to allocate Allen's potential deficit of $25,500 among Brown and Cox in their ratio of 3:2, respectively. The allocation would be as follows:

Partner	Deficit	% share =	$ amount
Brown	$25,500	3/5	$15,300
Cox	25,500	2/5	10,200
			$25,500

The new balances would then be:

Partner	Balance
Allen	– 0 – ($25,000 – $25,000)
Brown	$26,600 ($41,900 – $15,300)
Cox	$18,400 ($28,600 – $10,200)

4.5 The $45,000 cash would be distributed between Brown and Cox, based on their potential capital balances of $26,600 and $18,400. Allen would receive nothing from this first distribution because of his potential deficit.

Unofficial Answer
(Author Modified)

Problem 1 Partnership Liquidation

Part a.

Allen, Brown, & Cox Partnership
Schedule to Compute Safe Installment Payments
as of January 31, 1982

				Net investment in partnership		
	Cash Dr. (Cr.)	Other assets Dr. (Cr.)	Liabilities (Dr.) Cr.	Allen .5 (Dr.) Cr	Brown .3 (Dr.) Cr.	Cox .2 (Dr.) Cr.
Balances before liquidation	$18,000	$307,000	$53,000	$88,000[1]	$110,000[2]	$74,000
January Transactions						
Collection of A/R at loss of $15,000	51,000	(66,000)		(7,500)	(4,500)	(3,000)
Sale of inventory at loss of $14,000	38,000	(52,000)		(7,000)	(4,200)	(2,800)
Liquidation expenses paid	(2,000)			(1,000)	(600)	(400)
Share of credit memorandum			(3,000)	1,500	900	600
Payments to creditors	(50,000)		(50,000)			
Cash withheld[3]	(10,000)	10,000				
Balances 1/31/82	45,000	199,000	–0–	74,000	101,600	68,400
Distribution of potential losses		(199,000)		(99,500)	(59,700)	(39,800)
Potential balances	45,000	–0–	–0–	(25,500)	41,900	28,600
Share of Allen's potential deficit				25,500	(15,300)	(10,200)
Potential balances	45,000	–0–	–0–	–0–	26,600	18,400
Safe installment payment as of 1/31/82	($45,000)			$–0–	($26,600)	($18,400)

1 $118,000 capital less $30,000 loan.
2 $90,000 capital plus $20,000 loan.
3 Cash to be retained by partnership is treated as other asset. It is restricted in use and not available for distribution.

Multiple Choice Questions (1 - 39)

1. On January 15, 1981, Ward Company purchased 10,000 shares (10%) of the outstanding common stock of Diamond, Inc., for $25 per share. The purchase was appropriately recorded as a long-term investment and accounted for under the cost method. The market price of the stock was $24 per share on December 31, 1981. During 1982 Diamond experienced severe financial difficulties and Ward disposed of its entire investment in Diamond stock for $10 per share on November 10, 1982. Ward's effective income tax rate was 40% for 1982. In its income statement for the year ended December 31, 1982, how much should Ward report as unusual loss from disposal of the long-term investment?

a. $150,000
b. $140,000
c. $ 90,000
d. $ 84,000

2. On July 1, 1982, Diamond, Inc., paid $1,000,000 for 100,000 shares (40%) of the outstanding common stock of Ashley Corporation. At that date the net assets of Ashley totaled $2,500,000 and the fair values of all of Ashley's identifiable assets and liabilities were equal to their book values. Ashley reported net income of $500,000 for the year ended December 31, 1982, of which $300,000 was for the six months ended December 31, 1982. Ashley paid cash dividends of $250,000 on September 30, 1982. In its income statement for the year ended December 31, 1982, what amount of income should Diamond report from its investment in Ashley?

a. $ 80,000
b. $100,000
c. $120,000
d. $200,000

3. On January 2, 1981, Portela, Inc., bought 30% of the outstanding common stock of Bracero Corporation for $258,000 cash. Portela accounts for this investment by the equity method. At the date of acquisition of the stock, Bracero's net assets had a book and fair value of $620,000. The excess of Portela's cost of the investment over its share of Bracero's net assets has an estimated life of 40 years. Bracero's net income for the year ended December 31, 1981, was $180,000. During 1981, Bracero declared and paid cash dividends of $20,000. On December 31, 1981, Portela should have carried its investment in Bracero in the amount of

a. $234,000
b. $258,000
c. $304,200
d. $306,000

4. On January 2, 1980, Troquel Corporation bought 15% of Zafacon Corporation's capital stock for $30,000. Troquel accounts for this investment by the cost method. Zafacon's net income for the years ended December 31, 1980, and December 31, 1981, were $10,000 and $50,000 respectively. During 1981, Zafacon declared a dividend of $70,000. No dividends were declared in 1980. How much should Troquel show on its 1981 income statement as income from this investment?

a. $ 1,575
b. $ 7,500
c. $ 9,000
d. $10,500

5. On January 1, 1980, Rey Corporation paid $150,000 for 10,000 shares of Rio Corporation's common stock, representing a 15% investment in Rio. Rio declared and paid a dividend of $1 a share to its common stockholders during 1980. Rio's net income was $130,000 for the year ended December 31, 1980. At what amount should Rey's investment in Rio appear on Rey's balance sheet as of December 31, 1980?

a. $140,000
b. $150,000
c. $159,500
d. $169,500

6. Cash dividends declared out of current earnings are distributed to an investor. How will the investor's investment account be affected by those dividends under each of the following accounting methods?

	Cost method	*Equity method*
a.	Decrease	No effect
b.	Decrease	Decrease
c.	No effect	Decrease
d.	No effect	No effect

7. When an investor uses the equity method to account for investments in common stock, the equity in the earnings of the investee reported in the investor's income statement will be affected by which of the following?

	Cash dividends from investee	*Goodwill amortization related to purchase*
a.	No	Yes
b.	No	No
c.	Yes	No
d.	Yes	Yes

8. Ownership of 51 percent of the outstanding voting stock of a company would usually result in

a. The use of the cost method.

b. The use of the lower of cost or market method.
c. A pooling of interests.
d. A consolidation.

9. The equity method of accounting for an investment in the common stock of another company should be used when the investment
a. Is composed of common stock and it is the investor's intent to vote the common stock.
b. Ensures a source of supply such as raw materials.
c. Enables the investor to exercise significant influence over the investee.
d. Is obtained by an exchange of stock for stock.

10. On April 1, 1983, Union Company paid $1,600,000 for all the issued and outstanding common stock of Cable Corporation in a transaction properly accounted for as a purchase. The recorded assets and liabilities of Cable on April 1, 1983, were as follows:

Cash	$160,000
Inventory	480,000
Property, plant and equipment (net)	960,000
Liabilities	(360,000)

On April 1, 1983, it was determined that Cable's inventory had a fair value of $460,000, and the property, plant and equipment (net) had a fair value of $1,040,000. What is the amount of goodwill resulting from the business combination?
a. $0
b. $ 20,000
c. $300,000
d. $360,000

11. The Troy Corporation was organized to consolidate the resources of Able Company and Baker, Inc., in a business combination appropriately accounted for by the pooling of interests method. On January 1, 1980, Troy issued 65,000 shares of its $10 par value voting stock in exchange for all of the outstanding capital stock of Able and Baker. The equity account balances of Able and Baker on this date were:

	Able	*Baker*	*Total*
Par value of common stock	$150,000	$450,000	$600,000
Additional paid-in capital	20,000	55,000	75,000
Retained earnings	110,000	210,000	320,000
	$280,000	$715,000	$995,000

What is the balance in Troy's "Additional Paid-in Capital" account immediately after the business combination?
a. $0
b. $ 25,000
c. $ 75,000
d. $395,000

Items 12 and 13 are based on the following data:

On March 1, 1982, Agront Corporation issued 10,000 shares of its $1 par value common stock for all of the outstanding stock of Barcelo Corporation, when the fair market value of Agront's stock was $50 per share. In addition, Agront made the following payments in connection with this business combination:

Finder's and consultants' fees	$20,000
SEC registration costs	7,000

12. If this business combination is treated as a pooling of interests, how much should be recorded as business combination expenses in 1982?
a. $0
b. $ 7,000
c. $20,000
d. $27,000

13. If this business combination is treated as a purchase, Agront's acquisition cost would be capitalized at
a. $0
b. $500,000
c. $520,000
d. $527,000

Items 14 and 15 are based on the following data:

On January 1, 1981, Rolan Corporation issued 10,000 shares of common stock in exchange for all of Sandin Corporation's outstanding stock. Condensed balance sheets of Rolan and Sandin immediately prior to the combination are as follows:

	Rolan	Sandin
Total assets	$1,000,000	$500,000
Liabilities	$ 300,000	$150,000
Common stock ($10 par)	200,000	100,000
Retained earnings	500,000	250,000
Total equities	$1,000,000	$500,000

Rolan's common stock had a market price of $60 per share on January 1, 1981. The market price of Sandin's stock was not readily ascertainable.

14. Assuming that the combination of Rolan and Sandin qualifies as a purchase, Rolan's investment in Sandin's stock will be stated in Rolan's balance sheet immediately after the combination in the amount of

a. $100,000
b. $350,000
c. $500,000
d. $600,000

15. Assuming that the combination of Rolan and Sandin qualifies as a pooling of interests, rather than as a purchase, what should be reported as retained earnings in the consolidated balance sheet immediately after the combination?

a. $500,000
b. $600,000
c. $750,000
d. $850,000

16. The Action Corporation issued non-voting preferred stock with a fair market value of $4,000,000 in exchange for all of the outstanding common stock of Master Corporation. On the date of the exchange, Master had tangible net assets with a book value of $2,000,000 and a fair value of $2,500,000. In addition, Action issued preferred stock valued at $400,000 to an individual as a finder's fee in arranging the transaction. As a result of this transaction, Action should record an increase in net assets of

a. $2,000,000
b. $2,500,000
c. $2,900,000
d. $4,400,000

17. Alan Company purchased the net assets of Barry Company in a business combination accounted for as a purchase. As a result, goodwill was recorded. For tax purposes this combination was considered to be a tax-free merger.

One of Barry's assets that Alan purchased was a building with an appraised value of $150,000 at the date of the business combination. This asset had a cost of $90,000 which was net of accumulated depreciation for accounting purposes. The building had an adjusted tax basis to Barry (and to Alan as a result of the merger) of $100,000. Assuming a 48% income tax rate, at what amount should Alan record this building on its books after the purchase?

a. $100,000
b. $121,200
c. $126,000
d. $150,000

18. In order to report a business combination as a pooling of interests, the minimum amount of an investee's common stock which must be acquired during the combination period in exchange for the investor's common stock is

a. 100 percent.
b. 51 percent.
c. 80 percent.
d. 90 percent.

19. In a business combination how should plant and equipment of the acquired corporation generally be reported under each of the following methods?

	Pooling of interests	Purchase
a.	Fair value	Recorded value
b.	Fair value	Fair value
c.	Recorded value	Recorded value
d.	Recorded value	Fair value

20. Company X acquired for cash all of the outstanding common stock of Company Y. How should Company X determine in general the amounts to be reported for the inventories and long-term debt acquired from Company Y?

	Inventories	Long-term debt
a.	Fair value	Fair value
b.	Fair value	Recorded value
c.	Recorded value	Fair value
d.	Recorded value	Recorded value

21. A supportive argument for the pooling of interests method of accounting for a business combination is that

a. One company is clearly the dominant and continuing entity.
b. Goodwill is generally a part of any acquisition.

c. It was developed within the boundaries of the historical-cost system and is compatible with it.
d. A portion of the total cost is assigned to individual assets acquired on the basis of their fair value.

Items 22 and 23 are based on the following information:

On December 1, 1976, Company B was merged into Company A, with Company B going out of existence. Both companies report on a calendar year basis. This business combination should have been accounted for as a pooling of interests, but it was mistakenly accounted for as a purchase.

22. As a result of this error, what was the effect upon Company A's net earnings for the year ended December 31, 1976?
a. Overstated if B had a net loss from December 1, 1976, to December 31, 1976.
b. Understated if B had a net loss from January 1, 1976, to November 30, 1976.
c. Overstated if B had net earnings from December 1, 1976, to December 31, 1976.
d. Understated if B had net earnings from January 1, 1976, to November 30, 1976.

23. What was the effect of this error upon Company A's asset valuations at December 1, 1976?
a. Overstated under any circumstances.
b. Understated under any circumstances.
c. Overstated if the fair value of B's assets exceeded their book value.
d. Understated if the fair value of B's assets exceeded their book value.

24. Companies A and B have been operating separately for five years. Each company has a minimal amount of liabilities and a simple capital structure consisting solely of voting common stock. Company A, in exchange for 40 percent of its voting stock, acquires 80 percent of the common stock of Company B. This was a "tax free" stock for stock (type B) exchange for tax purposes. Company B assets have a total net fair market value of $800,000 and a total net book value of $580,000. The fair market value of the A stock used in the exchange was $700,000. The goodwill on this acquisition would be
a. Zero, this would be a pooling of interest.
b. $60,000.
c. $120,000.
d. $236,000.

25. Two calendar-year corporations combined on July 1, 1975. The combination is properly accounted for as a pooling of interests. How should the results of operations have been reported for the year ended December 31, 1975?
a. Combined from July 1 to December 31 and disclosed for the separate companies from January 1 to June 30.
b. Combined from July 1 to December 31 and disclosed for the separate companies for the entire year.
c. Combined for the entire year and disclosed for the separate companies from January 1 to June 30.
d. Combined for the entire year and disclosed for the separate companies for the entire year.

26. In a business combination accounted for as a pooling of interests, the combined corporation's retained earnings usually equals the sum of the retained earnings of the individual combining corporations. Assuming there is no contributed capital other than capital stock at par value, which of the following describes a situation where the combined retained earnings must be increased or decreased?
a. Increased if the par value dollar amount of the outstanding shares of the combined corporation exceeds the total capital stock of the separate combining companies.
b. Increased if the par value dollar amount of the outstanding shares of the combined corporation is less than the total capital stock of the separate combining companies.
c. Decreased if the par value dollar amount of the outstanding shares of the combined corporation exceeds the total capital stock of the separate combining companies.
d. Decreased if the par value dollar amount of the outstanding shares of the combined corporation is less than the total capital stock of the separate combining companies.

27. On January 1, 1980, Platt Company issued 200,000 additional shares of $5 par value voting common stock in exchange for all of Drew Company's voting common stock in a business combination ap-

propriately accounted for by the pooling of interests method. Immediately before the business combination the total stockholders' equity of Platt was $16,000,000 and of Drew was $4,000,000. Net income for the year ended December 31, 1980, was $1,500,000 for Platt, exclusive of any consideration of Drew, and $450,000 for Drew. During 1980, Platt paid $750,000 in dividends to stockholders. The consolidated stockholders' equity at December 31, 1980, should be

a. $17,750,000
b. $19,250,000
c. $21,200,000
d. $21,950,000

28. On June 30, 1979, Needle Corporation purchased for cash at $10 per share all 100,000 shares of the outstanding common stock of Thread Company. The total appraised value of identifiable assets less liabilities of Thread was $1,400,000 at June 30, 1979, including the appraised value of Thread's property, plant, and equipment (its only noncurrent asset) of $250,000. The consolidated balance sheet of Needle Corporation and its wholly owned subsidiary at June 30, 1979, should reflect

a. A deferred credit (negative goodwill) of $150,000.
b. Goodwill of $150,000.
c. A deferred credit (negative goodwill) of $400,000.
d. Goodwill of $400,000.

29. On December 1, 1978, Drew Company issued shares of its voting common stock in exchange for all of the voting common stock of Art Company in a business combination appropriately accounted for by the pooling of interests method. Net income for each company is as follows:

	Drew	Art
12 months ended December 31, 1978	$2,000,000	$1,200,000
1 month ended December 31, 1978	220,000	115,000

During 1978 Drew paid $900,000 in dividends to its stockholders. Art had paid $500,000 in dividends to its stockholders in September 1978. Assuming that the net income of Drew given above does not include the equity in net income of Art, the consolidated net income for the year ended December 31, 1978, should be

a. $ 335,000
b. $2,115,000
c. $2,700,000
d. $3,200,000

30. On November 1, 1982, Company X acquired all of the outstanding common stock of Company Y in a business combination accounted for as a pooling of interests. Both companies have a December 31 year end and have been in business for many years. Consolidated net income for the year ended December 31, 1982, should include net income for 12 months of

	Company X	Company Y
a.	Yes	Yes
b.	Yes	No
c.	No	No
d.	No	Yes

31. How would the retained earnings of a subsidiary acquired in a business combination usually be treated in a consolidated balance sheet prepared immediately after the acquisition?

a. Excluded for both a purchase and a pooling of interests.
b. Excluded for a pooling of interests but included for a purchase.
c. Included for both a purchase and a pooling of interests.
d. Included for a pooling of interests but excluded for a purchase.

32. Consolidated financial statements are typically prepared when one company has

a. Accounted for its investment in another company by the equity method.
b. Accounted for its investment in another company by the cost method.
c. Significant influence over the operating and financial policies of another company.
d. The controlling financial interest in another company.

33. A subsidiary may be acquired by issuing common stock in a pooling of interests transaction or by paying cash in a purchase transaction. Which of the following items would be reported in the consolidated financial statements at the same amount regardless of the accounting method used?

a. Minority interest.
b. Goodwill.
c. Retained earnings.
d. Capital stock.

34. Grant, Inc., has current receivables from affiliated companies at December 31, 1982, as follows:

- A $50,000 cash advance to Adams Corporation. Grant owns 30% of the voting stock of Adams and accounts for the investment by the equity method.

• A receivable of $160,000 from Bullard Corporation for administrative and selling services. Bullard is 100% owned by Grant and is included in Grant's consolidated statements.

• A receivable of $100,000 from Carpenter Corporation for merchandise sales on open account. Carpenter is a 90% owned, unconsolidated subsidiary of Grant.

In the current assets section of its December 31, 1982, consolidated balance sheet, Grant should report accounts receivable from investees in the total amount of

a. $ 90,000
b. $140,000
c. $150,000
d. $310,000

35. On January 1, 1978, Harry Corporation sold equipment costing $2,000,000 with accumulated depreciation of $500,000 to Anna Corporation, its wholly-owned subsidiary, for $1,800,000. Harry was depreciating the equipment on the straight-line method over twenty years with no salvage value, which Anna continued. In consolidation at December 31, 1978, the cost and accumulated depreciation, respectively, should be

a. $1,500,000 and $100,000.
b. $1,800,000 and $100,000.
c. $2,000,000 and $100,000.
d. $2,000,000 and $600,000.

36. Eltro Company acquired a 70% interest in the Samson Company in 1972. For the years ended December 31, 1973 and 1974, Samson reported net income of $80,000 and $90,000, respectively. During 1973, Samson sold merchandise to Eltro for $10,000 at a profit of $2,000. The merchandise was later resold by Eltro to outsiders for $15,000 during 1974. For consolidation purposes what is the minority interest's share of Samson's net income for 1973 and 1974, respectively?

a. $23,400 and $27,600.
b. $24,000 and $27,000.
c. $24,600 and $26,400.
d. $26,000 and $25,000.

May 1984 Questions

37. On January 1, 1983, Miller Company purchased 25% of Wall Corporation's common stock; no goodwill resulted from the purchase. Miller appropriately carries this investment at equity, and the balance in Miller's investment account was $190,000 at December 31, 1983. Wall reported net income of $120,000 for the year ended December 31, 1983, and paid common stock dividends totaling $48,000 during 1983. How much did Miller pay for its 25% interest in Wall?

a. $172,000
b. $202,000
c. $208,000
d. $232,000

38. On October 31, 1983, Simpson, Inc., purchased for cash of $40 per share all 250,000 of the outstanding common stock of Rex Corporation. Rex's balance sheet at October 31, 1983, showed a book value of $8,000,000. Additionally, the fair value of Rex's property, plant, and equipment on that date was $900,000 in excess of its book value. In the October 31, 1983, consolidated balance sheet of Simpson, Inc., and its wholly owned subsidiary, what amount should be reported as goodwill?

a. $0
b. $ 900,000
c. $1,100,000
d. $2,000,000

39. On January 4, 1982, Wynn, Inc., bought 15% of Parr Corporation's common stock for $60,000. Wynn appropriately accounts for this investment by the cost method. The following data concerning Parr are available for the years ended December 31, 1982 and 1983:

	1982	*1983*
Net income	$30,000	$90,000
Dividends paid	None	80,000

In its income statement for the year ended December 31, 1983, how much should Wynn report as income from this investment?

a. $ 4,500
b. $ 9,000
c. $12,000
d. $13,500

Repeat Question

(584,P2,29) Identical to item 29 above

Problems

Problem 1 Business Combinations (1179,T5)

(15 to 20 minutes)

When a business combination is effected by an exchange of common stock, the transaction is accounted for as a purchase or as a pooling of interests, depending on the circumstances. The methods are not optional and each yields significantly different results as to financial position and results of operations.

Required:

Discuss the **supportive** arguments for each of the following:

a. Purchase method.
b. Pooling of interests method.

Do **not** discuss in your answer the rules for distinguishing between a purchase and a pooling of interests.

Problem 2 Purchase Pooling Criteria (577,T3)

(20 to 25 minutes)

Hanover Company and Case Company, both of whom have only voting common stock, are considering a merger whereby Hanover would be the surviving company. The terms of the combination provide that the transaction would be carried out by Hanover exchanging one share of its stock for two shares of Case's stock. Prior to the date of the contemplated exchange, Hanover had purchased five percent of Case's stock which it holds as an investment. Case, at the same date, owns two percent of Hanover's stock. All of the remaining outstanding stock of Case will be acquired by Hanover in this contemplated exchange. Neither of the two companies has ever had any affiliation as a subsidiary or division of any other company.

Required:

a. Without enumerating specific criteria, how is a determination made as to whether a business combination is accounted for as a pooling of interests or as a purchase?

b. Based only on the facts above discuss the specific criteria which would qualify or disqualify this business combination as being accounted for as a pooling of interests.

c. What additional requirements (other than those discussed in b. above) must be met in order to account for this business combination as a pooling of interests?

Problem 3 Equity Method Accounting (1174,T3)

(25 to 30 minutes)

Hawkes Systems, Inc., a chemical processing company, has been operating profitably for many years. On March 1, 1974, Hawkes purchased 50,000 shares of Diversified Insurance Company stock for $2,000,000. The 50,000 shares represented 25% of Diversified's outstanding stock. Both Hawkes and Diversified operate on a fiscal year ending August 31.

For the fiscal year ended August 31, 1974, Diversified reported net income of $800,000 earned ratably throughout the year. During November 1973, February, May, and August 1974, Diversified paid its regular quarterly cash dividend of $100,000.

Required:

a. What criteria should Hawkes consider in determining whether its investment in Diversified should be classified as (1) a current asset (marketable security) or (2) a noncurrent asset (investment) in Hawkes' August 31, 1974, balance sheet? Confine your discussion to the decision criteria for determining the balance-sheet classification of the investment.

b. Assume that the investment should be classified as a long-term investment in the noncurrent asset section of Hawkes' balance sheet. The cost of Hawkes' investment equaled its equity in the recorded values of Diversified's net assets; recorded values were not materially different from fair values (individually or collectively). For the fiscal year ended August 31, 1974, how did the net income reported and dividends paid by Diversified affect the accounts of Hawkes (including Hawkes' income tax accounts)? Indicate each account affected, whether it increased or decreased, and explain the reason for the change in the account balance (such as Cash, Investment in Diversified, etc.). Organize your answer in the following format.

Account Name	Increase or Decrease	Reason for Change in Account Balance

c. Independent of your answers to parts a. and b. above, assume Hawkes had purchased 70% of Diversified's stock on March 1,1974.

1. Under certain circumstances Hawkes (the parent) should not accrue income taxes on all or part of its equity in the undistributed earnings of Diversified (its subsidiary). What are these circumstances and what evidence and other considerations must be evaluated to substantiate these circumstances?

2. What information should be disclosed in the notes to its financial statements if Hawkes does not accrue income taxes on all or part of its equity in the undistributed earnings of Diversified?

3. Would it be appropriate to prepare consolidated financial statements for Hawkes and its subsidiary, Diversified, for the fiscal year ended August 31, 1974? Explain.

Problem 4 Change to Equity Method (581,P4b)

(25 to 30 minutes)

Part b. On January 1, 1979, Jeffries, Inc., paid $700,000 for 10,000 shares of Wolf Company's voting common stock which was a 10% interest in Wolf. At that date the net assets of Wolf totaled $6,000,000. The fair values of all of Wolf's identifiable assets and liabilities were equal to their book values. Jeffries does not have the ability to exercise significant influence over the operating and financial policies of Wolf. Jeffries received dividends of $0.90 per share from Wolf on October 1, 1979. Wolf reported net income of $400,000 for the year ended December 31, 1979.

On July 1, 1980, Jeffries paid $2,300,000 for 30,000 additional shares of Wolf Company's voting common stock which represents a 30% investment in Wolf. The fair values of all of Wolf's identifiable assets net of liabilities were equal to their book values of $6,500,000. As a result of this transaction, Jeffries has the ability to exercise significant influence over the operating and financial policies of Wolf. Jeffries received dividends of $1.10 per share from Wolf on April 1, 1980, and $1.35 per share on October 1, 1980. Wolf reported net income of $500,000 for the year ended December 31, 1980, and $200,000 for the six months ended December 31, 1980. Jeffries amortizes goodwill over a forty-year period.

Required:

1. Prepare a schedule showing the income or loss before income taxes for the year ended December 31, 1979, that Jeffries should report from its investment in Wolf in its income statement issued in March 1980.

2. During March 1981 Jeffries issues comparative financial statements for 1979 and 1980. Prepare schedules showing the income or loss before income taxes for the years ended December 31, 1979, and 1980, that Jeffries should report from its investment in Wolf. Show supporting computations in good form.

Problem 5 Current and Noncurrent Marketable Equity Securities (1183,Q5)

(40 to 50 minutes)

At December 31, 1982, Winsor Corp. properly reported as current assets the following marketable equity securities:

Bea Corp., 1,000 shares, $2.40 convertible preferred stock	$ 40,000
Cha, Inc., 6,000 shares of common stock	60,000
Dey Co., 2,000 shares of common stock	55,000
Marketable equity securities at cost	$155,000
Less valuation allowance	7,000
Marketable equity securities at market	$148,000

On January 2, 1983, Winsor purchased 100,000 shares of Eddie Corp. common stock for $1,700,000, representing 30% of Eddie's outstanding common stock and an underlying equity of $1,400,000 in Eddie's net assets at January 2. Winsor, which had no other financial transactions with Eddie during 1983, amortizes goodwill over a 40-year period. As a result of Winsor's 30% ownership of Eddie, Winsor has the ability to exercise significant influence over Eddie's financial and operating policies.

During 1983, Winsor disposed of the following securities:

- January 18 – sold 2,500 shares of Cha for $13 per share.
- June 1 – sold 500 shares of Dey, after a 10% stock dividend, for $21 per share.
- October 1 – converted 500 shares of Bea's preferred stock into 1,500 shares of Bea's common stock, when the market price was $60 per share for the preferred stock and $21 per share for the common stock.

The following 1983 dividend information pertains to the stock held by Winsor:

- February 14 – Dey issued a 10% stock dividend, when the market price of Dey's common stock was $22 per share.
- April 5 and October 5 – Bea paid dividends of $1.20 per share on its $2.40 preferred stock, to stockholders of record on March 9 and September 9, respectively. Bea did not pay any dividends on its common stock during 1983.
- June 30 – Cha paid a $1.00 per share dividend on its common stock.
- March 1, June 1, September 1, and December 1 – Eddie paid quarterly dividends of $0.50 per share on each of these dates. Eddie's net income for the year ended December 31, 1983, was $1,200,000.

At December 31, 1983, Winsor's management intended to hold the Eddie stock as a long-term investment, with the remaining investments being considered as temporary. Market prices per share of the marketable equity securities were as follows:

	At December 31,	
	1983	*1982*
Bea Corp. – preferred	$56	$42
Bea Corp. – common	20	18
Cha, Inc. – common	11	11
Dey Co. – common	22	20
Eddie Corp. – common	16	18

All of the foregoing stocks are listed on major stock exchanges. Declines in market value from cost would not be considered as permanent declines.

Required:

a. Prepare a schedule of Winsor's *current* marketable equity securities at December 31, 1983, including any information necessary to determine the related valuation allowance and unrealized gross gains and losses.

b. Prepare a schedule to show the carrying amount of Winsor's *noncurrent* marketable equity securities at December 31, 1983.

c. Prepare a schedule showing all income, gains, and losses (realized and unrealized) relating to Winsor's investments, for the year ended December 31, 1983.

Problem 6 Purchase vs. Pooling Worksheet (1174,Q5)

(40 to 50 minutes)

Blue Corporation was merged into Ace Corporation on August 31, 1974, with Blue Corporation going out of existence. Both corporations had fiscal years ending on August 31, and Ace Corporation will retain this fiscal year. The enclosed worksheet contains a balance sheet for each corporation and a combined balance sheet as of August 31, 1974, immediately prior to the merger, and net income figures for each corporation for the fiscal year ended August 31, 1974. You have obtained the following additional information as of the date of the merger:

- The fair value of the assets and liabilities on August 31, 1974, of Ace Corporation and Blue Corporation was as follows:

	Ace	*Blue*
Current assets	$ 4,950,000	$ 3,400,000
Plant & equip. (net)	22,000,000	14,000,000
Patents	570,000	360,000
Plant rearrangement costs	150,000	40,000
Total assets	$27,670,000	$17,800,000
Liabilities	(2,650,000)	(2,100,000)
Net assets	$25,020,000	$15,700,000

- Ace Corporation capitalized its fiscal year 1974 plant rearrangement costs and has always amortized them over five years beginning with the year of expenditure. All plant rearrangement costs of Ace have been appropriately capitalized and amortized for the current and preceding years. Blue Corporation incurred $50,000 of plant rearrangement costs which were expensed during the fiscal year ending August 31, 1974. Blue did not have any plant rearrangement costs in any year before 1974. Blue will adopt Ace's method of accounting for plant rearrangement costs.
- Internally generated general expenses incurred because of the merger were $25,000 and are included in the current assets of Ace as a prepaid expense.
- There were no intercompany transactions during the year.
- Before the merger, Ace had 3,000,000 shares of common stock authorized; 1,200,000 shares issued; and 1,100,000 shares outstanding. Blue had 750,000 shares of common stock authorized, issued, and outstanding.

Required:

(See worksheet on following page.)

On the worksheet, prepare the balance sheet and determine the amount of net income under each of the following independent situations. Include explanations of adjustments on the worksheet. Cross-reference explanations to the adjustments. Do not prepare formal journal entries.

a. Ace Corporation exchanged 400,000 shares of previously unissued common stock and 100,000

Problem 6

Ace Corporation and Blue Corporation
Worksheet for Pooling of Interests and Purchase Accounting

	Ace Corporation	Blue Corporation	Combined	a. Adjustments Debit	a. Adjustments Credit	Pooling of interests	b. Adjustments Debit	b. Adjustments Credit	Purchase
Current assets	$ 4,350,000	$ 3,000,000	$7,350,000						
Plant & equipment (net)	18,500,000	11,300,000	29,800,000						
Patents	450,000	200,000	650,000						
Plant rearrangement costs	150,000	—	150,000						
	$23,450,000	$14,500,000	$37,950,000						
Liabilities	$ 2,650,000	$ 2,100,000	$ 4,750,000						
Common stock $10 par value	12,000,000	—	12,000,000						
Common stock $5 par value	—	3,750,000	3,750,000						
Paid-in capital in excess of par	4,200,000	—	4,200,000						
Paid-in capital in excess of par	—	3,200,000	3,200,000						
Retained earnings	5,850,000	—	5,850,000						
Retained earnings	—	5,450,000	5,450,000						
	24,700,000	14,500,000	39,200,000						
Less treasury stock at cost, 100,000 shares	1,250,000	—	1,250,000						
	$23,450,000	$14,500,000	$37,950,000						
Net income (no extraordinary items for fiscal year ended August 31, 1974)	$ 2,450,000	$ 1,300,000							

shares of treasury stock for all the outstanding common stock of Blue Corporation. All the conditions for pooling-of-interests accounting enumerated in APB Opinion No. 16 ("Business Combinations") were met.

b. Ace Corporation purchased the assets and assumed the liabilities of Blue Corporation by paying $3,100,000 cash and issuing debentures of $16,900,000 at face value.

Problem 7 Consolidated Financial Statement Worksheet (1183,P5)

(40 to 50 minutes)

Amboy Corporation acquired all of the outstanding $10 par voting common stock of Taft, Inc., on January 1, 1982, in exchange for 50,000 shares of its $10 par voting common stock. On December 31, 1981, Amboy's common stock had a closing market price of $15 per share on a national stock exchange. The acquisition was appropriately accounted for as a purchase. Both companies continued to operate as separate business entities maintaining separate accounting records with years ending December 31.

On December 31, 1982, after year-end adjustments but before the nominal accounts were closed, the companies had condensed general ledger trial balances as follows:

	Amboy Dr. (Cr.)	*Taft Dr. (Cr.)*
Net sales	$(1,900,000)	$(1,500,000)
Dividend income from Taft, Inc.	(40,000)	
Gain on sale of warehouse	(30,000)	
Cost of goods sold	1,180,000	870,000
Operating expenses (includes depreciation)	550,000	440,000
Cash	285,000	150,000
Accounts receivable (net)	430,000	350,000
Inventories	530,000	410,000
Land, plant & equipment	660,000	680,000
Accumulated depreciation	(185,000)	(210,000)
Investment in Taft, Inc. (at cost)	750,000	
Accounts payable & accrued expenses	(670,000)	(594,000)
Common stock ($10 par)	(1,200,000)	(400,000)
Additional paid-in capital	(140,000)	(80,000)
Retained earnings (1/1/82)	(220,000)	(156,000)
Dividends paid		40,000
Total	$ 0	$ 0

Additional information is as follows:

- There were no changes in the common stock and additional paid-in capital accounts during 1982 except the one necessitated by Amboy's acquisition of Taft.
- At the acquisition date the current value of Taft's machinery exceeded its book value by $54,000. The excess will be amortized over the estimated average remaining life of six years. The fair values of all of Taft's other assets and liabilities were equal to their book values. Any goodwill resulting from the acquisition will be amortized over a 20-year period.
- On July 1, 1982, Amboy sold a warehouse facility to Taft for $129,000 cash. At the date of sale Amboy's book values were $33,000 for the land and $66,000 for the undepreciated cost of the building. Taft allocated the $129,000 purchase price to the land for $43,000 and to the building for $86,000. Taft is depreciating the building over its estimated five-year remaining useful life by the straight-line method with no salvage value.
- During 1982 Amboy purchased merchandise from Taft at an aggregate invoice price of $180,000, which included a 100% markup on Taft's cost. At December 31, 1982, Amboy owed Taft $75,000 on these purchases, and $36,000 of the merchandise purchased remained in Amboy's inventory.

Required:

Complete the tear-out worksheet to prepare a consolidated income statement and retained earnings statement for the year ended December 31, 1982, and a consolidated balance sheet as at December 31, 1982, for Amboy Corporation and its subsidiary, Taft, Inc. Formal consolidated statements and journal entries are not required. Ignore income tax considerations. Supporting computations should be in good form. Include the completed tear-out worksheet in the proper sequence and turn in with other answer sheets.

Amboy Corporation and Subsidiary
Consolidating Statement Worksheet
December 31, 1982

	Amboy Corp.	Taft Inc.	Adjustments & eliminations Debit	Adjustments & eliminations Credit	Adjusted balance
Income Statement					
Net sales	$(1,900,000)	$(1,500,000)			
Dividends from Taft	(40,000)				
Gain on sale of warehouse	(30,000)				
Cost of goods sold	1,180,000	870,000			
Operating expenses (incl. deprec.)	550,000	440,000			
Net income	$ (240,000)	$ (190,000)			
Retained Earnings Statement					
Balance, 1/1/82	$ (220,000)	$ (156,000)			
Net income	(240,000)	(190,000)			
Dividends paid		40,000			
Balance, 12/31/82	$ (460,000)	$ (306,000)			
Balance Sheet					
Assets:					
Cash	$ 285,000	$ 150,000			
Accounts receivable (net)	430,000	350,000			
Inventories	530,000	410,000			
Land, plant & equipment	660,000	680,000			
Accumulated depreciation	(185,000)	(210,000)			
Investment in Taft (at cost)	750,000				
	$2,470,000	$1,380,000			
Liabilities & stockholders' equity:					
Accounts pay. & accrued exp.	$ (670,000)	$ (594,000)			
Common stock ($10 par)	(1,200,000)	(400,000)			
Additional paid-in capital	(140,000)	(80,000)			
Retained earnings	(460,000)	(306,000)			
	$(2,470,000)	$(1,380,000)			

Problem 8 Consolidated Balance Sheet (580,Q3)

(45 to 55 minutes)

The December 31, 1979, balance sheets of Encanto Corporation and its subsidiary, Norris Corporation, are presented below:

Assets:	*Encanto Corporation*	*Norris Corporation*
Cash	$ 167,250	$101,000
Accounts receivable	178,450	72,000
Notes receivable	87,500	28,000
Dividends receivable	36,000	
Inventories	122,000	68,000
Property, plant and equipment	487,000	252,000
Accumulated depreciation	(117,000)	(64,000)
Investment in Norris Corporation	240,800	
	$1,202,000	$457,000

Liabilities and stockholders' equity:		
Accounts payable	$ 222,000	$ 76,000
Notes payable	79,000	89,000
Dividend payable		40,000
Common stock, $10 par value:		
Encanto Corporation	400,000	
Norris Corporation		100,000
Retained earnings:		
Encanto Corporation	501,000	
Norris Corporation		152,000
	$1,202,000	$457,000

Additional information:

- Encanto initially acquired 60 percent of the outstanding common stock of Norris in 1977. This purchase resulted in no difference between cost and net assets acquired. As of December 31, 1979, the percentage owned is 90 percent. An analysis of the account "Investment in Norris Corporation" is as follows:

Date	*Description*	*Amount*
Dec. 31, 1977	Acquired 6,000 shares	$ 70,800
Dec. 31, 1978	60% of 1978 net income of $78,000	46,800
Sept. 1, 1979	Acquired 3,000 shares	92,000
Dec. 31, 1979	Subsidiary income for 1979:	67,200*
Dec. 31, 1979	90% of dividends declared	(36,000)
		$240,800

*Subsidiary income for 1979:	
60% of $96,000	$57,600
30% of 96,000 x 33-1/3%	9,600
	$67,200

Assume that Norris's net income is earned ratably during the year. Amortization of the excess of cost over the net assets acquired is to be recorded over sixty months.

- On December 15, 1979, Norris declared a cash dividend of $4 per share of common stock, payable to shareholders of January 7, 1980.
- During 1979, Encanto sold merchandise to Norris. Encanto's cost for this merchandise was $68,000, and the sale was made at 125% of cost. Norris's inventory at December 31, 1979, included merchandise purchased from Encanto at a cost to Norris of $35,000.
- In December 1978, Norris sold merchandise to Encanto for $67,000, which was at a markup of 35% over Norris's cost. On January 1, 1979, $54,000 of this merchandise remained in Encanto's inventory. This merchandise was subsequently sold by Encanto at a profit of $11,000 during 1979.
- On October 1, 1979, Encanto sold for $42,000, excess equipment to Norris. Data relating to this equipment is as follows:

Book value on Encanto's records	$36,000
Method of depreciation	Straight-line
Estimated remaining life on October 1, 1979	10 years

- Near the end of 1979, Norris reduced the balance of its intercompany account payable to Encanto to zero by transferring $8,000 to Encanto. This payment was still in transit on December 31, 1979.

Required:

Complete the consolidated balance sheet worksheet of Encanto Corporation and its subsidiary, Norris Corporation, as of December 31, 1979. Formal statements and journal entries are **not** required. Supporting computations should be in good form.

Encanto Corporation and Subsidiary
Consolidated Balance Sheet Worksheet
December 31, 1979

	Encanto Corporation	Norris Corporation	Total	Adjustments and eliminations: Debit	Adjustments and eliminations: Credit	Minority interest	Consolidated
Assets:							
Cash	$ 167,250	$101,000	$ 268,250				
Accounts receivable	178,450	72,000	250,450				
Notes receivable	87,500	28,000	115,500				
Dividends receivable	36,000		36,000				
Inventories	122,000	68,000	190,000				
Property, plant, and equipment	487,000	252,000	739,000				
Accumulated depreciation	(117,000)	(64,000)	(181,000)				
Investment in Norris Corp.	240,800		240,800				
Goodwill							
Total assets	$1,202,000	$457,000	$1,659,000				
Liabilities and stockholders' equity:							
Accounts payable	$ 222,000	$ 76,000	$ 298,000				
Notes payable	79,000	89,000	168,000				
Dividends payable		40,000	40,000				
Common stock							
Encanto Corp.	400,000		400,000				
Norris Corp.		100,000	100,000				
Retained earnings							
Encanto Corp.	501,000		501,000				
Norris Corp.		152,000	152,000				
Minority interest							
Total liabilities and stockholders' equity	$1,202,000	$457,000	$1,659,000				

Multiple Choice Answers

1.	a	9.	c	17.	c	25.	c	33.	a
2.	c	10.	c	18.	d	26.	c	34.	c
3.	c	11.	b	19.	d	27.	c	35.	d
4.	c	12.	d	20.	a	28.	a	36.	a
5.	b	13.	c	21.	c	29.	d	37.	a
6.	c	14.	d	22.	d	30.	a	38.	c
7.	a	15.	c	23.	c	31.	d	39.	c
8.	d	16.	d	24.	b	32.	d		

Multiple Choice Answer Explanations

A. & B. Concepts of Accounting and Investment Percentage, and Equity Method

1. (1183,P1,12) (a) The requirement is the amount to be reported in the 1982 income statement as an unusual loss from the disposal of a long-term investment. The realized loss on the sale of an investment is the difference between its cost and the selling price. The cost of this investment is $250,000 (10,000 x $25) and the selling price is $100,000 (10,000 x $10), resulting in a loss of $150,000 ($250,000 – $100,000). Per APB 30, such unusual items are **not** reported net of tax. Note that since the investment is accounted for under the **cost** method (appropriate for a nonmarketable security not accounted for by the equity method), it would **not** be written down to $24 per share at 12/31/81, unless that decline in market value was determined to be other than temporary when the 1981 financial statements were being prepared.

2. (1183,P2,26) (c) The requirement is the amount of income to be recognized in 1982 from a long-term investment in common stock. Since Diamond owns 40% of Ashley's common stock, the equity method is used from the date of investment (July 1) to year end. There is no excess of cost over book value, so Diamond would recognize 40% of Ashley's income during the last six months of the year (40% x $300,000, or $120,000). The cash dividends are not reflected in investor income under the equity method; they are recorded as a reduction of the investment account when received.

3. (582,Q1,2) (c) The requirement is the balance in the "Investment in Bracero" account at the end of the first year. The most efficient solutions approach is to use "T" account analysis. The first step is to enter $258,000 (initial cost) in the investment account. Recall that under the equity method the investment account is affected by three types of transactions each year. First, the account is increased by the investor's proportionate share of the investee's earnings ($180,000 x 30% = $54,000). Second, the investment account is decreased by dividends received by the investor ($20,000 x 30% = $6,000). Third, the account is decreased by the amortization of the excess of the cost over the book value of the investment. The excess is $172,000 [$258,000 – ($620,000 x 30%)], and the amortization each year is $1,800 ($172,000 ÷ 40 years).

Investment in Bracero

Cost	$258,000	$6,000	Dividends
Earnings	54,000	1,800	Amortization
End. bal.	$304,200		

4. (582,Q1,10) (c) The requirement is the amount that the investor company (Troquel) should show on its 1981 income statement as income from the investment in Zafacon. Since the investor has only a 15% interest in the investee, the investment is accounted for under the cost method. Per para 17 of APB 18, the cost method is appropriate for investments where ownership is less than 20% of the investee. Under the cost method, the investor records the long-term investment at cost and records dividends received as income. However, dividends received in excess of the investor's share of the investee's earnings since acquisition are recorded as a reduction in the investment account. Such distributions are treated as a return of capital (liquidating dividend). In this case, the investor's share of the dividend is $10,500 ($70,000 x 15%). The investor's share of earnings since acquisition is only $9,000 ($60,000 x 15%). Thus, only $9,000 can appropriately be recorded as investment income. The journal entry to record the receipt of the dividend is:

Cash	$10,500	
Dividend income		$9,000
Investment in Zafacon		1,500

5. (1181,Q1,11) (b) The requirement is the balance in the investment account at 12/31/80. APB 18, para 17 identifies the circumstances in which the equity method and the cost method are appropriate. Basically, the cost method is appropriate when the investor lacks significant influence over the investee which is typically quantified as being less than 20% ownership. Under the cost method, the investment is originally recorded at cost. It is appropriate to reduce the investment when dividends received represent a distribution of earnings retained in the business prior to the acquisition of the investment. Additionally, SFAS 12, requires that investments which are market-

able and are accounted for under the cost method be carried at the lower of aggregate cost or market. Since the dividend paid by Rey Corporation is not a liquidating dividend and there is no mention in the problem of a lower market value at 12/31/80, the investment would continue to be carried at its original cost.

6. (1183,T1,6) (c) The requirement is the effect of cash dividends declared and paid out of current earnings upon an investor's investment account, accounted for under both the cost and equity methods. Under the cost method, APB 18, para 6 states that dividends received are to be recognized as income to the investor and the investment account is unaffected. However, if dividends were received in excess of earnings subsequent to the investment date, they would be considered a return of the investment and would be recorded as a reduction in the investment account. In this case, dividends are paid from current earnings and are not, therefore, considered a return of capital. Under the equity method (APB 18, para 10), the receipt of dividends reduces the carrying amount of the investment. Therefore, answer (c) is correct.

7. (1183,T1,24) (a) According to APB 18, para 4b, the amortization of goodwill related to the purchase of the investment reduces the amount of equity in the earnings of the investee reported on the investor's income statement. Dividends received from the investee reduce the carrying value of the investment on the investor's books but do not reduce earnings recognized on the income statement. The entries to record the investor's equity in the earnings of the investee and the receipt of dividends by the investor, respectively, are as follows:

Investment	XXX	
Income from investee		XXX
Cash (from dividends)	XXX	
Investment		XXX

8. (582,T1,18) (d) APB 18 states that consolidated financial statements should generally be prepared when there is greater than 50% ownership of the outstanding voting stock of the company although there are circumstances in which reporting under the equity method or even the cost method is more appropriate. (Note that consolidation may also refer to a form of business combination where two or more entities form a new entity.) The exhibit below illustrates the accounting treatment for equity investments.

Financial reporting	*% owned*
Cost or LCM	20
Equity	20-50
Consolidated or Equity	51-100

Answers (a) and (b) are incorrect because the ownership in voting stock is greater than 20%. Pooling of interest [answer (c)] is incorrect because recording an acquisition of stock as a pooling requires at least 90% ownership of the voting stock.

9. (1180,T1,19) (c) The requirement is the appropriate circumstances in which to use the "equity method." The equity method should be used in those cases where "an investor has the ability to exercise significant influence over an investee." Choices (a) and (b) indicate that such influence may be present, but are not sufficient evidence in themselves. Choice (d) is a criteria for pooling of interests accounting.

G. Accounting for the Combination, and Sections H.–K.

10. (583,P1,4) (c) The requirement is the amount of goodwill resulting from a business combination properly accounted for as a purchase. In a purchase, the difference between the cost of an acquired company and the fair value of its net assets (fair value of tangible and identifiable intangible assets less liabilities) is recorded as goodwill. The cost of the acquired company is $1,600,000, and the fair value of its net assets is $1,300,000 ($160,000 + $460,000 + $1,040,000 – $360,000). Therefore, goodwill to be recorded is $1,600,000 less $1,300,000, or $300,000.

11. (580,P1,3) (b) The requirement is to compute the balance in Troy's paid-in capital account immediately after a business combination accounted for as a pooling of interests. One solutions approach is to make an entry to record the combination on the new entity's books to reflect the $995,000 book value of the net assets. In making the entry the objective is to carry forward the maximum amount of retained earnings (see APB 16, para 53).

Net assets	$995,000	
Common stock		$650,000
Paid-in capital		?
Retained earnings		?

Paid-in capital in this case will be equal to $995,000 minus the sum of common stock ($650,000) and retained earnings ($320,000). This difference is a credit to paid-in capital of $25,000. If the sum of the par value of the common stock and retained earnings had been greater than $995,000, there would be no credit to paid-in capital and retained earnings carried forward would be reduced.

The other approach to obtain the amount of paid-in capital is to subtract from combined paid-in capital ($75,000) the difference between the par value issued for the new corporation ($650,000) and the combined par value of the constituents ($600,000).

$75,000 – ($650,000 par value issued – $600,000 combined par value) = $25,000.

12. (1182,Q1,3) (d) The requirement is to determine the business combination expenses if the business combination is treated as a pooling of interests. APB 16, para 58 states that the pooling of interests method records neither the acquiring of assets nor the obtaining of capital. Costs incurred to effect a combination accounted for by the pooling of interests method are, therefore, expenses of the combined corporation rather than additions to assets or direct reductions of stockholders' equity. Accordingly, the entire $27,000 would be recorded as business combination expense.

13. (1182,Q1,4) (c) The requirement is to determine the amount that would be capitalized if the business combination was accounted for as a purchase. APB 16, para 76 states that the cost of a company acquired in a business combination accounted for by the purchase method includes the direct costs of acquisition. These direct costs are the incremental costs rather than recurring internal costs which may be directly related to an acquisition. Direct costs which are capitalized in a purchase would, therefore, include finder's fees and fees paid to outside consultants. The acquisition cost includes the FMV of the stock issued $500,000 (10,000 shares x $50) plus the $20,000 of costs directly related to the acquisition or total acquisition costs to be capitalized of $520,000. The SEC registration costs reduce the recorded amount of the common stock. The journal entry to record the combination is

Assets (listed separately)	$520,000	
Common stock (10,000 x 1)		$ 10,000
Additional paid-in capital (500,000 – 7,000)		483,000
Cash (20,000 + 7,000)		27,000

14. (1181,Q2,36) (d) The requirement is the balance in the investment account on the balance sheet immediately after a combination, assuming it qualifies as a purchase. When a stock acquisition is recorded as a purchase the investment in the stock of the subsidiary is recorded at the fair market value of the securities issued or the property received, whichever is more readily determinable. Since the market price of Rolan's (acquiror) stock has been determined, the investment would be recorded on that basis at $600,000 ($10,000 shares issued x $60 market value).

15. (1181,Q2,37) (c) The requirement is the consolidated retained earnings balance immediately after a combination assuming the combination qualifies as a pooling of interests. Normally, in a 100% pooling of interests the retained earnings of the two entities are simply added together. An exception occurs when the par or stated value of the shares issued exceeds the total paid-in capital (common stock and additional paid-in capital) of the company being combined with the issuer and there is not enough additional paid-in capital on issuer's balance sheet to cover the deficiency. Since the par value of the stock issued by Rolan in this problem is equal to the par value of the common stock on Sandin's balance sheet, the consolidated retained earnings would be the sum of the two companies' retained earnings before the combination ($500,000 + 250,000 = $750,000).

16. (1180,Q1,13) (d) The requirement is the increase in net assets to be recorded by Action as a result of acquiring all of the outstanding common stock of Master Corporation. This acquisition is a **purchase** because Action issued **nonvoting preferred stock** in exchange for all of Master's common stock. A purchase is accounted for under the basic historical cost principal; the net assets acquired are recorded at their fair value or the fair value of the stock issued, whichever is more objectively determinable. The tangible net assets acquired have a fair value of $2,500,000; the fact that the stock issued has a value of $4,000,000 indicates that intangible assets are also acquired. The total cost of acquiring the net assets is the fair value of the preferred stock ($4,000,000) plus the finders' fee of $400,000 of preferred stock.

17. (1179,Q1,18) (c) The requirement is the amount that Alan Company should record as cost of a building that was part of net assets purchased in a business combination accounted for as a purchase. While the building had an appraised value of $150,000, its adjusted tax basis was only $100,000. Accordingly, $50,000 of depreciation ($150,000 – $100,000) will be lost relative to the purchase of a similar asset for $150,000. Thus, the valuation of the asset should be $150,000 less the $24,000 of tax benefits ($50,000 x 48%). See para 89 of APB 16.

18. (1183,T1,34) (d) The requirement is the minimum amount of an investee's stock which must be acquired in order to report a business combination as a pooling of interests. APB 16, para 47 requires that one of the combining companies issues voting common stock in exchange for at least 90 percent of the voting stock of another combining company that is outstanding at the date the combination is consummated.

19. (583,T1,41) (d) The requirement is to determine the treatment of plant and equipment in a business combination reported under the pooling of interests and the purchase methods. Under the pooling of interests method, a business combination is viewed in substance as an arrangement among stockholders, since no corporate assets are disbursed, and stockholder groups retain their respective interest. Consequently, the recorded assets and liabilities of the separate companies become the recorded assets and liabilities of the combined corporation (APB 16, para 51). Thus, under the pooling of interests method, plant and equipment should be reported at recorded value. Conversely, the purchase method reports assets acquired in a business combination at fair value. Thus, answer (d) is correct.

20. (1182,T1,31) (a) The requirement is to determine the amounts to be reported for inventories and long-term debt acquired when a company purchases all the outstanding common stock of another company for cash. This situation is accounted for using the purchase method. APB 16, paras 72 and 88 state that, in general, all assets and liabilities (including inventories and long-term debt) should be reported at fair value [answer (a)]. Answer (d) is incorrect because it describes the treatment accorded to inventories and long-term debt when a combination is accounted for as a pooling of interests. However, since cash is used exclusively in the transaction, a pooling of interest is precluded (APB 16, para 47b).

21. (582,T1,32) (c) Pooling of interests accounting requires that assets acquired and liabilities assumed be carried forward at their recorded (book) values. Thus, pooling accounting is consistent with the historical-cost system. Answers (a), (b), and (d) are incorrect because they apply to the purchase method of accounting for a business combination (APB 16, paras 17-41).

22. (577,T1,14) (d) The requirement is the effect on earnings of accounting for a business combination as a purchase instead of a pooling. First review accounting for income per purchase and per pooling. Per purchase, the income of the acquiring corporation only includes income of the acquired company after the date of acquisition (para 94, APB 16). Per pooling, income is reported as if the companies had been combined as of the beginning of the period (para 56, APB 16). In this case, the combination was accounted for as purchase instead of a pooling. Under both purchase and pooling, December earnings of B are included in A's retained earnings. Thus, the concern must be with B's operation from the beginning of 1976 through November. Thus answer (b) is incorrect because if B had a net loss in the beginning of the year and this loss was not recognized in A's retained earnings due to purchase rather than pooling accounting, A's retained earnings are overstated. Answer (d) is correct because the net earnings in the beginning of the year should have been, but were not, included in A's retained earnings.

23. (577,T1,15) (c) The requirement is the effect of recording a combination as a purchase instead of a pooling on parent's asset valuations at the date of acquisition. Note that the requirement is the effect on asset valuations, not on total asset value. Under purchase accounting, assets are recorded at their fair value; under pooling accounting, assets are recorded at their book value. Thus relative to valuation under pooling accounting, the assets will be overstated at their fair value if their fair value exceeds their book value. Remember, under pooling accounting they would have been recorded at their book value. See para 51 and 87 of APB 16.

24. (1176,T1,9) (b) Acquisition of B by A is to be accounted for by the purchase method because less than 90% of B's stock is acquired by A (para 47b of APB 16). Company A acquires 80% of $800,000, or $640,000, of net fair market value for $700,000 of stock, resulting in $60,000 of goodwill (para 87 of APB 16). The book value of Company B is not relevant to determine the consideration given by A or the recording of the historical cost for the amount paid for by A.

25. (576,T1,6) (c) When a pooling takes place in mid-year, the income statement of the pooled company should reflect pooled operations for the entire year. The rationale is that the pooled company will report on a combined basis in the future. Also required are the revenue, extraordinary items, and net income for each of the separate companies from the beginning of the period to the date of the pooling. See para 56 and 64 of APB 16. Note that this is in contrast to purchase accounting wherein the consolidated income statement only includes the parent's share of the subsidiary's income from the date of acquisition of the subsidiary. However, under purchase accounting, consolidated income as if the purchase had occurred at the beginning of the period is required on a pro forma basis in the notes to the financial statements.

26. (576,T1,13) (c) In a pooling of interest, the balance sheets are simply added together. Only intercompany items such as receivables and payables

are eliminated. If the legal capital (capital stock) of the surviving company exceeds or is less than the sum of the legal capitals of the combining companies, an adjustment must be made to paid-in capital and/or retained earnings. If the legal capital of the surviving company exceeds the legal capital of the combining companies, paid-in capital first and then retained earnings is debited to make up this difference. If the legal capital of the surviving company is less than the legal capitals of the combining companies, a credit is required to paid-in capital from pooling. See para 53 of APB 16.

L. Consolidated Financial Statements, and Sections M.—O.

27. (1181,P1,13) (c) The requirement is the consolidated stockholders' equity at 12/31/80 after a pooling of interests on 1/1/80. The acquisition of a subsidiary in a pooling of interests is recorded at the book value of the subsidiary's net assets (stockholders' equity). Therefore, consolidated stockholders' equity at 1/1/80 would be the sum of Platt's and Drew's individual equity sections ($20,000,000). This amount would be increased by combined net income ($1,950,000) and decreased by dividends paid ($750,000), resulting in 12/31/80 consolidated stockholders' equity of $21,200,000.

Consolidated Stockholders' Equity

Platt dividends paid, 1980	$750,000	$16,000,000	Platt SE 1/1/80
		4,000,000	Drew SE 1/1/80
		1,500,000	Platt NI for 1980
		450,000	Drew NI for 1980
		$21,200,000	Balance 12/31/80

28. (580,P1,2) (a) The situation is a business combination accounted for as a purchase where the cost of the acquired company is less than the fair market value of the identifiable assets and liabilities of Thread Company. Per APB 16, para 91, the excess of fair market value over cost ($400,000) should be used first to reduce proportionately all noncurrent assets other than long-term investments in marketable securities. Any excess remaining is a deferred credit to be amortized to income over a period not to exceed forty years (see APB 16, para 91). In this case, $250,000 of the $400,000 excess is used to eliminate the entire amount of property, plant, and equipment. Additionally, $150,000 remains as a deferred credit.

$1,000,000	Cost
1,400,000	FMV of identifiable assets and liabilities
$ 400,000	Excess of FMV over cost
250,000	Reduction of PP&E
$ 150,000	Deferred credit

29. (1179,P1,3) (d) The requirement is the 1978 consolidated net income for two companies that combined as a pooling of interests on December 1, 1978. Per para 56 of APB 16, business combinations accounted for by the pooling of interest method should report results of operations as if the combination took place at the beginning of the year. Thus, the consolidated income would be $3,200,000 ($2,000,000 + $1,200,000). Note that the problem indicates that the surviving company (Drew) does not already include the equity in the net income of the combining company (Art). If Drew had been using the equity method, and if the $2,000,000 of Drew income already included the $1,200,000 of Art income, consolidated net income would be $2,000,000.

30. (1183,T1,33) (a) The requirement is the proper amount of consolidated net income under a pooling of interests. In a business combination accounted for as a pooling of interests, APB 16, para 56 states that the results of operations for the period in which the combination occurs should be reported as though the companies had been combined as of the beginning of the period. Consolidated net income, therefore, includes the results of operations both before the pooling and after. Therefore, the 12 months' net income for both Company X and Company Y would be included in consolidated net income.

31. (1182,T1,2) (d) In a consolidated balance sheet prepared immediately after the acquisition, the retained earnings of a subsidiary are included for a pooling of interests (APB 16, para 53) but excluded for a purchase (ARB 51, para 9).

32. (1182,T1,4) (d) Per ARB 51, para 2, consolidated financial statements are typically prepared when one company has the controlling financial interest in another company [answer (d)]. This control is usually direct or indirect ownership of over 50% of the outstanding voting stock. Significant influence [answer (c)], usually between 20% and 50% voting stock ownership, should be reported using the equity

method (APB 18, para 17). The method of accounting for a subsidiary [answers (a) and (b)] is irrelevent when determining whether consolidated financial statements should or should not be prepared because consolidated subsidiaries may be accounted for using either the cost or equity method.

33. (582,T1,12) (a) The percentage of stock not owned by the parent company represents the minority interest's share of the net assets of the subsidiary. Under both purchase and pooling accounting, minority interest income will be a deduction on the consolidated income statement for its portion of the subsidiary's income. Minority interest will be shown on the consolidated balance sheet in an amount determined by multiplying the owners' equity of the subsidiary by the minority's respective ownership percentage. Answer (b) is incorrect because goodwill is only recorded under the purchase method. Answer (c) is incorrect because under purchase accounting none of the subsidiary's retained earnings is carried over in the consolidated balance sheet whereas under pooling of interest accounting all or some of the subsidiary's retained earnings will be carried over. Answer (d) is incorrect because the additional stock issued by the parent in the pooling transaction will appear in the consolidated balance sheet.

P. Intercompany Transactions and Profit Confirmation, and Section Q.

34. (1183,P1,19) (c) The requirement is the amount to be reported as accounts receivable from investees in the December 31, 1982, consolidated balance sheet. The $160,000 receivable from the consolidated subsidiary would be eliminated on the consolidated worksheet and, therefore, not reported on the consolidated balance sheet. The receivables from the unconsolidated subsidiaries ($50,000 + $100,000) would **not** be eliminated and, therefore, would be reported as receivables in the consolidated balance sheet.

35. (579,Q1,8) (d) The requirement is the year-end consolidated balances of fixed assets and related accumulated depreciation after an intercompany sale as of the beginning of the year. The objective is to restate the accounts as if the intercompany transaction had not occurred. Since the $2,000,000 asset, which had $500,000 accumulated depreciation at January 1, was being depreciated over 20 years, the ending balances should be $2,000,000 of fixed assets and $600,000 of accumulated depreciation. On the consolidated books, depreciation expense must be adjusted since the subsidiary recorded $120,000 expense ($1,800,000 ÷ 15 remaining years), while consolidated expense would be $100,000 ($2,000,000 ÷ 20 years). The entry is:

Accum. depr.	$20,000	
Depr. exp.		$20,000

Also, the equipment must be debited for $200,000 to adjust the subsidiary's cost ($1,800,000) up to the parent's original cost ($2,000,000). $500,000 of accumulated depreciation must be recorded on the consolidated books to reflect the depreciation the parent had recorded. Finally, the gain on sale of $300,000 ($1,800,000 received less $1,500,000 book value) must be eliminated.

Equipment	$200,000	
Gain on sale	300,000	
Accum. depr.		$500,000

R. Minority Interest

36. (1175,Q1,7) (a) Without the intercompany transaction, the minority interest income from Samson in 1973 would be $24,000 (30% of $80,000). in 1974, the minority interest income would be $27,000 (30% of 90,000). On the consolidated statements in 1973 the $2,000 intercompany profit will be eliminated, because from a consolidated viewpoint an arms-length transaction has not occurred with third parties. The elimination entry will be to credit inventory (which is in effect on the books of Eltro) for $2,000 and debits will be made of $1,400 to majority interest income and $600 to minority interest income. In 1974 when Eltro sells the inventory to outsiders, the $2,000 profit has effectively been earned. In 1974 an entry will be made on the consolidated books to effectively recognize this profit and allocate it to the majority and minority interest. Thus the 1973 minority interest income will be reduced by $600 and 1974 minority interest income increased by $600.

1973	*1974*
24,000	27,000
− 600	+ 600
23,400	27,600

May 1984 Answers

37. (584,P1,4) (a) The requirement is to compute the amount paid for a 25% interest in an investee. The equity method is used to account for the investment, and no goodwill resulted from the acquisition. The solutions approach is to set up a T-account for the investment account remembering that under the equity method the investor debits the investment account

for the cost of the investment and its share of the earnings of the investee and credits the account for its share of dividends paid by the investee.

Investment in Wall			
Cost	X	12,000	Dividends (25% x $48,000)
Earnings (25% x $120,000)	30,000		
12/31/83	190,000		

The initial cost (purchase price) of $172,000 is computed by solving the following equation for X:

Beg. balance (cost)	+	Earnings	–	Dividends	=	End. balance
X	+	$30,000	–	$12,000	=	$190,000

X = $172,000

38. (584,P1,12) (c) The requirement is the amount to be reported as goodwill as the result of the consolidation. The cost of the investment is $10,000,000 (250,000 shares x $40 per share), and the fair value is $8,900,000 ($8,000,000 book value plus $900,000 fair value of property, plant, and equipment in excess of its book value). Per SFAS 16, para 87 goodwill is the excess of cost over fair value. Thus, goodwill is $1,100,000 [cost ($10,000,000) - fair value ($8,900,000)].

39. (584,P2,31) (c) The requirement is to determine the 1983 income to be reported from an investment accounted for under the cost method. Under the cost method, dividends are treated as income in the year received by the investor to the extent of the investee's earnings since acquisition (APB 18, para 6a). The investor does **not** recognize any portion of the investee's undistributed earnings. Therefore, the investor's reported income from the investment would be the dividends received of $12,000 (15% x $80,000). Note, if dividends were received in excess of earnings subsequent to the acquisition, a return of capital exists and a reduction in the investment account would be necessary.

Answer Outline

Problem 1 Business Combinations

a. Supportive arguments for the purchase method
   One company usually acquires another
   Identities of acquirer and acquiree are usually obvious
   One company is usually clearly dominant and others lose control of assets and liabilities
   Based on bargaining of independent parties
      Parties assess current status and future prospects of individual companies
      Agreed terms recognized bargained values
   Business acquisitions should be accounted for by recording
      1. All assets and liabilities comprising the bargained cost
      2. Bargained cost of assets acquired less liabilities assumed
      3. Fair value received for stock issued
      4. Retained earnings from operations since acquisition
      5. Expenses and net income based on bargained costs

b. Supportive arguments for the pooling method
   1. No corporate assets are disbursed
   2. Net assets of issuing corporation are enlarged
   3. No newly invested capital
   4. No assets withdrawn, since stock is not an asset
   5. Net assets and stockholder groups remain intact
   6. Aggregate income not changed
   7. Resources, talents, etc. combined
   8. Former investment risk elements are maintained

   Thus, in substance, an arrangement among stockholder groups and corporations are separate from their stockholders
   Pooling was developed within the historical cost system and is compatible therewith

Unofficial Answer

Problem 1 Business Combinations

a. Those who support the purchase method believe that one company acquires another company in almost every business combination. The acquisition of one company by another and the identities of the acquiring and acquired companies are usually obvious. Generally, one company in a business combination is clearly the dominant and continuing entity and one or more other companies cease to control their own assets and operations because control passes to the acquiring corporation.

Proponents of purchase accounting hold that a business combination is a significant economic event that results from bargaining between independent parties. Each party bargains on the basis of an assessment of the current status and future prospects of each constituent as a separate enterprise and as a contributor to the proposed combined enterprise. The agreed terms of the combination recognize primarily the bargained values and only secondarily the constituent's recorded costs of assets and liabilities.

Those who support the purchase method of accounting for business combinations effected by issuing stock believe that an acquiring corporation accounts for business combinations effected by issuing stock believe that an acquiring corporation accounts for the economic substance of the transaction by applying those principles and by recording

1. All assets and liabilities that compose the bargained cost of an acquired company, not merely those items previously shown in the financial statements of an acquired company.

2. The bargained costs of assets acquired less liabilities assumed, not the costs to a previous owner.

3. The fair value of the consideration received for stock issued, not the equity shown in the financial statements of an acquired company.

4. Retained earnings from the acquiring company's operations, not a fusion of its retained earnings and previous earnings of an acquired company.

5. Expenses and net income after an acquisition computed on the bargained cost of acquired assets less assumed liabilities, not on the costs to a previous owner.

b. Those who support the pooling of interests method believe that a business combination effected by issuing common stock is different from a purchase in that no corporate assets are disbursed to stockholders, and the net assets of the issuing corporation are enlarged by the net assets of the corporation whose stockholders accept common stock of the combined corporation. There is no newly invested capital nor have owners withdrawn assets from the group since the stock of a corporation is not one of its assets. Accordingly, the net assets of the constituents remain intact but combined; the stockholder groups remain intact but combined. Aggregate income is not changed since the total resources are not changed. Consequently, the historical costs and earnings of the separate corporations are appropriately combined. In a business combination effected by exchanging stock, groups of stockholders combine their resources, talents, and risks to form a new entity to carry on in combination the previous businesses and to continue their earnings streams. The sharing of risks by the constituent stockholder groups is an important element in a business combination effected by exchanging stock. By pooling equity interest, each group continues to maintain risk elements of its former investment, and they mutually exchange risks and benefits.

A pooling-of-interests transaction is regarded as, in substance, an arrangement among stockholder groups. A fundamental concept of entity accounting is that a corporation is separate and distinct from its stockholders.

Proponents of pooling-of-interests accounting point out that the pooling concept was developed within the boundaries of the historical-cost system and is compatible with it.

Answer Outline

Problem 2 Purchase Pooling Criteria

a. Purchase or pooling must be used, i.e., not alternatives
   Purchase method required unless all pooling characteristics met

b. The companies are autonomous
   - Have not been subsidiaries within past two years

   The companies are independent, i.e., less than 10% ownership in each other

   Substantially all of Case's common stock is exchanged
   - Only voting common is being exchanged
   - Substantial means greater than 90% as follows

	100%
Less 5% of Case previously held	– 5%
Less 4%* per Case investment in Hanover	– 4%
	91%

*2% investment converted to equivalent investment by Hanover (2:1 exchange ratio)

c. Additional characteristics required for pooling
   1. Combination effected in a single transaction or within one year under a specified plan
   2. No change in equity interests within past two years
   3. Reacquisitions of common must be per systematic plan
      I.e., not in contemplation of combination
   4. Maintenance of same relative interest by all stockholders
   5. No restrictions on common stock exchanged
   6. No contingent issuances

   The combined corporation cannot agree or intend
   1. To reacquire common issued in the combination
   2. To enter into other arrangements for benefits of former stockholders
   3. To dispose of a significant part of the newly combined company's assets within two years

Unofficial Answer

Problem 2 Purchase Pooling Criteria

a. Both the purchase method and pooling-of-interests method of reporting business combinations are in accordance with generally accepted accounting principles. However, the two methods are not interchangeable and a combination must be accounted for as a purchase unless all of the characteristics of a pooling of interest are present. In order for a business combination to be considered a pooling of interests it must have nine basic characteristics and not have entered into any of the three types of transactions that are inconsistent with a pooling of interests. If any of the characteristics are missing or any transaction that is inconsistent with a pooling of interests has taken place, the business combination must be accounted for as a purchase.

b. Because the information given is incomplete with respect to the business combination of Hanover and Case, a final determination of which accounting method must be used cannot be made. From the information given it can be determined that three of the requisite chracteristics have been met for a pooling of interests business combination. The three characteristics are as follows:

1. Hanover and Case are autonomous in that neither has been a subsidiary or division of another company within the preceding two years.
2. Each company is independent of the other company in that neither has an investment in the common stock of the other in excess of 10%.

3. Hanover is exchanging its common stock for substantially all of the common stock of Case. The Accounting Principles Board has defined "substantially" to mean 90% or greater of the outstanding common stock of the combining company (Case) at the date the plan is consummated. Hanover is to receive 100% of the outstanding common stock of Case, but for purposes of the 90% requirement this amount must be reduced by the amount of Case stock held by Hanover at the date the plan is initiated (5%). Also, the common shares of Hanover owned by Case must be converted to equivalent shares of Case using the exchange rate agreed upon by the terms of the combination and the resultant amount deducted from the amount of Case shares to be received by Hanover. The equivalent percentage of Case common stock is 4% (the 2% of Hanover stock held by Case converted at an exchange rate of one share for two shares). The sum of the two deductions is 9%, which results in a 91% exchange of Case stock.

c. In addition to the information given, the following six characteristics and the absence of three types of transactions must be considered in order to make a determination as to which accounting method must be employed in accounting for this combination.

1. The combination must be effected in a single transaction or within one year under a specified plan.
2. Within the preceding two years, and between the dates that a plan of combination was initiated and consummated the equity interests of the voting common stock was not changed in contemplation of the business combination. Changes in contemplation of effecting the combination may include distributions to stockholders and additional issuances, exchanges, and retirements of securities.
3. If either of the combining companies reacquires common stock, the acquisitions must be in accordance with a systematic pattern established over the prior two years (or in accordance with the adoption of a new stock option or compensation plan if less than two years) and not in contemplation of the business combination.
4. The shareholders within each combining company maintain the same relative interest with respect to the other shareholders within the combining company.
5. The common stock of the resulting combined company conveys immediate voting rights with no restrictions upon the shareholders.
6. There are no contingencies as to the number of shares to be issued in exchange for the substantial interest of the combining company after the date the plan of combination is initiated.

Further, the combination must not contain provision for the following three transactions:

1. The combined corporation agrees directly or indirectly to retire or reacquire all or part of the common stock issued to effect the combination.
2. The combined corporation agrees to enter into other financial arrangements for the benefit of the former stockholders of one of the combining companies, such as a guaranty of loans secured by stock issued in the combination, which in effect negates the exchange of equity securities.
3. The combined corporation intends to dispose of a significant part of the assets of the combining companies within two years after the combination other than disposals in the ordinary course of business of the formerly separate companies or to eliminate duplicate facilities or excess capacity.

Answer Outline

Problem 3 Equity Method Accounting

a. Primary criterion is intent of Hawkes' management
   - If a marketable security: current asset
     - Investment will be liquidated when needed
     - Investment made from idle cash
     - The investment is of a speculative nature
   - If a long-term investment: noncurrent asset
     - Held for dividend revenue
     - Held for long-term appreciation
     - For ownership control purposes

   Other factors to be considered in classifying investments
   - Degree of other ownership dispersion
   - Daily volume of shares traded
   - Stability of market price of stock

   Base decision on evaluation of all criteria

b. The investment accounts and effect thereon are described in outline form in the Unofficial Answer below

c1. Interperiod tax allocation is not required
  If undistributed earnings will not be remitted
    Or remitted in a tax-free liquidation
  Specific plans for reinvestment required past experience

c2. Disclosures required if interperiod taxes are not accrued
  Intention to reinvest undistributed earnings permanently
    Or earnings are to be remitted in a tax-free liquidation
  The amount of undistributed earnings on which taxes are not accrued

c3. Consolidated statements are not appropriate
  Diversified and Hawke are in dissimilar industries

Unofficial Answer

Problem 3 Equity Method Accounting

a. The primary criterion to be considered in ascertaining the appropriate classification of the investment is the intent of Hawkes' management.

If management intends to treat the investment as a marketable security in the current-asset section of the balance sheet, its reasoning should be substantiated by one or more of the following: the invested cash is considered contingency funds, to be liquidated, whenever the need may arise; the investment was made from cash temporarily idle because of the seasonality of the business; or the holding is of a speculative nature and will be liquidated as soon as appropriate.

The investment may be held for long-term purposes indicating that it should be classified as a noncurrent asset in the investments caption because of one or more of the following reasons: the investment is held for dividend revenue; long-term appreciation of the market price of the stock is the motivating factor for holding the investment; or the investment is held for ownership-control purposes.

Although the intent of Hawkes' management is a very important criterion, other criteria should also be considered in ascertaining the appropriate asset classification of the investment. For example, the degree of ownership dispersion of the remaining outstanding shares, average daily volume of shares traded, and the stability or volatility of the market price of the stock should be considered. If the stock is closely held (not publicly traded) there may be no market or a very limited market for the stock, indicating the investment probably should be classified as a noncurrent asset. Similar arguments could be presented indicating appropriate classification of the investment as noncurrent if the stock was traded infrequently in small lots.

Of the criteria discussed above no one criterion would necessarily be determinative, and any one might have varying degrees of significance in different cases. The presence or absence of specific criteria would be cumulative in effect for ascertaining the appropriate asset classification of the investment in Hawkes' balance sheet.

b.

Account name	*Increase or decrease*	*Reason for change in account balance*
Cash	Increase	Hawkes received \$50,000 (25% of \$200,000) of dividends paid by Diversified.
Investment in Diversified	Increase	The Investment account should increase by \$100,000 (25% of ½ of \$800,000) for Hawkes' equity in the reported earnings of Diversified and decrease by \$50,000 for dividends received by Diversified, when applying the equity method of accounting for the investee company. Following the guides of APB Opinions, the equity method must be applied unless it can be demonstrated that Hawkes does not have the ability to exercise significant influence over Diversified.
Estimated income taxes payable	Increase	This liability account should increase by the amount of estimated taxes to be paid on the taxable portion of dividends received from Diversified during the accounting period.

Account name	Increase or decrease	Reason for change in account balance
Deferred income taxes	Increase (or decrease, depending on its prior balance)	The deferred income taxes account will be credited for an indeterminate amount because only one-half of the earnings of Diversified was paid out as dividends during the fiscal year ended August 31, 1974. The difference between the taxable portion of Hawkes' equity in Diversified's earnings and its share of the taxable portion of Diversified's dividends paid represents a timing difference for income tax purposes.
Retained earnings	Increase	Hawkes' retained earnings will increase by the amount of its equity in the reported earnings of Diversified, less applicable income taxes.
Investment revenue from investee	Increase	Hawkes' equity in Diversified's earnings of the current accounting period, since acquisition, must be included in Hawkes' earnings when accounting for the investment by the equity method.
Income taxes expense	Increase	The appropriate amount of income taxes expense should be estimated and included on Hawkes' earnings statement. The expense computation should be based on the taxable portion of Diversified's earnings recognized by Hawkes. For reporting purposes, that portion of the expense which is payable currently (based on the taxable portion of dividends received) must be disclosed separately from that portion which is deferred (based on the taxable portion of undistributed earnings).

c. 1. The presumption that a pro rata portion of Diversified's undistributed earnings will be transferred to Hawkes may be overcome, and no income taxes should be accrued by Hawkes, if sufficient evidence shows that Diversified has invested or will invest the undistributed earnings indefinitely or that the earnings will be remitted in a tax-free liquidation.

Hawkes should have evidence of specific plans for reinvestment of Diversified's undistributed earnings which will demonstrate that remittance of the earnings will be postponed indefinitely. Experience of the companies and definite future programs of operations and remittances are examples of types of evidence required to substantiate Hawkes' representation of indefinite postponement of remittances from Diversified.

2. Hawkes should disclose, as a minimum, the following information in notes to its financial statements:

A declaration of an intention to reinvest Diversified's undistributed earnings to support the conclusion that remittance of those earnings has been indefinitely postponed, or a declaration that the undistributed earnings will be remitted in a tax-free liquidation.

The cumulative pro rata amount of Diversified's undistributed earnings on which Hawkes has not recognized income taxes.

3. The nature of Diversified Insurance Company's activities is sufficiently dissimilar to Hawkes' to preclude the preparation of consolidated financial statements. Based on all other facts given it would have been appropriate to consolidate, but because of dissimilar activities consolidated financial statements should not be published. Therefore, Hawkes should include the investment, accounted for by the equity method, in its separate financial statements.

Solution Guide

Problem 4 Change to Equity Method

1. Part b1. requires a schedule showing the income or loss before income taxes for the year ending 12/31/79 that an investor would show for a 10% investment in the common stock of another company.

1.1 The solutions approach is to determine whether or not Jeffries should account for its investment per the cost or equity method. Under the cost method, an investor in the common stock of another recognizes income only when dividends are received from the investee. Under the equity method, the investor recognizes income from its investment as its share of the investee's income for the period. Dividends do not affect the income recognition by the investor; they represent a reduction in the amount of the investment.

1.2 APB 18 established that an investment in the stock of another should be accounted for per the equity method if the investor has the ability to exercise "significant influence" over the operating and financial policies of the investee. An investor is presumed to have significant influence if it owns 20% or more of the voting stock of the investee, assuming no evidence to the contrary.

1.3 Since Jeffries owns only 10% of the voting stock of Wolf and the facts indicate that significant influence is not present, the cost method should be used; and income for the year is the $.90 per share of dividends. The difference between the cost of the investment ($700,000) and the fair value of the assets acquired (10% x $6,000,000) is not amortized under the cost method.

2. Part b2. requires schedules showing the income or loss before income taxes on a comparative basis for years ending 12/31/79 and 12/31/80.

2.1 During 1980 Jeffries increased its investment in the voting stock of Wolf from 10% to 40%, and the facts indicate that significant influence exists. Thus, the investment should be accounted for per the equity method. Per APB 18, para 19m, the investment, results of operations, and retained earnings of Jeffries should be adjusted retroactively.

2.2 APB 18 also requires that if comparative statements are prepared and issued, all prior-year statements presented must be restated to reflect the items listed in 2.1 above on an equity method basis.

2.3 The solutions approach is to go back and recompute the income or loss from the investment as if the equity method had been used from 1/1/79. Remember that during 1979, Jeffries only owned 10% of Wolf, and this is the percentage that should be used for restatement, **not** the 40% now held.

2.4 If Jeffries had recognized income from its investment in Wolf in 1979 on the equity method, 10% of Wolf Company's net income of $400,000, or $40,000, would have been recognized. Also, Jeffries must amortize 1/40 of the goodwill it purchased from Wolf, and the dividends have no effect on Jeffries' income.

2.5 For 1980, Jeffries would recognize as income its share of Wolf's net income for 1980. Since Jeffries still owns only 10% of Wolf for the first six months, it should only recognize 10% of the first six months of Wolf's income (10% of $500,000 – $200,000 = $30,000). During the last six months, Jeffries owns 40% of Wolf, and should thus recognize its share equal to 40% of the last six months' income ($200,000).

2.6 The goodwill acquired in the 1980 purchase of 30,000 additional shares of Wolf is equal to the difference between the cost of the additional 30% less Jeffries' share of net assets it acquired (30% x 6,500,000). This amount is amortized for one-half year in 1980 because the additional investment was not made until July 1, 1980. Also remember that 1/40 of the goodwill purchased in 1979 must be amortized this year.

Unofficial Answer

Problem 4 Change to Equity Method

Part b.

1.

Jeffries, Inc.
Schedule of Income or Loss from Investment
For Year Ending December 31, 1979

Income from investment in Wolf (10,000 shares x $.90 dividend/share)	$ 9,000

2.

Jeffries, Inc.
Schedule of Income or Loss from Investment
For Years Ending December 31, 1980 and 1979

	1980	1979 Restated
Income from investment in Wolf (Schedule 1)	$110,000	$40,000
Less: Goodwill amortization (Schedule 2)	6,875	2,500
Income from investment	$103,125	$37,500

Schedule 1

Jeffries' Share of Investee's Income

	1980	*1979*
Income for 1979 ($400,000 x 10%)		$40,000
Income for 1980		
First half ($300,000 x 10%)	$ 30,000	
Second half ($200,000 x 40%)	80,000	
	$110,000	$40,000

Schedule 2

Goodwill Amortization

	1980	*1979*
Goodwill on 1979 acquisition [$700,000 – (10% x $6,000,000) = $100,000 ÷ 40 years]	$ 2,500	$ 2,500
Goodwill on 1980 acquisition [$2,300,000 – (30% x $6,500,000) = ($350,000 ÷ 40 years) x ½]	4,375	
Total goodwill amortization	$ 6,875	$ 2,500

Solution Guide

Problem 5 Current and Noncurrent Marketable Equity Securities

1. Number five consists of three related requirements concerning a company's investments in marketable equity securities.

2. In part a., a schedule of Winsor's current marketable equity securities must be prepared. This schedule should include columns for cost, market, and unrealized gain or loss.

2.1 Winsor owned 1,000 shares of Bea preferred which cost $40,000, or $40 per share. 500 of these shares were converted into common stock. The 500 shares still held have a cost of $20,000 (500 x $40), and a market value of $28,000 (500 x $56).

2.2 Winsor converted 500 shares of Bea preferred into 1,500 shares of Bea common. The cost of the 1,500 shares of common acquired is the book value of the preferred stock surrendered (500 x $40 = $20,000). The market value of the common at year end is $30,000 (1,500 x $20).

2.3 Winsor owned 6,000 shares of Cha common which cost $60,000, or $10 per share. 2,500 of these shares were sold. The 3,500 still held have a cost of $35,000 (3,500 x $10), and a market value of $38,500 (3,500 x $11).

2.4 Winsor owned 2,000 shares of Dey common which cost $55,000. Dey issued a 10% stock dividend, which gave Winsor an additional 200 shares (2,000 x 10%) at no additional cost. Therefore, the 2,200 shares had an adjusted cost of $25 per share ($55,000 ÷ 2,200). Winsor sold 500 shares. The 1,700 still held have a cost of $42,500 (1,700 x $25), and a market value of $37,400 (1,700 x $22).

2.5 Since the market value exceeds the cost at year end, no valuation allowance is needed.

3. A schedule to show the carrying amount of Winsor's noncurrent investment in Eddie Corp. is required in part b. Winsor intends to hold this stock as a long-term investment. Since they own 30% of the voting stock and can exercise significant influence over Eddie, the use of the equity method is appropriate.

3.1 The original cost of the investment was $1,700,000.

3.2 The excess of investment cost ($1,700,000) over the book value of the net assets purchased ($1,400,000) is $300,000. This amount must be amortized over 40 years ($300,000 ÷ 40 = $7,500) and is a reduction of both investment revenue and the investment account.

Investment revenue	7,500	
Investment in Eddie		7,500

3.3 Using the equity method, the investment account is increased by the investor's share of investee earnings (30% x $1,200,000 = $360,000).

Investment in Eddie	360,000	
Investment revenue		360,000

3.4 The investment account is also reduced by dividends received when the equity method is used. Eddie paid quarterly dividends of $.50 a share, or a total of $50,000 each quarter to Winsor (100,000 x $.50). Therefore, Winsor received a total of $200,000 in dividends from Eddie (4 x $50,000).

Cash	200,000	
Investment in Eddie		200,000

4. In part c., a schedule showing all income, gains, and losses relating to Winsor's investments must be prepared.

4.1 Dividend income should be included in Winsor's income statement. The Bea preferred stock paid a $1.20 dividend on 1,000 shares twice during the year, for a total of $2,400. Note that the second dividend was received on October 5, after 500 shares of preferred were converted. However, the dividend was received for all 1,000 shares, since the date of record was September 9. A $1.00 per share dividend was received on the Cha common stock (3,500 shares x $1.00 per share, or $3,500). Note that the dividend received from Eddie is not recognized as income under the equity method. Also, the stock dividend is not reflected in income.

4.2 A $7,500 gain was realized on the sale of Cha common. The selling price was $32,500 (2,500 x $13), and the cost was $25,000 (2,500 x $10).

4.3 A $2,000 loss was realized on the sale of Dey common. It was sold for $10,500 (500 x $21) and had a cost of $12,500 (500 x $25).

4.4 Investment revenue of $352,500 is recognized on the long-term investment in Eddie. This consists of the investor's share of investee income (30% of $1,200,000, or $360,000) less the amortization of the excess of cost over book value ($300,000 ÷ 40, or $7,500).

4.5 A recovery of the unrealized loss must also be recognized in 1983. At 12/31/82, the valuation allowance was $7,000. However, at 12/31/83, the market value of the current portfolio exceeds its cost; therefore, the valuation account must be decreased to zero, and the recovery is reflected in the 1983 income statement.

Valuation allowance	7,000	
Recovery of unrealized loss		7,000

Unofficial Answer

Problem 5 Current and Noncurrent Marketable Equity Securities

a.

Winsor Company
Schedule of Current Marketable Equity Securities
December 31, 1983

	Number of shares	*Cost*	*Market price per share*	*Market value*	*Unrealized gross gain or (loss)*
Bea–preferred	500	$ 20,000	$56	$ 28,000	$ 8,000
Bea–common	1,500	20,000	20	30,000	10,000
Cha–common	3,500	35,000	11	38,500	3,500
Dey–common	1,700	42,500	22	37,400	(5,100)
		$117,500		$133,900	$16,400
Valuation allowance		–			
Carried at cost		$117,500			

The valuation allowance of $7,000 at December 31, 1982, for current marketable equity securities should be eliminated by a debit to valuation allowance–current, and a credit to recovery of unrealized loss on current marketable equity securities. This $7,000 recovery of unrealized loss should be included in Winsor's income statement for the year ended December 31, 1983.

b.

Winsor Company
Schedule of Noncurrent Marketable Equity Securities
December 31, 1983

Eddie Corp. – 100,000 shares of common stock:		
Cost:		
In underlying equity		$1,400,000
In excess of underlying equity	$300,000	
Less amortization of excess of cost over underlying equity	(7,500)	292,500
Net cost		1,692,500
Increase in equity during 1983:		
Equity in Eddie's earnings		360,000
Less dividends received		(200,000)
Carrying amount of Eddie Corp. investment		$1,852,500

c.

Winsor Corp.
Income Statement Items Resulting From Investments
1983

Dividend income (Schedule 1)	$ 5,900
Realized gain on sale (Schedule 2)	7,500
Realized loss on sale (Schedule 3)	(2,000)
Investment revenue (Schedule 4)	352,500
Recovery of unrealized loss (Schedule 5)	7,000
Total effect on income statement	$370,900

Schedule 1*

Dividend Income

Bea Corp., preferred [2 x (1,000 x $1.20)]	$2,400
Cha, Inc., common (3,500 x $1.00)	3,500
Dividend income	$5,900

Schedule 2*

Realized Gain on Sale

Selling price of Cha, Inc., common (2,500 x $13)	$32,500
Cost of Cha, Inc., common (2,500 x $10)	25,000
Realized gain on sale	$ 7,500

Schedule 3*

Realized Loss on Sale

Selling price of Dey Co., common (500 x $21)	$10,500
Cost of Dey Co., common (500 x $25)	12,500
Realized loss on sale	$ (2,000)

Schedule 4*

Investment Revenue

Share of investee earnings (30% x $1,200,000)	$360,000
Amortization of excess of cost over book value [($1,700,000 – $1,400,000) ÷ 40]	(7,500)
Investment revenue	$352,500

Schedule 5*

Recovery of Unrealized Loss

Valuation allowance at 12/31/82	$7,000
Valuation allowance needed at 12/31/83	0
Recovery of unrealized loss	$7,000

*The authors believe that inclusion of these schedules would allow the graders to follow your work if your answers do not agree with those of the AICPA.

Solution Guide

Alternate Solution follows this Solution Guide

Problem 6 Purchase vs. Pooling Worksheet

1. Ace Corporation acquires Blue Corporation at the end of the fiscal year ended August 31, 1974. You are to (1) complete worksheets and (2) determine net income under two different combination assumptions: purchase and pooling. Scan the text of the problem, studying the requirements, and review the accounts and amounts on the worksheet. Next, work through the text of the problem, paragraph by paragraph, taking notes and preparing intermediary solutions.

2.1 The first paragraph gives a general overview of the problem.

2.2 The fair value of the assets and liabilities of Blue are relevant to the purchase assumption. Under the purchase assumption the fair values rather than the book values of Blue will be recorded on the books of Ace.

2.3 If Blue Corporation had accounted for plant rearrangement costs in the same manner as Ace, Blue would have expensed $10,000 rather than $50,000 during fiscal year 1974. Blue also would have $40,000 of deferred plant rearrangement costs on the balance sheet at year-end. For the pooling assumption, the $40,000 of deferred plant rearrangement costs will have to be recorded as an asset with a corresponding credit to retained earnings. For purchase accounting the $40,000 will be recorded as an asset as indicated in 2.2 above.

2.4 The internally generated expenses incurred should not be deferred under either the pooling or purchase assumption. Under purchase accounting direct costs of acquisition of subsidiaries are considered costs of acquisition but not indirect and general expenses. They should be considered an expense of the period of acquisition. See paragraph 76 of APB 16. In pooling accounting, the expenses related to the combination are considered an expense of the period because the pooling method records neither the acquiring of assets nor the obtaining of capital. See paragraph 58 of APB 16.

2.5 The absence of intercompany transactions during the year precludes any possible elimination or adjusting entries at year-end. Note that if intercompany transactions had occurred during the year, adjustments may have been required to the combined income statement for both pooling and purchases. See paragraph 56 of APB 16 and paragraph 6 of ARB 51.

2.6 The shares outstanding and shares authorized data are redundant to the data provided in the worksheet.

3. Under the pooling assumption, the combined income for 1974 would be the sum of the reported income of both Ace and Blue. To this sum add the plant rearrangement expenditures that should have been capitalized and deduct the general expenses that were incorrectly deferred. The explanation of the pooling worksheet entries follows.

3.1 To defer $40,000 of plant rearrangement costs.

3.2 To record the expensing of indirect general expenses which were incorrectly deferred.

3.3 To record the issuance of 500,000 Ace shares for 750,000 Blue shares. This is a compound entry and consists of retiring the treasury stock to be later reissued, eliminating the par value of stock received, recording the stock issued, and making the net adjustment to paid-in capital. In pooling, the distribution of treasury stock requires it to be accounted for as retired. (See paragraph 54 of APB 16). The entry eliminates the cost of the treasury shares, eliminates Blue's paid-in capital, eliminates the par value of Blue's outstanding stock, records the additional issuance of $4,000,000 of Ace stock, and records the credit balance of the entry to Ace's paid-in capital.

4. The net income assuming a purchase combination is the parent's net income for the year less the adjustment for the erroneous deferral of $25,000 of expenses. In a similar vein, the consolidated financial statements at the time of acquisition will only reflect the retained earnings of the parent and not those of the subsidiary. The explanation of the purchase worksheet entries follows:

4.1 To adjust for the incorrect deferral of $25,000 of general and indirect expenses.

4.2 To record the payment of $3,100,000 in cash and issuance of $16,900,000 of debentures at face value as well as recording the fair market value of the assets received and $2,100,000 of liabilities assumed. Note that $4,300,000 of goodwill or excess of cost over book value arises because $20,000,000 ($16,900,000 plus $3,100,000) was paid for $15,700,000 of net assets.

Alternate Solution

Problem 6 Purchase vs. Pooling Worksheet

The entries shown in the adjustments columns for pooling of interests in the AICPA solution above are "worksheet entries" to give effect to the pooling. The following set of entries are the "ledger entries" that would be made on Ace's books. The debit and credit amounts in these entries would be added to Ace's account balances to get the totals in the Pooling of Interests column. The purchase entries on the worksheet are also the "ledger entries" on Ace's books.

Pooling Entries

(1)	Common stock	$ 1,000,000	
	Paid-in capital in excess of par	250,000	
	Treasury stock (a)		$1,250,000
(2)	Retained earnings	$ 25,000	
	Current assets		25,000
(3)	Current assets	$ 3,000,000	
	Plant & equipment	11,300,000	
	Patents	200,000	
	Plant rearrangement costs	40,000	
	Liabilities		$2,100,000
	Common stock (a)		5,000,000
	Paid-in capital in excess of par		1,950,000
	Retained earnings		5,490,000

(a) This treatment of treasury stock is an acceptable variation. See the AICPA Unofficial Answer on the worksheet.

Solution Guide

Problem 7 Consolidated Financial Statement Worksheet

1. This problem requires the completion of a consolidating worksheet. The worksheet incorporates the income statement, the retained earnings statement, and the balance sheet. In this approach, any postings to the income statement section are totalled and carried forward to the retained earnings section. Similarly, the postings in the retained earnings statement section are totalled and carried forward to the balance sheet section.

2. The solutions approach is to go through the information and prepare any entries necessary to be posted on the worksheet.

2.1 The primary elimination entry is simply the elimination of the investment account (at cost) and the subsidiary's equity accounts at the time of investment (1/1/82). Additionally, the excess of cost over book value must be allocated to the proper accounts. The investment account has a balance of $750,000. The equity purchased is 100% of the subsidiary's equity accounts at the time of investment, or $636,000. The difference ($114,000) is allocated first to machinery ($54,000), and then to goodwill ($60,000).

Common stock (Taft)	400,000	
APIC (Taft)	80,000	
Retained earnings (Taft)	156,000	
Machinery	54,000	
Goodwill	60,000	
Investment in Taft		750,000

Note that the debit to retained earnings is entered into the beginning balance line in the retained earnings statement section of the worksheet.

2.2 The secondary elimination entry amortizes the excess of cost over book value. Because the parent uses the cost method rather than the equity method, this entry becomes an adjusting entry rather than a reclassifying entry. The excess allocated to machinery ($54,000) is amortized over six years ($9,000 per year). The amount allocated to goodwill ($60,000) is amortized over twenty years ($3,000 per year).

Operating expenses	12,000	
Accumulated depreciation		9,000
Goodwill		3,000

Note that the depreciation is debited to operating expenses, since the problem indicates that the account includes depreciation. However, it can be argued that depreciation of machinery should be reflected in cost of goods sold.

2.3 The third elimination entry is necessary to eliminate the parent's income from subsidiary dividends.

Dividends from Taft	40,000	
Dividends paid		40,000

Note that the credit to dividends paid is entered on the appropriate line in the retained earnings statement section.

2.4 Next the gain on the intercompany fixed asset sale must be eliminated. The gain on land is $10,000 ($43,000 – $33,000) and the gain on the warehouse is $20,000 ($86,000 – $66,000). This $30,000 gain must be eliminated, and the assets written down to original cost.

Unofficial Answer

Problem 6 Purchase vs. Pooling Worksheet

Ace Corporation and Blue Corporation
Worksheet for Pooling of Interests and Purchase Accounting
August 31, 1974

	Ace Corporation	Blue Corporation	Combined	Part a. Adjustments Debit	Part a. Adjustments Credit	Pooling of interests	Part b. Adjustments Debit	Part b. Adjustments Credit	Purchase
Current assets	$ 4,350,000	$ 3,000,000	$ 7,350,000		$ 25,000 (2)	$ 7,325,000	$ 3,400,000 (2)	$ 25,000 (1) 3,100,000 (2)	$ 4,625,000
Plant and equipment (net)	18,500,000	11,300,000	29,800,000			29,800,000	14,000,000 (2)		32,500,000
Patents	450,000	200,000	650,000			650,000	360,000 (2)		810,000
Plant rearrangement costs	150,000	—	150,000	$ 40,000 (1)		190,000	40,000 (2)		190,000
Goodwill	—	—	—			—	4,300,000 (2)		4,300,000
	$23,450,000	$14,500,000	$37,950,000			$37,965,000			$42,425,000
Liabilities	$ 2,650,000	$ 2,100,000	$ 4,750,000			$ 4,750,000		16,900,000 (2) 2,100,000 (2)	$21,650,000
Common stock $10 par value	12,000,000	—	12,000,000		4,000,000 (3)	16,000,000			12,000,000
Common stock $5 par value	—	3,750,000	3,750,000	3,750,000 (3)					—
Paid-in capital in excess of par	4,200,000	—	4,200,000		1,700,000 (3)	5,900,000			4,200,000
Paid-in capital in excess of par	—	3,200,000	3,200,000	3,200,000 (3)					--
Retained earnings	5,850,000	—	5,850,000	25,000 (2)	40,000 (1)		25,000 (1)		5,825,000
Retained earnings	—	5,450,000	5,450,000			11,315,000			--
	24,700,000	14,500,000	39,200,000						43,675,000
Less treasury stock, at cost, 100,000 shares	1,250,000	—	1,250,000		1,250,000 (3)				1,250,000
	$23,450,000	$14,500,000	$37,950,000			$37,965,000			$42,425,000
Net income (no extraordinary items) for fiscal year ended August 31, 1974	$ 2,450,000	$ 1,300,000							

Calculation of Combined Net Income

Blue net income (before adjustment)	$1,300,000
Add plant rearrangement costs	40,000
Blue net income	1,340,000
Ace net income (before adjustment)	2,450,000
Total	3,790,000
Less general expenses	25,000
Combined net income	$3,765,000

Calculation of Net Income

Ace net income	$2,450,000
Less general expenses	25,000
Net income	$2,425,000

Gain on sale of warehouse	30,000	
Land, plant, and equipment		30,000

Taft has depreciated some of the extra $20,000 paid for the warehouse. Depreciation for a half-year would be $2,000 ($20,000 x 1/5 x 1/2). This depreciation must also be eliminated.

Accumulated depreciation	2,000	
Operating expenses		2,000

2.5 An intercompany sale of inventory has also occurred. Taft sold $180,000 of merchandise to Amboy. The original cost of the merchandise to Taft was $90,000 [$180,000 ÷ (100% + 100%)]. Amboy sold $144,000 of this merchandise ($180,000 – $36,000) to outside customers.

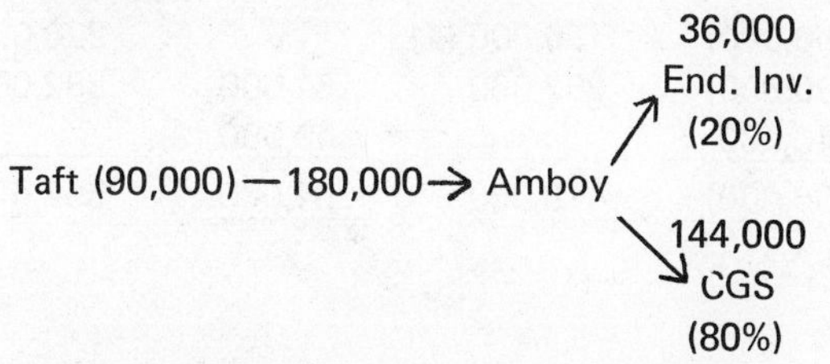

The intercompany sales of $180,000 must be eliminated. Additionally, cost of goods sold (CGS) and inventory must be adjusted. Since 80% of the inventory was sold, CGS should include 80% of Taft's original cost of $90,000, or $72,000. Since Taft recorded CGS of $90,000, and Amboy recorded CGS of $144,000, a total CGS of $234,000 was recorded. Therefore, CGS must be reduced by $162,000 ($234,000 – $72,000). Finally, inventory must be reduced by $18,000, from $36,000 to its original cost of $18,000 (20% x $90,000).

Net sales	180,000	
Cost of goods sold		162,000
Inventories		18,000

2.6 Since Amboy still owes Taft $75,000 on the purchases, the intercompany receivable/payable must also be eliminated.

Accounts payable	75,000	
Accounts receivable		75,000

3. The worksheet can now be totalled and completed.

3.1 The income statement adjustments total $262,000 debits and $164,000 credits. These amounts are entered on the net income lines in the retained earnings section.

3.2 The retained earnings adjustments total $418,000 debits and $204,000 credits. These amounts are entered on the retained earnings line in the balance sheet section.

3.3 The worksheet can now be totalled across.

Unofficial Answer

Problem 7 Consolidated Financial Statement Worksheet

Amboy Corporation and Subsidiary
Consolidating Statement Worksheet
December 31, 1982

	Amboy Corp.	Taft Inc.	Adjustments & eliminations Debit	Adjustments & eliminations Credit	Adjusted balance
Income Statement					
Net sales	$(1,900,000)	$(1,500,000)	180,000 (5)		3,220,000
Dividends from Taft	(40,000)		40,000 (3)		
Gain on sale of warehouse	(30,000)		30,000 (4)		
Cost of goods sold	1,180,000	870,000		162,000 (5)	1,888,000
Operating expenses (incl. deprec.)	550,000	440,000	12,000 (2)	2,000 (4)	1,000,000
Net income	$ (240,000)	$ (190,000)	262,000	164,000	332,000
Retained Earnings Statement					
Balance, 1/1/82	$ (220,000)	$ (156,000)	156,000 (1)		220,000
Net income	(240,000)	(190,000)	262,000	164,000	332,000
Dividends paid		40,000		40,000 (3)	
Balance, 12/31/82	$ (460,000)	$ (306,000)	418,000	204,000	552,000
Balance Sheet					
Assets:					
Cash	$ 285,000	$ 150,000			435,000
Accounts receivable (net)	430,000	350,000		75,000 (6)	705,000
Inventories	530,000	410,000		18,000 (5)	922,000
Land, plant & equipment	660,000	680,000	54,000 (1)	30,000 (4)	1,364,000
Accumulated depreciation	(185,000)	(210,000)	2,000 (4)	9,000 (2)	(402,000)
Investment in Taft (at cost)	750,000			750,000 (1)	
Goodwill			60,000 (1)	3,000 (2)	57,000
	$2,470,000	$1,380,000			3,081,000
Liabilities & stockholders' equity:					
Accounts pay. & accrued exp.	$ (670,000)	$ (594,000)	75,000 (6)		1,189,000
Common stock ($10 par)	(1,200,000)	(400,000)	400,000 (1)		1,200,000
Additional paid-in capital	(140,000)	(80,000)	80,000 (1)		140,000
Retained earnings	(460,000)	(306,000)	418,000	204,000	552,000
	$(2,470,000)	$(1,380,000)	1,089,000	1,089,000	3,081,000

Explanations of adjustments & eliminations:

(1) To eliminate the reciprocal elements in investment, equity, and property accounts. Amboy's investment is carried at cost at December 31, 1982.

(2) To record amortization of current value in excess of book value of Taft's machinery at date of acquisition ($54,000 ÷ 6) and amortization of goodwill ($60,000 ÷ 20) for the year ended December 31, 1982.

(3) To eliminate Amboy's dividend income from Taft.

(4) To eliminate the intercompany profit on the sale of the warehouse by Amboy to Taft and to eliminate the excess depreciation on the warehouse building sold by Amboy to Taft [($86,000 – $66,000) ÷ 5] x ½.

(5) To eliminate intercompany sales from Taft to Amboy and the intercompany profit in Amboy's ending inventory as follows:

	Total	On hand
Sales	$180,000	$36,000
Gross profit	90,000	18,000

(6) To eliminate Amboy's intercompany balance for merchandise owed to Taft.

Schedule 1*

Allocation of Excess of Cost Over Book Value

Cost of investment		$750,000
Equity purchased at time of investment		
Common stock	$400,000	
Addl. paid-in capital	80,000	
Retained earnings	156,000	(636,000)
Excess of cost over book value		114,000
Amount allocated to machinery		(54,000)
Amount allocated to goodwill		$60,000

Schedule 2*

Amortization of Excess of Cost Over Book Value

Amount allocated to machinery	$54,000
Remaining useful life	÷ 6 years
Amortization	$9,000/year
Amount allocated to goodwill	$60,000
Amortization period	÷ 20 years
Amortization	$3,000/year

Schedule 3*

Excess Depreciation Recorded on Warehouse

Purchase price of warehouse	$86,000
Original cost of warehouse	(66,000)
Excess cost recorded by subsidiary	$20,000
Remaining useful life	÷ 5 years
Depreciation per year	$4,000
Portion of year (July 1—Dec. 31)	x 6/12
Excess depreciation recorded in 1982	$2,000

Schedule 4*

Elimination of Cost of Goods Sold

Cost of goods sold recorded by Taft ($180,000 ÷ 200%)	$90,000
Cost of goods sold recorded by Amboy ($180,000 – $36,000)	144,000
Total cost of goods sold recorded	234,000
Consolidated cost of goods sold (80% x $90,000)	(72,000)
Cost of goods sold to be eliminated	$162,000

Schedule 5*

Restatement of Inventory to Original Cost

Inventory at sales price	$36,000
Inventory restated to cost ($36,000 ÷ 200%)	$18,000

*The authors believe that inclusion of these schedules would allow the graders to follow your work if your answers do not agree with those of the AICPA.

Solution Guide

Problem 8 Consolidated Balance Sheet

1. Problem 8 requires the completion of a consolidated **balance sheet** worksheet (which is given) with appropriate supporting schedules.

2. Since this is a balance sheet worksheet, not including the income statement accounts, all entries affecting nominal accounts will be debited or credited to Encanto's retained earnings (consolidated retained earnings). The combined account balances for Encanto and Norris are given to save time adding the individual balances.

3. The solutions approach is to analyze the balance sheets and additional information given to determine the required adjusting and eliminating entries. The detail of the investment in Norris Corporation should be analyzed for correctness. The equity pickup is correct for the mid-year purchase of an additional 30% interest in Norris. Note that Encanto is not using the full equity method of accounting for its investment in Norris. Otherwise, the investment account would reflect amortization of the "excess of cost over book value" and elimination of intercompany profits.

3.1 First, the investment account and subsidiary's stockholders' equity should be eliminated. Ninety percent of Norris' stockholders' equity will be eliminated. Two approaches exist for handling the minority interest. Either extend the balances remaining after eliminating 90% of the stockholders' equity balances to the minority interest column or eliminate 100% of the stockholders' equity and credit minority interest on the line labeled minority interest. The debit to balance the entry is the excess of cost over the book value of net assets acquired. Computation of this excess (at point of purchase) is shown below:

12/31/79 subsidiary stockholders' equity	$252,000
Less 1979 net income	(96,000)
Plus 1979 dividends	40,000
1/1/79 subsidiary stockholders' equity	$196,000
Plus 1979 net income thru Sept. 1 (2/3 x $96,000)	64,000
9/1/79 subsidiary stockholders' equity	$260,000
	x 30%
Net assets acquired (Book value)	78,000
Cost of investment	(92,000)
Excess cost over net assets acquired	$ 14,000

The information given does not indicate the nature of the $14,000. Therefore, it is necessary to assume that the fair values of the identifiable assets and liabilities are equal to their book values and that the excess is goodwill. The entry is presented below:

Common stock (Norris)	100,000	
Retained earnings (Norris)	152,000	
Goodwill	14,000	
Investment in Norris Corp.		240,800
Minority interest		25,200

Supporting computations:

Investment cost	$240,800
Net assets acquired [90% x (100,000 + 152,000)]	226,800
Goodwill	$ 14,000
Minority interest [10% x (100,000 + 152,000)]	$ 25,200

3.2 An entry must be made to amortize the goodwill recorded in Entry 1. The goodwill must be amortized for the 4 months which have elapsed since the Sept. 1 purchase.

Retained earnings (Encanto)	933	
Goodwill		933

Supporting computations:

Goodwill	$14,000
	x 4/60
1979 amortization	$ 933

3.3 The reciprocal accounts from the declaration of dividends must be eliminated:

Dividends payable	36,000	
Dividends receivable		36,000

3.4 The unrealized profit in the ending inventory sold to Norris by Encanto must be eliminated. The remainder of the merchandise sold between affiliates in 1979 has been sold to outsiders. Therefore, no adjustment is necessary for this portion. Since the intercompany sale was "downstream," the entire amount is charged to Encanto's retained earnings (consolidated retained earnings):

Retained earnings (Encanto)	7,000	
Inventories		7,000

Supporting computations:

Intercompany sales not resold, at selling price	$35,000
Intercompany sales not resold at cost (÷125%)	28,000
Unrealized profit	$ 7,000

3.5 No entry need be made for the unrealized profit in the beginning inventory since those goods were sold to third parties during the year. Remember this is a **balance sheet** worksheet, and although cost of sales and beginning retained earnings are overstated, ending retained earnings is correctly stated. The overstatement of retained earnings (caused by the overstatement of gross profit at the end of 1978) no longer exists because the gross profit was realized in 1979.

3.6 The unrealized gain on the intercompany sale of equipment and the related depreciation expense must be eliminated:

Retained earnings (Encanto)	6,000	
Property plant and equipment		6,000
Accumulated depreciation	150	
Retained earnings (Encanto)		150

Supporting computations:

Sale price of asset	$42,000
Book value of asset	36,000
Encanto's gain (excess cost to be depreciated by Norris)	6,000
	x 1/10
Yearly depreciation	600
	x 3/12
1979 excess depreciation	$ 150

3.7 Norris recorded the $8,000 transfer to Encanto with the following entry:

Accounts payable	8,000	
Cash		8,000

Since the payment was still in transit at year end Encanto should make an entry to pick up this cash.

Cash	8,000	
Accounts receivable		8,000

Encanto Corporation and Subsidiary
Adjusting and Elimination Entries
December 31, 1979
(Not Required)

	Debit	*Credit*
(1)		
Goodwill	$ 14,000	
Investment in Norris Corporation		$ 14,000
To reclassify excess of cost over net assets acquired $260,000*x30% = $78,000; 30% of investment 92,000; $14,000		
(2)		
Retained earnings — Encanto Corporation	933	
Goodwill		933
To record amortization for four months $14,000 ÷ 60 x 4		
(3)		
Common stock — Norris Corporation	90,000	
Retained earnings — Norris Corporation	136,800	
Investment in Norris Corporation		226,800
To eliminate reciprocal elements in investment and equity accounts		
(4)		
Common stock — Norris Corporation	10,000	
Retained earnings — Norris Corporation	15,200	
Minority interest in common stock of Norris Corporation		10,000
Minority interest in retained earnings of Norris Corporation		15,200
To record minority interest's share of common stock and retained earnings of Norris Corporation		
(5)		
Dividends payable	36,000	
Dividends receivable		36,000
To eliminate Encanto's share of intercompany dividends $40,000 x 90%		
(6)		
Retained earnings — Encanto Corporation	$7,000	
Inventory — Norris Corporation		$7,000
To eliminate intercompany profit in ending inventory of Norris Corporation $35,000 ÷ 125% = $28,000; $35,000 – $28,000 = $7,000 profit		

*[$100,000 + ($152,000 – 96,000 + 40,000) + 2/3 x 96,000]

(7)

Accumulated depreciation	150	
Retained earnings — Encanto Corporation	5,850	
Property, plant, and equipment		6,000

To eliminate intercompany gain and adjust accumulated depreciation on equipment sold by Encanto to Norris

	Equipment	*Depreciation*
Encanto's book value	$36,000	$ 900
Selling price	42,000	1,050
Excess	($ 6,000)	($ 150)

(8)

Cash	8,000	
Accounts receivable		8,000

To record payment in transit

Unofficial Answer

Problem 8 Consolidated Balance Sheet

Encanto Corporation and Subsidiary
Consolidated Balance Sheet Worksheet
December 31, 1979

	Encanto Corporation	*Norris Corporation*	*Total*	*Adjustments and eliminations* *Debit*	*Credit*	*Minority interest*	*Consolidated*
Assets:							
Cash	$ 167,250	$101,000	$ 268,250	$ 8,000 (7)			$ 276,250
Accounts receivable	178,450	72,000	250,450		$ 8,000 (7)		242,450
Notes receivable	87,500	28,000	115,500				115,500
Dividends receivable	36,000		36,000		36,000 (3)		
Inventories	122,000	68,000	190,000		7,000 (4)		183,000
Property, plant, and equipment	487,000	252,000	739,000		6,000 (5)		733,000
Accumulated depreciation	(117,000)	(64,000)	(181,000)	150 (6)			(180,850)
Investment in Norris Corp.	240,800		240,800		240,800 (1)		
Goodwill				14,000 (1)	933 (2)		13,067
Total assets	$1,202,000	$457,000	$1,659,000				$1,382,417
Liabilities and Stockholders' Equity:							
Accounts payable	$ 222,000	$ 76,000	$ 298,000				$ 298,000
Notes payable	79,000	89,000	168,000				168,000
Dividends payable		40,000	40,000	36,000 (3)			4,000
Common stock							
Encanto Corp.	400,000		400,000				400,000
Norris Corp.		100,000	100,000	100,000 (1)			
Retained earnings							
Encanto Corp.	501,000		501,000	7,000 (4)	150 (6)		487,217
				6,000 (5)			
				933 (2)			
Norris Corp.		152,000	152,000	152,000 (1)			
Minority interest					25,200 (1)	$25,200	25,200
Total liabilities and stockholders' equity	$1,202,000	$457,000	$1,659,000				$1,382,417

CHAPTER FIVE

COST ACCOUNTING PROBLEMS AND SOLUTIONS

Cost accounting questions appear with regularity on both the practice and theory sections. You may expect a series of multiple choice questions on both practice and theory as well as one cost essay question and one cost practice problem. A complete analysis of recent examinations and the *AICPA Content Specification Outlines* appear in Volume I, *Outlines and Study Guides*.

Each question is coded as to month, year, section, problem number, and multiple choice question number. For example, (1183,T1,27) indicates November 1983, Theory problem 1, and multiple choice question 27. Note that P = Practice I, Q = Practice II, and T = Theory.

COST ACCOUNTING PROBLEMS INDEX

Multiple Choice Questions (1–50)

1. Wages paid to factory machine operators of a manufacturing plant are an element of

	Prime cost	Conversion cost
a.	No	No
b.	No	Yes
c.	Yes	No
d.	Yes	Yes

2. Property taxes on a manufacturing plant are an element of

	Conversion cost	Period cost
a.	Yes	No
b.	Yes	Yes
c.	No	Yes
d.	No	No

3. Paulson Company had inventories at the beginning and end of 1982 as follows:

	1/1/82	12/31/82
Raw materials	$55,000	$65,000
Work in process	96,000	80,000
Finished goods	50,000	85,000

During 1982 the following costs were incurred:

Raw materials purchased	$400,000
Direct-labor payroll	220,000
Factory overhead	330,000

Paulson's cost of goods sold for 1982 was

a. $921,000
b. $956,000
c. $966,000
d. $979,000

Items 4 through 6 are based on the following information:

Wayne Company had the following inventories at the beginning and end of March 1983:

	3/1/83	3/31/83
Direct materials	$36,000	$30,000
Work in process	18,000	12,000
Finished goods	54,000	72,000

The following additional manufacturing cost data were available for the month of March 1983:

Direct materials purchased	$84,000
Direct-labor payroll	60,000
Direct-labor rate per hour	7.50
Factory overhead rate per direct-labor hour	10.00

4. During March 1983 prime cost added to production was

a. $ 90,000
b. $140,000
c. $144,000
d. $150,000

5. During March 1983 conversion cost added to production was

a. $ 60,000
b. $ 80,000
c. $140,000
d. $150,000

6. The cost of goods manufactured for March 1983 was

a. $212,000
b. $218,000
c. $230,000
d. $236,000

7. Regan Company operates its factory on a two-shift basis and pays a late-shift differential of 15%. Regan also pays a premium of 50% for overtime work. Since Regan manufactures only for stock, the cost system provides for uniform direct-labor hourly charges for production done without regard to shift worked or work done on an overtime basis. Overtime and late-shift differentials are included in Regan's factory overhead application rate. The May 1983 payroll for production workers is as follows:

Wages at base direct-labor rates	$325,000
Shift differentials	25,000
Overtime premiums	10,000

For the month of May 1983, what amount of direct labor should Regan charge to work-in-process?

a. $325,000
b. $335,000
c. $350,000
d. $360,000

8. During March 1983 Hart Company incurred the following costs on Job 109 for the manufacture of 200 motors:

Original cost accumulation:	
Direct materials	$ 660
Direct labor	800
Factory overhead (150% of direct labor)	1,200
	$2,660
Direct costs of reworking 10 units:	
Direct materials	$ 100
Direct labor	160
	$ 260

The rework cost were attributable to exacting specifications of Job 109 and the full rework costs were charged to this specific job. The cost per finished unit of Job 109 was

a. $15.80
b. $14.60
c. $14.00
d. $13.30

9. Blackwood uses a job order cost system and applies factory overhead to production orders on the basis of direct-labor cost. The overhead rates for 1982 are 200% for department A and 50% for department B. Job 123, started and completed during 1982, was charged with the following costs:

	Department	
	A	*B*
Direct materials	$25,000	$ 5,000
Direct labor	?	30,000
Factory overhead	40,000	?

The total manufacturing costs associated with Job 123 should be

a. $135,000
b. $180,000
c. $195,000
d. $240,000

Items 10 and 11 are based on the following information:

Harper Company's Job 501 for the manufacture of 2,200 coats was completed during August 1982 at the following unit costs:

Direct materials	$20
Direct labor	18
Factory overhead (includes an allowance of $1 for spoiled work)	18
	$56

Final inspection of Job 501 disclosed 200 spoiled coats which were sold to a jobber for $6,000.

10. Assume that spoilage loss is charged to all production during August 1982. What would be the unit cost of the good coats produced on Job 501?

a. $53.00
b. $55.00
c. $56.00
d. $58.60

11. Assume, instead, that the spoilage loss is attributable to exacting specifications of Job 501 and is charged to this specific job. What would be the unit cost of the good coats produced on Job 501?

a. $55.00
b. $57.50
c. $58.60
d. $61.60

12. Worrell Corporation has a job order cost system. The following debits (credits) appeared in the general ledger account work in process for the month of March 1982:

March 1, balance	$ 12,000
March 31, direct materials	40,000
March 31, direct labor	30,000
March 31, factory overhead	27,000
March 31, to finished goods	(100,000)

Worrell applies overhead to production at a predetermined rate of 90% based on the direct-labor cost. Job No. 232, the only job still in process at the end of March 1982, has been charged with factory overhead of $2,250. What was the amount of direct materials charged to Job No. 232?

a. $2,250
b. $2,500
c. $4,250
d. $9,000

13. In job order costing, what journal entry should be made for the return to the storekeeper of direct materials previously issued to the factory for use on a particular job?

a. Debit materials and credit factory overhead.
b. Debit materials and credit work in process.
c. Debit purchase returns and credit work in process.
d. Debit work in process and credit materials.

14. In job order costing, payroll taxes paid by the employer for factory employees are preferably accounted for as

a. Direct labor.
b. Factory overhead.
c. Indirect labor.
d. Administrative costs.

15. Accounting for factory overhead costs involves averaging in

	Job order costing	*Process costing*
a.	Yes	No
b.	Yes	Yes
c.	No	Yes
d.	No	No

16. In order to identify costs that relate to a specific product, an allocation base should be chosen that
   a. Does **not** have a cause and effect relationship.
   b. Has a cause and effect relationship.
   c. Considers variable costs but **not** fixed costs.
   d. Considers direct materials and direct labor but **not** factory overhead.

17. Worley Company has underapplied overhead of $45,000 for the year ended December 31, 1982. Before disposition of the underapplied overhead, selected December 31, 1982, balances from Worley's accounting records are as follows:

Sales	$1,200,000
Cost of goods sold	720,000
Inventories:	
Direct materials	36,000
Work in process	54,000
Finished goods	90,000

Under Worley's cost accounting system, over or underapplied overhead is allocated to appropriate inventories and cost of goods sold based on year-end balances. In its 1982 income statement, Worley should report cost of goods sold of
   a. $682,500
   b. $684,000
   c. $756,000
   d. $757,500

18. Hartwell Company distributes the service department overhead costs directly to producing departments without allocation to the other service department. Information for the month of January 1982 is as follows:

	Service departments	
	Maintenance	*Utilities*
Overhead costs incurred	$18,700	$9,000
Service provided to:		
Maintenance department	—	10%
Utilities department	20%	—
Producing department A	40%	30%
Producing department B	40%	60%
Total	100%	100%

The amount of utilities department costs distributed to producing department B for January 1982 should be
   a. $3,600
   b. $4,500
   c. $5,400
   d. $6,000

19. Barnett Company adds materials at the beginning of the process in department M. Conversion costs were 75% complete as to the 8,000 units in work in process at May 1, 1983, and 50% complete as to the 6,000 units in work in process at May 31. During May 12,000 units were completed and transferred to the next department. An analysis of the costs relating to work in process at May 1 and to production activity for May is as follows:

	Costs	
	Materials	*Conversion*
Work in process, 5/1	$ 9,600	$ 4,800
Costs added in May	15,600	14,400

Using the weighted-average method, the total cost per equivalent unit for May was
   a. $2.47
   b. $2.50
   c. $2.68
   d. $3.16

20. Assuming that there was no beginning work in process inventory, and the ending work in process inventory is 50% complete as to conversion costs, the number of equivalent units as to conversion costs would be
   a. The same as the units placed in process.
   b. The same as the units completed.
   c. Less than the units placed in process.
   d. Less than the units completed.

21. Walden Company has a process cost system using the FIFO cost flow method. All materials are introduced at the beginning of the process in department One. The following information is available for the month of January 1983:

	Units
Work in process, 1/1/83 (40% complete as to conversion costs)	500
Started in January	2,000
Transferred to Department Two during January	2,100
Work in process, 1/31/83 (25% complete as to conversion costs)	400

What are the equivalent units of production for the month of January 1983?

	Materials	*Conversion*
a.	2,500	2,200
b.	2,500	1,900
c.	2,000	2,200
d.	2,000	2,000

22. During April 1983 Clayton Company's department B equivalent unit product costs, computed under the weighted-average method, were as follows:

Materials	$1
Conversion	3
Transferred-in	5

Materials are introduced at the end of the process in department B. There were 2,000 units (40% complete as to conversion costs) in work in process at April 30, 1983. The total costs assigned to the April 30, 1983, work-in-process inventory should be

a. $12,400
b. $13,600
c. $14,400
d. $18,000

23. Barkley Company adds materials at the beginning of the process in department M. Data concerning the materials used in March 1983 production are as follows:

	Units
Work in process at March 1	16,000
Started during March	34,000
Completed and transferred to next department during March	36,000
Normal spoilage incurred	4,000
Work in process at March 31	10,000

Using the weighted-average method, the equivalent units for the materials unit cost calculation are

a. 30,000
b. 34,000
c. 40,000
d. 46,000

24. Lawton Company produces canned tomato soup and is budgeting sales of 250,000 units for the month of January 1983. Actual inventory units at January 1 and budgeted inventory units at January 31 are as follows:

	Units
Actual inventory at January 1:	
Work in process	None
Finished goods	75,000
Budgeted inventory at January 31:	
Work in process (75% processed)	16,000
Finished goods	60,000

How many equivalent units of production is Lawton budgeting for January 1983?

a. 235,000
b. 247,000
c. 251,000
d. 253,000

Items 25 and 26 are based on the following information:

Bronson Company had 6,000 units in work-in-process at January 1, 1982, which were 60% complete as to conversion costs. During January 20,000 units were completed. At January 31, 1982, 8,000 units remained in work in process which were 40% complete as to conversion costs. Materials are added at the beginning of the process.

25. Using the weighted-average method, the equivalent units for January for conversion costs were

a. 19,600
b. 22,400
c. 23,200
d. 25,600

26. How many units were started during January?

a. 18,000
b. 19,600
c. 20,000
d. 22,000

27. Information for the month of January 1982 concerning department A, the first stage of Ogden Corporation's production cycle, is as follows:

	Materials	Conversion
Work in process, beginning	$ 8,000	$ 6,000
Current costs	40,000	32,000
Total costs	$48,000	$38,000
Equivalent units using weighted-average method	100,000	95,000
Average unit costs	$ 0.48	$ 0.40
Goods completed		90,000 units
Work in process, end		10,000 units

Materials are added at the beginning of the process. The ending work in process is 50% complete as to conversion costs. How would the total costs accounted for be distributed, using the weighted-average method?

	Goods completed	Work in process, end
a.	$79,200	$6,800
b.	$79,200	$8,800
c.	$86,000	$0
d.	$88,000	$6,800

28. The Cutting Department is the first stage of Mark Company's production cycle. Conversion costs for this department were 80% complete as to the beginning work in process and 50% complete as to the ending

work in process. Information as to conversion costs in the Cutting Department for January 1980 is as follows:

	Units	Conversion costs
Work in process at January 1, 1980	25,000	$ 22,000
Units started and costs incurred during January	135,000	$143,000
Units completed and transferred to next department during January	100,000	

Using the FIFO method, what was the conversion cost of the work in process in the Cutting Department at January 31, 1980?

a. $33,000
b. $38,100
c. $39,000
d. $45,000

29. The percentage of completion of the beginning work-in-process inventory should be included in the computation of the equivalent units of production for which of the following methods of process costing?

	First-in, first-out	Weighted-average
a.	Yes	No
b.	Yes	Yes
c.	No	Yes
d.	No	No

30. Purchased materials are added in the second department of a three-department process; this increases the number of units produced in the second department and would always

a. Change the direct labor cost percentage in the ending work-in-process inventory.
b. Cause **no** adjustment to the unit cost transferred in from the first department.
c. Increase total unit costs.
d. Decrease total ending work-in-process inventory.

31. The units transferred in from the first department to the second department should be included in the computation of the equivalent units for the second department for which of the following methods of process costing?

	First-in first-out	Weighted-average
a.	Yes	Yes
b.	Yes	No
c.	No	Yes
d.	No	No

32. In a process costing system that assumes that normal spoilage occurs at the end of a process, the cost attributable to normal spoilage should be assigned to

a. Ending work-in-process inventory.
b. Cost of goods manufactured and ending work-in-process inventory in the ratio of units worked on during the period to units remaining in work-in-process inventory.
c. Cost of goods manufactured (transferred out).
d. A separate loss account in order to highlight production inefficiencies.

33. An error was made in the computation of the percentage-of-completion of the current year's ending work-in-process inventory. The error resulted in assigning a lower percentage-of-completion to each component of the inventory than actually was the case. What is the resultant effect of this error upon:

1. The computation of equivalent units in total?
2. The computation of costs per equivalent unit?
3. Costs assigned to cost of goods completed for the period?

	1	2	3
a.	Understate	overstate	overstate.
b.	Understate	understate	overstate.
c.	Overstate	understate	understate.
d.	Overstate	overstate	understate.

Items 34 and 35 are based on the following information:

Grafton Company produces joint products A and B in department One from a process which also yields by-product W. Product A and by-product W are sold after separation, but product B must be further processed in department Two before it can be sold. The cost assigned to the by-product is its market value less $0.40 per pound for delivery expense (net realizable value method). Information relating to a batch produced in July 1983 is as follows:

Product	Production (in pounds)	Sales price per pound
A	2,000	$4.50
B	4,000	9.00
W	500	1.50

Joint cost in department One	$18,000
Product B additional process cost in department Two	$10,000

34. For joint cost allocation purposes, what is the net realizable value at the split-off point of product B?
    a. $46,000
    b. $45,000
    c. $36,000
    d. $26,000

35. How much of the joint cost incurred in department One should be allocated to the joint products?
    a. $17,250
    b. $17,450
    c. $17,800
    d. $18,550

Items 36 and 37 are based on the following information:

Warfield Corporation manufactures products C, D and E from a joint process. Joint costs are allocated on the basis of relative-sales-value at split-off. Additional information is as follows:

	Product			
	C	*D*	*E*	*Total*
Units produced	6,000	4,000	2,000	12,000
Joint costs	$ 72,000	?	?	$120,000
Sales value at split-off	?	?	$30,000	$200,000
Additional costs if processed further	$ 14,000	$10,000	$ 6,000	$ 30,000
Sales value if processed further	$140,000	$60,000	$40,000	$240,000

36. How much of the joint costs should Warfield allocate to product D?
    a. $24,000
    b. $28,800
    c. $30,000
    d. $32,000

37. Assuming that the 2,000 units of product E were processed further and sold for $40,000, what was Warfield's gross profit on the sale?
    a. $ 4,000
    b. $14,000
    c. $16,000
    d. $22,000

38. Ohio Corporation manufactures liquid chemicals A and B from a joint process. Joint costs are allocated on the basis of relative-sales-value at split-off. It costs $4,560 to process 500 gallons of product A and 1,000 gallons of product B to the split-off point. The sales value at split-off is $10 per gallon for product A and $14 for product B. Product B requires an additional process beyond split-off at a cost of $1 per gallon before it can be sold. What is Ohio's cost to produce 1,000 gallons of product B?
    a. $3,360
    b. $3,660
    c. $4,040
    d. $4,360

39. Pendall Company manufactures products Dee and Eff from a joint process. Product Dee has been allocated $2,500 of total joint costs of $20,000 for the 1,000 units produced. Dee can be sold at the split-off point for $3 per unit, or it can be processed further with additional costs of $1,000 and sold for $5 per unit. If Dee is processed further and sold, the result would be
    a. A break-even situation.
    b. An additional gain of $1,000 from further processing.
    c. An overall loss of $1,000.
    d. An additional gain of $2,000 from further processing.

40. For purposes of allocating joint costs to joint products, the relative sales value at split-off method could be used in which of the following situations?

	No costs beyond split-off	*Costs beyond split-off*
a.	Yes	Yes
b.	Yes	No
c.	No	Yes
d.	No	No

Items 41 and 42 are based on the following data:

Earl Corporation manufactures a product that gives rise to a by-product called "Zafa." The only costs associated with Zafa are selling costs of $1 for each unit sold.

Earl accounts for Zafa sales by deducting its separable costs from such sales, and then deducting this net amount from cost of sales of the major product. In 1981, 1,000 units of Zafa were sold at $4 each.

41. If Earl changes its method of accounting for Zafa sales by showing the net amount as additional sales revenue, then Earl's gross margin would

a. Be unaffected.
b. Increase by $3,000.
c. Decrease by $3,000.
d. Increase by $4,000.

42. If Earl changes its method of accounting for Zafa sales by showing the net amount as "Other Income," then Earl's gross margin would

a. Be unaffected.
b. Increase by $3,000.
c. Decrease by $3,000.
d. Decrease by $4,000.

43. Which of the following is (are) acceptable regarding the allocation of joint product cost to a by-product?

	None allocated	*Some portion allocated*
a.	Acceptable	Not acceptable
b.	Acceptable	Acceptable
c.	Not acceptable	Acceptable
d.	Not acceptable	Not acceptable

May 1984 Questions

44. In a job order cost system, the incurrence of indirect labor costs would usually be included in the general ledger as a charge to

a. Factory department overhead control.
b. Factory overhead applied.
c. Work-in-process control.
d. Accrued payroll.

45. Which of the following is an element of prime cost?

	Direct materials	*Indirect materials*
a.	Yes	No
b.	Yes	Yes
c.	No	Yes
d.	No	No

46. Wages paid to a timekeeper in a factory are a

	Prime cost	*Conversion cost*
a.	No	No
b.	No	Yes
c.	Yes	No
d.	Yes	Yes

47. The fixed portion of the semivariable cost of electricity for a manufacturing plant is a

	Conversion cost	*Product cost*
a.	No	No
b.	No	Yes
c.	Yes	Yes
d.	Yes	No

48. Assuming that there was **no** beginning work-in-process inventory and the ending work-in-process inventory is 100% complete as to material costs, the number of equivalent units as to material costs would be

a. The same as the units placed in process.
b. The same as the units completed.
c. Less than the units placed in process.
d. Less than the units completed.

49. A standard cost system may be used in

a. Job order costing but **not** process costing.
b. Either job order costing or process costing.
c. Process costing but **not** job order costing.
d. Neither process costing nor job order costing.

50. For purposes of allocating joint costs to joint products, the sales price at point of sale reduced by cost to complete after split-off is assumed to be equal to the

a. Relative sales value at split-off.
b. Sales price less a normal profit margin at point of sale.
c. Joint costs.
d. Total costs.

Problems

Problem 1 Overhead Application Bases (582,T5a)

(10 to 15 minutes)

Part a. Stein Company is going to use a predetermined annual factory overhead rate to charge factory overhead to products. In conjunction with this, Stein Company must decide whether to use direct labor hours or machine hours as the overhead rate base.

Required:

Discuss the objectives and criteria that Stein Company should use in selecting the base for its predetermined annual factory overhead rate.

Problem 2 Equivalent Units; Indirect Manufacturing Costs (580,T5)

(15 to 25 minutes)

Part a. An important concept in process costing is that of equivalent units.

Required:

1. Describe the difference between units placed in process for a period and equivalent units for a period when there is no beginning work-in-process inventory and the ending work-in-process inventory is 50% complete.
2. Describe the difference between units completed for a period and equivalent units for a period when there is no beginning work-in-process inventory and the ending work-in-process inventory is 50% complete.
3. Describe how equivalent units for a period are used to compute the cost of the ending work-in-process inventory.

Part b. Indirect manufacturing costs (factory overhead) include indirect materials, indirect labor, and other indirect costs.

Required:

1. Describe indirect materials and give an appropriate example.
2. Describe indirect labor and give an appropriate example.
3. Describe fixed indirect manufacturing costs (factory overhead).
4. Describe variable indirect manufacturing costs (factory overhead).
5. Describe semivariable indirect manufacturing costs (factory overhead).

Problem 3 Process Cost Theory (1175,T6)

(25 to 30 minutes)

Presented below are four independent questions concerning a typical manufacturing company that uses a process-cost accounting system. Your response to each question should be complete, including simple examples or illustrations where appropriate.

Required:

a. What is the rationale supporting the use of process costing instead of job-order costing for product-costing purposes? Explain.

b. Define equivalent production (equivalent units produced). Explain the significance and use of equivalent production for product-costing purposes.

c. Define normal spoilage and abnormal spoilage. Explain how normal spoilage costs and abnormal spoilage costs should be reported for management purposes.

d. How does the first-in, first-out (FIFO) method of process costing differ from the weighted average method of process costing? Explain.

Problem 4 By-Product and Joint Product (582,Q5a)

(30 to 35 minutes)

Part a. Lares Confectioners, Inc., makes a candy bar called Rey, which sells for $.50 per pound. The manufacturing process also yields a product known as Nagu. Without further processing, Nagu sells for $.10 per pound. With further processing, Nagu sells for $.30 per pound. During the month of April, total joint manufacturing costs up to the point of separation consisted of the following charges to work in process:

Raw materials	$150,000
Direct labor	120,000
Factory overhead	30,000

Production for the month aggregated 394,000 pounds of Rey and 30,000 pounds of Nagu. To complete Nagu during the month of April and obtain a selling price of $.30 per pound, further processing of Nagu during April would entail the following additional costs:

Raw materials	$2,000
Direct labor	1,500
Factory overhead	500

Required:

Prepare the April journal entries for Nagu, if Nagu is:

1. Transferred as a by-product at sales value to the warehouse without further processing, with a corresponding reduction of Rey's manufacturing costs.

2. Further processed as a by-product and transferred to the warehouse at net realizable value, with a corresponding reduction of Rey's manufacturing costs.

3. Further processed and transferred to finished goods, with joint costs being allocated between Rey and Nagu based on relative sales value at the split-off point.

Problem 5 Cost of Goods Manufactured (1174,P4a)

(10 to 15 minutes)

Part a. The Helper Corporation manufactures one product and accounts for costs by a job-order-cost system. You have obtained the following information for the year ended December 31, 1973, from the Corporations's books and records:

Total manufacturing cost added during 1973 (sometimes called cost to manufacture) was $1,000,000 based on actual direct material, actual direct labor, and applied factory overhead on actual direct labor dollars.

Cost of goods manufactured was $970,000 also based on actual direct material, actual direct labor, and applied factory overhead.

Factory overhead was applied to work in process at 75% of direct labor dollars. Applied factory overhead for the year was 27% of the total manufacturing cost.

Beginning work-in-process inventory, January 1, was 80% of ending work-in-process inventory, December 31.

Required:

Prepare a formal statement of cost of goods manufactured for the year ended December 31, 1973, for Helper Corporation. Use actual direct material used, actual direct labor, and applied factory overhead. Show supporting computations in good form.

Problem 6 Weighted-Average Process Costing (579,Q4)

(50 to 60 minutes)

You are engaged in the audit of the December 31, 1978, financial statements of Spirit Corporation, a manufacturer of a digital watch. You are attempting to verify the costing of the ending inventory of work in process and finished goods which were recorded on Spirit's books as follows:

	Units	Cost
Work in process (50% complete as to labor and overhead)	300,000	$ 660,960
Finished goods	200,000	$1,009,800

Materials are added to production at the beginning of the manufacturing process and overhead is applied to each product at the rate of 60% of direct labor costs. There was no finished goods inventory on January 1, 1978. A review of Spirit's inventory cost records disclosed the following information:

		Costs	
	Units	Materials	Labor
Work in process 1/1/78 (80% complete as to labor and overhead)	200,000	$ 200,000	$ 315,000
Units started in production	1,000,000		
Material costs		$1,300,000	
Labor costs			$1,995,000
Units completed	900,000		

Required:

a. Prepare schedules as of December 31, 1978, to compute the following:

- Equivalent units of production using the weighted-average method.
- Unit costs of production of materials, labor, and overhead.
- Costing of the finished goods inventory and work-in-process inventory.

b. Prepare the necessary journal entry to correctly state the inventory of finished goods and work in process, assuming the books have not been closed. **(Ignore income tax considerations.)**

Problem 7 Process Costing (1176,Q3a)

(30 to 35 minutes)

Part a. The Dexter Production Company manufactures a single product. Its operations are a continuing process carried on in two departments—machining and finishing. In the production process, materials are added to the product in each department without increasing the number of units produced.

For the month of June, 1975, the company records indicated the following production statistics for each department:

	Machining department	*Finishing department*
Units in process, June 1, 1975	0	0
Units transferred from preceding department	0	60,000
Units started in production	80,000	0
Units completed and transferred out	60,000	50,000
Units in process, June 30, 1975*	20,000	8,000
Units spoiled in production	0	2,000
*Percent of completion of units in process at June 30, 1975:		
Materials	100%	100%
Labor	50%	70%
Overhead	25%	70%

The units spoiled in production had no scrap value and were 50% complete as to material, labor, and overhead. The company's policy is to treat the cost of spoiled units in production as a separate element of cost in the department in which the spoilage occurs.

Cost records showed the following charges for the month of June:

	Machining department	*Finishing department*
Materials	$240,000	$ 88,500
Labor	140,000	141,500
Overhead	65,000	25,700

Required:

For both the machining and finishing departments, prepare in good form complete production reports for the month of June, including the following information:

1. Physical flow of units
2. Equivalent units
3. Total costs
4. Unit costs
5. Summary of total costs

Round all computations to the nearest cent.

Problem 8 FIFO Process Costing (580,Q5)

(40 to 50 minutes)

The Adept Company is a manufacturer of two products known as "Prep" and "Pride." Incidental to the production of these two products, it produces a by-product known as "Wilton." The manufacturing process covers two departments, Grading and Saturating.

The manufacturing process begins in the Grading department when raw materials are started in process. Upon completion of processing in the Grading department, the by-product "Wilton" is produced, which accounts for 20% of the material output. This by-product needs no further processing and is transferred to finished goods.

The net realizable value of the by-product "Wilton" is accounted for as a reduction of the cost of materials in the Grading department. The current selling price of "Wilton" is $1.00 per pound and the estimated selling and delivery costs total ten cents per pound.

The remaining output is transferred to the Saturating department for the final phase of production. In the Saturating department, water is added at the beginning of the production process which results in a 50% gain in weight of the materials in production.

The following information is available for the month of November 1979:

Inventories	*November 1 Quantity (pounds)*	*Amount*	*November 30 Quantity (pounds)*
Work in process:			
Grading dept.	None	—	None
Saturating dept.	1,600	$17,600	2,000
Finished goods:			
Prep	600	14,520	1,600
Pride	2,400	37,100	800
Wilton	None	—	None

The work-in-process inventory (labor and overhead) in the Saturating department is estimated to be 50% complete both at the beginning and end of November.

Costs of production for November are as follows:

Costs of production	*Materials used*	*Labor and overhead*
Grading department	$265,680	$86,400
Saturating department	—	86,000

The material used in the Grading department weighed 36,000 pounds.

Adept uses the first-in, first-out method of process costing.

Required:

Prepare a cost of production report for both the Grading and Saturating departments for the month of November. Show supporting computations in good form.

The answer should include:

- Equivalent units of production (in pounds.)
- Total manufacturing costs.
- Cost per equivalent unit (pounds).
- Dollar amount of ending work in process.
- Dollar amount of inventory cost transferred out.

Multiple Choice Answers

1.	d	11.	b	21.	d	31.	a	41.	a
2.	a	12.	c	22.	a	32.	c	42.	c
3.	a	13.	b	23.	d	33.	a	43.	b
4.	d	14.	b	24.	b	34.	d	44.	a
5.	c	15.	b	25.	c	35.	b	45.	a
6.	d	16.	b	26.	d	36.	c	46.	b
7.	a	17.	d	27.	a	37.	c	47.	c
8.	a	18.	d	28.	c	38.	d	48.	a
9.	a	19.	c	29.	a	39.	b	49.	b
10.	c	20.	c	30.	a	40.	a	50.	a

Multiple Choice Answer Explanations

A. Cost of Goods Manufactured

1. (1183,T1,36) (d) The requirement is the classification of wages paid to factory machine operators. Wages of factory machine operators are considered direct labor. Prime cost is composed of direct materials and direct labor. Conversion cost is composed of direct labor and manufacturing overhead. Since direct labor is an element of both prime cost and conversion cost, answer (d) is correct.

2. (1183,T1,37) (a) The requirement is the classification of property taxes on a manufacturing plant. Property taxes are classified as manufacturing overhead. Overhead includes all costs associated with the manufacturing process that are not classified as direct materials or direct labor. All costs associated with the manufacture of goods are considered product (inventoriable) costs. In contrast, period costs are deducted as expenses in the period incurred without having been previously classified as inventoriable costs. Property taxes on a manufacturing plant are, therefore, not classified as a period cost. Conversion cost is composed of direct labor and manufacturing overhead. Property taxes on the plant (an element of overhead) are properly included in conversion cost. Answer (a) is, therefore, correct.

3. (583,P1,18) (a) The requirement is Paulson's cost of goods sold in 1982. Three computations must be performed: raw materials used, cost of goods manufactured, and cost of goods sold.

Beginning materials	$ 55,000
Materials purchases	400,000
Materials available	$455,000
Ending materials	(65,000)
Materials used	$390,000
Beginning WIP	$ 96,000
Materials used	390,000
Direct labor	220,000
Factory overhead	330,000
Costs to account for	$1,036,000
Ending WIP	(80,000)
Cost of goods manufact.	$ 956,000
Beginning finished goods	$ 50,000
Cost of goods manufact.	956,000
Cost of goods available	$1,006,000
Ending finished goods	(85,000)
Cost of goods sold	$ 921,000

4. (583,P2,26) (d) The requirement is the prime cost added to production during March. Prime cost includes direct materials and direct labor. Direct labor is $60,000. Direct materials used must be computed. The solutions approach is to enter the information given into the materials T-account.

Direct Materials

3/1/83 bal.	$36,000		
Purchases	84,000	?	Materials used
3/31/83	$30,000		

Therefore, $90,000 of direct materials were used. Prime cost added to production is $150,000 ($60,000 + $90,000).

5. (583,P2,27) (c) The requirement is the conversion cost added to production during March. Conversion cost includes direct labor ($60,000) and factory overhead. The factory overhead rate per direct-labor hour is $10.00. To compute the number of direct-labor hours worked, the direct-labor payroll ($60,000) is divided by the direct-labor rate per hour ($7.50), resulting in 8,000 direct-labor hours. Factory overhead applied is 8,000 hours at $10 per hour, or $80,000. Conversion cost added to production is $140,000 ($60,000 of direct labor and $80,000 of applied factory overhead).

6. (583,P2,28) (d) The requirement is the cost of goods manufactured for March. First, direct materials used ($90,000) and overhead applied ($80,000) must be computed. The materials computation is found in item 5 above, and the overhead computation is in item 4 above. Next, a cost of goods manufactured statement can be prepared.

BWIP	$18,000
DM used	90,000
DL	60,000
OH applied	80,000
Costs to account for	248,000
EWIP	(12,000)
Cost of goods manufactured	$236,000

B. Cost Flows

7. (1183,P3,43) (a) The requirement is the amount of direct labor to be charged to work in process. The base direct-labor wages, totaling $325,000, should be debited to work in process. The shift differentials ($25,000) and overtime premiums ($10,000) should be charged to factory overhead as incurred. These costs will be spread over production throughout the year via the overhead application rate.

C. Job-Order Costing

8. (1183,P3,54) (a) The requirement is the cost per finished unit of Job 109. Ten units from the production of Job 109 (200 units total) were reworked. The rework costs were attributable to the exacting specifications of Job 109, therefore, the **full** rework costs are to be charged to this specific job. The full rework costs include materials ($100), labor ($160), and overhead ($240), ($160 x 150%), for a total of $500. The total cost of Job 109 is $3,160 (original cost accumulation of $2,660 plus the rework costs of $500). The cost per finished unit is $15.80 ($3,160 ÷ 200).

9. (583,P2,32) (a) The requirement is the total manufacturing costs associated with Job 123. The total cost of any manufactured job includes direct materials used, direct labor, and factory overhead applied. In department A, the overhead rate is 200% of direct labor cost, so direct labor must be $20,000.

DL x 200% = OH applied
DL x 200% = $40,000
DL = $40,000 ÷ 200% = $20,000

In department B, the overhead rate is 50%, so overhead applied is 50% of $30,000, or $15,000. The cost of Job 123 totals $135,000:

DM used ($25,000 + $5,000)	$30,000
DL ($20,000 + $30,000)	50,000
OH applied ($40,000 + $15,000)	55,000
Total manufacturing cost of Job 123	$135,000

10. (1182,P2,28) (c) The requirement is the unit cost of good coats produced on Job 501, assuming that spoilage loss is charged to all of August production. Job 501 included 2,200 coats, of which 200 were spoiled and sold as inferior goods for $6,000. Note that factory overhead of $18 per unit includes an allowance of $1 per unit for spoiled work. It is through this allowance that the cost of spoiled goods is "spread" over the entire month's production. Therefore, if this spoilage is to be charged to all production during the month, the cost of good coats in Job 501 would be the full unit cost of $56, which includes the normal spoilage allowance. In this case the cost of spoiled units, less the $6,000 proceeds, would be charged to factory overhead.

11. (1182,P2,29) (b) The requirement is the unit cost of good coats produced on Job 501, assuming that the spoilage is attributable to the exacting specifications of Job 501 and is, therefore, charged to this specific job. In this case, since spoilage is a function of specific job requirements rather than general factory conditions, the overhead rate should not include the $1 allowance for spoiled work. Therefore, the cost of all coats, before adjustment for spoilage, is $55 ($56 – $1). The cost of the 2,000 good coats on Job 501 would be the total cost of all 2,200 coats, less the scrap value of the bad coats.

Cost of 2,200 coats (2,200 x $55)	$121,000
Scrap value of bad coats	(6,000)
Net cost of Job 501	$115,000
Cost per good coat ($115,000 ÷ 2,000)	$57.50

Note that the net cost of spoilage [(200 x $55) – $6,000] is charged to the good coats in Job 501. In this case, the net spoilage cost is included in the charge to finished goods along with the cost of good units.

12. (582,P2,23) (c) The requirement is the amount of direct materials charged to Job No. 232, which is the only job still in process at the end of March. The first step in the solutions approach is to determine the ending work-in-process inventory, which consists of total costs charged to Job No. 232 to date. The T-account analysis below indicates an ending WIP balance of $9,000.

Work in process		
3/1 balance	$12,000	
DM	40,000	
DL	30,000	
OH	27,000	
		$100,000 to finished goods
3/31 balance	$ 9,000	

The $9,000 WIP balance shows that the total cost of Job No. 232 to date is $9,000. This $9,000 amount consists of direct materials, direct labor, and overhead (given, $2,250). The overhead has been applied at a rate of 90% of direct labor cost, resulting in the equation below:

(90%) x (DL) = $2,250
DL = $2,250 ÷ 90%
DL = $2,500

Knowing both direct labor and manufacturing overhead, the amount of direct materials can be derived.

Total cost of job		$9,000
Less: DL ($2,250 ÷ 90%)	$2,500	
OH (given)	2,250	(4,750)
Cost of DM		$4,250

13. (582,T1,41) (b) When direct materials are issued the journal entry would require a debit to work in process and a credit to materials. When materials are returned to the storekeeper, materials will increase and work in process will decrease which will require a reversal of the original entry [answer (d)].

14. (579,T1,22) (b) In job order costing, payroll taxes on factory employee wages paid by the employer are preferably accounted for as factory overhead. While payroll taxes can be directly associated with direct labor, the taxes are not incurred at a constant rate. Both state and federal employer payroll taxes are taxed up to a certain amount of annual wages and not thereafter. Thus the taxes should be accounted for as factory overhead rather than direct labor. Thus answer (a) is incorrect. Answer (c) is incorrect because indirect labor is the cost of labor that cannot be associated with specific jobs, e.g., janitorial services. Answer (d), administrative costs, is incorrect because administrative costs are concerned with costs of administration rather than of factory production employees.

D. Accounting for Overhead

15. (1183,T1,39) (b) The requirement is to determine which product costing method involves averaging factory overhead costs. Answer (b) is correct since both job order and process costing use an averaging process. Unit costs for inventory purposes result from taking overhead costs and dividing by some measure of production. Job order costing divides overhead cost by the number of units produced per **batch** (usually a small number of units). Process costing allocates overhead cost to the units produced in each **processing center** (usually a much larger number of units).

16. (581,T1,43) (b) The requirement is to indicate the **characteristics** of an allocation base to be used for relating costs to specific products. The allocation base chosen to relate costs to a specific product should have a cause and effect relationship. Answer (c) is incorrect since fixed production costs are allocated to specific products. Answer (d) is incorrect since factory overhead is also allocated to specific products.

E. Disposition of Overhead

17. (1183,P3,44) (d) The requirement is the amount of cost of goods sold to be reported on the 1982 income statement. The balance in the cost of goods sold account is $720,000. This amount must be increased by the portion of underapplied overhead allocated to cost of goods sold. The underapplied overhead is appropriately allocated to work in process, finished goods, and cost of goods sold. No overhead is allocated to direct materials inventory, since this account contains only the cost of unused materials. The other three accounts contain the cost of materials, labor, and overhead. The amounts to be allocated to work in process, finished goods, and cost of goods sold are determined by each account's relative balance as compared to the total balance in the accounts. The total balance of the three accounts is $864,000 ($720,000 + $54,000 + $90,000). Therefore, the amount allocable to cost of goods sold is [$720,000/ $864,000 x (45,000)] or $37,500. Since overhead was underapplied, not enough costs were applied to production during the year. Thus, cost of goods sold is increased to $757,500 ($720,000 + $37,500).

F. Service Department Cost Allocation

18. (582,P2,21) (d) The requirement is the amount of utilities department costs to be distributed to producing department B for January 1982. The direct method is used. Under this method, service department costs are allocated directly to the producing departments based on relative services provided, and services to other service departments are ignored. Therefore, even though 10% of the utilities department services were used by maintenance, the 10% is ignored and no cost is allocated to maintenance. The $9,000 of utilities cost is allocated to departments A and B based on relative service performed: 30/90 to A and 60/90 to B, where 90 = 30 + 60. Department B would be allocated $6,000 of utilities cost.

A: (30/90)($9,000) = $3,000
B: (60/90)($9,000) = $6,000

G. Process Costing

19. (1183,P3,46) (c) The requirement is the total cost per equivalent unit using the weighted-average method. The solutions approach is to first visualize the physical flow of the units.

BWIP 8,000 —— 8,000 → 12,000 Completed
4,000 ↗
Started 10,000* —— 6,000 → 6,000 EWIP

*12,000 + 6,000 – 8,000

Next, the equivalent units (EU) are computed.

	Materials	*Conversion*
Units completed and transferred	12,000	12,000
Work on EWIP	6,000	3,000
Equivalent units	18,000	15,000

Note that under the weighted-average assumption, no distinction is made between work done last period and work done in the current period on BWIP. All BWIP is "averaged" together. In EWIP, all 6,000 units are included in EU for materials, since materials are added at the beginning of the process. However, the EWIP is only 50% complete as to conversion costs so only 3,000 (6,000 x 50%) units are included in EU for conversion costs. Under the weighted-average assumption BWIP costs and current period costs are combined. The cost per EU for materials is:

$$\frac{\$9,600 + \$15,600}{18,000} = \$1.40$$

While the cost per EU for conversion is:

$$\frac{\$4,800 + \$14,400}{15,000} = \$1.28$$

The total cost per equivalent unit is $1.40 + $1.28, or $2.68.

20. (1183,T1,40) (c) The requirement is to determine the number of equivalent units as to conversion costs. Answer (c) is correct since the existence of ending work in process, coupled with no beginning work in process, indicates that more units were placed into production than were completed during the period. Answer (a) is incorrect because the only way the equivalent units as to conversion costs would equal the number of units placed into production is when there is no change in the level of work in process (BWIP units = EWIP units). Answers (b) and (d) are incorrect since the equivalent units as to conversion would be greater than the units completed, because work was done on the ending work in process.

21. (583,P2,21) (d) The requirement is the equivalent units of production (EUP) for materials and conversion costs, using the FIFO cost flow method. First, visualize the physical flow of units.

BWIP 500 —— 500 → 2,100 Transferred
1,600 ↗
Started 2,000 —— 400 → 400 EWIP

Next, set up the FIFO EUP computation.

	Materials	*Conversion*
Work to complete, BWIP	0	300
Units started and transferred	1,600	1,600
Work to date on EWIP	400	100
EUP	2,000	2,000

Since materials are introduced at the beginning of the process, BWIP is already complete as to materials. All materials were added this month for any units started this month, whether those units were transferred or remain in EWIP. Since BWIP is 40% complete on 1/1/83 as to conversion costs, 60% of the work (60% x 500, or 300) must be done in January. EWIP is 25% complete at 1/31/83, which means 25% of the conversion work (25% x 400, or 100) was done in January. Remember, under the FIFO assumption, EUP measures only the work done in the current period.

22. (583,P2,29) (a) The requirement is the total cost assigned to the 4/30/83 work-in-process inventory. Unit product costs are given for transferred-in, conversion, and materials. The ending work-in-process (EWIP) inventory consists of 2,000 units. Transferred-in costs are assigned to the product in a preceding department. These costs come into the next department as the product is transferred in, so equivalent units of production (EUP) for transferred-in costs in EWIP are 2,000. The EWIP is 40% complete as to conversion costs, so EUP for conversion costs are 800 (40% of 2,000). Since materials are introduced at the end of the process, there are no materials in the EWIP, and EUP for materials is 0. Therefore, the total cost of the EWIP is $12,400 as calculated below.

Transferred-in	2,000 x $5	$10,000
Conversion	800 x $3	2,400
Materials	0 x $1	0
Total cost		$12,400

23. (583,P2,30) (d) The requirement is the equivalent units of production (EUP) for materials using the weighted-average method. The physical flow of units is:

BWIP 16,000 —— 16,000 → 40,000 Completed & spoiled
24,000 ↗
Started 34,000 —— 10,000 → 10,000 EWIP

In the weighted-average method, BWIP and units started are averaged together. The EUP computation is:

Units completed	36,000
Work to date on EWIP	10,000
EUP	46,000

Note that **normal** spoilage is disregarded in the EUP computation. Normal spoilage is a necessary cost in the production process and is therefore a product cost. By not including normal spoilage of 4,000 units in EUP, the cost of spoilage is spread over the good units produced and EWIP. However, if **abnormal** spoilage occurs, spoiled units are included in the EUP computation. The cost assigned to abnormal spoilage would be recognized as a loss in the period of occurrence.

24. (583,P2,31) (b) The requirement is the equivalent units of production (EUP) budgeted for January. First a production budget must be prepared.

Budgeted sales	250,000
Budgeted ending FG	60,000
Total units needed	310,000
Beginning FG	(75,000)
Units to be completed	235,000

Since there is no BWIP, the units started must cover both the units to be completed (235,000) and those budgeted, EWIP (16,000). Therefore, 251,000 units (235,000 + 16,000) must be started during January.

BWIP 0 ——— 0 ——→ 235,000 Completed
235,000
Started 251,000 ——— 16,000 ——→ 16,000 EWIP

EUP budgeted for January would be 235,000 units started and completed, plus 12,000 EUP (16,000 x 75%) in EWIP, for a total of 247,000 EUP. Note that the problem does not specify either the FIFO or weighted-average cost flow method. Since there is no BWIP, FIFO and weighted-average will give identical results.

25. (1182,P2,32) (c) The requirement is equivalent units for conversion costs for January using the weighted-average method. Equivalent units under the weighted-average method is equal to units completed plus equivalent units in ending work in process.

Units completed	20,000
EU in ending WIP (8,000 x 40%)	3,200
Equivalent units	23,200

Recall that under the weighted-average method, equivalent units in beginning WIP (included in units completed) are combined with the current period's work.

26. (1182,P2,33) (d) The requirement is the number of units started in January. The solutions approach is to prepare a schedule summarizing the physical flow of units.

	Units		*Units*
BWIP	6,000	Completed	20,000
Started	?	EWIP	8,000
To acct. for	28,000	Acctd. for	28,000

Since 28,000 units were either completed or left in ending work in process, 28,000 must be the total of units in beginning work in process and units started. Beginning WIP consisted of 6,000 units, so 22,000 units were started during January (28,000 – 6,000).

27. (582,P2,26) (a) The requirement is the allocation of manufacturing costs to goods completed and to ending work in process. The weighted average method of process costing is used, which means beginning work-in-process costs are merged with those of the current month, rather than being accounted for separately. The cost of goods completed is equal to the number of units completed times the weighted average unit cost.

Cost of goods completed = 90,000 x \$.88 = \$79,200

The cost of ending work in process must be computed separately for materials (added at the beginning of the process; 100% complete) and for conversion costs (50% complete).

Materials cost (10,000 x \$.48)	\$4,800
Conversion cost [(10,000 x 50%) x \$.40]	2,000
Cost of EWIP	\$6,800

Notice that the total cost to account for is \$86,000 (\$48,000 materials plus \$38,000 conversion). The cost allocated to goods completed and to ending work-in-process must also total \$86,000. Only choices (a) and (c) meet this requirement, and (c) allocates \$0 to ending work in process. Therefore, choice (a) can be selected by process of elimination without even performing the preceding calculations.

28. (1180,P2,33) (c) The requirement is the conversion cost of the ending work-in-process inventory using the FIFO method. The number of units in ending work in process must be computed:

Work in Process

BWIP	25,000	100,000	Units completed
Units started	135,000	?	EWIP
Units to account for	160,000	160,000	Units accounted for

EWIP = 160,000 units to account for – 100,000 units completed = 60,000 units.

The next step is to compute equivalent units of production under the FIFO method:

Units completed	100,000
EU in ending WIP (60,000)(50%)	30,000
	130,000
EU in beginning WIP (25,000)(80%)	(20,000)
EU of production	110,000

Conversion cost per unit for the current period is \$143,000/110,000 or \$1.30 per equivalent unit. With the FIFO method, the beginning WIP is assumed to be completed during the period; therefore the ending inventory consists solely of current period costs. The cost of the ending WIP is the equivalent units in ending WIP times the conversion cost/unit of \$1.30:

(30,000)(\$1.30) = \$39,000

29. (1182,T1,43) (a) The requirement is to identify which method would include the percentage of completion of beginning work-in-process inventory in the computation of equivalent units of production (EUP). Solving this question requires the "mechanical" approach and the phrase "included in the computation" is the key to the solution.

Units completed and transferred this period
\+ EUP in ending WIP
EUP on weighted-average basis
– EUP in beginning WIP
EUP on FIFO basis

The FIFO (first-in, first-out) method separates costs incurred last period (beginning WIP) from costs incurred in the current period. Thus, in computing FIFO EUP for the current period, EUP in beginning WIP are separated from the work done in the current period. The weighted-average method combines beginning WIP costs with costs incurred in the current period; i.e., all costs are lumped together. Thus, EUP in beginning WIP are not treated separately in the computation of weighted-average EUP.

30. (1181,T1,43) (a) As direct materials, direct labor, and factory overhead are added to a production process manufacturing costs increase. If material costs are added to a second process, it increases the percentage of material costs in ending work in process and reduces the percentages of labor costs and factory overhead costs. Answer (b) is incorrect because unit costs would change unless the increase in total costs was exactly offset by the increase in units produced. Answer (c) is incorrect because total unit costs could increase, decrease, or remain the same depending on the relationship between the added costs and the increase in the units produced. Answer (d) is incorrect because ending work in process cannot decrease because the added materials increase the manufacturing costs allocated to work in process.

31. (581,T1,46) (a) The requirement is for the proper treatment of transferred in costs in computing equivalent units. Units transferred into the second department should be taken into account in the equivalent units computation for the second department under both FIFO and weighted-average. They are treated the same as materials added at the beginning of a process.

32. (1178,T1,36) (c) The requirement is how to treat normal spoilage given that it occurs at the end of the production process. As the spoilage occurs at the end of the process, it cannot be detected until the goods are finished. All spoilage relates to goods that are complete. Thus all spoilage costs should be charged to finished goods. Answers (a) and (b) are incorrect because none of the work in process has a chance to spoil until completion. Answer (d) is incorrect because normal spoilage should not be charged to a separate loss account, but rather be included as cost of finished goods.

33. (1177,T2,34) (a) The requirement is to determine the effect of assigning a lower percentage-of-completion to ending work in process than was actually accomplished. The effect is to understate equivalent units of production, because the amount of work or production that was completed was understated. Since the costs of production remain constant, the cost per equivalent unit is overstated. In turn, the costs assigned to goods completed for the period will be overstated. Note that it makes no difference whether it is a FIFO or a weighted-average method, because the only difference between FIFO and weighted-average is that under FIFO, the EUP already completed at the beginning of the period is subtracted from the EUP in goods completed and ending work in process.

H. Joint Products

34. (1183,P3,51) (d) The requirement is the net realizable value at the split-off point of product B.

Product B must be processed further, beyond the split-off point, to become salable. Therefore, the net realizable value of product B at the split-off point is its estimated selling price, $36,000 (4,000 x $9.00) less any further processing costs ($10,000), or $26,000.

35. (1183,P3,52) (b) The requirement is the amount of joint cost to be allocated to the joint products, A and B. The total joint cost of $18,000 must be reduced by any cost allocated to by-product W. The by-product is accounted for using the net realizeable value method. The cost assigned to by-product W would be the market value of $750 (500 x $1.50), less delivery expenses of $200 (500 x $.40), or $550. Therefore, $17,450 of joint cost ($18,000 – $550) should be allocated to the joint products.

36. (583,P2,35) (c) The requirement is the amount of joint cost allocable to product D. Since joint costs are allocated based on relative sales values at split-off, the amount allocated to product E would be computed as follows:

$$\frac{\text{Sales value (E)}}{\text{Total sales value}} = \frac{\text{Joint costs (E)}}{\text{Total joint costs}}$$

$$\frac{\$30{,}000}{\$200{,}000} = \frac{\text{Joint costs (E)}}{\$120{,}000}$$

$$\$18{,}000 = \text{Joint costs (E)}$$

Therefore, $18,000 of joint costs would be allocated to product E. Joint costs allocated to product D would be $30,000 [$120,000 total, less $72,000 (C) and $18,000 (E)].

An alternate approach could be used. Total joint costs are $120,000, and total sales value at split-off is $200,000. Therefore, the ratio of joint costs to sales value at split-off is 60% ($120,000 ÷ $200,000). This ratio is valid for each individual product, since relative sales values at split-off are used to allocate joint costs. Therefore, product E should be allocated $18,000 of joint costs ($30,000 x 60%). Joint costs allocated to product D are $30,000 [$120,000 total, less $72,000 (C) and $18,000 (E)].

37. (583,P2,36) (c) The requirement is the gross profit on the sale of 2,000 units of product E after further processing. Gross profit is calculated as sales ($40,000), less the total costs (joint and additional) assigned to product E. The joint costs allocated to product E are $18,000 as calculated in the previous answer. The total costs assigned to E after further processing total $24,000 ($18,000 joint + $6,000 additional), yielding a gross profit of $16,000 ($40,000 – $24,000).

38. (1180,P2,32) (d) The requirement is Ohio's cost to produce 1,000 gallons of product B, one of two products resulting from a joint manufacturing process. The cost will include any joint cost allocated to product B, plus the additional processing cost of $1 per gallon. The joint cost of $4,560 is allocated based on relative sales value at split-off:

	Product A	*Product B*	*Total*
Units produced	500	1,000	
Sales value at split-off/unit	$ 10	$ 14	
Total sales value at split-off	$5,000	$14,000	$19,000

The joint costs to be allocated to Product B are ($14,000/$19,000)($4,560), or $3,360. Total cost of Product B, then is $3,360 + (1,000 units)($1), or $4,360.

39. (1182,Q2,26) (b) The requirement is to calculate the profit effect of further processing a product after the split-off point. The solutions approach is to calculate the incremental effects assuming product Dee is further processed past split-off. If product Dee was further processed, the sales price per unit would increase by $2 ($5 – $3); the $1,000 of additional processing costs allocated over the 1000 units produced mean that cost per unit would increase by $1 ($1,000 ÷ 1000 units). Therefore, a decision to further process product Dee would result in an additional gain of $1,000 [(1000 units) x ($2 – $1)].

40. (582,T1,44) (a) The relative sales value method allocates common costs to the joint products based on their sales value at split-off. It can be used whether or not there are processing costs beyond the split-off. When no sales value exists at the split-off, an estimated one is derived by subtracting the processing costs beyond the split-off from the selling price obtainable after additional processing.

I. By-Products

41. (1182,Q2,39) (a) The requirement is to calculate the effect on gross margin if the accounting treatment for a by-product is changed. The solutions approach is to determine what is currently being done, then calculate the effect of the accounting change. To facilitate understanding, **assume** that dollar amounts for sales and cost of sales for the major product are $10,000 and $8,000, respectively:

	Present method	Proposed method
Sales	$10,000	$10,000 + $3,000*
Cost of sales	$8,000 – $3,000*	$8,000
Gross Margin	$ 5,000	$5,000

*1,000 units x ($4 selling price – $1 separable costs)

Note that the change in accounting treatment has no effect on gross margin.

42. (1182,Q2,40) (c) The requirement is to find the effect on gross margin caused by treating the net amount realized from the by-product as "Other Income."

	Present method	Proposed method
Sales	$10,000	$10,000
Cost of sales	$8,000 – $3,000	$ 8,000
Gross margin	$ 5,000	$ 2,000
Other income	–0–	$ 3,000

Since cost of sales is increased by $3,000, gross margin is reduced by $3,000.

43. (1182,T1,45) (b) The requirement is to identify the acceptable treatment of allocating joint product cost to a by-product. Joint product costs are common costs of two or more products produced simultaneously, with each having significant sales value. A joint product with insignificant value relative to the other products is called a by-product. One method of accounting for by-products treats the net revenue from the by-product sold as a reduction in cost of the main product. No portion of the joint costs are allocated to the by-product. A second method treats the net realizable value of the by-product produced as a reduction in cost of the main product. Under the latter method, unsold by-product is carried forward as inventory at net realizable value on the balance sheet.

May 1984 Answers

44. (584,T1,36) (a) The requirement is to determine which general ledger account is charged for the incurrence of indirect labor. The correct answer is (a) since actual indirect labor costs are debited (charged) to the factory department overhead control account upon incurrence. Answer (b) is incorrect since factory overhead applied is credited (rather than debited) in the entry to apply overhead to production. Applied overhead is based upon estimated factory overhead costs, not actual costs. Answer (c) is incorrect because the WIP control account is charged only for direct materials used, direct labor costs incurred, and factory overhead applied to production. Answer (d) is incorrect because the accrued payroll account is credited upon the incurrence of labor costs (direct or indirect).

45. (584,T1,37) (a) The requirement is to determine which elements are included in prime cost. Prime cost includes direct materials and direct labor. Answer (a) is correct since indirect materials would be included in overhead which is excluded from prime cost.

46. (584,T1,38) (b) The requirement is the classification of a factory timekeeper's wages. Direct labor includes all costs that are directly traceable to the product. All other labor costs which are necessary for the operation of the factory are considered indirect labor. Since the wages of the timekeeper bear no direct relationship to the production process, they would be considered indirect labor. Prime cost includes direct materials and direct labor. Conversion costs are those costs associated with the conversion of direct materials into finished goods. Therefore, conversion costs include direct labor and overhead. The correct answer is (b) since indirect labor is excluded from prime cost but included in conversion cost (as a component of overhead).

47. (584,T1,39) (c) The requirement is to determine the classification of the cost of electricity for a manufacturing plant. The fact that the problem asks for the classification of the fixed portion of electricity is irrelevant. Electric costs (both variable and fixed) incurred in a manufacturing plant would be included in manufacturing overhead. Conversion costs are those costs incurred to convert direct materials into a finished product; therefore, they include both direct labor and overhead. Product costs attach to the physical unit produced and are charged to expense in the period in which the unit is sold. Accordingly, product costs include direct materials, direct labor, and manufacturing overhead. Answer (c) is correct since electricity would be included in overhead which is an element of both conversion cost and product cost.

48. (584,T1,42) (a) The requirement is to determine the equivalent units as to material costs. Since there was no beginning work in process (BWIP), only those units started during the period can qualify as completed units. Since ending work in process (EWIP) was 100% complete as to material costs, all units started during the period must be complete as to material costs. Thus, the equivalent units for materials must be equal to the number of units placed into process during the period [answer (a)]. Answers (b) and (d) are incorrect because they ignore the equivalent units included in

EWIP. Answer (c) is incorrect because all units started into production have been completed in the current period. Thus, the equivalent units of output must be at least as great as the units placed into process and would be greater if any BWIP units were on hand which were not fully complete as to material costs.

49. (584,T1,43) (b) The requirement is to determine when a standard cost system may be used. Answer (b) is correct since both job order costing and process costing may employ a standard cost system. The only difference between the two systems is that job order costing accumulates costs by individual job, while process costing accumulates costs by department. This difference does not preclude either system from being compatible with a standard cost system.

50. (584,T1,45) (a) The requirement is to determine what the sales price at the point of sale reduced by cost to complete after split-off represents. Joint costs are allocated based on their relative sales value at the split-off point. If an actual sales value at the split-off point is not available, then a hypothetical sales value at split-off is computed. This hypothetical sales value is equal to the sales price at the point of sale reduced by the cost to complete after the split-off point [answer (a)].

Answer Outline

Problem 1 Overhead Application Bases

Part a.

Factory overhead
- Must be incurred in order to produce goods
- Cannot be specifically identified with units produced
  - Applied to units using predetermined rate
  - Provides accurate product cost information

Predetermined rate
- Budgeted factory overhead, divided by
- Forecasted activity level (base)

Overhead rate base—objectives
- Cause-and-effect relationship
  - Base should cause incurrence of overhead costs
  - Accurate product cost information

Overhead rate base—criteria
- Relationship which can predict changes in cost
  - Correlation and significance of dependent variable on independent variable
  - Regression analysis or high-low
- Capital-intensive or labor-intensive
- Stability of relationship in past and plans for future
- Availability of data

Unofficial Answer

(Author Modified)

Problem 1 Overhead Application Bases

Part a.

Factory overhead costs such as depreciation, property taxes, and utilities must be incurred in order to produce goods. Yet by definition, these factory overhead costs cannot be specifically identified with the units produced, as can direct labor and direct materials costs. Therefore, in order to provide accurate product cost information, overhead costs must be applied to the units produced using a predetermined overhead rate.

The predetermined overhead rate is computed at the beginning of the period. The budgeted factory overhead is divided by the forecasted activity level, or base. Then as units are produced, the activity used in production is measured and multiplied by the rate to determine the amount of overhead applied to each batch of production. Selection of the overhead rate base is therefore an important step in the overhead allocation process. The primary objective of this selection is that the base should have a cause-and-effect relationship with the overhead costs. In other words, an increase in the base (for Stein Co., direct labor hours or machine hours) should cause incurrence of overhead cost. If a cause-and-effect relationship exists, the overall objective of accurate product cost information is more likely to be attained.

Although conceptually a cause-and-effect relationship is the ultimate goal, practically a pure relationship of this sort is usually not available. In absence of a cause-and-effect relationship, there should at least be a predictive relationship between the base and overhead costs. Changes in the base (independent variable) should predict changes in overhead costs (dependent variable); the base with the highest level of correlation would be preferable. Regression analysis or the high-low method could be used to analyze the relationships.

In choosing the base which would be the best predictor, an important consideration is whether the manufacturing process is capital-intensive or labor-intensive. A capital-intensive process would favor machine hours, while a labor-intensive process would favor labor hours. Other factors to consider concern how Stein's future plans will affect the stability of the past relationship and the ease of availability of data. For many firms, while direct labor hour information is readily available, machine hour information may be more difficult and costly to obtain.

Unofficial Answer*

Problem 2 Equivalent Units; Indirect Manufacturing Costs

Part a.

1. The units placed in process for a period represent the units started during a period. The equivalent units for a period when there is no beginning work-in-process inventory and the ending work-in-process inventory is 50 percent complete represent the units that are placed in process for a period and are fully completed during a period (units completed for a period), plus 50 percent of the units that are placed in process for a period and are included in the ending work-in-process inventory.

2. The units completed for a period when there is no beginning work-in-process inventory and the ending

**The format of the Unofficial Answer precludes the need for an Answer Outline.*

work-in-process inventory is 50 percent complete represent the units that are placed in process for a period and are fully completed during a period. The equivalent units for a period when there is no beginning work-in-process inventory and the ending work-in-process inventory is 50 percent complete represent the units that are completed for a period plus 50 percent of the units that are placed in process for a period and are included in the ending work-in-process inventory.

3. The equivalent units for a period are divided into the total costs for a period to compute the unit cost. The equivalent units in the ending work-in-process inventory are then multiplied by the unit cost to compute the cost of the ending work-in-process inventory.

Part b.

1. Indirect materials are those materials needed for the completion of the product but whose consumption is either so small or so complex that their treatment as direct materials would not be feasible. For example, nails used to make the product are indirect materials.

2. Indirect labor, in contrast to direct labor, is labor expended that does not affect the construction or the composition of the finished product. For example, the labor of custodians is indirect labor.

3. The total of fixed indirect manufacturing costs (factory overhead) remains unchanged over a given range of activity.

4. The total of variable indirect manufacturing costs (factory overhead) changes in proportion to changes in activity.

5. Semivariable indirect manufacturing costs (factory overhead) contain both fixed and variable elements.

Answer Outline

Problem 3 Process Cost Theory

a. Type of manufacturing will determine cost system
 Process system for continuous mass production
 Job-order for unique goods
 The process is center of attention in continuous production
 Unit costs by cost category are possible
 Process costing is often used for
 Chemicals, food processing, oil, mining, and rubber

b. Equivalent units of production (EUP) is work completed
 Assumes whole equivalent units finished
 I.e., units completed if no BWIP or EWIP
 EUP is a denominator in ratio for assigning costs
 Numerator is amount of work in FG, EWIP, spoilage, etc.
 Often done on a unit cost basis

c. Normal spoilage is expected
 Inherent in production process
 A normal cost of production
 Abnormal spoilage is unexpected
 Not per normal efficient operating conditions
 I.e., is avoidable, controllable, etc.
 Accounted for as a loss, not production cost
 For practical reasons there may be no distinction

d. FIFO and weighted-average differ due to treatment of BWIP
 Per FIFO, BWIP is separated from current period's cost
 Finished goods are separated into
 Started this period, completed this period
 And started last period, completed this period
 Weighted-average does not separate BWIP
 All costs are averaged

Unofficial Answer

Problem 3 Process Cost Theory

a. The type of cost system used by a company will be determined by the type of manufacturing operations performed. A manufacturing company should use a process cost system for product costing purposes when it continuously mass produces like units; while the production of custom-made or unique goods would indicate a job-order cost system to be more appropriate.

Because there is continuous mass production of like units in a process cost system, the center of attention is the individual process (usually a department). The unit costs by cost category as well as total unit cost for each process (department) are necessary for product costing purposes.

Process costing is often used in industries such as chemicals, food processing, oil, mining, rubber and electrical appliances.

b. "Equivalent production" (equivalent units produced) is the term used to identify the number of completed units that would have been produced if all the work performed during the period had been applied to units that were begun and finished during the period. Thus, equivalent production represents the total number of units that could have been started and finished during the period, given the same effort, assuming no beginning or ending work-in-process inventories.

The work of each producing department must be expressed in terms of a common denominator; this denominator represents the total work of a department or process in terms of fully completed units. Units in process of production at the beginning and end of the period should not be counted the same as units started and completed during the period when determining the equivalent amount of production for a period. Each partially completed unit has received only part of the attention and effort that a finished unit has received and, therefore, each partially completed unit should be weighted accordingly.

The equivalent production figure computed represents the number of equivalent whole units for which materials, labor, and overhead were issued, used, or incurred during a period. The cost of each element of materials, labor, and overhead is divided by the appropriate equivalent production figure to determine the unit cost for each element. Should units be at a different stage of completion with respect to each type of cost element, then a separate equivalent production figure must be completed for that cost element.

c. Normal spoilage is the spoilage that arises under normal efficient operating conditions, i.e., it is inherent in the production process and is uncontrollable in the short run. Abnormal spoilage is the spoilage that is not expected to arise under normal efficient operating conditions; i.e., it is not inherent in the production process and is usually considered as avoidable, or controllable, by management. Thus, by definition, the critical factor in distinguishing between normal and abnormal spoilage is the degree of controllability of units spoiled. Any spoilage that occurs during a production process functioning within the expected usual range of performance is considered to be normal spoilage. Any spoilage occurring in amounts in excess of the defined usual range is considered abnormal (controllable) spoilage.

Conceptually, the cost of normal spoilage should be included in the cost of good units produced because of its association with normal production. Likewise, cost of abnormal spoilage should be accounted for as a loss because of its abnormal (unusual) nature. The cost of abnormal spoilage should be separately identified as a loss on reports for management.

For practical reasons, there may be no distinction made between normal and abnormal spoilage in reports for management. The primary reason for not distinguishing between types of spoilage is that it is sometimes very difficult (or impossible) to distinguish between normal and abnormal spoilage. The production process may be relatively new or the process may be altered often enough to make it impractical or too costly to distinguish between normal or abnormal spoilage. Whenever possible, though, the distinction between types of spoilage should be made and accounted for as discussed in the preceding paragraphs.

d. The primary difference between the FIFO method and the weighted-average method of process costing is in the treatment of the cost of the beginning work-in-process inventory. When applying FIFO method the cost of the beginning work-in-process inventory is kept separate from the cost of production of the current period.

When determining the FIFO cost of units completed and transferred to the next department or to finished goods, the cost of the beginning work-in-process inventory plus the cost necessary to complete the beginning work-in-process units are added together. The sum of these two cost totals is the cost assigned to the units in the beginning work-in-process inventory that are transferred out. Units started and completed during the period are assigned costs on the basis of costs incurred during the period for the equivalent units produced during that period.

In applying the FIFO method, each department is regarded as a separate accounting unit. Thus, the application of the FIFO method in practice is modified to the extent that subsequent departments usually combine all transferred-in costs into one amount, even though they could identify and separately account for the costs relating to the preceding department's beginning inventory and the costs relating to the preceding department's units started and completed during the period.

The weighted-average method of process costing is simpler to apply than the FIFO method primarily because the beginning work-in-process inventory is considered to be part of current production. In applying the weighted-average method, the beginning work-in-process inventory costs are combined with current costs even though some of the production was begun prior to the current period. When equivalent units are determined, work done on the beginning inventory in a preceding period is regarded as if it were done in the current period.

The weighted-average method is applied by adding the beginning work-in-process inventory costs to the production costs incurred during the current period. Then unit costs are determined by dividing the sum of these costs by the equivalent units produced, including the units in the department's beginning work-in-process inventory. The cost of all units transferred out of a department (process) during the period is the product of the number of units completed multiplied by the average cost to produce a unit.

Solution Guide

Problem 4 By-Product and Joint Product

1. Part a. requires journal entries for a product accounted for as a by-product and also as a joint product.

2. Part a. describes a by-product which, if further processed, can be accounted for as either a by-product or a joint product. The "solutions approach" is to first study the requirements; second, quickly review mentally the concepts of accounting for joint products and by-products; third, read through the information given; and fourth, make the necessary calculations and prepare the required journal entries. Note that journal entries are required under three sets of circumstances:

- Nagu is transferred as a by-product without further processing;
- Nagu is further processed and transferred as a by-product;
- Nagu is further processed and transferred as a joint product.

2.1 In a.1, Nagu is transferred at sales value as a by-product. The first step is to calculate the sales value of Nagu at the split-off point. Without further processing, Nagu sells for $.10 per pound. To obtain the total sales value, this selling price must be multiplied by the total number of pounds of Nagu (30,000). Thus, the sales value at which Nagu is transferred to the warehouse as a by-product is $3,000 (30,000 x $.10). The account debited is "By-product-Nagu". The transfer reduces the manufacturing costs of Rey, the primary product. Therefore,the credit would be to the work-in-process account, where manufacturing costs are accumulated.

2.2 In a.2, Nagu is processed further and then transferred as a by-product at net realizable value (NRV). In this situation, the costs incurred to further process Nagu (given) must be recorded with a debit to work in process and credits to materials, factory payroll, and factory overhead control. Recall that NRV is calculated by deducting costs to complete, selling expenses, and disposal costs from the sales value of the product produced. The sales value of Nagu after further processing is $9,000 (30,000 pounds x $.30 per pound). The NRV at this point is also $9,000, since no **additional** costs are indicated in this problem.The diagram below illustrates NRV at different points in the process:

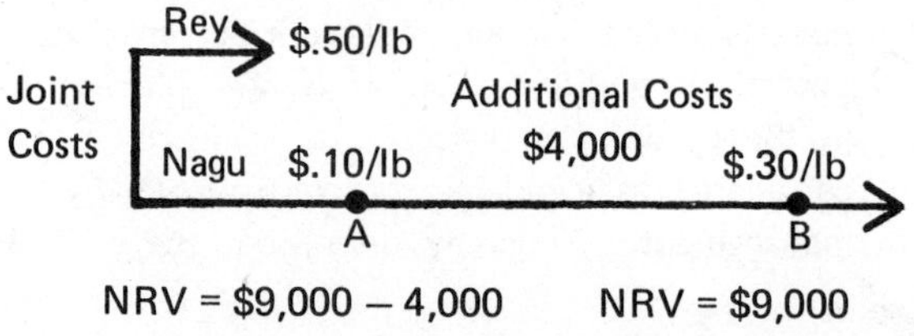

If Nagu was transferred out of work in process at point A, before further processing, NRV would be $5,000 because additional costs of $4,000 would be incurred in the future. In this problem, however, Nagu is transferred out of work in process at point B. At this point, NRV is simply the $9,000 selling price, since there are no **future** additional costs indicated. Again, the credit would be to work in process, where Rey's manufacturing costs are accumulated.

2.3 In part three, Nagu is further processed and transferred to finished goods as a joint product with joint costs being allocated between Rey and Nagu based on relative sales value at the split-off point. First, raw materials, direct labor, and factory overhead must be recorded for the additional costs incurred to further process Nagu, as was done in 2.2 above.

2.4 In order to record the transfer of Nagu to finished goods, the joint costs must be allocated between Nagu and Rey based on relative sales value at the split-off point. Recall that the first step in this approach is determination of the total sales value of each product. The total sales value of Nagu is $3,000 (30,000 pounds x $.10). The total sales value of Rey is $197,000 (394,000 pounds x $.50). The sales value of Nagu and Rey combined is $200,000 ($3,000 + $197,000). The total joint costs to be allocated are:

Raw materials	$150,000
Direct labor	120,000
Factory overhead	30,000
Total	$300,000

The joint costs allocated to Nagu are:

($3,000/$200,000) x $300,000 = $4,500

The cost at which Nagu is to be transferred to finished goods is $8,500 ($4,500 joint costs + $4,000 additional costs).

Unofficial Answer
(Author Modified)

Problem 4 By-Product and Joint Product

Part a.

1.

By-product—Nagu	$3,000	
Work in process		$3,000

To transfer the by-product to the warehouse at sales value (30,000 lbs x $.10/lb)

2.

Work in process	$4,000	
Materials		$2,000
Factory payroll		1,500
Factory overhead control		500

To record the further processing of the by-product.

By-product—Nagu	$9,000	
Work in process		$9,000

To transfer the by-product to the warehouse at net realizable value (30,000 lbs x $.30/lb).

3.

Work in process	$4,000	
Materials		$2,000
Factory payroll		1,500
Factory overhead control		500

To record the further processing of the by-product.

Finished goods—Nagu	$8,500	
Work in process		$8,500

To transfer 30,000 lbs of Nagu to finished goods (Schedule 1).

Note: An alternative in a.2 and a.3 above is to transfer the cost assigned to Nagu ($5,000 in a.2 and $4,500 in a.3) to another department, work in process: Nagu. The additional processing costs ($4,000) would also be charged to work in process: Nagu. The entry to transfer Nagu would be a credit to work in process: Nagu.

Schedule 1

Cost of Finished Goods—Nagu

Sales value of Rey at split-off (394,000 x $.50)	$197,000
Sales value of Nagu at split-off (30,000 x $.10)	3,000
Total sales value at split-off	$200,000
Joint costs ($150,000 + $120,000 + $30,000)	$300,000
Relative sales value of Nagu ($3,000/$200,000)	x .015
Joint costs allocated to Nagu	$4,500
Further processing costs	4,000
Total cost of finished goods—Nagu	$8,500

Solution Guide

Problem 5 Cost of Goods Manufactured

1. This problem consists of three separate topics: cost of goods manufactured statement; computation of equivalent units of production; and joint, by-product cost allocations.

2. The cost of goods manufactured statement is a summary of the work-in-process account.

Beg. WIP
+ Raw Materials
+ Labor
+ Overhead

Total Manufacturing Cost
−End. WIP

Cost of goods manufactured

Use T-account analysis for the work in process account.

WIP

BWIP	?	C of GM	970
RM	370		
L	360	EWIP	?
O/H	270		

The O/H was 27% of $1,000,000 and is 75% of L. Labor, therefore, is $360,000 and RM is $370,000, because RM, L, and O/H equal $1,000,000. The increase in WIP of $30,000 (1,000,000 – 970,000) is 20% of EWIP. Thus EWIP is $150,000 and BWIP is $120,000.

Unofficial Answer

Problem 5 Cost of Goods Manufactured

a.

Helper Corporation
Statement of Cost of Goods Manufactured
For the Year Ended December 31, 1973

Direct material used	$ 370,000
Direct labor	360,000
Factory overhead applied	270,000
Total manufacturing cost added during 1973	1,000,000
Plus beginning work-in-process inventory	120,000
Manufacturing costs to account for	1,120,000
Less ending work-in-process inventory	150,000
Cost of goods manufactured	$ 970,000

Supporting Computations

Factory overhead applied:
27% x total manufacturing cost (27% x $1,000,000)

Direct labor:
75% of direct labor equals $270,000 so direct labor was
$360,000 ($270,000 ÷ 75%)

Work-in-process inventories:
Let X = Ending work-in-process inventory
$1,000,000 + .8X – X = $970,000
X = $150,000
.8X = $120,000

Direct material used equals total manufacturing cost less direct labor and factory overhead applied [$1,000,000 – ($360,000 + $270,000)].

Solution Guide

Problem 6 Weighted-Average Process Costing

1. This problem is a process costing problem requiring equivalent units of production (weighted average method), unit costs for material, labor, overhead, and cost of ending inventories. Also, part b. requires journal entries to correct ending work in process and finished goods inventories.

2. The solutions approach is to analyze the work-in-process account for 1978. The left (dr) side of the account reflects the costs incurred. The costs incurred are allocated to finished goods and ending work-in-process inventories which appear as credits on the right hand side of the account.

2.1 The total costs incurred are $5,196,000 as detailed in this "T-account." Note that overhead is 60% of direct labor. The 200,000 units of beginning work in process are 100% complete as to material and 80% complete as to conversion costs (direct labor and overhead). During the period 1,000,000 units were started that had a material cost of $1,300,000. Also during the period $1,995,000 of direct labor and $1,197,000 of overhead were incurred.

2.2 The $5,196,000 of costs are allocated to FG and EWIP based on equivalent units of production (EUP). Compute the EUP by doing a "T-account" analysis of the work-in-process account as illustrated in this "T-account." Note that the "T-account" contains unit data only and is a simplified version of the 2.1 "T-account."

2.1 "T-Account"

Work In Process

BWIP (200,000 units)		FG (900,000 units)	$??
Conversion 80%		Conversion 100%	
Material 100 %		Material 100%	
Material	$ 200,000		
Labor	315,000		
Overhead	189,000		
Material (1,000,000 units added)	1,300,000		
Labor	1,975,000	EWIP (300,000 units)	$??
Overhead (60% of labor)	1,197,000	Conversion 50%	
		Material 100%	
	$5,196,000		$5,196,000

2.2 "T-Account"

Work In Process (Units Only)

BWIP	200,000	FG	900,000
Conversion 80%			
Material 100%			
		EWIP	300,000
Units added	1,000,000	Conversion 50%	
		Material 100%	
	1,200,000		1,200,000

2.3 The material EUP are 1,200,000 because there are 1,200,000 units of material to assign cost (900,000 of FG and 300,000 of EWIP). Since the total cost of material is $1,500,000 ($200,000 in BWIP and $1,300,000 of material added), the unit cost is $1.25 ($1,500,000 ÷ 1,200,000). Thus the material cost in FG is $1,125,000 (900,000 x $1.25), and the material cost in EWIP is $375,000 (300,000 x $1.25).

2.4 The direct labor EUP is 1,050,000 because 900,000 units were completely finished and 300,000 are only 50% complete. Thus the total direct labor cost of $2,310,000 ($315,000 in BWIP and $1,995,000 incurred this period) will be allocated 900/1,050 to FG and 150/1,050 to EWIP. Note that most cost textbooks allocate the cost by dividing 1,050,000 EUP into $2,310,000 to get a $2.20 EUP unit cost and multiply the $2.20 times 900,000 FG, EUP and 150,000 EWIP, EUP.

2.5 The overhead EUP is the same as direct labor as both are elements of "conversion." Divide the 1,050,000 EUP into overhead cost of $1,386,000 ($189,000 in BWIP plus $1,197,000 incurred this period) to obtain an overhead EUP unit cost of $1.32.

2.6 After the EUP unit costs are determined the cost of FG and EWIP can be determined, i.e., the total costs incurred, as above in 2.1, can be allocated to FG and EWIP.

FG (900,000 units at $4.77)			$4,293,000
Material	$1.25		
Direct labor	2.20		
Overhead	1.32		
	$4.77		
EWIP (300,000 units)			
Material, 300,000 at $1.25		$375,000	
Direct labor, 150,000 at $2.20		330,000	
Overhead, 150,000 at $1.32		198,000	903,000
			$5,196,000

3. Part b. requires a journal entry to correct ending inventory. Ending inventory consists of 300,000 units of work in process and 200,000 units of finished goods.

3.1 The books currently reflect EWIP at $660,960 while the above calculation shows the cost to be $903,000, i.e., debit work-in-process inventory for $242,040 ($903,000 – $660,960).

3.2 The books currently reflect FG at $1,009,800 while the 200,000 units priced at $4.77 (per above) should be $954,000, requiring a credit to finished goods inventory of $55,800 ($1,009,800 – $954,000). Note that there was no beginning FG inventory, i.e., the unit cost is $4.77.

3.3 Since the net adjustment is a $186,240 debit to inventory ($242,040 dr – $55,800 cr), cost of sales should be credited for $186,240.

Work in process	$242,040	
Finished goods inventory		$ 55,800
Cost of sales		186,240

Unofficial Answer

Problem 6 Weighted-Average Process Costing

a.

Spirit Corporation
Ending Inventory Schedules
December 31, 1978

Equivalent Units of Production (Weighted-Average Method):

	Materials	*Labor*	*Overhead*
Units completed during year	900,000	900,000	900,000
Units on hand at December 31, 1978 (50% complete as to labor and overhead)	300,000	150,000	150,000
Equivalent units of production	1,200,000	1,050,000	1,050,000

Unit Cost of Production:

	Total	*Materials*	*Labor*	*Overhead*
Beginning costs	$ 704,000	$ 200,000	$ 315,000	$ 189,000
Added costs	4,492,000	1,300,000	1,995,000	1,197,000
Total costs	$5,196,000	$1,500,000	$2,310,000	$1,386,000
Equivalent units of production	—	1,200,000	1,050,000	1,050,000
Unit costs of production	$ 4.77	$ 1.25	$ 2.20	$ 1.32

Costing of Inventories:

		Amounts		
	Units	*Total*	*Finished goods*	*Work in process*
Finished goods:				
200,000 X $4.77	200,000	$ 954,000	$ 954,000	
Work in process:	300,000			
Materials @ $1.25	—	375,000		$375,000
Labor @ $2.20 @ 50%	—	330,000		330,000
Overhead @ $1.32 @ 50%	—	198,000		198,000
Per costing test	500,000	1,857,000	954,000	903,000
Per books	500,000	1,670,760	1,009,800	660,960
Adjustment	—	$ 186,240	$ (55,800)	$242,040

b.

Spirit Corporation
Journal Entry to Correctly State Inventories
December 31, 1978

	Debit	Credit
Work-in-process inventory	$242,040	
Finished goods inventory		$ 55,800
Cost of sales		186,240
To adjust inventory accounts to correct cost		

Solution Guide

Problem 7 Process Costing

The requirement for part "a" of this problem has been modified, and an alternative solution has been substituted for the AICPA unofficial answer.

1. The requirement in part a is to prepare a cost of production report for both the machining and finishing departments.
2. The solutions approach is to prepare a complete production report first for the machining department, then for the finishing department.
3. The steps in the production report for the machining department are physical flow, equivalent units, total costs, unit costs, cost summary.

3.1 Physical flow is summarized in this T-account:

Machining	
Started 80,000 units	60,000 units completed
	20,000 units end. WIP

3.2 Equivalent units are computed for materials, labor, and overhead. Ending WIP is 100%, 50%, and 25% complete for these elements respectively.

3.3 Machining costs (given) are summarized for all three elements.

3.4 The costs (3.3) are divided by equivalent units (3.2) to obtain cost per equivalent unit for all three elements.

3.5 Finally, costs are summarized for units transferred (60,000 units x total per unit cost) and ending WIP (equivalent units for each element x per unit cost for each element).

4. The same five steps are used for the finishing department production report. There are two additional complications in this department: transferred-in costs and spoiled units.

4.1 Physical flow is summarized in this T-account:

Finishing	
Transferred in 60,000 units	50,000 units completed
	2,000 units spoiled
	8,000 units end. WIP

4.2 Equivalent units are computed for transferred-in costs, materials, labor, and overhead. Note that transferred-in costs are treated like materials added at the beginning of the process. Percentage of completion in ending WIP is 100%, 100%, 70%, and 70% for the four elements respectively. Separate percentages of completion (100%, 50%, 50% and 50%) are given for units spoiled.

4.3 Finishing costs (given) are summarized for all four elements. Note that transferred-in costs in the finishing dept. = transferred-out costs from the machining dept.

4.4 The costs (4.3) are divided by equivalent units (4.2) to obtain cost per equivalent unit for all four elements.

4.5 The most complicated part of this problem is summarizing costs for the finishing dept., because the cost of spoiled goods must be considered. It is important to think through this step carefully.

4.6 First, the cost of nonspoiled goods can be summarized for units completed (50,000 units x total per unit cost of $10.45) and ending WIP (equivalent units for each element x per unit cost for each element).

4.7 Finally, the cost of spoiled goods is allocated. The cost of these goods is the equivalent units spoiled x equivalent cost per unit [(2,000) ($6) + (1,000) ($1.50 + $2.50 + $ .45)]. This total cost ($16,450) is allocated to units completed and ending WIP based on good units in each category. Therefore, units completed are allocated 50,000/58,000, while ending WIP is allocated 8,000/58,000.

Unofficial Answer

Problem 7 Process Costing

The Dexter Products Company
MACHINING DEPARTMENT PRODUCTION COST REPORT
For the Month Ended June 30, 1976

Quantities	Physical Flow	Equivalent Units: Materials	Labor	Overhead	
WIP, beginning	0				
Units started	80,000				
Units to account for	80,000				
Units spoiled	0	0	0	0	
Units transferred	60,000	60,000	60,000	60,000	
WIP, ending	20,000	20,000	10,000	5,000	
Units accounted for	80,000	80,000	70,000	65,000	
Costs	**Totals**	**Materials**	**Labor**	**Overhead**	**Equivalent Whole Unit**
WIP, beginning	0	0	0	0	
Current costs	$445,000	$240,000	$140,000	$65,000	
Total costs to account for	$445,000	$240,000	$140,000	$65,000	
Divide by equivalent units		÷80,000 =	÷70,000 =	÷65,000 =	
Cost per equivalent unit		$3	$2	$1	$6

Summary of costs:

Units transferred	$360,000		60,000 x $6
WIP, ending	85,000	20,000 x $3 + 10,000 x $2 + 5,000 x $1	
Total costs accounted for	$445,000		

The Dexter Products Company
FINISHING DEPARTMENT PRODUCTION COST REPORT
For the Month Ended June 30, 1976

Quantities	Physical Flow	Transferred-in Costs	Materials	Labor	Overhead	
WIP, beginning	0					
Units transferred in	60,000					
Units to account for	60,000					
Units spoiled	2,000	2,000	1,000	1,000	1,000	
Units completed	50,000	50,000	50,000	50,000	50,000	
WIP, ending	8,000	8,000	8,000	5,600	5,600	
Units accounted for	60,000	60,000	59,000	56,600	56,600	
Costs	**Totals**	**Transferred-in Costs**	**Materials**	**Labor**	**Overhead**	**Equivalent Whole Unit**
WIP, beginning	0					
Current costs	$615,700	$360,000	$88,500	$141,500	$25,700	
Total costs to account for	$615,700	$360,000	$88,500	$141,500	$25,700	
Divided by equivalent units		÷60,000 =	÷59,000 =	÷56,600 =	÷56,600 =	
Cost per equivalent unit (EUP)		$6	$1.50	$2.50	$.45	$10.45

Summary of Costs:

Units completed[a] $$\$536{,}681.03 = (50{,}000 \times \$10.45) + \left[\$6\left(2{,}000 \times \frac{50{,}000}{58{,}000}\right) + \$4.45\left(1{,}000 \times \frac{50{,}000}{58{,}000}\right)\right]$$

WIP, ending $$78{,}788.97 = (8{,}000 \times \$6) + (8{,}000 \times \$1.50) + (5{,}600 \times \$2.50) + (4{,}600 \times \$.45)$$
$$+ \left[\$6\left(2{,}000 \times \frac{8{,}000}{58{,}000}\right) + \$4.45\left(1{,}000 \times \frac{8{,}000}{58{,}000}\right)\right]$$

Costs accounted for $615,470.00

[a] Spoilage allocated to units based on goods units
Good units = 60,000 total units – 2,000 spoiled units
Spoiled units have transferred-in costs plus materials, labor, and overhead costs

$$\text{Spoilage costs} = \text{EUP cost}\left(\text{EUP quantity} \times \frac{\text{units transferred}}{\text{good units}}\right)$$

Prepared by Professor David E. Keys, Northern Illinois Univ.

Solution Guide

Problem 8 FIFO Process Costing

1. The requirement is to prepare a cost of production report for both the Grading and Saturating departments using the FIFO (first-in, first-out) method of process costing.

2. The solutions approach is to prepare a complete production report for the Grading department first, then for the Saturating department.

3. Completing a cost of production report can be simplified by implementing a five-step approach: 1) visualize **physical flow** of units, 2) calculate **equivalent units of production (EUP)**, 3) determine **costs to allocate**, 4) calculate **unit costs**, 5) **allocate costs.** Note that the five steps can be memorized using the mnemonic: PECUA (Physical flow, Equivalent Units of Production, Costs to allocate, Unit costs, Allocate costs).

3.1 In solving process costing problems, it is beneficial to use a diagram to help visualize the **physical flow** of the production process.

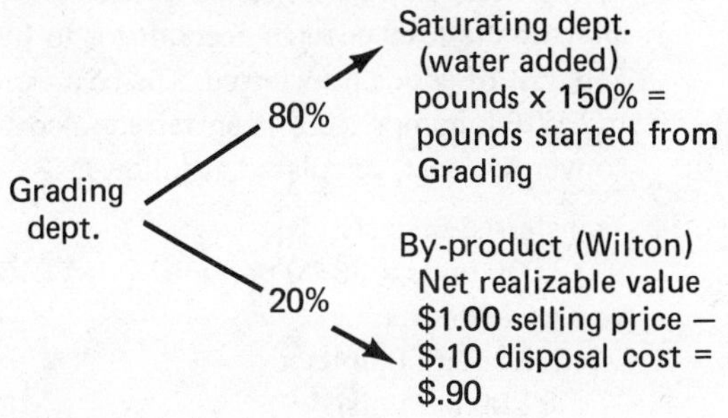

3.2 The **physical flow** of units in the Grading department is summarized in the work-in-process T-account which follows. The debit side of the T-account reflects units in or costs incurred. The credit side of the T-account reflects units out or costs allocated.

Grading (in Units)

BWIP	–	28,800	Transferred to Saturating
Started	36,000	7,200	By-product to FG (20% x 36,000 lbs.)
		–	EWIP
	36,000	36,000	

3.3 Since the by-product accounts for 20% of the material output, 7,200 pounds (36,000 pounds of material x 20%) of by-product were produced.

3.4 The units (pounds) transferred to Saturating are 28,800 [36,000 pounds to account for less 7,200 pounds of by-product and EWIP (0)]. The number of units which were started and completed, excluding the by-product, is also 28,800 because there was no BWIP.

3.5 Since there was no EWIP, **EUP** for materials (all added at the beginning of process) are the 28,800 units (pounds) started and completed during the period. The **EUP** for labor and overhead (conversion costs) are the same as for materials because there was no BWIP or EWIP requiring additional conversion work.

3.6 The **costs to allocate** are determined by tracing the flow of costs for the Grading department as follows:

Grading

BWIP	$ –	$345,600	Transferred to Saturating
Costs added:			
Materials	$265,680		By-product to FG ($.90 x 7,200 lbs.)
Conversion	86,400	6,480	
		–	EWIP
	$352,080	$352,080	

Note that the by-product is valued at net realizable value (NRV) of $.90 per pound ($1.00 selling price less $.10 delivery cost).

3.7 Next compute **unit costs** as follows:

Material	
[($265,680 cost added – $6,480 assigned to by-product) ÷ 28,800 EUP]	$ 9.00
Conversion costs	
[$86,400 (cost assigned to main products ÷ 28,800 EUP]	$ 3.00
Total cost per EUP	$12.00

Note that the NRV of the by-product is to be accounted for as a reduction of the cost of materials in the Grading department. Thus, the NRV of the by-product ($6,480) is subtracted from the cost of materials added ($265,680) before computing the materials cost per EUP.

3.8 Since there was no BWIP or EWIP, all costs are **allocated** to the cost of goods transferred to Saturating which consists of the total cost added ($352,080) less the NRV of the by-product ($6,480) or $345,600. The cost of goods transferred can also be computed as 28,800 units x $12/unit (above) = $345,600.

4. The same five steps are used for the production report in the Saturating department. There are two additional complications in this department: transferred-in costs and a 50% gain in weight of the materials in production. Recall that transferred-in costs are to be treated the same as material added at the beginning of a process in the next department.

4.1 The **physical flow** of units in the Saturating department is summarized in the following work-in-process T-account:

Saturating (in units)

Debit			Credit		
BWIP (50% complete)		1,600		1,600	Transferred to finished goods: From BWIP
Units added: From Grading	28,800		42,800	41,200	Started and completed
Water	14,400	43,200			
			2,000		EWIP (50% complete)
		44,800	44,800		

Note that the water added results in a 50% gain in weight of the units transferred in from Grading (50% x 28,800 units = 14,400 units).

4.2 The units completed and transferred to FG in the above account are the 44,800 units to account for (1,600 BWIP + 43,200 units added) less 2,000 units of EWIP, or 42,800 units. The units started and completed are 41,200 (42,800 units transferred less 1,600 BWIP).

4.3 **EUP** for transferred-in costs are computed by adding the 41,200 units started and completed and the 2,000 units of EWIP for a total of 43,200 equivalent units. **EUP** for the material added (water) would be computed on the same basis as for transferred-in costs (i.e., in terms of output units). EUP for materials is, therefore, 43,200.

4.4 **EUP** for conversion costs are calculated as follows:

BWIP (units)	[1,600 x 50%]	800
Units started and completed		41,200
EWIP (units)	[2,000 x 50%]	1,000
		43,000 EUP

4.5 The **costs to allocate** are determined by tracing the flow of costs for the Saturating department as follows:

Saturating

Debit			Credit	
BWIP (1,600 units)	$ 17,600			Transferred to finished goods: BWIP
Transferred in from Grading	345,600		$17,600	Costs from last period
		$ 19,200	1,600	Cost to complete
Costs added: Conversion	86,000	412,000		Started and completed
				EWIP (2,000 units)
			16,000	Transferred-in cost
		18,000	2,000	Conversion cost
	$449,200	$449,200		

4.6 Next compute **units cost** as follows:

Material (water)	$ –
Transferred-in cost ($345,600 total cost transferred this period ÷ 43,200 EUP)	8.00
Conversion ($86,000 added this period ÷ 43,000 EUP)	2.00
Total cost per EUP	$10.00

4.7 The last step in our five-step approach is to **allocate the total costs** to account for to EWIP and cost of goods transferred. The cost assigned to EWIP is comprised of transferred-in cost and conversion cost, calculated as follows:

Transferred-in costs (2,000 units x $8.00 per unit)	$16,000
Conversion costs (50% x 2,000 units x $2.00 per unit)	2,000
Cost assigned to EWIP	$18,000

Finally, calculate the cost of goods transferred out of Saturating. According to the FIFO cost flow assumption, the first batch of units transferred must be the 1,600 BWIP units. The remaining units transferred would be units started and completed this period. The total cost of goods transferred is calculated as follows:

BWIP	
Costs from last period	$ 17,600
Conversion cost added to complete units (50% x 1,600 units x $2.00 per unit)	1,600
	19,200
Units started and completed (41,200 units x $10.00 per unit)	412,000
Total cost of goods transferred	$431,200

Unofficial Answer

Problem 8 FIFO Process Costing

Adept Company
Grading Department
Cost of Production Report
For the Month of November 1979

Description	*Total*	*Material*	*Labor/overhead*
Physical units in pounds to be accounted for:			
(a) Beginning inventory	—		
(b) Added	36,000		
(c) Less by-product*	(7,200)		
Pounds to be accounted for (Prep and Pride)	28,800		
Equivalent units in pounds:			
(d) Beginning inventory	—	—	—
(e) Started and completed	28,800	28,800	28,800
(f) Ending inventory	—	—	—
(g) Equivalent units	28,800	28,800	28,800
Manufacturing costs:			
(h) Beginning inventory	—	—	—
(i) Current — November	$352,080	$265,680	$86,400
(j) Less net realizable value of by-product	(6,480)	(6,480)	—
(k) Current costs	$345,600	$259,200	$86,400
(l) Total costs	$345,600	$259,200	$86,400
Equivalent unit cost (m) = (k ÷ g)	$ 12.00	$ 9.00	$ 3.00
Amount of ending work in process (m x f)	—	—	—
Amount transferred out (m x e)	$345,600	$259,200	$86,400
Total manufacturing cost	$345,600	$259,200	$86,400

*36,000 x 20%

Adept Company
Saturating Department
Cost of Production Report
For the Month of November 1979

Description	*Total*	*Transferred in*	*Material*	*Labor/ overhead*
Physical units in pounds to be accounted for:				
(a) Beginning inventory	1,600			
(b) Transferred in	28,800			
(c) Water added (b) x 50%	14,400			
(d) Pounds to be accounted for	44,800			
Equivalent units in pounds:				
(e) Beginning inventory	1,600	–	–	800
(f) Started and completed*	41,200	41,200	41,200	41,200
(g) Ending inventory	2,000	2,000	2,000	1,000
(h) Equivalent units	44,800	43,200	43,200	43,000
Manufacturing costs:				
(i) Beginning inventory	$ 17,600			
(j) Current – November	431,600	$345,600	–	$86,000
(k) Total costs	$449,200			
Equivalent units cost (m) = (j) ÷ (h)	$ 10.00	$ 8.00	–	$ 2.00
Amount of ending work in process [(g) x (m)] or [$16,000 + $2,000]	$ 18,000	$ 16,000	–	$ 2,000
Amount transferred out:				
Beginning inventory	$ 17,600			
Completion cost (e) x (m)	1,600			
First layer (1,600 lbs.)	19,200			
Started and completed (f) x (m)	412,000			
Total transferred out	431,200			
Total cost	$449,200			

*44,800 – (1,600 + 2,000) or (43,200 – 2,000)

Multiple Choice Questions (1–39)

1. Jackson, Inc., is preparing a flexible budget for 1981 and requires a breakdown of the cost of steam used in its factory into the fixed and variable elements. The following data on the cost of steam used and direct-labor hours worked are available for the last six months of 1980:

Month	*Cost of steam*	*Direct-labor hours*
July	$ 15,850	3,000
August	13,400	2,050
September	16,370	2,900
October	19,800	3,650
November	17,600	2,670
December	18,500	2,650
Total	$101,520	16,920

Assuming that Jackson uses the high-low points method of analysis, the estimated variable cost of steam per direct-labor hour should be

a. $4.00
b. $5.42
c. $5.82
d. $6.00

2. Wilson Company prepared the following preliminary forecast concerning product G for 1982 assuming no expenditure for advertising:

Selling price per unit	$10
Unit sales	100,000
Variable costs	$600,000
Fixed costs	$300,000

Based on a market study in December 1981, Wilson estimated that it could increase the unit selling price by 15% and increase the unit sales volume by 10% if $100,000 were spent on advertising. Assuming that Wilson incorporates these changes in its 1982 forecast, what should be the operating income from product G?

a. $175,000
b. $190,000
c. $205,000
d. $365,000

3. Birney Company is planning its advertising campaign for 1981 and has prepared the following budget data based on a zero advertising expenditure:

Normal plant capacity	200,000 units
Sales	150,000 units
Selling price	$25.00 per unit
Variable manufacturing costs	$15.00 per unit
Fixed costs:	
Manufacturing	$800,000
Selling and administrative	$700,000

An advertising agency claims that an aggressive advertising campaign would enable Birney to increase its unit sales by 20%. What is the maximum amount that Birney can pay for advertising and obtain an operating profit of $200,000?

a. $100,000
b. $200,000
c. $300,000
d. $550,000

4. In planning its operations for 1981 based on a sales forecast of $6,000,000, Wallace, Inc., prepared the following estimated data:

	Costs and expenses	
	Variable	*Fixed*
Direct materials	$1,600,000	
Direct labor	1,400,000	
Factory overhead	600,000	$ 900,000
Selling expenses	240,000	360,000
Administrative expenses	60,000	140,000
	$3,900,000	$1,400,000

What would be the amount of sales dollars at the break-even point?

a. $2,250,000
b. $3,500,000
c. $4,000,000
d. $5,300,000

5. Warfield Company is planning to sell 100,000 units of product T for $12.00 a unit. The fixed costs are $280,000. In order to realize a profit of $200,000, what would the variable costs be?

a. $480,000
b. $720,000
c. $900,000
d. $920,000

6. The Seahawk Company is planning to sell 200,000 units of Product B. The fixed costs are $400,000 and the variable costs are 60% of the selling price. In order to realize a profit of $100,000, the selling price per unit would have to be

a. $3.75
b. $4.17
c. $5.00
d. $6.25

7. At a breakeven point of 400 units sold, the variable costs were $400 and the fixed costs were $200. What will the 401st unit sold contribute to profit before income taxes?

35

a. $0
b. $0.50
c. $1,00
d. $1.50

8. Koby Co. has sales of $200,000 with variable expenses of $150,000, fixed expenses of $60,000, and an operating loss of $10,000. By how much would Koby have to increase its sales in order to achieve an operating income of 10% of sales?

a. $400,000
b. $251,000
c. $231,000
d. $200,000

9. How would the following be used in calculating sales necessary to realize a projected profit?

	Projected profit	*Contribution margin ratio*
a.	Denominator	Numerator
b.	Denominator	Not used
c.	Numerator	Numerator
d.	Numerator	Denominator

10. If the fixed costs attendant to a product increase while variable costs and sales price remain constant, what will happen to (1) contribution margin and (2) breakeven point?

	Contribution margin	*Breakeven point*
a.	Increase	Decrease
b.	Decrease	Increase
c.	Unchanged	Increase
d.	Unchanged	Unchanged

11. Thomas Company sells products X, Y, and Z. Thomas sells three units of X for each unit of Z, and two units of Y for each unit of X. The contribution margins are $1.00 per unit of X, $1.50 per unit of Y, and $3.00 per unit of Z. Fixed costs are $600,000. How many units of X would Thomas sell at the break-even point?

a. 40,000
b. 120,000
c. 360,000
d. 400,000

12. The Ship Company is planning to produce two products, Alt and Tude. Ship is planning to sell 100,000 units of Alt at $4 a unit and 200,000 units of Tude at $3 a unit. Variable costs are 70% of sales for Alt and 80% of sales for Tude. In order to realize a total profit of $160,000, what must the total fixed costs be?

a. $ 80,000
b. $ 90,000
c. $240,000
d. $600,000

13. Walman Company is budgeting sales of 42,000 units of product Y for March 1983. To make one unit of finished product, three pounds of raw material A are required. Actual beginning and desired ending inventories of raw material A and product Y are as follows:

	3/1/83	*3/31/83*
Raw material A	100,000 pounds	110,000 pounds
Product Y	22,000 units	24,000 units

There is no work-in-process inventory for product Y at the beginning and end of March. For the month of March, how many pounds of raw material A is Walman planning to purchase?

a. 126,000
b. 132,000
c. 136,000
d. 142,000

14. In preparing its cash budget for July 1983, Reed Company made the following projections:

Sales	$1,500,000
Gross profit (based on sales)	25%
Decrease in inventories	$ 70,000
Decrease in accounts payable for inventories	$ 120,000

For July 1983 what were the estimated cash disbursements for inventories?

a. $ 935,000
b. $1,050,000
c. $1,055,000
d. $1,175,000

15. Eriksen Company has budgeted its activity for October 1982 based on the following information:

- Sales are budgeted at $300,000. All sales are credit sales and a provision for doubtful accounts is made monthly at the rate of 3% of sales.
- Merchandise inventory was $70,000 at September 30, 1982, and an increase of $10,000 is planned for the month.
- All merchandise is marked up to sell at invoice cost plus 50%.
- Estimated cash disbursements for selling and administrative expenses for the month are $40,000.
- Depreciation for the month is projected at $5,000.

Eriksen is projecting operating income for October 1982 in the amount of

a. $96,000
b. $56,000
c. $55,000
d. $46,000

16. In preparing its budget for July 1982, Robinson Company has the following accounts receivable information available:

Accounts receivable at June 30, 1982	$350,000
Estimated credit sales for July	400,000
Estimated collections in July for credit sales in July and prior months	320,000
Estimated write-offs in July for uncollectible credit sales	16,000
Estimated provision for doubtful accounts for credit sales in July	12,000

What is the projected balance of accounts receivable at July 31, 1982?

a. $402,000
b. $414,000
c. $426,000
d. $430,000

17. Sussex Company has budgeted its operations for February 1981. No change in inventory level during the month is planned. Selected data from estimated amounts are as follows:

Net loss	$100,000
Increase in accounts payable	40,000
Depreciation expense	35,000
Decrease in gross amount of trade accounts receivable	60,000
Purchase of office equipment on 45-day credit terms	15,000
Provision for estimated warranty liability	10,000

How much change in cash position is expected for February?

a. $15,000 decrease.
b. $25,000 decrease.
c. $30,000 increase.
d. $45,000 increase.

18. Mapes Corporation has estimated its activity for January 1981. Selected data from these estimated amounts are as follows:

- Sales $1,400,000
- Gross profit (based on sales) 30%
- Increase in trade accounts receivable during month $ 40,000
- Change in accounts payable during month $ 0
- Increase in inventory during month $ 20,000
- Variable selling, general and administrative expenses (S, G & A) include a charge for uncollectible accounts of 1% of sales.
- Total S, G & A is $142,000 per month plus 15% of sales.
- Depreciation expense of $80,000 per month is included in fixed S, G & A.

What are the estimated cash disbursements for January 1981?

a. $1,238,000
b. $1,252,000
c. $1,258,000
d. $1,272,000

19. Reid Company is developing a forecast of March 1980 cash receipts from credit sales. Credit sales for March 1980 are estimated to be $320,000. The accounts receivable balance at February 29, 1980, is $300,000; one-quarter of the balance represents January credit sales and the remainder is from February sales. All accounts receivable from months prior to January of 1980 have been collected or written off. Reid's history of accounts receivable collections is as follows:

In the month of sale	20%
In the first month after month of sale	50%
In the second month after month of sale	25%
Written off as uncollectible at the end of the second month after month of sale	5%

Based on the above information, Reid is forecasting March 1980 cash receipts from credit sales of

a. $176,500
b. $195,250
c. $253,769
d. $267,125

20. A flexible budget is

a. Not appropriate when costs and expenses are affected by fluctuations in volume limits.
b. Appropriate for any relevant level of activity.
c. Appropriate for control of factory overhead but **not** for control of direct materials and direct labor.
d. Appropriate for control of direct materials and direct labor but **not** for control of factory overhead.

21. Dean Company is preparing a flexible budget for 1982 and the following maximum capacity estimates for department M are available:

	At maximum capacity
Direct-labor hours	60,000
Variable factory overhead	$150,000
Fixed factory overhead	$240,000

Assume that Dean's normal capacity is 80% of maximum capacity. What would be the total factory overhead rate, based on direct-labor hours, in a flexible budget at normal capacity?

a. $6.00
b. $6.50
c. $7.50
d. $8.13

22. When using a flexible budget, what will occur to fixed costs (on a per unit basis) as production increases within the relevant range?

a. Fixed costs are **not** considered in flexible budgeting.
b. Fixed costs per unit will decrease.
c. Fixed costs per unit will increase.
d. Fixed costs per unit will remain unchanged.

23. Gordon Company began its operations on January 1, 1982, and produces a single product that sells for $10 per unit. Gordon uses an actual (historical) cost system. In 1982, 100,000 units were produced and 80,000 units were sold. There was no work-in-process inventory at December 31, 1982.

Manufacturing costs and selling and administrative expenses for 1982 were as follows:

	Fixed costs	*Variable costs*
Raw materials	—	$2.00 per unit produced
Direct labor	—	1.25 per unit produced
Factory overhead	$120,000	.75 per unit produced
Selling and administrative	70,000	1.00 per unit sold

What would be Gordon's operating income for 1982 under the variable (direct) costing method?

a. $114,000
b. $210,000
c. $234,000
d. $330,000

24. Operating income using direct costing as compared to absorption costing would be higher

a. When the quantity of beginning inventory equals the quantity of ending inventory.
b. When the quantity of beginning inventory is more than the quantity of ending inventory.
c. When the quantity of beginning inventory is less than the quantity of ending inventory.
d. Under **no** circumstances.

Items 25 and 26 are based on the following information:

Selected information concerning the operations of Kern Company for the year ended December 31, 1981, is available as follows:

Units produced	10,000
Units sold	9,000
Direct materials used	$40,000
Direct labor incurred	$20,000
Fixed factory overhead	$25,000
Variable factory overhead	$12,000
Fixed selling and administrative expenses	$30,000
Variable selling and administrative expenses	$ 4,500
Finished goods inventory, January 1, 1981	None

There were no work-in-process inventories at the beginning and end of 1981.

25. What would be Kern's finished goods inventory cost at December 31, 1981, under the variable (direct) costing method?

a. $7,200
b. $7,650
c. $8,000
d. $9,700

26. Which costing method, absorption or variable costing, would show a higher operating income for 1981 and by what amount?

	Costing method	*Amount*
a.	Absorption costing	$2,500
b.	Variable costing	$2,500
c.	Absorption costing	$5,500
d.	Variable costing	$5,500

27. A basic tenet of direct costing is that period costs should be currently expensed. What is the basic rationale behind this procedure?

a. Period costs are uncontrollable and should not be charged to a specific product.
b. Period costs are generally immaterial in amount and the cost of assigning the amounts to specific products would outweigh the benefits.

c. Allocation of period costs is arbitrary at best and could lead to erroneous decisions by management.
d. Period costs will occur whether or not production occurs and so it is improper to allocate these costs to production and defer a current cost of doing business.

28. The contribution margin decreases when sales volume remains the same and
a. Fixed costs increase.
b. Fixed costs decrease.
c. Variable cost per unit increases.
d. Variable cost per unit decreases.

29. Purvis Company manufactures a product that has a variable cost of $50 per unit. Fixed costs total $1,000,000, allocated on the basis of the number of units produced. Selling price is computed by adding a 10% markup to full cost. How much should the selling price be per unit for 100,000 units?
a. $55
b. $60
c. $61
d. $66

30. Controllable costs for responsibility accounting purposes are those costs that are directly influenced by
a. A given manager within a given period of time.
b. A change in activity.
c. Production volume.
d. Sales volume.

Items 31 and 32 are based on the following information:

Ajax Division of Carlyle Corporation produces electric motors, 20% of which are sold to Bradley Division of Carlyle and the remainder to outside customers. Carlyle treats its divisions as profit centers and allows division managers to choose their sources of sale and supply. Corporate policy requires that all interdivisional sales and purchases be recorded at variable cost as a transfer price. Ajax Division's estimated sales and standard cost data for the year ending December 31, 1982, based on the full capacity of 100,000 units, are as follows:

	Bradley	*Outsiders*
Sales	$ 900,000	$ 8,000,000
Variable costs	(900,000)	(3,600,000)
Fixed costs	(300,000)	(1,200,000)
Gross margin	$(300,000)	$ 3,200,000
Unit sales	20,000	80,000

Ajax has an opportunity to sell the above 20,000 units to an outside customer at a price of $75 per unit during 1982 on a continuing basis. Bradley can purchase its requirements from an outside supplier at a price of $85 per unit.

31. Assuming that Ajax Division desires to maximize its gross margin, should Ajax take on the new customer and drop its sales to Bradley for 1982, and why?
a. No, because the gross margin of the corporation as a whole would decrease by $200,000.
b. Yes, because Ajax Division's gross margin would increase by $300,000.
c. Yes, because Ajax Division's gross margin would increase by $600,000.
d. No, because Bradley Division's gross margin would decrease by $800,000.

32. Assume, instead, that Carlyle permits the division managers to negotiate the transfer price for 1982. The managers agreed on a tentative transfer price of $75 per unit, to be reduced based on an equal sharing of the additional gross margin to Ajax resulting from the sale to Bradley of 20,000 motors at $75 per unit. The actual transfer price for 1982 would be
a. $52.50
b. $55.00
c. $60.00
d. $67.50

Items 33 and 34 are based on the following data:

The following selected data pertain to the belt division of Allen Corp. for 1982:

Sales	$2,000,000
Average invested capital	500,000
Operating income	300,000
Capital turnover	4.0
Imputed interest rate	18%

33. How much is the return on investment?
a. 60%
b. 33%
c. 18%
d. 15%

34. How much is the residual income?
a. $0
b. $200,000
c. $210,000
d. $246,000

35. A company's return on investment (ROI) would generally increase when
   a. Assets increase.
   b. Selling prices decrease.
   c. Costs decrease.
   d. Costs increase.

May 1984 Questions

36. A flexible budget is appropriate for a

	Direct-labor budget	*Marketing budget*
a.	No	No
b.	No	Yes
c.	Yes	No
d.	Yes	Yes

37. If an income statement is prepared as an internal report, under which of the following methods would the term gross profit most likely appear?
   a. Both absorption costing and direct (variable) costing.
   b. Absorption costing but **not** direct (variable) costing.
   c. Direct (variable) costing but **not** absorption costing.
   d. Neither direct (variable) costing nor absorption costing.

38. The contribution margin ratio always increases when the
   a. Breakeven point increases.
   b. Breakeven point decreases.
   c. Variable costs as a percentage of net sales decrease.
   d. Variable costs as a percentage of net sales increase.

39. In using cost-volume-profit analysis to calculate the expected sales level expressed in units, a predicted operating loss would be
   a. Added to fixed costs in the numerator.
   b. Added to fixed costs in the denominator.
   c. Subtracted from fixed costs in the numerator.
   d. Subtracted from fixed costs in the denominator.

Problems

Problem 1 Breakeven Analysis (574,T7)

(25 to 30 minutes)

Cost-volume-earnings analysis (breakeven analysis) is used to determine and express the interrelationships of different volumes of activity (sales), costs, sales prices, and sales mix to earnings. More specifically, the analysis is concerned with what will be the effect on earnings of changes in sales volume, sales prices, sales mix, and costs.

Required:

a. Certain terms are fundamental to cost-volume-earnings analysis. Explain the meaning of each of the following terms:

1. Fixed costs.
2. Variable costs.
3. Relevant range.
4. Breakeven point.
5. Margin of safety.
6. Sales mix.

b. Several assumptions are implicit in cost-volume-earnings analysis. What are these assumptions?

c. In a recent period Zero Company had the following experience:

	Fixed	*Variable*	
Sales (10,000 units @ $200)			$2,000,000
Costs:			
Direct material	$ —	$ 200,000	
Direct labor	—	400,000	
Factory overhead	160,000	600,000	
Administrative expenses	180,000	80,000	
Other expenses	200,000	120,000	
Total costs	$540,000	$1,400,000	$1,940,000
Net income			$ 60,000

Each item below is independent.

1. Calculate the breakeven point for Zero in terms of units and sales dollars. Show your calculations.
2. What sales volume would be required to generate a net income of $96,000? Show your calculations.
3. What is the breakeven point if management makes a decision which increases fixed costs by $18,000? Show your calculations.

Problem 2 Direct Costing Concepts (1179,T6a)

(7 to 10 minutes)

Part a. Although direct costing is not a current generally accepted method of costing inventory for external reporting, it is useful for internal pruposes.

Required:

1. Describe the difference between direct costing and the current generally accepted method of costing inventory for external reporting.
2. Describe how a direct costing structure facilitates calculation of the contribution margin and the breakeven point.

Problem 3 Direct vs. Absorption Costing Theory (1182,T4a)

(10 to 15 minutes)

Part a. Grisp Company, a manufacturer with heavy investments in property, plant, and equipment, is presently using absorption costing for both its external and internal reporting. The management of Grisp Company is considering using the direct costing method for internal reporting only.

Required:

1. What would be the rationale for using the direct costing method for internal reporting?
2. Assuming that the quantity of ending inventory is higher than the quantity of beginning inventory, would operating income using direct costing be different from operating income using absorption costing? If so, specify if it would be higher or lower. Discuss the rationale for your answer.

Problem 4 Direct and Absorption Costing (576,Q5b)

(15 to 20 minutes)

Part b. Management of the Bicent Company uses the following unit costs for the one product it manufactures:

Direct material (all variable)	$30.00
Direct labor (all variable)	19.00
Manufacturing overhead:	
Variable cost	6.00
Fixed cost (based on 10,000 units per month)	5.00
Selling, general and administrative:	
Variable cost	4.00
Fixed cost (based on 10,000 units per month)	2.80

The projected selling price is $80 per unit. The fixed costs remain fixed within the relevant range of 4,000 to 16,000 units of production.

Management has also projected the following data for the month of June 1976:

	Units
Beginning inventory	2,000
Production	9,000
Available	11,000
Sales	7,500
Ending inventory	3,500

Required:

Prepare projected income statements for June 1976 for management purposes under each of the following product-costing methods:

1. Absorption costing with all variances charged to cost of goods sold each month.
2. Direct (variable) costing.

Supporting schedules calculating inventoriable production costs per unit should be presented in good form. Ignore income taxes.

Problem 5 Breakeven Computations (583,Q4)

(45 to 55 minutes)

Melford Hospital operates a general hospital, but rents space and beds to separately owned entities rendering specialized services such as pediatrics and psychiatric. Melford charges each separate entity for common services such as patients' meals and laundry, and for administrative services such as billings and collections. Space and bed rentals are fixed charges for the year, based on bed capacity rented to each entity.

Melford charged the following costs to pediatrics for the year ended June 30, 1982:

	Patient days (variable)	*Bed capacity (fixed)*
Dietary	$ 600,000	—
Janitorial	—	$ 70,000
Laundry	300,000	—
Laboratory	450,000	—
Pharmacy	350,000	—
Repairs and maintenance	—	30,000
General and administrative	—	1,300,000
Rent	—	1,500,000
Billings and collections	300,000	—
Totals	$2,000,000	$2,900,000

During the year ended June 30, 1982, pediatrics charged each patient an average of $300 per day, had a capacity of 60 beds, and had revenue of $6,000,000 for 365 days.

In addition, pediatrics directly employed the following personnel:

	Annual salaries
Supervising nurses	$25,000
Nurses	20,000
Aides	9,000

Melford has the following minimum departmental personnel requirements based on total annual patient days:

Annual patient days	*Aides*	*Nurses*	*Supervising nurses*
Up to 21,900	20	10	4
21,901 to 26,000	26	13	4
26,001 to 29,200	30	15	4

These staffing levels represent full-time equivalents. Pediatrics always employs only the minimum number of required full-time equivalent personnel. Salaries of supervising nurses, nurses, and aides are therefore fixed within ranges of annual patient days.

Pediatrics operated at 100% capacity on 90 days during the year ended June 30, 1982. It is estimated that during these 90 days the demand exceeded 20 patients more than capacity. Melford has an additional 20 beds available for rent for the year ending June 30, 1983. Such additional rental would increase pediatrics' fixed charges based on bed capacity.

Required:

a. Calculate the minimum number of patient days required for pediatrics to break even for the year ending June 30, 1983, if the additional 20 beds are not rented. Patient demand is unknown, but assume that revenue per patient day, cost per patient day, cost per bed, and salary rates will remain the same as for the year ended June 30, 1982.

b. Assume that patient demand, revenue per patient day, cost per patient day, cost per bed, and salary rates for the year ending June 30, 1983, remain the same as for the year ended June 30, 1982. Prepare a schedule of increase in revenue and increase in costs for the year ending June 30, 1983, in order to determine the net increase or decrease in earnings from the additional 20 beds if pediatrics rents this extra capacity from Melford.

Problem 6 Breakeven Theory (583,T4b)

(7 to 10 minutes)

Part b. Daly Company has determined the number of units of Product Y that Daly would have to sell in order to break even. However, Daly would like to attain a 20 percent profit on sales of Product Y.

Required:

1. Explain how breakeven analysis can be used to determine the number of units of Product Y that Daly would have to sell to attain a 20 percent profit on sales.

2. If variable cost per unit increases as a percentage of the sales price, how would that affect the number of units of Product Y that Daly would have to sell in order to break even and why?

3. Identify the limitations of breakeven analysis in managerial decision making.

Problem 7 Budgeted Cash Collections and Disbursements (582,Q5b)

(10 to 15 minutes)

Part b. The following information was available from Montero Corporation's books:

1982	*Purchases*	*Sales*
Jan.	$42,000	$72,000
Feb.	48,000	66,000
Mar.	36,000	60,000
Apr.	54,000	78,000

Collections from customers are normally 70% in the month of sale, 20% in the month following the sale, and 9% in the second month following the sale. The balance is expected to be uncollectible. Montero takes full advantage of the 2% discount allowed on purchases paid for by the tenth of the following month. Purchases for May are budgeted at $60,000, while sales for May are forecasted at $66,000. Cash disbursements for expenses are expected to be $14,400 for the month of May. Montero's cash balance at May 1 was $22,000.

Required:

Prepare the following schedules:

1. Expected cash collections during May.
2. Expected cash disbursements during May.
3. Expected cash balance at May 31.

Multiple Choice Answers

1.	a	9.	d	17.	d	25.	a	33.	a
2.	c	10.	c	18.	c	26.	a	34.	c
3.	a	11.	b	19.	d	27.	d	35.	c
4.	c	12.	a	20.	b	28.	c	36.	d
5.	b	13.	d	21.	c	29.	d	37.	b
6.	d	14.	d	22.	b	30.	a	38.	c
7.	b	15.	d	23.	b	31.	c	39.	c
8.	d	16.	b	24.	b	32.	c		

Multiple Choice Answer Explanations

A. High-Low Method

1. (1181,P2,25) (a) The requirement is to estimate the variable cost of steam using the high-low points method of analysis. The high-low method separates a mixed cost into its variable and fixed components. The initial step in the high-low method utilizes a formula to find the variable rate. The formula used in developing the variable rate is:

$$\frac{\text{Cost at high point} - \text{Cost at low point}}{\text{High activity point} - \text{Low activity point}} = \text{Variable rate}$$

In this problem, the cost of steam is given at several levels of the designated activity, direct labor hours (DLH). Substituting into the formula gives the variable cost of steam per direct labor hour:

$$\frac{\$19,800 - \$13,400}{3650 \text{ DLH} - 2050 \text{ DLH}} = \$4.00/\text{DLH}$$

B. Cost-Volume-Profit (CVP) Analysis

2. (1182,P2,39) (c) The requirement is the budgeted 1982 operating income. In the preliminary forecast, selling price was $10, variable expense $6 ($600,000 ÷ 100,000 units), fixed expense $300,000, and unit sales 100,000. However, changes are to be incorporated into budget which will alter some of these amounts. Selling price is to be increased by 15% to $11.50 ($10 x 115%). Unit sales volume will increase by 10% to 110,000 units (100,000 x 110%). Fixed costs will increase from $300,000 to $400,000 due to an additional $100,000 spent on advertising. After computing these changes, an income statement can be prepared.

Sales (110,000 x $11.50)	$1,265,000
Variable expenses (110,000 x $6)	(660,000)
Contribution margin	605,000
Fixed expenses	(400,000)
Net income	$205,000

3. (1181,P2,34) (a) The requirement is to calculate the maximum amount that the company can pay for advertising and obtain an operating profit of $200,000. Since advertising is assumed to be a fixed cost, the **first** step is to determine the maximum amount of fixed cost which can be incurred including advertising. Given that (sales = variable cost + fixed cost + profit), then (sales – variable cost – profit = fixed cost). With the advertising, sales will increase 20%, or 120% (150,000 units x $25/unit). If sales increase, the increase in variable costs will be a proportional 20%, or 120% (150,000 units x $15/unit). Given operating profit of $200,000, fixed cost will be:

Sales	$4,500,000	[1.20 (150,000 x $25)]
– Variable cost	(2,700,000)	[1.20 (150,000 x $15)]
– Profit	(200,000)	(given)
Fixed cost	$1,600,000	

Once the fixed cost is determined, the **second** step is to determine the increase in fixed cost:

Fixed cost with advertising	$1,600,000	(above)
Current fixed cost	(1,500,000)	($800,000 + $700,000)
Advertising (increase in fixed cost)	$ 100,000	

4. (1181,P2,35) (c) The requirement is the amount of sales dollars at the breakeven point. The solutions approach is to utilize a formula to find the breakeven point:

Sales = Fixed costs + Variable costs + Expected profit

$$\text{Sales} = \frac{\$6,000,000}{\$6,000,000} = 100\% = 1.00$$

$$\text{Variable costs} = \frac{\$3,900,000}{\$6,000,000} = 65\% = .65$$

Profit = Zero at breakeven

$$1.00X = \$1,400,000 + .65X + 0$$

Solving the equation:

$$1.00X - .65X = 1,400,000$$
$$.35X = 1,400,000$$
$$X = \$4,000,000 \text{ in sales dollars}$$

5. (581,P2,35) (b) The requirement is to compute variable costs. The solutions approach is to analyze the income statement equation : Sales – Variable Costs – Fixed Costs = Income. Rearranging terms gives Variable Costs = Sales – Fixed Costs – Income. Therefore, variable costs are ($100,000 x $12) – $280,000 – $200,000 = $720,000.

6. (579,P2,26) (d) The requirement is the selling price per unit for 200,000 units to realize a profit of $100,000. The solutions approach is to set up a breakeven formula in which 200,000 units of Product B times B (selling price of each B) equals $400,000 of fixed costs plus variable costs of 60% of the selling price plus $100,000 of profits. Solving the equation, one finds B (selling price of Product B) to be $6.25.

$$\begin{aligned} \text{Sales} &= \text{FC} + \text{VC} + \text{Desired NI} \\ 200{,}000\,B &= \$400{,}000 + .60\,(200{,}000\,B) + \$100{,}000 \\ 200{,}000\,B &= \$500{,}000 + 120{,}000\,B \\ 80{,}000\,B &= \$500{,}000 \\ B &= \$6.25 \end{aligned}$$

7. (1176,P2,21) (b) At the breakeven point of 400 units, there is $600 of total cost ($400 variables and $200 fixed) which equal sales. If 400 units create sales of $600, the unit selling price is $1.50. The variable cost per unit is $1.00 ($400 divided by 400). Thus, the contribution margin per unit is $.50 ($1.50 minus $1.00).

8. (1183,Q1,12) (d) The requirement is the **increase** in sales in order to achieve an operating income of 10% of sales (expressed as .10S below). The solutions approach is to use the standard breakeven formula and solve for S. Variable costs are $150,000 at a sales level of $200,000; therefore, variable costs are .75S ($150,000/$200,000).

$$\begin{aligned} S &= VC + FC + \text{Expected profit} \\ S &= .75S + \$60{,}000 + .10S \\ .15S &= \$60{,}000 \\ S &= \$400{,}000 \end{aligned}$$

Remember that the requirement was the **increase** in sales to achieve a profit of 10% of sales. The correct answer is $200,000 ($400,000 total sales needed less $200,000 present sales level).

9. (1183,T1,45) (d) The requirement is to determine how projected profit and the contribution margin ratio are used in calculating sales necessary to realize a projected profit. The solutions approach is to recall the formula to compute the required sales.

$$\text{Required sales} = \frac{\text{Fixed costs} + \text{Projected profit}}{\text{Contribution margin ratio}}$$

Answer (d) is correct since the projected profit is included in the numerator with fixed costs.

10. (580,T1,47) (c) When fixed costs increase, the breakeven point will also increase because more units must be sold in order to cover the fixed costs. Contribution margin is equal to sales less variable costs. Therefore, an increase in fixed costs will have no effect on the contribution margin.

C. Breakeven: Multi-Product Firm

11. (1180,P2,29) (b) The requirement is how many units of product X (one of three products) Thomas would sell at the breakeven point. The solutions approach is first to find the number of composite units to breakeven; a composite unit consists of the number of units of each of the three products in the mix. Since Thomas sells 3 units of X for each unit of Z and 2 units of Y for each unit of X they are selling 6 units of Y for each unit of Z; therefore a composite unit consists of 3X, 6Y, and 1Z. The total contribution margin for 1 composite unit is

$$\begin{aligned} X\,(3)\,(\$1.00) &= \$\ 3 \\ Y\,(6)\,(\$1.50) &= \$\ 9 \\ Z\,(1)\,(\$3.00) &= \$\ \underline{3} \\ &\quad \underline{\underline{\$15}} \end{aligned}$$

The breakeven point in terms of units of the product mix group is:

$$\$600{,}000 \div \$15 = 40{,}000 \text{ composite units}$$

Since there are three units of X in each composite unit, (40,000)(3) or 120,000 units of X are sold at breakeven.

12. (1179,P2,27) (a) The requirement is the amount of total fixed costs given the desired profit level, sales value, and variable costs. The solutions approach is to set up a formula equating profit to sales value minus variable costs minus fixed costs. As illustrated below, the profit of $160,000 is to be equal to $400,000 (100,000 units @ $4) from sales of Alt, less $280,000 for variable costs of Alt (variable costs are 70% of sales), plus $600,000 (200,000 units @ $3) from sales of Tude, less $480,000 of variable costs of Tude (variable costs are 80% of sales), minus the unknown fixed costs. Solving for fixed costs equals $80,000.

$$\begin{aligned} \$160{,}000 &= \$400{,}000 - \$280{,}000 + \\ &\quad \$600{,}000 - \$480{,}000 - FC \\ FC &= \$80{,}000 \end{aligned}$$

E. Budgeting

13. (1183,P3,41) (d) The requirement is the number of pounds of raw material A that Walman is planning to purchase. The first step is to prepare a production budget for product Y.

Sales	42,000
Desired ending inventory	24,000
Total units needed	66,000
Beginning inventory	(22,000)
Units of Y to be produced	44,000

Next, a purchases budget for raw material A should be prepared.

Production needs (44,000 x 3)	132,000
Desired ending inventory	110,000
Total pounds needed	242,000
Beginning inventory	(100,000)
Pounds of A to be purchased	142,000

Note that the production needs for material A are equal to the units of Y to be produced, multiplied by 3 (number of pounds of A per unit of Y).

14. (1183,P3,55) (d) The requirement is to determine cash disbursements for inventories for July. The solutions approach is to use T-accounts to arrive at cash disbursements for the month. Cash disbursements for inventory are found on the debit side of the accounts payable account. This debit is found using T-accounts for inventory and accounts payable.

Inventory

	Debit	Credit	
(3) Purchases of inventory	$1,055	$1,125	(1) Cost of goods sold
(2) Decrease	$ 70		

Accounts Payable

	Debit	Credit	
(5) Cash disbursements	X	$1,055	(3) Purchases of inventory
		$ 120	(4) Decrease

Begin by finding the credit to cost of goods sold (1). If gross profit is 25% of sales, then cost of goods sold must be 75%, or (.75)($1,500,000) = $1,125,000. If the inventory account has decreased by $70,000 (2), purchases of inventory on accounts must have been $1,125,000 – $70,000, or $1,055,000 (3), reflected as a debit to inventory and a credit to accounts payable. Finally, if the accounts payable account was decreased by $120,000 (4), payments on account (X) must be $1,055,000 + $120,000, or $1,175,000 (5).

15. (1182,P2,30) (d) The requirement is the budgeted operating income for October 1982. The solutions approach is to set up an income statement based on the information given.

Sales	$300,000
Cost of goods sold ($300,000 ÷ 150%)	(200,000)
Gross margin	100,000
Selling and admin. expenses	(40,000)
Depreciation expense	(5,000)
Bad debt expense ($300,000 x 3%)	(9,000)
Budgeted operating income	$ 46,000

Because inventory is sold at cost plus 50%, the following equation can be used to compute cost of goods sold

100% CGS + (50% x CGS) = Sales

100% CGS + (50% x CGS) = $300,000

150% x CGS = $300,000

CGS = $300,000 ÷ 150% = $200,000

Note that the budgeted increase in inventory, while affecting the production budget, would not affect the above CGS computation.

16. (1182,P2,38) (b) The requirement is the projected balance of accounts receivable at 7/31/82. The solutions approach is to enter the appropriate estimated amounts in an accounts receivable T-account.

Accounts Receivable

	Debit	Credit	
6/30/82	$350,000		
Credit sales	400,000	$320,000	Collections
		16,000	Write-offs
7/31/82 (estimated)	$414,000		

Note that the estimated provision for doubtful accounts for July credit sales ($12,000) is not entered in the above T-account. The entry would be to debit bad debt expense and credit the allowance for doubtful accounts. While this amount would affect "net accounts receivable" (accounts receivable – allowance for doubtful accounts), it does not affect "gross accounts receivable".

17. (1181,P2,28) (d) The requirement is to determine the change in cash position expected for February. One approach to the solution is to arrange the data in the format used for a cash from operations section of a statement of changes in financial position prepared on a cash basis. This approach converts accrual net income (loss) to cash flow as required in this problem.

Net loss		($100,000)
Add: Expenses not requiring cash:		
Depreciation	$35,000	
Warranty expense	10,000	45,000
Changes in receivables and payables:		
Decrease in A/R	$60,000	
Increase in A/P	40,000	100,000
Change in cash position from operations		$ 45,000

The purchase of office equipment will not affect cash during February.

18. (581,P2,34) (c) The requirement is to compute the estimated cash disbursements for January 1981. The solutions approach is to convert the estimated expenses from the accrual basis to the cash basis. The cash disbursements for purchases is computed as follows

CGS [$1,400,000 x (1.00 – .30)] =	$ 980,000
+ Increase in inventory	20,000
Cash disbursements for purchases	$1,000,000

No adjustment is necessary for accounts payable; there was no change in the beginning and ending balance. The cash disbursements for selling and general and administrative expenses can be computed as follows

Total S, G & A $142,000 + (.15 x $1,400,000) =	$ 352,000
– Bad debts exp. $1,400,000 x .01 =	(14,000)
– Depreciation expense	(80,000)
Cash disbursements for expenses	$ 258,000

The total cash disbursements for Mapes Corporation in January are $1,000,000 + $258,000 = $1,258,000. Note that Bad Debts Expense and Depreciation Expense are not cash outflows and must be subtracted from total S, G & A expenses to arrive at cash disbursements.

19. (1180,P2,23) (d) The requirement is Reid's forecast of March 1980 cash receipts from credit sales; credit sales for March will be $320,000; A/R at the end of February is $300,000, broken down as follows:

From January sales:	(¼)($300,000)	= $ 75,000
From February sales:	(¾)($300,000)	= $225,000

This problem must be read carefully; a key point is that the collection percentages given are *based on sales,* not on the A/R balance. The first step of the solutions approach is to compute January and February credit sales. January sales remaining in A/R are $75,000, but 70% of January sales have already been collected; therefore

(30%)(January sales)	= $ 75,000
January sales	= $250,000

February sales remaining in A/R are $225,000, but 20% of February sales have already been collected; therefore

(80%)(February sales)	= $225,000
February sales	= $281,250

Once the sales figures have been computed, estimated March collections can be obtained by applying the appropriate collection percentages:

Collections from	*Sales*	*%*	*Cash to be collected*
January sales	$250,000	25%	$ 62,500
February sales	$281,250	50%	$140,625
March sales	$320,000	20%	$ 64,000
			$267,125

F. Flexible Budgets

20. (583,T1,49) (b) The requirement is to determine when usage of a flexible budget is appropriate. A flexible budget is a budget adjusted for changes in volume. For cost control purposes, the flexible budget is used to analyze actual results by comparing actual results with the budget adjusted for the level of activity achieved [answer (b)]. Answer (a) is incorrect because the flexible budget is designed to control costs and expenses when volume fluctuates. Answers (c) and (d) are incorrect because a flexible budget is appropriate to use for controlling direct materials, direct labor, and factory overhead, since it is adjusted for fluctuations in actual output.

21. (1182,P2,21) (c) The requirement is the total factory overhead rate, based on direct-labor hours, in a flexible budget at normal capacity. The variable portion of the factory overhead rate can be computed by dividing variable factory overhead (at maximum capacity) by direct-labor hours (at maximum capacity).

$$\$150{,}000 \div 60{,}000 = \underline{\underline{\$2.50}}$$

Note that the variable overhead rate is constant over the relevant range of activity. Since **total** fixed overhead is constant over the relevant range, the budgeted fixed overhead is divided by direct-labor hours at 80% of maximum capacity, or 48,000 hours (60,000 x 80%).

$240,000 ÷ 48,000 = $5.00

The total factory overhead rate is $2.50 plus $5.00, or $7.50 per direct-labor hour.

22. (1182,T1,46) (b) The requirement is the effect on fixed costs per unit as production increases within the relevant range. Fixed costs **in total** are constant within the relevant range. Thus, as the production level increases the fixed costs on a per unit basis will decrease. Therefore, answers (c) and (d) are incorrect. Answer (a) is incorrect because a flexible budget should provide for both variable and fixed costs.

G. Direct (Variable) and Absorption (Full) Costing

23. (583,P2,33) (b) The requirement is Gordon's operating income for 1982 under the variable (direct) costing method. Under direct costing, fixed manufacturing costs are treated as period costs (expensed in full) rather than as product costs. Only variable manufacturing costs are inventoriable. Direct costing income for 1982 is $210,000.

Sales (80,000 x $10)	$800,000
Variable expenses (80,000 x $5)	(400,000)
Contribution margin	400,000
Fixed expenses ($120,000 + $70,000)	(190,000)
Operating income	$210,000

The variable expense per unit ($5) is obtained by adding together the variable costs per unit as given ($2 + $1.25 + $.75 + $1).

24. (583,T1,47) (b) Under direct costing, all fixed costs are expensed as incurred. Under absorption costing, fixed manufacturing costs attach to the product and become a part of inventory. If beginning inventory exceeds ending inventory, one must conclude that some of the units produced in a prior period were sold in the current period. As a result, absorption costing expenses not only the current period's fixed manufacturing costs, but also charges to expense some of the prior period's fixed manufacturing costs related to beginning inventory. Therefore, answer (b) is correct. Answer (a) will result in income being equal under both methods. Answer (c) will result in absorption income being higher. Answer (d) is incorrect because, per the discussion above, the operating incomes can differ.

25. (1182,P2,24) (a) The requirement is Kern's finished goods inventory at 12/31/81 under variable (direct) costing. Note that beginning and ending WIP, and beginning finished goods, are all zero. Under direct costing, only variable manufacturing costs are inventoriable. Variable manufacturing costs for 1981 total $72,000.

Direct materials	$40,000
Direct labor	20,000
Variable overhead	12,000
	$72,000

The direct costing unit cost is $72,000 divided by 10,000 units produced, or $7.20. Of the 10,000 units produced, 9,000 were sold, leaving 1,000 units in ending finished goods inventory at an assigned cost of $7,200 (1,000 x $7.20).

26. (1182,P2,25) (a) The requirement is which costing method (absorption/variable) would show a higher 1981 operating income, and by what amount. Recall that the only difference in these two costing methods is the treatment of fixed overhead. Since there was no beginning finished goods inventory, the treatment of 1981 fixed overhead is the only difference between the two methods. Under variable costing, the entire $25,000 fixed overhead is expensed as a period cost. Under absorption costing, a portion of the fixed overhead is assigned to ending finished goods inventory.

$25,000 ÷ 10,000 units = $2.50 per unit;
1,000 x $2.50 = $2,500

Under absorption costing, therefore, $2,500 of the fixed overhead is deferred while $22,500 is expensed as part of cost of goods sold. Absorption costing operating income is $2,500 higher than variable costing operating income.

27. (1178,T1,39) (d) The requirement is the best argument for expensing period costs per direct costing. The rationale is that period costs are incurred whether or not production occurs; the act of producing does not incur period costs. Thus period costs should not be allocated to the goods produced. Answer (a) is incorrect because period costs may be controllable, i.e., the foreman may be fired. Answer (b) is incorrect because period costs may be quite substantial, especially when capital outlays and resulting depreciation are high. Answer (c) is incorrect because allocation of period costs can be done systematically, i.e., not arbitrarily.

H. Contribution Margin

28. (1183,T1,46) (c) An increase in variable cost per unit [answer (c)] will cause contribution margin to decrease. Contribution margin is computed as follows:

Sales – Variable costs = Contribution margin

The question states that sales volume remains constant which means that any effect on contribution margin is due to a change in selling price per unit or variable cost per unit. Answers (a) and (b) are incorrect because fixed costs are not considered when calculating contribution margin. Answer (d) is incorrect because a decrease in the variable cost per unit will cause contribution margin to increase.

I. Product Pricing

29. (1182,Q2,33) (d) The requirement is to determine selling price per unit for 100,000 units. The solutions approach is to derive an equation from the information given and fill in the given dollar amounts:

$$\text{Selling price per unit} = (1 + 10\%\ \text{markup})\left(\text{Fixed costs per unit} + \text{Variable costs per unit}\right)$$

$$\text{Selling price per unit} = (1.10)[(\$1{,}000{,}000/100{,}000\ \text{units}) + \$50]$$

$$\text{Selling price per unit} = \$66$$

J. Responsibility Accounting

30. (1181,T1,51) (a) Controllable costs are defined as those costs which can be directly influenced by a given manager within a given time span.

K. Transfer Pricing

31. (1183,P3,57) (c) The requirement is to determine if Ajax should take on a new customer and why. As a profit center, Ajax will make the decision independent of the effects on the corporation as a whole. If Ajax sells to the new customer, its revenues will increase to $1,500,000 ($75 x 20,000), but its costs will remain the same at $1,200,000 ($900,000 + $300,000). This results in a positive gross margin of $300,000 ($1,500,000 – $1,200,000). The new gross margin is $600,000 [$300,000 – ⟨$300,000⟩] greater than the original gross margin. The shortcut (incremental) approach is to multiply 20,000 units times the $30 increase ($75 – $45) in Ajax's unit selling (transfer) price.

32. (1183,P3,58) (c) The requirement is to compute the transfer price per unit if the tentative transfer price of $75 is reduced by an equal sharing of the **additional** gross margin generated. The additional gross margin is equal to the difference between the gross margin computed using the tentative transfer (selling) price of $75, and the old gross margin of ⟨$300,000⟩, or $600,000 as computed in the previous question. The additional gross margin of $600,000 is split equally to result in a $300,000 reduction in total price. The total transfer price (revenue) of $1,200,000 ($1,500,000 – $300,000) divided by the 20,000 units yields a unit transfer price of $60. The shortcut (incremental) approach is to subtract one-half of the $30 [new unit selling price ($75) less original unit selling price ($45)] increase in revenue per unit from the new selling price ($75) to arrive at $60 per unit [$75 – ($30/2) = $60].

L. Performance Analysis

33. (1183,Q1,13) (a) The requirement is to calculate the return on investment. Return on investment (ROI) is the product of two components: operating income as a percentage of sales and capital turnover as shown below:

$$\text{ROI} = \frac{\text{Operating income}}{\text{Sales}} \times \frac{\text{Sales}}{\text{Avg. invested capital}}$$

$$\text{ROI} = \frac{\$\ 300{,}000}{\$2{,}000{,}000} \times \frac{\$2{,}000{,}000}{\$\ 500{,}000}$$

$$\text{ROI} = \frac{\$300{,}000}{\$500{,}000} = 60\%$$

As a shortcut approach, note that in the ROI formula the "sales" in both ratios cancel each other out leaving ROI equal to operating income divided by average invested capital.

34. (1183,Q1,14) (c) The requirement is to calculate the amount of residual income. The residual income method is an alternative to using return on investment for evaluating divisional performance. Residual income is equal to the operating income of $300,000 less the cost of capital on the division's assets of $90,000 (18% x $500,000), or $210,000. Under the residual income approach, a manager would be evaluated on how well s/he maximizes dollars of residual income instead of maximizing a profit percentage (ROI).

35. (1183,T1,49) (c) The requirement is to identify the factor which would cause return on investment (ROI) to increase. The solutions approach is to recall the formula to compute ROI.

$$\text{ROI} = \frac{\text{Net operating income}}{\text{Sales}} \times \frac{\text{Sales}}{\text{Net operating assets}}$$

$$\text{ROI} = \frac{\text{Net operating income}}{\text{Net operating assets}}$$

Answer (c) is correct because a decrease in cost will increase operating income (other factors held constant). As operating income increases and assets are held constant, ROI will increase. Answer (a) is incorrect because an increase in assets without a corresponding increase in operating income will cause ROI to decrease. Answers (b) and (d) are incorrect since a decrease in selling prices or an increase in costs will cause income to decline, and therefore, ROI to decrease.

May 1984 Answers

36. (584,T1,40) (d) The requirement is to determine whether a flexible budget is appropriate for direct-labor costs and/or for marketing costs. In the planning stage, a flexible budget is used to compare the effects of various activity levels on costs and revenues. A direct-labor budget would include the direct-labor hours expected at an anticipated level of activity, multiplied by the hourly rate to determine estimated direct-labor cost. A marketing budget would include salesmen's salaries, commissions, advertising, and other marketing costs. Although salesmen's salaries and advertising costs are generally fixed amounts (i.e., not dependent on planned activity), salesmen's commissions are variable and would be affected by changes in the activity level. Since both the direct-labor budget and the marketing budget include a variable element, a change in the activity level would affect both total direct-labor costs and total marketing costs. Therefore, a flexible budget would be appropriate for both direct-labor and marketing costs [answer (d)].

37. (584,T1,46) (b) The requirement is to identify which costing method (direct or absorption) would include the term gross profit on an income statement prepared for internal purposes. Direct (variable) costing, includes only **variable** manufacturing costs as product costs. Absorption costing includes **all** manufacturing costs (both fixed and variable) as product costs. When preparing a direct costing income statement, the emphasis is on cost behavior. A firm would deduct variable manufacturing costs from sales yielding manufacturing contribution margin. On an absorption costing income statement, the cost of goods sold figure (which includes all manufacturing costs) would be deducted from sales yielding gross profit [answer (b)].

38. (584,T1,47) (c) Contribution margin is equal to net sales less variable costs. The contribution margin ratio is calculated as contribution margin divided by net sales. A reduction in variable costs as a percentage of sales would increase contribution margin and thereby increase the contribution margin ratio [answer (c)]. Answers (a) and (b) are incorrect because a change in the breakeven point does not always imply a change in the contribution margin ratio (e.g., a change in the breakeven point may be caused by a change in fixed costs). Answer (d) is incorrect because an increase in variable costs would cause the contribution margin ratio to decrease.

39. (584,T1,48) (c) The requirement is to determine how a predicted operating loss would be handled when calculating the expected unit sales. The CVP formula for computing unit sales is expressed as:

$$\frac{\text{Fixed costs + Target net income}}{\text{Contribution margin per unit}} = \text{Sales in units}$$

A predicted loss should be treated as the opposite of a target net income and would result, therefore, in a subtraction from fixed costs in the numerator [answer (c)].

Unofficial Answer*

Problem 1 Breakeven Analysis

a. 1. Fixed costs are those which remain unchanged, over short time periods at least, regardless of changes in physical volume (sales or production volume).
2. Variable costs are those costs that vary in direct ratio (proportionately) to changes in physical volume.
3. The relevant range establishes the limits within which the volume of activity can vary and the sales and cost relationships remain valid. It is usually a range in which the entity has had some recent experience.
4. The breakeven point is the level of sales volume (assuming sales volume is equal to production volume) where total revenues equal total expenses and the business has neither earnings nor a loss.
5. The margin of safety is the excess of actual or budgeted sales over sales at the breakeven point. Expressed another way, the margin of safety reveals the amount by which sales could decrease before losses occur.
6. Sales mix is the composition of total sales broken down among various products, product mix, or product lines; it is the relative combination of the quantities of the variety of company products that compose total sales.

b. Assumptions which underlie cost-volume-earnings analysis include the following:

1. Cost can be classified as either fixed or variable.
2. Variable costs change at a linear rate.
3. Fixed costs remain unchanged over the relevant range of the breakeven chart.
4. Selling prices do not change as the physical sales volume changes.
5. There is only a single product; or, if there are multiple products, the sales mix remains constant.
6. Productive efficiency does not change.
7. There is synchronization between sales and production; i.e., inventories are either kept constant or are zero.
8. Volume is the only relevant factor affecting costs.
9. There is a relevant range of validity for all of the other underlying assumptions and concepts.

c. Basic formula:

$$\text{Breakeven sales} = \frac{\text{Fixed costs + Earnings}}{1-\dfrac{\text{Variable costs}}{\text{Corresponding sales}}}$$

1. $$\frac{\$540{,}000 + 0}{1-\dfrac{\$1{,}400{,}000}{\$2{,}000{,}000}} = \$1{,}800{,}000 \text{ (9,000 units @ \$200)}$$

2. $$\frac{\$540{,}000 + \$96{,}000}{1-\dfrac{\$1{,}400{,}000}{\$2{,}000{,}000}} = \$2{,}120{,}000 \text{ (10,600 units @ \$200)}$$

3. $$\frac{\$558{,}000 + 0}{1-\dfrac{\$1{,}400{,}000}{\$2{,}000{,}000}} = \$1{,}860{,}000 \text{ (9,300 units @ \$200)}$$

**The format of the Unofficial Answer precludes the need for an Answer Outline.*

Unofficial Answer*

Problem 2 Direct Costing Concepts

1. Under direct costing, only variable manufacturing costs are included in inventory; whereas, under absorption costing (the current generally accepted method of costing inventory for external reporting), all manufacturing costs, both variable and fixed, are included in inventory.

2. Direct costing charges the product with only those manufacturing costs that vary directly with volume. In order to do this, a direct-costing structure must separate variable (product) costs and fixed (period) costs. As a result, a direct-costing structure facilitates calculation of the contribution margin and breakeven point because sales less variable costs equals the contribution margin, and the contribution margin, as a percentage of sales divided into fixed costs, equals the breakeven point.

**The format of the Unofficial Answer precludes the need for an Answer Outline.*

Answer Outline

Problem 3 Direct vs. Absorption Costing Theory

Part a.

1. Rationale for using direct costing for internal reporting
   - Direct costing enhances decision making
     - Highlights impact of fixed costs on operating income
       - Income fluctuates with sales, not production
     - Highlights contribution margin (sales minus variable costs), thereby facilitating
       - Short-run decisions in which most fixed costs not relevant
         - E.g., Evaluation of special orders
       - Cost-volume-profit analysis
2. Yes, operating income under direct costing would be lower
   - Rationale
     - Direct costing expenses all fixed production costs
     - Absorption costing allocates all fixed production costs to units produced
     - When ending inventory is higher than beginning inventory
       - Amount of fixed costs allocated to ending inventory will be greater than amount in beginning inventory
       - Less fixed costs expensed as part of CGS under absorption costing
       - Therefore, operating income under direct costing will be less than absorption costing

Unofficial Answer
(Author Modified)

Problem 3 Direct vs. Absorption Costing Theory

Part a.

1. The rationale for using the direct costing method for internal reporting is that it enhances decision making. Under direct costing, fixed production costs are treated as a period cost rather than as a product cost thereby eliminating the need to allocate joint fixed costs and highlighting the impact of fixed costs on income. Also, income fluctuates only with sales thus eliminating the absorption costing anomaly of income fluctuating with production levels. Direct costing also highlights contribution margin (CM). CM is used to evaluate special orders and other short-run decisions where fixed costs are often considered irrelevant. CM also facilitates more efficient cost-volume-profit analysis, a technique used for short-run planning and control.

2. Yes, operating income under direct costing will be lower. Under direct costing all fixed production costs incurred in the period are expensed. However, when absorption costing is used fixed costs are allocated to the units produced, and the fixed costs so allocated are not expensed until the goods are sold. Since Grisp's inventory of finished units increased, a larger amount of current fixed costs remain in ending inventory than were included in the beginning inventory as a result of being allocated in the same manner last period. Therefore, the amount of fixed costs charged to income will be less than under direct costing. Consequently, operating income under direct costing will be less than under absorption costing.

Solution Guide

Problem 4 Direct and Absorption Costing

1. The requirement in part b. is a projected income statement per each direct and absorption costing.

1.1 The major differences between direct and absorption costing are that (1) direct costing inventories include only variable costs and absorption costing includes fixed as well as variable costs, and (2) on direct costing statements, variable costs (both manufacturing and administrative) are deducted from sales to obtain the contribution margin. Also fixed costs (both manufacturing and administrative) are deducted from the contribution margin to arrive at net income.

1.2 In this problem unit inventory cost per direct costing is $55 and per absorption costing is $60. The difference of $5/unit is fixed cost.

1.3 The only twist to the problem is underapplied overhead per absorption costing. Since only 9,000 units are being produced, only $45,000 of the $50,000 of fixed costs will be applied in June. The unofficial answer changes this $5,000 underapplied June overhead to the June operating results.

Unofficial Answer

Problem 4 Direct and Absorption Costing

1.

Bicent Company
Projected Income Statement
For the Month of June 1976
(Absorption Costing)

Sales (7,500 units x $80)		$600,000
Beginning inventory (2,000 units x $60) (Schedule 1)	$120,000	
Production (9,000 units x $60)	540,000	
Available	660,000	
Ending inventory (3,500 units x $60)	210,000	
Cost of goods sold before adjustment	450,000	
Adjustment for volume variance (production projected as 10,000 units as "normal"; 1,000 units underapplied x $5 fixed manufacturing overhead)	5,000	
		455,000
Gross margin		145,000
Variable selling, general, and administrative (7,500 units x $4)	30,000	
Fixed selling, general, and administrative (10,000 units x $2.80)	28,000	58,000
Projected income		$ 87,000

2.

Bicent Company
Projected Income Statement
For the Month of June 1976
(Direct Costing)

Sales (7,500 units x $80)		$600,000
Beginning inventory (2,000 units x $55) (Schedule 2)	$110,000	
Production (9,000 units x $55)	495,000	
Available	605,000	
Ending inventory (3,500 units x $55)	192,500	
Variable cost of goods sold	412,500	
Variable selling, general, and administrative (7,500 units x $4)	30,000	
Total variable costs		442,500
Contribution margin		157,500
Fixed manufacturing overhead (10,000 units x $5)	50,000	
Fixed selling, general, and administrative (10,000 units x $2.80)	28,000	
Total fixed costs		78,000
Projected income		$ 79,500

Note *(Not Required)*: The difference in the two projected income figures ($87,000 – $79,500) equals $7,500. This is accounted for as the increase in inventory (3,500 – 2,000) times the fixed manufacturing overhead application rate (1,500 units x $5). The $7,500 of fixed manufacturing overhead is included in ending inventory under absorption costing, but it is expensed under direct (variable) costing.

Schedule 1

Schedule of Inventoriable Production Costs Per Unit
(Absorption Costing)

Direct material	$30
Direct labor	19
Manufacturing overhead (variable)	6
Manufacturing overhead (fixed)	5
Total unit cost	$60

Schedule 2

Schedule of Inventoriable Production Costs Per Unit
(Direct Costing)

Direct material	$30
Direct labor	19
Manufacturing overhead (variable)	6
Total unit cost	$55

Solution Guide

Problem 5 Breakeven Computations

1. This problem involves the pediatrics ward of a hospital which rents space and beds at a fixed charge. Pediatrics is also charged for carryover services such as meals, billings, and collections. Part a. requires the calculation of minimum patient days (PD) for pediatrics to break even assuming that additional beds available are **not** rented.

2. The solutions approach is to utilize the unit contribution margin technique to compute breakeven as both fixed costs and the contribution margin (CM) per PD can be determined from the data provided.

$$\frac{\text{Total fixed costs}}{\text{CM per PD}} = \text{Breakeven point}$$

2.1 To determine the CM per PD, we subtract variable expenses per PD from average revenue per PD. Variable expenses per PD are computed by first dividing total revenue for the year by the average revenue per PD ($6,000,000 ÷ $300 = 20,000 PD) resulting in the current level of activity, 20,000 PD.

2.2 Next divide the current level of total variable costs by the number of patient days ($2,000,000 ÷ 20,000 = $100) to determine the variable costs per patient day.

2.3 Contribution margin per patient day is therefore $300 (revenue per PD) – $100 (variable costs per PD) = $200.

2.4 To determine total fixed costs at the breakeven point we need to consider the fixed charges based on capacity as given in the problem and the fixed costs of personnel.

2.5 The level of staffing necessary for the lowest level of activity given (up to 21,900 PD) is 20 aides, 10 nurses, and 4 supervising nurses from the data provided.
Total fixed costs at this level are:

Charges based on bed capacity	$2,900,000
Personnel	
Aides (20 x $9,000)	180,000
Nurses (10 x $20,000)	200,000
Supervisors (4 x $25,000)	100,000
Total fixed costs	$3,380,000

2.6 The breakeven point is 16,900 patient days ($3,380,000 ÷ $200 = 16,900).

2.7 As a proof, an income statement based on 16,900 patient days could be prepared:

Revenue (16,900 x $300)		$5,070,000
Variable costs (16,900 x $100)		1,690,000
Contribution margin		3,380,000
Fixed costs		
Bed capacity	$2,900,000	
Personnel	480,000	3,380,000
Operating income		$ 0

3. Part b. requires a schedule of increases in revenue and costs to determine the net increase or decrease in earnings if pediatrics rents 20 additional beds for the year. The solutions approach is to compare incremental revenue with incremental costs from renting the additional beds to determine the effect on earnings.

3.1 The 20 additional beds rented are expected to be occupied only 90 days during the year. The incremental revenue and variable costs from the rental are computed as $540,000 (20 beds x 90 days x $300) and $180,000 (20 beds x 90 days x $100), respectively.

3.2 Fixed costs based on capacity (charges for common and administrative services) will increase due to the rental of additional beds. The solutions approach is to determine the fixed charge per bed at 60 beds capacity and then calculate the incremental fixed costs for 20 additional beds.

$$\frac{\$2{,}900{,}000}{60 \text{ beds}} = \$48{,}333 \text{ fixed charge per bed}$$

Additional beds	x	Fixed chg. per bed	=	Incremental costs
20	x	$48,333	=	$966,667

3.3 The rental of the additional beds will not cause an increase in the personnel costs. The analysis in Part a indicated there were 20,000 patient days at 60 bed capacity. Adding 20 beds for 90 days adds 1,800 patient days to the 20,000, resulting in 21,800 patient days. This total is still 100 patient days less than that which would cause personnel costs to increase.

3.4 The comparison of incremental revenues with costs indicates costs greater than revenues by $606,667, as follows:

Incremental revenues	$ 540,000
Incremental costs	
Variable	180,000
Fixed	966,667
Total	$1,146,667
Excess of costs over revenues	$ 606,667

Unofficial Answer

Problem 5 Breakeven Computations

a. The breakeven point in patient days equals total fixed costs divided by contribution margin per patient day.

Pediatrics
Computation of Breakeven Point
in Patient Days
For the Year Ending June 30, 1983

Total fixed costs (Schedule 1)	$3,380,000
Divided by contribution margin per patient day (Schedule 2)	$ 200
Breakeven point in patient days	16,900

Schedule 1

Total Fixed Costs

Melford Hospital charges	$2,900,000
Supervising nurses ($25,000 x 4)	100,000
Nurses ($20,000 x 10)	200,000
Aides ($9,000 x 20)	180,000
Total fixed costs	$3,380,000

Schedule 2

Contribution Margin Per Patient Day

Revenue per patient day	$300
Variable costs per patient day ($6,000,000/$300 = 20,000 patient days) ($2,000,000/20,000 patient days)	100
Contribution margin per patient day	$200

b.

Pediatrics
Computation of
Loss from Rental of Additional 20 Beds
For the Year Ending June 30, 1983

Increase in revenue (20 additional beds x 90 days x $300 charge per day)	$ 540,000
Increase in expenses	
Variable charges by Melford Hospital (20 additional beds x 90 days x $100 per day)	180,000
Fixed charges by Melford Hospital ($2,900,000/60 beds = $48,333 per bed x 20 beds) (or, $2,900,000 x 20/60)	966,667
Salaries expense (20,000 patient days before additional 20 beds, + 20 additional beds x 90 days = 21,800, which does not exceed 21,900 patient days; therefore, no additional personnel are required)	–
Total increase in expenses	1,146,667
Net decrease in earnings from rental of additional 20 beds	$ 606,667

Answer Outline

Problem 6 Breakeven Theory

Part b.

1. Unit sales required to earn 20% profit on sales =

$$\frac{\text{Total fixed costs + Desired profit}}{\text{CM per unit}}$$

Desired profit = 20% x total sales
CM per unit = Selling price per unit – Variable cost per unit

2. If variable cost per unit increases, unit sales to breakeven increase
   Unit CM lower
   Must sell more to cover fixed costs
3. Limitations of breakeven analysis
   - Breakeven chart static analysis
     Changes shown only by drawing new chart
   - Slope of sales and variable cost lines and amount of fixed cost valid only in relevant range
   - Difficult to determine fixed/variable cost elements
   - Assumes following unchanged
     - Product mix
     - Product technology
     - Labor productivity
     - Selling price and other market factors

Unofficial Answer

Problem 6 Breakeven Theory

Part b.

1. Daly would determine the number of units of Product Y that it would have to sell to attain a 20 percent profit on sales by dividing total fixed costs plus desired profit (20 percent of the sales price per unit times the units to attain a 20 percent profit) by unit contribution margin (sales price per unit less variable cost per unit).

2. If variable cost per unit increases as a percentage of the sales price, Daly would have to sell more units of Product Y to break even. Because the unit contribution margin (sales price per unit less variable cost per unit) would be lower, Daly would have to sell more units to cover the fixed costs.

3. The limitations of breakeven analysis in managerial decision making are as follows:

- The breakeven chart is fundamentally a static analysis, and, in most cases, changes can only be shown by drawing a new chart or series of charts.
- The amount of fixed and variable cost, as well as the slope of the sales line, is meaningful in a defined range of activity and must be redefined for activity outside the relevant range.
- It is difficult to determine the fixed and variable components of cost.
- It is assumed that product mix will be unchanged.
- It is assumed that product technology will be unchanged.
- It is assumed that labor productivity will be unchanged.
- It is assumed that selling prices and other market conditions will be unchanged.

Solution Guide

Problem 7 Budgeted Cash Collections and Disbursements

3. Part b. requires three schedules computing expected cash balance at May 31.

3.1 The "solutions approach" is to study the requirements first; second, quickly review mentally the accounting concepts needed to prepare cash budgets; third, read through the information given; and fourth, make the necessary computations and prepare the required schedules.

3.2 Note that the January and February sales information is not needed. 9% of March sales are expected to be collected in May; 20% of April sales are expected to be collected in May; and 70% of May sales are to collected in May. Thus, collections from March sales are $5,400 ($60,000 x 9%); from April, $15,600 ($78,000 x 20%); and from May, $46,000 ($66,000 x 70%). The total expected cash collections would be $67,200 ($5,400 + $15,600 + $46,200). The 1% uncollectible does not enter into the computation; this schedule is only concerned with amounts collected.

3.3 For the second schedule, expected cash disbursements, note that purchases are paid for by the tenth of the following month, less a 2% discount. Assuming that **no** purchases are paid for until the month following the purchase (to take full advantage of the terms), the only relevant information concerning purchases is the amount for April. January, February, March, and May purchases can be ignored. Cash disbursements for purchases are calculated by deducting $1,080 (2% x $54,000) from April purchases of $54,000 to obtain $52,920. Alternatively, this amount can be obtained by multiplying $54,000 by 98%. Cash disbursements for expenses during May are expected to be $14,400. Thus, total cash disbursements would be $67,320 ($52,920 + $14,400).

3.4 To compute the third item, the expected cash balance at May 31, start with the May 1 cash balance of $22,000, add expected collections of $67,200 and subtract expected cash disbursements of $67,320 to arrive at an expected May 31st balance of $21,880.

Unofficial Answer

Problem 7 Budgeted Cash Collections and Disbursements

Part b.

1. **Montero Corporation**
Expected Cash Collections
May 1982

From March sales ($60,000 x 9%)	$ 5,400
From April sales ($78,000 x 20%)	15,600
From May sales ($66,000 x 70%)	46,200
Expected cash collections, May 1982	$67,200

2. **Montero Corporation**
Expected Cash Disbursements
May 1982

For April purchases ($54,000 x 98%)	$52,920
For May expenses	14,400
Expected cash disbursements, May 1982	$67,320

3. **Montero Corporatiion**
Expected Cash Balance
May 31, 1982

Cash balance, May 1	$22,000
Expected cash collections	67,200
Cash available	89,200
Expected cash disbursements	(67,320)
Expected cash balance, May 31	$21,880

Multiple Choice Questions (1–27)

1. The absolute minimum cost that would be possible under the best conceivable operating conditions is a description of which type of standard cost?
   a. Currently attainable (expected).
   b. Theoretical.
   c. Normal.
   d. Practical.

2. When performing input-output variance analysis in standard costing, "standard hours allowed" is a means of measuring
   a. Standard output at standard hours.
   b. Actual output at standard hours.
   c. Standard output at actual hours.
   d. Actual output at actual hours.

3. Information on Cox Company's direct-material costs for the month of January 1983 was as follows:

Actual quantity purchased	18,000
Actual unit purchase price	$ 3.60
Materials purchase price variance—unfavorable (based on purchases)	$ 3,600
Standard quantity allowed for actual production	16,000
Actual quantity used	15,000

For January 1983 there was a favorable direct-material usage variance of
   a. $3,360
   b. $3,375
   c. $3,400
   d. $3,800

4. Throop Company had budgeted 50,000 units of output using 50,000 units of raw materials at a total material cost of $100,000. Actual output was 50,000 units of product requiring 45,000 units of raw materials at a cost of $2.10 per unit. The direct-material price variance and usage variance were

	Price	*Usage*
a.	$ 4,500 unfavorable	$10,000 favorable
b.	$ 5,000 favorable	$10,500 unfavorable
c.	$ 5,000 unfavorable	$10,500 favorable
d.	$10,000 favorable	$ 4,500 unfavorable

5. Information on Kennedy Company's direct-material costs is as follows:

Standard unit price	$3.60
Actual quantity purchased	1,600
Standard quantity allowed for actual production	1,450
Materials purchase price variance—favorable	$ 240

What was the actual purchase price per unit, rounded to the nearest penny?
   a. $3.06
   b. $3.11
   c. $3.45
   d. $3.75

6. Perkins Company, which has a standard cost system, had 500 units of raw material X in its inventory at June 1, 1982, purchased in May for $1.20 per unit and carried at a standard cost of $1.00. The following information pertains to raw material X for the month of June 1982:

Actual number of units purchased	1,400
Actual number of units used	1,500
Standard number of units allowed for actual production	1,300
Standard cost per unit	$1.00
Actual cost per unit	$1.10

The unfavorable materials purchase price variance for raw material X for June was
   a. $0
   b. $130
   c. $140
   d. $150

7. The standard unit cost is used in the calculation of which of the following variances?

	Materials price variance	*Materials usage variance*
a.	No	No
b.	No	Yes
c.	Yes	No
d.	Yes	Yes

8. Which department is customarily held responsible for an unfavorable materials usage variance?
   a. Quality control.
   b. Purchasing.
   c. Engineering.
   d. Production.

9. Harper Company uses a standard cost system. Data relating to direct labor for the month of August 1983 is as follows:

Direct-labor efficiency variance—favorable	$5,250
Standard direct-labor rate	$ 7.00
Actual direct-labor rate	$ 7.50
Standard hours allowed for actual production	9,000

What are the actual hours worked for the month of August 1983?

a. 9,750
b. 8,400
c. 8,300
d. 8,250

10. Information on Barber Company's direct-labor costs for the month of January 1981 is as follows:

Actual direct-labor hours	34,500
Standard direct-labor hours	35,000
Total direct-labor payroll	$241,500
Direct-labor efficiency variance - favorable	$ 3,200

What is Barber's direct-labor rate variance?

a. $17,250 unfavorable.
b. $20,700 unfavorable.
c. $21,000 unfavorable.
d. $21,000 favorable.

11. Lion Company's direct-labor costs for the month of January 1980 were as follows:

Actual direct-labor hours	20,000
Standard direct-labor hours	21,000
Direct-labor rate variance-unfavorable	$ 3,000
Total payroll	$126,000

What was Lion's direct-labor efficiency variance?

a. $6,000 favorable.
b. $6,150 favorable.
c. $6,300 favorable.
d. $6,450 favorable.

12. Which of the following is the most probable reason a company would experience an unfavorable labor rate variance and a favorable labor efficiency variance?

a. The mix of workers assigned to the particular job was heavily weighted towards the use of higher paid experienced individuals.
b. The mix of workers assigned to the particular job was heavily weighted towards the use of new relatively low paid unskilled workers.
c. Because of the production schedule workers from other production areas were assigned to assist this particular process.
d. Defective materials caused more labor to be used in order to produce a standard unit.

13. Excess direct labor wages resulting from overtime premium will be disclosed in which type of variance?

a. Yield.
b. Quantity.
c. Labor efficiency.
d. Labor rate.

14. A debit balance in the labor-efficiency variance indicates that

a. Standard hours exceed actual hours.
b. Actual hours exceed standard hours.
c. Standard rate and standard hours exceed actual rate and actual hours.
d. Actual rate and actual hours exceed standard rate and standard hours.

15. Under the two-variance method for analyzing factory overhead, the volume variance is the difference between the

a. Budget allowance based on standard hours allowed and the budget allowance based on actual hours worked.
b. Budget allowance based on standard hours allowed and the factory overhead applied to production.
c. Actual factory overhead and the budget allowance based on standard hours allowed.
d. Actual factory overhead and the factory overhead applied to production.

16. Universal Company uses a standard cost system and prepared the following budget at normal capacity for the month of January 1983:

Direct-labor hours	24,000
Variable factory overhead	$ 48,000
Fixed factory overhead	$108,000
Total factory overhead per direct-labor hour	$ 6.50

Actual data for January 1983 were as follows:

Direct-labor hours worked	22,000
Total factory overhead	$147,000
Standard direct-labor hours allowed for capacity attained	21,000

Using the two-way analysis of overhead variances, what is the budget (controllable) variance for January 1983?

a. $ 3,000 favorable.
b. $ 5,000 favorable.
c. $ 9,000 favorable.
d. $10,500 unfavorable.

36

17. Under the two-variance method for analyzing factory overhead, the controllable (budget) variance is the difference between the

a. Budget allowance based on standard hours allowed and the factory overhead applied to production.
b. Budget allowance based on standard hours allowed and the budget allowance based on actual hours worked.
c. Actual factory overhead and the factory overhead applied to production.
d. Actual factory overhead and the budget allowance based on standard hours allowed.

18. Under the three-variance method for analyzing factory overhead, which of the following is used in the computation of the spending variance?

	Actual factory overhead	Factory overhead applied to production
a.	Yes	Yes
b.	Yes	No
c.	No	Yes
d.	No	No

Items 19 and 20 are based on the following information.

The following information relates to a given department of Herman Company for the fourth quarter 1974:

Actual total overhead (fixed plus variable)	$178,500
Budget formula	$110,000 plus $0.50/hr.
Total overhead application rate	$1.50/hr.
Spending variance	$8,000 unfavorable
Volume variance	$5,000 favorable

The total overhead variance is divided into three variances — spending, efficiency, and volume.

19. What were the actual hours worked in this department during the quarter?

a. 110,000
b. 121,000
c. 137,000
d. 153,000

20. What were the standard hours allowed for good output in this department during the quarter?

a. 105,000
b. 106,667
c. 110,000
d. 115,000

21. Geyer Company uses a standard cost system. For the month of April 1983, total overhead is budgeted at $80,000 based on the normal capacity of 20,000 direct-labor hours. At standard each unit of finished product requires 2 direct-labor hours. The following data are available for the April 1983 production activity:

Equivalent units of product	9,500
Direct-labor hours worked	19,500
Actual total overhead incurred	$79,500

What amount should Geyer credit to the applied factory overhead account for the month of April 1983?

a. $76,000
b. $78,000
c. $79,500
d. $80,000

22. Fawcett Company uses a flexible budget system and prepared the following information for 1982:

	Normal capacity	Maximum capacity
Percent of capacity	80%	100%
Direct-labor hours	32,000	40,000
Variable factory overhead	$ 64,000	$ 80,000
Fixed factory overhead	$160,000	$160,000
Total factory overhead rate per direct-labor hour	$7	$6

Fawcett operated at 90% of capacity during 1982. The actual factory overhead for 1982 was $252,000. What was the budget (controllable) overhead variance for the year?

a. $36,000 unfavorable.
b. $20,000 unfavorable.
c. $18,000 unfavorable.
d. $0.

23. What standard cost variance represents the difference between actual factory overhead incurred and budgeted factory overhead based on actual hours worked?

a. Volume variance.
b. Spending variance.
c. Efficiency variance.
d. Quantity variance.

24. How should a usage variance that is significant in amount be treated at the end of an accounting period?

a. Reported as a deferred charge or credit.
b. Allocated among work-in-process inventory, finished goods inventory, and cost of goods sold.

c. Charged or credited to cost of goods manufactured.

d. Allocated among cost of goods manufactured, finished goods inventory, and cost of goods sold.

25. The gross profit of Reade Company for each of the years ended December 31, 1981 and 1980, was as follows:

	1981	*1980*
Sales	$792,000	$800,000
Cost of goods sold	464,000	480,000
Gross profit	$328,000	$320,000

Assuming that selling prices were 10% lower during 1981, what would be the amount of decrease in gross profit due to the change in selling prices?

a. $ 8,000
b. $72,000
c. $79,200
d. $88,000

26. Garfield Company, which sells a single product, provided the following data from its income statements for the calendar years 1980 and 1979:

	1980
Sales (150,000 units)	$750,000
Cost of goods sold	525,000
Gross profit	$225,000

	1979 (Base year)
Sales (180,000 units)	$720,000
Cost of goods sold	575,000
Gross profit	$145,000

In an analysis of variation in gross profit between the two years, what would be the effects of changes in sales price and sales volume?

	Sales price	*Sales volume*
a.	$150,000 favorable	$120,000 unfavorable
b.	$150,000 unfavorable	$120,000 favorable
c.	$180,000 favorable	$150,000 unfavorable
d.	$180,000 unfavorable	$150,000 favorable

May 1984 Question

27. Under the three-variance method for analyzing factory overhead, which of the following is used in the computation of the spending variance?

	Budget allowance based on actual hours	*Budget allowance based on standard hours*
a.	Yes	No
b.	Yes	Yes
c.	No	Yes
d.	No	No

Problems

Problem 1 Standard Costs and Variances (581,Q5)

(40 to 50 minutes)

Vogue Fashions, Inc., manufactures ladies' blouses of one quality, produced in lots to fill each special order from its customers, comprised of department stores located in various cities. Vogue sews the particular stores' labels on the blouses. The standard cost for a dozen blouses are:

Direct materials	24 yards @ $1.10	$26.40
Direct labor	3 hours @ $4.90	14.70
Manufacturing overhead	3 hours @ $4.00	12.00
Standard cost per dozen		$53.10

During June 1980, Vogue worked on three orders, for which the month's job cost records disclose the following:

Lot no.	*Units in lot (dozens)*	*Materials used (yards)*	*Hours worked*
22	1,000	24,100	2,980
23	1,700	40,440	5,130
24	1,200	28,825	2,890

The following information is also available:

1. Vogue purchased 95,000 yards of material during June at a cost of $106,400. The materials price variance is recorded when goods are purchased. All inventories are carried at standard cost.

2. Direct labor during June amounted to $55,000. According to payroll records, production employees were paid $5.00 per hour.

3. Manufacturing overhead during June amounted to $45,600.

4. A total of $576,000 was budgeted for manufacturing overhead for the year 1980, based on estimated production at the plant's normal capacity of 48,000 dozen blouses annually. Manufacturing overhead at this level of production is 40% fixed and 60% variable. Manufacturing overhead is applied on the basis of direct labor hours.

5. There was no work in process at June 1. During June, lots 22 and 23 were completed. All material was issued for lot 24, which was 80% completed as to direct labor.

Required:

a. Prepare a schedule showing the computation of standard cost of lots 22, 23, and 24 for June 1980.

b. Prepare a schedule showing the computation of the materials price variance for June 1980. Indicate whether the variance is favorable or unfavorable.

c. Prepare a schedule showing, for each lot produced during June 1980, computations of the

1. Material quantity variance in yards.
2. Labor efficiency variance in hours.
3. Labor rate variance in dollars.

Indicate whether each variance is favorable or unfavorable.

d. Prepare a schedule showing computations of the total controllable and noncontrollable (volume) manufacturing overhead variances for June 1980. Indicate whether the variances are favorable or unfavorable.

Problem 2 Standard Costs (1177,T3)

(20 to 25 minutes)

Standards are used by many concerns to generate data relevant to the acquisition and utilization of the component cost elements in a manufacturing process. There are three basic types of standards that may be employed: 1. Fixed (basic), 2. Ideal, and 3. Attainable.

Required:

a. Define the three types of standards.

b. What do standards and related variances attempt to disclose with respect to acquisition and utilization within a manufacturing process? Limit the discussion to the two general categories: Variable costs and fixed factory overhead. Identify specific variances but do not discuss their computations.

c. How do standards relate to cost accumulation procedures?

Problem 3 Variance Analysis (582,T5b)

(10 to 15 minutes)

Part b. Meyer Company's cost accounting department has prepared a factory overhead variance analysis report using the two-variance method. The plant manager of Meyer Company is interested in understanding the managerial usefulness of this report.

Required:

1. What are the purposes of a factory overhead variance analysis report?

2. Identify and explain the underlying assumptions associated with the two-variance method. Discuss the significance of each variance.

Problem 4 Gross Profit (576,Q5a)

(15 to 20 minutes)

Part a. You have acquired the following data for the calendar years 1974 and 1975 for Celebration, Inc.:

	1974		1975		Dollar increase
Sales	$750,000	100%	$840,000	100%	$90,000
Cost of goods sold	495,000	66	560,000	$66\frac{2}{3}$	65,000
Gross margin	$255,000	34%	$280,000	$33\frac{1}{3}$%	$25,000
Unit selling price	$10		$12		

Required:

Prepare a statement in good form which analyzes the variations in sales and cost of goods sold between 1974 and 1975.

Problem 5 Standard Costing (1176,Q3b)

(20 to 25 minutes)

Part b. On May 1, 1975, Bovar Company began the manufacture of a new mechanical device known as "Dandy." The company installed a standard cost system in accounting for manufacturing costs. The standard costs for a unit of "Dandy" are as follows:

Raw materials	6 lbs. at $1 per lb.	$ 6.00
Direct labor	1 hour at $4 per hour	4.00
Overhead	75% of direct labor costs	3.00
		$13.00

The following data were obtained from Bovar's records for the month of May:

	Units
Actual production of "Dandy"	4,000
Units sold of "Dandy"	2,500

	Debit	Credit
Sales		$50,000
Purchases (26,000 pounds)	$27,300	
Material price variance	1,300	
Material quantity variance	1,000	
Direct labor rate variance	760	
Direct labor efficiency variance		800
Manufacturing overhead total variance	500	

The amount shown above for material price variance is applicable to raw materials purchased during May.

Required:

Compute each of the following items for Bovar for the month of May. Show computations in good form.

1. Standard quantity of raw materials allowed (in pounds).
2. Actual quantity of raw materials used (in pounds).
3. Standard hours allowed.
4. Actual hours worked.
5. Actual direct labor rate.
6. Actual total overhead.

Multiple Choice Answers

1. b	7. d	13. d	18. b	23. b
2. b	8. d	14. b	19. b	24. b
3. c	9. d	15. b	20. d	25. d
4. a	10. b	16. a	21. a	26. a
5. c	11. b	17. d	22. b	27. a
6. c	12. a			

Multiple Choice Answer Explanations

A. Variance Analysis

1. (1180,T1,48) (b) There are basically two types of standard costs, currently attainable [answer (a)] and theoretical [answer (b)]. A currently attainable cost is the target cost that employees are expected to acheive under efficient conditions. A theoretical standard cost is the absolute minimum cost that would be possible under the best conceivable operating conditions. Normal [answer (c)] and practical [answer (d)] are not terms used to describe the attainability of standard costs; they are alternative bases for determining budgeted fixed cost per hour or units.

2. (577,T2,38) (b) Standard hours allowed, as the title implies, are the standard hours permitted for a given level of production which is the actual output times standard hours. In other words, given the level of production, what are the standard hours budgeted?

B. Material Variances

3. (1183,P3,48) (c) The requirement is the favorable direct-material usage variance. The usage variance is the difference between AQ x SP and SQ x SP. The actual quantity used (AQ) is 15,000, and the standard quantity allowed (SQ) is 16,000. The standard price (SP) must be computed from the other given information. The materials purchase price variance (based on purchases) is $3,600 unfavorable. Since the actual quantity purchased was 18,000, the unfavorable price variance is $.20 per unit ($3,600 ÷ 18,000). The actual price per unit is $3.60; therefore, the standard price per unit must be $3.40. Now the usage variance can be computed as $3,400 favorable.

AQ x SP	SQ x SP
15,000 x $3.40	16,000 x $3.40
$51,000	$54,000

Usage, $3,400 favorable

4. (1181,P2,26) (a) The requirement is to determine the direct material price variance and usage variance. The direct material price variance is the difference between actual and standard prices times either the quantity of material purchased or used depending on when the variance is isolated. Since the quantity of material purchased is not specified in the problem, it must be assumed to be the same quantity as the quantity used to produce outputs, or alternatively, that the price variance is not isolated until usage occurs. In graphic form, the direct material price variance would appear as follows:

Actual quantity x Actual price — Actual quantity x Standard price

Material price variance

45,000 x $2.10 — 45,000 x $2.00

|<$4500 unfavorable>|

The direct material usage variance examines the difference between actual quantity of inputs and standard quantity of inputs for output achieved based on the quantity of material used. In graphic form, the direct material usage variance would appear as follows:

Actual quantity x Standard price — Standard quantity of inputs for output achieved x Standard price

Material usage variance

45,000 x $2.00 — 50,000 x $2.00

| ← $10,000 favorable → |

5. (1179,P2,38) (c) The requirement is the actual pruchase price per unit given a standard unit price of $3.60 and a favorable price variance of $240. Dividing the actual quantity purchased of 1,600 units into the $240 favorable variance results in a $.15 per unit favorable price variance. The actual cost per unit was $3.45 ($3.60 standard less $.15 favorable variance).

6. (1182,Q2,24) (c) The requirement is to calculate the unfavorable materials purchase price variance for June. Note that the information given concerning beginning inventory is not relevant in the determination of the purchase price variance for June. To properly evaluate the performance of the purchasing department, the actual number of units purchased rather than the actual number of units used in calculating the materials purchase variance should be used. Since 1,400 units were purchased at $.10 above standard

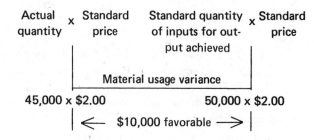

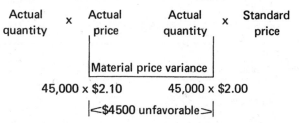

cost ($1.00 standard cost – $1.10 actual cost), the unfavorable materials purchase price variance is $140 (1,400 x $.10).

7. (1182,T1,50) (d) The materials price variance is computed as: Actual quantity (Actual price – Standard unit cost). The materials usage variance is computed as: Standard unit cost (Actual quantity – Standard quantity). Thus, the standard unit cost is used in the calculation of both the materials price and usage variances.

8. (581,T1,50) (d) The requirement is to identify the department cusomarily held responsible for an unfavorable materials usage variance. The department customarily held responsible for an unfavorable materials usage variance is the production department. Although the engineering and quality control departments may have some effect on the use of materials, they are not usually responsible for material usage variances. The purchasing department is usually responsible for material price variances.

C. Labor Variances

9. (1183,P3,49) (d) The requirement is the actual hours (AH) worked in August. The solutions approach is to set up a diagram computing the direct-labor efficiency variance (which is given) and fill in the given information.

AH x SR	SH x SR
? x $7.00	9,000 x $7.00
?	$63,000

Efficiency variance, $5,250 favorable

Since the variance is favorable, AH x SR must equal $63,000 less $5,250, or $57,750. The actual hours can then be computed by dividing $57,750 by $7.00, resulting in AH of 8,250. The diagram can be completed as follows:

AH x SR	SH x SR
8,250 x $7.00	9,000 x $7.00
$57,750	$63,000

Efficiency variance, $5,250 favorable

10. (581,P2,27) (b) The requirement is to compute the direct-labor rate variance for Barber Company. Since the standard-direct labor rate is not given in this situation, it is necessary to work from the direct labor efficiency variance to compute the standard direct labor rate. Set up a schedule and fill in the known variables.

Actual	*Budget*	*Applied*
	34,500 hrs.	35,000 hrs.
$241,500	x Std. DL rate = (2)	x Std. DL rate (1)

← (3) → ← $3,200 →

D.L. Rate Var. D.L. Effic. Var.

The unknowns are keyed (1) through (3).

(1) The standard direct labor rate is equal to:

$$\frac{\$3{,}200}{35{,}000 - 34{,}500} = \$6.40$$

(2) The budget at 34,500 hours is

$34,500 x $6.40 = $220,800

(3) Finally, the direct labor rate variance is:

$241,500 – $220,800 = $20,700

11. (580,P2,39) (b) The requirement is for the direct-labor efficiency variance. Since the standard direct-labor rate per hour is not given in this situation, it is necessary to work from the actual labor cost incurred and the unfavorable direct-labor rate variance to find the direct-labor rate. First, subtract the $3,000 unfavorable direct-labor rate variance from the actual labor cost incurred to find the $123,000 budgeted amount (standard cost of inputs) of labor cost at 20,000 hours of activity. Then divide $123,000 by 20,000 to find the standard direct-labor rate of $6.15. The $6,150 favorable labor efficiency variance is $6.15 times 1,000 hours (21,000 standard hours – 20,000 actual hours).

Actual labor cost	Act. hrs x std. rate	Std. hrs. x std. rate
$126,000	$123,000	21,000 x $6.15 =$129,150

$3,000 unfavorable $6,150 favorable

12. (1178,T1,43) (a) The requirement is the situation that would produce an unfavorable labor rate variance and a favorable labor efficiency variance. Unfavorable labor rate variances will be caused by higher-paid employees. Favorable labor efficiency variances can be caused by more experienced, better trained employees. Thus higher-paid, experienced individuals would tend to produce unfavorable labor rate variances and favorable labor efficiency variances. Answer (b) is incorrect because it is just the opposite of answer (a); low-paid unskilled workers will produce favorable labor rate variances and unfavorable labor efficiency variances. Answer (c) is incorrect because

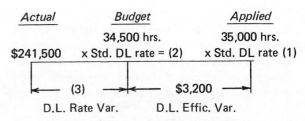

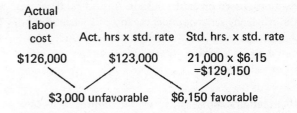

workers from other areas of production will probably result in unfavorable labor efficiency variances as they are unfamiliar with the task at hand. Answer (d) is incorrect because using more labor due to defective materials to produce a standard unit results in unfavorable labor efficiency variances.

13. (578,T2,43) (d) Overtime premiums increase the hourly wage to employees, and accordingly result in a labor rate variance. Recall that the labor rate variance has to do with the hourly rate of pay and the labor efficiency rate is concerned with the number of hours incurred.

14. (1176,T2,31) (b) The labor efficiency variance relates to the number of direct labor hours incurred. A debit balance indicates inefficiency or actual hours exceeded standard hours. Answer (a) describes a favorable efficiency variance. Answer (c) describes both a favorable rate variance and a favorable efficiency variance. Answer (d) describes both an unfavorable rate variance and an unfavorable efficiency variance.

E. Overhead Analysis: 2-Way

15. (1183,T1,42) (b) The requirement is the calculation of the volume variance, under the two-variance method. The volume variance is solely a **fixed** overhead variance. This variance occurs when actual activity differs from the budgeted (denominator) activity. Answer (b) is correct because the volume variance is the difference between budgeted costs and standard costs allowed (the amount applied to production), based on actual output. Answer (a) describes the efficiency variance under the three-variance method. Answer (c) describes the budget variance under the two-variance method. Answer (d) describes the total overhead variance.

16. (583,P2,39) (a) The requirement is the budget (controllable) variance for January 1983, using the two-way analysis of overhead variances. The controllable variance is the difference between actual overhead costs ($147,000), and overhead budgeted for the output achieved. When overhead is applied based on direct-labor hours, the budgeted amount is equal to budgeted fixed overhead ($108,000), plus standard direct-labor hours times the standard variable overhead rate (21,000 x $2 = $42,000). The standard variable rate is computed by dividing budgeted variable overhead by the budgeted activity level ($48,000 ÷ 24,000 = $2). The budget (controllable) variance is computed below.

Actual	Budget for output achieved
	$108,000 + (21,000 x $2)
$147,000	$150,000

← Budget variance, $3,000 F →

The variance is favorable because actual costs are less than budgeted costs.

17. (583,T1,48) (d) The requirement is the calculation of the controllable (budget) variance for the two-variance method. The two-variance method is diagrammed as:

Actual overhead	Budget for outputs achieved*	Applied overhead
	Fixed OH + (SQ x SVR)	SQ x STR

← Budget variance → ← Volume variance →

*Based on standard inputs allowed.

Thus, the difference between actual factory overhead costs and the budget allowance based on standard hours allowed [answer (d)] represents the controllable (budget) variance. Answer (a) describes the volume variance for factory overhead. Answer (b) is incorrect because this difference is not used in the two-variance method, although it is used in the three-variance method. Answer (c) is incorrect because it describes the **total** factory overhead variance.

F. Overhead Analysis: 3-Way

18. (1183,T1,43) (b) The requirement is the calculation of the spending variance under the three-variance method. The spending variance occurs when the actual amount spent for overhead items (both fixed and variable) differs from the budgeted amount based on actual direct labor hours. Answer (b) is correct because the factory overhead applied to production is excluded from the computation of the spending variance.

19. (575,P2,18) (b) First, note that there are three related questions on the same data. Study all of the requirements before beginning any question. Second, you should review overhead variances. Spending variance is the difference between the actual price and the standard price for items purchased. Efficiency variance is the difference between the actual input and the standard input at standard price. Fixed budget variance is the actual amount versus the budgeted amount spent. Volume variance is the difference between the budgeted fixed overhead and the amount actually applied based on the budgeted rate.

Variable variances:

Spending		Efficiency
Actual input	Actual input	Standard input
Actual price	Standard price	Standard price

Fixed variances:

Budget		Volume
Actual	Budget	Standard hours
		Budgeted rate

The requirement is the actual hours worked. In this problem there was no reported fixed budget variance. Thus the fixed overhead was $110,000 and the actual variable overhead was $68,500 ($178,500 – $110,000). Take the $8,000 of unfavorable spending variance from the $68,500, and the remaining $60,500 divided by $.50 equals 121,000 actual hours worked (i.e., the budgeted variable costs divided by the variable overhead rate).

20. (575,P2,19) (d) The standard hours of good output during the quarter were 115,000. The variable overhead rate is $.50 and the total overhead rate is $1.50 making the fixed overhead application rate $1.00/hr. Not only were all of the $110,000 of fixed overhead applied but also an additional $5,000 because there was a $5,000 favorable volume variance. Recall that the volume variance is based upon standard hours at the budgeted rate.

G. Overhead Analysis by Cost Behavior

21. (1183,P3,47) (a) The requirement is the amount to be credited to the applied factory overhead account for April 1983. The predetermined overhead rate is computed as follows:

$$\frac{\text{Est. OH costs}}{\text{Est. DL hours}} = \frac{\$80{,}000}{20{,}000} = \underline{\underline{\$4 \text{ per DL hour}}}$$

Under a standard cost system, overhead is applied on the basis of standard activity (in this case, DL hours) allowed. Production was 9,500 units with two hours per unit allowed at standard. Accordingly, there were 19,000 standard direct labor hours allowed (9,500 x 2) resulting in $76,000 of overhead (19,000 x $4) being applied to work in process.

22. (1183,P3,56) (b) The requirement is the budget (controllable) overhead variance for 1982. This variance is the difference between the actual overhead incurred ($252,000) and the overhead budgeted for the actual outputs achieved. Fawcett operated at 90% of capacity. A 90% level means that 36,000 direct-labor hours (40,000 x 90%) were worked. The variable overhead rate is $2 per DL hour [($64,000 ÷ 32,000) or ($80,000 ÷ 40,000)]. Therefore, total budgeted overhead consists of $160,000 fixed (given) and $72,000 variable (36,000 x $2), or $232,000. The budget variance is $252,000 (actual) less $232,000 (budgeted), or $20,000. The variance is unfavorable, since actual costs exceeded budgeted costs.

23. (575,T2,38) (b) The difference between actual factory overhead incurred and budgeted factory overhead is a spending variance. Answer (a), the volume variance, is the difference between the budgeted amount of fixed overhead and the actual fixed overhead applied based upon standard hours of production. The efficiency variance is the difference between the actual variable overhead incurred at standard prices and the standard input at standard prices, i.e., it is the usage variance of variable overhead. The quantity variance is the difference between actual materials used at standard and the standard materials at standard costs.

J. Disposition of Variances

24. (579,T1,25) (b) Significant usage variances (or any other variance) should be allocated to work-in-process inventory, finished goods inventory, and cost of goods sold at year-end. If significant variances exist, the inventory and cost of goods sold figures are not stated at actual costs, i.e., they are misstated. This may be the result of faulty standards, changed conditions, etc. If the variance is favorable, inventory and cost of goods sold have been overstated. If the variance is unfavorable, inventory and cost of goods sold have been understated. An additional allocation must be made between work-in-process and finished goods inventories. Answer (d) is incorrect because cost of goods manufactured refers to the amount of goods completed in the period and transferred from the work-in-process account to the finished goods (inventory) account, i.e., it represents a flow rather than a year-end balance.

M. Analysis of Variation in Gross Profit (AVGP)

25. (582,P2,32) (d) The requirement is the amount of decrease in gross profit caused by a 10% decrease in selling prices. If 1981 prices are 10% lower than 1980 prices, then 1981 sales are 90% of what they would have been had 1980 prices been in effect.

Taking 1981 sales of $792,000 and dividing by 90% gives a result of $880,000. Sales in 1981 were actually $792,000, but if there was no decrease in selling prices, 1981 sales would have been $880,000. Therefore, sales and gross profit are $88,000 less because of the 10% decrease in selling prices.

26. (1181,P2,31) (a) The requirement is to determine the effects of changes in sales price and sales volume between two years' data. Note that the requirement only requires use of the sales data. This problem is solved as a variance problem using the 1980 figures as actual price and quantity and the 1979 figures as standard price and quantity:

	1980 (actual)	*1979 (standard)*
Sales price	$750,000 sales ÷ 150,000 units = $5 per unit	$720,000 sales ÷ 180,000 units = $4 per unit
Sales quantity	150,000 units	180,000 units

Using these values, the variance analysis can be diagrammed as follows:

(Actual quantity x Actual price)	(Actual quantity x Standard price)	(Standard quantity x Standard price)
(150,000 x $5)	(150,000 x $4)	(180,000 x $4)

< $150,000 F >	< $120,000 U >
Sales price variance	Sales quantity (volume) variance

May 1984 Answer

27. (584,T1,44) (a) The requirement is to identify the information necessary to calculate the spending variance using the three-variance method. Under the three-variance method, the spending variance is diagrammed as follows:

Actual overhead	Budget for actual inputs Fixed OH + (AQ x SVR)*

|← Spending variance →|

*SVR = Standard variable rate

Answer (a) is correct because actual hours, not standard hours, are needed to calculate the spending variance.

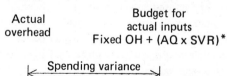

Solution Guide

Problem 1 Standard Costs and Variances

1. This problem consists of four parts which are based on common information. The requirements include computations of standard costs and various variances.

2. Part a. requires a schedule showing the computation of the standard cost of lots 22, 23, and 24 for June 1980.

2.1 The standard costs for a dozen blouses are summarized in the first table given in the problem. The standard costs per dozen are $26.40 (DM), $14.70 (DL), and $12.00 (MOH), or a total standard cost per dozen of $53.10.

2.2 Lots 22 and 23 were completed during June, so the standard cost of these lots is the number of units in each lot (1,000 and 1,700) multiplied by $53.10.

2.3 Lot 24 was complete as to material, but only 80% complete as to labor and overhead. Although the data given only mention the percentage of completion as to direct labor, the paragraph above mentions that overhead is applied on the basis of direct labor. Therefore, the number of units in lot 24 (1,200) would be multiplied by the standard cost of materials ($26.40). However, the standard direct labor cost ($14.70) and overhead cost ($12.00) are multiplied by only 80% of 1,200 units, or 960 equivalent dozens of production.

3. Part b. requires the computation of the materials price variance for June 1980 and an indication of whether that variance is favorable or unfavorable.

3.1 The solutions approach is to recall the format for computing materials variances. Since Vogue records the material price variance at the time of purchase, the price variance is computed by comparing the total actual price of the actual quantity purchased (AQ x AP) with the total standard price of the actual quantity purchased (AQ x SP).

AQ x AP	AQ x SP
	95,000 yards x $1.10/yard
$106,400	$104,500
$1,900 Unfav. price variance	

3.2 The price variance is unfavorable since the actual price resulted in a larger total cost than the standard price.

4. Part c. requires a schedule showing, for each lot, the computation of three different variances: materials quantity in yards, labor efficiency in hours, and labor rate in dollars. The required schedule should have either three columnar or three row headings for lots 22, 23, and 24.

4.1 The materials quantity variance is to be computed in yards, not dollars; therefore, this variance is simply the actual quantity of materials used less the standard quantity allowed (AQ – SQ). The actual quantity used for each lot is given in the second table (24,100; 40,440; 28,825). The standard quantity of materials allowed is the number of dozens in each lot multiplied by the standard material quantity of 24 yards per dozen. For example, lot 22 contains 1,000 dozens at 24 yards each, or 24,000 standard yards allowed. The same computation is repeated for lots 23 and 24 (note that lot 24 is complete as to materials). If the actual quantity is greater than standard, the variance is unfavorable; if actual is less than standard, the variance is favorable.

4.2 The labor efficiency variance is to be computed in hours, not dollars; therefore, this variance is simply the actual labor hours used less the standard hours allowed (AH – SH). The actual hours worked on each lot is given (2,980; 5,130; 2,890). The standard hours of direct labor allowed is the number of dozens in each lot multiplied by the standard hours per dozen (3). However, since lot 24 is only 80% complete as to direct labor, the number of dozens (1,200) must be multiplied by 80% to obtain 960 equivalent dozens; this is multiplied by 3 standard hours per unit resulting in 2,880 standard hours allowed for lot 24.

4.3 The labor rate variance is to be computed in dollars. The solutions approach is to recall the format for computing labor variances. The total labor rate variance is computed by comparing the actual direct labor cost (AH x AR) with the total standard cost of the actual direct labor hours used (AH x SR).

AH x AR	AH x SR
11,000 x $5.00	11,000 x $4.90
$55,000	$53,900
$1,100 Unfav. rate variance	

4.4 The total labor rate variance of $1,100 (Unfavorable) must be broken down for each of the three lots. This can be done by multiplying the actual hours for each lot by the difference between the actual and standard rates [AH(AR – SR)].

5. Part d. requires a schedule showing computations of the total controllable and noncontrollable (volume) variances for June 1980.

5.1 The only overhead variance which is considered noncontrollable is the fixed overhead volume variance. Therefore, the other three overhead variances commonly computed (variable overhead spending variance, efficiency variance, and fixed overhead budget variance) are included as the controllable variance.

5.2 The format used when performing two-way (controllable and noncontrollable) variance analysis of overhead is to compare actual overhead, budgeted overhead at standard hours, and applied overhead.

5.3 Actual overhead, variable and fixed, was given as $45,600. Since it is not broken down between fixed and variable, it is necessary to do a "combined analysis" to find the variances.

5.4 Total overhead was budgeted at $576,000 for 1980, based on normal activity of 48,000 dozen blouses per year. This budgeted amount consists of 40% fixed overhead ($230,400) and 60% variable overhead ($345,600). The budgeted fixed overhead for June is the yearly amount ($230,400) divided by 12, or $19,200. The budgeted variable overhead must be computed per direct labor hours, since this is the basis used to apply overhead. Three standard direct labor hours are allowed per dozen blouses, so 144,000 hours would be allowed for 48,000 blouses. Therefore, the budgeted variable overhead per standard direct labor hour is $345,600/144,000 hours = $2.40/hour. The total standard hours allowed for June was computed in part c2. as 10,980 hours; when multiplied by $2.40, this results in $26,352 variable overhead budgeted at standard hours allowed.

5.5 Applied overhead is equal to standard hours allowed (10,980) multiplied by the predetermined overhead rate. For variable overhead, the predetermined rate is the previously computed standard rate of $2.40/hour, so variable overhead applied is $26,352. The predetermined rate for fixed overhead is budgeted annual fixed overhead ($230,400) divided by normal annual activity (144,000 hours) or $1.60. Therefore, fixed overhead applied is (10,980 hours)($1.60), or $17,568.

5.6 Based on the calculations in 5.3–5.5, a diagram can be set up to analyze overhead.

	Actual	*Budgeted at standard*	*Applied*
Fixed	*	$19,200	$17,568
Variable	*	26,352	26,352
Total	$45,600	$45,552	$43,920
	$48 Unfav. Controllable		$1,632 Unfav. Noncontrollable

*not broken out in this problem

The controllable variance is unfavorable because actual cost was greater than budgeted cost. The noncontrollable (volume) variance is unfavorable because the plant was underutilized; 10,980 standard hours were worked in June, less than normal capacity of 12,000 hours (144,000 hours ÷ 12 months).

5.7 Notice that the noncontrollable variance consists solely of the fixed overhead volume variance (fixed OH budgeted less fixed OH applied). Variable overhead budgeted at standard is equal to variable overhead applied; therefore, variable overhead does not enter into this computation.

Unofficial Answer

Problem 1 Standard Costs and Variances

Part a.

Vogue Fashions, Inc.
Schedule of Standard Costs for Lots 22, 23, and 24
For Month of June 1980

	Dozens	*Direct materials*	*Direct labor*	*Manufacturing overhead*	*Total per dozen*	*Total standard cost*
Lot 22	1,000				$53.10	$ 53,100
Lot 23	1,700				$53.10	90,270
Lot 24	1,200	$26.40				31,680
	960*		$14.70	$12.00		25,632
Total standard cost						$200,682

*1,200 dozen x .80 = 960 equivalent dozens

Part b.

Vogue Fashions, Inc.
Schedule of Materials Price Variance
For Month of June 1980

Actual cost of materials purchased		$106,400
Standard cost of materials purchased:		
Yards	95,000	
Standard cost per yard	x $1.10	104,500
Materials price variance—Unfavorable		$ 1,900

Part c.

1.

Vogue Fashions, Inc.
Schedule of Materials Quantity Variances
for Lots 22, 23, and 24
For Month of June 1980

	Lot 22		Lot 23		Lot 24	
Actual Quantity		24,100		40,440		28,825
Standard Quantity						
Dozens	1,000		1,700		1,200	
Standard per dozen	x 24	24,000	x 24	40,800	x 24	28,800
Variance in yards		100 U		360 F		25 U

F = Favorable U = Unfavorable

2.

Vogue Fashions, Inc.
Schedule of Labor Efficiency Variances
for Lots 22, 23, and 24
For Month of June 1980

	Lot 22		Lot 23		Lot 24	
Actual hours		2,980		5,130		2,890
Standard hours						
Dozens	1,000		1,700		960*	
Standard per dozen	x 3		x 3		x 3	
Standard hours per lot		3,000		5,100		2,880
Variance in hours		20 F		30 U		10 U

*1,200 dozens, 80% complete

F = Favorable U = Unfavorable

3.

Vogue Fashions, Inc.
Schedule of Labor Rate Variances
for Lots 22, 23, and 24
For Month of June 1980

	Lot 22	Lot 23	Lot 24
Actual rate	$5.00	$5.00	$5.00
Standard rate	$4.90	$4.90	$4.90
	$ .10	$ .10	$ .10
Actual hours	2,980	5,130	2,890
Unfavorable	$ 298	$ 513	$ 289

Part d.

Vogue Fashions, Inc.
Schedule of Controllable and Uncontrollable Overhead Variances
For Month of June 1980

Total actual overhead		$45,600
Less overhead budgeted at standard hours allowed		
Fixed ($576,000)(40%)(1/12)	$19,200	
Variable (see Schedule 1)	26,352	45,552
Controllable variance—unfavorable		$ 48
Overhead budgeted at standard hours (above)		$45,552
Less overhead applied		
Fixed (see Schedule 2)	$17,568	
Variable (see Schedule 1)	26,352	43,920
Noncontrollable variance—unfavorable		$ 1,632

Schedule 1

Computation of Variable Overhead Budgeted at Standard

Variable overhead budgeted for 1980 (60% x $576,000 total budgeted)	$345,600
Standard hours at normal capacity (48,000 dozen x 3 hours per dozen)	÷ 144,000
Standard variable overhead rate	$ 2.40/ hr.
Standard hours allowed in June (see part c2.) (3,000 + 5,100 + 2,880)	x 10,980
Variable overhead budgeted and applied at standard hours allowed	$ 26,352

Schedule 2

Computation of Fixed Overhead Applied

Fixed overhead budgeted for 1980 (40%)($576,000)	$230,400
Standard hours at normal capacity (48,000 dozen x 3 hours per dozen)	÷144,000
Predetermined fixed overhead rate	$ 1.60/hr.
Standard hours allowed in June (see Schedule 1)	x 10,980
Fixed overhead applied	$ 17,568

Answer Outline

Problem 2 Standard Costs

a. Fixed standards do not change
   - May be originally ideal or attainable
   - Over time, value to management decreases

   Ideal standards assume 100% capacity
   - And 100% factory and labor efficiency
   - Also assume minimum material, labor, etc., costs

   Attainable standards reflect factory inefficiencies
   - E.g., normal spoilage
   - But above-average efficiency

b. Efficiencies in acquisition of product components
   - Material price variances
   - Labor rate variances
   - Overhead spending variances

   Efficiencies in usage of product components
   - Material usage variance
   - Labor efficiency variance
   - Variable overhead efficiencies

   Fixed overhead variances relate budgeted amounts to standard amounts applied to product

c. Standard costs are used for cost accumulation as well as cost accounting
   - Can be used in any cost accumulation framework
   - Are not a mandatory component of cost accumulation

Unofficial Answer

Problem 2 Standard Costs

a. A fixed or basic standard, once established, is unchanging. Such a standard may be ideal or attainable when established, but it is never altered once it has been set. Because of the obvious diminution of utility to management over a span of time, fixed standards are rarely used in manufacturing concerns.

An ideal standard is computed using utopian conditions for a given manufacturing process. Ideal standards presume that material, labor, and factory overhead items will be purchased at the minimum price in all cases. Ideal standards also are based upon the optimal usage of the material, labor, and factory overhead components at 100 percent manufacturing capacity. In reality, ideal standards cannot be met and will give rise to unfavorable variances.

Attainable standards are standards based on a high degree of efficiency, but differ from ideal standards in that they can be met or even surpassed by the employment of excellent management. Attainable standards consider that the component parts (material, labor, and factory overhead) can be purchased at a good overall price, not necessarily the lowest price at all times, but well below the expected highest price. Attainable standards also consider that (1) labor is not 100 percent efficient; (2) when material is used there will be some "normal" spoilage; and (3) a manufacturing concern cannot produce at 100 percent of theoretical capacity. Attainable standards are set above average levels of efficiency, but may be met or surpassed in efficient production situations.

b. All standards attempt to monitor costs and measure efficiency. In relation to the acquisition of goods or services related to a manufacturing situation, the variances (for example, spending variances) from standard disclose efficiencies in the "purchasing" function. With respect to the utilization of the component parts of a manufacturing process, standards and related variance reports are meant to disclose relative efficiency in the usage of the goods or services in the actual manufacturing process. For material, labor, and variable factory overhead variances, the efficiencies are measured by comparing actual operations with operations stated in standard units (dollars).

Fixed factory overhead is evaluated with reference to a budget amount that is compared to standard amounts of fixed factory overhead applied and actual amounts expended for fixed overhead items.

c. Standards are an integral part of a cost accumulation procedure (such as job order, process, direct) but do not comprise a system that could be utilized in lieu of one of the accumulation procedures mentioned above. Standards may be used within any cost accumulation procedure, but a cost accumulation procedure may be employed without the inclusion of standards.

Answer Outline

Problem 3 Variance Analysis

Part b.

1. Purpose of factory overhead variance analysis
    - Controlling costs
        - Pinpoints areas needing managerial attention
        - Indicates items both above and below budget
    - Motivating and measuring efficiency
        - Performance evaluation
        - Controllable vs. non-controllable
    - Encouraging possible cost reduction and/or quality control
2. Assumptions associated with the two-variance method
    - Separation of fixed and variable costs to enable preparation of flexible budget
    - Assignment of responsibility for controllable variances
    - Costs are perfectly positively correlated with overhead base
    - Causes of variances can be identified
    - Variances can be identified as controllable/uncontrollable

   Significance of variances
    - Flexible budget (controllable) variance
        - Actual costs compared with flexible budget for output achieved
        - Responsibility of department managers
    - Volume (noncontrollable) variance
        - Flexible budget for outputs acheived compared with overhead applied
        - Utilization of capacity (variation of actual from expected output)

Unofficial Answer
(Author Modified)

Problem 3 Variance Analysis

Part b.

1. A primary purpose of factory overhead variance analysis is controlling overhead costs. The variance report should pinpoint areas needing managerial attention (management by exception). Items which are significantly above or below budgeted amounts should be investigated to determine the cause of the variance. Other purposes of variance analysis are motivation and measurement of efficiency. The performance of department managers is measured and evaluated based on the variance analysis report. The variances must be categorized as either controllable by managers or non-controllable. A related purpose of variance analysis is the encouragement of possible cost reduction and/or quality control.

2. Five basic assumptions underly the two-variance method of analyzing factory overhead. First, the firm must be able to separate the fixed and variable components of overhead cost. This is necessary because both variable and fixed overhead have to be calculated on the flexible budget which is used to separate the two variances. Another assumption is that responsibility for controllable variances can be assigned to various departments. This is crucial if the variance analysis report is to be used to control, measure, evaluate and motivate. A third assumption is that overhead costs are perfectly positively correlated with the overhead base. A fourth assumption is that the causes of the variances can be identified. A fifth assumption is that the variances can be identified as controllable or noncontrollable. Both the fourth and fifth assumptions are necessary before benefits can be obtained from the variances analysis.

One of the variances computed in two-way overhead analysis is the flexible-budget, or controllable variance. This variance is the difference between actual overhead costs and the flexible budget overhead. This variance is generally controllable and is the responsibility of various department managers.

The other two-way variance is the volume, or noncontrollable variance. The volume variance is the difference between the overhead on the flexible budget and the overhead applied. Since variable overhead on the flexible budget (prepared on standard quantities) and variable overhead applied are always equal, the noncontrollable variance will be measured entirely in fixed overhead dollars. This variance is often not controllable in the short run. It is a measure of the extent of the variation of actual output from expected output.

Solution Guide

Problem 4 Gross Profit

1. The requirement in part a. is an analysis of variance of sales and cost of goods sold from 1974 to 1975. Like cost variance the change or variation is a function of changes in units and prices (costs).

1.1 Two way analysis of variance would be

Sales:		
Volume:		
5,000 units @ $10	=	$ (50,000)
Price:		
70,000 units @ $2	=	140,000
Net increase		$ 90,000
Cost of Sales		
Volume:		
5,000 units @ $6.60	=	$ (33,000)
Price:		
70,000 units @ $1.40	=	98,000
Net increase		$ 65,000

1.2 The unofficial solution presents three way analysis of variance. The difference is a price-volume variance in addition to the price and volume variances.

Unofficial Answer

Problem 4 Gross Profit

a.

Celebration, Inc.
Statement Accounting for Variation in Sales and Cost of Goods Sold Between the Years 1974 and 1975

Increase in net sales:	
Variation due to decrease in volume at the 1974 selling price (–5,000 x $10)	–$ 50,000
Variation due to increase in selling price at the 1974 volume (75,000 x $2)	150,000
Variation due to joint decrease in volume and increase in selling price (–5,000 x $2)	– 10,000
Increase in net sales	$ 90,000
Less increase in cost of goods sold:	
Variation due to decrease in volume at the 1974 costs (–5,000 x $6.60)	– 33,000
Variation due to increase in costs at the 1974 volume (75,000 x $1.40)	105,000
Variation due to joint decrease in volume and increase in costs	– 7,000
Increase in cost of goods sold	65,000
Increase in dollar gross margin	$ 25,000

Solution Guide

Problem 5 Standard Costing

1. **The requirement in part b is to compute six standard cost figures. The solutions approach is to calculate each amount separately.**

1.1 **The standard quantity of raw materials is the actual production of 4,000 units times the standard usage of 6 pounds per unit.**

1.2 **The actual quantity of raw materials used is the standard quantity of 24,000 lbs. (just computed above) plus the unfavorable material usage variance ($1,000 variance divided by $1.00 standard cost) of 1,000 lbs.**

1.3 **The standard hours of production is the actual production of 4,000 units times the standard labor usage of 1 hour.**

1.4 **The actual hours worked is the standard hours allowed of 4,000 less the favorable labor efficiency variance ($800 variance ÷ $4/hr.) of 200 hours.**

1.5 **The actual labor rate is the standard labor rate of $4 plus the unfavorable rate variance (760 ÷ 3,800 hours) of $ .20.**

1.6 **The actual total overhead is the standard overhead of $12,000 (4,000 units @ $3.00) plus the unfavorable overhead variance of $500.**

Unofficial Answer

Problem 5 Standard Costing

b.

1. Standard quantity of raw materials allowed:		
Actual production	4,000	units
Standard raw materials per unit	x6	pounds
Standard quantity of raw materials allowed	24,000	pounds
2. Actual quantity of raw materials used:		
Standard quantity	24,000	pounds
Unfavorable (debit) material quantity variance ($1,000 variance x $1 standard price per lb.)	+1,000	pounds
Actual quantity of raw materials used	25,000	pounds
3. Standard hours allowed:		
Actual production	4,000	units
Standard hours per unit	x1	hour
Standard hours allowed	4,000	hours
4. Actual hours worked:		
Standard hours allowed	4,000	hours
Favorable (credit) direct labor efficiency variance (800 variance ÷ $4 standard hrs. per unit)	(200)	hours
Actual hours worked	3,800	hours
5. Actual direct labor rate:		
Standard direct labor rate	$4.00	
Unfavorable (debit) direct labor rate variance ($760 variance ÷ 3,800 hrs. actually worked)	+ .20	
Actual direct labor rate	$4.20	
6. Actual total overhead:		
Standard overhead (4000 units produced x $3 standard overhead rate per unit)	$12,000	
Unfavorable (debit) overhead variance	500	
Actual total overhead	$12,500	

Multiple Choice Questions (1–31)

1. The manufacturing capacity of Jordan Company's facilities is 30,000 units of product a year. A summary of operating results for the year ended December 31, 1982, is as follows:

Sales (18,000 units @ $100)	$1,800,000
Variable manufacturing and selling costs	990,000
Contribution margin	810,000
Fixed costs	495,000
Operating income	$ 315,000

A foreign distributor has offered to buy 15,000 units at $90 per unit during 1983. Assume that all of Jordan's costs would be at the same levels and rates in 1983 as in 1982. If Jordan accepted this offer and rejected some business from regular customers so as not to exceed capacity, what would be the total operating income for 1983?

a. $390,000
b. $705,000
c. $840,000
d. $855,000

2. Rice Corporation currently operates two divisions which had operating results for the year ended December 31, 1982, as follows:

	West Division	*Troy Division*
Sales	$600,000	$300,000
Variable costs	310,000	200,000
Contribution margin	290,000	100,000
Fixed costs for the Division	110,000	70,000
Margin over direct costs	180,000	30,000
Allocated corporate costs	90,000	45,000
Operating income (loss)	$ 90,000	$(15,000)

Since the Troy Division also sustained an operating loss during 1981, Rice's president is considering the elimination of this division. Assume that the Troy Division fixed costs could be avoided if the division were eliminated. If the Troy Division had been eliminated on January 1, 1982, Rice Corporation's 1982 operating income would have been

a. $15,000 higher.
b. $30,000 lower.
c. $45,000 lower.
d. $60,000 higher.

3. Wagner Company sells product A at a selling price of $21 per unit. Wagner's cost per unit based on the full capacity of 200,000 units is as follows:

Direct materials	$ 4
Direct labor	5
Overhead (two-thirds of which is fixed)	6
	$15

A special order offering to buy 20,000 units was received from a foreign distributor. The only selling costs that would be incurred on this order would be $3 per unit for shipping. Wagner has sufficient existing capacity to manufacture the additional units. In negotiating a price for the special order, Wagner should consider that the minimum selling price per unit should be

a. $14
b. $15
c. $16
d. $18

4. Gandy Company has 5,000 obsolete desk lamps that are carried in inventory at a manufacturing cost of $50,000. If the lamps are reworked for $20,000, they could be sold for $35,000. Alternatively, the lamps could be sold for $8,000 to a jobber located in a distant city. In a decision model analyzing these alternatives, the sunk cost would be

a. $ 8,000
b. $15,000
c. $20,000
d. $50,000

5. Plainfield Company manufactures part G for use in its production cycle. The cost per unit for 10,000 units of part G are as follows:

Direct materials	$ 3
Direct labor	15
Variable overhead	6
Fixed overhead	8
	$32

Verona Company has offered to sell Plainfield 10,000 units of part G for $30 per unit. If Plainfield accepts Verona's offer, the released facilities could be used to save $45,000 in relevant costs in the manufacture of part H. In addition $5 per unit of the fixed overhead applied to part G would be totally eliminated. What alternative is more desirable and by what amount is it more desirable?

	Alternative	*Amount*
a.	Manufacture	$10,000
b.	Manufacture	$15,000
c.	Buy	$35,000
d.	Buy	$65,000

6. The Blade Division of Dana Company produces hardened steel blades. One-third of the Blade Division's output is sold to the Lawn Products Division of Dana; the remainder is sold to outside customers. The Blade Division's estimated sales and standard cost data for the fiscal year ending June 30, 1981, are as follows:

	Lawn products	*Outsiders*
Sales	$15,000	$40,000
Variable costs	(10,000)	(20,000)
Fixed costs	(3,000)	(6,000)
Gross margin	$ 2,000	$14,000
Unit sales	10,000	20,000

The Lawn Products Division has an opportunity to purchase 10,000 identical quality blades from an outside supplier at a cost of $1.25 per unit on a continuing basis. Assume that the Blade Division cannot sell any additional products to outside customers. Should Dana allow its Lawn Products Division to purchase the blades from the outside supplier, and why?

a. Yes, because buying the blades would save Dana Company $500.
b. No, because making the blades would save Dana Company $1,500.
c. Yes, because buying the blades would save Dana Company $2,500.
d. No, because making the blades would save Dana Company $2,500.

7. Light Company has 2,000 obsolete light fixtures that are carried in inventory at a manufacturing cost of $30,000. If the fixtures are reworked for $10,000, they could be sold for $18,000. Alternately, the light fixtures could be sold for $3,000 to a jobber located in a distant city. In a decision model analyzing these alternatives, the opportunity cost would be

a. $ 3,000
b. $10,000
c. $13,000
d. $30,000

8. The following standard costs pertain to a component part manufactured by Ashby Company:

Direct materials	$ 2
Direct labor	5
Factory overhead	20
Standard cost per unit	$27

Factory overhead is applied at $1 per standard machine hour. Fixed capacity cost is 60% of applied factory overhead, and is not affected by any "make or buy" decision. It would cost $25 per unit to buy the part from an outside supplier. In the decision to "make or buy," what is the total relevant unit manufacturing cost to be considered?

a. $ 2
b. $15
c. $19
d. $27

9. In deciding whether to manufacture a part or buy it from an outside vendor, a cost that is irrelevant to the short-run decision is

a. Direct labor.
b. Variable overhead.
c. Fixed overhead that will be avoided if the part is bought from an outside vendor.
d. Fixed overhead that will continue even if the part is bought from an outside vendor.

37

10. The discount rate (hurdle rate of return) must be determined in advance for the

a. Payback period method.
b. Time adjusted rate of return method.
c. Internal rate of return method.
d. Net present value method.

11. Which of the following capital budgeting techniques consider(s) cash flow over the entire life of the project?

	Internal rate of return	*Payback*
a.	Yes	Yes
b.	Yes	No
c.	No	Yes
d.	No	No

12. Maxwell Company has an opportunity to acquire a new machine to replace one of its present machines. The new machine would cost $90,000, have a five-year life, and no estimated salvage value. Variable operating costs would be $100,000 per year.

The present machine has a book value of $50,000 and a remaining life of five years. Its disposal value now is $5,000 but it would be zero after five years. Variable operating costs would be $125,000 per year.

Ignore present-value calculations and income taxes. Considering the five years in total, what would be the difference in profit before income taxes by acquiring the new machine as opposed to retaining the present one?

a. $10,000 decrease.
b. $15,000 decrease.
c. $35,000 increase.
d. $40,000 increase.

13. The minimum return that a project must earn for a company in order to leave the value of the company unchanged is the

a. Current borrowing rate.
b. Discount rate.
c. Capitalization rate.
d. Cost of capital.

14. Sensitivity analysis is used in capital budgeting to quantify the

a. Amount that an assumed factor used in evaluating a project could be varied and still produce acceptable results.
b. Reaction within the marketplace to a new product.
c. Type of capital that will have to be committed to an anticipated project.
d. Relationship between the payback period and the economic lives of the assets used in a project.

15. The weighted average cost of capital approach to decision making is not directly affected by the

a. Value of the common stock.
b. Current budget for expansion.
c. Cost of debt outstanding.
d. Proposed mix of debt, equity, and existing funds used to implement the project.

16. What capital-budgeting method assumes that funds are reinvested at the company's cost of capital?

a. Payback.
b. Accounting rate of return.
c. Net present value.
d. Time-adjusted rate of return.

17. Nelson Company is planning to purchase a new machine for $500,000. The new machine is expected to produce cash flow from operations, before income taxes, of $135,000 a year in each of the next five years. Depreciation of $100,000 a year will be charged to income for each of the next five years. Assume that the income tax rate is 40%. The payback period would be approximately

a. 2.2 years.
b. 3.4 years.
c. 3.7 years
d. 4.1 years.

18. The Polar Company is planning to purchase a new machine for $30,000. The pay-back period is expected to be five years. The new machine is expected to produce cash flow from operations, net of income taxes, of $7,000 a year in each of the next three years and $5,500 in the fourth year. Depreciation of $5,000 a year will be charged to income for each of the five years of the payback period. What is the amount of cash flow from operations, net of taxes, that the new machine is expected to produce in the last (fifth) year of the pay-back period?

a. $1,000
b. $3,500
c. $5,000
d. $8,500

19. Which of the following is necessary in order to calculate the pay-back period for a project?

a. Useful life.
b. Minimum desired rate of return.
c. Net present value.
d. Annual cash flow.

20. Heller Company purchased a machine for $500,000 with a useful life of five years and no salvage value. The machine is being depreciated using the straight-line method and it is expected to produce annual cash flow from operations, net of income taxes, of $150,000. The present value of an ordinary annuity of $1 for five periods at 14% is 3.43. The present value of $1 for five periods at 14% is 0.52. Assuming that Heller uses a time-adjusted rate of return of 14%, what is the net present value?

a. $280,000
b. $250,000
c. $180,000
d. $ 14,500

21. Garwood Company purchased a machine which will be depreciated on the straight-line basis over an estimated useful life of seven years and no salvage value. The machine is expected to generate cash flow from operations, net of income taxes, of $80,000 in each of the seven years. Garwood's expected rate of return is 12%. Information on present value factors is as follows:

Present value of $1 at 12% for seven periods	.0452
Present value of an ordinary annuity of $1 at 12% for seven periods	4.564

Assuming a positive net present value of $12,720, what was the cost of the machine?

a. $240,400
b. $253,120
c. $352,400
d. $377,840

22. How are the following used in the calculation of the net present value of a proposed project? Ignore income tax considerations.

	Depreciation expense	Salvage value
a.	Include	Include
b.	Include	Exclude
c.	Exclude	Include
d.	Exclude	Exclude

23. The net present value of a proposed project represents the

a. Cash flows less the present value of the cash flows.
b. Cash flows less the original investment.
c. Present value of the cash flows plus the present value of the original investment less the original investment.
d. Present value of the cash flows less the original investment.

24. Kipling Company invested in an eight-year project. It is expected that the annual cash flow from the project, net of income taxes, will be $20,000. Information on present value factors is as follows:

Present value of $1 at 12% for eight periods	0.404
Present value of an ordinary annuity of $1 at 12% for eight periods	4.968

Assuming that Kipling based its investment decision on an internal rate of return of 12%, how much did the project cost?

a. $160,000
b. $ 99,360
c. $ 80,800
d. $ 64,640

25. Hamilton Company invested in a two-year project having an internal rate of return of 12%. The project is expected to produce cash flow from operations, net of income taxes, of $60,000 in the first year and $70,000 in the second year. The present value of $1 for one period at 12% is 0.893 and for two periods at 12% is 0.797. How much will the project cost?

a. $103,610
b. $109,370
c. $116,090
d. $122,510

26. Tracy Corporation is planning to invest $80,000 in a three-year project. Tracy's expected rate of return is 10%. The present value of $1 at 10% for one year is .909, for two years is .826, and for three years is .751. The cash flow, net of income taxes, will be $30,000 for the first year (present value of $27,270) and $36,000 for the second year (present value of $29,736). Assuming the rate of return is exactly 10%, what will the cash flow, net of income taxes, be for the third year?

a. $17,268
b. $22,000
c. $22,994
d. $30,618

Items 27 and 28 are based on the following data:

Amaro Hospital, a nonprofit institution not subject to income taxes, is considering the purchase of new equipment costing $20,000, in order to achieve cash savings of $5,000 per year in operating costs. The equipment's estimated useful life is ten years, with no net residual value. Amaro's cost of capital is 14%. For ten periods at 14%, the present value of $1 is 0.270, while the present value of an ordinary annuity of $1 is 5.216.

27. What factor contained in or developed from the above information should be used in computing the internal rate of return for Amaro's proposed investment in the new equipment?

a. 5.216
b. 4.000
c. 1.400
d. 0.270

28. How much is the accounting rate of return based on Amaro's initial investment in the new equipment?

a. 27%
b. 25%
c. 15%
d. 14%

29. The Fudge Company is planning to purchase a new machine which it will depreciate on a straight-line basis over a ten-year period with no salvage value and a full year's depreciation taken in the year of acquisition. The new machine is expected to produce cash flow from operations, net of income taxes, of $66,000 a year in each of the next ten years. The accounting (book value) rate of return on the initial investment is expected to be 12%. How much will the new machine cost?

a. $300,000
b. $550,000
c. $660,000
d. $792,000

May 1984 Questions

30. Under the internal rate of return capital budgeting technique, it is assumed that cash flows are reinvested at the

a. Cost of capital.
b. Hurdle rate of return.
c. Rate earned by the investment.
d. Payback rate.

31. A company is deciding whether to exchange an old asset for a new asset. Within the context of the exchange decision, and ignoring income tax considerations, the undepreciated book balance of the old asset would be considered a(an)

	Sunk cost	*Irrelevant cost*
a.	No	No
b.	Yes	No
c.	No	Yes
d.	Yes	Yes

Problems

Problem 1 Special Order Decision (1174, T5)

(25 to 30 minutes)

Nubo Manufacturing, Inc., is presently operating at 50% of practical capacity producing about 50,000 units annually of a patented electronic component. Nubo recently received an offer from a company in Yokohama, Japan, to purchase 30,000 components at $6.00 per unit, FOB is Nubo's plant. Nubo has not previously sold components in Japan. Budgeted production costs for 50,000 and 80,000 units of output follow:

Units	50,000	80,000
Costs:		
Direct material	$ 75,000	$120,000
Direct labor	75,000	120,000
Factory overhead	200,000	260,000
Total costs	$350,000	$500,000
Cost per unit	$7.00	$6.25

The sales manager thinks the order sould be accepted even if it results in a loss of $1.00 per unit, because he feels the sales may build up future markets. The production manager does not wish to have the order accepted primarily because the order would show a loss of $.25 per unit when computed on the new average unit cost. The treasurer has made a quick computation indicating that accepting the order will actually increase gross margin.

Required:

a. Explain what apparently caused the drop in cost from $7.00 per unit to $6.25 per unit when budgeted production increased from 50,000 to 80,000 units. Show supporting computations.

b. 1. Explain whether (either or both) the production manager or the treasurer is correct in his reasoning.
   2. Explain why the conclusions of the production manager and the treasurer differ.

c. Explain why each of the following may affect the decision to accept or reject the special order.

1. The likelihood of repeat sales and/or all sales to be made at $6.00 per unit.
2. Whether the sales are made to customers operating in two separate, isolated markets or whether the sales are made to customers competing in the same market.

Problem 2 Capital Budgeting (1182,T4b)

(10 to 15 minutes)

Part b. The net present value method and the internal rate of return method are both sophisticated capital budgeting techniques.

Required:

1. State the advantages that both the net present value method and the internal rate of return method have over the payback method.
2. State the limitations of the net present value method.
3. State the limitations of the internal rate of return method.
4. How does each method (net present value and internal rate of return) handle depreciation? Discuss the rationale for your answer. Ignore income tax considerations in your answer.

Problem 3 Replacement Decision (577,Q4b)

(15 to 20 minutes)

Part b. The management of Essen Manufacturing Company is currently evaluating a proposal to purchase a new and innovative drill press as a replacement for a less efficient piece of similar equipment which would then be sold. The cost of the equipment including delivery and installation is $175,000. If the equipment is purchased, Essen will incur costs of $5,000 in removing the present equipment and revamping service facilities. The present equipment has a book value of $100,000 and a remaining useful life of 10 years. Due to new technical improvements which have made the equipment outmoded, it presently has a resale value of only $40,000.

Additional information:

- Management has provided you with the following comparative manufacturing cost tabulation:

	Present equipment	*New equipment*
Annual production-units	400,000	500,000
Annual costs:		
Labor	$30,000	$25,000
Operating costs:		
Depreciation (10% of asset book value)	10,000	17,500
Other	48,000	20,000
	58,000	37,500
Total	$88,000	$62,500

- Management believes that if the present equipment is not replaced now, it will have to wait 7 years before replacement is justifiable.
- Both pieces of equipment are expected to have a negligible salvage value at the end of 10 years.
- If the new equipment is purchased, the management of Essen would require a 15% return on the investment before income taxes.
- The following table lists the present value of an ordinary annuity of $1 at 15%:

Period	*Present value*
1	0.870
2	1.626
3	2.283
4	2.855
5	3.352
6	3.784
7	4.160
8	4.487
9	4.772
10	5.019

Required:

1. In order to assist the management of Essen in reaching a decision on the proposal, prepare schedules showing the computation of the following:
   - Net initial outlay before income taxes.
   - Net present value of investment before income taxes.
2. Would you recommend this investment, and why?

Note: Ignore any effects of net incremental cash flow from increased sales of units produced by the new machine.

Problem 4 Alternate Production Decisions (577,Q4a)

(25 to 30 minutes)

Part a. You have been engaged to assist the management of the Arcadia Corporation in arriving at certain decisions. Arcadia has its home office in Ohio and leases factory buildings in Texas, Montana and Maine, all of which produce the same product. The management of Arcadia has provided you with a projection of operations for 1977, the forthcoming year, as follows:

	Total	*Texas*	*Montana*	*Maine*
Sales	$4,400,000	$2,200,000	$1,400,000	$800,000
Fixed costs:				
Factory	1,100,000	560,000	280,000	260,000
Administration	350,000	210,000	110,000	30,000
Variable costs	1,450,000	665,000	425,000	360,000
Allocated home office costs	500,000	225,000	175,000	100,000
Total	3,400,000	1,660,000	900,000	750,000
Net profit from operations	$1,000,000	$ 540,000	$ 410,000	$ 50,000

The sales price per unit is $25.

Due to the marginal results of operations of the factory in Maine, Arcadia has decided to cease operations and sell that factory's machinery and equipment by the end of 1976. Arcadia expects that the proceeds from the sale of these assets would be greater than their book value and would cover all termination costs.

Arcadia, however, would like to continue serving its customers in that area if it is economically feasible and is considering one of the following three alternatives:

1. Expand the operations of the Montana factory by using space presently idle. This move would result in the following changes in that factory's operations:

	Increase over factory's current operations
Sales	50%
Fixed costs:	
Factory	20%
Administration	10%

Under this proposal, variable costs would be $8 per unit sold.

2. Enter into a long-term contract with a competitor who will serve that area's customers. This competitor would pay Arcadia a royalty of $4 per unit based upon an estimate of 30,000 units being sold.

3. Close the Maine factory and not expand the operations of the Montana factory.

Required:

In order to assist the management of Arcadia Corporation in determining which alternative is more economically feasible, prepare a schedule computing Arcadia's estimated net profit from total operations that would result from each of the following methods:

1. Expansion of the Montana factory.
2. Negotiation of long-term contract on a royalty basis.
3. Shutdown of Maine operations with no expansion at other locations.

Note: Total home office costs of $500,000 will remain the same under each situation.

Multiple Choice Answers

1. b	8. b	14. a	20. d	26. d
2. b	9. d	15. b	21. c	27. b
3. a	10. d	16. c	22. c	28. c
4. d	11. b	17. d	23. d	29. a
5. c	12. d	18. b	24. b	30. c
6. d	13. d	19. d	25. b	31. d
7. a				

Multiple Choice Answer Explanations

A. Short-Term Differential Cost Analysis

1. (1183,P3,50) (b) The requirement is the total operating income for 1983 if a special order is accepted. Since capacity is 30,000 units, acceptance of the special order for 15,000 units leaves only 15,000 units (30,000 – 15,000) of capacity for business from regular customers. Assuming the order is accepted, revenue would consist of 15,000 units at $100 per unit ($1,500,000) and 15,000 units at $90 per unit ($1,350,000), or a total of $2,850,000. Variable costs at $55 per unit ($990,000 ÷ 18,000) would total $1,650,000 (30,000 x $55). Fixed costs would remain at $495,000. The summary below indicates operating income would be $705,000 if the order is accepted.

Sales	$2,850,000
Variable costs	(1,650,000)
Contribution margin	1,200,000
Fixed costs	(495,000)
Operating income	$ 705,000

2. (1183,P3,59) (b) The requirement is the effect on corporate operating income if the Troy Division were eliminated. If the division were eliminated, $100,000 of contribution margin would be lost. $70,000 of divisional fixed costs would, however, be eliminated. The net effect on corporate income of eliminating the Troy Division would be a $30,000 ($70,000 of fixed costs avoided less $100,000 of contribution margin lost) decrease. Alternatively, the result could be computed as follows:

	Total (before elimination)	*Total (after elimination)*
Sales	$900,000	$600,000
Variable costs	510,000	310,000
Contribution margin	390,000	290,000
Fixed costs for the division	180,000	110,000
Margin over direct costs	210,000	180,000
Allocated corporate costs	135,000	135,000
Operating income	$75,000	$45,000

$30,000 decrease

3. (582,P2,24) (a) The requirement is the minimum selling price to be considered in negotiating for a special order. The minimum selling price, given sufficient existing capacity, should be at least equal to the incremental costs associated with the order. Fixed manufacturing costs of $4 per unit (2/3 x $6) are not incremental since they will be incurred regardless of the activity level within the relevant range. However, the selling price must at least cover the variable manufacturing costs and the variable shipping costs.

Direct materials	$ 4
Direct labor	5
Variable overhead (1/3 x $6)	2
Shipping	3
Minimum acceptable selling price	$14

4. (582,P2,30) (d) The requirement is the sunk cost in a decision involving the sale of obsolete inventory. A sunk cost is a past cost which has been previously incurred; it cannot be changed no matter what alternative is chosen. The $50,000 manufacturing cost of the inventory is a sunk cost. It was previously incurred and it cannot be changed in any alternative; thus it is irrelevant to the decision. The other items are differential. If the lamps are reworked, it will cost $20,000 and produce revenue of $35,000. If the lamps are scrapped, it will produce $8,000 revenue.

5. (581,P2,29) (c) The requirement is to compute the alternative (make or buy) that is most desirable and the amount by which that alternative is more desirable. The solutions approach is to list the relevant costs associated with each alternative.

Buy G		*Manufacture G*	
Purchase price of G 10,000 x $30 =	$300,000	Direct materials: 10,000 x $ 3 =	$ 30,000
		Direct labor: 10,000 x $15 =	150,000
Less cost savings on Product H	(45,000)	Variable OH: 10,000 x $ 6 =	60,000
		Fixed OH: 10,000 x $ 5*=	50,000
Total cost	$255,000	Total cost	$290,000

*The relevant (out of pocket) cost is the $5 cost which is avoided if part G is not manufactured.

Buying part G from Verona Company is the more desirable alternative; the net cost saving is $35,000.

6. (1180,P2,31) (d) The requirement is to determine whether or not Dana should let its Lawn Products

Division purchase the blades required for production from an outside supplier. The solutions approach is to identify any differential costs between the two alternatives.

	Differential costs		
	Make	Buy	Difference
Variable costs	(10,000)		
Cost to buy (10,000) ($1.25)	______	(12,500)	
	(10,000)	(12,500)	(2,500)

The cost of buying from an outside supplier is $2,500 more than making, so the Lawn Products Division should not buy the blades from the outsider. Note that fixed costs are not differential; they would be incurred under either alternative.

7. (580,P2,40) (a) The requirement is the opportunity cost in a decision model analysis of two alternatives. The opportunity cost is the $3,000 for which obsolete fixtures could be sold rather than reworking them.

8. (1182,Q2,35) (b) The requirement is to determine the total relevant manufacturing cost to be considered in a make or buy decision. Relevant costs are those future costs that differ between the alternatives under consideration. The direct material and direct labor are both relevant as these costs would not be incurred if a buy decision were made. Of the $20 of factory overhead, 60% is irrelevant because it is not affected by make or buy decisions. In other words, $12 (.60 x $20) would not change regardless of the make or buy decision. Therefore, total relevant manufacturing cost is $15 ($2 DM + $5 DL + $8 overhead avoided if the buy decision is made).

9. (1179,T1,32) (d) In the short run, a cost which is irrelevant in deciding whether to manufacture a part in-house or to buy it from an outside vendor is fixed overhead, which cannot be saved if the part is purchased from the outside vendor. In other words, costs that will continue in either case are irrelevant to the decision. Costs that can be avoided by purchasing the part outside are relevant. For example, answer (a), direct labor, answer (b), variable overhead, and answer (c) avoidable fixed overhead, will all be avoided if the part is purchased from an outside vendor.

B. Capital Budgeting

10. (1183,T1,47) (d) The requirement is to identify which capital budgeting technique requires the discount rate to be determined in advance. The net present value method [answer (d)] compares the present value of the future cash flows of a project with initial investment required. In order to determine the present value of the future cash flows, a discount rate must be determined in advance. Answer (a) is incorrect because the payback method ignores the time value of money and therefore does not require the use of a discount rate. The internal rate of return (time-adjusted) method determines the rate of discount at which the present value of the future cash flows will exactly equal the required investment. This rate is then compared to the minimum desired rate (hurdle rate) to determine if the investment should be made. Note that the hurdle rate could be selected after calculating the internal rate of return of the project. Therefore, answers (b) and (c) are incorrect.

11. (1183,T1,48) (b) The requirement is to determine the capital budgeting techniques which consider cash flow over the entire life of the project. The internal rate of return (IRR) is defined as the discount rate which equates the present value of the net cash inflows over the life of the project with the initial outlay. Payback measures the length of time it takes to recover (in the form of cash inflows) the initial investment in the project. Answer (b) is correct because the IRR considers all cash flows over the life of the project, whereas the payback method considers cash flows only to the point where the initial investment has been recouped (subsequent cash flows are ignored).

12. (1176,P2,22) (d) Ignoring present value and tax considerations, the new machine's depreciation over its 5-year period will decrease income by $40,000 (additional cost of new machine over old machine's book value). The operating costs savings will be $25,000 per year or $125,000. Also acquisition of the new machine will result in a $45,000 loss from the sale of the old machine. The journal entry would be:

Cash	$ 5,000	
Loss on sale	45,000	
Machine (old)		$50,000

The net effect is a $40,000 increase in income over the five-year period as calculated below:

$ −40,000	additional depreciation of new machine
−45,000	loss on sale (closed to I/S account)
+125,000	cost savings
$ 40,000	increase in income

13. (1181,T1,60) (d) Cost of capital, or desired rate of return, is defined as the rate of return that a project must earn to leave the market value of the firm unchanged, and is typically determined by a weighted average of the sources of funds (debt, preferred and common stock, and retained earnings).

14. (1177,T2,38) (a) Sensitivity analysis generally describes the process of determining the effect of varying the inputs in an optimization model, e.g., linear programming. Thus sensitivity analysis indicates what will happen to the profitability of a project if constraints are slightly tightened, increased, etc. Sensitivity analysis would be used in capital budgeting to determine the amount that an assumed input could be varied and still produce acceptable results. Sensitivity analysis does not accomplish any of the objectives specified in answers (b), (c), and (d).

15. (1177,T2,44) (b) The requirement is what does not directly affect the weighted-average cost of capital approach to decision making. The weighted-average cost of capital approach to decision making is to determine the proportionate share of financing to be done by different methods, e.g., debt, preferred stock, common stock, etc. Then weight the cost of each type of financing by the proportion to be thus financed to obtain a weighted-average of the cost of capital for various types of financing. Answer (a), value of common stock, is necessary to compute the cost of common stock, i.e., common dividends divided by common stock value. Answer (c), cost of debt outstanding, is the cost of debt. Answer (d), the proposed mix of debt, equity, etc., is necessary to determine the weighted-average of the cost of capital. Answer (b), the current budget for expansion, is a constraint upon the amount of investments to be made, but does not affect the relative ranking of desirability of investments.

16. (1176,T2,32) (c) The payback capital budgeting method measures the length of time for the investment to return the original investment, i.e., investment divided by net annual cash flow. The accounting rate of return (also book value and unadjusted rate of return) is the increase in dollars of accounting income over the average investment (occasionally with a denominator of the entire investment). The net present value method determines the present value of the investment given a discount (profit return) rate. Alternate investments are evaluated by comparing the present values of the alternate investment projects. Presumably the project with the highest present value is the most favorable. Unfortunately, this method assumes that investment flows are reinvested at the company's cost of capital. The time adjusted rate of return method determines the discount (investment return) rate by setting the future net cash flows of an investment project equal to the amount of the required investment. In contrast to the net present value approach, the rate of return method assumes that the cash flows from the investment project can be reinvested at the rate of return obtained from the original investment project.

B. Capital Budgeting: Payback

17. (1181,P2,36) (d) The requirement is to calculate the payback period for a machine. The payback period is that period of time over which the net cash inflows will equal the initial investment (cash outflow). The net cash inflows given in the problem are equal annual amounts. Therefore, the payback period can be computed by dividing the initial investment by the annual net cash inflow. The **first** step is to calculate the amount of each equal annual net cash inflow. The data given includes cash inflow before taxes and an income tax rate of 40%. Net cash inflow is:

Cash inflow before taxes	–	Taxes	=	Annual net cash inflow
\$135,000	–	Taxes	=	x
\$135,000	–	[(135,000–100,000).40]	=	x
\$135,000	–	\$14,000	=	x
		\$121,000	=	x

Note that depreciation is deducted in order to obtain the amount of income tax. The **second** step is to use the calculated value of annual net cash inflow in the formula to determine payback:

$$\frac{\text{Original investment cash outflow}}{\text{Annual net cash inflow}} = \text{Payback in years}$$

$$\frac{\$500{,}000}{\$121{,}000} = 4.1 \text{ years}$$

18. (1179,P2,23) (b) The requirement is the expected cash flow (net of taxes) from a machine in its fifth year. The machine will cost \$30,000 and has a 5-year payback. The payback period is the number of years required to recoup the original investment. Thus, \$30,000 will be returned from operating the machine in the first 5 years. The problem states that the payback (net of taxes) is \$7,000 a year for the first 3 years and \$5,500 in the fourth year. Thus, \$26,500 is paid back in years 1 through 4. Accordingly, the payback in the 5th year is \$3,500 (\$30,000 – \$26,500).

19. (1180,T1,33) (d) The payback method evaluates investments on the basis of the length of time until

the initial investment is returned. If annual cash flows are constant, the payback period is calculated as follows:

$$\frac{\text{Initial investment}}{\text{Annual cash flow}}$$

Answer (a) is incorrect because the payback period is not a function of useful life. Answers (b) and (c) are incorrect because the payback method ignores the time value of money.

B. Capital Budgeting: Net Present Value

20. (1182,P2,26) (d) The requirement is the net present value of an investment in a machine, using a discount or target rate of 14%*. The machine cost $500,000 and provides annual net-of-tax inflows of $150,000 a year for 5 years, with no salvage value. The annual cash inflow must be multiplied by the present value of an annuity factor. Then the cost is subtracted from the result to compute net present value.

PV of cash inflows ($150,000 x 3.43)	$514,500
Less initial investment	(500,000)
Net present value	$ 14,500

**Authors' note:*

Most textbooks use the terms "discount, target, or hurdle" to describe the rate used in the net present value method. The term "time-adjusted rate of return" is ordinarily used to identify the actual or implicit rate of return which is derived in applying the method known as the internal or time-adjusted rate of return.

21. (1181,P2,39) (c) The requirement is to solve for the cost of a machine, given annual net cash inflows and a specified positive net present value. Net present value is defined as the excess of the present value of the cash inflows over the initial net investment. In this case, the net present value is positive. Therefore, the present value of the outflow must be less than the present value of the inflows.

Cash inflows	x	Present value of an ordinary annuity for 8 per.	=	Present value of cash inflows
$80,000	x	4.564	=	$365,120
Present value of cash inflows	—	Initial net investment	=	Net present value
$365,120	—	X	=	$ 12,720
		Initial investment (X)	=	$352,400

22. (582,T1,49) (c) Net present value is the difference between the required investment and the present value of the future cash flows. Since all future cash flows are included in the analysis, the inflow of cash from the salvage value of the project is included in the calculation. Depreciation, however, does not enter directly into the net present value calculation. It is a determinant in computing the related income taxes (a cash flow item), but in this case, you are told to ignore income taxes. Therefore, depreciation is not to be used.

23. (1180,T1,32) (d) The net present value of a project represents the present value of the cash flows less the original investment. Answer (b) is incorrect because present value is not used. Answer (a) is incorrect because it is the amount of the discount on the cash flows. Answer (c) does not make sense.

B. Capital Budgeting: Internal (Time-Adjusted) Rate of Return

24. (1182,P2,40) (b) The requirement is the cost of a project which has been determined to provide a 12% internal rate of return (time-adjusted rate of return). This means that the present value of future net cash inflows, discounted at 12%, is exactly equal to the cost of the project. The project provides an annual inflow for eight years of $20,000 a year. The relationship can be shown as

Project cost	÷	Annual cash inflow	=	P.V. of ordinary annuity factor for 12%

Let X = Project cost

Then X	÷	$20,000	=	4.968

X = 4.968 x $20,000

X = $99,360

Note that in practice, the project cost is ordinarily known and the annuity factor is the unknown. Once the factor is derived, the rate is found in an ordinary annuity table.

25. (582,P2,38) (b) The requirement is the cost of a project having an internal (time-adjusted) rate of return of 12%. If the project has an IRR of 12%, its cost is equal to the present value of its cash inflows discounted at 12%. As shown below, the present value of the inflows is $109,370, which is also the cost of the project.

Year one inflow ($60,000 x .893)	$ 53,580
Year two inflow ($70,000 x .797)	55,790
PV of inflows	$109,370

26. (581,P2,21) (d) The requirement is to compute the cash flow, net of income taxes, for the third year. Assuming that the rate of return is exactly 10%,

then the $80,000 investment is the present value of the 3 future cash inflows discounted at 10%. The net cash flow in year three is computed as follows:

Total Present Value	$80,000
–PV year 1 cash flow	(27,270)
–PV year 2 cash flow	(29,736)
PV year 3 cash flow	$22,994

$22,994 = .751 x year 3 cash flow

$22,994 ÷ .751 (PV of $1 year 3) = $30,618 year 3 cash flow.

B. Capital Budgeting: Accounting Rate of Return

27. (1183,Q1,17) (b) The requirement is to determine the factor which should be used in computing the internal rate of return for Amaro's proposed investment in new equipment. The internal rate of return (IRR) is defined as the rate of discount which will cause the present value of the benefits to exactly equal the investment outlay. This discount rate represents "true" rate of return the project will generate. The IRR is then compared with the cost of capital to determine if the investment should be made. The IRR is determined by setting the investment outlay equal to the discounted value of future net cash inflows as illustrated below. The discount factor is the unknown.

$$\begin{pmatrix}\text{PV}\\ \text{investment}\\ \text{today}\end{pmatrix} = \begin{pmatrix}\text{TVMF}\\ \text{unknown rate}\\ \text{of return}\end{pmatrix} \times \begin{pmatrix}\text{Payments}\\ \text{annual cash}\\ \text{savings}\end{pmatrix}$$

$$\$20{,}000 = \text{TVMF} \times \$5{,}000$$

$$\text{TVMF} = 4.000$$

28. (1183,Q1,18) (c) The requirement is to calculate the accounting rate of return (ARR) based on Amaro's initial investment in the new equipment. The accounting rate of return is based on financial statements prepared on the accrual basis. Gauging profitability is an objective of this method; however, consideration of the time value of money is ignored. The solutions approach is to recall the formula below.

$$\text{ARR} = \frac{\text{Expected increase in annual net income}}{\text{Initial investment}}$$

$$\text{ARR} = \frac{\underset{\text{(annual cash savings)}}{\$5{,}000} - \underset{\text{(annual depreciation)}}{\$2{,}000}}{\$20{,}000}$$

$$\text{ARR} = 15\%$$

The problem could have required the accounting rate of return based on average investment, in which case the denominator would have been $10,000 ($20,000 ÷ 2).

29. (1179,P2,24) (a) The requirement is the initial investment in a machine if it has an accounting rate of return of 12% and will generate $66,000 of net cash flow (before depreciation). The accounting rate of return is net income over the initial investment. Net income would be the net cash flow (i.e., after taxes, operating expenses, etc.) less depreciation. The solutions approach is to set up an equation to determine the cost. 12% of cost is equal to $66,000 minus depreciation (10% of cost per year). As computed below the cost is $300,000.

$$\begin{aligned} .12 \text{ cost} &= \$66{,}000 - .10 \text{ cost} \\ .22 \text{ cost} &= 66{,}000 \\ \text{cost} &= \$300{,}000 \end{aligned}$$

May 1984 Answers

30. (584,T1,41) (c) The requirement is to ascertain the rate at which cash flows from an investment are assumed to be reinvested when using the internal rate of return technique. Answer (c) is correct since the internal rate of return method implicitly assumes that cash flows are reinvested at the same rate earned by the investment. Answers (a) and (b) are incorrect because the net present value method assumes that cash flows are reinvested at the hurdle rate of return (which should not be lower than the cost of capital). Answer (d) is incorrect because the payback rate is expressed as a period of time and does not consider the rate of return earned by the investment. The payback period is simply the length of time it takes to recoup the original investment in the form of cash flows.

31. (584,T1,49) (d) The requirement is to determine whether the undepreciated book balance of an old asset should be considered an irrelevant cost and/or a sunk cost. All costs incurred in the past are considered sunk costs and, as such, are irrelevant to the exchange decision unless they have future tax ramifications (i.e., taxable gain or tax-deductible loss on disposal of the asset). The question states, however, that any income tax considerations should be ignored. Therefore, answer (d) is correct.

Answer Outline

Problem 1 Special Order Decision

a. Unit cost dropped due to factory overhead averaging
 With increased volume, average unit cost decreased
 I.e., factory overhead contained fixed components

b1. Both the production manager and treasurer are correct
 New $6.25 cost is more than $6.00 purchase price
 Results in loss of $.25 per unit
 Totalling $7,500 on 30,000 units
 Regular sales profit increases $37,500
 $.75 cost per unit decrease times 50,000 units
 Net increase is $30,000 in gross profit

b2. Production manager evaluation based on unit cost
 Treasurer evaluation based on marginal costs
 Marginal costs are appropriate in the short run
 Average costs are appropriate in the long run

c1. If offer is accepted repeat business is likely
 This may establish a market price of $6.00 per unit
 Which cannot be maintained in the long run
 I.e., no possibility of profit from the present plant

c2. Yokohama may compete for customers of Nubo's regular customers
 I.e., decreasing demand to regular customers
 Reduces sales at regular price
 No effect if Yokohama operates in completely isolated market

Unofficial Answer

Problem 1 Special Order Decision

a. The difference in unit cost was caused by the difference in average unit cost of factory overhead. The computations for costs per unit follow:

	Cost per unit	
	50,000 units of output	*80,000 units of output*
Direct material:		
$75,000/50,000 units	$1.50	
$120,000/90,000 units		$1.50
Direct labor:		
$75,000/50,000 units	1.50	
$120,000/80,000 units		1.50
Factory overhead:		
$200,000/50,000 units	4.00	
$260,000/80,000 units		3.25
Cost per unit	$7.00	$6.25

The reason for the difference in average unit cost of factory overhead probably was caused by some of the overhead being fixed within the given levels of output. In this instance the fixed component of factory overhead may be estimated using the following reasoning.

$$\frac{\text{Change in cost } (\$260,000 - \$200,000)}{\text{Change in output } (80,000 - 50,000)} = \frac{\$60,000}{30,000}$$

Variable costs per unit = $ 2.00

If variable factory overhead is incurred at $2.00 per unit, the amount of fixed costs would be computed as follows:

$200,000 factory overhead – ($2.00 x 50,000 units) variable overhead = $100,000 fixed factory overhead

or

$260,000 factory overhead – ($2.00 x 80,000 units) variable overhead = $100,000 fixed factory overhead.

At 50,000 units of output the fixed portion of factory overhead is $2.00 per unit ($100,000 ÷ 50,000 units). And at 80,000 units of output the fixed portion of factory overhead is $1.25 per unit ($100,000 ÷ 80,000 units). Thus, the $.75 per unit decrease in average unit cost apparently resulted from spreading the fixed costs over an increased number of units of production.

b. 1. Both the production manager's and treasurer's statements are correct as given. The new average unit cost of $6.25 is certainly more than the offered purchase price of $6.00; thus, a $.25 per unit loss would result on this order. The resulting "book loss" on this order would be $7,500 ($.25 x 30,000 units) as indicated by the production manager. Not withstanding, the remaining 50,000 units of regular sales would show an increased margin (gain) of $.75 per unit because their average unit cost decreased from $7.00 to $6.25 per unit. Thus, regular sales would show an increased profit of $37,500 ($.75 x 50,000 units). The net result would be an increase of $30,000 in gross margin this period if the Yokohama Company offer was accepted. Accordingly, the treasurer's statement is also correct because gross margin for this period will increase if the offer is accepted.

The treasurer's reasoning can also be illustrated by application of the marginal-income or contribution-margin technique. The extra units will generate a unit sales price of $6.00 and a unit variable cost of $5.00 ($1.50 + $1.50 + $2.00); the result is a $1.00 per unit contribution margin to increase gross margin. Thus, by selling the extra 30,000 units gross margin will increase by $30,000 (30,000 units x $1.00 contribution margin per unit).

2. The primary reason for the difference in conclusions by the production manager and the treasurer is in their respective methods of analysis. The production manager is evaluating average unit costs in comparison with selling price to determine the profitability of the special order. The treasurer is comparing the difference in total costs at the two levels of output with the difference in total revenues at the two levels of output, in effect comparing marginal cost with marginal revenue, to determine the incremental effect of gross margin. The treasurer's reasoning is appropriate for the short run while the production manager's reasoning is inappropriate for a short-range decision but is appropriate for a long-range decision. In this instance the decision appears to be a one-time thing indicating that the treasurer's reasoning is most appropriate.

c. 1. Perhaps the most important consideration is the extent to which this short-range decision will have a long-range effect on Nubo. If the offer is rejected the chances of receiving another offer from the Yokohama Company is considerably reduced. But if the offer is accepted, a repeat order is more likely in the future.

By accepting the offer, Nubo may be inadvertently establishing a market price of $6.00 per unit for its product which cannot be maintained in the long run (average unit cost at 80,000 units is $6.25). If the customers who purchase the other 50,000 units become aware of the $6.00 units sales price charged the Yokohama firm they too may want a $6.00 unit price. If Nubo sold all 80,000 units at $6.00 each a negative gross margin of $20,000 would result, and it would have zero gross margin at 100,000 units, the practical capacity of the plant.

2. Even if the $6.00 unit selling price does not have an effect on the unit selling price to present customers, it may depress the quantity of sales of other units at the normal price. If the Yokohama firm plans to compete for the same customers as Nubo's regular customers, the ultimate effect of making the 30,000 unit sale to the Yokohama firm at $6.00 a unit may give it an unfair competitive advantage. Ultimately, a shift of customers from Nubo's regular customers to the Yokohama firm would cause a decrease in unit sales at the regular price.

If the Yokohama firm is operating in a completely isolated market from Nubo's regular customers, no undesirable effects should result from this one-time sale. An exception to this reasoning would result if Nubo's regular customers desired to expand into this isolated market but found that they were at a competitive disadvantage because of the 30,000 unit sale made by Nubo to the Yokohama firm.

Answer Outline

Problem 2 Capital Budgeting

1. Both techniques have following advantages over payback
   - Adjust for time value of money
   - Indicate relative profitability of competing investments by considering cash flows beyond payback period
2. Limitations of net present value (NPV) are
   - Assumes cash flows from competing alternatives reinvested at firm's minimum desired rate of return
     - Therefore, biased toward longer-lived projects
   - Discount rate (target rate of return) must be determined in advance
   - Difficulties of predicting future cash flows

3. Limitations of internal rate of return (IRR) are
    Assumes cash flows from competing alternatives reinvested at company's internal rate of return
        Therefore, biased toward shorter-lived projects
    Difficulties of predicting future cash flows
    Involves complex (trial-and-error) computations
4. Both techniques ignore depreciation
    Rationale
        Depreciation does not involve cash outlay
            Both methods discount future cash flows
        Depreciation is product of accrual basis accounting
            Allocates investment cost systematically and rationally to periods benefited
        Investment recovery is considered through single cash outflow at date investment made

Unofficial Answer
(Author Modified)

Problem 2 Capital Budgeting

1. Both the net present value (NPV) and internal rate of return (IRR) methods adjust for the time value of money whereas the payback method does not. Also, the NPV and IRR methods indicate the relative profitability of competing projects because they take into account cash flows beyond the payback period and adjust these cash flows for the time value of money.

2. When evaluating projects with differing lives and positive net present values, NPV tends to favor longer projects because it assumes that funds from shorter projects are reinvested at the minimum rate of return, when in fact, the reinvestment rate may be higher. Also, net present value is not easy to calculate because the discount or target rate of return must be determined in advance, and the prediction of future cash flows is difficult.

3. When evaluating projects with differing lives, the IRR tends to favor shorter projects because it assumes that the funds from those projects are reinvested at the internal rate of return when the reinvestment rate may, in fact, be lower. Another limitation of IRR relates to the difficulties of predicting future cash flows. Additionally, the IRR method requires complex (trial-and-error) calculations for all but the simplest situations.

4. Both of the discounted cash flow techniques (NPV and IRR) ignore depreciation which is a product of accrual accounting (i.e., it is a method of allocating a capital expenditure systematically and rationally over the periods benefited by the expenditure). Both NPV and IRR are concerned only with cash flows. Under these methods, the cost of an asset is considered as a single cash outflow at the time the investment is made. If depreciation was included, the cost would, in effect, be considered twice.

Solution Guide

Problem 3 Replacement Decision

1. The requirement of part b. is to determine the net initial outlay for some replacement equipment and the net present value of the investment, along with the recommendation as to whether or not the investment is worthwhile.

1.1 The solutions approach is to handle the three requirements (even though they are numbered as two) separately. The net initial outlay is the $175,000 equipment cost plus $5,000 of old machine removal cost less the $40,000 resale value of the old equipment. Thus, it is $140,000.

1.2 The net present value of the investment will be the excess of the present value of the annual cost savings during the next ten years over the net present outlay ($140,000 as computed just above). The annual savings will be $5,000 of labor costs plus $28,000 of other operating costs, a total of $33,000. The present value of $33,000 a year for the next ten years is $165,627 ($33,000 times 5.019). The net present value is the present value of the cost savings ($165,627) less the net initial outlay ($140,000) or $25,627.

1.3 Thus the investment should be made because in addition to the substantial net present value assuming a 15% return, there is also a 25% increase in production capacity.

Unofficial Answer

Problem 3 Replacement Decision

b. 1.

Net Initial Outlay Before Income Taxes

Cost of new equipment	$175,000
Cost of conversion	5,000
	180,000
Less resale value of present equipment	40,000
Net initial outlay	$140,000

Net Present Value of Investment Before Income Taxes

Annual operating costs excluding depreciation:	
With present equipment	$ 78,000
With new equipment	45,000
Annual cash savings before income taxes	$ 33,000
Present value of future savings (33,000 x 5.019)	$165,627
Net initial outlay	140,000
Net present value of investment	$ 25,627

b. 2. The investment in new equipment should be made as the present value of future savings is greater than the net initial outlay.

Solution Guide

Problem 4 Alternate Production Decisions

1. The requirement of part a is to compute the estimated net profit from total operations of Arcadia under three different assumptions. The solutions approach is to prepare each estimate separately, even though each of the solutions should be on the same schedule per the requirement. It should be noted that under all three alternatives, the Maine operations are going to cease. Furthermore, the problem indicates that the $100,000 of home office cost now allocated to Maine will continue to be incurred.

1.1 Expansion of the Montana factory will result in a 50% increase in sales to $2,100,000. The fixed factory costs will increase 20% to $336,000. The fixed administration costs will increase 10% to $121,000.

The variable costs will be $672,000, $8 per unit times 84,000 units ($2,100,000 divided by $25). The $175,000 of home office costs will continue. To the resulting $796,000 of Montana profit, add the $540,000 of Texas factory profit, and subtract the $100,000 of home office overhead that was allocated to Maine.

1.2 If a competitor pays $4 for each of the estimated 30,000 units sold, $120,000 in royalties will be received. These royalties, however, will not offset the previous $50,000 of Maine profit plus the $100,000 of home office cost allocated to Maine operations. In other words, the net effect will be to decrease total income by $30,000 ($150,000 – $120,000). Thus total income will be $970,000.

1.3 If Maine operations are shut down with no alternatives, the total income will be $850,000. This is the previous total estimated profit of $1,000,000 less the estimated Maine profit of $50,000 and less the $100,000 of home office cost allocated to Maine which will continue in the future.

Unofficial Answer

Problem 4 Alternate Production Decisions

a. 1. **Arcadia Corporation**
Computation Of Estimated Net Profit From Operations After Expansion of Montana Factory

Montana factory—	
Sales	$2,100,000
Fixed costs:	
Factory	336,000
Administration	121,000
Variable costs	672,000
Allocated home office costs	175,000
Total	1,304,000
Estimated net profit from operations	796,000
Texas factory—estimated net profit from operations	540,000
Home office expense allocated to Maine factory	(100,000)
Estimated net profit from operations	$1,236,000

a. 2. **Arcadia Corporation**
Computation Of Estimated Net Profit From Operations After Negotiation of Royalty Contract

Estimated net profit from operations:	
Texas factory	$ 540,000
Montana factory	410,000
Estimated royalties to be received (30,000 x $4)	120,000
	1,070,000
Less home office expense allocated to Maine factory	100,000
Estimated net profit from operations	$ 970,000

a. 3. **Arcadia Corporation**
Computation Of Estimated Net Profit From Operations After Shutdown Of Maine Factory

Estimated net profit from operations:	
Texas factory	$540,000
Montana factory	410,000
	950,000
Less home office expense allocated to Maine factory	100,000
Estimated net profit from operations	$850,000

CHAPTER SIX

QUANTITATIVE PROBLEMS AND SOLUTIONS

Quantitative methods questions appear on both the practice and theory sections of the examination. During the late Sixties and early Seventies the mechanics were emphasized (probably to encourage schools to teach the material), but this resulted in the criticism that such knowledge was not necessary for the practice of public accounting. As a result, the quantitative questions appearing on recent examinations have emphasized knowledge of the objectives, variables, and results of managerial quantitative techniques rather than mathematical calculations. An exception is the economic order quantity (EOQ) calculation which has been required on several examinations (you should memorize the formula). A complete analysis of recent examinations and the *AICPA Content Specification Outlines* appear in Volume I, *Outlines and Study Guides* (beginning of Chapter 10). Currently, the coverage of these topics on the exam has been very sparse.

For the majority of questions, knowledge of when, how, and why particular optimization techniques are used is required. Do not attempt to memorize formulas, etc. Rather, try to understand the concepts underlying the technique or model. Generally the techniques provide a means of maximizing revenue (profit) or minimizing costs.

Each question is coded as to month, year, section, problem number, and multiple choice question number. For example, (583,Q1,3) indicates May 1983, problem 1 of the Practice II section, multiple choice question number 3. Note that P = Practice I, Q = Practice II, and T = Theory.

QUANTITATIVE PROBLEM INDEX

Multiple Choice Questions (1–29)

1. Simple regression analysis
   a. Establishes a cause and effect relationship.
   b. Produces measures of probable error.
   c. Involves the use of independent variables only.
   d. Involves the use of more than two variables.

2. A scatter chart depicting the relationship between sales and salesmen's automobile expenses is set forth below:

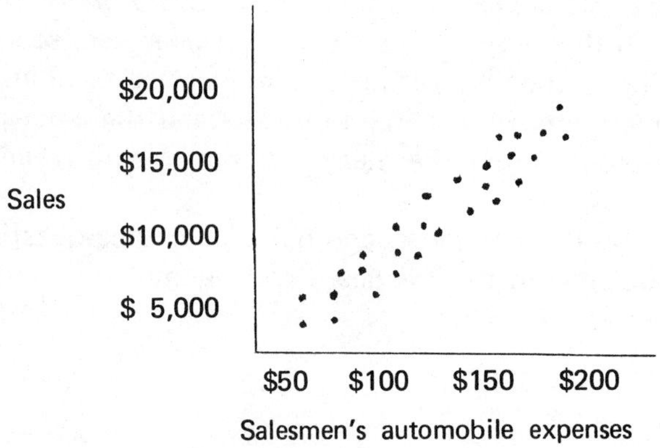

What can we deduce from the chart about the relationship between sales and salesmen's automobile expenses?
   a. A high degree of linear correlation.
   b. A high degree of nonlinear correlation.
   c. No apparent correlation.
   d. Both sales and salesmen's automobile expenses are independent variables.

3. What is the appropriate range for the coefficient of correlation (r)?
   a. $0 \leq r \leq 1$.
   b. $-1 \leq r \leq 1$.
   c. $-100 \leq r \leq 100$.
   d. $-\text{infinity} \leq r \leq \text{infinity}$.

4. Which of the following methods can be used to determine the fixed and variable elements of a semivariable expense?
   a. Statistical scattergraph method.
   b. Linear programming.
   c. Input-output analysis.
   d. Program evaluation review technique.

5. Regression analysis is superior to other cost behavior analysis techniques because it
   a. Produces measures of probable error.
   b. Examines only one variable.
   c. Proves a cause and effect relationship.
   d. Is not a sampling technique.

6. A measure of the extent to which two variables are related linearly is referred to as
   a. Cause-effect ratio.
   b. Coefficient of correlation.
   c. Sensitivity analysis.
   d. Input-output analysis.

7. Mori Company plans to begin production of a new product on July 1, 1983. An 80% learning curve is applicable to Mori's manufacturing operations. If it is expected to take 1,000 direct labor hours to produce the first unit, how many direct labor hours should it take to produce a total of four units?
   a. 4,000
   b. 3,200
   c. 2,560
   d. 2,048

8. Which of the following unfavorable variances would be directly affected by the relative position of a production process on a learning curve?
   a. Materials mix.
   b. Materials price.
   c. Labor rate.
   d. Labor efficiency.

9. Bolton Company produces a food product in 50 gallon batches. The basic ingredients used are material X costing $8 per gallon and material Y costing $12 per gallon. No more than 16 gallons of X can be used, and at least 18 gallons of Y must be used. How would the objective function (minimization of product cost) be expressed?
   a. $8X + 12Y$
   b. $8X + 18Y$
   c. $16X + 18Y$
   d. $16X + 34Y$

10. Probability (risk) analysis
   a. Ignores probability weights under fifty percent.
   b. Is only for situations in which there are three or fewer possible outcomes.
   c. Does **not** enhance the usefulness of sensitivity analysis data.
   d. Is an extension of sensitivity analysis.

11. A pay-off table (matrix) for evaluating alternative courses of action attempts to deal with
   a. Centralization.
   b. Uncertainty.
   c. Goal congruence.
   d. Motivation.

12. Barclay Company sells 20,000 pocket calculators evenly throughout the year. The cost of carrying one unit in inventory for one year is $4 and the purchase order cost per order is $64. What is the economic order quantity?

a. 400
b. 566
c. 800
d. 1,250

13. The economic order quantity formula can be used to determine the optimum size of a

	Production run	Purchase order
a.	Yes	No
b.	Yes	Yes
c.	No	Yes
d.	No	No

14. The following information relates to the Gerald Company:

Optimal production run	500
Average inventory in units	250
Number of production runs	10
Cost per unit produced	$5
Desired annual return on inventory investment	10%
Set up costs per production run	$10

Assuming that the units will be required evenly throughout the year, what are the total annual relevant costs using the economic-order-quantity approach?

a. $ 225
b. $ 350
c. $1,350
d. $2,625

15. The following information relates to Eagle Company's material A:

Annual usage in units	7,200
Working days per year	240
Normal lead time in working days	20
Maximum lead time in working days	45

Assuming that the units of material A will be required evenly throughout the year, the safety stock and order point would be

	Safety stock	Order point
a.	600	750
b.	600	1,350
c.	750	600
d.	750	1,350

16. Politan Company manufactures bookcases. Set up costs are $2.00. Politan manufactures 4,000 bookcases evenly throughout the year. Using the economic-order-quantity approach, the optimal production run would be 200 when the cost of carrying one bookcase in inventory for one year is

a. $0.05
b. $0.10
c. $0.20
d. $0.40

17. The Polly Company wishes to determine the amount of safety stock that it should maintain for Product D that will result in the lowest cost. The following information is available:

Stockout cost	$80 per occurrence
Carrying cost of safety stock	$2 per unit
Number of purchase orders	5 per year

The available options open to Polly are as follows:

Units of safety stock	Probability of running out of safety stock
10	50%
20	40%
30	30%
40	20%
50	10%
55	5%

The number of units of safety stock that will result in the lowest cost are

a. 20
b. 40
c. 50
d. 55

18. Siegal Company has correctly computed its economic order quantity as 500 units; however, management feels it would rather order in quantities of 600 units. How should Siegal's total annual purchase-order cost and total annual carrying cost for an order quantity of 600 units compare to the respective amounts for an order quantity of 500 units?

a. Higher purchase-order cost and higher carrying cost.
b. Lower purchase-order cost and lower carrying cost.
c. Higher purchase-order cost and lower carrying cost.
d. Lower purchase-order cost and higher carrying cost.

19. The order size determined by the economic order quantity formula minimizes the annual inventory cost which is comprised of ordering cost and

a. Safety-stock cost.
b. Stock-out cost.
c. Set-up cost.
d. Carrying cost.

20. Which of the following is a relevant factor in the determination of an economic order quantity?

a. Physical plant insurance costs.
b. Warehouse supervisory salaries.
c. Variable costs of processing a purchase order.
d. Physical plant depreciation charges.

21. Ridgefield, Inc., is considering a three-phase research project. The time estimates for completion of Phase 1 of the project are:

	Months
Optimistic	4
Most likely	8
Pessimistic	18

Using the Program Evaluation Review Technique (PERT), the expected time for completion of Phase 1 should be

a. 8 months.
b. 9 months.
c. 10 months.
d. 18 months.

22. In a program evaluation review technique system (PERT), reducing total time can be accomplished only by

a. Shortening a slack path.
b. Shortening the critical path.
c. Working overtime.
d. Using sensitivity analysis.

23. Gandy Company is considering a proposal to introduce a new product, RLX. An outside marketing consultant prepared the following payoff probability distribution describing the relative likelihood of monthly sales volume levels and related income (loss) for RLX:

Monthly sales volume	*Probability*	*Income (loss)*
6,000	0.10	$(70,000)
12,000	0.20	10,000
18,000	0.40	60,000
24,000	0.20	100,000
30,000	0.10	140,000

The expected value of the monthly income from RLX is

a. $ 48,000
b. $ 53,000
c. $ 60,000
d. $240,000

24. Johnson, Inc., manufactures product X and product Y which are processed as follows:

	Type A machine	*Type B machine*
Product X	6 hours	4 hours
Product Y	9 hours	5 hours

The contribution margin is $12 for product X and $7 for product Y. The available time daily for processing the two products is 120 hours for machine Type A and 80 hours for machine Type B. How would the restriction (constraint) for machine Type B be expressed?

a. $4X + 5Y$
b. $4X + 5Y \leq 80$
c. $6X + 9Y \leq 120$
d. $12X + 7Y$

25. The Hale Company manufactures products A and B, each of which requires two processes, polishing and grinding. The contribution margin is $3 for Product A and $4 for Product B. The graph below shows the maximum number of units of each product that may be processed in the two departments.

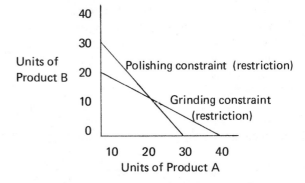

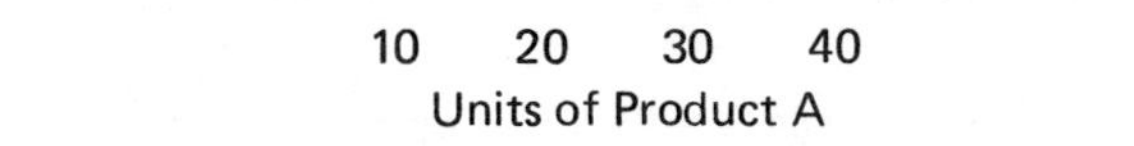

Considering the constraints (restrictions) on processing, which combination of products A and B maximizes the total contribution margin?

a. 0 units of A and 20 units of B.
b. 20 units of A and 10 units of B.
c. 30 units of A and 0 units of B.
d. 40 units of A and 0 units of B.

26. In a system of equations for a linear-programming model, what can be done to equalize an inequality such as $3X + 2Y \leqslant 15$?

a. Nothing.
b. Add a slack variable.
c. Add a tableau.
d. Multiply each element by −1.

27. When using the graphic method of solving a linear programming problem, the optimal solution will always be at

a. Minimum value of X.
b. X and Y intercept.
c. A corner point described by the feasible area.
d. Point of inception.

28. The use of the graphic method as a means for solving linear programming problems

a. Can be used when there are more than two restrictions (constraints).
b. Is limited to situations where there are two restrictions (constraints).
c. Is limited to situations where there is one restriction (constraint).
d. **Cannot** be used if there are any restrictions (constraints).

May 1984 Question

29. When using the graphic method of solving a linear-programming problem, which of the following would be depicted on the graph?

	Line of best fit	*Optimum corner point*
a.	No	No
b.	No	Yes
c.	Yes	No
d.	Yes	Yes

Multiple Choice Answers

1.	b	7.	c	13.	b	19.	d	25.	b
2.	a	8.	d	14.	a	20.	c	26.	b
3.	b	9.	a	15.	d	21.	b	27.	c
4.	a	10.	d	16.	d	22.	b	28.	a
5.	a	11.	b	17.	d	23.	b	29.	b
6.	b	12.	c	18.	d	24.	b		

Multiple Choice Answer Explanations

A. Analyzing Cost Behavior

1. (1183,T1,50) (b) Simple regression is a quantitative method used to analyze cost behavior. Answer (b) is correct since simple regression does produce measures of probable error such as the standard error of estimate. The standard error of the estimate is a measure of the dispersion of observations about the regression line. Answer (a) is incorrect because regression analysis does not imply a cause and effect relationship, but merely indicates whether a relationship between variables exists. Answer (c) is incorrect since regression analysis uses an independent variable to explain (predict) the change in a dependent variable. Answer (d) is incorrect since simple regression involves the use of only one independent variable. When there are two or more independent variables, the technique is known as multiple regression analysis.

2. (577,P2,31) (a) The scatter diagram indicates salesmen's automobile expenses increase as their sales increase. The relationship appears linear, i.e., a straight line. If it were a nonlinear correlation, the relationship or the line of dots would bend, i.e., not be straight. If there were no apparent correlation, there would be no trend in the line of dots, i.e., they would be all over. Answer (d) is incorrect because it is not apparent what is causing sales and automobile expenses. Independent variables are those which explain changes in dependent variables.

3. (576,P2,29) (b) Correlation coefficients range from minus 1 to positive 1. A minus 1 indicates a perfect inverse relationship, i.e., as one variable increases in size, the other variable decreases by the same amount. A correlation coefficient of one indicates a perfect positive or direct relationship, i.e., as one variable increases, the other variable increases a like amount. If there is no correlation between the two variables, the correlation coefficient is zero. Most correlation coefficients do not approach 1 as many variables affect a single given variable rather than one variable. Thus perfect correlation, positive or negative, is rarely found, especially in the social sciences.

4. (1180,T1,47) (a) Statistical scattergraph methods can be used to determine the fixed and variable elements of a semivariable expense. Linear programming [answer (b)] is a technique used to determine optimal use of limited resources. Input-output analysis [answer (c)] deals with the conversion ratio of input resources into output resources. Program evaluation review technique [answer (d)], known as PERT, is a map of the flow of work through a network of interdependent tasks.

5. (580,T1,46) (a) A major advantage of regression analysis over other cost analysis techniques is the fact that it does produce measures of probable error (such as the standard error of estimate). Another advantage is its ability to examine more than one variable, which eliminates answer (b). Regression analysis is a sampling technique [answer (d)], but does not prove cause and effect [answer (c)]. It merely indicates that variables move together.

6. (579,T1,27) (b) The linear relationship between two variables is called a coefficient of correlation. If there is absolutely no correlation between the two variables, the coefficient of correlation is said to be zero. If there is perfect direct correlation, i.e., both variables increase by the same amount, correlation is said to be +1. If on the other hand one variable decreases by the same amount that another variable increases, the coefficient of correlation is said to be −1. Answer (a) is incorrect because, while two variables may be highly correlated, one may not necessarily cause the other, e.g., they may both be caused by a third variable. Answer (c), sensitivity analysis, is incorrect because sensitivity analysis refers to analyzing the effect of changing variables on the results of an optimization model. Answer (d), input/output analysis, is incorrect because input/output analysis shows statistically how an economy's industries interact with each other.

B. Learning Curves

7. (1182,Q2,34) (c) The requirement is total direct labor hours (DLH) for production of four units, assuming an 80% learning curve. The learning curve describes the efficiencies arising from experience. The increased experience leads to productivity increases at decreasing rates. As cumulative output doubles, the cumulative average direct labor hours decline by the learning curve percentage:

Cumulative output	*Cumulative average DLH*	*Cumulative DLH*
1	1,000	1,000
2	800 (1,000 x 80%)	1,600
4	640 (800 x 80%)	2,560

Note that the cumulative hours for four units took 2,560 DLH; the first unit took 1,000 DLH, the second unit took 600 DLH (1,600 cumulative DLH – 1,000 DLH for the first unit) and the third and fourth units each took 480 DLH [(2,560 – 1,600) ÷ 2].

8. (1181,T1,53) (d) Learning curve refers to the effect of learning on output per labor-hour or machine-hour. As experience is gained in a production process the time needed per unit of product tends to become progressively smaller, which has an impact on the labor efficiency variance. The learning curve is not directly related to the variances in (a), (b) or (c).

C. Probability Analysis

9. (1183,P3,42) (a) The requirement is the specification of the objective function in a linear programming application. The objective function is the quantification of a goal to be maximized or minimized. In this case, the objective is the minimization of product cost, which is \$8 per gallon of X used and \$12 per gallon of Y used. Mathematically, the costs to be minimized are expressed as $8X + 12Y$. The constraint functions would be $X + Y = 50$, $X \leq 16$, and $Y \geq 18$.

10. (1181,T1, 58) (d) Sensitivity analysis is a method of coping with uncertainty in decision models by measuring how expected outcomes are affected if input variables are changed in the model. Probability (risk) analysis is an extension of this concept, because it is a method of measuring the degree of uncertainty of possible outcomes using mathematical techniques. Answers (a) and (b) can be eliminated because all probability weights must be considered for outcomes that can range from two to infinity.

11. (577,T2,42) (b) A payoff matrix for evaluating alternative courses of action is concerned with uncertainty, e.g., alternative courses of action with different payoffs. These different alternative courses of action and payoffs generally have different probabilities that can be associated with them. Centralization concerns the delegation or lack of delegation of control and authority. Goal congruence concerns the relationship of individual participants' goals to the goals of the overall entity. Motivation concerns individual interests in achieving output, performance, etc.

D. Inventory Models

12. (1183,P3,53) (c) The requirement is the economic order quantity (EOQ). The EOQ formula is:

$$EOQ = \sqrt{\frac{2aD}{k}}$$

In the above equation a = cost of placing one order, D = annual demand in units, and k = annual cost of carrying one unit in inventory for one year. Substituting the given information, the equation becomes:

$$EOQ = \sqrt{\frac{(2)\ (64)\ (20{,}000)}{4}} = \sqrt{640{,}000} = 800 \text{ units}$$

13. (583,T1,50) (b) The requirement is to determine the appropriate usage of the economic order quantity (EOQ) formula. The EOQ model is primarily used to obtain the optimal purchase order quantity by minimizing the sum of ordering and carrying costs. The EOQ model can also be adjusted to compute the optimal size of a production run by minimizing the sum of setup and carrying costs. Thus, answer (b) is correct.

EOQ for purchase order:

$$\sqrt{\frac{2(\text{annual quantity})\ (\text{cost per order})}{\text{annual carrying cost per unit}}}$$

EOQ for production run:

$$\sqrt{\frac{2(\text{setup cost})\ (\text{annual demand})}{(\text{variable mfg. cost per unit})\ (\text{annual carrying cost percentage})}}$$

14. (580,P2,31) (a) The requirement is the total annual relevant costs using the EOQ model. The two elements composing this annual cost are total annual set up cost and the total annual cost of carrying the average number of units in inventory for one year.

\$10 set costs per run x 10 production runs + 10%(250 units x \$5 cost per unit produced) = \$225

15. (580,P2,38) (d) The requirement is for the safety stock and order point. Safety stock is equal to the normal usage per day of 30 units times the difference between the maximum lead time and normal lead time, both expressed in terms of days. The order point is equal to safety stock plus the normal usage during the lead time.

Normal usage = 7,200 ÷ 240 = 30 units
Safety stock = 30 units (45 days – 20 days)
Safety stock = 750 units
Order point = (30 units x 20 days) + safety stock
Order point = 1,350 units

16. (1179,P2,31) (d) The requirement is to determine the cost of carrying one bookcase in inventory for 1 year using the EOQ model. The economic order quantity (EOQ) is a formula based on an inventory cost function. The objective of the formula is to minimize both carrying costs and total ordering costs. The formula is:

$$EOQ = \sqrt{\frac{2aD}{k}}$$

a = fixed order cost
D = annual demand
k = unit carrying cost

This problem requires you to calculate the value of k. The solutions approach is to plug the data in the problem into the formula above, as illustrated below. Squaring both sides of the equation gives 40,000k = \$16,000 or k = \$.40.

$$200 = \sqrt{\frac{2 \times \$2.00 \times 4{,}000}{k}}$$

$$40{,}000 = \frac{2 \times \$2.00 \times 4{,}000}{k}$$

$$40{,}000k = \$16{,}000$$

$$k = \$.40$$

17. (579,P2,28) (d) The requirement is the number of units of safety stock that will result in the lowest cost. The approach is to compute the total cost for each of the 4 alternative levels of safety stock as illustrated below. The carrying cost is \$2 for each unit of safety stock. The stock-out cost is the probability of running out times \$80 for each of the 5 reorders. The lowest total cost of both carrying safety stock and running out is \$130 [(55 units x \$2/unit) + (\$80 x 5% x 5 reorders)]. Thus 55 units of safety stock should be maintained.

Safety stock	*Carrying cost*	*Stockout cost/order*	*Stockout cost/5 orders*	*Total cost*
20	\$40	\$32	\$160	\$200
40	\$80	\$16	\$80	\$160
50	\$100	\$8	\$40	\$140
55	\$110	\$4	\$20	\$130

18. (1176,P2,34) (d) The economic order quantity (EOQ) model considers two costs—ordering costs and carrying costs. Ordering costs are considered to be a fixed cost for each order placed and carrying costs are based on the average level of inventory, i.e., the larger the order size, the smaller the annual order costs but the higher the carrying costs. In this case the standard order quantity is going to be raised from 500 units to 600 units. As a result, fewer orders will be placed resulting in a lower annual order cost. Conversely, a higher average inventory will be maintained, which will increase the carrying costs.

19. (1182,T1,49) (d) The requirement is the component of annual inventory cost in addition to ordering cost that is included in the economic order quantity (EOQ) model. Application of the EOQ formula provides the quantity to order in units. EOQ minimizes the sum of ordering cost and carrying costs. Safety-stock costs [answer (a)] are costs associated with maintaining some minimum level of inventory as a cushion to provide for usage beyond a reasonably expected rate. Stock-out costs [answer (b)] are the costs from losing an order because of insufficient inventory. When determining the optimal size of a production run, set-up cost [answer (c)] would replace the cost of placing an order in the EOQ formula.

20. (578,T2,32) (c) The EOQ model minimizes variable order costs and variable inventory carrying costs. For example, incremental (variable) order costs can be reduced by fewer orders, but this increases incremental (variable) carrying costs because a larger average inventory is required.

The requirement is the cost which effects the EOQ. Since only variable costs associated with carrying inventory and purchasing are reflected in the model, the answer is variable order processing costs. Answers (a) and (d) are incorrect because physical plant insurance and depreciation cover more than just inventory carrying costs, i.e., includes insurance and depreciation on production and other facilities. They are also fixed costs. Answer (b) is incorrect because only variable, not fixed, costs are considered by the EOQ. Supervisory salaries are fixed costs.

E. Network Problems

21. (1181,P2,29) (b) The requirement is to find the expected time for completion of phase one of a project using PERT. The expected time of completion of a particular phase of a project is governed by the formula:

$$\text{Expected time of completion} = \frac{A + 4m + B}{6}$$

A = Optimistic time estimate
m = Most likely time estimate
B = Pessimistic time estimate

$$\text{Expected time of completion} = \frac{4 + 4(8) + 18}{6} = 9 \text{ months}$$

Note that this question requires much more specific knowledge of quantitive method procedures than do the more general types of questions typically found on past examinations.

22. (1181,T1,55) (b) PERT is a technique used for analyzing, planning, and scheduling large complex projects by forecasting the time of completion, monitoring progress, and identifying parts of the project which are critical for the project to be completed on time. The critical path is the longest time path from the first event to the last event for the project, which must be reduced before total time required to complete the project can be reduced. Reducing a slack path [answer (a)] would not reduce the total time of the project because slack time is the excess time over the budgeted amount for an event which can be incurred without affecting the critical path time.

F. Linear Programming

23. (1183,P3,60) (b) The requirement is the expected value of the monthly income from a proposed new product. The expected value is a weighted average of the possible incomes (losses), using the associated probabilities as weights. The expected value of this product is $53,000, as computed below:

Income loss		*Probability*		*Expected value*
$(70,000)	x	.10	=	$(7,000)
10,000	x	.20	=	2,000
60,000	x	.40	=	24,000
100,000	x	.20	=	20,000
140,000	x	.10	=	14,000
				$53,000

24. (1180,P2,30) (b) The requirement is the constraint for the Type B machine in a linear programming problem. Type B is available for 80 hours of processing, so the time used must be less than or equal to 80. Product X requires 4 hours of machine B time and product Y requires 5 hours; the total time spent on the two products is subject to the 80 hour limit. Therefore, using X to signify units of X and Y to signify units of Y, the constraint is: $4X + 5Y \leq 80$.

25. (1177,P2,33) (b) The requirement is the optimum production level of Products A and B given their respective contribution margins of $3 and $4. The solution must be subject to the constraints, i.e., be within both the polishing and grinding constraints. For example, zero units of A and 20 units of B are within both constraints, but 40 units of A and zero units of B are not (the maximum number of A that can be polished is 30). The solutions approach is to first see whether each of the four answers is within both the polishing and grinding constraints, and second, to determine the level of income projection. The solutions approach is illustrated below; the maximum contribution margin possible is alternative (b).

	A	*B*	*Total*	*Within constraints*
a.	$0	$80	$80	Yes
b.	$60	$40	$100	Yes
c.	$90	$0	$90	Yes
d.	$120	$0	$120	No

26. (576,P2,28) (b) Inequalities in linear programming models are equalized by adding a slack variable to obtain normal equations. If a slack variable, Z, was added to the equation in this problem to form the equation $3X + 2Y + Z = 15$, Z would be the slack variable and would be the excess of 15 over $3X + 2Y$.

27. (1181,T1,59) (c) Linear programming is used in business as a technique for maximizing profits and minimizing losses. Using the graphic method the area of feasible combinations is restricted by the constraint functions. The optimal solution (i.e., profit maximization) occurs where the objective function intersects the feasible area at the farthest possible point from the origin which is a cornerpoint of the feasible area where the constraint lines intersect.

28. (1180,T1,41) (a) Linear programming is a technique used to determine optimal use of limited resources. The graphic method of linear programming can be used with any number of restraints. In solving these problems, all (restraint) constraint lines are drawn on the graph. While often only two restraints will apply, the graphic method will indicate which constraints do and do not apply.

May 1984 Answer

29. (584,T1,50) (b) The requirement is to determine which of the items listed would appear in a graphic solution to a linear programming problem. A line of best fit is associated with regression analysis, not linear programming. Linear programming is a technique used to determine the optimal use of limited resources. Constraint lines are drawn indicating the maximum output obtainable from each scarce resource. The optimum corner point lies at the intersection of the constraint equations. Therefore, answer (b) is correct since only the optimum corner point is associated with linear programming.

CHAPTER SEVEN

GOVERNMENTAL PROBLEMS AND SOLUTIONS

Governmental and not-for-profit accounting questions appear on both the theory and practice sections of the examination. The candidate should be familiar with accounting principles which relate to colleges and universities, hospitals, voluntary health and welfare organizations and other not-for-profit organizations. A complete analysis of recent examinations and the *AICPA Content Specification Outlines* appear in Volume I, *Outlines and Study Guides.*

Each question is coded as to month, year, exam section, problem number and multiple choice question number. For example, (583,T1,38) indicates May 1983 theory problem 1, and question number 38. Note the P = Practice 1, Q = Practice II, and T = Theory.

Several of the multiple choice questions from past examinations, or their answers, have been modified to reflect changes in law and practice since the questions appeared on the exam.

GOVERNMENTAL PROBLEM INDEX

Multiple Choice Questions (1–111)

1. One of the differences between accounting for a governmental (not-for-profit) unit and a commercial (for-profit) enterprise is that a governmental (not-for-profit) unit should

a. **Not** record depreciation expense in any of its funds.
b. Always establish and maintain complete self-balancing accounts for each fund.
c. Use only the cash basis of accounting.
d. Use only the modified accrual basis of accounting.

2. The Town of Newbold General Fund issued purchase orders to vendors and suppliers of $630,000. Which of the following entries should be made to record this transaction?

		Debit	Credit
a.	Encumbrances	$630,000	
	Reserve for encumbrances		$630,000
b.	Expenditures	630,000	
	Vouchers payable		630,000
c.	Expenses	630,000	
	Accounts payable		630,000
d.	Reserve for encumbrances	630,000	
	Encumbrances		630,000

3. The following balances are included in the subsidiary records of Burwood Village's Parks and Recreation Department at March 31, 1982:

Appropriations—supplies	$7,500
Expenditures—supplies	4,500
Encumbrances—supply orders	750

How much does the Department have available for additional purchases of supplies?

a. $0
b. $2,250
c. $3,000
d. $6,750

4. The Board of Commissioners of the City of Rockton adopted its budget for the year ending July 31, 1982, which indicated revenues of $1,000,000 and appropriations of $900,000. If the budget is formally integrated into the accounting records, what is the required journal entry?

		Dr.	Cr.
a.	Memorandum entry only		
b.	Appropriations	$ 900,000	
	General Fund	100,000	
	Estimated revenues		$1,000,000
c.	Estimated revenues	$1,000,000	
	Appropriations		$ 900,000
	Fund balance		100,000
d.	Revenues receivable	$1,000,000	
	Expenditures payable		$ 900,000
	General fund balance		100,000

5. Which of the following accounts of a governmental unit is credited when the budget is recorded?

a. Encumbrances.
b. Reserve for encumbrances.
c. Estimated revenues.
d. Appropriations.

6. Which of the following accounts of a governmental unit is debited when supplies previously ordered are received?

a. Encumbrances.
b. Reserve for encumbrances.
c. Vouchers payable.
d. Appropriations.

7. Which of the following funds of a governmental unit integrates budgetary accounts into the accounting system?

a. Enterprise.
b. Special revenue.
c. Internal service.
d. Nonexpendable trust.

8. Which of the following will increase the fund balance of a governmental unit at the end of the fiscal year?

a. Appropriations are less than expenditures and reserve for encumbrances.
b. Appropriations are less than expenditures and encumbrances.
c. Appropriations are more than expenditures and encumbrances.
d. Appropriations are more than estimated revenues.

9. Which of the following accounts of a governmental unit is credited to close it out at the end of the fiscal year?

a. Appropriations.
b. Revenues.
c. Reserve for encumbrances.
d. Encumbrances.

10. At the end of the fiscal year of a governmental unit, the excess of expenditures and encumbrances over appropriations

a. Increases the fund balance.
b. Decreases the fund balance.
c. Increases the reserve for encumbrances.
d. Decreases the reserve for encumbrances.

11. When the estimated revenue account of a governmental unit is closed out at the end of the fiscal year, the excess of revenues over estimated revenues is

a. Debited to fund balance.
b. Debited to reserve for encumbrances.
c. Credited to fund balance.
d. Credited to reserve for encumbrances.

12. Which of the following will increase the fund balance of a governmental unit at the end of the fiscal year?

a. Appropriations are less than expenditures and reserve for encumbrances.
b. Appropriations are less than expenditures and encumbrances.
c. Appropriations are more than estimated revenues.
d. Appropriations are more than expenditures and encumbrances.

13. What type of account is used to earmark the fund balance to liquidate the contingent obligations of goods ordered but not yet received?

a. Appropriations.
b. Encumbrances.
c. Obligations.
d. Reserve for encumbrances.

14. The comprehensive annual financial report (CAFR) of a governmental unit should contain a combined statement of changes in financial position for

	Governmental funds	*Proprietary funds*
a.	No	No
b.	No	Yes
c.	Yes	No
d.	Yes	Yes

15. Kingsford City incurred $100,000 of salaries and wages for the month ended March 31, 1982. How should this be recorded at that date?

		Dr.	*Cr.*
a.	Expenditures— salaries and wages	$100,000	
	Vouchers payable		$100,000
b.	Salaries and wages expense	$100,000	
	Vouchers payable		$100,000
c.	Encumbrances— salaries and wages	$100,000	
	Vouchers payable		$100,000
d.	Fund balance	$100,000	
	Vouchers payable		$100,000

Items 16 and 17 are based on the following information:

During the year ended December 31, 1981, Leyland City received a state grant of $500,000 to finance the purchase of buses, and an additional grant of $100,000 to aid in the financing of bus operations in 1981. Only $300,000 of the capital grant was used in 1981 for the purchase of buses, but the entire operating grant of $100,000 was spent in 1981.

16. If Leyland's bus transportation system is accounted for as part of the city's general fund, how much should Leyland report as grant revenues for the year ended December 31, 1981?

a. $100,000
b. $300,000
c. $400,000
d. $500,000

17. If Leyland's bus transportation system is accounted for as an enterprise fund, how much should Leyland report as grant revenues for the year ended December 31, 1981?

a. $100,000
b. $300,000
c. $400,000
d. $500,000

Items 18 and 19 are based on the following information:

On December 31, 1981, Madrid Township paid a contractor $2,000,000 for the total cost of a new firehouse built in 1981 on Township-owned land. Financing was by means of a $1,500,000 general obligation bond issue sold at face amount on December 31, 1981, with the remaining $500,000 transferred from the general fund.

18. What should be reported on Madrid's 1981 financial statements for the capital project fund?

a. Revenues, $1,500,000; Expenditures, $1,500,000.
b. Revenues, $1,500,000; Other financing sources, $500,000; Expenditures, $2,000,000.

c. Revenues, $2,000,000; Expenditures, $2,000,000.
d. Other financing sources, $2,000,000; Expenditures, $2,000,000.

19. What should be reported on Madrid's 1981 financial statements for the general fund?
a. Expenditures, $500,000.
b. Other financing uses, $500,000.
c. Revenues, $1,500,000; Expenditures, $2,000,000.
d. Revenues, $1,500,000; Other financing uses, $2,000,000.

Items 20 and 21 are based on the following information:

The following balances appeared in the City of Reedsbury's general fund at June 30, 1981:

Account	Balance Dr. (Cr.)
Encumbrances—current year	$ 200,000
Expenditures:	
Current year	3,000,000
Prior year	100,000
Fund balance reserved for encumbrances:	
Current year	(200,000)
Prior year	None

Reedsbury maintains its general fund books on a legal budgetary basis, requiring revenues and expenditures to be accounted for on a modified accrual basis. In addition, the sum of current year expenditures and encumbrances cannot exceed current year appropriations.

20. What total amount of expenditures (and encumbrances, if appropriate) should Reedsbury report in the general fund column of its combined statement of revenues, expenditures, and changes in fund balance for the year ended June 30, 1981?
a. $3,000,000
b. $3,100,000
c. $3,200,000
d. $3,300,000

21. What total amount of expenditures (and encumbrances, if appropriate) should Reedsbury report in the general fund "actual" column of its combined statement of revenues, expenditures, and changes in fund balance—budget and actual—for the year ended June 30, 1981?
a. $3,000,000
b. $3,100,000
c. $3,200,000
d. $3,300,000

22. When fixed assets purchased from general fund revenues were received, the appropriate journal entry was made in the general fixed asset account group. What account, if any, should have been debited in the general fund?
a. No journal entry should have been made in the general fund.
b. Fixed assets.
c. Expenditures.
d. Due from general fixed asset account group.

23. Which of the following funds of a governmental unit uses the modified accrual basis of accounting?
a. Debt service.
b. Internal service.
c. Enterprise.
d. Nonexpendable trust.

24. Fixed assets should be accounted for in the general fixed assets account group for

	Governmental funds	Proprietary funds
a.	No	Yes
b.	No	No
c.	Yes	No
d.	Yes	Yes

25. Which of the following accounts of a governmental unit is credited when taxpayers are billed for property taxes?
a. Estimated revenues.
b. Revenues.
c. Appropriations.
d. Reserve for encumbrances.

26. Which of the following funds of a governmental unit uses the same basis of accounting as the special revenue fund?
a. Internal service.
b. Expendable trust.
c. Nonexpendable trust.
d. Enterprise.

27. Revenues of a municipality should be recognized in the accounting period in which they become available and measurable for a

	Governmental fund	Proprietary fund
a.	Yes	No
b.	Yes	Yes

c.	No	Yes
d.	No	No

28. A debt service fund of a municipality is an example of which of the following types of fund?
    a. Fiduciary.
    b. Governmental.
    c. Proprietary.
    d. Internal service.

29. Revenues of a special revenue fund of a governmental unit should be recognized in the period in which the
    a. Revenues become available and measurable.
    b. Revenues become available for appropriation.
    c. Revenues are billable.
    d. Cash is received.

30. Which of the following funds of a governmental unit would use the general long-term debt account group to account for unmatured general long-term liabilities?
    a. Special assessment.
    b. Capital projects.
    c. Trust.
    d. Internal service.

31. Which of the following funds of a governmental unit could use the general fixed assets account group to account for fixed assets?
    a. Internal service.
    b. Enterprise.
    c. Trust.
    d. Special assessment.

32. A state governmental unit should use which basis of accounting for each of the following types of funds?

	Governmental	*Proprietary*
a.	Cash	Modified accrual
b.	Modified accrual	Modified accrual
c.	Modified accrual	Accrual
d.	Accrual	Accrual

33. Which of the following funds of a governmental unit recognizes revenues and expenditures under the same basis of accounting as the general fund?
    a. Debt service.
    b. Enterprise.
    c. Internal service (intragovernmental service).
    d. Nonexpendable pension trust.

34. Which of the following requires the use of the encumbrance system?
    a. Special assessment fund.
    b. Debt service fund.
    c. General fixed assets group of accounts.
    d. Enterprise fund.

35. When a capital project is financed entirely from a single bond issue, and the proceeds of the bond issue equal the par value of the bonds, the capital projects fund would record this transaction by debiting cash and crediting
    a. Bond issue proceeds.
    b. Fund balance.
    c. Appropriations.
    d. Bonds payable.

36. Taxes collected and held by a municipality for a school district would be accounted for in a (an)
    a. Enterprise fund.
    b. Intragovernmental (internal) service fund.
    c. Agency fund.
    d. Special revenue fund.

37. Under the modified accrual basis of accounting, which of the following taxes is usually recorded before it is received in cash?
    a. Property.
    b. Income.
    c. Gross receipts.
    d. Gift.

38. Interest expense on bonds payable should be recorded in a Debt Service Fund
    a. At the end of the fiscal period if the interest due date does not coincide with the end of the fiscal period.
    b. When bonds are issued.
    c. When legally payable.
    d. When paid.

39. Which of the following should be accrued as revenues by the general fund of a local government?
    a. Sales taxes held by the state which will be remitted to the local government.
    b. Parking meter revenues.
    c. Sales taxes collected by merchants.
    d. Income taxes currently due.

40. Which of the following expenditures is normally recorded on the accrual basis in the general fund?
    a. Interest.
    b. Personal services.
    c. Inventory items.
    d. Prepaid expenses.

41. The initial transfer of cash from the general fund in order to establish an internal service fund would require the general fund to credit cash and debit

a. Accounts receivable—internal service fund.
b. Unreserved fund balance.
c. Reserve for encumbrances.
d. Operating transfers out.

42. Which of the following funds frequently does not have a fund balance?

a. General fund.
b. Agency fund.
c. Special revenue fund.
d. Capital projects fund.

43. The City of Rover has two special-assessment funds. In the preparation of the statement of financial position for these funds as of the end of the fiscal year, these funds may be reported on

a. A combined basis which shows the total for both funds and has separate columns to present account balances for each fund.
b. A consolidated basis after eliminating the effects of interfund transactions.
c. A separate basis, but never together in the same statement.
d. A consolidated basis with the general fund after eliminating the effects of interfund transactions.

44. Premiums received on general obligation bonds are generally transferred to what fund or group of accounts?

a. Debt service.
b. General long-term debt.
c. General.
d. Special revenue.

45. Equipment in general governmental service that had been constructed ten years before by a capital-projects fund was sold. The receipts were accounted for as unrestricted revenue. Entries are necessary in the

a. General fund and capital-projects fund.
b. General fund and general fixed-assets group of accounts.
c. General fund, capital-projects fund, and enterprise fund.
d. General fund, capital-projects fund, and general fixed-assets group of accounts.

46. The Town of Boyd Electric Utility Fund, which is an enterprise fund, had the following:

Prepaid insurance paid in December 1976	$ 43,000
Depreciation for 1976	129,000
Provision for doubtful accounts for 1976	14,000

What amount should be reflected in the statement of revenues and expenses (income statement) of the Town of Boyd Electric Utility Fund for the above items?

a. $(43,000)
b. $0
c. $129,000
d. $143,000

47. Which of the following funds of a governmental unit would account for depreciation in the accounts of the fund?

a. General.
b. Internal service.
c. Capital projects.
d. Special assessment.

48. Which of the following funds of a governmental unit uses the same basis of accounting as an enterprise fund?

a. Special revenue.
b. Internal service.
c. Expendable trust.
d. Capital projects.

49. Fixed assets utilized in a city-owned utility are accounted for in which of the following?

	Enterprise fund	*General fixed assets group of accounts*
a.	No	No
b.	No	Yes
c.	Yes	No
d.	Yes	Yes

50. Which of the following funds of a governmental unit would include retained earnings in its balance sheet?

a. Expendable pension trust.
b. Internal service (intragovernmental service).
c. Special revenue.
d. Capital projects.

51. Which of the following accounts could be included in the balance sheet of an enterprise fund?

	Reserve for encumbrances	*Revenue bonds payable*	*Retained earnings*
a.	No	No	Yes
b.	No	Yes	Yes

c.	Yes	Yes	No
d.	No	No	No

52. Customers' meter deposits which cannot be spent for normal operating purposes would be classified as restricted cash in the balance sheet of which fund?
   a. Internal service (intragovernmental service).
   b. Trust.
   c. Agency.
   d. Enterprise.

53. Which fund is not an expendable fund?
   a. Capital projects.
   b. General.
   c. Special revenue.
   d. Internal service.

54. "Excess of net billings to departments over cost" would appear in the financial statement of which fund?
   a. Internal.
   b. Enterprise.
   c. Capital projects.
   d. Special revenue.

55. If a governmental unit established a data processing center to service all agencies within the unit, the data processing center should be accounted for as a (an)
   a. Capital projects fund.
   b. Internal service fund.
   c. Agency fund.
   d. Trust fund.

56. Recreational facilities run by a governmental unit and financed on a user-charge basis would be accounted for in which fund?
   a. General.
   b. Trust.
   c. Enterprise.
   d. Capital projects.

57. An "actuarial deficiency" would appear in which fund?
   a. Agency.
   b. Trust.
   c. General.
   d. Debt service.

58. Which type of fund can be either expendable or non-expendable?
   a. Debt service.
   b. Enterprise.
   c. Trust.
   d. Special revenues.

59. The following assets are among those owned by the City of Foster:

Apartment building (part of the principal of a nonexpendable trust fund)	$ 200,000
City Hall	800,000
Three fire stations	1,000,000
City streets and sidewalks	5,000,000

How much should be included in Foster's general fixed assets account group?
   a. $1,800,000 or $6,800,000.
   b. $2,000,000 or $7,000,000.
   c. $6,800,000, without election of $1,800,000.
   d. $7,000,000, without election of $2,000,000.

60. The following items were among Kew Township's expenditures from the general fund during the year ended July 31, 1981:

Minicomputer for tax collector's office	$22,000
Furniture for Township Hall	40,000

How much should be classified as fixed assets in Kew's general fund balance sheet at July 31, 1981?
   a. $0
   b. $22,000
   c. $40,000
   d. $62,000

61. Ariel Village issued the following bonds during the year ended June 30, 1981:

Revenue bonds to be repaid from admission fees collected by the Ariel Zoo enterprise fund	$200,000
General obligation bonds issued for the Ariel water and sewer enterprise fund which will service the debt	300,000

How much of these bonds should be accounted for in Ariel's general long-term debt account group?
   a. $0
   b. $200,000
   c. $300,000
   d. $500,000

62. Long-term liabilities of an enterprise fund should be accounted for in the

	Enterprise fund	Long-term debt account group
a.	No	No
b.	No	Yes
c.	Yes	Yes
d.	Yes	No

63. Which of the following funds of a governmental unit would account for long-term liabilities in the accounts of the fund?

a. Special assessment.
b. Special revenue.
c. Capital projects.
d. Debt service.

64. Which of the following accounts would be included in the asset section of the combined balance sheet of a governmental unit for the general long-term debt account group?

	Amount available in debt service funds	Amount to be provided for retirement of general long-term debt
a.	Yes	Yes
b.	Yes	No
c.	No	Yes
d.	No	No

65. "Investment in general fixed assets" accounts would appear in which fund or group of accounts?

a. General fixed assets.
b. Enterprise.
c. Capital projects.
d. General.

66. During the years ended June 30, 1980 and 1981, Sonata University conducted a cancer research project financed by a $2,000,000 gift from an alumnus. This entire amount was pledged by the donor on July 10, 1979, although he paid only $500,000 at that date. The gift was restricted to the financing of this particular research project. During the two-year research period, Sonata's related gift receipts and research expenditures were as follows:

	Year ended June 30 1980	1981
Gift receipts	$1,200,000	$ 800,000
Cancer research expenditures	900,000	1,100,000

How much gift revenue should Sonata report in the restricted column of its statement of current funds revenues, expenditures, and other changes for the year ended June 30, 1981?

a. $0
b. $ 800,000
c. $1,100,000
d. $2,000,000

67. On January 2, 1982, John Reynolds established a $500,000 trust, the income from which is to be paid to Mansfield University for general operating purposes. The Wyndham National Bank was appointed by Reynolds as trustee of the fund. What journal entry is required on Mansfield's books?

		Dr.	Cr.
a.	Memorandum entry only		
b.	Cash	$500,000	
	Endowment fund balance		$500,000
c.	Nonexpendable endowment fund	$500,000	
	Endowment fund balance		$500,000
d.	Expendable funds	$500,000	
	Endowment fund balance		$500,000

68. For the fall semester of 1981, Cranbrook College assessed its students $2,300,000 for tuition and fees. The net amount realized was only $2,100,000 because of the following revenue reductions:

Refunds occasioned by class cancellations and student withdrawals	$ 50,000
Tuition remissions granted to faculty members' families	10,000
Scholarships and fellowships	140,000

How much should Cranbrook report for the period for unrestricted current funds revenues from tuition and fees?

a. $2,100,000
b. $2,150,000
c. $2,250,000
d. $2,300,000

69. The current funds group of a not-for-profit private university includes which of the following subgroups?

	Term endowment funds	Life income funds
a.	No	No
b.	No	Yes
c.	Yes	Yes
d.	Yes	No

70. Tuition waivers for which there is **no** intention of collection from the student should be classified by a not-for-profit university as

	Revenue	*Expenditures*
a.	No	No
b.	No	Yes
c.	Yes	Yes
d.	Yes	No

71. Which of the following is utilized for current expenditures by a not-for-profit university?

	Unrestricted current funds	*Restricted current funds*
a.	No	No
b.	No	Yes
c.	Yes	No
d.	Yes	Yes

72. Which of the following should be used in accounting for not-for-profit colleges and universities?
   a. Fund accounting and accrual accounting.
   b. Fund accounting but **not** accrual accounting.
   c. Accrual accounting but **not** fund accounting.
   d. Neither accrual accounting nor fund accounting.

73. In the loan fund of a college or university, each of the following types of loans would be found except
   a. Student.
   b. Staff.
   c. Building.
   d. Faculty.

74. Which of the following receipts is properly recorded as restricted current funds on the books of a university?
   a. Tuition.
   b. Student laboratory fees.
   c. Housing fees.
   d. Research grants.

75. Glenmore Hospital's property, plant, and equipment (net of depreciation) consists of the following:

Land	$ 500,000
Buildings	10,000,000
Movable equipment	2,000,000

What amount should be included in the restricted fund grouping?
   a. $0
   b. $ 2,000,000
   c. $10,500,000
   d. $12,500,000

76. During the year ended December 31, 1981, Melford Hospital received the following donations stated at their respective fair values:

Employee services from members of a religious group	$100,000
Medical supplies from an association of physicians. These supplies were restricted for indigent care, and were used for such purpose in 1981	30,000

How much revenue (both operating and nonoperating) from donations should Melford report in its 1981 statement of revenues and expenses?
   a. $0
   b. $ 30,000
   c. $100,000
   d. $130,000

77. On July 1, 1981, Lilydale Hospital's Board of Trustees designated $200,000 for expansion of outpatient facilities. The $200,000 is expected to be expended in the fiscal year ending June 30, 1984. In Lilydale's balance sheet at June 30, 1982, this cash should be classified as a $200,000
   a. Restricted current asset.
   b. Restricted noncurrent asset.
   c. Unrestricted current asset.
   d. Unrestricted noncurrent asset.

78. Which of the following would normally be included in Other Operating Revenues of a voluntary not-for-profit hospital?
   a. Unrestricted interest income from an endowment fund.
   b. An unrestricted gift.
   c. Donated services.
   d. Tuition received from an educational program.

79. An unrestricted pledge from an annual contributor to a voluntary not-for-profit hospital made in December 1981 and paid in cash in March 1982 would generally be credited to
   a. Nonoperating revenue in 1981.
   b. Nonoperating revenue in 1982.
   c. Operating revenue in 1981.
   d. Operating revenue in 1982.

80. Donated medicines which normally would be purchased by a hospital should be recorded at fair market value and should be credited directly to
   a. Other operating revenue.
   b. Other nonoperating revenue.
   c. Fund balance.
   d. Deferred revenue.

81. Depreciation should be recognized in the financial statements of
   a. Proprietary (for-profit) hospitals only.
   b. Both proprietary (for-profit) and not-for-profit hospitals.
   c. Both proprietary (for-profit) and not-for profit hospitals, only when they are affiliated with a college or university.
   d. All hospitals, as a memorandum entry not affecting the statement of revenues and expenses.

82. A voluntary health and welfare organization received a pledge in 1979 from a donor specifying that the amount pledged be used in 1981. The donor paid the pledge in cash in 1980. The pledge should be accounted for as
   a. A deferred credit in the balance sheet at the end of 1979, and as support in 1980.
   b. A deferred credit in the balance sheet at the end of 1979 and 1980, and as support in 1981.
   c. Support in 1979.
   d. Support in 1980, and **no** deferred credit in the balance sheet at the end of 1979.

83. Which of the following funds of a voluntary health and welfare organization does not have a counterpart fund in governmental accounting?
   a. Current unrestricted.
   b. Land, building, and equipment.
   c. Custodian.
   d. Endowment.

May 1984 Questions

Items 84 through 86 are based on the following data:

Under Abbey Hospital's established rate structure, the hospital would have earned patient service revenue of $6,000,000 for the year ended December 31, 1983. However, Abbey did not expect to collect this amount because of charity allowances of $1,000,000 and discounts of $500,000 to third-party payors. In May 1983, Abbey purchased bandages from Lee Supply Co. at a cost of $1,000. However, Lee notified Abbey that the invoice was being cancelled and that the bandages were being donated to Abbey. At December 31, 1983, Abbey had board-designated assets consisting of cash $40,000, and investments $700,000.

84. For the year ended December 31, 1983, how much should Abbey record as patient service revenue?
   a. $6,000,000
   b. $5,500,000
   c. $5,000,000
   d. $4,500,000

85. For the year ended December 31, 1983, Abbey should record the donation of bandages as
   a. A $1,000 reduction in operating expenses.
   b. Nonoperating revenue of $1,000.
   c. Other operating revenue of $1,000.
   d. A memorandum entry only.

86. How much of Abbey's board-designated assets should be included in the unrestricted fund grouping?
   a. $0
   b. $ 40,000
   c. $700,000
   d. $740,000

Items 87 and 88 are based on the following data:

Community Service Center is a voluntary welfare organization funded by contributions from the general public. During 1983, unrestricted pledges of $900,000 were received, half of which were payable in 1983, with the other half payable in 1984 for use in 1984. It was estimated that 10% of these pledges would be uncollectible. In addition, Selma Zorn, a social worker on Community's permanent staff, earning $20,000 annually for a normal workload of 2,000 hours, contributed an additional 800 hours of her time to Community, at no charge.

87. How much should Community report as net contribution revenue for 1983 with respect to the pledges?
   a. $0
   b. $405,000
   c. $810,000
   d. $900,000

88. How much should Community record in 1983 for contributed service expense?
   a. $8,000
   b. $4,000
   c. $ 800
   d. $0

89. Cura Foundation, a voluntary health and welfare organization supported by contributions from the general public, included the following costs in its statement of functional expenses for the year ended December 31, 1983:

Fund-raising	$500,000
Administrative (including data processing)	300,000
Research	100,000

Cura's functional expenses for 1983 program services included

a. $900,000
b. $500,000
c. $300,000
d. $100,000

90. Fred Bosin donated a building to Palma City in 1983. Bosin's original cost of the property was $100,000. Accumulated depreciation at the date of the gift amounted to $60,000. Fair market value at the date of the gift was $300,000. In the general fixed assets account group, at what amount should Palma record this donated fixed asset?

a. $300,000
b. $100,000
c. $ 40,000
d. $0

Items 91 through 93 are based on the following data relating to Lely Township:

Printing and binding equipment used for servicing all of Lely's departments and agencies, on a cost-reimbursement basis	$100,000
Equipment used for supplying water to Lely's residents	900,000
Receivables for completed sidewalks to be paid for in installments by affected property owners	950,000
Cash received from federal government, dedicated to highway maintenance, which must be accounted for in a separate fund	995,000

91. How much should be accounted for in a special revenue fund or funds?

a. $ 995,000
b. $1,050,000
c. $1,095,000
d. $2,045,000

92. How much could be accounted for in an internal service fund?

a. $100,000
b. $900,000
c. $950,000
d. $995,000

93. How much could be accounted for in an enterprise fund?

a. $100,000
b. $900,000
c. $950,000
d. $995,000

Items 94 through 96 are based on the following data:

The Board of Commissioners of Vane City adopted its budget for the year ending July 31, 1985, comprising estimated revenues of $30,000,000 and appropriations of $29,000,000. Vane formally integrates its budget into the accounting records.

94. What entry should be made for budgeted revenues?

a. Memorandum entry only.
b. Debit estimated revenues receivable control, $30,000,000.
c. Debit estimated revenues control, $30,000,000.
d. Credit estimated revenues control, $30,000,000.

95. What entry should be made for budgeted appropriations?

a. Memorandum entry only.
b. Credit estimated expenditures payable control, $29,000,000.
c. Credit appropriations control, $29,000,000.
d. Debit estimated expenditures control, $29,000,000.

96. What entry should be made for the budgeted excess of revenues over appropriations?

a. Memorandum entry only.
b. Credit budgetary fund balance, $1,000,000.
c. Debit estimated excess revenues control, $1,000,000.
d. Debit excess revenues receivable control, $1,000,000.

97. The following funds were among those on Kery University's books at April 30, 1984:

Funds to be used for acquisition of additional properties for University purposes (unexpended at 4/30/84)	$3,000,000
Funds set aside for debt service charges and for retirement of indebtedness on University properties	5,000,000

How much of the above-mentioned funds should be included in plant funds?

a. $0
b. $3,000,000
c. $5,000,000
d. $8,000,000

98. On May 1, 1984, Lila Lee established a $50,000 endowment fund, the income from which is to be paid to Waller Hospital for general operating purposes. Waller does not control the fund's principal. Anders National Bank was appointed by Lee as trustee of this fund. What journal entry is required on Waller's books?

		Debit	*Credit*
a.	Memorandum entry only	—	—
b.	Nonexpendable endowment fund	$50,000	
	Endowment fund balance		$50,000
c.	Cash	50,000	
	Endowment fund balance		50,000
d.	Cash	50,000	
	Nonexpendable endowment fund		50,000

99. Ariel Village issued the following bonds during the year ended June 30, 1983:

For installation of street lights, to be assessed against properties benefitted	$300,000
For construction of public swimming pool; bonds to be paid from pledged fees collected from pool users	400,000

How much should be accounted for through debt service funds for payments of principal over the life of the bonds?

a. $0
b. $300,000
c. $400,000
d. $700,000

Items 100 and 101 are based on the following data:

Albee Township's fiscal year ends on June 30. Albee uses encumbrance accounting. On April 5, 1984, an approved $1,000 purchase order was issued for supplies. Albee received these supplies on May 2, 1984, and the $1,000 invoice was approved for payment.

100. What journal entry should Albee make on April 5, 1984, to record the approved purchase order?

		Debit	*Credit*
a.	Memorandum entry only	—	—
b.	Encumbrances control	$1,000	
	Fund balance reserved for encumbrances		$1,000
c.	Supplies	1,000	
	Vouchers payable		1,000
d.	Encumbrances control	1,000	
	Appropriations control		1,000

101. What journal entry or entries should Albee make on May 2, 1984, upon receipt of the supplies and approval of the invoice?

		Debit	*Credit*
a.	Appropriations control	$1,000	
	Encumbrances control		$1,000
	Supplies	1,000	
	Vouchers payable		1,000
b.	Supplies	1,000	
	Vouchers payable		1,000
c.	Fund balance reserved for encumbrances	1,000	
	Encumbrances control		1,000
	Expenditures control	1,000	
	Vouchers payable		1,000
d.	Encumbrances control	1,000	
	Appropriations control		1,000
	Fund balance	1,000	
	Vouchers payable		1,000

102. When the budget of a governmental unit is adopted and the estimated revenues exceed the appropriations, the excess is

a. Credited to fund balance.
b. Debited to fund balance.
c. Credited to reserve for encumbrances.
d. Debited to reserve for encumbrances.

103. The estimated revenues account of a governmental unit is credited when

a. The budget is closed out at the end of the year.
b. The budget is recorded.
c. Property taxes are recorded.
d. Property taxes are collected.

104. When supplies ordered by a governmental unit are received at an actual price which is less than the estimated price on the purchase order, the encumbrance account is

a. Credited for the estimated price on the purchase order.
b. Credited for the actual price for the supplies received.
c. Debited for the estimated price on the purchase order.
d. Debited for the actual price for the supplies received.

105. A capital projects fund of a municipality is an example of what type of fund?

a. Internal service.
b. Governmental.
c. Proprietary.
d. Fiduciary.

106. Which of the following funds of a governmental unit would account for general long-term debt in the accounts of the fund?

a. Special revenue.
b. Capital projects.
c. Internal service.
d. General.

107. The amount to be provided for retirement of general long-term debt is an account of a governmental unit that would be included in the

a. Asset section of the general long-term debt account group.
b. Asset section of the debt service fund.
c. Liability section of the general long-term debt account group.
d. Liability section of the debt service fund.

108. Customers' meter deposits which can **not** be spent for normal operating purposes would be classified in the balance sheet of the enterprise fund of a governmental unit as

a. Restricted cash or investments.
b. Nonrestricted cash or investments.
c. Due to general fund.
d. Due to special revenue fund.

109. Which of the following would be included in the Combined Statement of Revenues, Expenditures, and Changes in Fund Balances—Budget and Actual in the comprehensive annual financial report (CAFR) of a governmental unit?

	Enterprise fund	*General fixed asset account group*
a.	Yes	Yes
b.	Yes	No
c.	No	Yes
d.	No	No

110. Which of the following would be included in the unrestricted funds of a not-for-profit hospital?

a. Permanent endowments.
b. Term endowments.
c. Board designated funds orginating from previously accumulated income.
d. Plant expansion and replacement funds.

111. Which basis of accounting should a voluntary health and welfare organization use?

a. Cash basis for all funds.
b. Modified accrual basis for all funds.
c. Accrual basis for all funds.
d. Accrual basis for some funds and modified accrual basis for other funds.

Repeat Questions

(584,Q3,51) Identical to item 69 above

(584,Q3,57) Identical to item 61 above

Problems

Problem 1 Internal Service/General Fund (581,Q4)

(45 to 55 minutes)

Part a. The City of Merlot operates a central garage through an Internal (Intragovernmental) Service Fund to provide garage space and repairs for all city-owned and operated vehicles. The Central Garage Fund was established by a contribution of $200,000 from the General Fund on July 1, 1977, at which time the building was acquired. The after-closing trial balance at June 30, 1979, was as follows:

	Debit	*Credit*
Cash	$150,000	
Due from General Fund	20,000	
Inventory of materials and supplies	80,000	
Land	60,000	
Building	200,000	
Allowance for depreciation—building		$ 10,000
Machinery and equipment	56,000	
Allowance for depreciation—machinery and equipment		12,000
Vouchers payable		38,000
Contribution from General Fund		200,000
Retained earnings		306,000
	$566,000	$566,000

The following information applies to the fiscal year ended June 30, 1980:

1. Materials and supplies were purchased on account for $74,000.
2. The inventory of materials and supplies at June 30, 1980, was $58,000, which agreed with the physical count taken.
3. Salaries and wages paid to employees totaled $230,000, including related costs.
4. A billing was received from the Enterprise Fund for utility charges totaling $30,000, and was paid.
5. Depreciation of the building was recorded in the amount of $5,000. Depreciation of the machinery and equipment amounted to $8,000.
6. Billings to other departments for services rendered to them were as follows:

General Fund	$262,000
Water and Sewer Fund	84,000
Special Revenue Fund	32,000

7. Unpaid interfund receivable balances at June 30, 1980, were as follows:

General Fund	$ 6,000
Special Revenue Fund	16,000

8. Vouchers payable at June 30, 1980, were $14,000.

Required:

1. For the period July 1, 1979, through June 30, 1980, prepare journal entries to record all of the transactions in the Central Garage Fund accounts.
2. Prepare closing entries for the Central Garage Fund at June 30, 1980.

Part b. The following information was abstracted from the accounts of the General Fund of the City of Rom after the books had been closed for the fiscal year ended June 30, 1980:

	Post-Closing Trial Balance June 30, 1979	Transactions July 1, 1979 to June 30, 1980 Debit	Credit	Post-Closing Trial Balance June 30, 1980
Cash	$ 700,000	$1,820,000	$1,852,000	$ 668,000
Taxes receivable	40,000	1,870,000	1,828,000	82,000
	$ 740,000			$ 750,000
Allowance for uncollectible taxes	$ 8,000	8,000	10,000	$ 10,000
Vouchers payable	132,000	1,852,000	1,840,000	120,000
Fund balance:				
Reserved for encumbrances	—	1,000,000	1,070,000	70,000
Unreserved	600,000	140,000	60,000 30,000	550,000
	$ 740,000			$ 750,000

Additional information:

The budget for the fiscal year ended June 30, 1980, provided for estimated revenues of $2,000,000 and appropriations of $1,940,000.

Required:

Prepare journal entries to record the budgeted and actual transactions for the fiscal year ended June 30, 1980.

Problem 2 Municipality Journal Entries (580,Q4)

(45 to 55 minutes)

The Village of Dexter was recently incorporated and began financial operations on July 1, 1978, the beginning of its fiscal year.

The following transactions occurred during this first fiscal year, July 1, 1978, to June 30, 1979:

1. The village council adopted a budget for general operations during the fiscal year ending June 30, 1979. Revenues were estimated at $400,000. Legal authorizations for budgeted expenditures were $394,000.

2. Property taxes were levied in the amount of $390,000; it was estimated that 2% of this amount would prove to be uncollectible. These taxes are available as of the date of levy to finance current expenditures.

3. During the year a resident of the village donated marketable securities valued at $50,000 to the village under the terms of a trust agreement. The terms of the trust agreement stipulated that the principal amount is to be kept intact; use of revenue generated by the securities is restricted to financing college scholarships for needy students. Revenue earned and received on these marketable securities amounted to $5,500 through June 30, 1979.

4. A General Fund transfer of $5,000 was made to establish an Intragovernmental Service Fund to provide for a permanent investment in inventory.

5. The village decided to install lighting in the village park and a special assessment project was authorized to install the lighting at a cost of $75,000. The appropriation was formally recorded.

6. The assessments were levied for $72,000 with the village contributing $3,000 out of the General Fund. All assessments were collected during the year including the village's contribution.

7. A contract for $75,000 was let for the installation of the lighting. At June 30, 1979, the contract was completed but not approved. The contractor was paid all but 5 percent, which was retained to insure compliance with the terms of the contract. Encumbrances and other budgetary accounts are maintained.

8. During the year the Intragovernmental Service Fund purchased various supplies at a cost of $1,900.

9. Cash collections recorded by the General Fund during the year were as follows:

Property taxes	$386,000
Licenses and permits	7,000

10. The village council decided to build a village hall at an estimated cost of $500,000 to replace space occupied in rented facilities. The village does not record project authorizations. It was decided that general obligation bonds bearing interest at 6% would be issued. On June 30, 1979, the bonds were issued at their face value of $500,000, payable June 30, 1999.

No contracts have been signed for this project and no expenditures have been made.

11. A fire truck was purchased for $15,000 and the voucher approved and paid by the General Fund. This expenditure was previously encumbered for $15,000.

Required:

Prepare journal entries to properly record each of the above transactions in the appropriate fund(s) or group of accounts of Dexter Village for the fiscal year ended June 30, 1979. Use the following funds and groups of accounts:

- General Fund
- Capital Projects Fund
- Special Assessment Fund
- Internal Service Fund
- Trust Fund
- General Long-Term Debt Group of Accounts
- General Fixed Assets Group of Accounts

Each journal entry should be numbered to correspond with the transactions described above. Do **not** prepare closing entries for any fund.

Your answer sheet should be organized as follows:

Trans-action no.	Fund or group of accounts	Account title and explanation	Amounts Debit	Amounts Credit

Problem 3 Budget Theory (1181,T3)

(15 to 25 minutes)

Governmental accounting gives substantial recognition to budgets, with those budgets being recorded in the accounts of the governmental unit.

Required:

a. What is the purpose of a governmental accounting system and why is the budget recorded in the accounts of a governmental unit? Include in your discussion the purpose and significance of appropriations.

b. Describe when and how a governmental unit records its budget, and closes it out.

Problem 4 Municipal vs. Financial Accounting (575,T6)

(25 to 30 minutes)

William Bates is executive vice-president of Mavis Industries, Inc., a publicly held industrial corporation. Bates has just been elected to the city council of Gotham City. Prior to assuming office as a city councilman, he asks you as his CPA to explain the major differences that exist in accounting and financial reporting for a large city when compared to a large industrial corporation.

Required:

a. Describe the major differences that exist in the purpose of accounting and financial reporting and in the type of financial reports of a large city when compared to a large industrial corporation.

b. Why are inventories often ignored in accounting for local governmental units? Explain.

c. Under what circumstances should depreciation be recognized in accounting for local governmental units? Explain.

Problem 5 Capital Projects Fund (1180,Q5)

(40 to 50 minutes)

The City of Westgate's fiscal year ends on June 30. During the fiscal year ended June 30, 1979, the City authorized the construction of a new library and sale of general obligation term bonds to finance the construction of the library. The authorization imposed the following restrictions:

- Construction cost was not to exceed $5,000,000;
- Annual interest rate was not to exceed 8½%.

The City does not record project authorizations, but other budgetary accounts are maintained. The following transactions relating to the financing and construction of the library occurred during the fiscal year ended June 30, 1980:

1. On July 1, 1979, the City issued $5,000,000 of 30 year 8% general obligation bonds for $5,100,000. The semiannual interest dates are December 31 and June 30. The premium of $100,000 was transferred to the library debt service fund.
2. On July 3, 1979, the library capital projects fund invested $4,900,000 in short-term commercial paper. These purchases were at face value with no accrued interest. Interest on cash invested by the library capital projects fund must be transferred to the library debt service fund. During the fiscal year ending June 30, 1980, estimated interest to be earned is $140,000.
3. On July 5, 1979, the City signed a contract with F&A Construction Company to build the library for $4,980,000.
4. On January 15, 1980, the library capital projects fund received $3,040,000, from the maturity of short-term notes purchased on July 3. The cost of these notes was $3,000,000. The interest of $40,000 was transferred to the library debt service fund.
5. On January 20, 1980, F&A Construction Company properly billed the City $3,000,000 for work performed on the new library. The contract calls for 10% retention until final inspection and acceptance of the building. The library capital projects fund paid F&A $2,700,000.
6. On June 30, 1980, the Library Capital Projects Fund made the proper adjusting entries (including accrued interest receivable of $103,000) and closing entries.

Required:

1. Prepare in good form journal entries to record the six preceding sets of facts in the Library Capital Projects Fund. List the transaction numbers (1 to 6) and give the necessary entry or entries. Do not record journal entries in any other Fund or Group of Accounts.

2. Prepare in good form a Balance Sheet for the City of Westgate – Library Capital Projects Fund as of June 30, 1980.

Problem 6 University Journal Entries and Statement of Changes in Fund Balance (1183,Q4)

(45 to 55 minutes)

A partial balance sheet of Rapapo State University as of the end of its fiscal year ended July 31, 1982, is presented below.

Rapapo State University
Current Funds Balance Sheet
July 31, 1982

Assets:	
Unrestricted:	
Cash	$200,000
Accounts receivable— tuition and fees, less allowance for doubtful accounts of $15,000	360,000
Prepaid expenses	40,000
Total unrestricted	600,000
Restricted:	
Cash	10,000
Investments	210,000
Total restricted	220,000
Total current funds	$820,000
Liabilities and fund balances:	
Unrestricted:	
Accounts payable	$100,000
Due to other funds	40,000
Deferred revenue—tuition and fees	25,000
Fund balance	435,000
Total unrestricted	600,000
Restricted:	
Accounts payable	5,000
Fund balance	215,000
Total restricted	220,000
Total current funds	$820,000

The following information pertains to the year ended July 31, 1983:

1. Cash collected from students' tuition totaled $3,000,000. Of this $3,000,000, $362,000 represented accounts receivable outstanding at July 31, 1982; $2,500,000 was for current year tuition; and $138,000 was for tuition applicable to the semester beginning in August 1983.

2. Deferred revenue at July 31, 1982, was earned during the year ended July 31, 1983.

3. Accounts receivable at July 31, 1982, which were not collected during the year ended July 31, 1983, were determined to be uncollectible and were written off against the allowance account. At July 31, 1983, the allowance account was estimated at $10,000.

4. During the year, an unrestricted appropriation of $60,000 was made by the state. This state appropriation was to be paid to Rapapo sometime in August 1983.

5. During the year, unrestricted cash gifts of $80,000 were received from alumni. Rapapo's board of trustees allocated $30,000 of these gifts to the student loan fund.

6. During the year, investments costing $25,000 were sold for $31,000. Restricted fund investments were purchased at a cost of $40,000. Investment income of $18,000 was earned and collected during the year.

7. Unrestricted general expenses of $2,500,000 were recorded in the voucher system. At July 31, 1983, the unrestricted accounts payable balance was $75,000.

8. The restricted accounts payable balance at July 31, 1982, was paid.

9. The $40,000 due to other funds at July 31, 1982, was paid to the plant fund as required.

10. One quarter of the prepaid expenses at July 31, 1982, expired during the current year and pertained to general education expense. There was no addition to prepaid expenses during the year.

Required:

a. Prepare journal entries in summary form to record the foregoing transactions for the year ended July 31, 1983. Number each entry to correspond with the number indicated in the description of its respective transaction. Your answer sheet should be organized as follows:

		Current funds			
Entry		Unrestricted		Restricted	
no.	Accounts	Debit	Credit	Debit	Credit

b. Prepare a statement of changes in fund balances for the year ended July 31, 1983.

Problem 7 Hospital Statement of Revenues and Expenses (1182,Q5)

(40 to 50 minutes)

The following selected information was taken from the books and records of Glendora Hospital (a voluntary hospital) as of and for the year ended June 30, 1982:

- Patient service revenue totaled $16,000,000, with allowances and uncollectible accounts amounting to $3,400,000. Other operating revenue aggregated $346,000, and included $160,000 from specific purpose funds. Revenue of $6,000,000 recognized under cost reimbursement agreements is subject to audit and retroactive adjustment by third-party payors. Estimated retroactive adjustments under these agreements have been included in allowances.
- Unrestricted gifts and bequests of $410,000 were received.
- Unrestricted income from endowment funds totaled $160,000.
- Income from board-designated funds aggregated $82,000.
- Operating expenses totaled $13,370,000, and included $500,000 for depreciation computed on the straight-line basis. However, accelerated depreciation is used to determine reimbursable costs under certain third-party reimbursement agreements. Net cost reimbursement revenue amounting to $220,000, resulting from the difference in depreciation methods, was deferred to future years.
- Also included in operating expenses are pension costs of $100,000, in connection with a noncontributory pension plan covering substantially all of Glendora's employees. Accrued pension costs are funded currently. Prior service cost is being amortized over a period of 20 years. The actuarially computed value of vested and nonvested benefits at year-end amounted to $3,000,000 and $350,000 respectively. The assumed rate of return used in determining the actuarial present value of accumulated plan benefits was 8%. The plan's net assets available for benefits at year-end was $3,050,000.
- Gifts and bequests are recorded at fair market values when received.
- Patient service revenue is accounted for at established rates on the accrual basis.

Required:

1. Prepare a formal statement of revenues and expenses for Glendora Hospital for the year ended June 30, 1982.

2. Draft the appropriate disclosures in separate notes accompanying the statement of revenues and expenses, referencing each note to its respective item in the statement.

Problem 8 Journal Entries and All-Inclusive Activity Statement for Nonprofit Organization (583,Q5)

(40 to 50 minutes)

In 1950 a group of civic-minded merchants in Albury City organized the "Committee of 100" for the purpose of establishing the Community Sports Club, a nonprofit sports organization for local youth. Each of the Committee's 100 members contributed $1,000 towards the Club's capital, and in turn received a participation certificate. In addition, each participant agreed to pay dues of $200 a year for the Club's operations. All dues have been collected in full by the end of each fiscal year ending March 31. Members who have discontinued their participation have been replaced by an equal number of new members through transfer of the participation certificates from the former members to the new ones. Following is the Club's trial balance at April 1, 1982:

	Debit	*Credit*
Cash	$ 9,000	
Investments (at market, equal to cost)	58,000	
Inventories	5,000	
Land	10,000	
Building	164,000	
Accumulated depreciation—building		$130,000
Furniture and equipment	54,000	
Accumulated depreciation—furniture and equipment		46,000
Accounts payable		12,000
Participation certificates (100 at $1,000 each)		100,000
Cumulative excess of revenue over expenses		12,000
	$300,000	$300,000

Transactions for the year ended March 31, 1983, were as follows:

(1)	Collections from participants for dues	$20,000
(2)	Snack bar and soda fountain sales	28,000
(3)	Interest and dividends received	6,000
(4)	Additions to voucher register:	
	House expenses	17,000
	Snack bar and soda fountain	26,000
	General and administrative	11,000
(5)	Vouchers paid	55,000
(6)	Assessments for capital improvements not yet incurred (assessed on March 20, 1983; none collected by March 31, 1983; deemed 100% collectible during year ending March 31, 1984)	10,000
(7)	Unrestricted bequest received	5,000

Adjustment data:

(1) Investments are valued at market, which amounted to $65,000 at March 31, 1983. There were no investment transactions during the year.

(2) Depreciation for the year:

Building	$4,000
Furniture and equipment	8,000

(3) Allocation of depreciation:

House expenses	9,000
Snack bar and soda fountain	2,000
General and administrative	1,000

(4) Actual physical inventory at March 31, 1983, was $1,000, and pertains to the snack bar and soda fountain.

Required:

On a functional basis

a. Record the transactions and adjustments in journal entry form for the year ended March 31, 1983. Omit explanations.

b. Prepare the appropriate all-inclusive activity statement for the year ended March 31, 1983.

Multiple Choice Answers

1.	b	24.	c	46.	d	68.	c	90.	a
2.	a	25.	b	47.	b	69.	a	91.	a
3.	b	26.	b	48.	b	70.	c	92.	a
4.	c	27.	a	49.	c	71.	d	93.	b
5.	d	28.	b	50.	b	72.	a	94.	c
6.	b	29.	a	51.	b	73.	c	95.	c
7.	b	30.	b	52.	d	74.	d	96.	b
8.	c	31.	d	53.	d	75.	a	97.	d
9.	d	32.	c	54.	a	76.	d	98.	a
10.	b	33.	a	55.	b	77.	d	99.	a
11.	c	34.	a	56.	c	78.	d	100.	b
12.	d	35.	a	57.	b	79.	a	101.	c
13.	d	36.	c	58.	c	80.	a	102.	a
14.	b	37.	a	59.	a	81.	b	103.	a
15.	a	38.	c	60.	a	82.	b	104.	a
16.	c	39.	a	61.	a	83.	b	105.	b
17.	a	40.	b	62.	d	84.	a	106.	c
18.	d	41.	b	63.	a	85.	c	107.	a
19.	b	42.	b	64.	a	86.	d	108.	a
20.	b	43.	a	65.	a	87.	b	109.	d
21.	c	44.	a	66.	c	88.	a	110.	c
22.	c	45.	b	67.	a	89.	d	111.	c
23.	a								

Multiple Choice Answer Explanations

I.A. Fund Accounting

1. (1180,T1,51) (b) A major difference between governmental and commercial accounting is that governmental units maintain complete self-balancing accounts for each fund, while a commercial enterprise keeps one set of books for the entire entity. Answer (a) is incorrect because a not-for-profit entity should record depreciation expense in some funds, and answers (c) and (d) are incorrect because neither type of entity uses only the cash basis or modified accrual basis of accounting. A commercial enterprise uses accrual basis accounting, while a governmental unit uses different accounting bases for different funds, depending on the purpose of the fund.

I.B. Budgets and Their Impact Upon the Accounting System

2. (577,P1,15) (a) The entry to record issuance of purchase vouchers is to debit encumbrances and credit reserve for encumbrances. This is a budgetary entry which is reversed for the same amount upon payment of the invoice (after receipt of the goods or services). The entry is reversed for the same amount of dollars as originally recorded, even if the entry to record the actual expenditure is for a different amount of dollars. The entry to record the expenditure is to debit expenditures and credit the vouchers payable. The encumbering entry is made to control or hold expenditures within appropriations. Unencumbered appropriated funds available for spending are appropriations made at the beginning of the year, less expenditures and encumbrances to date.

3. (582,Q2,25) (b) The requirement is the funds available for additional purchases of supplies. GAAFR, STMT 1 states that appropriations constitute maximum expenditure authorizations during the fiscal year, and cannot legally be exceeded unless subsequently amended by the legislative body. An encumbrance reduces appropriation authority and is formally recorded in the accounting records.

Appropriations		$7,500
Less: Encumbrances	$ 750	
Expenditures	4,500	5,250
Unencumbered balance		$2,250

The unencumbered balance is the amount of resources that can still be obligated or expended without exceeding the legal or authorized limit.

4. (582,Q2,28) (c) The requirement is the accounting entry required to record the annual budget. Under current GAAFR, budgetary accounts (estimated revenues and appropriations) are incorporated into governmental accounting systems to provide legislative control over receipts and disbursements and to provide an assessment of managements' stewardship by facilitating a comparison of budget vs. actual. Upon adoption of the estimated revenues and appropriations budgets the following entry is made and posted to the general ledger:

Estimated revenues	XXX	
Appropriations		XXX
Fund balance		XXX

Estimated revenues and appropriations are temporary accounts which are closed against actual revenues and expenditures at year end. Differences between budget and actual are debited (credited) to fund balance.

5. (1183,T1,51) (d) The requirement is to determine the account credited when the budget is recorded on the books. The following entry should be made (assuming a surplus):

Estimated revenues	XXX	
Appropriations		XXX
Unreserved fund balance		XXX

Answers (a) and (b) are incorrect as encumbrances is debited and reserve for encumbrances is credited when goods are ordered; these accounts are included in the budget entry. Answer (c) is incorrect as it is the debit in the entry illustrated above.

6. (1183,T1,52) (b) The requirement is to determine the account debited when goods are received by a governmental unit. The typical entries to record the receipt are:

Reserve for encumbrances	XXX	
Encumbrances		XXX
Expenditures	XXX	
Vouchers payable		XXX

Answer (a) is incorrect because encumbrances is debited when the goods are ordered. Answer (c) is incorrect as vouchers payable is credited when goods are received and debited when the account is paid. Answer (d) is incorrect because appropriations is not debited until the end of the accounting period.

7. (1183,T1,54) (b) The requirement is to determine which fund integrates budgetary accounts into the accounting system. According to GAAFR, STMT 1, budgetary integration is essential in general, special revenue, and other annually budgeted governmental funds. Answers (a) and (c) are incorrect because they are proprietary funds which do not require the integration of budgets into the accounting system. Answer (d) is incorrect because nonexpendable trust funds (a type of fiduciary fund) have the same budgetary considerations as the proprietary funds described above.

8. (583,T1,51) (c) When appropriations are greater than actual expenditures and encumbrances, the fund has spent less than was budgeted. At the **end** of the fiscal year, this difference will be closed to (and will increase) unreserved fund balance. Answers (a) and (b) are incorrect because they will decrease the unreserved fund balance at year end. Additionally, reserve for encumbrances [included in answer (a)] is not closed out at year end because it is a real account. Answer (d) is incorrect because any difference between appropriations and estimated revenues in the initial budget entry will affect unreserved fund balance at the **beginning** of the year.

9. (583,T1,52) (d) The requirement is to determine which account is credited when it is closed out at the end of the fiscal year. The solutions approach is to prepare a typical closing entry:

Appropriations	XXX	
Expenditures		XXX
Encumbrances		XXX
Unreserved fund balance		XXX

The encumbrances account [answer (d)] is credited in the above entry. Answer (a) is incorrect because the appropriations account is debited in the closing entry. Answer (b) is incorrect because revenues are debited when revenues and estimated revenues are closed to unreserved fund balance. Answer (c) is incorrect because the reserve for encumbrances account is a real account and is not closed out at year end.

10. (582,T1,53) (b) The typical closing entry made at year end when appropriations exceed expenditures plus encumbrances is the following:

Appropriations	XXXX	
Unreserved fund balance		XX
Expenditures		XXX
Encumbrances		XXX

However, when expenditures and encumbrances exceed appropriations (which is a violation of the budget) the fund balance would decrease and be debited in the closing entry.

11. (581,T1,51) (c) The requirement is the treatment of the excess of revenues over estimated revenues when the estimated revenue account of a governmental unit is closed at the end of the fiscal year. At the beginning of the fiscal year, a governmental unit estimates the amount of revenue it will collect during the year from various sources. The account "Estimated Revenues" is debited at the beginning of the year. When preparing closing entries, then, the amount of actual revenues over estimated revenues would be credited to the fund balance account.

12. (580,T1,56) (d) If appropriations are greater than the actual expenditures and encumbrances, this means the fund has spent less than expected. This difference will be closed to (and will increase) unreserved fund balance. Answers (a) and (b) both state the opposite of answer (d), while answer (c) concerns only appropriations and estimated revenues, which would affect the unreserved fund balance at the beginning of the year.

13. (1175,T2,31) (d) When goods or services are ordered, appropriatioms are encumbered by debiting encumbrances and crediting reserve for encumbrances. If the goods and services are received in the period ordered, the foregoing entry is reversed when the expenditure is recorded. If the goods are not received in the period they are ordered, the encumbrance account is closed to the appropriations account at the end of the period (as is expenditures). The reserve for encumbrances, a real account, earmarks the fund balance to liquidate goods ordered in previous periods. Expenditures for goods ordered in previous periods are charged to the reserve for encumbrances account.

I.C. Financial Statements for State and Local Governments

14. (1183,T1,58) (b) According to GAAFR, STMT 1, the CAFR must include a comprehensive statement of changes in financial position for all proprietary funds. This is consistent with the nature of the proprietary funds and their similarity to commercial business. A statement of changes in financial position is **not** required for a general fund.

I.E. Governmental Funds

15. (582,Q2,29) (a) The requirement is the journal entry to record monthly salaries and wages. GAAFR, STMT 1 states that expenditures generally should be recognized in the accounting period in which the fund liability is incurred, if measurable. Thus, an expenditure and a corresponding liability are recorded at the time goods or services are received. Formal encumbrance accounting for expenditures such as salaries is unnecessary because these amounts are precisely measurable in advance and subject to additional alternative administrative and personnel controls, which effectively prevent overexpenditure. Answer (c) is inappropriate because encumbrances are not used for expenditures such as salaries. Answer (b) is incorrect because expenditures, rather than expenses, would be debited.

16. (582,Q2,32) (c) The requirement is the grant revenues to be recorded in the **general fund** for the year ended 12/31/81. GAAFR, STMT 2 states that grants, entitlements, or shared revenues recorded in **governmental funds** typically should be recognized as revenue in the accounting period when they become susceptible to accrual (i.e., both measurable and available). However, in applying this definition, legal and contractual requirements should be carefully reviewed. When expenditure is the prime factor for determining eligibility (as assumed in this case) revenue should be recognized in the period when the expenditures are made.

Purchase of buses	$300,000
Bus operations	100,000
Total revenue reported	$400,000

17. (582,Q2,33) (a) The requirement is the grant revenues to be recorded in the **enterprise fund** for the year ended 12/31/81. GAAFR, STMT 2 states that grants, entitlements, or shared revenues received for proprietary fund operating purposes, or which may be utilized for either operations or capital expenditures at the discretion of the recipient, should be recognized as "nonoperating" revenue in the accounting period in which they are earned and become measurable. Such resources restricted for the acquisition or construction of capital assets should be recorded as contributed equity. In this case $100,000 would be reported as revenue and $500,000 as contributed equity.

18. (582,Q2,36) (d) The requirement is the appropriate reporting in the financial statements for the **capital project fund**. GAAFR states that neither proceeds from a general obligation bond nor transfers from the general fund are revenues. Rather they are recognized as "other financing sources" when they become measurable and available as net current assets. Expenditures of governmental funds are generally recognized in the accounting period in which the fund liability is incurred, which is the current year in this question.

19. (582,Q2,37) (b) The requirement is the reporting in the financial statements of the **general fund**. GAAFR, STMT 1 states that transfers from the general fund to a capital projects fund should be considered operating transfers and be reported in the "other financing uses" section in general fund's statement of revenues, expenditures, and changes in fund balance.

20. (582,Q2,38) (b) The requirement is the total amount of expenditures to be reported in the general fund column of the combined statement of revenues, expenditures, and changes in fund balance. GAAFR, STMT 1 states that encumbrances outstanding at year end **may** not be reported as expenditures in GAAP financial statements. The prior year's expenditures being included in the current year's financial statements evolved as follows:

- Encumbrances from the preceding year were carried over in the account-fund balance reserved for encumbrances-prior year.
- When the expenditure actually took place during the current year it exceeded the reserved amount and the following entry was made:

Fund balance reserved for encumbrances-prior year	(reserved amount)	
Expenditures control	$100,000	
Vouchers payable		(actual amount)

Therefore, total expenditures reported for the current year would be:

Current year expenditures	$3,000,000
Prior year expenditures	100,000
Total	$3,100,000

21. (582,Q2,39) (c) The requirement is the total amount of expenditures to be reported in the general fund "actual" column of the combined statement of revenues, expenditures, and changes in fund balance-budget and actual. This statement is used to evaluate management's stewardship of the current fiscal budget. Per GAAFR, STMT 1, this statement should present comparisons of the legally adopted budget with actual data on the budgetary basis (which may include encumbrances). The problem indicates that the general fund books are maintained on a legal budgetary basis, and that current year expenditures and encumbrances **cannot** exceed current year appropriations. This implies that the budgetary comparison statements must include encumbrances and treat them like expenditures in the "actual" column. The "actual" data on this statement may be different from the GAAP presentations in the combined statement of revenues, expenditures, and changes in fund balance-all governmental fund types. In this case, the current year appropriations should be compared to:

Current year expenditures	$3,000,000
Add: current year encumbrances	200,000
Total "actual" expenditures	$3,200,000

The prior year's expenditures should not be included since they were appropriated in the previous year's budget.

22. (1183,T1,53) (c) The requirement is the treatment of a fixed asset purchase out of the general fund revenues. The fixed asset purchase results in a reduction in the fund balance or resource outflow. Resource outflows are recorded as a debit to expenditures and a credit to vouchers payable. Answer (a) is incorrect as no journal entry would result in an overstatement of the fund balance. Answer (b) is incorrect because per GAAFR, STMT 1, general fixed assets do not represent financial resources available for expenditure and, therefore, are not recorded in the general fund. Answer (d) is incorrect because transfers and the resulting "due froms" are a result of interfund transactions; the general fixed asset group is **not** a fund.

23. (1183,T1,55) (a) Per GAAFR, STMT 1, governmental fund revenues and expenditures should be recognized on the modified accrual basis of accounting; debt service funds are classified as governmental funds. Per GAAFR, STMT 1, proprietary fund revenues and expenses should be recognized on the accrual basis; internal service and enterprise funds [answers (b) and (c)] are classified as proprietary funds. A nonexpendable trust [answer (d)] is a fiduciary fund, and per GAAFR, STMT 1 should be accounted for on the accrual basis.

24. (1183,T1,57) (c) The general fixed assets account group is used to establish accounting control and responsibility for the government's general fixed assets. Per GAAFR, STMT 1, fixed assets related to proprietary funds or trust funds should be accounted for within these funds. Other fixed assets of a governmental unit should be accounted for through the general fund fixed assets account group.

25. (583,T1,53) (b) Per GAAFR, STMT 1, governmental funds should recognize revenues and expenditures on the modified accrual basis of accounting. Under this basis, revenues are recognized in the period in which they are both measurable and available to finance expenditures of the current fiscal period. GAAFR requires that property taxes, net of estimated uncollectibles, be recognized as revenues when the taxes are available [answer (b)]. Per GAAFR, STMT 1, "available" means collectible within the current period or soon enough thereafter, to be used to pay liabilities of the current period. However, if the property taxes are deemed measurable but not available, the property taxes, net of estimated uncollectibles, should be recorded as deferred revenues. Answer (a) is incorrect because estimated revenues is credited only during the year-end closing. Appropriations [answer (c)] is credited when the budget is formally recorded by the fund. Reserve for encumbrances [answer (d)] is credited when encumbrances are recorded.

26. (583,T1,56) (b) The requirement is to determine which fund of a governmental unit uses the same basis of accounting as the special revenue fund. Due to the absence of a capital maintenance objective (the preservation of capital), special revenue funds are expendable funds and are accounted for by the modified accrual basis of accounting. Expendable trust funds [answer (b)] are also accounted for on the modified accrual basis due to the lack of a capital maintenance objective. Answers (a), (c), and (d) are incorrect because they describe funds having a capital maintenance objective which, therefore, use the accrual basis of accounting.

27. (583,T1,59) (a) The requirement is to determine the type of funds for which revenues are recognized when they become **available** and **measurable.** These two criteria are used for revenue recognition under the modified accrual basis of accounting. Governmental funds lack the capital maintenance objective and, therefore, use the modified accrual basis. Proprietary funds use the accrual basis of accounting, recognizing revenues in the period in which they are **earned** and become **measurable** (GAAFR, STMT 1).

28. (1182,T1,54) (b) There are three types of funds used by state and local governments: governmental, proprietary, and fiduciary. Per GAAFR, STMT 1, a debt service fund is a governmental fund. Other governmental funds include general fund, special revenue fund, capital projects fund, and special assessment fund. Internal service fund [answer (d)] is classified as a proprietary fund.

29. (1182,T1,55) (a) A special revenue fund is a governmental fund. Per GAAFR, STMT 2, a governmental fund should recognize revenue in the period when it becomes susceptible to accrual, i.e., both "available" and "measurable." "Available" means collectible within the current period or soon enough thereafter to be used to pay liabilities of the current period.

30. (1182,T1,56) (b) GAAFR, STMT 1 states that general long-term liabilities of proprietary funds, special assessment funds, and trust funds should be accounted for in those funds. Other funds should use the general long-term debt account group to account for their general long-term liabilities. Therefore, such liabilities arising in connection with capital projects would be accounted for in the general long-term debt account group.

31. (1182,T1,58) (d) Per GAAFR, STMT 1, the general fixed assets account group should be used to account for fixed assets other than those related to specific proprietary funds or trust funds. The special assessments fund, a governmental fund, should use the general fixed assets account group to account for its fixed assets.

32. (1182,T1,59) (c) Per GAAFR, STMT 1, governmental funds should recognize revenues and expenditures on the modified accrual basis. Also, per STMT 1, proprietary funds revenues and expenses should be recognized on the accrual basis.

33. (582,T1,56) (a) The debt service fund is a governmental fund as is the general fund. Revenues and expenditures for governmental funds should be recognized on the modified accrual basis. In proprietary funds [answers (b) and (c)] revenues and expenses should be recognized on the accrual basis. Nonexpendable trust and pension trust funds [answer (d)] should also be accounted for on the accrual basis.

34. (582,T1,58) (a) Budgeting is important in the financial planning, control and evaluation processes of governmental units. Integration of budgetary accounts (including encumbrances) in the formal accounting system is essential in general, special revenue, and other annually budgeted governmental funds which have numerous types of revenues, expenditures and transfers. For example, full or partial budgetary account integration would be essential where numerous construction projects are being financed through a capital projects or special assessment fund. Budgetary accounts (including encumbrances) are not necessary in controlling most debt service funds [answer (b)], where the amounts required to be received and expended are set forth in bond indentures or sinking fund provisions and only a few transactions occur each year. Encumbrance accounting is inappropriate for nonfund account groups [answer (c)] and proprietary funds [answer (d)].

35. (1180,T1,56) (a) Capital projects funds account for the proceeds of a debt issue to be used for a capital project. When the bonds are issued, cash is debited and bond issue proceeds is credited. The fund balance account [answer (b)] is not affected until closing entries are prepared. An appropriations account [answer (c)] is not used, and bonds payable [answer (d)] are not recorded in this fund but instead are recorded in the general long term debt group of accounts.

36. (580,T1,53) (c) Agency funds are used to account for assets held by a governmental unit as an agent for individuals, private organizations, other governmental units, or other funds. Enterprise funds [answer (a)] are used to account for funds which are operated in a fashion similar to private business concerns. Internal service funds [answer (b)] are used to account for operations which provide goods or services for other departments. Special revenue funds [answer (d)] are used to account for proceeds that are restricted to expenditures for specified purposes, but these funds do not hold resources for another governmental unit.

37. (1179,T1,42) (a) Under the modified accrual basis, property taxes are usually recorded before they are received. The rationale is that collection of property taxes is reasonably assured (as the property can be liened and even sold for taxes). Answers (b), (c), and (d) (income taxes, gross receipts taxes, and gift taxes) are not as reasonably assured as property taxes, and, therefore, are not recorded as income until received.

38. (1179,T1,45) (c) Interest on bonds payable should be recorded in the debt service fund when the interest is legally payable. The debt service fund accounts for the monies used to repay debt. Thus, there

is no need to accrue the interest as suggested in answer (a). Answer (b) is incorrect because there is no interest payable upon issuance of the bonds. Answer (d) is incorrect because the payable is extinguished upon payment.

39. (1178,T1,26) (a) The requirement is the item that should be accrued as revenue by the general fund. The general fund, as well as the special revenue and debt service funds, uses the modified accrual basis. The modified accrual basis recognizes expenses when they are incurred and revenues when they are received, i.e., cash basis for revenues and accrual basis for expenses. The rationale is that most governmental revenues are not assured until received, e.g., license revenues which are dependent upon persons making a decision to purchase a license. The revenue recognition rule under the modified accrual basis, however, is modified to recognize taxes when levied. When taxes are levied, they are considered collectible. The same would be true of sales taxes that have already been collected by the state which will be remitted to the local government. Answers (b), (c), and (d), parking meter revenues, sales taxes, and income taxes, are accounted for on the cash basis and not accrued.

40. (1178,T1,33) (b) The requirement is the type of expenditure normally recorded on the accrual basis in the general fund. Personal services are expenses that are accounted for on an accrual basis, i.e., they are expensed and set up as a liability when incurred. In contrast, answers (c) and (d), inventory items and prepaid expenses, are deferrals (cash basis transaction occurs before accrual basis transactions) but are normally expensed as purchased. Answer (a) is incorrect because interest is normally expensed when paid by the general fund.

41. (1177,T2,23) (b) When the general fund transfers money to establish a new internal service fund, a residual equity transfer has occurred. This requires a debit to fund balance in the general fund. In the internal service fund, Cash is debited and "Contribution from general fund" is credited. Answer (c) is incorrect because "Reserve for encumbrances" is not debited for cash payments. Answer (d) is incorrect because the accounts "Operating transfers out" and "Operating transfers in" are used for interfund transfers which are not residual equity transfers.

42. (1177,T2,27) (b) Agency funds perform a holding operation for money, e.g., collection of union dues, employee wthholding, etc. Thus the assets are usually liquid and offset entirely by liabilities rather than a fund balance. The general, special revenue, and capital projects funds all use budgetary accounts, i.e., recording appropriations, estimated revenues, etc., which result in a fund balance account.

43. (1176,T2,42) (a) The accounts of similar funds, e.g., special assessment, special revenue, etc., can be combined into a total column. The accounts of different types of funds can be added together on a memorandum basis only as the funds are independent entities with no right of offset. Answer (b) is incorrect because the effect of interfund transactions may not be eliminated, as the right of offset does not exist. Answer (c) is incorrect because funds may be reported on a separate basis on the same statement (but not totaled together if they are not the same type of fund). Answer (d) is incorrect as the lack of the right of offset precludes eliminating the effects of interfund transactions.

44. (1175,T2,32) (a) The proceeds of general obligation bonds are accounted for in the capital projects fund, and the debt service fund usually handles the repayment of long-term debt (except repayment of special assessment debt) and interest payments. The premiums received on general obligation bonds are usually transferred from the capital projects fund to the debt service fund, because the premium represents an adjustment of the interest cost. If the general fund is paying the interest, the premium should be transferred to the general fund.

45. (1175,T2,40) (b) Upon sale of fixed assets, the cash is recorded in the general fund as a debit to cash and a credit to revenue. The entry to remove the fixed assets in the general fixed-assets group of accounts is to debit "investment in fixed assets – capital projects fund" and credit "equipment". The entry would be made for the original cost as no depreciation is recorded in the general fixed-assets group of accounts.

I.F. Proprietary Funds

46. (577,P1,16) (d) Enterprise funds use the same accrual accounting system and procedures as for-profit enterprises. Thus, only 1976 depreciation and 1976 bad debts expense would appear in the revenues and expenses statement. The prepaid insurance would be deferred in the statement of financial position.

47. (583,T1,55) (b) The internal service fund accounts for the provision of goods or services to other governmental funds on a cost-reimbursement basis. Capital maintenance is a primary objective of the internal service fund, and consequently, the accrual basis of accounting is employed. Per GAAFR, STMT 1, depreciation must be recorded in the internal service fund to determine fund expenses, charges to other funds, and changes in fund equity. Answers (a), (c) and (d) are incorrect because the general, capital projects, and special assessment funds are nonexpendable funds. Nonexpendable funds do not record depreciation since they lack the capital maintenance objective.

48. (1182,T1,57) (b) Both an enterprise fund and an internal service fund are classified as proprietary funds. Per GAAFR, STMT 1, proprietary fund revenues and expenses should be recognized on the accrual basis. Answers (a) and (d) are incorrect because special revenue and capital projects funds are classified as governmental funds. Per GAAFR, STMT 1, governmental fund revenues and expenditures should be recognized on the modified accrual basis. Answer (c) is incorrect because expendable trust funds are accounted for in essentially the same manner as governmental funds (i.e., on the modified accrual basis).

49. (582,T1,51) (c) GAAFR, STMT 1 states that fixed assets utilized in proprietary fund activities or in trust funds are accounted for within those funds. The activities of a city-owned utility which provides goods or services to the general public on a continuous basis and recovers the majority of costs incurred from charges to users should be accounted for in an enterprise fund (a proprietary fund). Enterprise fund fixed assets are capitalized in the enterprise fund accounts because the fixed assets are used in the production of the goods or services provided and sold. Fixed assets other than those accounted for in the proprietary funds or trust funds are general fixed assets and are accounted for in the general fixed assets account group rather than in the governmental funds.

50. (582,T1,57) (b) Government operations that are similar to commercial business operations, such as utilities or a central computer facility, are accounted for in proprietary funds. Financial accounting and reporting for these entities parallel accounting and reporting for profit-oriented enterprises. Special revenue and capital projects are governmental funds [answers (c) and (d)]. These funds are not concerned with capital maintenance or measuring net income. Rather they are concerned with the availability of resources to provide services, and the emphasis is on working capital flows. Expendable trust funds [answer (a)] and agency funds are also classified as governmental funds and are accounted for as such.

51. (581,T1,56) (b) The requirement is which accounts could be included in the balance sheet of an enterprise fund. Enterprise funds are used to account for operations that are financial and operated in a manner similar to a private business, where the provision of goods or services to the general public are on a continuing basis and where all or most costs incurred are recovered from charges to users. An example of an enterprise fund is a public utility. Accounting for the operations of enterprise funds closely parallels the accounting for profit-oriented enterprises and uses the same accounts. The two accounts which closely parallel those used in profit-oriented business are revenue bonds payable (bonds which are secured by the future revenues of the fund) and retained earnings. Reserve for Encumbrances is not used in profit-oriented accounting and is also not used in enterprise funds.

52. (581,T1,58) (d) The requirement is the fund in which customers' meter deposits, which cannot be spent for normal operating purposes, would be classified as restricted in the balance sheet. The meters are assumed to be those associated with public utilities, such as water meters or electric meters. Enterprise funds are used to account for the provision of goods or services to the general public on a continuing basis where all or most of the costs incurred are recovered from charges to users.

53. (1179,T1,43) (d) The internal service fund is not an expendable fund as are the general fund, capital projects funds, and special revenue funds. The internal service fund is established to provide services to other funds. Accounting for internal service funds follows normal profit accounting except "contribution from general fund" is used in lieu of the capital stock account. Answers (a), (b), and (c) are incorrect because the capital projects, general, and special revenue funds collect monies to be spent to provide services.

54. (1178,T1,29) (a) "Excess of net billings to departments over costs" would appear in the financial statements of internal service fund. The internal service fund provides services to other governmental funds. An excess of net billings to departments over cost would be the "income" figure of the fund. The objective of an internal service fund is not to create a profit, but rather to provide services at cost to other

funds. Small profits or losses can be expected from time to time; these would be closed to a retained earnings account.

55. (578,T2,29) (b) Governmental units that provide services to other governmental units are accounted for in the internal service fund. Internal service funds use accrual accounting and have accounting systems similar to for-profit organizations. The only difference is that the internal service fund attempts to price its service at cost rather than to make a profit. Answer (a) is incorrect because the capital projects fund is used to account for capital expenditures, e.g., issuance of bonds to build buildings or federal grants to construct streets. Answers (c) and (d) are incorrect because agency and trust funds provide a fiduciary capacity, i.e., holding funds for some future use. Agency funds usually involve short-term holdings, and trust funds involve long-term holdings.

56. (1176,T2,38) (c) The enterprise fund is appropriate for recreational and similar facilities for which one-half or more of the finances are obtained by user charges. If more than one-half of the finances come from taxes, a special revenue fund is used. The general fund accounts for all transactions not accounted for in other funds. The trust fund accounts for assets that are going to be held on behalf of others for long periods of time, e.g., pension funds. Capital project funds account for the proceeds of bond issues, federal grants, etc., which are used to construct capital projects such as schools, libraries, etc.

I.G. Fiduciary Funds – Trust and Agency

57. (1178,T1,28) (b) An actuarial deficiency would be the amount associated with an actuarial computation where a prior actuarial estimate was insufficient. Actuarial amounts have to do with pensions which would be accounted for in a trust fund. Answer (a) is incorrect because an agency fund has to do only with short-term holdings for others, e.g., payroll taxes to be remitted to the federal government or union dues to be remitted to a union. Answers (c) and (d) are incorrect because the general and debt service funds would not administer programs in which actuarial computations are necessary.

58. (1178,T1,31) (c) Trust funds are nonexpendable as to principal and expendable as to income. Frequently two trust funds are established: one for principal and the other for income. Then as income is earned by the nonexpendable fund, it is transferred to the expendable fund. The debt service fund [answer (a)], enterprise fund [answer (b)], and special revenues fund [answer (d)], all are exclusively expendable funds.

I.H. The GFA and GLTD Account Groups

59. (582,Q2,22) (a) The requirement is the fixed assets that should be included in the general fixed assets account group. GAAFR, STMT 1 states that general fixed assets are fixed assets other than those accounted for in the proprietary funds or trust funds. Reporting public domain or "infrastructure" fixed assets – roads, bridges, curbs and gutters, streets and sidewalks, drainage systems, lighting systems and similar assets that are immovable and of value only to the governmental unit – is optional.

City Hall	$ 800,000
Three fire stations	1,000,000
Option 1 total	$1,800,000
Add: City streets and sidewalks	5,000,000
Option 2 total	$6,800,000

60. (582,Q2,23) (a) The requirement is the expenditures that should be classified as fixed assets in the **general fund** balance sheet. GAAFR, STMT 1 states that general fixed assets are accounted for in the general fixed assets account group rather than in the governmental funds. General fixed assets do not represent financial resources available for expenditure, but are items for which financial resources have been used and for which accountability should be maintained. Their inclusion in the financial statements of a governmental fund would increase the fund balance, which could mislead users of the fund balance sheet. Therefore, none of the items listed would be classified as fixed assets in Kew Township's general fund balance sheet.

61. (582,Q2,35) (a) The requirement is the bonds to be accounted for in the general long-term debt account group. GAAFR, STMT 1 states that bonds, notes, and other long-term liabilities directly related to and expected to be paid from proprietary funds, special assessment funds, and trust funds should be included in the accounts of such funds. These are specific fund liabilities, even though the full faith and credit of the governmental unit may be pledged as further assurance that the liabilities will be paid.

62. (1183,T1,56) (d) According to GAAFR, STMT 1, long-term liabilities directly related to and expected to be paid from proprietary funds,

special assessment funds, and trust funds should be included in the accounts of such funds because they are specific fund liabilities. Other long-term debt of governmental units is accounted for in the general long-term debt account group. Long-term debt is **not** accounted for in both the fund and the account group.

63. (583,T1,57) (a) Special assessment funds [answer (a)] account for the financing of public improvements or services deemed to benefit the properties against which special assessments are levied. Per GAAFR, STMT 1, long-term liabilities should be included in the accounts of special assessment and trust funds, since they are considered liabilities of the **specific** funds, not general obligation debt. The long-term liabilities arising from special revenue and capital projects funds [answers (b) and (c)] are general obligations of the governmental unit and should be recorded in the GLTD group of accounts. Debt service funds [answer (d)] do not incur long-term liabilities, but rather, account for the repayment of long-term, general obligation interest and principal.

64. (583,T1,58) (a) The requirement is to determine which accounts are included in the asset section of the combined balance sheet of a governmental unit for the general long-term debt account group. The general long-term debt account group records the repayment of long-term debt incurred by the general fund, special revenue funds, and capital projects funds. When long-term debt is initially recorded, the following entry is made:

Amount to be provided for retirement of general long-term debt	XXX	
Bonds payable		XXX

As monies are set aside in the debt service fund for bond repayment, the following entry is made:

Amount available in debt service fund	XXX	
Amount to be provided for retirement of general long-term debt		XXX

Per GAAFR, the accounts debited in the entries above are to be included in the asset section of a governmental unit's combined balance sheet. Therefore, answer (a) is correct.

65. (1178,T1,32) (a) Investments in general fixed assets appear in the general fixed assets group of accounts. The general fixed assets goup of accounts is a self-balancing list of the costs of general fixed assets. All governmental assets are accounted for in a general fixed asset fund except for assets of the internal service and enterprise funds. Also depreciable assets held in trust are recorded in trust funds. When assets are acquired, each asset, e.g., land, building, equipment, etc., is debited in the general fixed assets account and the account "investment in general fixed assets – (fund acquiring)" is credited. When the assets are disposed of, the entry is reversed.

II.A. College and University Accounting

66. (582,Q2,24) (c) The requirement is the gift revenue that should be reported in the restricted column of the Statement of Current Fund Revenues, Expenditures, and Other Changes for the year ended 6/30/81. The AICPA College and University Audit Guide states that donor-restricted resources designated for specific operating purposes should be accounted for in a restricted fund or as defined revenue in the unrestricted fund. These resources should be reported as "other operating" revenue in the financial statements of the period in which expenditures are made for the purpose intended by the donor. In 1981 revenues would be recognized to the extent of the 1981 research expenditures – $1,100,000.

67. (582,Q2,31) (a) The requirement is the journal entry **required** on the books of the trust fund beneficiary. Funds held in trust by others are resources neither in the possession of nor under the control of the institution. They are held and administered by outside fiscal agents, with the institution deriving income from such funds. The AICPA Colleges and Universities Audit Guide states that funds held in trust by others **preferably should not** be included in the balance sheet with other funds administered by the institution, but should be disclosed parenthetically in the endowment and similar funds group in the balance sheet or in the notes to the financial statements.

68. (582,Q2,34) (c) The requirement is the unrestricted current funds revenues from tuition and fees. The AICPA Colleges and Universities Audit Guide states that current funds revenues include all tuition and fees assessed (net of refunds) against students for educational and general purposes. Tuition and fee remissions or exemptions should be assessed and reported as revenue even though there is no intention of collecting from the student.

Tuition and fee assessment	$2,300,000
Less: Refunds	(50,000)
Revenue from tuition and fees	$2,250,000

69. (1183,T1,59) (a) Per the AICPA Colleges and Universities Audit Guide, current funds are those which are expendable for **any** purpose in performing the primary objectives of the institution. Term endowment funds are those in which the principal is required to be kept intact in perpetuity until a certain event or condition (e.g., time passage) has been met, and then all or part of the principal may be expended. Life income funds receive gifts or amounts from donors which constitute principal, with the principal's earnings being paid to the donor annually while living. Upon the donor's death, the principal may then be transferred to the current funds group. Since the principal amount in the term endowment and life income funds is not readily available for expenditures, they may not be included within the current funds subgroups.

70. (583,T1,60) (c) Per the AICPA Colleges and Universities Audit Guide, tuition waivers for which there is no intention of collection from the student should be assessed and reported as revenue. The amount of the waiver should also be recorded as an expenditure and appropriately classified as student aid, or as staff benefits associated with the functional category to which the student personnel relate.

71. (582,T1,59) (d) Per the AICPA Colleges and Universities Audit Guide, both unrestricted and restricted current funds are utilized for current expenditures.

72. (1180,T1,59) (a) Per the AICPA Audit Guide prepared for CPAs to use in examining the financial statements of colleges and universities these institutions should use fund accounting and should recognize revenues and expenditures on the accrual basis.

73. (579,T1,42) (c) The requirement is the type of loan that would not be accounted for in a loan fund of a college or university. Loan funds typically account for loans to (a), students, (b), staff, and (d), faculty. Answer (c), building indebtedness, is usually shown as a liability in the "Investment in Plant" section of the plant fund of a college or university balance sheet.

74. (579,T1,45) (d) The requirement is the type of receipt to be accounted for in the restricted current funds of a university. Research grants are usually made with specific restrictions as to expenditure and accordingly are accounted for in current restricted funds. Tuition, laboratory fees, and housing fees are within the general operations of a university and thus are not restricted resources, i.e., they are used to fund general operations.

II.B. Hospital Accounting

75. (582,Q2,21) (a) The requirement is the portion of property, plant, and equipment that should be included in the **restricted** fund grouping. The AICPA Hospital Audit Guide states that property, plant, and equipment and related liabilities should be accounted for as a part of **unrestricted** funds, since segregation in a separate fund would imply the existence of restrictions on asset use. Therefore, Glenmore Hospital would not include any of its property, plant, and equipment in the restricted fund grouping.

76. (582,Q2,30) (d) The requirement is the revenue from donations to be reported on the 1981 statement of revenues and expenses. The AICPA Hospital Audit Guide states that donated services from a religious group should be reported as expense with the credit to nonoperating revenue. Gifts that are restricted to specific operating purposes should be reported as "other operating" revenue in the financial statements of the period in which expenditures are made for the purpose intended by the donor.

Nonoperating revenue	$100,000
Operating revenue	30,000
Total	$130,000

77. (582,Q2,40) (d) The requirement is how the designated funds should be classified on Lilydale's balance sheet at 6/30/82. The AICPA Hospital Audit Guide states that board-designated funds should be reported separately from donor-restricted funds. The term "restricted" should not be used in connection with board or other internal hospital appropriations or designation of funds. The funds would be classified as noncurrent because they will be expended in 1984.

78. (1183,T1,60) (d) Per the AICPA Hospital Guide, p. 33, other operating revenues include revenue from nonpatient care services to patients, and sales and activities to persons other than patients. Such revenues are normal to the day-to-day operations of a hospital and should be accounted for separately from patient revenues. Tuition received from an educational program [answer (d)] is an example of such a revenue. Answers (a), (b), and (c) are classified as nonoperating revenues because these revenues are not directly related to patient care, related patient services, or the sale of related goods.

79. (1182,T1,60) (a) Per the AICPA Hospital Audit Guide, an **unrestricted** pledge should appear as nonoperating revenue in the financial statements of the period in which the pledge is made. Answer (b) is

incorrect because unless the donor specifies that part or all of the pledge is to be applied to a future period(s) (if such a restriction were made, deferred or restricted revenue would be recorded in 1981), the entire amount should be recognized as nonoperating revenue in 1981. Answers (c) and (d) are incorrect because such pledges are not part of the revenue from operations, i.e., the revenue does not come from patients who receive care from the hospital.

80. (582,T1,60) (a) Per the AICPA Hospital Audit Guide donated medicines, linen, office supplies and other materials which normally would be purchased by a hospital should be recorded at fair market value and reported as other operating revenue.

81. (580,T1,60) (b) Generally accepted accounting principles are applicable to hospitals, except where they are clearly inappropriate, according to the AICPA Audit Guide. Therefore, depreciation should be recognized in the financial statements of both proprietary and not-for-profit hospitals.

II.C. Voluntary Health and Welfare Organizations

82. (1180,T1,60) (b) The requirement is to identify the proper period for recognizing support (revenue) from a pledge specifying that the amount pledged in 1979 should be used two periods later (1981). The AICPA's Audit Guide for Voluntary Health and Welfare Organizations specifies that such pledges are to be recorded as assets. The related credit is to a deferred revenue (credit) account. In this case, the asset is converted to cash when the pledge is paid in 1980 and the support (revenue) is recognized in 1981, the period which the donor specified.

83. (579,T1,46) (b) The land, building and equipment fund in voluntary health and welfare organizations is used to account for the net investment in fixed assets and also used to account for unexpended resources contributed specifically for the purpose of replacing land, building, and equipment. Mortgages or liabilities are also included in the fund, and depreciation is recorded on fixed assets. Thus there is no comparable fund in governmental accounting. Answer (a) is incorrect because unrestricted current funds are somewhat similar to special revenue funds in governmental accounting. Answer (c) is incorrect because custodian funds are similar to agency funds in governmental accounting. Answer (d) is incorrect because endowment funds in voluntary health and welfare organizations are similar to endowment funds in governmental accounting.

May 1984 Answers

84. (584,Q3,41) (a) The requirement is the amount of patient service revenue to be recognized. The *AICPA Hospital Audit Guide* defines patient service revenues as gross revenues earned by rendering patient services measured at standard rates. The Audit Guide requires allowances and discounts to be shown as deductions from patient service revenue. Answers (b), (c), and (d) include the adjustments for charity allowances and discounts which would be made to arrive at net patient service revenue and, therefore, are incorrect.

85. (584,Q3,42) (c) The requirement is the proper classification of the donated bandages. Per the *AICPA Hospital Audit Guide,* donations of materials which normally would be purchased by a hospital should be reported as other operating revenue. Answer (a) is incorrect because revenue must be recognized with the receipt of the gift. Answer (b) is incorrect because nonoperating revenue includes revenue not directly related to patient care, related patient services, or the sales of related goods. Answer (d) is incorrect because the bandages are recorded on Abbey's books.

86. (584,Q3,43) (d) Per the *AICPA Hospital Audit Guide*, any funds not restricted as to purpose when they were donated will be part of unrestricted funds. The board has the authority to designate these funds for a specific purpose. However, they still remain a part of the unrestricted fund balance. Thus, both cash and investments are part of the unrestricted fund balance.

87. (584,Q3,44) (b) The requirement is Community's net contribution revenue for 1983 with respect to the pledges. The *AICPA Voluntary Health and Welfare Organizations Audit Guide* requires that unless donors specify otherwise, donations and pledges should be recorded as support in the period received. Estimated uncollectible pledges should be treated as a reduction of such support, not as an expense. In this case, however, the half of the pledges receivable in 1984 are specified "for use in 1984." Therefore, the net contribution revenue for 1983 is [½($900,000 - .10($900,000)] or $405,000. Note that the $405,000 not recognized in 1983 would be recorded as a deferred credit in the balance sheet of the appropriate fund.

88. (584,Q3,45) (a) Per the *AICPA Voluntary Health and Welfare Organizations Audit Guide*, the fair market value of donated services should be reported both as a contributed service revenue and contributed service expense, provided an employer-employee rela-

tionship exists. Answer (b) is incorrect because it includes only one-half of the contributed services. Answer (c) is incorrect because it assumes a value less than market value. Answer (d) is incorrect because it would fail to recognize the true cost of Community's operation.

89. (584,Q3,46) (d) The requirement is Cura Foundation's amount of functional expenses for 1983 program services. The *AICPA Voluntary Health and Welfare Organizations Audit Guide* classifies expenses into two functional categories—those related to program services and those related to support services. Program service expenses are defined as direct costs of an organization's programs and allocations of clearly identifiable indirect costs. Research is the only item listed that is program-related. Answers (b), (c), and (d) are incorrect because they include costs of support services listed in the information given.

90. (584,Q3,47) (a) The rquirement is the amount at which Palma City should record a donated building. Gifts and donations received by governmental units are recognized at FMV (GAAFR, STMT 1). Answers (b), (c), and (d) all use some other basis for recognition and are, therefore, incorrect.

91. (584,Q3,48) (a) The requirement is the amount of the items listed that should be recorded in a special revenue fund. Special revenue funds are defined as funds established to receive funds from specific sources (e.g., city's share of state gasoline tax revenue) to be expended for a legally restricted purpose (e.g., street maintenance). Excluded from this definition are special assessments, expendable trusts, and major capital projects. The $995,000 relates to funds from the Federal government dedicated to highway maintenance. None of the other items in the information given would be recorded in a special revenue fund; thus, answers (b), (c), and (d) are incorrect.

92. (584,Q3,49) (a) The requirement is the amount to be accounted for in an internal service fund. Internal service funds are used to account for activities in which one department in a governmental unit provides services exclusively to other departments within the governmental unit, generally on a not-for-profit (cost--reimbursement) basis. An example is a motor pool. Among the items listed, only the printing/binding service qualifies for inclusion in an internal service fund.

93. (584,Q3,50) (b) The requirement is the amount to be accounted for in an enterprise fund. An enterprise fund is used to account for the activities of a governmental unit to which the government provides goods and services which are (1) rendered primarily to the general public, (2) financed substantially or entirely through user charges, and (3) intended to be self-supporting. Examples include city water works or a swimming pool.

94. (584,Q3,52) (c) The requirement is the entry made to record budgeted revenues. The entire entry is as follows:

Estimated revenue control	30,000,000	
Appropriations control		29,000,000
Unreserved fund balance		1,000,000

Answer (a) is incorrect because budgets are recorded. Answer (b) is incorrect because the estimated revenue account is not a receivable but a budgetary control account. Answer (d) is incorrect because the estimated revenues account is recorded as a debit.

95. (584,Q3,53) (c) The requirement is the entry to record budgeted appropriations. Appropriations has a balance opposite that of expenditures and encumbrances. Answer (a) is incorrect because budgets are recorded. Answer (b) is incorrect because estimated expenditures are not recorded as a liability. Answer (d) is incorrect because the account title should include the word appropriations and be credited, not debited, when the budget is recorded.

96. (584,Q3,54) (b) The requirement is the entry to account for the budgeted excess of revenues over appropriations. An excess of budgeted revenues over appropriations is recorded as an increase (credit) to the fund balance. Answer (a) is incorrect because budgets are recorded in governmental accounting. Both answers (c) and (d) are incorrect because the excess is a credit, and the account title should include the words **fund balance**.

97. (584,Q3,55) (d) The requirement is the amount of funds mentioned in the information given to be recorded in plant funds. Per the *AICPA Colleges and Universities Audit Guide*, resources in plant funds can be classified as:

1. Funds for acquisition of plant.
2. Funds for maintenance of plant.
3. Funds for servicing plant-related debt.
4. Funds previously expended on plant.

Thus, both the funds for acquisition ($3,000,000) and the funds for debt service ($5,000,000) are part of plant funds.

98. (584,Q3,56) (a) The requirement is the journal entry required on Waller Hospital's books. Per the *AICPA Hospital Audit Guide*, funds held in trust by outside parties should not be included in the hospital balance sheet. In the case given here, Anders National Bank was appointed as trustee of the fund. Therefore, the fund will not appear on Waller's books. However, the AICPA Audit Guide does encourage footnote disclosure of the endowment fund's existence and terms.

99. (584,Q3,58) (a) The requirement is the amount of bonds issued in 1983 to be accounted for in the debt service fund. The debt service fund is used to account for payments of principal of general obligation long-term debt (i.e., long-term debt for which the issue proceeds are recorded in the general fund, special revenue fund, and capital projects fund). The liability for bonds issued for installation of street lights would be accounted for in a special assessment fund, and the liability for bonds issued for construction of the swimming pool would be accounted for in an enterprise fund. In both of these types of funds, debt is serviced internally. Therefore, the debt service fund would not be used to accumulate funds for retirement of these bonds.

100. (584,Q3,59) (b) The requirement is the entry to record the approved purchase order. Per GAAFR, STMT 1, approved purchase orders should be recorded by debiting "encumbrances" and crediting "fund balance reserved for encumbrances." Answer (a) is incorrect because an encumbrance entry is required for a purchase order; only regular periodic expenditures (i.e., employee salaries) do not require an encumbrance entry. Answer (c) is incorrect because since the supplies have not yet been received, no entry is needed to reflect the liability, "vouchers payable." Answer (d) is incorrect because entries are made using the appropriations account only at the beginning of the year to record the budget and the end of the year to close the account.

101. (584,Q3,60) (c) The requirement is the entry to be made upon the receipt of supplies. When the supplies are received, the encumbrance entry made at the time the goods were ordered must be reversed, and an expenditure and related payable must be recognized. Answers (a), (b), and (d) are incorrect because they do not properly reverse the encumbrance entry made when the supplies were ordered, and they fail to debit expenditures control.

102. (584,T1,51) (a) The requirement is to determine the treatment of the excess when estimated revenues exceed appropriations in recording the budget. The solutions approach is to prepare the correct budgetary entry. Per GAAFR this entry is:

Estimated revenues	XXX	
Appropriations		XXX
Fund balance		XXX

Therefore, answer (a) is correct. Answer (b) is incorrect because it represents the proper treatment for an excess of appropriations over estimated revenues. Answers (c) and (d) are incorrect because the reserve for encumbrances is neither debited nor credited as part of the budgetary entry.

103. (584,T1,52) (a) The requirement is to determine when the estimated revenues account of a governmental entity is credited. The estimated revenues account of a governmental unit is credited when the following entry is made to close out the budget:

Revenues	XXX	
Estimated revenues		XXX
Fund balance		XXX

Therefore, answer (a) is correct. Answer (b) is incorrect because the estimated revenues account is debited when the budget is recorded. Answers (c) and (d) are incorrect because the recording and collection of property taxes require entries to actual revenue accounts.

104. (584,T1,53) (a) The requirement is the treatment of the encumbrance account upon receipt of supplies order by a governmental unit. When supplies are ordered, the encumbrance account is debited for the estimated price of the supplies by making the following entry:

Encumbrances	XXX	
Reserve for encumbrances		XXX

When supplies are received, the entry setting up the encumbrances is reversed for the original amount, and the actual expenditure is recorded using the **actual** amount. The following entries would be made when the order is received:

Reserve for encumbrances	XXX	
Encumbrances		XXX
Expenditures	XXX	
Vouchers payable (cash)		XXX

Therefore, answer (a) is correct.

105. (584,T1,54) (b) The requirement is the fund classification for a capital projects fund. The capital projects fund is a governmental fund. The National Council on Governmental Accounting recommends the use of eight different types of funds grouped into three different types of fund entities. General funds, special

revenue funds, **capital projects funds**, debt service funds, and special assessment funds are all grouped together as Governmental Funds. Enterprise funds and internal service funds [answer (a)] are classified as Proprietary Funds; trust and agency funds are classified as Fiduciary Funds [answer (d)].

106. (584,T1,55) (c) The requirement is to determine in which fund a governmental unit would account for general long-term debt. Per GAAFR, STMT 1, long-term liabilities directly related to and expected to be paid from proprietary funds, special assessment funds, and trust funds should be included in the accounts of these funds. All other unmatured long-term indebtedness is considered general long-term debt and should be accounted for in the general long-term debt group of accounts. The internal service fund [answer (c)] is a proprietary fund; and, therefore, long-term debt to this fund should be accounted for by the fund. Answers (a), (b), and (d) are all governmental funds.

107. (584,T1,56) (a) The requirement is to determine the appropriate classification of the amount to be provided for retirement of general long-term debt account. Per GAAFR, STMT 1, the accumulation of resources for the repayment of general long-term debt is accounted for in the debt service fund, while the debt itself is accounted for in the general long-term debt group of accounts. The entry to record the debt in the GLTD group of accounts is:

Amount to be provided for retirement of long-term debt	XXX	
Bonds payable		XXX

As monies are accumulated in the debt service fund, the amount to be provided account is credited, with a corresponding debit to amounts available for retirement of long-term debt. Therefore, answer (a) is correct. Answers (b) and (d) are incorrect because the amount to be provided account is not included in the books of a debt service fund. Answer (c) is incorrect because the account is included in the assets section, not the liability section of the GLTD account group.

108. (584,T1,57) (a) The requirement is to determine the correct balance sheet classification of customers' meter deposits held by an enterprise fund, which cannot be spent for normal operating purposes. Per GAAFR, customers' deposits held by an enterprise fund are still owned by its customers. Such deposits are to be classified as **restricted** [answer (a)] and reported separately on the balance sheet of the enterprise fund. These deposits would be reported with a corresponding liability account, customer deposits payable from restricted assets.

109. (584,T1,58) (d) The requirement is to determine whether the enterprise fund and the general fixed asset account group should be included in the Comprehensive Annual Financial Report as part of the Combined Statement of Revenues, Expenditures, and Changes in Fund Balances-Budget and Actual. Per GAAFR, STMT 1, the Combined Statement of Revenues, Expenditures, and Changes in Fund Balances-Budget and Actual should include general and special revenue fund types and similar governmental fund types for which annual budgets have been legally adopted. Answer (d) is correct because the enterprise fund and the general fixed asset account group are generally not legally required to adopt a budget and, therefore, are not similar fund types. All proprietary fund types (enterprise funds) are included in the Combined Statement of Revenues, Expenses, and Changes in Retained Earnings (or Equity), while the account groups are included in the Combined Balance Sheet.

110. (584,T1,59) (c) The requirement is to determine which of the alternatives is considered an unrestricted resource and, therefore, would be included in the unrestricted funds of a not-for-profit hospital. The *AICPA Hospital Audit Guide* states that "The term 'restricted' should not be used in connection with board or other internal hospital appropriations or designations of funds." The reasoning is that if the governing board can appropriate resources in such a manner, it can also rescind such action. Therefore, answer (c) is correct. The AICPA Audit Guide identifies three categories that represent restricted funds. These categories are: (1) funds for specific operating purposes, (2) funds for additions to property, plant, and equipment, and (3) endowment funds. Therefore, answers (a), (b), and (d) are incorrect because all fall into one of the categories identified.

111. (584,T1,60) (c) The requirement is to determine which basis of accounting a voluntary health and welfare organization should use. According to the *AICPA Audit Guide for Audits of Voluntary Health and Welfare Organizations*, Chapter 7, the accrual basis of accounting is required per generally accepted accounting principles and should be used for a fair presentation of financial position and results of operations of a voluntary health and welfare organization. Cash basis and modified accrual basis financial statements may be used only if the financial statements do not differ materially from accrual basis statements. If the results of such statements do differ materially from accrual basis statements, they should be treated as special reports. Therefore, answer (c) is the best answer.

Solution Guide

Problem 1 Internal Service/General Fund

1. This problem consists of two unrelated parts. Part a. requires (1) journal entries to record all of the transactions in the Central Garage Fund accounts for the fiscal year, and (2) closing entries for the fiscal year ending 6/30/80.

2. All of the journal entries will be determined from the additional information. The trial balance will be used to determine the appropriate account titles, opening account balances for reconciliation, and most importantly, to indicate the type of fund you are working with. Just by looking at the trial balance accounts, you see that there are no fund balance accounts. Remember that accounting for the internal service fund is almost like for-profit accounting, the journal entries being very similar.

2.1 The first entry is for the materials and supplies that were purchased on account. The words "on account" should tell you what account to credit. The inventory account is debited because the wording of information in item 2 implies use of the perpetual method.

Inventory of materials & supplies	74,000	
Vouchers payable		74,000

2.2 An adjusting entry is needed to bring the inventory account balance to $58,000 and to determine the appropriate amount of materials "expense." Note that the Internal Service Fund does not have "expenditures" but "expenses" because it is like for-profit accounting. Using a T-account, we have:

Inventory of Materials & Supplies

	Debit	Credit	
Beg. bal.	80,000		
From 2.1	74,000	96,000	Adjust.
	58,000		

Materials & supplies expense	96,000	
Inventory of materials & supplies		96,000

2.3 The salaries and wages were paid.

Salaries and wages expense	230,000	
Cash		230,000

2.4 The bill received from the enterprise fund can be handled in either one or two entries, depending on whether or not you initially set up a liability before paying the utility bill.

Utilities expense	30,000	
Due to enterprise fund		30,000
Due to enterprise fund	30,000	
Cash		30,000

2.5 The depreciation adjustments are identical to those of a for-profit entity.

Depreciation exp.—building	5,000	
Depreciation exp.—machinery & equipment	8,000	
Allowance for depreciation—building		5,000
Allowance for depreciation—machinery & equipment		8,000

2.6 Billings by an internal service fund are accounted for in that fund by charging an interfund receivable and crediting revenue.

Due from general fund	262,000	
Due from water & sewer fund	84,000	
Due from special revenue fund	32,000	
Service revenue		378,000

2.7 The cash collected from the other funds can be determined by using the billings in 2.6 above, the beginning balance for the General Fund from the trial balance, and the ending balances given in item 7. A T-account must be used for the General Fund receivable because this account had a beginning and ending balance.

Due from General Fund

	Debit	Credit	
Beg. bal.	20,000		
From 2.6	262,000	276,000	Cash collect.
	6,000		

The other two receivables had no beginning balances. The Water and Sewer Fund receivable had no ending balance. Therefore, the amount billed ($84,000) was all collected. The amount collected for the Special Revenue Fund is $32,000 billed less the $16,000 uncollected at 6/30/80.

Cash	376,000	
Due from General Fund		276,000
Due from Water and Sewer Fund		84,000
Due from Special Revenue Fund		16,000

2.8 The final transaction entry required is for the payment of vouchers during the year. Using a T-account, we have:

Vouchers Payable			
		38,000	Beg. bal.
Payments	98,000	74,000	From 2.1
		14,000	End. balance

Vouchers payable	98,000	
Cash		98,000

3. The closing entry required is identical to that of a for-profit entity. All the revenue and expense accounts are closed, and the difference is debited or credited to the retained earnings account. In this case, revenues exceed expenses by $9,000.

Service revenue	378,000	
Salaries and wages expense		230,000
Utilities expense		30,000
Materials & supplies expense		96,000
Depreciation expense—building		5,000
Depreciation expense—equipment		8,000
Retained earnings (plug)		9,000

Although an income summary account can be used, it is not required by the most recent GAAFR.

4. Part b. requires you to prepare journal entries to record the budgeted and actual transactions for the fiscal year ended June 30, 1980. The solutions approach is to examine the transaction effects shown in the two middle columns and the additional information given. Since the problem gives only a post-closing trial balance, the solution becomes somewhat more difficult because some of the account titles debited or credited when the transactions were recorded are not listed.

5. Work through the trial balance to gain familiarity with the accounts and to note the required entries. It is evident from the additional piece of information given that the budget entry needed at the beginning of the year was:

Estimated revenues	2,000,000	
Appropriations		1,940,000
Fund balance—unreserved		60,000

Notice that the first credit entry in the "transactions" for the unreserved fund balance was for $60,000. Thus, we have explained the transaction which caused that number. Now go through and explain the other 12 entries; put a mark beside each number as you explain it.

5.1 The entry to explain the debit to the "Taxes Receivable" account and the credit to the "Allowance" account was from recording the levy of taxes. Recall that in governmental funds, estimated uncollectible taxes are a reduction of revenue.

Taxes receivable	1,870,000	
Allowance for uncollectible taxes		10,000
Revenue		1,860,000

To record the collection of taxes, three account entries are explained as follows:

Cash	1,820,000	
Allowance for uncollectible taxes	8,000	
Taxes receivable		1,828,000

5.2 The debit and credit from the vouchers payable account require the following entries:

Expenditures	1,840,000	
Vouchers payable		1,840,000
Vouchers payable	1,852,000	
Cash		1,852,000

The above entries reconcile the vouchers payable account.

5.3 When you examine the "Reserved for encumbrances" account, it appears as though some of the expenditures had been previously encumbered, but only part of the contract completed (i.e., goods or services received).

Encumbrances	1,070,000	
Fund balance—reserve for encumbrances		1,070,000
Fund balance—reserve for encumbrances	1,000,000	
Encumbrances		1,000,000

5.4 All of the account balance entries have been explained except the $140,000 debit and the $30,000 credit to the unreserved fund balance. These entries are the result of closing the accounts created in the above transaction entries that are not shown in the post-closing trial balance. To close the revenue and estimated revenue accounts, the entry was:

Fund balance—unreserved	140,000	
Revenue	1,860,000	
Estimated revenue		2,000,000

To close the appropirations, expenditures, and encumbrances accounts, the entry was:

Appropriations	1,940,000	
Expenditures		1,840,000
Encumbrances*		70,000
Fund balance—unreserved		30,000

*Excess of entry debiting encumbrances over entry crediting encumbrances in 5.3 above.

Unofficial Answer

Problem 1 Internal Service/General Fund

Part a.

City of Merlot
Central Garage Fund
Journal Entries
July 1, 1979 to June 30, 1980

	Debit	Credit
1. Inventory of materials and supplies	$ 74,000	
Vouchers payable		$ 74,000
To record purchases on account		
2. Materials and supplies expense	96,000	
Inventory of materials and supplies		96,000
To record ending inventory and materials and supplies used		
3. Personal service expense	230,000	
Cash		230,000
To record personal service expense paid		
4. Utility expense	30,000	
Cash		30,000
To record payment of utility charges		
5. Depreciation expense—building	5,000	
Depreciation expense—machinery and equipment	8,000	
Allowance for depreciation—building		5,000
Allowance for depreciation—machinery and equipment		8,000
To record depreciation		
6. Due from General Fund	262,000	
Due from Water and Sewer Fund	84,000	
Due from Special Revenue Fund	32,000	
Service Revenue		378,000
To record billings to departments for services rendered		
7. Cash	376,000	
Due from General Fund		276,000
Due from Water and Sewer Fund		84,000
Due from Special Revenue Fund		16,000
To record collection of receivables		
8. Vouchers payable	98,000	
Cash		98,000
To record payment of vouchers		

2.

City of Merlot
Central Garage Fund
Closing Entries
June 30, 1980

	Debit	Credit
Service Revenue	$378,000	
Materials and supplies expense		$ 96,000
Personal service expense		230,000
Utility expense		30,000
Depreciation expense—building		5,000
Depreciation expense—machinery and equipment		8,000
Income summary		9,000
To close revenue and expense accounts		
Income summary	9,000	
Retained earnings		9,000
To close income summary to retained earnings		

Part b.

City of Rom
Journal Entries to Record
Budgeted and Actual Transactions
For the Year Ended June 30, 1980

	Debit	Credit
1. Estimated revenues (various subaccounts)	$2,000,000	
Appropriations (various subaccounts)		$1,940,000
Fund balance—unreserved		60,000
To record budget		
2. Taxes receivable	1,870,000	
Allowance for uncollectible taxes		10,000
Revenues—taxes		1,860,000
To record tax levy		
3. Cash	1,820,000	
Allowance for uncollectible taxes	8,000	
Taxes receivable		1,828,000
To record tax collections		
4. Encumbrances (various subaccounts)	1,070,000	
Fund balance—reserved for encumbrances		1,070,000
To record encumbrances		
5. Fund balance—reserved for encumbrances	1,000,000	
Encumbrances (various subaccounts)		1,000,000
To reverse encumbrances		
6. Expenditures (various subaccounts)	1,840,000	
Vouchers payable		1,840,000
To record expenditures		
7. Vouchers payable	1,852,000	
Cash		1,852,000
To record payment of vouchers		
8. Fund balance—unreserved	140,000	
Revenues—taxes	1,860,000	
Estimated revenues (various subaccounts)		2,000,000
To close actual and estimated revenues to fund balance		
9. Appropriations (various subaccounts)	1,940,000	
Expenditures (various subaccounts)		1,840,000
Encumbrances (various subaccounts)		70,000
Fund balance—unreserved		30,000
To close expenditures, encumbrances, and appropriations to fund balance		

Solution Guide

Problem 2 Municipality Journal Entries

1. Problem 2 requires journal entries (excluding closing entries) necessary for 7 funds or account groups based on 11 descriptive paragraphs of information. Each paragraph describes one or two transactions, and a particular transaction may require entries in more than one fund or account group. The solution format to be used is described in the requirement.

2. The solutions approach is to analyze each paragraph identifying in the margin the fund(s) or account group(s) affected. Be sure to glance at the list of funds and account groups given to avoid forgetting any affected funds or account groups. The next step is to make all the necessary entries.

2.1 Estimated revenues (anticipated resources) are $6,000 greater than appropriations (anticipated expenditures) resulting in a credit to fund balance-unreserved.

2.2 In governmental funds expected uncollectible property taxes are treated as a reduction of revenue. Revenue can be recognized because these taxes are available (i.e., they can be used as collateral if necessary).

2.3 The $50,000 gift of securities is to be maintained in a nonexpendable trust fund. The $5,500 earned on the securities is recorded as revenue.

2.4 The transfer of $5,000 to establish an intragovernmental (internal) service fund is recorded as a transfer out. Remember that transfers result from the shifting of resources between funds except for those transfers which would result in a revenue or expenditure if an outsider were involved.

The intragovernmental (internal) service fund account credited (contribution from general fund) is an equity account.

2.5 Although appropriations for special assessments are not usually recorded, this problem requires a formal entry.

2.6 The $72,000 special assessments levied are recorded as revenue, but the $3,000 contribution from the general fund is recorded as a transfer in. The next entry records receipt of all $75,000.

Entries are needed in the general fund to record the $3,000 as a transfer out and the payment of the interfund obligation created by the transfer.

An encumbrance in the amount of the contract should be recorded and reversed when the project is completed and the billing rendered, even though the project was not approved by the village. The expenditures should be recorded in the amount of $75,000 (since no other figure is given, expenditures are assumed to equal the contract price). Since 5% is to be withheld pending approval of the project, the cash payment is $71,250. Contracts payable-retained percentage is credited for 5% of $75,000. Finally, the cost of the project must be recorded in the general fixed asset group of accounts.

2.7 Credit vouchers payable or cash since the information does not indicate whether or not payment was made.

2.8 Property taxes collected exceed the net realizable value of the receivable recorded.

Taxes receivable – current	$390,000
Estimated amount uncollectible	–7,800
	$382,200
Amount collected to date	$386,000
Excess collected to date	$ 3,800

Since the revenue recognized from property taxes at the date of levy was net of the estimated amount uncollectible it is necessary to reduce the allowance by $3,800 and recognize this amount as additional revenue. There is no information given to indicate what portion of the remaining $4,000 ($390,000 – $386,000) of property taxes receivable are not likely to be collected. Therefore, nothing further can be done with respect to uncollectible taxes. Licenses and permits are recognized as revenue when collected.

2.9 Only an entry to record the sale of bonds is needed in the capital projects fund. The liability for the bonds is recorded in the general long-term debt group.

2.10 Entries are needed in the general fund to remove the encumbrance. Record the expenditure and the payment of the expenditure. An alternative is to credit vouchers payable in recording the expenditure and make a separate payment entry. In the general fixed asset group, an entry is needed to record the equipment and fund source of the acquisition.

Unofficial Answer

Problem 2 Municipality Journal Entries

Dexter Village
Transactions for the Fiscal Year
Ended June 30, 1979

Journal Entries

1.	General fund		
	Estimated revenues	$400,000	
	Appropriations		$394,000
	Unreserved fund balance		6,000
	To record budget		
2.	General fund		
	Taxes receivable – Current	390,000	
	Revenues		382,200
	Estimated uncollectible current taxes		7,800
	To record tax levy		
3a.	Trust fund		
	Investments	50,000	
	Fund principal balance		50,000
	To record value of securities donated in trust		
3b.	Trust fund		
	Cash	5,500	
	Revenues		5,500
	To record revenues earned		

4a. General fund		
Unreserved fund balance	5,000	
Cash		5,000
To record establishment of intragovernmental fund		
4b. Internal service fund		
Cash	5,000	
Contributions from general fund		5,000
To record contribution from general fund		
5. Special assessment fund		
Improvements authorized (or estimated revenue)	75,000	
Appropriations		75,000
To record authorization of assessment		
6a. Special assessment fund		
Assessments receivable — Current	72,000	
Due from general fund	3,000	
Revenue — Special assessments levied		72,000
Operating transfers in		3,000
To record assessment		
6b. Special assessment fund		
Cash	75,000	
Assessment receivable—Current		72,000
Due from general fund		3,000
To record cash received		
6c. General fund		
Operating transfers out	3,000	
Due to special assessment fund		3,000
6d. General fund		
Due to special assessment fund	3,000	
Cash		3,000
To record cash payment		
7a. Special assessment fund		
Encumbrances	75,000	
Reserve for encumbrances		75,000
To record contract for lighting		
7b. Special assessment fund		
Reserve for encumbrances	75,000	
Expenditures	75,000	
Cash		71,250
Contracts payable — Retained percentage		3,750
Encumbrances		75,000
To record payment and retained percentage		
7c. General fixed assets		
Improvements other than buildings	75,000	
Improvements in fixed assets		75,000
To record improvements		
8. Internal service fund		
Inventory	1,900	
Cash or vouchers payable		1,900
To record purchase of supplies		
9a. General fund		
Cash	393,000	
Taxes receivable — Current		386,000
Revenues		7,000
To record collections		
9b. General fund		
Estimated uncollectible current taxes	3,800	
Revenues		3,800
To correct tax revenues		
10a. Capital projects fund		
Cash	500,000	
Proceeds of general obligation bonds		500,000
To record issuance of bonds		
10b. General long-term debt		
Amount to be provided for retirement of bonds	500,000	
General obligation bonds payable		500,000
To record liability		
11a. General fund		
Reserve for encumbrances	15,000	
Encumbrances		15,000
To record cancellation of encumbrances upon payment for fire truck		

11b. General fund

Expenditures	15,000	
Cash		15,000
To record purchase of fire truck		

11c. General fixed assets

Fire truck	15,000	
Investment in fixed assets		15,000
To record acquisition		

Answer Outline

Problem 3 Budget Theory

a. Governmental accounting system must make it possible to
   - Present financial statements of the funds and account groups of a governmental unit
     - Fairly,
     - With full disclosure, and
     - In conformity with GAAP
   - Determine and demonstrate complicance with finance-related legal and contractual provisions
     - Budget is recorded in accounts of governmental unit because legislative body enacts budget into law
     - Enables governmental unit to show legal compliance with budget by providing accounting system that measures
       - Actual expenditures and obligations against amounts appropriated and
       - Actual revenues against estimated revenues
       - Appropriations enacted into law constitute maximum expenditure authorizations during fiscal year
         - These cannot legally be exceeded unless subsequently amended by legislative body

b. Once legislative body has enacted budget into law and as the new fiscal year begins, budget is recorded
   - Budgetary accounts are set up to record estimated revenues and appropriations in fund accounts
     - Debit estimated revenues and credit appropriations
   - If estimated revenues > appropriations or vice versa
     - Credit or debit unreserved fund balance
   - Subsidiary ledger accounts are maintained for estimated revenues by source and for appropriation/expenditure items
   - At year end, estimated revenues and appropriations are closed to unreserved fund balance

Unofficial Answer

Problem 3 Budget Theory

a. A governmental accounting system must make it possible to:

- Present fairly and with full disclosure, in conformity with generally accepted accounting principles, the financial position and results of financial operations of the funds and account groups of the governmental unit.
- Determine and demonstrate compliance with finance-related legal and contractual provisions.

Because the legislative body enacts the budget into law, the budget is recorded in the accounts of a governmental unit. This enables a governmental unit to show legal compliance with the budget by providing an accounting system that measures actual expenditures and obligations against amounts appropriated, and actual revenues against estimated revenues. Appropriations enacted into law constitute maximum expenditure authorizations during the fiscal year, and they cannot legally be exceeded unless subsequently amended by the legislative body.

b. As the new fiscal year begins, the budget, already enacted into law by the legislative body, is recorded. Budgetary accounts are set up to record the estimated revenues and appropriations in the fund accounts by debiting estimated revenues and crediting appropriations. If there is a difference between estimated revenues and appropriations, the excess or deficit is credited or debited, respectively, to fund balance. In addition, subsidiary ledger accounts are maintained for estimated revenues by source and for appropriation/expenditure items.

At the end of the fiscal year, the estimated revenues balance and the appropriations balance are closed out to fund balance.

Answer Outline

Problem 4 Municipal vs. Financial Accounting

a. Commercial enterprises emphasize earnings
   - Governmental units emphasize budgetary control
   - Governmental accounting controlled by legal provisions
     - Accounts organized on the basis of independent fund
   - Legal provisions take priority over GAAP
   - Budgetary accounts disclosed in statements
   - Commercial accounting not subject to these restrictions

Governmental units often use modified accrual method
Revenue reported when measurable and available for the financing of expenditures
Expenditures recorded essentially when incurred
Fund financial statements (Expendable funds)
Balance sheet
Statements of Revenues, Expenditures, and Changes in Fund Balance
Commercial enterprises have retained earnings instead of fund balance (and a Statement of Changes in Financial Position)

b. Budgeting is based on outlays rather than net income
I.e., inventories are often ignored
Except in enterprise and internal service funds
Inventories are considered when preparing budgets

c. Depreciation is computed in enterprise and internal service funds
To measure profit or efficiency
To charge users with actual cost

Unofficial Answer

Problem 4 Municipal vs. Financial Accounting

a. The most significant difference in purpose between municipal accounting and commercial accounting is that commercial enterprises are operated for profit, which places much emphasis on the proper determination of periodic earnings. Governmental units are primarily concerned with providing services to their citizens at minimum cost and reporting on the stewardship of public officials with respect to public funds, which places much emphasis on budgetary controls. However, some municipal units perform commercial services that are generally secondary to their tax-financed primary services.

Another difference in accounting purpose is that municipal accounting operations are controlled by legal provisions in constitutions, charters, and regulations having the force and effect of law. Because of these legal provisions and the diversity of its governmental operations, a municipality cannot use a single, unified set of accounts for recording and summarizing all financial transactions. If there is a conflict between legal provisions and generally accepted accounting principles applicable to governmental units, legal provisions should take precedence to the extent that the accounting system must enable the ready disclosure of compliance. However, for financial reporting purposes, generally accepted accounting principles must take precedence. Commercial enterprises usually are not controlled by charters that are as restrictive; therefore, their accounting systems are designed differently.

Legislative action may limit the use of certain tax revenues for expenditure on particular programs, the methods of tax collection, or the rates of tax assessment. Such provisions must be reflected in the accounting system and be appropriately disclosed in the municipality's financial statements as a report on the stewardship of public officials with respect to public funds.

In governmental accounting all required accounts are organized on the basis of funds, each of which is independent of the other. Each fund must be so accounted for that the identity of its resources, obligations, revenues, expenditures, and fund balance is continually maintained. These purposes are accomplished by providing a complete self-balancing set of accounts for each fund.

The basis of accounting for the reporting on governmental units is often different from that used by commercial enterprises. For example, the accrual basis of accounting is recommended for all funds except the general, special revenue, debt service fund, capital projects, special assessments, agency, and expendable trust funds. These funds should be accounted for by the modified accrual method. The modified accrual method is recommended for these funds because some of their revenue sources are difficult to measure in advance and frequently become available only a short time before cash receipt.

Generally, fair presentation of financial position and results of operations in conformity with generally accepted accounting principles requires that the financial statements of expendable funds (those that use the modified accrual basis) include a balance sheet and a statement of revenues, expenditures, and changes in fund balance. In contrast, however, a commercial enterprise would usually prepare a statement of financial position, an earnings statement, a statement of retained earnings, and a statement of changes in financial position. The statement of revenues and expenditures of the general fund and certain special revenue funds should include a comparison with a formal budget in order to conform with generally accepted accounting principles; there is no such requirement for a commercial enterprise.

b. Inventories are often ignored in governmental accounting because of an emphasis on budgeting revenues against outlays without looking behind the outlays to determine the extent to which they represent actual usage or consumption. Put another way, there is an emphasis on the cash or fiscal aspects rather than the operational aspects. This is easy to understand when one considers that general-fund expenditures for firemen's salaries and for the purchase of a new fire truck are accounted for in the same way.

However, inventories are not wholly ignored in governmental accounting. In those funds in which accounting parallels commercial accounting practice, such as enterprise funds, inventories are taken into consideration. Similarly, in an internal service fund concerned with rendering service involving the consumption of supplies or the delivery of stores to other funds and activities, the inventories of supplies or stores are taken into consideration in computing billings to departments serviced.

Inventories can and should be taken into consideration when preparing budgets. A fund, such as a general fund, having departments that possess large inventories at year end obviously has need for smaller appropriations for the coming year than it would if those departments had zero inventories.

c. In municipal accounting the assigning of cost of assets with lives extending over several years to accounting periods through depreciation is not followed except in enterprise funds or internal service funds. Because governmental general-obligation credit does not rest upon financial condition but upon the power to tax, valuation is not significant.

There are four reasons for computing depreciation for governmental units: (1) profit measurement for enterprise and internal service funds, (2) cost accounting for services and programs, (3) measurement of a cost to be included in the basis for reimbursements or grants, and (4) systematic amortization of cost to recognize use or obsolescence. Thus, the primary purposes of computing depreciation on fixed assets of municipalities are to charge users with their share of the cost of governmental services and to evaluate the efficiency of programs.

Solution Guide

Problem 5 Capital Projects Fund

1. This problem requires journal entries for a series of capital project fund transactions and a year-end balance sheet for the fund. It is not necessary to record the transactions in any other fund or group of accounts.

2. For requirement 1, the solutions approach is to analyze each transaction and prepare the journal entry or entries needed. Remember that not all of the customary budgetary accounts are used in the capital projects fund; e.g., no estimated revenue or appropriation accounts are used in the capital projects fund because a separate fund is created for each project. Proceeds from grants, bond sales, etc., are considered revenue which is closed to the fund balance at year end. Entries are usually made to encumbrances and reserve for encumbrances when commitments are made; the encumbrance entry is reversed when the related expenditure is recorded. At year end the expenditures and remaining encumbrances are closed to unreserved fund balance.

2.1 The \$5,100,000 proceeds from the issue of bonds is debited to cash and credited to proceeds from sale of bonds which is an "other financing source" account. The second entry associated with transaction 1 is to make an entry reflecting the transfer of the \$100,000 premium (\$5,100,000 – \$5,000,000) to the debt service fund from which the bonds will be retired. The debit is to operating transfers out.

2.2 The first entry associated with the second transaction is to reflect the investment in commercial paper by debiting investments and crediting cash. The AICPA solution records the $140,000 as a debit to estimated revenue and a credit to appropriations.

Authors' note: In light of the generalization made in 2 above, the entry for the estimated interest of $140,000 does not appear to be necessary.

2.3 The entry needed for the third transaction is to reflect the signing of the contract with F&A Construction Co. This event is recorded by debiting encumbrances and crediting reserve for encumbrances for $4,980,000.

2.4 Two entries are needed to reflect transaction 4. The first is to record the receipt of the $3,040,000 in cash consisting of principal and interest on the commercial paper investment. Since all of the interest income must be transferred to the debt service fund, an entry is needed to reflect the transfer by debiting operating transfers out and crediting cash.

2.5 Two entries are needed to reflect transaction 5. The first entry reflects the $3,000,000 expenditure on the library, a payment of $2,700,000 and a remaining $300,000 representing the amount retained. The second entry reverses $3,000,000 of the previous encumbrance entry made in transaction 3.

2.6 The first entry needed in transaction 6 is to accrue the $103,000 of interest receivable by debiting accrued interest receivable and crediting interest revenue. A second entry is needed to record the $103,000 obligation to the debt service fund; the debit is to operating transfers out.

The last three entries are needed to close the revenue, other financing sources, expenditure and encumbrance accounts to unreserved fund balance. The closing entries (one compound entry is acceptable) are made by going through all of the entries made and identifying the debits or credits to nominal accounts.

3. The second requirement is to prepare the ending Balance Sheet for the City of Westgate Library Capital Projects Fund.

3.1 The solutions approach is to simply post the transactions in the problem using "T-accounts" as needed and compute the ending balances. For example:

Cash

Debit		Credit		
(1)	5,100,000	(1)	100,000	
		(2)	4,900,000	
(4)	3,040,000	(4)	40,000	
		(5)	2,700,000	
			400,000	End bal.
	8,140,000		8,140,000	

Investments

Debit		Credit		
(2)	4,900,000	(4)	3,000,000	
			1,900,000	End. bal.
	4,900,000		4,900,000	

3.2 Finally prepare the Balance Sheet in good form.

Unofficial Answer

Problem 5 Capital Projects Fund

a.

City of Westgate
Library Capital Projects Fund
Journal Entries
July 1, 1979 to June 30, 1980

		Debit	*Credit*
1.	Cash	$5,100,000	
	Proceeds of general obligation bonds		$5,100,000
	To record issuance of bonds		
	Operating transfers out	100,000	
	Cash		100,000
	To record transfer of premium to library debt service fund		
2.	Investments	4,900,000	
	Cash		4,900,000
	To record purchase of commercial paper		
	Estimated revenues	140,000	
	Appropriations		140,000
	To record estimated interest on investments		
3.	Encumbrances	4,980,000	
	Reserve for encumbrances		4,980,000
	To record contract price for the building of the library		

4.	Cash	3,040,000	
	Investments		3,000,000
	Interest revenue		40,000
	To record maturing of commercial paper		
	Operating transfers out	40,000	
	Cash		40,000
	To record transfer of interest earned on commercial paper to library debt service fund		
5.	Expenditures	3,000,000	
	Cash		2,700,000
	Contracts payable—retained percentage		300,000
	Reserve for encumbrances	3,000,000	
	Encumbrances		3,000,000
	To record progress billing and pay contractor net of retained amount and reverse encumbrances.		
6.	Accrued interest receivable	103,000	
	Interest revenue		103,000
	Operating transfers out	103,000	
	Due to library debt service fund		103,000
	To record accrued interest receivable and related interfund payable		
	Proceeds of general obligation bonds	5,100,000	
	Interest revenue	143,000	
	Unreserved fund balance		5,103,000
	Estimated revenues		140,000
	Appropriations	140,000	
	Unreserved fund balance	3,103,000	
	Expenditures		3,000,000
	Operating transfers out		243,000
	Unreserved fund balance	1,980,000	
	Encumbrances		1,980,000
	To close temporary accounts		

b.

City of Westgate
Library Capital Projects Fund
Balance Sheet
June 30, 1980

Assets:	
Cash	$ 400,000
Accrued interest receivable	103,000
Investments	1,900,000
Total assets	$2,403,000
Liabilities and fund balance:	
Contracts payable—retained percentage	$ 300,000
Due to library debt service	103,000
Total liabilities	403,000
Fund balance:	
Reserved for encumbrances	1,980,000
Unreserved	20,000
Total fund balance	2,000,000
Total liabilities and fund balance	$2,403,000

Solution Outline

Problem 6 University Journal Entries and Statement of Changes in Fund Balance

1. Number 4 consists of two related parts requiring university journal entries and a financial statement.

2. Part a. requires journal entries for ten transactions of Rapapo State University. The entries are to be recorded in the current unrestricted and current restricted funds.

3. The solutions approach is to analyze each of the ten transactions and determine the fund affected and the appropriate journal entry or entries. The unrestricted current fund is used for all transactions not accounted for elsewhere, similar to the general fund in governmental accounting. The current restricted fund accounts for monies which have been externally restricted for specified current operating purposes. Note that by using the given 7/31/82 balance sheet and the additional information, you can find many "hints" as to which fund or accounts are to be used.

3.1 Tuition and fees are accounted for in the unrestricted fund. The $3,000,000 debit to cash is offset by a $362,000 credit to accounts receivable; a $2,500,000 credit to revenues for the current year tuition; and a $138,000 credit to deferred revenue for the tuition paid in advance.

3.2 The deferred revenue in the 7/31/82 balance sheet was earned during the year. Therefore, deferred revenue is debited and revenues are credited.

3.3 Accounts receivable at 7/31/82 which were not collected in item one are uncollectible. Note that \$375,000 of receivables were outstanding, since the \$360,000 listed in the balance sheet was net of a \$15,000 allowance for doubtful accounts. Therefore, \$13,000 of receivables (\$375,000 total less \$362,000 collected) must be written off by debiting the allowance account and crediting accounts receivable. Additionally, at year end the allowance account must be increased from \$2,000 (\$15,000 balance at 7/31/82 less \$13,000 of write-offs) to \$10,000. This results in the recording of bad debts of \$8,000.

3.4 The unrestricted state appropriation is recorded as revenue in the unrestricted fund on the accrual basis by debiting a receivable and crediting a revenue account.

3.5 Unrestricted cash gifts received are recorded as revenue in the unrestricted fund. Monies designated by the board of trustees to be transferred from unrestricted funds to nonoperating funds, such as the \$30,000 transfer in this problem, are called nonmandatory transfers. The transfer is recorded as a debit to fund balance.

3.6 The investments in the 7/31/82 balance sheet are held in the restricted fund. The \$6,000 (\$31,000 selling price less \$25,000 cost) is credited directly to the restricted fund balance account. This is a peculiarity of university accounting; the earnings of current restricted funds are credited to fund balance when received and recognized as revenue when expended for the specified purpose. Similarly, the investment income (\$18,000) is credited to fund balance. Investments purchased are recorded with a debit to investments and a credit to cash.

3.7 The unrestricted expenses recorded in the voucher system (\$2,500,000) are recorded in the unrestricted fund by debiting expenditures and crediting accounts payable. When a voucher system is used, all expenditures run through accounts or vouchers payable. Since the accounts payable totalled \$75,000 at year end, cash payments of \$2,525,000 (\$100,000 beginning balance plus \$2,500,000 expenditures, less \$75,000 ending balance) must also be recorded.

3.8 The restricted accounts payable at 7/31/82 (\$5,000) were paid; this is recorded by debiting accounts payable and crediting cash.

3.9 The \$40,000 due to other funds was a liability of the unrestricted funds on the 7/31/82 balance sheet. Payment is recorded by debiting the liability and crediting cash.

3.10 The prepaid expenses in the unrestricted portion of the 7/31/82 balance sheet amounted to \$40,000. Since one quarter of these prepayments expired, \$10,000 (¼ x \$40,000) must be debited to expenditures and credited to prepaid expenses.

4. Part b. requires a statement of changes in fund balances for the year ended 7/31/83.

4.1 The statement of changes in fund balances is a primary university financial statement, as it explains the activity (inflows and outflows) for the restricted and unrestricted current funds.

4.2 Unrestricted revenues include \$2,500,000 tuition, \$25,000 in deferred revenue earned during the current year, a \$60,000 appropriation from the state, and \$80,000 in gifts. These revenues total \$2,665,000. Additions to the restricted fund balance include the \$6,000 gain on sale of investments and the \$18,000 of investment income.

4.3 Unrestricted expenditures included \$2,500,000 for general expenses, \$10,000 of expired prepayments, and \$8,000 of bad debts for a total of \$2,518,000. There were no restricted expenditures.

4.4 The nonmandatory transfer is not similar to a normal expenditure and, therefore, is reported in a separate section near the bottom of the statement.

4.5 Finally, the beginning fund balance is added to the net increase during the year, to result in the ending fund balance.

Unofficial Answer

Problem 6 University Journal Entries and Statement of Changes in Fund Balance

Part a.

Rapapo State University
General Journal

Entry no.	Accounts	Current funds – Unrestricted Debit	Current funds – Unrestricted Credit	Current funds – Restricted Debit	Current funds – Restricted Credit
1.	Cash	3,000,000			
	Accounts receivable – Tuition and fees		362,000		
	Revenues – Tuition and fees		2,500,000		
	Deferred revenue – Tuition and fees		138,000		
2.	Deferred revenue – Tuition and fees	25,000			
	Revenues – Tuition and fees		25,000		
3.	Allowance for doubtful accounts	13,000			
	Accounts receivable – Tuition and fees		13,000		
	Provision for uncollectible tuition and fees	8,000			
	Allowance for doubtful accounts		8,000		
4.	State appropriation receivable	60,000			
	Revenues – State appropriation		60,000		
5.	Cash	80,000			
	Revenues – Private gifts, grants, and contracts		80,000		
	Fund balance	30,000			
	Cash (or due to student loan fund)		30,000		
6.	Cash			31,000	
	Investments				25,000
	Fund balance – Gain on sale of investments				6,000
	Investments			40,000	
	Cash				40,000
	Cash			18,000	
	Fund balance – Investment income				18,000
7.	Expenditures – General expenses	2,500,000			
	Accounts payable		2,500,000		
	Accounts payable	2,525,000			
	Cash		2,525,000		
8.	Accounts payable			5,000	
	Cash				5,000
9.	Due to other funds	40,000			
	Cash		40,000		
10.	Expenditures – Education and general	10,000			
	Prepaid expenses		10,000		

Part b.

Rapapo State University
Statement of Changes in Fund Balances
Year Ended July 31, 1983

	Current funds	
	Unrestricted	*Restricted*
Revenues and other additions:		
Tuition and fees	$2,525,000	
State appropriation	60,000	
Gifts	80,000	
Realized gains on investments – Restricted		6,000
Investment income – Restricted		18,000
Total revenues and other additions	$2,665,000	$24,000
Expenditures and other deductions:		
Unrestricted expenditures	$2,518,000	
Transfers among funds – additions/deductions:		
Nonmandatory transfer to student loan fund	(30,000)	
Net increase (decrease) for the year	$117,000	$ 24,000
Fund balance at beginning of year	435,000	215,000
Fund balance at end of year	$552,000	$239,000

Solution Guide

Problem 7 Hospital Statement of Revenues and Expenses

1. This problem consists of two parts requiring a formal statement of revenues and expenses for Glendora Hospital and the appropriate footnote disclosures accompanying the statement.

2. Hospital accounting is similar to profit-oriented financial accounting. Hospitals use the accrual basis for reporting and GAAP is applicable. Therefore, your knowledge of financial accounting and GAAP can aid in the solution of this problem. Preparing an income statement in accordance with GAAP would have assured the candidate a majority of the points for this problem. The footnote disclosures can be drafted directly from information given in the problem.

2.1 The requirement in part one is to prepare the formal statement of revenues and expenses.

3. The format of this statement is fairly straightforward. The first section lists operating revenue. From this is subtracted operating expenses to result in net revenue or net loss from operations. The final section is nonoperating revenue. The bottom line in the statement is labeled excess of revenues over expenses (or expenses over revenues), since the concept of net income is not emphasized in hospital accounting.

3.1 The first section of the statement is the operating revenue section. Patient service revenue is recorded on a gross charge basis, from which is subtracted allowances and uncollectible amounts. The allowances include such items as contracted adjustments by third-party payors, adjustments for charitable discounts, and estimated uncollectible accounts. The difference is the net patient service revenue which has been or will be collected. The last item in this section is other operating revenue. The amount which is transferred from specific purpose funds to cover current operations should be separately disclosed.

3.2 The next category on the statement is operating expenses which are generally listed by function (nursing services, administrative expenses, etc.). Except for depreciation expense, which is listed in total in this problem, the functional detail is not given. Therefore, only the provision for depreciation can be shown separately. Subtracting operating expenses from operating revenue results in a $424,000 loss from operations.

3.3 The final section in the statement lists nonoperating revenues, which are revenues not related to patient care. This includes unrestricted gifts and bequests, unrestricted income from endowment funds, and income from board-designated funds. The final result is a $228,000 excess of revenues over expenses.

4. The requirement in part two is the drafting of appropriate footnotes to accompany the statement prepared in part one. The solutions approach is to go through the statement and the problem narrative, noting any items requiring footnote disclosure.

4.1 The basis of accounting for patient service revenues should be disclosed.

4.2 Information concerning retroactive contractual adjustments by third-party payors should also be disclosed. Generally, this disclosure includes the amount of contractual adjustments included in the allowances subtracted from gross patient service revenue. However, this amount is not given in the problem.

4.3 Pension disclosures as required by SFAS 36 should also be included in the footnotes. These disclosures include the actuarial present value of both vested and nonvested benefits, net assets available for benefits, and the assumed rates of return.

4.4 Information concerning depreciation methods should also be disclosed, including the amount of net cost reimbursement revenue being deferred as the result of different depreciation methods being used for financial reporting and cost reimbursement purposes.

4.5 The basis of accounting for gifts and bequests also requires disclosure.

Unofficial Answer
(Author Modified)

Problem 7 Hospital Statement of Revenues and Expenses

Glendora Hospital
Statement of Revenues and Expenses
Year Ended June 30, 1982

Patient service revenue (note 1)	$16,000,000
Allowances and uncollectible accounts (note 2)	(3,400,000)
Net patient service revenue	$12,600,000
Other operating revenue (including $160,000 from specific purpose funds)	346,000
Total operating revenue	$12,946,000
Operating expenses:	
(Detailed by function) (note 3)	$12,870,000
Provision for depreciation (note 4)	500,000
Total operating expenses	$13,370,000
Loss from operations	$ (424,000)
Nonoperating revenue:	
Unrestricted gifts and bequests (note 5)	$410,000
Unrestricted income from endowment funds	160,000
Income from board-designated funds	82,000
Total nonoperating revenue	652,000
Excess of revenues over expenses	$228,000

Notes: (1) Patient service revenue is recorded at established rates for all patients on the accrual basis. All discounts for employees, third party payors, and welfare funding agencies are included in the allowances and uncollectible accounts.

(2) Patient service revenues of $6,000,000 recognized under cost reimbursement agreements is subject to audit and retroactive adjustment by third-party payors. An estimate of $____ in retroactive adjustments under these agreements has been included in the allowances and uncollectible accounts.

(3) Included in operating expenses are pension costs of $100,000, in connection with a noncontributory pension plan covering substantially all of Glendora's employees. Accrued pension costs are funded currently. Prior service cost is being amortized over a period of 20 years. The actu-

arially computed value of vested and nonvested benefits at year-end amounted to $3,000,000 and $350,000 respectively. The assumed rate of return used in determining the actuarial present value of accumulated benefits was 8%. The plan's net assets available for benefits at year-end were $3,050,000.

(4) Depreciation for the statement of Revenues and Expenses was computed using the straight-line basis. However, accelerated depreciation is used to determine reimbursable costs under certain third-party reimbursement agreements. Net cost reimbursement revenue amounting to $220,000, resulting from the difference in depreciation methods, was deferred to future years.

(5) Gifts and bequests are recorded at fair market value when received.

Solution prepared by John H. Engstrom, Northern Illinois University.

Solution Guide

Problem 8 Journal Entries and All-Inclusive Activity Statement for Nonprofit Organization

1. Number 5 requires (1) transaction and adjusting entries and (2) an activity statement for a nonprofit organization. Since this is not a Voluntary Health and Welfare Organization, the provisions of AICPA *Statement of Position 78-10*, Accounting Principles and *Reporting Practices for Certain Nonprofit Organizations*, would apply.

2. The solutions approach for the journal entries is to approach the transactions and adjustments consecutively, relating each situation to SOP 78-10 principles. Account titles for the balance sheet accounts are given, and revenue and expense accounts would be generated using the descriptive phrases given for each numbered item.

2.1 The $20,000 is recorded as a credit to membership dues, which is considered to be revenue for the current period and will be included on the activity statement.

2.2 The $28,000 is a revenue of the organization, and the account title used is simply: Snack bar and soda fountain sales.

2.3 The $6,000 represents another investment revenue of the organization for the period.

2.4 Under SOP 78-10 rules, expenses are recorded on the accrual basis. The titles used for the expenses listed are as given. The amounts should be credited to either vouchers payable or accounts payable.

2.5 Since accrual accounting is used, the entry to pay the vouchers simply reduces the liability.

2.6 Under SOP 78-10, "capital additions that are restricted for acquisition of plant assets should be treated as deferred capital support in the balance sheet until they are used for the indicated purpose." (para .052)

2.7 The $5,000 unrestricted bequest is considered to be a current revenue.

2.8 SOP 78-10 permits carrying certain investments at market. When investments are carried at market, increases and decreases in market value are to be recognized in the current period. The $7,000 increase is, accordingly, credited to a gain account, unrealized gain on investments.

2.9 Under SOP 78-10, depreciation of fixed assets is to be recognized and recorded. Also, the beginning trial balance includes accumulated depreciation accounts.

2.10 Nonprofit organizations report expenses by function in the statement of activity. Also, the necessity of a functional classification is suggested by the adjustment data given. This entry reclassifies depreciation expense to functional categories.

2.11 The beginning trial balance includes a $5,000 balance in the inventory account. The reduction of $4,000 would be charged to the snack bar and soda fountain expense account used in entry number 4.

3. SOP 78-10 contains several illustrative financial statements for nonprofit organizations, one of which is directly applicable to the organization described in this problem, i.e., a country club which is shown in para 131 of the SOP.

3.1 The title of the statement should be "Statement of revenues, expenses and charges in cumulative excess of revenues over expenses."

3.2 All the revenues are grouped together.

3.3 The expenses which are supported by the revenues are listed in the same fashion as they were recorded in Part a.

3.4 The unrealized gain on investments is shown separately after the revenues and expenses.

3.5 The beginning and ending balance amounts for the account "Cumulative excess of revenues over expenses" are shown at the end of the statement in order to tie into the balance sheet.

Unofficial Answer

Problem 8 Journal Entries and All-Inclusive Activity Statement for Nonprofit Organization

a.

Community Sports Club
Transactions
For the Year Ended March 31, 1983

		Debit	*Credit*
(1)	Cash	$20,000	
	Revenue—annual dues		$20,000
(2)	Cash	$28,000	
	Revenue—snack bar and soda fountain		28,000
(3)	Cash	6,000	
	Investment income		6,000
(4)	Expense—house	17,000	
	Expense—snack bar and soda fountain	26,000	
	Expense—general and administrative	11,000	
	Accounts payable		54,000
(5)	Accounts payable	55,000	
	Cash		55,000
(6)	Assessments receivable	10,000	
	Deferred capital support		10,000
(7)	Cash	5,000	
	Revenue—bequest (unrestricted revenue)		5,000

Adjustments
March 31,1983

(1)	Investments	7,000	
	Unrealized gain on investment		7,000
(2)	Expense—house	9,000	
&	Expense—snack bar and soda fountain	2,000	
(3)	Expense—general and administrative	1,000	
	Accumulated depreciation—building		4,000
	Accumulated depreciation—furniture and equipment		8,000
(4)	Expense—snack bar and soda fountain	4,000	
	Inventories		4,000

b.

Community Sports Club
Statement of Revenue, Expenses, and Changes in Cumulative Excess of Revenue over Expenses
For the Year Ended March 31, 1983

Revenue		
Snack bar and soda fountain sales		$28,000
Dues		20,000
Investment income		6,000
Bequest		5,000
Total revenue		59,000
Expenses		
Snack bar and soda fountain	$32,000	
House	26,000	
General and Administrative	12,000	
Total expenses		70,000
Deficiency of revenue over expenses before unrealized gain on investments		(11,000)
Unrealized gain on investments		7,000
Deficiency of revenue over expenses after unrealized gain on investments		(4,000)
Cumulative excess of revenue over expenses at April 1, 1982		12,000
Cumulative excess of revenue over expenses at March 31, 1983		$ 8,000

CHAPTER EIGHT

TAX PROBLEMS AND SOLUTIONS

Federal income taxation appears only in the practice sections. Interperiod and intraperiod tax allocation questions are presented in Chapter 4, Module 27: Deferred Taxes.

Recently, 2 of the multiple choice practice problems (20 multiple choice questions each) have tested federal income taxation. One generally tests individual taxation and the other tests corporate taxation. Occasionally, a section of another problem will require calculation of deferred taxes. A complete analysis of recent examinations and the *AICPA Content Specification Outlines* appear in Volume I, *Outlines and Study Guide.*

Since federal income taxation rules and regulations vary from year to year, some of the exam items have been changed so that the question, solution, and explanation reflect the current law for which you are responsible. Past coverage indicates that the tax law in effect during the immediately preceding calendar year is tested. Thus, it would appear that the 1983 tax law will be tested on both 1984 CPA examinations.

The month, year, exam section, problem number, and objective question are given for each question. For example, (583,Q2,37) indicates May 1983, problem 2 of the Practice II section, multiple choice question number 37. Note that P = Practice I and Q = Practice II.

TAX PROBLEMS INDEX

Note: Gift and Estate tax is listed in the Content Specification Outlines under taxes, (ref. XI,H). This topic has also been tested on the business law section of the exam. See Module 22, Trusts and Estates, for examples.

Multiple Choice Questions (1 - 107)

1. Richard Brown, who retired on May 31, 1979, receives a monthly pension benefit of $700 payable for life. The first pension check was received on June 15, 1979. During his years of employment, Brown contributed $14,700 to the cost of his company's pension plan. How much of the pension amounts received may Brown exclude from taxable income for the years 1979, 1980, and 1981?

	1979	*1980*	*1981*
a.	$0	$0	$0
b.	$4,900	$4,900	$4,900
c.	$4,900	$8,400	$1,400
d.	$4,900	$8,400	$8,400

2. Seymour Thomas named his wife, Penelope, the beneficiary of a $100,000 (face amount) insurance policy on his life. The policy provided that upon his death, the proceeds would be paid to Penelope with interest over her present life expectancy, which was calculated at 25 years. Seymour died during 1979 and Penelope received a payment of $5,200 from the insurance company. What amount should she include in her gross income for 1979?

a. $ 200
b. $1,200
c. $4,200
d. $5,200

3. David Hetnar is covered by a $90,000 group-term life insurance policy of which his wife is the beneficiary. Hetnar's employer pays the entire cost of the policy, for which the uniform annual premium is $8 per $1,000 of coverage. How much of this premium is taxable to Hetnar?

a. $0
b. $320
c. $360
d. $720

4. Howard O'Brien, an employee of Ogden Corporation, died on June 30, 1981. During July Ogden made employee death payments of $10,000 to his widow, and $10,000 to his 15-year-old son. What amounts should be included in gross income by the widow and son in their respective tax returns for 1981?

	Widow	*Son*
a.	$0	$0
b.	$5,000	$ 5,000
c.	$5,000	$10,000
d.	$7,500	$ 7,500

5. During the current year Mike Larsen sustained a serious injury in the course of his employment. As a result of the injury sustained, he received the following payments during the year:

Workmen's compensation	$1,200
Reimbursement from his employer's accident and health plan for medical expenses paid by Larson	900
Damages for personal injuries	4,000

The amount to be included in Larsen's gross income for the current year should be

a. $0
b. $ 900
c. $4,000
d. $6,100

6. James Martin received the following compensation and fringe benefits from his employer during 1978:

Salary	$50,000
Year-end bonus	10,000
Medical insurance premiums paid by employer	1,000
Allowance paid for moving expenses	5,000

What amount of the preceding payments should be included in Martin's 1978 gross income?

a. $60,000
b. $61,000
c. $65,000
d. $66,000

7. Mr. and Mrs. Carl Nido own 5,000 shares of common stock of Niagara Power Corporation, a qualified domestic public utility. Instead of receiving their dividends in cash on the Niagara stock, the Nidos have elected to receive common stock under Niagara's qualified dividend reinvestment plan. The Nidos earned $2,000 in dividends on their Niagara stock in 1982. What portion of these dividends could the Nidos exclude from gross dividend income (before other allowable dividend exclusions) on their 1982 joint return?

a. $2,000
b. $1,800
c. $1,500
d. $0

8. During 1980, Harry Gibbs, a resident of Florida, received the following dividends:

Source	*Amount*
Real estate investment trust	$1,000
Delaware corporation operating exclusively in Puerto Rico	500

The total amount of gross dividends eligible for the dividend exclusion on Gibbs' 1980 federal income tax return is

a. $0
b. $ 500
c. $1,000
d. $1,500

9. Jack and Joan Mitchell, married taxpayers and residents of a separate property state, elect to file a joint return for 1982 during which they received the following dividends:

	Received by	
	Jack	Joan
Alert Corporation (a qualified, domestic corporation)	$400	$ 50
Canadian Mines, Inc. (a Canadian Company)		300
Eternal Life Mutual Insurance Company (dividends on life insurance policy)	200	

For 1982 what amount should the Mitchells report on their joint return as dividend income net of the allowable dividend exclusion?

a. $550
b. $600
c. $750
d. $800

10. Daniel Kelly received interest income from the following sources in 1981:

New York Port Authority bonds	$1,000
Puerto Rico Commonwealth bonds	1,800

What portion of such interest is tax exempt?

a. $0
b. $1,000
c. $1,800
d. $2,800

11. In 1979 Uriah Stone received the following interest payments:

- Interest of $400 on refund of federal income tax for 1976.
- Interest of $300 on award for personal injuries sustained in an automobile accident during 1978.
- Interest of $1,500 on municipal bonds.
- Interest of $1,000 on United States savings bonds (Series H).

What amount, if any, should Stone report as interest income on his 1979 tax return?

a. $0
b. $ 700
c. $1,700
d. $3,200

12. For the year 1979 Frances Quinn had a time savings account with the Benevolent Savings Bank. The following entries appeared in her passbook for 1979.

March 30, 1979, interest credited	$150
June 19, 1979, interest credited	$160
July 25, 1879, penalty forfeiture because of premature withdrawal	$125
September 28, 1979, interest credited	$ 80
December 18, 1979, interest credited	$ 85

The above information should be reported by Ms. Quinn on her 1979 tax return as

a. Interest income of $350.
b. Interest income of $475.
c. Interest income of $475 and an itemized deduction for interest expense of $125.
d. Interest income of $475 and a deduction of $125 in arriving at adjusted gross income.

13. In 1981, Max Bayne filed a joint return with his wife, Lois, and excluded $400 of interest earned on an all-savers certificate held in Max's name alone. In 1982, Max and Lois were divorced. Neither spouse remarried in 1982. In 1982, Max received interest of $1,000 on his all-savers certificate. How much of this $1,000 interest could Max exclude in 1982?

a. $1,000
b. $ 800
c. $ 700
d. $ 600

14. On January 1, 1979, James Davis was awarded a post-doctorate fellowship grant of $4,500 by a tax-exempt educational organization. Davis is not a candidate for a degree and was awarded the grant to continue his research. The grant was awarded for the period March 1, 1979, through July 31, 1980.

On March 1, 1979, Davis elected to receive the full amount of the grant. What amount should be included in his gross income for 1979?

a. $0
b. $1,500
c. $3,000
d. $4,500

15. In July 1963 Dan Farley leased a building to Robert Shelter for a period of fifteen years at a monthly rental of $1,000 with no option to renew. At that time the building had a remaining estimated useful life of twenty years.

Prior to taking possession of the building, Shelter made improvements at a cost of $18,000. These improvements had an estimated useful life of twenty years at the commmencement of the lease period. The lease expired on June 30, 1978, at which point the improvements had a fair market value of $2,000. The amount that Farley, the landlord, should include in his gross income for 1978 is

a. $ 6,000
b. $ 8,000
c. $10,500
d. $18,500

16. The following information is available for Ann Drury for 1982:

Salary	$36,000
Premiums paid by employer on group-term life insurance in excess of $50,000	500
Proceeds from state lottery	5,000

How much should Drury report as gross income on her 1982 tax return?

a. $36,000
b. $36,500
c. $41,000
d. $41,500

17. Mr. and Mrs. Alvin Charak took a foster child, Robert, into their home in 1981. A state welfare agency paid the Charaks $3,900 during the year for related expenses. Actual expenses incurred by the Charaks during 1981 in caring for Robert amounted to $3,000. The remaining $900 was spent by the Charaks in 1981 towards their own personal expenses. How much of the foster child payments is taxable income to the Charaks in 1981?

a. $0
b. $ 900
c. $2,900
d. $3,900

18. Paul Bristol, a cash basis taxpayer, owns an apartment building. The following information was available for 1982:

- An analysis of the 1982 bank deposit slips showed recurring monthly rents received totaling $50,000.
- On March 1, 1982, the tenant in apartment 2B paid Bristol $2,000 to cancel the lease expiring on December 31, 1982.
- The lease of the tenant in apartment 3A expired on December 31, 1982, and the tenant left improvements valued at $1,000. The improvements were not in lieu of any rent required to have been paid.

In computing net rental income for 1982, Bristol should report gross rents of

a. $50,000
b. $51,000
c. $52,000
d. $53,000

19. Bill McDonald, a cash-basis taxpayer, is the owner of a house with two identical apartments. He resides in one apartment and rents the other apartment to a tenant under a five-year lease dated March 1, 1979, and expiring on February 29, 1984. The tenant made timely monthly rental payments of $500 for the months of January through November 1980. Rents for December 1980 and January 1981 were paid by the tenant on January 5, 1981. The following additional information for 1980 was available:

Fuel and utilities	$3,600
Depreciation of building	3,000
Maintenance and repairs (rental apartment)	400
Insurance on building	600

What amount should McDonald report as net rental income for 1980?

a. $2,200
b. $2,000
c. $1,700
d. $1,500

20. Richard and Alice Kelley lived apart during 1980 and did not file a joint tax return for the year. Under the terms of the written separation agreement they signed on July 1, 1980, Richard was required to pay Alice $1,500 per month of which $600 was designated as child support. He made six such payments in 1980. Additionally, Richard paid Alice $1,200 per month for the first six months of 1980, no portion of which was designated as child support. Assuming that Alice has no other income, her tax return for 1980 should show gross income of

a. $0
b. $ 5,400
c. $ 9,000
d. $12,600

21. Victor and Claire Anet, residents of a separate property state, were divorced in February 1978. Specific requirements of the divorce decree and Mr. Anet's performance of those requirements follow:

- Transfer title in their personal residence to Claire as part of a lump-sum property settlement. On the day of the transfer, Victor's basis in the house was $38,000, the fair market value was $42,000, and the property was subject to a mortgage of $20,000.

• Make the mortgage payments on the twenty-year mortgage. He paid $2,500 from March 1, 1978, through December 31, 1978.

• Repay to Claire a $3,000 loan which he did on April 1, 1978.

• Pay Claire $700 per month of which $200 is designated as child support. He made ten such payments in 1978.

Assuming that Claire has no other income, her 1978 gross income should be

a. $ 7,500
b. $ 9,500
c. $12,500
d. $16,000

22. Edward Ryan, who is single, had adjusted gross income, other than unemployment compensation, of $17,000 in 1983. Ryan had no disability income exclusion, but received $3,000 in unemployment compensation benefits during the year. How much of the unemployment compensation is taxable in 1983?

a. $0
b. $1,500
c. $2,500
d. $3,000

23. Dr. Berger, a physician, reports on the cash basis. The following items pertain to Dr. Berger's medical practice in 1982:

Cash received from patients in 1982	$200,000
Cash received in 1982 from third-party reimbursers for services provided by Dr. Berger in 1981	30,000
Salaries paid to employees in 1982	20,000
Year-end 1982 bonuses paid to employees in 1983	1,000
Other expenses paid in 1982	24,000

What is Dr. Berger's net income for 1982 from his medical practice?

a. $155,000
b. $156,000
c. $185,000
d. $186,000

24. Dr. Chester is a cash basis taxpayer. His office visit charges are usually paid on the date of visit or within one month. However, services rendered outside the office are billed weekly, and are usually paid within two months as patients collect from insurance companies. Information relating to 1982 is as follows:

Cash received at the time of office visits	$ 35,000
Collections on accounts receivable	130,000
Accounts receivable, January 1	16,000
Accounts receivable, December 31	20,000

Dr. Chester's gross income from his medical practice for 1982 is

a. $165,000
b. $169,000
c. $181,000
d. $185,000

25. Morris Babb, CPA, reports on the cash basis. In March 1983, Babb billed a client $1,000 for accounting services rendered in connection with the client's divorce settlement. No part of the $1,000 fee was ever paid. In July 1983, the client went bankrupt and the $1,000 obligation became totally worthless. What loss can Babb deduct on his 1983 tax return?

a. $0.
b. $1,000 short-term capital loss.
c. $1,000 business bad debt.
d. $1,000 nonbusiness bad debt.

26. During the 1982 holiday season, Palo Corp. gave business gifts to 17 customers. These gifts, which were not of an advertising nature, had the following fair market values:

4 @ $ 10
4 @ 25
4 @ 50
5 @ 100

How much of these gifts was deductible as a business expense for 1982?

a. $840
b. $365
c. $140
d. $0

27. Prior to 1981 Carlyle Corporation used the specific charge-off method for computing its bad debt deduction. During 1981 Carlyle filed a timely request for a change to the reserve method of accounting for its bad debt deduction. The following data are available from Carlyle's records:

	Accounts receivable at end of year	*Bad debts charged off*
1976	$ 420,000	$11,500
1977	470,000	14,500
1978	500,000	15,000
1979	480,000	13,500
1980	530,000	17,500
	$2,400,000	$72,000
1981	$ 600,000	$19,500

How much should Carlyle claim as a bad debt deduction on its 1981 tax return?

a. $18,000
b. $19,500
c. $21,300
d. $37,500

28. Paramount Corporation has consistently used the reserve method to compute the bad debt deduction on its tax returns. The year-end reserve for bad debts reported on the 1979 tax return was $11,200. Additional information is available as follows:

	Accounts receivable at end of year	*Bad debt*	
		Losses	*Recoveries*
1975	$ 255,000	$12,000	$1,150
1976	265,000	13,500	1,300
1977	270,000	11,500	1,450
1978	250,000	12,000	1,500
1979	280,000	14,000	1,920
1980	300,000	18,000	2,400
Totals	$1,620,000	$81,000	$9,720
% of receivables		5.0%	0.6%

In December 1980 one of Paramount's important customers experienced financial difficulties, which could result in a bad debt write-off of $10,000 during 1981 in respect of this customer. What is the maximum bad debt deduction that Paramount can claim on its tax return for 1980?

a. $13,200
b. $17,600
c. $19,400
d. $27,600

29. On March 1, 1981, Milford Corporation purchased for $70,000 machinery that was installed in its factory on April 1, 1981. The machinery was estimated to have a salvage value of $7,000 at the end of its estimated useful life which was 7 years. What is Milford's maximum depreciation allowance for 1981?

a. $ 9,450
b. $15,750
c. $10,500
d. $17,500

30. Charles Gilbert, a corporate executive, incurred business-related, unreimbursed expenses in 1982 as follows:

Entertainment	$900
Travel	700
Education	400

Assuming that Gilbert does not itemize deductions, how much of these expenses should he deduct on his 1982 tax return?

a. $ 700
b. $1,100
c. $1,300
d. $1,600

31. Herbert Mann is an engineer employed by a major chemical company. During 1981 he paid the following business related expenses:

Travel expenses incurred while away from home overnight	$2,500
Executive search consultant fees paid in securing a new job in same profession	1,500
Professional society dues	600
Transportation expenses	350

Mann received travel expense reimbursements totaling $2,300 from his employer during 1981. How much should Mann deduct as employee business expenses in arriving at his adjusted gross income for 1981?

a. $ 550
b. $2,050
c. $2,650
d. $2,850

32. Martin Hart, who is not an outside salesman, earned a salary of $30,000 during the current year. During the year, he was required by his employer to take several overnight business trips, and he received an expense allowance of $1,500 for travel and lodging. In the course of these trips he incurred the following expenses which were either adjustments to income or deductions from adjusted gross income.

Travel	$1,100
Lodging	500
Entertainment of customers	400

What is Hart's adjusted gross income?

a. $28,000
b. $29,500
c. $29,600
d. $29,900

33. Martin Dawson, who resided in Detroit, was unemployed for the last six months of 1981. In January 1982, he moved to Houston to seek employment, and obtained a full-time job there in February. He kept this job for the balance of the year. Martin paid the following expenses in 1982 in connection with his move:

Rental of truck to move his personal belongings to Houston	$ 800
Penalty for breaking the lease on his Detroit apartment	300
Total	$1,100

How much can Martin deduct in 1982 for moving expenses?

a. $0
b. $ 300
c. $ 800
d. $1,100

34. Richard Putney, who lived in Idaho for five years, moved to Texas in 1980 to accept a new position. His employer reimbursed him in full for all direct moving costs, but did not pay for any part of the following indirect moving expenses incurred by Putney:

Househunting trips to Texas	$800
Temporary housing in Texas	$900

How much of the indirect expenses can be deducted by Putney as moving expenses?

a. $0
b. $ 900
c. $1,500
d. $1,700

35. Ronald Birch, who is single, earned a salary of $30,000 in 1982 as a plumber employed by Lupo Company. Birch was covered for the entire year 1982 under Lupo's qualified pension plan for employees. In addition, Birch had a net income of $10,000 from self-employment in 1982. What is the maximum amount that Birch can deduct in 1982 for contributions to an individual retirement account (IRA)?

a. $4,500
b. $2,000
c. $1,500
d. $0

36. Under the provisions of ERISA, deductible contributions to a qualified retirement plan on behalf of a self-employed individual whose earned income is $20,000 are limited to

a. $1,500
b. $2,000
c. $3,000
d. $7,500

37. For the year 1982 Fred and Wilma Todd reported the following items of income:

	Fred	*Wilma*
Salary	$40,000	–
Interest income	1,000	$ 200
Cash prize won on T.V. game show	–	8,800
	$41,000	$9,000

Fred is not covered by any qualified retirement plan and he and Wilma established individual retirement accounts during the year. Assuming a joint return was filed for 1982, what is the maximum amount that they can be allowed for contributions to their individual retirement accounts?

a. $2,000
b. $2,250
c. $6,000
d. $7,500

38. Jill Nolan's filing status for 1982 was that of a single individual. Jill claimed itemized deductions of $5,000 on her 1982 income tax return. How much was Jill's zero bracket amount for 1982?

a. $1,700
b. $2,300
c. $2,700
d. $3,400

39. Jon Stenger, a cash basis taxpayer, had adjusted gross income of $35,000 in 1983. During the year he incurred and paid the following medical expenses:

Drugs and medicines prescribed by doctors	$ 300
Health insurance premiums	750
Doctors' fees	2,250
Eyeglasses	75
	$3,375

Stenger received $900 in 1983 as reimbursement for a portion of the doctors' fees. If Stenger were to itemize his deductions, what would be his allowable net medical expense deduction?

a. $ 425
b. $ 725
c. $1,125
d. $1,425

40. During 1979 Mr. and Mrs. Benson provided substantially all the support, in their own home, for their son John, age 26, and for Mrs. Benson's cousin Nancy, age 17. John had $1,100 of income for 1979, and Nancy's income was $500. The Bensons paid the following medical expenses during the year:

Medicines and drugs:	
For themselves	$400
For John	500
For Nancy	100
Doctors:	
For themselves	600
For John	900
For Nancy	200

What is the total amount of medical expenses (before application of any limitation rules) that would enter into the calculation of excess itemized deductions on the Benson's 1979 tax return?

a. $1,000
b. $1,300
c. $2,400
d. $2,700

41. Henry Warren did not itemize his deductions on his 1981 and 1980 federal income tax returns. However, Warren plans to itemize his deductions for 1982. The following information relating to his state income taxes is available:

Taxes withheld in 1982	$2,000
Refund received in 1982 of 1981 tax	300
Assessment paid in 1982 of 1980 tax	200

What amount should Warren utilize as state and local income taxes in calculating excess itemized deductions for his 1982 federal income tax return?

a. $1,700
b. $1,900
c. $2,000
d. $2,200

42. Sara Harding is a cash basis taxpayer who itemizes her deductions. The following information pertains to Sara's state income taxes for the taxable year 1981:

Withheld by employer in 1981		$2,000
Payments on 1981 estimate:		
4/15/81	$300	
6/15/81	300	
9/15/81	300	
1/15/82	300	1,200
Total paid and withheld		$3,200
Actual tax, per state return		3,000
Overpayment		$ 200

There was no balance of tax or refund due on Sara's 1980 state tax return. How much is deductible for state income taxes on Sara's 1981 federal income tax return?

a. $2,800
b. $2,900
c. $3,000
d. $3,200

43. During 1981 Jack and Mary Bronson paid the following taxes:

Taxes on residence (for period January 1 to September 30, 1981)	$2,700
State motor vehicle tax on value of the car	360

The Bronsons sold their house on June 30, 1981, under an agreement in which the real estate taxes were not prorated between the buyer and sellers. What amount should the Bronsons deduct as taxes in calculating excess itemized deductions for 1981?

a. $1,800
b. $2,160
c. $2,700
d. $3,060

44. The following information is available for Seymour and Ruth Atkinson, who reside in Pennsylvania, for 1981:

Adjusted gross income	$31,500
Tax-exempt interest received	$ 1,500
Exemptions (including exemption claimed for their son John, a full-time student at State University)	3

An abstract from the Optional Sales Tax Table for Pennsylvania is presented below:

	Sales tax	
Income	*Family size 1 & 2*	*Family size Over 2*
$30,001–$32,000	$219	$248
$32,001–$34,000	$230	$261

Assuming that the Atkinsons elect to use the Optional Sales Tax Table, what is the maximum amount of general sales taxes that they can utilize in calculating excess itemized deductions for 1981?

a. $219
b. $230
c. $248
d. $261

45. George Granger sold a plot of land to Albert King on July 1, 1981. Granger had not paid any realty taxes on the land since 1979. Delinquent 1980 taxes amounted to $600, and 1981 taxes amounted to $700. King paid the 1980 and 1981 taxes in full in 1981, when he bought the land. What portion of the $1,300 is deductible by King in 1981?

a. $ 353
b. $ 700
c. $ 953
d. $1,300

46. During 1980 Mr. and Mrs. West paid the following taxes:

Property taxes on residence	$1,800
Special assessment for installation of a sewer system in their town	1,000
State personal property tax on their automobile	600
Property taxes on land held for long-term appreciation	300

What amount can the Wests deduct as property taxes in calculating excess itemized deductions for 1980?

a. $2,100
b. $2,700
c. $3,100
d. $3,700

47. Robert and Judy Parker made the following payments during 1982:

Interest on a life insurance policy loan (the related policy on Robert's life was purchased in 1950)	$1,200
Interest on home mortgage for period January 1 to October 4, 1982	3,600
Penalty payment for prepayment of home mortgage on October 4, 1982	900

How much can the Parkers utilize as interest expense in calculating excess itemized deductions for 1982?

a. $5,700
b. $4,800
c. $4,500
d. $3,600

48. Charles Wolfe purchased the following long-term investments at par during 1981:

$20,000 general obligation bonds of Burlington County (wholly tax exempt)
$10,000 debentures of Arrow Corporation

Wolfe financed these purchases by obtaining a $30,000 loan from the Union National Bank. For the year 1981, Wolfe made the following interest payments:

Union National Bank	$3,600
Interest on home mortgage	3,000
Interest on credit card charges	500

What amount can Wolfe utilize as interest expense in calculating excess itemized deductions for 1981?

a. $3,500
b. $4,700
c. $5,400
d. $7,100

49. Phil and Joan Crawley make the following payments during 1980:

Interest on bank loan (loan proceeds were used to purchase United States savings bonds Series H)	$4,000
Interest on installment charge accounts	500
Interest on home mortgage for period April 1 to December 31, 1980	2,700
Points paid to obtain conventional mortgage loan on April 1, 1980	900

What is the maximum amount that the Crawleys can utilize as interest expense in calculating excess itemized deductions for 1980?

a. $4,100
b. $7,200
c. $7,600
d. $8,100

50. For the year ended December 31, 1979, David Roth, a married taxpayer filing a joint return, reported the following:

Investment income from dividends and interest	$24,000
Long-term capital gains	25,000
Investment expenses	4,000
Interest expense on funds borrowed in 1979 to purchase investment property	70,000

What amount can Roth deduct in 1979 as investment interest expense?

a. $20,000
b. $30,000
c. $45,000
d. $70,000

51. During 1979, William Clark was assessed a deficiency on his 1978 federal income tax return. As a result of this assessment he was required to pay $1,120 determined as follows:

Additional tax	$900
Late filing penalty	60
Negligence penalty	90
Interest	70

What portion of the $1,120 would qualify as itemized deductions for 1979?

a. $0
b. $ 70
c. $150
d. $220

52. Ruth Lewis has adjusted gross income of $100,000 for 1982 and itemizes her deductions. On September 1, 1982, she made a contribution to her church of stock held for investment for two years which cost $10,000 and had a fair market value of $70,000. The church sold the stock for $70,000 on the same date. Assume that Lewis made no other contributions during 1982 and made no special election in regard to this contribution on her 1982 tax return. How much should Lewis claim as a charitable contribution deduction for 1982?

a. $50,000
b. $30,000
c. $20,000
d. $10,000

53. On December 15, 1981, Donald Calder made a contribution of $500 to a qualified charitable organization, by charging the contribution on his bank credit card. Calder paid the $500 on January 20, 1982, upon receipt of the bill from the bank. In addition, Calder issued and delivered a promissory note for $1,000 to another qualified charitable organization on November 1, 1981, which he paid upon maturity six months later. If Calder itemizes his deductions, what portion of these contributions is deductible in 1981?

a. $0
b. $ 500
c. $1,000
d. $1,500

54. Judy Bishop had adjusted gross income of $35,000 in 1981 and itemizes her deductions. Additional information is available for 1981 as follows:

Cash contribution to church	$2,500
Purchase of an art object at her church bazaar (with a fair market value of $500 on date of purchase)	800
Donation of used clothes to Goodwill Charities (fair value evidenced by receipt received)	400

What is the maximum amount Bishop can claim as a deduction for charitable contributions in 1981?

a. $2,800
b. $3,200
c. $3,300
d. $3,400

55. Under a written agreement between Mrs. Norma Lowe and an approved religious exempt organization, a ten-year-old girl from Vietnam came to live in Mrs. Lowe's home on August 1, 1980, in order to be able to start school in the U.S. on September 3, 1980. Mrs. Lowe actually spent $500 for food, clothing, and school supplies for the student during 1980, without receiving any compensation or reimbursement of costs. What portion of the $500 may Mrs. Lowe deduct on her 1980 income tax return as a charitable contribution?

a. $0
b. $200
c. $250
d. $500

56. During 1978 Vincent Tally gave to the municipal art museum title to his private collection of rare books that was assessed and valued at $60,000. However, he reserved the right to the collection's use and possession during his lifetime. For 1978 he reported an adjusted gross income of $100,000. Assuming that this was his only contribution during the year, and that there were no carryovers from prior years, what amount can he deduct as contributions for 1978?

a. $0
b. $30,000
c. $50,000
d. $60,000

57. Henry Mitchell is a self-employed individual. During 1982 his car, which he used 75% for business and 25% for personal use, was totally destroyed in an accident. The car had a fair market value of $10,800 when destroyed, which was less than the car's adjusted basis. Mitchell received only $9,000 as a recovery from his insurance company. What amount can Mitchell utilize as a casualty loss in calculating excess itemized deductions for 1982?

a. $1,800
b. $ 450
c. $ 350
d. $0

58. Nelson Harris had adjusted gross income in 1983 of $60,000. During the year his personal summer home was completely destroyed by a cyclone. Pertinent data with respect to the home follows:

Cost basis	$39,000
Value before casualty	45,000
Value after casualty	3,000

Harris was partially insured for his loss and in 1983 he received a $15,000 insurance settlement. What is Harris' allowable casualty loss deduction for 1983?

a. $17,900
b. $18,000
c. $26,900
d. $27,000

59. On December 24, 1979, Otis Johnson was seriously injured in a collision while driving his car. The car, which cost Johnson $6,000 and was used solely for personal use, had an appraised value of $4,200 for trade-in purposes just before the accident. After his release from the hospital on January 25, 1980, Johnson traded in the car for a new car at an allowance of $2,200. Johnson also received a settlement of $1,500 under his collision insurance policy in February 1980. What amount can he deduct as a casualty loss on his tax return, and in which year should the deduction be taken?

a. $400 in 1979.
b. $400 in 1980.
c. $500 in 1979.
d. $500 in 1980.

60. Mr. & Mrs. Ben Bornn adopted a child in 1983. The child qualified for adoption assistance payments under the Social Security Act. In connection with the adoption, Bornn paid court costs and legal fees aggregating $1,600. These expenses were considered reasonable and were not reimbursed to Bornn. If Mr. and Mrs. Bornn itemize their deductions on their 1983 return, how much will they be permitted to deduct for adoption expenses?

a. $0
b. $1,000
c. $1,500
d. $1,600

61. Magda Micale, a public school teacher, paid the following items in 1980, for which she received no reimbursement:

Initiation fee for membership in teachers' union	$100
Dues to teachers' union	180
Voluntary unemploymnet benefit fund contributions to union-established fund	72

How much can Magda claim in 1980 as allowable miscellaneous deductions on Schedule A of Form 1040?

a. $180
b. $280
c. $252
d. $352

62. Gabriel Colon, a jet airplane mechanic, paid the following items in 1980, for which he received no reimbursement:

Tools used in connection with his work (bought on July 1, 1980; estimated useful life 5 years, no salvage value)	$600
Union dues	$180
Legal fee in connection with preparation of his will, 25% of which was attributable to income tax advice	$300

How much can Colon claim in 1980 as allowable miscellaneous deductions on Schedule A of Form 1040?

a. $ 315
b. $ 780
c. $ 855
d. $1,080

63. Harold Brodsky is an electrician employed by a contracting firm. During the current year he incurred and paid the following expenses:

Use of personal auto for company business (reimbursed by employer for $200)	$300
Specialized work clothes	550
Union dues	600
Cost of income tax preparation	150
Preparation of will	100

If Brodsky were to itemize his personal deductions, what amount should he claim as miscellaneous deductible expenses?

a. $1,300
b. $1,400
c. $1,500
d. $1,700

64. During 1982 Robert Moore, who is 50 years old and unmarried, maintained his home in which he and his widower father, age 75, resided. His father had $1,600 interest income from a savings account and also received $2,400 from social security during 1982. Robert provided 60% of his father's total support for 1982. What is Robert's filing status for 1982, and how many exemptions should he claim on his tax return?

a. Head of household and 2 exemptions.
b. Single and 2 exemptions.
c. Head of household and 1 exemption.
d. Single and 1 exemption.

65. During 1982 Mary Dunn provided 20% of her own support; the remaining 80% was provided by her three sons as follows:

Bill	15%
Jon	25%
Tom	40%
	80%

Assume that a multiple support agreement exists and that the brothers will sign multiple support declarations as required. Which of the brothers is eligible to claim the mother as a dependent for 1982?

a. None of the brothers.
b. Tom only.
c. Jon or Tom only.
d. Bill, Jon or Tom.

66. John and Mary Arnold are a childless, married couple who lived apart (alone in homes maintained by each) the entire year 1982. On December 31, 1982, they were legally separated under a decree of separate maintenance. Which of the following is the only filing status choice available to them when filing for 1982?

a. Single.
b. Head of household.
c. Married filing separate return.
d. Married filing joint return.

67. Mark Erickson, age 46, filed a joint return for 1981 with his wife Helen, age 24. Their son John was born on December 16, 1981. Mark provided 60% of the support for his 72-year-old widowed mother until April 10, 1981, when she died. His mother's only income was from social security benefits totaling $1,100 during 1981. How many exemptions should the Ericksons claim on their 1981 tax return?

a. 2
b. 3
c. 4
d. 5

68. Albert and Lois Stoner, age 66 and 64, respectively, filed a joint tax return for 1980. They provided all of the support for their blind 19-year-old son, who has no gross income. Their 23-year-old daughter, a full-time student until her graduation on June 14, 1980, earned $2,000, which was 40% of her total support during 1980. Her parents provided the remaining support. The Stoners also provided the total support of Lois' father, who is a citizen and life-long resident of Peru. How many examptions can the Stoners claim on their 1980 income tax return?

a. 4
b. 5
c. 6
d. 7

69. Jim Planter, who reached age 65 on January 1, 1980, filed a joint return for 1979 with his wife Rita, age 50. Mary, their 21-year-old daughter, was a full-time student at a college until her graduation on June 2, 1979. The daughter had $6,500 of income and provided 25% of her own support during 1979. In addition, during 1979 the Planters were the sole support for Rita's niece, who had no income. How many exemptions should the Planters claim on their 1979 tax return?

a. 2
b. 3
c. 4
d. 5

70. Mr. and Mrs. Vonce, both age 62, filed a joint return for 1981. They provided all the support for their daughter who is 19, legally blind, and who has no income. Their son, age 21 and a full-time student at a university, had $4,200 of income and provided 70% of his own support during 1981. How many exemptions should Mr. and Mrs. Vonce have claimed on their 1981 joint income tax return?

a. 2
b. 3
c. 4
d. 5

71. William Dalton, age 30 and single, provided the following information for his 1982 income tax return:

Salary	$30,000
Payment to an Individual Retirement Account	$ 2,000
Total itemized deductions	$ 3,400
Number of exemptions claimed	1

Dalton should report taxable income for 1982 of

a. $24,600
b. $25,900
c. $26,900
d. $27,900

72. Martin Dale, single, paid the entire cost of maintaining his dependent mother in a home for the aged, for the whole year 1980. How much is Martin's zero bracket amount for 1980?

a. $0
b. $1,700
c. $2,300
d. $3,400

73. During 1980 Howard Thomson maintained his home in which he and his sixteen-year-old son resided. The son qualifies as his dependent. Thomson's wife died in 1979, for which year a joint return was appropriately filed. Thomson remarried on March 15, 1981. What is Thomson's filing status for 1980?

a. Single.
b. Head of household.
c. Surviving spouse.
d. Married filing jointly.

74. Mrs. Irma Felton, by herself, maintains her home in which she and her unmarried son reside. Her son, however, does not qualify as her dependent. Mrs. Felton's husband died in 1977. What is Mrs. Felton's filing status for 1978?

a. Single.
b. Surviving spouse.
c. Head of household.
d. Married filing jointly.

75. Alex Berger, a retired building contractor, earned the following income during 1981:

Director's fee received from Keith Realty Corp.	$ 600
Executor's fee received from the estate of his deceased sister	7,000

Berger's self-employment income for 1981 is

a. $0
b. $ 600

c. $7,000
d. $7,600

76. William Linnett, a cash basis sole proprietor, had the following receipts and disbursements for 1981:

Gross receipts	$60,000
Dividend income (on personal investment)	400
Cost of sales	30,000
Other operating expenses	6,000
State business tax	600
Federal self-employment tax	1,600

What amount should Linnett report as net earnings from self-employment for 1981?

a. $24,000
b. $23,800
c. $23,400
d. $21,800

77. Orna Corp., a calendar-year taxpayer, had an unused investment credit of $8,000 at December 31, 1982, its first taxable year. For how many years can Orna carry over this unused investment credit?

a. 15
b. 7
c. 5
d. 3

78. Foster Corporation's tax liability for the year ended December 31, 1981, was $15,000 before claiming an investment tax credit. On July 1, 1981, Foster purchased a new truck for $180,000. The truck is appropriately categorized by Foster as five-year property under the accelerated cost recovery system. Foster's allowed investment tax credit for 1981 is

a. $ 9,000
b. $12,000
c. $15,000
d. $18,000

79. On July 1, 1981, Pemberton Corporation bought a new drill press for $20,000, which was placed in service the same day. The drill press qualifies as five-year accelerated cost recovery system property, for which an investment credit of $2,000 was claimed. If Pemberton disposes of this drill press on May 31, 1983, how much of the investment credit must be recaptured in 1983?

a. $0
b. $1,200
c. $1,600
d. $2,000

80. On October 1, 1981, Helma Corporation traded a business automobile with an adjusted basis of $1,500 for a new automobile to be used in the business. In addition Helma paid $3,000 in cash. The new automobile has an estimated life of four years and no estimated salvage. The corporation is on a calendar year and had 1981 taxable income of $80,000. The 1981 investment tax credit allowed on this acquisition should be

a. $300
b. $270
c. $210
d. $450

81. In 1981, Pianca Corporation bought the following new assets, both of which are in the five-year class under the accelerated cost recovery system:

Asset	*Cost*
Solar panels	$ 8,000
Shredder for recycling of aluminum cans	12,000

Pianca claimed the regular investment credit in 1981 for the qualifying property. What is the total amount of the above-mentioned assets eligible in 1981 for the business energy investment credit?

a. $0
b. $ 8,000
c. $12,000
d. $20,000

82. Melvin Crane is 66 years old, and his wife, Matilda, is 65. They filed a joint income tax return for 1980, reporting an adjusted gross income of $7,800, on which they paid a tax of $60. They received $1,250 from social security benefits in 1980. How much can they claim on Schedule R of Form 1040 in 1980, as a credit for the elderly?

a. $0
b. $ 60
c. $315
d. $375

83. Nora Hayes, a widow, maintains a home for herself and her two dependent preschool children. In 1982, Nora's earned income and adjusted gross income was $29,000. During 1982, Nora paid work-related expenses of $3,000 for a housekeeper to care for her children. How much can Nora claim for child care credit in 1982?

a. $0
b. $480
c. $600
d. $900

84. Robert and Mary Jason, filing a joint tax return for 1982, had a tax liability of $9,000 based on their tax table income and three exemptions. Robert and Mary had earned income of $20,000 and $12,000, respectively, during 1982. In order for Mary to be gainfully employed, the Jasons incurred the following employment-related expenses for their four-year-old son John in 1982:

Payee	*Amount*
Union Day Care Center	$1,500
Acme Home Cleaning Service	500
Wilma Jason, babysitter (Robert Jason's mother)	1,000

Assuming that the Jasons do not claim any other credits against their tax, what is the amount of the child care tax credit they should report on their tax return for 1982?

a. $300
b. $480
c. $500
d. $600

85. During 1980 Bell Corporation had worldwide taxable income of $675,000 and a tentative United Staes income tax of $270,000. Bell's taxable income from business operations in Country A was $300,000, and foreign income taxes imposed were $135,000 stated in United States dollars. How much should Bell claim as a credit for foreign income taxes on its United States income tax return for 1980?

a. $0
b. $ 75,000
c. $120,000
d. $135,000

86. Philip and Joan Sampson, filing a joint tax return for 1981, had a tax liability of $8,000 computed from the tax table. During 1981 Philip contributed $150 to a candidate for a local elective public office. Assuming that the Sampsons do not claim any other credits against their tax, what is the amount of the political contributions tax credit they should claim on their tax return for 1981?

a. $150
b. $100
c. $ 75
d. $ 50

87. In 1980, Alex Burgos paid $600 to Rita, his ex-wife, for child support. Under the terms of the divorce decree, Alex claims the exemption for his five-year-old son, William, who lived with Rita for the entire year. Alex's only income in 1980 was from wages of $5,500, resulting in an income tax of $172. How much is Alex's earned income credit for 1980?

a. $0
b. $328
c. $378
d. $500

88. For the year 1979 Roberta Collins, who is divorced, reported the following items of income:

Interest income	$ 100
Wages	4,000
Earnings from self-employment	3,000

She maintains a household for herself and her 5-year-old son who qualifies as her dependent. What is the maximum earned income credit available to her for 1979?

a. $310
b. $362.50
c. $400
d. $710

89. During 1980 William and Jane Conley made the following energy-conserving component additions to their personal residence (a five-year-old house purchased by them in July 1980):

Aluminum siding (on the north side of the house)	$1,000
Insulation	750
Automatic setback thermostat	150
Used storm windows (purchased from an unrelated third party)	300

Assuming that the Conleys have a tax liability of $3,000 without any other credits against their tax for 1980, what amount can they claim as a residential energy credit on their 1980 income tax return?

a. $135
b. $180
c. $300
d. $330

90. Harold Thompson, a self-employed individual, had income transactions for 1979 (duly reported on his return filed in April 1980) as follows:

Gross receipts	$400,000
Less cost of goods sold and deductions	320,000
Net business income	80,000
Capital gains	36,000
Gross income	$116,000

In March 1983 Thompson discovers that he had inadvertently omitted some income on his 1979 return and retains Mann, CPA, to determine his position under the statute of limitations. Mann should advise Thompson that the six-year statute of limitations would apply to his 1979 return only if he omitted from gross income an amount in excess of

a. $ 20,000
b. $ 29,000
c. $100,000
d. $109,000

91. Fred Wright filed his 1981 income tax return on March 15, 1982, showing gross income of $20,000. He had mistakenly omitted $6,000 of income which, in good faith, he considered nontaxable. By what date must the Internal Revenue Service assert a notice of deficiency?
a. March 15, 1985
b. April 15, 1985
c. March 15, 1988
d. April 15, 1988

May 1984 Questions

92. Earl Cook, who worked as a machinist for Precision Corp., loaned Precision $1,000 in 1980. Cook did not own any of Precision's stock, and the loan was not a condition of Cook's employment by Precision. In 1984, Precision declared bankruptcy, and Cook's note receivable from Precision became worthless. What loss can Cook claim on his 1984 income tax return?
a. $0.
b. $ 500 long-term capital loss.
c. $1,000 short-term capital loss.
d. $1,000 business bad debt.

Items 93 through 96 are based on the following data:

Laura Lewis has been legally separated from her husband, Herman, since 1982. Their three-year-old son, Ronald, lived with Laura for the entire year 1983. Under the written separation agreement between Laura and Herman, Herman was obligated to pay Laura $300 per month for alimony and $200 per month for child support, or a total of $6,000 annually. However, Laura received a total of only $300 from Herman during 1983. Laura's other income in 1983 was from the following sources:

Salary	$20,000
Interest on insurance dividends left on deposit with a life insurance company	100
Interest on federal income tax refund	60

In addition, Laura's father, Albert, gave Laura a gift of 500 shares of Liba Corporation common stock in 1983. Albert's basis for the Liba stock was $4,000. At the date of this gift, the fair market value of the Liba stock was $3,000.

The information above was originally followed by seven multiple choice questions, three of which concerned property transactions. Those three questions and the relevant information have been put in Module 41, Transactions in Property.

93. What was Laura's filing status for 1983?
a. Single.
b. Married filing separate return.
c. Unmarried head of household.
d. Married head of household.

94. How much alimony was includible in Laura's 1983 taxable income?
a. $0
b. $ 300
c. $3,600
d. $6,000

95. How much interest was includible in Laura's 1983 taxable income?
a. $0
b. $ 60
c. $100
d. $160

96. How much was includible in Laura's 1983 taxable income for the 500 shares of Liba stock?
a. $0
b. $3,000
c. $3,500
d. $4,000

Items 97 through 102 are based on the following data:

Roger Efron, who is single and has no dependents, earned a salary of $50,000 in 1983, and had an adjusted gross income of $60,000. Roger has been an active participant in a qualified noncontributory pension plan since 1972. Roger itemized his deductions on his 1983 income tax return. Among Roger's 1983 cash expenditures were the following:

Real estate taxes on Roger's condominium	$4,000
Contribution to an individual retirement account ($200 interest was earned on this IRA in 1983)	2,000
Dental expenses	700
Premium on Roger's life insurance policy	600
Medical insurance premiums	500
Contribution to candidate for public office	300
Legal fee for preparation of Roger's will	200
Customs duties	80
City dog license fee	10

In addition, Roger suffered a casualty loss of $400 in 1983 due to storm damage.

97. How much could Roger deduct for the contribution to his individual retirement account in arriving at his 1983 adjusted gross income?
    a. $0
    b. $1,500
    c. $1,800
    d. $2,000

98. How much could Roger deduct in 1983 for medical and dental expenses?
    a. $0
    b. $ 150
    c. $ 700
    d. $1,200

99. How much could Roger deduct in 1983 for taxes?
    a. $4,000
    b. $4,010
    c. $4,080
    d. $4,090

100. How much could Roger deduct in 1983 for miscellaneous deductions?
    a. $0
    b. $200
    c. $600
    d. $800

101. How much could Roger deduct in 1983 for the casualty loss?
    a. $0
    b. $100
    c. $300
    d. $400

102. How much of a credit could Roger offset against his 1983 income tax, for his contributions to a candidate for public office?
    a. $0
    b. $ 50
    c. $100
    d. $150

103. For the year ended December 31, 1983, Elmer Shaw earned $3,000 interest at Prestige Savings Bank, on a time savings account scheduled to mature in 1985. In January 1984, before filing his 1983 income tax return, Shaw incurred a forfeiture penalty of $1,500 for premature withdrawal of the funds from his account. Shaw should treat this $1,500 forfeiture penalty as a
    a. Penalty **not** deductible for tax purposes.
    b. Deduction from gross income in arriving at 1984 adjusted gross income.
    c. Deduction from 1984 adjusted gross income, deductible only if Shaw itemizes his deductions for 1984.
    d. Reduction of interest earned in 1983, so that only $1,500 of such interest is taxable on Shaw's 1983 return.

Items 104 through 107 are based on the following data:

John Budd, who was 58 at the date of his death on July 1, 1983, received $1,000 interest in 1983 on municipal bonds. John's wife, Emma, age 57, received a $300 television set in 1983 as a gift for opening a long-term savings account at a bank. Upon John's death, Emma received life insurance proceeds of $60,000 under a group policy paid for by John's employer. In addition, an employee death benefit of $7,500 was paid to Emma by John's employer. Emma did not remarry in 1983. Emma is executrix of John's estate.

The information above originally included other information concerning property transactions. That information and the question that related to it have been put in Module 41, Transactions in Property.

104. With regard to John's and Emma's filing status for 1983, Emma should file
    a. As a single individual, and a separate return should be filed for John as unmarried head of household.
    b. As a qualifying widow, and a separate return should be filed for John as married head of household.

c. As a qualifying widow, and a separate return should be filed for John as a single deceased individual.
d. A joint return including John, as married taxpayers.

105. How much taxable interest was received by John and Emma in 1983?
a. $0
b. $ 300
c. $1,000
d. $1,300

106. How much of the group life insurance proceeds should be excluded from 1983 taxable income?
a. $0
b. $ 5,000
c. $50,000
d. $60,000

107. How much of the employee death benefit should be excluded from 1983 taxable income?
a. $0
b. $4,500
c. $5,000
d. $7,500

Multiple Choice Answers

1.	c	23.	d	45.	a	66.	a	87.	a
2.	a	24.	a	46.	b	67.	c	88.	b
3.	b	25.	a	47.	a	68.	b	89.	a
4.	d	26.	b	48.	b	69.	d	90.	d
5.	a	27.	c	49.	d	70.	b	91.	d
6.	c	28.	b	50.	b	71.	b	92.	c
7.	c	29.	c	51.	b	72.	c	93.	c
8.	a	30.	a	52.	b	73.	c	94.	a
9.	a	31.	a	53.	b	74.	c	95.	d
10.	d	32.	d	54.	b	75.	b	96.	a
11.	c	33.	d	55.	b	76.	c	97.	d
12.	d	34.	c	56.	a	77.	a	98.	a
13.	b	35.	b	57.	c	78.	c	99.	a
14.	a	36.	c	58.	a	79.	c	100.	a
15.	a	37.	b	59.	b	80.	b	101.	a
16.	d	38.	b	60.	c	81.	d	102.	b
17.	b	39.	a	61.	b	82.	b	103.	b
18.	c	40.	d	62.	a	83.	c	104.	d
19.	d	41.	d	63.	a	84.	b	105.	b
20.	b	42.	b	64.	d	85.	c	106.	d
21.	a	43.	b	65.	d	86.	c	107.	c
22.	d	44.	d						

Multiple Choice Answer Explanations

I.B.3. Annuities

1. (580,P3,57) (c) The requirement is to determine the pension (annuity) amounts excluded from income during 1979, 1980, and 1981. This is an employee annuity subject to a special rule because Brown's contribution of $14,700 will be recovered within 36 months after payments begin. Under this special rule, all amounts received are excluded from income until the employee recovers his total contribution (i.e., cost); thereafter all amounts are included in income.

	Received	*Excluded*	*Included*
1979	$4,900	$ 4,900	$ –
1980	8,400	8,400	–
1981	8,400	1,400	7,000
		$14,700	

I.B.4. Life Insurance Proceeds

2. (1180,Q2,28) (a) The requirement is to determine the amount of life insurance payments to be included in a widow's gross income. Life insurance proceeds paid by reason of death are excluded from income if paid in a lump sum or in installments. If the payments are received in installments, the principal amount of the policy divided by the number of payments is excluded each year. In addition, a surviving spouse is entitled to a $1,000 per year exclusion. Therefore, only $200 of the $5,200 insurance payment is included in Penelope's gross income:

Annual installment	$5,200
Principal amount ($100,000 ÷ 25)	– 4,000
	$1,200
Surviving spouse's exclusion	– 1,000
Amount included in gross income	$ 200

I.B.5. Employee Benefits

3. (1182,P3,47) (b) The requirement is to determine the amount of group-term life insurance premium that is taxable to Hetnar. The cost of group-term life insurance provided by an employer must be included in an employee's income to the extent of the cost of life insurance coverage in excess of $50,000. The excess coverage is $90,000 – $50,000 = $40,000. At a cost of $8 per thousand, the amount taxable to Hetnar is $8 x 40 = $320.

4. (582,P3,47) (d) The requirement is to determine the amount of employee death payments to be included in gross income by the widow and the son. Up to $5,000 of an employee's death benefits is excluded from income. Note that there is only one $5,000 exclusion allowed. Since $10,000 was received by each beneficiary, the $5,000 exclusion is allocated proportionately to each beneficiary. Thus, each includes $10,000 – $2,500 = $7,500 in gross income.

5. (1180,Q2,37) (a) All three items that Larsen received as a result of his injury are excluded from gross income. Benefits received under workmen's compensation and compensation received for damages resulting from personal injury are always excluded. Amounts received from an employer's accident and health plan as reimbursement for medical expenses are excluded as long as the medical expenses were not previously deducted as itemized deductions.

6. (579,Q2,26) (c) James Martin's gross income is:

Salary	$50,000
Bonus	10,000
Allowance for moving expenses	5,000
	$65,000

Although the moving expense allowance must be included in income, Martin may deduct amounts spent on qualified moving expenditures. Medical insurance premiums paid by an employer are excluded from the employee's income.

I.B.9. Dividends

7. (1183,Q2,35) (c) The requirement is to determine the amount the Nidos can exclude for dividends received under a qualified public utility dividend reinvestment plan. Individuals may elect to exclude up to $750 ($1,500 on a joint return) of qualifying public utility dividends per year.

8. (1181,Q3,59) (a) The requirement is to determine the amount of dividends eligible for the dividend exclusion. Dividends **not** qualifying for exclusion include dividends from foreign corporations, exempt corporations and farmers' cooperative associations, real estate investment trusts, and corporations deriving at least 80% of their income from U.S. possessions and at least 50% from business activities there.

9. (579,Q2,23) (a) The requirement is to determine the amount of dividends (net of exclusion) to be reported by the Mitchells on a joint return. An individual may exclude up to $100 ($200 on a joint return) of dividends received from taxable domestic corporations. Dividends from foreign corporations do not qualify for exclusion. Since a joint return is being filed and at least $200 of dividends are received from a qualified corporation (Alert Corp.), a $200 dividend exclusion is allowed. The amount of dividends (net of exclusion) would be [($400 + $50) – $200 exclusion] + $300 = $550. The $200 dividend on the life insurance policy is not gross income, but is considered a reduction of the cost of the policy.

I.B.11. Interest Income

10. (1182,P3,44) (d) The requirement is to determine the amount of tax-exempt interest. Interest on obligations of a state or one of its political subdivisions (e.g., New York Port Authority bonds), or a possession of the U.S. (e.g., Puerto Rico Commonwealth bonds) is tax-exempt.

11. (580,P3,48) (c) Stone will report $1,700 of interest income. Interest on FIT refunds, personal injury awards, U.S. savings bonds, and most other sources is fully taxable. However, interest on state or municipal bonds is nontaxable.

12. (580,P3,49) (d) The requirement is to describe the reporting on Quinn's tax return of interest income and interest penalty forfeiture due to early withdrawal from a time savings account. Quinn must include in income the total gross amount of interest credited to his account, and then separately deduct the penalty forfeiture in arriving at AGI.

13. (1183,Q2,34) (b) The requirement is to determine the amount of all-savers certificate interest that Max can exclude for 1982. Individuals are entitled to a lifetime exclusion of $1,000 ($2,000 on a joint return). Of the $400 excluded on a joint return in 1981, half is treated as having been excluded by Max, and half by his wife, Lois. Thus, Max's exclusion on a separate return for 1982 is limited to $800 (i.e., $1,000 maximum exclusion less the $200 deemed to have been excluded by Max in 1981).

I.B.12. Scholarships

14. (1180,Q2,21) (a) The requirement is to determine the amount to be included in Davis' gross income for 1979 from the fellowship grant. Scholarships and fellowships are generally excluded. But if the recipient is not a candidate for a degree, the grant must be from a government or tax-exempt organization, and the exclusion is limited to $300 times the number of months for which the grant is received (maximum of 36 months). For the 17-month period of the grant (March 1, 1979 through July 31, 1980) up to $5,100 may be excluded, which is in excess of the amount received. Therefore, $0 is included in Davis' gross income for 1979.

I.B.16. Lease Improvements

15. (1179,Q2,31) (a) The requirement is to determine a lessor's 1978 gross income. A lessor excludes from income any increase in the value of property caused by improvements made by the lessee, unless the improvements were made in lieu of rent. In this case, there is no indication that the improvements were made in lieu of rent. Therefore, for 1978, Farley should only include the six rent payments in income: 6 x $1,000 = $6,000.

I.C. Items to be Included in Gross Income

16. (583,P3,45) (d) The requirement is to determine the amount of gross income. Drury's gross income includes the $36,000 salary, the $500 of premiums paid by her employer for group-term life insurance coverage in excess of $50,000, and the $5,000 proceeds received from a state lottery.

17. (1182,P3,46) (b) The requirement is to determine the amount of foster child payments to be included in income by the Charaks. Foster child payments are excluded from income to the extent they represent reimbursement for expenses incurred for care of the foster child. Since the payments ($3,900)

exceeded the expenses ($3,000), the $900 excess used for the Charaks' personal expenses must be included in their gross income.

I.C.6. Rents and Royalties

18. (583,P3,42) (c) The requirement is to determine the amount to be reported as gross rents. Gross rents include the $50,000 of recurring rents plus the $2,000 lease cancellation payment. The $1,000 of lease improvements are excluded from income since they were **not** required in lieu of rent.

19. (581,P3,53) (d) The requirement is to compute McDonald's net rental income. Since McDonald is a cash-basis taxpayer, his rental income consists of the eleven payments received. Since he resides in one apartment, only 50% of the expenses relating to both apartments can be allocated to the rental unit.

Rents (11 x $500)	$5,500
Less:	
Fuel and utilities (50% x $3,600)	(1,800)
Depreciation (50% x $3,000)	(1,500)
Repairs to rental unit	(400)
Insurance (50% x $600)	(300)
Net rental income	$1,500

I.C.8. Alimony and Separate Maintenance

20. (581,P3,42) (b) The requirement is to determine the amount of separate maintenance payments to be included in gross income. Periodic payments required by and received after a written separation agreement is executed are includible in income, except to the extent they are specifically designated as child support. Thus, ($1,500 – $600) x 6 = $5,400 is includible in income. The $1,200 per month paid for the first 6 months of 1980 are excluded from income because the payments were received prior to the signing of the written separation agreement.

21. (1179,Q2,25) (a) The requirement is the amount of gross income arising from a divorce settlement and alimony. Property settlements are treated as a division of capital and are not included in the recipient's income. To be a property settlement it must be a definite sum, and, if a series of payments, not over a period of more than 10 years. Child support is also excluded from the recipient's income. All other payments are taxable as alimony. Therefore, the transfer of title in the house is a property settlement while the mortgage payments are alimony, because they are for more than 10 years. Repayment of a loan is merely a return of capital and not taxable. While $200 of the $700 monthly payment is excluded as child support, the remaining $500 is alimony. Thus, Claire's gross income for 1978 is $7,500.

Mortgage payments	$2,500
Alimony ($500 x 10 mos.)	5,000
	$7,500

I.C.20. Unemployment Compensation

22. (1182,P3,50) (d) The requirement is to determine the amount of unemployment compensation (U/C) that is taxable for 1983. Since Ryan is single, the amount taxable will be the lesser of (a) the $3,000 U/C received, or (b) 50% x [($17,000 AGI + $3,000 U/C) – $12,000] = $4,000. All $3,000 of unemployment compensation received is taxable.

I.D.1. Cash Method or Accrual Method

23. (1183,Q2,36) (d) The requirement is to determine the 1982 medical practice net income for a cash basis physician. Dr. Berger's income consists of the $200,000 received from patients and the $30,000 received from third-party reimbursers during 1982. His 1982 deductions include the $20,000 of salaries and $24,000 of other expenses paid in 1982. The year-end bonuses will be deductible for 1983.

24. (583,P3,41) (a) The requirement is to determine Dr. Chester's gross income from his medical practice. Since Chester is a cash basis taxpayer, income is recognized at the time that cash is actually or constructively received, whichever is earlier. Since there was no constructive receipt, his 1982 income consists of the $35,000 received from office visits, plus the $130,000 collected on accounts receivable.

I.E. Business Income and Deductions

25. (1183,Q3,37) (a) The requirement is to determine the amount of business bad debt deduction for a cash basis taxpayer. Accounts receivable resulting from services rendered by a cash basis taxpayer have a zero tax basis, because the income has not yet been reported. Failure to collect the receivable results in a nondeductible loss.

26. (1183,Q3,59) (b) The requirement is to determine the amount of gifts deductible as a business expense. The deduction for business gifts is limited to $25 per recipient each year. Thus, Palo Corporation's deduction for business gifts would be [(4 x $10) + (13 x $25)] = $365.

27. (1182,Q3,45) (c) The requirement is to determine the bad debt deduction for the year in which Carlyle Corporation changed from the specific charge-off to the reserve method. The initial reserve for the year of change is found by (a) dividing the total accounts receivable at the close of the 5 preceding years into the total bad debts losses for those years ($72,000 ÷ $2,400,000 = 3%), and then (b) multiplying the outstanding accounts receivable at the end of the year of change by the % determined in (a), i.e., $600,000 x 3% = $18,000. The initial reserve is deducted ratably over a 10-year period. The bad debt deduction for the year of change will be the bad debts charged off during the year ($19,500), plus 1/10 of the $18,000 initial reserve; $19,500 + $1,800 = $21,300.

28. (1181,P3,42) (b) The requirement is to determine the maximum bad debt deduction that can be claimed for 1980 using the reserve method. The reserve for bad debts had a balance of $11,200 at 12/31/79, and was charged with $18,000 of losses and credited with $2,400 of recoveries during 1980. Since average net bad debt losses equal 4.4% of accounts receivable, 4.4% x $300,000 = $13,200 is the desired balance for the reserve for bad debts at 12/31/80. To arrive at the desired balance, the reserve must be credited and a bad debt deduction can be claimed for $17,600 computed as follows:

Beginning reserve	($11,200)
1980 losses	+ 18,000
1980 recoveries	(2,400)
Desired reserve	+ 13,200
1980 bad debt deduction	$17,600

I.F.2. Accelerated Cost Recovery System (ACRS)

29. (580,Q2,40) (c) The requirement is to determine the ACRS allowance for 1981. The salvage value of $7,000 is irrelevant since salvage value is disregarded in computing the ACRS allowance. The machinery is classified as 5-year property so the maximum allowance for 1981 would be:

$70,000 x .15 = $10,500

II.A.1. Reimbursed Expenses

30. (583,P3,46) (a) The requirement is to determine the amount of unreimbursed employee expenses that can be deducted by Gilbert if he does not itemize deductions. Since only travel, transportation, and employee reimbursed expenses can be deducted for AGI, Gilbert can deduct only the $700 of travel expenses if he does not itemize deductions. The unreimbursed entertainment and education expenses are deductible only as itemized deductions.

31. (582,P3,49) (a) The requirement is to determine the amount of employee business expenses deductible in arriving at adjusted gross income. Only the travel expenses of $2,500 less reimbursement of $2,300, and the transportation expense of $350 are deductible in arriving at AGI, a total of $550. The executive search fees and professional society dues are deductible **from** AGI.

32. (1180,Q2,31) (d) The requirement is to calculate adjusted gross income. First the expense allowance of $1,500 for travel and lodging must be combined with the salary of $30,000 to arrive at gross income of $31,500. Then one must determine whether deductions are **toward** AGI or **from** AGI. Travel and lodging expense are always deductible **toward** AGI. Therefore, a deduction of $1,600 ($1,100 travel expense + $500 lodging expense) results in AGI of $29,900. Entertainment expenses are deductible **toward** AGI only if reimbursed. Since the entertainment expenses of $400 were not reimbursed, they must be deducted **from** AGI.

II.B. Moving Expenses

33. (1182,P3,45) (d) The requirement is to determine Martin's deductible moving expenses. Moving expenses are deductible if closely related to the start of work at a new location and a distance (i.e., new job must be at least 35 miles from former residence) and time (i.e., employed at least 39 weeks out of 12 months following move) tests are met. Since the two tests are met, Martin's deductible moving expenses include both the $800 truck rental and the $300 penalty for breaking his apartment lease.

34. (1181,Q3,46) (c) The requirement is to determine the amount deductible as indirect moving expenses. The expenses of temporary housing (limited to a 30-day period) and househunting trips are deductible up to a maximum of $1,500.

II.D. Contributions to Certain Retirement Plans

35. (1182,P3,58) (b) Beginning in 1982, an individual is eligible to have an IRA even though he participates in a qualified employee pension plan. The maximum amount deductible for contributions to an IRA is the lesser of 100% of compensation, or $2,000.

36. (1179,Q2,34) (c) Before 1984, the maximum deduction for contributions by a self-employed person to a qualified retirement plan is limited to the lesser of $15,000 or 15% of earned income. Since 15% of $20,000 ($3,000) is less than $15,000, the deduction is limited to $3,000. Beginning in 1984, the maximum deduction for contributions to a self-employed retirement plan is limited to the lesser of $30,000, or 25% of earned income.

37. (579,Q2,25) (b) The Todds may contribute and deduct a total of $2,250 to their individual retirement accounts. The contribution limit when there is a nonworking spouse is the lesser of 15% of compensation or $2,250. In this case $2,250 is less than 15% of $40,000. The prize won on the TV game show does not qualify Wilma as a working spouse, nor is it compensation for purposes of computing the 15% limit.

III. Itemized Deductions from Adjusted Gross Income

38. (1183,Q2,24) (b) The requirement is to determine Jill's zero bracket amount for 1982. Since Jill is an unmarried individual, her zero bracket amount is $2,300.

III.A. Medical and Dental Expenses

39. (582,P3,50) (a) The requirement is to determine Stenger's net medical expense deduction for 1983. It would be computed as follows:

Drugs and medicine	$ 300
Less 1% of AGI ($35,000)	(350)
	$ 0
Medical insurance premiums	750
Doctors	1,350
Eyeglasses	75
	$2,175
Less 5% of AGI ($35,000)	1,750
Medical expense deduction for 1983	$ 425

If the medical expense deduction was instead being computed for 1984, the 1% floor on drugs and medicine would be eliminated and these expenses would be included in total medical expenses. However, only prescription drugs and insulin would be deductible.

Prescription drugs	$ 300
Medical insurance premiums	750
Doctors	1,350
Eyeglasses	75
	$2,475
Less 5% of AGI ($35,000)	1,750
Medical expense deduction for 1984	$ 725

40. (580,P3,53) (d) The requirement is to determine the total amount of deductible medical expenses for the Bensons before the application of any limitation rules. Deductible medical expenses include those incurred by a taxpayer, taxpayer's spouse, dependents of the taxpayer, or any person that a taxpayer could claim as a dependent except that the person had income of $1,000 or more, or filed a joint return. Thus, the Bensons may deduct medical expenses incurred for themselves, for John (i.e., not a dependent only because his income is $1,000 or more), and for Nancy (i.e., a dependent of the Bensons).

III.B. Taxes

41. (583,P3,51) (d) The requirement is to determine the amount of state income taxes deductible as an excess itemized deduction for 1982. The amount deductible includes the $2,000 of taxes withheld during 1982, plus the $200 assessment of 1980 tax paid in 1982. Note that the 1981 refund is **not** netted against the taxes paid in 1982.

42. (1182,P3,51) (b) The requirement is to determine Sara's deduction for state income taxes in 1981. Sara's deduction would consist of the $2,000 withheld by her employer in 1981, plus the three estimated payments (3 x $300 = $900) actually paid during 1981, a total of $2,900. Note that the 1/15/82 estimated payment would be deductible for 1982.

43. (582,P3,52) (b) The requirement is to determine the amount of **taxes** deductible as an excess itemized deduction. The $360 vehicle tax based on value is deductible. The real property tax of $2,700 must be apportioned between the Bronsons and the buyer for tax purposes even though they did not actually make an apportionment. Since the house was sold June 30, while the taxes were paid to September 30, the Bronsons would deduct 6/9 x $2,700 = $1,800. The buyer would deduct the remaining $900.

44. (582,P3,54) (d) The requirement is to determine the amount of deductible sales tax using the Optional Sales Tax Table provided. The deduction is based on:

Total available income, including nontaxable income (AGI of $31,500 plus tax-exempt interest of $1,500).

Family size based on number of exemptions claimed, including dependency exemptions.

Accordingly, the Income is $33,000, and the Family size is over 2 resulting in a maximum amount of $261.

45. (1181,Q3,56) (a) The requirement is to determine what portion of the $1,300 of realty taxes is deductible by King in 1981. The $600 of delinquent taxes charged to the seller and paid by King are not deductible, but are added to the cost of the property. The $700 of taxes deductible for 1981 are apportioned between the seller and King according to the number of days that each held the property during the year. King's deduction would be:

$$\frac{184}{365} \times \$700 = \underline{\underline{\$353}}$$

46. (581,P3,57) (b) The requirement is to determine the amount of property taxes deductible as excess itemized deductions. The property taxes on the residence and the land held for appreciation, together with the personal property taxes on the auto are deductible. The special assessment is not deductible, but would be added to the basis of the residence.

III.C. Interest Expense

47. (583,P3,50) (a) The requirement is to determine the amount of interest expense deductible as an excess itemized deduction. The $1,200 of interest on the life insurance policy loan, the $3,600 of home mortgage interest, and the $900 mortgage prepayment penalty are all deductible as interest expense in computing excess itemized deductions.

48. (582,P3,51) (b) The requirement is to determine the amount of interest deductible as an excess itemized deduction. Since 2/3 of the loan proceeds were used to purchase tax exempt bonds, 2/3 of the bank interest is nondeductible. Thus, the remaining $1,200 of bank interest, the home mortgage interest of $3,000, and the $500 interest on credit card charges are deductible as an excess itemized deduction.

49. (581,P3,41) (d) The requirement is to determine the amount of interest deductible in calculating excess itemized deductions. The $4,000 of interest on the bank loan is deductible since the proceeds were used to purchase U.S. Series H bonds which are taxable. The interest on installment charge accounts and the interest on the home mortgage also are deductible. "Points" are deductible as interest if they represent payment for the use of money. Points are fully deductible in the year paid if the loan was used to buy or improve a principal residence; otherwise, points are treated as interest paid in advance and are considered paid over the life of the mortgage.

50. (1180,Q2,30) (b) The requirement is to determine the amount deductible as investment interest expense. The deduction for investment interest is limited to $10,000 plus the amount of net investment income. Since the net investment income is $20,000 (dividends and interest of $24,000, less investment expense of $4,000), the deduction for investment interest expense is $30,000 ($20,000 + $10,000).

51. (1180,Q2,39) (b) Of the items listed relating to the tax deficiency for 1978, only the interest is deductible. The additional federal income tax, the late filing penalty, and the negligence penalty are not deductible. Therefore, only $70 relating to the tax deficiency is deductible as an itemized deduction for 1979.

III.D. Charitable Contributions

52. (583,P3,52) (b) The requirement is to determine Lewis' charitable contribution deduction. The donation of appreciated stock held more than one year is a contribution of intangible, long-term capital gain appreciated property. The amount of contribution is the stock's FMV of $70,000, but is limited in deductibility for 1982 to 30% of AGI. Thus, the 1982 deduction is $100,000 x 30% = $30,000. The amount of contribution in excess of the 30% limitation ($70,000 – $30,000 = $40,000) can be carried forward for up to 5 years, subject to the 30% limitation in the carryforward years.

53. (1182,P3,52) (b) The requirement is to determine the amount of contributions deductible in 1981. Charitable contributions are generally deductible in the year actually paid. The 12/15/81 $500 charge to his bank credit card is considered a payment, and is deductible for 1981. The $1,000 promissory note delivered 11/1/81 is not considered a contribution until payment of the note upon maturity in 1982.

54. (582,P3,53) (b) The requirement is to determine the maximum deduction for charitable contributions. The cash contribution of $2,500 and the $400 FMV of used clothing are deductible. The deduction for the art object is limited to the $300 excess of its cost ($800) over its FMV ($500).

55. (1181,Q3,45) (b) The requirement is to determine the amount of student expenses deductible as a charitable contribution. A taxpayer may deduct as a charitable contribution up to $50 per **school month** of unreimbursed expenses incurred to maintain a student (in the 12th or lower grade) in the taxpayer's home pursuant to a written agreement with a qualified organization. Since the student started school in September, the amount deductible as a charitable contribution is $50 x 4 = $200.

56. (1179,Q2,37) (a) Vincent Tally is entitled to no deduction for contributions in 1978 because he did not give up his entire interest in the book collection. By reserving the right to use and possess the book collection for his lifetime, Vincent Tally has made a gift of a future interest. Therefore, no deduction is available. The contribution will be deductible when all his interest in the books is transferred to the art museum.

III.E. Casualty and Theft Losses

57. (583,P3,54) (c) The requirement is to determine the amount of casualty loss deductible as an excess itemized deduction. Only nonbusiness casualty losses are deductible as itemized deductions. Since the car was used 25% for personal use, 25% of the insurance recovery must be subtracted from 25% of the FMV to determine the nonbusiness loss. The loss must then be reduced by the $100 **floor.**

	Personal (25%)
FMV ($10,800)	$2,700
Insurance settlement ($9,000)	(2,250)
Personal casualty loss	$ 450
Less $100 floor	(100)
Deductible casualty loss	$ 350

If the loss had occurred in 1983, the $350 loss would only be deductible to the extent in excess of 10% of Mitchell's AGI.

58. (581,P3,49) (a) The requirement is to compute the amount of casualty loss deduction. Beginning in 1983, the deduction for a nonbusiness casualty loss is computed as the lesser of (1) the adjusted basis of property, or (2) the decrease in FMV; reduced by any insurance recovery, $100, and 10% of the taxpayer's AGI.

Lesser of:		
Decrease in FMV		
($45,000 – $3,000) =	$42,000	
Adjusted basis	$39,000	$39,000
Decrease by:		
Insurance recovery		(15,000)
$100 exclusion		(100)
10% of $60,000		(6,000)
Casualty loss deduction		$17,900

59. (580,P3,54) (b) The requirement is to compute the amount of casualty loss deduction and indicate the year of deduction. Casualty losses are generally deductible only in the year in which they occur. However, where the loss is in part covered by insurance, the loss is deductible in the year in which the claim for insurance compensation is finally settled. The deductible loss must be reduced by any anticipated insurance recovery, even though payment won't be received until a later year. The amount of a nonbusiness casualty loss is the lesser of the decrease in the FMV of the property or the adjusted basis of the property. A nonbusiness casualty loss must be reduced by a $100 floor, any expected insurance recovery, and 10% of taxpayer's AGI (beginning in 1983).

Lower of basis ($6,000), or decrease in FMV ($4,200 – $2,200)	$2,000
Less expected insurance recovery	(1,500)
Less $100 per casualty	(100)
Loss deductible in year insurance claim is settled (1980)	$ 400

III.F. Miscellaneous Deductions

60. (1183,Q2,29) (c) The requirement is to determine the amount of adoption expenses deductible as an itemized deduction. Individual taxpayers may deduct up to $1,500 as an itemized deduction for qualified expenses in connection with the adoption of a "child with special needs" as defined in the Social Security Act.

61. (1181,Q3,52) (b) The requirement is to determine the amount that can be claimed as miscellaneous itemized deductions. Both the initiation fee and the union dues are fully deductible. The voluntary benefit fund contribution is not deductible.

62. (1181,Q3,55) (a) The requirement is to determine the amount allowable as miscellaneous itemized deductions for 1980. The union dues ($180) and the legal fee attributable to income tax advice (25% x $300 = $75) are deductible. The remainder of the legal fee is a personal expense and not deductible. The cost of the tools can be deducted over their useful life. $600 x 1/5 x 1/2 = $60 can be deducted in 1980.

63. (1180,Q2,38) (a) The requirement is to compute the amount of miscellaneous itemized deductions. The cost of uniforms not adaptable to general use (specialized work clothes), union dues, and the cost of income tax preparation are all miscellaneous itemized deductions. The excess of auto expense over the amount of reimbursement is always deductible **toward** AGI. The preparation of a will is personal in nature, and is not deductible. Thus, the computation of Brodsky's miscellaneous itemized deductions is as follows:

Specialized work clothes	$ 550
Union dues	600
Cost of income tax preparation	150
	$1,300

IV. Exemptions

64. (583,P3,56) (d) The requirement is to determine Robert's filing status and the number of exemptions that he should claim. Robert's father does not qualify as Robert's dependent because his father's gross income (interest income of $1,600) was not less than $1,000. Social security is not included in the gross income test. Since his father does not qualify as his dependent, Robert does not qualify for head-of-household filing status. Thus, Robert will file as single with one exemption.

65. (583,P3,57) (d) The requirement is to determine which of the brothers is eligible to claim the mother as a dependent through the use of a multiple support agreement. In the event no one person provides more than 50% of a dependent's support, any individual who contributes more than 10% is entitled to claim the exemption if each other person contributing more than 10% of the support signs a written consent not to claim the exemption. Thus, either Bill, Jon, or Tom may claim the mother as a dependent.

66. (583,P3,58) (a) The requirement is to determine the filing status of the Arnolds. Since they were legally separated under a decree of separate maintenance on the last day of the taxable year and do not qualify for head-of-household status, they must each file as single.

67. (582,P3,60) (c) The requirement is to determine the number of exemptions that can be claimed by the Ericksons. There is one exemption for Mr. Erickson and one exemption for his spouse. There is a dependency exemption for their son, and a dependency exemption for Mr. Erickson's mother. Note that a full exemption is allowed in the year of birth or death.

68. (581,P3,55) (b) Mr. and Mrs. Stoner are entitled to one exemption each, with one additional exemption for Mr. Stoner's age. They are entitled to one exemption for their daughter since they provided over 50% of her support and she was a full-time student not subject to the $1,000 gross income test. An exemption can be claimed for their son because they supported him and he made less than $1,000 in gross income. No exemption is allowable for Mrs. Stoner's father since he was neither a U.S. citizen nor resident of U.S., Canada, or Mexico.

69. (580,P3,60) (d) The requirement is to determine the number of exemptions the Planters may claim on their joint tax return. Since a taxpayer is considered to be 65 on the day before his 65th birthday, there are two exemptions for Mr. Planter, and one exemption for his spouse. In addition there is one dependency exemption for their daughter, and one dependency exemption for the niece. The dependency gross income test does not apply to their daughter since she was a full-time student for at least some part of at least 5 calendar months.

70. (1179,Q2,22) (b) The requirement is to determine the number of exemptions allowable in 1981. Mr. and Mrs. Vonce are entitled to one exemption each. They are also entitled to one exemption for their dependent daughter since they provide over one-half of her support and she had less than $1,000 of income. An additional exemption for blindness is only available if the taxpayer or spouse is blind, i.e., not available for their son because he provided over one-half of his own support.

V. Tax Computation

71. (583,P3,49) (b) Dalton's 1982 taxable income would be computed as follows:

Salary		$30,000
Less IRA contribution		(2,000)
Adjusted gross income		$28,000
Itemized deductions	$3,400	
Less ZBA	(2,300)	
Excess itemized deductions		(1,100)
Personal exemption		(1,000)
Taxable income		$25,900

V.B. Tax Rate Schedules

72. (1181,Q3,53) (c) The zero bracket amount for a taxpayer who is single or a head of household is $2,300.

73. (581,P3,44) (c) Thomson should file as a surviving spouse. A surviving spouse is taxed at the same rate as married taxpayers filing a joint return. Surviving spouse filing status is available for two taxable years after a spouse's death if a dependent child lives with the surviving spouse, the surviving spouse pays more than 50% of the costs of maintaining a household, and the surviving spouse does not marry before year end.

74. (579,Q2,21) (c) Mrs. Felton qualifies as a head of household because she is both unmarried and maintains a household for her unmarried child. The unmarried child for whom she maintains a household need not qualify as her dependent in order for Mrs. Felton to claim the head-of-household status. Answer (b) is incorrect because in order for Mrs. Felton to

qualify as a surviving spouse, her son must qualify as a dependent, which he does not. Although Mrs. Felton would have qualified as married filing jointly, answer (d), in 1977 (the year of her husband's death), the problem requirement is her 1978 status. Answer (a), single, is incorrect because although the widow is single, her circumstances make head of household her proper filing status.

V.E.3. Self-Employment Tax

75. (1182,P3,43) (b) The requirement is to determine Berger's self-employment income for 1981. Self-employment income represents the net earnings of an individual from a trade or business carried on as a proprietor or partner, or from rendering services as an independent contractor. The director's fee is self-employment income since it is related to a trade or business and Berger is not an employee. Fees received by a fiduciary (e.g., executor) are generally not related to a trade or business and not self-employment income. However, executor's fees may constitute self-employment if the executor is a professional fiduciary or carries on a trade or business in the administration of an estate.

76. (582,P3,48) (c) The requirement is to calculate Linnett's net earnings from self-employment. The gross receipts of $60,000 are reduced by the cost of sales ($30,000), other operating expenses ($6,000), and state business taxes ($600). The dividend income on personal investments is not included in earnings from self-employment, and the self-employment taxes are not deductible. Thus, the computation of Linnett's net earnings from self-employment is as follows:

Gross receipts	$60,000
Cost of sales	(30,000)
Gross margin	$30,000
Other operating expenses	(6,000)
State business taxes paid	(600)
Net self-employment earnings	$23,400

VI.A. Investment Tax Credit (ITC)

77. (1183,Q3,55) (a) Unused investment tax credit (ITC) is generally carried back 3 years and forward 15 years. Since 1982 was Orna Corporation's first taxable year, the unused ITC would be carried forward for up to 15 years.

78. (1182,Q3,57) (c) The requirement is to determine Foster's allowed investment tax credit for 1981. 100% of the cost of new 5-year ACRS property qualifies for the 10% ITC. However, the amount of credit ($180,000 x 10% = $18,000) allowed is limited to Foster's pre-credit tax liability of $15,000. The excess of $3,000 would be carried back 3 years and forward 15 years to offset tax liability in other years.

79. (582,Q3,60) (c) The requirement is to determine the amount of investment credit recapture. Each full year that ACRS property is held earns 1/5 of the ITC for 5, 10, and 15-year property. Since the drill press was 5-year property and was only held for one full year, only 1/5 of the ITC was earned, and 4/5 x $2,000 = $1,600 is recaptured.

80. (1174,P1,4) (b) The new automobile is three-year ACRS property so the qualifying investment tax credit percentage is .60. The computations for the investment tax credit are:

Trade-in	$1,500
Cash paid	3,000
Total investment	$4,500
Percentage	x .60
Qualified investment	$2,700
Investment credit rate	x .10
Investment tax credit allowed	$ 270

VI.B. Business Energy Credit

81. (582,Q3,54) (d) The requirement is to determine the total cost that will qualify for the business energy investment credit for 1981. Qualified investment in energy property is eligible for a business energy investment credit. If the energy property also qualifies for the regular investment tax credit, both credits can be taken. Since qualified energy property includes solar panels and recycling equipment, all $20,000 of cost qualifies.

VI.E. Credit for the Elderly

82. (1181,Q3,58) (b) The requirement is to determine the amount that can be claimed as a credit for the elderly. The credit is the lesser of (1) taxpayer's tax liability of $60, or (2) 15% ($3,750 – $1,250 social security) = $375.50.

VI.F. Child Care Credit

83. (1182,P3,57) (c) The requirement is to compute Nora's child care credit for 1982. Since she has two dependent preschool children, all $3,000 paid for child care qualifies for the credit. For 1982, the credit is 30% of qualified expenses, but is reduced by 1 percentage point for each $2,000 (or fraction thereof) of AGI over $10,000; down to a minimum of 20%. Since Nora's AGI is $29,000, her credit is 20% x $3,000 = $600.

84. (581,P3,59) (b) The requirement is to determine the amount of the child care credit allowable to the Jasons. The credit is from 20% to 30% of certain dependent care expenses limited to the lesser of (1) $2,400 for one qualifying individual, $4,800 for two or more; (2) taxpayer's earned income, or spouse's if smaller; or (3) actual expenses. The $1,500 paid to the Union Day Care Center qualifies, as does the $1,000 paid to Wilma Jason. Payments to relatives qualify if the relative is not a dependent of the taxpayer. Since Robert and Mary Jason only claimed three exemptions, Wilma was not their dependent. The $500 paid to Acme Home Cleaning Service does not qualify since it is **completely** unrelated to the care of their child. To qualify, expenses must be at least partly for the care of a qualifying individual. Since qualifying expenses exceed $2,400, the Jason's credit is 20% x $2,400 = $480.

VI.G. Foreign Tax Credit

85. (1181,P3,55) (c) The requirement is to determine the amount of foreign tax credit that may be claimed by Bell Corporation for 1980. The deduction of a credit for foreign income taxes is subject to an overall limit of:

$$\frac{\text{Foreign TI}}{\text{World-wide TI}} \times (\text{U.S. tax})$$

Thus, the $135,000 of foreign taxes are deductible as a credit for 1980 to the extent of:

$$\frac{\$300,000}{\$675,000} \times (\$270,000) = \underline{\underline{\$120,000}}$$

There would be a 2-year carryback and a 5-year carryover for the remaining $15,000 of foreign taxes.

VI.H. Political Contribution Credit

86. (582,P3,59) (c) The requirement is to determine the amount of political contributions credit that can be claimed on a joint return filed by the Sampsons. The political contributions credit is 50% of the contribution, limited to $50 on a single return, and $100 on a joint return.

VI.I. Earned Income Credit

87. (1181,Q3,57) (a) The requirement is to determine Alex's earned income credit for 1980. Alex is not eligible for the earned income credit because his dependent child did not live with him.

88. (1179,Q2,32) (b) The credit is 10% of the first $5,000 of earned income reduced by 12.5% of the greater of earned income ($7,000) or adjusted gross income ($7,100) in excess of $6,000.

$$\$500 - (12.5\% \times \$1,100) = \$362.50$$

VI.J. Residential Energy Credit

89. (581,P3,58) (a) The requirement is to determine the amount of residential energy credit available to the Conleys. The credit is 15% of the first $2,000 of qualified expenditures to save energy in a personal residence. Qualifying items must be new and be expected to last 3 years. The cost of the insulation ($750) and the automatic setback thermostat ($150) qualify. The aluminum siding does not qualify. The storm windows do not qualify because they were already "used" when purchased.

VII.B. Assessments

90. (583,P3,55) (d) A six-year statute of limitations applies if gross income omitted from the return exceeds 25% of the gross income reported on the return. For this purpose, gross income of a business includes total gross receipts before subtracting cost of goods sold and deductions. Thus, a six-year statute of limitations will apply to Thompson if he omitted from gross income an amount in excess of ($400,000 + $36,000) x 25% = $109,000.

91. (1182,P3,60) (d) The requirement is to determine the date by which the IRS must assert a notice of deficiency. The normal period for assessment is 3 years after the return is filed, or 3 years after the due date, whichever is later. However, since gross income omitted from the return ($6,000) exceeds 25% of the gross income stated on the return (25% x $20,000 = $5,000), the normal 3-year period is extended to 6 years (i.e., extended to 4/15/88).

May 1984 Answers

92. (584,Q2,21) (c) The requirement is to determine the loss that Cook can claim as a result of the worthless note receivable in 1984. Cook's $1,000 loss will be treated as a nonbusiness bad debt, deductible as a short-term capital loss. The loss is **not** a business bad debt because Cook was not in the business of lending money, nor was the loan required as a condition of Cook's employment. Since Cook owned no stock in Precision, the loss could **not** be deemed to be a loss from worthless stock, deductible as a long-term capital loss.

93. (584,Q2,22) (c) The requirement is to determine Laura's filing status for 1983. Laura is not considered married because she was legally separated from her husband. However, Laura does qualify as unmarried head of household because she is considered unmarried and provides more than half the cost of keeping up a household that was the principal home of her unmarried child.

94. (584,Q2,23) (a) The requirement is to determine the amount of alimony includible in Laura's 1983 taxable income. If both alimony and child support payments are called for by a separation agreement but less is paid than required by the agreement, then payments are applied first to child support and then to alimony. Since Laura received a total of only $300 during 1983, the $300 would be treated as child support and excluded from Laura's income.

95. (584,Q2,24) (d) The requirement is to determine the amount of interest includible in taxable income. Both the $100 interest on insurance dividends left on deposit with a life insurance company and the $60 interest on the federal income tax refund are includible in income.

96. (584,Q2,25) (a) The requirement is to determine the amount of income to be reported from the receipt of the gift of Liba stock. Property received as a gift is always excluded from gross income.

97. (584,Q2,29) (d) The requirement is to determine the amount that Roger can deduct for the $2,000 contribution to his individual retirement account (IRA). Any taxpayer (even if a participant in a qualified pension plan) may contribute to an IRA. For a single taxpayer, contributions are deductible up to the lesser of (1) $2,000, or (2) 100% of compensation.

98. (584,Q2,30) (a) The requirement is to determine the amount that Roger can deduct for medical and dental expenses in 1983. The dental expenses and medical insurance premiums are not deductible since their total does not exceed 5% of AGI:

Dental expenses	$ 700
Medical insurance premiums	500
	$1,200
Less 5% of AGI ($60,000)	−3,000
Amount deductible	$ 0

99. (584,Q2,31) (a) The requirement is to determine the amount that Roger can deduct in 1983 for taxes. Roger's real estate taxes of $4,000 are deductible. Roger cannot deduct the customs duties and city dog license fee since they are only deductible if incurred in a trade or business or in the production of income.

100. (584,Q2,32) (a) The requirement is to determine the amount that Roger can deduct for miscellaneous deductions. None of the items listed are deductible as miscellaneous deductions. The life insurance premiums and the legal fee for preparation of Roger's will are considered personal expenses and not deductible.

101. (584,Q2,33) (a) The requirement is to determine the amount that Roger can deduct as a casualty loss for 1983. Beginning in 1983, nonbusiness casualty and theft losses are deductible only to the extent the total amount of such losses (after reduction for the $100 floor for each loss) exceeds 10% of the taxpayer's AGI. Roger's casualty loss of $400 is not deductible because it, less the $100 floor, does not exceed 10% of Roger's AGI.

102. (584,Q2,34) (b) The requirement is to determine the amount of tax credit for Roger's $300 contribution to a candidate for public office. A taxpayer may take a credit equal to 50% of political contributions limited to $50 ($100 on a joint return). Roger's political contribution credit is limited to $50.

103. (584,Q2,35) (b) The requirement is to determine how the $1,500 interest forfeiture penalty should be reported. An interest forfeiture penalty for making a premature withdrawal from a time savings account should be deducted from gross income in arriving at adjusted gross income in the year in which the penalty is incurred.

104. (584,Q2,36) (d) The requirement is to determine John and Emma's filing status for 1983. If a taxpayer's spouse dies during the year, the taxpayer is considered married for the entire year. If the taxpayer does not remarry before the end of the tax year, the taxpayer may file a joint return with the deceased spouse.

105. (584,Q2,37) (b) The requirement is to determine the amount of taxable interest received in 1983. Interest from state and municipal bonds is excluded from gross income. The fair market value of gifts or services received for making long-term deposits or for opening an account in a savings institution is treated as interest income when received. Thus, the $1,000 of municipal bond interest is excluded, while the $300 television set is reported as taxable interest for 1983.

106. (584,Q2,38) (d) The requirement is to determine the amount of life insurance proceeds to be excluded from taxable income. Life insurance proceeds paid by reason of death are fully excluded from taxable income regardless of the amount paid.

107. (584,Q2,39) (c) The requirement is to determine the amount of employee death benefit to be excluded from taxable income. Up to $5,000 of an employee's death benefit can be excluded from a beneficiary's taxable income.

Multiple Choice Questions (1 - 36)

1. In January 1979, Melvin Axel bought 100 shares of a listed stock for $4,000. In March 1980, when the fair market value was $3,000, Melvin gave this stock to his cousin, Ellen. No gift tax was paid. Ellen sold this stock in June 1982 for $3,500. How much is Ellen's reportable gain or loss in 1982 on the sale of this stock?

a. $0.
b. $ 500 loss.
c. $ 500 gain.
d. $3,500 gain.

2. On January 10, 1970, Martin Mayne bought 3,000 shares of Hance Corporation stock for $300,000. The fair market values of this stock on the following dates were as follows:

Dec. 31, 1980	$210,000
Mar. 31, 1981	240,000
June 30, 1981	270,000

Martin died on December 31, 1980, bequeathing this stock to his son, Philip. The stock was distributed to Philip on March 31, 1981. The alternate valuation date was elected for Martin's estate. Philip's basis for this stock is

a. $210,000
b. $240,000
c. $270,000
d. $300,000

3. Martin Rowe died on January 5, 1982, bequeathing his entire $1,000,000 estate to his brother, Art. The alternate valuation date was elected by the executor of Martin's estate, and the estate tax return was timely filed. Martin's estate included 1,000 shares of a listed stock for which Martin's basis was $190,000. This stock was distributed to Art nine months after Martin's death. Fair market values of this stock were as follows:

As of the date of Martin's death	$200,000
Six months after Martin's death	225,000
Nine months after Martin's death	240,000

What is Art's basis for this stock?

a. $190,000
b. $200,000
c. $225,000
d. $240,000

4. On July 1, 1978, William Greene paid $45,000 for 450 shares of Acme Corporation common stock. Greene received a nontaxable stock dividend of 50 new common shares in December 1979. On December 15, 1981, Greene sold the 50 new shares of common stock for $5,500. In respect of this sale Greene should report on his 1981 tax return

a. No gain or loss since the stock dividend was nontaxable.
b. $500 of long-term capital gain before capital gain deduction.
c. $1,000 of long-term capital gain before capital gain deduction.
d. $5,500 of long-term capital gain before capital gain deduction.

5. On January 5, 1979, Norman Harris purchased for $6,000, 100 shares of Campbell Corporation common stock. On July 8, 1979, he received a nontaxable stock dividend of 10 shares of Campbell Corporation $100 par value preferred stock. On that date, the market values per share of the common and preferred stock were $75 and $150, respectively. Harris's tax basis for the common stock after the receipt of the dividend is

a. $2,000
b. $4,500
c. $5,000
d. $6,000

6. Stanley Garret purchased 1,000 shares of Pat Corporation common stock at $5 per share in 1972. On September 19, 1975, he received 1,000 stock rights entitling him to buy 250 additional shares of Pat Corporation common stock at $10 per share. On the day that the rights were issued, the fair market value of the stock was $12 per share ex-rights and that of the rights was $1 each. Garret did not exercise the rights; he let them expire on November 28, 1975.

What should be the loss that Garret can report for 1975?

a. A long-term capital loss of $250.
b. A short-term capital loss of $250.
c. A long-term capital loss of $1,000.
d. A short-term capital loss of $1,000.
e. None of the above.

7. On July 1, 1982, Riley exchanged investment real property, with an adjusted basis of $160,000 and subject to a mortgage of $70,000, and received from Wilson $30,000 cash and other investment real property having a fair market value of $250,000. Wilson assumed the mortgage. What is Riley's recognized gain in 1982 on the exchange?

a. $ 30,000
b. $ 70,000
c. $ 90,000
d. $100,000

8. On October 1, 1981, Donald Anderson exchanged an apartment building, having an adjusted basis of $375,000 and subject to a mortgage of $100,000, for $25,000 cash and another apartment building with a fair market value of $550,000 and subject to a mortgage of $125,000. The property transfers were made subject to the outstanding mortgages. What amount of gain should Anderson recognize in his tax return for 1981?

a. $0
b. $ 25,000
c. $125,000
d. $175,000

9. James Harper, a self-employed individual, owned a truck driven exclusively for business use. The truck had an original cost of $8,000 and had an adjusted basis on December 31, 1980, of $3,600. On January 2, 1981, he traded it in for a new truck costing $10,000 and was given a trade-in allowance of $2,000. The new truck will also be used exclusively for business purposes and will be depreciated with no salvage value. The basis of the new truck is

a. $ 8,000
b. $ 8,400
c. $10,000
d. $11,600

10. Joseph Kurtz exchanged land that he held for four years as an investment, with a tax basis of $36,000, for similar land valued at $40,000 which was owned by Adrian Flemming. In connection with this transaction, Kurtz assumed Flemming's $10,000 mortgage and Flemming assumed Kurtz's $12,000 mortgage. As a result of this transaction Kurtz should report a long-term capital gain of

a. $0
b. $2,000
c. $4,000
d. $6,000

11. An office building owned by Elmer Bass was condemned by the state on January 2, 1982. Bass received the condemnation award on March 1, 1983. In order to qualify for nonrecognition of gain on this involuntary conversion, what is the last date for Bass to acquire qualified replacement property?

a. August 1, 1984.
b. January 2, 1985.
c. March 1, 1986.
d. December 31, 1986.

12. On January 8, 1982, Sam Meyer, age 62, sold for $210,000 his personal residence which had an adjusted basis of $60,000. On May 1, 1982, he purchased a new residence for $80,000. Meyer elected the exclusion of realized gain available to taxpayers over age 55.

For 1982, Meyer should recognize a gain on the sale of his residence of

a. $0
b. $ 5,000
c. $ 30,000
d. $130,000

13. On March 10, 1975, James Rogers sold 300 shares of Red Company common stock for $4,200. Rogers acquired the stock in 1972 at a cost of $5,000.

On April 4, 1975, he repurchased 300 shares of Red Company common stock for $3,600 and held them until July 18, 1975, when he sold them for $6,000.

How should Rogers report the above transactions for 1975?

a. A long-term capital loss of $800.
b. A long-term capital gain of $1,000.
c. A long-term capital gain of $1,600.
d. A long-term capital loss of $800 and a short-term capital gain of $2,400.

14. Murd Corporation, a domestic corporation, acquired a 90% interest in the Drum Company in 1971 for $30,000. During 1974, the stock of Drum was declared worthless. What type and amount of deduction should Murd take for 1974?

a. Long-term capital loss of $1,000.
b. Long-term capital loss of $15,000.
c. Ordinary loss of $30,000.
d. Long-term capital loss of $30,000.

15. On July 1, 1982, Daniel Wright owned stock (held for investment) purchased two years earlier at a cost of $10,000 and having a fair market value of $7,000. On this date he sold the stock to his son, William, for $7,000. William sold the stock for $6,000 to an unrelated person on November 1, 1982. How should William report the stock sale (before any deduction) on his 1982 tax return?

a. As a short-term capital loss of $1,000.
b. As a long-term capital loss of $1,000.
c. As a short-term capital loss of $4,000.
d. As a long-term capital loss of $4,000.

16. On January 1, 1977, Hubert Toast sold stock with a cost of $4,000 to his sister Melba for $3,500, its fair market value. On July 30, 1977, Melba sold the same stock for $4,100 to a friend, in a bona fide transaction. In 1977 as a result of these transactions

a. Neither Hubert nor Melba has a recognized gain or loss.
b. Hubert has a recognized loss of $500.
c. Melba has a recognized gain of $100.
d. Melba has a recognized gain of $600.

17. Jerry owns 60% of the outstanding stock of Mitch Corporation. During 1973, Jerry sold Mitch a machine for $60,000 that had an adjusted tax basis of $68,000. For tax purposes, what should Jerry report for 1973?

a. $0 recognized loss.
b. $8,000 ordinary loss.
c. $8,000 Section 1231 loss.
d. $8,000 capital loss.

18. For the year 1982 Diana Clark had salary income of $38,000. In addition, she had the following capital transactions during the year:

Long-term capital gain	$14,000
Short-term capital gain	6,000
Long-term capital loss	(4,000)
Short-term capital loss	(8,000)

There were no other items includible in her gross income. What is her adjusted gross income for 1982?

a. $38,000
b. $41,200
c. $42,800
d. $46,000

19. Paul Beyer, who is unmarried, has taxable income of $30,000 exclusive of capital gains and losses and his personal exemption. In 1980, Paul incurred a $1,000 net short-term capital loss and a $5,000 net long-term capital loss. His long-term capital loss carryover to 1981 is

a. $0
b. $1,000
c. $2,500
d. $5,000

20. Alan Kupper had the following transactions during 1980:

- Gain of $7,000 on sale of common stock purchased on June 15, 1978, and sold on April 15, 1980.
- Gain of $5,000 on sale of common stock purchased on October 15, 1979, and sold on July 25, 1980.
- Receipt of a $10,000 installment payment on an installment contract created in 1977 when Kupper sold for $100,000 (exclusive of 6% interest on installments) land acquired in 1975 for $20,000.

The contract provides for ten equal annual principal payments of $10,000 beginning on July 1, 1977, and ending on July 1, 1986.

What is the taxable amount of Kupper's long-term capital gain for 1980?

a. $8,000
b. $7,500
c. $6,800
d. $6,000

21. Wonder Inc., had 1979 taxable income of $200,000 exclusive of the following:

Gain on sale of land used in business	$25,000
Loss on sale of machinery used in business	(13,000)
Loss on sale of securities held three years	(4,000)
Loss on sale of securities held three months	(3,000)

Wonder uses the regular method for computing its federal income tax. On what amount of taxable income should this tax be computed?

a. $200,000
b. $202,500
c. $205,000
d. $212,000

22. In 1981 Studley Corporation, not a dealer in securities, realized taxable income of $80,000 from the operation of its business. Additionally in 1981, Studley realized a long-term capital loss of $12,000 from the sale of marketable securities. Studley did not realize any other capital gains or losses since it began operations. What is the proper treatment for the $12,000 long-term capital loss in Studley's income tax returns?

a. Use $3,000 of the loss to reduce taxable income for 1981, and carry $9,000 of the long-term capital loss forward five years.
b. Use $6,000 of the loss to reduce taxable income by $3,000 for 1981, and carry $6,000 of the long-term capital loss forward five years.
c. Use $12,000 of the long-term capital loss to reduce taxable income by $6,000 for 1981.
d. Carry the $12,000 long-term capital loss forward five years, treating it as a short-term capital loss.

23. Don Mott was the sole proprietor of a high-volume drug store which he owned for 15 years before he sold it to Dale Drug Stores, Inc., in 1982. Besides the $900,000 selling price for the store's tangible assets and goodwill, Mott received a lump sum of $30,000 in 1982 for his agreement not to operate a competing

enterprise within ten miles of the store's location, for a period of six years. The $30,000 will be taxed to Mott as

a. $30,000 ordinary income in 1982.
b. $30,000 short-term capital gain in 1982.
c. $30,000 long-term capital gain in 1982.
d. Ordinary income of $5,000 a year for six years.

24. In June 1982, Olive Bell bought a house for use partially as a residence and partially for operation of a retail gift shop. In addition, Olive bought the following furniture:

Kitchen set and living room pieces for the residential portion	$ 8,000
Showcases and tables for the business portion	12,000

How much of this furniture comprises capital assets?

a. $0
b. $ 8,000
c. $12,000
d. $20,000

25. The following assets were among those owned by Yolanda Corporation at December 31, 1982:

Delivery truck	$12,000
Land used as parking lot for customers	20,000

The capital assets amount to

a. $0
b. $12,000
c. $20,000
d. $32,000

26. On December 31, 1980, Day Corporation sold machinery for $48,000. The machinery which had been purchased on January 1, 1976, for $40,000 had an adjusted basis of $28,000 on the date of sale. For 1980 Day should report

a. Ordinary income of $20,000.
b. Section 1231 gain of $20,000.
c. Section 1231 gain of $12,000 and ordinary income of $8,000.
d. Section 1231 gain of $8,000 and ordinary income of $12,000.

27. Thayer Corporation purchased an apartment building on January 1, 1980, for $200,000. The building was depreciated on the straight-line basis. On December 31, 1983, the building was sold for $220,000, when the asset balance net of accumulated depreciation was $170,000. On its 1983 tax return, Thayer should report

a. Section 1231 gain of $42,500 and ordinary income of $7,500.
b. Section 1231 gain of $45,500 and ordinary income of $4,500.
c. Ordinary income of $50,000.
d. Section 1231 gain of $50,000.

28. For the year ended December 31, 1979, Murray Corporation, a calendar-year corporation, reported book income before income taxes of $120,000. Included in the determination of this amount were the following items:

Loss on sale of building depreciated on the straight-line method	($12,000)
Gain on sale of land used in business	7,000
Loss on sale of investments in marketable securities (long-term)	(8,000)

For the year ended December 31, 1979, Murray's taxable income was

a. $113,000
b. $120,000
c. $125,000
d. $128,000

29. David Price owned machinery which he had acquired in 1972 at a cost of $100,000. During 1975, the machinery was destroyed by fire. At that time it had an adjusted basis of $86,000. The insurance proceeds awarded to Price amounted to $125,000, and he immediately acquired a similar machine for $110,000.

What should Price report as ordinary income resulting from the involuntary conversion for 1975?

a. $14,000
b. $15,000
c. $25,000
d. $39,000

May 1984 Questions

30. Rose Budd owns 55% of the outstanding stock of Kee Corp. During 1983 Kee sold a machine to Rose for $80,000. This machine had an adjusted tax basis of $92,000 and had been owned by Kee for three years. What is the allowable loss that Kee can claim in its 1983 income tax return?

a. $12,000 Section 1245 loss.
b. $12,000 Section 1231 loss.
c. $12,000 ordinary loss.
d. $0.

31. Arch Corp. sold machinery for $80,000 on December 31, 1983. This machinery was purchased on January 2, 1979, for $68,000 and had an adjusted basis of $40,000 at the date of sale. For 1983 Arch should report

a. Ordinary income of $12,000 and Section 1231 gain of $28,000.
b. Ordinary income of $28,000 and Section 1231 gain of $12,000.
c. Ordinary income of $40,000.
d. Section 1231 gain of $40,000.

32. The following accounts are among those appearing on the books of Nilon, Inc.:

Goodwill	$1,000
Treasury stock, at cost	5,000

The capital assets amount to

a. $6,000
b. $5,000
c. $1,000
d. $0

Items 33 through 35 are based on the following data:

Laura's father, Albert, gave Laura a gift of 500 shares of Liba Corporation common stock in 1983. Albert's basis for the Liba stock was $4,000. At the date of this gift, the fair market value of the Liba stock was $3,000.

These facts and the following three questions were part of a larger set of facts which was followed by seven multiple choice questions. We have included the other information and the four multiple choice questions which pertain to it in Module 40, Individual Taxation.

33. If Laura sells the 500 shares of Liba stock in 1984 for $5,000, her basis is

a. $5,000
b. $4,000
c. $3,000
d. $0

34. If Laura sells the 500 shares of Liba stock in 1984 for $2,000, her basis is

a. $4,000
b. $3,000
c. $2,000
d. $0

35. If Laura sells the 500 shares of Liba stock in 1984 for $3,500, what is the reportable gain or loss in 1984 before the long-term capital gain deduction?

a. $3,500 gain.
b. $ 500 gain.
c. $ 500 loss.
d. $0.

A month before John died, John and Emma sold their house for $225,000. They had lived in this house since 1970 and held the property as tenants by the entirety. Their basis for this property was $100,000. No replacement property was purchased, and Emma does not intend to buy another residence.

These facts and the following question were part of a larger set of facts which was followed originally by five multiple choice questions. We have included the other information and the four multiple choice questions which pertain to it in Module 40, Individual Taxation.

36. How much of the gain on the sale of the residence should be excluded from 1983 taxable income?

a. $125,000
b. $100,000
c. $ 75,000
d. $0

Multiple Choice Answers

1. a	9. d	16. c	23. a	30. d
2. b	10. b	17. a	24. b	31. b
3. c	11. d	18. b	25. a	32. c
4. c	12. b	19. b	26. d	33. b
5. c	13. c	20. d	27. b	34. b
6. e	14. c	21. c	28. d	35. d
7. d	15. a	22. d	29. a	36. a
8. b				

Multiple Choice Answer Explanations

A.1.b. Gift

1. (1183,Q2,28) (a) The requirement is to determine Ellen's reportable gain (loss) from the sale of stock received as a gift. There is no gain (loss) to be reported since the sale price ($3,500) is less than the basis for gain ($4,000), and more than the basis for loss ($3,000).

A.1.c. Acquired from Decedent

2. (1182,P3,59) (b) The requirement is to determine the basis of stock acquired from a decedent. Since the alternate valuation date (6/30/81) was elected for Martin's estate but the property was distributed to Philip before that date, Philip's basis is the $240,000 FMV of the stock on date of distribution (3/31/81).

3. (1183,Q2,27) (c) The requirement is to determine Art's basis for the stock inherited from Rowe. The basis of property received from a decedent is generally the property's FMV at date of the decedent's death, or FMV on the alternate valuation date (6 months after death). Since the executor of Rowe's estate elected to use the alternate valuation date for estate tax purposes, the stock's basis to Art is its $225,000 FMV six months after Martin's death.

A.1.d. Stock Received as a Dividend

4. (582,P3,42) (c) The requirement is to determine the amount of gain to be reported from the sale of stock that was received as a **nontaxable** stock dividend. After the stock dividend, the basis of each share is determined as follows:

$$\left(\begin{array}{c}\text{New}\\ \text{basis}\\ \text{per share}\end{array}\right)=\frac{\text{Basis}}{\text{Shares}\left(\begin{array}{c}\text{current}\\ \text{shares}\end{array}+\begin{array}{c}\text{shrs. received}\\ \text{as stock}\\ \text{dividend}\end{array}\right)}=\frac{\$45{,}000}{450+50}=\left(\begin{array}{c}\$90\\ \text{per}\\ \text{share}\end{array}\right)$$

Since the holding period of the new shares includes the holding period of the old shares, the sale of the new shares for $5,500 results in a LTCG of $1,000 [$5,500 – (50 x $90)].

5. (1180,Q2,22) (c) The requirement is to establish Harris' tax basis of the common stock **after** receipt of a nontaxable preferred stock dividend. Harris' original common stock basis must be allocated between the preferred and common stock according to relative market values:

Common stock	
Market value = $ 75 x 100 shares =	$7,500
Preferred stock	
Market value = $150 x 10 shares =	1,500
Total value	$9,000

The ratio of the common stock to total value is 7,500/9,000 or 5/6. This ratio multiplied by the original common stock basis of $6,000, results in a basis for the common stock of $5,000. Note that the basis of the preferred stock is 1/6 x $6,000 = $1,000.

6. (576,Q2,18) (e) If nontaxable stock rights are received and allowed to expire, they are considered to have no basis; and thus no loss is recognized.

A.4.a. Like-Kind Exchange

7. (583,P3,47) (d) The requirement is to determine the amount of recognized gain resulting from a like-kind exchange of investment property. In a like-kind exchange, gain is recognized to the extent of the lesser of (1) "boot" received, or (2) gain realized.

FMV of property received	$250,000
Cash received	30,000
Mortgage assumed	70,000
Amount realized	$350,000
Basis of property exchanged	(160,000)
Gain realized	$190,000

Since the "boot" received includes both the cash and the assumption of the mortgage, gain is recognized to the extent of the $100,000 of "boot" received.

8. (582,P3,56) (b) The requirement is to determine the amount of gain recognized to Anderson on the like-kind exchange of apartment buildings. Anderson's realized gain is computed as follows:

FMV of building received		$550,000
Mortgage on old building		100,000
Cash received		25,000
Total consideration received		$675,000
Less:		
Basis of old building	$375,000	
Mortgage on new building	125,000	
		500,000
Realized gain		$175,000

Since the boot received in the form of cash cannot be offset against boot given in the form of an assumption of a mortgage, the realized gain is recognized to the extent of the $25,000 cash received.

9. (582,P3,41) (d) The requirement is to determine the basis of a truck acquired in a like-kind exchange. The basis of the new truck is the adjusted basis of the old truck of $3,600 plus the additional cash paid of $8,000 ($10,000 – $2,000), a total of $11,600.

10. (1179,Q2,27) (b) The requirement is to determine the gain to be recognized on exchange of like-kind property subject to a mortgage. The exchange of property, held for productive use or investment, for property of a like-kind is a tax-free exchange. However, to the extent boot is received, gain is recognized. Boot is cash or other property, including the assumption of a mortgage. If both properties exchanged are subject to mortgages, these mortgages are netted. Since Kurtz was relieved of a $12,000 mortgage and took a $10,000 mortgage, he will recognize gain of $2,000.

11. (1183,Q2,39) (d) The requirement is to determine the end of the replacement period for nonrecognition of gain following the condemnation of real property. For a condemnation of real property held for productive use in a trade or business or for investment, the replacement period ends three years after the close of the taxable year in which the gain is first realized. Since the gain was realized in 1983, the replacement period ends December 31, 1986.

A.4.c. Sale or Exchange of Residence

12. (1180,Q2,23) (b) Taxpayers age 55 or older may make a once in a lifetime election to exclude up to $125,000 of the realized gain on the sale of a principal residence. Deducting the excluded gain of $125,000 from the selling price of $210,000 results in an adjusted selling price of $85,000. Reinvesting $80,000 in the new residence leaves $5,000 to be recognized as gain.

A.5. Sales and Exchanges of Securities

13. (576,Q2,16) (c) The purchase of substantially identical stock within 30 days of the sale of stock at a loss is known as a wash sale. The $800 loss incurred in the wash sale ($5,000 basis less $4,200 amount realized) is disallowed. The basis of the replacement (substantially identical) stock is its cost ($3,600) plus the disallowed wash sale loss ($800). The holding period of the replacement stock includes the holding period of the wash sale stock. The amount realized ($6,000) less the basis ($4,400) yields a long-term gain of $1,600.

14. (1175,Q2,19) (c) Worthless securities generally receive capital loss treatment. However, if the loss is incurred by a corporation on its investment in an affiliated corporation (80% or more ownership), the loss is treated as an ordinary loss.

A.6. Losses, Expenses, and Interest Between Related Taxpayers

15. (583,P3,48) (a) Losses are disallowed on sales between related parties, including family members. Thus, Daniel's loss of $3,000 is disallowed on the sale of stock to his son, William. William's basis for the stock is his $7,000 cost. Since William's stock basis is determined by his cost (not by reference to Daniel's cost), there is no "tack-on" of Daniel's holding period. Thus, a later sale of the stock for $6,000 on November 1 generates a $1,000 STCL for William.

16. (578,Q2,20) (c) Losses are disallowed on sales between related parties (including members of a family). Therefore, Hubert does not recognize the $500 loss on the sale to Melba. On the subsequent sale by Melba, the gain is recognized only to the extent it exceeds the previously disallowed loss of $500. Therefore, Melba only recognizes a gain of $100 ($600 gain less $500 previously disallowed loss).

17. (1174,P1,10) (a) No loss is allowed on transactions between an individual and a corporation if the individual owns more than 50% of the corporation's stock.

B. Capital Gains and Losses

18. (583,P3,44) (b) Clark's adjusted gross income would be computed as follows:

Salary income			$38,000
LTCG	$14,000		
LTCL	(4,000)		
NLTCG		$10,000	
STCG	$6,000		
STCL	(8,000)		
NSTCL		(2,000)	
NLTCG–NSTCL		$8,000	
Less 60% capital gain deduction		(4,800)	3,200
Adjusted gross income			$41,200

19. (1181,Q3,41) (b) The requirement is to determine the amount of long-term capital loss carryover to 1981. A net capital loss is deducted from ordinary income up to a maximum of $3,000. STCLs reduce ordinary income dollar-for-dollar and are applied first. It then takes $2 of LTCL to reduce ordinary income by $1. Beyer's $1,000 STCL is deducted first, then it takes $4,000 of his $5,000 LTCL to bring the deduction up to $3,000. This leaves a $1,000 LTCL to carryover to 1981.

20. (581,P3,51) (d) The requirement is to compute the taxable amount of LTCG. The $7,000 gain is a LTCG since the stock was held more than 1 year. The $5,000 gain on sale of stock held 9 months is a STCG. Since the gross profit on the installment sale of land held more than 1 year is $80,000 and the payments to be received total $100,000, $80,000/$100,000 or 80% of the $10,000 installment received in the current year is a LTCG. The taxable LTCG is:

NLTCG	$15,000
Less 60% of NLTCG – NSTCL (60% x $15,000)	(9,000)
Taxable LTCG	$ 6,000

Of course the taxpayer would also report the STCG of $5,000.

21. (1176,Q2,24) (c) Under the regular method of corporate tax computation, net capital gain is included in taxable income on which the corporate tax is computed. Wonder has a net capital gain of $5,000 which consists of a Section 1231 gain of $12,000 ($25,000 – $13,000), a long-term capital loss of $4,000, and a short-term capital loss of $3,000. Therefore, the amount of taxable income under the regular method is $205,000 ($200,000 plus $5,000). The alternative method is computed by adding 28% of the net capital gain ($5,000) to the corporate tax on taxable income exclusive of the net capital gain ($200,000).

22. (1182,Q3,43) (d) The requirement is to determine the proper treatment for a $12,000 NLTCL for Studley Corporation. A corporation's net capital loss is not currently deductible, but is generally carried back 3 years and forward 5 years as a STCL to offset capital gains in those years. Since Studley had not realized any capital gains since it began operations, the $12,000 LTCL can only be carried forward for 5 years as a STCL.

B.1. Capital Assets

23. (1183,Q2,21) (a) The requirement is to determine how a lump sum of $30,000 received in 1982, for an agreement not to operate a competing enterprise, should be treated. A **covenant not to compete** is not a capital asset. Thus, the $30,000 received as consideration for such an agreement must be reported as ordinary income in the year received.

24. (1183,Q2,33) (b) The requirement is to determine the amount of furniture classified as capital assets. The definition of capital assets includes investment property and property held for personal use (e.g., kitchen and living room pieces), but excludes property used in a trade or business (e.g., showcases and tables).

25. (583,Q3,50) (a) The requirement is to determine the amount of capital assets owned by the Yolanda Corporation. The term **capital assets** means assets held for investment purposes. All property that is used in the conduct of a trade or business is specifically excluded from the definition of capital assets. Thus, the delivery truck and the land used as a parking lot for customers are not capital assets.

C. Gains and Losses on Business Property

26. (1181,P3,57) (d) The requirement is to determine the nature and amount of gain from the sale of machinery to be reported by Day Corporation. Since the sale of machinery is subject to Sec. 1245 recapture, Day's realized gain of $20,000 ($48,000 – $28,000) is treated as ordinary income to the extent of the depreciation deducted of $12,000 ($40,000 – $28,000). The remaining $8,000 ($20,000 – $12,000) is Sec. 1231 gain.

27. (1180,P3,44) (b) The requirement is to determine the proper treatment of the $50,000 gain on the sale of the building, which is Sec. 1250 property. Sec. 1250 recaptures gain as ordinary income to the extent of "excess" depreciation (i.e., depreciation deducted in excess of straight-line). The total gain less any depreciation recapture is Sec. 1231 gain. Since straight-line depreciation was used, there is no Sec. 1250 recapture. However, beginning in 1983, Sec. 291 requires that the ordinary income element on the disposition of Sec. 1250 property by corporations *be increased by 15% of the additional amount that would have been ordinary income if the property had been Sec. 1245 property*. Thus, the ordinary income is $30,000 x 15% = $4,500. The remaining $45,000 is Sec. 1231 gain.

28. (580,Q2,32) (d) The requirement is to determine Murray Corporation's TI given book income plus additional information. The gain on sale of land ($7,000) and loss on sale of building ($12,000) are Sec. 1231 gains and losses. The resulting Sec. 1231 net loss of $5,000 is an ordinary tax deduction which has already been deducted in computing book income of $120,000. The loss on sale of investments results in a net capital loss which is not deductible for 1979 (carryback 3 and forward 5 years to offset capital gains in other years).

Book income before taxes	$120,000
Add back net capital loss	+ 8,000
Taxable income	$128,000

29. (576,Q2,26) (a) The realized gain resulting from the involuntary conversion ($125,000 insurance proceeds – $86,000 adjusted basis = $39,000) is recognized only to the extent that the insurance proceeds are not reinvested in similar property ($125,000 – $110,000 = $15,000). Since the machinery was Sec. 1245 property, the recognized gain of $15,000 is recaptured as ordinary income to the extent of the $14,000 of depreciation previously deducted. The remaining $1,000 is Sec. 1231 gain.

May 1984 Answers

30. (584,Q1,3) (d) The requirement is to determine the allowable loss on a property transaction between a corporation and a 55% shareholder. A loss is disallowed if it results from a transaction between a corporation and a person who owns **more than** 50% of its stock.

31. (584,Q1,5) (b) The requirement is to determine the proper treatment of the $40,000 gain on the sale of the machinery. Since the machinery is subject to Sec. 1245 recapture, gain will be treated as ordinary income to the extent of all depreciation deducted.

Selling price		$80,000
Cost	$68,000	
Depreciation	–28,000	
Adjusted basis		40,000
Recognized gain		$40,000
Sec. 1245 ordinary income		–28,000
Sec. 1231 gain		$12,000

32. (584,Q1,7) (c) The requirement is to determine the amount of capital assets. The definition of capital assets includes goodwill. Treasury stock is not considered an asset but is treated as a reduction of stockholder's equity.

33. (584,Q2,26) (b) The requirement is to determine the basis of the Liba stock if it is sold for $5,000. If property acquired by gift is sold at a gain, its basis is the donor's basis ($4,000), increased by any gift tax paid attributable to the net appreciation in value of the gift ($0).

34. (584,Q2,27) (b) The requirement is to determine the basis of the Liba stock if it is sold for $2,000. If property acquired by gift is sold at a loss, its basis is the lesser of (1) its gain basis ($4,000 above), or (2) its FMV at date of gift ($3,000).

35. (584,Q2,28) (d) The requirement is to determine the amount of reportable gain or loss if the Liba stock is sold for $3,500. No gain or loss is recognized on the sale of property acquired by gift if the basis for loss ($3,000 above) results in a gain and the basis for gain ($4,000 above) results in a loss.

36. (584,Q2,40) (a) The requirement is to determine the amount of the $125,000 realized gain on sale of the residence that can be excluded from taxable income. Taxpayers age 55 or older may make a once-in-a-lifetime election to exclude from income up to $125,000 of the gain on a sale of a principal residence. To qualify, a taxpayer must have owned and occupied the residence for at least 3 of the 5 years ending at date of sale.

Multiple Choice Questions (1 - 28)

1. Harry Arch, an attorney, rendered legal services in organizing an oil and gas partnership in 1983. Instead of submitting a bill for his services, Arch accepted a 10% interest in the partnership. Arch's normal charge for the services performed would have been $10,000. The fair market value of the 10% interest received by Arch was $12,000. How much should Arch report on his 1983 income tax return?

a. $12,000
b. $10,000
c. $ 2,000
d. $0

2. On July 1, 1982, Clark acquired a 20% interest in the partnership of Davis & Denny, by contributing a parcel of land for which his basis was $8,000. At July 1, 1982, the land had a fair market value of $20,000 and was subject to a mortgage of $4,000. Payment of the mortgage was assumed by the partnership. The basis of Clark's interest in the partnership is

a. $ 4,000
b. $ 4,800
c. $16,000
d. $16,800

3. On July 1, 1981, Bertram Bryant acquired a 30% interest in Windward Company, a partnership, by contributing property with an adjusted basis of $5,000 and a fair market value of $12,000. The property was subject to a mortgage of $8,000, which was assumed by Windward. What is Bryant's basis of his interest in Windward?

a. $0
b. $4,000
c. $5,000
d. $6,400

4. On September 1, 1981, James Elton received a 25% capital interest in Bredbo Associates, a partnership, in return for services rendered plus a contribution of assets with a basis to Elton of $25,000 and a fair market value of $40,000. The fair market value of Elton's 25% interest was $50,000. How much is Elton's basis for his interest in Bredbo?

a. $25,000
b. $35,000
c. $40,000
d. $50,000

5. In computing the ordinary income of a partnership reportable on the partnership return, a deduction is allowed for

a. Contributions to charitable organizations.
b. The net operating loss deduction.
c. A net short-term capital loss.
d. Guaranteed payments to partners.

6. The partnership of Felix and Oscar had the following items of income during the taxable year ended December 31, 1980:

Income from operations	$156,000
Tax-exempt interest income	8,000
Dividends from foreign corporations	6,000
Net rental income	12,000

What is the total ordinary income of the partnership for 1980?

a. $170,000
b. $174,000
c. $176,000
d. $182,000

7. The Troika Partnership has an ordinary operating loss of $48,000 for the current year. The partnership had assets of $58,500 and liabilities of $15,000 at the end of the year. Before allocation of the loss, partner Ashford's one-third interest had an adjusted basis of $10,000 at the end of the current year. Ashford may deduct on his income tax return as his share of the loss

a. $14,500
b. $10,000
c. $16,000
d. $15,000

8. Crater Partnership had 1979 net ordinary income of $45,000 and a net long-term capital gain of $5,000. Mr. Abbott who has a 20% interest in the profits and losses of the partnership, had 1979 drawings of $12,500 from the partnership. The other partners withdrew $27,500 during 1979. The partnership agreement does not provide for partner salaries or bonuses. Mr. Abbott had no other capital gains or losses during 1979. By how much will Mr. Abbott's 1979 adjusted gross income increase because of his interest in Crater Partnership?

a. $ 2,000
b. $ 8,000
c. $ 9,400
d. $10,000

9. At December 31, 1979, Burns and Cooper were equal partners in a partnership with net assets having a tax basis and fair market value of $100,000. On January 1, 1980, Todd contributed securities with a fair market value of $50,000 (purchased in 1978 at a cost

of $35,000) to become an equal partner in the new firm of Burns, Cooper and Todd. The partnership agreement provided that Todd would report all gain attributable to the precontribution appreciation in the securities and that postcontribution appreciation is to be shared equally by the partners. The securities were sold on December 15, 1980, for $65,000. How much of the partnership's capital gain from the sale of these securities should be allocated to Todd?

a. $ 5,000
b. $10,000
c. $15,000
d. $20,000

10. Gilroy, a calendar-year taxpayer, is a partner in the firm of Adams and Company which has a fiscal year ending June 30. The partnership agreement provides for Gilroy to receive 25% of the ordinary income of the partnership. Gilroy also receives a guaranteed payment of $1,000 monthly which is deductible by the partnership. The partnership reported ordinary income of $88,000 for the year ended June 30, 1980, and $132,000 for the year ended June 30, 1981. How much should Gilroy report on his 1980 return as total income from the partnership?

a. $25,000
b. $30,500
c. $34,000
d. $39,500

11. On December 31, 1981, Edward Baker gave his son, Allan, a gift of a 50% interest in a partnership in which capital is a material income-producing factor. For the year ended December 31, 1982, the partnership's ordinary income was $100,000. Edward and Allan were the only partners in 1982. There were no guaranteed payments to partners. Edward's services performed for the partnership were worth a reasonable compensation of $40,000 for 1982. Allan has never performed any services for the partnership. What is Allan's distributive share of partnership income for 1982?

a. $20,000
b. $30,000
c. $40,000
d. $50,000

12. Clark and Lewis are partners who share profits and losses 60% and 40%, respectively. The tax basis of each partner's interest in the partnership as of December 31, 1978, was as follows:

Clark	$24,000
Lewis	$18,000

During 1979, the partnership had ordinary income of $50,000 and a long-term capital loss of $10,000 from the sale of securities. There were no distributions to the partners during 1979. What is the amount of Lewis' tax basis as of December 31, 1979?

a. $33,000
b. $34,000
c. $38,000
d. $42,000

13. Debra Wallace and Joan Pedersen are equal partners in the capital and profits of Wallace & Pedersen, but are otherwise unrelated. On August 1, 1981, Wallace sold 100 shares of Kiandra Mining Corporation stock to the partnership for its fair market value of $7,000. Wallace had bought the stock in 1975 at a cost of $10,000. What is Wallace's recognized loss in 1981 on the sale of this stock?

a. $0.
b. $1,500 long-term capital loss.
c. $3,000 long-term capital loss.
d. $3,000 ordinary loss.

14. On December 1, 1980, Alan Younger, a member of a three-man equal partnership, bought securities from the partnership for $27,000, their market value. The securities were acquired by the partnership for $15,000 on March 1, 1980. By what amount will this transaction increase Younger's taxable income for 1980?

a. $0
b. $ 1,600
c. $ 4,000
d. $12,000

15. Irving Aster, Dennis Brill, and Robert Clark were partners who shared profits and losses equally. On February 28, 1973, Aster sold his interest to Phil Dexter. On March 31, 1973, Brill died, and his estate held his interest for the remainder of the year. The partnership continued to operate and for the fiscal year ending June 30, 1973, it had a profit of $45,000. Assuming that partnership income was earned on a pro rata monthly basis and that all partners were calendar-year taxpayers, the distributive shares to be included in 1973 gross income should be

a. Aster $10,000, Brill $0, Estate of Brill $15,000, Clark $15,000, and Dexter $5,000.
b. Aster $10,000, Brill $11,250, Estate of Brill $3,750, Clark $15,000, and Dexter $5,000.

c. Aster $0, Brill $11,250, Estate of Brill $3,750, Clark $15,000, and Dexter $15,000.
d. Aster $0, Brill $0, Estate of Brill $15,000, Clark $15,000, and Dexter $15,000.

16. Axel, Banner & Carr, a calendar-year partnership, had the following partners since 1970:

	Partnership interest (%)
Axel	20
Banner	20
Carr	60

On October 20, 1982, Axel and Banner sold their partnership interests to Carr and withdrew from participation in the partnership's affairs. At what date was the partnership terminated for tax purposes?

a. October 1, 1982.
b. October 20, 1982.
c. October 31, 1982.
d. December 31, 1982.

17. David Beck and Walter Crocker were equal partners in the calendar-year partnership of Beck & Crocker. On July 1, 1982, Beck died. Beck's estate became the successor in interest and continued to share in Beck & Crocker's profits until Beck's entire partnership interest was liquidated on April 30, 1983. At what date was the partnership considered terminated for tax purposes?

a. April 30, 1983.
b. December 31, 1982.
c. July 31, 1982.
d. July 1, 1982.

18. On April 1, 1980, George Hart, Jr., acquired a 25% interest in the Wilson, Hart and Company partnership by gift from his father. The partnership interest had been acquired by a $50,000 cash investment by Hart, Sr., on July 1, 1965. The tax basis of Hart, Sr.'s partnership interest was $60,000 at the time of the gift. Hart, Jr., sold the 25% partnership interest for $85,000 on December 17, 1980. What type and amount (before consideration of the capital gain deduction) of capital gain should Hart, Jr., report on his 1980 tax return?

a. A long-term capital gain of $25,000.
b. A short-term capital gain of $25,000.
c. A long-term capital gain of $35,000.
d. A short-term capital gain of $35,000.

19. On June 30, 1982, James Roe sold his interest in the calendar-year partnership of Roe & Doe for $30,000. Roe's adjusted basis in Roe & Doe at June 30, 1982, was $7,500 before apportionment of any 1982 partnership income. Roe's distributive share of partnership income up to June 30, 1982, was $22,500. Roe acquired his interest in the partnership in 1970. How much long-term capital gain should Roe report in 1982 on the sale of his partnership interest?

a. $0
b. $15,000
c. $22,500
d. $30,000

20. On November 30, 1981, Diamond's adjusted basis for his one-third interest in the capital and profits of Peterson and Company was $95,000 ($80,000 capital account plus $15,000 share of partnership liabilities). On that date Diamond sold his partnership interest to Girard for $120,000 cash and the assumption of Diamond's share of the partnership liabilities. What amount and type of gain should Diamond recognize in 1981 from the sale of his partnership interest?

	Amount	*Type of gain*
a.	$25,000	Ordinary income
b.	$25,000	Capital gain
c.	$40,000	Ordinary income
d.	$40,000	Capital gain

21. Atley had an adjusted basis of $11,000 for his interest in the Atley and Donald partnership on December 31, 1979. On this date, Atley received from the partnership, in complete liquidation of his interest, $10,000 cash and land with a basis to the partnership of $2,000 and a fair market value of $3,000. What is Atley's basis for the land distributed to him?

a. $0
b. $1,000
c. $2,000
d. $3,000

22. Magda Shaw's adjusted basis for her partnership interest in Shaw & Zack was $60,000. In complete liquidation of her interest in Shaw & Zack, Shaw received cash of $44,000 plus the following assets:

	Adjusted basis to Shaw & Zack
Land—Tract "A"	$24,000
Land—Tract "B"	8,000

How much is Shaw's basis for Tract "B"?

a. $16,000
b. $15,000
c. $ 8,000
d. $ 4,000

23. Fred Elk's adjusted basis of his partnership interest in Arias & Nido was $30,000. Elk received a current nonliquidating distribution of $12,000 cash, plus property with a fair market value of $26,000 and an adjusted basis to the partnership of $24,000. How much is Elk's basis for the distributed property?

a. $18,000
b. $24,000
c. $26,000
d. $30,000

24. At December 31, 1982, Max Curcio's adjusted basis in the partnership of Maduro & Motta was $36,000. On December 31, 1982, Maduro & Motta distributed cash of $6,000 and a parcel of land to Curcio in liquidation of Curcio's entire interest in the partnership. The land had an adjusted basis of $18,000 to the partnership and a fair market value of $42,000 at December 31, 1982. How much is Curcio's basis in the land?

a. $0
b. $12,000
c. $30,000
d. $36,000

25. John Albin is a retired partner of Brill & Crum, a personal service partnership. Albin has not rendered any services to Brill & Crum since his retirement in 1975. Under the provisions of Albin's retirement agreement, Brill & Crum is obligated to pay Albin 10% of the partnership's net income each year. In compliance with this agreement, Brill & Crum paid Albin $25,000 in 1982. How should Albin treat this $25,000?

a. Not taxable.
b. Ordinary income.
c. Short-term capital gain.
d. Long-term capital gain.

May 1984 Questions

26. Gladys Peel owns an 80% interest in the capital and profits of the partnership of Peel & Poe. On July 1, 1983, Peel bought surplus land from the partnership at the land's fair market value of $10,000. The partnership's basis in the land was $16,000. For the year ended December 31, 1983, the partnership's net income was $94,000 after recording the $6,000 loss on the sale of land. Peel's distributive share of ordinary income from the partnership for 1983 was

a. $70,400
b. $75,200
c. $78,200
d. $80,000

27. Morris Babb, sole proprietor of Babb Fabrics, hired Ken Ryan on January 1, 1981, for an agreed salary and the promise of a 10% partnership capital interest if Ryan continued in Babb's employ until December 31, 1983. On January 1, 1984, when the enterprise's net worth was $100,000, the partnership was formed as agreed. Ryan should treat the receipt of his partnership interest in 1984 as

a. Nontaxable.
b. $10,000 ordinary income.
c. $10,000 short-term capital gain.
d. $10,000 long-term capital gain.

28. In 1984 Peggy Pink contributed property to a new partnership in return for a 50% interest in capital and profits. The property had a fair market value of $10,000, an adjusted basis of $6,000, and was subject to a $9,000 mortgage which was assumed by the partnership. What was Pink's basis in the partnership as a result of this contribution?

a. $5,500
b. $1,500
c. $ 500
d. $0

Multiple Choice Answers

1. a	7. d	13. c	19. a	24. c
2. b	8. c	14. c	20. d	25. b
3. a	9. d	15. a	21. b	26. d
4. b	10. c	16. b	22. d	27. b
5. d	11. b	17. a	23. a	28. b
6. b	12. b	18. a		

Multiple Choice Answer Explanations

A. Partnership Formation

1. (1183,Q3,53) (a) The requirement is to determine the amount of income to be reported by Arch. An individual must recognize compensation income when a partnership interest is received in exchange for services rendered. The amount to be reported by Arch is the $12,000 fair market value of the partnership interest received.

2. (583,Q3,58) (b) The requirement is to determine the basis of Clark's 20% partnership interest. Clark's basis consists of the $8,000 basis of the land that he contributed to the partnership, less the reduction in his individual liability resulting from the partnership's assumption of the mortgage (80% x $4,000 = $3,200). Thus, Clark's basis is $8,000 – $3,200 = $4,800.

3. (582,Q3,57) (a) The requirement is to determine the basis of Bryant's 30% interest in the Windward partnership. Bryant's basis is the $5,000 adjusted basis of property contributed reduced (but not below zero) by the decrease in his individual liability resulting from the assumption by the partnership of his liability (70% x $8,000 = $5,600). Thus, Bryant's basis for his partnership interest is zero. Note that Bryant must recognize gain of $5,600 – $5,000 = $600.

4. (582,Q3,58) (b) The requirement is to determine Elton's basis for his 25% interest in the Bredbo partnership. Since Elton received a capital interest with a FMV of $50,000 in exchange for property worth $40,000 and services, Elton must recognize compensation income of $10,000 ($50,000 – $40,000) on the transfer of services for a capital interest. Thus, Elton's basis for his partnership interest consists of the $25,000 basis of assets transferred plus the $10,000 of income recognized on the transfer of services, a total of $35,000.

B. Partnership Income and Loss

5. (1182,Q3,47) (d) Guaranteed payments to partners are deductible in computing ordinary income. Since the deductibility of charitable contributions and a NSTCL are subject to special limitations, they must be separately allocated to partners and cannot be included in computing ordinary income. There would be no NOL deduction since prior losses would have already been passed through to partners.

6. (581,Q3,49) (b) The requirement is to determine the ordinary income of the partnership. Income from operations is considered ordinary income as is net rental income. Dividends from foreign corporations also are included in the partnership's ordinary income since they are not eligible for the dividend exclusion. Tax-exempt income remains tax-exempt and is excluded from the computation of ordinary income. Thus, ordinary income is:

Income from operations	$156,000
Dividends from foreign corporations	6,000
Net rental income	12,000
Partnership ordinary income	$174,000

7. (1176,P1,15) (d) The amount of partnership loss which may be deducted by a partner is limited to his tax basis in the partnership at the end of the partnership taxable year. Ashford's share of the loss is 1/3 of $48,000, or $16,000. However, his loss deduction is limited to his basis of $15,000 ($10,000 + 1/3 of $15,000 liabilities). The remaining $1,000 may be carried over and taken when the partner's basis has been built up. For purposes of determining the amount of deductible loss, liabilities are included in basis only if the partner is personally liable (i.e., at risk) for them.

8. (575,Q2,19) (c) Abbott's distributive share is 20% of $45,000 ordinary income and 20% of $5,000 LTCG. The LTCG is subject to a 60% capital gains deduction. Thus his adjusted gross income is increased by $9,400 ($9,000 ordinary income plus $400 LTCG).

C. Partnership Agreements

9. (1181,P3,53) (d) The requirement is to determine the amount of the partnership's capital gain from the sale of securities to be allocated to Todd. The partnership's gain from the sale of securities was $65,000 – $35,000 = $30,000. The pre-contribution gain ($50,000 – $35,000) plus 1/3 of the post-contribution gain ($65,000 – $50,000) is allocated to Todd, a total of $20,000.

10. (1181,P3,58) (c) The requirement is to determine the amount that Gilroy should report for 1980 as total income from the partnership. Gilroy's income will consist of his share of the partnership's ordinary income for the fiscal year ending June 30, 1980 (the partnership year that ends within his year), plus the 12 monthly guaranteed payments that he received for that period of time.

25% x $88,000 =	$22,000
12 x $ 1,000 =	12,000
Total income =	$34,000

11. (1183,Q3,42) (b) The requirement is to determine Allan's distributive share of the partnership income. In a family partnership, services performed by family members must first be reasonably compensated before income is allocated according to the capital interests of the partners. Since Edward's services were worth $40,000, Allan's distributive share of partnership income is ($100,000 – $40,000) x 50% = $30,000.

D. Partner's Basis in Partnership

12. (1180,P3,60) (b) The requirement is to determine the tax basis of Lewis' partnership interest as of December 31, 1979. Since Lewis' share of profits and losses is 40%, Lewis' December 31, 1978, basis of $18,000 is increased by $20,000 (40% of $50,000) and decreased by $4,000 (40% of $10,000) resulting in a basis of $34,000 at December 31, 1979.

E. Transactions Between Partnership and Partners

13. (582,Q3,55) (c) The requirement is to determine the amount and nature of recognized loss resulting from the sale of stock by Wallace to a partnership in which she has a 50% capital and profits interest. Although losses incurred in transactions between a partnership and its partners are generally recognized, a loss is disallowed if incurred in a transaction between a partnership and a partner owning (directly or constructively) **more** than a 50% capital or profits interest. Since Wallace's interest does not exceed 50%, her realized loss of $3,000 is fully recognized. It is a LTCL because the stock was a capital asset and was held more than 12 months.

14. (1181,P3,54) (c) The requirement is to determine the increase in Younger's TI resulting from his purchase of the securities from the partnership. The sale of the securities resulted in a $27,000 – $15,000 = $12,000 STCG to the partnership. This gain would increase Younger's TI by 1/3 x $12,000 = $4,000.

F. Taxable Year of Partnership and Partners

15. (574,Q2,31) (a) Brill received nothing due to his death, but his estate is entitled to his 1/3 share ($15,000). Clark was a partner for the full year and receives his 1/3 share ($15,000). Aster was a partner for 2/3 of the year and, therefore, 2/3 of the 1/3 partnership income is includable by him ($10,000). Dexter must report the remaining 1/3 of the 1/3 partnership income ($5,000). The split between Aster and Dexter is based on the assumption that income was earned on a pro rata monthly basis.

G. Sale of a Partnership Interest

16. (583,Q3,56) (b) The requirement is to determine the date on which the partnership was terminated for tax purposes. The partnership was terminated on October 20, 1982, the date on which Axel and Banner sold their interests to Carr. On that date, the business ceased to operate as a partnership because the operation of a partnership requires two or more partners.

17. (583,Q3,57) (a) The requirement is to determine the date on which the partnership was terminated. A partnership generally does not terminate for tax purposes upon the death of a partner, since the deceased partner's estate or successor in interest continues to share in partnership profits and losses. Here, the partnership was terminated on April 30, 1983, when Beck's entire partnership interest was liquidated, and the business ceased to exist as a partnership.

H. Pro Rata Distributions from Partnership

18. (1181,P3,56) (a) The requirement is to determine the amount and type of capital gain to be reported by Hart, Jr. from the sale of his partnership interest. Since the partnership interest was acquired by gift from Hart, Sr., Jr.'s basis would be the same as Sr.'s basis at date of gift, $60,000. Since Jr.'s basis is determined from Sr.'s basis, Jr.'s holding period includes the period the partnership interest was held by Sr. Thus, Hart, Jr. will report a LTCG of $85,000 – $60,000 = $25,000.

19. (583,Q3,53) (a) The requirement is to determine the amount of LTCG to be reported by Roe on the sale of his partnership interest. Roe's basis for his partnership interest of $7,500 must first be increased by his $22,500 distributive share of partnership income, to $30,000. Since the selling price also was $30,000, Roe will report no gain or loss.

20. (1182,Q3,60) (d) The requirement is to determine the amount and type of gain that Diamond should report on the sale of his partnership interest. The amount realized from the sale is the $120,000 cash plus the $15,000 of liabilities assumed by the buyer, a total of $135,000. Since a partnership interest is usually a capital asset and generally results in capital gain or loss, Diamond will report a $135,000 – $95,000 = $40,000 capital gain.

I. Pro Rata Distributions from Partnership

21. (1180,P3,59) (b) The requirement is to calculate the basis of the land distributed to Atley in liquidation of his interest in the Atley and Donald partnership. Since the cash distribution first reduces Atley's basis in the partnership to $1,000, Atley's basis for the land is limited to $1,000, which represents his remaining partnership basis after the cash distribution. Note that even though the FMV of the property is $3,000, Atley recognizes no gain, since gain is only recognized on a distribution if the money received exceeds basis.

22. (1183,Q3,58) (d) The requirement is to determine the basis of the Tract "B" land received in complete liquidation of Shaw's partnership interest. Shaw's basis for her partnership interest of $60,000 is first reduced by the $44,000 of cash received, to $16,000. This remaining basis of $16,000 is then allocated to Tracts "A" and "B" according to their relative adjusted bases. Thus, the basis of the Tract "B" land to Shaw is (8/32 x $16,000) = $4,000.

23. (583,Q3,54) (a) The requirement is to determine Elk's basis for the property distributed to him. In nonliquidating distributions, a partner's basis in distributed property is the partnership's former basis in the property, limited to the partner's basis for his partnership interest less any cash received. Here, Elk's partnership basis of $30,000 is first reduced by the $12,000 cash, to $18,000. Since the partnership's basis for the property is greater than $18,000, the property's basis to Elk will be limited to $18,000, reducing the basis of Elk's partnership interest to zero.

24. (583,Q3,59) (c) The requirement is to determine the basis of the land distributed to Curcio. In a liquidating distribution, a partner's basis for his partnership interest is reduced by the amount of money received and the partnership's basis for any unrealized receivables and inventory received. Any remaining basis is then allocated to other property received. Here, Curcio's partnership basis of $36,000 is reduced by the $6,000 cash, to $30,000. This $30,000 becomes the basis for the distributed property.

25. (583,Q3,60) (b) The requirement is to determine the treatment for the payments received by Albin. Payments to a retired partner that are determined by partnership income are distributive shares of partnership income, regardless of the period over which they are paid. Here, they are taxable to Albin as ordinary income.

May 1984 Answers

26. (584,Q1,14) (d) The requirement is to determine Peel's distributive share of ordinary income from the partnership. Since a loss is disallowed on a sale or exchange between a partnership and a more than 50% partner, the $6,000 loss on the sale of land to Peel must be added back to the partnership's net income of $94,000. Peel's distributive share of partnership ordinary income is then ($94,000 + $6,000) x 80% = $80,000.

27. (584,Q1,17) (b) The requirement is to determine the amount and type of income to be recognized on a transfer of services for a 10% interest in partnership capital. Ordinary income is recognized if services are transferred in exchange for an interest in partnership capital. The amount recognized is 10% of the $100,000 net worth of the partnership, or $10,000.

28. (584,Q1,19) (b) The requirement is to determine the basis of Pink's 50% partnership interest. Pink's basis is the $6,000 adjusted basis of property contributed less the decrease in her individual liability resulting from the partnership's assumption of the mortgage (50% x $9,000 = $4,500). Thus, Pink's basis is $6,000 - $4,500 = $1,500.

Multiple Choice Questions (1 - 66)

1. In 1982, Dr. Ernest Griffiths, a cash basis taxpayer, incorporated his medical practice. No liabilities were transferred. The following assets were transferred to the corporation:

Cash	$ 20,000
Equipment:	
Adjusted basis	140,000
Fair market value	180,000

Immediately after the transfer, Griffiths owned 100% of the corporation's stock. The corporation's total basis for the transferred assets is

a. $140,000
b. $160,000
c. $180,000
d. $200,000

2. On July 1, 1981, Alan Rees, sole proprietor of Kee Nail, transferred all of Kee's assets to Merit, Inc., a new corporation, solely in exchange for a certain percentage of Merit's stock. Al Clyde, who is not related to Rees, bought the rest of Merit's stock on July 1. Merit's outstanding capital stock consisted of 1,000 shares of common stock with a par value of $100 per share. For the transfer of Kee's assets to be tax-free, what is the minimum number of shares of Merit's stock that must be owned by Rees immediately after the exchange?

a. 500
b. 501
c. 800
d. 801

3. Roberta Warner and Sally Rogers formed the Acme Corporation on October 1, 1980. On the same date Warner paid $75,000 cash to Acme for 750 shares of its common stock. Simultaneously, Rogers received 100 shares of Acme's common stock for services rendered. How much should Rogers include as taxable income for 1980, and what will be the basis of her stock?

	Taxable income	*Basis of stock*
a.	$0	$0
b.	$0	$10,000
c.	$10,000	$0
d.	$10,000	$10,000

4. On July 1, 1979, Mr. Grey formed Dover Corporation. The same date Grey paid $100,000 cash and transferred property with an adjusted basis of $50,000 to Dover in exchange for 3,000 shares of its common stock. The property had a fair market value of $85,000 on the date of the exchange. Dover had no other shares of common stock outstanding on July 1, 1979. As a result of the above transaction, Grey's basis in his stock and Dover's basis in the property, respectively, are:

a. $150,000 and $50,000.
b. $150,000 and $85,000.
c. $185,000 and $50,000.
d. $185,000 and $85,000.

5. Finbury Corporation's taxable income for the year ended December 31, 1982, was $2,000,000, on which its tax liability was $900,250. In order for Finbury to escape the estimated tax underpayment penalty for the year ending December 31, 1983, Finbury's 1983 estimated tax payments must equal at least

a. 60% of the 1983 tax liability.
b. 65% of the 1983 tax liability.
c. 75% of the 1983 tax liability.
d. The 1982 tax liability of $900,250.

6. When Kile Corp. was organized in 1975, it received $100,000 from the sale of 10,000 shares of its $10 par value common stock. In 1980, Kile reacquired 300 of these shares as treasury stock, at a cost of $6,000. In 1983, Kile sold the 300 shares of treasury stock to an unrelated party for $7,500. How much capital gain should Kile report in its 1983 tax return in connection with the sale of these 300 shares?

a. $4,500
b. $3,000
c. $1,500
d. $0

7. Lara Corporation's stock is owned by Toty, Inc., a Delaware corporation. At December 31, 1982, the close of Lara's taxable year, Lara had earnings and profits of $90,000. In December 1982, Lara made a distribution of land to Toty. Lara's adjusted basis for this land was $25,000, while the land's fair market value at the date of distribution was $40,000. Lara had no recognized gain or loss on this property distribution. How much of this property distribution should be treated as a dividend in 1982?

a. $0
b. $15,000
c. $25,000
d. $40,000

8. During 1983 Wyld Corp., in need of additional factory space, exchanged 10,000 shares of its common stock with a par value of $50,000 for a building with a fair market value of $60,000. On the date of the exchange the stock had a fair market value of $65,000.

For 1983, how much and what type of gain or loss should Wyld report on this transaction?

a. $10,000 section 1231 gain.
b. $10,000 capital gain.
c. $ 5,000 capital loss.
d. No gain or loss.

9. Sportsworld, Inc., issued $500,000 face amount of bonds in 1976 and established a sinking fund to pay the debt. An independent trustee was appointed by the bondholders to administer the sinking fund. In 1981, the sinking fund earned $30,000 in interest on bank deposits, and $2,000 in net short-term capital gains. How much of this income is taxable to Sportsworld?

a. $0
b. $ 2,000
c. $30,000
d. $32,000

10. Delve Co., Inc., issued $1,000,000 of 8-year convertible bonds on October 1, 1980, for $880,000. The amount of bond discount deductible on Delve's income tax return for the year ended March 31, 1981, is

a. $0
b. $ 7,500
c. $ 15,000
d. $120,000

11. On December 31, 1960, Homer Corporation issued $2,000,000 of fifty-year bonds for $2,600,000. On December 31, 1980, Homer issued new bonds with a face value of $3,000,000 for which it received $3,400,000 and used part of the proceeds to repurchase for $2,320,000 the bonds issued in 1960. No elections were made to adjust the basis of any property. What is the taxable income to Homer on the repurchase of the 1960 bonds?

a. $0
b. $ 40,000
c. $280,000
d. $360,000

12. Shaney Corporation repurchased its own outstanding bonds in the open market for $258,000 on May 31, 1976. The bonds were originally issued on May 5, 1974, at face value of $250,000. For its tax year ending December 31, 1976, Shaney should report

a. Neither income nor a deduction.
b. A deduction of $4,000.
c. A capital gain of $4,000.
d. A deduction of $8,000.

13. Yuki Corp., which began business in 1982, incurred the following costs in 1982 in connection with organizing the corporation:

Printing of stock certificates	$ 5,000
Underwriters' commissions on sale of stock	100,000

What portion of these costs qualifies as amortizable organization expenses deductible ratably over a period of not less than 60 months?

a. $105,000
b. $100,000
c. $ 5,000
d. $0

14. Filo, Inc., began business on July 1, 1980, and elected to file its income tax returns on a calendar-year basis. The following expenditures were incurred in organizing the corporation:

August 1, 1980	$300
September 3, 1980	$600

The maximum allowable deduction for amortization of organization expense in 1980 is

a. $60
b. $65
c. $81
d. $90

15. Richards Corporation had taxable income of $280,000 before deducting charitable contributions for its tax year ended December 31, 1982. The dividends received deduction was $34,000. Richards made cash contributions of $35,000 to charitable organizations. How much can Richards deduct as contributions for 1982?

a. $28,000
b. $31,400
c. $32,000
d. $35,000

16. Norwood Corporation is an accrual-basis taxpayer. For the year ended December 31, 1982, it had book income before tax of $500,000 after deducting a charitable contribution of $100,000. The contribution was authorized by the Board of Directors in December 1982, but was not actually paid until March 1, 1983. How should Norwood treat this charitable contribution for tax purposes to minimize its 1982 taxable income?

a. It cannot claim a deduction in 1982, but must apply the payment against 1983 income.

b. Make an election claiming a deduction for 1982 of $50,000 and carry the remainder over a maximum of five succeeding tax years.
c. Make an election claiming a deduction for 1982 of $60,000 and carry the remainder over a maximum of five succeeding tax years.
d. Make an election claiming a 1982 deduction of $100,000.

17. Pym Corp. received the following dividends in 1982:

From a mutual savings bank	$1,000
From an unaffiliated domestic taxable corporation	5,000

How much of these dividends qualifies for the 85% dividends-received deduction?

a. $0
b. $1,000
c. $5,000
d. $6,000

18. For the year ended December 31, 1981, Atkinson, Inc., had gross business income of $160,000 and dividend income of $100,000 from unaffiliated domestic corporations. Business deductions for 1981 amounted to $170,000. What is Atkinson's dividends received deduction for 1981?

a. $0
b. $76,500
c. $85,000
d. $90,000

19. For the year ended December 31, 1982, Haya Corp. had gross business income of $600,000 and expenses of $800,000. Contributions of $5,000 to qualified charities were included in expenses. In addition to the expenses, Haya had a net operating loss carryover of $9,000. What was Haya's net operating loss for 1982?

a. $209,000
b. $204,000
c. $200,000
d. $195,000

20. Dorsett Corporation's income tax return for 1981 shows deductions exceeding gross income by $56,800. Included in the tax return are the following items:

Net operating loss deduction (carryover from 1980)	$15,000
Dividends received deduction	6,800

What is Dorsett's net operating loss for 1981?

a. $56,800
b. $50,000
c. $41,800
d. $35,000

21. Bishop Corporation reported taxable income of $700,000 on its federal income tax return for calendar year 1981. Selected information for 1981 is available from Bishop's records as follows:

Provision for federal income tax per books	$280,000
Depreciation claimed on the tax return	130,000
Depreciation recorded in the books	75,000
Life insurance proceeds on death of corporate officer	100,000

Bishop reported net income per books for 1981 of

a. $855,000
b. $595,000
c. $575,000
d. $475,000

22. Cooma Corporation's book income before income taxes for the year ended December 31, 1981, was $260,000. The company was organized three years earlier. Organization costs of $130,000 are being written off over a ten-year period for financial statement purposes. For tax purposes these costs are being written off over the minimum allowable period. For the year ended December 31, 1981, Cooma's taxable income was

a. $234,000
b. $247,000
c. $260,000
d. $273,000

23. For the year ended December 31, 1980, Apollo Corporation had net income per books of $1,200,000. Included in the determination of net income were the following items:

Interest income on municipal bonds	$ 40,000
Gain on settlement of life insurance policy (death of officer)	200,000
Interest paid on loan to purchase municipal bonds	8,000
Provision for federal income tax	524,000

What should Apollo report as its taxable income for 1980?

a. $1,492,000
b. $1,524,000
c. $1,684,000
d. $1,692,000

24. Barbaro Corporation's retained earnings at January 1, 1982, was $600,000. During 1982 Barbaro paid cash dividends of $150,000 and received a federal income tax refund of $26,000 as a result of an IRS audit of Barbaro's 1979 tax return. Barbaro's net income per books for the year ended December 31, 1982, was $274,900 after deducting federal income tax of $183,300. How much should be shown in the reconciliation schedule M-2, of Form 1120, as Barbaro's retained earnings at December 31, 1982?

a. $443,600
b. $600,900
c. $626,900
d. $750,900

25. Olex Corporation's books disclosed the following data for the calendar year 1981:

Retained earnings at beginning of year	$50,000
Net income for year	70,000
Contingency reserve established at end of year	10,000
Cash dividends paid during year	8,000

What amount should appear on the last line of reconciliation Schedule M-2 of Form 1120?

a. $102,000
b. $120,000
c. $128,000
d. $138,000

26. Hill Corporation and its wholly-owned subsidiary, Dale Corporation, file a consolidated return on a calendar-year basis. On March 28, 1976, Hill sold land, which it had used in its business for ten years, to Dale for $60,000. Hill's basis in the land on March 28th was $40,000. Dale held the land until June 2, 1977, whereupon it sold the property for $75,000 to an unrelated third party. What amount of income should Hill report in the consolidated return filed for 1976?

a. $0.
b. $20,000 Section 1250 gain.
c. $20,000 long-term capital gain.
d. $20,000 ordinary income.

27. On June 30, 1980, Ral Corporation had retained earnings of $100,000. On that date, it sold a plot of land to a stockholder for $50,000. Ral had paid $40,000 for the land in 1975, and it had a fair market value of $80,000 when the stockholder bought it. The amount of dividend income taxable to the stockholder in 1980 (before the dividend exclusion) is

a. $0
b. $10,000
c. $20,000
d. $30,000

28. The Guardian Corporation, not a dealer in securities, owned marketable securities that had an adjusted basis of $150,000. On June 30, 1977, when the market value of these securities rose to $180,000, Guardian distributed these securities to its shareholders. As a result of this distribution, Guardian should report

a. No gain on the distribution.
b. Ordinary income of $30,000.
c. A capital gain of $30,000.
d. A capital gain of $180,000.

29. On December 1, 1976, Gelt Corporation distributed to its sole shareholder, as a dividend in kind, a parcel of land that was not an inventory asset. On the date of the distribution, the following data were available.

Adjusted basis of land	$ 6,500
Fair market value of land	14,000
Mortgage on land	5,000

For the year ended December 31, 1976, Gelt had earnings and profits of $30,000 without regard to the dividend distribution. By how much should the dividend distribution reduce the earnings and profits for 1976?

a. $ 1,500
b. $ 6,500
c. $ 9,000
d. $14,000

30. Eazy Corporation's earnings and profits for 1974, its first year of operations, were $22,000. In December of 1974, it distributed to its individual stockholders, cash of $10,000 and land with a basis of $14,000 and a fair market value of $25,000 at the date of distribution. Prior to the distribution, the stockholders' tax basis of their investment in the corporation was $76,000.

What was the stockholders' adjusted basis at the end of 1974?

a. $51,000
b. $52,000
c. $63,000
d. $74,000

31. At January 1, 1983, Pearl Corp. owned 90% of the outstanding stock of Seso Corp. Both companies were domestic corporations. Pursuant to a plan of liquidation adopted by Seso in March 1983, Seso distributed all of its property in September 1983, in complete redemption of all its stock, when Seso's accumulated earnings equalled $18,000. Seso had never been insolvent. Pursuant to the liquidation, Seso

transferred to Pearl a parcel of land with a basis of $10,000 and a fair market value of $40,000. How much gain must Seso recognize in 1983 on the transfer of this land to Pearl?

a. $0
b. $18,000
c. $27,000
d. $30,000

32. Carmela Corporation had the following assets on January 2, 1982, the date on which it adopted a 12-month complete liquidation plan:

	Adjusted basis	*Fair market value*
Land	$ 75,000	$150,000
Inventory	43,500	66,000
Totals	$118,500	$216,000

The land was sold on June 30, 1982, to an unrelated party at a gain of $75,000. The inventory was sold to various customers during 1982 at an aggregate gain of $22,500. On December 10, 1982, the remaining asset (cash) was distributed to Carmela's stockholders, and the corporation was liquidated. What is Carmela's recognized gain in 1982?

a. $0.
b. $22,500 ordinary income.
c. $75,000 capital gain.
d. $97,500 capital gain.

33. Edgewood Corporation was liquidated in 1981 by Roberts, its sole shareholder. Pursuant to the liquidation, Roberts' stock in Edgewood was cancelled and he received the following assets on July 15, 1981:

	Basis to Edgewood	*Fair market value*
Cash	$ 40,000	$ 40,000
Accounts receivable	20,000	20,000
Inventory	30,000	45,000
Land	50,000	75,000
	$140,000	$180,000

How much gain should be recognized by Edgewood Corporation on the liquidation?

a. $0
b. $15,000
c. $25,000
d. $40,000

34. John Gerry, the sole shareholder in Rockville Corporation, elected to liquidate the corporation in a one-month liquidation which was begun and completed within the month of October 1980. Gerry received a liquidating distribution during October 1980 as follows:

- Cash of $6,000.
- Machinery (subject to a $13,000 lien) with a fair market value of $40,000.

At the time of liquidation, the basis of Gerry's stock investment in Rockville was $20,000, and the accumulated earnings and profits of the corporation amounted to $5,000. How much of the liquidating distribution is taxable to Gerry as ordinary income and as capital gain in 1980?

	Ordinary income	*Capital gain*
a.	$0	$6,000
b.	$5,000	$0
c.	$5,000	$1,000
d.	$6,000	$7,000

35. Will Benton owned all of the stock of a corporation that has been determined to be collapsible. The basis of the stock to Benton was $25,000, and the corporation had accumulated earnings and profits of $1,000. Benton sold his stock for $40,000. As a result of the sale, Benton must report

a. $15,000 ordinary gain.
b. $1,000 ordinary income and $14,000 capital gain.
c. $14,000 capital gain.
d. $15,000 capital gain.

Items 36 and 37 are based on the following statements which pertain *either* to the accumulated earnings tax, *or* to the personal holding company tax, *or* to both:

(1) Imposition of the tax depends on a stock ownership test specified in the statute.
(2) Imposition of the tax can be mitigated by sufficient dividend distributions.
(3) The tax should be self-assessed by filing a separate schedule along with the regular tax return.

36. Which of the foregoing statements pertain to the accumulated earnings tax?

a. (1) only.
b. (2) only.
c. (3) only.
d. (1), (2), and (3).

37. Which of the foregoing statements pertain to the personal holding company tax?

a. (1) only.
b. (2) only.
c. (3) only.
d. (1), (2), and (3).

38. The minimum accumulated earnings credit beginning in 1982 is
   a. $150,000 for all corporations.
   b. $150,000 for nonservice corporations only.
   c. $250,000 for all corporations.
   d. $250,000 for nonservice corporations only.

39. Daystar Corp., which is not a mere holding or investment company, derives its income from consulting services. Daystar had accumulated earnings and profits of $45,000 at December 31, 1982. For the year ended December 31, 1983, it had earnings and profits of $115,000 and a dividends-paid deduction of $15,000. It has been determined that $20,000 of the accumulated earnings and profits for 1983 is required for the reasonable needs of the business. How much is the allowable accumulated earnings credit at December 31, 1983?
   a. $105,000
   b. $205,000
   c. $150,000
   d. $250,000

40. Cromwell Investors, Inc., has ten unrelated equal stockholders. For the year ended June 30, 1980, Cromwell's adjusted gross income comprised the following:

Dividends from domestic taxable corporations	$10,000
Dividends from savings and loan associations on passbook savings accounts	1,000
Interest earned on notes receivable	5,000
Net rental income	3,000

The corporation paid no dividends during the taxable year. Deductible expenses totaled $4,000 for the year. Cromwell's liability for personal holding company tax for the year will be based on undistributed personal holding company income of
   a. $0
   b. $ 3,500
   c. $ 6,500
   d. $15,000

41. Luba Corp. was organized in 1983 with the intention of operating as an S corporation (Subchapter S). What is the maximum number of stockholders allowable for eligibility as an S corporation (Subchapter S)?
   a. 35
   b. 15
   c. 9
   d. 5

42. Which of the following is **not** a requirement for a corporation to elect S corporation status (Subchapter S)?
   a. Must be a member of a controlled group.
   b. Must confine stockholders to individuals, estates, and certain qualifying trusts.
   c. Must be a domestic corporation.
   d. Must have only one class of stock.

43. For the year ended December 31, 1983, Harlan, Inc., an S corporation, had net income per books of $108,000, which included $90,000 from operations and an $18,000 net long-term capital gain. During 1983, $45,000 was distributed to Harlan's three equal shareholders, all of whom are on a calendar-year basis. On what amounts should Harlan compute its income and capital gain taxes?

	Ordinary income	*Long-term capital gain*
a.	$0	$0
b.	$0	$18,000
c.	$45,000	$0
d.	$63,000	$0

44. Brooke, Inc., an S corporation, was organized on January 2, 1983, with two equal stockholders. Each stockholder invested $5,000 in Brooke's capital stock, and each loaned $15,000 to the corporation. Brooke then borrowed $60,000 from a bank for working capital. Brooke sustained an operating loss of $90,000 for the year ended December 31, 1983. How much of this loss can each stockholder claim on his 1983 income tax return?
   a. $ 5,000
   b. $20,000
   c. $45,000
   d. $50,000

45. Drury Corporation, an S corporation, had income of $45,000 for the year ended December 31, 1983. Included in the above is $42,000 excess net long-term capital gain over net short-term capital losses. Drury paid $4,760 in capital gains taxes for 1983. Cash distributions to Mr. Hoyt, the sole shareholder, totaled $60,000 during 1983. On December 31, 1982, Drury had accumulated earnings and profits of $50,000. What amount should Hoyt report on his individual income tax return for 1983 as long-term capital gain passed through from Drury?
   a. $37,240
   b. $42,000
   c. $45,000
   d. $46,760

46. For the year ended December 31, 1983, the Dab Corporation, an S corporation, had net income per books of $60,000 which included $70,000 from operations and a $10,000 net long-term capital loss. During 1983, $30,000 was distributed to the corporation's ten equal shareholders, all of whom are calendar-year taxpayers.

For 1983, each shareholder should report as his or her share of the corporation's income

a. $3,000 ordinary income.
b. $6,000 ordinary income.
c. $7,000 ordinary income.
d. $7,000 ordinary income; $1,000 long-term capital loss.

47. Claudio Corporation and Stellar Corporation both report on a calendar-year basis. Claudio merged into Stellar on June 30, 1982. Claudio had an allowable net operating loss carryover of $270,000. Stellar's taxable income for the year ended December 31, 1982, was $360,000 before consideration of Claudio's net operating loss carryover. How much of Claudio's net operating loss carryover can be used to offset Stellar's 1982 taxable income?

a. $0
b. $135,000
c. $180,000
d. $270,000

48. Pursuant to a plan of reorganization adopted in 1981, Summit Corporation exchanged 1,000 shares of its common stock and paid $40,000 cash for Hansen Corporation assets with an adjusted basis of $200,000 (fair market value of $300,000). The 1,000 shares of Summit common stock had a fair market value of $260,000 on the date of the exchange. What is the basis to Summit of the assets acquired in the exchange?

a. $200,000
b. $240,000
c. $260,000
d. $300,000

49. Pursuant to a tax-free reorganization in 1981, Sandra Peel exchanged 100 shares of Lorna Corporation for 100 shares of Wood Corp. and, in addition, received $1,000 cash, which was not in excess of Peel's ratable share of Lorna's undistributed earnings and profits. Peel paid $20,000 in 1975 for the Lorna stock. The Wood stock had a fair market value of $24,000 on the date of the exchange. What is the recognized gain to be reported by Peel in 1981?

a. $0.
b. $1,000 dividend.
c. $1,000 long-term capital gain.
d. $5,000 long-term capital gain.

50. In 1976, Celia Mueller bought a $1,000 bond issued by Disco Corporation, for $1,100. Instead of paying off the bondholders in cash, Disco issued 100 shares of preferred stock in 1981 for each bond outstanding. The preferred stock had a fair market value of $15 per share. What is the recognized gain to be reported by Mueller in 1981?

a. $0.
b. $400 dividend.
c. $400 long-term capital gain.
d. $500 long-term capital gain.

51. On July 1, 1980, in connection with a recapitalization of Yorktown Corporation, Robert Moore exchanged 1,000 shares of stock which cost him $95,000 for 1,000 shares of new stock worth $108,000 and bonds in the principal amount of $10,000 with a fair market value of $10,500. What is the amount of Moore's recognized gain during 1980?

a. $0
b. $10,500
c. $23,000
d. $23,500

52. Pursuant to a plan of corporate reorganization adopted in 1980, Bart Smith exchanged 1,000 shares of Talbot Corporation common stock that he had purchased for $150,000, for 1,800 shares of Mark Corporation common stock having a fair market value of $172,000. As a result of this exchange, Smith's recognized gain and his basis in the Mark Corporation common stock should be

	Recognized gain	*Basis*
a.	$0	$150,000
b.	$0	$172,000
c.	$22,000	$150,000
d.	$22,000	$172,000

May 1984 Questions

53. Dale Corporation's book income before federal income taxes was $520,000 for the year ended December 31, 1983. Dale was organized three years earlier. Organization costs of $260,000 are being written off over a ten-year period for financial statement purposes. For tax purposes these costs are being written off over the minimum allowable period. For the year ended December 31, 1983, Dale's taxable income was

a. $468,000
b. $494,000
c. $520,000
d. $546,000

54. Roper Corp. had operating income of $200,000, after deducting $12,000 for contributions, but not including dividends of $20,000 received from nonaffiliated domestic taxable corporations. How much is the base amount to which the percentage limitation should be applied in computing the maximum allowable deduction for contributions?

a. $212,000
b. $215,000
c. $220,000
d. $232,000

55. Pursuant to a plan of corporate reorganization adopted in 1983, Emil Gow exchanged 2,000 shares of Bly Corp. common stock for 3,600 shares of Rolf Corp. common stock. Gow had paid $75,000 for the Bly stock. The fair market value of the Rolf stock was $86,000 on the date of the exchange. As a result of this exchange, how much was Gow's recognized gain and his basis in the Rolf stock?

	Recognized gain	*Basis*
a.	$11,000	$86,000
b.	$11,000	$75,000
c.	$0	$86,000
d.	$0	$75,000

56. Tyson Corp. distributed marketable securities in redemption of its stock in a complete liquidation. These securities had a basis of $300,000 and a fair market value of $450,000. What gain does Tyson have as a result of the distribution?

a. $0.
b. $150,000 capital gain.
c. $150,000 Section 1231 gain.
d. $150,000 ordinary gain.

Items 57 through 59 are based on the following data:

Pym, Inc., which had earnings and profits of $100,000, distributed land to Alex Rowe, a stockholder, as a dividend in kind. Pym's adjusted basis for this land was $3,000. The land had a fair market value of $12,000 and was subject to a mortgage liability of $5,000, which was assumed by Rowe.

57. How much was Pym's gain on the distribution?

a. $9,000
b. $4,000
c. $2,000
d. $0

58. Before the dividend exclusion, how much of the distribution was taxable to Rowe as a dividend?

a. $9,000
b. $7,000
c. $4,000
d. $3,000

59. If the distribution of the dividend in kind had been made to Kile Corporation instead of to Alex Rowe (an individual), how much of the distribution would be reportable by Kile as a dividend, before the dividends-received deduction?

a. $0
b. $ 3,000
c. $ 7,000
d. $12,000

60. In computing a corporation's taxable income, a net capital loss is

a. Deductible in full in the year sustained.
b. Deductible to a maximum extent of 50% in the year sustained.
c. Not deductible at all in the year sustained.
d. Limited to a maximum deduction of $3,000 in the year sustained.

61. The accumulated earnings tax does **not** apply to corporations that

a. Have more than one class of stock.
b. Are personal holding companies.
c. Are members of a controlled group.
d. Are manufacturing enterprises.

62. Ace Corp. files a consolidated return with its wholly-owned subsidiary, Barr Corp. During 1983 Barr paid a cash dividend of $10,000 to Ace. How much of this dividend is taxable on the 1983 consolidated return?

a. $0
b. $ 1,500
c. $ 8,500
d. $10,000

63. In a corporation that has **no** cash and does **not** own any stock or securities, the one-month liquidation under Code Section 333

a. Is available only if the corporation is collapsible.
b. Can be in partial redemption of the corporation's capital stock.
c. Results in the corporation's earnings and profits being taxed as an ordinary dividend to noncorporate stockholders.
d. Is required to take effect in the same month in which the election was made.

64. Lindal Corp., organized in 1984, immediately filed an election for S corporation status under the rules of Subchapter S. What is the maximum amount of passive investment income that Lindal will be allowed to earn and still qualify as an S corporation (Subchapter S)?

a. 80% of gross receipts.
b. 50% of gross receipts.
c. 20% of gross receipts.
d. No limit on passive investment income.

65. The personal holding company tax

a. Is imposed on corporations having 50 or more equal stockholders.
b. Applies regardless of the extent of dividend distributions.
c. Should be self-assessed by filing a separate schedule along with the regular tax return.
d. May apply if at least 20% of the corporation's gross receipts constitute passive investment income.

66. James Bell, CPA, a sole practitioner reporting on the cash basis, incorporated his accounting practice in 1984, transferring the following assets to the newly formed corporation:

Cash	$ 5,000
Office furniture and equipment:	
Adjusted basis	35,000
Fair market value	45,000

No liabilities were transferred, and there were no other stockholders. The corporation's total basis for the transferred assets is

a. $35,000
b. $40,000
c. $45,000
d. $50,000

Multiple Choice Answers

1.	b	15.	b	28.	a	41.	a	54.	d
2.	c	16.	c	29.	a	42.	a	55.	d
3.	d	17.	c	30.	c	43.	a	56.	a
4.	a	18.	b	31.	a	44.	b	57.	c
5.	c	19.	d	32.	b	45.	a	58.	b
6.	d	20.	c	33.	a	46.	d	59.	a
7.	c	21.	c	34.	c	47.	c	60.	c
8.	d	22.	b	35.	a	48.	b	61.	b
9.	d	23.	a	36.	b	49.	b	62.	a
10.	b	24.	d	37.	d	50.	a	63.	c
11.	b	25.	a	38.	d	51.	b	64.	d
12.	d	26.	a	39.	b	52.	a	65.	c
13.	d	27.	d	40.	a	53.	b	66.	b
14.	d								

Multiple Choice Answer Explanations

A. Transfers to a Controlled Corporation

1. (583,Q3,46) (b) The requirement is to determine the corporation's total basis for the assets transferred from its sole shareholder. The cash and equipment were transferred by Griffiths in a nontaxable, Sec. 351 transfer to a controlled corporation. The corporation's basis for the assets would be the same as Griffiths' basis, increased by any gain recognized by Griffiths. Since Griffiths did not receive any boot, no gain was recognized by him. Thus, the corporation's total basis for the assets transferred is $20,000 + $140,000 = $160,000.

2. (582,Q3,45) (c) The requirement is to determine the minimum number of Merit shares that must be owned by Rees for the transfer of Rees' assets to be tax-free. No gain or loss is recognized if assets are transferred to a corporation controlled after the exchange. Control is the ownership of at least 80% of the outstanding stock. Since Merit has 1,000 shares outstanding, Rees must own at least 800.

3. (1181,P3,46) (d) The requirement is to determine the taxable income to Rogers and the basis of her stock. Since services are excluded from the definition of "property,"Rogers' transfer does not fall under the nonrecognition provision of Sec. 351, but instead is a taxable exchange. Rogers reports $10,000 of income and the basis for the stock is $10,000, the amount reported as income.

4. (1180,P3,43) (a) The requirement is to determine Grey's basis for his stock and Dover's basis for the property following a nontaxable transfer to a controlled corporation. Grey's basis in the stock equals the $50,000 adjusted basis of property plus the $100,000 cash transferred, a total of $150,000. Dover's basis for the property equals Grey's adjusted basis plus any gain recognized on the transfer. Since no gain was recognized by Grey, the basis of the property to Dover is $50,000.

C.1. Payment of Tax

5. (583,Q3,45) (c) The requirement is to determine the minimum estimated tax payments that must be made by Finbury Corporation to avoid the estimated tax underpayment penalty for 1983. Since Finbury is a large corporation (i.e., a corporation with TI of $1,000,000 or more in any of its three preceding tax years), its estimated tax payments must be at least equal to 75% of its 1983 tax liability (90% for 1984).

C.3. Gross Income

6. (1183,Q3,50) (d) The requirement is to determine the amount of capital gain recognized by a corporation on the sale of its treasury stock. No gain (loss) is recognized by a corporation on the sale of its stock (including treasury stock). The excess of selling price over cost is treated as an addition to paid-in capital.

7. (1183,Q3,60) (c) The requirement is to determine the amount of property distribution that should be treated as a dividend to Toty, Inc. The amount of distribution to a corporate distributee is the lesser of the property's (1) FMV ($40,000), or (2) adjusted basis ($25,000), plus gain recognized to the distributing corporation ($0). Since Lara's earnings and profits exceed $25,000, all $25,000 will be treated as a dividend to Toty, Inc.

8. (583,Q3,43) (d) No gain or loss is recognized by a corporation on the receipt of money or other property in exchange for its stock (including treasury stock).

9. (582,Q3,42) (d) The requirement is to determine the amount of sinking fund income taxable to Sportsworld. Since the property in the sinking fund is owned by Sportsworld, all income and gain from the sinking fund is taxable to Sportsworld.

10. (581,Q3,56) (b) The requirement is to determine the amount of bond discount deductible for the fiscal year ended March 31, 1981. Bond discount must be amortized ratably over the life of the bonds. Thus, the deduction for bond discount is $120,000 x 6/96 = $7,500.

11. (581,Q3,44) (b) The requirement is to compute the taxable income to Homer Corporation resulting from the repurchase of its bonds. Ordinary income or loss is recognized on the repurchase of a corporation's own bonds determined by the difference between the repurchase price and the net carrying value of the bonds (issue price plus or minus the discount or premium amortized). In this case, the bonds were issued at a $600,000 premium which was amortized at the rate of $12,000 ($600,000 ÷ 50 years) per year. The carrying value of the bonds on December 31, 1980, is $2,600,000 – ($12,000 x 20) = $2,360,000. Since Homer retired the bonds for $2,320,000, a gain of $40,000 is recognized.

12. (1177,Q2,22) (d) Gains and losses are recognized on the repurchase of a corporation's bonds in the year of the repurchase. The gain or loss is determined by the relationship of the repurchase price to the net carrying value of the bonds (face value plus or minus unamortized premium or discount). In this case the bonds were issued at face value, so the loss is the amount paid to repurchase ($258,000) less the face value of the bonds ($250,000) which is $8,000 and deductible as an expense.

C.4.b. Organization Expenditures

13. (1183,Q3,44) (d) The requirement is to determine the amount qualifying as amortizable organization expenses. Expenses incurred for printing and selling stock certificates are neither deductible, nor amortizable as organization expenses. These expenses of issuing stock are treated as a reduction of paid-in capital.

14. (581,Q3,55) (d) The requirement is to determine the maximum deduction for amortization of organization expense for 1980. A corporation's organizational expenditures can be amortized ratably over a period of not less than 60 months, beginning with the month in which a corporation begins business. Thus, the maximum deduction for 1980 is $900 x 6/60 = $90.

C.4.c. Charitable Contributions

15. (1182,Q3,41) (b) The requirement is to determine the contributions deduction for Richards Corporation given charitable contributions of $35,000, and TI of $280,000 before the contributions deduction. Since contributions are limited to 10% of TI before the contributions and DRD, the DRD of $34,000 must be added back to TI to arrive at the contributions base against which to apply the 10% limitation.

TI before CC	$280,000
Add back DRD	34,000
TI before CC and DRD	$314,000
% limitation	10%
Allowable contributions	$ 31,400

16. (581,Q3,48) (c) The requirement is to determine the maximum charitable contribution deduction for 1982. An accrual-basis corporation can elect to deduct a charitable contribution paid within 2-1/2 months of the close of its taxable year if its board of directors authorize the contribution during the taxable year. Thus, the $100,000 charitable contribution is deductible in 1982, but is limited to 10% of taxable income before the charitable contribution deduction. The maximum amount deductible in 1982 is:

Book income	$500,000
+ Charitable contribution	100,000
TI before CC deduction	$600,000
	x 10%
Maximum CC deduction	$ 60,000

The remaining $40,000 can be carried over a maximum of 5 years.

C.4.d. Dividend Received Deduction

17. (1183,Q3,43) (c) The requirement is to determine the amount that qualifies for the 85% dividends-received deduction. Corporations generally can deduct an amount equal to 85% of the dividends received from unaffiliated, domestic taxable corporations. Dividends from a mutual savings bank do not qualify for the deduction.

18. (1182,Q3,50) (b) The requirement is to determine Atkinson's DRD for dividends received from unaffiliated domestic corporations. The DRD (normally 85% of dividends) may be limited to 85% of TI before the DRD.

Gross business income	$160,000
Dividend income	100,000
	$260,000
Less business deductions	(170,000)
TI before DRD	$ 90,000
DRD ($90,000 x 85%)	(76,500)
TI	$13,500

Since the full deduction (85% x $100,000 = $85,000) would not create a NOL, the limitation applies.

C.4.e.5. Net Operating Loss

19. (1183,Q3,47) (d) The requirement is to determine Haya Corporation's net operating loss (NOL) for 1982. A deduction for a net operating loss carryover is not allowed in computing NOL. Furthermore, a deduction for charitable contributions is generally not allowed, since the charitable contributions deduction is limited to 10% of taxable income before the charitable contributions and dividends-received deductions. Thus, Haya's NOL for 1982 would be computed as follows:

Gross income	$ 600,000
Less expenses	(800,000)
	$(200,000)
Add back contributions included in expenses	5,000
NOL for 1982	$(195,000)

20. (1182,Q3,48) (c) The requirement is to determine the NOL for 1981 given that deductions in the tax return exceed gross income by $56,800. In computing the NOL for 1981, the DRD of $6,800 would be fully allowed, but the $15,000 NOL deduction (carryover from 1980) would not be allowed. $56,800 – $15,000 = $41,800.

C.6. Reconcile Book and Taxable Income

21. (1182,Q3,53) (c) The requirement is to determine net income per books given TI of $700,000.

Taxable income	$700,000
Provision for federal income tax	–280,000
Depreciation on tax return	+130,000
Depreciation per books	– 75,000
Life insurance proceeds	+100,000
Net income per books	$575,000

The provision for federal income tax is not deductible in computing TI but must be deducted per books. The life insurance proceeds are tax exempt, but must be included per books.

22. (582,Q3,41) (b) The requirement is to convert Cooma Corporation's book income of $260,000 to taxable income. Organization expenses may be amortized over 60 months or longer for tax purposes; therefore, the minimum period is 60 months. Adding back the book amortization or organization expenses of $13,000 ($130,000 ÷ 10 years), and then deducting the maximum amount of $26,000 ($130,000 x 12/60), results in taxable income of $247,000.

23. (581,Q3,42) (a) The requirement is to compute Apollo's taxable income for 1980. None of the income/expense items listed are includible in the computation of taxable income. Taxable income is computed as follows:

Book income	$1,200,000
– Municipal bond interest	(40,000)
– Proceeds of life insurance	(200,000)
+ Nondeductible interest expense (to produce tax-exempt interest income)	8,000
+ Provision for federal income tax	524,000
Taxable income	$1,492,000

C.6.d. Schedule M-2

24. (583,Q3,49) (d) The requirement is to determine the amount to be shown on schedule M-2 of Form 1120 as Barbaro's retained earnings at December 31, 1982. Beginning with the balance at January 1, 1982, the end of year balance would be computed as follows:

Balance, 1/1/82	$600,000
Net income for year	+ 274,900
Federal income tax refund	+ 26,000
Cash dividends	– 150,000
Balance, 12/31/82	$750,900

25. (582,Q3,50) (a) The requirement is to determine the amount that should appear on the last line of Schedule M-2 of Form 1120. Schedule M-2 is an "Analysis of Unappropriated Retained Earnings Per Books." Its first line is the balance at the beginning of the year and its last line is the balance at the end of the year. The end of year balance would be computed as follows:

Retained earnings, beginning	$ 50,000
Net income for year	+70,000
Contingency reserve	–10,000
Cash dividends	– 8,000
Retained earnings, end of year	$102,000

D. Affiliated and Controlled Corporations

26. (1177,Q2,21) (a) Recognition of gains and losses on the sale or exchange of property between affiliated corporations is deferred when a consolidated return is filed. Therefore, none of the $20,000 gain on sale of land to Dale Corporation will be recognized in 1976. In 1977 when the property is sold to an unrelated third party, i.e., one outside the affiliated group, a $35,000 gain will be recognized by Hill Corporation.

E. Dividends and Distributions

27. (581,Q3,57) (d) The requirement is to determine the amount of dividend income taxable to the shareholder. If a corporation sells property to a shareholder for less than fair market value, a noncorporate distributee is considered to have received a constructive dividend to the extent of the differences between the fair market value of the property and the price paid. Thus, the shareholder's dividend income is $80,000 – $50,000 = $30,000. Note the question states "before the dividend exclusion" which indicates that the shareholder was a noncorporate distributee.

28. (1178,Q2,21) (a) Corporations generally do not recognize gains or losses on the distribution of property to shareholders. (Gains may be recognized on distribution of LIFO inventory, depreciable property, and property with a basis less than related liability.) Guardian Corporation would recognize no gain on the distribution of the marketable securities to its shareholders.

29. (1177,Q2,31) (a) Distributions of property to shareholders reduce earnings and profits (E&P) by the adjusted basis of the property distributed. The reduction of E&P must be adjusted by any liabilities to which the property being distributed is subject. Therefore, E&P is reduced by $1,500 ($6,500 basis of land less $5,000 mortgage).

30. (1175,Q2,18) (c) The amount of the distribution is the amount of money plus the fair market value of any property received ($10,000 plus $25,000). Distributions, to the extent of earnings and profits ($22,000), are dividends to shareholders. The portion of the distribution that is not a dividend ($13,000) is a return of capital and will reduce shareholders' basis in their stock accordingly. The $13,000 return of capital distribution will reduce their basis from $76,000 to $63,000.

E.5. Complete Liquidations

31. (1183,Q3,51) (a) The requirement is to determine the amount of gain recognized to Seso Corporation on the transfer of appreciated land in complete liquidation of Seso. A solvent, 80% or more owned subsidiary corporation never recognizes a gain (loss) on the distribution of its assets in complete liquidation. Since Pearl Corporation owned 90% of Seso at the time of liquidation, complete nonrecognition of gain (loss) for Seso is assured.

32. (583,Q3,48) (b) The requirement is to determine Carmela's recognized gain from the sale of assets during a complete liquidation. No gain or loss is recognized by a corporation on the sale of **property** following the adoption of a plan of complete liquidation if the corporation then distributes all of its assets within 12 months after the plan of liquidation is adopted. The term **property** includes the land, but excludes inventory (unless sold in bulk). Thus, ordinary income of $22,500 is recognized on the sale of inventory.

33. (1182,Q3,59) (a) The requirement is to determine the amount of gain recognized by Edgewood Corporation on its liquidation. A corporation generally recognizes no gain or loss on the distribution of its assets in liquidation. Exceptions include a distribution of installment obligations or property subject to recapture, but these exceptions do not apply here.

34. (1181,P3,48) (c) The requirement is to determine the amount of liquidating distribution taxable to Gerry as ordinary income and as capital gain in a one-month liquidation of Rockville Corporation. In a Sec. 333 (one-month) liquidation, a noncorporate shareholder's realized gain is recognized as ordinary dividend income to the extent of his ratable share of earnings and profits. The shareholder will have capital gain to the extent that the total amount of cash, stock, and securities received exceeds the amount reported as ordinary income. Gerry realized a gain of $13,000 ($6,000 + $40,000 – $13,000 – $20,000). Gerry will recognize $5,000 of ordinary income (the extent of Rockville's earnings and profits), and $1,000 of capital gain ($6,000 cash – $5,000 reported as ordinary income). The remainder of the realized gain is deferred.

F. Collapsible Corporations

35. (1172,P1,6) (a) A shareholder owning more than 5% of the stock of a corporation which has been determined to be collapsible is generally denied long-term capital gain treatment on a sale of stock or on the liquidation of the corporation. Instead, the shareholder must report all gain as ordinary income.

Sale price	$40,000
Basis	–25,000
Ordinary income	$15,000

G. Personal Holding Company and Accumulated Earnings Tax

36. (1183,Q3,56) (b) The imposition of the accumulated earnings tax (AET) does **not** depend on a stock ownership test, nor is the tax self-assessing. The

AET is imposed on a corporation's retention of earnings in excess of reasonable business needs, but may be mitigated by sufficient dividend distributions.

37. (1183,Q3,57) (d) The personal holding company (PHC) tax is self-assessed by a corporation filing a Schedule PH along with its regular Form 1120 tax return. The PHC tax may be imposed if more than 50% of a corporation's stock is owned by 5 or fewer individuals, **and** 60% or more of the corporation's adjusted ordinary gross income is PHC income. The tax (at a rate of 50%) is assessed against undistributed PHC income, which may be reduced by dividend distributions.

38. (583,Q3,42) (d) Beginning in 1982, the minimum accumulated earnings credit is $250,000 for nonservice corporations; $150,000 for service corporations.

39. (582,Q3,44) (b) The requirement is to determine Daystar's allowable accumulated earnings credit for 1983. The credit is the greater of (1) the earnings and profits of the tax year retained for reasonable business needs of $20,000; or, (2) $250,000 less the accumulated earnings and profits at the end of the preceding year of $45,000. Thus, the credit is $250,000 – $45,000 = $205,000.

40. (581,Q3,60) (a) The requirement is to determine the undistributed personal holding company income for Cromwell Investors, Inc. Cromwell does not meet the "stock ownership test" that is required to be classified as a personal holding company. The "stock ownership test" requires that **more** than 50% of the outstanding stock must be owned directly or indirectly by five or fewer individuals. Cromwell has ten **equal unrelated** shareholders. Thus, Cromwell is not classified as a personal holding company and therefore, has no undistributed PHC income.

H. S Corporations

41. (1183,Q3,41) (a) For taxable years beginning after 1982, an S corporation may have a maximum of 35 shareholders.

42. (1183,Q3,46) (a) The requirement is to determine which is **not** a requirement for a corporation to elect S corporation status. An S corporation must generally have only one class of stock, be a domestic corporation, and confine shareholders to individuals, estates, and certain trusts. An S corporation need **not** be a member of a controlled group.

43. (583,Q3,51) (a) The requirement is to determine the amount upon which an S corporation should compute its income and capital gain tax. An S corporation never pays any regular federal income tax, and is only subject to a capital gain tax if certain requirements are met. Since one requirement is that the NLTCG exceed $25,000, the corporation will not be subject to the capital gain tax.

44. (582,Q3,52) (b) The requirement is to determine the amount of loss from an S corporation that can be deducted by each of two equal shareholders. An S corporation loss is passed through to shareholders and is deductible to the extent of a shareholder's basis for stock plus the basis for any debt owed the shareholder by the corporation. Here, each shareholder's allocated loss of $45,000 ($90,000 ÷ 2) is deductible to the extent of stock basis of $5,000 plus debt basis of $15,000, or $20,000. The remainder of the loss ($25,000 for each shareholder) can be carried forward indefinitely by each shareholder and deducted when there is basis to absorb it.

45. (1180,P3,45) (a) The requirement is to calculate the amount of LTCG passed through to Mr. Hoyt, the sole shareholder. An S corporation's NLTCG is passed though to shareholders as LTCG after being reduced by any capital gain and minimum taxes paid. Thus, the $42,000 LTCG minus the capital gains tax of $4,760, equals $37,240, the amount to be reported as LTCG by Mr. Hoyt.

46. (1176,Q2,21) (d) The requirement is to determine each shareholder's income from an S corporation. Shareholders of an S corporation must report their pro rata share of all items of income or loss, whether distributed or not. Thus, each shareholder should report ordinary income of $7,000 ($70,000 ÷ 10), and long-term capital loss of $1,000 ($10,000 ÷ 10).

I. Corporate Reorganizations

47. (583,Q3,52) (c) The requirement is to determine the amount of Claudio's net operating loss (NOL) carryover that can be used to offset Stellar's 1982 taxable income. The amount of Claudio's NOL ($270,000) that can be utilized by Stellar for 1982 is limited to the taxable income of Stellar for its full taxable year (before a NOL deduction) multiplied by the fraction:

$$\frac{\text{Days after acquisition date}}{\text{Total days in the taxable year}}$$

Here, you must use calendar months, and the deduction for the NOL carryover would be limited to (6/12) x $360,000 = $180,000.

48. (1182,Q3,55) (b) The requirement is to determine the basis to Summit of assets acquired in a reorganization. The basis of assets acquired in a reorganization equals the transferor's (Hansen's) adjusted basis, increased by any gain recognized to the transferor. Hansen's realized gain [($260,000 + $40,000) – $200,000 = $100,000] is recognized to the extent of the $40,000 cash boot received. Thus, Summit's basis for the acquired assets is $200,000 + $40,000 = $240,000.

49. (582,Q3,46) (b) The requirement is to determine the amount and nature of recognized gain to be reported by Peel as a result of a reorganization. A recognized gain resulting from a reorganization is generally treated as a dividend to the extent of the shareholder's ratable share of earnings and profits. Here, Peel's realized gain of $5,000 [($24,000 – $20,000) + $1,000] is recognized to the extent of the $1,000 cash (boot) received. Since $1,000 is not in excess of Peel's ratable share of Lorna's earnings and profits, all $1,000 is reported as dividend income.

50. (582,Q3,53) (a) The requirement is to determine the recognized gain to be reported by Mueller on the exchange of her Disco bond for Disco preferred stock. The issuance by Disco Corporation of its preferred stock in exchange for its bonds is a nontaxable "Type E" reorganization (i.e., a recapitalization). Since Mueller did not receive any boot, no part of her $400 realized gain is recognized.

51. (1181,P3,41) (b) The requirement is to determine the amount of recognized gain in a recapitalization. Since a recapitalization is a reorganization, a realized gain is recognized only to the extent that consideration other than stock or securities is received, including the FMV of an excess of the principal amount of securities received over the principal amount of securities surrendered. Since no securities were surrendered, the excess principal amount of securities received is $10,000, and Moore's realized gain of $23,500 is recognized to the extent of the $10,500 FMV of the excess principal amount of securities received.

52. (581,Q3,50) (a) The requirement is to determine the recognized gain and basis of stock received in a corporate reorganization. No gain or loss is recognized if stock is exchanged **solely** for stock in a corporation that is a party to the reorganization. Smith's basis in the Mark Corporation stock received is the same as his basis in the Talbot Corporation stock ($150,000).

May 1984 Answers

53. (584,Q1,1) (b) The requirement is to determine Dale Corporation's taxable income, given book income of $520,000. Organization expenditures may be amortized over a minimum period of 60 months. Adding back the book amortization of organization costs of $26,000 ($260,000 ÷ 10 years), and then deducting the maximum amount of $52,000 ($260,000 x 12/60) results in taxable income of $494,000 ($520,000 + $26,000 – $52,000) for the Dale Corporation.

54. (584,Q1,2) (d) The requirement is to determine the base amount for computing the maximum allowable deduction for charitable contributions. A corporations's charitable contribution deduction is limited to 10% of a base amount comprised of TI before the contributions deduction, the dividend received deduction, a net operating loss carryback, and a capital loss carryback. The base amount would be computed as follows:

Operating income after deducting contributions	$200,000
Dividend income	+20,000
Charitable contributions	+12,000
TI before contributions deduction	$232,000

55. (584,Q1,4) (d) The requirement is to determine the recognized gain and basis of stock received in a corporate reorganization. No gain or loss is recognized if stock is exchanged **solely** for stock in a corporate reorganization. Gow's basis in the Rolf Corp. stock received is the same as his former basis in the Bly Corp. stock ($75,000).

56. (584,Q1,6) (a) The requirement is to determine the gain recognized by Tyson Corp. on the distribution of marketable securities in complete liquidation. A corporation generally recognizes no gain or loss on the distribution of its property in complete liquidation.

57. (584,Q1,8) (c) The requirement is to determine the amount of gain recognized by Pym on the dividend distribution of land to a shareholder. Although a corporation generally recognizes no gain or loss on the distribution of property to a shareholder, gain is recognized if property is distributed with a liability in excess of the property's basis. The amount of gain recognized is $2,000, the excess of the liability ($5,000) over the property's basis ($3,000).

58. (584,Q1,9) (b) The requirement is to determine the amount of the taxable dividend for an individual shareholder on a property distribution. A noncorporate distributee is considered to have received a dividend equal to the fair market value of the property distributed less any liabilities assumed. In this case, Rowe received a taxable dividend of $7,000 ($12,000 – $5,000).

59. (584,Q1,10) (a) The requirement is to determine the amount of dividend reportable by a corporate shareholder on a property distribution. The amount of the dividend to be reported by a corporate distributee is the lesser of (1) the fair market value, or (2) the distributor's basis plus any gain recognized by the distributor, less the liability assumed. Thus, the amount of the dividend for Kyle Corporation is the lesser of (1) $12,000, or (2) [$3,000 + $2,000] – $5,000 = $0. Kyle's reportable dividend is zero.

60. (584,Q1,11) (c) The requirement is to determine the treatment of a **net** capital loss by a corporate taxpayer. A corporation's capital losses are deductible only to the extent of its capital gains. Therefore, a **net** capital loss indicates an excess of capital losses over capital gains and is **not** deductible in the year sustained. Instead, it is carried back three years and forward five years as a STCC to offset capital gains in those years.

61. (584,Q1,12) (b) The requirement is to determine the applicability of the accumulated earnings tax (AET). The AET is an additional tax assessed because corporations accumulate earnings as a means of tax avoidance. The AET is applicable to all corporations **except** personal holding companies.

62. (584,Q1,13) (a) The requirement is to determine the taxability of a dividend between affiliated corporations filing a consolidated return. A dividend distribution from one member to another member of an affiliated group during a consolidated return year is eliminated in determining taxable income. Note, that even if a consolidated return is not filed, members of an affiliated group (80% or more ownership) are entitled to a 100% dividends received deduction.

63. (584,Q1,15) (c) In a one-month Sec. 333 liquidation, a noncorporate shareholder's realized gain is recognized as dividend income to the extent of his ratable share of earnings and profits. Sec. 333 only applies to a **complete** liquidation and is generally not applicable to collapsible corporations. To be eligible for Sec. 333, all property must be distributed within one calendar month, but it need not be the same month in which the election was made.

64. (584,Q1,16) (d) For an S corporation organized after 1983, there is no limit on the amount of passive investment income that can be earned and still qualify as an S coroporation. If a corporation was in existence prior to 1984 **and** has Subchapter C earnings and profits, an S corporation election will be terminated if passive investment income exceeds 25% of gross receipts for three consecutive taxable years. Subchapter C earnings and profits accumulated during a taxable year for which a Subchapter S election was not in effect.

65. (584,Q1,18) (c) The personal holding company (PHC) tax is self-assessed by a corporation filing Schedule PH along with its regular Form 1120 tax return. The PHC tax may be imposed if more than 50% of the value of a corporation's stock is owned by 5 or fewer individuals and 60% or more of the corporation's adjusted ordinary gross income is PHC income. The tax (at a rate of 50%) is assessed against undistributed PHC income, which may be reduced (and even eliminated) by dividend distributions.

66. (584,Q1,20) (b) The requirement is to determine the corporation's total basis for the transferred assets. The cash and office furniture and equipment were transferred by Bell in a nontaxable Sec. 351 transfer to a controlled corporation. The corporation's basis for the transferred assets would be the same as Bell's basis, increased by any gain recognized by Bell. Since Bell did not receive any boot, no gain was recognized by him. Thus, the corporation's total basis for the transferred assets would be $5,000 + $35,000 = $40,000.

Multiple Choice Questions (1–2)

1. Mr. & Mrs. John Hance jointly gave a $100,000 outright gift in 1982 to an unrelated friend, Fred Green, who needed the money to pay medical expenses. In filing their gift tax returns for 1982, Mr. & Mrs. Hance were entitled to exclusions aggregating

   a. $0
   b. $ 6,000
   c. $10,000
   d. $20,000

2. In 1970, Edwin Ryan bought 100 shares of a listed stock for $5,000. In June 1982, when the stock's fair market value was $7,000, Edwin gave this stock to his sister, Lynn. No gift tax was paid. Lynn died in October 1982, bequeathing this stock to Edwin, when the stock's fair market value was $9,000. Lynn's executor did not elect the alternate valuation. What is Edwin's basis for this stock after he inherits it from Lynn's estate?

   a. $0
   b. $5,000
   c. $7,000
   d. $9,000

Multiple Choice Answers

1. d 2. b

Multiple Choice Answer Explanations

1. (1183,Q2,25) (d) The requirement is to determine the amount of gift tax exclusions allowable to the Hances for 1982. In computing a donor's gift tax, there is an annual exclusion of $10,000 per donee. Since the $100,000 gift was jointly made by Mr. & Mrs. Hance, each would be entitled to a $10,000 exclusion, a total of $20,000.

2. (1183,Q2,26) (b) The requirement is to determine Edwin's basis for the stock inherited from Lynn's estate. A special rule applies if a decedent (Lynn) acquires appreciated property as a gift within one year of death, and this property passes to the donor (Edwin) or donor's spouse. Then the donor's (Edwin's) basis is the basis of the property in the hands of the decedent (Lynn) before death. Since Lynn had received the stock as a gift, Lynn's basis before death ($5,000) becomes the basis of the stock to Edwin.

SAMPLE CPA EXAMINATION

The following sample CPA Examination is presented to enable students to gain experience in taking a "realistic" exam. Selection of multiple choice items and problems was based on a statistical analysis of recent exams. This examination consists of five sections - Auditing, Business Law, Practice I and II and Theory.

Candidates will benefit most from this sample exam if they work each of the five parts in one sitting within the time limits allowed. Prepare your solutions as thoroughly as if you were actually taking the exam.

Unofficial answers are presented immediately following the examination.

EXAMINATION IN AUDITING

NOTE TO CANDIDATES: Suggested time allotments are as follows:

All questions are required:	*Estimated Minutes* Minimum	Maximum
No. 1	90	110
No. 2	15	25
No. 3	15	25
No. 4	15	25
No. 5	15	25
Total	150	210

Number 1 (Estimated time – 90 to 110 minutes)

Select the **best** answer for each of the following items.

1. Most of the independent auditor's work in formulating an opinion on financial statements consists of
   a. Studying and evaluating internal control.
   b. Obtaining and examining evidential matter.
   c. Examining cash transactions.
   d. Comparing recorded accountability with assets.

2. The principal auditor is satisfied with the independence and professional reputation of the other auditor who has audited a subsidiary but wants to indicate the division of responsibility. The principal auditor should
   a. Modify the scope paragraph of the report.
   b. Modify the scope and opinion paragraphs of the report.
   c. Not modify the report except for inclusion of an explanatory middle paragraph.
   d. Modify the opinion paragraph of the report.

3. The auditor is **least** concerned with which of the following?
   a. Administrative controls.
   b. Application controls.
   c. Safeguarding of assets.
   d. Access to assets.

4. Analytical review procedures may be classified as being primarily
   a. Compliance tests.
   b. Substantive tests.
   c. Tests of ratios.
   d. Detailed tests of balances.

5. Which of the following is **not** a typical analytical review procedure?
   a. Study of relationships of the financial information with relevant nonfinancial information.
   b. Comparison of the financial information with similar information regarding the industry in which the entity operates.
   c. Comparison of recorded amounts of major disbursements with appropriate invoices.
   d. Comparison of the financial information with budgeted amounts.

6. An individual just entering upon an auditing career must obtain professional experience primarily in order to achieve a
   a. Positive quality control review.
   b. Seasoned judgment.
   c. Favorable peer review.
   d. Specialty designation by the AICPA.

7. A conceptually logical approach to the auditor's evaluation of accounting controls consists of the following four steps:

I. Determine the accounting control procedures that should prevent or detect errors and irregularities.
II. Evaluate any weakness to determine its effect on the nature, timing or extent of auditing procedures to be applied and suggestions to be made to the client.
III. Determine whether the necessary procedures are prescribed and are being followed satisfactorily.
IV. Consider the types of errors and irregularities that could occur.

What should be the order in which these four steps are performed?

a. I, II, III, and IV.
b. I, III, IV, and II.
c. III, IV, I, and II.
d. IV, I, III, and II.

8. The third general standard states that due care is to be exercised in the performance of the examination. This standard should be interpreted to mean that a CPA who undertakes an engagement assumes a duty to perform

a. With reasonable diligence and without fault or error.
b. As a professional who will assume responsibility for losses consequent upon error of judgment.
c. To the satisfaction of the client and third parties who may rely upon it.
d. As a professional possessing the degree of skill commonly possessed by others in the field.

9. An auditor is confronted with an exception considered sufficiently material as to warrant some deviation from the standard unqualified auditor's report. If the exception relates to a departure from generally accepted accounting principles, the auditor must decide between expressing a (an)

a. Adverse opinion and a "subject to" opinion.
b. Adverse opinion and an "except for" opinion.
c. Adverse opinion and a disclaimer of opinion.
d. Disclaimer of opinion and a "subject to" opinion.

10. Where computers are used, the effectiveness of internal accounting control depends, in part, upon whether the organizational structure includes any incompatible combinations. Such a combination would exist when there is no separation of the duties between

a. Documentation librarian and manager of programming.
b. Programmer and console operator.
c. Systems analyst and programmer.
d. Processing control clerk and keypunch supervisor.

11. An auditor's working papers will generally be **least** likely to include documentation showing how the

a. Client's schedules were prepared.
b. Engagement had been planned.
c. Client's system of internal control had been reviewed and evaluated.
d. Unusual matters were resolved.

12. During the review of an EDP internal control system an auditor may review decision tables prepared by the client. A decision table is usually prepared by a client to supplement or replace the preparation of

a. An internal control questionnaire when the number of alternative responses is large.
b. A narrative description of a system where transactions are not processed in batches.
c. Flowcharts when the number of alternatives is large.
d. An internal control questionnaire not specifically designed for an EDP installation.

13. An important statistic to consider when using a statistical sampling audit plan is the population variability. The population variability is measured by the

a. Sample mean.
b. Standard deviation.
c. Standard error of the sample mean.
d. Estimated population total minus the actual population total.

14. Mavis, CPA, has audited the financial statements of South Bay Sales Incorporated for several years and had always been paid promptly for services rendered. Last year's audit invoices have not been paid because South Bay is experiencing cash flow difficulties, and the current year's audit is scheduled to commence in one week. With respect to the past due audit fees Mavis should

a. Perform the scheduled audit and allow South Bay to pay when the cash flow difficulties are alleviated.
b. Perform the scheduled audit only after arranging a definite payment schedule and securing notes signed by South Bay.

c. Inform South Bay's management that the past due audit fees are considered an impairment of auditor independence.
d. Inform South Bay's management that the past due audit fees may be considered a loan on which interest must be imputed for financial statement purposes.

15. With respect to consistency, which of the following should be done by an independent auditor, who has not examined a company's financial statements for the preceding year but is doing so in the current year?
a. Report on the financial statements of the current year without referring to consistency.
b. Consider the consistent application of principles within the year under examination but not between the current and preceding year.
c. Adopt procedures, that are practicable and reasonable in the circumstances to obtain assurance that the principles employed are consistent between the current and preceding year.
d. Rely on the report of the prior year's auditors if such a report does not take exception as to consistency.

16. The purpose of tests of compliance is to provide reasonable assurance that the
a. Accounting treatment of transactions and balances is valid and proper.
b. Accounting control procedures are functioning as intended.
c. Entity has complied with disclosure requirements of generally accepted accounting principles.
d. Entity has complied with requirements of quality control.

17. A sales cutoff test of billings complements the verification of
a. Sales return.
b. Cash.
c. Accounts receivable.
d. Sales allowances.

18. In performing an audit, Jackson, CPA, discovers that the professional competence necessary for the engagement is lacking. Jackson informs management of the situation and recommends another local CPA firm, and management engages this other firm. Under these circumstances
a. Jackson may request compensation from the other CPA firm for any professional services rendered to it in connection with the engagement.
b. Jackson may accept a referral fee from the other CPA firm.
c. Jackson has violated the AICPA Code of Professional Ethics because of nonfulfillment of the duty of performance.
d. Jackson's lack of competence should be construed to be a violation of generally accepted auditing standards.

19. Under which of the following set of circumstances might an auditor disclaim an opinion?
a. The financial statements contain a departure from generally accepted accounting principles, the effect of which is material.
b. The principal auditor decides to make reference to the report of another auditor who audited a subsidiary.
c. There has been a material change between periods in the method of the application of accounting principles.
d. There are significant uncertainties affecting the financial statements.

20. The client's EDP exception reporting system helps an auditor to conduct a more efficient audit because it
a. Condenses data significantly.
b. Highlights abnormal conditions.
c. Decreases the EDP compliance testing.
d. Is an efficient EDP input control.

21. Once a CPA has determined that accounts receivable have increased due to slow collections in a "tight money" environment, the CPA would be likely to
a. Increase the balance in the allowance for bad debts account.
b. Review the going concern ramifications.
c. Review the credit and collection policy.
d. Expand tests of collectibility.

22. The AICPA Code of Professional Ethics would be violated if a CPA accepted a fee for services and the fee was
a. Fixed by a public authority.
b. Based on a price quotation submitted in competitive bidding.
c. Determined, based on the results of judicial proceedings.
d. Payable after a specified finding was obtained.

23. At which point in an ordinary sales transaction of a wholesaling business would a lack of specific authorization be of **least** concern to the auditor in the conduct of an audit?
 a. Granting of credit.
 b. Shipment of goods.
 c. Determination of discounts.
 d. Selling of goods for cash.

24. On February 13, 1978, Fox, CPA, met with the audit committee of the Gem Corporation to review the draft of Fox's report on the company's financial statements as of and for the year ended December 31,1977. On February 16, 1978, Fox completed all remaining field work at the Gem Corporation's headquarters. On February 17, 1978, Fox typed and signed the final version of the auditor's report. On February 18, 1978, the final report was mailed to Gem's audit committee. What date should have been used on Fox's report?
 a. February 13, 1978.
 b. February 16, 1978.
 c. February 17, 1978.
 d. February 18, 1978.

25. If the size of the sample to be used in a particular test of attributes has **not** been determined by utilizing statistical concepts, but the sample has been chosen in accordance with random selection procedures
 a. No inferences can be drawn from the sample.
 b. The auditor has committed a nonsampling error.
 c. The auditor may or may **not** achieve desired precision at the desired level of confidence.
 d. The auditor will have to evaluate the results by reference to the principles of discovery sampling.

26. Some firms which dispose of only a small part of their total output by consignment shipments fail to make any distinction between consignment shipments and regular sales. Which of the following would suggest that goods have been shipped on consignment?
 a. Numerous shipments of small quantities.
 b. Numerous shipments of large quantities and few returns.
 c. Large debits to accounts receivable and small periodic credits.
 d. Large debits to accounts receivable and large periodic credits.

27. For the purpose of proper accounting control, postdated checks remitted by customers should be
 a. Restrictively endorsed.
 b. Returned to customer.
 c. Recorded as a cash sale.
 d. Placed in the joint custody of two officers.

28. In pursuing a CPA firm's quality control objectives, a CPA firm may maintain records indicating which partners or employees of the CPA firm were previously employed by the CPA firm's clients. Which quality control objective would this be **most** likely to satisfy?
 a. Professional relationship.
 b. Supervision.
 c. Independence.
 d. Advancement.

29. Comparative financial statements include the financial statements of a prior period which were examined by a predecessor auditor, whose report is **not** presented. If the predecessor auditor's report was qualified, the successor auditor must
 a. Express an opinion on the current year statements alone and make **no** reference to the prior year statements.
 b. Disclose the reasons for any qualification included in the predecessor auditor's opinion.
 c. Obtain written approval from the predecessor auditor, to include the prior year's financial statements.
 d. Issue a standard short-form comparative report indicating the division of responsibility.

30. A continuing auditor would update his opinion on prior financial statements by issuing a "subject to" opinion for the
 a. Subsequent resolution of an uncertainty in the current period.
 b. Discovery of an uncertainty in the current period.
 c. Discovery of an uncertainty in the current period that relates to the prior-period statements being reported on.
 d. Restatement of prior-period statements in conformity with generally accepted accounting principles.

31. When outside firms of nonaccountants specializing in the taking of physical inventories are used to count, list, price and subsequently compute the total

dollar amount of inventory on hand at the date of the physical count, the auditor will ordinarily

a. Consider the report of the outside inventory-taking firm to be an acceptable alternative procedure to the observation of physical inventories.
b. Make or observe some physical counts of the inventory, recompute certain inventory calculations and test certain inventory transactions.
c. **Not** reduce the extent of work on the physical count of inventory.
d. Consider the reduced audit effort with respect to the physical count of inventory as a scope limitation.

32. The auditor's count of the client's cash should be coordinated to coincide with the

a. Study of the system of internal controls with respect to cash.
b. Close of business on the balance sheet date.
c. Count of marketable securities.
d. Count of inventories.

33. A basic objective of a CPA firm is to provide professional services to conform with professional standards. Reasonable assurance of achieving this basic objective is provided through

a. Continuing professional education.
b. A system of quality control.
c. Compliance with generally accepted reporting standards.
d. A system of peer review.

34. Which of the following is an effective internal accounting control over accounts receivable?

a. Only persons who handle cash receipts should be responsible for the preparation of documents that reduce accounts receivable balances.
b. Responsibility for approval of the write-off of uncollectible accounts receivable should be assigned to the cashier.
c. Balances in the subsidiary accounts receivable ledger should be reconciled to the general ledger control account once a year, preferably at year-end.
d. The billing function should be assigned to persons other than those responsible for maintaining accounts receivable subsidiary records.

35. A major customer of an audit client suffers a fire just prior to completion of year-end field work. The audit client believes that this event could have a significant direct effect on the financial statements. The auditor should

a. Advise management to disclose the event in notes to the financial statements.
b. Disclose the event in the auditor's report.
c. Withhold submission of the auditor's report until the extent of the direct effect on the financial statements is known.
d. Advise management to adjust the financial statements.

36. A CPA examining inventory may appropriately apply sampling for attributes in order to estimate the

a. Average price of inventory items.
b. Percentage of slow-moving inventory items.
c. Dollar value of inventory.
d. Physical quantity of inventory items.

37. An auditor will use the EDP test data method in order to gain certain assurances with respect to the

a. Input data.
b. Machine capacity.
c. Procedures contained within the program.
d. Degree of keypunching accuracy.

38. An auditor has withdrawn from an audit engagement of a publicly-held company after finding irregularities which may materially affect the financial statements. The auditor should set forth the reasons and findings in correspondence to the

a. Securities and Exchange Commission.
b. Client's legal counsel.
c. Stock exchanges where the company's stock is traded.
d. Board of directors.

39. The physical count of inventory of a retailer was higher than shown by the perpetual records. Which of the following could explain the difference?

a. Inventory items had been counted but the tags placed on the items had not been taken off the items and added to the inventory accumulation sheets.
b. Credit memos for several items returned by customers had not been prepared.
c. No journal entry had been made on the retailer's books for several items returned to its suppliers.
d. An item purchased "FOB shipping point" had not arrived at the date of the inventory count and had not been reflected in the perpetual records.

40. With respect to issuance of an audit report which is dual dated for a subsequent event occurring after the completion of fieldwork but before issuance of the auditor's report, the auditor's responsibility for events occurring subsequent to the completion of fieldwork is

a. Extended to include all events occurring until the date of the last subsequent event referred to.
b. Limited to the specific event referred to.
c. Limited to all events occurring through the date of issuance of the report.
d. Extended to include all events occurring through the date of submission of the report to the client.

41. When a contingency is resolved immediately subsequent to the issuance of a report which was qualified with respect to the contingency, the auditor should

a. Insist that the client issue revised financial statements.
b. Inform the audit committee that the report cannot be relied upon.
c. Take no action regarding the event.
d. Inform the appropriate authorities that the report cannot be relied upon.

42. Propex Corporation uses a voucher register and does not record invoices in a subsidiary ledger. Propex will probably benefit most from the additional cost of maintaining an accounts payable subsidiary ledger if

a. There are usually invoices in an unmatched invoice file.
b. Vendors' requests for confirmation of receivables often go unanswered for several months until paid invoices can be reviewed.
c. Partial payments to vendors are continuously made in the ordinary course of business.
d. It is difficult to reconcile vendors' monthly statements.

43. The auditor should insist that a representative of the client be present during the physical examination of securities in order to

a. Lend authority to the auditor's directives.
b. Detect forged securities.
c. Coordinate the return of all securities to proper locations.
d. Acknowledge the receipt of securities returned.

44. In order to efficiently establish the correctness of the accounts payable cutoff, an auditor will be **most** likely to

a. Coordinate cutoff tests with physical inventory observation.
b. Compare cutoff reports with purchase orders.
c. Compare vendors' invoices with vendors' statements.
d. Coordinate mailing of confirmations with cutoff tests.

45. Cortney has moved to a distant city but desires to continue to retain Blake, CPA, to prepare his personal federal tax return. Blake telephones Cortney after receiving his written list of information to be used in the preparation of the tax return because it appears to contain an understatement of interest expense. Based upon the conversation Blake learns that the interest expense should be double the amount indicated on the written list. Blake, who asked Cortney to send a photocopy of the supporting evidence indicating the correct amount of the interest expense, has not received the correspondence and the filing deadline is five days away. Under the circumstances Blake should

a. Prepare the return based upon the written information received and **not** sign the preparer's declaration.
b. Prepare the return based upon the written information received, clearly indicating that an amended return will follow.
c. Prepare the return based upon the written and oral information received.
d. Send Cortney a telegram indicating that no tax return will be prepared until all requested data are received.

46. To strengthen the system of internal accounting control over the purchase of merchandise, a company's receiving department should

a. Accept merchandise only if a purchase order or approval granted by the purchasing department is on hand.
b. Accept and count all merchandise received from the usual company vendors.
c. Rely on shipping documents for the preparation of receiving reports.
d. Be responsible for the physical handling of merchandise but not the preparation of receiving reports.

47. A representation letter issued by a client

a. Is essential for the preparation of the audit program.

b. Is a substitute for testing.
c. Does **not** reduce the auditor's responsibility.
d. Reduces the auditor's responsibility only to the extent that it is relied upon.

48. In performing a compilation of financial statements of a nonpublic entity, the accountant decides that modification of the standard report is not adequate to indicate deficiencies in the financial statements taken as a whole, and the client is not willing to correct the deficiencies. The accountant should therefore
a. Perform a review of the financial statements.
b. Issue a special report.
c. Withdraw from the engagement.
d. Express an adverse audit opinion.

49. In the audit of which of the following types of profit-oriented enterprises would the auditor be most likely to place special emphasis on testing the internal controls over proper classification of payroll transactions?
a. A manufacturing organization.
b. A retailing organization.
c. A wholesaling organization.
d. A service organization.

50. A CPA certificate is evidence of
a. Recognition of independence.
b. Basic competence at the time the certificate is granted.
c. Culmination of the educational process.
d. Membership in the AICPA.

51. The objective of precision in sampling for compliance testing on an internal control system is to
a. Determine the probability of the auditor's conclusion based upon reliance factors.
b. Determine that financial statements taken as a whole are not materially in error.
c. Estimate the reliability of substantive tests.
d. Estimate the range of procedural deviations in the population.

52. Which of the audit procedures listed below would be **least** likely to disclose the existence of related party transactions of a client during the period under audit?
a. Reading "conflict-of-interest" statements obtained by the client from its management.
b. Scanning accounting records for large transactions at or just prior to the end of the period under audit.
c. Inspecting invoices from law firms.
d. Confirming large purchase and sales transactions with the vendors and/or customers involved.

53. An example of a transaction which may be indicative of the existence of related parties is
a. Borrowing or lending at a rate of interest which equals the current market rate.
b. Selling real estate at a price that is comparable to its appraised value.
c. Making large loans with specified terms as to when or how the funds will be repaid.
d. Exchanging property for similar property in a nonmonetary transaction.

54. Which of the following would not be included in a CPA's report based upon a review of the financial statements of a nonpublic entity?
a. A statement that the review was in accordance with generally accepted auditing standards.
b. A statement that all information included in the financial statements are the representations of management.
c. A statement describing the principal procedures performed.
d. A statement describing the auditor's conclusions based upon the results of the review.

55. Which of the following statements with respect to required auditor communication of weaknesses in internal accounting controls is correct?
a. Such communication is required to be in writing.
b. Such communication must include a description of all weaknesses.
c. Such communication is the principal reason for testing and evaluating internal controls.
d. Such communication is incidental to the auditor's study and evaluation of the system of internal accounting control.

56. The most efficient and least costly method of dumping information for purposes of maintaining a backup file is from disk to
a. Dump.
b. Printout.
c. Cards.
d. Tape.

57. The SEC has strengthened auditor independence by requiring that management
   a. Engage auditors to report in accordance with the Foreign Corrupt Practices Act.
   b. Report the nature of disagreements with former auditors.
   c. Select auditors through audit committees.
   d. Acknowledge their responsibility for the fairness of the financial statements.

58. An auditor who was engaged to perform an examination of the financial statements of a nonpublic entity has been asked by the client to refrain from performing various audit procedures and change the nature of the engagement to a review of the financial statements in accordance with standards established by the AICPA. The client's request was made because the cost to complete the examination was significant. Under the circumstances the auditor would most likely
   a. Qualify the auditor's report and refer to the scope limitation.
   b. View the request as an indication of a possible irregularity.
   c. Complete the examination which was in progress.
   d. Honor the client's request.

59. A corporate balance sheet indicates that one of the corporate assets is a patent. An auditor will **most** likely obtain evidence regarding the continuing validity and existence of this patent by obtaining a written representation from
   a. A patent attorney.
   b. A regional State Patent Office.
   c. The patent inventor.
   d. The patent owner.

60. The objective of a review of the interim financial information of a publicly held company is to
   a. Provide the accountant with a basis for the expression of an opinion.
   b. Estimate the accuracy of financial statements based upon limited tests of accounting records.
   c. Provide the accountant with a basis for reporting to the board of directors or stockholders.
   d. Obtain corroborating evidential matter through inspection, observation and confirmation.

Number 2 (Estimated time -- 15 to 25 minutes)

Dunbar Camera Manufacturing, Inc., is a manufacturer of high-priced precision motion picture cameras in which the specifications of component parts are vital to the manufacturing process. Dunbar buys valuable camera lenses and large quantities of sheetmetal and screws. Screws and lenses are ordered by Dunbar and are billed by the vendors on a unit basis. Sheetmetal is ordered by Dunbar and are billed by the vendors on the basis of weight. The receiving clerk is responsible for documenting the quality and quantity of merchandise received.

A preliminary review of the system of internal control indicates that the following procedures are being followed:

Receiving Report

1. Properly approved purchase orders, which are prenumbered, are filed numerically. The copy sent to the receiving clerk is an exact duplicate of the copy sent to the vendor. Receipts of merchandise are recorded on the duplicate copy by the receiving clerk.

Sheetmetal

2. The company receives sheetmetal by railroad. The railroad independently weighs the sheetmetal and reports the weight and date of receipt on a bill of lading (waybill), which accompanies all deliveries. The receiving clerk only checks the weight on the waybill to the purchase order.

Screws

3. The receiving clerk opens cartons containing screws, then inspects and weighs the contents. The weight is converted to number of units by means of conversion charts. The receiving clerk then checks the computed quantity to the purchase order.

Camera lenses

4. Each camera lens is delivered in a separate corrugated carton. Cartons are counted as they are received by the receiving clerk and the number of cartons are checked to purchase orders.

Required:

a. Explain why the internal control procedures as they apply individually to receiving reports and the receipt of sheetmetal, screws, and camera lenses are adequate or inadequate. **Do not discuss recommendations for improvements.**

b. What financial statement distortions may arise because of the inadequacies in Dunbar's system of internal control and how may they occur?

Number 3 (Estimated time – 15 to 25 minutes)

During the year Strang Corporation began to encounter cash flow difficulties, and a cursory review by management revealed receivable collection problems. Strang's management engaged Stanley, CPA, to perform a special investigation. Stanley studied the billing and collection cycle and noted the following:

The accounting department employs one bookkeeper who receives and opens all incoming mail. This bookkeeper is also responsible for depositing receipts, filing remittance advices on a daily basis, recording receipts in the cash receipts journal, and for posting receipts in the individual customer accounts and the general ledger accounts. There are no cash sales. The bookkeeper prepares and controls the mailing of monthly statements to customers.

The concentration of functions and the receivable collection problems caused Stanley to suspect that a systematic defalcation of customers' payments through a delayed posting of remittances (lapping of accounts receivable) is present. Stanley was surprised to find that no customers complained about receiving erroneous monthly statements.

Required:

Identify the procedures which Stanley should perform to determine whether lapping exists. **Do not discuss deficiencies in the system of internal control.**

Number 4 (Estimated time – 15 to 25 minutes)

Sturdy Corporation owns and operates a large office building in a desirable section of New York City's financial center. For many years the management of Sturdy Corporation has modified the presentation of their financial statements by:

1. Reflecting a write-up to appraisal values in the building accounts.
2. Accounting for depreciation expense on the basis of such valuations.

Wyley, a successor CPA, was asked to examine the financial statements of Sturdy Corporation, for the year ended December 31, 1980. After completing the examination Wyley concluded that, consistent with prior years, an adverse opinion would have to be expressed because of the materiality of the apparent deviation from the historical-cost principle.

Required:

a. **Describe** in detail the form of presentation of the middle paragraph of the auditor's report on the financial statements of Sturdy Corporation for the year ended December 31, 1980, clearly identifying the information contained in the paragraph. **Do not discuss deferred taxes.**

b. **Write a draft** of the opinion paragraph of the auditor's report on the financial statements of Sturdy Corporation for the year ended December 31, 1980.

Number 5 (Estimated time – 15 to 25 minutes)

Roger Peters, CPA, has examined the financial statements of the Solt Manufacturing Company for several years and is making preliminary plans for the audit for the year ended June 30, 1972. During this examination Mr. Peters plans to use a set of generalized computer audit programs. Solt's EDP manager has agreed to prepare special tapes of data from Company records for the CPA's use with the generalized programs.

The following information is applicable to Mr. Peters' examination of Solt's accounts payable and related procedures:

1. The formats of pertinent tapes are on the following page.
2. The following monthly runs are prepared:
   a. Cash disbursements by check number.
   b. Outstanding payables.
   c. Purchase journals arranged (1) account charged and (2) by vendor.
3. Vouchers and supporting invoices, receiving reports and purchase order copies are filed by vendor code. Purchase orders and checks are filed numerically.
4. Company records are maintained on magnetic tapes. All tapes are stored in a restricted area within the computer room. A grandfather-father-son policy is followed for retaining and safeguarding tape files.

Required:

a. Explain the grandfather-father-son policy. Describe how files could be reconstructed when this policy is used.

b. Discuss whether Company policies for retaining and safeguarding the tape files provide adequate protection against losses of data.

c. Describe the controls that the CPA should maintain over:

1. Preparing the special tape.
2. Processing the special tape with the generalized computer audit programs.

d. Prepare a schedule for the EDP manager outlining the data that should be included on the special tape for the CPA's examination of accounts payable and related procedures. This schedule should show the:

1. Client tape from which the item should be extracted.
2. Name of the item of data.

Master File—Vendor Name

Vendor Code	Recd Type	Space	Blank	Vendor Name	Blank	Card Code 100

Master File—Vendor Address

Vendor Code	Recd Type	Space	Blank	Address—Line 1	Address—Line 2	Address—Line 3	Blank	Card Code 120

Transaction File—Expense Detail

Vendor Code	Recd Type	Voucher Number	Blank	Batch	Voucher Number	Voucher Date	Vendor Code	Invoice Date	Due Date	Invoice Number	Purchase Order Number	Debit Account	Prd Type	Product Code	Blank	Amount	Quantity	Card Code 160

Transaction File—Payment Detail

Vendor Code	Recd Type	Voucher Number	Blank	Batch	Voucher Number	Voucher Date	Vendor Code	Invoice Date	Due Date	Invoice Number	Purchase Order Number	Check Number	Check Date	Blank	Amount	Blank	Card Code 170

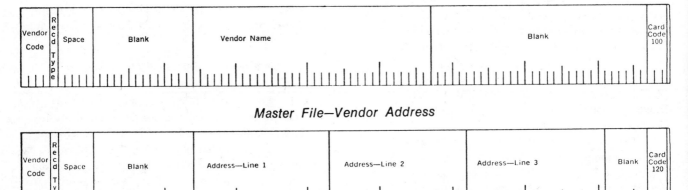

ANSWERS TO SAMPLE EXAMINATION AUDITING

Answer 1

1. b	11. a	21. d	31. b	41. c	51. d
2. b	12. c	22. d	32. c	42. c	52. d
3. a	13. b	23. d	33. b	43. d	53. d
4. b	14. c	24. b	34. d	44. a	54. a
5. c	15. c	25. c	35. a	45. c	55. d
6. b	16. b	26. c	36. b	46. a	56. d
7. d	17. c	27. a	37. c	47. c	57. b
8. d	18. a	28. c	38. d	48. c	58. d
9. b	19. d	29. b	39. b	49. a	59. a
10. b	20. b	30. c	40. b	50. b	60. c

Answer 2

a. The adequacy of internal control is questionable whenever quantities are not blocked out on the copy of the purchase order that is sent to the receiving department, because this practice may cause the receiving clerk to bypass the counting and inspection procedures. The receiving clerk may only compare the purchase order and packing slip (or other document accompanying the shipment) and prepare a receiving report based on these documents. As a result of this weakness, incorrect quantities of merchandise or inferior quality merchandise may be received and accepted. However, in the case of Dunbar Manufacturing, Inc., in certain areas there are compensating controls.

Receipt of sheetmetal. Although the receiving clerk may only compare quantities on the purchase order and the bill of lading, there is a compensating control over quantities of sheetmetal received. This compensating control is the independent verification of weights received and date of receipt, which are provided in the bill of lading. However, sheetmetal with unacceptable quality specifications may still be received and accepted.

Receipt of screws. Since the receiving clerk weighs the screws upon receipt and the weight is converted to units, control over quantities received is adequate. Furthermore, screws of an unacceptable specification may be expected to be detected during the weighing and inspecting process.

Receipt of camera lenses. Because there are no controls that compensate for the weakness in checking actual receipt of camera lenses, there is inadequate control over the quantity and quality of lenses received.

b. Inventory may be overstated and the cost of merchandise sold and income may be misstated because additions to inventory may be based on suppliers' invoices, which may include nonusable items or items that were not received. Further, because the company may have erroneously accrued the cost of nonusable items or items not received, accounts payable may be overstated.

Answer 3

The procedures that the auditor (Stanley) should perform to determine whether lapping exists are:

1. Compare names, amounts, and dates on remittance advice with entries in the cash receipts journal.
2. Trace the detailed amounts from the cash receipts journal to the accounts receivable subsidiary ledger to ensure that receipts are being posted to the proper account.
3. Compare details of the cash receipts journal entries with authenticated duplicate deposit slips received directly from the bank.
4. On a surprise basis, trace detail of undeposited cash receipts (counted by the auditor) to postings in the accounts receivable subsidiary ledger.
5. Compare details of cutoff statement (received directly by the auditor) deposits with postings in the subsidiary ledger.
6. Compare the monthly statement sent to customers with the balances in the accounts receivable subsidiary ledger.
7. Confirm positively month end balances with customers. Perform alternative procedures for those accounts not returning positive confirmations. Investigate all exceptions noted on confirmations.
8. Verify approvals of credits to accounts receivable for uncollectible accounts, sales discounts and sales returns and allowances.
9. Foot the cash receipts journal, accounts receivable control and customer's ledger accounts.
10. Reconcile the control account balance with the sum of the customer balances.

Answer 4

a. A separate (middle) paragraph should set forth reasons for the expression of an adverse opinion and the principal effects of the subject matter of the adverse opinion. The separate paragraph should state the following, providing dollar amounts where practicable:

- The company carries its building accounts at appraisal values and provides for depreciation on the basis of such values.
- Buildings, accumulated depreciation, and equity (attributed to appraisals) are overstated.
- Net income is understated.
- Depreciation expense is overstated.

b. The opinion paragraph should contain a reference to the separate paragraph and state that the financial statements do not present fairly the financial position, results of operations, and changes in financial position. No reference to consistency should be made in the opinion paragraph. It should be worded as follows:

> In our opinion, because of the effects of the matters discussed in the preceding paragraph, the financial statements referred to above do not present fairly, in conformity with generally accepted accounting principles, the financial position of Sturdy Corporation as of December 31, 1980, or the results of its operations and changes in its financial position for the year then ended.

Answer 5

a. A grandfather-father-son tape retention policy is one under which two predecessor tape files are held as back-up for the current file. This provides a method for reconstruction of the tape files in the event of accidental destruction of a tape used during processing. The use of this concept is illustrated as follows: At the end of period 3, a company holds master tapes as of the ends of periods 1 (grandather) and 2 (father) and transaction tapes for periods 2 and 3. Transactions for period 3 are then processed with the father tape to form a son tape. Following the processing of period 3 transactions, the company holds master tapes as of the end of periods 1 (grandfather), 2 (father) and 3 (son) and transaction tapes for periods 2 and 3. The father tape can be replicated by processing the grandfather tape with period 2 transactions, and the son tape can be replicated by processing the father tape with period 3 transactions. Period 4 transactions are processed at the end of period 4 with the son tape (master file at the end of period 3) to form a new son file. The old son tape becomes the new father tape, the old father tape becomes the new grandfather tape and the old grandfather tape (end of period 1) together with the transaction tape for period 2 may be released. Should anything happen to the old son tape during the updating with period 4 transactions, it may be replicated from the father tape and the period 3 transactions.

b. Holding two generations of backup tapes generally provides adequate protection. An additional generation might be maintained if the tape file is crucial or if there is a high rate of tape destruction. Since all tapes are stored together, they are vulnerable to loss through a common catastrophe—fire, theft or malicious act. Reconstruction from predecessor tapes can only be effected if the predecessor tapes are in existence. For this reason it is desirable that at least one generation of backup tapes be maintained in a separate location that is well protected from environmental hazards such as fires or magnetic interference. Access to both storage areas should be limited, and the librarianship function should be specifically assigned.

c.

1. The extent of the CPA's participation in preparation of the special tape and of his review of the tape will depend upon his assessment of computer department capabilities and his evaluation of EDP controls, particularly the separation of data processing from the purchasing, accounts payable and disbursement functions. As a minimum, he should clearly indicate tape format and the data that he requires and must perform some testing to satisfy himself that all items have been included on the special tape. He may accomplish this by tracing items on a test basis from Company records to a print-out of the special tape and comparing print-out totals to Company records.
2. The CPA should maintain physical control over the special tape, the general computer audit programs and any print-outs prepared for him. He should take his programs and data directly to the machine operators and be present during the processing. He should keep confidential the transactions selected for review and the method for selecting them.

d. Solt Manufacturing Company

Schedule of Data to be Retained on the Special Tape

Source—Client Tape	*Item of Data*
Master file—vendor name	Vendor code
	Vendor name
Transaction file—expense detail	Voucher number
	Voucher date
	Invoice date
	Invoice number
	Purchase order number
	Debit account
	Amount
Transaction file—payment detail	Check number
	Check date

If the auditor plans to circularize vendors, he may also request addresses, either on this tape or in another listing.

EXAMINATION IN BUSINESS LAW
(Commercial Law)

NOTE TO CANDIDATES: Suggested time allotments are as follows:

All questions are required:	Estimated Minutes: Minimum	Maximum
No. 1	110	130
No. 2	15	20
No. 3	15	20
No. 4	15	20
No. 5	15	20
Total	170	210

Number 1 (Estimated time — 110 to 130 minutes)

Select the **best** answer for each of the following items.

1. Bigelow manufactures mopeds and sells them through franchised dealers who are authorized to resell them to the ultimate consumer or return them. Bigelow delivers the mopeds on consignment to these retailers. The consignment agreement clearly states that the agreement is intended to create a security interest for Bigelow in the mopeds delivered on consignment. Bigelow wishes to protect itself against the other creditors of and purchasers from the retailers who might assert rights against the mopeds. Under the circumstances, Bigelow

   a. Must file a financing statement and give notice to certain creditors in order to perfect his security interest.
   b. Will have rights against purchasers in the ordinary course of business who were aware of the fact that Bigelow had filed.
   c. Need take no further action to protect himself, since the consignment is a sale or return and title is reserved in Bigelow.
   d. Will have a perfected security interest in the mopeds upon attachment.

2. Carter Corporation loaned $500,000 to Devon Corporation pursuant to an oral agreement granting a security interest in certain shares of stock held by Devon. Carter sought to have Devon sign a security agreement granting a security interest in the shares. Devon refused to sign any agreement, but instead delivered the stock certificates in question to Carter.

   a. The security interest of Carter is not perfected until Devon signs the security agreement or Carter files a financing statement, whichever first occurs.
   b. Carter must file a financing statement, or a copy of a security agreement, signed by the debtor to perfect its security interest.
   c. Carter has a perfected security interest in the collateral.
   d. Carter must sign the agreement, and a financing statement, and file either one of them to perfect its security interest in the shares of stock.

3. As a secured creditor under the Uniform Commercial Code, Dawson has invariably perfected a security interest in goods which provide the underlying security for various loans. Under the circumstances, which of the following is correct?

   a. Dawson is assured that the debts will be repaid.
   b. Dawson's security interest can not be perfected by possession.
   c. Dawson is entitled to "resort to" or obtain the property even as against a trustee in bankruptcy.
   d. Dawson has a priority in bankruptcy and therefore is entitled to defeat the claims of all creditors which are asserted against the goods.

4. Mansfield Financial lends money on the strength of negotiable warehouse receipts. Its policy is always to obtain a perfected security interest in the receipts against the creditors of the borrowers and to maintain

it until the loan has been satisfied. Insofar as this policy is concerned, which of the following is correct?

a. Mansfield can **not** transfer the warehouse receipts to another lending institution without the debtor's consent.
b. Relinquishment of the receipts is **not** permitted under any circumstances without the loss of the perfected security interest in them.
c. Mansfield has a perfected security interest in goods which the receipts represent.
d. If the receipts are somehow wrongfully duly negotiated to a holder, Mansfield's perfected security interest will **not** be prejudiced.

5. On June 10, Central Corporation sold goods to Bowie Corporation for $5,000. Bowie signed a financing statement containing the names and addresses of the parties and describing the collateral. Central filed the financing statement on June 21, noting the same in its accounting books.

a. Central need not sign the financing statement to perfect its security interest in the collateral.
b. Central must file the financing statement prior to the sale if a security interest is to be perfected.
c. Central must sign the financing statement in order to perfect its security interest.
d. Central had a perfected security interest in the collateral even before the financing statement was filed.

6. Workmen's compensation laws are

a. Governed by federal regulation.
b. Applicable to all types of employment.
c. Designed to eliminate the usual defenses by the employer, such as contributory negligence, when an employee is injured.
d. Not applicable if the employee signs a waiver and consents to his noncoverage under workmen's compensation at the time he is hired.

7. Nebor Industries, Inc., manufactures toys which it sells throughout the United States and Europe. Europe accounts for 25% of sales. Among its 5,000 employees in 1980 were 490 young males aged 14 and 15 who are paid at the rate of $3.50 per hour. Under the general rules of the Fair Labor Standards Act, Nebor

a. Was exempt from regulations because less than 10% of its employees were children.
b. Did not violate the law since it was paying more than the minimum wage.
c. Violated the law by employing children under 16 years of age.
d. Is exempt from regulation because more than 20% of its sales are in direct competition with foreign goods.

8. Markum was grossly negligent in the operation of a forklift. As a result he suffered permanent disability. His claim for workmen's compensation will be

a. Denied.
b. Limited to medical benefits.
c. Reduced by the percentage share attributable to his own fault.
d. Paid in full.

9. Badger Corporation engaged Donald Keller as one of its sales representatives to sell automotive parts. Keller signed an employment contract which required him to obtain home-office approval on any contract in excess of $500 entered into by Keller on Badger's behalf. The industry custom and most of Badger's agents had authority to make such contracts if they did not exceed $1,000. Keller signed a contract on Badger's behalf with Zolar Garages, Inc. for $850. Badger rejected the contract and promptly notified Zolar of its decision. Under these circumstances

a. Keller is a del credere agent.
b. Keller did not have express authority to make the Zolar contract.
c. Keller had the implied authority to make the contract.
d. Badger's prompt disaffirmance of Keller's action retroactively terminated any liability it might have had.

10. Star Corporation dismissed Moon, its purchasing agent. Star published a notice in appropriate trade journals which stated: "This is to notify all parties concerned that Moon is no longer employed by Star Corporation, and the corporation assumes no further responsibility for his acts." Moon called on several of Star's suppliers with whom he had previously dealt, and when he found one who was unaware of his dismissal, he placed a substantial order for merchandise to be delivered to a warehouse in which Moon rented space. Star had rented space in the warehouse in the past when its storage facilities were crowded. Moon also called on several suppliers with whom Star had never dealt and made purchases from them on open account in the name of Star. The mer-

chandise purchased by Moon was delivered to the warehouse. Moon then sold all the merchandise and absconded with the money. Which of the following most accurately describes the legal implications of this situation?

a. Moon had apparent authority to make contracts on Star's behalf with suppliers with whom Moon was currently dealing as Star's agent if they had no actual knowledge of his dismissal.
b. The suppliers who previously had no dealings with Star can enforce the contracts against Star if the suppliers had no actual knowledge of Moon's lack of authority.
c. Star is liable on the Moon contracts to all suppliers who had dealt with Moon in the past as Star's agent and who have not received personal notice, even though they had read the published notice.
d. Constructive notice by publication in the appropraite trade journals is an effective notice to all third parties regardless of whether they had previously dealt with Moon or read the notice.

11. Wishing to acquire a site for its factory without provoking a rise in price, Peter Corporation engaged Argus Realty Company to purchase land without disclosing Peter's name. Argus did so and signed a contract in its own name with Tyrone to purchase Tyrone's land. Under these circumstances

a. The transaction is fraudulent.
b. Argus is not personally liable on the contract.
c. Peter Corporation must formally ratify the contract if it is to hold Tyrone liable.
d. Tyrone may obtain recourse against either Peter or Argus if the contract is not performed.

12. Adams, Baker, and Carter are co-sureties on a $250,000 loan by the Wilson National Bank to Marathon Motors, Inc. Adams is a surety for the full amount of the debt; Baker's obligation is limited to $100,000; and Carter has agreed to pay $50,000 upon default. In the event of default by Marathon on the entire $250,000 loan, what is the liability of Adams, Baker, and Carter?

a. Baker is liable for the first $100,000; Carter, the next $50,000; and Adams, the balance.
b. Baker and Adams are each liable for $100,000 and Carter for $50,000.
c. If both Baker and Carter know of Adams' obligation for the full amount, then they are not liable unless Adams can not satisfy the debt.
d. Adams is liable for $156,250; Baker, $62,500; and Carter, $31,250.

13. Filbert is the surety on a loan made by Holmes to Watson. Which statement describes Filbert's legal relationship or status among the respective parties?

a. Filbert is a fiduciary insofar as Holmes is concerned.
b. As between Watson and Filbert, Filbert has the ultimate liability.
c. Filbert is not liable immediately upon default by Watson, unless the agreement so provides.
d. Upon default by Watson and payment by Filbert, Filbert is entitled to subrogation to the rights of Holmes or to obtain reimbursement from Watson.

14. Marbury Surety, Inc., agreed to act as a guarantor of collection of Madison's trade accounts for one year beginning on April 30, 1980, and was compensated for same. Madison's trade debtors are in default in payment of $3,853, as of May 1, 1981. As a result

a. Marbury is liable to Madison without any action on Madison's part to collect the amounts due.
b. Madison can enforce the guarantee even if it is **not** in writing since Marbury is a *del credere* agent.
c. The relationship between the parties must be filed in the appropriate county office since it is a continuing security transaction.
d. Marbury is liable for those debts for which a judgment is obtained and returned unsatisfied.

15. Marigold, Inc., was in extreme financial difficulty. Hargrove, one of its persistent creditors, insisted upon payment of the entire amount due on the shipments of goods to Marigold over the past four months or it would sue Marigold and obtain a judgment against it. In order to dissuade Hargrove from taking such action, Marigold persuaded Hargrove to accept its note which was secured by a second mortgage on Marigold's warehouse. Hargrove filed the mortgage on November 1, 1978, the same day that the note and mortgage were executed. On February 1, 1979, Marigold concluded that things were hopeless and filed a voluntary petition in bankruptcy. The trustee in bankruptcy is attacking the

validity of the mortgage as a voidable preference. Which of the following is correct?

a. The mortgage is not a voidable preference since it was filed the same day it was obtained.
b. The fact that Marigold was delinquent on its payment to Hargrove establishes that Hargrove knew that Marigold was insolvent in the bankruptcy sense.
c. The antecedent indebtedness requirement necessary to establish a voidable preference has not been satisfied under the facts given.
d. The mortgage given to Hargrove was a voidable preference.

16. Your client is insolvent under the federal bankruptcy law. Under the circumstances

a. As long as the client can meet current debts or claims by its most aggressive creditors, a bankruptcy proceeding is not possible.
b. Such information, i.e., insolvency, need not be disclosed in the financial statements reported upon by your CPA firm as long as you are convinced that the problem is short lived.
c. An assignment for the benefit of creditors will constitute an act of bankruptcy.
d. Your client may file a voluntary petition for bankruptcy.

17. In which of the following situations would an oral agreement without any consideration be binding under the Uniform Commercial Code?

a. A renunciation of a claim or right arising out of an alleged breach.
b. A firm offer by a merchant to sell or buy goods which gives assurance that it will be held open.
c. An agreement which is a requirements contract.
d. An agreement which modifies an existing sales contract.

18. Keats Publishing Company shipped textbooks and other books for sale at retail to Campus Bookstore. An honest dispute arose over Campus's right to return certain books. Keats maintained that the books in question could not be returned and demanded payment of the full amount. Campus relied upon trade custom which indicated that many publishers accepted the return of such books. Campus returned the books in question and paid for the balance with a check marked "Acount Paid in Full to Date." Keats cashed the check. Which of the following is a correct statement?

a. Keats is entitled to recover damages.
b. Keats' cashing of the check constituted an accord and satisfaction.
c. The pre-existing legal duty rule applies and Keats is entitled to full payment for all the books.
d. The custom of the industry argument would have no merit in a court of law.

19. Marco Auto Inc., made many untrue statements in the course of inducing Rockford to purchase a used auto for $3,500. The car in question turned out to have some serious faults. Which of the following untrue statements made by Marco should Rockford use in seeking recovery from Marco for breach of warranty?

a. "I refused a $3,800 offer for this very same auto from another buyer last week."
b. "This auto is one of the best autos we have for sale."
c. "At this price the auto is a real steal."
d. "I can guarantee that you will never regret this purchase."

20. If a seller repudiates his contract with a buyer for the sale of 100 radios, what recourse does the buyer have?

a. He can "cover," i.e., procure the goods elsewhere and recover the difference.
b. He must await the seller's performance for a commercially reasonable time after repudiation.
c. He can obtain specific performance by the seller.
d. He can recover punitive damages.

21. A dispute has arisen between two merchants over the question of who has the risk of loss in a given sales transaction. The contract does not specifically cover the point. The goods were shipped to the buyer who rightfully rejected them. Which of the following factors will be the most important factor in resolving their dispute?

a. Who has title to the goods.
b. The shipping terms.
c. The credit terms.
d. The fact that a breach has occurred.

22. On July 14, 1976, Seeley Corp. entered into a written agreement to sell to Boone Corp. 1,200

cartons of certain goods at $.40 per carton, delivery within 30 days. The agreement contained no other terms. On July 15, 1976, Boone and Seeley orally agreed to modify their July 14 agreement so that the new quantity specified was 1,500 cartons, same price and delivery terms. What is the status of this modification?

a. Enforceable.
b. Unenforceable under the statute of frauds.
c. Unenforceable for lack of consideration.
d. Unenforceable because the change is substantial.

23. The partnership of Maxim & Rose, CPAs, has been engaged by their largest client, a limited partnership, to examine the financial statements in connection with the offering of 2,000 limited-partnership interests to the public at $5,000 per subscription. Under these circumstances, which of the following is true?

a. Maxim & Rose may disclaim any liability under the federal securities acts by an unambiguous, bold-faced disclaimer of liability on its audit report.
b. Under the Securities Act of 1933, Maxim & Rose has responsibility only for the financial statements as of the close of the fiscal year in question.
c. The dollar amount in question is sufficiently small so as to provide an exemption from the Securities Act of 1933.
d. The Securities Act of 1933 requires a registration despite the fact that the client is not selling stock or another traditional "security."

24. One of the major purposes of federal security regulation is to

a. Establish the qualifications for accountants who are members of the profession.
b. Eliminate incompetent attorneys and accountants who participate in the registration of securities to be offered to the public.
c. Provide a set of uniform standards and tests for accountants, attorneys and others who practice before the Securities and Exchange Commission.
d. Provide sufficient information to the investing public who purchases securities in the marketplace.

25. Of the following securities transactions, which is exempt from federal securities regulations?

a. An offering of $100,000 of corporate bonds.
b. The sales of $2,000,000 of limited partnership interest.
c. A secondary offering of stock which had been previously registered.
d. The sale of $500,000 of common stock to a single sophisticated purchaser for investment purposes.

26. Dowling is a promoter and has decided to use a limited partnership for conducting a securities investment venture. Which of the following is unnecessary in order to validly create such a limited partnership?

a. All limited partners' capital contributions must be paid in cash.
b. There must be a state statute which permits the creation of such a limited partnership.
c. A limited partnership certificate must be signed and sworn to by the participants and filed in the proper office in the state.
d. There must be one or more general partners and one or more limited partners.

27. In the course of your audit of Harvey Fox, doing business as Harvey's Apparels, a sole proprietorship, you discovered that in the past year Fox had regularly joined with Leopold Morrison in the marketing of bathing suits and beach accessories. You are concerned whether Fox and Morrison have created a partnership relationship. Which of the following factors is the most important in ascertaining this status?

a. The fact that a partnership agreement is not in existence.
b. The fact that each has a separate business of his own which he operates independently.
c. The fact that Fox and Morrison divide the net profits equally on a quarterly basis.
d. The fact that Fox and Morrison did not intend to be partners.

28. Jon and Frank Clarke are equal partners in the partnership of Clarke & Clarke. Both Jon Clarke and the partnership are bankrupt. Jon Clarke personally has $150,000 of liabilities and $100,000 of assets. The partnership's liabilities are $450,000 and its assets total $250,000. Frank Clarke, the other partner, is solvent with $800,000 of assets and $150,000 of lia-

bilities. What are the rights of the various creditors of Jon Clarke, Frank Clarke and the partnership?

a. Jon Clarke must divide his assets equally among his personal creditors and firm creditors.
b. Frank Clarke will be liable in full for the $200,000 partnership deficit.
c. Jon Clarke's personal creditors can recover the $50,000 deficit owed to them from Frank Clarke.
d. Frank Clarke is liable only for $100,000, his equal share of the partnership deficit.

29. In determining the liability of a partnership for the acts of a partner purporting to act for the partnership without the authorization of his fellow partners, which of the following actions will bind the partnership?

a. A written admission of liability in a lawsuit brought against the partnership.
b. Signing the partnership name as a surety on a note for the purchase of that partner's summer home.
c. An assignment of the partnership assets in trust for the benefit of creditors.
d. The renewal of an existing supply contract which the other partners had decided to terminate and which they had specifically voted against.

30. Lantz sold his moving and warehouse business, including all the personal and real property used therein, to Mallen Van Lines, Inc. The real property was encumbered by a duly-recorded $300,000 first mortgage upon which Lantz was personally liable. Mallen acquired the property subject to the mortgage but did not assume the mortgage. Two years later, when the outstanding mortgage was $260,000, Mallen decided to abandon the business location because it had become unprofitable and the value of the real property was less than the outstanding mortgage. Mallen moved to another location and refused to pay the installments due on the mortgage. What is the legal status of the parties in regard to the mortgage?

a. Mallen breached its contract with Lantz when it abandoned the location and defaulted on the mortgage.
b. Mallen took the real property free of the mortgage.
c. If Lantz pays off the mortgage, he will be able to successfully sue Mallen because Lantz is subrogated to the mortgagee's rights against Mallen.
d. Lantz must satisfy the mortgage debt in the event that foreclosure yields an amount less than the unpaid balance.

31. Winslow conveyed a 20-acre tract of land to his two children, George and Martha, "equally as tenants in common." What is the legal effect of this form of conveyance?

a. George and Martha are joint owners with a right of survivorship.
b. Each must first offer the other the right to purchase the property before he or she can sell to a third party.
c. Neither may convey his or her interest in the property unless both join in the conveyance.
d. Each owns an undivided interest in the whole, which he or she may dispose of by deed or by will.

32. Fitz decided to purchase a two-acre tract in an industrial park from Expansion, Inc., the developer. The usual contract of sale was drafted and signed by the parties. However, it was silent in respect to marketable title and the type of deed to be delivered at the closing. What effect does the omission of these items from the contract have?

a. The contract is subject to an implied covenant that Fitz will receive marketable title at the closing.
b. Expansion must deliver a warranty deed with full covenants.
c. In the event Expansion decides to withdraw the property from the market because of rising land prices, Fitz could obtain damages but not specific performance.
d. Fitz should have a title search within 30 days after the closing in order to make sure the title is clear.

33. Harper died and his will was admitted to probate. It named his son Harris and his daughter Jean as co-executors. Under the terms of the will, he left 60% of his estate outright to his wife, Martha, after all expenses, taxes, and fees were paid. The balance was equally divided among his children, Harris, Jean, Tobey, and Lydia. The value of the gross estate is $400,000. Which of the following is correct?

a. Martha would be better off electing to take under the intestate succession laws.
b. The estate will be able to take a $250,000 statutory marital deduction.

c. Tobey and Lydia are also entitled to qualify as executors since Harris and Jean are residuary takers as well as executors.
d. All the property bequeathed to Martha will be deducted from Harper's estate for federal estate tax purposes.

34. Hacker is considering the creation of either a lifetime (intervivos) or testamentary (by his will) trust. In deciding what to do, which of the following statements is correct?
a. An intervivos trust must meet the same legal requirements as one created by a will.
b. Property transferred to a testamentary trust upon the grantor's (creator's) death is not included in the decedent's gross estate for federal tax purposes.
c. Hacker can retain the power to revoke an intervivos trust.
d. If the trust is an intervivos trust, the trustee must file papers in the appropriate state office roughly similar to those required to be filed by a corporation.

35. A group of real estate dealers has decided to form a Real Estate Investment Trust (REIT) which will invest in diversified real estate holdings. A public offering of $10,000,000 of trust certificates is contemplated. Which of the following is an incorrect statement?
a. Those investing in the venture will not be insulated from personal liability.
b. The entity will be considered to be an "association" for tax purposes.
c. The offering must be registered under the Securities Act of 1933.
d. If the trust qualifies as a REIT and distributes all its income to the investors, it will not be subject to federal income tax.

36. Montbanks' son, Charles, was seeking an account executive position with Dobbs, Smith, and Fogarty, Inc., the largest brokerage firm in the United States. Charles was very independent and wished no interference by his father. The firm, after several weeks deliberation, decided to hire Charles. They made him an offer on April 12, 1979, and Charles readily accepted. Montbanks feared that his son would not be hired. Being unaware of the fact that his son had been hired, Montbanks mailed a letter to Dobbs on April 13 in which he promised to give the brokerage firm $50,000 in commission business if the firm would hire his son. The letter was duly received by Dobbs and they wish to enforce it against Montbanks. Which of the following statements is correct?
a. Past consideration is no consideration, hence there is no contract.
b. The pre-existing legal duty rule applies and makes the promise unenforceable.
c. Dobbs will prevail since the promise is contained in a signed writing.
d. Dobbs will prevail based upon promissory estoppel.

37. Martin, a wholesale distributor, made a contract for the purchase of 10,000 gallons of gasoline from the Wilberforce Oil Company. The price was to be determined in accordance with the refinery price as of the close of business on the delivery date. Credit terms were net/30 after delivery. Under these circumstances which of the following is true?
a. If Martin pays upon delivery, he is entitled to a 2% discount.
b. The contract being silent on the place of delivery, Martin has the right to expect delivery at his place of business.
c. Although the price has some degree of uncertainty, the contract is enforceable.
d. Because the goods involved are tangible, specific performance is a remedy available to Martin.

38. Major Steel Manufacturing, Inc., signed a contract on October 2, 1978, with the Hard Coal & Coke Company for its annual supply of coal for three years commencing on June 1, 1979, at a price to be determined by taking the average monthly retail price per ton, less a ten cent per ton quantity discount. On March 15, 1979, Major discovered that it had made a bad bargain and that it could readily fulfill its requirements elsewhere at a much greater discount. Major is seeking to avoid its obligation. Which of the following is correct?
a. The pricing term is too indefinite and uncertain hence there is no contract.
b. Since the amount of coal required is unknown at the time of the making of the contract, the contract is too indefinite and uncertain to be valid.
c. Major is obligated to take its normal annual coal requirements from Hard or respond in damages.
d. There is no contract since Major could conceivably require no coal during the years in question.

39. Potter orally engaged Arthur as a salesman on April 5, 1978, for exactly one year commencing on

May 1, 1978. Which of the following is correct insofar as the parties are concerned?

a. If Arthur refuses to perform and takes another job on April 14, 1978, he will not be liable if he pleads the statute of frauds.
b. The contract need not be in writing since its duration is exactly one year.
c. Potter may obtain the remedy of specific performance if Arthur refuses to perform.
d. The parol evidence rule applies.

40. Milbank undertook to stage a production of a well-known play. He wired Lucia, a famous actress, offering her the lead in the play at $2,000 per week for six weeks from the specified opening night plus $1,000 for a week of rehearsal prior to opening. The telegram also said, "offer ends in three days." Lucia wired an acceptance the same day she received it. The telegram acceptance was temporarily misplaced by the telegraph company and did not arrive until five days after its dispatch. Milbank, not hearing from Lucia, assumed she had declined and abandoned the production. Which of the following is correct if Lucia sues Milbank?

a. The contract was automatically terminated when Milbank decided not to proceed.
b. Lucia has entered into a valid contract and is entitled to recover damages if Milbank fails to honor it.
c. Lucia may not take any other engagement for the period involved if she wishes to recover.
d. Milbank is excused from any liability since his action was reasonable under the circumstances.

41. Which of the following offers for the sale of the Lazy L Ranch is enforceable?

a. Owner tells buyer she will sell the ranch for $35,000 and that the offer will be irrevocable for ten days.
b. Owner writes buyer offering to sell the ranch for $35,000 and stating that the offer will remain open for ten days.
c. Owner telegraphs buyer offering to sell the ranch for $35,000 and promises to hold the offer open for ten days.
d. Owner writes buyer offering to sell the ranch for $35,000 and stating that the offer will be irrevocable for ten days if buyer will pay $1.00. Buyer pays.

42. The parol evidence rule prohibits contradiction of a written contract through the proof of

a. A previous oral contract.
b. A subsequent written contract.
c. The meaning or clarification of the contract's terms.
d. A subsequent oral contract.

43. Higgins orally contracted to pay $3,500 to Clark for $4,000 of thirty-day accounts receivable that arose in the course of Clark's office equipment leasing business. Higgins subsequently paid the $3,500. What is the legal status of this contract?

a. The contract is unenforceable by Higgins since the statute of frauds requirement has not been satisfied.
b. If Higgins failed to notify the debtors whose accounts were purchased, they will, upon payment in good faith to Clark, have no liability to Higgins.
c. The contract in question is illegal because it violates the usury laws.
d. Higgins will be able to collect against the debtors free of the usual defenses which would be assertable against Clark.

44. Anderson agreed to purchase Parker's real property. Anderson's purchase was dependent upon his being able to sell certain real property that he owned. Anderson gave Parker an instrument for the purchase price. Assuming the instrument is otherwise negotiable, which one of the statements below, written on the face of the instrument, will render it non-negotiable?

a. A statement that Parker's cashing or indorsing the instrument acknowledges full satisfaction of Anderson's obligation.
b. A statement that payment of the instrument is contingent upon Anderson's sale of his real property.
c. A statement that the instrument is secured by a first mortgage on Parker's property and that upon default in payment the entire amount of the instrument is due.
d. A statement that the instrument is subject to the usual implied and constructive conditions applicable to such transactions.

45. A formal protest of dishonor must be made in order to hold the drawer or indorsers liable for all of the following foreign instruments except

a. Drafts.
b. Promissory notes.
c. Trade acceptances.
d. Checks.

46. A holder in due course will take an instrument free from which of the following defenses?
   a. Claims of ownership on the part of other persons.
   b. Infancy of the maker or drawer.
   c. Discharge in insolvency proceedings.
   d. The forged signature of the maker or drawer.

47. Path stole a check made out to the order of Marks. Path forged the name of Marks on the back and made the instrument payable to himself. He then negotiated the check to Harrison for cash by signing his own name on the back of the instrument in Harrison's presence. Harrison was unaware of any of the facts surrounding the theft or forged indorsement and presented the check for payment. Central County Bank, the drawee bank, paid it. Disregarding Path, which of the following will bear the loss?
   a. The drawer of the check payable to Marks.
   b. Central County Bank.
   c. Marks.
   d. Harrison.

48. There are several legally significant differences between a negotiable instrument and a contract right and the transfer of each. Which of the following statements is correct?
   a. A negotiable instrument is deemed prima facie to have been issued for consideration whereas a contract is not deemed prima facie to be supported by consideration.
   b. Generally, the transferee of a negotiable instrument and the assignee of a contract right take free of most defenses.
   c. Neither can be transferred without a signed writing or by a delivery.
   d. The statute of frauds rules apply to both.

49. Davidson bore a remarkable physical resemblance to Ford, one of the town's most prominent citizens. He presented himself one day at the Friendly Finance Company, represented himself as Ford, and requested a loan of $500. The manager mistakenly, but honestly, believed that Davidson was Ford. Accordingly, being anxious to please so prominent a citizen, the manager required no collateral and promptly delivered to Davidson a $500 check payable to the order of Ford. Davidson took the check and signed Ford's name to it on the back and negotiated it to Robbins, who took in the ordinary course of business (in good faith and for value). Upon learning the real facts, Friendly stopped payment on the check. Robbins now seeks recovery against Friendly. Under these circumstances, which of the following statements is correct?
   a. Friendly could not validly stop payment on the check.
   b. Davidson's signature of Ford's name on the check constitutes a forgery and is a real defense which is valid against Robbins.
   c. Since both Friendly and Robbins were mistaken as to Davidson's real identity, they will share the loss equally.
   d. Davidson's signature of Ford's name on the check is effective and Robbins will prevail against Friendly.

50. Your client, Commercial Factors, Inc., discounted a $2,000 promissory note, payable in two years, for $1,500. It paid $500 initially and promised to pay the balance ($1,000) within 30 days. Commercial paid the balance within the 30 days, but before doing so learned that the note had been obtained originally by fraudulent misrepresentations in connection with the sale of land which induced the maker to issue the note. For what amount will Commercial qualify as a holder in due course?
   a. None because the 25% discount is presumptive of prima facie evidence that Commercial is not a holder in due course.
   b. $500.
   c. $1,500.
   d. $2,000.

51. Glick was the owner of a factory valued at $100,000. He procured a fire insurance policy on the building for $40,000 from Safety Insurance Company, Inc. The policy contained an 80% coinsurance clause. The property was totally destroyed by fire. How much will Glick recover from the insurance company?
   a. $20,000.
   b. $32,000.
   c. $40,000.
   d. Glick will recover nothing because he did not meet the coinsurance requirements.

52. DuBary and Young were business partners. They agreed that each would insure the life of the other for his own benefit (cross insurance). On the application for insurance, DuBary stated that he had never had any heart trouble when, in fact, he had suffered a mild heart attack some years before. Young's policy on DuBary's life contained a two-year incontestability clause. Three years later, after the partnership had been dissolved but while the policy on his life was still in force, DuBary was killed when his car was struck by a car negligently driven by Peters.

The insurer has refused to pay the policy proceeds to Young, asserting that Young at the time DuBary died had no insurable interest in DuBary's life and that DuBary's misrepresentation voided the policy. Which of the following statements is correct?

a. The misrepresentation in the application is a bar to recovery.
b. If DuBary and Young were never partners, recovery will be denied.
c. Dissolution of the partnership eliminated any possible insurable interest and is a bar to recovery.
d. If the insurance company has to pay, it will be subrogated to DuBary's rights against Peters.

53. Mammoth Furniture, Inc., is in the retail furniture business and has stores located in principal cities in the United States. Its designers created a unique coffee table. After obtaining prices and schedules, Mammoth ordered 2,000 tables to be made to its design and specifications for sale as a part of its annual spring sales promotion campaign. Which of the following represents the earliest time Mammoth will have an insurable interest in the tables?

a. Upon shipment of conforming goods by the seller.
b. When the goods are marked or otherwise designated by the seller as the goods to which the contract refers.
c. At the time the contract is made.
d. At the time the goods are in Mammoth's possession.

54. The "incontestable clause" in a life insurance policy usually provides that

a. The insured is covered on delivery of the policy regardless of any misstatement in the application.
b. If death occurs after a specified period of time, a misstatement in the application will not constitute a defense by the insurer.
c. Suicide of the named insured will not constitute a defense by the insurer.
d. Only the estate of the insured may contest the named beneficiary's rights to proceeds of the policy.

55. A corporation may not redeem its own shares when it

a. Is currently solvent but has been insolvent within the past five years.
b. Is insolvent or would be rendered insolvent if the redemption were made.
c. Has convertible debt that is publicly traded.
d. Has mortgages and other secured obligations equal to 50 percent of its stated capital.

56. The consideration for the issuance of shares by a corporation may not be paid in

a. Services actually performed for the corporation.
b. Services to be performed for the corporation.
c. Tangible property.
d. Intangible property.

57. Nicks is a troublesome chain store furniture dealer. He constantly engaged in price cutting on widely advertised name products in order to lure customers to his store so that he could sell them other products. The "big three" manufacturers agreed that Nicks could no longer sell their products unless he ceased and desisted from such practices. Nicks refused and the three manufacturers promptly cut off his supply of their branded products. Which of the following is a correct statement?

a. Since a businessman has the freedom to choose with whom he will deal, the conduct in question is not illegal under the antitrust laws.
b. If the harm to the public was minor, and the products were readily available from other appliance dealers in a market marked by free and open competition, there would be no violation of the law.
c. The conduct described is a joint boycott, and as such is illegal per se.
d. Since the conduct described was unilateral, and Nicks did not agree to stop his price cutting, the manufacturers' conduct is illegal.

58. Zebra Acquisitions, Inc., has been steadily acquiring the assets and stock of various corporations manufacturing brass. It also has been purchasing the stock of its customers and others who purchase substantial quantities of brass. It now has 8% of the brass manufacturing facilities in the United States and 22% in the tri-state area in which it is located. Which of the following claims is the United States Department of Justice likely to assert?

a. The relevant market in question is the entire United States.
b. It is illegal per se to purchase the stock of competitors.

c. It is illegal per se to purchase the stock of customers and other potential buyers.
d. The most recent acquisition substantially lessens competition in the tri-state area.

59. Drummond Company manufactures and sells distinctive clocks. Its best selling item is a reproduction of a rare antique grandfather clock. Adams purchased 100 of the clocks from Drummond at $79.50. Much to Adam's chagrin it discovered that Young, one of its competitors, had purchased the same clock at $74.50 per clock. Adams has complained and threatened legal action. In the event the issue is litigated

a. Drummond will prevail if it can show it did not intend to harm Adams.
b. Adams has a presumption in its favor that it has been harmed by price discrimination.
c. Drummond will prevail if it can show that it sold the clocks at the lower price to all customers such as Young who had been doing business with it continuously for ten years or more.
d. Drummond will prevail if it can establish that there were several other clock companies with which Adams could deal if Adams were dissatisfied.

60. Research Development Corporation has made a major breakthrough in the development of a super TV antenna. It has patented the product and is seeking to maximize the profit potential. In this effort, Research can legally

a. Require its retailer to take stipulated quantities of its other products in addition to the antennas.
b. Require its retailers to sell only Research's products including the antennas, and not sell similar competing products.
c. Sell the product to its retailers upon condition that they do not sell the antennas to the public for less than a stated price.
d. Sell the product at whatever price the traffic will bear even though it has a monopoly.

Number 2 (Estimated time — 15 to 20 minutes)

During the course of your year-end audit for a new client, Otis Corporation, you discover the following facts. Otis was incorporated in 1974 and is owned 94% by James T. Parker, President; 1% by his wife; and 5% by Wilbur Chumley. These three individuals were incorporators and are officers and directors of the corporation.

Otis manufactures and sells telephone equipment. In 1974, it sold approximately $350,000 of its various products almost exclusively in the state of its incorporation. In 1975, it began to branch out and sold $550,000 of its products throughout that state and $50,000 of its products in a neighboring state. Otis expanded rapidly, and 1976 was a banner year with sales of $1,250,000 and profits of $175,000. Otis constructed a small office building on a tract of land it had purchased for expansion purposes in the neighboring state and used the top floor to establish a regional sales office and rented the balance of the building.

During the course of your audit for the year 1976, you discover that Parker commingles his personal funds with those of the corporation, keeps very few records of board and shareholder meetings, and at his convenience disregards corporate law regarding separatness of personal and corporate affairs. The corporation had 1976 sales in excess of $300,000 in the neighboring state. The corporation has not filed any papers with the Secretary of State of that state in connection with these operations.

In light of the above discoveries, it was deemed prudent to examine the original incorporation papers which were filed by Parker in 1974. The following irregularities were discovered. The powers and purposes clause states that the geographical territory in which the newly created corporation was to do business was solely the state of incorporation. Next, a certified copy of the corporate charter was not obtained and filed in the county in which the corporation's principal place of business is located, as required by state law. Additionally, Mr. Chumley and Mrs. Parker did not sign the articles of incorporation, and prior to the effective date of incorporation, a lease was taken out and a car purchased in the corporate name.

Required:

Answer the following, setting forth reasons for any conclusions stated.

Discuss the legal problems which Otis may face as a result of the above facts. **Do not consider any tax implications.**

Number 3 (Estimated time -- 15 to 20 minutes)

The CPA firm of Martinson, Brinks & Sutherland, a partnership, was the auditor for Masco Corporation, a medium-sized wholesaler. Masco leased warehouse facilities and sought financing for leasehold improvements to these facilities. Masco assured its bank that the leasehold improvements would result in a more efficient and profitable operation. Based on these assurances, the bank granted Masco a line of credit.

The loan agreement required annual audited financial statements. Masco submitted its 1975 audited financial statements to the bank which showed an operating profit of $75,000, leasehold improvements of $250,000, and net worth of $350,000. In reliance thereon, the bank loaned Masco $200,000. The audit report which accompanied the financial statements disclaimed an opinion because the cost of the leasehold improvements could not be determined from the company's records. The part of the audit report dealing with leasehold improvements reads as follows:

> Additions to fixed assets in 1975 were found to include principally warehouse improvements. Practically all of this work was done by company employees and the cost of materials and overhead were paid by Masco. Unfortunately, fully complete detailed cost records were not kept of these leasehold improvements and no exact determination could be made as to the actual cost of said improvements. The total amount capitalized is set forth in note 4.

In late 1976 Masco went out of business, at which time it was learned that the claimed leasehold improvements were totally fictitious. The labor expenses charged as leasehold improvements proved to be operating expenses. No item of building material cost had been recorded. No independent investigation of the existence of the leasehold improvements was made by the auditors.

If the $250,000 had not been capitalized, the income statement would have reflected a substantial loss from operations and the net worth would have been correspondingly decreased.

The bank has sustained a loss on its loan to Masco of $200,000 and now seeks to recover damages from the CPA firm, alleging that the accountants negligently audited the financial statements.

Required: Answer the following, setting forth reasons for any conclusions stated.

a. Will the disclaimer of opinion absolve the CPA firm from liability?

b. Are the individual partners of Martinson, Brinks & Sutherland, who did not take part in the audit, liable?

Part b. A CPA firm has been named as a defendant in a class action by purchasers of the shares of stock of the Newly Corporation. The offering was a public offering of securities within the meaning of the Securities Act of 1933. The plaintiffs alleged that the firm was either negligent or fraudulent in connection with the preparation of the audited financial statements filed with the SEC. Specifically, they alleged that the CPA firm either intentionally disregarded, or failed to exercise reasonable care to discover, material facts which occurred subsequent to January 31, 1978, the date of the auditor's report. The securities were sold to the public on March 16, 1978. The plaintiffs have subpoenaed copies of the CPA firm's working papers. The CPA firm is considering refusing to relinquish the papers, asserting that they contain privileged communication between the CPA firm and its client. The CPA firm will, of course, defend on the merits irrespective of the questions regarding the working papers.

Required:

Answer the following, setting forth reasons for any conclusions stated.

1. Can the CPA firm rightfully refuse to surrender its working papers?

2. Discuss the liability of the CPA firm in respect to events which occur in the period between the date of the auditor's report and the effective date of the public offering of the securities.

Number 4 (Estimated time – 15 to 20 minutes)
Number 4 consists of 2 unrealted parts

Part a. Davidson was one of Fenner Corporation's chief stock clerks. His net weekly salary was $125. Unfortunately, he lost a substantial sum of money betting on sports events, and he owed $2,000 to the loan sharks. Under these circumstances, he decided to raise the amount of his paychecks to $725 per week. His strategem was to wait until the assistant treasurer, in whose office the paymaster check imprinting machine was located, was away from his desk. He would then go into the office and artfully strike the number 7 over the number 1 and raise the paycheck amount from $125 to $725. The checks were promptly negotiated to Smith, a holder in due course, who cashed them at his own bank, and the checks were subsequently paid by Fenner's bank, Beacon National. The fraudulent scheme was discovered within a week after Beacon returned Fenner's canceled checks for the month. By that time five weekly paychecks had been raised by Davidson and cashed by Smith. Fenner promptly notified Beacon of the fraud.

Required:

Answer the following, setting forth reasons for any conclusions stated.

1. To whom is Davidson liable?
2. What are the rights and liabilities of Fenner?
3. What are the rights and liabilities of Beacon?
4. What are the rights and liabilities of Smith?

Part b. Sill Corporation operates a retail appliance store. About a year ago, Sill borrowed $3,000 from Castle to supplement its working capital. At that time it granted to Castle a security interest in its present and future inventory pursuant to a written security agreement signed by both parties. Castle duly filed a properly executed financing statement a few days later. In the ordinary course of business, a customer purchased a $500 television set from Sill. The customer knew of the existence of Castle's security interest.

Required:

What rights does Castle have against Sill's customer? Explain.

Number 5 (Estimated time — 15 to 20 minutes)
Number 5 consists of 2 unrelated parts)

Part a. Granville Motors, Inc., wished to acquire a 4-acre tract of land owned by Bonanza Realty Developers in an industrial city. Granville did not want to waste time and money considering the suitability of the property unless assured that the plant site would be available if studies indicated that the proposed purchase would be desirable. Granville did not discuss this concern with Bonanza but proposed to Bonanza that an option be drafted granting Granville 30 days in which to purchase the plant site for $62,950. Bonanza agreed and mailed to Granville the following written option:

> For ONE DOLLAR ($1.00) and other valuable consideration, Bonanza Realty Developers hereby grants to Granville Motors, Inc., the exclusive option to purchase for SIXTY-TWO THOUSAND NINE HUNDRED FIFTY DOLLARS ($62,950) the 4-acre tract of land known as the N.E. corner site . . . (*assume legal description included*) for THIRTY (30) days. This option is exclusive and irrevocable and will automatically expire on September 15, 1977.
>
> *Joseph T. Verona*
> Joseph T. Verona, President
> Bonanza Realty Developers

The letter containing the option was mailed on August 14, but due to a delay in the mails, did not reach Granville until August 18. Upon receipt Granville promptly engaged an expert to do a feasibility study with respect to the location and began to solicit bids on the construction of the proposed plant. Bonanza had no knowledge of these facts. Granville had no further correspondence with Bonanza after the receipt of the option, and Granville neither paid the $1.00 nor gave any other bargained for consideration.

On September 15, Jordon, Granville's President, telephoned Verona intending to accept the offer for Granville. However, before Jordon could accept, Verona stated that the property had already been sold at a higher price. The purchaser had no actual knowledge of the above facts. Jordon nevertheless accepted on Granville's behalf. The next day Jordon sent a written confirmation which stated that Granville expected performance by Bonanza, and that if Bonanza failed to perform, Granville would be forced to sue to protect its interests. Jordon also reminded Verona that the offer was irrevocable and that substantial time, money, and effort had been expended in a feasibility study. In addition Jordon noted the adverse effect which a refusal would have on Granville's future profits in that plans had been finalized calling for the plant to be on line by April 1978 to supply the increased demand of its customers.

Required:

Answer the following, setting forth reasons for any conclusions stated.

1. Is the option legally binding on Bonanza?
2. Assuming Granville will prevail, is specific performance available to Granville?
3. Assuming Granville will prevail, what would Granville be entitled to recover if it seeks damages as a form of relief?

Part b. The Minlow, Richard, and Jones partnership agreement is silent on whether the partners may assign or otherwise transfer all or part of their partnership interests to an outsider. Richard has assigned his partnership interest to Smith, a personal creditor, and as a result the other partners are furious. They have threatened to remove Richard as a partner, not admit Smith as a partner, and bar Smith from access to the firm's books and records.

Required:

Answer the following, setting forth reasons for any conclusions stated.

Can Minlow and Jones successfully implement their threats? Discuss the rights of Richard and Smith and the effects of the assignment on the partnership.

ANSWERS TO SAMPLE EXAMINATION

BUSINESS LAW

Answer 1

1. a	11. d	21. d	31. d	41. d	51. c
2. c	12. d	22. b	32. a	42. a	52. b
3. c	13. d	23. d	33. d	43. b	53. b
4. c	14. d	24. d	34. c	44. b	54. b
5. a	15. d	25. c	35. a	45. b	55. b
6. c	16. d	26. a	36. a	46. a	56. b
7. c	17. d	27. c	37. c	47. d	57. c
8. d	18. b	28. b	38. c	48. a	58. d
9. b	19. a	29. d	39. a	49. d	59. b
10. a	20. a	30. d	40. b	50. b	60. d

Answer 2

The facts pose the following legal problems.

(1) Is there a valid corporate entity? There are two two separate aspects of this problem. First, the incorporation was irregular. Second, there is a question whether the corporation is a mere sham.

It is possible that the irregularities in the original incorporation procedures would be of sufficient gravity to result in a finding that Otis was neither a corporation *de jure* nor *de facto.* This issue would not arise unless Otis encountered financial difficulty and it became necessary for a party to try to impose personal liability against Parker or others associated with him, such as directors, owners, and managers of Otis. When deciding the problem of *de jure, de facto,* or *no corporation,* the key legal factor that often is not clearly articulated by the courts is the question of deciding on what basis the plaintiff dealt with the corporation. Obviously, from a practical standpoint, all of the irregularities should be remedied by the corporation's attorney. Any existing contracts which were made prior to incorporation should be adopted by or re-executed in the corporate name.

By and large, courts are reluctant to disregard the corporate entity. This is so because the very purpose of incorporation is to permit the avoidance of personal liability. However, Parker has treated the corporation as his alter ego and has ignored its existence; consequently, a court may not respect the corporate entity in view of the fact that Parker himself has not. Certainly the commingling of funds and near total disregard for the formalities required by law would create problems for the corporation and Mr. Parker.

(2) What is the effect of doing business in the neighboring state without having first qualified to do business in that state?

The volume of business, the frequency of contact, and, most important, the fact that it has established a facility in the neighboring state is conclusive evidence that Otis is doing business in that state. Under the circumstances, Otis was obligated to file the appropriate papers necessary to qualify for doing business in the neighboring state. Failure to do so can have serious legal consequences. Although the law varies from jurisdiction, the corporation may be subject to fines, penalties, or injunction proceedings to prohibit its carrying on business in the state. Furthermore, the corporation may be denied the right of access to the courts of the neighboring state. This has the effect of making its contracts legally unenforceable.

(3) What is the effect of doing business outside the state of incorporation, where the corporate charter is narrowly drafted and does not permit engaging in business outside of that state?

This question has not been adjudicated frequently by the courts in recent times. Current practice is to draft purposes and powers clauses in such a manner that virtually anything can be done at any time and anywhere by the corporation. Consequently, the charter under which Otis is operating, in this fact situation, raises the question of *ultra vires.* Currently the courts by and large take a practical and sensible view of the matter. Although the contracts made in the neighboring state exceed the corporate purposes and powers as stated in the charter they are a *fait accompli;* therefore, they should be recognized as valid except in extraordinary circumstances which would not appear to be present in the facts given. From a practical standpoint, it is obvious that the corporate charter should be amended immediately to permit the corporation to do busness anywhere and everywhere.

Answer 3

a. No. The disclaimer of opinion will not absolve the CPA firm from liability. The auditor was negligent by failing either to take adequate measures to determine whether the leasehold improvements existed or to give notice that their existence had not been verified. As a result of such negligence and the bank's reliance upon the report, the CPA firm would be liable to the bank.

An auditor generally will not be held responsible for limitations on the audit if the auditor's report gives adequate notice of them. A disclaimer of opinion is the means used by the auditor to give adequate notice of limitations. Although the CPA firm attempted to disclaim an opinion on the financial statements, the wording in the auditor's report was sufficiently unclear that it is doubtful a court would find the report accomplished its intended purpose. The disclaimer said only that the "actual cost" of the improvements could not be determined, and the explanation strongly implied that the improvements actually existed and had substantial value (by use of such phrases as "were found" and "work was done") when in fact they did not exist. Consequently, the report was misleading.

b. Yes. The individual partners of the CPA firm are liable even though they did not take part in the audit. A partnership is an entity that is an association of two or more persons as co-owners to carry on a business for profit. All partners are jointly and severally liable and therefore personally responsible for the firm's liability to the bank. The individual partners may have to satisfy the bank's claim from their personal assets, even though they did not personally take part in the audit.

Part b.

1. No. Neither federal nor common law recognizes the validity of the privilege rule insofar as accountants are concerned. Furthermore, even where the privilege rule is applicable, it can only be claimed by the client. Only a limited number of jurisdictions recognize the rule, and these jurisdictions have by statute overridden the common law rule which does not consider such communications to be within the privilege rule. The privilege rule applies principally to the attorney-client and doctor-patient relationships.

2. The Securities Act of 1933 requires a review by the auditor who reported on the financial statements accompanying the registration statement of events in the period between the date of the auditor's report and the date of the public sale of the securities. The auditors must show that they made a reasonable investigation, had a reasonable basis for their belief, and they did believe the financial statements were true as of the time the registration statement became effective. The auditor defendants have the burden of proving that the requisite standard was met. Therefore, unless the auditors can satisfy the foregoing tests, they will be liable.

Answer 4

Part a.

1. The embezzler, Davidson, is liable to whichever party bears the ultimate loss.

2. Fenner Corporation would normally be able to recover $600 per check from Beacon National because it has a real defense (material alteration), which is valid even against a holder in due course. However, Beacon National has a possible defense of contributory negligence by Fenner on the basis that Fenner did not exercise proper safeguards to prevent improper use of the check-imprinting machine. The Uniform Commercial Code provides that any person who by his negligence substantially contributes to a material alteration of the instrument is precluded from asserting the alteration against a holder in due course or against a drawee or other payor who pays the instrument in good faith and in accordance with the reasonable commercial standards of the drawee's or payor's business. In any event, Fenner is still liable to the extent of the original amount of $125 per check.

3. Normally, Beacon National must credit Fenner's account for the overpayments. It in turn has an action against the parties endorsing the instruments based upon a breach of their warranty that there were no material alterations. However, as discussed above, the possible defense of contributory negligence would be equally applicable here.

4. Smith, as a holder in due course, has the same rights and liabilities as Beacon National as they are given above.

Part b.

None. The Uniform Commercial Code provides that a retail customer in the ordinary course of business takes free of a security interest created by his seller even though the security interest is perfected and even though the buyer knows of its existence. A buyer in the ordinary course of business is, generally, a person who, in good faith and without knowledge that the sale to him is in violation of the ownership rights or security interest of a third party in the goods, buys goods from someone in the business of selling them.

By duly filing a financing statement, Castle perfects its security interest in then-existing as well as after-acquired inventory. Even though Castle held a perfected security interest in Sill's inventory, the customer who purchased the television set from Sill in the ordinary course of business took the property free of Castle's security interest.

Answer 5

Part a.

1. The option is not legally binding on Bonanza. The issue is whether the option fails for want of legal consideration. The option involved here must meet the necessary common law requirements to establish a legally enforceable contract. Since land is the subject matter of the option, it is tested under the common law rules as contrasted with the more liberal Uniform Commercial Code rule on options. The main pitfall is the lack of consideration. Despite the facts that the promise was written and was signed by the offeror, and that it recited consideration, and manifested a clear intent that it be irrevocable for 30 days, it is not legally binding. It is not supported by actual consideration and, therefore, fails to meet the requirements necessary to establish a valid contract under common law principles.

Neither the signed written offer, nor the expenditures made by Granville constitute consideration. With respect to the feasibility study, the parties did not bargain for the performance of such acts and expenditures by Granville in exchange for the promise contained in the option. The facts indicate that Bonanza had no knowledge that Granville was incurring the expense of a feasibility study prior to reaching a decision whether to exercise the option.

Although the courts generally are receptive to a formal satisfaction of the consideration requirement by the actual payment of $1.00 or some other bargained for token consideration, they do not accept fictional statements of receipt of consideration. If the option were valid, the acceptance would of course be timely even if made orally on September 15, provided the fact of acceptance could be established. One need not use the same means of communication in order to have a valid acceptance, provided it is received prior to the termination of the offer.

2. No. Although specific performance generally is not available as a remedy for breach of contract, there is a notable exception with respect to contracts for the sale of real property. Real property is deemed to be unique, and therefore, specific performance usually is available. However, when there has been a subsequent sale to a good faith third-party purchaser, the courts will let the title rest where they find it. Thus, Granville would fail unless the third party had actual or constructive notice of the option granted by Bonanza to Granville. If this option agreement had been recorded, the third party would be deemed to have constructive notice.

3. Granville would be limited to recovery of the typical contract measure of damages, that is, the difference between the fair market value and the contract price at the date the contract was to be performed. The sale at the higher price to the third party will have strong evidentiary value as to the fair market value. Recovery for the expenditures made it possible but not probable unless these facts were known to the seller and thus was within the contemplation of the parties at the time the contract was made. Such does not appear to be the case. This would also apply to the lost future profits. In addition, the lost future profits are at best speculative and would appear to be unattainable as damages.

Part b.

Unless there is an express prohibition against the assignment of a partner's partnership interest stated in the partnership agreement, it is assignable. This rule applies whether all or part of the partnership interest is assigned. Probably the most common situation in which a partner assigns his partnership interest is in connection with collateralizing a personal loan. Therefore, barring an express prohibition or a clause requiring the consent of the other partners, Richard may assign his interest.

As a result of the above assignment, Richard remains a partner. Although Richard has assigned his partnership interest he still remains a partner and rerains all of the rights, privileges, perquisites, duties, and liabilities he formerly had vis-a-vis the partnership and his fellow partners. The assignee (Smith) has only the right to Richard's share of the profits in the event of a default. He would succeed to Richard's rights, in whole or in part, upon the dissolution and winding up of the partnership or upon its bankruptcy. Smith does not, however, succeed to Richard's right to access to the partnership's books and records.

EXAMINATION IN ACCOUNTING PRACTICE – PART I

NOTE TO CANDIDATES: Suggested time allotments are as follows:

All questions are required:	Estimated Minutes Minimum	Estimated Minutes Maximum
No. 1	45	55
No. 2	45	55
No. 3	45	55
No. 4	40	50
No. 5	45	55
Total	220	270

Number 1 (Estimated time - 45 to 55 minutes)

Select the **best** answer for each of the following items relating to a **variety of financial accounting problems.**

1. Chip Company operates in four different industries, each of which is appropriately regarded as a reportable segment. Total sales for 1978 for all the segments combined were $1,000,000. Sales for Segment No. 2 were $400,000 and traceable costs were $150,000. Total common costs for all the segments combined were $500,000. Chip allocates common costs based on the ratio of a segment's sales to total sales, an appropriate method of allocation. The operating profit presented for Segment No. 2 for 1978 should be
   a. $ 50,000
   b. $125,000
   c. $200,000
   d. $250,000

2. Stark, Inc., has $1,000,000 of notes payable due June 15, 1981. At the financial statement date of December 31, 1980, Stark signed an agreement to borrow up to $1,000,000 to refinance the notes payable on a long-term basis. The financing agreement called for borrowings not to exceed 80% of the value of the collateral Stark was providing. At the date of issue of the December 31, 1980, financial statements the value of the collateral was $1,200,000 and was not expected to fall below this amount during 1981. On the December 31, 1980, balance sheet, Stark should classify
   a. $40,000 of notes payable as short-term and $960,000 as long-term obligations.
   b. $200,000 of notes payable as short-term and $800,000 as long-term obligations.
   c. $1,000,000 of notes payable as short-term obligations.
   d. $1,000,000 of notes payable as long-term obligations.

3. Minor Baseball Company had a player contract with Doe that was recorded in its accounting records at $145,000. Better Baseball Company had a player contract with Smith that was recorded in its accounting records at $140,000. Minor traded Doe to Better for Smith by exchanging each player's contract. The fair value of each contract was $150,000. What amount should be shown in the accounting records after the exchange of player contracts?

	Minor	Better
a.	$140,000	$140,000
b.	$140,000	$145,000
c.	$145,000	$140,000
d.	$150,000	$150,000

Items 4 and 5 are based on the following information:

Information concerning the capital structure of the Petrock Corporation is as follows:

	December 31, 1975	December 31, 1976
Common stock	90,000 shares	90,000 shares
Convertible preferred stock	10,000 shares	10,000 shares
8% convertible bonds	$1,000,000	$1,000,000

During 1976, Petrock paid dividends of $1.00 per share on its common stock and $2.40 per share on its preferred stock. The preferred stock is convertible into 20,000 shares of common stock; but is not considered a common stock equivalent. The 8% convertible bonds are convertible into 30,000 shares of common stock and are considered common stock equivalents. The net income for the year ended December 31, 1976, was $285,000. Assume that the income tax rate was 50%.

4. What should be the primary earnings per share for the year ended December 31, 1976, rounded to the nearest penny?
   a. $2.38.
   b. $2.51.
   c. $2.84.
   d. $3.13.

5. What should be the fully diluted earnings per share for the year ended December 31, 1976, rounded to the nearest penny?
   a. $2.15.
   b. $2.32.
   c. $2.61.
   d. $2.74.

6. The capital accounts for the partnership of Lance and Dey at October 31, 1975, are as follows:

Lance, capital	$ 80,000
Dey, capital	40,000
	$120,000

The partners share profits and losses in the ratio of 6:4, respectively.

The partnership is in desperate need of cash, and the partners agree to admit Carey as a partner with a one-third interest in the capital and profits and losses upon his investment of $30,000. Immediately after Carey's admission, what should be the capital balances of Lance, Dey, and Carey, respectively, assuming goodwill is not to be recognized?
   a. $50,000; $50,000; $50,000.
   b. $60,000; $60,000; $60,000.
   c. $66,667; $33,333; $50,000.
   d. $68,000; $32,000; $50,000.

7. In January 1980 Farley Corporation acquired 20% of the outstanding common stock of Davis Company for $800,000. This investment gave Farley the ability to exercise significant influence over Davis. The book value of the acquired shares was $600,000. The excess of cost over book value was attributed to an identifiable intangible asset which was undervalued on Davis' balance sheet and which had a remaining useful life of ten years.

For the year ended December 31, 1980, Davis reported net income of $180,000 and paid cash dividends of $40,000 on its common stock. What is the proper carrying value of Farley's investment in Davis at December 31, 1980?
   a. $772,000.
   b. $780,000.
   c. $800,000.
   d. $808,000.

8. In January 1977, Hunter, Inc., estimated that its year end bonus to executives would be $240,000 for 1977. The actual amount paid for the year end bonus for 1976 was $224,000. The estimate for 1977 is subject to year-end adjustment. What amount, if any, of expense should be reflected in Hunter's quarterly income statement for the three months ended March 31, 1977?
   a. $0.
   b. $56,000.
   c. $60,000.
   d. $240,000.

9. Growing, Inc., had net income for 1977 of $10,600,000 and earnings per share on common stock of $5.00. Included in the net income was $1,000,000 of bond interest expense related to its long-term debt. The income tax rate for 1977 was 50%. Dividends on preferred stock were $600,000. The dividend-payout ratio on common stock was 40%. What were the dividends on common stock in 1977?
   a. $3,600,000.
   b. $3,800,000.
   c. $4,000,000.
   d. $4,240,000.

10. The Park Company is disposing of a segment of its business. At the measurement date the net loss from the disposal is estimated to be $950,000. Included in the $950,000 are severance pay of $100,000 and employee relocation costs of $50,000, both of which are directly associated with the decision to dispose of the segment; and estimated net losses from operations from the measurement date to the expected disposal date of $200,000. Net losses from operations of $150,000 from the beginning of the year to the measurement date are not included in the estimated net loss from the disposal. Park's income statement should report a loss on discontinued operations (a separate component of income below the caption "Income From Continuing Operations") of

a. $750,000.
b. $850,000.
c. $900,000.
d. $1,100,000.

11. A company was formed on January 1, 1975. Selected balances from the historical-dollar balance sheet at December 31, 1975, were:

Accounts Receivable	$ 70,000
Accounts Payable	60,000
Long-term debt	110,000
Common stock	100,000

At what amounts should these selected accounts be shown in a constant dollar balance sheet at December 31, 1975, if the general price-level index was 100 at December 31, 1974, and 110 at December 31, 1975?

	Accounts Receivable	Accounts Payable	Long-term Debt	Common Stock
a.	$70,000	$60,000	$110,000	$100,000
b.	$70,000	$60,000	$110,000	$110,000
c.	$70,000	$60,000	$121,000	$110,000
d.	$77,000	$66,000	$121,000	$110,000

12. Tob Corporation purchased certain machinery on January 1, 1973. At the date of acquisition, the machinery had an estimated useful life of ten years with no salvage. The machinery was being depreciated using the double-declining-balance method for both financial statement reporting and income tax reporting. On January 1, 1978, Tob changed to the straight-line method for depreciation of the machinery for financial statement reporting but not for income tax reporting. Assume that Tob can justify the change.

The accumulated depreciation from January 1, 1973, through December 31, 1977, under the double-declining-balance method was $200,000. If the straight-line method had been used, the accumulated depreciation from January 1, 1973, through December 31, 1977, would have been $140,000. Assuming that the income tax rate for the years 1973 through 1978 is 50%, the amount shown in the 1978 income statement for the cumulative effect of changing from the double-declining-balance method to the straight-line method would be

a. $0.
b. $30,000 credit.
c. $60,000 credit.
d. $60,000 debit.

13. In January 1977 Action Corporation entered into a contract to acquire a new machine for its factory. The machine, which had a cash price of $150,000, was paid for as follows:

Down payment	$ 15,000
Notes payable in 10 equal monthly installments	120,000
500 shares of Action common stock with an agreed value of $50 per share	25,000
Total	$160,000

Prior to the machine's use, installation costs of $4,000 were incurred. The machine has an estimated useful life of 10 years and an estimated salvage value of $5,000. What should Action record as depreciation expense for 1977 under the straight-line method?

a. $15,900.
b. $15,500.
c. $15,000.
d. $14,900.

Items 14 and 15 are based on the following information:

The Nugget Company's balance sheet on December 31, 1976, is as follows:

Assets

Cash	$ 100,000
Accounts receivable	200,000
Inventories	500,000
Property, plant and equipment	900,000
	$1,700,000

Liabilities and Stockholders' Equity

Current liabilities	$ 300,000
Long-term debt	500,000
Common stock (par $1 per share)	100,000
Additional paid-in capital	200,000
Retained earnings	600,000
	$1,700,000

On December 31, 1976, the Bronc Company purchased all of the outstanding common stock of Nugget for $1,500,000 cash. On that date, the fair (market) value of Nugget's inventories was $450,000 and the fair value of Nugget's property, plant and equipment was $1,000,000. The fair values of all other assets and liabilities of Nugget were equal to their book values.

14. As a result of the acquisition of Nugget by Bronc, the consolidated balance sheet of Bronc and Nugget should reflect goodwill in the amount of

a. $500,000.
b. $550,000.
c. $600,000.
d. $650,000

15. Assuming that the balance sheet of Bronc (unconsolidated) at December 31, 1976, reflected retained earnings of $2,000,000, what amount of retained earnings should be shown in the December 31, 1976, consolidated balance sheet of Bronc and its new subsidiary, Nugget?

a. $2,000,000.
b. $2,600,000.
c. $2,800,000.
d. $3,150,000

16. The Blue Department Store uses the retail inventory method. Information relating to the computation of the inventory at December 31, 1976, is as follows:

	Cost	Retail
Inventory at January 1, 1976	$ 16,000	$ 40,000
Sales		290,000
Purchases	135,000	300,000
Freight-in	3,800	
Net markups		20,000
Net markdowns		10,000

What should be the ending inventory at cost at December 31, 1976, using the retail inventory method?

a. $21,500.
b. $22,500.
c. $25,800.
d. $27,000.

17. Tackle Company sells football helmets. In 1977 Tackle discovered a defect in the helmets which has produced lawsuits that are reasonably estimated to result in losses of $900,000. Based on its own experience and the experience of other enterprises in the business, Tackle considers it probable that additional lawsuits that are reasonably estimated to result in losses of $1,600,000 will occur even though the particular parties that will bring suit are not identifiable at this time. What amount of loss, if any, should be accrued by a charge to income in 1977?

a. $0.
b. $900,000.
c. $1,600,000.
d. $2,500,000.

18. An inventory loss from market decline of $600,000 occurred in May 1978. The Kup Company recorded this loss in May 1978 after its March 31, 1978, quarterly report was issued. None of this loss was recovered by the end of the year. How should this loss be reflected in Kup's quarterly income statements?

	Three Months Ended			
	March 31, 1978	June 30, 1978	September 30, 1978	December 31, 1978
a.	$ 0	$ 0	$ 0	$600,000
b.	$ 0	$200,000	$200,000	$200,000
c.	$ 0	$600,000	$ 0	$ 0
d.	$150,000	$150,000	$150,000	$150,000

19. Donahue Corporation purchased a machine in 1976 when the general price-level index was 180. The price-level index was 190 in 1977 and 200 in 1978. The price-level indexes above are stated in terms of the 1958 base year. Donahue prepares supplemental constant dollar financial statements (restated for changes in the general purchasing power of the dollar), as recommended by SFAS 33. Depreciation is $100,000 a year. In Donahue's constant dollar income statement for 1978, the amount of depreciation would be stated as

a. $ 90,000.
b. $ 95,000.
c. $105,263.
d. $111,111.

20. On April 30, 1979, Standard, Inc., purchased Dynamo Corporation, 10-year, 9% bonds with a face value of $120,000 for $133,600, which includes $3,600 accrued interest. The bonds mature on January 1, 1986, and pay interest on January 1 and July 1. Standard uses the straight-line method of amortization. The amount of income Standard should report for the year ended December 31, 1979, as a result of this long-term bond investment, is

a. $6,200.
b. $6,393.
c. $6,533.
d. $8,200.

Number 2 (Estimated time - 45 to 55 minutes)

Select the **best** answer for each of the following items relating to a **variety of managerial accounting and quantitative method problems.**

21. On November 1, 1977, Yankee Company had 20,000 units of work in process in Department No. 1 which were 100% complete as to material costs and 20% complete as to conversion costs. During November, 160,000 units were started in Department No. 1 and 170,000 units were completed and transferred to Department No. 2. The work in process on November 30, 1977, was 100% complete as to material costs and 40% complete as to conversion costs. By what amount would the equivalent units for conversion costs for the month of November differ if the first-in, first-out method were used instead of the weighted-average method?
    a. 20,000 decrease.
    b. 16,000 decrease.
    c. 8,000 decrease.
    d. 4,000 decrease.

22. Keller Company, a manufacturer of rivets, uses absorption costing. Keller's 1981 manufacturing costs were as follows:

Direct materials and direct labor	$800,000
Depreciation of machines	100,000
Rent for factory building	60,000
Electricity to run machines	35,000

How much of these costs should be inventoried?
    a. $800,000
    b. $835,000
    c. $935,000
    d. $995,000

23. Walsh, Inc., is preparing its cash budget for the month of November. The following information is available concerning its inventories:

Inventories at beginning of November	$180,000
Estimated cost of goods sold for November	900,000
Estimated inventories at end of November	160,000
Estimated payments in November for purchases prior to November	210,000
Estimated payments in November for purchases in November	80%

What are the estimated cash disbursements for inventories in November?
    a. $720,000.
    b. $914,000.
    c. $930,000.
    d. $1,042,000.

24. O'Connor Company manufactures Product J and Product K from a joint process. For Product J, 4,000 units were produced having a sales value at split-off of $15,000. If Product J were processed further, the additional costs would be $3,000 and the sales value would be $20,000. For Product K, 2,000 units were produced having a sales value at split-off of $10,000. If Product K were processed further, the additional costs would be $1,000 and the sales value would be $12,000. Using the relative-sales-value at split-off approach, the portion of the total joint product costs allocated to Product J was $9,000. What were the total joint product costs?
    a. $14,400.
    b. $15,000.
    c. $18,400.
    d. $19,000.

25. Helen Corp. manufactures products W, X, Y, and Z from a joint process. Additional information is as follows:

Product	Units Produced	Sales Value at Split-off	If Processed Further: Additional Costs	If Processed Further: Sales Value
W	6,000	$ 80,000	$ 7,500	$ 90,000
X	5,000	60,000	6,000	70,000
Y	4,000	40,000	4,000	50,000
Z	3,000	20,000	2,500	30,000
	18,000	$200,000	$20,000	$240,000

Assuming that total joint costs of $160,000 were allocated using the relative-sales-value at split-off approach, what were the joint costs allocated to each product?

	W	X	Y	Z
a.	$40,000	$40,000	$40,000	$40,000
b.	$53,333	$44,444	$35,556	$26,667
c.	$60,000	$46,667	$33,333	$20,000
d.	$64,000	$48,000	$32,000	$16,000

26. The Wiring Department is the second stage of Flem Company's production cycle. On May 1, the beginning work in process contained 25,000 units which were 60% complete as to conversion costs. During May, 100,000 units were transferred in from the first stage of Flem's production cycle. On May 31, the ending work in process contained 20,000 units

which were 80% complete as to conversion costs. Material costs are added at the end of the process. Using the weighted-average method, the equivalent units were

	Transferred-in costs	*Materials*	*Conversion costs*
a.	100,000	125,000	100,000
b.	125,000	105,000	105,000
c.	125,000	105,000	121,000
d.	125,000	125,000	121.000

Items 27. and 28. are based on the following information:

The January 31, 1976, balance sheet of Shelpat Corporation follows:

Cash	$ 8,000
Accounts receivable (net of allowance for uncollectible accounts of $2,000)	38,000
Inventory	16,000
Property, plant and equipment (net of allowance for accumulated depreciation of $60,000)	40,000
	$102,000
Accounts payable	$ 82,500
Common stock	50,000
Retained earnings (deficit)	(30,500)
	$102,000

Additional information:

* Sales are budgeted as follows:
  February $110,000
  March $120,000
* Collections are expected to be 60% in the month of sale, 38% the next month, and 2% uncollectible.
* The gross margin is 25% of sales. Purchases each month are 75% of the next month's projected sales. The purchases are paid in full the following month.
* Other expenses for each month, paid in cash, are expected to be $16,500. Depreciation each month is $5,000.

27. What are the budgeted cash collections for February 1976?
  a. $63,800.
  b. $66,000.
  c. $101,800.
  d. $104,000.

28. What is the pro forma income (loss) before income taxes for February 1976?
  a. ($3,700).
  b. ($1,500).
  c. $3,800.
  d. $6,000.

29. Davis Company has budgeted its activity for April 1980. Selected data from estimated amounts are as follows:

Net income	$120,000
Increase in gross amount of trade accounts receivable during month	35,000
Decrease in accounts payable during month	25,000
Depreciation expense	65,000
Provision for income taxes	80,000
Provision for doubtful accounts receivable	45,000

On the basis of the above data, Davis has budgeted a cash increase for the month in the amount of
  a. $ 90,000.
  b. $195,000.
  c. $250,000.
  d. $300,000.

30. The Aron Company requires 40,000 units of Product Q for the year. The units will be required evenly throughout the year. It costs $60 to place an order. It costs $10 to carry a unit in inventory for the year. What is the economic order quantity?
  a. 400.
  b. 490.
  c. 600.
  d. 693.

31. During January 1981 Gable, Inc., produced 10,000 units of product F with costs as follows:

Direct materials	$40,000
Direct labor	22,000
Variable overhead	13,000
Fixed overhead	10,000
	$85,000

What is Gable's unit cost of product F for January 1981 calculated on the direct costing basis?
  a. $6.20.
  b. $7.20.
  c. $7.50.
  d. $8.50.

32. A company uses the first-in, first-out method of costing in a process-costing system. Material is added at the beginning of the process in Department A, and conversion costs are incurred uniformly throughout the process. Beginning work-in-process inventory on April 1 in Department A consisted of 50,000 units estimated to be 30% complete. During April, 150,000 units were started in Department A, and 160,000 units were completed and transferred to Department B. Ending work-in-process inventory on April 30 in Department A was estimated to be 20% complete. What were the total equivalent units in Department A for April for materials and conversion costs, respectively?

a. 150,000 and 133,000.
b. 150,000 and 153,000.
c. 200,000 and 133,000.
d. 200,000 and 153,000.

33. Lab Corp. uses a standard cost system. Direct labor information for Product CER for the month of October is as follows:

Standard rate	$6.00 per hour
Actual rate paid	$6.10 per hour
Standard hours allowed for actual production	1,500 hours
Labor efficiency variance	$600 unfavorable

What are the actual hours worked?

a. 1,400.
b. 1,402.
c. 1,598.
d. 1,600.

34. Information on Overhead Company's overhead costs is as follows:

Standard applied overhead	$80,000
Budgeted overhead based on standard direct-labor hours allowed	$84,000
Budgeted overhead based on actual direct-labor hours allowed	$83,000
Actual overhead	$86,000

What is the total overhead variance?

a. $2,000 unfavorable.
b. $3,000 favorable.
c. $4,000 favorable.
d. $6,000 unfavorable.

35. Cardinal Company needs 20,000 units of a certain part to use in its production cycle. The following information is available:

Cost to Cardinal to make the part:	
Direct materials	$ 4
Direct labor	16
Variable overhead	8
Fixed overhead applied	10
	$38
Cost to buy the part from the Oriole Company	$36

If Cardinal buys the part from Oriole instead of making it, Cardinal could not use the released facilities in another manufacturing activity. 60% of the fixed overhead applied will continue regardless of what decision is made.

In deciding whether to make or buy the part, the total relevant costs to make the part are

a. $560,000.
b. $640,000.
c. $720,000.
d. $760,000.

36. Sun Company's tentative budget for product H for 1981 is as follows:

Sales	$600,000
Variable manufacturing costs	360,000
Fixed costs:	
Manufacturing	90,000
Selling and administrative	110,000

Mr. Johnston, the marketing manager, proposes an aggressive advertising campaign costing an additional $50,000 and resulting in a 30% unit sales increase for product H. Assuming that Johnston's proposal is incorporated into the budget for product H, what should be the increase in the budgeted operating profit for 1981?

a. $ 12,000.
b. $ 22,000.
c. $ 72,000.
d. $130,000.

37. Jarvis Co. has fixed costs of $200,000. It has two products that it can sell, Tetra and Min. Jarvis sells these products at a rate of 2 units of Tetra to 1 unit of Min. The contribution margin is $1 per unit for Tetra and $2 per unit for Min. How many units of Min would be sold at the breakeven point?

a. 44,444.
b. 50,000.

c. 88,888.
d. 100,000.

38. Dallas Corporation wishes to market a new product for $1.50 a unit. Fixed costs to manufacture this product are $100,000 for less than 500,000 units and $150,000 for 500,000 or more units. The contribution margin is 20%. How many units must be sold to realize net income from this product of $100,000?

a. 333,333.
b. 500,000.
c. 666,667.
d. 833,333.

Items 39 and 40 are based on the following information:

Flemming, Inc., is planning to acquire a new machine at a total cost of $36,000. The estimated life of the machine is six years with no salvage value. The straight-line method of depreciation will be used. Flemming estimates that the annual cash flow from operations, before income taxes, from using this machine will be $9,000. Assume that Flemming's cost of capital is 8% and the income tax rate is 40%. The present value of $1 at 8% for six years is .630. The present value of an annuity of $1 in arrears at 8% for six years is 4.623.

39. What would the payback period be?

a. 4.0 years.
b. 4.6 years.
c. 5.7 years.
d. 6.7 years.

40. What would the net present value be?

a. $59.
b. $5,607.
c. $10,800.
d. $13,140.

Number 3 (Estimated time –– 45 to 55 minutes)

Select the **best** answer for each of the following items relating to **the federal income taxation of individuals.**

41. In January 1983, Sharon Lee was awarded a post-graduate grant of $5,000 by a tax-exempt educational foundation. Ms. Lee is not a candidate for a degree and was awarded the grant to continue her research. The grant is for the period April 1, 1983, through November 30, 1984.

On April 1, 1983, she elected to receive the full amount of the grant. What amount should be included in her gross income for 1983?

a. $0
b. $2,300
c. $2,700
d. $5,000

42. During 1983, Albert Mason purchased the following long-term investments at par:

$10,000 general obligation bonds of Tulip County (wholly tax exempt)
$10,000 debentures of Laxity Corporation

He financed these purchases by obtaining a loan from the Community Bank for $20,000. For the year 1983, he paid the following amounts as interest expense:

Community Bank	$1,600
Interest on mortgage	3,000
Interest on installment purchases	300
	$4,900

What amount can Mason deduct as interest expense in 1983?

a. $4,900
b. $4,100
c. $3,600
d. $3,300

43. Harold Shore was the owner of a parcel of vacant land that cost him $50,000 when he acquired it in 1970. On January 1, 1977, when the property was valued at $10,000, he made a bona fide gift of the property to his niece, Matilda River. Ms. River held the property until December 15, 1983, and then sold it for $20,000. What is the amount of the gain or loss that Ms. River should include in her adjusted gross income for 1983?

a. $0.
b. $10,000 gain.
c. $30,000 loss.
d. $40,000 loss.

44. Sam Mitchell, a calendar year taxpayer, purchased an annuity contract for $3,600 that would pay him $120 a month beginning on January 1, 1983. His expected return under the contract is $10,800. How much of this annuity is excludable from gross income for the 1983 calendar year?

a. $0
b. $ 480
c. $ 960
d. $1,440

45. Gilbert Quinn loaned a friend $2,000 in 1976 and it had not been repaid in 1983 when the friend died insolvent. For 1983 Quinn should account for the nonpayment of the loan as a (an)

a. Ordinary loss.
b. Long-term capital loss.
c. Short-term capital loss.
d. Deduction from adjusted gross income.

46. John Abel, whose wife died in December 1982, filed a joint tax return for 1982. He did not remarry but continued to maintain his home in which his two dependent children lived. In the preparation of his tax return for 1983, Abel should file as a

a. Single individual.
b. Surviving spouse.
c. Head of household.
d. Married individual filing separately.

47. Al Rivers, a cash basis taxpayer, died on September 30, 1983. From January 1 until his death he received a salary of $15,000. In addition, he earned commissions of $6,500 which were not received, although a check for $2,000 had been available since September 15, 1983. On December 15, 1983, Mr. Rivers' widow, Paula, received a $6,000 death benefit from his employer in consideration of his past services rendered. Assuming a joint return is properly filed, gross income of Mrs. Rivers and the decedent for 1983 should be

a. $27,500
b. $23,000
c. $18,000
d. $16,000

48. Sergio Morris, age 35, single with no dependents, is a self-employed individual. For the year 1983, his business sustained a net loss from operations of $18,000. There was no net operating loss in any prior year. The following additional information was obtained from his personal records for 1983:

Interest income	$2,000
Dividend income (after exclusion)	500
Itemized deductions, including a net casualty loss of $700	4,000
Personal exemption	1,000

Based upon the above information, what is his net operating loss for 1983?

a. $18,000
b. $18,700
c. $20,500
d. $22,000

49. Irving Press died on December 2, 1983. In his will, he left 5,000 shares of Vichy Corporation common stock to his daughter Celia. The stock was acquired by Press in 1971 for $20,000. At the time of his death, the stock had a fair market value of $25,000. The executor of the will elected to value the stock at the date of Press's death. On January 21, 1984, the stock was distributed to Press's daughter, when the fair market value was $26,000.

What should be the basis of the stock to Press's daughter?

a. $ 5,000
b. $20,000
c. $25,000
d. $26,000

50. During 1983, Jack Howard, an engineer, had the following items of income and expense:

Salary	$30,000
Interest income	1,200
Short-term capital gains	200
Long-term capital losses	(800)

In addition, Howard failed to make a claim for reimbursement to his employer for reimbursable travel expenses of $100 incurred by him. What should Howard report as his adjusted gross income for 1983?

a. $30,500
b. $30,600
c. $30,800
d. $30,900

51. During 1983 Seth Parker, a self-employed individual, paid the following taxes:

Federal income tax	$5,000
State income tax	2,000
Real estate taxes on land in South America (held as an investment)	900
State sales taxes	500
Federal self-employment tax	800
State unincorporated business tax	200

What amount can Parker claim for 1983 as an itemized deduction for taxes paid?

a. $7,500
b. $4,400
c. $3,600
d. $3,400

52. Mort Gage, a cash basis taxpayer, is the owner of an apartment building containing 10 identical apartments. Gage resides in one apartment and rents out the remaining units. For 1983 the following information was available:

Gross rents	$21,600
Fuel	2,500
Maintenance and repairs (rental apartments)	1,200
Advertising for vacant apartments	300
Depreciation of building	5,000

What amount should Gage report as net rental income for 1983?

a. $12,600
b. $13,350
c. $13,500
d. $17,600

53. In January 1983, Luther Miller sold stock with a cost basis of $26,000 to his brother, Marvin, for $24,000, the fair market value of the stock on the date of sale. Five months later, Marvin sold the same stock through his broker for $27,000. The tax effect for 1983 of these transactions would be a

a. Nondeductible loss to Luther of $2,000; gain to Marvin of $1,000.
b. Nondeductible loss to Luther of $2,000; gain to Marvin of $3,000.
c. Deductible loss to Luther of $2,000; gain to Marvin of $3,000.
d. Nonrecognized loss to Luther of $2,000; gain to Marvin of $1,000.

54. During 1983 Mary Culbert paid the following expenses:

Prescription drugs	$470
Aspirin and over-the-counter cold capsules	130
Hospital and doctors (net of insurance reimbursements under plan paid for by her employer)	700
Premiums for a policy to reimburse her for lost income due to illness	350

What is the total amount of medical expenses (before application of any limitation rules) that would enter into the calculation of excess itemized deductions on Culbert's 1983 tax return?

a. $1,170
b. $1,300
c. $1,520
d. $1,650

55. During 1983 Anthony and Cleo Patra received the following dividends on their jointly held investments:

- Dividends of $600 from Hall Corporation, a taxable domestic corporation.
- A liquidating dividend of $500 from Tell Corporation.
- A dividend of $1,400 from Roe Corporation, a domestic corporation whose earnings consisted entirely of interest on municipal bonds.

Assuming that the Patras file a joint return for 1983, what amount should they report as dividend income after the allowable exclusion?

a. $ 900
b. $1,800
c. $2,300
d. $2,500

56. John Morris, single, had adjusted gross income of $16,000 in 1983. Morris is 66 and has two dependents. In examining his records, the following allowable deductions were compiled:

Medical expenses (in excess of 5% limitation)	$1,100
Contributions	200
State and local taxes paid	700
	$2,000

What should be his taxable income for 1983, using the maximum deductions allowable?

a. $ 9,700
b. $10,000
c. $11,975
d. $12,000

57. The following information is available for Jack and Jill Moore, who reside in Indiana, for 1983:

Adjusted gross income	$10,500
Exemptions (including 2 exemptions claimed for being over 65)	4
Social Security benefits received	$3,000

An abstract from the Optional Sales Tax Table for Indiana is presented below:

	Sales tax	
Income	*Family size 1&2*	*Family size 3&4*
$10,001–$12,000	$124	$148
$12,001–$14,000	$138	$165

Assuming that the Moores elect to use the Optional Sales Tax Table, what is the maximum amount of general sales taxes that they can utilize in calculating excess itemized deductions for 1983?

a. $124
b. $138
c. $148
d. $165

58. For the year 1983 Peter Paul had the following capital transactions:

$3,000 net long-term capital gain
$1,000 net short-term capital loss

What is the amount of Paul's long-term capital gain deduction for 1983?

a. $ 600
b. $ 800
c. $1,200
d. $1,800

59. On July 1, 1981, the original date of issue David Karp purchased for $9,520, a $10,000 ten-year bond of the Expoxy Corporation. The bond was issued for long-term financing. On January 31, 1983, he sold the bond to an unrelated party for $9,800. What amount should Karp report as a long-term capital gain from this transaction?

a. $ 76
b. $204
c. $200
d. $280

60. Roger Goodfriend's adjusted gross income was $50,000 in 1983. He made the following contributions to qualified charitable organizations during the year:

- $10,000 cash
- 1,000 shares of common stock of Electronics Corporation (bought in 1974 for $5,000) with a fair market value of $17,000 on the date of the contribution.

What is the maximum amount Goodfriend can claim as a deduction for charitable contributions in 1983?

a. $15,000
b. $21,000
c. $22,200
d. $25,000

Number 4 (Estimated time — 40 to 50 minutes)

Part a. The controller of the Investor Corporation, a retail company, made three different schedules of gross margin for the first quarter ended September 30, 1974. These schedules appear below.

	Sales ($10 per Unit)	Cost of Goods Sold	Gross Margin
Schedule A	$280,000	$118,550	$161,450
Schedule B	280,000	116,900	163,100
Schedule C	280,000	115,750	164,250

The computation of cost of goods sold in each schedule is based on the following data:

	Units	Cost per Unit	Total Cost
Beginning inventory, July 1	10,000	$4.00	$40,000
Purchase, July 25	8,000	4.20	33,600
Purchase, August 15	5,000	4.13	20,650
Purchase, September 5	7,000	4.30	30,100
Purchase, September 25	12,000	4.25	51,000

The president of the corporation cannot understand how three different gross margins can be computed from the same set of data. As controller, you have explained to him that the three schedules are based on three different assumptions concerning the flow of inventory costs; i.e., first-in, first-out; last-in, first-out; and weighted average. Schedules A, B, and C were not necessarily prepared in this sequence of cost-flow assumptions.

Required:

Prepare three separate schedules computing cost of goods sold and supporting schedules showing the composition of the ending inventory under each of the three cost-flow assumptions.

Part b. The Grand Department Store, Inc. uses the retail-inventory method to estimate ending inventory for its monthly financial statements. The following data pertain to a single department for the month of October, 1974.

Inventory, October 1, 1974:	
At cost	$ 20,000
At retail	30,000
Purchases (exclusive of freights and returns):	
At cost	100,151
At retail	146,495
Freight-in	5,100
Purchase returns:	
At cost	2,100
At retail	2,800
Additional markups	2,500
Markup cancellations	265
Markdowns (net)	800
Normal spoilage and breakage	4,500
Sales	135,730

Required:

1. Using the conventional retail method, prepare a schedule computing estimated lower-of-cost-or-market inventory for October 31, 1974.

2. A department store using the conventional retail-inventory method estimates the cost of its ending inventory as $29,000. An accurate physical count reveals only $22,000 of inventory at lower of cost or market.

List the factors that may have caused the difference between the computed inventory and the physical count.

Number 5 (Estimated time – 45 to 55 minutes)

The management of Hatfield Corporation, concerned over a decrease in cash, has provided you with the following comparative analysis of changes in account balances between December 31, 1976, and December 31, 1977:

	December 31,		
Debit Balances	1977	1976	Increase (Decrease)
Cash	$ 145,000	$ 186,000	$ (41,000)
Accounts receivable	253,000	273,000	(20,000)
Inventories	483,000	538,000	(55,000)
Securities held for plant expansion purposes	150,000	—	150,000
Machinery and equipment	927,000	647,000	280,000
Leasehold improvements	87,000	87,000	—
Patents	27,800	30,000	(2,200)
	$2,072,800	$1,761,000	$311,800
Credit Balances			
Allowance for uncollectible accounts receivable	$ 14,000	$ 17,000	$ (3,000)
Accumulated depreciation of machinery and equipment	416,000	372,000	44,000
Allowance for amortization of leasehold improvements	58,000	49,000	9,000
Accounts payable	232,800	105,000	127,800
Cash dividends payable	40,000	—	40,000
Current portion of 6% serial bonds payable	50,000	50,000	—
6% serial bonds payable	250,000	300,000	(50,000)
Preferred stock	90,000	100,000	(10,000)
Common stock	500,000	500,000	—
Retained earnings	422,000	268,000	154,000
Totals	$2,072,800	$1,761,000	$311,800

Additional Information

During 1977 the following transactions occurred:

- Accounts receivable of $12,000 were written off during the year and an estimate was recorded for uncollectible accounts expense in the amount of $9,000.
- New machinery was purchased for $386,000. In addition, certain obsolete machinery, having a book value of $61,000, was sold for $48,000. No other entries were recorded in Machinery and Equipment or related accounts other than provisions for depreciation.
- Hatfield paid $2,000 legal costs in a successful defense of a new patent. Amortization of patents amounting to $4,200 was recorded.
- Preferred stock, par value $100, was purchased at 110 and subsequently cancelled. The premium paid was charged to retained earnings.
- On December 10, 1977, the board of directors declared a cash dividend of $0.20 per share payable to holders of common stock on January 10, 1978.
- A comparative analysis of retained earnings as of December 31, 1977 and 1976, is presented below:

	December 31, 1977	December 31, 1976
Balance, January 1	$268,000	$131,000
Net income	195,000	172,000
	463,000	303,000
Dividends declared	(40,000)	(35,000)
Premium on preferred stock repurchased	(1,000)	–
	$422,000	$268,000

Required:

Prepare a statement of changes in financial position of Hatfield Corporation for the year ended December 31, 1977, based upon the information presented above. The statement should be prepared using a cash basis format.

ANSWERS TO SAMPLE EXAMINATION

ACCOUNTING PRACTICE – PART I

Answer 1		Answer 2		Answer 3	
1. a	11. b	21. d	31. c	41. a	51. d
2. a	12. b	22. d	32. b	42. b	52. b
3. c	13. d	23. b	33. d	43. a	53. a
4. b	14. b	24. b	34. d	44. b	54. b
5. b	15. a	25. d	35. b	45. c	55. b
6. d	16. c	26. c	36. b	46. b	56. c
7. d	17. d	27. d	37. b	47. c	57. b
8. c	18. c	28. c	38. d	48. b	58. c
9. c	19. d	29. c	39. b	49. c	59. b
10. d	20. a	30. d	40. a	50. d	60. d

Answer 4

a. *Investor Corporation*

SCHEDULES OF COST OF GOODS SOLD

For the First Quarter Ended September 30, 1974

	First-in, First-out	*Last-in, First-out*	*Weighted Average*
Beginning inventory	$ 40,000	$ 40,000	$ 40,000
Plus purchases	135,350	135,350	135,350
Cost of goods available for sale	175,350	175,350	175,350
Less ending inventory	59,600	56,800	58,450
Cost of goods sold	$115,750	$118,550	$116,900

Schedules Computing Ending Inventory

	Units
Beginning inventory	10,000
Plus purchases	32,000
Units available for sale	42,000
Less sales ($280,000 ÷ $10)	28,000
Ending inventory	14,000

Unit computation is the same for all three assumptions.

First-in, First-out

12,000	at $4.25	=	$51,000
2,000	at 4.30	=	8,600
14,000			$59,600

Last-in, First-out

10,000	at $4.00	=	$40,000
4,000	at 4.20	=	16,800
14,000			$56,800

Weighted Average

14,000 at $4.175 = $58,450

Cost of goods available for sale ($175,350) divided by units available for sale (42,000) equals weighted-average cost.

b.1. *Grand Department Store, Inc.*

A Single Department

SCHEDULE OF ENDING INVENTORY

October 31, 1974

	At Cost	*At Retail*
Inventory, October 1, 1974	$ 20,000	$ 30,000
Purchases	100,151	146,495
Freight-in	5,100	–
Purchase returns	(2,100)	(2,800)
Additional markups	–	2,500
Markup cancellations	–	(265)
Available for sale	$123,151	175,930

Ratio: $\frac{\$123,151}{\$175,930} = 70\%$

Markdowns (net)		(800)
Normal spoilage and breakage		(4,500)
Sales		(135,730)
Inventory, October 31, 1974 (Retail)		$ 34,900
Inventory, October 31, 1974 at lower of cost or market (estimated): $34,900 x 70%	$ 24,430	

2. The difference between the inventory estimate per retail method and the amount per physical count may be due to:

(1) Theft losses (shoplifting or pilferage).

(2) Spoilage or breakage above normal.

(3) Differences in cost/retail ratio for purchases during the month, beginning inventory, and ending inventory.

(4) Markups on goods available for sale inconsistent between cost of goods sold and ending inventory.

(5) A wide variety of merchandise with varying cost/retail ratios.

(6) Incorrect reporting of markdowns, additional markups or cancellations.

Answer 5

Hatfield Corporation
Statement of Changes in Financial Position—Cash Basis
For the Year Ended December 31, 1977

Financial resources provided:		
Cash provided:		
Net income		$195,000
Add (deduct) items to change to cash basis:		
Decrease in accounts receivable (net)	$17,000	
Decrease in inventories	55,000	
Increase in accounts payable	127,800	
Loss on sale of machinery	13,000	
Depreciation expense	89,000	
Amortization of leasehold improvements	9,000	
Amortization of patents	4,200	$315,000
Cash provided from operations		$510,000
Other sources		
Sale of machinery		48,000
Total cash provided		558,000
Financial resources provided not affecting cash:		
Liability for dividends declared but not paid		40,000
Decrease in cash		41,000
Total financial resources provided		$639,000

Financial resources used:	
Cash used:	
Repurchase and retirement of preferred stock	$ 11,000
Payment of legal fees in defense of patent	2,000
Purchase of securities for plant expansion	150,000
Purchase of machinery	386,000
Payment of current portion of 6% serial bonds	50,000
Total cash used	$599,000
Financial resources used not providing cash:	
Cash dividends declared but not paid	40,000
Total financial resources used	$639,000

EXAMINATION IN ACCOUNTING PRACTICE – PART II

NOTE TO CANDIDATES: Suggested time allotments are as follows:

All questions are required:	Estimated Minutes Minimum	Estimated Minutes Maximum
No. 1	45	55
No. 2	45	55
No. 3	45	55
No. 4	45	55
No. 5	40	50
Total	220	270

Number 1 (Estimated time - 45 to 55 minutes)

Select the **best** answer for each of the following items relating to a **variety of financial accounting problems.**

1. An analysis and aging of the accounts receivable of the Franklin Company at December 31, 1979, revealed the following data:

Accounts receivable	$450,000
Allowance for uncollectible accounts per books	25,000
Accounts deemed uncollectible	32,000

Based upon the above data, the net realizable value of the accounts receivable at December 31, 1979, was

a. $393,000
b. $418,000
c $425,000
d. $443,000

2. The Madden Company had 600,000 shares of common stock issued and outstanding at December 31, 1977. During 1978, no additional common stock was issued. On January 1, 1978, Madden issued 400,000 shares of nonconvertible preferred stock. During 1978, Madden declared and paid $200,000 cash dividends on the common stock and $110,000 on the nonconvertible preferred stock. Net income for the year ended December 31, 1978, was $750,000. What should be Madden's 1978 earnings per common share, rounded to the nearest penny?

a. $0.73.
b. $0.92.
c. $1.07.
d. $1.25.

3. During 1977, Hollin Company determined, as a result of additional information, that machinery that was previously depreciated over a seven-year life had a total estimated useful life of only five years. An accounting change was made in 1977 to reflect this additional information. If the change had been made in 1976, the allowance for accumulated depreciation would have been $2,600,000 at December 31, 1976, instead of $2,100,000. As a result of this change, 1977 depreciation expense was $200,000 greater than it would have been if the change had not been made. Assume that the direct effects of this change are limited to the effect on depreciation and the related tax provision, and that the income tax rate was 50% in both years. What should be reported in Hollin's income statement for the year ended December 31, 1977, as the cumulative effect on prior years of changing the estimated useful life of the machinery?

a. $0.
b. $250,000.
c. $350,000.
d. $500,000.

4. The Raff Company purchased a machine on January 1, 1978, for $5,500,000. The machine has an estimated useful life of ten years with no salvage. The machine is being depreciated using the sum-of-the-years digits method for income tax reporting and the straight-line method for financial statement reporting. Assuming that the income tax rate is 50%, the amount of deferred taxes charged to Raff's 1978 income statement would be

a. $225,000.
b. $275,000.
c. $450,000.
d. $550,000.

5. Jenny Corporation was organized on January 1, 1978, with an authorization of 500,000 shares of common stock with a par value of $5 per share.

During 1978 the corporation had the following capital transactions:

January 5 – issued 100,000 shares @ $5 per share

April 6 – issued 50,000 shares @ $7 per share

June 8 – issued 15,000 shares @ $10 per share

July 28 – purchased 25,000 shares @ $4 per share

December 31 – sold the 25,000 shares held in treasury @ $8 per share

Jenny used the par value method to record the purchase and reissuance of the treasury shares.

What is the amount of paid-in capital in excess of par value as of December 31, 1978?

a. $175,000
b. $200,000
c. $250,000
d. $275,000

6. The stockholders' equity section of Sola Corporation as of December 31, 1976, was as follows:

Common stock, $20 par value, authorized 150,000 shares, issued and outstanding 100,000 shares	$2,000,000
Capital in excess of par value	400,000
Retained earnings	200,000
	$2,600,000

On March 1, 1977, Sola reacquired 10,000 shares for $240,000. The following transactions occurred in 1977 with respect to treasury stock acquired:

June 1 – Sold 3,000 shares for $84,000.
August 1 – Sold 2,000 shares for $42,000.
September 1 – Retired remaining 5,000 shares.

Sola accounts for treasury stock on the cost method. As a result of these transactions

a. Stockholders' equity remained unchanged.
b. Common stock decreased $100,000 and retained earnings decreased $14,000.
c. Common stock decreased $100,000 and capital in excess of par decreased $14,000.
d. Common stock decreased $126,000.

7. The following condensed balance sheet is presented for the partnership of Fisher, Taylor and Simon who share profits and losses in the ratio of 6:2:2, respectively:

Cash	$ 40,000
Other assets	140,000
	$180,000
Liabilities	$ 70,000
Fisher, capital	50,000
Taylor, capital	50,000
Simon, capital	10,000
	$180,000

The assets and liabilities are fairly valued on the above balance sheet, and it was agreed to by all the partners that the partnership would be liquidated after selling the other assets. What would each of the partners receive at this time if the other assets are sold for $80,000?

	Fisher	Taylor	Simon
a.	$12,500	$37,500	$0
b.	$13,000	$37,000	$0
c.	$14,000	$38,000	$ 2,000
d.	$50,000	$50,000	$10,000

8. During 1979 Criterion Corporation issued at 105, two hundred $1,000 bonds due in ten years. One detachable stock purchase warrant entitling the holder to buy 20 shares of Criterion's common stock was attached to each bond. Shortly after issuance, each bond had a market value of $940, and each warrant was quoted at $60. What amount, if any, of the proceeds from the bond issuance should be recorded as part of Criterion's stockholders' equity?

a. $0
b. $12,000
c. $12,600
d. $13,404

9. During 1978, Red, Incorporated, purchased $2,000,000 of inventory. The cost of goods sold for 1978 was $2,200,000, and the ending inventory at December 31, 1978, was $400,000. What was the inventory turnover for 1978?

a. 4.0.
b. 4.4.
c. 5.5.
d. 11.0.

10. On December 1, 1978, Chest Corporation purchased 200,000 shares representing 45% of the outstanding stock of Park Company for cash of $2,500,000. As a result of this purchase, Chest has the ability to exercise significant influence over the operating and financial policies of Park. 45% of the net income of Park amounted to

$20,000 for the month of December and $350,000 for the year ended December 31, 1978. The appropriate amount of goodwill amortization to be recorded by Chest in 1978 as a result of its purchase of Park stock would be $10,000. On January 15, 1979, cash dividends of $0.30 per share were paid to stockholders of record on December 31, 1978. Chest's long-term investment in Park should be shown in Chest's December 31, 1978, balance sheet at

a. $2,450,000.
b. $2,460,000.
c. $2,500,000.
d. $2,510,000.

Items 11 and 12 are based on the following information:

Hamilton Company uses job order costing. Factory overhead is applied to production at a predetermined rate of 150% of direct-labor cost. Any over or underapplied factory overhead is closed to the cost of goods sold account at the end of each month. Additional information is available as follows:

Job 101 was the only job in process at January 31, 1982, with accumulated costs as follows:

Direct materials	$4,000
Direct labor	2,000
Applied factory overhead	3,000
	$9,000

- Jobs 102, 103, and 104 were started during February.
- Direct materials requisitions for February totaled $26,000.
- Direct-labor cost of $20,000 was incurred for February.
- Actual factory overhead was $32,000 for February.
- The only job still in process at February 28, 1982, was Job 104, with costs of $2,800 for direct materials and $1,800 for direct labor.

11. The cost of goods manufactured for February 1982 was

a. $77,700
b. $78,000
c. $79,700
d. $85,000

12. Over or underapplied factory overhead should be closed to the cost of goods sold account at February 28, 1982, in the amount of

a. $ 700 overapplied.
b. $1,000 overapplied.
c. $1,700 underapplied.
d. $2,000 underapplied.

Items 13 and 14 are based on the following data:

Morton Company's manufacturing costs for 1981 were as follows:

Direct materials	$300,000
Direct labor	400,000
Factory overhead:	
Variable	80,000
Fixed	50,000

13. Prime cost totaled

a. $300,000
b. $380,000
c. $700,000
d. $830,000

14. Conversion cost totaled

a. $400,000
b. $480,000
c. $530,000
d. $830,000

15. Indiana Corporation began its operations on January 1, 1979, and produces a single product that sells for $9.00 per unit. Indiana uses an actual (historical) cost system. 100,000 units were produced and 90,000 units were sold in 1979. There was no work-in-process inventory at December 31, 1979.

Manufacturing costs and selling and administrative expenses for 1979 were as follows:

	Fixed costs	*Variable costs*
Raw materials	–	$1.75 per unit produced
Direct labor	–	1.25 per unit produced
Factory overhead	$100,000	.50 per unit produced
Selling and administrative	70,000	.60 per unit sold

What would be Indiana's operating income for 1979 using the direct-costing method?

a. $181,000
b. $271,000
c. $281,000
d. $371,000

Items 16 and 17 are based on the following information:

Summit Company provided the following inventory balances and manufacturing cost data for the month of January 1983:

Inventories:	1/1/83	1/31/83
Direct materials	$30,000	$40,000
Work in process	15,000	20,000
Finished goods	65,000	50,000

	Month of January 1983
Cost of goods manufactured	$515,000
Factory overhead applied	150,000
Direct materials used	190,000
Actual factory overhead	144,000

Under Summit's cost system, any over or underapplied overhead is closed to the cost of goods sold account at the end of the calendar year.

16. What was the total amount of direct-material purchases during January 1983?
  a. $180,000
  b. $190,000
  c. $195,000
  d. $200,000

17. How much direct-labor cost was incurred during January 1983?
  a. $170,000
  b. $175,000
  c. $180,000
  d. $186,000

18. Elliott Company manufactures tools to customer specifications. The following data pertain to Job 1501 for February 1983:

Direct materials used	$4,200
Direct-labor hours worked	300
Direct-labor rate per hour	$ 8.00
Machine hours used	200
Applied factory overhead rate per machine hour	$15.00

What is the total manufacturing cost recorded on Job 1501 for February 1983?
  a. $ 8,800
  b. $ 9,600
  c. $10,300
  d. $11,100

19. Simpson Company manufactures electric drills to the exacting specifications of various customers. During April 1983, Job 403 for the production of 1,100 drills was completed at the following costs per unit:

Direct materials	$10
Direct labor	8
Applied factory overhead	12
	$30

Final inspection of Job 403 disclosed 50 defective units and 100 spoiled units. The defective drills were reworked at a total cost of $500 and the spoiled drills were sold to a jobber for $1,500. What would be the unit cost of the good units produced on Job 403?
  a. $33
  b. $32
  c. $30
  d. $29

20. Crowley Company produces joint products A and B from a process which also yields a by-product, Y. The by-product requires additional processing before it can be sold. The cost assigned to the by-product is its market value less additional costs incurred after split-off (net realizable value method). Information concerning a batch produced in January 1983 at a joint cost of $40,000 is as follows:

Product	Units produced	Market value	Costs after split-off
A	800	$44,000	$4,500
B	700	32,000	3,500
Y	500	4,000	1,000

How much of the joint cost should be allocated to the joint products?
  a. $35,000
  b. $36,000
  c. $37,000
  d. $39,000

Number 2 (Estimated time - 45 to 55 minutes)

Select the **best** answer for each of the following items relating to a **variety of financial accounting problems.**

21. The Shamus Company was organized on January 2, 1975, and issued the following stock:

•200,000 shares of $5 par value common stock at $12 per share (authorized 200,000 shares).

•50,000 shares of $10 par value fully participating 4% cumulative preferred stock at $25 per share (authorized 150,000 shares).

The net income for 1975 was $420,000 and cash dividends of $72,000 were declared and paid in 1975.

What were the dividends paid on the preferred and common stock, respectively?
  a. $20,000 and $52,000.
  b. $24,000 and $48,000.
  c. $46,000 and $26,000.
  d. $72,000 and $0.

22. On June 30, 1973, Leaf Corporation granted compensatory stock options for 10,000 shares of its $24 par value common stock to certain of its key employees. The market price of the common stock on that date was $31 per share and the option price was $28. The options are exercisable beginning January 1, 1976, providing those key employees are still in the employ of the Company at the time the options are exercised. The options expire on June 30, 1977.

On January 4, 1976, when the market price of the stock was $36 per share, all 10,000 options were exercised.

What should be the amount of compensation expense recorded by Leaf Corporation for the calendar year 1975?

a. $0.
b. $7,500.
c. $12,000.
d. $30,000.

23. The Miller Corporation was established in 1970. In 1978 it adopted a pension plan for its employees. On December 31, 1978, the past service cost was determined to be $500,000. Miller had elected to amortize past service cost over ten years and to fund past service cost over fifteen years. The past service cost of $500,000 as of December 31, 1978, should be accounted for as a charge to

a. Prior periods as a prior-period adjustment.
b. Operations in 1978.
c. Operations ratably from 1978 through 1987.
d. Operations ratably from 1978 through 1992.

24. For calendar year 1981 Steiner Corporation reported depreciation of $300,000 in its income statement. On its 1981 income tax return Steiner reported depreciation of $500,000. Additionally, Steiner's income statement included interest income of $50,000 on municipal obligations. Assuming an income tax rate of 40%, the amount of deferred taxes reported on Steiner's 1981 income statement should be

a. $ 60,000
b. $ 80,000
c. $100,000
d. $120,000

18. Seed Company has a receivable from a foreign customer which is payable in the local currency of the foreign customer. On December 31, 1976, this receivable was appropriately included in the accounts receivable section of Seed's balance sheet at $450,000. When the receivable was collected on January 4, 1977, Seed converted the local currency of the foreign customer into $440,000. Seed also owns a foreign subsidiary from which a translation adjustment credit of $45,000 resulted as a consequence of translation in 1977. What amount, if any, should be included as an exchange gain or loss in Seed's 1977 consolidated income statement (assume the functional currency is the foreign currency)?

a. $0.
b. $10,000 exchange loss.
c. $35,000 exchange gain.
d. $45,000 exchange gain.

26. The owners of the Zoot Suit Clothing Store are contemplating selling the business to new interests. The cumulative earnings for the past five years amounted to $450,000 including extraordinary gains of $10,000. The annual earnings based on an average rate of return on investment for this industry would have been $76,000. If excess earnings are to be capitalized at 10%, then implied goodwill should be

a. $120,000.
b. $140,000.
c. $440,000.
d. $450,000.

27. Royal Company's net accounts receivable were $500,000 at December 31, 1977, and $600,000 at December 31, 1978. Net cash sales for 1978 were $200,000. The accounts receivable turnover for 1978 was 5.0. What were Royal's total net sales for 1978?

a. $2,950,000.
b. $3,000,000.
c. $3,200,000.
d. $5,500,000.

28. The balance sheet for the partnership of Lang, Monte, and Newton at April 30, 1975, follows. The partners share profits and losses in the ratio of 2:2:6, respectively.

Assets, at cost	$100,000
Lang, Loan	$ 9,000
Lang, capital	15,000
Monte, capital	31,000
Newton, capital	45,000
Total	$100,000

Lang is retiring from the partnership. By mutual agreement, the assets are to be adjusted to their fair value of $130,000 at April 30, 1975. Monte and Newton agree that the partnership will pay Lang $37,000 cash for his partnership interest, exclusive of his loan which is to be paid in full. No goodwill is to be recorded. What is the balance of Newton's capital account after Lang's retirement?

a. $51,000.
b. $53,400.
c. $59,000.
d. $63,000.

29. Jackson Corporation provides an incentive compensation plan under which its president is to receive a bonus equal to 10% of Jackson's income in excess of $100,000 before deducting income tax but after deducting the bonus. If income before income tax and the bonus is $320,000, the amount of the bonus should be

a. $44,000.
b. $32,000.
c. $22,000.
d. $20,000.

30. On January 1, 1973, Ben Corporation issued $600,000 of 5% ten-year bonds at 103. The bonds are callable at the option of Ben at 104. Ben has recorded amortization of the bond premium on the straight-line method (which was not materially different from the interest method).

On December 31, 1977, when the fair market value of the bonds was 97, Ben repurchased $300,000 of the bonds in the open market at 97. Ben has recorded interest and amortization for 1977. Ignoring income taxes and assuming that the gain is material, Ben should report this reacquisition as

a. A gain of $13,500.
b. An extraordinary gain of $13,500.
c. A gain of $21,000.
d. An extraordinary gain of $21,000.

31. The Thoughtful Corporation adopted an employee pension plan on January 1, 1976, for all of its eligible employees. Thoughtful has agreed to make annual payments to a designated trustee at the end of each year. Data relating to the plan follow:

Normal cost	$100,000
Past-service cost on January 1, 1976	500,000
Funds held by trustee are expected to earn a 5% return.	

In accordance with APB No. 8 what is the maximum provision for pension cost that Thoughtful can record for 1976?

a. $105,000.
b. $125,000.
c. $150,000.
d. $175,000.

32. On January 1, 1977, Wilson, Inc., issued 100,000 additional shares of $10 par value voting common stock in exchange for all of Thomson Company's voting common stock in a business combination appropriately accounted for by the pooling of interests method. Net income for the year ended December 31, 1977, was $400,000 for Thomson and $1,300,000 for Wilson, exclusive of any consideration of Thomson. During 1977, Wilson paid $900,000 in dividends to its stockholders and Thomson paid $250,000 in dividends to Wilson. What should be the consolidated net income for the year ended December 31, 1977?

a. $1,150,000.
b. $1,450,000.
c. $1,550,000.
d. $1,700,000.

33. On January 1, 1975, The Jonas Company sold equipment to its wholly-owned subsidiary, Neptune Company, for $1,800,000. The equipment cost Jonas $2,000,000; accumulated depreciation at the time of sale was $500,000. Jonas was depreciating the equipment on the straight-line method over 20 years with no salvage value, a procedure which Neptune continued. On the consolidated balance sheet at December 31, 1975, the cost and accumulated depreciation, respectively, should be

a. $1,500,000 and $600,000.
b. $1,800,000 and $100,000.
c. $1,800,000 and $500,000.
d. $2,000,000 and $600,000.

34. On January 1, 1979, the Carpet Company lent $100,000 to its supplier, Loom Corporation, evidenced by a note, payable in 5 years. Interest at 5% is payable annually with the first payment due on December 31, 1979. The going rate of interest for this type of loan is 10%. The parties agreed that Carpet's inventory needs for the loan period will be met by Loom at favorable prices. Assume that the present value (at the going rate of interest) of the $100,000 note is $81,000 at January 1, 1979. What amount of interest income, if any, should be included in Carpet's 1979 income statement?

a. $0.
b. $4,050.

c. $5,000.
d. $8,100.

35. Certain balance sheet accounts in a foreign subsidiary of the Brogan Company at December 31, 1977, have been transated into United States dollars as follow:

	Translated at Current Rates	Translated at Historical Rates
Marketable equity securities carried at cost	$100,000	$110,000
Marketable equity securities carried at current market price	120,000	125,000
Inventories carried at cost	130,000	132,000
Inventories carried at net realizable value	80,000	84,000
	$430,000	$451,000

What amount should be shown in Brogan's balance sheet at December 31, 1977, as a result of the above information (assume the functional currency is the U.S. dollar)?

a. $430,000.
b. $436,000.
c. $442,000.
d. $451,000.

36. The Robert Construction Corporation uses the percentage-of-completion method of accounting. In 1975, Robert began work on a contract it had received which provided for a contract price of $8,000,000. Other details follow:

	1975
Costs incurred during the year	$1,200,000
Estimated costs to complete as of December 31	4,800,000
Billings during the year	1,440,000
Collections during the year	1,000,000

What should be the gross profit recognized in 1975?

a. $160,000.
b. $240,000.
c. $400,000.
d. $1,600,000.

37. The Hint Corporation granted stock options for 10,000 shares of its $20 par value common stock to certain of its key employees on January 1, 1975, when the fair market value of the common stock was $35 per share. The options, which can be exercised at $38 per share, became exercisable on January 1, 1976, and expire on December 31, 1978. Those employees receiving the options must be employed by the corporation at the time the options are exercised. What amount of additional compensation should Hint record in 1975?

a. $0.
b. $7,500.
c. $10,000.
d. $30,000.

38. Flex Company owns a machine that was bought on January 2, 1977, for $94,000. The machine was estimated to have a useful life of five years and a salvage value of $6,000. Flex uses the sum-of-the-years digits method of depreciation. At the beginning of 1980, Flex determined that the useful life of the machine should have been four years and the salvage value $8,800. For the year 1980, Flex should record depreciation expense on this machine of

a. $11,100.
b. $14,800.
c. $17,600.
d. $21,300.

39. For financial statement reporting, the Lexington Corporation recognizes royalty income in the period earned. For income tax reporting, royalties are taxed when collected. At December 31, 1976, unearned royalties of $400,000 were included in Lexington's balance sheet. All of these royalties had been collected in 1976. During 1977, royalties of $600,000 were collected. Unearned royalties in Lexington's December 31, 1977, balance sheet amounted to $350,000. Assuming that the income tax rate was 50%, the amount reported in the provision for deferred income taxes in Lexington's income statement for the year ended December 31, 1977, should be a

a. $25,000 debit.
b. $175,000 credit.
c. $200,000 debit.
d. $300,000 credit.

40. The Lake Company sold some machinery to the View Company on January 1, 1976, for which the cash selling price was $758,200. View entered into an installment sales contract with Lake at an interest rate of 10%. The contract required payments of $200,000 a year over five years with the first payment due on December 31, 1976. What amount of interest income, if any, should be included in Lake's 1977 income statement (the second year of the contract), using the "interest method"?

a. $0.
b. $63,402.
c. $75,820.
d. $100,000.

Number 3 (Estimated time—-45 to 55 minutes)

Select the **best** answer for each of the following items relating to **the federal income taxation of corporations and partnerships.**

41. During the 1983 holiday season, Barmin Corporation gave business gifts to 16 customers. The value of the gifts, which were not of an advertising nature, was as follows:

4 @ $ 10
4 @ $ 25
4 @ $ 50
4 @ $100

For 1983, Barmin can deduct as a business expense
- a. $0
- b. $140
- c. $340
- d. $740

42. Sher Corporation's tax liability for 1983 was $125,000 before claiming an investment tax credit. In January 1983, Sher purchased new qualified Section 38 equipment for $2,000,000 with a recovery period of ten years. The investment tax credit allowable for 1983 is
- a. $ 25,000
- b. $110,000
- c. $125,000
- d. $200,000

43. The Cresap Corporation, an accrual basis taxpayer, was formed and began operations on May 1, 1983. The following expenses were incurred during its first tax period, May 1—December 31, 1983:

Expenses of temporary directors and of organizational meetings	$500
Fee paid to state for incorporation	100
Accounting services incident to organization	200
Legal services for drafting the corporate charter and bylaws	400
Expenses of printing stock certificates	420

If Cresap Corporation makes an appropriate and timely election, the maximum organization expense that it can properly deduct for 1983 would be
- a. $160
- b. $216
- c. $324
- d. $0

44. Soft Cream sells franchises to independent operators. In 1983 it sold a franchise to Edward Trent, charging an initial fee of $20,000 and a monthly fee of 2% of sales. Soft Cream retains the right to control such matters as employee and management training, quality control and promotion, and the purchase of ingredients. Mr. Trent's 1983 sales amounted to $200,000. From the transactions with Trent, Soft Cream, an accrual basis taxpayer, would include in its computation of 1983 taxable income
- a. Long-term capital gain of $24,000.
- b. Long-term capital gain of $20,000, ordinary income of $4,000.
- c. Long-term capital gain of $4,000, ordinary income of $20,000.
- d. Ordinary income of $24,000.

45. Jesse Jenkins in a bona fide transaction transferred land worth $50,000 to his controlled corporation for stock of the corporation worth $20,000 and cash of $20,000. The basis of the property to him was $15,000, and it was subject to a $10,000 mortgage which the corporation assumed. Jenkins must report a gain of
- a. $10,000
- b. $20,000
- c. $30,000
- d. $35,000

46. In March 1983, Davis entered a partnership by contributing to the partnership $10,000 cash and machinery which had an adjusted basis to him of $6,000 and a fair market value of $9,000. Davis acquired the machinery in 1980 at a cost of $12,000. His capital account was credited for $20,000, which constituted one-fourth of total partnership capital, and goodwill was recorded for the difference. What should be the tax effects to Davis of this transaction?
- a. $0.
- b. Long-term capital gain of $3,000.
- c. Long-term capital gain of $3,000; ordinary income of $1,000.
- d. Ordinary income of $3,000; long-term capital gain of $1,000.

47. In computing the taxable income of a partnership a deduction is allowed for
- a. Fixed salaries paid to partners for services determined without regard to the income of the partnership.
- b. The net operating loss deduction.
- c. Contributions to charitable organizations.
- d. Personal exemptions of the partners.

48. Gary Corporation had 1983 gross income of $90,000 including $50,000 of dividends received from

a nonaffiliated domestic corporation. Gary had business deductions of $43,000 and a net operating loss carryover of $5,000. What is Gary's 1983 dividends received deduction?

a. $35,700
b. $39,950
c. $42,500
d. $50,000

49. Vacconey Corporation's taxable income for 1983 was $120,000. All taxable income resulted from regular operations of the corporation. Vacconey's tax liability before credits for 1983 would be

a. $35,950
b. $34,950
c. $35,450
d. $44,100

50. During the current year, a corporation retired obsolete equipment purchased in 1979 having an adjusted basis of $30,000 and sold it as scrap for $1,000. The only other transactions affecting taxable income resulted in $50,000 net income from operations. The taxable income of the corporation was

a. $21,000.
b. $35,000.
c. $49,000 with a capital loss carryover of $27,000.
d. $50,000 with a capital loss carryover of $14,500.

51. The Market Corporation had taxable income in 1983 of $40,000 before deducting contributions to qualified charitable organizations. During 1983 it gave $5,000 cash to a charitable organization. Market also had a contribution carryover from 1982 of $1,000. What is Market's contribution deduction for 1983?

a. $2,000
b. $4,000
c. $5,000
d. $6,000

52. Orville Company had earnings and profits of $82,000 for the year ended December 31, 1983, before distribution of dividends. On December 31, 1983, the company distributed as a dividend to its sole individual stockholder, Orville, inventory with a fair market value of $16,000 and an adjusted basis of $12,000. The company values its inventory by the first-in, first-out method. What should be the earnings and profits after distribution of the dividend for the year ended December 31, 1983?

a. $66,000
b. $70,000
c. $74,000
d. $82,000

53. For the year ended December 31, 1983, the partnership of Charles and Paul had book income of $75,000 which included the following:

Short-term capital loss	$(3,100)
Long-term capital gain (on sale of securities)	4,300
Section 1231 gain	1,500
Ordinary income (Section 1245 recapture)	600
Dividends qualifying for exclusion	200

The partners share profits and losses equally. What should be each partner's share of partnership income (excluding all partnership items which must be accounted for separately) to be reported as taxable for 1983?

a. $35,700
b. $36,050
c. $36,150
d. $37,500

54. For the year ended December 31, 1983, the partnership of Bicent and Tennial reported ordinary income of $260,000, which included the following items of expenses and losses:

Salaries paid (other than to partners)	$70,000
Interest paid (other than to partners)	4,000
Real estate taxes	8,000
Charitable contributions	2,000
Repairs	1,000
Foreign income taxes	5,000
Loss on sale of machinery held 7 years	12,000

As a result of the above items, the partnership should increase its ordinary income and report separately on its tax return

a. $19,000
b. $23,000
c. $24,000
d. $74,000

55. On July 17, 1983, Porter Corp. purchased a new delivery truck (list price, $4,300) for $4,000 by trading in an old truck with a fair market value of $2,500 and paying $1,500 cash. The old truck had been purchased for $3,500 cash on January 12, 1981, and had $2,100 of undepreciated cost on the date of trade-in. The tax effect of this transaction to Porter Corp. would be

a. No recognized gain or loss and basis of new truck, $4,000.
b. Recognized gain of $400 and basis of new truck, $4,000.

c. No recognized gain or loss and basis of new truck, $3,600.
d. Recognized gain of $400 and basis of new truck, $4,300.

56. Rambo Corporation owns 10% of the stock of Duntulum Corporation with a basis of $8,000 and a market value of $50,000. Rambo uses the Duntulum stock to redeem approximately 1%, or $10,000 par value, of its own outstanding stock from noncorporate shareholders. As a result of this transaction, Rambo must report

a. $42,000 gain.
b. No gain or loss.
c. $2,000 gain.
d. $50,000 gain.

57. Pursuant to a plan of reorganization in 1983, Mr. Jack exchanged 500 shares of Zee Corporation common stock that he had purchased for $50,000 for 850 shares of Dal Corporation common stock having a fair market value of $58,000. What is Mr. Jack's recognized gain on this exchange, and what is his basis for the Dal stock, respectively?

a. $0 and $50,000.
b. $8,000 and $50,000.
c. $0 and $58,000.
d. $8,000 and $58,000.

58. For its year ended December 31, 1983, Valor Corporation, an S corporation, had net income per books of $216,000 which included $180,000 from operations and a $36,000 net long-term capital gain. During 1983, $90,000 was distributed to the corporation's nine equal shareholders, all of whom are on a calendar-year basis. Each shareholder should report for 1983

a. $10,000 ordinary income.
b. $20,000 ordinary income.
c. $20,000 ordinary income and $4,000 long-term capital gain.
d. $24,000 ordinary income.

59. In 1983, the partnership of Al, Gus, and Lew realized an ordinary loss of $90,000. The partnership and partners are on a calendar year basis. At December 31, 1983, Lew had an adjusted basis of $30,000 for his interest in the partnership before taking the 1983 loss into consideration. Lew has a 40% interest in the profits and losses of the partnership. On his personal income tax return for 1983, what should Lew deduct relative to his partnership interest?

a. An ordinary loss of $30,000.
b. An ordinary loss of $36,000.
c. An ordinary loss of $30,000 and a capital loss of $6,000.
d. A capital loss of $36,000.

60. Barker owns a 40% interest in the capital and profits of the Murphy and Barker partnership. During 1983 Barker sold securities to the partnership for their fair market value of $36,000. Barker's adjusted tax basis in the securities was $24,000. How much gain (before any long-term capital gain deduction) should Barker recognize on this transaction on his 1983 tax return?

a. $0
b. $ 4,800
c. $ 7,200
d. $12,000

Number 4 (Estimated time - 45 to 55 minutes)

Number 4 consists of two unrelated parts.

Part a. The Dahlia Company has two divisions, the Astor Division which started operating in 1973 and the Tulip Division which started operating in 1974. The Astor Division leases medical equipment to hospitals. All of its leases are appropriately recorded as operating leases for accounting purposes except for a major lease entered into on January 1, 1975, which is appropriately recorded as a sale for accounting purposes.

Under long-term contracts, Tulip constructs waste water treatment plants for small communities throughout the United States. All of its long-term contracts are appropriately recorded for accounting purposes under the percentage-of-completion method except for two contracts which are appropriately recorded for accounting purposes under the completed-contract method because of a lack of dependable estimates at the time of entering into these contracts.

For the year ended December 31, 1975, the following information is available.

Astor Division:

Operating Leases

Revenues from operating leases were $800,000. The cost of the related leased equipment is $3,700,000 which is being depreciated on a straight-line basis over a five-year period. The estimated residual value of the leased equipment at the end of the five-year period is $200,000. No leased quipment was acquired or constructed in 1975. Maintenance and other related costs and the costs of any other services rendered under the provisions of the leases were $70,000 in 1975.

Lease Recorded as a Sale

The January 1, 1975, lease recorded as a sale is for a six-year period expiring December 31, 1980. The cost of this leased quipment is $3,500,000. This leased equipment is estimated to have no residual value at the end of the lease. Maintenance and other related costs and the costs of any other services rendered under the provisions of this lease, all of which were paid by the lessee, were $120,000 in 1975. Equal annual payments under the lease are $750,000 and are due on January 1. The first payment was made on January 1, 1975. The present value of an annuity of $1 in advance at 10% is as follows:

Required:

Prepare an income statement of the Dahlia Company for the year ended December 31, 1975, stopping at income (loss) before income taxes. Show supporting schedules and computations in good form. Ignore income tax and deferred tax considerations. Footnotes are not required.

Part b. Homer, Inc. has two fire insurance policies. Policy A covers the office building at a face value of $360,000 and the furnitures and fixtures at a face value of $108,000. Policy B covers only the office building at an additional face value of $140,000. Each policy is with a different insurance company. A fire caused losses to the office building and the furniture and fixtures. The relevant data are summarized below:

	Furniture and Fixtures	Office Building	
Insurance policy	A	A	B
Fair market value of the property before fire	$150,000	$700,000	$700,000
Fair market value of the property after fire	$ 20,000	$420,000	$420,000
Face of insurance policy	$108,000	$360,000	$140,000
Co-insurance requirement	80%	80%	80%

Required:

Compute the amount due from each insurance company for the loss on each asset category. Show computations in good form.

Number 5 (Estimated time – 40 to 50 minutes)

The following summary of transactions was taken from the accounts of the Annaville School District General Fund before the books had been closed for the fiscal year ended June 30, 1983:

	Post-closing balances June 30, 1982	*Pre-closing balances June 30, 1983*
Cash	$400,000	$ 700,000
Taxes receivable	150,000	170,000
Estimated uncollectible taxes	(40,000)	(70,000)
Estimated revenues	–	3,000,000
Expenditures	–	2,840,000
Encumbrances	–	91,000
	$510,000	$6,731,000
Vouchers payable	$ 80,000	$ 408,000
Due to other funds	210,000	142,000
Fund balance reserved for encumbrances	60,000	91,000
Fund balance unreserved	160,000	180,000
Revenues from taxes	–	2,800,000
Miscellaneous revenues	–	130,000
Appropriations	–	2,980,000
	$510,000	$6,731,000

Additional information:

- The estimated taxes receivable for the year ended June 30, 1983, were $2,870,000, and taxes collected during the year totaled $2,810,000.
- An analysis of the transactions in the vouchers payable account for the year ended June 30, 1983, follows:

	Debit (Credit)
Current expenditures	$(2,700,000)
Expenditures for prior year	(58,000)
Vouchers for payment to other funds	(210,000)
Cash payments during the year	2,640,000
Net change	$ (328,000)

- During the year the General Fund was billed $142,000 for services performed on its behalf by the enterprise fund.
- On May 2, 1983, commitment documents were issued for the purchase of new textbooks at a cost of $91,000.
- Annaville school encumbers all of its expenditures.

Required:

Based upon the data presented above, reconstruct the original detailed journal entries that were required to record all transactions for the fiscal year ended June 30, 1983, including the recording of the current year's budget. Do not prepare closing entries at June 30, 1983.

ANSWERS TO SAMPLE EXAMINATION

ACCOUNTING PRACTICE – PART II

Answer 1		Answer 2		Answer 3	
1. b	11. a	21. b	31. c	41. c	51. b
2. c	12. d	22. b	32. d	42. b	52. b
3. a	13. c	23. c	33. d	43. a	53. b
4. a	14. c	24. b	34. d	44. d	54. a
5. d	15. b	25. b	35. c	45. b	55. c
6. c	16. d	26. a	36. c	46. a	56. a
7. a	17. c	27. a	37. a	47. a	57. a
8. c	18. b	28. a	38. b	48. b	58. c
9. b	19. b	29. d	39. a	49. b	59. a
10. a	20. c	30. b	40. b	50. a	60. d

Answer 4

Part a.

Dahlia Company
INCOME STATEMENT
For the Year Ended December 31, 1975

Operating revenues:	
Sales from lease recorded as a sale *(Schedule 1)*	$3,593,250
Revenues from operating leases	800,000
Revenues recognized on long-term contracts *(Schedule 2)*	3,169,090
Total operating revenues	7,562,340
Costs and expenses:	
Cost of sales on lease recorded as a sale	3,500,000
Cost of sales on long-term contracts *(Schedule 3)*	3,550,000
Selling, general, and administrative expenses *(Schedule 4)*	1,370,000
Total costs and expenses	8,420,000
Operating (loss)	(857,660)
Other income *(Schedule 5)*	334,325
(Loss) before income taxes	$ (523,335)

Schedule 1

Computation of Sales from Lease Recorded as a Sale

Equal annual payment	$ 750,000
Present value of an annuity of $1 in advance at 10% for 6 periods	x 4.791
	$3,593,250

Schedule 2

Computation of Revenues Recognized on Long-Term Contracts

Costs incurred in 1974	$1,500,000
Costs incurred in 1975	3,000,000
Costs incurred to date	(A) 4,500,000
Estimated additional costs to complete contracts	1,000,000
Total estimated costs at December 31, 1975	(B) $5,500,000
Contract price	(C) $6,000,000
Revenues recognized to date (A) $4,500,000 / (B) $5,500,000 x (C) $6,000,000	$4,909,090
Revenues recognized in 1974	(1,740,000)
	$3,169,090

Schedule 3

Computation of Cost of Sales on Long-Term Contracts

Percentage-of-Completion Method:	
Costs incurred in 1975	$3,000,000
Completed-Contract Method:	
Establishment of accrual for estimated losses in 1975	550,000
	$3,550,000

Schedule 4

Computation of Selling, General, and Administrative Expenses

Operating Leases:		
Depreciation on leased equipment:		
Cost of leased equipment	$3,700,000	
Estimated residual value of leased equipment	(200,000)	
	3,500,000	
Depreciation rate	20%	
		700,000
Maintenance and other related costs		70,000
		770,000
Selling, general, and administrative expenses		600,000
		$1,370,000

Schedule 5

Computation of Other Income

Interest Income from Lease Recorded as a Sale:	
Sales from lease recorded as a sale	$3,593,250
Payment made on January 1, 1975	(750,000)
	2,843,250
Interest rate	10%
	284,325
Other income	50,000
	$ 334,325

Notes *(Not Required)*:

Lease Recorded as a Sale

The $120,000 paid by the lessee should not appear in the income statement of Dahlia.

Long-Term Contracts–Percentage-of-Completion Method

The amounts billed and collected on these contracts only affected the balance sheet of Dahlia.

Long-Term Contracts–Completed-Contract Method

The amounts billed and collected on these contracts only affected the balance sheet of Dahlia. Furthermore, no revenues or cost of sales on these contracts (except for the establishment of an accrual for estimated losses of $550,000 on one of the contracts) should appear in the income statement of Dahlia since neither of the two contracts has been completed.

Part b.

Computation of Amount Due for Fire Loss

	Furniture and Fixtures	*Office Building*	
Insurance policy	A	A	B
Fair market value of the property **before** fire	$150,000	$700,000	$700,000
Less: fair market value of the property **after** fire	20,000	420,000	420,000
Fire loss	$130,000	$280,000	$280,000
Face of insurance policy	$108,000	$360,000	$140,000
Co-insurance requirement	80%	80%	80%
Co-insurance formula	$117,000	$180,000	$ 70,000
Due from insurance company	$108,000	$180,000	$ 70,000

Amount due from insurance company is lowest of the fire loss, face of policy, or co-insurance formula.

Co-insurance formula is as follows:

Face of policy ÷ (80% times fair market value of property **before** fire) times the fire loss.

$108,000 ÷ ($150,000 x.8) x $130,000 = $117,000
$360,000 ÷ ($700,000 x.8) x $280,000 = $180,000
$140,000 ÷ ($700,000 x.8) x $280,000 = $ 70,000

Answer 5

1. The requirement is to prepare all journal entries (except closing entries) during fiscal 1983 for the school district general fund. Thus, your objective is to reconcile the beginning and ending account balances with journal entries, i.e., prepare the journal entries required to change the beginning balance of each account to the ending balance.

2. Work through the trial balance to gain familiarity with the accounts and to note required entries. For example: it is evident that the budgetary entry at the beginning of the year was:

Estimated revenues	$3,000,000	
Appropriations		$2,980,000
Fund balance unreserved		20,000

Upon journalizing this entry you have explained the change in the estimated revenues and the appropriations account.

3. Work through the additional information recording required journal entries. The objective is to explain the entries in each account as is provided in the second paragraph for the vouchers payable account.

3.1 The entry to record the estimated taxes receivable is

Taxes receivable	$2,870,000	
Revenues from taxes		$2,800,000
Estimated uncollectible taxes		70,000

The entry to record the taxes collected is

Cash	$2,810,000	
Taxes receivable		$2,810,000

The increase in taxes receivable account is $20,000 ($170,000 – $150,000) rather than $60,000 ($2,870,000 – $2,810,000), because $40,000 of taxes receivable were written off.

Estimated uncollectible taxes	$ 40,000	
Taxes receivable		$ 40,000

The entries described in these two paragraphs explain the changes in both the taxes receivable and the estimated uncollectable taxes accounts.

3.2 The data from the vouchers payable account allows you to make the following entries.

Expenditures	$2,700,000	
Vouchers payable		$2,700,000
Fund balance reserved for encumbrances	60,000	
Fund balance reserved for encumbrances–prior year		60,000
Fund balance reserved for encumbrances–prior year	60,000	
Vouchers payable		58,000
Expenditures		2,000
Due to other funds	210,000	
Vouchers payable		210,000
Vouchers payable	2,640,000	
Cash		2,640,000

Above entries reconcile the beginning and ending vouchers payable balance. Also suggested by the above entries are entries to record encumbrances and to reverse them for $2,700,000. Additionally, the entries rename the reserve account for those goods encumbered in the prior year. This account is then reversed with the difference between the original encumbrance and the actual expenditure credited to the current year's expenditures account.

Encumbrances	$2,700,000	
Fund balance reserved for encumbrances		$2,700,000
Fund balance reserved for encumbrances	2,700,000	
Encumbrances		2,700,000

3.3 The $142,000 is recorded in due to other funds with the debit to expenditures. At this point, the expenditures account and the due to other funds account have been reconciled.

Expenditures	$ 142,000	
Due to other funds		$ 142,000

3.4 Record the purchase commitment which completes the reconciliation of both the encumbrances and reserve for encumbrances accounts.

Encumbrances	$ 91,000	
Fund balance reserved for encumbrances		$ 91,000

4. After making all of the apparent entries from 1) working through the trial balance, and 2) analyzing the additional information, work through the trial balance once again to make sure the change in every account has been reconciled.

4.1 The only accounts not reconciled by the above entries are cash and miscellaneous which can be completed by recording the miscellaneous revenues (the general fund is on a modified accrual basis where only tax revenue is accrued; other revenues are on the cash basis).

Cash	$ 130,000	
Miscellaneous revenue		$ 130,000

Answer 5

The Annaville School District
General Fund Transactions
July 1, 1982 through June 30, 1983

	Debit	Credit
(1)		
Estimated revenues	$3,000,000	
Appropriations		$2,980,000
Fund balance unreserved		20,000
(2)		
Taxes receivable	2,870,000	
Revenues from taxes		2,800,000
Estimated uncollectible taxes		70,000
(3)		
Cash	2,810,000	
Taxes receivable		2,810,000
(4)		
Estimated uncollectible taxes	40,000	
Taxes receivable		40,000
(5)		
Expenditures	2,700,000	
Vouchers payable		2,700,000
(6)		
Fund balance reserved for encumbrances	60,000	
Fund balance reserved for encumbrances-prior year		60,000
(7)		
Fund balance reserved for encumbrances-prior year	60,000	
Vouchers payable		58,000
Expenditures		2,000
(8)		
Due to other funds	210,000	
Vouchers payable		210,000
(9)		
Vouchers payable	2,640,000	
Cash		2,640,000
(10)		
Encumbrances	2,700,000	
Fund balance reserved for encumbrances		2,700,000
(11)		
Fund balance reserved for encumbrances	2,700,000	
Encumbrances		2,700,000
(12)		
Expenditures	142,000	
Due to other funds		142,000
(13)		
Encumbrances	91,000	
Fund balance reserved for encumbrances		91,000
(14)		
Cash	130,000	
Miscellaneous revenues		130,000

EXAMINATION IN ACCOUNTING THEORY

NOTE TO CANDIDATES: Suggested time allotments are as follows:

All questions are required:	*Estimated Minutes* *Minimum*	*Maximum*
No. 1	90	110
No. 2	10	15
No. 3	15	30
No. 4	15	25
No. 5	20	30
Total	150	210

Number 1 (Estimated time — 90 to 110 minutes)

Select the **best** answer for each of the following items relating to **a variety of issues in accounting.**

1. The accrued balance in a revenue account represents an amount which is

	Earned	*Collected*
a.	Yes	Yes
b.	Yes	No
c.	No	Yes
d.	No	No

2. The amortization of bond discount on long-term debt should be presented in a statement of changes in financial position as a (an)
   a. Addition to net income.
   b. Deduction from net income.
   c. Use of funds.
   d. Source and use of funds.

3. How should a gain from the sale of treasury stock be reflected when using the cost method of recording treasury stock transactions?
   a. As ordinary earnings shown on the earnings statement.
   b. As paid-in capital from treasury stock transactions.
   c. As an increase in the amount shown for common stock.
   d. As an extraordinary item shown on the earnings statement.

4. Abbot Co. is being sued for illness caused to local residents as a result of negligence on the company's part in permitting the local residents to be exposed to highly toxic chemicals from its plant. Abbot's lawyer states that it is probable that Abbot will lose the suit and be found liable for a judgment costing Abbot anywhere from $500,000 to $2,500,000. However, the lawyer states that the most probable cost is $1,000,000. As a result of the above facts, Abbot should accrue
   a. A loss contingency of $500,000 and disclose an additional contingency of up to $2,000,000.
   b. A loss contingency of $1,000,000 and disclose an additional contingency of up to $1,500,000.
   c. A loss contingency of $1,000,000 but not disclose any additional contingency.
   d. No loss contingency but disclose a contingency of $500,000 to $2,500,000.

5. When bad debt expense is estimated on the basis of the percentage of past actual losses from bad debts to past net credit sales, and this percentage is adjusted for anticipated conditions, the accounting concept of
   a. Matching is being followed.
   b. Matching is not being followed.
   c. Substance over form is being followed.
   d. Going concern is not being followed.

6. Which of the following requires intraperiod tax allocation?
   a. That portion of dividends reduced by the dividends received deduction by corporations under existing federal income tax law.
   b. The excess of accelerated depreciation used for tax purposes over straight-line depreciation used for financial reporting purposes.
   c. Extraordinary gains or losses as defined by the Accounting Principles Board.
   d. All differences between taxable income and financial statement earnings.

7. When a company purchases land with a building on it and immediately tears down the building so that the land can be used for the construction of a plant, the costs incurred to tear down the building should be
   a. Expensed as incurred.
   b. Added to the cost of the plant.
   c. Added to the cost of the land.
   d. Amortized over the estimated time period between the tearing down of the building and the completion of the plant.

8. Under which of the following conditions would flood damage be considered an extraordinary item for financial reporting purposes?
   a. Only if floods in the geographical area are unusual in nature and occur infrequently.
   b. Only if floods are normal in the geographical area but do not occur frequently.
   c. Only if floods occur frequently in the geographical area but have been insured against.
   d. Under any circumstance flood damage should be classified as an extraordinary item.

9. In accounting for a long-term construction-type contract using the percentage-of-completion method, the gross profit recognized during the first year would be the estimated total gross profit from the contract multiplied by the percentage of the costs incurred during the year to the
   a. Total costs incurred to date.
   b. Total estimated cost.
   c. Unbilled portion of the contract price.
   d. Total contract price.

10. Which of the following costs is not a part of the defined maximum for pension cost determination?
   a. Normal cost.
   b. Provision for vested benefits.
   c. Interest on overfunding.
   d. 10% of prior service costs.

11. For a compensatory stock option plan for which the date of the grant and the measurement date are the same, what account is credited at the date of the grant?
   a. Retained earnings.
   b. Stock options outstanding.
   c. Deferred compensation cost.
   d. Compensation expense.

12. In theory (disregarding any other marketplace variables) the proceeds from the sale of a bond will be equal to
   a. The face amount of the bond.
   b. The present value of the principal amount due at the end of the life of the bond plus the present value of the interest payments made during the life of the bond discounted at the prevailing market rate of interest.
   c. The fact amount of the bond plus the present value of the interest payments made during the life of the bond discounted at the prevailing market rate of interest.
   d. The sum of the face amount of the bond and the periodic interest payments.

13. A foreign exchange gain on a transaction which is denominated in other than the functional currency should be
   a. Included in net income in the period it occurs.
   b. Deferred and amortized over a period not to exceed forty years.
   c. Deferred until a subsequent year when a loss occurs and offset against that loss.
   d. Included as a separate item in the equity section of the balance sheet.

14. Q, R, S, and T are partners sharing profits and losses equally. The partnership is insolvent and is to be liquidated; the status of the partnership and each partner is as follows:

	Partnership Capital Balance	Personal Assets (Exclusive of Partnership Interest)	Personal Liabilities (Exclusive of Partnership Interest
Q	$ 15,000	$100,000	$40,000
R	$ 10,000	30,000	60,000
S	(20,000)	80,000	5,000
T	(30,000)	1,000	28,000
Total	$(25,000)		

Assuming the Uniform Partnership Act applies, the partnership creditors
   a. Must first seek recovery against S because he is solvent personally and he has a negative capital balance.

b. Will not be paid in full regardless of how they proceed legally because the partnership assets are less than the partnership liabilities.
c. Will have to share R's interest in the partnership on a pro rata basis with R's personal creditors.
d. Have first claim to the partnership assets before any partner's personal creditors have rights to the partnership assets.

15. Which of the following cost items would be matched with current revenues on a basis other than association of cause and effect?
a. Goodwill
b. Sales commissions.
c. Cost of goods sold.
d. Purchases on account.

16. A company is required to disclose, usually in the footnotes to its financial statements, two main points regarding income taxes. First, it must disclose the factors causing a deferred tax expense, if any. Second, it must disclose the factors causing a difference, if any, between a tax expense figure computed at the statutory rates and its actual tax expense.

Which of the following would cause a deferred tax expense?
a. Amortization of goodwill.
b. Use of equity method where undistributed earnings of a 30% owned investee are related to probable future dividends.
c. Premiums paid on insurance carried by company (beneficiary) on its officers or employees.
d. Income taxed at capital gains rates.

17. A change in accounting entity is actually a change in accounting
a. Principle.
b. Estimate.
c. Method.
d. Concept.

18. Interperiod income tax allocation is justified by the basic theory that income taxes should be treated as which of the following?
a. An expense.
b. A distribution of earnings.
c. A distribution of earnings for the current portion and an expense for the deferred portion.
d. An expense for the current portion and a distribution of earnings for the deferred portion.

19. The appropriate valuation of an operating lease on the statement of financial position of a lessee is
a. Zero.
b. The absolute sum of the lease payments.
c. The present value of the sum of the lease payments discounted at an appropriate rate.
d. The market value of the asset at the date of the inception of the lease.

20. A company changed its method of inventory pricing from last-in, first-out to first-in, first-out during the current year. Generally accepted accounting principles require that this change in accounting method be reported by
a. Disclosing the reason for the change in the current year's footnotes along with pro forma effects on future earnings for the succeeding five years.
b. Showing the cumulative effect of the change in the current year's financial statements and pro forma effects on prior year's financial statements in an appropriate footnote.
c. Disclosing the reason for the change in the "significant accounting policies" footnote for the current year but not restating prior year financial statements.
d. Applying retroactively the new method in restatements of prior years and appropriate footnote disclosures.

21. What are the three types of period costs that a lessee experiences with capital leases?
a. Lease expense, interest expense, amortization expense.
b. Interest expense, amortization expense, executory costs.
c. Amortization expense, executory costs, lease expense.
d. Executory costs, interest expense, lease expense.

22. For a marketable equity securities portfolio included in noncurrent assets, which of the following should be included in net income of the period?
a. Realized gains during the period.
b. Unrealized losses during the period.

c. Accumulated changes in the valuation allowance.
d. Increases in the valuation allowance during the period.

23. In a business combination what is the appropriate method of accounting for an excess of fair value assigned to net assets over the cost paid for them?
a. Record as negative goodwill.
b. Record as additional paid-in capital from combination on the books of the combined company.
c. Proportionately reduce values assigned to nonmonetary assets and record any remaining excess as a deferred credit.
d. Proportionately reduce values assigned to noncurrent assets and record any remaining excess as a deferred credit.

24. An example of a special change in accounting principle that should be reported by restating the financial statements of prior periods is the change from the
a. Straight-line method of depreciating plant equipment to the sum-of-the-years-digits method.
b. Sum-of-the-years-digits method of depreciating plant equipment to the straight-line method.
c. LIFO method of inventory pricing to the FIFO method.
d. FIFO method of inventory pricing to the LIFO method.

25. Which of the following is the appropriate basis for valuing fixed assets acquired in a business combination accounted for as a purchase carried out by exchanging cash for common stock?
a. Historic cost.
b. Book value.
c. Cost plus any excess of purchase price over book value of asset acquired.
d. Fair value.

26. Gilbert Corporation issued a 40% stock split-up of its common stock which had a par value of $10 before and after the split-up. At what amount should retained earnings be capitalized for the additional shares issued?
a. There should be no capitalization of retained earnings.
b. Par value.
c. Market value on the declaration date.
d. Market value on the payment date.

27. When translating foreign currency financial statements, which of the following accounts would be translated using current exchange rates? Assume the foreign currency is the functional currency.

	Property, plant, and equipment	*Inventories carried at cost*
a.	Yes	Yes
b.	No	No
c.	Yes	No
d.	No	Yes

28. The sale of a depreciable asset resulting in a loss, indicates that the proceeds from the sale were
a. Less than current market value.
b. Greater than cost.
c. Greater than book value.
d. Less than book value.

29. A parent corporation which uses the equity method of accounting for its investment in a 40% owned subsidiary, which earned $20,000 and paid $5,000 in dividends, made the following entries:

Investment in subsidiary	$8,000	
Equity in earnings of subsidiary		$8,000
Cash	2,000	
Dividend revenue		2,000

What effect will these entries have on the parent's statement of financial position?
a. Financial position will be fairly stated.
b. Investment in subsidiary overstated, retained earnings understated.
c. Investment in subsidiary understated, retained earnings understated.
d. Investment in subsidiary overstated, retained earnings overstated.

30. The terminal funding method and pay-as-you-go method of accounting for pension plans are not generally accepted accounting methods because
a. They do not require the funding of past service costs.
b. They are not actuarially sound.
c. They do not recognize pension costs prior to the retirement of employees.
d. They are not acceptable methods for federal income tax purposes.

31. The concept of objectivity is complied with when an accounting transaction occurs that
  a. Involves an arm's-length transaction between two independent interests.
  b. Furthers the objectives of the company.
  c. Is promptly recorded in a fixed amount of dollars.
  d. Allocates revenues or expense items in a rational and systematic manner.

32. When a fixed asset with a five-year estimated useful life is sold during the second year, how would the use of the sum-of-the-years-digits method of depreciation instead of the straight-line method of depreciation affect the gain or loss on the sale of the fixed asset?

	Gain	*Loss*
a.	Decrease	Increase
b.	Increase	Decrease
c.	No effect	No effect
d.	No effect	Decrease

33. An increase in inventory balance would be reported in a statement of changes in financial position as a
  a. Use of working capital.
  b. Source of working capital.
  c. Source of cash.
  d. Use of cash.

34. The vested benefits of an employee in a pension plan represent
  a. Benefits to be paid to the retired employee in the current year.
  b. Benefits to be paid to the retired employee in the subsequent year.
  c. Benefits accumulated in the hands of an independent trustee.
  d. Benefits that are not contingent on the employee's continuing in the service of the employer.

35. How should the balances of progress billings and construction in progress be shown at reporting dates prior to the completion of a long-term contract?
  a. Progress billings as deferred income, construction in progress as a deferred expense.
  b. Progress billings as income, construction in progress as inventory.
  c. Net, as a current asset if debit balance and current liability if credit balance.
  d. Net, as income from construction if credit balance, and loss from construction if debit balance.

36. The granting by a company to its shareholders of the opportunity to buy additional shares of stock within a specified future time at a specified price is an example of a
  a. Dividend reinvestment plan.
  b. Stock right.
  c. Stock dividend.
  d. Stock option.

37. In accounting for income taxes, interest received on municipal obligations is an example of
  a. Intraperiod tax allocation.
  b. Interperiod tax allocation.
  c. A permanent difference.
  d. A timing difference.

38. What is the proper time or time period over which to match the cost of an intangible asset with revenues if it is likely that the benefit of the asset will last for an indeterminate but very long period of time?
  a. Forty years.
  b. Fifty years.
  c. Immediately.
  d. At such time as diminution in value can be quantitatively determined.

39. If the conventional (lower of cost or market) retail inventory method is used, which of the following calculations would include (exclude) net markdowns?

	Cost ratio (percentage)	Ending inventory at retail
a.	Include	Include
b.	Include	Exclude
c.	Exclude	Include
d.	Exclude	Exclude

40. Which of the following is a potential abuse that can arise when a business combination is accounted for as a pooling of interests?
  a. Assets of the investee may be overvalued when the price paid by the investor is allocated among specific assets.
  b. Liabilities may be undervalued when the price paid by the investor is allocated to the specific liabilities.
  c. An undue amount of cost may be assigned to goodwill, thus potentially allowing for an overstatement of pooled earnings.
  d. Earnings of the pooled entity may be increased because of the combination only and not as a result of efficient operations.

41. Wages of the security guard for a small plant would be an example of

	Indirect labor	Fixed factory overhead
a.	No	No
b.	Yes	Yes
c.	Yes	No
d.	No	Yes

42. The contribution margin increases when sales volume remains the same and
   a. Variable cost per unit decreases.
   b. Variable cost per unit increases.
   c. Fixed costs decrease.
   d. Fixed costs increase.

43. The beginning work-in-process inventory was 60 percent complete as to conversion costs, and the ending work-in-process inventory was 45 percent complete as to conversion costs. The dollar amount of the conversion cost included in the ending work in process inventory (using the weighted-average method) is determined by multiplying the average unit conversion costs by what percentage of the total units in the ending work-in-process inventory?
   a. 100 percent.
   b. 60 percent.
   c. 55 percent.
   d. 45 percent.

44. The direct (variable) costing method includes in inventory
   a. Direct materials cost, direct labor cost, but **no** factory overhead cost.
   b. Direct materials cost, direct labor cost, and variable factory overhead cost.
   c. Prime cost but **not** conversion cost.
   d. Prime cost and all conversion cost.

45. A useful tool in financial statement analysis is termed "common size financial statements." What does this tool enable the financial analyst to do?
   a. Evaluate financial statements of companies within a given industry of the approximate same value.
   b. Determine which companies in a similar industry are at approximately the same stage of development.
   c. Compare the mix of assets, liabilities, capital, revenue, and expenses within a company over a period of time or between companies within a given industry without respect to relative size.
   d. Ascertain the relative potential of companies of similar size in different industries.

46. The minimum return that a project must earn for a company in order to leave the value of the company unchanged is the
   a. Current borrowing rate.
   b. Discount rate.
   c. Cost of capital.
   d. Capitalization rate.

47. Which type of cost is a vital part of decision making but omitted from conventional accounting records?
   a. Out-of-pocket cost.
   b. Sunk cost.
   c. Opportunity cost.
   d. Direct cost.

48. If the fixed costs attendant to a product increase while variable costs and sales price remain constant what will happen to (1) contribution margin and (2) break-even point?

	Contribution margin	Breakeven point
a.	Unchanged	increase
b.	Unchanged	unchanged
c.	Increase	decrease
d.	Decrease	increase

49. Which of the following quantitative methods will separate a semi-variable cost into its fixed and variable components with the highest degree of precision under all circumstances?
   a. High-low method.
   b. Simplex method.
   c. Least squares method.
   d. Scattergraph method.

50. A company buys a certain part for its manufacturing process. In order to determine the optimum size of a normal purchase order, the formula for the economic order quantity (EOQ) is used. In addition to the annual demand, what other information is necessary to complete the formula?
   a. Cost of placing an order, and annual cost of carrying a unit in stock.
   b. Cost of the part, and annual cost of carrying a unit in stock.
   c. Cost of placing an order.
   d. Cost of the part.

51. When the budget of a governmental unit is adopted and the estimated revenues exceed the appropriations, the excess is
    a. Debited to reserve for encumbrances.
    b. Credited to reserve for encumbrances.
    c. Debited to fund balance.
    d. Credited to fund balance.

52. Which of the following funds should use the modified accrual basis of accounting?
    a. Capital projects.
    b. Internal service.
    c. Enterprise.
    d. Nonexpendable trust.

53. What is not a major concern of governmental units?
    a. Budgets.
    b. Funds.
    c. Legal requirements.
    d. Consolidated statements.

54. A reason for a voluntary health and welfare organization to adopt fund accounting is that
    a. Restrictions have been placed on certain of its assets by donors.
    b. It provides more than one type of program service.
    c. Fixed assets are significant.
    d. Donated services are significant.

55. When a truck is received by a governmental unit, it should be recorded in the General Fund as a (an)
    a. Appropriation.
    b. Encumbrance.
    c. Expenditure.
    d. Fixed asset.

56. Within a governmental unit, three funds that are accounted for in a manner similar to a for-profit entity are
    a. General, Debt Service, Special Assessment.
    b. Special Assessment, Enterprise, Internal Service.
    c. Internal Service, Enterprise, Nonexpendable Trust.
    d. Enterprise, General, Debt Service.

57. What is the recommended method of accounting to be used by colleges and universities?
    a. Cash.
    b. Modified cash.
    c. Restricted accrual.
    d. Accrual.

58. Under the modified accrual method of accounting used by a local governmental unit, which of the following would be a revenue susceptible to accrual?
    a. Income taxes.
    b. Business licenses.
    c. Property taxes.
    d. Sales taxes.

59. The accounting for special revenue funds is most similar to which type of fund?
    a. Capital projects.
    b. General.
    c. Enterprise.
    d. Special assessment.

60. Which governmental fund would account for fixed assets in a manner similar to a "for-profit" organization?
    a Enterprise.
    b. Capital projects.
    c. General fixed asset group of accounts.
    d. General.

Number 2 (Estimated time — 10 to 15 minutes)

The following is the complete set of financial statements prepared by Oberlin Corporation:

Oberlin Corporation
STATEMENT OF EARNINGS AND RETAINED EARNINGS
For the Fiscal Year Ended August 31, 1976

Sales		$3,500,000
Less returns and allowances		35,000
Net sales		3,465,000
Less cost of goods sold		1,039,000
Gross margin		2,426,000
Less:		
Selling expenses	$1,000,000	
General and administrative expenses (Note 1)	1,079,000	2,079,000
Operating earnings		347,000
Add other revenue:		
Purchase discounts	10,000	
Gain on increased value of investments in real estate	100,000	
Gain on sale of treasury stock	200,000	
Correction of error in last year's statement	90,000	400,000
Ordinary earnings		747,000
Add extraordinary item — gain on sale of fixed asset		53,000
Earnings before income tax		800,000
Less income tax expense		380,000
Net earnings		420,000
Add beginning retained earnings		2,750,000
		3,170,000
Less:		
Dividends (12% stock dividend declared but not yet issued)		120,000
Contingent liability (Note 4)		300,000
Ending unappropriated retained earnings		$2,750,000

Oberlin Corporation
STATEMENT OF FINANCIAL POSITION
August 31, 1976

Assets		
Current Assets		
Cash	$ 80,000	
Accounts receivable, net	110,000	
Inventory	130,000	
Total current assets		$ 320,000
Other Assets		
Land and building, net	4,000,000	
Investments in real estate (current value)	1,508,000	
Investment in Gray, Inc., at at cost (Note 2)	160,000	
Goodwill (Note 3)	250,000	
Discount on bonds payable	42,000	
Total other assets		5,960,000
Total assets		$6,280,000
Liabilities and Stockholders Equity		
Current Liabilities		
Accounts payable	$ 140,000	
Income taxes payable	320,000	
Stock dividend payable	120,000	
Total current liabilities		$ 580,000
Other Liabilities		
Due to Grant, Inc. (Note 4)	300,000	
Liability under employee pension plan	450,000	
Bonds payable (including portion due within one year)	1,000,000	
Deferred taxes	58,000	
Total other liabilities		1,808,000
Total liabilities		2,388,000
Stockholders' Equity		
Common stock	1,000,000	
Paid-in capital in excess of par	142,000	
Unappropriated retained earnings	2,750,000	
Total stockholders' equity		3,892,000
Total liabilities and stockholders' equity		$6,280,000

Footnotes to the Financial Statements

1. Depreciation expense is included in general and administrative expenses. During the fiscal year, the Company changed from the straight-line method of depreciation to the sum-of-the-years'-digits method.

2. The company owns 40% of the outstanding stock of Gray, Inc. Because the ownership is less than 50%, consolidated financial statements with Gray cannot be presented.

3. As per federal income tax laws, goodwill is not amortized. The goodwill was "acquired" in 1973.

4. The amount due to Grant, Inc., is contingent upon the outcome of a lawsuit which is currently pending. The amount of loss, if any, is not expected to exceed $300,000.

Required:

Identify and explain the deficiencies in the presentation of Oberlin's financial statements. There are no arithmetical errors in the statements. Organize your answer as follows:

a. Deficiencies in the statement of earnings and retained earnings.

b. Deficiencies in the statement of financial position.

c. General comments.

If an item appears on both statements, identify the deficiencies for each statement separately.

Number 3 (Estimated time — 15 to 30 minutes)

Incurring long-term debt with an arrangement whereby lenders receive an option to buy common stock during all or a portion of the time the debt is outstanding is a frequently used corporate financing practice. In some situations the result is achieved through the issuance of convertible bonds; in others the debt instruments and the warrants to buy stock are separate.

Required:

a. 1. Describe the differences that exist in current accounting for original proceeds of the issuance of convertible bonds and of debt instruments with separate warrants to purchase common stock.

2. Discuss the underlying rationale for the differences described in a.1. above.

3. Summarize the arguments which have been presented for the alternative accounting treatment.

b. At the start of the year AB Company issued $6,000,000 of 7% notes along with warrants to buy 400,000 shares of its $10 par value common stock at $18 per share. The notes mature over the next ten years starting one year from date of issuance with annual maturities of $600,000. At the time, AB had 3,200,000 shares of common stock outstanding and the market price was $23 per share. The company received $6,680,000 for the notes and the warrants. For AB Company, 7% was a relatively low borrowing rate. If offered alone, at this time, the notes would have been issued at a 20 to 24 percent discount. Prepare journal entries for the issuance of the notes and warrants for the cash consideration received.

Number 4 (Estimated time — 15 to 25 minutes)

You were requested to personally deliver your auditor's report to the board of directors of Sebal Manufacturing Corporation and answer questions posed about the financial statements. While reading the statements one director asked, "What are the precise meanings of the terms cost, expense and loss? These terms sometimes seem to identify similar items and other times seem to identify dissimilar items."

Required:

a. Explain the meanings of the terms (1) cost, (2) expense, and (3) loss as used for financial reporting in conformity with generally accepted accounting principles. In your explanation discuss the distinguishing characteristics of the terms and their similarities and interrelationships.

b. Classify each of the following items as a cost, expense, loss or other category and explain how the classification of each item may change:

1. Cost of goods sold.
2. Bad debts expense.
3. Depreciation expense for plant machinery.
4. Organization costs.
5. Spoiled goods.

c. The terms "period cost" and "product cost" are sometimes used to describe certain items in financial statements. Define these terms and distinguish between them. To what types of items do each apply?

Number 5 (Estimated time — 20 to 30 minutes)

Part a. Standard costs are being used increasingly by modern manufacturing companies. Many advocates of standard costing take the position that standard costs are a proper basis for inventory valuation for external reporting purposes. Accounting Research Bulletin No. 43, however, reflects the widespread view that standard costs are not acceptable unless "adjusted at reasonable intervals to reflect current conditions so that at the balance-sheet date standard costs reasonably approximate costs computed under one of the recognized (actual cost) bases."

Required:

1. Discuss the conceptual merits of using standard costs as the basis for inventory valuation for external reporting purposes.

2. Prepare general-journal entries for three alternative dispositions of a $1,500 unfavorable variance where all goods manufactured during the period are included in the ending finished-goods inventory. Assume a formal standard-cost system is in operation, that $500 of the variance resulted from actual costs exceeding attainable standard cost, and that $1,000 of the variance resulted from the difference between the "ideal-standard" and an attainable standard.

3. Discuss the conceptual merits of each of the three alternative methods of disposition requested in 2 above.

Part b. Cost for inventory purposes should be determined by the inventory cost flow method most clearly reflecting periodic income.

Required:

1. Describe the fundamental cost flow assumptions of the average cost, FIFO, and LIFO inventory cost flow methods.
2. Discuss the reasons for using LIFO in an inflationary economy.
3. Where there is evidence that the utility of goods, in their disposal in the ordinary course of business, will be less than cost, what is the proper accounting treatment and under what concept is that treatment justified?

ANSWERS TO SAMPLE EXAMINATION

ACCOUNTING THEORY

Answer 1

1. b	11. b	21. b	31. a	41. b	51. d
2. a	12. b	22. a	32. b	42. a	52. a
3. b	13. a	23. d	33. d	43. d	53. d
4. b	14. d	24. c	34. d	44. b	54. a
5. a	15. a	25. d	35. c	45. c	55. c
6. c	16. b	26. b	36. b	46. c	56. c
7. c	17. a	27. a	37. c	47. c	57. d
8. a	18. a	28. d	38. a	48. a	58. c
9. b	19. a	29. d	39. c	49. c	59. b
10. b	20. d	30. c	40. d	50. a	60. a

Answer 2

a. Deficiencies in the Statement of Earnings and Retained Earnings

Purchase discounts—These should preferably be shown as a reduction of purchases in the cost-of-goods-sold computation. While some accountants treat purchase discounts as financing revenue, most accountants would argue that a company theoretically cannot generate revenue by purchasing goods.

Gain on increased value of investments in real estate—This is an unrealized gain that does not appropriately belong on a corporation's earnings statement.

Gain on sale of treasury stock—This is not part of an earnings statement, but it should be treated as an increase to a paid-in capital account.

Correction of error in last year's statement—This should be treated as a prior-period adjustment; it should be added, net of applicable income tax effect, as an adjustment to the beginning retained earnings.

Gain on sale of fixed asset—Two possible deficiencies are identified. First this type of gain is not an extraordinary item because it does not meet the conditions of being unusual and infrequent; it should be shown among the ordinary items. Second, assuming an item is properly classified as an extraordinary item, it should be shown net of the applicable income tax effect as per requirements of intraperiod tax allocation.

Income tax expense—One can logically assume that there were timing differences during the fiscal year necessitating the use of interperiod tax allocation procedures. Under this condition, the components of income tax expense relating to amounts currently payable and to tax effects of timing differences should be separately disclosed per disclosure requirements of Accounting Principles Board opinions.

Depreciation expense (Note 1)—Oberlin changed its method of depreciation. Such a change should be accounted for as a change in accounting principle requiring the following steps:

> The cumulative effect of the change on the beginning retained earnings should be included in net earnings of the period of the change. This cumulative effect should be shown separately between earnings before extraordinary items and net earnings.
>
> The effect of adopting the new accounting principle on earnings before extraordinary items and on net earnings (and related per-share amounts) of the period of the change should be disclosed.

Equity method—The investment in Gray should be accounted for under the equity method. Oberlin's earnings should reflect its share of Gray's earnings for the year because the ownership exceeds 20%, per APB Opinion 18.

Earnings per share—These amounts must be shown on the face of the earnings statement.

They have been omitted from Oberlin's statement. Because there is a simple capital structure in this situation, only a single series (primary) or earnings-per-share figures are required rather than a series of figures for primary and fully diluted earnings per share.

b. Deficiencies in the Statement of Financial Position

Accounts receivable, net—The allowance for doubtful accounts should be shown either parenthetically or as a contra-asset account for disclosure.

Inventory—the basis for valuation of the inventory needs to be disclosed.

Land and Building, net—Two deficiencies are identified. First, land and building accounts should be shown separately because land is not depreciable. Second, the accumulated depreciation on the building must be disclosed.

Investments in real estate (current value)—Assets are appropriately valued at historical cost with the current value indicated parenthetically or in a footnote if management so desires.

Investment in Gray, Inc.—This should be reported based on the equity method rather than the cost method because the ownership exceeds 20%, per APB Opinion 18.

Goodwill—This should be amortized as an expense each period for financial accounting purposes in accordance with APB Opinion 17.

Discount on bonds payable—This should be a contra-liability account rather than an asset because the discount is a valuation adjustment of the liability.

Stock dividend payable—This should be classified as part of stockholders' equity rather than as a liability because it does not involve a distribution of corporate assets.

Due to Grant, Inc.—This is a possible loss contingency but does not meet the conditions of Statement of Financial Accounting Standards Board No. 5 that requires accrual by a charge to earnings. Therefore the contingency should be disclosed in a footnote, or management may appropriate a portion of retained earnings, as it did. Such appropriation, however, should be included in the stockholders' equity section and not shown as a liability.

Liability under employee pension plan—A footnote should be added disclosing facts about the plan, the funding policies, and the annual provision for pension cost. Apparently such cost is included in the general and administrative expenses on the earnings statement.

Bonds payable (including portion due within one year)—The interest rate and maturity date should be disclosed. The portion due within one year should be reclassified as a current liability so that working capital will not be distorted.

Common stock—The number of shares authorized, issued, and outstanding, and the par (or stated) value should be disclosed.

c. General Comments

Statement of changes in financial position—Oberlin Corporation should also prepare a statement of changes in financial position, including a summary of changes in each element of working capital or cash depending on which approach is more appropriate. Such a statement of changes in financial position is required if the corporation issues an earnings statement and a statement of financial position because it discloses certain information not readily attainable from these other statements.

Supporting schedules—Oberlin could prepare schedules showing the composition of cost of goods sold, selling expenses, and general administrative expenses. The schedules could be attached to the earnings statement for better disclosure.

Accounting policies—A corporation is required to disclose its accounting policies, e.g., inventory method. This is usually done as a footnote.

Answer 3

a. 1. When the debt instrument and the option to acquire common stock are inseparable, as in the case of convertible bonds, the entire proceeds of the bond issue should be allocated to the debt and the related premium or discount accounts.

When the debt and the warrants are separable, the proceeds of their sale should be allocated between them. The basis of allocation is their relative fair values. As a practical matter, these relative values are usually determined by reference to the price at which the respective instruments are traded in the open market. Thus, if the debt alone would bring six times as much as would the stock purchase warrants, if sold separately, one-seventh of the total proceeds should be apportioned to the warrants and six-sevenths to the debt securities. That portion of the proceeds assigned to the warrants should be accounted for as paid-in capital. The result may be that the debt is issued at a reduced premium or at a discount.

2. In the case of convertible debt there are two principal reasons why all the proceeds should be ascribed to the debt. First, the option is inseparable from the debt. The investor in such securities has two mutually exclusive choices: He may be a creditor and later receive cash for his security; or, he may give up his right as a creditor and become a stockholder. There is no way to retain one right while selling the other. Second, the valuation of the conversion option presents practical problems. For example, in the absence of separate transferability, no separate market values are established and the only values which could be assigned to each would be subjective.

Separability of the debt and the warrants and the establishment of a market value for each results in an objective basis for allocating proceeds to the two different equities—creditors' and stockholders'—involved.

3. Arguments have been advanced that accounting for convertible debt should be the same as for debt issued with detachable stock purchase warrants. Convertible debt has features of debt and stockholders' equity, and separate recognition should be given to those characteristics at the time of issuance. Difficulties encountered in separating the relative values of the features are not insurmountable and, in any case, should not result in a solution which ignores the problem. In effect, the company is selling a debt instrument and a call on its stock. Coexistence of the two features in one instrument is no reason why each cannot receive its proper accounting recognition. The practical difficulties of estimation of the relative values may be overcome with reliable professional advice. Allocation is a well recognized accounting technique and could be applied in this case once reliable estimates of the relative values are known. If the convertible feature was added in order to sell the security at an acceptable price, the value of the convertible option is obviously material and recognition is essential. The question of whether or not the purchaser will exercise his option is not relevant to reflecting the separate elements at the time of issuance.

b.

	Debit	Credit
Cash	$6,680,000	
Discount on notes payable	1,320,000	
Notes payable		$6,000,000
Paid-in capital (option to buy common stock)		2,000,000

To record issuance of notes at 22% discount with options to buy 400,000 shares of the company's no-par common stock at a price of $5 a share below the current market value. Debt matures in ten years in equal annual installments of $600,000 and options, if not exercised, lapse as notes mature.

Answer 4

a. 1. Cost is the amount measured by the current monetary value of economic resources given up or to be given up in obtaining goods and services. Economic resources may be given up by transferring cash or other property, issuing capital stock, performing services, or incurring liabilities.

Costs are classified as unexpired or expired. Unexpired costs are assets and apply to the production of future revenues. Examples of unexpired costs are inventories, prepaid expenses, plant and equipment, and investments. Expired costs, which most costs become eventually, are those that are not applicable to the production of future revenues and are deducted from current revenues or charged against retained earnings.

2. Expense in its broadest sense includes all expired costs, i.e., costs which do not have any potential future economic benefit. A more precise definition limits the use of the term expense to the expired costs arising from using or consuming goods and services in the process of obtaining revenues, e.g., cost of goods sold, and selling and administrative expenses.

3. A loss is an unplanned cost expiration and for this reason is often included in the broad definition of expenses. A more precise definition restricts the use of the term loss to cost expirations which do not benefit the revenue-producing activities of the firm. Examples include the unrecovered book value on the sale of fixed assets and the write-off of goodwill due to unusual events within an accounting period.

The term loss is used also to refer to the amount by which expenses and extraordinary items exceed revenues during an accounting period.

b. 1. Cost of goods sold is an expired cost and may be referred to as an expense in the broad sense of the term. On the income statement it is most often identified as a cost. Inventory held for sale which is destroyed by an abnormal casualty should be classified as a loss.

2. Bad debts expense is usually classified as an expense. However, some authorities believe that it is more desirable to classify bad debts as a direct reduction of sales revenue (an offset of revenue). A material bad debt which was not provided for in the annual adjustment, such as bankruptcy of a major debtor, may be classified as a loss.

3. Depreciation expense for plant machinery is a component of factory overhead and represents the reclassification of a portion of the machinery cost to product cost (inventory). When the product is sold, the depreciation becomes a part of the cost of goods sold which is an expense. Depreciation of plant machinery during an unplanned and unproductive period of idleness such as during a strike, should be classified as a loss. The term expense should preferably be avoided when making reference to production costs.

4. Organization costs are those costs that benefit the firm for its entire period of existence and are most appropriately classified as a non-current asset. When there is initial evidence that a firm's life is limited the organization costs should be allocated over the firm's life as an expense, or amortized as a loss when a going concern foresees termination.

In practice, however, organization costs are often written off in the early years of a firm's existence.

5. Spoiled goods resulting from normal manufacturing processing should be treated as a cost of the product manufactured. When the product is sold the cost becomes an expense. Spoiled goods resulting from an abnormal occurrence should be classified as a loss.

c. Period costs and product costs are usually differentiated under one of two major concepts. One concept identifies a cost as a period or a product cost according to whether the cost expires primarily with the passage of time or directly for the production of revenue. The other concept identifies a cost as a product or a period cost according to whether or not the cost is included in inventory.

Under the first concept period costs are all costs which expire within the accounting period and are only indirectly related to the production of revenue within the period and product costs are those costs associated with the manufacture of a firm's product and that generated revenue in the period of its sale. Some costs are easily associated with the production of revenue, such as the manufacturing or purchase cost of a product sold, and are designated as product costs. Other costs may be incurred as costs of doing business and are more difficult to relate to the production of revenue, such as general and administrative costs, and are classified as period costs. Costs which cannot be readily identified with the production of revenue in any particular period, such as the company president's salary which may produce revenue in many distant future accounting periods, are also classified as period costs because they cannot be specifically identified with any future accounting period.

Under the second concept product costs include only the costs which are carried forward to future accounting periods in inventory and all expired costs are period costs.

Answer 5

a. 1. The quotation implies that "actual" manufacturing costs form the ideal basis for inventory valuation because they were incurred in producing the inventory.

The notion that actual costs are the only acceptable costs for inventory purposes has been challenged by advocates of standard costs. Accountants who advocate using standard costs for reporting purposes believe that standard costs are more representative of the true cost of the product than actual costs. They maintain that variances are measures of abnormal inefficiencies or abnormal efficiencies. Therefore, variances cannot be inventoried and should be immediately recognized in determining net income of the period rather than prorated to inventories and cost of goods sold. Thus, the costs attached to the product are the costs that should have been incurred, not the costs that were incurred.

Many accountants believe that variances do not have to be inventoried as long as standards are currently attainable. But if standards are not up to date, or if they reflect ideal performance rather than expected performance under reasonably efficient conditions, then conceptually the variances should be split between the portion which reflects departures from currently attainable standards and that portion which does not.

Most accountants agree that unfavorable variances resulting from the difference between standards based on ideal performance and standards based on practical performance should be treated as product costs and prorated to inventories and cost of goods sold. There is less agreement relating to variances resulting from the difference between actual performance and standards based on practical (attainable) performance. Standard-cost advocates believe these variances should be expensed because they represent abnormal conditions. Many other accountants believe these variances represent part of the actual cost of producing the goods and, therefore, should be treated as product costs and prorated to inventories and cost of goods sold.

2. The three most appropriate alternative methods of variance disposition would require the following entries:

		Debit	Credit
a.	Cost of Goods Sold (or Expense and Revenue Summary)	$ 500	
	Finished Goods Inventory	1,000	
	Variance		$1,500
b.	Cost of Goods Sold (or Expense and Revenue Summary)	$1,500	
	Variance		1,500
c.	Finished Goods Inventory	1,500	
	Variance		1,500

3. The first journal entry presented is in accordance with the discussion in part a. 1. above as the most appropriate method of handling

variances. Cost of goods sold (or other expense account) is charged with the excess cost above what it should have taken to complete the project based on an attainable standard. The costs (variance) resulting from the difference between the ideal standard and the practical standard should be prorated to cost of goods sold and inventories based on the relative proportion of the associated cost contained in each. In the situation presented, the entire $1,000 is charged to finished-goods inventory instead of being prorated to inventories and cost of goods sold because the production is included solely in the finished-goods inventory.

The second journal entry, b., can be justified as an appropriate method for disposition of the variance primarily on practical consideration but has little theoretical justification. The practice of charging all variances to cost of goods sold (or against current revenue in some other manner) has often been justified on the grounds of simplicity, convenience, and immateriality.

The last entry would be appropriate where it is desired to adjust the standard-cost inventory to actual costs. Many accountants would advocate this entry in the circumstances presented because the inventory would then be stated at actual costs of production. However, it must be remembered that when following this method of variance disposition the asset inventory will be carried on the financial statements at an amount that exceeds the cost of what should have been incurred. Thus, inefficiencies in operations are being capitalized, as assets in the financial statements when this method is applied.

Part b.

1. The average cost method is based on the assumption that the average costs of the goods in the beginning inventory and the goods purchased during the period should be used for both the inventory and the cost of goods sold.

The FIFO (first-in, first-out) method is based on the assumption that the first goods purchased are the first sold. As a result, the inventory is at the most recent purchase prices, while cost of goods sold is at older purchase prices.

The LIFO (last-in, first-out) method is based on the assumption that the latest goods purchased are the first sold. As a result, the inventory is at the oldest purchase prices, while cost of goods sold is at more recent purchase prices.

2. In an inflationary economy, LIFO provides a better matching of current costs with current revenue because cost of goods sold is at more recent purchase prices. Net cash inflow is generally increased because taxable income is generally decreased, resulting in payment of lower income taxes.

3. Where there is evidence that the utility of goods to be disposed of in the ordinary course of business will be less than cost, the difference should be recognized as a loss in the current period, and the inventory should be stated at market value in the financial statements. In accordance with the concept of conservatism, inventory should be valued at the lower of cost or market.

OTHER ACCOUNTING TEXTBOOKS FROM JOHN WILEY & SONS

Arpan and Radebaugh: INTERNATIONAL ACCOUNTING AND MULTINATIONAL ENTERPRISES
Burch and Sardinas: COMPUTER CONTROL AND AUDIT
Burch, Strater, and Grudnitski: INFORMATION SYSTEMS: THEORY AND PRACTICE, 3rd edition
DeCoster, Ramanathan, and Sundem: ACCOUNTING FOR MANAGERIAL DECISION MAKING, 2nd edition
DeCoster and Schafer: MANAGEMENT ACCOUNTING: A DECISION EMPHASIS, 3rd edition
Gross and Jablonsky: PRINCIPLES OF ACCOUNTING AND FINANCIAL REPORTING FOR NONPROFIT ORGANIZATIONS
Guy: AN INTRODUCTION TO STATISTICAL SAMPLING IN AUDITING
Haried, Imdieke, and Smith: ADVANCED ACCOUNTING, 2nd edition
Helmkamp, Imdieke, and Smith: PRINCIPLES OF ACCOUNTING
Kell and Ziegler: MODERN AUDITING, 2nd edition
Kieso and Weygandt: INTERMEDIATE ACCOUNTING, 4th edition
Laughlin: FINANCIAL ACCOUNTING
Loeb: ETHICS IN THE ACCOUNTING PROFESSION
McCullers and Schroeder: ACCOUNTING THEORY, 2nd edition
Mock and Grove: MEASUREMENT, ACCOUNTING, AND ORGANIZATIONAL INFORMATION
Moscove and Simkin: ACCOUNTING INFORMATION SYSTEMS, 2nd edition
Ramanathan: MANAGEMENT AND CONTROL IN NONPROFIT ORGANIZATIONS: TEXT AND CASES
Ramanathan and Hegstad: READINGS IN MANAGEMENT CONTROL IN NONPROFIT ORGANIZATIONS
Sardinas, Burch, and Asebrook: EDP AUDITING: A PRIMER
Taylor and Glezen: AUDITING: Integrated Concepts and Procedures, 2nd edition
Taylor and Glezen: CASE STUDY IN AUDITING, 2nd edition
Tricker and Boland: MANAGEMENT INFORMATION AND CONTROL SYSTEMS, 2nd edition
Wilkinson: ACCOUNTING AND INFORMATION SYSTEMS

BUSINESS LAW TEXTBOOKS FROM JOHN WILEY AND SONS

Atteberry, Pearson, and Litka: REAL ESTATE LAW, 3rd edition
Cataldo, Kempin, Stockton, and Weber: INTRODUCTION TO LAW AND THE LEGAL PROCESS, 3rd edition
Deaver: THE COMPLETE LAW SCHOOL COMPANION
Delaney and Gleim: CPA REVIEW: BUSINESS LAW
Dunfee and Gibson: AN INTRODUCTION TO GOVERNMENT AND BUSINESS, 3rd edition
Dunfee, Gibson, Lamber, and McCarty: MODERN BUSINESS LAW: INTRODUCTION TO THE LEGAL ENVIRONMENT OF BUSINESS
Dunfee and Gibson: AN INTRODUCTION TO CONTRACTS, 2nd edition
Erickson, Dunfee, and Gibson: ANTITRUST AND TRADE REGULATION: CASES AND MATERIALS
Gleim and Delaney: CPA EXAMINATION REVIEW: VOLUME I OUTLINES AND STUDY GUIDES
Gleim and Delaney: CPA EXAMINATION REVIEW: VOLUME II PROBLEMS AND SOLUTIONS
Griffith: THE LEGAL ENVIRONMENT OF BUSINESS, 3rd edition
Henszey and Friedman: REAL ESTATE LAW, 2nd edition
Inman: THE REGULATORY ENVIRONMENT OF BUSINESS
Litka and Inman: THE LEGAL ENVIRONMENT OF BUSINESS, 3rd edition
Litka and Jennings: BUSINESS LAW, 3rd edition
Rothenberg and Blumenkrantz: PERSONAL LAW
Walder: PASS THIS BAR
Wolfe and Naffziger: THE LAW OF AMERICAN BUSINESS ASSOCIATIONS: AN ENVIRONMENTAL APPROACH

Fold here

NO POSTAGE
NECESSARY
IF MAILED
IN THE
UNITED STATES

BUSINESS REPLY MAIL

FIRST CLASS PERMIT NO. 2277 NEW YORK, N.Y.

POSTAGE WILL BE PAID BY

JOHN WILEY & SONS, INC.
1 Wiley Drive
Somerset, N.J. 08873

Staple or tape closed

CPA PUBLICATIONS ORDER FORM

The **TWO VOLUME SET** consists of **Volume I** containing outlines and study guides for each section of the exam and **Volume II** with multiple choice questions, problems, and essay questions—with accompanying solutions.

☐ Quantity	Gleim/Delaney CPA EXAMINATION REVIEW Set, 11th Edition	1-80081-3	$63.90
☐ Quantity	Gleim/Delaney CPA EXAMINATION REVIEW, Vol I, 11th Edition	1-80083-X	$31.95
☐ Quantity	Gleim/Delaney CPA EXAMINATION REVIEW, Vol II, 11th Edition	1-80082-1	$31.95

The **THREE PART FORMAT** lets students purchase **THEORY and PRACTICE, AUDITING** or **BUSINESS LAW** separately. Each of these new volumes combines outlines and study guides with problems and solutions.

☐ Quantity	Delaney/Gleim: CPA EXAMINATION REVIEW: CPA Set 1984	1-88220-8	$75.85
☐ Quantity	Delaney/Gleim: CPA EXAMINATION REVIEW: Theory & Practice 1984	1-88221-6	$31.95
☐ Quantity	Delaney/Gleim: CPA EXAMINATION REVIEW: Business Law 1984	1-88219-4	$21.95
☐ Quantity	Delaney/Gleim: CPA EXAMINATION REVIEW: Auditing 1984	1-88222-4	$21.95

Delaney/Gleim CPA EXAMINATION SOLUTIONS features all the multiple choice questions from each exam with Delaney & Gleim's clear, concise explanations of the answers; solutions for each Accounting Practice problem along with detailed Solution Guides for applying the authors' solutions approach; and the answers for each Essay problem along with answer outlines.

☐ Quantity	Delaney/Gleim CPA Examination Solutions: Nov 1982*	1-89821-X	$15.95
☐ Quantity	Delaney/Gleim CPA Examination Solutions: May 1983*	1-89825-2	$15.95

*For complete most recent examination answers and explanations we recommend you investigate the National Association of State Boards of Accountancy (NASBA) CPA Examination Critque Program, 545 Fifth Avenue, Suite 506, New York, New York 10017.

For prompt service check with your local bookstore, or remove and complete this form and return it to John Wiley and Sons, Inc., One Wiley Drive, Somerset, NJ 08873, or call our hotline (815)756-8486.

Full credit is guaranteed, if not satisfied, when books are returned within 30 days in saleable condition. We normally ship within ten days. If payment accompanies order and shipment cannot be made within 90 days, full payment will be refunded. Complete the following information and mail it (**by envelope if sending check**) to the address above.

☐ Check Enclosed ☐ Bill Me ☐ Charge to my Credit Card

☐☐ Charge Card Expiration Date

☐☐☐☐☐☐☐☐☐☐☐☐☐☐☐ Credit Card No. (All Digits Please)

Mastercard ☐ Visa ☐ American Express ☐

______________________ signature

Note:

1. If ordering by credit card, list complete card number, expiration date and sign order with full signature. Mastercard, Visa, and American Express honored.
2. If your order totals $126.00 or more, please attach a company purchase order or enclose 25% partial payment.
3. **Proprietary Schools Note:** To expedite orders at time of need, if you do not already have an account established at Wiley, contact in advance, **Marvin Willig, Credit Manager, John Wiley and Sons, Inc., One Wiley Drive, Somerset, NJ 08873**. Provide bank name and three credit references.

BILL TO ______________________ SHIP TO ______________________

ADDRESS ______________________ ADDRESS ______________________

CITY ______________________ CITY ______________________

STATE ______________ ZIP ______ STATE ______________ ZIP ______

For details regarding future issues and advance purchase plans write or call CPA Examination Review, P.O. Box 886, DeKalb, Illinois 60115, (815) 756-8486.

081-5-1107

PRICES SUBJECT TO CHANGE WITHOUT NOTICE

Fold here

Cut Here

NO POSTAGE
NECESSARY
IF MAILED
IN THE
UNITED STATES

BUSINESS REPLY MAIL

FIRST CLASS PERMIT NO. 2277 NEW YORK, N.Y.

POSTAGE WILL BE PAID BY

JOHN WILEY & SONS, INC.
1 Wiley Drive
Somerset, N.J. 08873

Staple or tape closed